THE ROUGH GUIDE TO
SOUTH AFRICA
LESOTHO & SWAZILAND

This ninth edition updated by
James Bainbridge, Hilary Heuler, Barbara McCrea,
Greg de Villiers, Louise Whitworth and Lizzie Williams

ROUGH
GUIDES

Contents

Introduction to
South Africa

South Africa is a large, diverse and incredibly beautiful country. The size of France and Spain combined, and roughly twice the size of Texas, it varies from the picturesque Garden Route towns of the Western Cape to the raw subtropical coast of northern KwaZulu-Natal, with the vast Karoo semi-desert across its centre and one of Africa's premier safari destinations, Kruger National Park, in the northeast. In addition, its big cities attract immigrants from across Africa, making them great, bubbling cultural crucibles.

Many visitors are pleasantly surprised by South Africa's excellent **infrastructure**, which, especially in the Western Cape, is comparable with developed nations. Good air links and bus routes, excellent roads and plenty of first-class B&Bs and guesthouses make South Africa perfect for touring. If you're on a budget, the network of hostels and backpacker buses provide cost-efficient means of exploring.

Yet, despite all these facilities, South Africa is also something of an enigma; after 25 years of democracy, the "**rainbow nation**" is still struggling to find a new identity. Apartheid is dead, but its heritage still shapes South Africa in very physical ways. This is all too evident in the layout of the towns and cities, where the historically poorer African areas are usually tucked away from the centre.

South Africa's **population** doesn't reduce simply to black and white. The majority are black **Africans** (over 80 percent of the population); **white people** make up just under nine percent, as do **coloured people** – the mixed-race descendants of white settlers, slaves from Southeast Asia and Africans, who speak English and Afrikaans and comprise the majority in the Western Cape. The rest are mostly **Indians** (2.5 percent), resident mainly in KwaZulu-Natal and descended from indentured labourers, who came to South Africa at the beginning of the twentieth century.0

But perhaps a better indication of South Africa's diversity is the plethora of official languages, most of which represent distinct cultures with rural roots in different corners of the country. Each region has its own particular style of architecture, craftwork, food and

ABOVE KNYSNA, WESTERN CAPE **RIGHT** TSITSIKAMMA NATIONAL PARK

sometimes dress. Perhaps more exciting still are the cities, where the whole country comes together in an alchemical blend of rural and urban, traditional and thoroughly modern.

Crime isn't the indiscriminate phenomenon that press reports suggest, but it is an issue. Really, it's a question of perspective – taking care, but not becoming paranoid. The odds of becoming a victim are highest in downtown Johannesburg, where violent crime is a daily reality; there is less risk in other cities.

Where to go

While you could circuit South Africa in a matter of weeks, it's more satisfying to focus on a specific region. Each of the nine provinces has compelling reasons to visit, although, depending on the time of year and your interests, you'd be wise to concentrate on either the **west** or the **east**.

The **west**, best visited in the warmer months (Nov–April), has the outstanding attraction of **Cape Town**, worth experiencing for its unbeatable location beneath Table Mountain. Half a day's drive from here can take you to any other destination in the **Western Cape**, a province that owes its character to the longest-established colonial heritage in the country. You'll find gabled Cape Dutch architecture, historic towns and vineyard-covered mountains in the **Winelands**; forested coast along the **Garden Route**; and a dry interior punctuated by Afrikaner *dorps* (towns) in the **Little Karoo**.

If the west sounds too pretty and you're after a more "African" experience, head for the **eastern** flank of the country, best visited in the cooler months (May–Oct). **Johannesburg** is

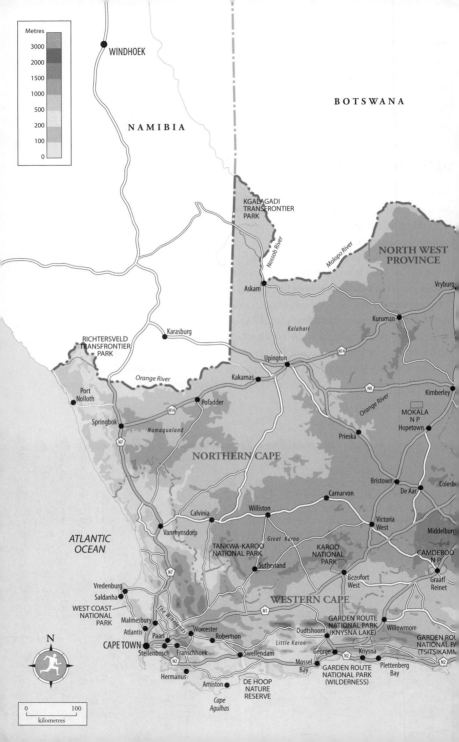

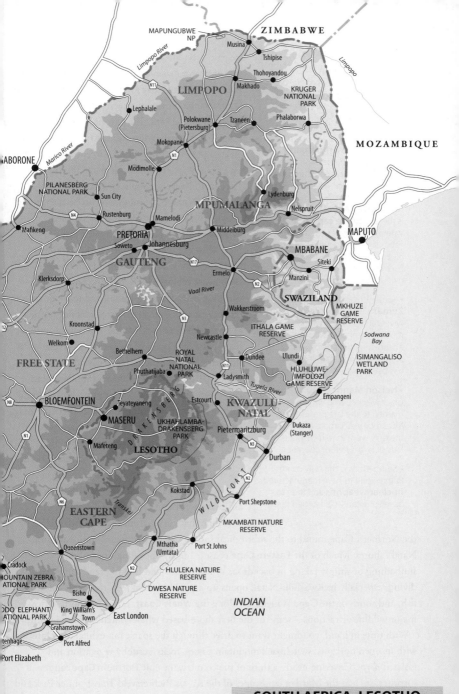

SOUTH AFRICA, LESOTHO
AND SWAZILAND

likely to be your point of entry to this area: its frenetic street life, soaring office blocks and lively mix of people make it quite unlike anywhere else in the country. Half a day away by car lie **Limpopo** and **Mpumalanga** provinces, which share the mighty **Kruger National Park**. The king of South Africa's roughly two dozen major parks, Kruger is one of the greatest places on the continent to encounter the Big Five (lion, leopard, buffalo, elephant and rhino).

A visit to Kruger combines perfectly with KwaZulu-Natal to the south, and an excellent route between the two is through tiny, landlocked **Swaziland**, which has a distinct Swazi culture and a number of well-managed game parks. **KwaZulu-Natal** itself offers superb game and birdlife; **Hluhluwe-iMfolozi Park** is the best place in the world to see endangered rhinos, and there are several other outstanding small game reserves nearby, such as Ithala, Mkhuze and Ndumo. For hiking and nature, the high point of the province – literally – is the soaring **Drakensberg**, half a day's drive from Durban. **Durban** is one of the few South African cities worth visiting in its own right: a busy cultural melting pot with a bustling Indian district and lively beachfront. The long strip of beaches north and south of Durban is the most developed in the country, but north towards the Mozambique border lies one of South Africa's wildest stretches of coast.

Long sandy **beaches**, developed only in pockets, are characteristic of much of the 2798km of shoreline that curves from the cool Atlantic along the Northern Cape round to the subtropical Indian Ocean that foams onto KwaZulu-Natal's shores. Much of the **Eastern Cape** coast is hugely appealing: for walking, sunbathing or simply taking in backdrops of mountains and hulking sand dunes. **Scuba diving**, especially in KwaZulu-Natal, opens up a world of coral reefs rich with colourful fish, and south of the Cape Winelands, along the **Whale Coast**, is one of South Africa's major wildlife attractions – some of the best shore-based **whale-watching** in the world.

With time in hand, you might want to drive through the sparse but exhilarating **interior**, with its open horizons, switchback mountain passes, rocks, scrubby vegetation and isolated *dorps*. Covering nearly a third of the country, the epic **Northern Cape** can reveal surprises, such as the Martian landscapes of the Ai-Ais Richtersveld Transfrontier Park and the lion country of the remote but thrilling Kgalagadi Transfrontier Park. The

FROM TOP WHITE RHINOS, EASTERN CAPE; BEAD DISPLAY, GREENMARKET SQUARE, CAPE TOWN

neighbouring North West Province has a few accessible and excellent wildlife reserves and Sun City, a surreal casino theme park in the bushveld.

From the open fields and Afrikaner heartland of the **Free State**, you're well poised to visit the undeveloped kingdom of **Lesotho**, set in the mountains between Free State and KwaZulu-Natal. Lesotho has few vestiges of royalty left, but does offer plenty of spectacular highland scenery, best explored on a sturdy, sure-footed Basotho pony.

When to go

South Africa is predominantly sunny, but when it does get cold you feel it, since everything is geared to fine weather. **Midwinter** in the southern hemisphere is in June and July, while **midsummer** is during December and January, when the country shuts down for its annual holiday.

South Africa has distinct climatic zones. In **Cape Town** and the **Garden Route** coastal belt, summers tend to be warm, mild and unpredictable; rain can fall at any time of the year and winter days can be cold and wet. Many Capetonians regard March to May as the perfect season, when the summer winds drop; it's mild, autumnal and the tourists have gone along with the stifling February heat. Subtropical **KwaZulu-Natal** has warm, sunny winters and tepid seas; in common with the **Lesotho** highlands, the province's Drakensberg range has misty days in summer and mountain snow in winter. **Johannesburg** and **Pretoria** lie on the highveld plateau and have a near-perfect climate; summer days are hot and frequently broken by dramatic thunder showers; winters are dry with chilly nights. East of Johannesburg, the **lowveld**, the low-lying wedge along the Mozambique border that includes the **Kruger National Park** and much of **Swaziland**, is subject to similar summer and winter rainfall patterns to the highveld, but experiences far greater extremes of temperature because of its considerably lower altitude.

HOUSE OF THE SPIRITS

For thousands of years, San Bushman shamans in South Africa decorated rock faces with powerful religious images. These finely realized paintings, found in mountainous areas across South Africa, include animals, people, and humans changing into animals. Archeologists now regard the images as metaphors for religious experiences, one of the most significant of which is the healing trance dance, still practised by the few surviving Bushman communities. Rock faces can be seen as portals between the human and spiritual worlds: when we gaze at Bushman rock art, we are looking into the house of the spirits.

ABOVE LILAC-BREASTED ROLLER, KRUGER NATIONAL PARK

Author picks

Our authors have visited every corner of South Africa, Lesotho and Swaziland – from the vineyards of the Cape to baobab-dotted Limpopo, via the tumbleweed-strewn Karoo and the peaks of the Drakensberg – to bring you some unique travel experiences. These are some of their favourite spots.

Beach break A favourite family holiday spot is Nature's Valley, with its lagoon and Tsitsikamma forests overlooking the beach. It's quieter than more westerly parts of the Garden Route and its tree-lined lanes are reminiscent of an English village (p.232).

Best wine estate There are so many to choose from, but two outstanding wineries are *Ataraxia* (p.188), with its chapel tasting room near Hermanus, and *Babylonstoren* (p.174) – a perennial favourite for its gardens and restaurants.

Go out on a limb The beautiful timber-and-steel "Boomslang" walkway twists through the forest canopy at Cape Town's *Kirstenbosch National Botanical Garden* (p.111), providing stunning views of Table Mountain and the Southern Suburbs.

Love the dorp An unsung South African pleasure is road tripping through the Karoo to elegantly decaying *dorps* (towns), affectionately known as *dorpies*, to enjoy country hospitality, Cape Dutch architecture and hurl-your-phone-from-the-car relaxation. Meander slowly to the likes of Prince Albert (p.248) and Nieu Bethesda (p.327).

Mountain marvels Built by intrepid colonials such as Andrew and Thomas Bain, South Africa's mountain passes are engineering feats. Crowned by a nineteenth-century British fort, Montagu's scenic Cogman's Kloof Pass cuts through the wrinkly Langeberg Mountains to the Little Karoo (p.237).

Favourite park For scenery it's KwaZulu-Natal's *Royal Natal National Park* (p.398), which offers epic hikes in the Northern Drakensberg, and the nearby *Golden Gate Highlands National Park* (p.438) in the Free State. For wildlife, it's a tough choice, but spotting Kalahari lions purring between the dunes of *Kgalagadi Transfrontier Park* (p.277) is certainly memorable.

> Our author recommendations don't end here. We've flagged up our favourite places – a perfectly sited hotel, an atmospheric café, a special restaurant – throughout the Guide, highlighted with the ★ symbol.

FROM TOP PRINCE ALBERT, WESTERN CAPE; TREE CANOPY WALKWAY, KIRSTENBOSCH; WINE CELLAR, BABYLONSTOREN

28

things not to miss

It's not possible to see everything that South Africa, Lesotho and Swaziland has to offer in one trip – and we don't suggest you try. What follows is a selective and subjective taste of the country's highlights, including outstanding national parks, spectacular wildlife, adventure sports and beautiful architecture. All entries have a page reference to take you straight into the Guide, where you can find out more. Coloured numbers refer to chapters in the Guide section.

1

1 THE WILD COAST
Page 337
This part of the Eastern Cape offers peace and seclusion along a remote and spectacular subtropical coastline.

2 HLUHLUWE-IMFOLOZI PARK
Page 401
KwaZulu-Natal's finest game reserve provides an unsurpassed variety of wildlife-spotting activities, from night drives to guided wilderness walks.

3 SOWETO
Page 467
A tour around the vast, sprawling township – South Africa's largest – gives visitors a vivid insight into how the majority of black South Africans live.

4 INDIAN CULTURE
Page 372
Durban, sub-Saharan Africa's busiest port, boasts a large Indian population, brightly coloured Hindu temples, buzzing markets and zinging curries.

10 THE SANI PASS
Page 390

The most precipitous pass in Southern Africa, connecting Lesotho to KwaZulu-Natal.

11 GAME TRAILS
Page 542

Spot wildlife on a guided hike in Kruger National Park.

12 CAPE POINT
Page 127

The rocky promontory south of Cape Town is one of the most dramatic coastal locations on the continent.

13 STORMS RIVER MOUTH
Page 233

Cross the spectacular Storms River Mouth by footbridge.

14 KGALAGADI TRANSFRONTIER PARK
Page 277

View cheetahs, meerkats and other desert dwellers amid the harsh beauty of the Kalahari.

15 WILD FLOWERS
Page 285

Following the winter rains, Namaqualand's normally bleak landscape explodes with colour.

16 THE BO-KAAP
Page 99

On the slopes of Signal Hill, meander through Cape Town's most colourful quarter with its pastel Cape Dutch and Georgian houses.

21

17 PONY TREKKING
Page 586

The perfect way to experience the ruggedly beautiful "mountain kingdom" of Lesotho.

18 KRUGER NATIONAL PARK
Page 538

Get spine-tinglingly close to hippos and other big game at South Africa's ultimate wildlife destination.

19 RAFTING
Page 631

Swaziland's Great Usutu River offers exhilarating whitewater rafting.

20 CANOPY TOURS
Page 236

From the Garden Route to the Drakensberg, swing through the treetops among the arboreal giants of South Africa's indigenous forests.

21 LIVE MUSIC
Page 479

Johannesburg offers the best nightlife in South Africa, attracting top musical performers from around the country and abroad.

22 TABLE MOUNTAIN AERIAL CABLEWAY
Page 106

The most spectacular way to ascend Cape Town's famous landmark is also the easiest – the revolving cable car.

22

23 MADIKWE GAME RESERVE

Page 512

This massive game park sees remarkably few visitors, yet boasts excellent lodges and superb wildlife-spotting opportunities, from wild dogs to lions and elephants.

24 DE HOOP NATURE RESERVE

Page 194

Monumental dunes, zebras, bontebok and whales by the dozen make this one of the Western Cape's most compelling reserves. See it all on the five-day Whale Trail.

25 BULUNGULA LODGE

Page 344

The most memorable lodge on the Wild Coast's beautiful river mouths, this backpacker community-run lodge offers an all-too-rare opportunity to experience rural African life.

26 ROBBEN ISLAND

Page 104

Just half an hour from Cape Town is the notorious offshore jail where political prisoners, including Nelson Mandela, were incarcerated.

27 WHALE-WATCHING

Page 186

Regularly visiting Hermanus and the southern Cape coast, whales often approach surprisingly close to the shore.

28 NEIGHBOURHOOD MARKETS

Pages 155 & 480

In Cape Town and Johannesburg, taste the products of the local fields, vineyards, brewers, distillers and artisan foodies, with craft and design thrown in.

23

24

25

Itineraries

The following itineraries take you from South Africa's southwestern corner to its northeastern extent, covering the classic attractions – such as Cape Town and Kruger National Park – as well as far less-visited sights. Stitched together, the three itineraries could constitute a two-month grand tour, sweeping across the country's major themes, from safaris, beaches and epic landscapes to ethnic art and culture, colonial architecture and urban life.

WESTERN CAPE CIRCUIT

South Africa's oldest urban centres are in the Western Cape, a province that packs a huge variety. You could cover its highlights in three weeks, but four would be better.

❶ Cape Town Southern Africa's oldest, most beautiful and most unmissable city has it all: an extraordinary natural setting, beautiful historic architecture and a buzzing urban life. **See p.82**

❷ The Winelands Limewashed Cape Dutch manors surrounded by vineyards beneath mauve mountains house some of the country's best restaurants and guesthouses. **See p.164**

❸ Whale Coast Monumental dunes and wild surf are reason enough to visit De Hoop Nature Reserve, but it's also one of the world's top spots for land-based whale-watching. **See p.179**

❹ Garden Route South Africa's quintessential route takes in pretty coastal towns, such as Knysna, as well as a national park with ancient forests and dramatic coastline. **See p.210**

❺ Little Karoo The R62 cuts through the semi-arid Little Karoo's mountain passes, taking in sculptural rock formations, hot springs and some lovely historic villages. **See p.237**

❻ Swartland The closest place to Cape Town to see the veld glowing with wild flowers in spring is Darling. **See p.195**

❼ Cederberg San rock-art sites and grotesque gargoyle-like rock formations give the Western Cape's mountain wilderness its otherworldly atmosphere. **See p.204**

THE EAST

The eastern flank of the country boasts game reserves, beaches and ethnic culture. You'll need at least three weeks for this tour.

❶ Johannesburg Africa's economic powerhouse buzzes with a thriving arts scene, well-established café culture and Soweto, the country's most populous township. **See p.448**

❷ Kruger National Park The size of a small country and brimming with wildlife, Kruger is up there with the continent's top game reserves. **See p.538**

❸ Swaziland One of the world's few remaining absolute monarchies retains its tribal traditions through a number of ceremonies. **See p.612**

❹ iSimangaliso Wetland Park UNESCO World Heritage Site that offers scuba diving in the subtropical waters of Sodwana Bay and where loggerhead and leatherback turtles come ashore to nest in summer. **See p.404**

❺ KwaZulu-Natal game reserves Hluhluwe-iMfolozi is the province's premier game reserve, roamed by big cats, rhinos and elephants;

ABOVE ROCK FORMATIONS, CEDERBERG MOUNTAINS; MSWATI III, KING OF SWAZILAND

a number of minor reserves such as Ithala, Mkhuze and Phinda also have a lot to offer. **See p.401, p.416, p.408 & p.410**

❻ **Zulu heartland** Geometrically patterned basketry and several festivals, including Shaka Day, keep alive the proud traditions of KwaZulu-Natal's dominant ethnic group. **See p.417**

❼ **uKhahlamba-Drakensberg** The dramatic landscapes make for breathtaking hikes and the chance to see the rock art of the San. **See p.388**

❽ **Durban** The subtropical vegetation, popular beachfront and cocktail of Zulu, Indian, South African and English cultures make Durban a compelling stay for a couple of days. **See p.355**

THE FRONTIER

Allow three weeks to explore the dry interior of the Great Karoo and the contrastingly verdant Wild Coast.

❶ **Port Elizabeth** Four thousand English settlers made landfall here in 1820, and today their descendants' families are drawn to its safe sandy beaches. **See p.302**

❷ **Big Game Country** Addo, the only Big Five national park in the southern half of the country, is also close to Shamwari and Kwande, two of the top private game reserves. **See p.308**

❸ **Graaff-Reinet** Totally surrounded by the mountainous Camdeboo National Park, whose highlight is the deep Valley of Desolation, this eighteenth-century Cape-Dutch Karoo outpost is perfect for exploring on foot. **See p.324**

❹ **Cradock** The atmospherically dusty frontier town sits on the banks of the Great Fish River, the fractious nineteenth-century border between the English-governed Cape Colony and the traditional Xhosa chiefdoms. **See p.322**

❺ **Grahamstown** Edgy blend of cultured university town and rural backwater, this Settler City glories in extensive Georgian- and Victorian-colonial streetscapes. **See p.317**

❻ **Hogsback** A lush Afromontane highland resort with alternatively minded locals and forest walks to waterfalls, elevated above baking valleys. **See p.332**

❼ **Madiba Country** Boys still herd cattle, just as Nelson Mandela did, around Qunu, the village where he grew up; museums here and in nearby Mthatha tell the story of his life. **See p.345**

❽ **Wild Coast** Immerse yourself in Xhosa culture and life at lodges such as Mdumbi and Buccaneers, in an unspoilt region of traditional villages, undulating hills, lush forests and undeveloped sandy beaches. **See p.337**

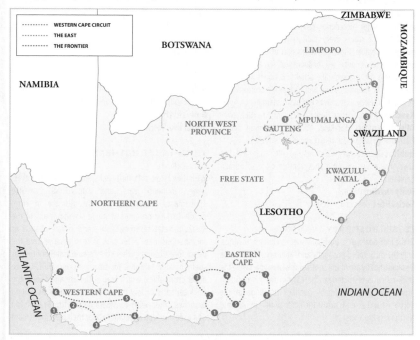

Wildlife

Apart from the likes of Kruger, Kgalagadi Transfrontier, Hluhluwe-iMfolozi, Addo Elephant, the Pilanesberg and a number of private parks, where you'll see the Big Five (lion, leopard, buffalo, elephant and rhino), more than a hundred other reserves offer numerous smaller predators and dozens of herbivores, including endangered species, in invariably beautiful settings.

This field guide provides a quick reference to help you identify some of the **mammals** most likely to be encountered in South Africa. It includes species found throughout the country as well a number whose range is more restricted. The photos show easily identified markings and features. The notes give pointers about the kind of habitat in which you are likely to see each mammal; its daily rhythm; the kind of social groups it usually forms; and some of the reserves you're most likely to find it in.

PRIMATES

Southern Africa has the lowest diversity of primates on the continent, a mere five species excluding *Homo sapiens*. They include two varieties of bushbaby, two monkeys and one species of baboon – the largest and most formidable of the lot. Great apes such as gorillas and chimpanzees aren't found in the wild in Southern Africa.

CHACMA BABOON *PAPIO (URSINUS) CYNOCEPHALUS*
Apart from humans, baboons are the primates most widely found in South Africa. Males can be intimidating and are bold enough to raid vehicles or accommodation in search of food, undeterred by the presence of people. Troops are led by a dominant male and are governed by complex social relations in which gender, precedence, physical strength and family ties determine status. Every adult male enjoys dominance over every female. Grooming forms part of the social glue and you'll commonly see baboons lolling about while performing this massage-like activity. Baboons are highly opportunistic omnivores and will tuck into a scorpion or a newborn antelope as readily as raid a citrus farm for oranges.
Reserves Addo, Garden Route (Tsitsikamma), Hluhluwe-iMfolozi, Kruger, Marakele, Mkhuze, Mountain Zebra, Pilanesberg, Table Mountain (Cape of Good Hope).
Habitat Open country with trees and cliffs; adaptable, but always near water; sometimes venture close to human habitation.
Daily rhythm Diurnal.
Social life Troops of 15–100.

LESSER BUSHBABY *GALAGO MOHOLI*
Of the half-dozen or so bushbaby species endemic to Africa, only the thick-tailed bushbaby and, about half its size, the lesser bushbaby are found south of the Limpopo. While the thick-tailed is restricted to the eastern fringes of South Africa, the lesser bushbaby overlaps its range in the northeast and extends across the north of the country into North West Province.

Reserves Kruger and Pilanesberg.
Habitat Woodland savanna and riverine woodland.
Daily rhythm Nocturnal.
Social life Small family groups.

SAMANGO (OR SYKES') MONKEY
CERCOPITHECUS MITIS
In striking contrast with the cheekier, upfront disposition of vervets, the rarer samango monkeys are shy and may only give themselves away through their loud explosive call or the breaking of branches as they go about their business. Samangos are larger than vervets and have long cheek hair. Like vervets, they're highly social and live in troops of females under the proprietorship of a dominant male, but unlike their relatives they are more inclined to fan out when looking for food.
Reserves Hluhluwe-iMfolozi, iSimangaliso Wetland and Ndumo.
Habitat Prefer higher reaches of gallery forest; occasionally venture into the open to forage.
Daily rhythm Diurnal.
Social life Troops.

THICK-TAILED BUSHBABY *OTOLEMUR CRASSICAUDATUS*
With their large, soft, fluffy pelts, huge, saucer-like eyes, large, rounded ears and superficially cat-like appearance, bushbabies are the ultimate in cute, cuddly-looking primates. If you're staying at any of the KwaZulu-Natal reserves, you stand a fair chance of seeing a bushbaby after dark as they emerge from the dense forest canopy, where they rest in small groups, for spells of lone foraging for tree gum and fruit. Unlike other bushbabies, which leap with ease and speed, the thick-tailed is a slow mover that hops or walks along branches, often with considerable stealth. Even if you don't see one, you're bound to hear their piercing scream

cut through the sounds of the night. Bushbabies habituate easily to humans and will sometimes come into lodge dining rooms, scavenging for titbits.

Reserves Hluhluwe-iMfolozi, iSimangaliso Wetland, Kruger.

Habitat Dry and riverine woodland; arboreal.

Daily rhythm Nocturnal.

Social life Small groups of a mating pair or one or two females with young; males territorial with ranges that overlap several female ranges.

VERVET MONKEY *CERCOPITHECUS AETHIOPS*

A widespread primate you may see outside reserves, living around nearby farms and even on suburban fringes, where opportunities for scavenging are promising. Vervets are principally vegetarians but are not averse to eating invertebrates, small lizards, nestlings and eggs, as well as biscuits and sweets. Vervet society is made up of family groups of females and young, defended by associate males, and is highly caste-ridden. A mother's rank determines that of her daughter from infancy, and lower-ranking adult females risk being castigated if they fail to show due respect to these "upper-crust" youngsters.

Reserves Eastern half of South Africa: virtually every game reserve in KwaZulu-Natal, Limpopo, Mpumalanga and North West Province, as well as along the coast from Mossel Bay to northern KwaZulu-Natal.

Habitat Will forage in grasslands, but rarely far from woodland; particularly along river courses; arboreal and terrestrial.

Daily rhythm Diurnal.

Social life Troops.

DOG RELATIVES AND ALLIED SPECIES

AARDWOLF *PROTELES CRISTATUS*

The hyena-like aardwolf is far smaller than the spotted hyena and far lighter, as well as being less shaggy, with vertical dark stripes along its tawny body. It is further distinguished from other hyenas by its insectivorous diet and its particular preference for harvester termites, which it laps up en masse (up to 200,000 in one night) with its broad sticky tongue. Far more widely distributed in South Africa than hyenas, but shy and not often seen.

Reserves Addo, Bontebok, iSimangaliso Wetland, Kruger and Pilanesberg.

Habitat Most habitats, except dense forest.

Daily rhythm Nocturnal; sometimes active in the cooler hours just before dusk or after dawn.

Social life Solitary.

BAT-EARED FOX *OTOCYON MEGALOTIS*

The bat-eared fox can easily be distinguished from the jackals by its outsized ears, its shorter, pointier muzzle and its considerably smaller size. The bat-eared fox's black Zorro mask helps distinguish it from the similar-sized Cape fox, *Vulpes chama*, which inhabits an overlapping range. Like other dogs, the bat-eared fox is an omnivore, but it favours termites and larvae, which is where its large radar-like ears come in handy. With these it can triangulate the precise position of dung-beetle larvae up to 30cm underground and dig them out.

Reserves Addo, Bontebok, Karoo, Kgalagadi, Kruger, Mountain Zebra and Pilanesberg.

Habitat Open countryside; scrubland; lightly forested areas.

Daily rhythm Nocturnal and diurnal.

Social life Family groups of 2–6.

BLACK-BACKED JACKAL *CANIS MESOMELAS*

The member of the dog family you're most likely to see is the black-backed jackal, found especially in the country's reserves. It bears a strong resemblance to a small, skinny German Shepherd, but with a muzzle more like that of a fox, and is distinguished from the grey, side-striped jackal (see below) by the white-flecked black saddle on its back, to which it owes its name. Jackals are omnivorous scavenger-hunters, who get most of their food from catching small creatures such as insects, lizards, snakes or birds, but will also tackle baby antelope and larger birds, and they are cheeky enough to steal pieces of prey from under the noses of lions or hyenas at a kill.

Reserves Addo, Hluhluwe-iMfolozi, Karoo, Kgalagadi, Kruger, Mkhuze, Mountain Zebra, Pilanesberg.

Habitat Broad range, from moist mountain regions to desert; avoids dense woodland.

Daily rhythm Normally nocturnal, but diurnal in safety of game reserves.

Social life Mostly monogamous pairs, but also seen singly and in small family groups.

SIDE-STRIPED JACKAL *CANIS ADJUSTUS*

Like its black-backed relative, the side-striped jackal is omnivorous, with a diet that takes in carrion, small animals, reptiles, birds and insects, as well as wild fruit and berries. The fact that the black-backed jackal seeks a drier habitat, in contrast to the side-striped's preference for well-watered woodland, is an identification pointer.

Reserves iSimangaliso Wetland, Kruger.

Habitat Well-watered woodland.

Daily rhythm Mainly nocturnal.

Social life Solitary or pairs.

SPOTTED HYENA *CROCUTA CROCUTA*

The largest carnivores after lions are hyenas, and apart from the lion, the spotted hyena is the meat-eater you will see most often. Although considered a scavenger *par excellence*, the spotted hyena is a formidable hunter, most often found where antelope and zebra are present. Exceptionally efficient consumers, with immensely strong teeth and jaws, spotted hyenas eat virtually every part of their prey, including bones and hide, and, where accustomed to humans, often steal shoes, unwashed pans and refuse from tents. They are most active at night, when they issue their unnerving whooping cries. Clans of twenty or so are dominated by females, who are larger than the males and compete with each other for rank.

Reserves Addo, Hluhluwe-iMfolozi, Kgalagadi and Kruger.

Habitat Wide variety of habitat apart from dense forest.

Daily rhythm Generally nocturnal from dusk, but diurnal in many parks.

Social life Highly social, usually living in extended family groups.

WILD DOG *LYCAON PICTUS*

Once the widely distributed hunters of the African plains, wild dogs have been brought to the edge of extinction. The world's second-most threatened dog relative, the South African population consists of just five hundred individuals, half of which are in the Kruger National Park. For many years they were shot on sight, having gained an unjustified reputation as cruel and wanton killers of cattle and sheep. More recent scientific evidence reveals them to be economical and efficient hunters – and more successful at it than any other African species. Capable of sustaining high speeds (up to 50km/h) over long distances, wild dogs lunge at their prey en masse, tearing it to pieces – a gruesome finish, but no more grisly than the suffocating muzzle-bite of a lion. The entire pack of ten to fifteen animals participates in looking after the pups, bringing back food and regurgitating it for them.

Reserves Kruger (best place) as well as Hluhluwe-iMfolozi, Madikwe, Marakele, Mkhuze, Pilanesberg and Tswalu.

Habitat Open savanna in the vicinity of grazing herds.

Daily rhythm Diurnal.

Social life Nomadic packs.

CATS

Apart from lions, which notably live in social groups, cats are solitary carnivores. With the exception of the cheetah, which is anatomically distinct from the other cats, the remaining members of the family are so similar, says mammal ecologist Richard Estes, that big cats are just "jumbo versions" of the domestic cat, "distinguished mainly by a modification of the larynx that enables them to roar".

CARACAL *CARACAL CARACAL*

Although classified as a small cat, the caracal is a fairly substantial animal. An unmistakeable and awesome hunter, with great climbing agility, it's able to take prey, such as adult impala and sheep, which far exceed its own weight of 8–18kg. More commonly it will feed on birds, which it pounces on, sometimes while still in flight, as well as smaller mammals, including dassies (see p.40).

Reserves Addo, Karoo, Kgalagadi, Kruger, Mountain Zebra (one of the best places), Table Mountain (Cape of Good Hope).

Habitat Open bush and plains; occasionally arboreal.

Daily rhythm Mainly nocturnal.

Social life Solitary.

CHEETAH *ACINONYX JUBATUS*

In the flesh the cheetah is so different from the leopard that it's hard to see how there could ever be any confusion. Cheetahs are the greyhounds of the big-cat world, with small heads, long legs and an exterior decor of fine spots. Unlike leopards, cheetahs never climb trees, being designed rather for activity on the open plains. Hunting is normally a solitary activity, down to keen eyesight and an incredible burst of speed that can take the animal up to

100km/h for a few seconds. Because they're lighter than lions and less powerful than leopards, cheetahs can't rely on strength to bring down their prey. Instead they resort to tripping or knocking the victim off balance by striking its hindquarters, and then pouncing.

Reserves Addo, Hluhluwe-iMfolozi, Kgalagadi, Kruger and Mountain Zebra.

Habitat Savanna in the vicinity of plains game.

Daily rhythm Diurnal.

Social life Solitary or temporary nuclear family groups.

LEOPARD *PANTHERA PARDUS*

The lion may be king, but most successful and arguably most beautiful of the large cats is the leopard, which survives from the southern coastal strip of Africa all the way to China. Highly adaptable, they can subsist in extremes of aridity or cold, as well as in proximity to human habitation, where they happily prey on domestic animals – which accounts for their absence in the sheep-farming regions of central South Africa, due to extermination by farmers. Powerfully built, they can bring down prey twice their weight and drag an impala (see p.34) their own weight up a tree. The chase is not part of the leopard's tactical repertoire; they hunt by stealth, getting to within 2m of their target before pouncing.

1 SERVAL; 2 LION; 3 CARACAL; 4 LEOPARD; 5 CHEETAH >

Reserves Kruger, Hluhluwe-iMfolozi, Kruger, Marakele and Pilanesberg; best places are the private reserves in Sabi Sands, abutting Kruger, which trade on their leopards being highly accustomed to humans; also present in rugged, mountainous southern Western Cape, but secretive and rarely seen.

Habitat Highly adaptable; frequently arboreal.

Daily rhythm Nocturnal; also cooler daylight hours.

Social life Solitary.

LION *PANTHERA LEO*

The most compelling and largest of the cats for most safari-goers are lions, the largest predators in Africa. It's fortunate then that, despite having the most limited distribution of any cat in South Africa, lions are the ones you're most likely to see. Lazy, gregarious and sizeable, lions rarely attempt to hide, making them relatively easy to find, especially if someone else has already found them – a gathering of stationary vehicles frequently signals lions. Their fabled reputation as cold, efficient hunters is ill-founded, as lions are only successful around thirty percent of the time, and only if operating as a group. Males don't hunt at all if they can help it and will happily enjoy a free lunch courtesy of the females of the pride.

Reserves Healthy populations in Kgalagadi and Kruger; limited numbers in Addo, Hluhluwe-iMfolozi, Mapungubwe, Marakele and Pilanesberg.

Habitat Wherever there's water and shade except thick forest.

Daily rhythm Diurnal and nocturnal.

Social life Prides of three to forty, more usually around twelve.

SERVAL *FELIS SERVAL*

Long legged and spotted, servals bear some resemblance to, but are far smaller than, cheetahs and are more rarely seen. Efficient hunters, servals use their large rounded ears to pinpoint prey (usually small rodents, birds or reptiles), which they pounce on with both front paws after performing impressive athletic leaps.

Reserves Hluhluwe-iMfolozi, Ithala, Kruger, Pilanesberg, uKhahlamba-Drakensberg.

Habitat Reed beds or tall grasslands near water.

Daily rhythm Normally nocturnal, but can be seen during daylight hours.

Social life Usually solitary.

SMALLER CARNIVORES

CIVET *CIVETTICTIS CIVETTA*

The civet (or African civet) is a stocky animal resembling a large, terrestrial genet. Civets were formerly kept in captivity for their musk (once an ingredient in perfume), which is secreted from glands near the tail. Civets aren't often seen, but they're predictable creatures, wending their way along the same path at the same time, night after night. Civets are omnivores that will scavenge for carrion and feed on small rodents, birds, reptiles and even fruit. Found in Northern South Africa, Mpumalanga and extreme north of KwaZulu-Natal.

Reserves Kruger and Pilanesberg.

Habitat Open, especially riverine, woodland.

Daily rhythm Nocturnal.

Social life Solitary.

HONEY BADGER *MELLIVORA CAPENSIS*

The unusual honey badger, related to the European badger, has a reputation for defending itself extremely fiercely. Primarily an omnivorous forager, it will tear open bees' nests (to which it is led by a small bird, the honey guide), its thick, loose hide rendering it impervious to stings.

Reserves Addo, Hluhluwe-iMfolozi, Karoo, Kgalagadi, Kruger and Pilanesberg.

Habitat Wide range except forest.

Daily rhythm Mainly nocturnal.

Social life Solitary, sometimes pairs.

SMALL-SPOTTED GENET *GENETTA GENETTA*

Small-spotted genets are reminiscent of slender elongated cats, and were once domesticated around the Mediterranean (but cats turned out to be better mouse hunters). In fact, they are viverrids, related to mongooses, and are frequently seen after dark around national-park lodges, where some live a semi-domesticated existence. They're difficult to distinguish from the less widely distributed, large-spotted genet, *Genetta tigrina*, which has bigger spots and a black (instead of white) tip to its tail.

Reserves Addo, Bontebok, Karoo, Kgalagadi, Kruger, Mountain Zebra, Pilanesberg, Table Mountain (Cape of Good Hope).

Habitat Wide range: light bush country, even arid areas; partly arboreal.

Daily rhythm Nocturnal. But becomes active at dusk.

Social life Solitary.

WATER MONGOOSE *ATILAX PALUDINOSUS*

Most species of mongoose, of which there are nearly a dozen in South Africa, are also tolerant of humans and, even when disturbed, can usually be observed for some time. If you keep your eyes peeled when driving on the open road, you'll often see mongooses darting across your path. Social arrangements differ from species to species, some being solitary while others live in packs. The water mongoose, one of the most widely distributed of the

mongooses, resembles an otter, but is a lot smaller and lighter. Foragers, they'll root for anything edible – mostly crabs and amphibians, but also invertebrates, eggs, lizards and small rodents. Water mongooses are found in a deep swathe across Southern Africa, sweeping down from Mpumalanga in the northeast to the Cape Peninsula in the southwest.

Reserves Bontebok, Hluhluwe-iMfolozi, Karoo, Kruger, Mkhuze, Table Mountain (Cape of Good Hope).
Habitat Well-watered areas, such as alongside streams, rivers and lakes.
Daily rhythm Mainly nocturnal, but also active at dusk and dawn.
Social life Solitary.

ANTELOPE

South Africa has roughly a third of all antelope species in Africa, and antelope are the most frequently seen family of animals in the country's game reserves. You'll even spot some on farmland along the extensive open stretches that separate interior towns. South African antelope are subdivided into a number of tribes, and like buffalo, giraffe and domestic cattle, they are ruminants – animals that have four stomachs and chew the cud.

BLACK WILDEBEEST *CONNOCHAETES GNOU*
Black wildebeest were brought to the edge of extinction in the nineteenth century and now number around three thousand in South Africa, though you will find them in a handful of parks in the country. You can tell them apart from their blue relatives by their darker colour (brown rather than the black suggested by their name) and long white tail. Black Wildebeest (1–1.2m high at the shoulder; 160–180kg) are also significantly shorter and lighter than their blue cousins (1.7m; 380kg). Black wildebeest appear to be under threat again, this time not from hunting, but hybridization, since black and blue wildebeest can interbreed and produce fertile offspring. Conservationists fear that the rarer black species will be bred out of existence. The problem is taken so seriously by KwaZulu-Natal wildlife authorities that no park in the province is stocked with both species.
Reserves Karoo, Mountain Zebra and uKhahlamba-Drakensberg.
Habitat Low scrub and open grassland.
Daily rhythm Diurnal.
Social life Cows and offspring wander freely through bull territories; during rutting bulls try to keep females within their territory.

BLUE DUIKER *PHILANTOMBA MONTICOLA*
The smallest South African antelope, the blue duiker weighs in at around 4kg, has an arched back and stands 35cm at the shoulder (roughly the height of a domestic cat). Pairs stick together and remain vigilant as a defence against predators, which can include leopards, baboons and even large birds of prey. Duiker are found in the forested areas of the coastal strip from George in the Western Cape to northern KwaZulu-Natal, but are extremely shy and seldom seen.
Reserves Garden Route (Knysna), iSimangaliso Wetland and Ndumo.
Habitat Forests and dense bushland.
Daily rhythm Mainly diurnal.
Social life Monogamous couples.

BLUE WILDEBEEST *CONNOCHAETES TAURINUS*
All wildebeest are sociable but the exemplar of this is the blue wildebeest (sometimes known as the brindled gnu), which, in East Africa, gather in hundreds of thousands for their annual migration. You won't see these numbers in South Africa, but you'll see smaller herds. Blue wildebeest are often seen in association with zebra.
Reserves Hluhluwe-iMfolozi, Ithala, Kgalagadi, Kruger, Mapungubwe and Mkhuze.
Habitat Grasslands.
Daily rhythm Diurnal, occasionally nocturnal.
Social life Intensely gregarious in a wide variety of associations from small groups to sizeable herds.

BONTEBOK *DAMALISCUS DORCAS DORCAS*
Better-looking version of the tsessebe, from which it's distinguished by its chocolate-brown colouring and white facial and rump markings. Bontebok, which were historically limited to a small range in the southern Cape, teetered on the edge of extinction, but their survival is now secured on several reserves and farms. A subspecies, the blesbok, *Damaliscus dorcas phillipsi*, is found in the Free State and northern Eastern Cape.
Reserves Bontebok, De Hoop, Table Mountain (Cape of Good Hope), West Coast.
Habitat Coastal plain where Cape *fynbos* occurs.
Daily rhythm Diurnal.
Social life Rams hold territories; ewes and lamb herds numbering up to ten wander freely between territories.

BUSHBUCK *TRAGELAPHUS SCRIPTUS*
Despite a distinct family resemblance, you could never confuse a kudu with a bushbuck, which is considerably shorter and, in the males, has a single twist to its horns, in contrast to the kudu's two or three turns. They also differ in being the only solitary members of the tribe, one reason you're less likely to spot them. Often seen in thickets or heard crashing through them. Not to be confused with the larger nyala.

1 BUSHBUCK; 2 NYALA; 3 ELAND >

Reserves Addo, Garden Route (Wilderness and Knysna), iSimangaliso Wetland, Kruger, Mapungubwe, Pilanesberg; also most reserves (even minor ones) in KwaZulu-Natal.

Habitat Thick bush and woodland near water.

Daily rhythm Mainly nocturnal, but also active during the day when cool.

Social life Solitary, but casually sociable; sometimes grazes in small groups.

COMMON (OR GREY) DUIKER *SYLVICAPRA GRIMMIA*

Of the duikers, the one you're most likely to see is the common duiker (sometimes called the grey duiker, reflecting its colouring), which occurs all over South Africa and is among the antelopes most tolerant of human habitation. When under threat it freezes in the undergrowth, but if chased will dart off in an erratic zigzagging run designed to throw pursuers off balance. The common duiker has a characteristic rounded back, is about 50cm high at the shoulder, and rams have short, straight horns.

Reserves Addo, Bontebok, Hluhluwe-iMfolozi, Ithala, Karoo, Kruger, Mkhuze, Mountain Zebra, Pilanesberg and Table Mountain (Cape of Good Hope).

Habitat Adaptable; prefers scrub and bush.

Daily rhythm Nocturnal and diurnal.

Social life Mostly solitary, but sometimes in pairs.

ELAND *TAUROTRAGUS ORYX*

Eland, the largest living antelope, is built like an ox and moves with the slow deliberation of one, though it's also a superb jumper. Once widely distributed, herds now survive only in pockets of northeast South Africa and protected areas of the Drakensberg in KwaZulu-Natal; also small introduced populations in numerous other reserves.

Reserves Addo, Ithala, Karoo, Kgalagadi, Kruger, Marakele, Mountain Zebra, Pilanesberg and Table Mountain (Cape of Good Hope).

Habitat Highly adaptable; semi-desert to mountains, but prefers scrubby plains.

Daily rhythm Nocturnal and diurnal.

Social life Non-territorial herds of up to sixty.

GEMSBOK (OR ORYX) *ORYX GAZELLA*

If you encounter a herd of these highly gregarious grazers, you should be left in no doubt as to what they are. Gemsbok are highly adapted for survival in the arid country they inhabit, able to go for long periods without water, relying instead on melons and vegetation for moisture. They tolerate temperatures above 40°C by raising their normal body temperature of 35°C above that of the surrounding air, losing heat by conduction and radiation; their brains are kept cool by a supply of blood from their noses.

Reserves Addo, Augrabies, Karoo, Kgalagadi, Mokala, Pilanesberg and Tankwa Karoo.

Habitat Open grasslands; waterless wastelands; tolerant of prolonged drought.

Daily rhythm Nocturnal and diurnal.

Social life Highly hierarchical mixed herds of up to fifteen, led by a dominant male.

IMPALA *AEPYCEROS MELAMPUS*

Larger and heavier than springbok, which they superficially resemble, impala are elegant and athletic. Prodigious jumpers, they have been recorded leaping distances of 11m and heights of 3m. Only the males carry the distinctive lyre-shaped pair of horns. They are so common in the reserves of the northeast and of KwaZulu-Natal that some jaded rangers look on them as the goats of the savanna – a perception that carries more than a germ of truth, as these flexible feeders are both browsers and grazers.

Reserves Hluhluwe-iMfolozi, Ithala, Kruger, Mapungubwe, Marakele, Mkhuze and Pilanesberg.

Habitat Open savanna, near light woodland cover.

Daily rhythm Diurnal.

Social life Large herds of females overlap with several male territories; during the rut (first five months of the year) dominant males will cut out harem herds of around twenty and expend considerable amounts of effort driving off any potential rivals.

KLIPSPRINGER *OREOTRAGUS OREOTRAGUS*

Another dwarf antelope (about 60cm at the shoulder) you might see is the stocky klipspringer, whose Afrikaans name (meaning "rock hopper") reflects its goat-like adaptation to living on *koppies* and cliffs – the only antelope to do so, making it unmistakable. It's also the only one to walk on the tips of its hooves. They occur sporadically throughout South Africa where there are rocky outcrops.

Reserves Addo, Augrabies, Garden Route (Tsitsikamma), Karoo, Kruger, Mapungubwe, Mkhuze, Mountain Zebra, Pilanesberg and Table Mountain (Cape of Good Hope).

Habitat Rocky terrain.

Daily rhythm Diurnal; most active in morning and late afternoon.

Social life Monogamous pairs or small family groups.

KUDU *TRAGELAPHUS STREPSICEROS*

The magnificent kudu is more elegantly built than the eland, and males are adorned with sensational spiralled horns that can reach well over 1.5m in length. Known for their athleticism, kudu can vault over a 2m fence with no difficulty.

Reserves Northern Limpopo and North West Province reserves, and those in Mpumalanga and northeastern KwaZulu-Natal; Addo, Ithala, Hluhluwe-iMfolozi, Karoo,

1 BLUE WILDEBEEST; 2 TSESSEBE; 3 BLACK WILDEBEEST; 4 SABLE; 5 ROAN >

Kgalagadi, Kruger, Marakele, Mountain Zebra and Pilanesberg.

Habitat Semi-arid, hilly or undulating bush country; tolerant of drought.

Daily rhythm Diurnal when secure, otherwise nocturnal.

Social life Males usually solitary or in small transient groups; females in small groups with young.

NYALA *TRAGELAPHUS ANGASII*

Nyalas are midway in size between the kudu and bushbuck, with which they could be confused at first glance. Telling pointers are their size, the sharp vertical white stripes on the side of the nyala (up to fourteen on the male, eighteen on the female), orange legs, and, in the males, a short stiff mane from neck to shoulder. Females tend to group with their two last offspring and gather with other females in small herds, rarely exceeding ten. Males become more solitary the older they get.

Reserves Kruger and around three dozen reserves in KwaZulu-Natal, of which Hluhluwe-Imfolozi, Mkhuze and Ndumo have the largest populations.

Habitat Dense woodland near water.

Daily rhythm Mainly nocturnal with some diurnal activity.

Social life Non-territorial; basic unit is female and two offspring.

ROAN *HIPPOTRAGUS EQUINUS*

The roan looks very similar to but is larger than a sable (it's Africa's second-largest antelope), with less impressive horns and lighter colouring. You're more likely to see them in open savanna than sables.

Reserves Kruger NP.

Habitat Tall grassland near water.

Daily rhythm Nocturnal and diurnal; peak afternoon feeding.

Social life Small herds led by dominant bull; herds of immature males; sometimes pairs in season.

SABLE *HIPPOTRAGUS NIGER*

The magnificent sable has a sleek, black upper body set in sharp counterpoint to its white underparts and facial markings, as well as its massive backwardly curving horns, making it the thoroughbred of the ruminants, particularly when galloping majestically across the savanna.

Reserves Kruger and Marakele.

Habitat Open woodland with medium to tall grass near water.

Daily rhythm Nocturnal and diurnal.

Social life Highly hierarchical female herds of up to three dozen; territorial bulls divide into sub-territories, through which cows roam.

SPRINGBOK *ANTIDORCAS MARSUPIALIS*

Springboks are South Africa's national animal. Their characteristic horns and dark horizontal patch on their sides, separating their reddish tawny upper body from their white underparts, are definitive identifiers. Springbok are recorded as having reached nearly 90km/h and are noted for "pronking", a movement in which they arch their backs and straighten their legs as they leap into the air. Indigenous to the (often arid) northern reaches of South Africa, where they were once seen in their hundreds, they are now more widespread in reserves and on farms where they are raised for their venison and hides.

Reserves Addo, Augrabies, Chelmsford NR (biggest population in KZN), Golden Gate, Karoo, Kgalagadi, Mountain Zebra, Pilanesberg, Tankwa Karoo and West Coast.

Habitat Wide range of open country, from deserts to wetter savanna.

Daily rhythm Seasonally variable, but usually cooler times of day.

Social life Highly gregarious, sometimes in huge herds of hundreds or even thousands; various herding combinations of males, females and young.

TSESSEBE *DAMALISCUS LUNATUS*

Somewhat ungainly in appearance because, according to legend, it arrived late when the Creator was dishing out the goodies, the tsessebe turns out to be a thoroughbred when it comes to speed. One of the fastest antelope on the African plains, a fleeing tsessebe can reach 70km/h. Males often stand sentry on termite hills, marking territory against rivals (rather than defending it against predators). Tricky customers, tsessebe bulls will sometimes falsely give an alarm signal to deter females from wandering out of their territory.

Reserves Restricted to northern extremities of South Africa; best place is Kruger NP; also present in Ithala, Marakele and Pilanesberg.

Habitat Savanna woodland.

Daily rhythm Diurnal.

Social life Females and young form permanent herds usually of about half a dozen, but up to thirty individuals with a territorial bull.

WATERBUCK *KOBUS ELLIPSIPRYMNUS*

Waterbuck are largest of the near-aquatic Kob tribe, which live close to water. They are sturdy animals – 1.3m at the shoulder, and a distinctive white horseshoe marking on their rump. Only the males have horns. Unable to reach or sustain significant speed, they rely on cover to evade predators. It is also claimed that the oily, musky secretion and powerful odour waterbuck emit from their hair is distasteful to predators and acts as a deterrent. They are common and rather tame where they occur, predominantly in KwaZulu-Natal, Limpopo and Mpumalanga.

Reserves Hluhluwe-iMfolozi, iSimangaliso Wetland, Ithala, Kruger, Mapungubwe, Marakele and Mkhuze.
Habitat Open woodland and savanna, near permanent water.

Daily rhythm Nocturnal and diurnal.
Social life Sociable animals, they usually gather in small herds of up to ten, and occasionally up to thirty.

OTHER HOOFED RUMINANTS

Alongside cattle, sheep, goats and antelope, buffalo and giraffe are also hoofed ruminants. Bacteria in their digestive systems process plant matter into carbohydrates, while the dead bacteria are absorbed as protein – a highly efficient arrangement that makes them economical consumers, far more so than non-ruminants such as elephants, which pass vast quantities of what they eat as unutilized fibre. Species that concentrate on grasses are grazers; those eating leaves are browsers.

BUFFALO *SYNCERUS CAFFER*
You won't have to be in the Kruger or most of the other reserves in South Africa for long to see buffalo, a common safari animal that, as one of the Big Five, appears on every hunter's shopping list. Don't let their resemblance to domestic cattle or water buffalo (to which they are not at all closely related) or their apparent docility lull you into complacency; lone bulls, in particular, are noted and feared even by hardened hunters as dangerous and relentless killers. Herds consist of clans and you'll be able to spot distinct units within the group: at rest, clan members often cuddle up close to each other. There are separate pecking orders among females and males, the latter being forced to leave the herd during adolescence (at about three years) or once they're over the hill, to form bachelor herds, which you can recognize by their small numbers. To distinguish males from females, look for their heavier horns bisected by a distinct boss, or furrow. Once found throughout South Africa, natural populations survive in the Eastern Cape, KwaZulu-Natal and Mpumalanga and have been widely reintroduced elsewhere.
Reserves Addo, Hluhluwe-iMfolozi, iSimangaliso Wetland, Karoo, Kruger and Mountain Zebra.
Habitat Wide range of habitats, always near water.
Daily rhythm Nocturnal and diurnal, but inactive during heat of the day.

Social life Buffalo are non-territorial and gather in large herds of hundreds or even sometimes thousands. Herds under one or more dominant bulls consist of clans of a dozen or so related females under a leading cow.

GIRAFFE *GIRAFFA CAMELOPARDALIS*
Giraffe are among the easiest animals to spot because their long necks make them visible above the low scrub. The tallest mammals on earth, they spend their daylight hours browsing on the leaves of trees too high up for other species; combretum and acacias are favourites. Their highly flexible lips and prehensile tongues give them almost hand-like agility and enable them to select the most nutritious leaves while avoiding deadly-sharp acacia thorns. At night they lie down and spend the evening ruminating. If you encounter a bachelor herd, look out for young males testing their strength with neck wrestling. When the female comes into oestrus, which can happen at any time of year, the dominant male mates with her. She will give birth after a fourteen-month gestation. Over half of all young, however, fall prey to lions or hyenas in their early years.
Reserves Hluhluwe-iMfolozi, Ithala, Kgalagadi, Kruger, Mapungubwe, Mkhuze and Pilanesberg.
Habitat Wooded savanna and thorn country.
Daily rhythm Diurnal.
Social life Loose, non-territorial, leaderless herds.

NON-RUMINANTS

Non-ruminating mammals have more primitive digestive systems than animals that chew the cud. Although both have bacteria in their gut that convert vegetable matter into carbohydrates, the less efficient system of the non-ruminants means they have to consume more raw material and process it faster. The upside is they can handle food that's far more fibrous.

AFRICAN ELEPHANT *LOXODONTA AFRICANA*
Elephants were once found throughout South Africa. Now you'll only see them in a handful of reserves. When encountered in the flesh, elephants seem even bigger than you would imagine. You'll need little persuasion from those flapping warning ears to back off if you're too close, but they are at the same time amazingly graceful. In a matter of moments a large herd can merge into the trees and disappear, silent on their padded, carefully placed feet, their presence betrayed only by the noisy cracking of branches as they strip trees and uproot saplings. Elephants are the most engaging of animals to watch, perhaps because their interactions, behaviour patterns and personality have so many human parallels. Like people,

1 GIRAFFE; 2 BUFFALO >

they lead complex, interdependent social lives, growing from helpless infancy through self-conscious adolescence to adulthood. Babies are born with other cows in close attendance, after a 22-month gestation. Calves suckle for two to three years. Basic family units are composed of a group of related females, tightly protecting their young and led by a venerable matriarch. Bush mythology has it that elephants become ashamed after killing a human, covering the body with sticks and grass. They certainly pay much attention to the disposal of their own dead relatives, often dispersing the bones and spending time near the remains. Old animals die in their 70s or 80s, when their last set of teeth wears out so that they are no longer able to feed themselves.

Reserves Addo (the only population to survive naturally in the southern two-thirds of the country), Hluhluwe-iMfolozi, Ithala, Kruger, Mkhuze, Pilanesberg and Tembe.

Habitat Wide range of habitats, wherever there are trees or water.

Daily rhythm Nocturnal and diurnal; sleeps as little as four hours a day.

Social life Highly complex; cows and offspring in herds headed by matriarch; bulls solitary or in bachelor herds.

ROCK DASSIE (OR HYRAX) *PROCAVIA CAPENSIS*
Dassies look like they ought to be rodents but, amazingly, despite being fluffy and rabbit-sized, their closest relatives (admittedly from some way back) are elephants. Their name (pronounced like "dusty" without the "t") is the Afrikaans version of *dasje*, meaning "little badger", given to them by the first Dutch settlers. Like reptiles, hyraxes have poor body control systems and rely on shelter against both the cold and hot sunlight. They wake up sluggish and seek out rocks to catch the early morning sun – this is one of the best times to look out for them. One adult stands sentry against predators and issues a low-pitched warning cry in response to a threat. Dassies are found throughout South Africa and are frequently sighted.

Reserves Bontebok, Garden Route (Tsitsikamma), Karoo, Kruger, Mountain Zebra, Pilanesberg, Table Mountain (Cape of Good Hope), uKhahlamba-Drakensberg.

Habitat Rocky areas, from mountains to isolated outcrops and coastal cliffs.

Daily rhythm Diurnal.

Social life Colonies of a dominant male and eight or more related females and their offspring.

RHINOS AND HIPPOS

"Hook-lipped" and "square-lipped" are technically more accurate terms for the two species of rhino. "Black" and "white" are based on a linguistic misunderstanding – somewhere along the line, the German *"weid"*, which refers to the square-lipped's wide mouth, was misheard as "white". The term has stuck, despite both rhinos being a greyish muddy colour. The shape of their lips is highly significant as it indicates their respective diets and consequently their favoured habitat. Rhinos give birth to a single calf after a gestation period of fifteen to eighteen months, and the baby is not weaned until it is at least a year old, sometimes two. Their population grows slowly compared with most animals, another factor contributing to their predicament.

BLACK RHINO *DICEROS BICORNIS*
The cantankerous, far rarer and smaller black rhino has the narrow prehensile lips of a browser, suited to picking leaves off trees and bushes. A solitary animal, it relies on the camouflage of dense thickets, which is why they are so much more difficult to see. South Africa's two thousand individuals make up forty percent of Africa's remaining black rhinos.

Reserves Addo, Augrabies, Hluhluwe-iMfolozi, iSimangaliso Wetland, Ithala, Karoo, Kruger, Marakele, Mkhuze and Pilanesberg.

Habitat Thick bush.

Daily rhythm Active day and night, resting between periods of activity.

Social life Solitary.

WHITE RHINO *CERATOTHERIUM SIMUM*
Twice as heavy as its black counterpart, the white rhino is also aggressive. Diet and habitat account for the greater sociability of the white rhino, which relies on safety in numbers under the exposure of open grassland, while its wide, flatter mouth is well suited to chomping away at grasses like a lawnmower. By the end of the nineteenth century, the only place white rhinos survived was the Hluhluwe-iMfolozi reserve (where they still thrive), but they have since been introduced to a number of reserves.

Reserves Hluhluwe-iMfolozi, Ithala, Kruger, Marakele, Mkhuze, Ndumo, Pilanesberg and Tembe.

Habitat Savanna.

Daily rhythm Active day and night, resting between periods of activity.

Social life Mother/s and calves, or small same-sex herds of immature animals; old males solitary.

HIPPOPOTAMUS *HIPPOPOTAMUS AMPHIBIUS*
Hippos are highly adaptable animals that once inhabited South African waterways from the Limpopo in the north to the marshes of the Cape Peninsula in the south. Today they're far more restricted. You'll see them elsewhere, in

1 ROCK HYRAX; 2 AFRICAN ELEPHANT >

RHINOS: LAST CHANCE TO SEE?

Two species of **rhinoceros** are found in Africa: the hook-lipped or black rhino and the much heavier square-lipped or white rhino. Both have come close to extinction and have all but disappeared in the African wild. South Africa has the biggest populations in Africa by far, with more than 18,000 white and roughly 2000 black rhinos, making it the best place on earth to view these ancient mammals.

Sadly, **rhino poaching** in South Africa is escalating annually, with over a thousand animals falling to poachers every year from 2013 onwards (up from thirteen in 2007). The main market for rhino horn is in Asia, where it is used as an ingredient in traditional medicine. Here, a single 3kg horn can fetch up to US$300,000, making it more expensive per kilo than gold. So lucrative is the trade that sophisticated criminal syndicates have moved in, using helicopters and night-vision equipment to slaughter the mammals under cover of night.

Efforts are being made to protect the rhinos – 2016 saw the arrest of over 650 poachers, who also have to risk shoot-outs with anti-poaching units – but this is insufficient to save the animals, who are now being killed faster than they can reproduce. Tactics such as removing the rhinos' horns have proved unsuccessful, because even the remaining stumps are still hugely valuable, and some conservationists argue that more resources need to be thrown at the problem. Ongoing conservation programmes include moving one hundred rhinos across South Africa's border into Botswana, whose vast and remote wildernesses, it is hoped, will prove inaccessible to poachers. Indeed, there is reason to be positive about such projects – since its creation 25 years ago, Botswana's Khama Rhino Sanctuary has relocated sixteen rhinos to different parts of the country from a foundation population of four animals, thanks to protection from anti-poaching units and the military. In South Africa, the increase in poacher arrests has brought down rhino-poaching figures from a peak of over 1200 in 2014.

places where they've been reintroduced. Hippos need fresh water deep enough to submerge themselves, with a surrounding of suitable grazing grass. By day, they need to spend most of their time in water to protect their thin, hairless skin. After dark, hippos leave the water to spend the whole night grazing, often walking up to 10km in one session. Their grunting and jostling in the water may give the impression of loveable buffoons, but throughout Africa they are feared, and rightly so, as they are reckoned to be responsible for more human deaths on the continent than any other animal. When disturbed, lone bulls and cows with calves can become extremely aggressive. Their fearsomely long incisors can slash through a canoe with ease; on land they can charge at speeds up to 30km/h, with a tight turning circle.

Reserves Addo, iSimangaliso Wetland, Kruger and Pilanesberg.

Habitat Slow-flowing rivers, dams and lakes.

Daily rhythm Principally nocturnal, leaving the water to graze at night.

Social life Bulls solitary; others live in family groups known as pods, headed by a matriarch.

ZEBRAS

Zebras are closely related to horses and, together with them, donkeys and wild asses, form the equidae family. Of the three species of zebra, two live in South Africa. Zebras congregate in family herds of a breeding stallion and two mares (or more) and their foals. Unattached males will often form bachelor herds. Among plains zebras, offspring leave the family group after between one and two years, while mountain zebras are far more tolerant in allowing adolescents to remain in the family.

BURCHELL'S ZEBRA *EQUUS QUAGGA*

A highly successful herbivore that can survive in a variety of grassland habitats, which accounts for its geographical range, the Burchell's or plains zebra has small ears and thick, black stripes, with lighter "shadows".

Reserves Addo, Hluhluwe-iMfolozi, iSimangaliso Wetland, Ithala, Kruger, Mapungubwe, Mkhuze, Pilanesberg.

Habitat Savanna, with or without trees.

Daily rhythm Active day and night, resting intermittently.

Social life Harems of several mares and foals, led by a dominant stallion, usually group together in large herds; harems highly stable and harem mares typically remain with the same male for life.

CAPE MOUNTAIN ZEBRA *EQUUS ZEBRA ZEBRA*

The Cape mountain zebra only narrowly escaped extinction, but now survives in healthy if limited numbers in several reserves in the southern half of South Africa, wherever there is suitably mountainous terrain. Characteristics that

distinguish the two zebras are the dewlap on the mountain zebra's lower neck, its absence of shadow stripes, its larger ears, and stripes that go all the way down to its hooves – the Burchell's stripes fade out as they progress down its legs.
Reserves Bontebok, De Hoop, Karoo, Mountain Zebra, Table Mountain (Cape of Good Hope) and Tankwa Karoo.

Habitat Mountainous areas and their immediate surrounds.
Daily rhythm Active by day.
Social life Harems of stallions with four or five mares and their foals.

OTHER MAMMALS

AARDVARK *ORYCTEROPUS AFER*
One of Africa's – indeed the world's – strangest animals, a solitary mammal weighing up to 70kg. Its name, Afrikaans for "earth pig", is an apt description, as it holes up during the day in large burrows that are excavated with remarkable speed and energy. It emerges at night to visit termite mounds within a radius of up to 5km, digging for its main diet. It's most likely to be common in bush country that's well scattered with termite mounds. Found throughout South Africa, but rarely seen.
Reserves Addo, Hluhluwe-iMfolozi, Karoo, Kgalagadi, Kruger, Mapungubwe and Mountain Zebra.
Habitat Open or wooded termite country; softer soil preferred.
Daily rhythm Nocturnal.
Social life Solitary.

PANGOLIN *MANIS TEMMINCKII*
Equally unusual – scale-covered mammals, resembling armadillos and feeding on ants and termites. Under attack they roll themselves into a ball. Pangolins occur widely in South Africa, north of the Orange River.
Reserves Kgalagadi and Kruger.
Habitat Wide range apart from desert and forest.
Daily rhythm Nocturnal.
Social life Solitary.

PORCUPINE *HYSTRIX AFRICAEAUSTRALIS*
The most singular and largest (up to 90cm) of the African rodents is the porcupine, which is quite unmistakeable with its coat of many quills. Porcupines are widespread and present in most reserves but, because they're nocturnal, you may only see shed quills. Rarely seen, but common away from croplands, where it is hunted as a pest.

Reserves Virtually all.
Habitat Adaptable to a wide range of habitats.
Daily rhythm Nocturnal; sometimes active at dusk.
Social life Family groups.

SPRINGHARES *PEDETES CAPENSIS*
If you go on a night drive in the Kruger or one of several other reserves in the north of the country, you'd be most unlucky not to see the glinting eyes of springhares which, despite their resemblance to rabbit-sized kangaroos, are in fact true rodents.
Reserves Kgalagadi, Kruger, Mountain Zebra and Pilanesberg.
Habitat Savanna; softer soil areas preferred.
Daily rhythm Nocturnal.
Social life Burrows, usually with a pair and their young; often linked into a network, almost like a colony.

WARTHOG *PHACOCHOERUS AETHIOPICUS*
If you're visiting the Kruger, Pilanesberg or the KwaZulu-Natal parks, families of warthogs will become a familiar sight, trotting across the savanna with their tails erect like communications antennae. Boars join family groups only to mate; they're distinguished from sows by their prominent face warts, which are thought to be defensive pads protecting their heads during often violent fights.
Reserves Addo, Hluhluwe-iMfolozi, iSimangaliso Wetland, Ithala, Kruger, Mkhuze and Pilanesberg.
Habitat Savanna.
Daily rhythm Diurnal.
Social life Family groups usually consist of a mother and her litter of two to four piglets, or occasionally two or three females and their young.

TRAIN CROSSING THE KAAIMANS RIVER

Basics

Getting there

As sub-Saharan Africa's economic and tourism hub, South Africa is well served with flights from London and the rest of Europe. The majority of these touch down at Johannesburg's OR Tambo International, but there are also frequent flights into Cape Town. From North America there are a relatively small number of nonstop flights into Johannesburg.

Airfares depend on the **season**, with the highest prices and greatest demand in July, August, September, December and the first week of January. Prices drop during April (except for around Easter), May and November, while the rest of the year is "shoulder season".

Flights from the UK and Ireland

From London there are nonstop flights with British Airways (🕸 ba.com), South African Airways (SAA, 🕸 flysaa.com) and Virgin Atlantic (🕸 virgin-atlantic .com) to Johannesburg and Cape Town. Flying time from the UK is around eleven hours to Joburg, about an hour longer to Cape Town; to the latter, average high-season scheduled direct fares from London start around £1000. It's generally cheaper to fly to Cape Town via Joburg; you can make major savings by flying via mainland Europe, the Middle East or Asia, and enduring at least one change of plane.

There are no direct flights from the **Republic of Ireland**, but a number of European and Middle Eastern carriers fly to South Africa via their hub airports.

Flights from the US and Canada

From the US there are regular direct **flights** from New York (JFK) and Washington (IAD) operated by South African Airways in partnership with United Airlines (🕸 united.com). Stopping in West Africa to refuel, these take between fifteen and seventeen hours. Most other flights stop off in Europe, the Middle East or Asia and involve a change of plane.

There are no direct flights **from Canada**; you'll have to change planes in the US, Europe or Asia, with journey times that can last over thirty hours.

For flights from New York to Cape Town via Joburg, expect high-season return fares to start around $1200; you will make major savings if you fly via Europe, the Middle East or Asia. High-season return fares from Toronto to Cape Town are similarly priced to those from the US east coast.

Flights from Australia and New Zealand

There are nonstop flights **from Sydney** (which take 14hr) and **Perth** (11hr) to Johannesburg, with onward connections to Cape Town. Flights **from New Zealand** tend to be via Sydney too. South African Airways and Qantas (🕸 qantas.com) fly nonstop to Joburg from Perth and Sydney respectively; several Asian, Middle Eastern and European airlines fly to South Africa via their hub cities, and tend to be less expensive, but their routings often entail long stopovers.

Cape Town is not a cheap destination for travellers from Australia and New Zealand; high-/low-season fares start around Aus$2000/1600 for an indirect return flight **from Sydney** to Cape Town with one change. A flight to Europe with a stopover in South Africa, or even a RTW ticket, may represent better value than a straightforward return. The most affordable return flights tend to travel via Dubai, Doha, Singapore and Kuala Lumpur, with the likes of Qatar Airways and Emirates.

Entry requirements

Nationals of the US, Canada, Australia, New Zealand, Japan, Argentina and Brazil don't require a **visa** to enter South Africa. Most EU nationals don't need a visa, the exceptions being citizens from Bulgaria, Croatia, Estonia, Latvia, Lithuania, Romania, Slovakia and Slovenia, who need to obtain one at a South African diplomatic mission in their home country.

As long as you carry a passport that is valid for at least thirty days from the date of exit from South

---

A BETTER KIND OF TRAVEL

At Rough Guides we are passionately committed to travel. We believe it helps us understand the world we live in and the people we share it with – and of course tourism is vital to many developing economies. But the scale of modern tourism has also damaged some places irreparably, and climate change is accelerated by most forms of transport, especially flying. All Rough Guides' flights are carbon-offset, and every year we donate money to a variety of environmental charities.

Africa, with at least two empty pages, you will be granted a **temporary visitor's permit**, which allows you to stay in South Africa for up to ninety days for most nationals, and thirty days for EU passport holders from Cyprus, Hungary and Poland. All visitors should have proof of a valid return ticket or another form of onward travel; immigration officers rarely ask to see it, but airlines will often check. Likewise, visitors should have a bank statement showing that they have sufficient funds to cover their stay, but, again, officials seldom ask to see it.

Cross-border "visa runs" are not possible, but you can **extend your visitor's visa** for up to ninety days, or apply to stay for longer periods for purposes such as study. Applications should be made through VFS Global (☎012 425 3000, ⓦvfsglobal.com/south africa), which will ask to see paperwork including proof of sufficient funds to cover your stay.

The easiest option is to use a **consultant** such as the immigration division of the International English School (☎021 852 8859, ⓦenglish.za .net/immigration-services) in Somerset West, just outside Cape Town. Their services are recommended, and paying such a consultant's fees is preferable to bureaucratic headaches.

AGENTS AND OPERATORS

Abercrombie & Kent Australia ☎ 1300 851 800, ⓦ abercrombiekent.com.au; UK ☎ 01242 547 760, ⓦ abercrombiekent.co.uk; US ☎ 1800 554 7016, ⓦ abercrombiekent.com. Classy operator whose packages feature Cape Town and luxury rail travel with Rovos Rail.

Absolute Africa UK ☎ 020 8742 0226, ⓦ absoluteafrica.com. Safaris and adventure camping overland trips.

Acacia Africa Australia ☎ 02 8011 3686, UK ☎ 020 7706 4700, South Africa ☎ 021 556 1157, ⓦ acacia-africa.com. Camping and accommodated trips along classic Southern African routes.

Adventures Abroad US ☎ 1 800 665 3998, ⓦ adventures-abroad .com. Small-group and activity tours, including family-friendly trips.

Africa Travel UK ☎ 020 7843 3500, ⓦ africatravel.com. Experienced Africa specialists, offering flights and packages including a thirteen-day Cape Town, Garden Route and Victoria Falls itinerary.

Classic Safari Company Australia ☎ 1300 130 218, ⓦ classicsafari company.com.au. Luxury tailor-made safaris to Southern Africa.

Cox & Kings UK ☎ 020 7873 5000, ⓦ coxandkings.co.uk; US ☎ 323 271 4317, ⓦ coxandkingsusa.com. Stylish operator with classic luxury journeys, including an eleven-day itinerary geared towards families. Also deluxe safaris.

Exodus Travels UK ☎ 0203 553 0654, ⓦ exodus.co.uk; US ☎ 1844 227 9087, ⓦ exodustravels.com. Small-group adventure tour operator with itineraries in and around Cape Town, overland trips taking in Kruger National Park and themed packages including activities such as cycling. Offices worldwide.

Expert Africa New Zealand ☎ 04 976 7585; UK ☎ 020 3405 6666; US ☎ 1 800 242 2434, ⓦ expertafrica.com. Mostly self-drive safari packages, including Addo Elephant National Park and with the option of incorporating flights from the UK.

Explore Worldwide UK ☎ 01252 883 503, ⓦ explore.co.uk; US ☎ 1 800 715 1746, ⓦ exploreworldwide.com. Good range of small-group tours, expeditions and safaris, staying mostly in small hotels and taking in Cape Town and beyond.

Goway Travel US ☎ 1 888 414 0246, ⓦ goway.com. Wide range of packages from two days on the Blue Train to six weeks overland, including eleven days in Cape Town, the Winelands, the Garden Route and a private game reserve.

Joe Walsh Tours Ireland ☎ 01 241 0800, ⓦ joewalshtours.ie. Budget fares as well as hotels, golf packages and holidays from the Western Cape to Kruger. Also has offices in the UK.

Journeys International US ☎ 1 800 255 8735, ⓦ journeys.travel. Small-group trips with a range of safaris.

Journeys Worldwide Australia ☎ 07 3221 4788, ⓦ journeys worldwide.com.au. Small-group tours of Southern Africa.

Kuoni Travel UK ☎ 0800 422 0799, ⓦ kuoni.co.uk. Flexible package itineraries, including tailor-made tours, self-drive holidays and escorted small-group excursions, with a nine-night trip covering the classic sights around Cape Town. Good ideas for families too.

North South Travel UK ☎ 01245 608 291, ⓦ northsouthtravel .co.uk. Discounted fares worldwide. Profits are used to support projects in the developing world, especially the promotion of sustainable tourism.

CHILDREN TRAVELLING TO SOUTH AFRICA

It is important to be aware of the **paperwork requirements** relating to kids aged under eighteen; failure to provide all the documents required has caused families to miss flights.

Children travelling into or out of South Africa will be asked to show an **unabridged (full) birth certificate**, showing both parents' details, in addition to their passport. This is not to be confused with the shorter and equally common abridged birth certificate.

Where only one parent is accompanying a child, parental or legal consent for the child to travel (such as an affidavit from the other parent or a court order) is required. There are other requirements for children travelling unaccompanied or with adults who are not their parents. The Department of Home Affairs has more details at ⓦdha.gov.za, while the British Foreign and Commonwealth Office (ⓦgov.uk/foreign-travel-advice/south-africa/entry-requirements) offers clear guidance and helpful links.

Oasis Overland UK ☎ 01963 530 113, ⓦ oasisoverland.co.uk. One of the smaller overland companies, running a range of good-value trips through Africa.

Okavango Tours and Safaris UK ☎ 07721 387 738, ⓦ okavango .com. Top-notch outfit with on-the-ground knowledge of sub-Saharan Africa, offering fully flexible and individual tours across the country, including the Western Cape and family-focused packages.

On the Go Tours UK ☎ 020 7371 1113; US ☎ 1866 377 6147, ⓦ on thegotours.com. Group and tailor-made tours to South Africa including a two-week overland safari from Cape Town to Namibia. Offices worldwide.

Rainbow Tours UK ☎ 020 3131 2831, ⓦ rainbowtours.co.uk. Knowledgeable Africa specialists whose trips include a sixteen-day Cape Town, Garden Route and Kruger holiday.

Safari Consultants UK ☎ 01787 888 590, ⓦ safari-consultants .co.uk. Company offering individually tailored upmarket holidays across southern and eastern Africa, and specializing in activity-based trips, including walking safaris.

STA Travel UK ☎ 0333 321 0099; US ☎ 1800 781 4040; Australia ☎ 134 782; New Zealand ☎ 0800 474 400; South Africa ☎ 0861 781 781, ⓦ statravel.co.uk. Worldwide specialists in independent travel; also student IDs, travel insurance, car rental and more. Discounts for students and youth travellers.

Trailfinders UK ☎ 0207 368 1200, Ireland ☎ 01 677 7888; ⓦ trailfinders.com. A well-informed and efficient agent for independent travellers, with numerous holiday packages on offer.

Travel Cuts Canada ☎ 1 800 667 2887, ⓦ travelcuts.com. Canadian youth and student travel firm.

Tribes UK ☎ 01473 890 499, ⓦ tribes.co.uk; US ☎ 1800 608 4651. Unusual and off-the-beaten-track sustainable safaris and cultural tours, including Cape Town itineraries.

USIT Ireland ☎ 01 602 1906; ⓦ usit.ie. Ireland's main student and youth travel specialists.

Wilderness Travel US ☎ 1 800 368 2794, ⓦ wildernesstravel .com. Hiking, cultural and wildlife adventures.

Wildlife Worldwide UK ☎ 01962 302 086, ⓦ wildlifeworldwide .com; US ☎ 1800 972 3982. Tailor-made trips for wildlife and wilderness enthusiasts, covering the Cape and the great reserves.

Getting around

Despite the large distances, travelling around most of South Africa is fairly straightforward, with a reasonably well-organized network of public transport, a good range of car rental companies, the best road system in Africa, and the continent's most comprehensive network of internal flights. The only weak point is public transport in urban areas, which is mostly poor and dangerous with the exceptions of Johannesburg's Gautrain and Cape Town's MyCiTi bus and Metrorail Southern Line. Urban South Africans who can afford to do so tend to use private transport, and renting a vehicle is the easiest and safest option (notwithstanding South African drivers). It's virtually impossible to get to the national parks and places off the beaten track by public transport; even if you do manage, you're likely to need a car once you're there.

Buses

South Africa's three established **intercity bus** companies are Greyhound (☎ 083 915 9000, ⓦ greyhound.co.za), Intercape (☎ 021 380 4400, ⓦ intercape.co.za) and Translux (☎ 086 158 9282, ⓦ translux.co.za); between them, they reach most towns in the country. Travel on these buses is safe, reasonable value and comfortable, and the vehicles are invariably equipped with air conditioning and toilets. Keep your valuables close on overnight journeys, when lone women should find a seat at the front near the driver.

Fares vary according to the time of year, with peak fares corresponding approximately to school holidays. As a rough indication, expect to pay the following Greyhound fares for single journeys from Cape Town: Paarl (1hr) from R320; Mossel Bay (7hr) from R430; and Port Elizabeth (12½hr) from R595.

Translux and Greyhound also operate the no-frills budget bus lines City to City (ⓦ www.citytocity.co.za) and Citiliner (ⓦ citiliner.co.za) respectively, which run along a range of routes around the country: check their websites for schedules and prices. You'll also find a host of small private companies running certain routes – your best bet is to enquire at the bus station the day before you travel.

Baz Bus (☎ 0861 229 287, ⓦ bazbus.com) operates an extremely useful hop-on/hop-off bus network aimed at backpackers and budget travellers, with minibuses stopping off at backpacker accommodation en route. Its services run up and down the coast in both directions between Cape Town and Port Elizabeth via the Garden Route (five days weekly), and between Port Elizabeth and Durban via the Wild Coast (four days weekly). Inland, it runs buses between Durban and Johannesburg via the Northern Drakensberg (four days weekly). A number of independently run **shuttle services** connect with the Baz Bus and go to Stellenbosch, Hermanus and Oudtshoorn in the Western Cape; to Hogsback and several Wild Coast backpackers in the Eastern Cape; to the Southern Drakensberg in KwaZulu-Natal; and to Pretoria in Gauteng.

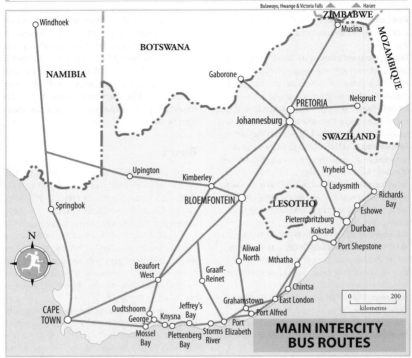

Bulawayo, Hwange & Victoria Falls ▲ ▲ Harare

MAIN INTERCITY BUS ROUTES

The Cape Town–Port Elizabeth fare is R2300 one way, though there are also better-value seven-, fourteen- and 21-day passes costing R2600, R4100 and R5100. Bookings can be made through the website, by email, telephone or SMS (☎ 076 427 3003).

Minibus taxis

Minibus taxis provide transport to the majority of South Africans, travelling everywhere in the country, covering relatively short hops from town to town, commuter trips from township to town and back, and routes within larger towns and cities. However, their associated problems – dangerous drivers and violent feuds between the different taxi associations competing for custom – mean that you should take local advice before using them. This is particularly true in cities, where minibus taxi ranks tend to be a magnet for petty criminals. The other problem with minibus taxis is that there is rarely much room to place **luggage**. Despite the drawbacks, minibus taxis are often the only option for getting around **remote areas**, where you're unlikely to encounter trouble, although it would be inadvisable for lone women. You should be prepared for some long waits in the countryside, due to the taxis' infrequency.

Fares are low and comparable to what you might pay on the inexpensive intercity buses. Try to have the exact change (on shorter journeys particularly), and pass your fare to the row of passengers in front of you; eventually all the fares end up with the conductor, who dishes out any change. It's a good idea to check with locals which taxi routes are safe to use.

Trains

Travelling by **train** is just about the slowest way of getting around South Africa: the trans-Karoo journey from Johannesburg to Cape Town, for example, takes 27 hours – compared with 19 hours by bus. **Overnighting** on the train, though, is more comfortable than the bus and saves you the cost of a night's accommodation. Families with children get a private compartment on the train, and under-3s travel free, while under-9s receive a 20 percent discount.

Shosholoza Meyl (☎ 086 000 8888 or ☎ 011 774 4555, ⓦ shosholozameyl.co.za) runs most of the intercity rail services, offering comfortable and good-value **Tourist Class** travel in lockable two-person coupés and four-person compartments equipped with washbasins. There are showers and a dining car serving passable food and alcoholic drinks. Seats are comfortable and convert into **bunks**; you can rent sheets and blankets for the night (R40 per person), which are brought around by a bedding attendant who'll make up your bed. It's best to buy your bedding voucher when you book your train ticket. Services run between Johannesburg and Cape Town, Port Elizabeth, East London and Durban; and between Cape Town and Queenstown and East London. Tourist class **fares** from Johannesburg range from R330 per person to Durban (the shortest route) to R690 to Cape Town (the longest route) but vary slightly depending on the time of year. Tickets must be booked in advance at train stations, over the phone or online. As the system can be prone to gremlins, a less stressful option is to pay a small commission and purchase tickets through travel agent **African Sun Travel** (☎ 086 584 6404, 🌐 africansuntravel.com).

If you are travelling alone, buy two tickets to ensure you get a private two-person coupé; otherwise you may end up sharing in a four-person compartment.

Shosholoza Meyl's upmarket, air-conditioned weekly **Premier Classe** (🌐 premierclasse.co.za) service connects Johannesburg and Cape Town. It also runs three times a week between Johannesburg and Durban. The trains offer a choice of single, double, triple and four-person compartments, with gowns, slippers and towels provided, plus high teas and five-course dinners served in a luxury dining car – all included in the fare. The **fare** from Johannesburg to Cape Town is R3120, and to Durban R1230.

South Africa also offers a handful of **luxury trains**, with plush carriages and pricey fares. The celebrated **Blue Train** (🌐 bluetrain.co.za) runs between Cape Town and Pretoria weekly, with fares starting at R15,500 per person sharing a double berth for the 27-hour journey; between Hoedspruit (for Kruger National Park) and Pretoria, fares start at R9995 per person sharing for the monthly 19-hour journey. Bookings can be made online, or with Blue Train in Pretoria (☎ 012 334 8459) or Cape Town (☎ 021 449 2672).

Rovos Rail (Cape Town ☎ 021 421 4020; Pretoria ☎ 012 315 8242; 🌐 rovos.com) also runs luxury rail trips between Pretoria and Cape Town (from R16,230 per person sharing), Durban (R16,230) and Victoria Falls in Zimbabwe (R21,250), at three levels of luxury, with prices to match.

A word of warning about **security** on trains: never leave valuables unattended in your compartment unless it is locked, and always close the window if leaving your carriage.

Visit The Man in Seat 61 (🌐 seat61.com/South Africa) for more ideas.

Domestic flights

Flying between destinations in South Africa compares favourably with the cost of covering long distances in a rental car and overnighting en route. With several competing **budget airlines**, you can also pick up good deals.

The biggest airline offering **domestic flights** is **South African Airways** (SAA), with its subsidiaries **SA Airlink** and **SA Express** (reservations for all three go through SAA). SAA's main competitor is British Airways Comair, while the budget airlines Kulula, Mango and FlySafair have more limited networks, but generally offer better deals on the major routes. For the coastal towns of Margate and Plettenberg Bay, Cemair runs a limited service from Johannesburg.

On SAA and its associates, one-way economy-class fares from Cape Town to Johannesburg cost from R1000, while the budget airlines generally charge around R800 for the same route, provided you book well ahead.

Computicket Travel (☎ 0861 915 4000, 🌐 computickettravel.com) is a useful booking engine for flights, buses and car rental.

SOUTH AFRICAN DOMESTIC AIRLINES

British Airways Comair ☎ 010 344 0130, 🌐 ba.com. Domestic flights serving Johannesburg, Cape Town, Durban, Port Elizabeth and Nelspruit (for Kruger National Park) with links to the rest of Africa, including Harare, Livingstone and Windhoek.

Cemair ☎ 011 395 4473, 🌐 flycemair.co.za. Links Johannesburg to the coastal resorts of Plettenberg Bay in the Western Cape and Margate in KwaZulu-Natal, with additional routes including Bloemfontein–Port Elizabeth.

FlySafair ☎ 087 135 1351, 🌐 flysafair.co.za. Budget airline with a useful network including Johannesburg and all the major coastal cities.

Kulula ☎ 086 158 5852, 🌐 kulula.com. Budget network covering Cape Town, Durban, George, East London, Johannesburg, Nairobi, Victoria Falls, Mauritius and beyond.

Mango ☎ 086 100 1234, 🌐 flymango.com. SAA's budget airline provides cheap flights including Johannesburg to Cape Town, Durban, George, Port Elizabeth and Zanzibar; and Cape Town to Bloemfontein, Durban and Joburg.

South African Airways ☎ 086 160 6606, 🌐 flysaa.com. Together with SA Airlink and SA Express, SAA serves the major hubs of Johannesburg, Cape Town and Durban. Other destinations include Bloemfontein, East London, George, Kimberley, Mthatha, Nelspruit, Phalaborwa (for Kruger National Park), Polokwane, Port Elizabeth, Pretoria, Richards Bay and Upington.

DISTANCE CHART
Figures are given in kilometres

	Bloemfontein	Cape Town	Durban	East London	George	Graaff-Reinet	Johannesburg
Bloemfontein	–	998	628	546	764	422	396
Cape Town	998	–	1660	1042	436	672	1405
Durban	628	1660	–	667	1240	945	598
East London	546	1042	667	–	630	388	992
George	764	436	1240	630	–	342	1168
Graaff-Reinet	422	672	945	388	342	–	826
Johannesburg	396	1405	598	992	1168	826	–
Kimberley	175	960	842	722	734	501	467
Maseru	150	1187	476	516	837	503	415
Mbabane	614	1483	394	802	1189	922	310
Mthatha	527	1181	436	231	851	509	866
Nelspruit	754	1779	689	1214	1509	1167	358
Port Elizabeth	676	756	927	300	330	251	1062
Pretoria	454	1324	656	322	1226	895	58
Skukuza	880	1888	809	1334	1616	1274	478
Upington	576	821	1243	958	857	667	875

Driving

Short of joining a tour, the only way to get to national parks and the more remote coastal areas is by **car**. Likewise, some of the most interesting places off the beaten track are only accessible in your own vehicle, as buses tend to ply just the major routes.

South Africa is ideal for driving, with a generally **well-maintained** network of highways and a high proportion of secondary and tertiary roads that are tarred and can be driven at a reasonable speed. **Renting a vehicle** is not prohibitively expensive, and for a couple or small group it can work out to be a cheap option.

Filling stations are frequent on the major routes of the country, and usually open 24 hours. Off the beaten track, though, stations are less frequent, so fill up whenever you get the chance. Stations are rarely self-service; instead, poorly paid attendants fill up your car, check oil, water and tyre pressure if you ask them to, and often clean your windscreen even if you don't. A **tip** of R5–10 is appropriate.

Parking is pretty straightforward, but due to the high levels of car break-ins, attendants, known as "**car guards**", are present virtually anywhere you'll find parking, for example at shopping malls. A tip of R2–5 during the day and around R10 at night is generally appreciated.

Rules of the road and driving tips

Foreign driving licences are valid in South Africa provided they are printed in English. If you don't have such a licence, you'll need to get an **International Driving Permit** (available from national motoring organizations) before arriving in South Africa. When driving, you are obliged by law to carry your driving **licence** and (unless you're a South African resident) your passport (or certified copies) at all times; in reality, in the rare event of your being stopped, showing one of these documents or uncertified photocopies should satisfy most police officers. Leaving these documents lying in your glove box or elsewhere is not recommended.

South Africans drive on the **left-hand side** of the road; speed limits range from 40km/h in wildlife parks and reserves and 60km/h in built-up areas to 100km/h on open roads and 120km/h on highways and major arteries. In addition to roundabouts, which follow the British rule of giving way to the right, there are four-way stops, where the rule is that the person who got there first leaves first. Traffic lights are often called **robots** in South Africa.

The main danger you'll face on the roads is other drivers. South Africa has among the world's worst road **accident** statistics – the result of recklessness, drunken drivers (see p.73) and unroadworthy, overloaded vehicles. Keep your distance from cars in front, as cars behind you often won't and

Kimberley	Maseru	Mbabane	Mthatha	Nelspruit	Port Elizabeth	Pretoria	Skukuza	Upington
175	150	614	527	754	676	454	880	576
960	1187	1483	1181	1779	756	1324	1888	821
842	476	394	436	689	927	656	809	1243
722	516	802	231	1214	300	322	1334	958
734	837	1189	851	1509	330	1226	1616	857
501	503	922	509	1167	251	895	1274	667
467	415	310	866	358	1062	58	478	875
–	326	684	779	832	763	525	952	401
326	–	326	402	620	660	473	707	734
684	489	–	626	96	1001	300	257	1008
779	402	626	–	983	490	903	1099	1178
832	620	96	983	–	1373	328	120	1144
763	660	1001	490	1373	–	1119	1459	902
525	473	300	903	328	1119	–	436	813
952	707	257	1099	120	1459	436	–	1252
401	734	1008	1178	1144	2902	813	1252	–

domino-style pile-ups are common. Watch out also for overtaking traffic coming towards you: overtakers often assume that you will head for the **hard shoulder** to avoid an accident (it is customary to drive on the hard shoulder, but be careful as pedestrians frequently use it). If you pull into the hard shoulder to let a car behind overtake, the other driver will probably thank you by flashing their hazard lights. It's wise to do so when it's safe, as aggressive and impatient South African drivers will soon start driving dangerously close to your back bumper to encourage you to give way. If oncoming cars flash their headlights at you, it probably means there is a speed trap or hazard ahead.

Another potential **hazard** is animals on the roads in rural areas – from livestock to baboons – so drive slowly even on quiet routes. Also, the large distances between major towns mean that falling asleep at the wheel, especially when travelling through long stretches of flat landscape in the Karoo or the Free State, is a real danger. Plan your car journeys to include breaks and stopovers. Finally, in urban areas, there's a small risk of being car-jacked; you should follow safety advice (see box, p.73).

South Africa's motoring organization, the **Automobile Association** (AA; ☎086 100 0234, ⓦaa.co.za), provides information about road conditions as well as free maps.

Car rental

Prebooking your **rental car** is the cheapest option, and will provide more favourable terms and conditions (such as unlimited mileage and lower insurance excesses). Don't rely on being able to just arrive at the airport and pick up a vehicle without reserving.

As a rough guideline, for a **one-week rental** expect to pay from R255 a day with a R7500 insurance excess and unlimited mileage. Many companies stipulate that drivers must be 23 or over and have been driving for at least two years. Note that to collect your vehicle, you will need to produce a credit (not debit) card.

Major rental companies usually allow you to return the car to a different city from where you rented it, though they will usually levy a charge for this. If you're planning to cross a border, for example to **Lesotho** or **Swaziland**, check that the company allows it and will provide a letter of permission. **Insurance** often doesn't cover you if you drive on unsealed roads, so check for this too. Local firms such as Around About Cars (ⓦaroundaboutcars.com) are almost always cheaper than chains, but may include limited mileage of around 200km per day and restrictions on how far you can take the vehicle.

Camper vans and **4WD vehicles** equipped with rooftop tents are a good idea for camping trips and self-drive safaris. For a 4WD, expect to pay from R1200 a day for a week's rental. Some companies

---

ENGLISH/AFRIKAANS STREET NAMES

Many towns have **bilingual street names** with English and Afrikaans alternatives sometimes appearing along the same road. This applies particularly in Afrikaans areas away from the large cities, and often the Afrikaans name bears little resemblance to the English one – something to be aware of when trying to map read. Some terms you may encounter on Afrikaans signage are listed in Language (see p.667).

---

knock fifteen to twenty percent off the price if you book at short notice. Vans generally come fully equipped with crockery, cutlery and linen, and usually a toilet and shower. The downside of camper vans and 4WDs is that they struggle up hills and guzzle a lot of fuel (15 litres per 100km in the smaller vans), which could partly offset any savings on accommodation.

CAMPER VAN AND 4WD RENTAL AGENCIES

Britz Ⓦ britz.co.za Bakkies, 4WDs and SUVs, geared towards safari holidays.
Cheap Motorhome Rental Ⓦ cheapmotorhomes.co.za. Booking agency that sources competitive motorhome rentals.
Drive Africa Cape Town ☎ 021 447 1144, Ⓦ driveafrica.co.za. Camper van, 4WD and car rental. They offer long-term deals and rent vehicles to drivers under 21.
Kea Travel Ⓦ kea.co.za. Motorhome and 4WD rental.
Maui ☎ 011 230 5200, Ⓦ maui.co.za. One of the biggest rental outlets for camper vans and 4WDs.

Cycling

It's easy to see why **cycling** is popular in South Africa: you can get to stunning destinations on good roads unclogged by traffic, many towns have decent cycle shops for spares and equipment, and many backpacker hostels rent out mountain bikes for reasonable rates, so you don't have to transport your bike into the country. You'll need to be fit though, as South Africa is a hilly place, and many roads have punishing gradients. The **weather** can make life difficult, too: if it isn't raining, there is a good chance of it being very hot, so carry plenty of liquids. Cycling in built-up areas and on the main intercity roads is not recommended due to dangerous drivers.

Hitching

Hitching is risky and not recommended, particularly in large towns and cities, and you should never pick up hitchhikers. If you must hitchhike, avoid hitching alone and being dropped off in isolated areas between settlements. Ask drivers where they are going before you say where you want to go, and keep your **bags** with you: having them locked

in the boot makes a hasty escape more difficult. Making a contribution towards petrol is often expected. Check the **notice boards** in backpacker lodges for people offering or looking to share lifts – that way, you can meet the driver in advance.

Accommodation

Accommodation in South Africa can be expensive compared with other African countries, but standards are generally high and you get exceptional value for money. Even modest backpacker lodges provide a minimum of fresh sheets and clean rooms. Other than in the very cheapest rooms, a private bath or shower is almost always provided, and you'll often have the use of a garden or swimming pool. South Africa also has some outstanding boutique hotels, luxury guesthouses, lodges and country retreats – invariably in beautiful settings – at fairly reasonable prices. The country's national parks and reserves feature a range of accommodation, from fairly basic restcamps to incredibly slick game lodges (see p.67), while you'll also find a backpacker hostel in most areas, plus no shortage of camping and self-catering options.

ACCOMMODATION PRICES

Accommodation prices given in the Guide for **hotels, guesthouses** and **B&Bs** are for the cheapest double room with breakfast in high season, unless otherwise stated. In the case of luxury **safari lodges**, such as those around Kruger National Park, prices are per person sharing a double room and include meals and two safari activities (for example, game drives or guided walks) per day. **Camping prices** are per tent, unless otherwise stated.

Advance booking is vital if you're travelling in high season or if you plan to stay in a national park or in popular areas such as Cape Town and the Garden Route. South Africa's **peak season** is during the midsummer Christmas school holiday period, when South African families migrate to the coast and inland resorts. The Easter school holiday is also busy. At Christmas and Easter, **prices** rise sharply across the spectrum, particularly in the mid-range and top-end categories, and most places get booked up months ahead (see p.77).

Hotels

Most of South Africa's **budget hotels** are throwbacks to the 1950s and 1960s, and little more than watering holes that earn their keep from the bar.

Mid-range hotels usually charge from R1000 a room. Along the coastal holiday strips such as the Garden Route, southern KwaZulu-Natal and the major seaside towns in between, these hotels are ubiquitous and frequently offer rooms on the **beachfront**. Many of the mid-priced hotels – especially those on main routes in the interior – are fully booked during the week by travelling salesmen, but over the weekend, when they're often empty, you can often negotiate **discounts**.

A large number of mid-range and **upmarket establishments** belong to hotel **chains**, which offer reliable but sometimes soulless accommodation. Big players include the Marriott-owned Protea Hotels (Ⓦproteahotels.com), Tsogo Sun (Ⓦtsogosunhotels.com), Holiday Inn (Ⓦihg .com) and Aha (Ⓦaha.co.za).

Country lodges and boutique hotels

You will find incredible value and a memorable stay at South Africa's many small, characterful establishments – something the country excels at. You'll find hip **boutique hotels** in the cities; cosy guesthouses in the *dorps* (small towns); and luxurious **country lodges** in exceptional natural surroundings, including eco-lodges in the middle of forests, properties perched on the edges of cliffs, and magical hideaways in the middle of nowhere. At these places you can expect to be pampered and there will often be a spa on-site. There are also numerous first-rate **safari camps** and **game lodges**, which fulfil your most romantic African fantasies (see p.67). You might pay anything from R3000 to R10,000 or more for a double, though this may include meals and guided wildlife-watching activities.

B&Bs and guesthouses

The most ubiquitous form of accommodation in South Africa is **B&Bs** and **guesthouses**. The official difference between the two is that the owner lives on-site at a B&B. The most basic B&Bs are just one or two rooms in a private home, perhaps with washing facilities shared with the owners in township accommodation. In reality, the distinction is a little hazy once you move up a notch to B&Bs and guesthouses that provide en-suite rooms (as is usually the case). **Rates** for en-suite rooms in both start at around R500, for which you can expect somewhere clean, comfortable and relaxed, but usually away from the beach or other action. Moving up another notch, you'll pay from R800 for a room with extra facilities, space or style, and tariffs from R1200 upwards should offer the works: a great location, comfort and good service. Prices are steeper in Cape Town, Johannesburg and the Garden Route.

Since the late 1990s, **township tours** have become popular, with township dwellers offering **B&B** accommodation to tourists in their homes; expect to pay from R500 per room per night for an authentic South African experience.

Along many roads in the countryside you will see signs for "**Bed en Ontbyt**" (Afrikaans for "bed and breakfast"), signalling **farmstay** accommodation, with rooms in the main homestead, in a cottage in its garden or out on the farm. Some also offer hiking trails, horseriding and other **activities**. Tourist offices have lists of farms in their area that rent out rooms or cottages.

Caravan parks, resorts and camping

Caravanning was once the favourite way to have a cheap family holiday in South Africa, and this accounts for the large number of caravan parks dotted across the length and breadth of the country. However, their popularity has declined and with it the standard of many of the country's municipal caravan parks and campsites. Today, **municipal campsites** are generally pretty scruffy, unsafe and not recommended. You may find the odd pleasant one in rural areas, or near small *dorps*.

All in all, you're best off heading for the privately owned **resorts**, where for roughly the same price you get greater comfort, facilities and safety. Although private resorts sometimes give off a holiday-camp vibe, they usually provide good washing and cooking **facilities**, self-catering chalets, shops selling basic goods, braai stands and swimming pools.

ONLINE ACCOMMODATION RESOURCES

B&BS, GUESTHOUSES AND SELF-CATERING

Ⓦ **budget-getaways.co.za** A great resource for affordable (under R400/person) self-catering accommodation in the Western Cape.

Ⓦ **greenwoodguides.com/south-africa** Although properties pay to be listed, this site's hand-picked selection is interesting and quirky.

Ⓦ **portfoliocollection.com** Again, properties pay to be listed, but they also have to meet fairly rigorous standards.

Ⓦ **safarinow.com** One of the oldest and best South African online booking sites covers all types of accommodation, with user reviews and rankings.

BACKPACKERS

Ⓦ **bazbus.com** Website of South Africa's biggest backpacker bus service also provides links to lodges with an online booking facility.

Ⓦ **hihostels.com** Hostelling International acts as a booking agent for over a dozen of South Africa's backpacker lodges.

Ⓦ **hostelbookers.com** International website with clear navigation and good coverage of South African hostels, including detailed reviews and ratings.

Ⓦ **travelnownow.com** Website of SAYTC (South African Youth Travel Confederation) has links to hostel members.

CAMPING AND CARAVAN PARKS

Ⓦ **campsa.co.za** Comprehensive online directory of Southern African campsites and caravan parks.

Virtually all **national parks** – and many provincial reserves – have well-maintained campsites, and in some of the really remote places, such as parts of KwaZulu-Natal, camping may be your only option. Use of a **campsite** generally costs from R265 per site depending on the popularity of the park and the facilities. At national parks you can expect sinks and draining boards for washing dishes; often communal kitchen areas or, at the very least, a braai stand and running water; and a decent toilet and shower block (known locally as "ablutions").

Camping rough is not recommended anywhere in the country.

Backpacker lodges

The cheapest beds in South Africa are in **dormitories** at backpacker lodges (or hostels), which cost from R150 per person. These are generally well-run operations with clean linen and helpful staff, although standards may slip during busy periods. In the cities and tourist resorts you'll have a number of places to choose from and almost all towns of any significance have at least one.

Apart from dorm beds, most also have **private rooms** (double R450–700) – sometimes even with private bathrooms – and an increasing number have **family rooms** that work out at around R180 per person. They usually have communal kitchens, an on-site café, TV, internet access and other facilities such as bike rental. When choosing a hostel, it's worth checking out the **ambience**, as some are party joints, while others have a quieter atmosphere.

The lodges are invariably good meeting points, with a constant stream of travellers passing through, and **notice boards** filled with advertisements for lifts, hostels and backpacker facilities throughout the

country. Many lodges operate reasonably priced **excursions** into the surrounding areas, and will pick you up from train stations or bus stops (especially Baz Bus stops) if you phone in advance.

Self-catering cottages and apartments

Self-catering accommodation in cottages, apartments, cabins and small complexes can provide cheap accommodation in a variety of locations – on farms, near beaches, in forests and wilderness areas, as well as in practically every town and city.

There's a wide range of this type of accommodation, with prices depending on facilities, location and level of luxury: expect to pay from R350 a night for something basic to R1000 or over for a luxurious beach stay. **Apartments** often sleep up to six, so this can be very economical if you're travelling as a family or in a small group. You can save a lot of money by cooking for yourself, and you'll get a sense of **freedom** and **privacy** which is missing from even the nicest guesthouse or B&B. Standards are high: cottages and apartments generally come fully equipped with crockery and cutlery, and even microwaves and TVs in the more modern places. Linen and towels are often provided; check before you book in.

Food and drink

With its myriad culinary influences, South Africa doesn't really have a coherent indigenous cuisine, although Cape Malay dishes come close to this status in the Western Cape. Meat is a big feature of meals nationwide, as is the

vast array of available seafood, which includes a wide variety of fish, lobster (crayfish), oysters and mussels. Locally grown fruit and vegetables are generally of a high standard.

Apart from Cape Malay street food such as salomes (savoury wraps) and samosas, people on the move tend to pick up a pie, burger or chicken and chips. The fast-food chains still have novelty status here, having steadily appeared since the end of apartheid. Drinking is dominated by the Western Cape's often superb wines and by a handful of unmemorable lagers; order a crisp Namibian Windhoek lager or a craft beer, as the recent upsurge of local microbreweries has dramatically improved the quality of beers on offer. In the cities, and to a lesser extent beyond them, there are numerous excellent restaurants serving local and international dishes.

Breakfast, lunch and dinner

B&Bs, hotels, guesthouses and some backpackers serve a **breakfast** of eggs with bacon and usually some kind of sausage. Muesli, fruit, yoghurt, croissants and pastries are increasingly popular. **Lunch** is eaten around 1pm and **dinner** in the evening around 7pm or 8pm; the two are pretty much interchangeable on more limited menus, usually along the lines of meat, chicken or fish and veg.

Styles of cooking

Traditional African food tends to focus around stiff grain **porridge** called *mielie pap* or *pap* (pronounced: "pup"), made of maize meal and accompanied by meat or vegetable-based sauces. Among white South Africans, Afrikaners have evolved a style of cooking known as **boerekos** (see below), which can be heavy-going if you're not used to it.

Some of the best-known South African **foods** are mentioned below, while there's a list of South African culinary terms, including other local foods, in the Language section (see p.672).

Braais

Braai (which rhymes with "dry") is an abbreviation of *braaivleis*, an Afrikaans word translated as "meat grill". More than simply the process of cooking over an outdoor fire, however, a braai is a cultural event that is central to the South African identity. A braai is an intensely social event, usually among family and friends and accompanied by plenty of **beer**. It's also probably the only occasion you'll catch an unreconstructed South African man cooking.

You can braai anything, but a traditional barbecue meal consists of huge slabs of **steak**, **lamb cutlets** and **boerewors** ("farmer's sausage"), with ostrich and venison becoming increasingly popular. Potatoes, onions and butternut squash wrapped in aluminium foil and placed in the embers are the usual accompaniment.

Potjiekos and boerekos

A variant on the braai is **potjiekos**, pronounced "poy-key-kos": pot food, in which meat and vegetables are cooked in a three-legged cast-iron cauldron (the *potjie*), preferably outdoors over an open fire. In a similar vein, but cooked indoors, **boerekos** (literally "farmer's food") is a style of cooking enjoyed mainly by Afrikaners. Much of it is similar to English food, but taken to cholesterol-rich extremes, with even the vegetables prepared with butter and sugar. *Boerekos* comes into its own in its variety of over-the-top **desserts**, including *koeksisters* (plaited doughnuts saturated with syrup) and *melktert* ("milk tart"), a solid, rich custard in a flan case.

Cape Malay

Styles of cooking brought to South Africa by **Asian** and **Madagascan** slaves have evolved into **Cape Malay** cuisine. Characterized by mild, semi-sweet **curries** with strong Indonesian influences, Cape Malay food is worth sampling, especially in Cape Town, where it developed and is associated with the Muslim community. Dishes include *bredie* (stew), of which *waterblommetjiebredie*, made using water hyacinths, is a speciality; **bobotie**, a spicy minced dish served under a savoury custard; and *sosaties*, a local version of kebabs. For **dessert**, dates stuffed with almonds make a light and delicious end to a meal, while *malva* pudding is a rich combination of milk, sugar, cream and apricot jam.

Although Cape Malay cuisine can be delicious, few restaurants specialize in it. Despite this, most of the dishes considered as Cape Malay have crept into the South African diet, many becoming part of the Afrikaner culinary vocabulary.

Other ethnic and regional influences

Although South Africa doesn't really have distinct **regional** cuisines, you will find local specialities in different parts of the country. KwaZulu-Natal, for instance, is especially good for **Indian** food. South African's contribution to this multifaceted tradition is the humble **bunny chow**, a cheap takeaway consisting of a hollowed-out half-loaf of white bread originally filled with curried beans, but nowadays with anything from curried chicken to sardines.

Portuguese food made early inroads into the country because of South Africa's proximity to Mozambique. The Portuguese influence is predominantly seen in the use of hot and spicy peri-peri seasoning, which goes extremely well with braais. The best-known example of this is peri-peri chicken, which you will find all over the country.

Eating out

Restaurants in South Africa offer good value compared with Britain or North America. In every city you'll find places where you can eat a decent main course for under R150, while for R250 you can splurge on the best. All the cities and larger towns boast some restaurants with imaginative menus. As a rule, restaurants are licensed, though Muslim establishments don't allow alcohol.

An attractive phenomenon in the big cities, especially Cape Town, has been the rise of continental-style cafés – easy-going places where you can eat as well as in a regular restaurant, or just drink coffee all night without feeling obliged to order food. A reasonable meal in one of these cafés is unlikely to set you back more than R100.

Don't confuse these with traditional South African cafés, found in even the tiniest country town. The equivalent of corner stores elsewhere, they commonly sell a few Afrikaans magazines, soft drinks, sweets and assorted tins and dry goods.

If popularity is the yardstick, then South Africa's real national cuisine is to be found in its franchise restaurants, which you'll find in every town of any size. The usual international names like KFC, McDonald's and Wimpy are omnipresent, as are South Africa's own home-grown offerings, such as the American-style steakhouse chain, Spur, and the much-exported Nando's chain, which serves Portuguese-style grilled chicken under a variety of spicy sauces. Expect to pay from around R60 for a burger and chips or chicken meal at any of these places, and twice that for a good-sized steak.

Drinking

White South Africans do a lot of their drinking at home, so pubs and bars are not quite the centres of social activity they are in the US or the UK, though in the African townships shebeens (unlicensed bars) do occupy this role. Sports bars with huge screens draw in crowds when there's a big match on, while many drinking spots in city centres and suburbs conform more to European-style café-bars than British pubs, serving coffee and

VEGETARIAN FOOD

While not quite a **vegetarian** paradise, South Africa is nevertheless vegetarian-savvy and you'll find at least one vegetarian dish in most restaurants. Even steakhouses will have something palatable on the menu and generally offer good salad bars. If you're self-catering in the larger cities, delicious dips and breads can be found at delis and Woolworths and Pick 'n Pay supermarkets, as can the range of frozen vegetarian sausages and burgers made by Fry's (**@** frysvegetarian.co.za).

light meals as well as alcohol. The closest things to British-style pubs are the themed bar-restaurant chains, such as Cape Town's *Slug & Lettuce*, while the city has a few longstanding watering holes with an old-world ambience. Johannesburg and Cape Town in particular have a growing range of hipster bars with eclectic decor and craft beers.

Beer, wines and spirits can by law be sold from Monday to Saturday between 9am and 6pm at liquor stores (the equivalent of the British off-licence) and at most supermarkets, although you'll still be able to drink at restaurants and pubs outside these hours.

There are no surprises when it comes to soft drinks, with all the usual names available. One proudly South African drink you will encounter is locally produced rooibos (or redbush) tea, made from the leaves of an indigenous plant (see box, p.208).

Beer

Although South Africa is a major wine-producing country, beer is indisputably the national drink. As much an emblem of South African manhood as the braai, it cuts across all racial and class divisions. As in most countries, South Africans tend to be fiercely loyal to their brand of beer, though they are somewhat interchangeable given that the enormous South African Breweries (SAB) produces most of the country's mainstream beers. A number of international labels supplement the local offerings dominated by Castle, Hansa and Carling Black Label lagers, which taste a bit thin and bland to a British palate, but are certainly refreshing when drunk ice-cold on a sweltering day. The SAB offerings are given a good run for their beer money by Windhoek Lager, produced by Namibian Breweries. Widely available international brands include Peroni, Miller Genuine Draft, Grolsch and Heineken.

In recent years, there has been a rapid growth in the number of **microbreweries** across the country, which produce **craft beers and ciders**. Brew Masters (Ⓦ brewmasters.co.za) lists breweries large and small throughout South Africa with a useful map, while the Brew Mistress (Ⓦ brewmistress.co.za) is a good blog.

Wine and spirits

South Africa is one of the world's top ten **winemaking** countries by volume. Despite having the longest-established New World wine-making tradition (going back over 350 years), this rapid rise has taken place within the past two post-apartheid decades. Before that, South Africa's stagnant wine industry produced heavy Bordeaux-style wines. After the arrival of democracy in 1994, wine-makers began producing fresher, fruitier New World wines, and now develop highly quaffable vintages that combine the best of the Old and New Worlds.

South Africa produces wines from a whole gamut of major cultivars. Of the **whites**, the top South African Chenin and Sauvignon Blancs can stand up to the best the New World has to offer, and among the **reds** it's the blends that really shine. Also look out for robust reds made from Pinotage grapes, a cross between Pinot Noir and Cinsaut unique to South Africa. **Port** is also made, with the best vintages from the Little Karoo town of Calitzdorp along the R62 (see p.247). There are also numerous excellent **sparkling wines**, including Champagne-style, fermented-in-the-bottle bubbly, known as **Méthode Cap Classique** (MCC).

Wine is available throughout the country, although the cost rises as you move out of the Western Cape. **Prices** start at under R30 a bottle, and you can get an easy-drinking, entry-level wine by the likes of Worcester's Alvi's Drift for a little over R40. Just another R20 or so will buy you something pretty decent – the vast bulk of wines cost less than R100 – but you can spend hundreds of rand for a truly great vintage. All this means that anyone with an adventurous streak can indulge in a bacchanalia of sampling without breaking the bank.

The best way to sample wines is by visiting **wineries**; some charge a small tasting fee, which is often waved if you buy a bottle. The oldest and most rewarding wine-producing regions are Cape Town's **Constantia** (see p.112) and the region known as **the Winelands** around the towns of Stellenbosch (see p.169), Paarl (see p.174) and Franschhoek (see p.179), which all have well-established **wine routes**. Other wine-producing areas include **Robertson** (see p.239), the **Orange River** (see p.272) and **Hermanus** (see box, p.188).

WINING AND FINE DINING

Focused around the towns of Stellenbosch, Franschhoek, Paarl and Somerset West, the Western Cape **Winelands** (see p.164) has established itself as one of South Africa's culinary centres, with numerous fine-dining restaurants in a small area. Many restaurants are on wine estates, and offer multi-course menus with wine pairings for each course – and superb views too. Restaurants in the Winelands regularly win the majority of South Africa's annual **Eat Out Restaurant Awards** (six out of the top ten in 2016, compared with three in Cape Town and one in Pretoria). *Eat Out* magazine provides restaurant reviews of establishments across South Africa (available from bookshops or online at Ⓦ eatout.co.za).

South Africa produces the world's largest volume of brandy – **Klipdrift** ("Klippie") is a popular local brand – and the Western Cape turns out spirits including Bain's Whisky and Inverroche fynbos-infused gin.

The media

South Africa has a stronger tradition of regional newspapers than nationals. Television delivers a mix of imported programmes and home-grown soaps, as well as distinctively South African reality TV shows and hard-hitting documentaries. Radio is where the South African media best serves the diverse and scattered audience, and deregulation of the airwaves in the late 1990s brought to life scores of small new stations.

Newspapers

Of the roughly twenty daily **newspapers**, most of which are published in English, Afrikaans or Zulu, the two most prominent nationals are *Business Day* (Ⓦ businesslive.co.za), which is a good source of serious national and international news, and the ANC-aligned *New Age* (Ⓦ thenewage.co.za).

Each of the larger cities has its own English-language **broadsheet**, most of them published by South Africa's largest newspaper publisher, **Independent Media**. In Johannesburg, **The Star** (Ⓦ thestar.co.za), the group's flagship, attracts a multi-racial readership of over 650,000 with its populist coverage of national and Gauteng news. Stable-mates the **Cape Times** (ⓦcapetimes.co.za) and **Cape Argus** (ⓦcapeargus.co.za) follow broadly the same formula, as do the **Pretoria News** (ⓦpretoria news.co.za), Port Elizabeth's **Herald** (ⓦheraldlive .co.za) and Durban's **Daily News** (ⓦdailynews.co.za).

The country's biggest-selling paper is the **Daily Sun** (ⓦdailysun.co.za), a Joburg-based tabloid that taps into the concerns of township dwellers, with a giddy cocktail of gruesome crime stories, tales of witchcraft and the supernatural, and coverage of the everyday problems of ordinary people. Another Joburg tabloid, the **Sowetan** (ⓦsowetan.co.za), has been going since the 1980s, but is a far more serious publication than the *Sun*. In Cape Town, the **Daily Voice** (ⓦdailyvoice.co.za) emulates the *Sun* in the coloured community, with a trashy mix of crime, sport and gossip.

Unquestionably the country's intellectual heavy-weight, the **Mail & Guardian** (ⓦmg.co.za), published every Friday, delivers nonpartisan and fearless investigative journalism, but frequently struggles to escape its own earnestness.

Of the Sunday papers, the **Sunday Times** (ⓦtimeslive.co.za) can attribute its circulation – over 300,000 copies – to a well-calculated mix of solid investigative reporting, gossip and material from the British press and foreign tabloids, while **City Press** (ⓦcitypress.co.za), which sells around half its copies in Gauteng, dishes up independently minded, politically savvy copy to its predominantly urban black readership.

The liveliest of all South Africa's news publications is the boundary-breaking free online **Daily Maverick** (ⓦdailymaverick.co.za), which is brim-full of news and analysis with a stable of some of South Africa's most provocative columnists.

The easiest places to buy newspapers are corner stores, newsagents and bookshop chains. These also sell **international publications** such as *Time*, *The Economist* and the weekly overseas editions of the British *Daily Mail*, *Telegraph* and *Express*.

Television

The South Africa Broadcasting Corporation's three main TV channels churn out a mixed bag of domestic dramas, game shows, sport, soaps and documentaries, filled out with familiar imports. **SABC 1, 2 and 3** (ⓦsabc.co.za) share the unenvi-able task of delivering an integrated service, while having to split their time between the eleven official languages. English is the best represented, with SABC 3 broadcasting almost exclusively in the

language, while SABC 2 and SABC 1 cover the remaining languages, with a fair amount of English creeping in even here. In the Afrikaans-dominated Western Cape, you will also come across much programming in that language.

A selection of movies, news, American programming and specialist channels is available to subscribers to the **M-Net** (ⓦm-net.dstv.com) satellite service, which is piped into many hotels. South Africa's first free-to-air independent commercial channel **e.tv**, launched in 1998, broad-casts both local productions and popular imports.

There is no cable TV in South Africa, but **DSTV** (ⓦdstv.co.za) offers a **satellite television** subscrip-tion service with a selection of sports, movies, news (including BBC, CNN and Al Jazeera) and specialist channels, some of which are available in hotels. Sports fans should surf to **SuperSport** (ⓦsuper sport.com) and everyone should catch an episode of KykNet's "Boer Soek 'n Vrou" (Farmer Seeks a Wife), an Afrikaans dating reality show for Boers from remote farms.

Radio

Given South Africa's low literacy rate and widespread poverty, it's no surprise that **radio** is a highly popular medium. The SABC operates a national radio station for each of the eleven official language groups, including the interesting English-language national service, **SAfm** (104–107FM, ⓦsafm.co.za). Heavily laden with phone-in shows interlaced with news bulletins, SAfm broadcasts current affairs programmes on weekdays from 6am to 9am ("AM Live"), midday to 1pm ("Midday Live") and 4pm to 6pm ("PM Live").

To get a taste of what makes South Africans tick, tune into the Primedia-owned **Gauteng talk station 702** (in Joburg 92.7 FM and in Pretoria 106 FM; ⓦ702.co.za) or its Cape Town sister station **Cape Talk** (567 AM; ⓦcapetalk.co.za), both of which are livelier than the state stations and broadcast news, weather, traffic and sports reports. Apart from these, there are innumerable regional, commercial and community stations, broadcasting a range of music and chat, which make surfing the airwaves an enjoyable experience nationwide.

Festivals

South Africa has no shortage of events – there are scores of annual music festivals and concert series in city parks. In

addition, countless small towns host umpteen diverting minor events. Although Johannesburg and Cape Town tend to dominate, the country's two biggest cultural events, the National Arts Festival and the Klein Karoo Nasionale Kunstefees, take place in (and take over) the far-flung towns of Grahamstown and Oudtshoorn respectively.

JANUARY

Cape Town Minstrel Carnival Cape Town. The city's longest-running and most raucous annual party, the carnival brings thousands of spectators to watch the parade through the city centre. It culminates on Jan 2 with the Tweede Nuwe Jaar or "Second New Year" celebrations – an extension of New Year's Day unique to the Western Cape. Central to the festivities are the brightly decked-out coloured minstrel troupes that vie for supremacy in singing and dancing contests. Arrive early to get a spot with a good view. **Jan 2.**

Shakespeare in the Park Wynberg, Cape Town Ⓦ maynardville .co.za. A usually imaginative production of one of the Bard's plays is staged each year in the beautiful setting of the Maynardville Open-Air Theatre in Maynardville Park. **Late Jan to late Feb.**

FEBRUARY

Cape Town Pride Pageant Cape Town Ⓦ capetownpride.org. Series of gay-themed events over a week, kicking off with a pageant at which Mr and Miss Cape Town are crowned, and taking in a bunch of parties and a street parade. **End of the month.**

MARCH

Dance Umbrella Johannesburg Ⓦ danceforumsouthafrica.co.za. The country's leading contemporary dance festival showcases a variety of local dance forms. **First half of the month.**

Cape Town Cycle Tour Cape Town Ⓦ capetowncycletour.org.za. The world's largest, and arguably most spectacular, individually timed bike race: some 40,000 participants on the 109km course – much of it along the ocean's edge – draw many thousands of spectators along the route. You can enter the Cape Argus (most locals still use its old name) online, and booking early is recommended, although sadly the event is often cancelled due to strong winds. **First half of the month.**

Cape Town Carnival Cape Town Ⓦ capetowncarnival.com. A Rio-style street extravaganza that kicked off in 2010, the carnival is centred on Green Point's Fan Walk with floats, parades and general euphoria intended to celebrate Cape Town's cultural diversity and richness. Festivities start at 3pm, and the parade at 7pm. **Middle of the month.**

Cape Town International Jazz Festival Cape Town Ⓦ capetown jazzfest.com. Initiated in 2000 as the Cape Town counterpart of the world-famous North Sea Jazz Festival (Rotterdam), Africa's largest jazz festival has come of age and acquired a local identity. Notable past performers have included Courtney Pine, Herbie Hancock, and African greats such as Jimmy Dludlu, Moses Molelekwa, Youssou N'Dour, Miriam Makeba and Hugh Masekela. **Last weekend of the month.**

APRIL

Two Oceans Marathon Cape Town Ⓦ twooceansmarathon.org.za. Another of the Cape's big sports events, this is in fact an ultramarathon (56km), with huge crowds lining the route to cheer on the participants. A less scenic half-marathon is held at the same time. **Easter Saturday.**

Fashion Week Cape Town Cape Town Ⓦ africanfashion international.com. Multiple catwalk shows over two days are aimed at showcasing new collections from leading South African designers, including the likes of Craig Port and Stefania Morland. **First half of the month.**

Afrika Splashy Fen Music Festival Underberg, KwaZulu-Natal Ⓦ splashyfen.co.za. South Africa's oldest music festival draws thousands of punters to a beautiful farm in the Drakensberg foothills, with a spread of mainstream and alternative rock and pop, trail running, glamping and a kids' programme. **Middle of the month.**

Pink Loerie Mardi Gras & Arts Festival Knysna, Garden Route Ⓦ pinkloerie.co.za. Gay pride celebration of parties, contests, cabaret, drag shows and performance over a long weekend in South Africa's oyster capital. **End of the month.**

AfrikaBurn Tankwa Karoo, Northern Cape Ⓦ afrikaburn.com. South Africa's official spinoff of Nevada's Burning Man festival is a spectacular week-long explosion of performance, creativity, revelry and controlled pyromania in the Karoo desert. **End of the month.**

MAY

Franschhoek Literary Festival Franschhoek, Western Cape Ⓦ flf.co.za. Three-day celebration of books, writers and wine in the Winelands food capital, featuring leading local and international writers, editors and cartoonists. **Middle of the month.**

JUNE

Good Food & Wine Show Cape Town Ⓦ goodfoodandwineshow .co.za. Celebrity chefs from around the world are just one of the compelling attractions that make this South Africa's foodie event of the year. There are hands-on workshops, kids' events, delicious nibbles and wine, as well as kitchen implements and books for sale. **Start of the month.**

Comrades Marathon Durban/Pietermaritzburg, KwaZulu-Natal Ⓦ comrades.com. This world-famous ultramarathon, run along the 89km between Durban and Pietermaritzburg, attracts around twenty thousand runners, many of them international competitors. **Beginning of the month.**

Encounters South African International Documentary Festival Johannesburg and Cape Town Ⓦ encounters.co.za. Fortnight-long showcase of documentary film-making from South Africa and the world. **Middle of the month.**

JULY

National Arts Festival Grahamstown, Eastern Cape (see box, p.320). Africa's largest arts jamboree, with its own fringe festival – ten days of jazz, classical music, dance, cabaret and theatre spanning every conceivable type of performance.

Knysna Oyster Festival Knysna, Western Cape Ⓦ oysterfestival .co.za. Ten days of carousing and oyster eating on the Garden Route, kicked off by the Knysna Cycle Tour and closed by the Knysna Forest Marathon. **First half of the month.**

Good Food & Wine Show Johannesburg See June. **End of the month.**

AUGUST

Jive Cape Town Funny Festival Cape Town ⓦ www.baxter.co.za.
Month-long comedy festival at the Baxter Theatre, beginning in mid-July and attracting both local and international names. **Beginning of the month.**

SEPTEMBER

Arts Alive Johannesburg ⓦ arts-alive.co.za. Joburg's largest arts event features a month of dance, theatre, poetry and music at venues in Newtown, the cultural precinct in the inner city.
Hermanus Whale Festival Hermanus, Western Cape
ⓦ whalefestival.co.za. To coincide with peak whale-watching season, the town of Hermanus stages a weekend festival of arts and the environment. Attractions include marine displays, children's areas, a treasure hunt and live music. **End of the month.**
Joy of Jazz Johannesburg ⓦ joyofjazz.co.za. Joburg's flagship jazz festival offers three days of varied music, including big names such as Abdullah Ibrahim and Salif Keita. **End of the month.**

OCTOBER

Oppikoppi Northam, Limpopo ⓦ oppikoppi.co.za. South Africa's answer to Woodstock, Oppikoppi (Afrikaans for "on the hill") brings the bushveld hills alive with the sound of music, as some sixty local and foreign bands rock the *bundu* (outback) for three days and nights.
Beginning of the month.
Rocking the Daisies Darling, Western Cape ⓦ rockingthedaisies
.com. South Africa's premier rock and pop fest, featuring local and international acts as well as much theatricality and debauchery. Held on Cloof Wine Estate, most people make a long weekend of it, camping for a few nights. **Beginning of the month.**
Good Food & Wine Show Durban See June. **End of the month.**

NOVEMBER TO APRIL

Kirstenbosch Summer Concerts Kirstenbosch National Botanical Garden, Cape Town ⓦ sanbi.org. Among the musical highlights of Cape Town's calendar are the popular concerts held on Kirstenbosch's magnificent lawns at the foot of Table Mountain. Performances begin at 5.30pm and cover a range of genres, from local jazz to classical music. American rockers the Pixies played their first African gig here in 2017. Come early to find a parking place and picnic spot with a good view of the stage - and bring some Cape fizz. Tickets available online or at the gate. **Every Sun evening from end of the month to early April.**

DECEMBER

Franschhoek Cap Classique and Champagne Festival
Franschhoek, Western Cape ⓦ www.franschhoekmcc.co.za. Popular two-day bacchanalia of bubbly sampling – a vast selection of local and French sparkling wine is on hand – and gourmandizing in the Cape Winelands. **Beginning of the month.**
Mother City Queer Project Cape Town ⓦ mcqp.co.za.
A hugely popular party attracting thousands of revellers, gay and otherwise. Outlandish get-ups, multiple dancefloors and a mood of sustained delirium make this event a real draw. **Mid-month.**
Christmas Carols at Kirstenbosch Cape Town ⓦ sanbi.org.
Kirstenbosch National Botanical Garden's annual carol singing and nativity tableau is a local institution, drawing crowds of families with their picnic baskets. The gates open at 6pm and the singing kicks off at 7.45pm.
Thurs–Sun before Christmas.

Activities and outdoor pursuits

South Africa's diverse landscape of mountains, forests, rugged coast and sandy beaches, as well as kilometres of veld and national parks, makes the country supreme outdoor terrain for sport and recreation. South Africans have been playing outdoors for decades, resulting in a well-developed infrastructure for activities, an impressive national network of hiking trails and plenty of operators selling adventure sports.

Hiking trails

South Africa has a comprehensive system of **footpaths**, of various distances and catering to all levels of fitness. Wherever you are – even in the middle of Johannesburg – you won't be far from some sort of trail. The best ones are in wilderness areas, where you'll find **waymarked paths**, from half-hour strolls to major hiking expeditions of several days that take you right into the heart of some of the most beautiful parts of the country.

Overnight trails are normally well laid out, with painted route markers, and campsites or huts along the way. Numbers are limited on most, and some trails are so popular that you need to book several months in advance to use them.

There are also **guided wilderness trails**, where you walk in game country accompanied by an armed ranger. These walking safaris are an excellent way to get a feel for the wild, although you are likely to see fewer animals on foot than from a vehicle. Specialist trails cover **mountain biking**, canoeing and horseriding, while a handful of trails have been set up specifically for people with disabilities, mostly for the **visually impaired** or those in wheelchairs.

Watersports

South Africa has some of the world's finest **surfing** breaks. The perfect waves of Jeffrey's Bay were immortalized in the 1966 cult movie *The Endless Summer*, but any surfer will tell you that there are equally good breaks all the way along the coast from Namibia to Mozambique.

The South African surfing community is among the friendliest in the world, and you should find plenty of advice on offer. Some world-class shapers work here, and you can pick up an excellent **board** at a fraction of the European or US price. **Boogie-boarding** and **body-surfing** make easy alternatives to the real thing, require less skill and dedication, and are great fun. **Windsurfing** is another popular sport you'll find at many resorts, where you can rent gear, while kitesurfing has taken off in Cape Town and elsewhere.

On inland waterways, South African holiday-makers are keen **speedboaters**, an activity that goes hand in hand with **waterskiing**. **Kayaking**, **canoeing** and stand-up paddleboarding (SUP) are also popular, and you can often rent craft at resorts or national parks that lie along rivers and lagoons. For the more adventurous, there's **whitewater rafting**, with some decent trips along the Tugela River in KwaZulu-Natal and on the Orange River.

Diving and snorkelling

Scuba diving is popular, and South Africa is an affordable country to get an internationally recognized open-water certificate. **Courses** start around R3500 (including gear) and are available in most coastal cities as well as a number of resorts. Some of the most rewarding diving is in the iSimangaliso Wetland Park area on the northern KwaZulu-Natal coast, which hosts 100,000 dives every year for its coral reefs and fluorescent fish.

You won't find corals and bright colours along the Cape coast, but the huge number of sunken vessels makes **wreck diving** popular, and you can encounter the swaying rhythms of giant kelp forests. Gansbaai (near Hermanus) is the most popular place to go **shark-cage diving** and come face to face with deadly great whites, with more options on the Garden Route.

KwaZulu-Natal is also good for **snorkelling**, and there are some underwater trails elsewhere in the country, most notably in the Garden Route's Tsitsikamma National Park.

Other activities

Fishing is a well-developed South African activity, and the coasts yield 250 species caught through rock, bay or surf angling. Inland you'll find plenty of rivers and dams stocked with freshwater fish, while trout fishing is extremely well established in Mpumalanga, the northern mountains of the Eastern Cape and the KwaZulu-Natal Midlands.

There are ample opportunities for aerial activities. In the Winelands you can go **ballooning**, while **paragliding** offers a thrilling way to see Cape Town – by diving off Lion's Head and riding the thermals. More down-to-earth options include **mountaineering** and **rock climbing**, both of which have a huge following in South Africa. In a similar vein is **kloofing** (or canyoning), in which participants trace the course of a deep ravine by climbing, scrambling, jumping, abseiling or using any other means.

If you can't choose between being airborne and being earthbound, you can always bounce between the two by **bungee jumping** 216m off the Garden Route's Bloukrans Bridge – one of the world's highest jumps.

Horseriding is available in most tourist towns, whether inland or on the coast, for trips of two hours or two days. **Birdwatching** can also be enjoyed almost anywhere, either on your own, or on a guided trip with an expert. Among the best birdwatching spots are Mkhuze and Ndumo game reserves in KwaZulu-Natal, where the Zululand Birding Route (🅦 zululandbirdingroute.co.za) is one of several routes and associations nationwide.

BEACH CONDITIONS

Don't expect balmy Mediterranean seas in South Africa: of its 2500km of coastline, only the stretch along the Indian Ocean seaboard of KwaZulu-Natal and the northern section of the Eastern Cape can be considered **tropical**, and along the entire coast an energetic surf pounds the shore. In Cape Town, sea bathing is only comfortable between November and March, and False Bay is generally warmer than the Atlantic. Generally, the further east you go from here, the warmer the water becomes and the longer the **bathing season**. Sea temperatures that rarely drop below 18°C make the KwaZulu-Natal coast balmy enough for a dip at most times of year.

A word of warning: dangerous **undertows** and **riptides** are present along the coast and you should try to bathe where lifeguards are present. Failing that (and guards aren't that common away from the main resorts out of season), follow local advice, never swim alone, and always treat the ocean with respect.

Golf courses are numerous and frequently in stunningly beautiful locations. Finally, you can **ski** at two resorts in the Eastern Cape and Lesotho, gaining a quirky and unusual experience of Africa.

Spectator sports

South Africa is a sports-mad nation, especially when local or international teams take to the field. Winning performances, controversial selections and scandals commonly dominate the front and back pages of newspapers. The major spectator sports are football, rugby and cricket, and big matches involving the international team or heavyweight local clubs are well worth seeing live.

Football

Football is the country's most popular game, with a primarily black and coloured following, and it is starting to attract serious money.

The professional **season** runs from August to May, with teams competing in the **Premier Soccer League** (PSL; Ⓦpsl.co.za) and a couple of knock-out cup competitions. Unlike rugby teams, football teams often share grounds with other local squads, or just rent them for specific fixtures. This has prevented the development of the kind of terrace fan culture found elsewhere, and football **crowds** are generally witty and good-spirited. Johannesburg is the heartland of South African football, and the biggest games normally involve the city's two major teams, **Kaizer Chiefs** and **Orlando Pirates**. Although the Chiefs and Pirates are both Sowetan clubs, they have a nationwide following, and their matches are the highlight of the PSL's fixture list. In recent years the dominance of these long-time rivals has been challenged by the Pretoria-based Mamelodi Sundowns and SuperSport United, both of which are regular champions of the PSL's Premier Division.

The **national squad**, nicknamed Bafana Bafana (literally "boys boys" but connoting "our lads"), is imaginative and strong on spectacular athletic feats, but less impressive when it comes to teamwork and resilience. Indeed, at the 2010 World Cup, host Bafana delivered an entertaining draw against Mexico in the opening match, but against Uruguay suffered the worst defeat (3–0) for a host nation since 1970, and was eliminated in the group stages. Sadly, Bafana failed even to qualify for the 2014 World Cup in Brazil.

Rugby

Rugby is hugely popular with white people, though attempts to broaden its appeal for a black audience have struggled. South Africa's victory against England at the 2007 World Cup final in Paris briefly brought the whole country together. The strength of emotion almost matched that shown in 1995 when South Africa hosted the event. Coming shortly after the advent of democracy, it attracted fanatical attention nationwide, particularly when national team the Springboks (or Boks) triumphed and President **Nelson Mandela** donned a green Springbok jersey (long associated exclusively with whites) to present the cup to the winning side – as depicted in Clint Eastwood's 2009 film *Invictus*.

Following that, the goodwill dissipated, to be replaced by an acrimonious struggle to transform traditionally white sports (cricket and rugby) into something more representative of all race groups, particularly following the government's policy of enforcing **racial quotas** in national squads.

Despite these problems, the country's two World Cup victories testify to South Africa's enduring skill at rugby, and you are likely to witness high-quality play when you watch either inter-regional or international games. The main domestic competition is the **Currie Cup**, with games played on weekends from June to October; admission to these matches starts at R50.

Recently this has been overshadowed by the **SuperRugby** competition, involving fifteen regional teams from **South Africa**, **New Zealand**, **Australia**, **Argentina** and **Japan**. You'll catch a fair bit of SuperRugby action in the major centres of Pretoria, Johannesburg, Cape Town and Durban, though smaller places such as Bloemfontein and Port Elizabeth sometimes get a look-in.

International fixtures involving the **Springboks** are dominated by visiting tours by northern-hemisphere teams and by the annual **Rugby Championship** competition, in which South Africa plays home and away fixtures against Australia, New Zealand and Argentina. These are normally played from August to October, and you will need to buy tickets well in advance. South Africa won in 1998, 2004 and 2009, but New Zealand and Australia are the teams that usually triumph.

Cricket

Cricket was for some years seen as the most progressive of the former white sports, with development programmes generating support and discovering talent among black and coloured communities. The sport was rocked to its foundations in 2000, however, when it was revealed that the South African national captain, the late **Hansie Cronje**, had received money from betting syndicates to influence the outcome of one-day matches. Cronje was banned for life, the credibility of the sport took a dive and the national team, the **Proteas**, struggled for years to recover. In 2012 the South Africans finally achieved the number one test spot, becoming the only team to simultaneously win all three premier international competitions, including the One Day International (ODI) and Twenty20 (T20) cricket. Talented batsman Hashim Amla (ranked in the world's top ten) subsequently made history as the first South African of colour to be appointed Proteas test captain.

The **domestic season** of inter-regional games runs from late September to March, with the main competitions being the four-day **Sunfoil Series**, the series of one-day, fifty-overs matches, the **Momentum One Day Cup**, and the shorter twenty-overs **Ram Slam T20 Challenge**. The contests see six regional squads slogging it out for national dominance. Games are played throughout the week, and admission is from R60. In the international standings, South Africa is one of the world's top teams, and you stand a good chance of being around for an international test or one-day series if you're in the country between October and March. Expect to pay from R120 for international matches, which are played in all the major cities.

Running and cycling

South Africa is strong at long-distance **running**, a tradition that reached its apotheosis at the 1996 Atlanta Olympics when Josiah Thugwane won the marathon, becoming the first black South African to bag Olympic gold. The biggest single athletics event in South Africa, the **Comrades Marathon**, attracts around twenty thousand participants. The 90km course crosses the hilly country between Durban and Pietermaritzburg, with a drop of almost 800m between the town and the coast. Run annually at the beginning of June, the race alternates direction each year and is notable for having been non-racial since 1975, although it wasn't until 1989 that a black South African, Samuel Tshabalala, won it. Since then, **black athletes** have dominated the front rankings. Almost as well known is the **Two Oceans ultra-marathon**, which attracts ten thousand competitors each April to test themselves on the 56km course that spectacularly circuits the Cape Peninsula.

Traversing a 109km route, the **Cape Town Cycle Tour** (aka the Argus) also includes the Cape Peninsula in its routing. The largest individually timed cycle race anywhere, it attracts some 40,000 participants from around the world each year in March.

Horse racing

You'll find huge interest among rich and poor South Africans in **horse racing**, with totes and tracks in the main cities. Its popularity is partly due to the fact that for decades this was the only form of public gambling allowed in the country – on the pretext that it involved skill not chance. The highlight of the racing calendar is the **Durban July** held at Durban's Greyville Racecourse. A flamboyant event, it attracts huge crowds, massive purses, socialites in outrageous headgear and vast amounts of media attention.

Parks, reserves and wilderness areas

No other African country has as rich a variety of parks, reserves and wilderness areas as South Africa. Hundreds of game reserves and state forests pepper the terrain, creating an enticing breadth of choice. While there are dozens of unsung treasures among these, the big destinations amount to some two dozen parks geared towards protecting the country's wildlife and wilderness areas.

With a few exceptions, these are run by **Ezemvelo KZN Wildlife** (☎033 845 1000, ⓦwww.kznwildlife .com), which controls public reserves in KwaZulu-Natal, and **South African National Parks** (☎012 428 9111, ⓦsanparks.org), which covers the rest of the country. In addition to the state-run parks there are **private reserves**, frequently abutting them and sharing the same wildlife population. Only some of the national parks are game reserves (see box, p.68).

While most people come for the superb **wildlife**, don't let the **Big Five** (buffalo, elephant, leopard, lion and rhino) blinker you into missing out on the marvellous wilderness areas that take in great landscapes and less publicized animal life. There are parks protecting coastal areas, wetlands, endangered species, forests, deserts and mountains, usually with the added attraction of assorted animals, birds, insects, reptiles or marine mammals

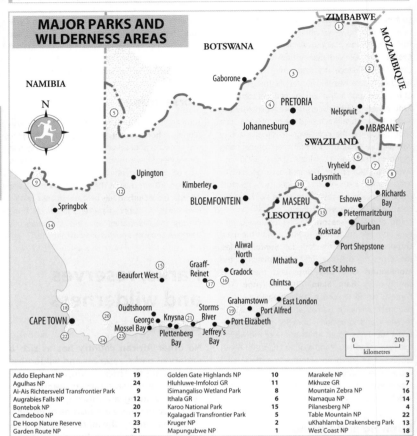

MAJOR PARKS AND
WILDERNESS AREAS

Addo Elephant NP	19	Golden Gate Highlands NP	10	Marakele NP	3
Agulhas NP	24	Hluhluwe-Imfolozi GR	11	Mkhuze GR	7
Ai-Ais Richtersveld Transfrontier Park	9	iSimangaliso Wetland Park	8	Mountain Zebra NP	16
Augrabies Falls NP	12	Ithala GR	6	Namaqua NP	14
Bontebok NP	20	Karoo National Park	15	Pilanesberg NP	4
Camdeboo NP	17	Kgalagadi Transfrontier Park	5	Table Mountain NP	22
De Hoop Nature Reserve	23	Kruger NP	2	uKhahlamba Drakensberg Park	13
Garden Route NP	21	Mapungubwe NP	1	West Coast NP	18

– South Africa is one of the top destinations for land-based **whale watching**.

If you had to choose just one of the country's top national parks, **Kruger**, stretching up the eastern flanks of Mpumalanga and Limpopo provinces, would lead the pack for its sheer size (almost as big as Wales), its range of animals, its varied lowveld habitats and its game-viewing opportunities. The **Tsitsikamma** section of the Western Cape's Garden Route National Park also attracts large numbers of visitors for its ancient forests, rugged sea cliffs and dramatic Storms River Mouth, as well as the multiday Otter Trail, South Africa's most popular hike. For epic mountain landscapes, nowhere in the country can touch the **uKhahlamba-Drakensberg Park**, which takes in a series of reserves on the KwaZulu-Natal border with Lesotho and offers scenic hikes as well as ambitious mountaineering for serious climbers.

The unchallenged status of Kruger for sighting the Big Five and a cast of thousands of animals tends to put the KwaZulu-Natal parks in the shade, quite undeservedly. As well as offering some of the world's best **rhino** viewing, these parks feel less developed than Kruger, and often provide superior accommodation at comparable prices. Both Kruger and the KwaZulu-Natal parks offer walking safaris, accompanied by a gun-toting guide, and **night drives**, a popular way to catch sight of the elusive denizens that creep around after dark.

Addo Elephant National Park in the Eastern Cape is the third-largest national park in South Africa, and still being expanded. The only major Big Five reserve in the southern half of the country, Addo has one of the most diverse **landscapes**, encompassing five biomes and protecting over six hundred elephants. A day's drive from Cape Town, it is also the country's only major **malaria-free** game reserve.

Park accommodation

Accommodation at national parks includes **campsites** (expect to pay R200–350 per site); **safari tents** at some of the Kruger and KwaZulu-Natal restcamps (clusters of accommodation in game reserves, including chalets, safari tents, cottages and campsites; from R580 per tent); one-room **huts** with shared washing and cooking facilities (from R500); one-room en-suite **bungalows** with shared cooking facilities (from R800); and self-contained family **cottages** with private bath or shower and cooking facilities (from R1500). In national parks accommodation (excluding campsites) you're supplied with bedding, towels, a fridge and basic cooking utensils. Some restcamps have a **shop** selling supplies for picnics or braais, as well as a **restaurant**.

The ultimate wilderness accommodation is in the **private game reserves**, with high concentrations of these around Kruger and Addo. Here you pay big bucks for accommodation, which is almost always luxurious, in large en-suite walk-in tents, small thatched **rondavels** or – in the larger and most expensive lodges – plush rooms with air conditioning. A few places have "bush showers" (a hoisted bucket of hot water with a shower nozzle attached) behind reed screens but open to the sky – one of the great treats of the bush. Some chalets and tents have gaslights or lanterns in the absence of **electricity**. Food is usually good and plentiful, and vegetarians can be catered for. Expect to pay upwards of R3000 per person per night, rising well over R10,000 at the most fashionable spots. High as these **prices** are, all meals and game drives are included, and as numbers are strictly limited, you get an exclusive experience of the bush.

Game viewing

Spotting wild animals takes skill and **experience**. It's easier than you'd think to mistake a rhino for a large boulder, or to miss the king of the beasts in the tall grass – African wildlife has, after all, evolved with **camouflage** in mind. Don't expect the volume of animals you get in wildlife documentaries: what you see is always a matter of **luck**, patience and skill. If you're new to the African bush and its wildlife, consider shelling out for at least two nights at one of the luxurious lodges on a private reserve (for example, those abutting Kruger); they're staffed by well-informed **rangers** who lead game-viewing outings in open-topped 4WDs.

The section on Kruger National Park (see box, p.547) gives more advice on spotting game and enjoying and understanding what you see – whether it's a brightly coloured lizard in a restcamp, head-butting giraffes at a waterhole or dust-kicking rhinos. Numerous **books** are available that can enhance your visit to a game reserve – especially if you plan a self-drive safari (see below).

Self-drive safaris

The least expensive way of experiencing a game reserve is by **renting a car** and driving around a national park, taking advantage of the self-catering and camping facilities. Most parks have easily navigable tarred and gravel roads. You'll have the thrill of spotting game at your own pace rather than relying on a ranger, and for people with **children**, a self-drive safari is the usual option, as most upmarket lodges don't admit under-12s. The disadvantage of self-driving is that you can end up jostling with other cars to get a view, especially when it comes to lion watching. Also, you may not know what spoor (animal signs) to look for, and unless you travel in a minibus or 4WD vehicle you're unlikely to be high enough off the ground to see across the veld.

The KwaZulu-Natal game reserves, including Hluhluwe-iMfolozi, Mkhuze and Ithala, offer rewarding opportunities for **self-drive touring**, as does Pilanesberg in North West Province, while the remote Kgalagadi Transfrontier Park that stretches into Botswana promises truly exciting wilderness driving. You might choose to cover a route that combines the substantial Kruger National Park with the more intimate reserves of KwaZulu-Natal.

If you plan to self-drive, consider investing in good animal and bird **field guides**, and a decent pair of **binoculars** – one pair per person is recommended. Whether you're self-catering or not, it's worth taking a flask for tea and a cool bag to keep drinks cold. Finally, remember that the best times to spot animals are **dawn and dusk**, when they are most active.

Escorted safaris

It's possible to book places on a **safari excursion** – such packages are often organized by backpacker lodges located near reserves, and occasionally by hotels and B&Bs. On the downside, these don't give you the experience of waking up in the wild, and entail spending more time on the road than if you were based inside a reserve. But during South African school holidays, when Kruger, for example, is booked to capacity, you may have no other option. You can also organize guided wildlife drives through national park offices.

Mostly, you get what you pay for as regards game-viewing packages. Be wary of cheap deals on

MAJOR PARKS AND WILDLIFE AREAS

PARK	FOCUS	DESCRIPTION AND HIGHLIGHTS
Addo Elephant NP (see p.308)	Game reserve	The only Big Five national park in the southern half of the country
Agulhas NP (see p.191)	Marine and coastal	Rugged southernmost tip of Africa with rich plant biodiversity and significant archeological sites
Ai-Ais Richtersveld Transfrontier Park (see p.291)	Mountain and desert	Craggy *kloofs*, high mountains and dramatic landscapes, sweeping north from the Orange River, which sustain a remarkable range of reptiles, birds, mammals and plant life
Augrabies Falls NP (see p.280)	Desert reserve	Notable for the dramatic landmark from which the park takes its name, where the Orange River plummets down a deep ravine; also great for desert scenery, antelopes and profuse birdlife
Bontebok NP (see p.183)	Endangered species	At the foot of rugged mountains, the park provides refuge to bontebok and Cape mountain zebra
Camdeboo NP (see p.326)	Desert reserve	Karoo semi-desert landscape in the foothills of the Sneeuberg range with 120m-high dolerite pillars plus 43 mammal species
De Hoop Nature Reserve (see p.194)	Marine and coastal, endangered species, and coastal vegetation	One of the world's top spots for land-based whale watching, with epic coastline and fynbos grazed by rare mountain zebras
Garden Route National Park (see p.218, p.224 & p.232)	Marine and coastal/ endangered species	Focused on three sections: wetlands and coast around Wilderness; Knysna's forests and lagoon; and Tsitsikamma's cliffs, gorges and ancient forests
Golden Gate Highlands NP (see p.438)	Mountain enclave	Photogenic grasslands and sandstone formations in the foothills of the Maluti Mountains
Hluhluwe-iMfolozi Park (see p.401)	Game reserve	KwaZulu-Natal's hillier, smaller answer to Kruger is among the top African spots for rhinos

"**safari farms**" in the vicinity of Kruger. Essentially huge zoos, these offer an overnight stop en route to Kruger, but are no substitute for a real wilderness experience – sooner or later you hit fences and gates on your game drive. Some of the better places in this category are listed in the relevant chapters.

Safaris on private reserves

If you choose well, the ultimate South African game experience has to be a **private reserve**. You can relax in comfort while your game-viewing activities are organized, and because you spend time in a small group, you get a stronger sense of the wild than at one of the big Kruger restcamps. Best of all, you have the benefit of knowledgeable **rangers**, who can explain the terrain and small-scale wildlife as they drive you around looking for game.

Privately run safari lodges in concessions inside Kruger and some other national parks, such as Addo, operate along similar lines. The smaller private reserves accommodate between ten and sixteen guests; larger **camps** often cater for two or three times as many people, and resemble hotels in

iSimangaliso Wetland Park (see p.404)	Coastal wetland	Vast patchwork of wetlands, wilderness, coast and game reserves
Ithala GR (see p.416)	Game reserve	Lesser-known small gem of a game reserve in mountainous country
Karoo NP (see p.253)	Desert reserve	Arid mountainous landscape with fossils, herbivores and succulents
Kgalagadi Transfrontier Park (see p.277)	Desert/ game reserve	Remote desert with rust-red dunes, Kalahari lions, shy leopards and thousands of antelope
Kruger NP (see p.538)	Game reserve	The largest, best-stocked and most popular game reserve in Southern Africa
Mapungubwe NP (see p.570)	Archeology/ game reserve	World Heritage Site listed for its significance as the location of a highly developed Iron Age culture. Also noted for its landscape and biodiversity, which supports a large variety of mammals
Marakele NP (see p.565)	Game reserve	Striking landscape of peaks, plateaus and cliffs, home to lions, elephants, leopards and a variety of other mammals
Mkhuze GR (see p.408)	Game/bird reserve	Top birding venue and excellent for rhinos and other herbivores, plus walks in wild fig forest
Mountain Zebra NP (see p.324)	Endangered species	Dramatic hilly landscape in otherwise flat country with rare Cape mountain zebras, cheetahs and other mammals
Namaqua NP (see p.286)	Marine and coastal	Mountainous and coastal region renowned for its estimated 3500 plant varieties, among them beautiful spring wildflowers
Pilanesberg NP (see p.508)	Game reserve	Mountain-encircled grassland trampled by the Big Five, accessible from Johannesburg
Table Mountain NP (see p.106)	The natural areas of the peninsula	Extraordinarily rich and diverse flora and fauna that thrives in the wilderness that is Cape Town's back yard
uKhahlamba-Drakensberg Park (see p.388)	Mountain reserve	A series of parks covering the highest, most stirring and most dramatic peaks in South Africa
West Coast NP (see p.198)	Marine and coastal	Wetland wilderness with birding and watersports

the bush. Many safari lodges have their own **waterholes**, overlooked by the bar or restaurant, from which you can watch animals drinking. Nowhere are the private reserves more developed than along the west flank of the Kruger, where you'll find the top-dollar prestigious lodges as well as some more affordable places.

A typical day at a private camp or lodge starts at **dawn** for tea or coffee, followed by guided **game viewing** on foot, or driving. After a mid-morning brunch/breakfast, there's the chance to spend time on a **viewing platform** or in a **hide**, quietly watching the passing scene. Late-afternoon game viewing is a repeat of early morning but culminates with **sundowners** as the light fades, and often turns into a **night drive** with spotlights looking for nocturnal creatures.

Prices, which include accommodation, meals and game-spotting activities, vary widely. The ultra-expensive camps offer more luxury and social cachet, but not necessarily better game viewing. You might find the cheaper camps in the same areas more to your taste, their plainer and wilder atmosphere more in keeping with the bush.

PARK FEES, RESERVATIONS AND ENQUIRIES

Fees given in our park accounts are generally daily conservation fees, which are essentially the entrance fees. The most expensive places are Kruger National Park and Kgalagadi Transfrontier Park, for which foreign visitors pay a conservation fee of R304 per adult (R152 per child), followed by Addo Elephant National Park where the adult fee is R248. The majority of the rest charge under R200, and small parks such as Bontebok charge R100. As a rule of thumb, visitors aged under 12 pay half the adult rate.

Accommodation at most national parks can be booked in advance through South African National Parks (in high season, you should try and book several months in advance). Exceptions include Pilanesberg (see p.508) and the KwaZulu-Natal reserves, for which you book through Ezemvelo KZN Wildlife. Booking with South African National Parks by phone usually involves a long wait; reserving online is the better option (see p.65).

Health

You can put aside most of the health concerns that may be justified in some parts of Africa; run-down hospitals and bizarre tropical diseases aren't typical of South Africa. All tourist areas boast generally high standards of hygiene and safe drinking water. The main hazard you're likely to encounter, and the one the majority of visitors are most blasé about, is the sun. In some parts of the country there is a risk of malaria, and you will need to take precautions.

Public **hospitals** are often well equipped and staffed, but the huge pressure they are under undermines their attempts to maintain standards. Expect long waits and frequently indifferent treatment. **Private hospitals** or clinics are a much better option for travellers and are well up to British and North American standards. You'll get to see a doctor quickly and costs are not excessive, unless you require an operation, in which case health insurance is a must.

Dental care in South Africa is also well up to British and North American standards, and is generally less expensive. You'll find dentists in most towns.

Inoculations

No specific inoculations are compulsory if you arrive in South Africa from the West, although the USA's *CDC* suggests several immunizations as routine for adults. In addition, it recommends inoculations against **typhoid** and **hepatitis A**, both of which can be caught from contaminated food or water. This is a worst-case scenario, however, as typhoid is eminently curable and few visitors to South Africa ever catch it. Vaccination against **hepatitis B** is essential only for people involved in health work; the disease is spread by the transfer of blood products – usually dirty needles.

A **yellow fever** vaccination certificate is necessary if you've come from a country where the disease is endemic, such as Kenya, Tanzania or tropical South America.

It's best to start organizing to have jabs **six weeks** before departure, and some clinics will not administer inoculations less than a fortnight before departure. If you're going to another African country first and need the yellow fever jab, note that a yellow fever certificate only becomes valid ten days after you've had the shot.

MEDICAL RESOURCES FOR TRAVELLERS

Canadian Society for International Health ☎ 613 241 5785, ⓦ csih.org. Extensive list of travel health centres.

CDC (Centers for Disease Control and Prevention) ☎ 800 232 4636, ⓦ cdc.gov/travel. Official US government travel health site.

Hospital for Tropical Diseases Travel Clinic ⓦ www.thehtd .org. Health advice for travellers, with a link to the British government's online travel health advice, and a shop selling goods such as first-aid kits, mosquito nets and suncream.

International Society for Travel Medicine US ☎ 1 404 373 8282, ⓦ istm.org. Has a global directory of travel health clinics.

MASTA (Medical Advisory Service for Travellers Abroad) ⓦ masta-travel-health.com. The UK's largest network of private travel clinics.

The Travel Doctor ⓦ traveldoctor.co.nz. Travel clinics in New Zealand and an online shop.

Travel Doctor ☎ 0861 300 911, ⓦ traveldoctor.co.za. Travel clinics in Cape Town, Stellenbosch, George and beyond.

Travel Doctor ⓦ traveldoctor.com.au. Travel clinics in Australia.

Tropical Medical Bureau ☎ 086 0728 999, ⓦ tmb.ie. Offers extensive advice for travellers, with a number of clinics in Ireland.

Stomach upsets

Stomach upsets from food are rare. Salad and ice – risky items in some developing countries – are bot█

perfectly safe. As with anywhere, don't keep food for too long, and be sure to wash fruit and vegetables as thoroughly as possible. Tap water is generally fine to drink, but bacteria levels rise as dam levels drop during the increasingly common droughts, when you may prefer to stick to bottled water.

If you do get a **stomach bug**, the best cure is lots of water and rest. Most chemists should have nonprescription anti-diarrhoea remedies and rehydration salts.

Avoid jumping for **antibiotics** at the first sign of illness. Instead keep them as a last resort – they don't work on viruses and they annihilate your gut flora (most of which you want to keep), making you more susceptible next time round. Taking probiotics helps to alleviate the latter side effect. Most tummy upsets will resolve themselves if you adopt a sensible **fat-free diet** for a couple of days, but if they do persist without improvement (or are accompanied by other unusual symptoms), see a doctor as soon as possible.

The sun

The **sun** is likely to be the worst hazard you'll encounter in Southern Africa, particularly if you're fair-skinned. Short-term effects of **overexposure** to the sun include burning, nausea and headaches. Make sure you wear **high-protection sunscreen**, a broad-brimmed hat and sunglasses, and don't stay too long in the sun – especially when you first arrive.

Extreme cases of overexposure to the sun, accompanied by dehydration, overexertion and intoxication, can lead to **heat exhaustion** or heatstroke.

Take particular care with **children**, who should be kept well covered at the seaside, preferably with UV-protective sun suits. Don't be lulled into complacency on **cloudy days**, when UV levels can still be high.

Bilharzia

One ailment that you need to take seriously throughout sub-Saharan Africa is **bilharzia** (schistosomiasis), carried in many freshwater lakes and rivers in northern and eastern South Africa except in the mountains. Bilharzia is spread by tiny, parasitic worm-like flukes which leave their water-snail hosts and burrow into human skin to multiply in the bloodstream; they then work their way to the walls of the intestine or bladder, where they lay **eggs**.

The chances are you'll avoid bilharzia even if you swim in a suspect river, but it's best to avoid **swimming** in dams, rivers and slow-moving water where possible. If you go **canoeing** or can't avoid the water, have a test for bilharzia when you return home.

Symptoms may be no more than a feeling of lassitude and ill health. Once the infection is established, abdominal pain and blood in the urine and stools are common, occasionally leading to kidney failure and bowel damage. Fortunately, bilharzia is easily and effectively treatable.

Malaria

Most of South Africa is free of **malaria**, a potentially lethal disease that is widespread in tropical and subtropical Africa, where it's a major killer. However, **protection** against malaria is essential if you're planning to travel to any of these areas: northern and northeastern Mpumalanga, notably the Kruger National Park; northern KwaZulu-Natal; or the border regions of Limpopo and, to a lesser degree, North West Province and the Northern Cape. The highest **risk** is during the hot, rainy months between October and May. The risk is reduced during the cooler, dry months from June to September, when some people decide not to take prophylactic medication.

Malaria is caused by a parasite carried in the saliva of the female anopheles mosquito. It has a variable incubation period of a few days to several weeks, so you can become ill long after being bitten. The first symptoms of malaria can be mistaken for **flu**, starting off relatively mildly with a variable combination that includes fever, aching limbs and shivering, which come in waves, usually beginning in the early evening. Deterioration can be rapid as the parasites in the bloodstream proliferate. Malaria is not **infectious**, but can be fatal if not treated quickly: get medical help without delay if you go down with flu-like symptoms a week after entering, or within three months of leaving, a malarial area.

Doctors can advise on which kind of **antimalarial tablets** to take. It's important to keep to the prescribed dose, which covers the period before and after your trip. Consult your **doctor** or **clinic** several weeks before you travel, as you should start taking medication a week or two before entering the affected region – depending on the particular drug you're using.

Whatever you decide to take, be aware that no antimalarial drug is totally effective – the most sure-fire protection is to **avoid getting bitten**. Malaria-carrying mosquitoes are active between **dusk** and **dawn**, so try to avoid being out at this time, or at least cover yourself well. Sleep under a **mosquito net** when possible, making sure to tuck it under the mattress, and burn **mosquito coils** (which you can buy everywhere) for a peaceful, if noxious, night. If you have access to a power supply, electric mosquito destroyers, which you fit with a pad, are less pungent than coils. Mosquito "buzzers" are useless. Whenever the mosquitoes are particularly bad, cover your exposed parts with **insect repellent**; those containing diethyltoluamide (DEET) work best. Other locally produced repellents such as Peaceful Sleep are widely available.

Bites and stings

Bites, **stings** and **rashes** in South Africa are comparatively rare. **Snakes** are present, but rarely seen as they move out of the way quickly. The aggressive puff and berg adders are the most dangerous, because they often lie on paths and don't move when humans approach. The best **advice** if you get bitten is to note what the snake looked like and get yourself to a clinic or hospital. Most bites are not fatal and the worst thing is to panic: desperate measures with razor blades and tourniquets can do more harm than good. It's more helpful to immobilise the bitten limb with a splint and apply a bandage over the bite.

Tick-bite fever is occasionally contracted from walking in the bush, particularly in long wet grass. The offending ticks can be minute and you may not spot them. **Symptoms** appear a week later – swollen glands and severe aching of the joints, backache and fever – and the disease should run its course in three or four days, but it is worth visiting the doctor for antibiotics. Ticks you may find on yourself are not dangerous – just make sure you pull out the head as well as the body (it's not painful). A good way of removing small ones is to press down with tweezers, grab the head and gently pull upwards.

Scorpion stings and **spider bites** are painful but almost never fatal, contrary to popular myth. Scorpions and spiders abound, but they're hardly ever seen unless you turn over logs and stones. If you're collecting wood for a campfire, knock or shake it before picking it up. Another simple **precaution** when camping is to shake out your shoes and clothes in the morning before you get dressed. Seek medical attention for scorpion stings if your condition deteriorates.

Rabies is present throughout Southern Africa, with **dogs** posing the greatest risk, although the disease can be carried by other animals. If you are bitten you should go immediately to a clinic or hospital. Rabies can be treated effectively with a course of **injections**. If you plan to spend time in remote areas without medical facilities close at hand, you can get pre-trip jabs, which will buy you more time to reach a clinic or hospital in the event of being bitten.

Sexually transmitted diseases

HIV/AIDS and venereal diseases are widespread in Southern Africa among both men and women, and the danger of catching the virus through sexual contact is very real. Avoid one-night stands with locals and follow the usual precautions regarding **safe sex**. There's very little risk from treatment in private medical facilities, but unsterilized equipment could be an issue in remote public hospitals. If you're travelling overland and want to play it safe, take your own well-stocked first-aid kit, including equipment such as needles.

Tuberculosis

TB is a serious problem in South Africa, but most travellers are at low risk. At higher risk are healthcare workers, long-term travellers and anyone with an impaired immune system, such as people infected with HIV. A **BCG vaccination** is routinely given to babies in South Africa, but its use elsewhere varies. Take medical advice on the question of **immunization** if you feel there may be a risk.

Crime and personal safety

Despite horror stories of sky-high crime rates, most people visit South Africa without incident; be careful, but not paranoid. This is not to underestimate the issue – crime is probably the most serious problem facing the country. But some perspective is in order: crime is disproportionately concentrated in the poor African and coloured townships. Violent crime is a problem throughout Johannesburg, from the city centre to the townships, and travellers are most at risk here. However, the greatest peril facing most visitors is navigating South Africa's roads, which claim well over ten thousand lives a year.

Protecting property and "**security**" are major national obsessions, and often a topic of conversation at dinner parties. A substantial percentage of middle-class homes subscribe to the services of armed private security firms. The other obvious manifestation of this obsession is the huge number of **alarms**, high walls and electronically controlled gates you'll see, not just in the suburbs, but even in less deprived areas of some townships. **Guns** are openly carried by police.

Drugs and drink-driving

Alcohol and **cannabis** in dried leaf form are South Africa's most widely used and abused drugs. The latter, known as dagga (pronounced like "dugger" with the "gg" guttural, as in the Scottish pronunciation of "loch"), is grown in hot regions like KwaZulu-Natal (the source of Durban Poison), Swaziland (Swazi Gold) and the Wild Coast. It is fairly easily available and the quality is generally good – but this doesn't alter the fact that it is **illegal**. If you do decide to partake, take particular care when scoring, as visitors have run into trouble dealing with unfamiliar local conditions.

Strangely, for a country that sometimes seems to be on one massive binge, South Africa has laws that prohibit **drinking** in public – not that anyone pays any attention. The drink-drive laws are routinely and brazenly flouted, making the country's **roads** the one real danger you should be concerned about. People routinely stock up their cars with booze for long journeys and levels of alcohol consumption

---

SAFETY TIPS

IN GENERAL:

- Dress down and try not to look too like a tourist.
- Avoid wearing expensive jewellery, eye gear and timepieces, carrying a camera or waving your phone around in cities.
- Use hotel safes.
- If you are accosted, remain calm and cooperative.

WHEN ON FOOT:

- Grasp bags firmly under your arm.
- Don't carry excessive sums of money on you.
- Don't put your wallet in your back trouser pocket.
- Always know where your valuables are.
- Don't leave valuables exposed (on a seat or the ground) while having a meal or drink.
- Don't let strangers get too close to you – especially people in groups.
- Travel around in pairs or groups and avoid isolated areas.
- Don't walk alone at night.

ON THE ROAD:

- Lock all your car doors, especially in cities.
- Keep rear windows sufficiently rolled up to keep out opportunistic hands.
- Never leave anything worth stealing in view when your car is unattended.
- If you've concealed valuables in the boot, don't open it after parking.

AT ATMS:

Cash machines are favourite hunting grounds for con men. Never underestimate their ability and don't get drawn into any interaction at an ATM, no matter how well spoken, friendly or distressed the other person appears. If they claim to have a problem with the machine, tell them to contact the bank. Don't let people crowd you or see your personal identification number (PIN) when you withdraw money; if in doubt, go to another machine. Finally, if your card gets swallowed, report it without delay.

WHEN PAYING WITH A CARD:

- Never let your plastic out of your sight.
- At a restaurant, ask for a portable card reader to be brought to your table.
- At the till, keep an eye on your card.
- If the transaction fails, don't try a second time; pay with cash or another card.

go some way to explaining why, during the Christmas holidays, over a thousand people die in an annual period of road carnage. Don't risk drinking and driving yourself, as nocturnal roadblocks are common in urban areas.

Sexual harassment

South Africa's extremely high incidence of **rape** doesn't as a rule affect tourists. However, sexism is more common and attitudes are not as progressive as in Western countries, especially in black communities. Sometimes your eagerness to be friendly may be taken as a sexual overture – always be sensitive to potential crossed wires and unintended signals.

Women should take care while travelling on their own, and never hitchhike or walk alone in deserted areas. This applies equally to cities, the countryside or anywhere after dark. Minibus taxis should be ruled out as a means of transport after dark, especially if you're not sure of the local geography.

The police

Poorly paid, shot at (and frequently hit), underfunded, badly equipped, barely respected and demoralized, the **South African Police Service** (SAPS) keeps a low profile. If you ever get stopped, at a **roadblock** for example (one of the likeliest

encounters), always be courteous. And if you're driving, note that under South African law you are required to carry your driver's **licence** at all times. If you are fined and you suspect corruption, asking to be issued with a receipt will discourage foul play or at least give you a record of the incident.

If **robbed**, you need to report the incident to the police, who should give you a case reference. Keep all paperwork for insurance purposes.

Travel essentials

Climate

Although South Africa is predominantly a dry, sunny country, bear in mind that the chart below shows average maximums. **June and July** temperatures can drop below zero in some places; be prepared for average minimums of 4°C in Johannesburg, 7°C in Cape Town and 11°C in Durban.

Costs

For budget and mid-range travellers, the most expensive thing about visiting South Africa is getting there. Once you've arrived, you're likely to find it a relatively **inexpensive** and good-value destination. This will depend partly on exchange

AVERAGE DAILY MAXIMUM TEMPERATURES

CAPE TOWN

	Jan	Feb	Mar	Apr	May	Jun	Jul	Aug	Sep	Oct	Nov	Dec
Max (°C)	27	27	26	23	20	19	17	18	19	22	24	26
Max (°F)	81	81	79	73	68	66	63	64	66	72	75	79

DURBAN

	Jan	Feb	Mar	Apr	May	Jun	Jul	Aug	Sep	Oct	Nov	Dec
Max (°C)	27	28	27	26	24	23	22	22	23	24	25	26
Max (°F)	81	82	81	79	75	73	72	72	73	75	77	79

JOHANNESBURG

	Jan	Feb	Mar	Apr	May	Jun	Jul	Aug	Sep	Oct	Nov	Dec
Max (°C)	26	26	24	22	19	16	16	20	23	25	25	26
Max (°F)	79	79	75	72	66	61	61	68	73	77	77	79

SKUKUZA (KRUGER NATIONAL PARK)

	Jan	Feb	Mar	Apr	May	Jun	Jul	Aug	Sep	Oct	Nov	Dec
Max (°C)	31	31	30	29	27	25	25	26	29	29	30	30
Max (°F)	88	88	86	84	81	77	77	79	84	84	86	86

MASERU (LESOTHO)

	Jan	Feb	Mar	Apr	May	Jun	Jul	Aug	Sep	Oct	Nov	Dec
Max (°C)	20	17	14	11	9	7	7	9	11	14	17	20
Max (°F)	68	63	57	52	48	45	45	48	52	57	63	68

rates at the time of your visit – since becoming fully convertible (after the advent of democracy in South Africa), the rand has seen some massive fluctuations against sterling, the dollar and the euro.

When it comes to daily budgets, your biggest expense is likely to be **accommodation**. If you limit yourself to backpacker dorms and self-catering, you should be able to sleep and eat for under R500 a day. If you stay in B&Bs and guesthouses, eat out once a day, and have a snack or two, budget for around double that. In top-end hotels expect to pay upwards of R2750 for a double, while luxury safari lodges in major game reserves charge from R3000 to over R10,000, with packages available including **extras** such as safaris, car rental, horseriding and other outdoor activities. While most museums and art galleries impose an **entry fee**, it's usually quite low: only the most sophisticated attractions charge more than R50.

Electricity

South Africa's electricity supply runs at 220/230V, 50Hz AC. Most **sockets** take unique plugs with three fat, round pins, although sockets taking European-style two-pin plugs are common. Most hotel rooms have sockets that will take 110V electric shavers, but for other appliances US visitors will need an **adaptor**.

Insurance

It's wise to take out an **insurance** policy to cover against theft, loss and illness or injury. A typical travel insurance policy usually provides cover for the loss of baggage, valuables and – up to a certain limit – cash and bank cards, as well as cancellation or curtailment of your journey. Most of them exclude so-called dangerous sports unless an extra **premium** is paid: in South Africa this can mean scuba diving, whitewater rafting, windsurfing, horseriding, bungee jumping and paragliding. In addition to these, check whether you are covered by your policy if you're hiking, kayaking, pony trekking or game viewing on safari, all activities people commonly take part in when visiting South Africa. Many policies can be chopped and changed to exclude **coverage** you don't need – for example, sickness and accident benefits can often be excluded or included at will.

If you do take **medical coverage**, ascertain whether benefits will be paid as treatment proceeds or only after you return home, if there's a 24-hour medical emergency number and if medical evacuation will be covered. When buying **baggage**

cover, make sure that the per-article limit will cover your most valuable possession. If you need to make a **claim**, you should keep receipts for medicines and medical treatment, and in the event of having anything stolen, you must obtain an official statement from the **police**.

Internet

Finding somewhere to access the **internet** will seldom be a problem in all but the most rural areas: cybercafés are found even in small towns, and most backpacker hostels and hotels have internet facilities, albeit sometimes too slow for Skype calls. It's easiest to bring your own device, enabling you to use the paid or free **wireless hotspots** of varying functionality at airports, cafés, malls and accommodation.

Bring your **smartphone** too, as South Africa is similar to the West in its increasing reliance on apps for ordering everything from taxis to takeaway food. It's wise and reassuring from a security point of view to have access to apps such as Google Maps, so you may wish to buy a local SIM with data or ensure your home SIM will work in the event of an emergency.

LGBT travellers

South Africa has the world's first gay- and lesbian-friendly constitution, and Africa's most developed and diverse gay and lesbian scene. Not only is homosexuality **legal** for consenting adults of 16 or over, but the constitution outlaws any **discrimination** on the grounds of sexual orientation. Outside the big cities, however, South Africa remains a **conservative** place, where open displays of public affection by gays and lesbians are unlikely to go down well. It's still especially hard for African and coloured men and women to come out, and homophobic attacks are a threat whatever your ethnicity, so be discreet and take care outside the city centres.

The tourist industry, on the other hand, is well aware of the potential of pink spending power and actively woos **gay travellers** – an effort that is evidently paying off, with Cape Town ranking among the world's top gay destinations (see box, p.148). The gay scene is typically multiracial in Johannesburg, especially the clubs, while Pretoria has a few gay and lesbian nightspots. There are also small gay scenes in Port Elizabeth and Durban, and you'll find gay-run or gay-friendly establishments in small towns. There are **gay pride** festivals in Cape Town in February and December (see p.148), Knysna in April and Joburg in October (Ⓦ johannesburgpride.co.za).

The **gay lifestyle magazine** Mamba (Ⓦ mambaonline.com) is one of the useful online resources, and you can download the app or listen online to **GaySA Radio** (Ⓦ gaysaradio.co.za).

Mail

The familiar feel of South African post offices can lull you into expecting an efficient British- or US-style service. In fact, mail within the country can be slow and unreliable, and certainly not safe for sending money or valuables. Expect domestic delivery times from one city to another of about a week – longer if a rural town is involved at either end.

International airmail deliveries are often quicker, thanks to direct flights to London. A letter or package sent by surface mail can take up to six weeks to get to London. Delivery is even less reliable and trustworthy coming into the country, when items frequently disappear or take weeks to arrive.

Most towns of any size have a **post office**, generally open Monday to Friday 8.30am to 4.30pm and Saturday till noon (closing earlier in some places). The ubiquitous private **PostNet** outlets (Ⓦ postnet.co.za) are a better option, offering many of the same postal services as the post office and more, including **courier services**. Courier companies like FedEx (Ⓣ 0800 033 339, Ⓦ fedex .com/za) and DHL (Ⓣ 086 034 5000, Ⓦ dhl.co.za) – operating only in the larger towns – are far more reliable than the mail.

Stamps are available at post offices and from newsagents such as the CNA chain. Postage is relatively inexpensive – it costs about R8 to send a postcard by airmail to anywhere in the world, while a small letter costs just over R9. You can open a **post box** at most post offices and PostNet branches.

Maps

Many **place and street names** in South Africa have been changed since the 1994 elections, so if you buy a **map**, make sure it's up to date. Bartholomew produces an excellent map of South Africa, including Lesotho and Swaziland, as part of its World Travel Map series. **MapStudio** (Ⓦ mapstudio.co.za) produces and sells a range of excellent maps, while Cape Town's **Slingsby Maps** (Ⓦ slingsbymaps.com) publish the best hiking and touring maps of the **Western Cape** and beyond. Slingsby's maps, which include the Cape Peninsula, Winelands and Garden Route, are available at South Africa bookshops.

South Africa's motoring organization, the **Automobile Association** (Ⓦ aa.co.za), has free maps available to download from its website.

Money

South Africa's currency is the **rand** (R), often called the "buck", divided into 100 **cents**. Notes come in R10, R20, R50, R100 and R200 denominations and there are coins of 5, 10, 20 and 50 cents, as well as R1, R2 and R5. The **exchange rate** fluctuates frequently; at the time of writing, it averaged around R17 to the pound sterling, R13 to the US dollar, R14 to the euro and R10 to the Australian dollar.

All but the tiniest settlement will have a **bank**, where you can withdraw and change money, or an ATM. **Banking hours** vary, but are at least from Monday to Friday 9am to 3.30pm, and Saturday 8.30am to 11am; banks in smaller towns usually close for lunch. In major cities, large hotels and banks operate **bureaux de change**. Outside banking hours, some hotel receptions will change money, although this entails a fairly hefty **commission**.

You can also change money at branches of American Express (Ⓦ americanexpressforex.co.za). **Keep exchange receipts**, which you'll need to show to convert your leftover rand at the end of your trip.

Cards and travellers' cheques

Credit and **debit cards** are the most convenient way to access your funds in South Africa. Most international cards can be used to withdraw money at **ATMs**. Plastic comes in very handy for paying for more mainstream and upmarket tourist facilities, and is essential for car rental. **Visa** and **Mastercard** are most widely accepted.

American Express, Visa and Thomas Cook **travellers' cheques** are widely accepted. US dollar and sterling cheques are accepted, and better to carry than cheques in the weaker rand.

In remoter areas, you'll need to carry **cash** to tide you between ATMs, which are unreliable in rural regions. Stash it in a safe place, or even better in a few places on your person and baggage.

Opening hours and holidays

The **working day** starts and finishes early in South Africa: shops and businesses generally open on **weekdays** around 8.30am and close at 4.30pm. In small towns, many places close for an hour over **lunch**. Many shops and businesses close around noon on Saturdays, and most shops are closed on Sundays. However, in urban neighbourhoods, you'll find small shops and supermarkets where you can buy groceries and essentials after hours. Some establishments have different opening times in summer (September to March) and winter (April to August).

School holidays can disrupt your plans, especially if you want to camp, or stay in the national parks and the budget end of accommodation (self-catering, cheaper B&Bs, etc). All are likely to be booked solid during holiday periods, especially along the coast. If you travel to South Africa over a school holiday, book accommodation well in advance, particularly for the national parks.

SOUTH AFRICAN PUBLIC HOLIDAYS

Many tourist-related businesses and some shops remain open over public holidays, although often with shorter opening hours. Most of the country shuts down on Christmas Day and Good Friday. The main holidays are:

New Year's Day (Jan 1)
Human Rights Day (March 21)
Good Friday, Easter Monday (variable)
Freedom Day (April 27)
Workers' Day (May 1)
Youth Day (June 16)
National Women's Day (Aug 9)
Heritage Day (Sept 24)
Day of Reconciliation (Dec 16)
Christmas Day (Dec 25)
Day of Goodwill (Dec 26)

EMERGENCY NUMBERS

Police ☎ 10111; fire and state ambulance ☎ 10177; cellphone emergency operator ☎ 112; ER24 private ambulance and paramedic assistance ☎ 084 124; Netcare911 ☎ 082 911.

The longest and busiest holiday period is **Christmas** (summer), which for schools stretches from early December to mid-January. Flights and train berths can be hard to get from mid-December to early January, when many businesses and offices close for their annual break. You should book your **flights** – long-haul and domestic – six months in advance for the Christmas period.

The remaining school holidays roughly cover the following periods: **Easter**, late March to mid-April; **winter**, late June to mid-July; and **spring**, late September to early October. Exact **dates** for each year are listed at ⊛ gov.za/about-sa/school-calendar.

Phones

South Africa's **telephone** system, dominated by Telkom, generally works well. Public phone booths are found in every city and town, and are either coin- or card-operated. While international calls can be made from virtually any phone, it helps to have a **phone card** such as Telkom WorldCall. Prepaid WorldCall vouchers and recharge cards are available at Telkom offices, supermarkets, banks and more in denominations of R10 upwards.

Mobile phones (referred to locally as cell phones) are widely used in South Africa, with more mobiles than landlines in use. The competing networks – Vodacom, MTN, Cell C and Virgin Mobile – cover all main areas and the national roads connecting them.

You can use 2G, 3G and 4G phones from outside South Africa, but you will need a **roaming** agreement with your provider at home. A far cheaper alternative is to buy an inexpensive prepaid **local SIM card**. These can be bought for about R20 from the ubiquitous mobile phone shops and various other outlets, including supermarkets. You will need your ID and a proof of address, which can be a hotel receipt or a signed letter from your accommodation or host. You can subsequently purchase data bundles as well as call credit.

INTERNATIONAL CODES

South Africa's international country code is ☎ 27. To dial out of South Africa, the **access code** is ☎ 00. In both cases, remember to omit the initial zero in the number of the place you're phoning.

Taxes

Value-added tax (**VAT**) of fourteen percent is levied on most goods and services, though it's usually already included in any quoted price. Foreign visitors can claim back VAT on goods over R250 total. To do this, present an official tax receipt, which should carry your name and address in the case of purchases over R5000, along with a proof of payment for purchases over R10,000, a non-South African passport and the purchased goods themselves, at the **airport** just before you fly out. You will also need to fill in a form, which can be obtained at the airport. For more information, call 📞 011 979 0055 or visit 🌐 taxrefunds.co.za.

Time

There is only one **time zone** in South Africa, two hours ahead of GMT year-round. If you're flying from Europe, you shouldn't experience any jet lag.

Tipping

Ten to fifteen percent of the tab is the normal **tip**, while taxi fares are generally rounded up. Don't feel obliged to tip if service has been shoddy, but bear in mind that many of the people who'll be serving you rely on tips to supplement a meagre wage on which they support huge extended families. Hotel **porters** normally get about R10 per bag. At petrol stations, someone will always be on hand to fill your vehicle, clean your windscreen and check your oil, water and tyre pressure, for which you should tip R5–10. Car guards meanwhile expect around R2–5. It is also usual at **hotels** to leave some money for the person who services your room. Many establishments, especially private game lodges, take (voluntary) communal tips when you check out – by far the fairest system, which ensures that all the low-profile staff behind the scenes get their share.

Tourist information

Given South Africa's booming tourism industry, it's not surprising that you'll have no difficulty finding **maps**, **books** and **brochures** before you leave. South African Tourism, the official organization promoting the country, is reasonably efficient: if there's an office near you, it's worth visiting for free maps, **information** and inspiration. Alternatively, check its **website** 🌐 southafrica.net.

In South Africa itself, nearly every town, right down to the sleepiest *dorp*, has some sort of **tourist office**

– sometimes connected to the museum, municipal offices or library – where you can pick up local maps, lists of B&Bs and local advice. In larger cities such as Cape Town, you'll find several branches offering everything from accommodation reservations to game park bookings. We've listed the business hours of tourist offices in the Guide, though they generally open at least Monday to Friday 8.30am to 4.30pm, with some also open shorter hours over weekends.

In this fast-changing country the best way of finding out what's happening is often by word of mouth, and for this, backpacker **hostels** are invaluable. If you're seeing South Africa on a budget, their useful notice boards, constant traveller traffic and largely helpful and friendly staff will smooth your travels.

To find out what's on, check out the entertainment pages of the daily **newspapers** or better still buy the *Mail & Guardian* (🌐 mg.co.za), which comes out every Friday and lists the coming week's offerings in a comprehensive pullout supplement.

TRAVEL ADVISORIES

Australian Department of Foreign Affairs 🌐 dfat.gov.au.
British Foreign & Commonwealth Office 🌐 fco.gov.uk.
Canadian Global Affairs 🌐 international.gc.ca.
Irish Department of Foreign Affairs 🌐 foreignaffairs.gov.ie.
New Zealand Ministry of Foreign Affairs 🌐 mfat.govt.nz.
US State Department 🌐 state.gov.

Travellers with disabilities

Facilities for **disabled travellers** are not as sophisticated as those you might find in developed countries, but they're sufficient to ensure you have a satisfactory visit. You will often find good **accessibility** to many buildings, as South Africans tend to build low (single-storey bungalows are the norm). As the car is king, you'll frequently find that you can drive to, and park right outside, your destination. There are organized **tours** and **holidays** for people with disabilities, and activity-based packages are available. These offer the possibility for wheelchair-bound visitors to take part in safaris and a range of adventure **activities**. Tours can either be taken as self-drive trips or as packages for groups.

USEFUL CONTACTS

🌐 **brandsouthafrica.com/tourism-south-africa/travel /advice/disabled** Useful overview and links.
🌐 **capetown.travel** Cape Town Tourism has a page on wheelchair-friendly activities.
🌐 **disabledtravel.co.za** Website of occupational therapist Karin Coetzee aimed at disabled travellers, with listings of accommodation,

restaurants and attractions personally evaluated for accessibility, as well as links to car rental, tours and orthopaedic equipment.

ⓦ **epic-enabled.com** Accommodation, tours and safaris.

ⓦ **flamingotours.co.za** Flamingo Tours and Disabled Ventures specialize in tours for visitors with special needs.

ⓦ **rollingsa.co.za** Accommodation, tours and safaris.

ⓦ **sanparks.org/groups/disabilities/general.php** Lists what wheelchair and mobility-impaired access and facilities are available at South African National Parks.

Travelling with children

Travelling with **children** is straightforward in South Africa, whether you want to explore a city, relax on the beach, or head for the tranquillity of the mountains. You'll find local people friendly, attentive and accepting of babies and young children. The major complication is the **paperwork requirements** for children entering South Africa (see box, p.48).

The following information is aimed mainly at families with under-5s. Although children up to 24 months only pay ten percent of the adult **airfare**, they get no seat allowance. Given this, you'd be well advised to secure bulkhead seats and reserve a basinet or sky cot, which can be attached to the bulkhead. **Basinets** are often allocated to babies under about nine months, though many airlines use weight (under 10kg) as the criterion.

Given the size of the country, you're likely to **drive** long distances. Go slowly and plan a route that allows frequent stops – or take flights or trains between centres. The Garden Route, for example, is an ideal drive, with easy stops for picnics between Mossel Bay and Storms River. The route between Johannesburg and Cape Town, conversely, is long, dangerous and tedious.

Game viewing can be boring for young children, since it too involves a lot of driving – and disappointment, should the promised beasts fail to appear. Toddlers also won't particularly enjoy watching animals from afar and through a window. If they are old enough to enjoy the experience, make sure they have their own **binoculars**. To get in closer, some animal parks, such as Tshukudu Bush Camp (ⓦtshukudubushcamp.co.za) near Kruger, have semi-tame animals, while snake and reptile parks are an old South African favourite.

Family accommodation is plentiful, and hotels, guesthouses, B&Bs and a growing number of backpacker lodges have rooms with extra beds or interconnecting rooms. Kids usually stay for half-price. Self-catering options, such as farmstays, generally have a good deal of space to play in, and there'll often be a **pool**. A number of resorts cater to families with older children, with suitable activities offered. Among these, the **Forever** chain (ⓦforeversa.co.za) has resorts in beautiful settings including Keurboomstrand near Plettenberg Bay, and two close to the Blyde River Canyon in Mpumalanga. Another option is full-board family hotels, of which there are a number along the Wild Coast (see p.337), with playgrounds and canoes for paddling about lagoons, and often **nannies** to look after the kids. Note that many **safari lodges** don't allow children under 12, so you'll have to self-cater or camp in many parks and reserves.

Eating out with a baby or toddler is easy, with many outdoor venues where they can get on unhindered with their exploration of the world. Some restaurants have highchairs and offer small portions. If in doubt, try the ubiquitous family-oriented **chains** such as Spur, Nando's or Wimpy.

Breast-feeding is practised by the majority of African mothers wherever they are, though you won't see many white women doing it in public. Be discreet, especially in more conservative areas – which is most of the country outside middle-class Cape Town, Johannesburg and Durban. There are relatively few **baby rooms** in public places for changing or feeding, although the situation is improving and you shouldn't have a problem at shopping malls in the cities. You can buy disposable **nappies** wherever you go, as well as wipes, bottles, formula and dummies. High-street chemists and the Clicks chain are the best places to buy baby goods. If you run out of **clothes**, the Woolworths chain has good-quality stuff, while the ubiquitous Pep stores, present in even the smallest towns, are an excellent source of cheap, functional clothes.

Malaria (see p.71) affects only a small part of the country, but think carefully about visiting these areas as some preventatives aren't recommended for babies or pregnant or breastfeeding women. Avoid many of the northeastern **game reserves**, particularly Kruger National Park and those in KwaZulu-Natal, Limpopo and the North West Province; opt instead for malaria-free reserves, such as Addo Elephant National Park. Malarial zones have a reduced risk in winter.

USEFUL CONTACTS

ⓦ **capetownkids.co.za** Resources for parents and children in Cape Town.

ⓦ **childmag.co.za** South African parenting guide.

ⓦ **jozikids.co.za** Resources for parents and children in Johannesburg.

ⓦ **sitters4u.co.za** Babysitters in Cape Town and Gauteng.

ⓦ **supersitters.net** Babysitters in Cape Town.

Cape Town and the Cape Peninsula

VIEW OF LION'S HEAD AND THE TWELVE APOSTLES

1

Cape Town and the Cape Peninsula

Cape Town is one of Africa's most beautiful, most romantic and most visited cities. Its physical setting is extraordinary, something its pre-colonial Khoikhoi inhabitants acknowledged when they referred to Table Mountain, the city's famous landmark, as Hoerikwaggo – the mountain in the sea. Even more extraordinary is that so close to the national park that extends over much of the peninsula, there's a vibrant metropolis with nightlife to match the city's wildlife. You can swim with penguins at Boulders Beach and see the continent's southwestern tip at Cape Point, enjoy a lingering lunch on the chichi Atlantic seaboard and taste fine wines on a historic Constantia estate, before partying the night away in a Long Street club. It's all in a Mother City day.

More than a scenic backdrop, **Table Mountain** is the solid core of Cape Town, dividing the city into distinct zones with public gardens, wilderness, forests, hiking routes, vineyards and desirable residential areas trailing down its lower slopes. Standing on the table top, you can look north for a giddy view of the **city centre**, its docks lined with matchbox ships. To the west, beyond the mountainous Twelve Apostles, the drop is sheer and your eye sweeps across Africa's priciest real estate, clinging to the slopes along the chilly but spectacularly beautiful **Atlantic seaboard**. To the south, the mountainsides are forested and several historic vineyards and the marvellous Kirstenbosch Gardens creep up the lower slopes. Beyond the oak-lined suburbs of Newlands and Constantia lies the **False Bay seaboard**, which curves around towards **Cape Point**. Finally, relegated to the grim and windblown Cape Flats, are the coloured neighbourhoods and black **townships** – a stark introduction to Cape Town when driving in from the airport towards the alluring Table Mountain, and an immediate reminder that you are visiting an unequal, divided city.

To appreciate Cape Town you need to spend time **outdoors**, as Capetonians do: they hike, picnic or sunbathe, often choose mountain bikes in preference to cars, and turn **adventure activities** into an obsession. Sailboarders from around the world

LONG STREET NIGHTLIFE

Highlights

❶ South African National Gallery Check out the sculpture *Butcher Boys* by Jane Alexander, the epitome of surreal menace. **See p.96**

❷ Bo-Kaap One of Cape Town's oldest residential areas, its hilly streets characterized by colourful nineteenth-century Cape Dutch and Georgian terraces. **See p.99**

❸ Robben Island The infamous island prison where Nelson Mandela lived for nearly two decades, breaking rocks in the quarry and planning the end of apartheid. See p.104

❹ Rotate up Table Mountain The revolving cable car is the city's easiest route to some breathtaking views. **See p.106**

❺ Kirstenbosch National Botanical Garden Picnic or hike in one of the world's loveliest botanical gardens. **See p.111**

❻ Boulders Beach The False Bay beach offers wonderful bathing and is home to an African penguin colony. **See p.126**

❼ Cape Point The dramatically rocky southernmost section of the Cape Peninsula offers spectacular views and walks. **See p.127**

❽ Township tour See where most Capetonians live and visit an artist's home gallery in Langa, the city's oldest township. **See p.129**

❾ Long Street nightlife Party till the early hours along the city centre's nightlife hub. **See p.145**

HIGHLIGHTS ARE MARKED ON THE MAP ON P.84

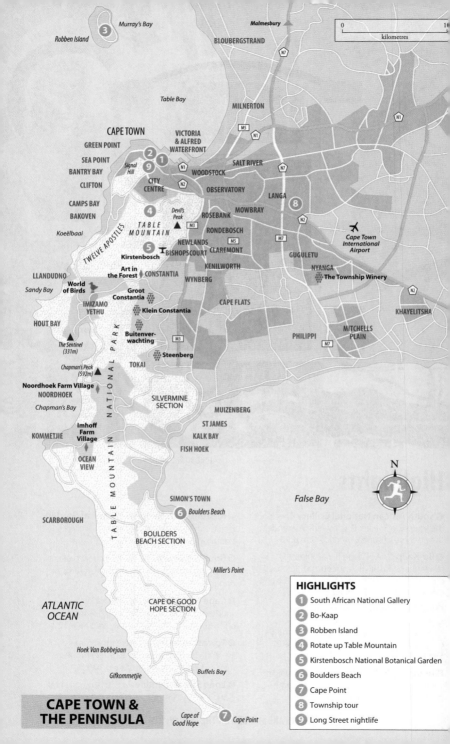

Murray's Bay
Robben Island ③

Malmesbury
BLOUBERGSTRAND

N7

Table Bay
MILNERTON

N1

N5
CAPE TOWN
GREEN POINT
VICTORIA
& ALFRED
WATERFRONT
SEA POINT ②
② ①
N1
WOODSTOCK
SALT RIVER
N7
BANTRY BAY
Signal
Hill
⑨
CLIFTON
CITY
CENTRE
N2
OBSERVATORY
LANGA ⑧
CAMPS BAY
④
Devil's
Peak
ROSEBANK
MOWBRAY
N2
BAKOVEN
TABLE
MOUNTAIN
M3
Koeëlbaai
TWELVE APOSTLES
NEWLANDS
RONDEBOSCH
M5
Cape Town
International
Airport
⑤ Kirstenbosch
BISHOPSCOURT
CLAREMONT
M7
GUGULETU
LLANDUDNO
Art in
the Forest
CONSTANTIA
KENILWORTH
NYANGA
The Township Winery
Sandy Bay
World
of Birds
WYNBERG
N2
Groot
Constantia
IMIZAMO
YETHU
Klein Constantia
CAPE FLATS
KHAYELITSHA
HOUT BAY
NATIONAL
Buitenver-
wachting
M3
PHILIPPI
MITCHELLS
PLAIN
The Sentinel
(331m)
Steenberg
M7
Chapman's Peak
(592m)
TOKAI
Noordhoek Farm Village
NOORDHOEK
PARK
SILVERMINE
SECTION
Chapman's Bay
Imhoff
Farm
Village
MUIZENBERG
KOMMETJIE
ST JAMES
OCEAN
VIEW
KALK BAY
FISH HOEK
TABLE MOUNTAIN
N
SIMON'S TOWN
False Bay
SCARBOROUGH
⑥ Boulders Beach
BOULDERS
BEACH SECTION
Miller's Point

ATLANTIC
OCEAN
CAPE OF GOOD
HOPE SECTION

Hoek Van Bobbejaan

Gifkommetjie
Buffels Bay

CAPE TOWN &
THE PENINSULA
Cape of
Good Hope
⑦ Cape Point

0   10
kilometres

HIGHLIGHTS
① South African National Gallery
② Bo-Kaap
③ Robben Island
④ Rotate up Table Mountain
⑤ Kirstenbosch National Botanical Garden
⑥ Boulders Beach
⑦ Cape Point
⑧ Township tour
⑨ Long Street nightlife

head to the Atlantic seaboard for windsurfing and kiteboarding, and the brave jump off Lion's Head and paraglide down close to the Camps Bay or Clifton beachfront. But the city offers sedate pleasures as well, along its hundreds of paths and 150km of beaches.

Cape Town's rich urban texture is immediately apparent in its varied **architecture**: the signature Cape Dutch style, rooted in northern Europe, is seen at its grandest on the Constantia wine estates and typified by whitewashed gables. Muslim dissidents and slaves, freed in the nineteenth century, added their minarets to the skyline, while the English, who invaded and freed the slaves, introduced Georgian and Victorian buildings. In the tightly packed terraces of the present-day Bo-Kaap and the tenements of District Six, coloured descendants of slaves evolved a unique, evocatively Cape brand of jazz, which is well worth catching live if you can.

Brief history

San hunter-gatherers, South Africa's first human inhabitants, moved freely through the Cape Peninsula for tens of millennia before being edged into the interior some two thousand years ago by the arrival of sheep-herding **Khoikhoi** migrants from the north. Over the following 1600 years, the Khoikhoi held sway over the Cape pastures. **Portuguese** mariners, in search of a route to East Africa and the East Indies, first rounded the Cape in the 1480s, and named it Cabo da Boa Esperança (Cape of Good Hope), but their attempts at trading with the Khoikhoi were short-lived.

The Cape goes Dutch

The Europeans did not seriously attempt to create a permanent stopping-off point at the Cape until the **Dutch East India Company** cruised into Table Bay in 1652 and set up shop. The Dutch East India Company, the world's largest corporation at the time, planned little more than a halfway house, to provide fresh produce to their ships trading between Europe and the East. Their small landing party, led by **Jan van Riebeeck**, built a mud fort where the Grand Parade now stands and established **vegetable gardens**, which they hoped to work with indigenous labour.

The Khoikhoi were understandably none too keen to swap their freedom for servitude, so Van Riebeeck began to import **slaves** in 1658, first from West Africa and later the East Indies. The growth of the Dutch settlement alarmed the Khoikhoi, who in 1659 tried to drive the Europeans out; however, they were defeated and had to cede the peninsula to the colonists. By 1700, the settlement had grown into an urban centre, referred to as "Kaapstad" (Cape Town).

During the early eighteenth century, Western Cape Khoikhoi society disintegrated, **German** and **French** religious refugees swelled the European population, and slavery became the economic backbone of the colony, now a minor colonial village of canals and low, whitewashed, flat-roofed houses. By 1750, however, Cape Town was a town of over a thousand buildings, with 2500 inhabitants.

Goodbye slavery, hello segregation

In 1795, **Britain**, deeply concerned by Napoleonic expansionism, grabbed Cape Town to secure the strategic sea route to the East. This displaced the settlement's Calvinist Dutch burghers, but was better news for the substantially Muslim slave population,

---

WINDY CITY

Weather is an abiding obsession of Capetonians, particularly the **southeaster** or Cape Doctor, the cool summer wind that blows in across False Bay. It can singlehandedly determine the kind of day you're going to have, and when it gusts at over 60km/h you won't want to be outdoors, let alone on the beach. Equally, the **Cape Doctor** brings welcome relief on humid summer days, and lays the famous cloudy **tablecloth** on top of Table Mountain.

1

as Britain ordered the **emancipation of slaves** in 1834. The British also allowed **freedom of religion**, and South Africa's first mosque was soon built by freed slaves, in Dorp Street in the Bo-Kaap.

By the turn of the nineteenth century, Cape Town had become one of the most cosmopolitan places in the world and a seaport of major significance, growing under the influence of the British Empire. The Commercial Exchange was completed in 1819, followed by department stores, banks and insurance company buildings. In the 1860s the docks were begun, Victoria Road was built from the city to Sea Point, and the suburban railway line to Wynberg, one of the Southern Suburbs, was laid. Since slavery had been abolished, Victorian Cape Town had to be built by **convicts** and prisoners of war transported from the colonial frontier in the Eastern Cape (see p.300). Racial segregation wasn't far behind, and an outbreak of bubonic plague in 1901 gave the town council a pretext to establish **Ndabeni**, Cape Town's first black location, near Maitland.

In 1910, Cape Town was drawn into the political centre of the newly federated South Africa when it became the **legislative capital** of the Union (see p.641). Black Africans and coloured people, excluded from the cosy deal between the Boers and the British, had to find expression in the workplace. In 1919, they flexed their collective muscle on the docks, forming the mighty **Industrial and Commercial Workers Union**, which boasted two hundred thousand members in its heyday.

Competing nationalisms

Increasing industrialization brought an influx of black workers to the city, who were housed in the locations of **Guguletu** and **Nyanga**, both built in the mid-twentieth century. In 1948, the whites-only National Party came to power, promising a fearful white electorate that it would reverse the flow of Africans to the cities. In Cape Town it introduced a policy favouring coloured people for employment, rather than black Africans; in the latter group, only men who had jobs were admitted to Cape Town, women were excluded altogether, and the construction of family accommodation for Africans was forbidden.

Langa township, just east of the suburb of Pinelands, became a stronghold of the exclusively black **Pan Africanist Congress** (PAC), which organized a peaceful anti-pass demonstration in Langa on March 30, 1960. As a result of the march and the subsequent unrest, the government declared a state of emergency and banned anti-apartheid opposition groups, including the PAC and ANC.

In 1966, the notorious **Group Areas Act** was used to uproot whole coloured communities from District Six and move them to the desolate **Cape Flats**. Here, rampant gangsterism took root and remains one of Cape Town's most pressing problems today. To compound the issue, the National Party stripped away coloured representation on the town council in 1972.

THE LANGUAGE OF COLOUR

It's striking just how un-African Cape Town looks and sounds. Halfway between East and West, Cape Town drew its population from Africa, Asia and Europe, and traces of all three continents are found in the genes, language, culture, religion and cuisine of South Africa's coloured population. **Afrikaans** (a close relative of Dutch) is the mother tongue of more than half the city's population. Having said that, about thirty percent of Capetonians are born English-speakers, and **English** punches well above its weight as the local lingua franca, which, in this multilingual society, virtually everyone can speak and understand.

Afrikaans is the mother tongue of a large proportion of the city's **coloured** residents, as well as Afrikaners. The term "coloured" is contentious, but in South Africa it doesn't have the same tainted connotations as in Britain and the US, referring simply to South Africans of mixed race. Over forty percent of Capetonians are coloured, with Asian, African and Khoikhoi ancestry.

Resistance resumes

Eleven years later, at a huge meeting on the Cape Flats, the extra-parliamentary opposition defied government repression and re-formed as the **United Democratic Front**, heralding a period of intensified opposition to apartheid. In 1986, one of the major pillars crumbled when the government was forced to scrap influx control; blacks began pouring into Cape Town seeking work and erecting shantytowns, making Cape Town one of the fastest-growing cities in the world. On February 11, 1990, the city's history took a neat twist when, just hours after being released from prison, **Nelson Mandela** made his first public speech from the balcony of City Hall to a jubilant crowd spilling across the Grand Parade, the very site of the first Dutch fort. Four years later, he entered the formerly whites-only Parliament, 500m away, as South Africa's first democratically elected president.

Transformation

One of the anomalies of the 1994 election was that while most of South Africa delivered an **ANC landslide**, the Western Cape returned the **National Party**, the party that invented apartheid, as its provincial government. Politics in South Africa were not, it turned out, divided along a fault line that separated whites from the rest of the population, as many had assumed; the majority of coloured people had voted for the party that had once stripped them of the vote, regarding it with less suspicion than they did the black-dominated ANC. The Western Cape and its capital have consistently bucked South Africa's national trend of overwhelming ANC dominance. Since 2006 both have been governed by the liberal Democratic Alliance (DA), which maintains Cape Town as the city in the country with the least corruption and best infrastructure and facilities, though there have been violent protests in the townships about non-delivery of services. The city also suffers from a slew of other problems – poverty, unemployment, rampant crime and high infection rates for HIV and TB – with housing one of the biggest issues facing the metropolis (and, indeed, the whole of South Africa). Planners project that within the next twenty years the city's **population** will grow from its present 3.8 million to anywhere between five and seven million inhabitants. Cape Town remains a divided city, and one where inequality is extreme.

The City Centre

Strand Street marks the edge of Cape Town's original beachfront (though you'd never guess it today), and all urban development to its north stands on reclaimed land. To its southwest is the **Upper City Centre**, containing the remains of the city's 350-year-old historic core, which has survived the ravages of modernization and apartheid-inspired urban clearance, and emerged with enough charm to make it South Africa's most pleasing city centre. The entire area from Strand Street to the northern foot of Table Mountain is a collage of Georgian, Cape Dutch, Victorian and twentieth-century architecture, as well as being the place where Europe, Asia and Africa meet in markets, alleyways and mosques. Among the drawcards here are **Parliament**, the **Company's Garden** and many of Cape Town's major **museums**. North of Strand Street to the shore, the **Lower City Centre** takes in the still-functional **Duncan Dock**.

The Upper City Centre

Adderley Street, running southwest from the train station to the Company's Garden, is a useful orientation axis here. To its east, and close to each other just off Strand Street, are the **Castle of Good Hope**, the site of **District Six**, the **Grand Parade** and the **City Hall**. The district to the west of Adderley Street is the closest South Africa gets to a European

1

CITY CENTRE & SUBURBS

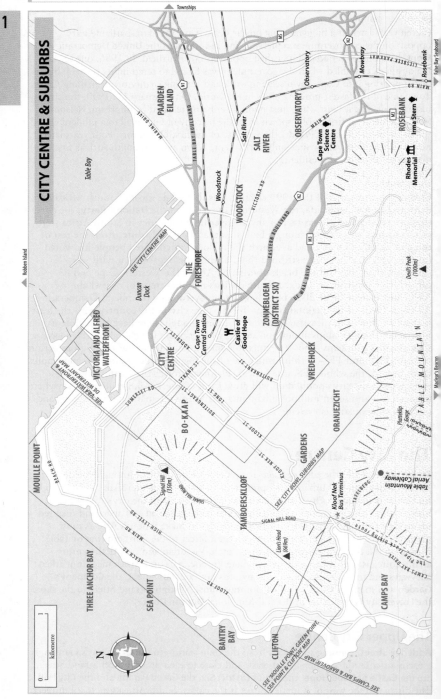

Townships

Table Bay

Robben Island

Mouille Point

BEACH RD

MAIN RD

HIGH LEVEL RD

SIGNAL HILL ROAD

Signal Hill (350m)

Lion's Head (669m)

THREE ANCHOR BAY

SEA POINT

BANTRY BAY

CLIFTON

KLOOF RD

CAMPS BAY

CAMPS BAY DRIVE

The Pipe Track Hiking Route

TAMBOERSKLOOF

BO-KAAP

SOMERSET RD

STRAND ST

BUITENGRACHT ST

LONG ST

KLOOF ST

KLOOF NEK ST

GARDENS

ORANJEZICHT

Kloof Nek Bus Terminus

Table Mountain Aerial Cableway

TAFELBERG RD

Platteklip Gorge

Maclear's Beacon

TABLE MOUNTAIN

VREDEHOEK

BUITENKANT ST

ADDERLEY ST

CITY CENTRE

Cape Town Central Station

Castle of Good Hope

THE FORESHORE

Duncan Dock

VICTORIA AND ALFRED WATERFRONT

SEE 'V&A WATERFRONT & DE WE WATERFRONT' MAP

SEE 'CITY CENTRE MAP

ZONNEBLOEM (DISTRICT SIX)

DE WAAL DRIVE

Devil's Peak (1000m)

VICTORIA RD

EASTERN BOULEVARD

WOODSTOCK

Woodstock

Salt River

SALT RIVER

TABLE BAY BOULEVARD

MARINE DRIVE

PAARDEN EILAND

M5

W1

N2

M3

OBSERVATORY

Observatory

Cape Town Science Centre

Rhodes Memorial

ROSEBANK

Irma Stern

Mowbray

Rosebank

LIESBEEK PARKWAY

MAIN RD

False Bay Seaboard

SEE 'CITY BOWL SUBURBS' MAP

SEE 'MOUILLE POINT, GREEN POINT, SEA POINT & CLIFTON' MAP

N

0   1
kilometre

THE NAMING OF ADDERLEY STREET

Although the Dutch used Robben Island as a political prison (see p.104), the South African mainland only narrowly escaped becoming a second Australia, a **penal colony** where British felons and enemies of the state could be dumped. By the 1840s, "respectable Australians" were lobbying for a ban on the transportation of criminals to the Antipodes, and the British authorities responded by trying to divert convicts to the Cape.

In 1848, the British ship *Neptune* set sail from Bermuda for Cape Town carrying 282 prisoners. When news of its departure reached Cape Town there was outrage; five thousand citizens gathered on the Grand Parade the following year to hear prominent liberals denounce the British government. When the ship docked in September 1849, governor Sir Harry Smith forbade any criminal from landing while, back in London, politician **Charles Adderley** successfully addressed the House of Commons in support of the Cape colonists. In February 1850, the *Neptune* set off for Tasmania with its full complement of convicts, and grateful Capetonians renamed the city's main thoroughfare **Adderley Street**.

quarter – a tight network of streets with cafés, buskers, craft markets, street stalls and antique shops congregating around the pedestrianized **St George's Mall** and **Greenmarket Square**. A few blocks further west across Buitengracht (which means Outer Canal; the canal here, like many that once earned Cape Town the nickname Little Amsterdam, was buried underground in the nineteenth century) is the **Bo-Kaap**, or Muslim quarter. This district is a piquant contrast with its colourful houses, minarets, spice shops and stalls selling curried snacks.

Southwest of the top of Adderley Street, where it takes a sharp right into Wale Street, is the symbolic heart of Cape Town, with **Parliament**, museums, archives and De Tuynhuys – the Western Cape office of the President – arranged around the **Company's Garden**.

Adderley Street

Once the place to shop in Cape Town, **Adderley Street**, lined with handsome buildings from several centuries, is still worth a stroll today. Its attractive streetscape has been blemished by a series of large 1960s and 1970s shopping centres, but, just minutes from these crowded malls, among the streets and alleys around Greenmarket Square, you can find a more human element and historic texture. One of the ugliest buildings erected in the 1970s is the **Golden Acre** shopping complex, facing Cape Town central train station across Strand Street – this area is a public transport hub.

Trafalgar Place Flower Market

Trafalgar Pl • Mon–Sat 9am–4pm

Local coloured people, originally from Constantia and more recently from the Bo-Kaap, have run this **flower market** for well over a century. Look out for Cape classics such as proteas, petunias and daisies at the market, which spills onto Adderley Street.

The Slave Lodge

Cnr Adderley and Wale sts • Mon–Sat 10am–5pm • R30 • ⓦ iziko.org.za/museums/slave-lodge

The Slave Lodge was built in 1679 to house the human chattels of the Dutch East India Company – the Cape's largest single slaveholder – and by the 1770s, almost a thousand slaves were held here. Under Dutch East India Company administration (see p.85), the lodge also became the Cape Colony's main brothel, its doors thrown open for an hour each night. From 1810, following the British takeover, the lodge variously housed government offices, the **Supreme Court**, the country's first library and first post office, finally becoming a museum in 1966.

The Slave Lodge has redefined itself as a museum of slavery and a human rights centre, with displays showing the family roots, ancestry and peopling of South Africa, and changing exhibitions, which have covered the likes of Steve Biko and slavery in

1

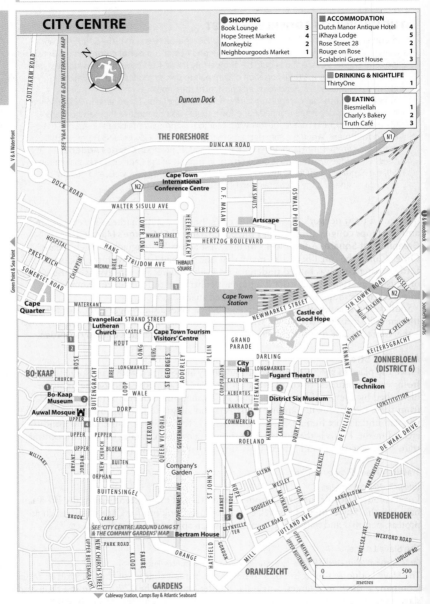

CITY CENTRE

Brazil. Taking an audio headset allows you to follow the footsteps of German salt trader Otto Menzl as he is taken on a tour of the lodge in the 1700s, giving a good idea of the miserable conditions at the time. Look out for the alcove, lit by a column of light, where the names of slaves are marked on rings that resemble tree trunks, symbolic of the **Slave Tree** under which slaves were bought and sold. Though the actual Slave Tree is long gone, the spot is marked by a simple and inconspicuous plinth behind the lodge on the traffic island in Spin Street.

SLAVERY AT THE CAPE

For nearly two centuries – more than half Cape Town's existence as an urban settlement – the city's economic and social structures depended on **slavery**. Although it was officially **abolished** at the Cape in 1834, its legacy lives on in South Africa. The country's coloured inhabitants, who make up over forty percent of Cape Town's population, are largely descendants of slaves, political prisoners from the East Indies and indigenous Khoisan people. The darkest elements of apartheid recalled the days of slavery, as did labour practices, such as the Dop System, in which workers on wine farms were partially paid in rations of cheap wine.

By the end of the eighteenth century, the almost 26,000-strong slave population of the Cape exceeded that of the free burghers (citizens, mostly of European extraction). Despite the profound impact this had on the development of social relations in South Africa, it remained one of the most neglected topics of the country's history, until the publication in the 1980s of a number of studies on slavery. Although many coloured people are still reluctant to acknowledge their slave origins, common **coloured surnames**, such as January and September, generally indicate these roots, as they refer to the month the slave was acquired.

Few, if any, slaves were captured at the Cape for export, making the colony unique in the African trade. Paradoxically, while people were being captured elsewhere on the continent for export to the Americas, the Cape administration, forbidden by the Dutch East India Company from enslaving the local indigenous population, had to look further afield. Of the 63,000 slaves imported to the Cape before 1808, most came from East Africa, Madagascar, India and Indonesia, representing one of the broadest cultural mixes of any slave society. This diversity initially worked against the establishment of a unified group identity, but eventually a **Creolized culture** emerged which, among other things, played a major role in the development of the Afrikaans language.

Long Street

Parallel to Adderley Street, buzzing one-way **Long Street** is one of Cape Town's most diverse thoroughfares, best known as the city's **main nightlife strip**. When Muslims first settled here some three hundred years ago, Long Street marked Cape Town's boundary; by the 1960s, it had become a sleazy strip of drinking holes and brothels. The libation and raucousness are certainly still here, but with a whiff of gentrification and a wad of fast-food joints, and the street deserves exploration roughly from the Greenmarket Square area upwards.

Mosques still coexist with bars, *dagga* (weed) is available, and antique dealers, craft shops, bookshops and cafés occupy the attractive Victorian buildings with New Orleans-style wrought-iron balconies. The street is packed with backpacker hostels and a few hotels, though it can be noisy into the early hours from the nightclubs. Until the area quietens down for the night, it's relatively safe to pub or club crawl on foot, with pickpockets being the main danger, and you'll always find taxis and street food.

Long Street Baths

Cnr Long and Orange sts • Daily 7am–7pm, women only Tues 10am–4pm • Pools R22, Turkish baths R60 per hour • ☏ 021 422 0100

The **Long Street Baths** is an unpretentious and relaxing historic Cape Town institution, established in 1908 in an Edwardian building. Though shabby, behind its Art Nouveau facade are a 25m heated pool and a children's pool, overlooked by murals of city life. Call ahead to use the Turkish baths, which have a sauna and steam room with massages available.

Palm Tree Mosque

185 Long St • Not open to the public

The diminutive **Palm Tree Mosque** was named after two palm trees that stood outside; the fronds of one still caress the building's upper storey. It's South Africa's second-oldest mosque and the street's only surviving eighteenth-century building, bought in 1807 by members of the local Muslim community, who turned the upper storey into a mosque and the lower floor into living quarters.

1

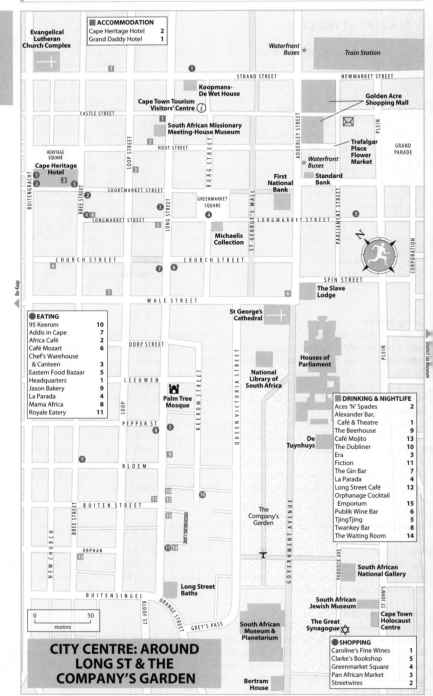

Evangelical Lutheran Church Complex

ACCOMMODATION
Cape Heritage Hotel	2
Grand Daddy Hotel	1

Waterfront Buses

Train Station

STRAND STREET

NEWMARKET STREET

Koopmans-De Wet House

Cape Town Tourism Visitors' Centre ⓘ

Golden Acre Shopping Mall

CASTLE STREET

South African Missionary Meeting-House Museum

ADDERLEY STREET

PLEIN

Trafalgar Place Flower Market

GRAND PARADE

HERITAGE SQUARE

HOUT STREET

BURG STREET

Cape Heritage Hotel

LOOP STREET

Waterfront Buses

BUITENGRACHT

BREE STREET

SHORTMARKET STREET

First National Bank

Standard Bank

PARLIAMENT STREET

LONGMARKET STREET

LONG STREET

GREENMARKET SQUARE

ST GEORGE'S MALL

LONGMARKET STREET

CORPORATION

Bo-Kaap

CHURCH STREET

Michaelis Collection

CHURCH STREET

N

SPIN STREET

The Slave Lodge

WALE STREET

St George's Cathedral

EATING
95 Keerom	10
Addis in Cape	7
Africa Café	2
Café Mozart	6
Chef's Warehouse & Canteen	3
Eastern Food Bazaar	5
Headquarters	1
Jason Bakery	9
La Parada	4
Mama Africa	8
Royale Eatery	11

DORP STREET

Houses of Parliament

PLEIN

National Library of South Africa

QUEEN VICTORIA STREET

LEEUWEN

De Tuynhuys

LOOP

Palm Tree Mosque

KEEROM STREET

PEPPER ST

BLOEM

BREE STREET

DRINKING & NIGHTLIFE
Aces 'N' Spades	2
Alexander Bar, Café & Theatre	1
The Beerhouse	9
Café Mojito	13
The Dubliner	10
Era	3
Fiction	11
The Gin Bar	7
La Parada	4
Long Street Café	12
Orphanage Cocktail Emporium	15
Publik Wine Bar	6
TjingTjing	5
Twankey Bar	8
The Waiting Room	14

BUITEN STREET

VREDENBURG LANE

GOVERNMENT AVENUE

PADDOCK AVE

South African National Gallery

NEW CHURCH

ORPHAN

The Company's Garden

ST JOHN'S

BUITENSINGEL

Long Street Baths

KLOOF ST

ORANGE STREET

GREY'S PASS

South African Jewish Museum

The Great Synagogue

Cape Town Holocaust Centre

0		50
	metres	

South African Museum & Planetarium

SHOPPING
Caroline's Fine Wines	1
Clarke's Bookshop	5
Greenmarket Square	4
Pan African Market	3
Streetwires	2

CITY CENTRE: AROUND LONG ST & THE COMPANY'S GARDEN

Bertram House

Pan African Market

76 Long St · Oct–March Mon–Fri 8.30am–5.30pm, Sat 9am–3.30pm; April–Sept Mon–Fri 9am–5pm, Sat 9am–3pm · ☎ 021 426 4478

Behind the yellow facade of the **Pan African Market**, one of Cape Town's most enjoyable places to buy African crafts, is a three-storey warren of passageways and rooms bursting at the seams with traders selling art and artefacts from all over the continent. With a team of in-house seamstresses at the ready, this is also the place to get kitted out in African garb.

South African Missionary Meeting-House Museum

40 Long St · Mon–Fri 8.30am–4pm · Free · ☎ 021 423 6755

The **South African Missionary Meeting-House Museum** was the first missionary church in the country, where slaves were taught literacy and instructed in Christianity. This exceptional building, completed in 1804 by the South African Missionary Society, has one of the most beautiful frontages in Cape Town. Inside, an impressive Neoclassical timber **pulpit** perches on a pair of columns, framing an inlaid image of an angel in flight.

Greenmarket Square

Turning east from Long Street into Shortmarket or Longmarket street, you'll skim the edge of **Greenmarket Square**, its cobblestones fringed by grand Art Deco buildings and coffee shops. As its name suggests, the square started as a vegetable market and is now home to a colourful flea market selling a range of crafts, including jewellery, and African masks and carvings.

Michaelis Collection

Old Town House, Greenmarket Square · Mon–Sat 10am–5pm · R20 · ☎ 021 481 3933, ⊛ iziko.org.za

On the southern corner of Greenmarket Square are the solid limewashed walls and small shuttered windows of the **Old Town House**, entered from Longmarket Street. Built in 1775, this beautiful example of Cape Rococo architecture houses the **Michaelis Collection** of predominantly minor but still significant seventeenth-century Dutch and Flemish portrait, townscape, interior and landscape paintings.

St George's Mall

East of Greenmarket Square is **St George's Mall**, a pedestrianized road that runs northeast from Wale Street to Thibault Square, near the train station. Coffee shops, snack bars and lots of street traders and buskers make this a pleasant route between the station and the Company's Garden.

Church Street

Crossing St George's Mall towards its southern end, **Church Street** and the surrounding area abound with antique dealers, selling Africana and bric-a-brac. In the pleasant pedestrianized section, between Long and Burg streets, art galleries mingle with the smell of coffee, and you can rest your legs sitting at an outdoor table at *Café Mozart* (see p.140).

Bree Street

Humming with design shops, boutiques, restaurants, cafés and bars, **Bree Street** has become the favourite haunt of hipsters, fashionistas and well-heeled Capetonians. The conversion of old buildings into new spaces enhances the lovely architecture, adding charm to equal Long Street's Victorian edifices, and even the car-loving locals are enticed to wander the pavements. The upper end of Bree, roughly between Buitensingel Street and Heritage Square, is your best bet to get a feel for this vibrant strip.

St George's Cathedral

5 Wale St · Mon–Fri 9am–4.30pm, Sat 9am–noon; services Mon–Fri 7.15am & 1.15pm, also Tues–Thurs 8am & 4pm, Wed 10am, Sat 8am, Sun 7am, 8am, 9.30am & 6pm · Free · ☎ 021 424 7360, ⊛ sgcathedral.co.za

St George's Cathedral is interesting as much for its history as for Herbert Baker's

1

Victorian Gothic design; **Desmond Tutu** hammered on its doors symbolically on September 7, 1986, when he was enthroned as South Africa's first black archbishop. Three years later, he heralded the last days of apartheid by leading thirty thousand people from the cathedral to the City Hall, where he coined his now-famous slogan for the new order: "We are the rainbow people!" he told the crowd, "We are the new people of South Africa!"

The cathedral hosts choral performances, classical concerts, exhibitions, walks around its labyrinth, daily services and **live jazz** in the atmospheric setting of its **crypt** (ⓦ thecryptjazz.com).

Government Avenue and around

A leisurely stroll down oak-lined, pedestrianized **Government Avenue**, the southwest extension of Adderley Street, makes for one of the most serene walks in central Cape Town. The leafy boulevard runs past the rear of Parliament through the Company's Garden, and its benches host everyone from office workers to *bergies* (homeless inhabitants of Cape Town).

National Library of South Africa
5 Queen Victoria St • Mon–Fri 8am–6pm • Free • ☎ 021 424 6320, ⓦ nlsa.ac.za

If you head south from the top of Government Avenue, you'll soon come across the **National Library of South Africa** on your right. The building houses one of the country's best collections of antiquarian historical and natural history books, covering Southern Africa. Built with the revenue from a tax on wine, it opened in 1822 as one of the world's first free libraries.

Company's Garden
19 Queen Victoria St • Daily: March–Nov 7am–9pm; Dec–Feb 7.30am–8.30pm • Free • ☎ 021 426 1357

Stretching from the National Library of South Africa to the South African Museum, the **Company's Garden** was the initial *raison d'être* for the Dutch settlement at the Cape. Established in 1652 to supply fresh greens to Dutch East India Company ships travelling between the Netherlands and the East, the gardens were initially worked by imported slave labour. At the end of the seventeenth century, the gardens were turned over to botanical horticulture for Cape Town's growing colonial elite. Ponds, lawns, landscaping and a crisscross web of oak-shaded walkways were introduced.

Today the gardens are full of local plants, the result of long-standing European interest in Cape botany. In recent years, the **vegetable patches** have been revived to evoke the agricultural diversity and splendour of the Dutch East India Company era, when Government Avenue was lined with citrus trees to supply the scurvy-ridden sailors. The garden-come-park is a pleasant place to meander, with a good outdoor café situated under massive trees.

De Tuynhuys
Government Ave • Not open to the public

Peer through an iron gate to see the grand facade and tended flowerbeds of **De Tuynhuys**, the Cape Town office (but not residence) of the president. In 1992, President F.W. de Klerk announced outside this beautiful eighteenth-century building that South Africa had "closed the book on apartheid".

Originally a Dutch building, it was remodelled during the governorship of **Lord Charles Somerset** (1814–26). The energy Somerset put into implementing an official policy of Anglicization at the Cape was matched only by his private obsession with architecture. Among the features he introduced to the building was the Colonial Regency veranda sheltering under an elegantly curving canopy, supported on slender iron columns.

1

South African National Gallery

Government Ave, Company's Garden (entrance on Paddock Ave) • Daily 10am–5pm • R30 • ⓦ iziko.org.za/museums/south-african
-national-gallery

The **South African National Gallery** is an essential port of call for anyone interested in
the local art scene, with a small but excellent permanent collection of contemporary
South African art. Be sure to take in Jane Alexander's sculpture *Butcher Boys* (1985–86),
which figuratively portrays South Africa's inherent menace and violence.

Another example of **Resistance Art**, which exploded in the 1980s, broadly as a
response to the growing repression of apartheid, is Willie Bester's *Challenges Facing the
New South Africa* (1990). Bester uses paint and found objects to depict the
multicultural chaos of the Cape Town squatter camps.

Since the 1990s, and especially in the post-apartheid period, the gallery has
engaged in a process of redefining what constitutes contemporary **indigenous art**.
Material that would previously have been treated as ethnographic, such as a major
bead collection as well as carvings and **craft objects**, is now finding a place alongside
oil paintings and sculptures.

The permanent collection also includes minor works by British artists, including
George Romney, Thomas Gainsborough, Joshua Reynolds and some Pre-Raphaelites.

South African Jewish Museum

88 Hatfield St • Mon–Thurs & Sun 10am–5pm, Fri 10am–2pm • R60 • Bring ID • ☎ 021 465 1546, ⓦ sajewishmuseum.org.za

The **South African Jewish Museum** is partially housed in South Africa's first synagogue,
built in 1863. One of Cape Town's most ambitious permanent exhibitions, it tells the
story of South African Jewry from its beginnings over 150 years ago to the present – a
narrative that starts in the Old Synagogue, from which visitors cross, via a gangplank,
to the upper level of a two-storey building, symbolically re-enacting the arrival by boat
of the first Jewish immigrants at Table Bay in the 1840s. Multimedia interactive
displays, models and artefacts explore Judaism in South Africa, drawing parallels
between the religion and the ritual practices and beliefs of South Africa's other
communities.

The **basement level** houses a walk-through reconstruction of a Lithuanian *shtetl* or village
(most South African Jews have their nineteenth-century roots in Lithuania). The museum
complex also has a restaurant, shop and noteworthy collection of ivory, staghorn and wood
Japanese Netsuke figures. During the time of the Samurai, the affluent Japanese merchant
classes used these miniature carvings to hang containers from their kimonos.

Cape Town Holocaust Centre

88 Hatfield St • Mon–Thurs & Sun 10am–5pm, Fri 10am–2pm • Free • Bring ID • ☎ 021 462 5553, ⓦ ctholocaust.co.za

Opened in 1999, the **Cape Town Holocaust Centre**, Africa's first centre of its kind,
features one of the city's most moving and brilliantly constructed displays. The
Holocaust Exhibition resonates sharply in a country that endured half a century of
systematic racial oppression – a connection that the exhibition makes explicitly.

Exhibits trace the history of anti-Semitism in Europe, culminating with the Nazis' Final
Solution; they also look at South Africa's Greyshirts, who were motivated by Nazi
propaganda during the 1930s and were later absorbed into the National Party. A
twenty-minute video tells the story of the Holocaust survivors who settled in Cape Town.

The Great Synagogue

88 Hatfield St • Mon–Thurs & Sun 10am–4pm • Free • Bring ID • ☎ 021 465 1405, ⓦ gardensshul.org

The **Great Synagogue** or Gardens Shul is one of Cape Town's outstanding religious
buildings. Designed by the Scottish architects Parker & Forsyth and completed in
1905, it features an impressive dome and two soaring towers in the style of Central
European Baroque churches. The elegant neo-Egyptian interior has a carved teak
pulpit, gold-leaf friezes and stained-glass windows.

1

South African Museum

25 Queen Victoria St (accessed from Museum Rd) • Daily 10am–5pm • R30, under 19s R15, under 6s free • ⓦ iziko.org.za/museums/south-african-museum

The nation's premier museum of natural history and human sciences, the **South African Museum** is notable for its **ethnographic galleries**, which contain some good displays on the traditional arts and crafts of several African groups and some exceptional examples of rock art. Upstairs, the **natural history galleries** display mounted mammals, dioramas of prehistoric Karoo reptiles and Table Mountain flora and fauna. A highlight is the four-storey "whale well", a hanging collection of beautiful whale skeletons, including a 20.5m blue whale skeleton, accompanied by recordings of the eerie strains of their song.

Planetarium

25 Queen Victoria St, accessed from Museum Rd • Shows daily noon, 1pm, 2pm, 3pm, 7pm and 8pm; times change during school holidays, check the website for schedules • R40 • ⓦ iziko.org.za/museums/planetarium

Housed in the South African Museum building is the **Planetarium**, in which you can see the constellations of the southern hemisphere, with an informed commentary. The changing programme of daily shows covers topics such as San sky myths, with some geared towards children and others to teenagers and adults, and you can buy a monthly chart of the current night sky.

Bertram House

University of Cape Town Hiddingh Campus (accessed from Orange St) • Daily 10am–5pm • Donation • ⓦ iziko.org.za/museums/bertram-house

At the southernmost end of Government Avenue, you'll pass **Bertram House**, whose beautiful two-storey brick facade looks out across a fragrant herb garden. The museum is significant as Cape Town's only surviving brick Georgian-style house, and displays typical furniture and objects of a well-to-do colonial British family in the first half of the nineteenth century.

The house was built in 1839 by John Barker, a Yorkshire attorney who came to the Cape in 1823 and named the building in memory of his late wife, Ann Bertram Findlay. The reception rooms are decorated in the Regency style, while the **porcelain** is predominantly nineteenth-century English, although there are also some very fine Chinese pieces.

Houses of Parliament

Public entrance 120 Plein St • **Guided tours** hourly tours Mon–Fri 9am–4pm, 1hr • Free • Book ahead and bring ID • ☏ 021 403 2266, ⓦ www.parliament.gov.za • **Debating sessions** Tues, Wed & Thurs afternoons, also occasionally Fri mornings • Free • Book at least a day in advance on ☏ 021 403 8219 or ✉ mtsheole@parliament.gov.za

South Africa's **Houses of Parliament** are a complex of interlinking buildings, with labyrinthine corridors connecting hundreds of offices, debating chambers and miscellaneous other rooms. Many of these are relics of the 1980s reformist phase of apartheid, when, in the interests of racial segregation, three distinct legislative complexes catered to people of different "race".

The original wing, completed in 1885, is an imposing Victorian Neoclassical building that first served as the legislative assembly of the Cape Colony. After the Boer republics and British colonies amalgamated in 1910, it became the parliament of the Union of South Africa. This is the old parliament, where over seven decades of repressive legislation, including apartheid laws, were passed. It's also where 1960s prime minister **Hendrik Verwoerd**, the arch-theorist of apartheid, was stabbed to death by unstable parliamentary messenger Dimitri Tsafendas. The assassin reputedly claimed that he was following the orders of a tapeworm in his stomach, although police may have concocted this story to detract attention from his crime's political motivation.

1

The new chamber was built in 1983 as part of the **Tricameral Parliament**, P.W. Botha's attempt to avert majority rule by trying to co-opt Indians and coloured people – but in their own separate debating chambers. The tricameral chamber, where the three non-African races occasionally met together, is now bicameral, made up of the directly elected **National Assembly** and the **National Council of Provinces** (elected by the provinces). One-hour tours take in the old and new debating chambers, the library and museum, and you can get free day-tickets for debating sessions in both chambers.

Castle of Good Hope

Castle St • Daily 9am–4pm • **Guided tours** Mon–Sat 11am, noon & 3pm • **Cannon firing & key ceremony** Mon–Fri 10am & noon, Sat 11am & noon • Adults R30 including optional tour, children R15 • ☎ 021 787 1249, ⓦ castleofgoodhope.co.za

Despite its unprepossessing pentagonal exterior, South Africa's oldest official building is one of the city's most worthwhile historical sights. Built in 1666, the **Castle of Good Hope** still serves as a (significantly downscaled) military barracks site and is considered the best-preserved example of a Dutch East India Company fort. For a hundred and fifty years, this was the symbolic heart of the Cape administration and a sense of self-importance lingers in its grand rooms and courtyards.

Finished in 1679, complete with the essentials of a moat and torture chamber, the castle replaced Jan van Riebeeck's earlier mud-and-timber fort, which stood on the site of the Grand Parade. The building was designed along seventeenth-century European principles of fortification, comprising strong bastions from which the outside walls could be protected by crossfire. Its entrance gate displays the coat of arms of the United Netherlands and those of the six Dutch cities in which the Dutch East India Company chambers were situated.

Still hanging from its original wooden beams in the tower above the entrance is a **bell** cast in 1697 by Claude Fremy in Amsterdam. It was used variously as an alarm signal, which could be heard from 10km away, and as a summons to residents to receive pronouncements.

Inside the castle are three main collections. At the castle's original, seaward gate, the **Castle Military Museum** exhibits South African military uniforms and delves into the Anglo-Boer War (often referred to as the South African War); the **Secunde's House** has furnishings, paintings and *objets d'art* that filled the living space of the deputy governor; and the **William Fehr Collection**, one of the country's most important exhibits of decorative arts, includes paintings of the early settlement, some fine examples of elegantly simple eighteenth-century Cape furniture, and seventeenth- and eighteenth-century Chinese and Japanese porcelain.

Guided tours take you to the prison cells and dungeons, where you can still see the touching centuries-old graffiti carved into the walls by prisoners, and visit the inner courtyard, where families of slaves would stand together as they were divided, bought and sold.

The Grand Parade and the City Hall

The **Grand Parade** is a large open area, just northwest of the Castle of Good Hope, which was originally built for military parades, but has since been used for markets, parking and political rallies.

On February 11, 1990, the Grand Parade appeared on TV screens throughout the world when over 60,000 people gathered to hear **Nelson Mandela** make his first speech after being released from prison, from the balcony of the adjoining **City Hall**. This grand Edwardian building dating to 1905, dressed in Bath stone, looks impressive against the backdrop of Table Mountain.

District Six

South of the Castle of Good Hope, in the shadow of Devil's Peak, is a vacant lot shown on maps as the suburb of **Zonnebloem**. Before being demolished by the apartheid authorities, it was an inner-city neighbourhood known as **District Six**, an impoverished but lively community of 55,000 predominantly coloured people. Later mythologized as the erstwhile soul of Cape Town, the district harboured a rich cultural life in its narrow alleys and crowded tenements.

In 1966, apartheid ideologues declared District Six a white area under the **Group Areas Act** and the bulldozers moved in, taking fifteen years to drive its presence from the skyline, leaving only the mosques and churches. The accompanying **forced removals** saw the coloured inhabitants moved to the Cape Flats. But, in the wake of the demolition, international and domestic outcry was so great that the area was never developed, apart from a few residential projects on its fringes and the hefty **Cape Technikon** college. After years of negotiation, a few of the original residents have moved back under a scheme to develop low-cost housing in the area.

A fertile place in the South African imagination, District Six has inspired novels, poems and jazz, often with more than a hint of nostalgia, anger and pain of displacement. A case in point are the musicals of **David Kramer**, which are often staged at the resident Fugard Theatre (see p.152).

District Six Museum

25A Buitenkant St • Mon–Sat 9am–4pm • Entry R30; tours R15 • ☎ 021 466 7200, ⓦ districtsix.co.za

Few places in Cape Town speak more eloquently of the effect of apartheid on the day-to-day lives of ordinary people than the **District Six Museum**. On the northern boundary of District Six, the museum occupies the former **Central Methodist Mission Church**, which offered solidarity and ministry to the victims of forced removals right up to the 1980s, and became a venue for anti-apartheid gatherings. Today, it houses a series of fascinating displays that include everyday household items and tools of trades, such as hairdressing implements, as well as **documentary photographs**, evoking the lives of the individuals who once lived here.

Occupying most of the floor is a huge map of District Six as it was, annotated by former residents who describe their memories, reflections and incidents associated with places and buildings that no longer exist. There's also a collection of original street signs, secretly retrieved at the time of demolition by the man entrusted with dumping them into Table Bay.

You can tour the museum with an ex-resident for an extra R15, and **guided walks** around the area can be organized. The coffee shop offers a variety of snacks, including traditional, syrupy *koeksisters*.

Bo-Kaap

On the slopes of Signal Hill, the **Bo-Kaap** is one of Cape Town's oldest and most fascinating residential areas. Its streets are characterized by brightly coloured nineteenth-century Cape Dutch and Georgian terrace houses, concealing a network of alleyways that are the arteries of its **Muslim community**. The Bo-Kaap harbours its own strong identity, made all the more unique by the destruction of District Six, with which it had much in common. Some long-standing residents have sold off family properties and a number of fashionable outsiders have moved in, starting up guesthouses that capitalize on the outstanding central city position and views of Table Mountain.

Bo-Kaap residents are descended from slaves, dissidents and Islamic leaders brought over by the Dutch in the sixteenth and seventeenth centuries. They became known collectively as **Cape Malay**, although the term is a misnomer: as well as the Dutch colonies in present-day Malaysia and Indonesia, many came from Africa, India, Madagascar and Sri Lanka.

The easiest way to get to the Bo-Kaap is by foot along Wale Street, which trails up from the south end of Adderley Street and across Buitengracht to become the neighbourhood's main drag. You might also consider a walking tour (see box, p.100).

BO-KAAP TOURS

The best way to explore the Bo-Kaap is by joining one of the **walking tours** of the district that also take in the Bo-Kaap Museum, with Cape Malay snacks or lunch along the way. A number of these combine walking with a **cooking tour**.

The Bo-Kaap Cooking Tour (meet at Bo-Kaap Museum; R500 including lunch; ☎074 130 8124, ⓦbokaapcookingtour.co.za) offers a two-hour tour including a forty-minute walk and three-course lunch in culinary guru Zainie's home. From Tuesday to Thursday, the same outfit offers a three-hour tour (R750) featuring an interactive cooking lesson, in which Zainie teaches you to mix masala and produce a Cape Malay meal.

Cape Malay cooking "safaris" are offered by Cooking With Love (109 Wale St; ☎072 483 4040; ⓦfacebook.com/Faldela1), run by the charismatic Faldela Tolker; Lekka Kombuis (☎079 957 0226; ⓦlekkakombuis.co.za); and Andulela (see p.134).

Bo-Kaap Museum

71 Wale St • Mon–Sat 10am–5pm • R20 • ☎021 481 3938, ⓦiziko.org.za/museums/bo-kaap-museum

If you're exploring the Bo-Kaap without a guide, a good place to start is the **Bo-Kaap Museum**. Occupying one of the neighbourhood's oldest houses, the museum explains the local culture and illustrates the lifestyle of a nineteenth-century Muslim family. It also explores the local form of Islam, which has its own unique traditions and two dozen *kramats* (shrines) dotted about the peninsula.

Auwal Mosque

39 Dorp St • Closed to the public

The **Auwal Mosque** is South Africa's first official mosque, founded in 1797 by Tuan Guru, a Moluccan prince and Muslim activist who was exiled to Robben Island in 1780 for opposing Dutch rule in the Indies. While on the island, he transcribed the Koran from memory and wrote several important Islamic commentaries, which provided a basis for the religion at the Cape for a century.

What is left of the mosque's original structure, distinguished only by its large minaret, blends in with the adjoining multicoloured terraced houses. It's one of ten mosques serving the Bo-Kaap's Muslim residents, their minarets punctuating the quarter's skyline.

De Waterkant

An atmospheric central neighbourhood within easy striking distance of the city centre, the Waterfront and the Bo-Kaap, **De Waterkant**'s mid-eighteenth-century terraces line cobbled streets on the lower flanks of Signal Hill. The district plays up its assets for all they're worth, with many of its houses turned over to guesthouses and self-catering flats. Within easy wandering distance of everything are restaurants, delis, clubs, art dealers and interior design boutiques, many clustered in and around the **Cape Quarter** (see p.156), an upmarket shopping mall. With a clutch of **gay-friendly nightclubs and bars** (see p.148) on both sides of main drag Somerset Road, the area is unofficially known as the **Pink Village**.

Strand Street

A major artery from the N2 freeway to the central business district, **Strand Street** neatly separates the upper from the lower city centre. Between the mid-eighteenth and mid-nineteenth centuries, it was one of the most fashionable streets in Cape Town because of its proximity to the shore. Its former cachet is now only discernible from a handful of quietly elegant national monuments left standing amid the traffic.

Evangelical Lutheran Church

98 Strand St, at Buitengracht • Mon–Fri 10am–2pm • Free • ☎021 421 5854, ⓦlutheranchurch.org.za

Converted around 1780 from a warehouse, the **Evangelical Lutheran Church** is South Africa's oldest church in permanent service and forms part of the country's oldest city block. Its facade includes Classical details such as a broken pediment perforated by the clock tower, as well as Gothic features including arched windows. Inside, the magnificent **pulpit**, supported by two life-size Herculean figures, is one of the masterpieces of the eighteenth-century German woodcarver Anton Anreith.

The establishment of a Lutheran church in Cape Town in the late eighteenth century struck a significant blow against the extreme religious intolerance that was rife in the city. Previously, Protestantism had been the only form of worship allowed, with the Dutch Reformed Church holding an absolute monopoly over saving people's souls.

Koopmans-De Wet House

35 Strand St • Mon–Fri 10am–5pm • R20 • ☎ 021 481 3935, Ⓦ iziko.org.za/museums/koopmans-de-wet-house

Sandwiched between two office blocks, **Koopmans-De Wet House** is an outstanding eighteenth-century pedimented Neoclassical townhouse and museum, which exhibits a fine collection of antique furniture and rare porcelain. The earliest sections of the house were built in 1701 by **Reyner Smedinga**, a well-to-do goldsmith who imported the building materials from Holland. After changing hands more than a dozen times over the following two centuries, the building eventually became the home of **Marie Koopmans-De Wet** (1834–1906), a prominent figure on the Cape social and political circuit.

The house represents a fine synthesis of Dutch elements (sash windows and large entrance doors) with the demands of local conditions; the huge rooms, lofty ceilings and shuttered windows reflect the high summer temperatures, while the front *stoep* has plastered masonry seats at each end. The **lantern** in the fanlight of the entrance was a common feature of Cape Town houses in the eighteenth and early nineteenth centuries, its purpose to shine light onto the street and thus hinder slaves from gathering at night to plot.

V&A Waterfront

Ⓦ waterfront.co.za • The V&A Waterfront is served by MyCiTi bus routes #104 from Sea Point and #T01 from the Civic Centre via Cape Town Stadium, as well as the City Sightseeing bus, which runs two routes around the city's main sights from outside the Two Oceans Aquarium (see p.131)

The **Victoria & Alfred Waterfront**, known locally as the Waterfront, is Cape Town's original Victorian harbour and incorporates the city's most popular central shopping area. The busy pedestrianized complex includes shops, restaurants, cinemas, waterside walkways, museums, markets and a yacht marina. The retail focus is the enormous flashy Victoria Wharf **mall** (daily 9am–9pm) on two levels, extending along Quays 5 and 6. The restaurants and cafés on the mall's southeast side, with their outdoor seating, have fabulous views of Table Mountain across the busy harbour.

Wandering south from the Victoria Wharf, you'll pass the **Amphitheatre**, where local musicians regularly perform. Look out, too, for **Nobel Square**, with its bronze statues of South Africa's four Nobel Peace Prize winners: Archbishop Desmond Tutu (1984); Nelson Mandela and F.W. de Klerk (both 1993); and the less familiar, Chief Albert John Lutuli (1960), former president of the African National Congress (ANC) and the first African to receive the award.

There are a few excellent markets nearby: the Watershed (see p.155) for craft shopping and the V&A Food Market (see p.156) – both open daily – and the Oranjezicht City Farm Market (see p.156), a Saturday foodie extravaganza.

The Waterfront is also where you set sail for Robben Island (see p.105), embarking at the same spot as many of South Africa's anti-apartheid activists on their way to incarceration and hard labour.

HISTORY OF THE WATERFRONT

Throughout the first half of the nineteenth century, arguments raged in Cape Town over the need for a proper dock. The Cape was often known as the **Cape of Storms** because of its tempestuous weather, which left Table Bay littered with wrecks. Clamour for a harbour grew in the 1850s with the increase in sea traffic arriving at the Cape, reaching its peak in 1860, when Lloyd's of London insurance company refused to cover ships dropping anchor in Table Bay.

The British colonial government dragged its heels because of the costs involved, but eventually conceded and, at a huge ceremony in September 1860, the teenage Prince Alfred (Queen Victoria's second son) tipped the first batch of stones into Table Bay to begin the **breakwater**, the harbour's westernmost arm. In 1870, the dock – consisting of two main basins – was completed.

Two Oceans Aquarium

Dock Rd • Daily 9.30am–6pm, feeding times 11.30am, noon, 2pm, 2.30pm • R160, under-17s R115, under-13s, R75, under-4s free • ☎ 021 418 3823, ⓦ aquarium.co.za

An excellent rainy-day option, the **Two Oceans Aquarium** showcases the Cape's unique marine environment, where the warm Indian Ocean mingles with the cold Atlantic. Its biggest and newest attraction is the **Ocean Exhibit**, which houses rays, striped bonito, turtles, a giant guitarfish and more in 1.6 million litres of seawater, with an atmospheric **jellyfish gallery** on the way in. The popular **shark exhibit** and the **Kelp Forest**, where fish glide through the swaying fronds of elongated kelp plants, will hopefully both reopen by 2018.

There is much hands-on fun for children, including the basement **Children's Play Centre**, with free organized activities, such as puppet shows, face painting, and arts and crafts. The play centre is combined with an observation area with tall windows through which the resident rockhopper penguins can be seen frolicking underwater during the day.

The top floor, accessed via a ramp, accommodates the **Penguin Exhibit**, featuring the rockhopper penguins and a small breeding colony of endangered African penguins, which you can see in their natural habitat at Boulders Beach (see p.126).

Chavonnes Battery Museum

Clock Tower Precinct • Mon–Wed 9am–4pm, Thurs–Sun 9am–6pm • R70, under-16s R30; **guided tours** R100, under-16s R50 • ☎ 021 416 6230, ⓦ chavonnesbattery.co.za

The Dutch East India Company built this **fortification**, named after an early eighteenth-century governor of the Cape, to protect Table Bay from European rivals. Along with the Castle of Good Hope, it was part of a line of fortifications around the bay, built by the Dutch and later used by the British. Rediscovered in the 1990s during the development of the Clock Tower Precinct, the two levels of ruined walls, artefacts and informative displays provide much historical interest. The guided tour is well worth the small extra outlay (the price includes admission and tours depart on demand).

Zeitz Museum of Contemporary Art Africa (Zeitz MOCAA)

Silo District • Check website for opening times • R180, under-18s free • ☎ 021 418 7855, ⓦ zeitzmocaa.museum

Occupying a historic grain silo, the ambitious **Zeitz MOCAA** is the world's leading museum dedicated to contemporary art from across Africa and its diaspora. The main collection was amassed by the German sustainable business guru and philanthropist Jochen Zeitz, who turned around the fortunes of the footwear brand Puma in the 1990s. At the time of writing, excitement was mounting in advance of the nine-floor, eighty-gallery institution's opening. Fourteen inaugural exhibitions are set to include spotlights on young artists from Zimbabwe, Angola and Swaziland. Towering 57m

V&A WATERFRONT & DE WATERKANT

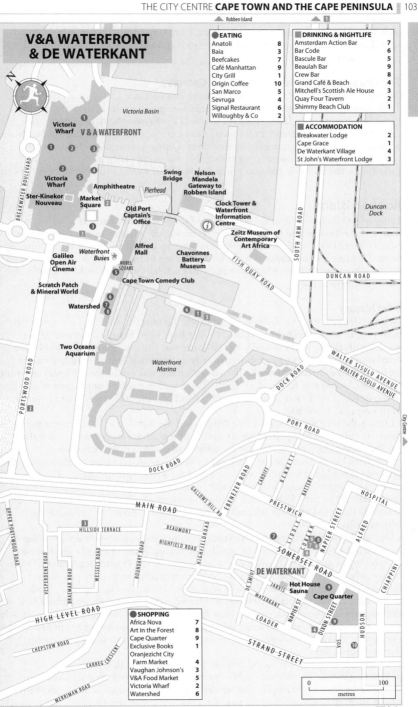

● EATING

Anatoli	8
Baia	3
Beefcakes	7
Café Manhattan	9
City Grill	1
Origin Coffee	10
San Marco	5
Sevruga	4
Signal Restaurant	6
Willoughby & Co	2

■ DRINKING & NIGHTLIFE

Amsterdam Action Bar	7
Bar Code	6
Bascule Bar	5
Beaulah Bar	9
Crew Bar	8
Grand Café & Beach	4
Mitchell's Scottish Ale House	3
Quay Four Tavern	2
Shimmy Beach Club	1

■ ACCOMMODATION

Breakwater Lodge	2
Cape Grace	1
De Waterkant Village	4
St John's Waterfront Lodge	3

● SHOPPING

Africa Nova	7
Art in the Forest	8
Cape Quarter	9
Exclusive Books	1
Oranjezicht City Farm Market	4
Vaughan Johnson's	3
V&A Food Market	5
Victoria Wharf	2
Watershed	6

Map labels: Robben Island, Victoria Basin, Victoria Wharf, V & A WATERFRONT, Breakwater Boulevard, Victoria Wharf, Ster-Kinekor Nouveau, Market Square, Amphitheatre, Pierhead, Swing Bridge, Old Port Captain's Office, Nelson Mandela Gateway to Robben Island, Clock Tower & Waterfront Information Centre, Zeitz Museum of Contemporary Art Africa, Duncan Dock, South Arm Road, Galileo Open Air Cinema, Waterfront Buses, Nobel Square, Alfred Mall, Chavonnes Battery Museum, Fish Quay Road, Duncan Road, Scratch Patch & Mineral World, Cape Town Comedy Club, Watershed, Two Oceans Aquarium, Waterfront Marina, Walter Sisulu Avenue, Dock Road, Port Road, City Centre, Portswood Road, Upper Portswood Road, Main Road, Gallows Hill Rd, Ebenezer Road, Cardiff, Bennett, Battery, Prestwich, Hospital, Hillside Terrace, Beaumont, Highfield Road, Highfield Road, Boundary Road, Wessels Road, Braemar Road, Vesperdene Road, Somerset Road, Napier Street, Alfred, Chiappini, De Waterkant, Hot House Sauna, Cape Quarter, Jarvis, Napier St, Dixon Street, Hudson, Vos, Loader, Waterkant, High Level Road, Chepstow Road, Carreg Crescent, Merriman Road, Strand Street, Bo-Kaap

0 — 100 metres

1

above a public plaza, the dynamic new addition to Cape Town's burgeoning cultural scene has regenerated this area of the Waterfront, attracting new hotels, shops and private galleries.

The Clock Tower and Nelson Mandela Gateway

Clock Tower Precinct • Daily 7.30am–5.30pm • Free • ☏ 021 413 4200, ⓦ robben-island.org.za

The imposing **Clock Tower** by the Waterfront's swing bridge was built as the original Port Captain's office in 1882. Adjacent to this is the **Nelson Mandela Gateway**, the embarkation point for ferries to Robben Island (see opposite), where the Robben Island Museum has installed a number of exhibitions. Displays cover the individual and collective struggles of those who went through this portal on their way to prison, including accounts by ex-political prisoners, ex-prison warders and the families of both.

Robben Island

Lying a few kilometres from the commerce of the Waterfront, flat and windswept **Robben Island** is suffused by a meditative, otherworldly silence. This key site of South Africa's liberation struggle was intended to silence apartheid's domestic critics, but instead became an international focus for opposition to the regime. Measuring just six square kilometres and sparsely vegetated by low scrub, it was Nelson Mandela's "home" for almost twenty years.

Brief history

Nelson Mandela may be Robben Island's most famous prisoner, but he wasn't the first: people who offended the political order have been banished here since the seventeenth century. The island's first prisoner was the indigenous Khoikhoi leader **Autshumato**, who learnt English in the early seventeenth century and became an emissary of the British. After the Dutch settlement was established, he was jailed on the island by Jan van Riebeeck in 1658. The rest of the seventeenth century saw a succession of East Indies political prisoners and Muslim holy men exiled here for opposing Dutch colonial rule.

During the nineteenth century, the **British** used the island as a dumping ground for deserters, criminals and political prisoners. Captured **Xhosa leaders** who defied the empire during the Frontier Wars of the early to mid-nineteenth century were transported by sea from the Eastern Cape to be imprisoned here. In 1846, the island's brief was extended to include a whole range of the **socially marginalized**; criminals and political detainees were joined by vagrants, prostitutes, and the mentally and chronically ill. In the 1890s, a leper colony numbering hundreds of sufferers existed alongside the social outcasts. Mentally ill patients were removed in 1921 and the leprosy sufferers in 1930.

During World War II, the **Defence Force** took over the island to set up defensive guns against a feared Axis invasion, which never came. Robben Island's greatest era of notoriety began in 1961, when it was taken over by the **Prisons Department**. When Nelson Mandela arrived in 1963, it had become a maximum security prison, and inmates were only allowed to send and receive one letter every six months. Harsh conditions, including routine beatings and forced hard labour, were exacerbated by the geographical location: icy winds blew in from the South Pole yet inmates wore only shorts and flimsy jerseys. Like every other prisoner, Mandela slept on a thin mat on the floor and was kept in a solitary confinement cell measuring two metres square for sixteen hours a day.

Amazingly, the prisoners found ways of **protesting**, through hunger strikes, publicizing conditions when possible (by visits from the International Committee of the Red Cross, for example) and, remarkably, by taking legal action against the prison authority to stop arbitrary punishments. They won improved conditions over

1

ROBBEN ISLAND TOURS

The ferry from the Waterfront's **Nelson Mandela Gateway** (May–Aug daily 9am, 11am & 1pm; Sept–April daily 9am, 11am, 1pm & 3pm) takes 30min–1hr to reach Robben Island. Tours are sometimes cancelled due to bad weather or boat problems and refunds are issued, so check ahead.

Visits to the island are by guided tour only, led by former political prisoners who share their experiences. The 4hr tours are of varying quality. Although a number of vendors sell tickets for cruises that may go close to Robben Island, the only ones that will get you onto it (R320, under-18s R180, including voyage, entry and tour) must be bought through the Nelson Mandela Gateway (see opposite). Bookings must be made well in advance, as the boats are often full, especially around December and January (📞021 413 4200, 🌐www.robben-island .org.za). For online sales, the website links to 🌐webtickets.co.za, which accepts credit and (most) debit cards, and you must print out your tickets. Although tickets are non-refundable if you cancel, tours can be rescheduled at least 48hrs in advance.

the years, and the island also became a university behind bars, where people of different political views and generations met; it was not unknown for prisoners to give academic help to their warders. The last political prisoners were released from Robben Island in 1991 and the remaining common-law prisoners were transferred to the mainland in 1996. A year later, the island was established as a museum, becoming a **UNESCO World Heritage Site** in 1999.

The island

Robben Island visits consist of a **bus tour** around the island followed by a **walking tour of the prison**. The bus tour stops off at several historical landmarks, including the **Moturu Kramat**, a shrine built in memory of Sayed Abdurahman Moturu. One of Cape Town's first imams, the Dutch exiled the Indonesian prince to the island, where he died in the mid-eighteenth century. The tour also passes a **leper graveyard** and a **church** designed by Sir Herbert Baker.

Robert Sobukwe's house is perhaps the most affecting relic of incarceration on the island. It was here that Sobukwe (see box, p.326), leader of the Pan Africanist Congress (a radical offshoot of the ANC), was held in solitary confinement for nine years. No other political prisoners were allowed to speak to him, but he would sometimes gesture his solidarity with them by letting sand trickle through his fingers as they walked past. After his release in 1969, Sobukwe was restricted to Kimberley under house arrest, until his death from cancer in 1978.

Another stopoff is the **lime quarry** where Nelson Mandela and his fellow inmates spent countless hours of hard labour.

The Maximum Security Prison

The **Maximum Security Prison**, a forbidding complex of unadorned H-blocks on the island's eastern edge, is introduced with a tour through the famous **B-Section**. Your ex-inmate guide will likely share their poignant memories of hunger strikes, solitary confinement and hardship alongside the great struggle heroes. **Mandela's cell** has been left exactly as it was, without embellishments or display, and the rest are locked and empty.

In the nearby **A-Section**, the Cell Stories exhibition skilfully shows the sparseness of prison life, with the tiny isolation cells containing personal artefacts loaned by former prisoners, plus quotations, recordings and photographs.

Towards the end of the 1980s, cameras were sneaked onto the island, and inmates took snapshots of each other, which have been enlarged and mounted as the **Smuggled Camera Exhibition** in the D-Section communal cells. The **Living Legacy** tour in F-Section involves ex-political prisoner guides describing their lives here and answering questions.

1

> **SACRED CIRCLE**
>
> During the late seventeenth and early eighteenth centuries, the Dutch exiled a number of **Muslim holy men and princes** from the East Indies to the Cape, where some became revered as **auliyah** or Muslim saints. The **kramats**, of which there are around two dozen in Cape Town and the Winelands, are their burial sites, shrines and places of pilgrimage. The Signal Hill *kramat* is a shrine to **Mohamed Gasan Galbie Shah**, a follower of Sheik Yusuf, an Indonesian Sufi scholar deported to the Cape in 1694 with a 49-strong retinue. According to tradition, Yusuf conducted Muslim prayer meetings in private homes and slave quarters, becoming the founder of Islam in South Africa. His *kramat* on the Cape Flats is said to be one of a sacred circle of six, including those on Signal Hill and Robben Island (see p.105), which **protect Cape Town** from natural disasters.

Table Mountain

Table Mountain, a 1086m flat-topped massif with dramatic cliffs and eroded gorges, dominates the northern end of the Cape Peninsula. Its north face overlooks the city centre with the distinct formations of **Lion's Head** and **Signal Hill** to the west and **Devil's Peak** to the east. The massif's west face is made up of a series of gable-like formations known as the **Twelve Apostles**; the southwest face towers over Hout Bay; and the east face over the Southern Suburbs. The mountain is a compelling feature in the middle of the city, a wilderness where you'll find wildlife and 1400 species of flora. Indigenous mammals include baboons, dassies (see box opposite) and porcupines.

One of the world's most-climbed mountains, Table Mountain has suffered under the constant pounding of **hikers** – although the damage isn't always obvious. Every year the mountain strikes back, taking its toll of lives. One of the commonest causes of difficulties is people losing the track (often due to sudden mist falling) and getting stuck or falling. If you plan to tackle one of its hundreds of walks or climbs, go properly prepared, or take a **guided hike** tailored to your level of fitness (see p.153). You may choose to come back the easy way by cable car.

Table Mountain Aerial Cableway

Lower Cableway Station, Tafelberg Rd • Daily every 10–15min: Jan–April 8am–8.30pm, Feb till 8pm, March till 7.30pm; May–Nov 8.30am–6pm, Sept & Oct till 7pm, Nov till 8.30pm • One way R135, return R255; children 4–17 one way R65, return R125; return tickets half price after 6pm Nov to mid-Dec & Jan–Feb • Last car up departs 1hr before last car down; operations can be disrupted by bad weather or maintenance work; for information on current schedules call ☎ 021 424 8181, or check ⓦ tablemountain.net • From the Waterfront and the Civic Centre respectively, the City Sightseeing Red City Tour route (see p.131) and MyCiTi buses #106 & #107 (see p.131) serve the cableway; alternatively take an Uber or normal metered taxi to the Lower Cableway Station, where taxis wait to take you home at the end. Drivers can park along Tafelberg Rd

The least challenging, but certainly not least interesting, way up and down the mountain is via the highly popular **cable car** at the western table, which offers dizzying views across town to Table Bay and the Atlantic. The state-of-the-art Swiss system completes a 360-degree rotation during the five-minute journey, giving passengers a full panorama. At the top, if you don't want to walk far, you can wander the concrete paths stopping at the viewpoints, and grab a meal or beer in the **cafeteria** (open from 8am until 30min before the last car down). The upper-station area is of course one of the city's best spots to watch the sun go down.

People start queuing early and finish late in summer, and weekends and public holidays tend to be very busy; shorten your queuing time by buying your ticket online.

Walks and viewpoints

Climbing the mountain will give you a greater sense of achievement than being ferried up by the cable car, but proceed with extreme caution: it may look sunny and clear when you leave, but conditions at the top could be very different. There are fabulous hikes up and along Table Mountain (see p.152), but consider hiring a guide, both for mountain safety and because there have been occasional and random muggings of tourists.

Signal Hill and Lion's Head

From the roundabout at the top of **Kloof Nek**, a road leads all the way along **Signal Hill** to a car park and lookout, with good views over Table Bay and the city. A cannon was formerly used for sending signals to ships at anchor in the bay, and the **Noon Gun**, still fired from its slopes daily, sends a thunderous rumble through the Bo-Kaap and city centre below. Halfway along Signal Hill Road is a sacred Islamic *kramat* (see box opposite), one of several dotted around the peninsula which are said to protect the city.

You can also walk up **Lion's Head**, a relatively non-strenuous 2km ascent (three hours return max) that seems to bring out half the population of Cape Town every **full moon**. It's a local ritual, not just for the beautiful nocturnal views of the city below and the silvery procession of head torches snaking up the mountain, but for the camaraderie and the novelty of climbing the peak after dark.

Be warned that Lion's Head gets extremely busy on and around full moon; the nights before and after are slightly quieter. Walk with others if possible, as muggings have occurred even on these busy nights.

Platteklip Gorge

The first recorded ascent to the summit of Table Mountain was by the Portuguese captain Antonio de Saldanha, in 1503. He wisely chose **Platteklip Gorge**, the gap visible from the front table (the north side), which, as it turned out, is the most accessible way up. A short and easy extension will take you to Maclear's Beacon which, at 1086m, is the **highest point** on the mountain. The Platteklip route starts at the Lower Cableway Station and ends near the upper station, so you can descend in a cable car.

From the lower station, walk east along Tafelberg Road until you see a sign pointing to Platteklip Gorge. A steep fifteen-minute climb brings you onto the **Upper Contour Path**. About 25m east along this, take the path indicated by a sign reading "Contour Path/Platteklip Gorge". The path zigzags from here onwards and is very clear. The gorge is the biggest chasm on the whole mountain, leading directly and safely to the top, but it's a very steep slog that will take around three hours total if you're reasonably fit. Once on top, turn right and ascend the last short section onto the **front table** for a breathtaking view of the city. A sign points to the Upper Cableway Station – a fifteen-minute walk along a concrete path thronging with visitors.

Maclear's Beacon

Maclear's Beacon is about 35 minutes from the top of the Platteklip Gorge on a path leading eastward, with white squares on little yellow footsteps guiding you all the way. The path crosses the front table with Maclear's Beacon visible at all times. From the top you'll get views of False Bay and the Hottentots Holland Mountains.

DASSIES

The outsized fluffy guinea pigs you'll encounter at the top of Table Mountain are **dassies** or rock hyraxes (*Procavia capensis*), which, despite their appearance, aren't rodents at all, but the closest living relatives of elephants. Their name (pronounced like "dusty" without the "t") is the Afrikaans version of *dasje*, meaning "little badger", a name given to them by the first Dutch settlers. Dassies are very widely distributed, having thrived in South Africa with the elimination of predators, and can be found in rocky habitats all over the country, often warming themselves in groups in the early morning sun, as they have poor body temperature control.

1

Skeleton Gorge and Nursery Ravine

You can combine a visit to the gardens at Kirstenbosch National Botanical Garden (see p.111) with an ascent of Table Mountain, returning via a different path and ending at the Kirstenbosch tea room. From just inside Gate 2, follow the **Skeleton Gorge** signs, which lead you onto the **Contour Path**. At the Contour Path, a plaque indicates that this forms part of the **Smuts Track**, the route to Maclear's Beacon favoured by Jan Smuts, the Boer leader and South African prime minister. The plaque marks the start of a broad-stepped climb up Skeleton Gorge, involving wooden steps, stone steps, wooden ladders and loose boulders. Be prepared for steep ravines and rock scrambles – and under no circumstances stray off the path. This route requires reasonable fitness, and takes about two hours to ascend.

Skeleton Gorge is not recommended for the descent, as it can be very slippery; rather use **Nursery Ravine**. From the top of Skeleton Gorge, a half-hour walk on the flat leads past the **Hely-Hutchinson Reservoir** to the head of Nursery Ravine. This descent returns you to the Contour Path, which leads back to Kirstenbosch. This entire walk lasts about five hours.

The Southern Suburbs

Away from Table Mountain and the city centre, the bulk of Cape Town's suburban sprawl extends inland towards the Cape Flats and the Winelands. The most appealing part of this sprawl is the **Southern Suburbs**, the formerly whites-only residential areas stretching down the east side of Table Mountain, ending at Muizenberg on the False Bay coast, with Claremont and Newlands acting as the central pivotal point. The area offers a quick escape from the city into forests, gardens and vineyards, all hugging the eastern slopes of the mountain and its extension, the Constantiaberg.

The quickest way of reaching the Southern Suburbs **by car** from the city centre, Waterfront or City Bowl suburbs is via the M3 highway. Alternatively, you can travel **by train** from Cape Town Station to Woodstock, Salt River, Observatory, Mowbray, Rosebank, Rondebosch, Newlands, Claremont and beyond, all the way south to Muizenberg, Kalk Bay, Fish Hoek and Simon's Town. The hop-on, hop-off City Sightseeing **buses** (see p.131) serve Kirstenbosch, the Constantia wine estates and Hout Bay.

Woodstock and Salt River

Windblown and gritty, **Woodstock** and **Salt River** are Cape Town's oldest suburbs, and retain memories of their manufacturing beginnings among the gentrification. Old folk conversing on their *stoeps*, keeping an eye on children playing on the crumbling pavement, give a hint of what nearby District Six (see p.98) must have been like before the forced evictions to the Cape Flats. Slowly but surely, these predominantly working-class coloured areas are morphing into Cape Town's premier design district, with clusters of design shops, artisan coffee houses and art galleries sitting alongside car dealers and secondhand furniture shops. The two suburbs blend imperceptibly, though Salt River remains poorer and more industrial, while Woodstock's pretty old Victorian houses have been snapped up by new arrivals and renovated.

Albert Road is the best place to head in Woodstock, with the **Old Biscuit Mill** hosting **Neighbourgoods**, a terrific Saturday morning organic and artisanal food market (see p.156). The complex is also home to two of Cape Town's best contemporary restaurants, *Test Kitchen* (see p.143) and *Pot Luck Club* (see p.143), and several craft and design shops. Nearby, the **Woodstock Foundry** fills a renovated

1

IRMA STERN

Born in South Africa's North West Province in 1894 to German-Jewish parents, **Irma Stern** studied at Germany's Weimar Academy. In reaction to the academy's conservatism, she adopted **expressionist distortion** in her paintings, and exhibited alongside the German Expressionists in Berlin. Returning to Cape Town in 1920, over the following decades she went on several expeditions to Zanzibar and the Congo, where she found the colourful and exotic inspiration for her intensely **sensuous paintings**, which shocked conservative South Africa.

Although Stern's work was appreciated in Europe, South African critics initially derided her style as simply a cover for technical incompetence; "ugliness as a cult", said one headline. South African art historians now regard her as the towering figure of her generation, and at Bonhams London in 2011, her *Arab Priest* (1945) fetched £3.1 million, the **highest auction price** ever achieved by a South African artwork. Stern's portraits range from the much-reproduced *The Eternal Child* (1916), a simple but vibrant depiction of a young girl, to her many later portrayals of African women.

heritage building with a creative mix of shops, Tribe coffee roastery and studio space. To discover more local creativity, join **Juma's Tours** (see p.129) on a walking tour of the area's street art and galleries.

Observatory

Abutting the southeastern end of Woodstock, "Obs" is generally regarded as Cape Town's **bohemian hub**, a reputation fuelled by its proximity to the University of Cape Town, Groote Schuur Hospital medical school and a number of NGOs. With their wrought-iron balconies, the attractively dilapidated and peeling buildings on Observatory's Lower Main Road, and the streets off it, have some inviting neighbourhood cafés, bars and shops. The huge Groote Schuur Hospital, which overlooks "hospital bend" on the N2 highway as it sweeps through Obs, was the site of the world's first heart transplant in 1967.

Irma Stern Museum

Cecil Rd, Rosebank • Tues–Fri 10am–5pm, Sat 10am–2pm • R10 • ⓦ irmastern.co.za

Irma Stern (see box above) is lauded as one of South Africa's greatest artists, for her vividly expressive and sensual portraits, still lifes and landscapes, which brought modern European ideas to South Africa in the twentieth century and now sell for millions of dollars. The **Irma Stern Museum** was the famously larger-than-life artist's home and studio for 38 years, until her death in 1966, and is definitely worth visiting to see her collection of African, Iberian, oriental and ancient artefacts. The whole house, in fact, reflects Stern's fascination with exoticism, from her own Gauguinesque paintings of African figures to the fantastic carved doors she brought back from Zanzibar. Even the garden brings a touch of the tropics to Cape Town, with its exuberant bamboo thickets and palm trees.

The Rhodes Memorial

Rhodes Memorial St • Restaurant and tea garden daily 9am–5pm • ☎ 021 687 0000, ⓦ rhodesmemorial.co.za • Leave the M3 (Rhodes Dr) at exit 8

The suburb of Rondebosch is home to the University of Cape Town (UCT), whose nineteenth-century buildings, handsomely festooned with creepers, sit grandly on the mountainside, overlooking the M3 freeway. Next to the campus, the conspicuous **Rhodes Memorial**, built to resemble a Greek temple, celebrates Cecil Rhodes, prime minister of the Cape (1890–96) and much-maligned colonial poster boy. A towering set of stairs climbs from a sculpture of a wildly rearing horse to the empire builder's bust. Herds of wildebeest and zebra nonchalantly graze on the slopes around the Memorial, and its **restaurant and tea garden** offer terrific views of Cape Town.

Below the Memorial, alongside the M3, you'll see the incongruous Mostert's Mill, a windmill built two centuries ago when the landscape was planted with wheat fields.

Newlands and Claremont

South of Rondebosch are some of Cape Town's most established, genteel suburbs, including **Newlands**, home to the city's famous rugby and cricket stadiums. Further south, well-heeled **Claremont** is an alternative focus to the city centre for shopping, with a cinema, restaurants, high-quality shops and an adjoining street market at **Cavendish Square Mall**.

Kirstenbosch National Botanical Garden

Rhodes Drive, signposted off the M3 • Daily: April–Aug 8am–6pm, Sept–March 8am–7pm; open-air concerts late Nov–early April • R60, under-17s R15, under-6s free; concert tickets R125–190 • Free walking tours (10am, 11am & 2pm Mon–Fri, 10am Sat) and shuttle-car tours (on the hour 9am–3pm daily; R70) depart from Visitors' Centre, Gate 1 • The City Sightseeing bus (see p.131) stops at the garden every 20min on its Blue Mini Peninsula Tour; the closest train station is Claremont

Thirteen kilometres south of the city centre, the unmissable **Kirstenbosch National Botanical Garden** was established in 1913, and is one of the planet's great natural treasure troves. In 2004, the biodiverse Cape Floristic Region, which Kirstenbosch showcases, became South Africa's sixth UNESCO World Heritage Site – making Kirstenbosch the world's first botanical garden to achieve this. The listing recognizes the international significance of the *fynbos* (see box below) vegetation and the Cape plant kingdom that predominate here, attracting botanists from all over the world.

Allow a good couple of hours to visit the garden, which has signboards and paved paths to guide you through its highlights, and labels to identify the trees and plants.

An exciting feature is the **Centenary Tree Canopy Walkway**, or "Boomslang", an elevated steel-and-timber walkway that snakes its way up and through the trees of the **Arboretum**, providing panoramic views of the garden and surrounding mountains. Five trails of varying difficulty explore the garden, including the **Braille Trail** starting at the **Fragrance Garden**; created for blind visitors, it has information signs in Braille and an abundance of aromatic and textured plants.

The garden trails off into **wild vegetation** covering a huge expanse of the rugged eastern slopes and wooded ravines of Table Mountain – its setting is breathtaking. Two popular paths, Nursery Ravine and Skeleton Gorge (see p.108), climb the mountain from the **Contour Path** above Kirstenbosch; while the garden itself is safe from crime, if you are hiking up Table Mountain, or along the Contour Path to **Constantia Nek**, take

---

FYNBOS

Early Dutch settlers were alarmed by the lack of good timber on the Cape Peninsula's hillsides, which were covered by nondescript, scrubby bush they described as *fijn bosch* (literally "fine bush") and which is now known by its Afrikaans name **fynbos** (pronounced "fayn-bos"). The settlers planted exotics, like the oaks that now shade central Cape Town, and over the ensuing centuries their descendants established pine forests on the sides of Table Mountain in an effort to create a landscape that fulfilled their European idea of the picturesque. It's only relatively recently that Capetonians have proudly claimed *fynbos* as part of the peninsula's heritage. Amazingly, many plant blooms in Britain and the US, including varieties of geraniums, freesias, gladioli, daisies, lilies and irises, are hybrids grown from indigenous Cape plants.

Fynbos is remarkable for its astonishing variety of plants, its 8500 mostly endemic species making the Cape Floristic Region one of the world's biodiversity hot spots. The Cape Peninsula alone, measuring less than 500 square kilometres, has 2256 plant species (nearly twice as many as Britain, which is five thousand times bigger). The four basic types of *fynbos* plants are **proteas** (South Africa's national flower); **ericas**, amounting to six hundred species of heather; **restios** (reeds); and **geophytes**, including ground orchids and the startling flaming red disas, which can be seen in flower on Table Mountain in late summer.

the usual safety precautions. The northern route to Newlands Forest and the Rhodes Memorial is not recommended following a spate of muggings.

The garden has a pleasant **tea room** (see p.143), serving breakfast, lunch and picnics just inside Gate 2, as well as a Vida e Caffè **coffee shop** just outside Gate 1 and a Moyo **restaurant** between the two gates. In summer, one of the city's delights is to bring a picnic for the Sunday evening **open-air concert**, where you can lie back on the lawn, sip Cape wine and savour the mountain air and sunset. Try to catch a local act such as Hugh Masekela, Jeremy Loops, Goldfish or Freshlyground, and arrive early to secure a good spot for your blanket.

Bishopscourt and Wynberg

South of Kirstenbosch Gardens, affluent **Bishopscourt** is home to the Anglican Archbishop of Cape Town and full of luxurious mansions with enormous grounds. Further south still, the suburb of **Wynberg** is known for its Shakespearean **Maynardville Open-Air Theatre** (see p.152) in the park of the same name. On Maynardville Park's western side, **Wynberg Village's** quaint row of galleries and restaurants is known as Little Chelsea. By contrast, Wynberg's Main Road offers a more African shopping experience: street vendors and fabric shops ply a lively trade as minibus taxis and pedestrians hustle along the thoroughfare.

Constantia and its winelands

South of Kirstenbosch lie the elegant suburb of **Constantia** and the Cape's oldest **winelands**. Luxuriating on the lower slopes of Table Mountain and the Constantiaberg, with tantalizing views of False Bay, Constantia's nine wine estates are off the M3, an easy thirty-minute drive from town.

The winelands started cultivated life in 1685 as the farm of **Simon van der Stel**, the governor charged with opening up the fledgling Dutch colony to the interior. Thrusting himself wholeheartedly into the task, he selected for his own use an enormous tract of the choicest land set against the Constantiaberg, the section of the peninsula just south of Table Mountain. It is thought that he named the estate after either his friend's daughter, Constancia, or a Dutch East India Company ship then anchored in Table Bay.

Constantia grapes have been used for wine-making since Van der Stel's first output in 1705. After his death in 1712, the estate was divided up and sold off as the modern **Groot Constantia**, **Klein Constantia** and **Buitenverwachting**. The major wine estates are open to the public and offer tastings; they're definitely worth visiting, even if you're heading out of town to the Cape Winelands proper.

Groot Constantia

Groot Constantia Rd • **Grounds** Daily 9am–6pm • Free • **Wine tasting** Daily 9am–5.30pm • R75 including five wines to taste and a souvenir glass • **Cellar tours** Daily on the hour 10am–4pm • R100; booking essential • **Museum** Daily 10am–5pm • R30 • ☏ 021 794 5128, ⓦ grootconstantia.co.za • The Purple Wine Tour bus, operated by City Sightseeing, circles from Constantia Nek (a stop on its Blue Mini Peninsula Tour) to Groot Constantia and two other wine estates

A terrific example of Cape Dutch grandeur, **Groot Constantia** is the largest wine estate in Constantia and the one most geared to tourists. Its big pull is that it retains the rump of Van der Stel's original estate, as well as the original buildings, which powerfully evoke life on an estate in the early Cape. The **manor house**, a quintessential eighteenth-century Cape Dutch homestead rebuilt from Van der Stel's original home, forms part of the museum. Walking straight through the house and across the yard, you'll come to the **Cloete Cellar**, fronted by a pediment carved by Anton Anreith and depicting a riotous bacchanalia, which represents fertility.

The substantial grounds of Groot Constantia are serene and orderly, and make for good walks among the vines. There's also a coach house, wine cellar and **orientation centre**, the latter covering the estate's history including the role of slavery.

1

The estate has two restaurants and a deli offering **picnics**. Its Visitors Route Experience offers access to the manor house, the Cloete Cellar, a wine tasting and two audio walking tours for R95. Tickets are available at Groot Constantia or through Webtickets (ⓦwebtickets.co.za).

Klein Constantia

Klein Constantia Rd • Mon–Fri 10am–5pm, Sat 10am–4.30pm, Sun 10am–4pm • R50 • ☎ 021 794 5188, ⓦ kleinconstantia.com

Smaller than Groot Constantia, **Klein Constantia** offers more casual wine tastings than at the bigger estate and, although the buildings are humbler, the setting is equally beautiful. Klein Constantia produces several fine wines, most famously its **Vin de Constance**, a re-creation of a historic Constantia wine that was a favourite of Napoleon, Frederick the Great and Bismarck. The poet Baudelaire compared its sweet delights to his lover's lips. It's a delicious **dessert wine**, packaged in a replica of the original bottle, and makes an original souvenir.

Buitenverwachting

Klein Constantia Rd • **Tastings** Mon–Fri 9am–5pm, Sat 9am–3pm • R50 • ☎ 021 794 5190, ⓦ buitenverwachting.co.za

Buitenverwachting (roughly pronounced "bay-tin-fur-vuch-ting" with the "ch" as in the Scottish rendition of loch) is a bucolic place tucked away in the Constantia suburbs, with sheep and cattle grazing in the fields as you approach the main buildings. The architecture and setting at the foot of the Constantiaberg are as lovely as any, while their wines have attracted accolades including a five-star rating in *Platter's Wine Guide 2015*.

Overlooking the vineyards and backing onto the garden, the late eighteenth-century homestead features an unusual gabled pediment broken by an urn motif. The original **wine cellar** and adjoining terrace are the venue for tastings and cheese and pâté platters, and the estate has a **restaurant** and a **coffee shop**.

The Atlantic seaboard

Table Mountain's steep drop into the ocean along much of the western peninsula forces the suburbs along the **Atlantic seaboard** into a ribbon of developments clinging dramatically to the slopes. The sea washing this side of the peninsula can be very chilly, far colder than on the False Bay seaboard. Although not ideal for bathing, the Atlantic seaboard offers mind-blowing views from some of the most incredible coastal roads in the world, particularly beyond **Sea Point**, and there are opportunities for whale spotting. The coast itself consists of a series of bays and white-sand beaches edged with smoothly sculpted bleached rocks. Inland, the Twelve Apostles, a series of rocky buttresses, gaze down on the surf. The beaches are ideal for sunbathing or sunset picnics – it's from this side of the peninsula that you can watch the sun sink into the

---

CAPE TOWN STADIUM

Described by British architecture critic Jonathan Glancey as "a stunning white apparition…in a sublime setting", **Cape Town Stadium**, on Fritz Zonneneberg Rd in Green Point, was arguably the jewel in South Africa's 2010 World Cup crown. The towering, 68,000-seater stadium relies on natural light, and at night the open-meshed roof can light up to resemble an ethereal UFO. Controversy surrounded its high building costs, which were funded by taxpayers, while the revelation of **corruption** during the tender process for its construction further tainted the stadium's reputation. Today, local teams use the stadium for **football matches** and it hosts **concerts** by major international rock and pop artists: tickets for both can be bought at ⓦ computicket.com. Hour-long stadium tours are also available (Mon–Fri 10am, noon & 2pm; R45, under-12 R17; ☎ 021 417 0120; ⓦ capetown.gov.za).

1

ocean, creating fiery reflections on the sea and mountains behind. Make the most of the views, and beautiful-people watching, in some of the city's most glamorous outdoor cafés and bars.

Mouille Point and Green Point

Just to the west of the V&A Waterfront, Mouille Point and neighbouring Green Point are among the suburbs closest to the city centre. **Mouille** (moo-lee) **Point** is known principally for its squat rectangular lighthouse, commissioned in the 1820s and painted like a children's picture-book lighthouse, with diagonal red and white stripes.

The larger suburb of **Green Point** is home to **Cape Town Stadium** and – thanks to its proximity to the Waterfront, an easy ten or so minutes' walk away, and the coast – plenty of good accommodation and cafés.

Sea Point

Nudging the western edge of Green Point, **Sea Point** is a **cosmopolitan area** known for its gay and Jewish communities, seafront apartment blocks, tourist accommodation and restaurants. The **Sea Point promenade** is the best way to appreciate the rocky coastline and salty air, along with pram-pushing mothers, grannies, power-walkers and joggers. People picnic or play ball games on the grassy parkland beside the walkway. Most restaurants and shops are along Main Road, a busy thoroughfare one block inland.

Sea Point Pavilion Swimming Pool

Lower Beach Rd • Daily: May–Nov 9am–5pm; Dec–April 7am–7pm • R22, children R11 • ☎ 021 434 3341

At the southwestern end of the Sea Point promenade is this set of four unheated filtered **saltwater pools**, beautifully located alongside the crashing surf. The largest of the four is Olympic-sized, making it a popular training tank for Cape Town's long-distance swimmers. There are also two children's splash pools and a fully equipped diving pool for the brave.

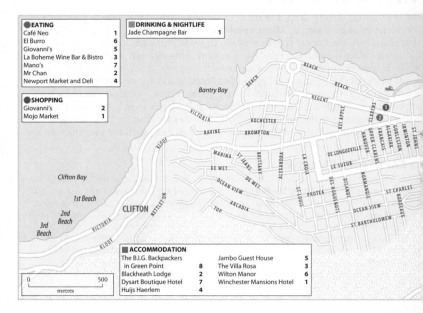

●EATING	
Café Neo	1
El Burro	6
Giovanni's	5
La Boheme Wine Bar & Bistro	3
Mano's	7
Mr Chan	2
Newport Market and Deli	4

■DRINKING & NIGHTLIFE	
Jade Champagne Bar	1

●SHOPPING	
Giovanni's	2
Mojo Market	1

■ACCOMMODATION			
The B.I.G. Backpackers in Green Point	8	Jambo Guest House	5
Blackheath Lodge	2	The Villa Rosa	3
Dysart Boutique Hotel	7	Wilton Manor	6
Huijs Haerlem	4	Winchester Mansions Hotel	1

Bantry Bay

At the southwestern-most edge of Sea Point lies **Bantry Bay**, combining the density of Sea Point with the wealth of Clifton; mansions rake back from the Atlantic shore on steep slopes, guarded by the granite boulders of Lion's Head. The upmarket resort hotels, guesthouses and self-catering apartment blocks are pleasantly removed from the hubbub of Sea Point, but close enough to walk to a restaurant.

Clifton

Fashionable **Clifton**, on the next cove along Victoria Road (the M6) from Bantry Bay, occupies some of Africa's most expensive real estate, studded with fabulous seaside apartments and four sandy **beaches**, reached via steep stairways and separated by clusters of granite boulders. The sea here is good for surfing and safe for swimming, but bone-chillingly cold. The four beaches – imaginatively named First, Second, Third and Fourth – are sheltered from the wind and popular with muscular ball players and families alike. Clifton Third is the gay choice and Fourth has a mellow mood on summer evenings, when groups of young people with candles hang out from sunset onwards.

Camps Bay

The suburb of **Camps Bay** climbs the slopes of Table Mountain, scooped into a ridiculously scenic amphitheatre by Lion's Head and the Twelve Apostles. With views across the Atlantic in the other direction, this is one of the city's most affluent and downright gorgeous neighbourhoods. The coast-hugging main drag, **Victoria Road**, is packed with trendy restaurants, a couple of nightspots and some upmarket accommodation, while the wide, sandy beach is enjoyed by families of all shapes and colours. However, the beach is exposed to the southeasterly wind, and there's the usual Atlantic chill and an occasional dangerous backwash.

Llandudno

There's little development between Camps Bay and the exclusive cove of **Llandudno**, 20km from Cape Town along Victoria Road. A steep and narrow road winds down past

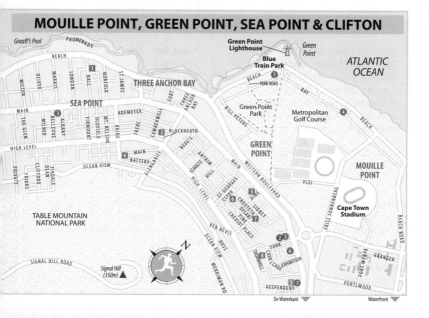

1

CAPE TOWN FOR KIDS

Cape Town and the nearby Winelands are an excellent place to travel with children, with plenty of outdoorsy activities. A good **website** for finding out what's on is Cape Town Kids (w capetownkids.co.za). For **babysitters**, or even nannies, to accompany you on trips, try Sitters4U (t 074 656 0469, w sitters4u.co.za) or Super Sitters (t 021 551 7082, w supersitters .net). Car rental companies will provide **child seats**, if booked in advance.

BEACHES AND SWIMMING POOLS

Cape Town's **beaches** offer a classic summer weekend family outing, though the water is not warm. Most are pretty undeveloped, so it's best to take what you need in the way of food and drink, although you may come across vendors. Arrive as early as possible so you can leave by 11am; on summer afternoons, the sun is too strong and the wind can get very gusty.

On the False Bay seaboard, **Boulders Beach** (see p.126) is one of the few beaches to visit when the southeaster is blowing and is gorgeous at any time. It has safe, flat water, making it ideal for kids – and its resident penguin colony is an added attraction. **Fish Hoek** (see p.123) is another great peninsula beach, with a long stretch of sand and a playground. The paved **Jager's Walk**, which runs along the rocky coast here, is suitable for pushchairs. **St James** (see p.122) boasts a safe tidal pool with a small sandy beach and photogenic bathing chalets, but gets overcrowded on summer weekends. From here you can walk to **Muizenberg** and its water park (see p.121) along a pushchair-friendly coastal pathway.

The **Atlantic seaboard** is too cold for serious swimming, but does have some lovely stretches of sand, boulders and rock pools – and astonishing scenery. The beaches here are excellent for picnics and are idyllic at sunset on calm summer evenings. The closest stretch of coast to the centre, ideal for prams – and rollerblading – is the paved **Sea Point promenade** (see p.114), stretching 3km from the lighthouse in Mouille Point to Sea Point Pavilion, with the draw of playgrounds en route. The tidal pool and small rock pools of **Camps Bay** (see p.115) make this popular beach very child-friendly, and it's easily reached from the centre by car or bus. Finally, the 8km stretch of white sand from **Noordhoek** to **Kommetjie** (see p.120) provides fine walking and horseriding opportunities, with stupendous views of Chapman's Peak. If you're heading for Kommetjie you can go camel riding at **Imhoff Farm Village** (see p.117).

As regards child-friendly swimming pools, **Newlands Pool** (see p.154) has a kids' paddling pool and large grounds, while the marvelous **Sea Point Pavilion Pool** (see p.114) has two splash pools for children and lawns to laze on, but go early or late to avoid the crowds on warm weekends.

INDOORS AND ENTERTAINMENT

Cape Town Science Centre 370B Main Rd, Observatory t 021 300 3200, w ctsc.org.za. Kids will love the interactive displays on science, new technologies and inventions here, which appeal to their innate sense of curiosity with things to touch, push and create. Highlights include a gyroscope, the brain-teasing Puzzling Things exhibits and an inflatable planetarium. Entry R50. Mon–Sat 9am–4.30pm, Sun 10am–4.30pm.

Planet Kids 3 Wherry Rd, Muizenberg t 021 788 3070, w planetkids.co.za. A great indoor play centre for kids up to 13, designed by an occupational therapist, which is loads of fun, as well as offering healthy snacks and a calmer environment than the usual plastic, sugar-crazed scene (R35/hr, parents free entry). With assistants on hand, you can drop off your child for 1hr (R30–55) or have a cup of tea while you wait. All abilities welcome, with facilities for kids with special needs. Thurs–Sun 10am–5pm.

smart homes to the shore, where the sandy beach is punctuated at either end by magnificent granite boulders and rock formations. It's a great spot for sunbathing and sunset-watching alike. MyCiTi buses #108 and #109 pass the entrance to Llandudno, from where it's a steep 20min walk down to the beach.

Sandy Bay

Isolated **Sandy Bay**, Cape Town's main nudist beach and a popular gay and lesbian hangout, can only be reached via a twenty-minute walk from Llandudno. The path

Scratch Patch and Mineral World Dido Valley Rd, off Main Rd, Simon's Town ☎ 021 786 2020; Dock Rd, V&A Waterfront ☎ 021 419 9429, ⦿ scratchpatch .co.za. Over-3s can search for jewels, filling a bag (R17–95) with the colourful polished gemstones that cover the floor. At the Simon's Town venue you can also see Topstones (⦿ topstones.co.za), one of the world's biggest gemstone-tumbling plants, in operation (Mon–Fri only). Simon's Town daily 9am–4.45pm; V&A Waterfront daily 9am–6pm.

South African Museum and Planetarium See p.97. The four-storey "whale well", African animal dioramas and dinosaur displays always please, while the hands-on Discovery Room features live ants, pinned and preserved spiders and a crocodile display. The planetarium's daily shows cover topics such as San sky myths, with some geared towards children. Daily 10am–5pm.

Two Oceans Aquarium See p.102. One of Cape Town's most rewarding attractions, the aquarium features loads to interest a wide range of ages. As well as looking at the weird and wonderful sea creatures, children can handle species such as anemones and crabs in the touch pool. The Children's Play Centre usually has puppet shows, face-painting and craft activities, as well as a window on the penguin pool. Daily 9.30am–6pm.

OUTDOORS AND PICNICS

Blue Train Park Beach Rd, Mouille Point ☎ 084 314 9200, ⦿ thebluetrainpark.com. Take a trip on Cape Town's favourite miniature train (R20) for a view of the sea, passing ships and Robben Island. There's also plenty to wear kids out afterwards in the park including a jungle gym, climbing rock, outdoor obstacles, basketball net, ice rink and toddler push-bike track. Tues–Sun 9.30am–6pm.

Deer Park Café See p.142. The most central outdoor family venue, adjoining a popular enclosed park (sadly no deer) with a good selection of jungle gyms, swings and so on, all overlooked by the towering massif of Table Mountain. There are outdoor tables with easy access to the park, and a children's menu. Daily 8am–8pm.

Green Point Park Bill Peters Dr, Green Point ⦿ gprra .co.za/green-point-urban-park. Offering vistas over the city and stadium, this grassy park has an educational Biodiversity Showcase Garden, tracks for jogging and cycling, a play park for small children and an outdoor gym for those a little older. Go for a picnic or join the 5km Saturday-morning Parkrun (⦿ parkrun .co.za/greenpoint). Free entry. Daily 7am–7pm.

Imhoff Farm Village Kommetjie Rd ⦿ imhofffarm .co.za. Activities here include camel rides, horseriding on the beach, paintball, a farmyard petting zoo and reptile park. There's also a good café, restaurant and farmers' shop with fabulous cheeses. Daily 9am–5pm.

Kirstenbosch National Botanical Garden See p.111. Top of the list for a family outing, with extensive lawns for running about, trees and rocks to climb, streams for paddling and the "Boomslang" treetop walkway. There's no litter, no dogs, it's extremely safe and you can push a pram all over the walkways; it's also great for picnics or to have tea outdoors at the café. For older kids there are short waymarked walks. Daily 8am–6pm.

Noordhoek Farm Village See p.120. A small, grassy green, surrounded by cafés, a deli, crafts stores and a gift shop, with gentle country charm. At the Weds food market (4–8pm) kids can tear around and enjoy the playground while their parents choose between stalls offering Mexican, Italian, craft beer and more. Daily 9am–5pm.

Oude Molen Eco Village Alexandra Rd, Pinelands ☎ 021 448 9442, ⦿ oudemolenecovillage.co.za. A working model of a sustainable eco-village in a suburban area. You can sample home-grown organic produce and wood-fired bread at the *Millstone Farmstall and Café* before taking the kids to play in the garden treehouse, swing and play area. Children are encouraged to feed the horses and pigs, while horseriding and nature walks can be organized. Tues–Sun 9am–5pm.

Silvermine Nature Reserve See p.122. A good place to see *fynbos* vegetation at close quarters while strolling around the lake and picnicking with small children; however, it is exposed, and not recommended in heavy winds or mist. For older children there are some mountain walks with relatively gentle gradients, which give spectacular views. Daily 8am–5pm.

here leads from the Sunset Rocks car park, at the southern end of Llandudno, through *fynbos* vegetation and over rocks.

Hout Bay

Although no longer the quaint fishing village it once was, **Hout Bay** still has a functioning fishing harbour and is the centre of the local crayfish industry. Some 20km from the centre of Cape Town, it's a favourite **day-trip** for fish and chips at Mariner's Wharf (see p.144) or the lively **Bay Harbour Market** (see p.156), with a

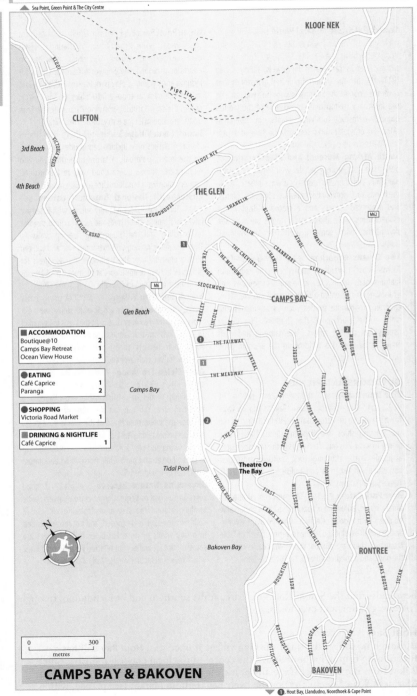

Sea Point, Green Point & The City Centre

KLOOF NEK

Pipe Track

CLIFTON

3rd Beach

4th Beach

THE GLEN

KLOOF NEK

ROUNDHOUSE

SHANKLIN

SHANKLIN

BLAIR

CRANBERRY

SHANKLIN

ATHOL

COMRIE

GENEVA

ATHOL

THE CHEVIOTS

THE MEADOWS

7TH GRANGE

SEDGEMOOR

CAMPS BAY

BERKLEY

LINCOLN

PARK

THE FAIRWAY

CENTRAL

THE MEADWAY

GENEVA

QUEENS

CRAMOND

MEDBURN

WOODFORD

FILLIANS

HALF HUTCHINSON

TRIMA

Glen Beach

Camps Bay

THE DRIVE

RONALD

STRATHEARN

UPPER TREE

ACCOMMODATION
Boutique@10   **2**
Camps Bay Retreat   **1**
Ocean View House   **3**

EATING
Café Caprice   **1**
Paranga   **2**

SHOPPING
Victoria Road Market **1**

DRINKING & NIGHTLIFE
Café Caprice   **1**

Tidal Pool

Theatre On The Bay

FIRST

CAMPS BAY

FINCHLEY

DUNKELD

WILLESDEN

INGLESIDE

KENILWORTH

EISKAAL

Bakoven Bay

HOUGHTON

JOCH

ROTTINGDEAN

TOTNESS

FELSHAM

FAIRHAM

PITLOCHRY

BAKOVEN

CHAS BOOTH

SUSAN

RONTREE

RONTREE

0   300
metres

CAMPS BAY & BAKOVEN

Hout Bay, Llandudno, Noordhoek & Cape Point

DUIKER ISLAND CRUISES

The best way to take in the dramatic ocean and mountain environment is on a short cruise from Hout Bay harbour to **Duiker Island**, sometimes called "seal island" because it's home to a massive **colony** of South African, or Cape, fur seals, the largest of the fur seals. Of the operators running tours (45min; R85) **Nauticat Charters** (☎021 790 7278, ⓦnauticatcharters.co.za) is one of the best, offering six daily departures in glass-bottomed boats that allow you to see the seals and kelp underwater.

stunning bay overlooked by the Sentinel and Chapman's Peak. Highly unusual for Cape Town with its legacy of apartheid town planning, poor black areas nose up to wealthy white neighbourhoods.

Imizamo Yethu township

As you head towards Constantia Nek from Hout Bay, you pass the township of **Imizamo Yethu**, a tightly packed shack-land settlement crawling up the hillside. Imizamo Yethu was first settled during the late 1980s, in the dying days of apartheid, by Xhosa job-seekers from the Eastern Cape. Its population grew to tens of thousands before the terrible fire of March 2017, which destroyed over 3000 homes and displaced 15,000-plus people. Although conditions are pretty dire, it is an easy township for visitors to visit and feel welcome on a **walking tour** (see p.120).

World of Birds

Valley Rd • Daily 9am–5pm, monkey jungle daily 11.30am–1pm & 2–3.30pm • Feeding times: penguins 11.30am & 3.30pm, pelicans 12.30pm, cormorants 1.30pm, birds of prey 4.15pm • R95, children R45 • ⓦworldofbirds.org.za

The **World of Birds** is home to more than three thousand birds, housed in surprisingly pleasant and peaceful walk-through **aviaries**, as well as small mammals and reptiles; allow at least two hours for a visit. The birds include indigenous species such as cranes, vultures and pelicans, as well as a number of feathered **exotics**. The large walk-in **monkey jungle** includes cute squirrel monkeys, which visitors are allowed to pet. There are also the popular meerkats, and the lush gardens with a mountain backdrop make for a tranquil outing.

Chapman's Peak Drive

Toll charge R42 • ☎021 791 8222, ⓦchapmanspeakdrive.co.za

Thrilling **Chapman's Peak Drive**, which winds along a cliff edge south of Hout Bay to Noordhoek, is one of the world's great ocean drives. There are a number of safe viewpoints along the route, some of which have picnic sites, so bring snacks and refreshments and stop to enjoy the spectacular view. The road is occasionally closed due to rockfalls, so phone or check the website in advance.

Noordhoek

This desirable, alternatively minded settlement (it even has a **hemp house**) at the southern end of Chapman's Peak Drive, a 35km drive from the city centre, consists of smallholdings and riding stables in a gentle valley planted with oaks. When Chapman's Peak is closed, Noordhoek is accessible via the M3 south over Oukaapseweg.

Noordhoek Beach

On the right as you come in from Chapman's Peak is the turning for Avondrust Circle, which leads to **Noordhoek Beach**, whose immense, white, kelp-strewn sands stretch towards Kommetjie. Each morning between 7.30am and 9am, **racehorses** gallop along the sand, and you will invariably see riders (see p.153) sharing the wide beach with local dog walkers. The sea is cold, wild and spectacular, framed by Chapman's Peak, though strong winds can sometimes turn the beach into a sandblaster. The nearby

1

TOURS OF IMIZAMO YETHU

Although it is unsafe to wander into Imizamo Yethu alone, you can take a fun, two-hour **walking tour** (daily at 10.30am, 1pm & 4pm; R75; ☎ 083 719 4870, ⓦ suedafrika.net/imizamoyethu) with enthusiastic and accomplished guide Afrika Moni, who knows the place and its history inside out. He walks you through his home township, stopping to chat to proprietors of informal *spaza* shops, sipping traditional beer at a *shebeen*, as well as popping into shacks and brick houses. Tours start from the police station at the entrance to the township, where there are reserved parking places for visitors; the City Sightseeing bus (see p.131) stops here too.

Monkey Valley Resort (see p.138) welcomes non-guests for reasonably priced meals with great views, its groves of milkwood trees offering shelter from the wind.

Noordhoek Farm Village

Village Lane • Opening hours vary for the different establishments, food market Wed 4–8pm • ⓦ noordhoekvillage.co.za

Noordhoek Farm Village, close to the signposted entrance to Chapman's Peak drive, is an excellent place for refuelling or entertaining children. The Cape Dutch-style complex is home to the excellent *Foodbarn* restaurant, deli and tapas bar (see p.144), as well as a pub, café, sushi bar, children's playground, craft shops and more. The weekly outdoor **market** features food by the Village traders ranging from Italian to Mexican.

Kommetjie

Although only a few kilometres' walk south of Noordhoek along the beach, getting to the tiny settlement of **Kommetjie** by road involves a detour inland to avoid the wetlands. Facilities are limited and one of the main reasons to come here is for the superb walks, either around the rocky shore near Slangkop lighthouse or across the extensive sands of Long Beach back towards Noordhoek.

Scarborough

The idyllic village of **Scarborough** is the most far-flung settlement along the peninsula, with cold, turquoise water and white sands. It's a lovely, easy drive to/from Simon's Town, winding over the spine of the peninsula, with a turning to **Cape Point** en route.

The False Bay seaboard

In summer the waters of **False Bay** are several degrees warmer than those on the Atlantic seaboard, which is why Cape Town's oldest and most popular seaside towns line this flank of the peninsula. A series of historic, village-like suburbs, backing onto the mountains, each served by a Metrorail station, is dotted all the way south from **Muizenberg**, through **St James**, **Kalk Bay**, **Fish Hoek** and down to **Simon's Town**. Each has its own character with restaurants, shops and places to stay, while Simon's Town, one of South Africa's oldest settlements, makes either a pleasant day-trip or a relaxing base for visiting **Boulders Beach** and the Cape of Good Hope Nature Reserve (see p.126).

ARRIVAL AND DEPARTURE   FALSE BAY SEABOARD

By car From central Cape Town, the best route is along the M3 south to Muizenberg. Boyes Drive, a mountainside alternative to coastal Main Rd, runs for about 7km between the suburbs of Lakeside at the southern end of the M3 and Kalk Bay, and offers spectacular views.

By train The train ride to Simon's Town is reason enough to visit, with most stations from Muizenberg onwards situated close to the shore. From Cape Town,

Metrorail (☎ 021 449 6478, ⓦ www.metrorail.co.za, ⓦ cttrains.co.za) runs roughly three trains an hour to Simon's Town (Mon–Fri 5.10am–9.15pm; 1hr 15min; R16.50), with four an hour as far as Fish Hoek (58min; R13.50). Trains travel via Muizenberg (48min; R13.50), St James (51min; R13.50) and Kalk Bay (55min; R13.50). On weekends, services are reduced to roughly one an hour to Simon's Town.

1

ALL ABOARD

These beachfront surf shops offer surfing lessons and equipment rental for those who want to try their skills on Muizenberg's breakers.

Gary's Surf School 34 Balmoral Building, Beach Rd ⊙ 021 788 9839, ⓦ garysurf.com. R450 for a two-hour lesson including gear rental.

Surf Shack York Rd, Muizenberg ⊙ 021 788 9286, ⓦ surfshack.co.za. Various lesson packages available or just board and wetsuit rental R100 for 90min.

Muizenberg

Once boasting South Africa's most fashionable seaside resort, **Muizenberg** is rising from the doldrums with the beautification of its seafront, while the brightly coloured Victorian **bathing chalets** on the beach are cheerful reminders of its more elegant heyday. The long, safe and fabulous **beach**, which shelves gently, is one of the peninsula's most popular spots for swimming. *National Geographic* named Muizenberg one of the world's top twenty surf towns in 2017, and you can rent boards and organize lessons at the **surf shops** on Beach Road (see above).

Don't take anything **valuable** to the beach and don't leave anything unguarded while you're there, as opportunist **theft** is rife. Guards are present at the car park, so preferably leave valuables in your car boot – and place them there discreetly.

The Historical Mile

A short stretch of the shore, stretching south from Muizenberg station, is known as the **Historical Mile**, dotted with notable buildings and easily explored on foot. **Muizenberg Station**, a late Edwardian-style edifice completed in 1913, with its lovely ornate clock tower, is now a National Monument, while the nearby **Posthuys** was once a lookout for ships entering the bay. The rugged whitewashed and thatched building dating from 1673 is a fine example of the Cape vernacular style – and purportedly the oldest European building in South Africa. **Rhodes' Cottage Museum**, 246 Main Road (Mon–Sat 10am–2pm; admission by donation), was bought in 1899 by the millionaire empire builder, who died here in 1902, and contains some personal memorabilia and period furniture.

Casa Labia Cultural Centre

192 Main Rd · Tues–Sun 10am–4pm · Free · ⊙ 021 788 6068, ⓦ casalabia.co.za

The most idiosyncratic of the buildings along the Historical Mile, **Casa Labia** was completed in 1930 as the residence of the Italian consul, Count Natale Labia. Built in eighteenth-century Venetian style, it's a glorious piece of architectural bling and worth popping into just for the *palazzo's* film-set **interiors**. It also houses a **cultural centre** that puts on concerts and talks, a **gallery** of modern and contemporary South African art, an opulent **café** and a craft shop.

CAPE TOWN'S TOP WHALE SPOTS

The commonest whales around Cape Town are southern rights, and the best **whale-watching spots** are on the warmer **False Bay** side of the peninsula from August to November. Along the False Bay seaboard, whale signboards indicate good places for sightings. **Boyes Drive**, running along the mountainside behind Muizenberg and Kalk Bay, provides an outstanding vantage point, and there are often whales off the coast at St James. Alternatively, sticking close to the shore along Main Road, the stretch between **Fish Hoek** and **Simon's Town** is recommended, with a particularly nice spot above the rocks at the south end of Fish Hoek Beach. Even better vantage points can be found further down the coast between Simon's Town and **Smitswinkelbaai**, where the road goes higher along the mountainside. Without a car, you can catch the train to Fish Hoek or Sunny Cove and whale-spot from the **Jager's Walk** beach path that runs along the coast between the two, just below the railway line.

1

St James

St James is more upmarket than neighbouring Muizenberg, its mountainside homes accessed mostly up long stairways between Main Road and Boyes Drive. The best reason to hop off the train here is for the **sheltered tidal pool** and the twenty-minute walk along the **paved coastal path** that runs along the rocky shore to Muizenberg – one of the peninsula's easiest and most rewarding walks, with panoramas of the full sweep of False Bay. Look out for seals and, in season, whales.

The compact St James beach draws considerable character from its much-photographed Victorian-style bathing chalets, whose bright, primary colours catch your eye as you pass by road or rail. The beach tends to be overcrowded at weekends and during school holidays; far fewer visitors stroll south on the short footpath to the adjacent sandy stretch of **Danger Beach**, an excellent spot for sunbathing and building sandcastles.

Kalk Bay

One of Cape Town's smallest and most southerly suburbs, **Kalk Bay** centres around a lively working harbour with wooden fishing vessels, mountain views, and a strip of shops packed with collectibles, antique dealers, trendy cafés and excellent restaurants. Kalk Bay managed to resist the Group Areas Act, making it one of the few places on the peninsula with an intact coloured community. As well as coloured fishermen, the 275-year-old settlement is home to numerous artists and creative types, who thrive on Kalk Bay's village atmosphere and natural beauty.

The settlement is arranged around the small **harbour**, where you can watch the boats come in; you can also buy fresh fish, which are flung onto the quayside, sold in spirited auctions, gutted for a small fee and the innards then thrown to waiting seals. Kalk Bay is busiest over weekends, when Capetonians descend to brunch at the excellent cafés, wander the shops and harbour, or have a drink at the water's edge.

Silvermine Nature Reserve

Ou Kaapse Weg, signposted at the southern end of the M3 • Daily: May–Aug 8am–5pm; Sept–April 7am–6pm • R50

Don't miss the beautiful **Silvermine Nature Reserve**, part of the Table Mountain National Park with walks offering fabulous views of both sides of the peninsula, as well

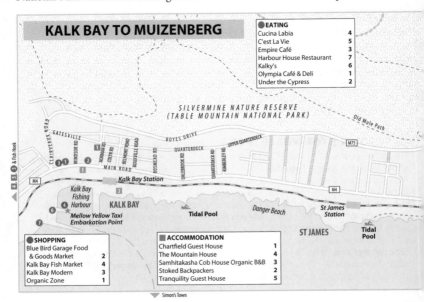

1

as a dam to swim in and picnic by. At the entrance, you'll be given a sketchy map of the reserve with the walks marked, though Slingsby's excellent *Silvermine & Hout Bay* (⊛slingsbymaps.com) is by far the best map.

Fish Hoek

Fish Hoek boasts one of the peninsula's finest family **beaches** along the False Bay coast. The best and safest swimming is at its southern end, where the surf is moderately warm, tame and much enjoyed by boogie boarders. Thanks to the beach, there's a fair amount of accommodation (see p.139), but this is otherwise one of the dreariest suburbs along the False Bay coast. An obscure bylaw banning the sale of alcohol in supermarkets or bottle stores has cast Fish Hoek as the peninsula puritan, but liquor is now available in bars and restaurants.

Simon's Town

Despite being the South African Navy's headquarters, having been a British Royal Navy base, historic **Simon's Town** isn't a hard-drinking port town. It's exceptionally pretty, with a well-preserved streetscape bearing testament to its history as one of the country's oldest European settlements. The domineering **naval dockyard** mars the aesthetics, but this — and glimpses of naval squaddies square-bashing behind high walls or strolling to the station in their crisp white uniforms — adds to Simon's Town's distinct nautical flavour.

Just 40km from Cape Town, roughly halfway down the peninsula to Cape Point, Simon's Town is a favourite stop-off point on guided tours, but it also makes a good base for a mellow seaside break. A few kilometres to the south is **Boulders Beach**, with its colony of cute **African penguins** — reason enough alone for a Simon's Town visit.

Brief history

Founded in 1687 as the winter anchorage of the Dutch East India Company, Simon's Town was one of several places in and around Cape Town modestly named by **Governor Simon van der Stel** after himself. Its most celebrated visitor was Lord Nelson, who convalesced here as a midshipman while returning home from the East Indies in 1776. Nineteen years later, the British sailed into Simon's Town and occupied it as a

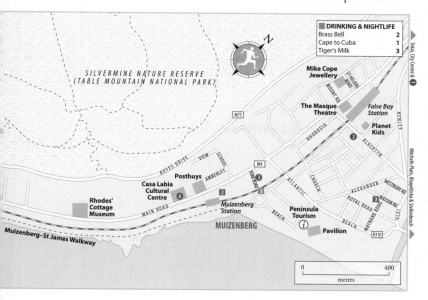

■ DRINKING & NIGHTLIFE	
Brass Bell	2
Cape to Cuba	1
Tiger's Milk	3

SILVERMINE NATURE RESERVE
(TABLE MOUNTAIN NATIONAL PARK)

Mike Cope Jewellery

The Masque Theatre

False Bay Station

Planet Kids

Posthuys

Casa Labia Cultural Centre

Rhodes' Cottage Museum

Muizenberg Station

MUIZENBERG

Peninsula Tourism

Pavilion

Muizenberg–St James Walkway

1

FALSE BAY WATER TAXI

In summer, **the Mellow Yellow Water Taxi** runs across False Bay between Kalk Bay and Simon's Town (☎073 473 7684, ⓦwatertaxi.co.za; R100 one-way, R150 return). The trip is highly recommended, and one of the few ways to get on the water in False Bay; book ahead as the vessel takes a maximum of ten passengers and only goes if weather conditions are favourable.

bridgehead for their first invasion and occupation of the Cape. They left after just seven years, only to return in 1806. Simon's Town remained a British base until 1957, when it was handed over to South Africa.

There are fleeting hints, such as the two mosques at the eastern end of Thomas Street, that the town's predominantly white appearance isn't the whole story. In fact, the first **Muslims** arrived from the East Indies in the early eighteenth century, imported as slaves to build the Dutch naval base. After the British banned the slave trade in 1807, ships were compelled to disgorge their human cargo at Simon's Town, where one district became known as Black Town.

In 1967, when Simon's Town was declared a White Group Area, there were 1200 well-established coloured families living here, who were descended from these slaves. By the early 1970s, the majority had been forcibly removed under the Group Areas Act to the township of **Ocean View**, whose inspiring name belies its desolation.

Simon's Town Museum

Court Rd • Mon–Fri 10am–4pm, Sat 10am–1pm • R20 • ⓦsimonstown.com/museum/index.html

Simon's Town Museum occupies the Old Residency, built in 1777 as the winter residence of the Governor of the Dutch East India Company, whose slave quarters (later a jail) can be seen in the basement. The museum's motley collection includes maritime material, militaria and an inordinate amount of information and exhibits on **Able Seaman Just Nuisance**, a much-celebrated seafaring Great Dane. The dog enjoyed drinking beer with the sailors he accompanied into Cape Town and was adopted as a mascot by the Royal Navy in World War II.

Jubilee Square and the Marina

In the centre of Simon's Town, a little over 1km south of the station, lies **Jubilee Square**, a palm-shaded car park just off St George's Street. Flanked by some cafés and shops, the square has on its harbour-facing side a broad walkway with a statue of the ubiquitous Able Seaman Just Nuisance and a few curio sellers. A couple of sets of stairs lead down to the **Marina**, a modest development of shops and restaurants set right on the waterfront.

SPOTTING MARINE LIFE IN FALSE BAY

False Bay is one of the best places in the country to see **great white sharks**, and you can also go **whale watching** and visit **seals**. One of the best shark-trip operators is **Apex Shark Expeditions** (☎021 786 5717, ⓦapexpredators.com; Feb–March R1750, April–May R1900, June–Aug R2400), run by naturalists Chris and Monique Fallows, who have worked with National Geographic and the BBC. They operate a range of marine excursions from Simon's Town pier between February and September, including shark-cage diving. Their emphasis is on observing the sharks' behaviour and that of other marine creatures you'll encounter on the trip out to Seal Island. Passenger numbers are strictly limited to twelve, which means everyone gets a good stint in the cage. The long-established **Simon's Town Boat Company** (☎083 257 7760, ⓦboatcompany.co.za) runs whale-watching trips (R900, under-12s R600), plus cruises around Cape Point (R600, under-12s R500) and tours to Seal Island (R450, under-12s R350).

FROM TOP STREET CRICKET IN LANGA TOWNSHIP (P.129); PENGUINS AT BOULDERS BEACH (P.126) >

1

Boulders Beach and the Penguin Reserve

2km from Jubilee Sq • Daily: Jan & Dec 7am–7.30pm; Feb, March, Oct & Nov 8am–6.30pm; April–Sept 8am–5pm • R70, child R35 • HGTS Tours (☎ 021 786 5243, ✆ hgtravel.co.za) runs a taxi service from Simon's Town Station to Boulders Beach (one-way R30).

Boulders Beach takes its name from the huge granite rocks, which create a cluster of little coves with sandy beaches and clear sea pools that are wonderful for swimming. However, the main reason people come to Boulders' fenced seafront reserve is for the 2000-plus **African penguins** (also known as jackass penguins for their distinctive bray). African penguins usually live on islands off the Southern African coast, including Robben Island, and the Boulders birds form one of only two mainland colonies. The reserve offers a rare opportunity to get a close look – and to hear that bray at its loudest, during the **breeding season** from March to May.

Access to the Boulders reserve is through two gates, one at the Boulders Beach (eastern) end, at the bottom Bellevue Road, and the other at the **Seaforth Beach** (western) side, off Seaforth Road. Both entrances are signposted along Main Road between Simon's Town and Cape Point. At the Seaforth end, there's a small visitors' centre and deck, from which two boardwalks lead to either end of Foxy Beach where you'll see hundreds of penguins. Most people walk from Seaforth to Boulders, looking at all the penguins in the bushes along the paths, where there are masses of burrows for nesting. At Seaforth itself, there is safe swimming on the beach, which is bounded on one side by the looming grey mass of the naval base. There's also plenty of lawn shaded by palm trees, and a **restaurant** with outdoor seating and fresh fish on the menu.

Cape of Good Hope

Daily: April–Sept 7am–5pm; Oct–March 6am–6pm • R135, child R70 • ☎ 021 780 9010, ✆ tmnp.co.za, ✆ capepoint.co.za

Most people visit the **Cape of Good Hope Nature Reserve**, which is part of Table Mountain National Park, to see the southernmost tip of Africa at **Cape Point**. In fact, the continent's real tip is at Cape Agulhas, some 300km southeast of here (see p.191); Cape Point is Africa's southwestern-most point, as well as being much easier to reach and a hugely dramatic spot. The reserve sits atop massive sea cliffs with huge views, strong seas, and an even wilder wind that whips off caps and sunglasses as visitors gaze southwards from the old **lighthouse** buttress.

If you don't bring any food, you can take in the views from Cape Point at the touristic *Two Oceans* restaurant (see p.145).

ARRIVAL AND INFORMATION
CAPE OF GOOD HOPE

By guided tour There's no public transport to the reserve, but numerous tours take it in as part of a package of peninsula highlights (see p.132). Day Trippers (☎ 021 511 4766, ✆ daytrippers.co.za) runs fun hiking and cycling tours for R850 (including entrance and picnic lunch). However you get there, go as early as you can in the day – the chances of the crowds and of the wind gusting up increase as the day progresses.

Tourist information Buffelsfontein Visitors' Centre, 8km from the entrance gate, has displays on the local fauna and flora as well as video screenings on the area's ecology (daily 9.30am–5.30pm).

FURRY FELONS

Baboons may look amusing, but be warned: they can be a menace. Keep your car windows closed, as it's not uncommon for them to invade vehicles, and they're adept at swiping picnics. You should lock your car doors even if you only plan to get out for a few minutes, as baboons have opened unlocked doors while the vehicle owner's back is turned. Avoid unwrapping food or eating or drinking anything if baboons are in the vicinity. Feeding them is illegal and provocative and can incur a fine. Authorized baboon chasers are in evidence in several places, warding off the animals.

1

CAPE FAUNA

Along with indigenous plants and flowers, you may well spot some of the animals living in the *fynbos* habitat on Cape Point. **Ostriches** stride through the low *fynbos*, and occasionally **African penguins** come ashore. A distinctive bird on the rocky shores is the **black oystercatcher** with its bright red beak, jabbing limpets off the rocks. You'll also see **Cape cormorants** in large flocks on the beach or rocks, often drying their outstretched wings. Running up and down the water's edge, littered with piles of shiny brown *Ecklonia* kelp, are **white-fronted plovers** and **sanderlings**, probing for food left by the receding waves.

As for mammals, **baboons** lope along the rocky shoreline, while grazing on the heathery slopes you'll see **bontebok**, **eland** and **red hartebeest**, as well as the smaller **grey rhebok** and **grysbok**. If you're very lucky, you may even see the rare **Cape mountain zebras**. What you will undoubtedly see are rock agama lizards, black zonure lizards and rock hyraxes (*dassies*).

Cape Point and around

From the Cape Point car park, it's a short, steep walk up a series of stairs to the famous viewpoint, the original **lighthouse**. The **Flying Dutchman Funicular** (R65 return) runs to the top, leaving every three minutes.

Cape Point is the treacherous promontory of rocks, winds and swells braved by navigators since the Portuguese first "rounded the Cape" in the fifteenth century. The lighthouse, built in 1860, was often dangerously shrouded in cloud and failed to keep ships off the rocks, so another was built lower down in 1914. You can walk to this quieter **second lighthouse** from the base of the first, near the lower funicular station.

Walking

Most visitors make a beeline for Cape Point, seeing the rest of the reserve through a vehicle window, but walking is the best way to appreciate the windswept coastline and **fynbos**.

There are several waymarked **walks** in the Cape of Good Hope reserve. If you're planning a big hike it's best to set out early and take plenty of water, as shade is rare and the wind can be foul. One of the most straightforward **hiking routes** is the signposted forty-minute walk from the car park at Cape Point to the more westerly **Cape of Good Hope**. For exploring the shoreline, a clear path runs down the Atlantic side, which you can join at **Gifkommetjie**, signposted off Cape Point Road. From the car park, several sandy tracks drop quite steeply down the slope across rocks, and through bushes and milkwood trees to the shore, along which you can walk in either direction. You can access several of the wrecks along this treacherous coast; visit the **Shipwreck Trails** page of the Cape Point website for more details (Ⓦcapepoint.co.za).

The beaches

You'll find the **beaches** along signposted side roads branching out from the main Cape Point road through the reserve. The sea here is too dangerous for swimming, but there are safe tidal pools at the adjacent **Buffels Bay** and **Bordjiesrif**, midway along the east shore. Both have braai stands, but more southerly Buffels Bay is nicer, with plentiful grassy banks and some sheltered spots to have a picnic – but don't produce any food if there are baboons in the vicinity (see box opposite).

The Cape Flats and the townships

Stretching east of the M5 highway and sprawling out past the airport, the windswept Cape Flats are Cape Town's largest residential area, taking in the **coloured districts**, **African townships** and **informal settlements** (shantytown **squatter camps**). Once the apartheid dumping ground for black and coloured people, these township-covered flatlands now offer rewarding experiences of everyday African life and are best visited on a tour.

1

Brief history

The African townships were historically set up as dormitories to provide labour for white Cape Town, not as places to build a life, which is why they had no facilities and no real hub. The **men-only hostels**, another apartheid relic, are at the root of many of the area's social problems. During the 1950s, the government set out a blueprint to turn the tide of Africans flooding into Cape Town. No African was permitted to settle permanently in the Cape west of a line near the Fish River, the old frontier over 1000km east of Cape Town; women were entirely banned from seeking work in Cape Town and men prohibited from bringing their wives to join them. By 1970 there were ten men for every woman in Langa.

In the end, apartheid failed to prevent the influx of job seekers desperate to come to Cape Town. Where people couldn't find legal accommodation, they set up **squatter camps** of makeshift iron, cardboard and plastic sheeting. During the 1970s and 1980s, the government attempted to demolish these – but no sooner had the police left than the camps reappeared, and they remain a permanent feature of the Cape Flats.

One of the best known of all South Africa's squatter camps is **Crossroads**, whose inhabitants suffered campaigns of harassment that included killings by apartheid collaborators and police, and continuous attempts to bulldoze it out of existence. Through sheer determination and desperation its residents hung on, eventually winning the right to stay. Today, the government is making attempts to improve

---

TOWNSHIP HIGHLIGHTS

While we don't recommend independent trips to the townships, you can ask to visit these highlights on your guided tour.

Gugulethu Seven Memorial and Amy Biehl Memorial, Gugulethu Steve Biko St ⓦamybiehl .co.za. Seven solid and powerful granite statue-like constructions honour the struggle and death of the Gugulethu Seven, an anti-apartheid group who were shot and killed by members of the South African police force in 1986. Nearby, a cross marks the site where Amy Biehl, a white American anti-apartheid activist, was murdered by local residents in 1993. A moving tribute to her courageous, all-too-short life.

★Guga S'Thebe Arts & Cultural Centre, Langa Cnr King Langalibalele/Washington Dr and Church St ☎021 695 3493. With art studios, a shop, an outdoor amphitheatre and a theatre constructed from recycled materials, this dynamic community centre nurtures creativity from drumming, theatre and pottery to sand art, beadwork and mosaics. There's free wi-fi, and *Kaffa Hoist Café* (see p.140) serves locally roasted Deluxe Coffeeworks coffee. The centre's location just off the N2 makes it easy to visit with your own wheels, although you will get more out of the experience on a guided tour; a car guard watches vehicles parked outside. Jazz in the Native Yards concerts (facebook.com/nativeyards) take place here from time to time. Daily 8.30am–6pm; free.

Ikhaya Le Langa Cnr Ndabeni and Rubuasna sts ⓦikhayalelanga.co.za. Part of the Langa Quarter scheme to regenerate the neighbourhood, this social

enterprise in an old primary school has attractions including a craft shop, café and "old-skool toilets" with piped music. Facing it, ten homes with brightly painted facades have opened up their front rooms as art galleries. When we visited, the centre and home galleries were not running, but there were hopes of reopening, so make enquiries if you visit the nearby Guga S'Thebe Arts & Cultural Centre.

★Langa Heritage Museum Cnr King Langalibalele/Washington Dr and Lerotholi Ave ☎084 949 2153, ☎072 975 5442. Cape Town's only major township museum is dedicated to the *dompas*, or pass system, which, during the apartheid years, required black citizens to carry a pass to enter "white-only" areas for work. The museum is located in the Old Pass Court, where people were tried for transgressing the pass laws. Mon–Fri 9am–4pm, Sat 9am–1pm, Sun by appointment; free.

The Township Winery, Philippi ☎021 447 4476, ⓦtownshipwinery.com. This is Cape Town's first township- and black-owned winery, situated in an area where patches of farmland exist amid mass housing. The winery aims to increase community ownership by giving hundreds of individual homesteads Sauvignon Blanc vines to grow at their homes. Once harvested, they will go towards production of a wine called "Township Winery". Tastings by appointment.

conditions in the shantytowns by introducing electricity, running water and sanitation, as well as building tiny brick houses to replace the shacks. In addition, myriad projects encourage tourists into the townships, focusing on positive social and economic developments and responsible tourism.

Visiting the townships

The safest, easiest and most informative way to experience the townships is on a **guided tour**. Most visit **Langa**, the oldest (established 1927) and most central township, located across the M17 from the middle-class suburb of Pinelands; **Gugulethu** ("Gugs"), dating to the 1960s; or **Khayelitsha** (established 1983), one of South Africa's largest and fastest-growing townships, with a population of around 2.5 million.

Tours typically last half a day, cover one or two townships and include a visit to a local home for some food, as well as a crèche, church or community centre, and often a *sangoma* (traditional healer). Book ahead and check that the price includes transport from your city-centre accommodation. It's possible, too, to gain a deeper understanding of the daily lives of the majority of South Africans by **staying overnight** in a township homestay or B&B (see box, p.136).

Visiting the townships under your own steam is not recommended: besides the threat of possible opportunistic crime, road signage is poor and opening and closing times erratic, so it's hard to find your way around.

TOURS

Andulela Tours (see p.134). Recommended cultural tour company offering themed explorations, some in the centre of Cape Town but mostly of Langa. Excursions include the African Cooking Safari, gospel music tour (with church visit) and more general township tour.

Awol Tours ☎ 021 418 3803, ⓦ awoltours.co.za. Walking tours of Gugulethu or the gardens of Seawinds (Muizenberg) and a cycling tour of Masiphumelele (Kommetjie).

CoffeeBeans Routes (see p.134). The cultural tour company offers day tours including Township Futures, which visits Khayelitsha CBD and Langa, with a positive focus on township projects and potential. Night tours include the Jazz Safari.

THE CAPE FLATS AND THE TOWNSHIPS

Juma's Tours ☎ 073 400 4064, ⓦ townshiparttours .co.za. Zimbabwean artist Juma Mkwela offers tours focused on the street art of Khayelitsha or Woodstock, with a Sunday itinerary incorporating lunch at a *shisa nyama* (township braai).

Maboneng Township Arts Experience ☎ 021 824 1773, ⓦ maboneng.com. The winner of an African Responsible Tourism Award 2017 (for engaging people and culture), Maboneng's Langa Home Gallery Tour of art galleries in township homes also includes the Guga S'Thebe Arts & Cultural Centre (see opposite), as well as street art and the Langa Heritage Museum (see opposite). One-hour, half- and full-day experiences are available, with African home cooking offered on longer itineraries.

ARRIVAL AND DEPARTURE

CAPE TOWN AND THE CAPE PENINSULA

BY PLANE

Cape Town International Airport Cape Town's international and domestic airport (CPT; ⓦ www .airports.co.za) lies 22km east of the city centre and is served by all South Africa's domestic airlines, plus a variety of international ones. Its bureau de change opens to coincide with international arrivals, and there are also ATMs here and a tourist information desk. The major car rental firms also have desks here; prebooking a vehicle is recommended, especially during the week and over the mid-December to mid-January and Easter peak seasons.

Taxis into the city Metered 24-hour taxis operated by Touch Down Taxis (☎ 082 569 7555), the airport's officially authorized taxi service, wait in ranks

outside both terminals and charge around R250 for the trip into the city.

Buses into the city The cheapest transport from the airport to the centre is the MyCiTi bus (every 30min; 5am–9.30pm; R88; ☎ 0800 65 64 63, ⓦ myciti.org.za), which goes to the Civic Centre on Hertzog Boulevard, near the central train and bus stations, with comprehensive connections further afield (see p.131). More expensive but considerably more convenient are the door-to-door shuttle services, such as the Backpacker Bus (☎ 082 809 9185, ⓦ backpackerbus.co.za).

BY TRAIN

Cape Town Station The city's mainline train station is in the centre of town on the corner of Strand and Adderley

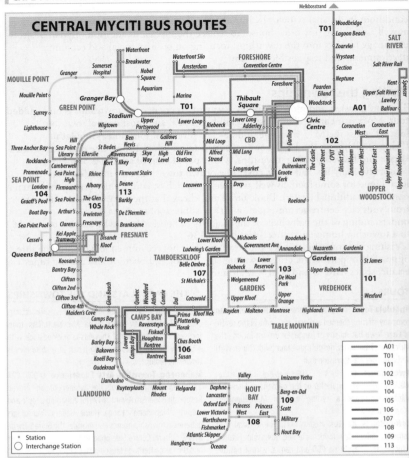

streets, with five trains a week between Cape Town and Johannesburg (27hr) via Kimberley, plus services to/from Queenstown and East London in the Eastern Cape. Book online at Shosholoza Meyl (w shosholozameyl.co.za) or, more reliably, through an agent such as African Sun Travel (w africansuntravel.com). The luxury Blue Train (w www .bluetrain.co.za) and Rovos Rail (w rovos.com) services also stop here (see p.51).

BY BUS

Intercity buses Serving most towns in the country between them, South Africa's three intercity bus companies are Greyhound (☎ 083 915 9000, w greyhound .co.za), Intercape (☎ 021 380 4400, w intercape.co.za) and Translux (☎ 086 158 9282, w translux.co.za). Buses mostly leave from Old Marine Drive, off Adderley St on the northeast side of Cape Town train station. For a single Greyhound fare from Cape Town, expect to pay from

around R320 to Paarl, R430 to Mossel Bay, and R595 to Port Elizabeth.

Baz Bus The useful hop-on, hop-off Baz Bus (☎ 0861 229 287, w bazbus.com) runs five days a week between Cape Town and Port Elizabeth in both directions, via Mossel Bay, George, Knysna, Plettenberg Bay, Storms River and Jeffrey's Bay, with other stops possible along the N2. The service is aimed at backpackers, with buses stopping off at hostels en route. The Cape Town to Port Elizabeth fare is R2330 one way; it's better value to buy a pass, available in seven-day (R2600), fourteen-day (R4100) and 21-day (R5100) versions. Book online, by telephone or SMS (☎ 076 427 3003).

SA Connection Faster and less cumbersome than the large Intercity buses, SA Connection (☎ 086 110 2426, w saconnection.co.za) is a daytime minibus shuttle service linking Cape Town with Port Elizabeth and East London via the Garden Route (4 weekly).

USEFUL MYCITI BUS ROUTES

#A01 Airport–Civic Centre
#101 Vredehoek–Gardens–Civic Centre
#102 Salt River Rail–Walmer Estate–Civic Centre
#103 Oranjezicht–Gardens–Civic Centre
#104 Sea Point–Waterfront–Civic Centre
#105 Sea Point–Fresnaye–Civic Centre

#106 Civic Centre–Camps Bay (clockwise)
#107 Civic Centre–Camps Bay (anticlockwise)
#108 Hangberg–Hout Bay–Sea Point–Adderley St
#109 Hout Bay–Imizamo Yethu–Sea Point–Adderley St

GETTING AROUND

Although Cape Town's city centre is compact enough to get around on foot, many of the major attractions are spread along the considerable length of the peninsula and require transport to get there. Between them, the MyCiTi rapid bus service and Metrorail, a single train line down the False Bay side of the peninsula, offer a useful, if not comprehensive, coverage of Cape Town, while the City Sightseeing bus routes are useful for visiting the city's main tourist sights. All rail, most bus transport (both intercity and from elsewhere in the city) and most minibus taxis converge around the main train station and the Golden Acre shopping complex, at the junction of Strand and Adderley streets in the heart of Cape Town: it's a confusing muddle, but everything you need for your next move is within two or three blocks of here, including tourist information (see p.134).

BY BUS

MyCiTi Bus A safe commuter system, the MyCiTi bus (☎ 0800 65 64 63, ⓦ myciti.org.za) runs daily from 5am to 10pm, with stations along dedicated trunk roads. Frequent buses reliably serve the city centre, City Bowl suburbs, Atlantic seaboard and Northern Suburbs, with buses every 10–20min during peak periods (6.45–8am & 4.15–5.30pm) and every 20–30min during the off-peak period and at weekends. Importantly it is the only safe public transport option in the evening. Cash is not accepted on the buses, so you'll need a myconnect card, which you can preload with credit; cards can be bought for R30 from MyCiTi stations and various retailers, or you can buy a single-trip card at some stations (R90 at the airport). When you board the bus, tap your card against validators marked "in", and again on one marked "out" when you get off. Fares include around R10 for routes within the city centre, R20 from the centre to Hout Bay or Table View and R88 to the airport. The MyCiTi website has user-friendly and up-to-date information on fares, routes and timetables.

City Sightseeing Bus The open-top, hop-on, hop-off red City Sightseeing buses (☎ 0861 733 287, ⓦ citysightseeing .co.za; 1-day ticket R170, children R90) leave from the Two Oceans Aquarium 0at the Waterfront, and run along a few useful routes, with the Red City Tour visiting the main city centre attractions (including the Table Mountain cable-car station) and the Blue Mini Peninsula Tour heading to sights along the peninsula. The buses are a convenient, informative and, on a fine day, fun way of getting to the major sights, especially with kids. The Blue Mini Peninsula Tour (daily 9am–3.25pm: May to late Sept every 35min; late Sept to early May every 25min) stops on Long Street, *Mount Nelson Hotel*, Kirstenbosch, World of Birds, Imizamo

Yethu township, Mariner's Wharf in Hout Bay, Camps Bay and Sea Point. The Red City Centre Tour (daily 8.40am–4.45pm: May to late Sept every 20min; late Sept to early May every 15min) stops on Long Street before crossing Kloof Nek to Camps Bay, Sea Point and Green Point.

BY TRAIN

Metrorail Cape Town's suburban train service is run by Metrorail (☎ 021 449 6478, ⓦ metrorail.co.za, ⓦ cttrains .co.za). Four lines run from Cape Town station to the Northern Suburbs, the Winelands and the Cape Flats, but these journeys aren't recommended, as they run through some less safe areas. The Southern Line to the False Bay seaboard from Cape Town station, however, is one of the world's great urban train journeys, reaching the coast at Muizenberg and continuing south to Simon's Town, sometimes so spectacularly close to the ocean that you can feel the spray and peer into rock pools. The trains are regular, though not especially reliable, and you should travel during daylight and avoid boarding an empty carriage. You should be aware that there are often no signposts to the stations on the streets. Tickets must be bought at the station before boarding, and you're best off in the MetroPlus (nominal first class) carriages, which are reasonably priced (for example, Cape Town–Muizenberg is R13.50 one way).

BY TAXI

METERED TAXIS

Regulated metered taxis don't cruise up and down looking for fares; you'll need to go to the taxi ranks around town, which include the Waterfront, the train station and Long Street, or phone to be picked up (see p.132). Taxis must have the driver's name and identification clearly on display

1

TOP 5 SCENIC DRIVES

Atlantic seaboard Chapman's Peak Drive; see p.119
City views Signal Hill Road; see p.107
False Bay seaboard Boyes Drive; see p.121
Leafy affluence Rhodes Drive and Constantia Nek; see p.111
Mountain pass Kloof Nek; see p.107

and the meter clearly visible. Fares work out at around R10 per kilometre, with minimum charges from R20, and rates go up after dark.

Excite Taxis ☎ 021 448 4444, ⓦ excitetaxis.co.za. Fares are R9 per kilometre within the city centre to southern suburbs, but there may be an additional charge for further-flung destinations.

Rikkis ☎ 0861 745 547, ⓦ rikkis.co.za. Long-running Rikki's charges R10 per kilometre and offers cheaper ride shares and airport shuttles.

Uber ⓦ uber.com/en-ZA/cities/cape-town. A popular and convenient option, with rates from R7 per kilometre (and R0.70 per minute) with a R5 base fare and a minimum charge of R20. Download the app to your phone.

MINIBUS TAXIS

Minibus taxis are cheap, frequent and race up and down the main routes at tearaway speeds. They can be hailed from the street or boarded at the central taxi rank, above the Cape Town train station. You'll recognize them from the hooting, booming music and touting. Once you've boarded, pay the assistant, who sits near the driver, and say where you want to get off. Fares for most trips should be under R15. As well as dangerous driving, be prepared for pickpockets working the taxi ranks.

BY CAR AND MOTORBIKE

Roads and rules Cape Town has good roads and several fast freeways that, outside peak hours (7–9am & 4–6pm), can whisk you across town in next to no time. The obvious landmarks of Table Mountain and the two seaboards make orientation straightforward, though driving in and around Cape Town presents a few peculiarities all of its own. An unwritten rule of the road is that minibus taxis have the right of way – and will push in front of you and routinely run through amber lights as they change to red – as will many Capetonians, to whom amber means speed up.

Vehicle rental As well as the usual international car rental companies, such as Avis (ⓦ avis.co.za), Budget (ⓦ budget .co.za), Europcar (ⓦ europcar.co.za), Hertz (ⓦ hertz .co.za) and Thrifty (ⓦ thrifty.co.za), which mostly have offices at the airport, there are plenty of local operators, including Around About Cars (ⓦ aroundaboutcars .co.za), Cheap Motorhome Rental (ⓦ cheapmotorhomes .co.za), Drive South Africa (ⓦ drivesouthafrica.co.za), Tempest (ⓦ tempestcarhire.co.za) and Vineyard Car Hire

(ⓦ vineyardcarhire.co.za). Many of them will bring you vehicle to the airport (or pick you up) if you book in advance Alternatively, you can rent scooters from Cape Town Scooter Hire (ⓦ capetownscooter.co.za) for R250 a day, o more powerful BMW and Harley-Davidson bikes with ful protective gear from Cape Bike Travel (ⓦ capebiketrave .com) from R1300 for one day, including comprehensive insurance and roadside assistance.

BY GUIDED TOUR

Cape Town is awash with guided tours, from general tour taking in all the main sights to niche cultural tours. The most popular in the latter category are township tours (se p.129), which are the safest way to visit the African and coloured areas that were created under apartheid.

WALKING TOURS

One of the best ways to orientate yourself is on a walking tour through central Cape Town. Tours run by the two companies below depart mid-morning at least three days a week, and last roughly three hours. You need to book in advance. Alternatively, check out Voice Maps (ⓦ voicemap .me), where you can download an app walking tour of various areas in the city, narrated by local Capetonians who are knowledgeable and passionate about their own districts. There are also free guided city walking tours; visi ⓦ bit.ly/CapeTownCityWalks for listings.

Cape Town on Foot ☎ 086 547 6833, ⓦ wanderlus .co.za. Run by writer Ursula Stevens, the historical tour (R250 per person) explore the city centre as well as the Bo-Kaap, and can be taken in English or German.

Footsteps to Freedom ☎ 083 452 1112, ⓦ footstepst freedom.co.za. Historical and Mandela-themed tours (one to four guests R1760) that take in sights, buildings and local stories in the Company's Garden area.

GENERAL TOURS

Cape Convoy ☎ 076 146 8577, ⓦ capeconvoy.com Tours with popular, passionate and fun Brit Rob Salmon t Cape Point (R999 including entrance fees) and the Winelands, along with cage diving to view great whit sharks.

Day Trippers ☎ 021 511 4766, ⓦ daytrippers.co.za. A excellent company if you want an active peninsula and Cape Point day tour that includes cycling and hiking (R85 including entrance fees and picnic lunch). They also g

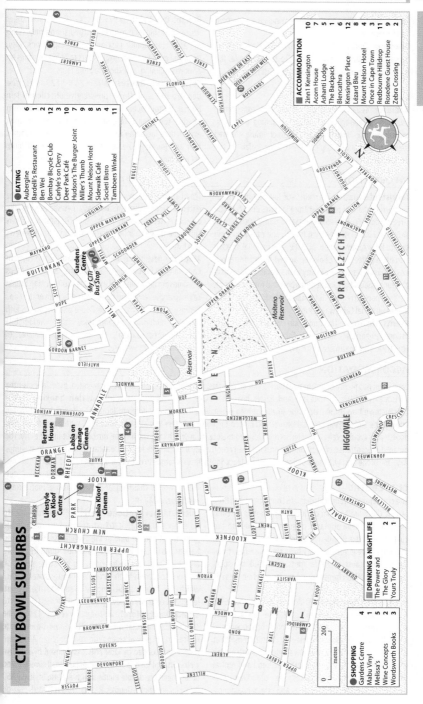

CITY BOWL SUBURBS

■ ACCOMMODATION

2inn1 Kensington	10
Acorn House	7
Ashanti Lodge	5
The Backpack	1
Blencathra	6
Kensington Place	12
Lézard Bleu	8
Mount Nelson Hotel	4
Once in Cape Town	3
Redbourne Hilldrop	11
Rosedene Guest House	9
Zebra Crossing	2

● EATING

Aubergine	6
Bardelli's Restaurant	1
Ben Wei	2
Bombay Bicycle Club	12
Carlyle's on Derry	10
Deer Park Café	7
Hudson's The Burger Joint	9
Miller's Thumb	8
Mount Nelson Hotel	5
Sidewalk Café	4
Societi Bistro	11
Tamboers Winkel	

■ DRINKING & NIGHTLIFE

The Power and The Glory	2
Yours Truly	1

● SHOPPING

Gardens Centre	4
Mabu Vinyl	1
Melissa's	5
Wine Concepts	2
Wordsworth Books	3

0 — 200 metres

1

further afield to hike and cycle in the Winelands, Cederberg and Eastern Cape.

Discovery Tours ☎ 078 161 7818, 🖥 discoverytours .co.za. Specializing in private tours to the peninsula, the Winelands (two people R1400) and the West Coast.

CULTURAL TOURS

Andulela ☎ 021 790 2592, 🖥 andulela.com. Small selection of interactive adventures including a walking township tour, cookery- and gospel music-themed township tours and a Cape Malay cooking "safari" in the Bo-Kaap.

Bonani Our Pride ☎ 021 531 4291, 🖥 bonanitours .co.za. Township tours to meet local people and understand the areas' tumultuous past and future aspirations. Also, township evening tours, gospel tours to Xhosa churches on a Sunday morning, and Xhosa folklore tours.

Coffeebeans Routes ☎ 021 813 9829, 🖥 coffee beansroutes.com. Under the creative direction of Iain Harris, this tour operator is a pioneer in cultural tourism in the townships, offering hands-on, eye-opening experiences including the Jazz Safari, Township Futures tour and journeys themed around beer, food, fashion, art and more.

INFORMATION

Tourist Information The main Cape Town Tourism Visitor Centre is in the city centre, at The Pinnacle, Burg & Castle streets (Mon–Fri 8am–5.30pm, Sat & Sun 8.30am–1pm; ☎ 086 132 2223, 🖥 capetown.travel), and runs a booking service for accommodation, activities and national parks; it also has a coffee shop, bookshop and wi-fi, and dishes out lots of brochures and cheap city maps. Cape Town Tourism also runs smaller bureaux at the airport and the Waterfront, with a non-accredited information desk at the Table Mountain Aerial Cableway station.

Events listings To find out what's on, check listings websites such as *Cape Town Magazine* (🖥 capetownmagazine.com) or *What's On in Cape Town*

(🖥 whatsonincapetown.com). Alternatively, look at the entertainment pages of the daily newspapers, or the excellent events listings in the *Mail & Guardian*'s Friday supplement, which injects some attitude into its reviews and listings.

Maps The best hiking and touring maps of the Western Cape are published by Cape Town's Slingsby Maps (🖥 slingsbymaps.com) and available through Map Studio (🖥 mapstudio.co.za) and bookshops. Maps cover the Cape Peninsula, Winelands, Garden Route and beyond. South Africa's motoring organization, the Automobile Association (🖥 aa.co.za), has free maps available to download from its website.

ACCOMMODATION

Cape Town has plenty of accommodation to suit all budgets, though booking ahead is recommended, especially over the Christmas (mid-Dec to mid-Jan) and Easter holidays – Cape Town Tourism's **accommodation booking** service (🖥 capetown.travel) can help. Cape Town is a long peninsula offering many different locations, all with hotly debated advantages and varying physical beauty. You'll need to choose whether you want to be central, with nightlife on your doorstep, or would prefer a quieter setting closer to the ocean, in which case you'll travel further to get into the city. The greatest concentration of accommodation is in the city centre, City Bowl and the Atlantic seaside strip as far south as Camps Bay. One of the best ways to experience everyday black South Africa is to stay in one of the African townships.

CITY CENTRE

The city centre's liveliest streets are Long Street and Bree Street. There are backpacker lodges and hotels on Long St itself, plus several places in quieter locations to the east, around the Company's Garden and the museums. From these areas you can walk to all the museums, trawl Cape Town's best nightlife spots, and find transport easily to the Waterfront. Expect rooms fronting Long St to be noisy.

★ **Cape Heritage Hotel** 90 Bree St ☎ 021 424 4646, 🖥 capeheritage.co.za; map p.92. An exceptionally stylish, elegant and tastefully restored boutique hotel located in the redeveloped eighteenth-century complex at Heritage Square, where a walkway shaded by South Africa's oldest fruit-bearing grapevine links the hotel and central courtyard. The spacious rooms are decorated with contemporary handcrafted objects and original paintings.

The service is charming and there's also a roof terrace and Jacuzzi. R2850

Dutch Manor Antique Hotel 158 Buitengracht, Bo-Kaap ☎ 021 422 4767, 🖥 dutchmanor.co.za; map p.90. Travel back in time in this townhouse, which dates back to 1812 and is filled with period furniture, lavish tapestries and four-poster beds. Its pervasive sense of history is spoilt only by the proximity of busy Buitengracht, which the hotel's small balcony overlooks. The central location is certainly handy. R2200

Grand Daddy Hotel 38 Long St ☎ 021 424 7247, 🖥 granddaddy.co.za; map p.92. The *Grand Daddy* has a rooftop trailer park of seven retro-cool American Airstream caravans, decorated by local artists and linked by wooden walkways. Opt for one of these novel but small silver trailers or for one of the double rooms, which are also imaginative, colourful and funky. Doubles R2895, trailers R3695

iKhaya Lodge Dunkley Square, Wandel St ☎ 021 461 8880, ⓦ www.ikhayalodge.co.za; map p.90. This small hotel is on a pretty square, right by the Company's Garden and the museums, and close to a few good restaurants and bars in the regenerated East City area. There's a fun African theme throughout, and accommodation ranges from rooms with balconies overlooking the square to singles, doubles and triple loft apartments. Doubles R1225, loft apartments R1700

Rose Street 28 28 Rose St, Bo-Kaap ☎ 021 424 3813, ⓦ rosestreet28.co.za; map p.90. This affordable and good-value B&B consists of three townhouses on Rose and perpendicular Wale St, simply but stylishly decorated with shared kitchen and courtyard and a friendly, laidback atmosphere. The main lodge occupies a grey-painted house in a row of typically colourful Bo-Kaap residences, with three dinky rooms inside. R890

Rouge on Rose 25 Rose St, at Hout St ☎ 021 426 0298, ⓦ rougeonrose.co.za; map p.90. Nine modern, comfortable suites with bohemian studio chic reflecting the pastel Bo-Kaap facades outside. Beaded artworks liven up the muted urban decor and the suites are certainly spacious, with freestanding bathtubs, great views and self-catering facilities in some. R1800

Scalabrini Guest House 47 Commercial St ☎ 021 465 6433, ⓦ scalabrini.org.za; map p.90. This backpackers with a difference is attached to the Scalabrini Centre, which provides protection and support to vulnerable immigrants. Spacious, wooden-floored dorms and rooms, a kitchen, lounge and laundry service are on offer, and proceeds fund the centre's work – which guests can learn about in reception. It's an interesting area on the edge of the creative East City district, with numerous pubs and cafés nearby. Dorms R260, doubles R660

V&A WATERFRONT AND DE WATERKANT

Accommodation here tends to be upmarket; there are, however, a couple of reasonably priced places to stay. Staying at the Waterfront is a good idea if you like shopping in a self-contained safe area, and you want to walk to restaurants and cafés, with transport readily available. On a hillside, less than 1km from the Waterfront, adjacent to the Bo-Kaap and a short hop to Green Point or the city centre, De Waterkant is a desirable place to stay, full of restored Victorian terraces on narrow, well-kept cobbled streets.

Breakwater Lodge Portswood Rd, Waterfront ☎ 021 406 1911, ⓦ www.breakwaterlodge.co.za; map p.103. One of the Waterfront's more affordable options occupies a "historic nineteenth-century building" according to owner Marriott's website – a prison, to be exact. The modern hotel inside this sturdy shell offers a bar, restaurant, secure parking, and accommodation from studios to family rooms. R2150

★**Cape Grace** West Quay Rd ☎ 021 410 7100, ⓦ capegrace.com; map p.103. Among the Waterfront's many top-end hotels, the Cape Grace stands out for its sheer style, amenities and gracious customer service. Bascule Bar (see p.149) is here, as are Signal Restaurant (see p.141) with its Cape tasting menu, plus a range of luxurious rooms and suites, and sumptuous public areas overlooking the yacht marina and Zeitz MOCAA. R9948

De Waterkant Village 137 Waterkant St, De Waterkant ☎ 021 409 2500, ⓦ dewaterkant.com; map p.103. These comfortable and contemporary self-catering properties include studios and one- to three-bedroom apartments and houses, dotted around De Waterkant's hilly streets. Guests can use the café, travel desk and services at affiliated guesthouse the Charles. Apartments (two person) R1400

St John's Waterfront Lodge 6 Braemar Rd, Green Point ☎ 021 439 1404, ⓦ stjohns.co.za; map p.103. A 15min walk from the Waterfront, this solid, no-frills choice occupies a salmon-hued suburban house on a hillside street. Accommodation includes dorms and private rooms, all with shared ablutions, while the communal facilities include a swimming pool, an outdoor BBQ area, a sun deck and a travel centre. Dorms R140, doubles R530

CITY BOWL SUBURBS

The City Bowl suburbs are popular for accommodation, as they are central yet quieter and leafier than the city centre proper, especially the further up the mountainside you go. The more comfortable guesthouses often have gardens, good views and a swimming pool. A few backpacker lodges can be found on and around Kloof St, the continuation of Long St, with some great cafés and restaurants.

GARDENS

Ashanti Lodge 11 Hof St ☎ 021 423 8721, ⓦ ashanti .co.za; map p.133. This massive two-storey Victorian mansion has marbling and ethnic decor, soaring ceilings, a nicely kept front garden and a swimming pool with sun terrace. The private double and twin rooms and six- to eight-bed mixed and female-only dorms are simple, colourful affairs, while campers can pitch tents outside. The bar is very lively, so if you are not a party animal, you might prefer their nearby guesthouse. Camping R140, dorms R250, doubles R780

★**Mount Nelson Hotel** 76 Orange St (rear entrance on Kloof St) ☎ 021 483 1000, ⓦ mountnelson.co.za; map p.133. Cape Town's grande dame: a fine and famous high-colonial Victorian hotel, built in 1899 (and extended in the late 1990s). Perfectly located, the building is set in extensive gardens with a majestic palm-lined driveway leading to the main entrance. Behind its jolly pink facade, the Nellie reflects its historical clout in the rates for its rooms, suites and garden cottages. R9185

★**Once in Cape Town** 73 Kloof St ☎ 021 424 6169, ⓦ stayatonce.com; map p.133. One of the most exciting backpackers to open in recent years, hip Once offers four-bed mixed and female-only dorms, doubles and twins, all

1

AFRICAN TOWNSHIP HOMESTAYS

One of the best ways to get a taste of the African townships is to spend a night there, which is made possible by the growing number of township residents offering **B&B accommodation**. You'll have a chance to experience the warmth of **ubuntu** – traditional African hospitality – by staying with a family and sitting down to eat with them. They will often take you around their local area to **shebeens** (unlicensed bars), music venues, church, or just to meet the neighbours. **Prices** start around R400 for a double or twin room, which is considerably cheaper than the centre of Cape Town, and you'll get to experience something totally different.

Some B&Bs will send someone to meet you at the airport; if you're driving, they'll most likely give you detailed directions or meet you at a convenient and obvious landmark. Many properties are listed on **Airbnb** and you can make bookings through Khayelitsha Travel (📞 021 361 4505, 🌐 khayelitshatravel.com).

GUGULETHU

Liziwe's Guest House 121 NY 111 📞 021 794 1619, 🌐 mycapetownstay.com/Liziwe_s_Guest_House. Experience "Gugs" while staying in one of Liziwe Ngcokoto's seven en-suite rooms, which have simple African decor and, in three cases, balconies with views of Table Mountain across the jumble of township roofs. Traditional African meals are on offer, as are township tours and visits to Gugulethu's memorials (see p.128). R700

KHAYELITSHA

Kopanong B&B C329 Velani Crescent 📞 021 361 2084 or 📞 082 476 1278, 🌐 kopanong-township.co.za. One of the townships' most dynamic B&B operations, run by the tireless Thope Lekau. This well-travelled Khayelitsha tourism guru and her daughter will treat you to a history of the city's largest township, introduce you to local music and dish up a hearty breakfast. A traditional dinner is available with advance notice, as is a guided tour. R780

Majoro's B&B 69 Helena Crescent 📞 021 794 1619, 🌐 mycapetownstay.com/MajorosBB. The charming Maria Maile hosts guests in her family home, which has

a double and a twin sharing a bathroom and kitchen, in an upmarket part of the township. Meals made by this seasoned cook include traditional dishes, after which you can watch TV with the family or visit a local shebeen. R900

Malebo's 18 Mississippi Way 📞 021 361 2391, 🌐 airbnb.com/rooms/2156844. This B&B consists of five rooms, three en-suite, in the welcoming family home of chef Lydia Masoleng and husband Alfred. Her generous breakfast and traditional Xhosa meals are a treat, and activities include *shebeen* outings, township tours and Sunday church visits. R550

LANGA

Nomase's Guesthouse Cnr King Langalibalele /Washington Dr and Sandile Ave 📞 021 694 3904 or 📞 083 482 8377, 🌐 bit.ly/NomaseGuesthouse. Just a few hundred metres from Langa train station, the Langa Heritage Museum (see p.128) and Guga S'Thebe Arts & Cultural Centre (see p.128), the matriarchal Nomase offers four clean, homely and secure en-suite rooms, plus a kitchen with fridge and microwave. Breakfast is R30, dinner can be arranged and minibus taxis pass along the main drag outside. R450

---

with en-suite bathroom, safes, universal chargers, reading lights and breakfast included. The adjoining café-bar has a stunning terrace and there's always something going on, from free walking tours to market visits. Dorms R315, doubles R1135

TAMBOERSKLOOF

★**The Backpack** 74 New Church St 📞 021 423 4530, 🌐 backpackers.co.za; map p.133. An excellent backpackers made up of four interconnected houses, where the interior has a spacious maze-like effect. *The Backpack* has some of the best communal and outdoor spaces in town, including a pool terrace, lounge area, restaurant, bar, courtyard, travel desk and craft shop. Choose between three- to eight-bed mixed and female-only dorms,

including an en-suite option, as well as private rooms and self-catering studios. Dorms R390, doubles R920

Blencathra 4 Cambridge Ave, at De Hoop 📞 021 424 9571, 🌐 blencathra.co.za; map p.133. A large, relaxed family house with a sunny garden and stunning views on the slopes of Lion's Head, 2km from the city centre. Rooms are peaceful and spacious; many are en suite, and options include a four-bed women-only dorm. Dorms R200, doubles R500

Zebra Crossing 82 New Church St 📞 021 422 1265, 🌐 zebra-crossing.co.za; map p.133. A no-frills backpacker lodge, with a leafy garden and limited off-street parking – perfect if you are looking for something affordable that's close to town. Amenities including a travel desk and a café-bar, pleasant courtyards and terraces under vines. Dorms R190, doubles R690

ORANJEZICHT

2Inn1 Kensington 21 Kensington Crescent ☎ 021 423 1707, ⓦ 2inn1.com; map p.133. Entering from a broad, quiet street into these two adjacent renovated houses, with bright, sleek furnishings and quiet music drifting over the lounge and dining area, gives the feel of walking into a soothing urban hideaway. The building backs onto a 10m swimming pool and deck area with sunbeds, complimentary sundowners and mountain views. R2700

★**Acorn House** 1 Montrose Ave ☎ 021 461 1782, ⓦ acornhouse.co.za; map p.133. High on the slopes of Table Mountain, this century-old residence has maintained its grandeur with a sweeping lawn, colonial furnishings and elegant lounge, and added comforts such as the pool and sun-loungers. Each room is unique; those at the front of the house offer great city views, while the back shows off Table Mountain. R1700

Lézard Bleu 30 Upper Orange St ☎ 021 461 4601, ⓦ lezardbleu.co.za; map p.133. This guesthouse offers six en-suite rooms, furnished with maple beds and private patio or balcony in a spacious open-plan 1960s house. The cosy lounge is perfect for reading, and a wall of sliding doors opens onto an outside deck. R1800

Redbourne Hilldrop 12 Roseberry Ave ☎ 021 461 1394, ⓦ redbourne.co.za; map p.133. This small and intimate B&B, with just a few rooms in a house dating to 1928, oozes hospitality and the quiet charm of being a guest in someone's home. There's an outside plunge pool and a small breakfast room with a panoramic view of the city. R1750

HIGGOVALE

Kensington Place 38 Kensington Crescent ☎ 021 424 4744, ⓦ kensingtonplace.co.za; map p.133. High on the side of Table Mountain, this stylish eight-room boutique hotel has a dazzling little pool and sweeping city views from its contemporary lounge, which is adorned with artworks and coffee-table books. R4200

★**Rosedene Guest House** 28 Upper Kloof St ☎ 021 424 3290, ⓦ rosedene.co.za; map p.133. Long-running Rosedene has struck a good balance of relative affordability in this exclusive area and of lofty views with restaurants nearby and the city centre below. The rooms up top feel far removed from the urban bustle. R1850

SOUTHERN SUBURBS

Cape Town's gracious Southern Suburbs – Rosebank, Claremont, Newlands and Rondebosch, on the forested side of the mountain – are home to Kirstenbosch Gardens as well as the Newlands cricket and rugby grounds and the University of Cape Town. Bohemian Observatory is a few minutes' drive from the city centre and offers buzzing cafés, a couple of backpacker lodges and lively nightlife.

African Heart 27 Station Rd, Observatory ☎ 021 447 3125, ⓦ backpackersincapetown.co.za. This creatively decorated hostel is set in a cheerful green Victorian house with wooden floors, comfy couches, bold murals and mosaics. There are several chill-out areas and an outdoor braai area, and main drag Lower Main Road is a few blocks away. Dorms R175, doubles R600

Carmichael Guesthouse 11 Wolmunster Rd, Rosebank ☎ 021 689 8350, ⓦ carmichaelhouse.co.za. Round the corner from the Irma Stern Museum, a Swiss-French couple offers six spacious rooms in a grand yellow two-storey Victorian mansion, among stained-glass windows, Oregon pine floors and period fireplaces. There's a peaceful garden, a swimming pool and secure parking. R1800

★**Vineyard Hotel** Colinton Rd, off Protea Rd, Newlands ☎ 021 657 4500, ⓦ vineyard.co.za. One of the city's top stays, with luxurious rooms in a grand 120-year-old hotel, on the site of a cottage built in 1799 by Georgian diarist Lady Anne Barnard. The extensive gardens are like those of a peaceful country estate, offering guided walks, children's activities, a spa and indoor and outdoor pools. R4040

ATLANTIC SEABOARD

Historically Cape Town's hotel and seafront apartment block area, you'll find a range of accommodation in Sea Point, a good alternative to the City Bowl if you want to be close to both the city centre and the ocean. Green Point is another appealing choice, as it's the closest suburb to the Waterfront, city centre and De Waterkant, although it's not directly on the water. The well-heeled mountainside suburb of Camps Bay offers soaring views over the Atlantic, with an upmarket Californian feel to its laidback restaurants and bars, and it's just a hop over Kloof Nek to the Table Mountain Aerial Cableway and city centre. Neighbouring Clifton has similar appeal. Hout Bay is the main urban concentration along the lower half of the peninsula, with a harbour, pleasant waterfront development and bus lines to town. Below Chapman's Peak, Noordhoek and Kommetjie offer coastal seclusion with mountain views.

GREEN POINT

★**The B.I.G. Backpackers in Green Point** 18 Thornhill Rd ☎ 021 434 0688, ⓦ bigbackpackers .com; map p.114. A backpacker lodge with a light, clean, modern feel, catering to a quieter crowd with three fully equipped self-catering kitchens, computer facilities, a library and two games rooms with big-screen TV, while outside are a sunny garden with braai facilities, a plunge pool and parking. The rooms and four-bed dorms are spacious, stylish and include breakfast and en-suite bathroom. Dorms R380, doubles R1200

Dysart Boutique Hotel 17 Dysart Rd ☎ 021 439 2832, ⓦ dysart.de; map p.114. This luxury boutique hotel is styled in Afro chic, with artworks dotting the slick and polished interior. Outside are two infinity pools, and wooden decking with sunbeds, umbrellas and tables – perfect for relaxing with a cocktail. R2000

Jambo Guest House 1 Grove Rd ☎ 021 439 4219, ⓦ jambo.co.za; map p.114. In a quiet cul-de-sac off Main Rd, this small, atmospheric establishment offers four luxury en-suite rooms, each decorated in a unique style, and one garden suite. R1900

Wilton Manor 15 Croxteth Rd ☎ 021 434 7869, ⓦ wilton guesthouses.co.za; map p.114. This beautifully renovated Victorian guesthouse is set on a quiet street, close to Cape Town Stadium and the Waterfront. Outside is a spacious and sunny deck with a homely atmosphere, breakfast tables and a plunge pool to cool off in. R1800

SEA POINT

Blackheath Lodge 6 Blackheath Rd ☎ 021 439 2541, ⓦ blackheathlodge.co.za; map p.114. Down a quiet backstreet, but close to the Sea Point action, this superb guesthouse just gets everything right. The sixteen rooms in the Victorian home are large and airy (some with views of Lion's Head and sea views), and the king-size beds are the most comfortable you'll find in Cape Town. R3200

Huijs Haerlem 25 Main Drive ☎ 021 434 6434, ⓦ huijshaerlem.co.za; map p.114. This elegant and gay-friendly guesthouse is made up of two adjacent houses furnished with antiques and separated by a pool. R2100

The Villa Rosa 277 High Level Rd ☎ 021 434 2768, ⓦ villa-rosa.com; map p.114. A friendly guesthouse in a rusty-red two-storey Victorian house on the lower slopes of Signal Hill, 500m from the beachfront promenade. Decorated with simplicity and style, all rooms have TV, phone and safe, but only some, on the upper floor, have sea views. R1300

★ Winchester Mansions Hotel 221 Beach Rd ☎ 021 434 2351, ⓦ winchester.co.za; map p.114. In a prime spot across the road from the seashore, this 1920s hotel has an atmosphere straight from the pages of Agatha Christie, though the rooms are fresh and contemporary. A cool Italianate courtyard restaurant is overlooked by balconies draped in luxuriant creepers. R2850

CAMPS BAY AND BAKOVEN

★ Boutique@10 10 Medburn Rd, Camps Bay ☎ 021 438 1234, ⓦ boutique10.co.za; map p.118. A stay in one of these four suites is as if you're a welcome guest at a friend's lavishly appointed house. Restored with reclaimed timber from an old hotel, the light and airy open-plan lounge features French doors that open onto the outside decking area, which is complete with sunbeds, plunge pool and a stunning view of the Atlantic Ocean and Lion's Head. Airport shuttles can be arranged. R3295

★ Camps Bay Retreat 7 Chilworth Rd, Camps Bay ☎ 021 437 8300, ⓦ campsbayretreat.com; map p.118. The secluded Earls Dyke Manor, set on a four-acre nature reserve, is located a 5min walk away from the beach. Stay in the mansion dating from 1929, with its plush colonial furnishings, lounge, reading room, fine-dining restaurant and bar, or cross the ravine on a rope bridge to the contemporary Deck House and Villa. R5000

★ Ocean View House 33 Victoria Rd, Bakoven ☎ 021 438 1982, ⓦ oceanview-house.com; map p.118. A mountain stream runs through the grounds of this boutique hotel, set among ancient milkwood trees and koi ponds in a gorgeous garden bordering a *fynbos* reserve. R2650

HOUT BAY, NOORDHOEK AND KOMMETJIE

Eco Wave Lodge 11 Gladioli Way, Kommetjie ☎ 073 927 5644, ⓦ ecowave.co.za. A short stroll from the beach, *Eco Wave* offers simple and stylish backpacker accommodation in a two-storey house with balconies overlooking the sea as well as a TV lounge and small garden. R600

Hout Bay Hideaway 37 Skaife St, Hout Bay ☎ 021 790 8040, ⓦ houtbay-hideaway.com. An outstanding guesthouse bursting with luxurious touches and decorative verve, from the Persian rugs and Art Deco armchairs to the huge beds and meranti shutters. At the back, there's a curvy saltwater pool surrounded by a *fynbos* garden that climbs the mountainside. R2100

Houtkapperspoort Hout Bay Main Rd, Constantia Nek, around 4km from Hout Bay and 17km from the city centre ☎ 021 794 5216, ⓦ houtkapperspoortresort .co.za. These rustic one- to three-bedroom, stone-and-brick self-catering cottages sit right by the Table Mountain National Park in the valley between Hout Bay and Constantia. R1470

Monkey Valley Resort Mountain Rd, Noordhoek ☎ 021 789 8000, ⓦ monkeyvalleyresort.com. An attractive group of mainly wooden-and-thatched rooms and cottages spread over several acres of Chapman's Peak, some 40km south of the city centre. Overlooking Noordhoek Beach, the site is surrounded by indigenous vegetation and has a restaurant. Doubles R1480, cottages R2360

Sunbird Mountain Retreat & Lodge Boskykloof Rd, Hout Bay ☎ 021 790 7758, ⓦ sunbirdlodge.co.za. Four pleasant, spacious, self-catering cabins and a guesthouse that includes a family unit, all nestled in a forest high up on the mountainside. Cabins R800, doubles R1200

★ Tintswalo Atlantic Chapman's Peak Drive, Hout Bay ☎ 021 201 0025, ⓦ tintswalo.com/atlantic. Perched on the rocks below Chapman's Peak, with a dramatic view of Hout Bay and the Sentinel peak, this stunning luxury lodge is the only hotel in Table Mountain National Park. The large bedrooms are lavishly furnished with tropical beach-house chic, each with ocean views and unique in style, and you might spot whales from the wooden deck as you wander to the pool, lounge, bar and restaurant. R107,80

FALSE BAY SEABOARD

This is a great area if you want to swim every day, surf or walk on the beach, and enjoy eating in some excellent restaurants. Once hugely popular because of its stunning beach and bay views, Muizenberg, 25km from the centre, is coming up after a period in the doldrums, and its peeling beachfront hotels have given way to surf schools and cafés. The real crown jewel is Kalk Bay with its working harbour, antique shops and arty cafés. Accommodation here is limited, but you have a good chance of finding a self-catering apartment through websites such as ⓦ safarinow .com. Fish Hoek, further south, is recommended for its beach but not much else; a better option is pretty Simon's Town, 40km from the city centre. The historic seafaring town is now technically part of the Cape Town metropolis, but still regarded by many as a separate entity.

MUIZENBERG

Samhitakasha Cob House Organic B&B 13 Watson Rd, Muizenberg ⓣ 021 788 6613, ⓦ cobhouse.co.za; map p.122. One of Cape Town's greenest B&Bs, this mud-and-straw cob house is run by a friendly couple and located 200m from the beach. It contains just one, comfy guest room, which works as a double or can sleep up to four guests, and the rate includes a room-service organic breakfast. Double R750, family R950

Stoked Backpackers 175 Main Rd, Muizenberg ⓣ 082 679 3651, ⓦ stokedbackpackers.com; map p.122. This vibey, well-run backpackers next to the station has a vegetarian café and a travel centre. There's a range of quality in the four- to twelve-bed dorms and the best en-suite rooms are on the upper levels with sunrise sea views; the upstairs terrace area overlooking the beach is stunning too. Dorms R200, doubles R865

KALK BAY AND FISH HOEK

★ **Chartfield Guest House** 30 Gatesville Rd, Kalk Bay ⓣ 021 788 3793, ⓦ chartfield.co.za; map p.122. This well-kept, rambling house sits halfway up the hill overlooking the harbour, with terrific sea views from some rooms and a hop and a skip down the cobbled road or steps to some of the peninsula's finest restaurants. R900

The Mountain House 7 Mountain Rd, Clovelly ⓣ 083 455 5664, ⓦ themountainhouse.co.za; map p.122. Built in the garden of local architect Carin Hartford, this beautiful two-bedroom self-catering cottage has windows on all sides to capitalize on the incredible mountain setting, and the living space flows out to a timber deck. R1100

Tranquility Guest House 25 Peak Rd, Fish Hoek ⓣ 021 782 2060, ⓦ tranquil.co.za; map p.122. This warm and welcoming place, walking distance to the beach, is situated on Fish Hoek mountainside and offers good ocean views. There are four flowery B&B en-suite rooms, and guests can soak in the outdoor Jacuzzi. R1800

SIMON'S TOWN

Simon's Town Boutique Backpackers 66 St George's St ⓣ 021 786 1964, ⓦ capepax.co.za. Conveniently located in the heart of Simon's Town, 1km south of the station, this boutique backpacker joint offers bunk-bed dorms and fairly spacious doubles, plus there's a large balcony with a view of the waterfront. You can rent bicycles and ride to Cape Point, or arrange a kayak tour to paddle past the penguin colony. Dorms R220, doubles R660

Whale View Manor Main Rd ⓣ 021 786 3291, ⓦ whaleviewmanor.co.za. In the guesthouse area on the south side of town, this imposing white villa houses a four-star boutique hotel and spa. It's right next to the surf, and the contemporary public spaces are sunny and relaxing. R1950

EATING

Eating out is one of the highlights of visiting this world-class culinary destination, where the Mediterranean climate nurtures farms, vineyards and small producers galore. The city has a bottomless selection of relaxed and convivial restaurants serving imaginative food of a high standard. Prices are inexpensive compared with Western countries; for the cost of an unmemorable meal back home, you can eat innovative dishes by outstanding chefs in an upmarket restaurant. This is the place to splash out on whatever takes your fancy, and you'll find the quality of meat, from steaks to springbok is high, with many vegetarian options available as well. There are a couple of restaurants dedicated to **Cape Malay** or **African cuisine** (see box, p.140), though other genres are generally prepared more skilfully. You can expect fresh **Cape fish** at every good restaurant as well as seafood from warmer waters – try one of the delicious local fish such as yellowtail, which is not endangered. Also check out the fun **neighbourhood markets**, where you can get a craft beer and something tasty to eat from a stall (see p.156).

CITY CENTRE

95 Keerom 95 Keerom St ⓣ 021 422 0765, ⓦ 95keerom.com; map p.92. Flash, fabulous and expensive, 95 Keerom offers fresh and light Italian nouvelle

cuisine, with dishes such as grilled beef, butternut ravioli, seared tuna (average mains R250). In 2013, the Italian chef Giorgio Nava won gold in the World Pasta Championship in Parma. Mon–Sat 6.30–10pm.

1

AFRICAN FOOD

Around the centre of Cape Town you will find a couple of restaurants offering African food, but these are geared towards tourists – most Xhosa locals would scoff at Long Street's prices. The best way to try African food in the **townships** is by staying over in a B&B (see box, p.136) or taking a tour that incorporates a township meal or a drink in a *shebeen* (see p.58). The following offer African eating experiences.

Dinner at Mandela's Departing from 259 Long St or accommodation ☎021 790 5817, ⚲dinneratmandelas.co.za. Priced at R395 including transfers (from your accommodation and back), this evening of African singing, dancing and food in Imizamo Yethu township near Hout Bay is a fun way to learn more about township culture. Book ahead. Mon & Thurs 6.15–11pm.

Kaffa Hoist Café Guga S'Thebe Arts & Cultural Centre, King Langalibalele/Washington Dr, Langa ☎071 120 6345, ✉kaffa.hoist@gmail.com. *Kaffa Hoist* is situated at the back of Langa's Guga S'Thebe Arts & Cultural Centre (see p.128), adjoining an amphitheatre made of shipping containers. Xhosa owner Chris serves locally roasted Deluxe Coffeeworks coffee (R19), muffins (R5), sweet or savoury pancakes (R30), tasty sandwiches (R30) and burgers (R50), and the courtyard café has free wi-fi. Daily 8.30am–5.30pm May–Sept, 7am–7pm Oct–April.

Addis in Cape 41 Church St ☎021 424 5722, ⚲addisincape.co.za; map p.92. This friendly and authentic restaurant has a lovely laidback atmosphere, with traditional furnishings and coffee ceremonies available. You'll find delicious Ethiopian dishes on the menu, such as spicy red lentils (R137), served on tasty *injera* (sourdough flatbread) to soak up the flavours and eat with your fingers. Set menus cost R105–260. Mon–Sat noon–10.30pm.

Africa Café 108 Shortmarket St ☎021 422 0221, ⚲africacafe.co.za; map p.92. This enduringly popular tourist restaurant is a good place to try African cuisine. Given that you're served a communal feast of sixteen dishes, and the evening includes a performance of African song and dance, the R250/head price tag is pretty reasonable. Booking essential. Mon–Sat 6–11pm.

Biesmiellah Cnr Wale and Pentz sts, Bo-Kaap ☎021 423 0850, ⚲biesmiellah.co.za; map p.90. This is one of the oldest restaurants to sample traditional Cape Malay cuisine (see p.57), serving halal mains such as *bobotie* (beef mince topped with a milk egg glaze; R95) and tomato *bredie* (cubes of lamb cooked in sweet-sour tomato sauce; R99). Alternatively, join local residents in the queue for takeaway samosas and delicious savoury wraps called *salomes*. Mon–Sat noon–10pm.

★**Café Mozart** 37 Church St ☎021 424 3774, ⚲themozart.co.za; map p.92. Sit under trees on cute Church St or in the quaint interior among printed wallpaper, porcelain and antiques, for hearty breakfasts, burgers (R90), sandwiches (R75) or a glass of Cape wine. A little like a cross between a twee English teahouse and a bohemian boudoir. Mon–Fri 8am–3.30pm, Sat 9am–3pm.

Charly's Bakery 38 Canterbury St, East City ☎021 461 5181, ⚲charlysbakery.co.za; map p.90. For three decades, this fun-loving bakery in a psychedelically painted heritage building has produced Cape Town's most spectacular and decorative cakes. Try the red velvet cupcakes or wheat- and gluten-free lemon meringue cupcakes (R30). They also do breakfasts and light lunches (from R50). Tues–Fri 8am–5pm, Sat 8.30am–2pm.

★**Chef's Warehouse & Canteen** 92 Bree St, Heritage Square ☎021 422 0128, ⚲chefswarehouse.co.za; map p.92. Alongside a culinary wonderland selling everything from coffee machines to pink Himalayan salt, chef Liam Tomlin serves a foodie tapas feast (R650 for two) in a casual setting. Featuring a global mix of French and Asian flavours, the three-course small-plate banquet takes up to one hour. They don't take reservations, so arrive early or head downstairs to the dinky basement bar. Mon–Fri noon–2.30pm & 4.30–8pm, Sat noon–2.30pm.

Eastern Food Bazaar 96 Longmarket St ☎021 461 2458, ⚲easternfoodbazaar.co.za; map p.92. Bustling food court with a dozen stalls selling hearty dishes from India, China, the Bo-Kaap and beyond (mains R50). You buy a token before queuing at your chosen counter, and there are often long waits at lunchtime. Mon–Sat 11am–10pm.

Headquarters 100 Shortmarket St, Heritage Square ☎021 424 6373, ⚲hqrestaurant.co.za; map p.92. There is only one main dish on the menu at *Headquarters* – prime free-range Namibian sirloin steak and Café de Paris butter sauce with perfect matchstick chips and salad (R198). Snack boards and tapas are also offered (R100), and the drinks menu compensates for its short culinary counterpart. Check the website for regular specials and events, including two steaks for the price of one on Monday evenings. Mon–Sat noon–midnight.

Jason Bakery 185 Bree St ☎021 424 5644, ⚲www.jasonbakery.com; map p.92. Baker Jason Lilley is renowned for his pastries, pies and sourdough rye bread. Lunch favourites at the fashionable spot include pulled pork shoulder (R75) and curried Chalmar beef burger (R90), while the menu also features numerous breakfasts, salads and sandwiches. Look out, too, for *Bardough* by Jason at 33 Loop St. Mon–Fri 7am–3.30pm, Sat 8am–2pm.

La Parada 107 Bree St ☎021 426 0330; map p.92 ⓦlaparada.co.za. Cape Town has fallen heavily for tapas, and this open-fronted restaurant with street seating offers some of the most authentic Spanish nibbles around (R55–89), as well as mains (R300) and cocktails, all served at long, wooden communal tables. There are also branches in Camps Bay and Constantia Nek. Daily 7am–2am.

Mama Africa 178 Long St ☎021 424 8634, ⓦmama africarestaurant.co.za; map p.92. With food from around the continent, the menu here includes *bobotie* and a wild-game mixed grill of springbok, kudu, ostrich and crocodile (mains R150). You can also sit in the *Snake Bar* and listen to live marimba music from 8pm. Mon & Sat 6.30–11pm, Tues–Fri noon–3pm & 6.30–11pm.

★**Royale Eatery** 273 Long St ☎021 422 4536, ⓦroyaleeatery.com; map p.92. A hip hangout serving inexpensive gourmet burgers, including lamb, beef, pork, ostrich and eight vegetarian cheeseburgers. The Miss Piggy burger with bacon and guacamole (R92) is a favourite. Book ahead, especially if you would like a balcony seat with Long St views. Mon–Sat noon–11.30pm.

★**Truth Café** 36 Buitenkant St, East City ☎021 200 0440, ⓦtruthcoffee.com; map p.90. These artisan coffee roasters supply a great caffeine kick at this hip café with its creative industrial interior centred on a cast-iron vintage roaster drum. They also do breakfast and lunch (mains R100), and the "steampunk" decor moved the UK *Telegraph* to proclaim this one of the world's best coffee shops in 2016. Mon–Fri 7am–6pm, Sat 8am–6pm, Sun 8am–2pm.

V&A WATERFRONT AND DE WATERKANT
THE WATERFRONT

Baia Upper Level, Victoria Wharf, Quay 6 ☎021 421 0935, ⓦbaiarestaurant.co.za; map p.103. Sit on the terrace and take in the views of Table Mountain while dining on masterfully cooked fresh fish and seafood, including a few *kingklip* dishes (R200). Daily noon–3pm & 7–11pm.

City Grill Shop 155, Victoria Wharf, Quay 5 ☎021 421 9820, ⓦcitygrill.co.za; map p.103. An excellent, if rather touristy and pricey, steakhouse, celebrating the meaty heart of South African cuisine. From the appetizer plate of beef biltong and dry sausage (R99) to the ostrich kebab (R245), numerous dishes offer local flavours (helpfully accompanied by South African flags on the menu). Daily 11am–11pm.

San Marco Lower Level, Victoria Wharf ☎021 418 5434, ⓦsanmarco.co.za; map p.103. This bar-restaurant with outdoor seating offers a breakfast menu, good sandwiches on Italian breads (R85), wraps and fresh salads. Mains range from grilled calamari (R129) to fillet steak (R175). Daily 8am–11pm.

★**Sevruga** Quay 5 ☎021 421 5134, ⓦsevruga restaurant.co.za; map p.103. *Sevruga* impresses everyone from local sushi-lovers to the *New York Times*, which called it the "only reason to go to the V&A Waterfront". Book a shaded outdoor table for some people-watching while you enjoy your sushi platter (R200), dim sum or seafood main (R200). Daily noon–11pm.

Signal Restaurant Cape Grace, West Quay Rd ☎021 410 7100, ⓦcapegrace.com; map p.103. In a quietly elegant dining room, the *Cape Grace* hotel's restaurant serves seven-course tasting menus (from R625, including wine from R945) and dinner mains such as *bobotie*-spiced springbok (R280). Lunch is a lighter affair (fish and chips R95), and you can enjoy a cream tea (R75) or full afternoon tea (R185) in the adjoining library. Daily 6.30am–10.30pm.

Willoughby & Co Lower Level, Victoria Wharf ☎021 418 6115, ⓦwilloughbyandco.co.za; map p.103. Despite its lack of sea views, many locals rate this as the Waterfront's best fish restaurant. It serves fantastic sushi (platters R85–309) and seafood (mains around R200). Daily noon–10.30pm.

DE WATERKANT

Anatoli 24 Napier St ☎021 419 2501, ⓦanatoli.co.za; map p.103. This Turkish restaurant has transformed an early twentieth-century coach house into a culinary caravanserai. It's great for vegetarians: the excellent meze selection includes *dolmades* (vine leaves stuffed with rice, pine nuts, blackcurrants and spices), with at least twenty other meze to choose from (R26–53). For a meaty main, look no further than the kebabs (R149). Mon–Sat 6.30–10.30pm.

★**Origin Coffee** 28 Hudson St ☎021 421 1000, ⓦoriginroasting.co.za; map p.103. These coffee devotees serve single-origin, home-roasted beans from across Africa and beyond, and their range of teas is equally appealing. The converted warehouse is popular among savvy city workers for breakfast (R60) and lunch (R90). Mon–Fri 7am–5pm, Sat & Sun 9am–2pm.

CITY BOWL SUBURBS
GARDENS

Aubergine 39 Barnet St ☎021 465 0000, ⓦaubergine .co.za; map p.133. This is an unbeatable choice for an elegant five-star dinner, with a courtyard to sit in and enjoy German chef Harald Bresselschmidt's fusions of African, Asian and European flavours (three-course lunch menu R445). There's a strong emphasis on fresh and local ingredients, and vegetarians will find inspired dishes. Mon, Tues & Sat 6–10pm, Wed–Fri noon–2pm & 6–10pm.

Bardelli's Restaurant 18 Kloof St ☎021 423 1502; map p.133. This reliable, bustling Italian restaurant occupies a historic Cape Dutch building. The

1

wood-fired pizzas such as the Pablo (bacon, feta, rosemary and fresh tomatoes; R95) are some of the best around. Daily 8am–10pm.

★ **Ben Wei** Wembley Square, Solan St ☎ 021 461 2966, ☼ facebook.com/BenWeiSushi; map p.133. This intimate sushi and Asian fusion restaurant offers some of the City Bowl's freshest, most flavoursome and visually striking dishes. Mains are available (around R75), but the best option is to share several bites such as the "rainbow reloaded" (California roll with salmon, tuna and avocado, topped with seven-spice seasoning, mayo and teriyaki sauce; R109). Mon–Sat 11.30am–9pm.

★ **Bombay Bicycle Club** 158 Kloof St ☎ 021 423 6805, ☼ thebombay.co.za; map p.133. A fun place for an evening out, offering things to play with in every area, whether you're sitting at a table with swings or wearing silly hats. Food includes grills, pastas and decadent desserts (average mains R150). Booking essential. Mon–Sat 6–11pm (bar 4–11pm).

Carlyle's on Derry 17 Derry St ☎ 021 461 8787, ☼ carlyles.co.za; map p.133. A friendly neighbourhood Italian restaurant where you'll need to book in advance for a table. They serve a great selection of thin-based, gourmet pizzas (R65–135), as well as meat dishes (R70–180), pasta (R80–120) and salads (R80–92). Tues–Fri 5.30–10.30pm, Sat & Sun noon–10.30pm.

Hudson's The Burger Joint 69 Kloof St ☎ 021 426 5974, ☼ theburgerjoint.co.za; map p.133. This Kloof St joint is a good choice for gourmet burgers (R44–97), with trendy young patrons, loud rock music, craft beer, decent salads, home-made lemonade and Bar One milkshakes (R49). There are also branches in Green Point, Claremont and Stellenbosch. Daily noon–11pm.

★ **Mount Nelson Hotel** 76 Orange St ☎ 021 483 1000, ☼ mountnelson.co.za; map p.133. Colonial-style afternoon tea, with a smart-casual dress code, in Cape Town's gracious hospitality legend is a slow-paced culinary delight. You can skip dinner after this R325 feast. Book in advance online. Tea at 1.30pm & 3.30pm.

★ **Societi Bistro** 50 Orange St ☎ 021 424 2100, ☼ societi.co.za; map p.133. This popular bistro serves good Italian and South African food, in a lovely restored building and garden near the *Mount Nelson Hotel* (see p.135) and *Labia* cinema (see p.152), with a fireplace for winter evenings. Mains include risotto (R66–85), Karoo lamb shank (R206), free-range ostrich burger (R94) and, generally, a vegan dish. Mon–Sat noon–10pm.

★ **Tamboers Winkel** 3 De Lorentz St ☎ 021 424 0521, ☼ facebook.com/Tamboerswinkel; map p.133. Like most residents of Gardens, this café seems to be suggesting it lives in posher Tamboerskloof, but we can forgive it for its excellent coffee and craft beer. The menu offers rustic tastes of the Cape *platteland* (farmland) with a creative twist, making this *winkel* (shop) a top choice for bloggers, media

types, models and all discerning Capetonians. Breakfast around R60, lunch mains around R90. Mon & Wed–Sun 8am–10pm, Tues 8am–6pm.

TAMBOERSKLOOF AND VREDEHOEK

Deer Park Café 2 Deer Park Drive, Vredehoek ☎ 021 462 6311, ☼ deerparkcafe.co.za; map p.133. On the lower slopes of Table Mountain, and with an enclosed park and playground sloping below its outdoor tables, this is the best central place to take children. The kids' menu features dishes from fruit salad to spaghetti bolognaise, and everyone will enjoy the fresh, well-priced soups, salads, sandwiches and more (mains average R80). Daily 8am–8pm.

Miller's Thumb 10b Kloof Nek Rd, Tamboerskloof ☎ 021 424 3838, ☼ millersthumb.co.za; map p.133. The *Thumb* serves consistently good seafood dishes, with a selection of line fish prepared in various ways from Cajun to Moroccan. If you're not into fish, you can try their juicy 300g rump steak (mains R125–185). Mon & Sat 6.30–10.30pm, Tues–Fri 12.30–2pm & 6.30–10.30pm.

★ **Sidewalk Café** 33 Derry St, Vredehoek ☎ 021 461 2839, ☼ sidewalk.co.za; map p.133. This modern, funky café has large windows and an enticing and imaginative menu (mains around R120). There's a good vegetarian selection, too – from quinoa salad to aubergine and spiced lentil moussaka. Mon–Sat 8am–10.30pm, Sun 9am–2pm.

SOUTHERN SUBURBS

Bistro Sixteen82 Steenberg Estate, Constantia ☎ 021 713 2211, ☼ steenberghotel.com. On the historic and scenic Steenberg wine estate, this chic and contemporary bistro is popular for decadent weekend breakfasts (mains R90) – followed by a visit to the adjoining tasting room or a wander across the lawns dotted with sculptures by South African-Italian artist Edoardo Villa. Tapas (plate R65) are served from 5pm. Daily 9–11am, noon–3pm & 5–8pm.

Catharina's Steenberg Estate, Constantia ☎ 021 713 2222, ☼ steenberghotel.com. Serving beautifully plated food on Steenberg estate, *Catharina's* is an elegant choice for a special occasion, with imposing windows making the most of the vineyard views. Seafood and venison regularly feature on the menu, while game and steaks appear alongside vegetarian options (mains R200). Daily 7–10am, noon–3pm & 6.30–9.30pm.

Common Ground Café 23 Milner Rd, Rondebosch ☎ 021 686 0154. Attached to a church, Common Ground offers reasonably priced breakfasts (around R50) and gourmet sandwiches, whole-wheat wraps, burgers, salads and quesadillas for lunch (average R60). The baristas are true artists, who make an excellent double-shot cup using locally roasted beans from Origin Coffee, and the terrace has stunning views of Devil's Peak across Rondebosch Common. Mon–Fri 7am–4pm, Sat 8am–2pm, Sun 8.30am–2pm.

The Dining Room 117 Sir Lowry Rd, Woodstock ☎ 021 461 0463, ⊛ dining-room.co.za. From Karen Dudley, the culinary brains behind Woodstock's famous *The Kitchen* (see below), this restaurant focuses on fresh seasonal produce among the whimsical array of screens, mirrors and portraits in its stylish vintage interior. Lunch R100, three-course dinner R350. Mon, Wed & Fri 8.30am–4pm, Tues & Thurs 8.30am–4pm & 7–10pm.

Kirstenbosch Tea Room Restaurant Kirstenbosch National Botanical Garden, Rhodes Drive, Newlands ☎ 021 797 4883, ⊛ ktr.co.za. The gorgeous setting in one of the world's greatest botanical gardens (see p.111) complements the pleasing, Cape country food. They serve some good vegetarian options and tea for two (R280). You can also order a gourmet picnic (R210/person) and even rent a picnic blanket (R30). It's located just inside Gate 2. Daily 8.30am–5pm.

★ **The Kitchen** 111 Sir Lowry Rd, Woodstock ☎ 021 462 2201, ⊛ lovethekitchen.co.za. Famously visited by former US First Lady Michelle Obama, chef Karen Dudley's fun but food-obsessed deli-café uses the freshest ingredients to create inventive breakfasts and lunches. The "love sandwiches" on artisanal bread (R60) are especially popular, and there is an ever-changing range of salads (R70). This is one of the best lunch stops around, especially if you are vegetarian, but arrive early (or come for a quieter breakfast). Mon–Fri 8am–3.30pm.

★ **Pot Luck Club** Top Floor, Silo Building, Old Biscuit Mill, 375 Albert Rd, Woodstock ☎ 021 447 0804, ⊛ thepotluckclub.co.za. Perched atop a converted silo, British chef Luke Dale-Roberts' second South African restaurant is all about inventive and tantalizing tapas dishes (around R100 each). The menu is arranged according to sweet, sour, salty, bitter and *umami* (savoury or meaty) flavours; order several to share with friends. You'll need to book at least a few weeks in advance and will be allocated a seating time. Mon–Sat 12.30–2.30pm & 6–8.30pm, Sun 11am–12.30pm.

★ **Test Kitchen** Old Biscuit Mill, 375 Albert Rd, Woodstock ☎ 021 447 2337, ⊛ thetestkitchen.co.za. For a table at South Africa's top, award-winning fine-dining contemporary restaurant you'll need to book months in advance. Should you be lucky enough to get in, prepare to be overwhelmed by the sensual feast of tastes, smells and colours provided by the astonishing creative mastery of chef Luke Dale-Roberts, whose innovative dishes on the ever-changing menu are rich in unusual ingredients and combinations. Menus range from R1200 to R2650; enjoy one in the industrial-style setting with its contemporary art and casual ambience. Tues–Sat 6.30–8.30pm.

ATLANTIC SEABOARD
GREEN POINT

El Burro 81 Main Rd ☎ 021 433 2364, ⊛ elburro.co.za; map p.114. This fun, casual spot offers Mexican food without too much cheese and grease (mains R130), plus a good view of Green Point Stadium from the balcony. There are a few vegetarian options. Mon–Sat noon–11.30pm.

Giovanni's 103 Main Rd ☎ 021 434 6893; map p.114. With both indoor and pavement seating, this lively Italian deli and coffee shop is right across from the stadium and has its own screen for watching sports. It offers delicious coffee, excellent made-to-order sandwiches, salads and prepackaged meals (R45–65). Daily 7.30am–8.30pm.

Mano's 39 Main Rd ☎ 021 434 1090, ⊛ mano.co.za; map p.114. Popular with Capetonian glitterati, chic *Mano's* serves seafood, grills and pasta from an unpretentious menu featuring Caesar salads, Prego rolls, lemon chicken and lamb chops (mains R100). After dinner, the party continues in champagne bar *Jade,* upstairs (see p.149). Mon–Sat noon–2am.

MOUILLE POINT

★ **Café Neo** 129 Beach Rd ☎ 021 433 0849; map p.114. *Neo* serves up deli-style food with a Greek influence, with mains going for around R80. There are tasty breakfast options, as well as meze platters, salads and sandwiches, and the umbrella-shaded outdoor seating area offers views of the stripy lighthouse. Vegetarians can do well here, too. Daily 7am–7pm.

★ **Newport Market and Deli** Amalfi, 125 Beach Rd ☎ 021 439 1538, ⊛ newportdeli.co.za; map p.114. This two-floor deli, with views onto Table Bay, serves coffee, juices, gourmet sandwiches (R80), tasty salads (R80), and hot dishes including macaroni cheese (R70) and burgers. The smoothies are packed with interesting blends (R38) – just right if you are walking or jogging along the Sea Point promenade. Daily 6.30am–6.30pm.

SEA POINT

La Boheme Wine Bar & Bistro 341 Main Rd ☎ 021 434 6539, ⊛ labohemebistro.co.za; map p.114. Great for an enjoyable and good-value night out, *La Boheme*'s menu is full of interesting, well-presented rural French food. Dishes, which are around the R100 mark, include the likes of confit rabbit and slow-braised pork belly. There's pavement seating for people-watching too, and next door is their sister espresso and tapas bar, *La Bruixa*. Mon–Sat noon–11pm.

Mr Chan 17 Regent Rd ☎ 021 439 2239, ⊛ mrchan.co.za; map p.114. This Cantonese restaurant has been keeping customers happy for years with excellent Hong Kong-style beef, seafood, roast duck, braised bean curd and mixed vegetables. Mains are around R90, with set dinner menus also available. Daily noon–2.30pm & 6–10.30pm.

CAMPS BAY

Café Caprice 37 Victoria Rd, Camps Bay ☎ 021 438 8315, ⊛ cafecaprice.co.za; map p.118. Across the road from Camps Bay Beach, this lively, albeit pretentious, Mediterranean-style restaurant's pavement tables are a time-honoured place to soak up the chichi suburb's street life, sunshine and sunsets. You can get nibbles (R45), more substantial meat, pasta or seafood dishes (R90), and sexy cocktails (R85). Mon 12.30pm–midnight, Tues–Sun 9.30am–midnight.

Paranga Shop 1, The Promenade, Victoria Rd, Camps Bay ☎021 438 0404, ⓦparanga.co.za; map p.118. This popular beach hangout is a place to see and be seen while you pick at salads, seafood, sushi or burgers (mains R130). Choose between a variety of champagnes and local MCC bubblies, plus all sorts of wines, single malts and cocktails while you watch the sun sinking into the ocean. Daily 9am–midnight.

HOUT BAY

★Kitima 140 Main Rd, Hout Bay ☎021 790 8004, ⓦkitima.co.za. One of Cape Town's best Asian-fusion restaurants, with a definite Thai slant, is situated in a lovely Cape Dutch homestead, where you can enjoy sushi and sashimi, dim sum and a plethora of seafood, meat stir-fries and curries. *Kitima* is best known for its sumptuous Sunday buffet (R250), for which you'll need to book. Tues–Sat 5.30–10.30pm, Sun noon–3.30pm.

La Cuccina Victoria Mall, Victoria Rd, Hout Bay ☎021 790 8008, ⓦfacebook.com/lacuccina. This high-quality deli and café occupies a roomy and appealing space, despite its mall location. On the main road through town, it makes a great pit stop for wholesome breakfasts (R70), quiches, salads, lasagne and the like, with a pay-by-weight lunch buffet offered from noon to 3pm (R195 for 1kg). Daily 7.30am–5pm.

Wharfette Bistro Mariner's Wharf, Harbour Rd, Hout Bay ☎021 790 1100, ⓦmarinerswharf.com. A relaxed and popular seafood restaurant, decorated with nostalgic passenger-liner photographs and memorabilia. The harbour views from the terrace seating outshine the food, but it's a fine spot to eat 'n' chips (R70) while sipping a cold beer. Daily 10am–8.30pm.

NOORDHOEK

Café Roux Noordhoek Farm Village ☎021 789 2538; ⓦcaferoux.co.za. This chilled-out café offers wholesome and healthy food with a contemporary feel, as well as regular evenings of live music or comedy. They serve breakfasts (R70) and lunch mains such as a Cape Malay *roti* wrap (R85), with a menu and garden catering to children. Sit under umbrellas with a butternut and goat's cheese salad (R85), and gaze at Noordhoek's surrounding mountains. The kitchen closes at 3.30pm, and there's another branch in town at 74 Shortmarket St. Daily 8.30am–5pm.

★The Foodbarn Noordhoek Farm Village ☎021 789 1390, ⓦthefoodbarn.co.za. Gourmet French food from acclaimed chef Franck Dangereux is served at reasonable prices here, compared to the top restaurants in the city centre. Starters include fish tartare (R95), and mains (R180) range from fish and vegetarian choices to Karoo lamb rack and seared duck breast. Booking is essential. Check out the deli or tapas bar for something more casual. Mon & Sun noon–2.30pm, Tues–Sat noon–2.30pm & 7–9.30pm.

KOMMETJIE AND SCARBOROUGH

★Blue Water Café Imhoff Farm, Kommetjie Rd, opposite the Ocean View turn-off ☎021 783 4545, ⓦimhofffarm.co.za. A great stop if you are on a Cape Point round route, *Blue Water* offers good seafood dishes (mussels R115), pastas (R100), wood-fired pizzas (R100) and local wines, as well as breakfast and tea. Set in a handsome Cape Dutch homestead, there are good views onto the wetlands and ocean, and there's a fire in winter. You can book outdoor tables next to the large lawn, where children can play – plus there's plenty at the farm to keep them occupied. Tues 9am–5pm, Wed–Sun 9am–9pm.

FALSE BAY SEABOARD
MUIZENBERG

Cucina Labia Casa Labia, 192 Main Rd ☎021 788 6062, ⓦcasalabia.co.za; map p.122. At *Casa Labia* (see p.121), you can expect contemporary Italian food and English-style high teas in seafront *palazzo* surroundings. Lavish breakfasts are on the menu and classical pianist Jean-Paul Grimaldi-Lasserre adds to the pervading elegance on weekends between 1pm and 3pm. There's usually a good art exhibition upstairs, and the small craft shop sells carefully chosen pieces. Tues–Sun 10am–4pm.

Empire Café 11 York Rd ☎021 788 1250, ⓦempirecafe .co.za; map p.122. Enjoy Woodstock-roasted Tribe coffee and munch on fresh pastries while sitting upstairs at this local hangout, gazing at passing trains and waiting for the surf to come up. A popular breakfast spot, its ever-changing lunch menu features burgers, fish and chips, pastas, salads, sticky pork ribs and chicken wraps, while drinks range from craft beer to gourmet milkshakes. Mon–Thurs & Sat 7am–4pm, Fri 7am–9pm, Sun 8am–4pm.

KALK BAY

Harbour House Restaurant Kalk Bay Harbour ☎021 788 4133; map p.122; Quay 4, Ground Floor, V&A Waterfront ☎021 418 4744; Hout Bay Rd, Constantia Nek ☎021 795 0688, ⓦharbourhouse.co.za. This memorable restaurant serves seafood and Mediterranean dishes (mains around R200), in a spectacular setting on the breakwater of Kalk Bay harbour. Seafood options including Mozambique grilled prawns are the obvious choice, but the menu also features lamb, beef and salads. Portions small, but rich and beautifully plated. Booking is essential.

They also have branches at the Waterfront and Constantia Nek. Daily noon–4pm & 6–10pm; V&A Waterfront & Constantia Nek daily noon–10pm.

Kalky's On the harbour ☎ 021 788 1726; map p.122. For years, this no-frills seafood cabin has served the peninsula's best traditional fish and chips (R55), as well as calamari, *snoek*, crayfish, prawns and good-value platters (R215). Fish is hauled off the boats and straight into the frying pan, before being eaten at benches; wait a bit longer and you can have your catch grilled. Daily 10am–8pm.

★ **Olympia Café & Deli** 134 Main Rd ☎ 021 788 6396, ⓦ olympiacafe.co.za; map p.122. Good enough to draw uptown Capetonians to the False Bay seaboard, *Olympia* is always buzzing, thanks to the harbour views, great coffee and freshly baked goods. Gourmet lunch menus are chalked on a board, with local fish and mussels often featured (mains around R100). They don't take bookings, so arrive early for dinner. Their bakery is round the corner, where you can get bread, pastries, takeaway coffee and sandwiches. Daily 7am–9pm, bakery 7am–7pm.

Under the Cypress 124 Main Rd, above Kalk Bay Books ☎ 021 788 2453, ⓦ underthecypress.co.za; map p.122. Formerly the *Annex* restaurant, this historic building has a terrace with superb views of the harbour and bay beyond. Enjoy local craft beers, ciders, wines and bar snacks such as fried calamari and squid heads (R65), or mains from Kalk Bay line fish (R145) to smoked and barbecued Greek lamb (R125). Mon–Sat 8am–9pm, Sun 8am–4pm.

FISH HOEK

C'est La Vie 2 Recreation Rd, Fish Hoek ☎ 083 676 7430; map p.122. This unassuming and tiny French-style bakery is popular locally for its pavement breakfasts and sandwiches (R55), breadsticks, muffins, croissants, coffee and orange juice. Tues–Sun 7.30am–3pm.

SIMON'S TOWN AND THE DEEP SOUTH

Black Marlin Main Rd, south of Simon's Town ☎ 021 786 1621, ⓦ blackmarlin.co.za. Every kind of sea denizen is on the menu at this popular place on the road to Cape Point. Don't expect culinary pyrotechnics, but the clifftop views (and possible whale sightings) from the outdoor tables certainly compensate. Catch of the day costs R145, and the breakfasts are good value (around R35). Daily 9am–10pm.

Salty Sea Dog 2 Wharf St, Waterfront, Simon's Town ☎ 021 786 1918, ⓦ saltyseadog.co.za. There's nothing fancy about this small restaurant on the wharf, but they do plain old fish and chips (R70) extremely well, and they serve beer and wine. With indoor and alfresco seating, it makes a great lunch stop on a Cape Point outing. Mon–Sat 8.30am–9pm, Sun 8.30am–4.30pm.

Two Oceans Cape Point ☎ 021 780 9200, ⓦ two -oceans.co.za. This touristic restaurant should more accurately be called "Two Ocean Currents", as the Benguela and Agulhas currents meet hereabouts, rather than the actual Atlantic and Indian oceans. Still, this quibble seems irrelevant when you reach the stunning clifftop alfresco deck that overlooks the ocean, taking in the whole of False Bay and its mountains. It's also a great place to see whales in season. As well as seafood including fish and sushi, they serve some meaty options (mains from R145), plus gourmet breakfasts (R70) till 10.45am. Daily 9am–11am & noon–4.30pm.

DRINKING AND NIGHTLIFE

Being a hedonistic city – especially in the summer – Cape Town has a range of great places to drink and party, particularly along **Long Street**, which is relatively safe and busy, and there are taxis to get you home. In the summer, the Atlantic seaboard, notably **Camps Bay**, is a great option, especially for sundowners. When the dust has settled after Saturday's hedonism, Sunday nights can be quiet, though there are a few welcoming options. An excellent monthly event is First Thursday (ⓦ first-thursdays.co.za), which sees galleries opening late, pop-up bars, and crowds thronging the restaurants and bars of the city centre, especially around Bree and Shortmarket streets. Unsurprisingly, it takes place on the first Thursday of every month.

Most liquor **licences** stipulate that the last round is served at 2am, though some places stay open until 4am. Laws prohibit the sale of alcohol in shops from 6pm on Saturday and all day Sunday. Drink **prices** obviously depend on the venue – a beer in a sports bar might set you back R25, while local craft brews cost upwards of R45. A smart bar will charge well over R50 for a cocktail or a glass of delicious Cape wine or bubbly. **Clubs** get going after 10pm and are pretty international in flavour, with **DJs** mixing house hits you're bound to recognize. Most have a **cover charge**, generally under R100, while other venues may charge when they have live music on. It's not a good idea to walk around late at night, so take a **taxi number** out with you (see p.131). Many bars and clubs offer food as well. When it comes to **live music**, the best-known South African musicians are sadly better appreciated, and better paid, abroad than in their own country. Look out for posters and listings magazines; if any local stars such as Abdullah Ibrahim or Hugh Masekela are in town, it is well worth catching them. Cape Town is known for its brand of Cape jazz, but there is nowhere regular to pick that up, though the **Cape Town International Jazz Festival** in late March is Africa's largest jazz festival, attracting performers from Courtney Pine to Youssou N'Dour. The Baxter and Artscape (see p.151) are both likely venues for any good musical offerings.

NEW YEAR, NEW YEAR – SO GOOD THEY DO IT TWICE

A long-standing tradition in Cape Town is **Tweede Nuwe Jaar** (Second New Year) on January 2 – once an official public holiday. Historically, this was the only day of the year slaves were allowed off, and the occasion has persisted as a celebration of epic proportions. *Tweede Nuwe Jaar* sees Cape Minstrels from the coloured community dancing through the streets of the city centre performing a traditional form of singing and riotous banjo playing, with each troupe dressed in matching outfits, often featuring outrageous colour combinations. Some roads in the centre are blocked off during the day for the festivities, which normally start at the Grand Parade and progress through the city.

CITY CENTRE

Aces 'N' Spades 62 Hout St ☎076 070 4474, Ⓦacesnspades.com; map p.92. This place is usually packed from the bar (craft beers R35), where chic meets grunge, to the heaving dancefloor. Rock 'n' roll (or electronic on Wednesdays) sets the tempo, with nightly DJs and live bands on Thursdays. Wed–Sat 6pm–2am.

Alexander Bar, Café & Theatre 76 Strand St ☎021 300 1088, Ⓦalexanderbar.co.za; map p.92. Handsomely furnished in old-world decor, this is a good spot for a quiet conversation or a nightcap, with old rotary phones to call the cutie at the next table – or order a single malt (R40) from the bar. Upstairs is an intimate theatre space that hosts music, comedy and plays. Mon–Sat 11am–1am, Sun 3pm–midnight.

The Beerhouse 223 Long St ☎021 424 3370, Ⓦbeerhouse.co.za; map p.92. With a beer menu comprising 25 beers on tap and 99 bottles, most of which are local craft brews, this industrial-styled beer hall also benefits from a large balcony overlooking Long St. Beers cost R30–70, with tastings, food and regular events adding to the appeal. Daily 11am–2am.

Cafe Mojito 265 Long St ☎021 422 1095, Ⓦfacebook .com/Cafe.Mojito.Cpt; map p.92. *Mojito* dishes up Cuban, Latin American and Caribbean cuisine and attitude. Pictures of Che Guevara and Ernest Hemingway overlook the tables spilling onto the pavement, where cocktails (from R45), daily happy hours (4–7pm) and tapas keep the comrades happy. Daily 11am–2am.

The Dubliner 251 Long St ☎021 424 1212, Ⓦdubliner .co.za; map p.92. Crammed, wildly popular Irish pub with Guinness on tap (R30), a good selection of single malts and pub meals (burgers R80), as well as live music from 10pm every night, flatscreens for sporting events and a nightclub upstairs. Daily 11–4am.

★**Era** 71 Loop St ☎021 422 0202, Ⓦeracapetown .com; map p.92. Rated one of the world's best clubs by *Mixmag*, *Era* promotes up-and-coming electronic DJs alongside seasoned artists, spinning tunes from house flavours to devious techno cuts, with killer aesthetics and a café serving tapas. Cover charge R50–100, drinks R40. Men must be over 23, women over 21. Thurs–Sat 10pm–4am.

Fiction 226 Long St ☎021 422 0400, Ⓦfacebook.com /Fictiondjbar; map p.92. Hosting standout electronic music nights since 2006, *Fiction* never fails to bring in high-quality local and international DJs, attracting names from Skrillex to Spoek Mathambo. Weekly nights range from Untamed Youth (indie) on Tuesday to It Came from the Jungle (drum and bass) on Thursday. Drinks R30; cover charge R50–70. Tues–Sat 10pm–4am.

The Gin Bar 64 Wale St ☎060 606 6014, Ⓦwww .theginbar.co.za; map p.92. This single-minded bar from the guys behind *Honest Chocolate Café*, with which it shares a courtyard, offers four artisan gin cocktails. Serious G&T fans can also design their own drink from a long list of gins and tonic waters (from R50). Mon–Sat 5pm–2am.

★**La Parada** 107 Bree St ☎021 426 0330, Ⓦlaparada .co.za; map p.92. With its open frontage, vibrant atmosphere and Spanish tapas menu, well-heeled Capetonians fill *La Parada's* long, sociable tables until late. Cocktails go for R55–65, while a glass of wine will set you back R35. Downstairs in the basement, DJs spin in *Catacombs Bar* from 7pm to 2am Wednesday to Saturday. Daily 7am–2am.

Long Street Café 259 Long St ☎021 424 2464; map p.92. This people-watching favourite near the top of Long St, identified by its neon sign and Art Deco windows, is popular for its great-value cocktails (R40), bar food and outside tables. Daily noon–1am.

Orphanage Cocktail Emporium Cnr Bree and Orphan sts ☎021 244 1995, Ⓦtheorphanage.co.za; map p.92. This concept cocktail bar's drinks are every bit as remarkable as its styling, which sends the roaring '20s down the rabbit hole. Gargoyles watch over as the bar serves up artisan elixirs, twisted classics and tantalizing intoxications (from R70), as well as gourmet snacks. Daily 4pm–late.

Publik Wine Bar 81 Church St Ⓦpublik.co.za; map p.92. This wine bar focuses on the more interesting and unusual products of the Cape's vineyards, which it also sells online. Settle in for a glass (R45–85), perhaps a red accompanied by some biltong from the adjoining artisan butcher, Frankie Fenner Meat Merchants. There's also a good charcoal restaurant, *Ash*, on-site. Mon–Sat noon–11pm.

CLOCKWISE FROM TOP ZEITZ MUSEUM OF CONTEMPORARY ART AFRICA (P.102); PARANGA (P.144); FOOD AT QUAY FOUR TAVERN (P.149) >

1

LGBT CAPE TOWN

Cape Town is South Africa's – and indeed, the African continent's – LGBT capital. The city has long had a vibrant gay culture, attracting gay travellers from across the country and the globe. The centrally located **Pink Village**, as the gay-friendly De Waterkant is known, offers excellent LGBT-orientated cafés, nightlife, accommodation and a sauna, with most options just off thoroughfare Somerset Rd, and more scattered across neighbouring Green Point and Sea Point. Despite South Africa's progressive constitution legalizing same-sex marriages, outside the city attitudes remain conservative and there is a great deal of homophobia. Homosexuals are regularly harassed and attacked in the African townships, so be discreet outside the city centre.

Cape Town hosts a hugely popular annual **gay costume party**, organized by Mother City Queer Project (ⓦmcqp.co.za), a one-day extravaganza held each December. People dress as outrageously as possible according to the official yearly theme (past themes include Space Cowboys) and the event is the Cape's answer to Sydney's Mardi Gras. There's also an annual **gay pride festival**, running for a week starting in late February (ⓦcapetownpride.org).

RESOURCES AND INFORMATION

For travel Information and inspiration, check out ⓦpinksa.co.za, ⓦgaycapetown4u.com, ⓦmapmyway.co.za/printed-maps, ⓦwww.mambaonline.com, ⓦwww.mambagirl.com and ⓦgaysaradio.co.za. Look out for monthly newspaper *The Pink Tongue* (ⓦlunchboxmedia.co.za) in bars and restaurants in De Waterkant.

GAP Leisure (ⓦgapleisure.com) is a travel agency specializing in gay holiday accommodation in both De Waterkant and countrywide. It's on the corner of Napier and Waterkant streets. **The Triangle Project** (ⓦtriangle.org.za) and **Health4Men** (ⓦhealth4men.co.za) provide sexual health services.

The event company **MISS** (Make It Sexy Sisters; ⓦmissmakeitsexysisters.wordpress.com) is the best platform for lesbian DJs, performers and parties. Check their Facebook page (ⓦbit.ly /missmakeitsexysisters) for details of upcoming events, such as the monthly **Unofficial Pink Parties** (ⓦfacebook.com/pinkpartyza) and the **Rouge Revue Burlesque Company**'s performances and classes (ⓦtherougerevue.co.za, ⓦfacebook.com/TheRougeRevue).

BARS AND CLUBS

Amsterdam Action Bar 10–14 Cobern St, off Somerset Rd, De Waterkant ⓦamsterdambar.co.za; map p.103. Old-school gay bar (men only) with a more mature crowd, keen on full leathers. There's a pool table, discreet booths and a small balcony overlooking the Pink Village, as well as topless barmen and shower shows in the neighbouring *Backroom Bar*. Daily 4pm–2am.

Bar Code 18 Cobern St, De Waterkant ☎021 421 5305, ⓦleatherbar.co.za; map p.103. Men-only leather, rubber, uniform and jeans bar with dark rooms and an outdoor deck. There is a different theme every night, from underwear to fetish pig. Cover charge R80. Wed–Sun 10pm–3am.

Beaulah Bar Cnr Somerset Rd & Cobern St, De Waterkant ☎021 418 5244, ⓦfacebook.com /Beaulahbar; map p.103. Popular with lesbians and (to a lesser degree) gays for its fun nights, *Beaulah Bar* has all the frills with disco lights, a dancefloor, screens showing music videos and a DJ playing all the latest tracks. Cover charge R30. Fri & Sat 9pm–4am.

Crew Bar 30 Napier St, De Waterkant ⓦfacebook .com/CrewBarCapeTown; map p.103. This stylish bar's topless barmen and dancing table-top hunks fill the house every weekend with gays and their fun-loving straight friends, with pop music downstairs and harder beats upstairs. Daily 7pm–4am.

CAFÉS AND RESTAURANTS

Beefcakes 40 Somerset Rd, De Waterkant ☎021 425 9019, ⓦbeefcakes.co.za; map p.103. This is one seriously camp burger bar, where Capetonians of all persuasions don a sequinned cowboy hat and build their own juicy burger (R80). There's nightly live entertainment, attracting a R80–250 cover charge. Mon–Sat 7–11.30pm.

Café Manhattan 74 Waterkant St, De Waterkant ☎021 421 6666, ⓦmanhattan.co.za; map p.103. A stalwart of the gay scene since 1994, this buzzing bar-restaurant with an attractive oak-shaded terrace offers an affordable and largely meat-orientated menu (R100) and a great drinks list. Mon–Fri 4–11pm, Sat & Sun noon–11pm.

SAUNA

Hot House 18 Jarvis St, De Waterkant ☎021 418 3888, ⓦhothouse.co.za; map p.103. A luxurious, men-only pleasure and relaxation complex, with all manner of Jacuzzis and steam rooms, a sundeck boasting superb views, a bar and an adult store. Entrance R90–180 depending on days and times. Mon–Wed noon–2am, Thurs noon–4am, Fri & Sat 24hr, Sun noon–midnight.

ThirtyOne 31st floor, ABSA Centre, 2 Riebeek St ☎021 421 0581, ⓦfacebook.com/thirtyone.capetown; map p.90. Take the lift to the thirty-first floor of the ABSA Centre, one of Cape Town's landmark towers, to feel on top of the world amid this club's wraparound views. Cover charge R100, drinks R50. Men must be over 23, women over 21. Fri & Sat 10pm–3am.

★**TjingTjing** 165 Longmarket St ☎021 422 4374, ⓦtjingtjing.co.za; map p.92. This rooftop cocktail bar is a low-key favourite for young professionals with its indie and electronica soundtrack and tempting menu of cocktails (R58–95) – expect unusual ingredients such as candyfloss-infused vodka. Tapas are offered, while *Torii* serves Asian food downstairs, and free wine tastings take place from 5pm to 7pm on Wednesdays. Tues–Fri 4pm–2am, Sat 6.30pm–2am.

Twankey Bar Cnr Wale and Adderley sts ☎021 819 2000, ⓦtajcapetown.co.za; map p.92. Run by the neighbouring *Taj Hotel*, *Twankey* is an elegant spot specializing in cocktails (R85) devised by a local mixologist. Every infusion, syrup and garnish is made from scratch, and unusual cocktail-making methods are employed, from wood-chip smoking to teapot brewing. Champagne (R60), craft beers on tap (R40) and snacks are also served in the historic marbled interior. Mon–Sat 3–11pm.

★**The Waiting Room** 273 Long St ☎021 422 4536, ⓦfacebook.com/WaitingRoomCT; map p.92. This long-running club above *Royale Eatery* (see p.141) is a good bet for live music and a boogie. Bands play on Tuesdays, Wednesdays and Thursdays; hip hop DJs hit the decks on Fridays; and Saturdays are all about house and disco. Cover charge R50–70, drinks R25. Tues–Sat 7pm–2am.

V&A WATERFRONT

★**Bascule Bar** Cape Grace, West Quay Rd ☎021 410 7100, ⓦbasculebar.com; map p.103. The *Cape Grace* hotel's whisky bar is one of the best stocked south of the equator. The whisky-tasting experiences are recommended and, with its terrace alongside the yacht marina, the bar is equally good for a beer or cocktail (R65). Daily 10am–midnight.

★**Grand Café & Beach** Haul Rd, Granger Bay ☎021 425 0551, ⓦwww.grandafrica.com; map p.103. This chichi beach paradise hidden between the Waterfront and Cape Town Stadium has sun-loungers on the sand and a bulging menu of exquisite cocktails (R80). Book ahead for a prime sundowner spot. Sept–June Mon–Sat noon–2am, Sun noon–5pm.

Quay Four Tavern Quay Four ☎021 419 2008, ⓦquay4.co.za; map p.103. The *Tavern* is an old favourite for a pint of tap beer or a cocktail (R50) on the terrace overlooking the Waterfront. Enjoy a hearty pub meal and catch the nightly free live music. Daily 7am–2am.

Shimmy Beach Club 12 South Arm Rd ☎021 200 7778, ⓦshimmybeachclub.com; map p.103. With a

private beach, outdoor deck and infinity plunge pool, the luxurious *Shimmy Beach Club* is draped with beautiful people day and night. Come to enjoy the upmarket restaurant, indoor dancefloor, cocktail menu (R80) and live electronic-music acts every Sunday during summer. Cover charge R150–250. Daily 11am–2am.

CITY BOWL SUBURBS

The Power and The Glory 13d Kloof Nek Rd ☎021 422 2108; map p.133. This diminutive bar-restaurant is a magnet for hipsters. The stylish bistro, kitted out with old-school metal chairs and botanical drawing prints, serves coffee during the day and morphs from 5pm into a cosy bar serving craft beers and local wine (R40). Mon–Sat 9am–1am.

★**Yours Truly** 73 Kloof St ☎021 426 2587, ⓦyours trulycafe.co.za; map p.133. Attracting hillside hipsters and backpackers from adjoining *Once in Cape Town* (see p.135) to its elongated terrace, *Yours Truly's* draught beer (R40) and iced coffee, pizzas and wraps are accompanied by city views and a dependably uplifting soundtrack. Daily 6am–11pm.

SOUTHERN SUBURBS

Foresters Arms 52 Newlands Ave, Newlands ☎021 689 5949, ⓦforries.co.za. Locals from students to families gather to quaff beer at the popular and busy "Forries", a big wood-panelled pub dating to 1852. There's a hedged-in courtyard with a playground and benches for a lazy afternoon pizza (R90) and pint (R30). Mon–Sat 11am–11pm, Sun 9am–10pm.

ATLANTIC SEABOARD

★**Café Caprice** 37 Victoria Rd, Camps Bay ☎021 438 8315, ⓦcafecaprice.co.za; map p.118. This beach-facing hangout, popular with local celebs and wannabes, is just right for cocktails (R85). Families are welcome for breakfast and lunch (see p.143), but the pace increases at sunset and the pavement tables are like gold dust. Tues–Sun 9.30am–midnight, Mon 12.30pm–midnight.

Dunes 1 Beach Rd, Hout Bay ☎021 790 1876, ⓦdunesrestaurant.co.za. Right on Hout Bay beach, this whitewashed restaurant is popular with families on sunny weekend afternoons, when kids enjoy the jungle gym. Savour the sea view over a cocktail (R50) or a glass of bubbly (R50). Daily 9am–10pm.

Jade Champagne Bar 39 Main Rd above Mano's restaurant, Green Point ☎021 758 4008, ⓦjade lounge.co.za; map p.114. Classy lounge-bar with DJs, plush sofas, chandeliers and a semi-enclosed balcony to relax on with a cocktail (from R80). Entry for over 23 years only; reservations recommended. Thurs & Sun 10pm–4am.

1

ALL ABOUT THE BEER

While the bulk of South African **beer** production is monopolized by the huge South African Breweries (SAB; tours Mon 11am and 3pm, Tues–Sat 10am and noon, with additional tours on some days; R80; ☎021 658 7440, ⊛newlandsbrewery.co.za), one of the world's largest beer-makers and the oldest brewery in Africa, the country's beer landscape has undergone a small transformation. Propelled by the global **microbrew** renaissance, microbreweries have popped up nationwide, making excellent versions of popular American and European beer styles such as weiss, IPA, amber and pale ales. Look out for the Western Cape's **Jack Black**, Boston Breweries, Darling Brew, Mitchell's and Cape Brewing Company. An interesting trend is the beer-wine hybrids and experimental beers aged in wine barrels, produced by Cape Town microbreweries such as Devil's Peak and **Triggerfish**, which are taking cues from the local wine-making industry.

Many of the microbreweries offer tours and tastings, and you can dip into the world of South African craft beer and find out about the latest festivals at ⊛brewmistress.co.za. Good places to sample **craft beer** in Cape Town include:

Banana Jam Cafe 157 2nd Avenue, Kenilworth ☎021 674 0186, ⊛bananajamcafe.co.za. Although not centrally located, this Caribbean-themed restaurant is the place to go for a relaxed introduction to South African beer, with an impressive selection of local and imported beers (330ml from R22). Try the six-sample tasting plate. Offering Caribbean food, rum cocktails (happy hour daily 5–6pm) and reggae music, it's next to Kenilworth train station, served by the Southern Line to/from Simon's Town. Tues–Sun 11am–10pm.

★**Devil's Peak Taproom** 95 Durham Ave, Salt River ☎021 200 5818, ⊛devilspeakbrewing.co.za.

Sample the Devil's Peak range in this eclectic bar-restaurant (beers R21–42), adjacent to the brewery. As well as an excellent menu, they offer beer and food pairing (R110). Mon–Sat 11am–2am, Sun noon–6pm.

Mitchell's Scottish Ale House Cnr East Pier & Dock Rd, V&A Waterfront ☎021 419 5074, ⊛mitchells-ale-house.com; map p.103. This no-frills pub serves the half-dozen ales made by the country's oldest microbrewery, Mitchell's of Knysna (established 1983). Mon–Sat 11am–2am, Sun 11am–midnight.

FALSE BAY SEABOARD

★**Brass Bell** Kalk Bay Station, Main Rd, Kalk Bay ☎021 788 5455, ⊛brassbell.co.za; map p.122. The *Brass Bell* has arguably the best location on the peninsula, with False Bay's waves breaking against the wall of its outdoor terrace. There are twin decks overlooking a beach and kids' tidal pool. Drinks include a range of draught beers and wines by the glass (R40), and there's decent fish and chips. Daily 11.30am–10pm.

Cape to Cuba 165 Main Rd, Kalk Bay ☎021 788 1566, ⊛capetocuba.com; map p.122. Bringing Cuban panache to False Bay, this rambling bar-restaurant is crammed to the rafters with a hodgepodge of chandeliers, devotional objects, vases and references to Guevara and Hemingway. It's an atmospheric setting for cocktails (R45) and live music (Sat & Sun 4–7pm). Daily 9am–midnight.

Tiger's Milk Cnr Beach and Sidmouth rds, Muizenberg ☎021 788 1860, ⊛tigersmilk.co.za; map p.122. With a sweeping view of Muizenberg Beach, this coastal outpost of Cape Town cool fills to the gills beneath its exposed beams and high ceiling. Burgers and pizzas are on offer (R100). Drinks around R40. There's also a city-centre branch at 44 Long St. Daily 11am–2am.

ENTERTAINMENT

There is a satisfying and easily accessible range of dramatic and musical performances on offer in Cape Town, and tickets are affordable compared with London or New York. Despite the dearth of government arts funding, there is a creative and lively cultural scene. Check out the offerings at the major venues, the **Baxter**, **Artscape** and the **Fugard Theatre**, where you are likely to find something appealing, be it a play, a classical concert, some opera, contemporary dance or comedy. The daily *Cape Times* and *Argus* carry listings and reviews.

CLASSICAL MUSIC AND AFRICAN OPERA

Classical music has a relatively small but faithful following, with symphony concerts at the City Hall and Baxter Theatre. There are free lunchtime concerts, showcasing the work of students and staff from the University of Cape Town's South African College of Music, on Thursdays at 1pm during term time. These take place in the Baxter's Concert Hall or nearby in the college's Chisholm Recital Room (☎021 650 2626, ⊛music.uct.ac.za). Recitals by visiting soloists and chamber ensembles are put on by an

CAPE JAZZ

1

One of Cape Town's musical treasures is **Cape jazz**, a local take on the jazz genre with distinctive African flavours. Its greatest exponent is the internationally acclaimed **Abdullah Ibrahim**, formerly known as Dollar Brand. Born and raised in District Six, Ibrahim is a supremely gifted pianist and composer, who has for decades produced a hypnotic fusion of African, American and Cape idioms. Some of his renowned recordings include *Mannenberg* and *African Marketplace*, combining the fluttering rhythms of **ghoema** – traditional Cape carnival music – with the call-and-answer structure of African gospel. Other Cape jazz legends include a triumvirate of distinctive (and now-departed) saxophonists: Basil Coetzee, a phenomenal tenor saxophonist; Robbie Jansen, alto player with a raunchy and original style; and Winston "Mankunku" Ngozi, another tenor player, schooled on Coltrane and Wayne Shorter, with his unique brand of African inflections. The annual **Cape Town International Jazz Festival** (late March; ⓦ capetownjazzfest.com) features some of the world's most renowned musicians. Jazz was the soundtrack to the struggle against **apartheid**, with dissenters listening all night in illegal clubs and stars such as Ibrahim, Miriam Makeba and Hugh Masekela going into exile. Jazz-themed township **tours** run by the likes of Coffeebeans Routes (see p.129) tell this story and include performances in musicians' homes. Popular jazz venues are **The Crypt Jazz Restaurant** (1 Wale St; ☎ 079 683 4658, ⓦ thecryptjazz.com), atmospherically located in the crypt beneath St George's Cathedral, and **The Piano Bar** (Cnr Napier and Jarvis sts, De Waterkant ☎ 021 418 1096, ⓦ thepianobar.co.za).

organization called Cape Town Concert Series (ⓦ ctconcerts .co.za), and there are excellent performances in different churches by Cape Town's only Baroque ensemble, Camerata Tinta Barocca (ⓦ bit.ly/2rCamJJ). It's a treat to catch a performance by Cape Town Opera (ⓦ capetownopera .co.za) to hear black South Africans, who dominate opera in South Africa, injecting some powerful new voices and energy into a programme that still predominantly features European works.

THEATRES

Tickets for most of the venues and performances listed are available from Computicket (☎ 0861 915 8000, ⓦ computicket.com) or Webtickets (☎ 086 111 0005, ⓦ webtickets.co.za). Most ticket prices are very reasonable at R100–200.

Alexander Bar, Café & Theatre 76 Strand St ☎ 021 300 1088, ⓦ alexanderbar.co.za; map p.92. An intimate 45-seat space which hosts music, comedy, play readings and theatre, giving a real taste of the South African arts scene. From R40.

Artscape D.F. Malan St, Foreshore ☎ 021 410 9838, ⓦ artscape.co.za; map p.90. Cape Town's most central and largest arts venue, where you can catch contemporary dance, ballet, opera, orchestral music, comedy, musicals and adventurous new dramas.

THE CAPE'S FINEST

Athol Fugard is historically the best-known South African playwright internationally, who continues to produce a steady trickle of innovative plays. Concerned with forging a new African or fusion theatre, Fugard's powerful and nuanced plays evolved from didactic protest theatre; his critically acclaimed, anti-apartheid work includes *Boesman and Lena* (1969) and *"Master Harold" and the Boys* (1982). Director Gavin Hood turned Fugard's novel **Tsotsi** (1980) into the Oscar-winning film of the same name (2005).

More visceral is the brilliant **Brett Bailey**, who creates electrifying, chaotic visual and physical theatre with his company **Third World Bunfight** (ⓦ thirdworldbunfight.co.za). The company does theatre productions, installations, house music shows and opera, mostly concerned with the post-colonial landscape of Africa. The city's most famous son is Cape Town-born Royal Shakespeare Company actor **Sir Antony Sher**, who regularly returns home to appear in fabulous productions.

David Kramer and the late **Taliep Petersen** produced several hit **musicals**, including *District Six – The Musical* (1987). Kramer (ⓦ davidkramer.co.za) is well known for his show *Karoo Kitaar Blues* (2001), presenting the unique finger picking and guitar tunings of marginalized people in the South African hinterland; pick up the soundtrack or DVD from ⓦ takealot.com.

1

CAPE TOWN'S FILM FESTIVALS

Although Cape Town is booming as a film-production centre, local feature films are scarce, though some excellent documentaries are produced. There are several film festivals of note: the **Cape Town International Animation Festival** (ⓦctiaf.com) screens animations from far and wide in March; each June, South Africa's leading film school shows films by students at the **AFDA Experimental Film Festival** (ⓦafda.co.za); the **Encounters South African International Documentary Festival** (ⓦencounters.co.za) in June or July features riveting South African documentaries as well as award winning international films; the **TRI Continental Film Festival** (ⓦtcff.org.za) in October has a strong sociopolitical emphasis on the developing world; and you can catch screenings of around thirty new South African short films and documentaries at the **Cape Town & Winelands Film Festival** (ⓦfilms-for-africa .co.za) in November.

Baxter Theatre Centre Main Rd, Rondebosch ☎021 685 7880, ⓦbaxter.co.za. This mammoth brick theatre complex is the cultural heart of Cape Town, mounting an eclectic programme of innovative plays, comedy festivals, jazz and classical concerts and kids' theatre.

Fugard Theatre Caledon St & Buitenkant St, East City ☎021 461 4554, ⓦthefugard.com. Named after South Africa's greatest living playwright (see p.151), the Fugard runs a cross section of interesting productions in the historic Sacks Futeran building in the old District Six.

Maynardville Open-Air Theatre Wolfe St, Wynberg ☎021 410 9838, ⓦmaynardville.co.za. From late January to late February, an imaginative production of a Shakespeare play is staged under the stars in Maynardville Park. Tickets R80–180. Take a picnic and something warm to wear as the evening wears on.

Moyo Branches at Kirstenbosch Gardens & Bloubergstrand beach ☎021 762 9585, ⓦmoyo.co.za. These African-themed restaurants offer a theatrical experience, with face-painting, colourful costumes, and song and dance to accompany your meal.

Theatre On The Bay 1 Link St, Camps Bay ☎021 438 3301, ⓦpietertoerien.co.za/venues. Puts on Liberace-esque performances of drama, musicals, comedy, cabaret, music and dance. The bistro and bar make it a pleasant venue for an evening out.

COMEDY

Comedy has a well-established following, particularly among coloured Capetonians, making the mix of Afrikaans slang and cultural references educating, if potentially bewildering, for outsiders. A great place to see comedians is the Baxter Theatre (see above) from late July to late August, when Jive Cape Town Funny Festival hosts local and international comedians. Look out for performances by Trevor Noah, Evita Bezuidenhout (aka Pieter-Dirk Uys), Marc Lottering, Nik Rabinowitz, Riaad Moosa and Loyiso Gola.

★**Cape Town Comedy Club** The Pumphouse, 6 Dock Rd, V&A Waterfront ☎021 418 8880, ⓦcapetowncomedy.com. The city's only major dedicated comedy venue, run by comedian Kurt Skoonraad, the former Jou Ma Se Comedy Club features both established and up-and-coming South African comedians. The stone-walled nineteenth-century building with a full restaurant menu available makes for a great evening out.

★**Evita se Perron** Old Darling Station, 8 Arcadia St, Darling ☎022 492 2831, ⓦevita.co.za. Just over an hour's drive north of Cape Town, the town of Darling is well worth visiting for its campily converted train station, which plays host to the satirical shows of Evita Bezuidenhout aka Tannie Evita (South Africa's answer to Dame Edna Everage, created by Pieter-Dirk Uys). It makes for a fantastic day out; check the website for dates.

CINEMAS

Galileo Open Air Cinema Croquet Lawn, Dock Rd, V&A Waterfront ☎071 471 8728, ⓦthegalileo.co.za. Catch an all-time classic under the stars at the Waterfront. Other locations include the Castle of Good Hope, Kirstenbosch Gardens and Cape Winelands. Tickets cost R80–160. Nov–April.

★**Labia** 68 Orange St, Gardens ☎021 424 5927, ⓦthelabia.co.za. The retro Labia (Lah-bia), named after the Italian family that converted it to a theatre, screens an intelligent mix of art-house films, mainstream features and cult classics. Tickets cost R50.

Pink Flamingo Grand Daddy Hotel, 38 Long St ☎021 424 7247, ⓦgranddaddy.co.za. The urban rooftop setting, complete with vintage Airstream trailers and a bar, makes this a memorable option for open-air cinema, with tickets from R125. Mondays at sunset.

Ster-Kinekor Nouveau Victoria Wharf, Waterfront ☎086 166 8473, ⓦsterkinekor.co.za. One of two cinemas in the Victoria Wharf mall, this art-house cinema shows films throughout the day (tickets R65–90).

OUTDOOR ACTIVITIES AND SPORTS

One of Cape Town's most remarkable features is its seamless fusion with Table Mountain National Park, a patchwork of mountains, forests and coastline – all on the city's doorstep. There are few, if any, other cities in the world where outdoor pursuits are so easily available and affordable. You can try activities such as sea kayaking, abseiling, paragliding and scuba diving for considerably less than you might pay in a Western country. Alternatively, hit the spa, swing a golf iron or sink a few beers and watch the cricket, rugby or football – to find out what major fixtures are on, and to buy tickets, visit Ⓦ computicket.com.

SPECTATOR SPORTS

Cricket Keenly followed by a range of Capetonians. The city's cricketing heart is Newlands Cricket Ground, Campground Rd, Newlands (☎ 021 657 2003, Ⓦ cricket .co.za), one of the world's most beautiful grounds. Nestling beneath venerable oaks and the elegant profile of Devil's Peak, it plays host to provincial, test and one-day international matches.

Football Though football matches aren't as well attended as cricket or rugby fixtures, Cape Town football is burgeoning with talent and received a boost from the 2010 FIFA World Cup. The dusty streets of the Cape Flats have produced superb young footballers, including Benni McCarthy (Porto, Ajax Amsterdam, Celta Vigo) and Quinton Fortune (Atlético Madrid, Manchester United). The city's most ambitious and professional club is Ajax (pronounced "I-axe") Cape Town (Ⓦ ajaxct.com), majority owned by its Amsterdam namesake. The most exciting games to attend are those between a local outfit and one of the Soweto glamour teams, Orlando Pirates and Kaizer Chiefs. Matches take place at Cape Town Stadium (see p.113) in Green Point and at Athlone Stadium, off Klipfontein Rd (M18) in the Cape Flats. For fixtures and results visit Ⓦ psl.co.za.

Rugby The Western Cape is one of the world's rugby heartlands, and the game is followed religiously here. Provincial, international and Super Rugby contests are fought on the hallowed turf of Newlands Rugby Stadium, Boundary Rd, Newlands (☎ 021 659 4600, Ⓦ wprugby.co.za).

PARTICIPATION SPORTS AND OUTDOOR ACTIVITIES

Abseiling You can abseil off Table Mountain with Abseil Africa (☎ 021 424 4760, Ⓦ abseilafrica.co.za) for R995. A guided walk up Platteklip Gorge to the plateau costs R495. Canyoning (or kloofing) is also on offer.

Birdwatching The peninsula boasts over four hundred species of birds, with open-water boat trips offering sightings of the area's seven species of albatross. Good places for birdwatching include Lion's Head, Kirstenbosch Gardens and the Cape of Good Hope Nature Reserve, as well as at Kommetjie and Hout Bay; you can find out about birding tours from Birding Africa (☎ 021 531 4592, Ⓦ www.birdingafrica.com) and about boat trips from Cape Town Pelagics (☎ 021 531 4592, Ⓦ www.capetownpelagics.com).

Cycling A great way to take in the scenery, but be vigilant about intolerant car drivers. Africa's biggest social bike ride, the Moonlight Mass (Ⓦ moonlightmass.co.za), heads out once a month at 9pm from the Green Point Circle: this casual night ride began on Twitter to promote cycling and has been gaining popularity ever since. The annual, spectacular Cape Town Cycle Tour travels 109km around the peninsula with forty thousand riders (☎ 087 820 7223, Ⓦ capetowncycletour.co.za). The March event is often cancelled due to strong winds. Pedal Power Association (Ⓦ pedalpower.org.za) organizes and lists road- and mountain-biking events throughout the Cape. Mountain and road bikes can be rented from Downhill Adventures (Shop 1, Overbeek Building, Cnr Kloof and Orange sts ☎ 021 422 0380, Ⓦ downhilladventures.co.za) from R300 a day. It also offers organized cycle outings including trips to Devil's Peak, while Day Trippers (see p.132) offers mountain-bike adventures including Cape Point.

Golf Milnerton Golf Club, Bridge Rd, Milnerton (☎ 021 552 1047 Ⓦ milnertongolf.co.za), is tucked between a lagoon and Table Bay, with classic views of Table Mountain. Another popular course is at Westlake Golf Club, Westlake Ave, Westlake (☎ 021 788 2020, Ⓦ westlakegolfclub .co.za), at the southern end of the Constantia Valley where the M3 south ends. At both, nonmembers pay about R700 to play eighteen holes.

Gyms Virgin Active clubs (☎ 086 020 0911, Ⓦ virginactive .co.za) runs upmarket, well-appointed gyms dotted around the peninsula, all with large swimming pools and spotless changing rooms. Prices vary between gyms, but a month membership at the Netcare Christiaan Barnard Memorial Hospital branch costs R1200.

Hiking The safest and most accessible places to walk are Kirstenbosch Gardens, Table Mountain's Pipe Track, along the Sea Point promenade and the beaches. For hikes up Table Mountain, in Silvermine Nature Reserve and the Cape Point area, contact experienced mountaineer and rock climber Mike Wakeford (☎ 079 772 9808, Ⓦ guidedbymike .co.za; half-day hike R1500, full day R2200) or Margaret Curran, a registered Table Mountain Guide (☎ 021 715 6136, Ⓦ tablemountainwalks.co.za), who offers a classic Table Mountain ascent for R650/person.

Horseriding Cape Town Horse Riding, Sea Cottage Dr, Noordhoek (☎ 021 856 2246, Ⓦ capetownhorseriding .co.za) offers rides in spectacular locations from the Cape

1

Winelands to Noordhoek Beach. Sleepy Hollow Horse Riding, Sleepy Hollow Lane, Noordhoek (☎021 789 2341, ⓦsleepyhollowhorseriding.co.za), also covers Noordhoek Beach, as does Imhoff Farm Village (☎082 774 1191, ⓦimhofffarm.co.za). Charges start around R500 for two hours.

Kayaking Real Cape Adventures (☎082 556 2520, ⓦseakayak.co.za) offers a range of half- and full-day sea-kayaking tours out of Hout Bay and Simon's Town, plus longer packages further afield. Downhill Adventures (see p.153) runs trips from Mouille Point, Simon's Town and Hermanus from R650 per half day. Kayak Cape Town (☎082 501 8930, ⓦkayakcapetown.co.za) offers two-hour trips from Simon's Town to the Boulders Beach penguin colony (R300).

Paragliding Cape Town has great air thermals for paragliding: the usual spot is from Lion's Head, drifting down to Camps Bay. Cape Town Tandem Paragliding (☎076 892 2283, ⓦwww.paraglide.co.za) offers tandem flights from R1150. Wallend-Air School of Paragliding (☎021 762 2441, ⓦwallendair.com), run by Peter Wallenda (one of SA's paragliding champs), offers tandem flights and courses to get your paragliding licence.

Rock climbing High Adventure Africa (☎021 689 1234, ⓦhighadventure.co.za) will take you to unusual and unique locations depending on your ability; packages start at R550/person, for a minimum of two climbers. Try also Mike Wakeford (see p.153). For indoor climbing walls, head to City Rock, 21 Anson Rd, Observatory (☎021 447 1326, ⓦcityrock.co.za).

Running The best places to jog are the Sea Point promenade and Table Mountain's Pipe Track. The Two Oceans Marathon, every Easter Saturday (ⓦwww .twooceansmarathon.org.za), is an international event, where athletes run the arduous 56km ultra-marathon around the peninsula. Trail runs (ⓦtrailrunning.co.za) and Parkruns (ⓦparkrun.co.za) are both popular.

Sandboarding Downhill Adventures (see p.153) is one of the pioneers of this sandy adventure sport. Boards, boots and bindings are all provided, as well as expert instruction for beginners (half day R950, full day R1100). Sunscene Outdoor Adventures (☎021 783 0203, ⓦsunscene.co.za) offers a day's sandboarding (R1200) and combinations with paragliding (R2500), surfing (R1600) or skydiving (R3000).

Scuba diving While the Cape waters are cold, they're also good for seeing wrecks, reefs and magnificent kelp forests. Scuba Shack, Kommetjie (☎072 603 8630, ⓦscubashack.co.za), offers PADI courses, boat and shore dives and snorkelling with Cape fur seals off Kommetjie or Hout Bay.

Skydiving The ultimate way to see Table Mountain and Robben Island is from a tandem jump 3000m up; contact Skydive Cape Town, situated a 40min drive north of Cape Town (☎082 800 6290, ⓦskydivecapetown.za.net; R2300).

Surfing Top surf spots include Big Bay at Bloubergstrand (competitions are held here every summer), Llandudno, Muizenberg and Long Beach near Kommetjie and Noordhoek. Muizenberg is the best place to learn to surf; try Gary's or Surf Shack (see box, p.121). Check out ⓦwavescape.co.za for more information.

Swimming Sea swimming is best on the warmer side of the peninsula at Muizenberg, St James and Fish Hoek beaches. For pools, try Long St Baths, Long St (☎021 422 0100; daily 7am–7pm; R22), a heated 25m indoor pool; or Newlands Swimming Pool (Cnr Main and San Souci rds, Newlands ☎021 444 2828; daily 10am–5pm; R22), an Olympic-sized outdoor pool. The unheated, ocean-side Sea Point Pavilion Swimming Pool (see p.114) is an Olympic-sized filtered seawater pool, with lawns to laze on.

Windsurfing and kiteboarding While most Capetonians moan about the howling southeasterly wind in summer, it's heaven if you're into windsurfing; Langebaan, a 90min drive north of town, is one of the best spots, as the enormous lagoon offers better conditions than the choppier ocean around Cape Town, which has a bigger swell. Cape Sports Centre, Langebaan (☎022 772 1114, ⓦcapesports.co.za), offers a variety of watersports and has a range of accommodation available. Lessons cost R400/hr or R3550/10hr. Surfstore Africa, Muizenberg (☎021 788 5055, ⓦsurfstore.co.za), offers kiteboarding lessons (three-day lessons R4800; tandem ride R1600) as well as stand-up paddleboarding and surfing. On the other side of Cape Town, Cabrinha Kiteboarding, Eden on the Bay Mall, Big Bay (☎021 554 1729, ⓦcabrinha.co.za), provides kitesurfing, surfing and stand-up paddleboarding gear rental and lessons (2hr kitesurfing introduction from R990).

SHOPPING

The **V&A Waterfront** is the city's most popular shopping venue; it has a vast range of shops, the setting on the harbour is lovely and there's a huge choice of places to eat and drink. Nearby, the **Cape Quarter**, accessed off Somerset Road on the border of Der Waterkant and Green Point, is smaller and more exclusive. While most South African malls tend to follow the American model, offering a safe, sterile indoor environment for browsing, banking and eating, the city centre offers much variety: **Long Street** is good for crafts, antiques and secondhand books, while **Bree Street** and **Kloof Steet** are perfect for unique designer goods. For something edgier, the increasingly gentrified city-fringe districts of **Woodstock** (see p.108) and the **East City** have clusters of cutting-edge design shops, markets and some of the city's best restaurants and cafés. Cape Town's Green Map (ⓦgreenmap.org) is a great source of information about ethical shopping, organic markets, delis and health shops.

BOOKS

★**Book Lounge** 71 Roeland St ⓦbooklounge.co.za; map p.90. The most congenial central bookshop, with comfy sofas and a downstairs café, stocks an excellent selection of local books and an imaginative list of imported titles, as well as hosting launches and stimulating events. Mon–Fri 8.30am–7.30pm, Sat 9am–5pm, Sun 10am–4pm.

Clarke's Bookshop 199 Long St ⓦclarkesbooks .co.za; map p.92. The best place for Africana, with well-informed staff and a huge selection of local titles covering literature, history, politics, natural history, the arts and more. It also deals in out-of-print and collectors' editions of South African books. Mon–Fri 9am–5pm, Sat 9.30am–1pm.

Exclusive Books Victoria Wharf, V&A Waterfront ⓦexclus1ves.co.za; map p.103. This chain's well-stocked shelves include magazines and coffee-table books on Cape Town and South African topics. Daily 9am–9pm.

Kirstenbosch Shop Gate 1 & Gate 2, Kirstenbosch National Botanical Gardens, Rhodes Dr, Newlands ⓦsanbi.org. A good selection of natural-history books, field guides and travel guides covering Southern Africa, as well as a range of titles for kids. Gate 1 daily 9am–6pm; Gate 2 daily 9am–4.30pm.

Wordsworth Books Gardens Shopping Centre, off Mill St, Gardens ⓦwordsworth.co.za; map p.133. A good general bookshop, with a strong selection of literature and travel. There's another branch in Sea Point. Mon–Fri 9am–7pm, Sat 9am–5pm, Sun 9am–2pm.

CERAMICS

Art In The Forest Off Constantia Nek Circle, Rhodes Drive, Constantia Nek; Watershed, V&A Waterfront; map p.103. ⓦartintheforest.com. Perched within a hillside forest with sweeping views, this studio and gallery, run by ceramicist Anthony Shapiro, offers workshops, hosts exhibitions of leading South African ceramicists and showcases their Forestware range. Also in the Watershed at the Waterfront. Constantia Nek Mon–Fri 9am–4.30pm, Sat 10am–3pm; Watershed daily 10am–7pm.

Clementina Ceramics The Old Biscuit Mill, 375 Albert Rd, Woodstock. ⓦclementina.co.za. Specializing in ceramics by Clementina van der Walt and other leading South African ceramicists, the shop also stocks unusual cards and other designer crafts. Mon–Fri 9am–5pm, Sat 9am–3pm.

CRAFT MARKETS

★**Greenmarket Square** Burg St; map p.92. City-centre open-air market on a cobbled square, where you can pick presents from all over the continent. To the sound of

bongo drums, marketers tout items from beaded rhinos to batik. Mon–Sat 9am–4pm.

★**Pan African Market** 76 Long St; map p.92. A multicultural hothouse of township and contemporary art, artefacts, curios and crafts. There's also a café specializing in African cuisine, a bookshop, a Cameroonian hair-braider and a West African tailor. Mon–Fri 9am–5pm, Sat 9am–3pm.

Victoria Road Market Between Camps Bay and Llandudno; map p.118. Carvings, beads, fabrics and baskets sold from a roadside market spectacularly sited on a clifftop overlooking the Atlantic. No set times, but usually daily 9am–4pm.

Watershed Dock Rd, V&A Waterfront ⓦwaterfront .co.za; map p.103. A creatively converted warehouse space with more than 150 shops and stalls selling local art, craftwork, fashion, jewellery and more. Daily 10am–7pm.

CRAFT SHOPS

★**Africa Nova** 72 Waterkant St, De Waterkant; map p.103; Watershed, V&A Waterfront ⓦafricanova.co.za. An excellent selection of ethnic crafts and curios as well as contemporary African textiles and artwork, with an emphasis on the individual and handmade. In the Cape Quarter mall, it is a dependable stop for quality souvenirs. There's another branch in the Watershed at the Waterfront. Both branches Mon–Fri 9am–5pm, Sat 10am–5pm, Sun 10am–2pm.

Ethno Bongo 35 Main Rd, Hout Bay ⓦandbanana .com. A charming shop selling quirky and well-priced crafts, jewellery and accessories made from reclaimed wood and recycled metal, as well as textile masks and bags. Mon–Fri 10am–5.30pm, Sat & Sun 10am–4pm.

Kalk Bay Modern 136 Main Rd, Kalk Bay ⓦkalkbay modern.co.za; map p.122. Contemporary photography, ceramics and jewellery as well as fine art and San textiles, with solo and group shows. Daily 9.30am–5pm.

Monkeybiz 61 Wale St, Bo-Kaap ⓦmonkeybiz.co.za; map p.90. A nonprofit income-generating project that sells unique, handmade items by 450 bead artists, aiming to create sustainable employment, particularly for women. Mon–Fri 9am–5pm, Sat 9.30am–1pm.

★**Montebello Design Centre** 31 Newlands Ave, Newlands ⓦmontebello.co.za. A great selection of South African crafts – jewellery, beadwork, ceramics, sculptures and even musical instruments – is created here by small studios, many training people from townships to become artisans. There's also a restaurant under the oaks and occasional night markets. Mon–Fri 9am–5pm, Sat 9am–4pm, Sun 9am–3pm.

1

★**Streetwires** 77 Shortmarket St, Bo-Kaap Ⓦ streetwires.co.za; map p.92. At this shop and working artists' studio, you can try your hand at beading, purchase wire and bead-craft artworks from lion heads to minibus taxis or get something custom made. Mon–Fri 9am–5pm, Sat 9am–1pm.

FOOD AND DRINK
The most convenient supermarkets in central Cape Town are Woolworths (daily 9am–9pm) and Pick n Pay (daily 8am–10pm), both at the Waterfront and elsewhere, and with longer trading hours than most shops.

DELIS
Giovanni's 103 Main Rd, Green Point; map p.114. Excellent breads and Italian foods to take away, and the tempting option of sitting down for a pavement coffee with a view of Cape Town Stadium. Daily 7.30am–8.30pm.
Melissa's 94 Kloof St, Gardens Ⓦ melissas.co.za; map p.133. Delectable imported and local specialities at this popular gourmet deli with the option of eating in. Three Southern Suburbs branches include Constantia Village Courtyard mall. Mon–Sat 7am–7pm, Sun 8am–6pm.
Organic Zone Lakeside Shopping Centre, Main Rd, Lakeside Ⓦ organizone.co.za; map p.122. Always fresh and well-stocked organic fruit and vegetables, as well as grains, honey, breads and dairy products. Mon–Fri 9am–6pm, Sat 8am–5pm, Sun 9am–5pm.

FRESH FISH
Fish Market Mariner's Wharf, Hout Bay Harbour. Fresh seafood from South Africa's original waterfront emporium, although it's less atmospheric than Kalk Bay Harbour. Daily 10am–8.30pm.
Kalk Bay Fish Market Kalk Bay Harbour, off Main Rd, Kalk Bay; map p.122. Buy fresh fish directly from the fishermen and have it gutted and scaled on the spot. Your best bet is during the morning, especially at weekends, though catches are dependent on several factors including the weather. Yellowtail fish are excellent cooked on a braai. Daily 9am–5pm.

MARKETS
Bay Harbour Market 31 Harbour Rd, Hout Bay Ⓦ bayharbour.co.za. Fills a cavernous old fish factory with stalls selling African crafts and local designer clothes, alongside artisan food traders and live acoustic acts. Fri 5–9pm, Sat & Sun 9.30am–4pm.
Blue Bird Garage Food & Goods Market 39 Albertyn Rd, Muizenberg Ⓦ bluebirdgarage.co.za; map p.122. Stalls sell food, wine, craft beer, clothing and jewellery, often accompanied by live music, in a former aeroplane hangar next to the railway line. Fri 4–10pm.

Hope Street (City Bowl) Market 14 Hope St Ⓦ citybowlmarket.co.za; map p.90. This indoor market is as much about meeting for a beer as grazing, with jam-packed stalls laden with everything from curries to burgers and a live band creating a bubbly atmosphere. Thurs 4.30–8.30pm.
Mojo Market 30 Regent Rd, Sea Point Ⓦ facebook .com/TheMojoMarket; map p.114. Beneath Sea Point's colourful *Mojo Hotel*, this market has 45 craft, design and fashion stalls in addition to twenty food vendors, a fresh produce section, 24hr coffee shop, three bars and live entertainment. Daily 8am–11pm.
★**Neighbourgoods Market** Old Biscuit Mill, 373–375 Albert Rd Ⓦ neighbourgoodsmarket.co.za; map p.90. This Victorian warehouse is one of the best places to experience the Cape's serious foodie credentials. Arrive when it opens to beat the devoted crowds, and wander around marvelling at the array of artisanal cheese, wood-fired bread, coffee, beer, fresh flowers, fruit and vegetables. There are also exceptional local designer crafts, homewares and clothing. Sat 9am–3pm.
★**Oranjezicht City Farm Market** Beach Rd, Granger Bay Ⓦ waterfront.co.za/Shop/markets; map p.103. Despite its relocation from the mountainside farm to the Waterfront, locals pick up fabulously fresh organic produce at this market, stopping for a coffee and breakfast or lunch with a beer and sea views. Sat 9am–2pm, though produce sells out fast.
V&A Food Market Dock Rd, V&A Waterfront Ⓦ waterfrontfoodmarket.com; map p.103. An enjoyable if commercialized lunch choice with forty stalls selling food from empanadas to ice cream in the historical Pumphouse. Daily 10am–6pm.

WINE
Caroline's Fine Wines 62 Strand St; map p.92 Ⓦ carolineswine.com. Caroline Rillema has been in the wine business for decades and stocks the Cape's finest and most exclusive wines. Mon–Fri 9am–5.30pm, Sat 9am–1pm.
Vaughan Johnson's Dock Rd, V&A Waterfront Ⓦ vaughanjohnson.co.za; map p.103. One of Cape Town's best-known wine shops, with a range of South African wines, although it can be pricey. Mon–Fri 9am–6pm, Sat 9am–5pm, Sun 10am–5pm.
Wine Concepts Lifestyle on Kloof Centre, 50 Kloof St Gardens Ⓦ wineconcepts.co.za; map p.133. An excellent selection of South African and foreign wines, with local estates often offering tastings. Mon–Fri 10am–7pm, Sat 9am–5pm.

MALLS AND SHOPPING CENTRES
Blue Route Mall Tokai Rd, Tokai Ⓦ blueroutemall .co.za. Major retailers and supermarkets are represented

here, handy if you're staying in Constantia or along False Bay. Mon–Sat 9am–7pm, Sun 9am–5pm.

Cape Quarter 27 Somerset Rd, De Waterkant ⓦcapequarter.co.za; map p.103. This upmarket centre has a range of shops and boutiques selling everything from everyday essentials to quality souvenirs. It's also a pleasant coffee stop with cafés including a branch of the Bootlegger chain. Mon–Fri 9am–6pm, Sat 9am–4pm, Sun 10am–2pm.

Cavendish Square Vineyard Rd, Claremont ⓦcavendish.co.za. An upmarket multistorey complex, the major shopping focus for the Southern Suburbs. Mon–Sat 9am–7pm, Sun 10am–5pm.

Constantia Village Main Rd, Constantia ⓦconstantia village.co.za. Small, exclusive mall including two supermarkets, a post office and general, practical shopping facilities. Next door is the similar Constantia Village Courtyard mall (ⓦconstantiavillagecourtyard.co.za). Mon–Fri 9am–6pm, Sat 9am–5pm, Sun 9am–2pm.

Gardens Centre off Mill St, Gardens ⓦgardens shoppingcentre.co.za; map p.133. This is a good-sized shopping mall with a broad selection of shops in most categories, including two large supermarkets, a bookshop and South African craft and fashion stores. Mon–Fri 9am–7pm, Sat 9am–5pm, Sun 9am–2pm.

Victoria Wharf Breakwater Boulevard, V&A Waterfront ⓦwaterfront.co.za; map p.103. This upmarket mall offers a vast range of shops including the major South African chains, selling books, clothes, food and crafts, as well as two cinemas. Daily 9am–9pm.

MUSIC

African Music Store 62 Lower Main Rd, Observatory ⓦfacebook.com/TheAfricanMusicStore. This small shop specializes in African music from around the continent. It also has a modest collection of instruments, such as shakers and thumb pianos. Mon–Sat 10.30am–5.30pm.

Mabu Vinyl 2 Rheede St, Gardens ⓦmabuvinyl.co.za; map p.133. The aficionado's choice for a great selection of both new and secondhand CDs, vinyl and even cassettes. Since it featured in *Searching for Sugarman*, the Oscar-winning documentary about Sixto Rodriguez, it has made a splash with tourists who drop by to see some musical history. Mon–Fri 9am–7pm, Sat 9am–6pm, Sun 11am–3pm.

Musica Cavendish Square, Claremont ⓦmusica.co.za. A musical megastore for mainstream pop purchases, as well as African music, classical, jazz, rock, DVDs and video games. Mon–Sat 9am–7pm, Sun 9am–5pm.

DIRECTORY

Banks and exchange Main bank branches with ATMs are easy to find in the shopping areas of the city. For currency exchange try American Express (ⓦamericanexpressforex.co.za), with branches including the Gardens Centre (Mon–Fri 9am–5.30pm, Sat 9am–2pm) and, for currency purchases only, the international arrivals hall at Cape Town International Airport (daily 5am–11pm).

Consulates Most embassies are in Pretoria, but countries including Canada (ⓦsouthafrica.gc.ca), the Netherlands (ⓦbit.ly/NetherlandsWorldwideSA), the UK (ⓦbit.ly /BritishConsulateCapeTown) and the USA (ⓦza .usembassy.gov) also have a consulate in Cape Town.

Hospitals The two largest private hospital groups, Netcare (emergency response ☎082 911, ⓦwww.netcare.co.za) and Mediclinic (emergency response operated by ER24 ☎084 124, ⓦmediclinic.co.za), have hospitals all over the Cape Peninsula. Cape Town Mediclinic, 21 Hof St, Oranjezicht (☎021 464 5500; emergency ☎021 464 5555), is close to the city centre in the City Bowl; Christiaan Barnard Memorial Hospital, Cnr D.F. Malan and Rua Bartholomeu Dias Plain (☎021 441 0000), is Netcare's most central private hospital; and Constantiaberg Mediclinic, Burnham Rd, Plumstead, Southern Suburbs (☎021 799 2911; emergency ☎021 799 2196), is the closest private hospital to the False Bay seaboard. The state

ambulance emergency number is ☎10177; from cellphones, ☎112. For more routine medical care, Netcare runs over two dozen private Medicross medical centres (ⓦmedicross.co.za) across the Western Cape, which are not open 24 hours, but do operate extended hours.

Laundry Most backpacker hostels have laundry facilities, while guesthouses, hotels and B&Bs usually offer a laundry service for a charge.

Mobile phone rental Available at the airport and elsewhere from car-rental companies as well as B4i.travel (ⓦb4i.travel) and Vodacom Rentals (ⓦvodacomrentals .co.za).

Pharmacies There are chemists with extended opening hours throughout the city. A dependable chain is Clicks (ⓦclicks.co.za), which has branches in Victoria Wharf (daily 9am–9pm; ☎021 418 3800) and Gardens Centre (Mon–Fri 8.30am–8pm, Sat 8am–5pm, Sun 9am–5pm; ☎021 418 3800) malls, both offering a clinic as well as a pharmacy.

Police The central police station is at 28 Buitenkant St (☎021 467 8001, ⓦwww.saps.gov.za). For emergencies, call ☎10 111; from cellphones, ☎112.

Post office The main post office is on the corner of Plein and Darling streets (Mon, Tues, Thurs & Fri 8am–4.30pm, Wed 8.30am–4.30pm, Sat 8am–1pm).

The Western Cape

OSTRICH FARM, OUDTSHOORN

The Western Cape

The most mountainous and arguably the most beautiful of South Africa's provinces, the Western Cape is also the most popular area for foreign tourists to visit, with the best roads and infrastructure in the country. Curiously, it's the least African province. Visitors spend weeks here without exhausting its attractions, but may leave slightly disappointed, never having quite experienced an African beat. Of South Africa's nine provinces, only the Western Cape and the Northern Cape do not have an African majority; one person in five here is black African, and the largest community, making up 55 percent of the population, are coloureds – people of mixed race descended from white settlers, indigenous Khoisan people and slaves from the East.

Although the Western Cape appears to conform more closely to the developed world than any other part of the country, the impression is superficial. Behind the prosperous feel of the Winelands and the Garden Route lies the reality of people living in poverty in shacks on the outskirts of well-to-do towns, and farm workers on minimum wages. Nevertheless, it's hard not to be moved by the sensuous beauty of the province's mountains, valleys and beaches. A short drive from Cape Town, **the Winelands** are a gourmet's paradise – a place to enjoy fine food and wine while visually feasting on verdant valleys, dramatic mountains and handsome Cape Dutch architecture. Another popular outing is the **Whale Coast**, centred around Hermanus, the best area in the country for shore-based whale-watching in the winter months. Further east takes you to the **Overberg** – roughly the area between Cape Agulhas

DE HOOP NATURE RESERVE

Highlights

❶ Wine estate lunches Eat alfresco and quaff fine vintages at the top restaurants in South Africa, while gazing out at beautiful vineyards and mountains. **See p.167 & p.178**

❷ De Hoop Nature Reserve Massive dunes and edge-to-edge whales make this the most exciting coastal nature reserve in the country. **See p.194**

❸ Rooibos tea tours See where rooibos tea is grown, and enjoy a tea tasting. **See p.208**

❹ Oudrif An exceptional and remote retreat lodge on the edge of a gorge in the dry and

dramatic redstone back country of the Cederberg. **See p.210**

❺ Ocean safaris Learn about whales and dolphins on an excursion around Plettenberg Bay. **See p.230**

❻ Storms River Mouth A dramatic section of coast, where hillside forests drop away to rocky coastline and the Storms River surges out of a gorge into the thundering ocean. **See p.233**

❼ Route 62 This mountainous inland route takes you via dozy villages, across spectacular passes and through semi-desert. **See p.237**

HIGHLIGHTS ARE MARKED ON THE MAP ON P.162

and Mossel Bay along the coast, and inland to Swellendam – a region that remains hidden behind the mountains.

North of Cape Town, the less popular, remote and windswept **West Coast** is usually explored during the wild-flower months of August and September, when visitors converge on its centrepiece, the West Coast National Park. Its other major draw, 200km north of Cape Town on the N7, is the **Cederberg**, a rocky wilderness with hikes and hidden rock-art sites – the work of indigenous **San**

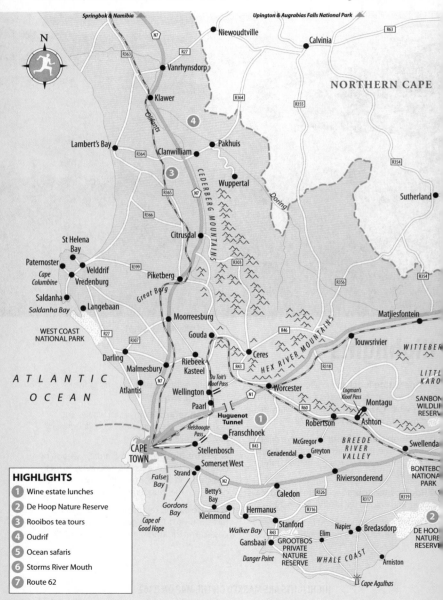

HIGHLIGHTS

1 Wine estate lunches
2 De Hoop Nature Reserve
3 Rooibos tea tours
4 Oudrif
5 Ocean safaris
6 Storms River Mouth
7 Route 62

people, who were virtually extinguished in the nineteenth century. In marked contrast, the best-known feature of the Western Cape is the **Garden Route**, a drive along the N2 that extends between Cape Town and Port Elizabeth (see p.302). **Public transport** along the route is better than anywhere else in the country, partly because it's a single stretch of freeway, and tour operators have turned it into South Africa's most concentrated strip for packaged **adventure sports** and **outdoor activities**. At its heart is the busy town of **Knysna**, with its magnificent surrounding

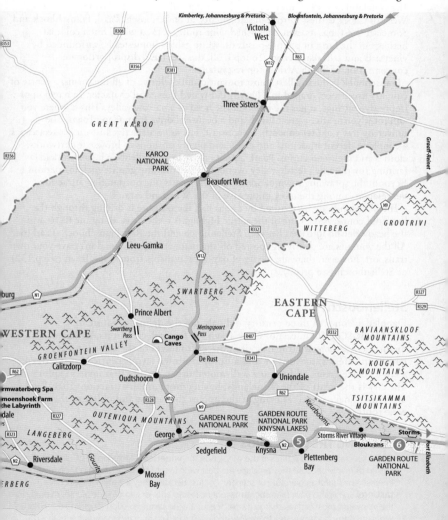

WESTERN CAPE

woodland. Even more rewarding is **Route 62**, the inland counterpart to the Garden Route, which takes you through the well-preserved small towns and dramatic mountain scenery of **Little Karoo**.

The Winelands

The Winelands are all about indulgence – eating, drinking and relaxing. Each of the Western Cape's earliest European settlements, at Stellenbosch, Paarl, Franschhoek and Somerset West, has its own established wine route, packed with Dutch colonial heritage in the form of picture-postcard, white gabled homesteads, surrounded by vineyards and tall, slatey crags. To top it all, the area has a disproportionate concentration of South Africa's top restaurants.

Franschhoek is the smallest, most romantic and exclusive of all the towns: a centre of culinary excellence, draped in a heavily cultivated Provençal character. In a region of impressive settings, it has the best – at the head of a narrow valley. This is where you aim for if you're after a great lunch and a beautiful drive from Cape Town. The university town of **Stellenbosch**, by contrast, has some attractive historical streetscapes, a couple of decent museums and cafés, and plenty of shops to browse for artworks, clothes and high-end curios. **Paarl**, a pretty drive from Stellenbosch, is a workaday farming town set in a fertile valley overlooked by stunning granite rock formations. Beyond, the sprawling town of **Somerset West** boasts one outstanding attraction, **Vergelegen**, among the most impressive of the Wineland estates.

The Winelands are best visited by car, as half the pleasure is driving through the beautiful countryside. One of the scenic highlights is the drive along the **R310** over the heady **Helshoogte Pass** between Stellenbosch and the R45 Franschhoek–Paarl road. All the wineries are clearly signposted off the main arteries. If you don't have your own transport, however, there are plenty of day-trips available from Cape Town (see p.132) or Stellenbosch (see p.167).

Stellenbosch

Dappled avenues of three-century-old oaks are the defining feature of **STELLENBOSCH**, 46km east of Cape Town – a fact reflected in its Afrikaans nickname *Die Eikestad* (the oak city). Street frontages of the same vintage, pavement cafés, water furrows and a European town layout centred on the Braak, a large village green, add up to a well-rooted urban texture that invites exploration. The city is the heart of the Winelands, having more urban attractions than Paarl or Franschhoek, as well as being at the hub of the largest and oldest of the Cape **wine routes**.

TACKLING THE WINELANDS

Of the several hundred estates in the Winelands, the **wineries** selected in this Guide were not picked primarily because they produce the best wine (although some do), but for general interest – beautiful architecture or scenery – or just because they are fun. While all offer **tastings**, some also have fantastic, atmospheric restaurants, or can provide picnics to enjoy in the vineyards; most estates charge a small fee for a wine-tasting session (anything up to R60). When visiting, choose an area to explore and don't try to cram in too many wineries in a day unless you want to return home in a dizzy haze; note, too, that several wineries are closed on Sundays, or have shorter opening hours in winter.

The definitive and widely available John Platter's **South African Wine Guide** (also available as an iPhone app) is a useful companion, which provides ratings of the produce of pretty well every winery in the country.

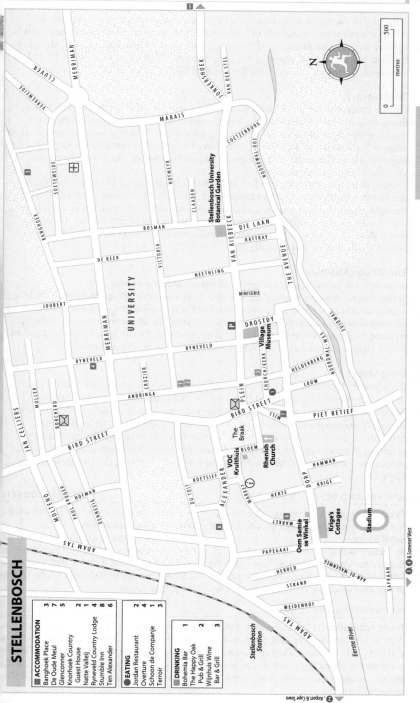

STELLENBOSCH

ACCOMMODATION

Banghoek Place	3
De Oude Meul	7
Glencomner	5
Knorhoek Country Guest House	2
Natte Valleij	1
Ryneveld Country Lodge	4
Stumble Inn	8
Ten Alexander	6

EATING

Jordan Restaurant	2
Overture	4
Schoon de Companje	1
Terroir	3

DRINKING

Bohemia Bar	1
The Happy Oak Pub & Grill	2
Wijnhuis Wine Bar & Grill	3

Stellenbosch University Botanical Garden

Stellenbosch University Botanical Garden

Drostdy

Village Museum

The Braak

VOC Kruithuis

Rhenish Church

Oom Samie se Winkel

Krige's Cottages

Stadium

Stellenbosch Station

Eerste River

N

500 metres

Airport & Cape Town

S. Somerset West

2

The city is also home to Stellenbosch University, but even the heady promise of plentiful alcohol and thousands of students hasn't changed the fact that at heart this is a rather conservative place, home to some notable intellectual and cultured Afrikaner families. It was once the engine room of apartheid, and fostered the likes of Dr H.F. Verwoerd, the prime minister who dreamed up Grand Apartheid.

Brief history

One of **Simon van der Stel**'s first actions after arriving at the Cape in 1679 to assume the governorship was to explore the area along the Eerste River (literally "the first river"), where he came upon an enchanting little valley. Within a month it appeared on maps as Stellenbosch ("Stel's bush"), the first of several places around the Cape that he was to name after himself or members of his family; another was Simonsberg, the mountain overlooking the town.

Charged by the Dutch East India Company with opening up the Cape interior, Van der Stel soon settled the first **free burghers** in Stellenbosch. Within eight years, sixty freehold grants had been made, and within two decades Stellenbosch was a prosperous, semi-feudal society dominated by landowners. By the end of the century there were over a thousand houses and some substantial burgher estates in and around Stellenbosch, many of which still exist.

The Village Museum

18 Ryneveld St · Mon–Sat 9am–5pm, Sun 10am–4pm · R25 · ⓦ stelmus.co.za/village_museum.htm

Stellenbosch's museum highlight is the extremely enjoyable **Village Museum**, which cuts a cross section through the town's architectural and social heritage by means of four adjacent dwellings from different periods, including the **Blettermanhuis**, an archetypal eighteenth-century Cape Dutch house. They're beautifully conserved and furnished in period style, and you'll meet the odd worker dressed in period costume.

Dorp Street

Dorp Street, Stellenbosch's best-preserved historic axis, is well worth a stroll just to soak up the ambience of buildings, gables, oaks and roadside water furrows. **Krige's Cottages**, an unusual terrace of historic townhouses at nos. 37–51, between Aan-de-Wagenweg and Krige Street, were built as Cape Dutch cottages in the first half of the nineteenth century; Victorian features were added subsequently, resulting in an interesting hybrid, with gables housing Victorian attic windows and decorative Victorian verandas with filigree ironwork fronting the elegantly simple Cape Dutch facades.

ARRIVAL AND DEPARTURE
STELLENBOSCH

By car All the wineries are an easy hour's drive from Cape Town; if you're not staying overnight, you can easily visit several in a day.

By train Metrorail trains (☎0800 65 64 63, ⓦ capemetrorail.co.za) run between Cape Town and Stellenbosch roughly every ninety minutes during the day, and take about an hour; use this line with caution – trains run through some rough areas of the Cape Flats and the service can be slow and unreliable.

By bus The Baz Bus (ⓦ bazbus.com) runs daily from Cape Town to Somerset West, where it drops passengers off at the BP filling station next to the *Lord Charles Hotel*. Some hostels operate shuttle services from there, but you need to arrange this in advance.

INFORMATION AND TOURS

Tourist information The tourist office, at 36 Market St (Mon–Fri 8am–5pm, Sat 9am–2pm, Sun 9am–2pm; ☎021 883 3584, ⓦ stellenbosch.travel), can reserve accommodation, though you'll need to book well in advance in summer, when rooms can be hard to find, and the weather is at its best.

Walking tours Leaving from the tourist office in the morning and afternoon, a walking tour is a great way to see the architectural highlights and get a feel of the town (by appointment with Sandra Krige ☎021 887 9150; R100 per person; minimum of six in a group).

WINE TOURS

If you want to visit the vineyards, ask at the tourist office, which represents a number of wine tour operators and can steer you towards the right one, depending on your time and budget. Expect to pay a minimum of R350 for a half-day tour and R550 for a full-day tour, including tasting fees. Recommended companies include:

Bikes n Wines 074 186 0418, bikesnwines.com. If you are feeling energetic, you can tour the vineyards by bicycle. Bikes n Wines offer a half-day tour (R550) with an overnight mountain bike trail option (R1950).

Easy Rider Wine Tours 021 886 4651, winetour .co.za. Based at *Stumble Inn* backpackers (see below), Easy Rider Wine Tours offers packages to four wineries (R500), with lunch at Franschhoek thrown in.

Equine Sport Centre 071 597 2546, equine sportcentre.co.za. Explore the vineyards on horseback, with rides at Morgenhof, Knorhoek and Remhoogte

Wine Estates. Beginners and experienced riders are catered for; shorter rides cover one wine estate (R220), half-day rides cover two (R600) and full-day outings (R900) visit all three – with stops for tastings and great views of the sea and Table Mountain on some rides.

The Vine Hopper 084 492 4992, vinehopper .co.za. A convenient hop-on-hop-off bus, which stops at a dozen wineries, including the Van Ryn's Brandy Cellar. Call in advance for their days and routes, which vary depending on the season and demand (day-ticket R240).

ACCOMMODATION

Accommodation can be hard to find in Stellenbosch in the summer months, when you can expect to find many places full, so book well in advance. The tourist office can be helpful in finding you a place.

Banghoek Place 193 Banghoek Rd 021 887 0048, banghoek.co.za; map p.165. Slightly more upmarket sister hostel to *Stumble Inn* (see below), with mostly en-suite double, twin and triple rooms that offer terrific value, and three small dorms. There are discount packages available, which include two nights' accommodation plus a wine tour. Dorms R180, doubles R600

De Oude Meul 10A Mill St, off Dorp St 021 887 7085, deoudemeul.com; map p.165. Located in the middle of town on a fairly busy street, above an antique shop, these pleasant rooms are good value. Ask for one at the back to ensure a quiet night's sleep. R1400

Glenconner Jonkershoek Rd, 4km from the centre 021 886 5120 or 082 354 3510, glenconner @icon.co.za; map p.165. Self-catering and B&B options are available at these pretty farm cottages with horses grazing in the fields below. The tranquil valley setting is spectacular, close to the walks in the Jonkershoek Nature Reserve. Breakfast can be taken under an old oak tree. R1200

Knorhoek Country Guest House Knorhoek Wine Estate, off the R44, 7km north of town 021 865 2114, knorhoek.co.za; map p.165. With a bucolic setting in a snug valley, these old farm buildings have been turned into modern guest rooms and cottages. Each has a sunny patio, a lawn, and a feeling of calm luxury, plus guests can wander the gardens and vineyard. Doubles R1200

Natte Valleij On the R44, 12km north of town 021 875 5171, nattevalleij.co.za; map p.165. Guests have a choice of a large cottage sleeping six, a smaller one-bedroom unit attached to an old wine cellar or an en-suite room with its own entrance. There's a swimming pool, and breakfast is served on the veranda. R900

Ryneveld Country Lodge 67 Ryneveld St 021 887 4469, ryneveldlodge.co.za; map p.165. Elegant late nineteenth-century building, now a National Monument furnished with Victorian antiques. The rooms are spotless, with the two best upstairs and leading onto a wooden deck. There are also two family cottages, which sleep up to four, and a pool. R1700

Stumble Inn 12 Market St 021 887 4049, stumbleinnbackpackers.co.za; map p.165. The town's best and longest-standing hostel, spread across two houses and run by friendly, switched-on staff. Just down the road from the tourist office, the hostel is also noted for its good-value tours. Dorms R150, doubles R410

Ten Alexander 10 Alexander St 021 887 4414, 10alexander.co.za; map p.165. This guesthouse is functional, quiet and pleasant, and very well run by the chatty owner. Rooms are small and spotless, plus there's a nice garden and pool. Facilities exist for self-catering, and there's a minimum stay requirement of two nights. R1850

EATING

Lunch or dinner at a vineyard is one of best eating experiences in South Africa, and almost every wine estate has a restaurant or does pre-booked picnics. Several of the **vineyard restaurants** are among the top ten in the country, so you'll need to reserve a table weeks or months in advance, particularly in the summer. In Stellenbosch there are some good **pavement cafés** and restaurants along Dorp and Church streets, with a nice crop in the leafy De Wet Square. On Saturday mornings (9am–2pm), it's worth visiting the fabulous and

2

very popular **farmers' market** (ⓦslowmarket.co.za) in the Oude Libertas Estate grounds, off the R310 just south of the centre, where you'll find a good range of locally produced food.

Jordan Restaurant Jordan Wine Estate, 11.5km west of Stellenbosch, off the R310 ☎021 881 3612, ⓦjordanwines.com; map p.165. One of the country's top chefs rules the roost here and never fails to please. Expect exquisite food, service and wines, which can be enjoyed on a deck overlooking a lake and distant mountains. The set menu is based on seasonal ingredients (R350 for two courses, R425 for three), and you can even visit the cheese-tasting room in between courses. *The Bakery at Jordan* (ⓦthebakery.co.za) does interesting breakfasts, lighter meals and cheese and charcuterie platters (R200). Restaurant summer Mon–Wed & Sun noon–2pm, Thurs–Sat noon–2pm & 6.30–8.30pm; winter Tues & Wed noon–2pm, Thurs–Sat noon–2pm & 6.30–9pm; Bakery daily 8am–4pm.

Overture Hidden Valley Wine Estate, Annandale Rd ☎021 880 2646, ⓦdineatoverture.co.za; map p.165. Top of the town in more ways than one, *Overture* looks down from the hills into the Annandale Valley – and it consistently wins awards as one of the country's top restaurants. Based on classical French cuisine, the dishes are made from scratch with fresh ingredients and interesting contemporary twists.

Sample the works with the six-course tasting menu (R690). Book way in advance. Wed & Sun noon–3pm, Thurs–Sat noon–2.30pm & 7–11pm.

★**Schoon de Companje** Corner of Bird & Church streets ☎021 883 2187, ⓦdecompanje.co.za; map p.165. A café combined with a deli, with various nooks to settle down in with some good coffee and croissants. The pavement seating is one of the big draws in summer, as are the artisan ice creams and locally brewed Stellenbrau craft beer. For lunch try the quinoa tabbouleh salad (R75), and a variety of sandwiches. Mon 7am–1.30pm, Tues–Sun 7.30am–5pm.

Terroir Kleine Zalze Wine Estate, Strand Rd (R44) ☎021 880 0717, ⓦkleinezalze.com; map p.165. Some 8km from Stellenbosch on a wine and golf estate, *Terroir* has a surprisingly relaxed dining room (for a nationally acclaimed restaurant) and tables outside under shady oaks. The fairly expensive French-inspired chalkboard menu is based as far as possible on local seasonal produce, including appealing desserts like marinated mango with coconut, vanilla brioche and banana (R110). Mon–Sat noon–2.30pm & 6.30–9pm, Sun noon–2.30pm.

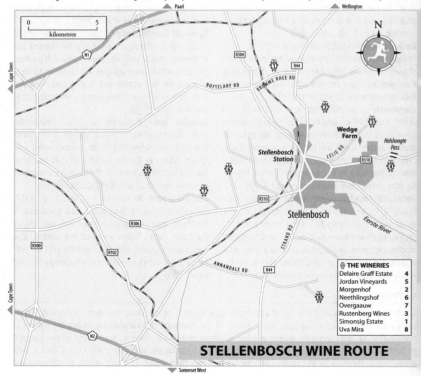

⚐ THE WINERIES	
Delaire Graff Estate	4
Jordan Vineyards	5
Morgenhof	2
Neethlingshof	6
Overgaauw	7
Rustenberg Wines	3
Simonsig Estate	1
Uva Mira	8

STELLENBOSCH WINE ROUTE

WINERIES AROUND STELLENBOSCH

Stellenbosch was the first locality in the country to wake up to the marketing potential of a **wine route**, launching its first in 1971. Although the region accounts for a small fraction of South Africa's land under vine, its wine route is the most extensive, with around three hundred establishments. If you're planning your own route, all the wineries are clearly signposted off the main arteries. Several offer sit-down luxury meals or picnic baskets (reserve in advance), but many only lay on tastings. Opening hours may be shorter in the winter.

Delaire Graff Estate On the Helshoogte Pass, 6km east of Stellenbosch along the R310 to Franschhoek ☎021 885 8160, ⓦdelairewinery.co.za. The highly regarded *Delaire Graff* restaurant has possibly the best views in the Winelands, looking through pin oaks across the Groot Drakenstein and Simonsig mountains and down into the valley. Outstanding wines aren't hard to find here: the majority are whites, but they also produce a great red blend. A tasting of three wines costs R50. Mon–Sat 10am–5pm, Sun 10am–4pm; restaurant (Mon–Sat noon–2pm & 6.30–9pm, Sun noon–2pm).

Jordan Vineyards 11.5km west of Stellenbosch off the R310 ☎021 881 3441, ⓦjordanwines.com. A pioneer among the new-wave Cape wineries, Jordan's high-tech cellar and modern tasting room is complemented by its friendly service. The drive there is half the fun, taking you into a *kloof* bounded by vineyards that get a whiff of the sea from both False Bay and Table Bay, which has clearly done something for its output – it has a list of outstanding wines as long as your arm and a highly rated restaurant (see opposite). Tasting R120 for six premier wines, redeemable against purchases. Daily 9am–4pm.

Morgenhof 4km north of Stellenbosch on the R44 ☎021 889 2007, ⓦmorgenhof.com. A French-owned chateau-style complex on the slopes of the Simonsberg, Morgenhof has a bright and airy tasting room and bar, with delicious light lunches served outside. They produce the excellent Morgenhof Estate red blend and a few brilliant whites (including a Chenin Blanc, Chardonnay and Sauvignon Blanc) under the same label, while the Fantail range is their second, more affordable, label. Tasting R35 for five wines. Mon–Fri 9am–5pm, Sat & Sun 9am–4pm; restaurant daily 9am–4pm.

Neethlingshof 6.5km west of Stellenbosch on Polkadraai Rd (the R306) ☎021 883 8988, ⓦneethlingshof.co.za. Centred around a beautifully restored Cape Dutch manor dating back to 1814, and reached down an avenue of stone pines, Neethlingshof's first vines were planted in 1692. Their flagship wines include the Caracal (a Bordeaux-style red blend) and the Pinotage Old Post. Tasting R40 for five wines. Mon–Fri 9am–4.30pm, Sat & Sun 10am–4pm; restaurant Mon, Tues & Sun 9am–5pm, Wed–Sat 9am–9pm.

Overgaauw 6.5km west of Stellenbosch, off the M12 ☎021 881 3815, ⓦovergaauw.co.za. Notable for its elegant Victorian tasting room, this pioneering estate was the first winery in the country to produce Merlots, and it's still the only one to make a wine with Sylvaner grapes, a well-priced, easy-drinking dry white. Tasting R30 for five wines, redeemable against purchase. Mon–Fri 9am–4pm, by appointment only.

Rustenberg Wines Off Lelie Rd, Ida's Valley ☎021 809 1200, ⓦrustenberg.co.za. One of the closest estates to Stellenbosch, Rustenberg is also one of the most attractive, reached after a drive through orchards, sheep pastures and tree-lined avenues. An unassuming working farm, it has a romantic pastoral atmosphere, which contrasts with its architecturally stunning tasting room in the former stables. Their high-flyers include the Peter Barlow Cabernet Sauvignon, and Five Soldiers Chardonnay. Tasting R25 for six wines, redeemable against purchase. Mon–Fri 9am–4.30pm, Sat 10am–3.30pm, Sun 10am–3pm.

Simonsig Estate 9.5km north of Stellenbosch, off Kromme Rhee Rd, which runs between the R44 and the R304 ☎021 888 4900, ⓦsimonsig.co.za. This winery has a relaxed outdoor tasting area under vine-covered pergolas, offering majestic views back to Stellenbosch of hazy stone-blue mountains and vineyards. The first estate in the country to produce a bottle-fermented bubbly nearly fifty years ago, it also makes a vast range of first-class still wines. Tasting R75 for five bubblies and R50 for three wines. Mon–Fri 8.30am–4.30pm, Sat 8.30am–3.30pm, Sun 11.30am–2.30pm.

★**Uva Mira** About 8km south of Stellenbosch, off Annandale Rd, which spurs off the R44 ☎021 880 1683, ⓦuvamira.co.za. Enchanting boutique winery that punches above its weight, worth visiting just for the winding drive halfway up the Helderberg. The highly original tasting room, despite being fairly recently built, gives the appearance of a gently decaying historic structure, and there are unsurpassed views from the deck across mountainside vineyards to False Bay some 50km away. Their 2006 Chardonnay stands out as an international winner and their flagship Bordeaux-style red blend is also noteworthy. Tasting R50 for three wines. Daily 10am–6pm.

2

DRINKING

The pavement cafés of Stellenbosch, especially those in Church Street, have some great places to drink, while in the evenings the student presence ensures a relaxed (and occasionally raucous) drinking culture.

Bohemia Bar 1 Victoria St ☎ 021 887 8375, Ⓦ facebook.com/bohemiabar; map p.165. There's a good chance of catching local live music here (usually alternative punk rock), with Thursday as the most reliable night. During the day, there is a pleasant wrap-around veranda with tables, looking onto the street. Food, such as pizzas and toasties, is exceptionally cheap, or try an egg and bacon breakfast (R30). Daily 11am–2am.

The Happy Oak Pub & Grill 62 Andringa St ☎ 021 882 9672, Ⓦ thehappyoak.co.za; map p.165. Central and cheap, this vintage-style place is where you can get a variety of beers and ciders, a bottle of decent local wine (R80) and meals like steak and egg (R70, but there's not much on offer for vegetarians. Popular with students. Daily 11am–2am.

Wijnhuis Wine Bar & Grill Cnr Church & Andringa sts ☎ 021 887 5844, Ⓦ wijnhuis.co.za; map p.165. Dazzling array of local wines sold by the glass, and artisanal beers to sample (R50), in a clean-cut environment with rather stylish wooden tables and fittings. It's a good place for steaks, bruschetta, salads, pasta, fish, and game dishes. Daily 8am–11pm.

Somerset West and around

The only compelling reasons to trawl out to the unpromising town of **SOMERSET WEST**, 50km east of Cape Town along the N2, are for **Vergelegen** on Lourensford Road, and its immediate neighbour **Morgenster**, which are officially part of the Helderberg wine route, but can easily be visited from Stellenbosch, just 14km to the north.

Vergelegen

Daily 9.30am–4pm • R20 • Wine tasting R50 for six wines • ☎ 021 847 2100, Ⓦ vergelegen.co.za

An architectural treasure as well as producing a stunning range of wines, **Vergelegen** represents a notorious episode of corruption at the Cape in the early years of Dutch East India Company rule. Built by Willem Adriaan van der Stel, who became governor in 1699 after his father Simon retired, the estate formed a grand Renaissance complex in the middle of the wild backwater that was the Cape at the beginning of the eighteenth century. Willem Adriaan acquired the land illegally and used Company slaves and resources to build Vergelegen and farm vast tracts of surrounding land. He also abused his power as governor to corner most of the significant markets at the Cape. When the Company became aware of this, they sacked him and ordered Vergelegen to be destroyed. It's believed that the destruction wasn't fully carried out and the current building is thought to stand on the original foundations.

Vergelegen was the only wine estate visited by Queen Elizabeth II during her 1995 state visit to South Africa – a good choice, as there's enough here to occupy even a monarch for an easy couple of hours. The **interpretive centre**, just across the courtyard from the shop at the building entrance, provides a useful history and background to the estate. Next door, the **wine-tasting centre** offers professionally run sampling with a brief talk through each label. The **homestead**, which was restored in 1917 to its current state by Lady Florence Phillips, wife of a Johannesburg mining magnate, can also be visited. The massive grounds, planted with chestnuts and camphor trees and with ponds around every corner, make this one of the most serene places in the Cape.

EATING   VERGELEGEN

★Vergelegen ☎ 021 847 2131, Ⓦ vergelegen .co.za. One of the best ways to enjoy the surroundings at Vergelegen is to order a gourmet picnic basket (R250 per person; summer only), which will be laid out under the camphor trees, complete with checked table cloth and wicker basket. *The Stables* offers breakfast, lunch and coffees in a bistro environment, while *Camphors Restaurant* is one of the top Winelands eating experiences – the seasonal menu might include steak tartare from their own Nguni cattle (R395 for three courses). Booking well in advance is absolutely essential. The Stables daily 9.30am–4pm; Camphors Restaurant Wed, Thurs & Sun noon–2.30pm, Fri & Sat noon–2.30pm & 6.30–9.30pm.

Morgenster

Mon–Sat 10am–5pm, Sun 10am-4pm • R65 for wine & chocolate tastings, R40 for olive oil tasting • ☎ 021 852 1738, ⓦ morgenster.co.za

Vergelegen's immediate neighbour, **Morgenster** sits in an exquisite rustic setting and has a tasting room with a veranda looking onto a lovely lake and hazy mountains in the distance. As well as producing two stellar blended reds, the estate offers the unusual addition of olive tasting, with three types of olive, three types of oil (including an award-winning cold-pressed extra virgin olive oil) and some delicious olive paste.

Paarl

Although **PAARL** is attractively ensconced in a fertile valley brimming with historic buildings, at heart it's a parochial *dorp*, lacking the sophistication of Stellenbosch or the striking setting of Franschhoek. It can claim some virtue, however, from being a prosperous farming centre that earns its keep from the agricultural industries – grain silos, canneries and flour mills – on the north side of town, and the cornucopia of grapes, guavas, olives, oranges and maize grown on the surrounding farms.

Brief history

In 1657, five years after the establishment of the Cape settlement, a party led by **Abraham Gabbema** arrived in the Berg River Valley to look for trading opportunities with the Khoikhoi, and search for the legendary gold of Monomotapa. With treasure on the brain, they awoke after a rainy night to see the silvery dome of granite dominating the valley, which they dubbed Peerlbergh (pearl mountain); its modified form, **Paarl**, became the name of the town.

Thirty years later, the commander of the Cape, Simon van der Stel, granted strips of the Khoikhoi lands on the slopes of Paarl Mountain to French Huguenot and Dutch settlers. By the time Paarl was granted town status in 1840, it was still an outpost at the edge of the Drakenstein Mountains, a flourishing wagon-making and last-stop provisioning centre. The town holds deep historical significance for the two competing political forces that forged modern South Africa. **Afrikanerdom** regards Paarl as the hallowed ground on which their language movement was born in 1875 (see box, p.173), while the **ANC** and everyone else remember it as the place from which Nelson Mandela made the final steps of his long walk to freedom, when he walked out of **Groot Drakenstein Prison** (then called Victor Verster) in 1990.

Paarl Museum

303 Main St • Mon–Fri 9am–4pm, Sat 9am–1pm • R5 • ☎ 021 872 2651

Housed in a handsome Cape Dutch building, originally a parsonage that was rebuilt in 1787, the contents of the **Paarl Museum** don't quite match up to its exterior. There are some good examples of Cape Dutch antique furniture (including a fine linen press), and an interesting collection of ceramics and silver, all of which reflect the early life of the town. There's also some coverage of the indigenous Khoisan populations of the area and the changes that came with European colonization, including slavery, and regular temporary exhibitions.

Taal Monument

Daily 9am–5pm • Free • To get here, drive south along Main St past the head office of the KWV, and follow the signs to your right up the slope of the mountain

The other sight of interest in Paarl is the grandiose **Taal Monument**, an apartheid-era memorial to the Afrikaans language, standing just outside the centre on top of Paarl Mountain. Designed by architect Jan van Wijk and erected in 1975, it consists of a highly abstract arrangement of domes, columns and obelisks made from cement and granite, and was once as important a place of pilgrimage for Afrikaners as the Voortrekker Monument in Pretoria. From the coffee and curio shop you can admire a

2

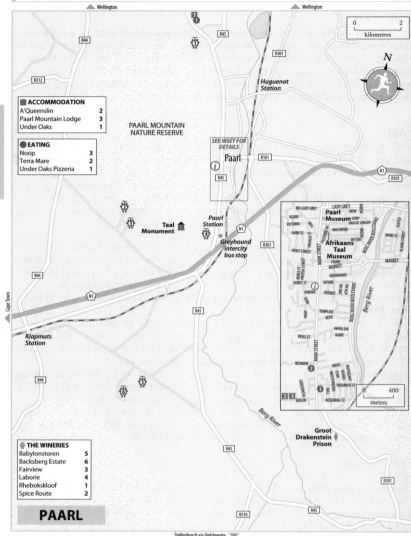

ACCOMMODATION
A'Queenslin	2
Paarl Mountain Lodge	3
Under Oaks	1

EATING
Noop	3
Terra Mare	2
Under Oaks Pizzeria	1

THE WINERIES
Babylonstoren	5
Backsberg Estate	6
Fairview	3
Laborie	4
Rhebokskloof	1
Spice Route	2

PAARL

truly magnificent panorama across to the Cape Peninsula and False Bay in one direction and the Winelands ranges in the other.

Groot Drakenstein (Victor Verster) Prison

Roughly 9km south of the N1 as it cuts through Paarl, along the R301 (the southern extension of Jan van Riebeeck St)

The **Victor Verster Prison**, renamed **Groot Drakenstein** in 2000, was Nelson Mandela's last place of incarceration. It was through the gates at Victor Verster that he walked to his freedom on February 11, 1990, and it was here that the first images of him in 27 years were broadcast (under the Prisons Act, not even old pictures of him could be published during his imprisonment). The working jail looks rather like a boys' school fronted by rugby fields beneath hazy mountains, and there are no tours given. Outside the entrance, a large statue of Mandela – with defiantly raised fist – was erected in 2008.

ARRIVAL AND DEPARTURE
PAARL

By bus Daily Greyhound intercity buses from Cape Town (1hr) stop at the Monument Shell Garage, on the corner of Main Road and South Street, about 2km from the tourist office.

By train Metrorail and Spoornet services from Cape Town (18 daily; 1hr 15min) pull in at Huguenot Station in Lady Grey Street at the north end of town, near to the central shops. Use the trains with caution.

INFORMATION AND ACTIVITIES

Tourist information The office at 216 Main St (Mon–Fri 8am–5pm, Sat 9am–1pm & Sun 10am–1pm ☎ 021 872 4842, ⓦ paarlonline.com) has a good selection of maps, including the wine routes, and can help with booking accommodation.

Horse and quad-bike trails Based at the Rhebokskloof wine estate (see box, p.174), Wine Valley

Horse Trails (☎ 083 226 8735 or ☎ 083 657 5135, ⓦ horsetrails-sa.co.za) offers one- to four-hour equestrian trails for novices and experts through the surrounding countryside. Prices start from R450 for a one-hour trail. For experienced riders, there is a 3hr beach trail at Grotto Bay, from R1500 per person. They also do quad-bike trips which start at R450 for 1hr.

ACCOMMODATION

A'Queenslin 2 Queen St ☎ 021 863 1160, ⓦ queenslin .co.za; map opposite. Two en-suite rooms with their own entrances and garden spaces, and three doubles that share a bathroom, in a split-level family home set in a quiet part of town, bounded on one side by vineyards and towered over by Paarl Rock. The rooms are large, each with a deck or patio, and private and limited self-catering is possible – there's a fridge and microwave. R900

Paarl Mountain Lodge 21 Enslin St ☎ 021 869 8045, ⓦ paarlmountainlodge.co.za; map opposite. Four simple, clean white en-suite bedrooms in a large house on a quiet street on the slopes of the Paarl mountain, 2km from the centre. There's secure parking, a deck with mountain views where you can drink your complimentary wine on arrival, and a swimming pool. Breakfasts are done buffet-style. R900

THE HISTORY OF AFRIKAANS

Afrikaans is South Africa's third mother tongue, spoken by fifteen percent of the population and outstripped only by Zulu and Xhosa. English, by contrast, is the mother tongue of only nine percent of South Africans.

Signs of the emergence of a new Southern African dialect appeared as early as 1685, when a Dutch East India Company official from the Netherlands complained about a "distorted and incomprehensible" version of Dutch being spoken around modern-day Paarl. By absorbing English, French, German, Malay and indigenous words and expressions, the language continued to diverge from mainstream Dutch, and by the nineteenth century was widely used in the Cape by both white and coloured speakers, but was looked down on by the elite.

In 1905, **Gustav Preller**, a young journalist from a working-class Boer background, set about reinventing Afrikaans as a "white man's language". He aimed to eradicate the stigma of its "coloured" ties by substituting Dutch words for those with non-European origins. Preller began publishing the first of a series of populist magazines written in Afrikaans and glorifying Boer history and culture. Pressure grew for the recognition of Afrikaans as an official language, which came in 1925.

When the **National Party** took power in 1948, its apartheid policy went hand in hand with promoting the interests of its Afrikaans-speaking supporters. Afrikaners were installed throughout the civil service and filled most posts in the public utilities. Despite there being more coloured than white Afrikaans speakers, the language quickly became associated with the apartheid establishment. This led directly to the **Soweto uprising** of 1976, when the government attempted to enforce Afrikaans as the sole language of instruction in African schools. At the same time, the repression of the 1970s and 1980s and the forced removals under the Group Areas Act led many coloured Afrikaans-speakers to adopt English in preference to their tainted mother tongue.

There are few signs that Afrikaans will die out. Under the new constitution, existing language rights can't be diminished, which effectively means that Afrikaans will continue to be almost as widely used as before. But it is now as much with coloured as with white people that the future of the **taal** (language) rests.

Under Oaks Off R45, 8km north of Paarl ☎021 869 8045, ⓦunderoaks.co.za; map p.172. Good-value, luxurious rooms, with comfy beds and plush linen, in a purpose-built, modern guesthouse. Breakfast is served in a historic wine-estate dining room overlooking pastures, while dinner is at their pizzeria (see opposite). You can try their flagship Sauvignon Blanc or Cabernet Sauvignon at the adjoining boutique winery. **R1350**

WINERIES AROUND PAARL

There are a couple of notable wineries in Paarl itself, but most are on farms in the surrounding countryside. Boschendal, one of the most popular of these, is officially on the Franschhoek wine route (see p.179), but is within easy striking distance of Paarl. Most of the wineries have a good-quality restaurant and some have accommodation in beautiful rooms – often a more appealing option than staying in central Paarl.

★ **Babylonstoren** Simondium Rd ☎021 863 3852, ⓦbabylonstoren; map p.172. Popular with tourists, and for good reason, Babylonstoren is beautifully set against the high Drakenstein mountains, with extensive gardens, ducks, chickens and olive trees as well as many acres of vineyard; there's also a shop selling South African cookery books and upmarket crafts. They're the new kid on the block in terms of wine, but are already winning a reputation for their red blend, Babel, and their Viognier. Of the two restaurants, the *Green House* is less formal while *Babel* is known for more traditional South African food. Entry to the estate costs R20. Estate daily 9am–5pm (last entry 4pm; Green House daily 10am–4pm; Babel Mon & Tues 7–8.30pm, Wed–Sun noon–3.30pm & 7–8.30pm.

Backsberg Estate 22km south of Paarl on Simondium Rd (WR1) ☎021 875 5141, ⓦbacksberg .co.za; map p.172. Notable as the first carbon-neutral wine estate in South Africa, Backsberg produces some top-ranking red blends, especially the Cabernet and Merlot, and a delicious Chardonnay in its Black Label ranges. Outdoor seating, with views of the rose garden and vineyard on the slopes of the Simonsberg, makes this busy estate a nice place to while away some time. There's also a restaurant and a maze to get lost in. Tasting R40 for five wines. Tasting Mon–Fri 8am–5pm, Sat 8.30am–4pm, Sun 9.30am–4.30pm; restaurant daily 11.30am–3pm.

The Fairview Estate Suid-Agter Paarl Rd, on the southern fringes of town ☎021 863 2450, ⓦfairview.co.za; map p.172. One of the most enjoyable of the Paarl estates (especially for families), with a resident population of goats who clamber up the spiral tower, featured in the estate's emblem, at the entrance. A deli sells breads and preserves, and you can sample and buy the goats', sheep's and cows' cheeses made on the estate, while wine tasting costs R40 for six wines and a cheese selection. Fairview is an innovative, family-run place, but it can get a bit hectic when the tour buses roll in. The *Goatshed* restaurant offers a cheese platter with ten cheeses, bread and preserves (R115) and is well known for its Sunday lunch. Tasting and restaurant daily 9am–5pm.

Laborie Taillefert St ☎021 807 3390, ⓦlaboriewines.co.za; map p.172. One of the most impressive Paarl wineries, all the more remarkable for being right in town. The beautiful manor is fronted by a rose garden, acres of close-cropped lawns, historic buildings and oak trees – with the Taal Monument towering neaby. There's a truly wonderful tasting room with a balcony that juts out over the vineyards trailing up Paarl Mountain, as well as a great restaurant with terrace seating offering good views. Their flagship is the Jean Taillefert Shiraz, but their brandy is also worth investigating. Tasting R25 for five wines. Mon–Sat 9am–5pm, Sun 11am–5pm.

Rhebokskloof Signposted off the R45, 11.5km northwest of Paarl ☎021 869 8386, ⓦrhebokskloof.co.za; map p.172. A highly photogenic wine estate, Rhebokskloof sits at the foot of sculptural granite *koppies* overlooking a lake with a shaded terrace for summer lunches and gourmet meals. Meat is the house speciality, with exciting combinations of flavours that are both Cape and international. It's also a good place for morning or afternoon teas, and they can prepare picnics on the lawns outside (R400 for two), while Sunday lunch buffets (R225) are a tremendous draw. In terms of wine, Shiraz is where they make their mark. Wine tasting R20 for five wines. Daily 9am–5pm.

Spice Route Suid-Agter Paarl Rd ☎021 863 5222, ⓦspiceroute.co.za; map p.172. The Spice Route farm offers unusual tastings drawn from several artisanal producers who have grouped together in different buildings on the same premises. You can try beer at the *Cape Brewing Company*, hand-made chocolate tasting at the *DV Artisan Chocolate* (R150), or local grappa at *La Grapperia Pizza and Tapas Bar*, the only place open after 5pm. Other residents include an art gallery, glass blowers and farm shop. It's very popular with groups, so book in advance for tastings. Daily 9am–5pm.

EATING

A working town, Paarl has none of the Winelands foodie pretensions of Franschhoek or Stellenbosch, but you'll find a number of places along the main street for a decent coffee or a meal, as well as a couple of outstanding places in the surrounding vineyards.

Noop 127 Main St ☎ 021 863 3925, ⓦ noop.co.za; map p.172. This cool pavement wine bar and restaurant, in a period house, has an extensive list of wines by the glass, and is well regarded for its steaks (R140) and seafood. Vegetarians can find at least one starter, salad or main. Risotto with truffle oil is a favourite (R120). Mon–Sat 11am–9.30pm.

★ **Terra Mare** 90A Main St ☎ 021 863 4805; map p.172. Italian- and Mediterranean-influenced dishes, such as three-mushroom risotto for starters (R95) and chalkboard specials like ostrich fillet (R170), which use local ingredients and are made with considerable flair. The glass-and-steel restaurant has great sweeping views of the Paarl Mountain. Mon–Sat 11am–2pm & 6–10pm.

Under Oaks Pizzeria Paarl Main Rd, 8km from the centre ☎ 021 869 8962; map p.172. The best thing about eating a delicious wood-fired pizza (R80) here, and drinking wine from grapes grown on the farm, is the setting beneath majestic oaks. The relaxed vibe has made it very popular with local families. Tues–Sat 11.30am–8.30pm, Sun noon–3.30pm.

Franschhoek

If eating, drinking and sleeping is what the Winelands is really about, then **FRANSCHHOEK** is the place that does it best. Its late Victorian and more recent Frenchified rustic architecture, the terrific setting (hemmed in on three sides by mountains), the vineyards down every other backstreet, have created a place you can really lose yourself in, a set piece that unashamedly draws its inspiration from Provence.

Between 1688 and 1700, about two hundred **French Huguenots**, desperate to escape religious persecution in France, accepted a Dutch East India Company offer of passage to the Cape and the grant of lands. They made contact with the area's earliest settlers, groups of **Khoi herders**, whom the white settlers gradually dispossessed. By 1713 white hegemony was established and the area was known as *de france hoek* (the French corner). Though French-speaking died out within a generation, many of the estates are still known by their original French names. Franschhoek itself occupies parts of the original farms of La Cotte and Cabrière and is relatively young, having been established around a church built in 1833.

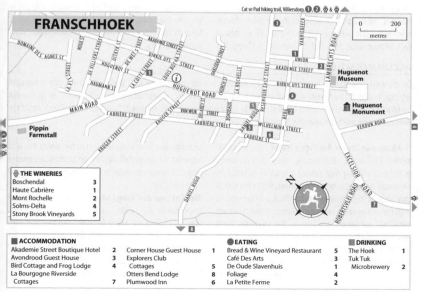

FRANSCHHOEK

THE WINERIES

Boschendal	3
Haute Cabrière	1
Mont Rochelle	2
Solms-Delta	4
Stony Brook Vineyards	5

■ ACCOMMODATION

Akademie Street Boutique Hotel	2	Corner House Guest House	1
Avonrood Guest House	3	Explorers Club	
Bird Cottage and Frog Lodge	4	Cottages	5
La Bourgogne Riverside		Otters Bend Lodge	8
Cottages	7	Plumwood Inn	6

● EATING

Bread & Wine Vineyard Restaurant	5
Café Des Arts	3
De Oude Slavenhuis	1
Foliage	4
La Petite Ferme	2

■ DRINKING

The Hoek	1
Tuk Tuk	
Microbrewery	2

Huguenot Memorial Museum and Huguenot Monument

Lambrechts Rd • Mon–Sat 9am–5pm, Sun 2–5pm • R10 • ☎ 021 876 2532

If you drive through Franschhoek, you can't really miss the **Huguenot Memorial Museum** because it's adjacent to the town's most obvious landmark, the **Huguenot Monument**, in a prime position at the head of Huguenot Road, the main road through town. The monument is dominated by three tall, interlocking arches, symbolizing the Holy Trinity, in front of which is a statue of a young woman standing on top of a terrestrial globe. The museum provides comprehensive coverage of Huguenot history and culture, and of their contribution to modern South Africa.

Museum van de Caab

Solms-Delta Wine Estate, 12km north of Franschhoek along the R45 • Sun–Thurs 9am–5pm, Fri & Sat 9am–6pm • Free •
ⓦ solms-delta.co.za/museums-archaeology

The highly recommended **Museum van de Caab** gives a condensed and riveting slice through South African vernacular history as it happened on the Solms-Delta farm and its surroundings. Housed alongside the atmospherically understated tasting room in the original 1740s gabled Cape Dutch cellar, the display begins with Stone Age artefacts found on the site and goes on to trace the arrival of the aboriginal Khoisan people, their colonization by Europeans, the introduction of slavery and how this eventually evolved into the apartheid system, and its eventual demise. There's a separate music museum outlining the history of Cape music, with a display of indigenous instruments and regular performances and demonstrations.

INFORMATION AND ACTIVITIES   FRANSCHHOEK

Tourist information Just north of the junction with Kruger St, the tourist office, 62 Huguenot Rd (Mon–Fri 8am–5pm, Sat 9am–6pm, Sun 9am–4pm; ☎ 021 876 2861, ⓦ franschhoek.org.za), has some excellent maps of the village and its winelands.

Equestrian wine tours Paradise Stables, Roberstsvlei Rd (☎ 021 876 2160 or ☎ 084 586 2160, ⓦ paradisestables .co.za) runs tours that visit Rickety Bridge and Mont Rochelle wineries: wine tasting is included in the price, though lunch is not (2hr 30min in the saddle, 30–45min stop at each winery; R850; Mon–Sat 8.45am and 1.15pm). The

well-behaved Arabian horses are ridden with halters, and beginners can be accommodated. The farm itself, where you begin the ride, has a couple of cottages for rent (R500).
Hiking The best hike in the vicinity is the Cat se Pad (Cat's Path), which starts as you head out of town up the Franschhoek Pass. The walk leads into *fynbos* with proteas, and gives instant access to the mountains surrounding the valley, with good views. The first 2km section gets you to the top of the pass, and you can keep going for another 10km in the direction of Villiersdorp (though you don't actually reach it).

ACCOMMODATION

On the whole, guesthouse accommodation here is pricey, but the rooms are of high quality and frequently in beautiful settings; budget accommodation is hard to find, but there are a couple of reasonably priced self-catering cottages and a backpackers. It can be hard to find a bed in Franschhoek during the summer, so book as far ahead as possible. Some of the wine estates outside town also offer luxury rooms.

★ **Akademie Street Boutique Hotel** 5 Akademie St ☎ 082 517 0405, ⓦ aka.co.za; map p.175. Luxury guesthouse offering total privacy in each of its tastefully decorated suites set in beautiful gardens, with a number of striking artworks. Facilities include DVDs, a fridge stocked with free drinks and a saltwater swimming pool. Gourmet breakfasts are served poolside by the charming hosts who'll happily recommend a restaurant and book a table for you. **R5000**
Avondrood Guest House 39 Huguenot St ☎ 021 876 2881, ⓦ avondrood.com; map p.175. A guesthouse with

six rooms in a beautifully restored home, which has won accolades for the level of comfort and aesthetic experience offered. There are extensive lawns, a manicured garden and a pool. **R2850**
Bird Cottage and Frog Lodge Verdun Rd, 4.5km from town ☎ 021 876 2136, ✉ graham@radionet.co.za; map p.175. Two artistically furnished cottages that each sleep four, surrounded by beautiful gardens close to the mountains, with a dam to swim in. It's as remote as you'll get this close to Franschhoek, as well as being thoroughly laidback and exceptional value. **R800**

RIGHT VINEYARD IN THE WINELANDS >

2

La Bourgogne Riverside Cottages Excelsior Rd ☎ 021 876 3245, ⍟ labourgogne.co.za; map p.175. Six simply but very tastefully furnished converted labourers' cottages set in gardens along a river. They are self-catered but you can get breakfast and coffee from the deli/farmshop on the property. The working farm presses its own olive oil and produces wines, including the highly rated Progeny Sémillon (R250); there's free wine tasting for guests. **R900**

Corner House Guest House Cnr Riebeeck & Union sts ☎ 021 876 4729, ⍟ thecornerhouse.co.za; map p.175. One of the few moderately priced popular guesthouses, Dutch-run *Corner House* offers six bright and spotless rooms, and a pretty garden with pool. It's a good base from which to explore the area. **R1400**

★**Explorers Club Cottages** Cabrière St ☎ 021 876 4229, ⍟ explorersclub.co.za; map p.175. A collection of centrally located self-catering houses – all luxurious, modern and tasteful. Each house sleeps two to ten people. *The Map Room* is ideally suited to couples, with a living space upstairs and folding glass doors opening onto a terrace with vineyard and mountain views. Their portfolio now includes cottages on La Cotte wine farm, 7km from Franschhoek. *Explorers Club* can also arrange meals to be delivered to you, or the services of a private chef. **R2850**

Otters Bend Lodge Dassenberg Rd ☎ 021 876 3200, ⍟ ottersbendlodge.co.za; map p.175. Rustic lodge with double and twin-bedded cabins, dorms, and camping on the lawn, 5min drive from town and surrounded by orchards and vineyards. There is an inviting communal area, complete with a roaring fire in winter, a well-equipped kitchen and an outside braai area. Camping **R200**, dorms **R200**, doubles **R550**

Plumwood Inn 11 Cabrière St ☎ 021 876 3883, ⍟ plumwoodinn.com; map p.175. Unfailingly excellent boutique guesthouse with smart, clean and modern furnishings. There's a close attention to detail throughout – from the custom-made cotton tablecloths to the luxurious beds and bathrooms, and the impeccable service. **R3000**

EATING

Eating and drinking is what Franschhoek is all about, and its **restaurants** rate among the country's best. The cuisine tends to be French-inspired, but with an emphasis on local ingredients. Restaurants in town are concentrated along Huguenot Rd, but there are a number of excellent alternatives in the surrounding wine estates, several of which do picnics in their beautiful grounds. Booking is essential, particularly for the smarter places, and winter opening hours are reduced. Every Saturday (9am–3pm) there is a Farmers' Market in the churchyard on Main Rd.

Bread & Wine Vineyard Restaurant Moreson Farm, Happy Valley Rd ☎ 021 876 3692, ⍟ moreson.co.za; map p.175. Signposted off the R45 and surrounded by lemon orchards and vineyards, this is a genial and child-friendly venue, consistently in the top twenty restaurants in the country. The two- or three-course menus (R300) change with the seasons, and the chef Neil smokes the meat and fish himself, while his wife Tina bakes outstanding bread. Daily noon–3pm.

Café Des Arts 7 Reservoir St, next to the library ☎ 021 876 2952, ⍟ cafedesarts.co.za; map p.175. Service and food are consistently good here, with unfussy but flavoursome dishes, all made from fresh, local ingredients. It's a relaxed spot, good for coffee and something delicious from their small bakery, or one of their excellent breakfasts – check out the truffled scrambled eggs with wilted baby spinach (R95). Mon–Sat 8am–3pm & 6.30–10pm.

De Oude Slavenhuis Huguenot Museum, Huguenot St ☎ 021 876 2192; map p.175. Reasonably priced and uncomplicated food served both indoors and outdoors under umbrellas, with plenty of play space on the lawns for children. Dishes include smoked salmon and scrambled egg (R65), salads, tea and scones. Daily 8am–4pm.

★**Foliage** 11 Huguenot Rd ☎ 021 876 2328, ⍟ foliage .co.za; map p.175. Sophisticated comfort food, with a forest-to-plate philosophy showcasing the chef's skills in foraging, pickling and preserving, using free-range meat, wild vegetables and herbs. The pan-fried angel fish with river greens and Cape Malay veloute (R150) is especially good. Mon–Sat noon–3pm & 6–9pm.

La Petite Ferme Franschhoek Pass Rd ☎ 021 876 3016, ⍟ lapetiteferme.co.za; map p.175. With gorgeous views across a vineyard-covered valley, this restaurant is a Franschhoek institution, and sets the bar extremely high. Slow-roasted lamb has been on the menu for thirty years and never fails to please (R190). Daily: summer noon–4pm & 7–9pm; winter noon–4pm. Daily noon–4pm, plus dinner from 6.30pm on Fridays in summer.

DRINKING

The Hoek 36 Huguenot St ☎ 079 451 3019; map p.175. This is the go-to place for coffee fanatics, being the only pure espresso bar in town – and it's a double-shot unless you request otherwise. There's excellent ice cream too, a friendly atmosphere, and relaxed seating at wooden tables. Mon–Sat 7am–3pm, Sun 8am–3pm.

Tuk Tuk Microbrewery 14 Huguenot Rd ☎ 021 492 2207, ⍟ tuktukbrew.com; map p.175. Delicious craft beers with a European café feel. Their Mexican bites, like a plate of cheese quesadillas with chicken, tomato and cream sauce and guacamole, will go down well (R100). Daily 11am–10pm.

WINERIES AROUND FRANSCHHOEK

Franschhoek's wineries are small enough and sufficiently close together to make it a breeze to visit two or three in a morning. Heading north through town from the Huguenot Monument, you'll find most of the wineries signposted off Huguenot Rd and its extension, Main Rd; the rest are off Excelsior Rd and the Franschhoek Pass Rd.

Boschendal Pniel Rd, just after the junction of the R45 and R310 to Stellenbosch ☏021 870 4274, ⓦboschendalwines.com; map p.175. One of the world's longest-established New World wineries, Boschendal draws around 200,000 visitors a year with its impressive Cape Dutch buildings, tree-lined avenues, beautiful gardens, restaurants and cafés and, of course, its wines. Of their six labels, the Pavilion range delivers high-class, well-priced plonk (Shiraz–Cabernet Sauvignon, Rosé and a white blend), while the top ranges include wines such as the Cecil John Reserve Shiraz and Sauvignon Blanc. Tastings cost R50. Try one of their famous picnic baskets (R360 for two) on the extensive lawns or, in the summer, their full-moon picnics. Daily 9am–4.30pm.

Haute Cabrière About 2km from town along the Franschhoek Pass Rd ☏021 876 8500, ⓦcabriere .co.za; map p.175. Atmospheric winery notable for its Pinot Noirs and colourful wine-maker Achim von Arnim, whose presence guarantees an eventful visit; try to catch him or, more commonly now, his son Takuan, when they demonstrate *sabrage* – slicing off the upper neck of a bubbly bottle with a French cavalry sabre. Cabrière is noted for its top-notch Pierre Jourdan range of sparkling wines. Tasting R30 for five wines and R60 for five bubblies. Mon–Fri 9am–5pm, Sat 10am–4pm, Sun 11am–4pm.

★**Mont Rochelle** Dassenberg Rd ☏021 876 2770, ⓦmontrochelle.co.za; map p.175. Set against the Klein Dassenberg, Mont Rochelle has one of the most stunning settings in Franschhoek – one seized upon by Sir Richard Branson and given a contemporary and vibrant makeover. Chardonnay is what they do best here, but don't overlook their stellar Sauvignon Blanc and Syrah. It is best visited in the evening (bar and restaurant open until 10pm) to catch the sunset or moonrise. They also offer very comfortable accommodation and have two restaurants and picnics available (R360 for two). Tasting for five wines R45. Daily 10am–6pm.

★**Solms-Delta** 13km north of Franschhoek along the R45 ☏021 874 3937, ⓦsolms-delta.co.za; map p.175. Pleasantly bucolic Solms-Delta produces unusual and consistently outstanding wines, which, on a summer's day, you can taste under ancient oaks at the edge of the vineyards with a picnic (R365 for two people). Half the profits from the wines produced go into a trust that benefits residents of the farm and the Franschhoek Valley. The Solms-Wijn de Caab range includes the excellent Hiervandaan (an unusual blend dominated by Shiraz, and including Carignan, Mourvèdre and Viognier grapes) and the even more highly rated Amalie (vine-dried Grenache Blanc and Viognier). Tasting R25 for five wines. Daily 9am–5pm.

Stony Brook Vineyards About 4km from Franschhoek, off Excelsior Rd ☏021 876 2182, ⓦstonybrook.co.za; map p.175. Family-run boutique winery, with just 140,000 square metres under vine, that produces first-rate wines, including its acclaimed flagship Ghost Gum Cabernet Sauvignon, which takes its name from a magnificent old tree outside the rather informal tasting room. Tastings are convivial affairs conducted by the owners and are by appointment only (R35). Mon–Fri 10am–5pm, Sat 10am–1pm.

The Overberg interior and the Whale Coast

East of the Winelands lies a vaguely defined region known as the **Overberg** (Afrikaans for "over the mountain"). In the seventeenth century, when Stellenbosch, Franschhoek and Paarl were remote outposts, everywhere beyond them was, to the Dutch settlers, a fuzzy hinterland drifting off into the arid sands of the Karoo.

Of the two main routes through the Overberg, the **N2** strikes out across the interior, a four- to five-hour stretch of sheep, wheat and mountains. Just north of the N2 is **Greyton**, a charming, oak-lined village used by Capetonians as a relaxing weekend retreat, and the starting point of the **Boesmanskloof Traverse** – a terrific two-day trail across the mountains into the Karoo. The historic Moravian mission station of **Genadendal**, ten minutes down the road from Greyton, has a strange Afro-Germanic ambience that offers an hour's pleasant strolling. **Swellendam**, with its well-preserved streetscape with serene Cape Dutch buildings and superb country museum, is favoured for the first night's stop on a Garden Route tour.

CALEDON SPA

The thermal springs at **Caledon Spa and Casino** (Tues–Sun 10am–7pm; R150; ⓣ028 214 5100), signposted off the N2, make a fun day-trip out of Cape Town, or a restorative stop off the N2. The Victorians built a pool filled with steamy, naturally brown water where the Khoi people had once had wallowing holes, and now there is a series of pools of varying temperatures to luxuriate in. There's also a steam room and sauna, but bring your own towel and robe.

2

The real draw of the area is the **Whale Coast**, close enough for an easy outing from Cape Town. **Hermanus**, the main town in the area, has good swimming beaches and plentiful accommodation, but owes its fame to its status as the whale-watching capital of South Africa. The whole of this southern Cape coast is, in fact, prime territory for land-based whale-watching. Also along this section of coast is **Cape Agulhas**, the southernmost point on the continent, where rocks peter into the ocean. Nearby, and more exclusive, is **Arniston**, one of the best-preserved fishing villages in the country, and a little to its east the **De Hoop Nature Reserve**, an exciting wilderness of bleached dunes, craggy coast and more whales.

Greyton

Tucked away at the edge of the Riviersonderend (meaning "river with no end") Mountains, the small, peaceful village of **GREYTON** is a favourite weekend destination for well-heeled Capetonians, based around a core of thatched Georgian and Victorian buildings with pretty gardens and shaded by grand old oaks. It offers good guesthouses, outdoor cafés, craft beer, hand-made chocolate, craft shops and places to walk, most notably the **Boesmanskloof Traverse** hike, which crosses the mountains to a point 14km from McGregor. Less arduous are the strolls through the **Greyton Nature Reserve** at the edge of town.

ARRIVAL AND INFORMATION — GREYTON

By car Greyton is 145km from Cape Town, a journey of around two and a half hours. Turn off the N2, just west of Caledon, and follow the signposted, sealed R406 for 30km – ignore any other signs to Greyton on the N2 as they are for unsealed, difficult roads. There is no organized public transport.

Tourist information The tourist office is at 29 Main St, along the main road as you come into town (Mon–Fri 9am–5pm, Sat & Sun 10am–1pm; ⓣ028 254 9564 or ⓣ028 254 9414, ⓦgreytontourism.com), where you can get help with accommodation.

ACCOMMODATION

If you're here in winter, it's advisable to stay somewhere with a fireplace as it can get really cold in this mountainous terrain; conversely, look for shady gardens in summer when the valley bakes.

Anna's Cottages 1 Market St ⓣ084 764 6012, ⓦgreyton-accommodation.com. A treehouse with an oak tree growing through it, and three lovely self-catering garden cottages, all attractively and eclectically furnished. Mark Cottage is a large space with two double-bed alcoves, indoor and outdoor cooking facilities, fairy lights and fireplaces. A minimum stay of two nights is a requirement. Cottages R800, treehouse R1400

High Hopes 89 Main Rd ⓣ028 254 9898, ⓦhighhopes.co.za. One of the best B&Bs in town, in a beautiful country-style retreat centre, set in large gardens with a swimming pool. There are five rooms, one of which, Camellia, is a self-contained unit with a kitchen, which can be taken on a B&B or self-catering basis. They also offer a variety of therapies, including massage. R1800

EATING

On Saturdays there's a morning **market** at the corner of Main Road and Cross Market Street, opposite the church (10am–noon), to which locals bring produce, including organic vegetables, and well-priced cheeses, decadent cakes, breads, biscuits and preserves.

Abbey Rose Main Rd ⓣ028 254 9470, ⓦabbeyrose.co.za. A nice garden and streetside-setting, with a delightful rose garden and hearty but uncomplicated food; try the oxtail stew (R150) and the *malva* pudding (R40).

THE BOESMANSKLOOF TRAVERSE

The 14km **Boesmanskloof Traverse** (ⓦ boesmanskloofmcgregor.com) takes you from Greyton across the Riviersonderend mountain range to the glaring Karoo scrubland around the town of McGregor (see p.239). No direct roads connect the two towns; to drive from one to the other involves a circuitous two-hour journey.

The classic way to cover the Traverse is to walk from Greyton to **Die Galg** (14km from McGregor), where people commonly spend the night, returning the same way to Greyton the following day. The Traverse rises and falls a fair bit, so you'll have to contend with a lot of strenuous uphill walking. If you're based in Greyton and don't want to do the whole thing, walk to **Oak Falls**, 9km from Greyton, and back. Composed of a series of cascades, it's the highlight of the route, its most impressive feature being a large pool where you can rest and swim in cola-coloured water.

TRAIL PRACTICALITIES

You're free to walk the first 5km of the trail and back, but you'll need a permit (R50 per person per day) to walk to Oak Falls, or to complete the whole route from Greyton to Die Galg: book in advance at the Greyton tourist office (see opposite).

Wed 6–10pm, Thurs–Sat 11.30am–3pm & 6–10pm, Sun 11.30am–3pm.
Oak and Vigne Café DS Botha St ☎ 028 254 9037. An extremely popular restaurant situated in an old cottage with an oak-shaded terrace. Fresh bread and croissants are baked daily, plus cooked breakfasts (R50) and good cocktails, such as the Greyton Mule (vodka, ginger beer and lime; R40) – service can sometimes be slow. Daily 8am–5pm.

★**Peccadillos Bistro** 23 Main Rd ☎ 028 254 9066, ⓦ peccadillos.co.za. With the reputation for the best fine dining in town, *Peccadillos* serves up food with a strong Mediterranean influence; try the local trout dishes, pork belly or wood-fired pizza (R100). It's also a good place to try out some local wines. Booking ahead is recommended. Mon & Thurs–Sun noon–3pm & 6–10pm.

Genadendal

Just 6km from Greyton, **GENADENDAL**, whose name means "valley of grace", was founded in 1737 by Georg Schmidt, a German missionary of the Moravian church. The village's focus is around **Church Square**, dominated by the imposing church – the third to be built on the site – completed in 1893. The original church bell, which now stands outside, became the centre of a bitter row, when Schmidt annoyed the local white farmers by forming a small Christian congregation with impoverished Khoi (who were on the brink of extinction) and giving refuge to maltreated labourers from local farms. What really annoyed the farmers was the fact that while they, white Christians, were illiterate, Schmidt was teaching native people, whom they considered uncivilized, to read and write. The Dutch Reformed Church, under the control of the Dutch East India Company, waded in when Schmidt began baptizing converts, and prohibited the mission from ringing the bell that called the faithful to prayer.

In 1838, the mission established the first teacher training college in the country, which the government closed in 1926, on the grounds that coloured people didn't need tertiary education and should be employed as workers on local farms – a policy that effectively ground the community into poverty. In 1995, in recognition of the mission's role in education, Nelson Mandela renamed his official residence in Cape Town "Genadendal".

Swellendam

SWELLENDAM is an attractive historic town at the foot of the Langeberg, 220km from Cape Town. With one of the best country museums in South Africa, it's a congenial stop along the N2 between Cape Town and the Garden Route. And because of its ample supply of good accommodation and its position – poised between the coastal De Hoop Nature Reserve and the Langeberg – it's a suitable base for spending a day or two exploring this part of the Overberg, with the Bontebok National Park close at hand to the south, home to a once-endangered antelope and other peaceful wildlife. The town is built along a very long main road with no traffic lights; it's most attractive at either end, with a mundane shopping area in the middle. The eastern end is dominated by the museum complex, which serves as a tourist centre of sorts.

Brief history

South Africa's third-oldest white settlement, Swellendam was established in 1745 by Baron Gustav van Imhoff, a visiting Dutch East India Company bigwig. He was deeply concerned about the "moral degeneration" of burghers who were trekking further and further from Cape Town and out of Company control. Of no less concern to the Baron was the loss of revenue from these "vagabonds" who were neglecting to pay the Company for the right to hold land and were fiddling their annual tax returns. The town grew into a prosperous rural centre known for its wagon-making, and for being the last "civilized" port of call for *trekboers* heading out into the interior. The income generated from this helped build Swellendam's gracious homes, many of which went up in smoke in a fire in 1865, which razed much of the town centre.

Oefeningshuis

36 Voortrek St

The only building in the centre to survive the town's 1865 fire was the Cape Dutch-style **Oefeningshuis**. Built in 1838, it was first used as a place for religious activity, then as a school for freed slaves. At either end, there are two surreal-looking clocks with frozen hands carved into the top of each gable, with a real clock beneath one of them.

Dutch Reformed church

Voortrek St

The imposing **Dutch Reformed church**, dating from 1910, incorporates an array of differing styles – Gothic windows, a Baroque spire, and Cape Dutch gables – into a wedding cake of a building that agreeably holds its own against the odds. There's a dramatic sweep of a gallery and dark wooden pews on the inside, and the church still draws a good crowd on Sundays.

Drostdy Museum

18 Swellegrebel St • Mon–Fri 9am–4.45pm, Sat & Sun 10am–2.45pm • R25 • ☎ 028 514 1138, ⊛ drostdy.com

On the east side of town, a short way from the centre, is the excellent **Drostdy Museum**, a collection of historic buildings arranged around large grounds, with a lovely nineteenth-century Cape garden. The centrepiece is the *drostdy* itself, built in 1747 as the seat of the *landdrost*, a magistrate-cum-commissioner sent out by the Dutch East India Company to control the outer reaches of its territory. The building conforms to the beautiful limewashed, thatched and shuttered Cape Dutch style of the eighteenth century, and houses a fine collection of eighteenth- and nineteenth-century Cape furniture.

ARRIVAL AND DEPARTURE   SWELLENDAM

By car Swellendam is 220km (about a 3hr drive) from Cape Town, on the N2, and 533km from Port Elizabeth, a 7hr drive up the Garden Route.

By bus Coaches, including the Baz Bus, run between Cape Town and Port Elizabeth via Swellendam, dropping off at the *Swellengrebel Hotel*, in the centre of town.

INFORMATION AND TOURS

Tourist information The tourist office is at 2 Swellengrebel St, in one of the Drostdy Museum buildings (Mon–Fri 9am–5pm, Sat & Sun 9am–2pm; ☎ 028 514 2770, ⊛ capetraderoute.co.za).

Horseriding tours Two Feathers Horse Trails (☎ 082 494 8279, ⊛ twofeathers.co.za) offers short trips for all levels (R400), and two hours for experienced riders (R600) in the foothills of the Langeberg Mountains.

ACCOMMODATION

★Augusta de Mist 3 Human St ☎028 514 2425, ⓦaugustademist.com. This 200-year-old homestead has three beautifully renovated cottages, two garden suites and a family unit (all with percale linen), and is altogether very luxurious and stylish. There's a rambling terraced garden and pool, plus a good restaurant on-site, though you need to book meals in advance. R2000

★Cypress Cottage 3 Voortrek St ☎028 514 3296, ⓦcypress-cottage.co.za. There are seven charming rooms, decorated with antiques: two in the old homestead and five (including a two-room family suite) in the converted stables. The house is one of the oldest in town and the friendly owner is a brilliant gardener. R900

Eenuurkop Huisie 8km from town on the Ashton Rd ☎028 514 1447, ⓦeenuurkop.co.za. Two self-catering cottages, one with three bedrooms, the other with one, in a stunning setting with great views, access to mountain walks, and the farm dam to swim in. R800

Hermitage Huisies 3km from town on R60 to Ashton ☎061 660 2138 or ☎061 660 2649, ⓦhermitage-huisies.co.za. Two restored labourers' cottages, sleeping four or five people, and two flats, all self-catering and in a beautiful location – a berry farm with duck pond, grazing sheep and horses – ideal for families. R750

Swellendam Backpackers 5 Lichtenstein St ☎028 514 2648 or ☎082 494 8279, ⓦswellendambackpackers.co.za. Swellendam's only hostel is well situated near the Marloth Nature Reserve, and close to the Drostdy Museum, with a large campsite, and decent twins and doubles. No dorms, so if you are on your own, you can have a room to yourself. Friendly staff can arrange activities including horseriding and hiking permits for Marloth. Camping R130, doubles R550

Swellendam Country Lodge 237 Voortrek St ☎028 514 3629, ⓦswellendamlodge.com. Six garden rooms with separate entrances, reed ceilings and elegant, uncluttered decor in muted hues. There's a veranda for summer days, as well as a swimming pool and well-kept garden. R1300

EATING

De Companjie 5 Voortrek St ☎083 399 0299. Set in a pleasing historic building that also functions as a guesthouse, it offers good teatime eats and hearty dinners. Well known for its steaks (R160) and venison dishes. Mon, Tues, Thurs & Sun 4–10pm.

La Belle Alliance 1 Swellengrebel St ☎028 514 2924. Conveniently located just off the N2 near the Drostdy Museum, with a restful garden setting and outdoor seating next to the river, this is ideal if you are simply passing through Swellendam and want tasty but uncomplicated food, such as a Ploughman's Platter (R85), or fish with a salad (R110). Daily 8am–5pm.

★La Sosta 145 Voortrek St ☎028 514 1470, ⓦlasostaswellendam.com. This elegant establishment is one of the best restaurants in the Western Cape and needs advance booking. Serving contemporary Italian food, it offers three set menus: one for fish eaters (R450), one for carnivores, and one (named Garden) for vegetarians (R350). Tues–Sat 6.30–10pm.

The Old Gaol Coffee Shop Church Square, 8A Voortrek St ☎028 514 3847. A great place where you can get milk tart in a copper pan and a traditional bread, *roosterkoek*, made on an open fire, with nice fillings (R70). The outdoor play area makes this an ideal choice for kids. Mon, Tues, Sat & Sun 8.30am–5pm, Wed–Fri 7.30am–10pm.

Woodpecker Deli 270 Voortrek St ☎028 514 2924. A relaxed and reasonably priced restaurant that serves tasty pizzas, pasta, soups and burgers. A good choice if you are in town for just one night and want something simple. Mon–Sat 11.30am–9pm, Sun 11.30am–5pm.

Bontebok National Park

6km south of Swellendam • Daily: May–Sept 7am–7pm; Oct–June 7am–6pm • R100 • ☎028 514 2735, ⓦsanparks.org/parks/bontebok

Bontebok National Park is a compact 28-square-kilometre reserve at the foot of the Langeberg range that makes a relaxing overnight stop between Cape Town and the Garden Route. The park was established in 1931 to save the Cape's dwindling population of bontebok, an attractive antelope with distinctive cappuccino, chocolate-brown and white markings on its forehead and hindquarters. By 1930, hunting in the area had reduced the number of animals to a mere thirty. Their survival has happily been secured and there are now three hundred of them in the park, as well as populations in other game and nature reserves in the province. There are no big cats in the park, but **mammals** you might encounter include rare Cape mountain zebra, red hartebeest and grey rhebok, and there are more than 120 **bird species**. It's also a rich environment for **fynbos**, with nearly five hundred species here, including erica, gladioli and proteas. Apart from game viewing, there are opportunities to swim in the Breede River, hike a couple of short nature trails and fish.

★**Bontebok National Park** ☎ 028 514 2735, ⓦ san parks.org/parks/bontebok. Self-catering accommodation is available in ten fully equipped chalets, the best of which have river views. There are lovely grassy areas and antelope wandering about grazing. There is also a campsite with good washing facilities – the pitches without electricity are cheaper. Stock up with food in Swellendam before you arrive. Camping R245, chalets R1100

Pringle Bay and Betty's Bay

2

The coastal drive along the R44 from Cape Town to Hermanus is spectacular – one of the most beautiful drives in the country – though this stretch is home to a series of rather unattractive, ever developing settlements, including **Pringle Bay** and **Betty's Bay**. The main reason to visit Betty's Bay is for its Botanical Garden (see below) and its colony of African (jackass) penguins at **Stony Point Penguin Colony** (daily 8am–4.30pm; R20), which can be seen from the well-signposted wooden boardwalk.

Harold Porter National Botanical Garden

Off the R44, Betty's Bay • Mon–Fri 8am–4.30pm, Sat & Sun 8am–5pm • R25 • ☎ 028 272 9311, ⓦ sanbi.org/gardens/harold-porter

Harold Porter National Botanical Garden is a wild sanctuary of coastal and montane *fynbos* that makes a good stop along the R44, if only to picnic or have tea at its outdoor café. The relatively compact botanical garden extends over two square kilometres from the mountains, through marshland down to coastal dunes. Once here, you'll probably get lured at least some of the way up the *kloof* that runs through the reserve; as you get higher up, you're treated to sea views in one direction and rugged mountains in the other.

Although there's wildlife present, in the form of small **antelope**, **baboons** and **leopards**, these are rarely sighted and it's more worthwhile looking out for the birds and blooms. Four **trails** of between one and three hours meander through the gardens, but you can just as easily take yourself off on an impromptu stroll, up and across the red-stained waters (the colour stems from phenols and tannins leaching from the *fynbos*) running through Disa Kloof.

Hook, Line and Sinker Off Pass Rd, Pringle Bay ☎ 028 273 8688. This is the best place to eat in the area, with a menu made up of seasonal fish and steak, which is cooked on an open fire by larger-than-life Stephan. Reservations and booking confirmation are essential. Mon 7–11pm, Tues–Sun noon–3pm & 7–11pm.

★**Moonstruck on Pringle Bay** 264 Hangklip Rd, Pringle Bay ☎ 028 273 8162, ⓦ moonstruck .co.za. This romantic and palatial modern guesthouse has four huge rooms with sea-facing balconies. It's a short walk from the guesthouse to a bay with good swimming. R2400

Hermanus

On the edge of rocky cliffs and backed by mountains, **HERMANUS**, 112km east of Cape Town, sits at the northernmost end of Walker Bay, an inlet whose protective curve attracts calving whales as it slides south to the promontory of Danger Point. From about July, southern right whales (see box, p.186) start appearing in the warmer sheltered bays of the Western Cape, and the town trumpets itself as the **whale capital** of South Africa. To prove it, an official whale crier (purportedly the only one in the world) struts around armed with a mobile phone and a dried kelp horn through which he yells the latest sightings. There's even an annual **whale festival** during the last week in September, when the town puts on events ranging from ecology talks to classical music recitals.

There is still the barest trace of a once-quiet, cliff-edge fishing village around the historic harbour and in some understated seaside cottages, but for the most part the town has gorged itself on its whale-generated income. An almost continuous 5km cliff path through coastal *fynbos* hugs the rocky coastline from the old harbour to Grotto Beach in the eastern suburbs, and it's from this path that you will spot whales.

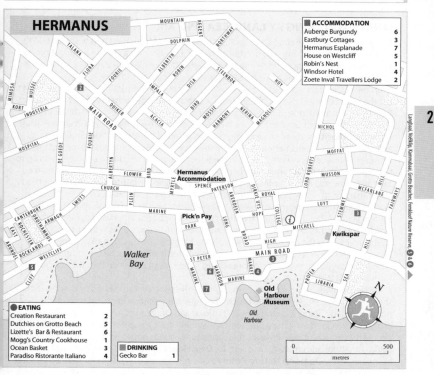

HERMANUS

ACCOMMODATION

Auberge Burgundy	6
Eastbury Cottages	3
Hermanus Esplanade	7
House on Westcliff	5
Robin's Nest	1
Windsor Hotel	4
Zoete Inval Travellers Lodge	2

EATING

Creation Restaurant	2
Dutchies on Grotto Beach	5
Lizette's Bar & Restaurant	6
Mogg's Country Cookhouse	1
Ocean Basket	3
Paradiso Ristorante Italiano	4

DRINKING

Gecko Bar	1

Main Road, the continuation of the R43, meanders through Hermanus, briefly becoming Seventh Street. Market Square, just above the old harbour and to the south of Main Street, is the closest thing to a centre, and it's here you'll find the heaviest concentration of restaurants, craft shops and flea markets – the principal forms of entertainment in town when the whales are taking time out.

Old Harbour Museum

At the Old Harbour • Mon–Sat 9am–4.30pm, Sun noon–4pm • R20 • ☏ 028 312 1476, ⓦ old-harbour-museum.co.za

The **Old Harbour Museum**, just below Market Square, is home to some uncompelling displays, among which you'll find lots of fishing tackle and sharks' jaws. Outside, a few colourful boats, used by local fishermen from the mid-eighteenth to mid-nineteenth centuries, create a photogenic vignette in the tiny harbour.

New Harbour

A couple of kilometres west of town along Westcliff

The **New Harbour** is a working fishing harbour, dramatically surrounded by steep cliffs, projecting a gutsy counterpoint to the more manicured central area. The whales sometimes enter the harbour – and there's nowhere better to base yourself for a spot of whale-watching than the *Gecko Bar* (see p.185).

Beaches and swimming

Just below the *Marine Hotel* on Marine Drive, a beautiful tidal pool offers the only sea swimming around the town centre's craggy coast. For sandy beaches, you have to head out east to the suburbs, where you'll find a decent choice, starting with secluded Langbaai, closest to town, a cove beneath cliffs at the bottom of Sixth Avenue that has

2

WHALE-WATCHING BY LAND, SEA AND AIR

The Southern Cape, including Cape Town, provides some of the easiest and best places in the world for **whale-watching**. You don't need to rent a boat or take a pricey tour to get out to sea; if you come at the right time of year, whales are often visible from the shore, although a good pair of binoculars will come in useful for when they are far out.

All nine of the great whale species of the southern hemisphere pass by South Africa's shores, but the most commonly seen off Cape Town are **southern right whales** (their name derives from being the "right" one to kill because of their high oil and bone yields and the fact that they float when dead). Southern right whales are black and easily recognized from their pale, brownish **callosities**. These unappealing patches of raised, roughened skin on their snouts and heads have a distinct pattern on each animal, which helps scientists keep track of them.

Female whales come inshore to calve in sheltered bays, and stay to nurse their young for up to three months. **July to October** is the best time to see them, although they start appearing in June and some stay around until December. When the calves are big enough, the whales head off south again, to colder, stormy waters, where they feed on enormous quantities of plankton, making up for the nursing months when the females don't eat at all. Though you're most likely to see females and young, you may see **males** early in the season boisterously flopping about the females, though they neither help rear the calves nor form lasting bonds with females.

What gives away the presence of a whale is the blow or spout, a tall smoky plume which disperses after a few seconds and is actually the whale breathing out before it surfaces. If luck is on your side, you may see whales **breaching** – the movement when they thrust high out of the water and fall back with a great splash.

The best vantage points for whale-watching are the concrete cliff paths that ring the rocky shore from New Harbour to Grotto Beach. There are interpretation boards at three of the popular vantage points (Gearing's Point, Die Gang and Bientang's Cave). These are the most congested venues during the whale season – at their worst, the paths can be lined with people two or three deep. However, there are equally good spots elsewhere along the Walker Bay coast. Aficionados make great claims for **De Kelders** (see p.190) some 39km east of Hermanus, while **De Hoop Nature Reserve** (see p.194), east of Arniston, is reckoned by some to be the ultimate whale-watching location along the entire Southern African coast.

Several **operators** run boat trips from Hermanus, all essentially offering the same service. Boats must give a 50m berth to whales, but if a whale approaches a boat, the boat may stop and watch it for up to twenty minutes. Hermanus Whale Cruises (☎028 313 2722, ⓦhermanus -whale-cruises.co.za) runs a two-hour boat trip for 87 passengers four times daily from the New Harbour (June–Dec; R800). Further around Walker Bay, close to Gansbaai, Dyer Island Cruises, on Geelbek St (☎082 801 8014 or ☎076 555 5520, ⓦwhalewatchsa.com), provides whale cruises in the Dyer Island area, with a marine biologist on hand to answer questions. Trips depart daily from Kleinbaai (2hr 30min; R1100), with times dependent on weather conditions. Book in advance.

Arguably the best way to see whales is from the air. David Austin, based in Hermanus (African Wings; ☎082 555 7605, ⓦafricanwings.co.za), flies a maximum of three people in a small plane over the bay to see whales, dolphins, sharks and other sea life. Flights range from thirty minutes (R3850 for 3 people) to an hour (R7300 for 3 people), and sightings are guaranteed in season, with the chance to observe mothers and baby whales interacting.

a narrow strip of beach and is excellent for swimming. Voelklip, at the bottom of Eighth Avenue, has grassed terraces, which are great for picnics, toilets and a nearby café for tea. Adjacent is Kammabaai, with the best surfing break around Hermanus, and, 1km further east, Grotto Beach, which marks the start of a 12km curve of dazzlingly white sand that stretches all the way to De Kelders.

Fernkloof Nature Reserve

On the east side of town, off Main Rd on Theron St · Daily dawn–dusk · Free · ☎028 313 0819, ⓦfernkloof.org.za

The **Fernkloof Nature Reserve** encompasses fifteen square kilometres of mountainous terrain and offers sweeping views of Walker Bay. It has some 40km of **waymarked** footpaths, including a 4.5km circular nature trail. Visiting is an excellent way to get close to the astonishing variety of delicate *fynbos* (over a thousand species have been identified in the reserve), much of it flowering species that attract scores of birds, including the brightly coloured sunbirds and sugarbirds endemic to the area.

ARRIVAL AND INFORMATION
HERMANUS

By car The most direct route to Hermanus, 125km from Cape Town, is to take the N2 then head south onto the R43 at Bot River (a 1hr 30min drive), though the winding road that leaves the N2 just before Sir Lowry's Pass hugs the coast from Strand and is one of the most scenic coastal drives in South Africa (2hr).

By bus The Baz Bus (☏ 021 422 5202, ⍟ bazbus.com) from Cape Town and Port Elizabeth drops off at Bot River 34km northeast of Hermanus on the R43, from where you can arrange to be collected by your hostel. Two shuttles – Bernadus (☏ 028 316 1093 or ☏ 083 658 7848) and Splash (☏ 028 316 4004) – also ply the route between Hermanus and Cape Town (1hr 30min). This is effectively a taxi service, operating on demand, so you need to book in advance. A

one-way trip to the airport or the centre of Cape Town costs R400–800 per person, depending on the number of people taking the shuttle. Bernadus also covers the 45km trip round the coast to Gansbaai for about R900 per person.

Tourist information The tourist office, at the old station building in Mitchell St (May–Aug Mon–Sat 9am–5pm & Sun 9am–2pm; Sept–April Mon–Sat 8am–6pm; ☏ 028 312 2629, ⍟ hermanustourism.info), provides maps and brochures about the area, and can book accommodation, whale-watching, and shark-cage diving trips.

Festival During the last week in September, the town puts on a lively show of almost anything with a whale connection, however tenuous (⍟ hermanuswhale festival.co.za).

ACCOMMODATION

As the most popular coastal destination outside Cape Town, Hermanus is awash with places to stay. If you want something a little more countrified, head off to Stanford, a 20min drive away around the curve of the bay. Alternatively, head further along the coast to Gansbaai (see p.190) and enjoy great whale viewing (in season) from the windows of any sea-facing accommodation.

Auberge Burgundy 16 Harbour Rd ☏ 028 313 1201, ⍟ auberge.co.za; map p.185. A Provençal-style country house in the town centre, close to the water, with a stylish Mediterranean atmosphere and a lavender garden. The rooms are light and airy and decorated with imported French fabrics. R1870

Eastbury Cottages 36 Luyt St ☏ 028 312 1258, ⍟ eastburycottage.co.za; map p.185. Four fully equipped self-catering cottages close to the *Marine Hotel*. Prices vary depending on group size, and breakfast can be ordered for an extra R100. R800

Hermanus Esplanade 63 Marine Drive ☏ 028 312 3610, ⍟ hermanusesplanade.co.za; map p.185. Self-catering apartments of varying sizes, facing onto the sea or onto a courtyard. It is worth opting for the more expensive ones that have views of the bay. R1000

House on Westcliff 96 Westcliff Rd ☏ 028 313 2388, ⍟ westcliffhouse.co.za; map p.185. This homely B&B is situated just out of the centre near the new harbour and boasts six bedrooms in a classic Cape-style house with a protected, tranquil garden and swimming pool. All rooms are en suite and have their own

entrance off the garden; there is also a three-bed family room. R1000

Robin's Nest 10 Meadow Ave ☏ 028 316 1597, ⍟ robinsnest-guesthouse.co.za; map p.185. Three fully equipped, but plain, self-catering studio flats above a garage in a garden, 4km west of the centre. Reached through the Hemel-en-Aarde shopping village, these purpose-built, two-storey flats sleep two and have good mountain views. R700

Windsor Hotel 49 Marine Drive ☏ 028 312 3727, ⍟ windsorhotel.co.za; map p.185. This old, but popular, seafront hotel offers a full range of accommodation right on the cliff edge. It's ideally situated in the centre of town and guests can enjoy sea views from the dining room, lounges and almost half of the bedrooms. R1500

Zoete Inval Traveller's Lodge 23 Main Rd ☏ 028 312 1242, ⍟ zoeteinval.co.za; map p.185. A quiet and relaxing hostel, with a distinct lack of party vibe, comprising dorms, doubles and family suites, with extras like good coffee, a Jacuzzi and a fireplace. They can organize baby beds, if you need one, as well as tours and outings in the area. Dorms R225, doubles R600, family room R1200

EATING

Seafood is the obvious thing to eat in Hermanus, though the sea views are often better than the food. There are a couple of excellent restaurants in the wine estate valley of Hemel-en-Aarde (see p.188), west of town, and further field in Stanford. Book well ahead at weekends and in summer. Head to the **market** at the Hermanus Cricket

Grounds (Sat 8am–noon; ⓦhermanus.co.za/hermanus-market) for excellent Bot River cheeses, as well as fresh pasta, pesto, muffins, hummus and baked goods.

HERMANUS

Dutchies on Grotto Beach 10th Ave, Grotto Beach, Voelklip ⓣ028 314 1392, ⓦdutchies.co.za; map p.185. The only place to eat on the beach, and a good one at that. There isn't much Dutch character to the menu, but the management and service sparkle. Prices are reasonable – a "health" breakfast (hot drink, fresh orange juice, fruit salad, Greek yoghurt and muesli) will set you back just R70, while a Dutch cheese and ham ciabatta sandwich is R80. Book ahead, especially to get outdoor seating. Daily 9am–9pm.

★**Lizette's Bar & Restaurant** 20 8th St, Voelklip ⓣ028 314 0308, ⓦlizetteskitchen.com; map p.185. Well-known chef Lizette Crabtree cooks up a storm in this spacious restored house, which has plenty of outdoor seating, a play area for kids, water bowls for dogs and a cosy interior. With her experience of cooking in Asia, you can expect Vietnamese street food (R100), as well as Moroccan dishes, some South African favourites with a twist, and burgers. Takeaways are available, too. Daily 9am–10pm.

Ocean Basket Fashion Square, Village Square ⓣ028 312 1313; map p.185. Part of a reasonably priced and consistently reliable seafood chain, this restaurant is popular thanks in no small part to its fabulous setting; the menu includes cheap fish and chips (R70) and a variety of salads and other fish dishes. Mon–Sat noon–9pm, Sun noon–8pm.

Paradiso Ristorante Italiano 83 Marine Drive ⓣ028 313 1153; map p.185. Situated behind Village Square, near the water in a zone of tourist restaurants, this reliable Italian place serves seafood dishes and chicken, alongside delicious pizza (R100) and pasta. Daily 11am–9.30pm.

HEMEL-EN-AARDE

★**Creation Restaurant** Hemel-en-Aarde Valley ⓣ028 212 1107, ⓦcreationwines.com; map p.185. A fabulous contemporary, elegant, yet informal, restaurant with tables, both inside and out, and looking onto the *fynbos*-clad mountains. The antipasto dishes and canapés are sublime, and the food is created to complement the wines (food and wine pairing R335). Children are well catered for, with their own tasting menu of five dishes paired with five surprise drinks (R75). Booking essential. Daily 11am–4pm.

★**Mogg's Country Cookhouse** Hemel-en-Aarde Valley, 12km from Hermanus along the R320 to Caledon ⓣ076 314 0671, ⓦmoggscookhouse.com;

HERMANUS WINE ROUTE

Hermanus is a great destination for estate visits and wine tasting, and it's in a landscape quite different to Stellenbosch and Franschhoek. Some of South Africa's top wines come from the **Hemel-en-Aarde (heaven and earth) Valley**, 2km west of the town, and can be explored in a day, with some notable restaurants and tasting rooms to tempt you along the 25km stretch. The journey is sometimes called **Wine Route 320**, as the estates are strung along the R320, a minor road that branches off the main road from Hermanus to Cape Town, and ends up in Caledon.

Hamilton Russell Winery 8km along the R320 ⓣ028 312 3595, ⓦhamiltonrussellvineyards.com. The longest established of the Walker Bay wineries, Hamilton Russell produces some of South Africa's most expensive wines. They are especially renowned for their Pinot Noir and outstanding Chardonnay. Mon–Fri 9am–5pm, Sat 9am–1pm.

Bouchard Finlayson 10km along the R320 ⓣ028 312 3515, ⓦbouchardfinlayson.co.za. This establishment has a formidable reputation, and produces a wider range of wines than its neighbours. Their award-winning Galpin Peak Pinot Noir is grown on the slopes of Galpin Peak, while the name of their dry white blend, Blanc de Mer, alludes to the fact that these wines are hugely influenced by their proximity to the cool ocean. Mon–Fri 9.30am–5pm, Sat 9.30am–12.30pm.

Ataraxia Wines 19km along the R320 ⓣ028 212 2007, ⓦataraxiawines.co.za. Contemporary and stylish, this newish winery offers mountain views from its wine-tasting lounge, which is built like a chapel to contemplate the heavenly wines, which include an excellent Pinot Noir. Mon–Fri 9am–4pm, Sat 10am–5pm.

★**Creation** 23km along the R320 ⓣ028 212 1107, ⓦwww.creationwines.com. One of the very best wineries, Creation produces fabulous wines and is known for its gourmet food and wine pairings (daily 11am–4pm), as well as chocolate- and tea-tasting. Its best wines are the Creation Syrah and Syrah Grenache, which are dark, fruity and aromatic. A wine tutor will help you to appreciate their complex and delicious wines, all served in the most elegant imported glassware. Book well in advance at weekends. Daily 10am–5pm.

map p.185. A farm cottage with superb views across the valley, Mogg's is an intimate place that's always full and unfailingly excellent, serving whatever takes the fancy of chefs Jenny Mogg and her daughter Julia. Mains, which might include pan-fried line fish on red pepper risotto with a mushroom sauce (R125), are followed by a selection of great desserts. Booking is essential and kids are welcome. Wed–Sun noon–2.30pm.

DRINKING

Gecko Bar 24a Still St, New Harbour ⊕028 312 2920; map p.185. With great harbour views, this packed, noisy bar has excellent cocktails, along with pizzas, burgers and other pub grub, and makes an ideal spot for a sundowner (R60). Smoking is permitted in some parts of the bar and it's also a regular venue for live music, showcasing local artists. If it's seafood you want, head next door to the classy *Harbour Rock* grill. Daily 12.30pm–midnight.

Stanford

East of Hermanus, the R43 takes a detour inland around the attractive Klein River Lagoon, past the pretty riverside hamlet of **STANFORD**. Despite its proximity to hyped-up Hermanus, this historic village, established in 1857, has become something of a refuge for arty types seeking a tranquil escape from the urban rat race. Stanford's principal attraction is its streetscape of simple **Victorian architecture** that includes limewashed houses and sandstone cottages, and the simple Anglican church whose thatched roof glows under the late afternoon sun. The town's northern boundary is the attractive **Klein River**, where rich birdlife inhabits the rustling reed beds lining the riverbanks, and where you stand a good chance of spotting the flashy malachite kingfisher.

ARRIVAL, INFORMATION AND TOURS   STANFORD

By car Stanford is 173km from Cape Town. Take the Hermanus turning from the N2 (about 90km from Cape Town), and follow the R43 for another 33km through Hermanus to Stanford.

Information The tourist office, on Main Rd (Mon–Thurs 8.30am–4.30pm, Fri 8.30am–5pm, Sat 9am–4pm, Sun 9am–1pm; ⊕028 341 0340, ⊕stanfordtourism.co.za), can help with booking accommodation, and can provide a brochure for a walking tour of the village that takes in the various historical houses.

Boat trips The town's northern boundary is the attractive Klein River, which can be explored on a boat trip or solo in a kayak. For trips on the river contact Ernie (⊕083 310 0952); a two-to-three-hour boat trip costs R150, while canoe and kayak rental is R100 – book in advance, especially at the weekend. The price is for the entire day.

ACCOMMODATION

X's Cottage 17 Morton St ⊕028 341 0430 or ⊕083 293 2512, ⊕www.stanford-accommodation.co.za. A small, open-plan, self-catering thatched house, with an English-style country garden. It sleeps two upstairs, and one on the couch in the downstairs living room. Its central location makes it popular, so book well ahead. Weekend bookings are for two nights only. R750

Mosaic Farm 10km from the centre, exit from Queen Victoria St ⊕028 313 2814, ⊕mosaicsouthafrica.com. In a natural setting with access to a wild part of the lagoon, this farm has 4km of lagoon frontage, with stone, canvas and thatched self-catering chalets, plus the luxury, full-board, lagoon-side safari camp *Lagoon Lodge* on the same site (R6200). R900

★**Stanford River Lodge** 4km from the centre, exit from Queen Victoria St ⊕028 341 0444, ⊕stanfordriverlodge.co.za. Sunny, spacious and modern self-catering cottages with river and mountain views. It's a lovely, upmarket place with river swimming and canoeing in summer. Bring all you need by way of supplies, though it's possible to order a breakfast basket 24hr in advance. R900

EATING

As well as some good restaurants, Stanford has a Saturday morning **market** (9am–noon). Located on the veranda of the *Stanford Hotel*, in Queen Victoria Street, this is the place to buy ready-made meals, bread, pastries, quiches and ingredients for picnics and self-catering.

★**Madre's Kitchen** Robert Stanford Estate, 1km west of Stanford ⊕028 341 0647, ⊕www.madreskitchen stanford.co.za. Located on the edge of town, this is the best place for breakfast, while the fabulous lunches include

2

A KLEIN RIVER GOURMET TOUR

Just outside Stanford, along the Klein River, there are several places providing yet more outstanding eating and drinking opportunities. Four of the best experiences are listed below.

Birkenhead Brewery Just across the R43 from Stanford along the R326 ☎028 341 0013, ⓦwalkerbayestate.com. Although it bills itself as a "craft brewery estate", the gleaming stainless-steel pipes and equipment inside soon reveal this to be an extremely slick operation. A great place for a pub lunch, or for sampling some outstanding craft beers – such as the malty Honey Blonde or rich Chocolate Stout. It's part of the Walker Bay Estate, which also produces some excellent wines. Daily 10am–5pm.

Klein River Cheese Farmstead 2km beyond Birkenhead Brewery, and 7km from Stanford on the R326 ☎028 341 0693, ⓦkleinrivercheese.co.za. Sample tastings of their famous Gruyère, Leiden, Colby and Dando cheeses, or put together a picnic basket at the *Picnic Shed* deli and enjoy it under the trees by the river. The farm has been helping to restore the forest along the river to its original condition, and visitors can contribute by purchasing a tree. Mon–Sat 9am–4pm.

Raka Wine 17km from Stanford on the R326 ☎028 341 0676, ⓦrakawine.co.za. *Raka* produces some of the finest wines in the region; its flagship red Quinary is particularly outstanding. Even if you don't make it out this far, be sure to try some of the Raka wines on your travels – it is served up across the region. Mon–Fri 9am–5pm, Sat 10am–2.30pm.

Springfontein Wine Estate 5km from Stanford on the Queen Victoria St extension ☎028 341 0651, ⓦwww.springfontein.co.za. *Springfontein* is the perfect destination for combining wine tasting with great food, with *The Barn* tasting room (R25) doubling up as a German-style pub with excellent cheese, salad and sausages on offer. A separate, extremely good, restaurant is open for lunch (Thurs–Sun from 12.30pm) and dinner (Wed–Sun from 6.30pm) and provides sophisticated three- or six-course meals cooked by Michelin Star chef Jürgen Schneider. Book in advance. Daily 11am–9pm.

platters of home-made bread, pâtés and cheeses, plus herbs and veggies from the garden, complemented by wines from their own estate (R130). It is great for children, with lawns, a jungle gym and ducks to feed. Thurs–Sun 8am–4pm.

★**Mariana's at Owls Barn** 12 Du Toit St ☎028 341 0272. The innovative and reasonably priced country food served at this Victorian cottage is good enough to draw Cape Town gourmets out for a long lazy lunch, and is a food

highlight of the region. Food and wines are local, and many of the vegetables are picked from the garden of the owners who host in a warm and engaged way, and can advise on food and wine choices. Vegetarians can enjoy chèvre tart or home-made ricotta in vine leaves (R90). You'll need to book well in advance, though cancellations may be a possibility. Try for a table on the *stoep* for a long lazy lunch. No children under 10. Thurs–Sun noon–4pm.

Gansbaai and De Kelders

GANSBAAI, 39km from Hermanus, is a workaday place, economically dependent on its fishing industry and the seafood canning factory at the harbour, which gives the place a gutsier feel than the surrounding holiday lands, but there's little reason to spend time here unless you want to engage in **great white shark safaris** (see box opposite), Gansbaai's other major industry. It is an appropriately competitive and cut-throat business, with operators engaged in a blind feeding frenzy to attract punters.

DE KELDERS, a couple of kilometres further east, is a suburb of Gansbaai. The De Kelders holiday homes and mansions are for the most part bland and ostentatious, but its rocky coast provides outstanding whale-watching and there is access to a beautiful, long sandy beach at the Walker Bay Nature Reserve, known by everyone as "Die Plat", where you can clamber over rocky sections and walk for many kilometres. Swimming can be dangerous however, so it is best not to venture in more than knee-high.

ARRIVAL AND INFORMATION   GANSBAAI AND DE KELDERS

By car Take the Hermanus off-ramp from the N2 (about 90km from Cape Town), and follow the R43 for another 85km through Hermanus and Stanford.

Tourist information The tourist office is at Great White Junction, Kapokblom St (Mon–Fri 8.30am–5.30pm, Sat 9am–4pm, Sun 10am–2pm; ☎028 384 1439, ⓦgansbaaiinfo.com).

DYER ISLAND AND SHARK ALLEY

How a black American came to be living on an island off South Africa in the early nineteenth century is something of a mystery. But, according to records, **Samson Dyer** arrived here in 1806 and made a living collecting guano on the island that subsequently took his name. **Dyer Island** is home to substantial **African penguin** and **seal breeding colonies**, both of which are prized morsels among great white sharks. So shark-infested is the channel between the island and the mainland at some times of year that it is known as **Shark Alley**, and these waters are used extensively by operators of **great white shark viewing trips**. If you go on a trip, you'll be safely contained within a sturdy boat or cage, and do not need to be able to dive.

2

CCOMMODATION

Cliff Lodge 6 Cliff St, De Kelders ☏ 028 384 0983, ▸ clifflodge.co.za. An elegant seafront guesthouse, erched on the cliffs of De Kelders, with breathtaking views om all four luxurious bedrooms and the spacious enthouse suite; there's also a deck for whale-watching nd a swimming pool. R2500

★ **Crayfish Lodge** Killarney St, De Kelders ☏ 028 384 1898, ⊚ crayfishlodge.net. This is the top stay in town, a palatial guesthouse with sea views and an individual patio or courtyard for all five rooms. The upstairs suites have jacuzzis (R3000). A path leads to a rocky beach with a channel for bathing, and there's a heated pool. R2800

ATING

lue Goose 12 Franken St, Gansbaai ☏ 028 384 1106. esh, locally sourced seafood and meat, complemented by gional wines. Their spicy fish curry (R150) and tempura awns are recommended, and there is always pasta for getarians. Daily 7am–10pm.

oat House Restaurant and Pub Gansbaai Harbour ▸ 071 657 5421. This is the place to come for over-the-unter traditional fresh fish and chips (R70) in big irtions, or enjoy a beer sitting on the veranda while atching the fishing boats come in. Daily 9am–5pm.

offee on the Rocks Cliff St, De Kelders ☏ 028 384 17, ⊚ coffee-on-the-rocks.com. A small bistro that

does great coffee, cakes and light meals, with a deck in an unsurpassed position for whale-watching; there's also a good choice for leisurely Sunday roasts (R130). Booking is essential. Wed–Sun 10am–5pm.

★ **Grootbos Nature Reserve** 8km west of Gansbaai, off the R43 ☏ 028 384 8008. This delightful eco-lodge is one of the culinary highlights of the area, offering fine-dining traditional cuisine with a modern twist. They only have a set menu, which is very reasonable for the quality; a three-course lunch costs R300, while the dinner is R460. Arrive early before dinner and enjoy a sundowner while taking in the view. Daily 1–3pm & 7–9pm.

:ape Agulhas and around

long the east flank of the Danger Point promontory, the rocky and shallow coastline ith heavy swells and strong currents makes this one of South Africa's most treacherous retches of coast – one that has claimed over 250 wrecks and around 2500 lives. Its ough terrain also accounts for the lack of a coastal road from Gansbaai and Danger oint to **Cape Agulhas**, the southernmost tip of Africa.

The plain around the southern tip of South Africa has been declared the **Agulhas ational Park** to conserve its estimated two thousand species of indigenous plant, marine nd intertidal life as well as a cultural heritage which includes shipwrecks and archeological tes – stone hearths, pottery and shell middens have all been discovered here.

The actual tip of the continent is marked by a rock and plaque about 1km below the ndmark of Agulhas Lighthouse, towards Suiderstrand, now part of the Agulhas lational Park. You may need to queue if you want your photo taken at the famous oot, which is definitely worth seeing, if undramatic – Africa simply tails off into a few ocks in the sea. Following the dirt road to **Suiderstrand** takes you to some beautiful ndeveloped beaches, and the National Park beach cottages, but the road is very neven and rough.

L'AGULHAS, referred to simply as Agulhas, is the rather windblown, treeless settlement ssociated with the southern tip. Consisting of a small collection of holiday houses and few shops, it's a much quieter coastal destination than anywhere along the Garden

Route. The centre of Agulhas, if you can call it a centre, is along Main Road, where you'll find a couple of restaurants, a small supermarket and a craft shop. There is a large tidal pool on the left, just before you reach the lighthouse, which is perfect if you fancy a swim.

Struisbaai, 4km from Agulhas, is worth considering as a place to stay, if you want access to sandy beaches (the coastline around Agulhas is very rocky). It has the added attraction of a small harbour and a couple of restaurants.

Agulhas Lighthouse

Daily 9am–4.30pm • R40

The red-and-white **Agulhas Lighthouse**, commissioned in 1849, offers vertiginous views from its top, reached by a series of steep ladders. The appeal of lonely lighthouses on rocky edges beaming out signals to ships at night is explored here through some interesting exhibits about lighthouses around South Africa.

Struisbaai

East of Agulhas is **STRUISBAAI** (pronounced strace-bye, often simply referred to as Strace), notable for its endless white-sand beach. The further you walk from the uninspiring holiday homes and camping site, the better it gets, with marvellous (and safe) swimming to be had in the dark, turquoise-coloured waters.

It is also worth investigating Struisbaai's small harbour where giant stingrays are frequently sighted, gracefully gliding through the water and under the wooden struts of the slipway looking for fish scraps. The resident ray, Parrie, has become something of a favourite and even has his own Facebook page. From the jetty, there is a lovely wooden walkway that takes you along the coast to some rocky beaches where you can fossick endlessly for small shells.

ARRIVAL AND INFORMATION
CAPE AGULHA

By car Agulhas is 230km from Cape Town. Take the N2 to Caledon (115km) then the R316 to Bredasdorp; here, the westerly branch of the R319 will take you down to Agulhas (43km). The drive takes you through vast rolling farmlands where you are almost certain to see South Africa's national bird, the elegant and endangered blue crane, feeding in the fields.

By taxi Mrs Marie Johannes runs a daily door-to-door tax company from Cape Town, which can drop you in Agulha or Struisbaai for R350 (☎ 082 691 9075).

Tourist information The tourist office at Agulha Lighthouse (daily 9am–5pm; ☎ 028 435 7185, ⓦ discove capeagulhas.co.za) is very helpful and provides comprehensive map of the area with useful listings.

ACCOMMODATION

Agulhas National Park Rest Camp Suiderstrand, 7km west of Agulhas ☎ 028 435 6078, ⓦ sanparks.org /parks/agulhas. If you want a remote beach experience, and some hiking, opt for one of the seaview chalets in Suiderstrand, all fully equipped for self-catering. You will need to collect the key from the National Park office near the Lighthouse before 6pm during the week, or 5pm at th weekend, and pay the R150 per person conservation fe Take everything with you, as you won't want to be bumpin along the rough road to the shops. R1100

Cape Agulhas Backpackers 17 Duiker St, Struisba ☎ 082 372 3354, ⓦ capeagulhasbackpackers.com. Th

---

ELIM MISSION STATION

Some 40km northwest of Agulhas, the Moravian mission station of **ELIM** was founded in 1824, its streets lined with thatched, whitewashed houses and fig trees. This central area is the most attractive part of the village, though the rest of it feels rather run-down and forsaken. You can wander about the central area, which is the most attractive part, and take in the architecture and history by visiting the church, the restored water mill (where wheat is still ground) and the memorial commemorating the **emancipation of slaves** in 1834 – the only such monument in South Africa. Its presence reflects the fact that numerous freed slaves found refuge in mission stations like Elim.

only budget place around Agulhas has camping, dorms and doubles, all with good bedding, plus a pool and garden. It's run by a couple who are big on helping you enjoy the outdoors and will organize fishing, surfing lessons, kite-surfing or horseriding. Camping R100, dorms R160, doubles R450

Langezandt Fishermen's Village Murex St, Struisbaai ☎028 435 7547, ⓦlangezandt.co.za. Self-catering, exclusive beach villas on an estate that's been built to look like traditional whitewashed, thatched local houses. They are geared to families, but there are some smaller units.

The fabulous location, right at the edge of town, has direct access to long stretches of sandy beach for walking or swimming. R1200

Southermost B&B On the corner of Van Breda and Lighthouse sts, Agulhas ☎028 435 6565, ⓦsouthermost.co.za. A well-loved and rather dilapidated historic beach cottage, opposite the tidal pool with a garden of native flowers sloping down to the water's edge. It is an easy walk from here to the centre to get an evening meal. Closed in winter. R800

EATING

L'Agulhas Seafoods Main Rd, Agulhas ☎028 435 7207. The best fish and chips (R65) in the region – people even travel from as far as Cape Town to enjoy them. As well as local fish, they also serve calamari and sushi, accompanied by a selection of wines and beers. Mon–Sat 10am–7pm, Sun 10am–3pm.

Pelican's Harbour Café Struisbaai Harbour ☎028 435 6526. Straightforward fish and chips café with wooden tables and benches. This may be the place to try

legitimately farmed and harvested Abalone (R190), a delicacy normally associated with poaching, otherwise go for mussels or the locally caught line fish. Daily 10am–9pm.

Twisted Fork Restaurant and Bar 184 Main Rd, Agulhas ☎028 435 6291. Enjoy a night out at the pub, and the food is not bad either. The Thai chicken and prawn curry is recommended (R120), and the catch of the day is served with excellent chips. Daily 11am–2am.

SHOPPING

Wine Boutique Main Rd, Agulhas ☎028 567 7858, ⓦwineboutiqueagulhas.co.za. If you want to taste and buy wines from the region, the infallibly excellent Wine Boutique, across the road from *Seagulls Pub and Restaurant*,

stocks an excellent selection, with daily tastings, and offers advice on the very best vintages. Opening times may be different in winter. Mon–Fri 9am–5.30pm, Sat 9am–5pm, Sun 11am–5pm.

Arniston

After the cool deep blues of the Atlantic to the west, the azure of the Indian Ocean at **ARNISTON** is startling, made all the more dazzling by the white dunes interspersed with rocky ledges. If you want nothing more than beach life, this is one of the best places to stay in the Overberg. The colours may be tropical, but the wind can howl as unpredictably here as anywhere else along the Cape coast, and when it does, there's nothing much to do. The village is known to locals by its Afrikaans name, Waenhuiskrans ("wagon-house cliff"), after a cliff containing a huge cave 1500m south of town, which *trekboers* reckoned was spacious enough for a wagon and span of oxen. The English name derives from a British ship, the *Arniston*, which hit the rocks here in 1815.

The shallow seas, so treacherous for vessels, provide Arniston with safe swimming waters. You can swim next to the slipway or at **Roman Beach**, the main swimming beach, just along the coast as you head south from the harbour. Apart from sea bathing, the principal attraction is **Kassiesbaai**, a district of starkly beautiful limewashed cottages, now declared a National Monument and home to coloured fishing families that have made their living here for generations. Although it is a living community, Kassiesbaai is also a bit of a theme park with visitors stalking the streets with their cameras. Heading north through Kassiesbaai at low tide, you can walk along an unspoilt beach for 5km.

Heading south of the harbour for 1500m along spectacular cliffs, you'll reach the vast cave after which the town is named. From the car park by the cave, it's a short signposted walk down to the *fynbos*-covered dunes and the cave, which can only be reached at low tide. The rocks can be slippery and have sharp sections, so be sure to wear shoes with tough soles and a good grip.

ARRIVAL AND DEPARTURE

By car The town is reached on the R316, 24km southeast of Bredasdorp, and 220km from Cape Town on the N2 before you reach the R316. There's no scheduled public transport to Arniston.

ACCOMMODATION

Arniston Lodge 23 Main Rd ☎ 028 445 9175, ⓦ arnistonlodge.co.za. In the residential area, this B&B offers four rooms in a two-storey thatched home with a pool. The upstairs rooms have views and better bathrooms than those downstairs. R1300

Arniston Seaside Cottages Huxham St, signposted as you arrive from Bredasdorp ☎ 028 445 9772, ⓦ arnistonseasidecottages.co.za. A series of attractive and modern self-catering establishments built in the style of traditional fishermen's cottages with limewashed walls and thatched roofs. Clean and bright, they're in a good position just a few minutes' walk from the beach and come fully equipped. R760

★ **Arniston Spa Hotel** Beach Rd ☎ 028 445 9000, ⓦ arnistonhotel.com. Dominating the seafront, this luxurious spa hotel boasts every comfort, including a spa with massage and beauty treatments. The best rooms have a fireplace, or a balcony with sea views. It is one of the best-set beach hotels in the country, and the only one in town. It's expensive, but cheaper during the week or in winter. R2550

EATING

Arniston Spa Hotel Beach Rd ☎ 028 445 9000, ⓦ arnistonhotel.com. Pleasing fresh fish dinners (R140), with outdoor seating to take in the sea views. It also has the town's only bistro bar, which serves burgers and the like, and a TV showing sport. Daily 10am–9.30pm.

Willeen's Meals Arts and Crafts House C26, Kassiesbaai ☎ 028 445 9995. An authentic fisherman's cottage serving traditional Cape Malay meals – try the *bobotie* (R60) or fried fish. You can also have tea and cakes in the garden while enjoying the sea views. Daily 9am–9pm.

De Hoop Nature Reserve

Daily 7am–6pm • R40

De Hoop is the **wilderness highlight** of the Western Cape and one of the best places in the world for land-based whale-watching from July to October, with the greatest numbers of whales to be seen in August and September. There's no need to take a boat or use binoculars; in season you'll see whales blowing or breaching – leaping clear of the water – or perhaps slapping a giant tail. Although the reserve could technically be done as a day-trip from Agulhas, Arniston or Swellendam, you'll find it far more rewarding to come here for a night or more. The **Whale Trail** hike is one of South Africa's best walks and among the finest wildlife experiences in the world (6 days; 54km).

The breathtaking coastline is edged by bleached sand dunes – standing 90m high in places – and rocky formations that at one point open to the sea in a massive craggy arch. The flora and fauna are impressive, too, encompassing 86 species of mammal, 260 different birds and 1500 varieties of plants. Inland, rare **Cape mountain zebra**, **bontebok** and other **antelope** congregate on a plain near the reserve accommodation.

ARRIVAL AND INFORMATION

By car The quickest route from Cape Town is along the N2; De Hoop is signposted off it, 13km west of Swellendam. Alternatively, if you are in the Overberg, take the signposted dirt road that spurs off the R319 as it heads out of Bredasdorp, 50km to its west.

Tourist information The information office (daily 7am–6pm; ☎ 028 542 1114) is at De Opstel, a 20min drive from the coast. Next door is the reserve's only restaurant and a small shop selling basics, so stock up in Swellendam or Bredasdorp before you come.

ACCOMMODATION

All accommodation within the National Park is available through the privately run De Hoop Collection (ⓦ dehoopcollection .co.za), and ranges from **camping** to luxurious **cottages**. The accommodation and **restaurant** are some 20min drive from the sea along roughish dirt roads.

★ **De Hoop Cottages** De Hoop Nature Reserve ☎ 021 422 4522, ⓦ dehoopcollection.co.za. You'll find an array of accommodation here, none of it especially cheap, but all appealing and comfortable. At the top end, you can enjoy

a bed and breakfast stay, with dinner included, in the converted manor house, with food at the next-door restaurant. Camping is the cheapest way to visit the reserve, and there are also a number of appealing self-catering properties of varying sizes – from basic rondavels with outdoor showers to a fully equipped cottage. Camping R375, rondavels R1050, cottages R1600, manor house R3000
Verfheuwel Guestfarm Potberg Rd, in the direction of Malgas ☏ 028 542 1038 or ☏ 082 767 0148,

Ⓦ verfheuwelguestfarm.co.za. This cottage accommodation, attached to the main farmhouse, is run by hospitable Afrikaner farming folk, with dinner brought to your cottage if you ask in advance. It accommodates a couple, with beds in the living area for children, and there's a beautiful garden with a swimming pool. If *Verfheuwel* is full, owner Matti will direct you to others in the area offering farm accommodation. R850

2

EATING

Fig Tree On the reserve, close to reception ☏ 021 422 4522. De Hoop's only restaurant uses local ingredients complementing the Elim wines, with good-value set-menu dinners, usually including fish (R275), plus a children's menu. Reservations are required. Picnic baskets can be ordered (R275 for two), and that is a lovely spot outside that is ideal for sundowners after a good day at the beach. Daily 8–11am, noon–3pm & 7–9pm.

The West Coast

The **West Coast** of South Africa – remote, windswept and bordered by the cold Atlantic – demands a special appreciation. For many years the black sheep of Western Cape tourism, it has been set upon by developers who seem all too ready to spoil the bleached, salty emptiness. The sandy soil and dunes harbour a distinctive coastal *fynbos* vegetation, while the coastline is almost devoid of natural inlets or safe harbours, with fierce southeasterly summer winds and dank winter fogs, though in spring **wild flowers** miraculously appear in the veld. The southern 200km of the region, by far the most densely populated part of the coast, has many links to Namaqualand to the north (see p.283) – not least the flowers.

Outside the flower months of August and September, this part of the West Coast has a wide range of attractions, particularly in summer when the lure of the sea and the cooler coast is strong. The area is well known for its variety of activities, most popularly watersports, hiking and some excellent **birdwatching** (see box, p.196).

Swartland

The N7 highway north from Cape Town leads quickly into the pleasing and fertile **Swartland** landscape. Swartland means "black country", but while the rolling countryside takes on some attractive hues at different times of year, it's never really black. The accepted theory is that, before the area was cultivated, the predominant vegetation was a grey-coloured bush called **renosterbos** (rhinoceros bush) which, seen from the surrounding ranges of hills, gave the area a complexion sufficiently dark to justify the name.

Bordered to the west by the less fertile coastal strandveld and to the east by the tall mountain range running from Wellington to the Cederberg, Swartland is known best as a wheat-growing area, although it also supports dairy farms, horse studs, tobacco crops and vineyards famous for earthy red wines. The N7 skirts a series of towns on its way north, including the largest in the region, **Malmesbury**. If you're travelling south towards Cape Town, look out for some unusual views of Table Mountain, and also for tortoises, which you should take care to avoid as they cross the road.

Darling and around

The small country town of **DARLING** is famous for its rolling countryside, vineyards and dairy products, as well as displays of wild flowers in spring. The town boasts some

BIRDWATCHING ON THE WEST COAST

The **West Coast** is a twitchers' dream, where you can tick off numerous wetland species. The most rewarding viewing time is just after **flower season** in early summer, which heralds the arrival of around 750,000 migrants on their annual pilgrimage from the northern hemisphere, many from as far as the Arctic Circle. They spend about eight months fattening up on delicacies from the tidal mudflats before their arduous journey back to their breeding grounds. **Langebaan** in the West Coast National Park is the best place in the country for such sightings and is considered the fifth most important wetland in the world, hosting over 250 bird species, more than a quarter of South Africa's total. The Berg River estuary and saltworks at **Velddrif** are another vital feeding ground for waders.

The coastal lake of **Verlorenvlei**, meaning "the lost marsh", is another important South African wetland, stretching 13.5km from its mouth at Eland's Bay (25km south of Lambert's Bay) to its headwaters near Redelinghuys. Here species more fond of arid conditions merge with the waders, and there have been some rare sightings including a black egret and a palm-nut vulture. More common are the purple gallinule – a colourful but shy wader – and the African marsh harrier. At **Bird Island**, Lambert's Bay, a sunken hide provides a fantastic view of a garrulous breeding colony of Cape gannets.

handsome old buildings and is something of an **artists' colony**, though it's far better known as the home of one of South Africa's best-loved comedians, **Pieter-Dirk Uys**, who regularly performs here at weekends.

Evita se Perron
At the old train station in the centre of town • Mon 9am–1pm, Tues–Sun 9am–4pm • ☎ 022 492 3930, ⓦ evita.co.za

Pieter-Dirk Uys, South Africa's internationally known comedian, has established his best-loved character, **Evita Bezuidenhout** (South Africa's answer to Dame Edna Everage), as the hostess of a weekend cabaret show. Taking in lunch and a show here is one of the best days out from Cape Town you can have. Book in advance.

!Khwa ttu San Culture and Education Centre
Some 20km west of Darling, along the R27, 70km from Cape Town • Daily 9am–5pm • Free • Tours daily at 10am & 2pm; R195 • ☎ 022 492 2998, ⓦ www.khwattu.org

!Khwa ttu San Culture and Education Centre is the place to visit if you want to find out about "bushmen" or San culture. The centre is run by descendants of Northern Cape San people in partnership with a Swiss NGO, with profits returned to San communities. There is an excellent exhibition of photographs, authentic crafts for sale and a restaurant, all appealingly situated on a hilltop. With a couple of hours in hand, you can take one of the tours to a replica San village and see tracking and hunting techniques. It's also possible to stay overnight (see below).

ARRIVAL AND INFORMATION

DARLING AND AROUND

By car Darling is easily reached from Cape Town (75km away) on a day-trip, via the coastal R27 route.

Tourist information The tourist office on Pastorie St

(Mon–Fri 9am–1pm & 2–4pm, Sat & Sun 10am–3pm ☎ 022 492 3361, ⓦ darlingtourism.co.za) can book accommodation in Darling and on surrounding farms.

ACCOMMODATION

!Khwa Ttu San Some 20km west of Darling, along the R27 ☎ 022 492 2998, ⓦ www.khwattu.org. Accommodation comprises a tented camp, with communal facilities, and a self-catering house with a fireplace. The centre, on a lovely farm, makes a good base for an exploration of Darling and the West Coast National Park. Breakfast included. Tented camp **R325**, house doubles **R1000**

Maison de l'Amour 21 Mount Pleasant St ☎ 022 492 3995, ⓦ maisondelamour.net. A romantic, Provençal style guesthouse in a town called Darling! The two bedrooms have four-poster beds, luxurious linen and en-suite bathrooms, and a cooked breakfast is served in the garden. There is also the adjacent *Gardener's Cottage* for added privacy. Doubles **R1750**, cottage **R1500**

WEST COAST FLOWERS

During August and September you'll see **wild flowers** across the West Coast region, with significant displays starting as far south as **Darling**. Excellent flowers are also found in the **West Coast National Park** and the hazy coastal landscapes around **Cape Columbine** and **Lambert's Bay**, while inland **Clanwilliam** is the centre of some good routes. Around four thousand species are found in the region, mostly of the daisy and mesembryanthemum groups. For advice and guidance, contact the helpful tourist offices in Darling, Saldanha and Clanwilliam; and follow the same wild-flower tips as for Namaqualand (see box, p.285).

EATING

Bistro Seven 7 Main Rd ☏022 492 3626, ⓦbistrosevendarling.com. *Bistro Seven* combines a country pub-style restaurant, offering delicious steaks, line fish, salads and Malay beef curry (R90); a coffee shop serving cakes, tarts, pasties and sandwiches; and a sports bar (see below). Restaurant Mon & Wed–Sat 11am to late, Sun 11am–3pm.

The Cloof Kitchen Cloof Wine Estate, a 20min drive from Darling towards Malmesbury on the R315 ☏022 492 2839, ⓦcloof.co.za. Reasonably priced light lunches – using fresh, local ingredients – including salads, the popular

"Trailblazer" beef burger with secret sauce (R70), and a children's menu; book in advance. Tues–Sat 10am–3pm.

★ **Hilda's Kitchen** Groote Post Wine Estate, Darling Hills Rd, off the R27 ☏022 492 2825 ⓦwww.grootepost.com. Modern, award-winning country cooking in a beautiful eighteenth-century house. The seasonal menu includes hearty soups, fish cakes with Asian flavours, vegetarian dishes, and rich meaty dishes like slow-roast pork belly with plum sauce and noodles (R145), complemented by wines from the estate; booking essential. Children are welcome to roam in the extensive grounds. Wed–Sun noon–2pm.

DRINKING

CJ's Sports Bar 7 Main Rd ☏022 492 3626, ⓦbistrosevendarling.com. This lively and convivial local, attached to *Bistro Seven*, is the place to go for a relaxing

drink, especially if you're a rugby fan and wish to fraternize with the locals. Mon & Wed–Fri 5–11.30pm, Sat & Sun from noon.

Langebaan

Once the home of the largest whaling station in the southern hemisphere, and for a while Cape Town's long-haul passenger flight terminus (when seaplanes from Europe touched down on the lagoon during World War II), **LANGEBAAN** now sells itself as the gateway to the **West Coast National Park**, though it has become depressingly overdeveloped. If you're after a small-town West Coast experience, Paternoster (see p.200) is a better bet. However, if you want to spend time in the small but precious West Coast National Park itself, where there is almost zero accommodation, or if you're into windsurfing, kitesurfing or sailing and have been wondering how to harness the big southeasterly summer winds, the excellent conditions here could mean Langebaan is just your thing. Right off the beach the water is flat, the sailing winds – as the ragged flags above the centre testify – are anywhere from fresh to fearsome, and, unless you catch a fast-running tide out towards the Atlantic, it's all reasonably safe.

ARRIVAL AND INFORMATION
LANGEBAAN

By bus A daily bus, run by Elwierda (☏021 557 9002, ⓦelwierda.com), leaves Cape Town Station at 5pm (Sat 2pm); the journey takes 2hr. Book in advance.

Tourist information The tourist office is in the West Coast National Park HQ on Oostewal Rd (Mon–Fri 9am–5pm, Sat 9am–2pm; ☏022 772 1515, ⓦlangebaan-info.co.za).

ACCOMMODATION

Friday Island Next to Cape Sport, on the beach ☏022 772 2506, ⓦfridayisland.co.za. Perfect for watersports enthusiasts, the units have small kitchenettes, wooden decks, outdoor courtyards to hang up wet gear, and an in-house restaurant. Sea-view rooms cost an extra R300. **R880**

Puza Moya Cnr of North and Suffern sts ☏022 772 1114, ⓦcapesport.co.za. Cheerful en-suite rooms with a shared kitchen and courtyard for braais. A good option if you like to socialize in a relaxed environment after an active day. Breakfast is available (R90). **R880**

HITTING THE WATER IN LANGEBAAN

If you want to try your hand at any of the **watersports** on offer in Langebaan, the friendly Cape Sports Centre (98 Main St; daily 8.30am–5.30pm; ☎ 022 772 1114, ⓦ capesports.co.za), on the beach on the northern edge of town, is the place to head to for **windsurfing**, **hobiecat sailing** and **kitesurfing** tuition. **Sailing courses** on the Langebaan Lagoon are run by Ocean Sailing Academy based in Cape Town (☎ 021 425 7837, ⓦ oceansailing.co.za).

2

EATING

★ **Die Strandloper Restaurant and Beach Bar** On the beach just beyond the Cape Sport Centre on the road to Saldanha ☎ 022 772 2490 or ☎ 083 227 7195, ⓦ www.strandloper.com. A good example of the West Coast's lively open-air seafood restaurants, with sand beneath your feet and fishing nets above. Committed to sustainable seafood, this is a good place to try West Coast fish delicacies like *harders* and dried *snoek*: it's R295 for a ten-course set menu, and booking is essential. Always check their website for opening hours as they vary from season to season, but are open every day in the peak summer months.

Pearly's On the beach, Bree St ☎ 022 772 2734 ⓦ pearlys.co.za. Crowded eating, drinking and people watching spot with outside tables in a great location for enjoying uncomplicated pizza, pasta (R90), seafood or grilled steak – not to mention the wonderful sunsets. Mon–Thurs 9am–10.30pm, Fri & Sat 9am–11pm, Sun 8.30am–10pm.

DRINKING

Kalmer Karma Craft Beer & Restaurant 98 Main St ☎ 022 707 9116. A beautiful location on the beach with outside tables, this is the best place in town for sundowners. There's a good selection of craft beers (R45) on offer, as well as pub meals, with fish often on the menu. Closed in the winter. Wed–Sun 11am–11pm.

West Coast National Park

Daily: April–Aug 7am–6pm; Sept–March 7am–7pm • R75 (outside flower season), R150 (in flower season Aug & Sept) • ☎ 012 428 9111 • ⓦ sanparks.org/parks/west_coast

The **West Coast National Park** is one of the best places to savour the charm of the area, which elsewhere is being devoured by housing developments. The park protects over 40 percent of South Africa's remaining pristine strandveld and 35 percent of the country's salt marshes, and incorporates most of Langebaan Lagoon and a Y-shaped area of land immediately around and below it.

Much of the park's appeal lies in the uplifting views over the still lagoon to an olive-coloured, rocky hillside, the sharp, saline air, and the calling gulls and Atlantic mists vanishing in the harsh sunlight. This isn't a game park – a few larger antelope are located in the Postberg section of the park, an area open only during the spring flower season, but there are huge numbers of **birds**, including ostriches and thousands of migrating waders, plus tortoises galore. A number of well-organized interpretive walking trails lead through the dunes to the long, smooth, wave-beaten Atlantic coastline, offering plenty of opportunity to learn about the hardy *fynbos* vegetation that so defines the look and feel of the West Coast region. The best time to visit the park is in **spring**, when the sun is shining and the flowers are out, although this is, inevitably, the busiest period. Like much of the West Coast, the national park is chilly and wet in winter, and hot and wind-blasted in summer.

On the southern tip of the lagoon is the effective centre – a large old farmhouse called **Geelbek**. From here, continue up the peninsula on the western side of the lagoon and you'll pass the entrance to **Churchhaven**, a tiny exclusive and beautiful village (gated to prevent day visitors), and two signposted beaches with picnic areas, Priekstool and Kraalbaai.

A little further on is the demarcated **Postberg area**, open only during flower season (see box, p.197), but worth visiting at that time to see **zebra**, **gemsbok** and **wildebeest** wandering through fields of wild flowers.

ARRIVAL AND INFORMATION

By car The park is 90km from Cape Town, and there are two entrance gates to the park: one on the R27, roughly 10km north of the turning to Yzerfontein, and the other south of Langebaan. The park isn't huge – if you're driving you'll cover the extent of the roads in a couple of hours.

WEST COAST NATIONAL PARK

Information Staff at the Geelbek Information Centre in the Geelbek Cape Dutch House (Mon–Fri 8.30am–4pm, Sat & Sun 9am–1pm; ☎ 022 772 2144/45) can direct you to the bird hides nearby, or give you information about walks in the area.

ACCOMMODATION

Churchaven Beach Houses Churchaven ☎ 021 790 0972, ⓦ perfecthideaways.co.za. A couple of stunning, if very pricey, self-catering beach houses (sleeping 2–10) in sought-after Churchaven. They are contemporary in design, with top-quality beds and linen, secluded outdoor showers and patios with incomparable views. R5500

Duinepos Chalets 1km from Geelbek (signposted) ☎ 022 707 9900, ⓦ duinepos.co.za. Eleven self-catering chalets, set in *fynbos*, designed to have a low environmental impact by using minimal water and electricity. There's a swimming pool on-site, or lagoon swimming at Priekstool or Kraalbaai some 12–15km away. R1150

EATING

Geelbek Restaurant Geelbek ☎ 022 772 2134. Magnificent setting in a graceful Cape Dutch building on the lagoon, where you can sit outside and watch flamingos – if you are lucky. South African dishes, such as *bobotie*

(R125), ostrich burgers, *snoek* salad and Cape Malay curries, are the speciality, though the surroundings are rather more appealing than the food. Booking essential during flower season. Daily 9am–5pm.

Vredenburg

North of Saldanha lies a sizeable inland farming centre, **VREDENBURG**, an unremarkable town in a featureless setting. However, it's a useeful place to visit for its well-stocked supermarkets and is a good place to buy fuel, since many of the smaller towns nearby don't have filling stations.

West Coast Fossil Park

About 10km southeast of Vredenburg, on the R45 • Mon–Fri 8am–4pm, Sat & Sun opening times vary, so phone first • R45 • Guided tours on the hour from 10am–3pm Mon–Fri and 10am–1pm Sat & Sun; R80 • ☎ 022 766 1606, ⓦ fossilpark.org.za

Founded in 1998 on the site of a decommissioned phosphate mine, and still being developed, the interesting **West Coast Fossil Park** is a relatively low-key affair, but highly recommended nevertheless. Displays include thousands of fossils and modern animal bones, as well as information panels about the extinct species that were found on-site, which date back some five million years. Finds include fossils from sabre-toothed cats, two species of extinct elephant, and sivatheres – long-horned, short-necked, giraffe-like browsers. Perhaps strangest of all are the extinct giant bears, *Agriotherium africanum*, which weighed in at 750kg (compared to 150kg for a large lion), making them the heftiest predators – and the only known bears – to have roamed sub-Saharan Africa in the past 65 million years. The guided tours are recommended, though you can wander around by yourself.

ARRIVAL AND INFORMATION

By bus A daily bus, operated by Elwierda (☎ 021 557 9002, ⓦ elwierda.com), leaves Cape Town Station for Vredenburg at 5pm (Sat 2pm) and leaves Vredenberg for Cape Town at 5.55am (Fri & Sun 12.55pm). The journey time is 3hr.

VREDENBURG

Information The West Coast Peninsula Tourism Bureau is in the Atrium Building on the corner of Piet Retief and Main Sts (Mon–Fri 9am–5pm; ☎ 022 715 1142, ⓦ capewestcoastpeninsula.co.za).

ACCOMMODATION

Windstone Backpackers Just past the main crossroads of the R45 from Vredenburg, and the R27 from Cape Town ☎ 022 766 1645 or ☎ 083 477 1756, ⓦ windstone.co.za. Straightforward and

unpretentious, *Windstone* makes a friendly base for exploring the region. The accommodation consists of four- and six-bed dorms, and two doubles. Dorms R150, doubles R350

Paternoster

The best of the West Coast is to be found at the village of **PATERNOSTER**, a favourite weekend seaside destination for Capetonians. Besides tourism, small-scale angling and crayfish netting is the principal economic activity of the village, and most of the fishermen live in the whitewashed cottages of the coloured district to the west of the hotel. When they're not out at sea, their small, brightly painted boats lie beached at the water's edge.

Unfortunately, Paternoster has become increasingly developed, and it's also a place (like many others) for opportunistic theft from unsuspecting tourists. Nevertheless, the coast itself is beautiful, saved from development by the Columbine Nature Reserve, 3km to the west (see below), where huge waves smash against large granite rocks as smooth as whales' backs.

Columbine Nature Reserve

3km to the west of Paternoster, along an unpaved road • Nature reserve daily sunrise to sunset • R20 • ☎ 022 752 2718

A small area set aside to conserve the sandveld-*fynbos* heathland indigenous to the region, the **Columbine Nature Reserve** makes a stunning change from the salty flats that typify the West Coast. Large vegetated dunes sweep down to a shoreline of massive pink granite boulders and little coves, with beaches that are blue-tinged, a result of mussel shells being washed up and finely crushed into the sands. It's best to park at **Tieties Bay** (camping is allowed here, right by the ocean), from where you can simply follow the marked path over the rocks and along the dunes to explore the area.

Besides rambling, there are some excellent coastal **hikes** through the reserve, including two long day-trails: Vredenburg tourist office (see p.199) can provide details of these. Along the road from Paternoster to the reserve you'll pass the **Cape Columbine lighthouse** (☎ 022 752 2705, open Mon–Fri 10am–noon and 12.30–3pm, entry R20), built in 1936 on Castle Rock. It emits a single white flash every fifteen seconds, and is usually the first lighthouse to be sighted by ships from Europe rounding Africa.

ARRIVAL AND INFORMATION

PATERNOSTER

By car Paternoster is 15km northwest of Vredenburg and 160km from Cape Town, on the R27.

By bus The daily Elwierda Bus (☎ 021 557 9002, ⓦ elwierda.com), which runs between Cape Town and Saldanha, stops at nearby Vredenburg (see p.199).

Tourist information The tourist office is next to the fish market at the beach, signposted from the main road as you enter town (Mon–Fri 9am–5pm, Sat 9am–2pm; ☎ 022 752 2323, ⓦ capewestcoastsa.co.za).

ACCOMMODATION

Baywatch Villa Collection 6 Ambyl Rd ☎ 022 752 2039, ⓦ baywatchvilla.co.za. A guesthouse offering four en-suite bedrooms and four luxurious self-catering thatched fisherman-style cottages, just a 2min walk from Long Beach, in the quiet part of town to the north. Doubles R1790, cottages R1200

Cape Columbine Lighthouse Guesthouse Cape Columbine Reserve ☎ 022 752 2705. Self-catering is offered in three former lighthouse keepers' cottages around the lighthouse, on a prominent headland in the Cape Columbine reserve. The cottages are kitted out with all mod cons, and have two or three bedrooms. R600

Die Opstal Sonkwas St ☎ 083 988 4645, ⓦ paternoster-villas.co.za. Five self-catering cottages, all with separate entrances. The building is one row behind the beachfront properties, and it's cheaper than other options because it lacks sea views, though you can reach the beach in two minutes. R850

Mosselbank On the corner of Trappiesklip and Mosselbank sts ☎ 022 752 2027, ⓦ weskus.com. A hospitable B&B in a suburban development in the northern part of town, close to Long Beach. There are five en-suite rooms, some with sea views. R1300

★**Oystercatchers' Haven** 48 Sonkwas St ☎ 022 752 2193, ⓦ oystercatchershaven.com. A top-quality guesthouse with four tastefully furnished rooms, situated on the beach at the edge of Columbine Reserve. The views are wonderful, and there's a swimming pool plus loungers close to the beach. R1950

★**Paternoster Dunes** 18 Sonkwas St ☎ 022 752 2217, ⓦ paternosterdunes.co.za. A gorgeous guesthouse with contemporary beachhouse-style rooms and one self-catering cottage leading onto the sand – everything designed to inspire and delight the senses. Make sure you have a seaview room, rather than a courtyard-facing one. The pool, in the central courtyard, is protected from the wind. R1500

SEA KAYAKING IN PATERNOSTER

An adventure highlight of Paternoster is guided **sea kayaking**. Kayak Paternoster (☎082 584 1907, ⓦkayakpaternoster.co.za; no under 7s) runs one-hour trips (R200), which are as much about observing and learning about birds, whales, dolphins and seals as about paddling. The kayaks launch from the Main Beach, but won't go out if the swell is too big.

Seashack Just below the lighthouse in Cape Columbine Reserve ☎082 824 8917, ⓦseashack .co.za. Ten small wooden cabins right on the beach, all self-catering and each one styled slightly differently by local artist Theo Kleynhans. The cabins are solar- and gas-powered, beds have fresh linen, but you should bring your own towels. A sociable place to stay – join other guests around the firepit at night to cook and chat. R750

EATING

★**Gaaitjie Salt Water Restaurant** Off Sampson Rd ☎022 752 2242, ⓦsaltcoast.co.za. The top-notch chef here produces creative seafood-based dishes in a great beachside location – try the Saldanha Bay mussels (R75). Book in advance for a sea-facing table; you'll be provided with a rug for the chill sea breezes. Delicious vegetarian dishes can be provided on request. Thurs–Mon noon–3pm & 6–9pm; closed in winter.

Noisy Oyster St Augustine Rd ☎022 752 2196. An informal restaurant just off the main drag where the speciality is fish – the raw oysters (R18 each) are reputedly "to die for" – but there also great meat and vegetarian options. What it lacks in setting, it makes up for in ambience and good food. Wed–Sat noon–3pm & 6–9pm, Sun noon–3pm; closed June & July.

Oep Ve Koep St Augustine Rd ☎022 752 2105. Served in the wind-sheltered garden, the set 3-course lunch (R295) consists of mussel soup starter, a fresh fish main and home-made ice-cream dessert, made by the talented chef whose repertoire is inspired by local fare. It also serves local craft beers and wines. Mon–Sat 9am–4pm; Sun 9am–3pm.

Paternoster Hotel St Augustine Rd ☎022 752 2703, ⓦpaternosterhotel.co.za/restaurant. Known for their West Coast seafood platters (R595 for two), and if you book in advance they can organize a seafood braai. Daily 8am–9.30pm.

DRINKING

The Panty Bar Paternoster Hotel, St Augustine Rd ☎022 752 2703, ⓦpaternosterhotel.co.za/pub. Down a beer or two under a ceiling festooned with assorted female lingerie – mostly knickers plus the odd trophy bra. This is something of a Paternoster landmark but (it's safe to say) will not appeal to everyone. Daily 11am–10pm.

Velddrif

At the northern end of the R27 from Cape Town is **VELDDRIF**, a fishing town situated at the point where the Great Berg River meets the sea. Each year the Berg River **canoe marathon** (which starts near Ceres, 49km north of Worcester) ends here at a marina development called Port Owen. Over the last couple of decades, the town has outgrown its fishing industry origins and is now dominated by a modern suburbia of brick bungalows. However, the town's setting on the meandering Berg and the surrounding wetlands – as well as the vision of some locals, who have managed to stay the eager hand of the demolition crews – have resulted in Velddrif retaining a little of its historic character, and there is a wealth of **birdlife**, including pelicans and flamingos, along both banks of the river (see box, p.196).

In the quieter backwaters near the Velddrif bridge, you can still see individual fishermen in small boats landing catches of mullet or horse mackerel. The fish are then dried and salted to make *bokkoms*, thought of as a delicacy, but essentially a source of cheap protein for fishermen and farm workers on the West Coast. To see the rickety wooden jetties where the boats tie up, and the frames and sheds by the shore where *bokkoms* are strung up to dry, turn right at the roundabout just over the bridge coming into town on the R27, and after 1km or so take the first right-hand turn down to the riverside. Turning left over the same bridge takes you to Pelican Harbour, where a number of coffee and craft shops are housed in a renovated fish factory.

INFORMATION AND TOURS

Information The tourist office is in the Municipal Building on Voortrekker Rd (Mon–Fri 8.30am–1pm, 2–5pm, Sat 10am–1pm; ☎ 022 783 1821, ⓦ velddriftourism.co.za).
Boat trips Take a pleasant boat trip into the wetlands with well-informed birder Dan Ahlers (☎ 082 951 0447; 60min trip R150), who organizes excursions up the Berg River. He also leads bay cruises on which you may get to see marine mammals.

ACCOMMODATION

★**Kersefontein Guest Farm** 25km south of Velddrif on the Berg River ☎ 083 454 1025, ⓦ kersefontein .co.za. A highlight of the West Coast region, this is a working farm grazed by wild horses that dates back to the eighteenth century. The farm includes several handsome Cape Dutch listed buildings, complete with antiques. Some of the buildings have been converted into stylish accommodation. Julian Melck, the eighth-generation owner, treats guests to lively tales of life on a South African farm. Dinner is available (R270). B&B R1220

Kuifkopvisvanger 5km from town on the other side of the river ☎ 022 783 0818, ⓦ kuifkop.co.za. There are just seven charming, rustic fishermen's cottages here, with views of the river and marshlands, and great for birdwatching. Camping is also available, and in the summer you can use the canoes to explore or swim in the river. Camping R120, cottages R1000

Riviera 136 Voortrekker Rd ☎ 022 783 1137, ⓦ eigevis .com. The *Riviera* has double rooms, plus well-equipped self-catering chalets sleeping four (from R950), each with a patio and set on the water's edge. There's also a restaurant and bar serving good food, with a balcony from which you can observe flamingos and other water birds. R850

EATING

The Laaiplek Hotel Jameson St ☎ 022 783 1116. This long-established, old-fashioned harbour hotel overlooks the Berg River and has great views of boats, fish factories and cranes, as well as birds. They specialize in seafood and steaks (R130), good solid fare though not particularly inspired. Daily 7am–9pm.

★**Die Vishuis** Vye St, about 3km west of Velddrif along the riverside dirt road ☎ 022 783 1183, ⓦ dievishuis.co.za. Housed in a restored traditional fish-drying factory, with outdoor seating offering views across the wetlands, *Die Vishuis* serves the best fish and chips (R105) in Velddrif. Mon–Sat 8am–8pm.

Elands Bay

Elands Bay (more commonly known as Elands) is a popular weekend destination, with a couple of guesthouses and restaurants, some fine bushman rock paintings on the south-side cliffs, and exceptional birdwatching. It's probably a place to catch before it's developed, though, like most of the West Coast, the water is freezing, and the coastline spare, windswept and harsh – the tide spewing mounds of kelp, shells and dried-out seal bones onto the deserted beaches. The spring flowers in this vicinity are also phenomenal.

Elands is divided into north and south sides by the **Verlorenvlei** ("lost wetland"), which supports over two hundred bird species. The nicer side is the south, where the surfers hang out. Above here, the Bobbejaanberg ridge runs into the sea. Where the road ends beneath the cliffs is the harbour. Nearby a path leads up to a large cave with rock art, including some large eland and hundreds of small handprints, thought to be connected to adolescent rites of passage.

ARRIVAL AND INFORMATION

By car It's a lonely 70km drive from Velddrif to Elands Bay, though the road is tarred all the way. It's approximately 200km from Cape Town (2hr 30min to drive).

Information There is no tourist office at Elands Bay, but the one at Lambert's Bay can help with information (☎ 027 432 1000, ⓦ lambertsbay.co.za).

ACCOMMODATION

Elands Bay Guest House 184 Kreef Rd, South Side ☎ 022 972 1755, ⓦ elandsbayguesthouse.co.za. No frills self-catering accommodation, sleeping up to four people. It's principally geared to groups of surfers, with a communal kitchen and wetsuits drying in the sun. R1200

Elands Bay Hotel North Side Beachfront ☎ 022 972 1640, ⓦ elandsbayhotel.co.za. Reasonably priced place right by the beach, with double rooms – go for the sea-facing ones – as well as backpackers' rooms and camping. Camping R250, dorms R180, B&B doubles R1490

★**Vensterklip** 5km from Elands Bay ☎ 022 972 1340, ⓦ vensterklip.co.za. A farm on the *vlei* with self-catering in restored, historic farm buildings and cottages, as well as camping (with tents for rent) and an excellent restaurant on-site. Kayaks, free for guests, can be rented by day visitors for nosing around the *vlei*. Guided horse trails are also available, and there's a swimming pool. Camping R150, cottages R920

EATING

Elands Bay Hotel North Side Beachfront ☎ 022 972 1640. The only central option for reasonably priced seafood meals, grills and steak (R125), or pop in for a drink while enjoying the brilliant views. Popular for breakfasts after a long surfing bout. Daily 8am–9pm.

Tin Kitchen Country Restaurant Vensterklip Farm, 5km from Elands Bay ☎ 022 972 1340. The best bet for food, though only available at weekends, with meals using mostly organic ingredients, farm meat, local seafood and seasonal vegetables. Friday nights are their popular and lively pizza nights (R90). The restaurant is in a 300-year-old barn, but you can also eat outside in the garden. Fri & Sat 9am–10pm, Sun 9am–3pm.

Lambert's Bay

The rather forlorn town of **LAMBERT'S BAY** is the only settlement of any note between Velddrif and Port Nolloth, the latter close to the Namibian border. It's an important fishing port, although judging by the sights and sounds of the harbour even the fishermen have to stand aside for the impressive colony of **gannets** on **Bird Island**, in the centre of the bay.

Lambert's Bay Bird Island Nature Reserve

Daily 8am–6pm • R40 • ☎ 021 483 0190, ⓦ capenature.co.za/reserves/bird-island-nature-reserve

It's possible to walk out to the island on the causeway for a closer look at the tightly packed, ear-piercing mass of petulant gannets from the bird hide, along with a few disapproving-looking penguins and cormorants, though viewing is not always guaranteed outside of the breeding season. The bay plays host to a resident pod of around seven **humpback whales** during their breeding season from July to November. This is also the southernmost area ranged by **Heaviside's dolphins** – small, friendly mammals with wedge-shaped beaks and white, striped patterning reminiscent of killer whales. You may be lucky and view the cavorting dolphins on trips from the fishing port.

ARRIVAL AND INFORMATION   LAMBERT'S BAY

By car Lambert's Bay is some 27km north of Elands Bay, and 70km due west of Clanwilliam by tarred road.

Information The tourist office is in the Medical Centre on Main Rd (Mon–Fri 9am–5pm, Sat 9am–12.30pm; ☎ 027 432 1000, ⓦ lambertsbay.co.za).

ACCOMMODATION

Grootvlei Guest Farm On the R365, 6km south of Lambert's Bay ☎ 027 432 2716 or ☎ 076 592 6541, ⓦ grootvleiguestfarm.co.za. There are two venues to choose from at *Grootvlei*: a luxurious guesthouse in a two-storey homestead or, for something very different, one of the shell-shaped rooms in an elegant, eco-friendly B&B set amid the dunes and just a step away from the ocean. No children or pets allowed. R1600

Lambert's Bay Hotel Voortrekker St ☎ 027 432 1126, ⓦ lambertsbayhotel.co.za. Smack in the centre of town, this conventional and rather old-fashioned hotel offers neat and reasonably priced rooms, a swimming pool at the back, and help with organizing activities such as boat trips, birding, beach riding or spring flower trips. There is a restaurant open for breakfast, lunch and dinner, and a ladies' bar. R1350

EATING

Isabella's Restaurant and Coffee Shop At the harbour ☎ 027 432 1177, ⓦ isabellas-restaurant.co.za. A popular hangout, largely because of its location right on the waterfront, with outside tables and chairs that take in the harbour atmosphere and views. It offers the whole range of meals, from coffee and cake to fish and chips, prawns or a pot of mussels, but is particularly renowned for its blowout West Coast breakfast (R80). Daily 8am–9pm.

★**Muisbosskerm** Elands Bay Rd, 5km from Lambert's Bay ☎ 027 432 1017, ⓦ muisbosskerm.co.za. The original West Coast open-air seafood restaurant scores on location – it's right at the edge of the ocean, on a deserted beach – and is rated by many as one of the top ten things to do on a visit to South Africa. A massive buffet (R250) is on offer, with baked, smoked or grilled fish, potato bread cooked in a clay oven and traditional *waterblommetjie* stew, complete with Afrikaans *boeremusiek* in the background. It's not open every day (phone to check before coming), and you will need to book in advance. Lunch from 12.30pm, dinner from 6.30pm.

2 The Cederberg

A bold and jagged outcrop of the Western Cape fold escarpment, the **Cederberg range** is one of the most magical wilderness areas in the Western Cape. Rising with a striking presence on the eastern side of the Olifants River Valley, around 250km north of Cape Town, these high sandstone mountains and long, dry valleys manage to combine accessibility with remote harshness, offering something for hikers, campers, naturalists and rock climbers.

The **Cederberg Wilderness Area**, flanking the N7 between Citrusdal and Clanwilliam, was created to protect the silt-free waters of the Cederberg catchment area, but it also provides a recreational sanctuary with over 250km of hiking trails. In a number of places, the red-hued sandstone has been weathered into grotesque, gargoyle-like shapes and a number of memorable natural features. Throughout the area there are also numerous **San rock-art** sites, an active array of Cape mountain fauna – from baboon and small antelope to leopard, caracal and aardwolf – and some notable montane *fynbos* flora, including the gnarled and tenacious Clanwilliam cedar and the rare snow protea.

The Cederberg is accessed from Cape Town on the N7. Its two main, but small, towns, **Citrusdal** and **Clanwilliam**, lie just off the highway near, respectively, the southern and northern tips of the mountain range. They are not in the mountains themselves, and are not the places to base yourself if you want to hike. The main route into the Cederberg is along a dirt road marked **Algeria**, which branches off the N7 between the two towns; it's 18km from the turn-off to Algeria campsite. The eastern side of the Cederberg, known as the **Koue Bokkeveld**, is not accessed from the N7, but from the N1 and Ceres.

Citrusdal

North of Piketberg on the N7, a long, flat plain reaches out to the line of Olifants River Mountains, which the highway crosses by way of the impressive **Piekenierskloof Pass**, forged in 1857 by the indomitable road engineer Thomas Bain. **CITRUSDAL** appears in the rolling countryside of the Olifants River Valley, with the dramatic mountainscape of the Cederberg behind. The river was named by early Dutch explorers who saw huge herds of elephants here as they travelled north towards Namaqualand (see p.283).

One of the principal attractions of this area is the natural **hot springs** 16km from Citrusdal, which you can visit as a day visitor or stay overnight (see below). Another draw is the jolly wayside farm stalls along the N7, which offer fruit from the area – especially citrus (as the town's name suggests) – plus dried fruit, vegetables, biltong, dates, nuts and rusks.

ARRIVAL AND INFORMATION   CITRUSDAL

By car Citrusdal is a couple of kilometres off the N7, 170km from Cape Town.
Information The tourist office, at 39 Voortrekker St

(Mon–Fri 9am–5pm, Sat 9am–1pm; ☎022 921 3210, ⓦ citrusdal.info), has a list of self-catering and B&B accommodation in the area.

ACCOMMODATION

The Baths South off the road leading into Citrusdal from the N7, then 16km down a good tarred road

☎022 921 8026, ⓦthebaths.co.za. A pleasantly old-fashioned mineral spa resort with one large hot pool

INTO THE MOUNTAINS

You have to **hike** to actually get into the Cederberg mountains themselves; short walks are possible from a few properties, but if you want to do any serious walking you should be properly equipped and experienced as this is rough country, and weather conditions can be harsh throughout the year.

One of the best ways to get into the mountains is with **professional mountaineer** Mike Wakeford (☎ 079 772 9808, ✪ guidedbymike.co.za), who offers tailor-made trekking trips that depart from Cape Town and take 2–5 days (R1500 per day).

2

(43°C), a cold pool and some stunning hot mineral spring water pools nestled in the trees. Day visitors pay R100 and must book one day in advance to use the amenities, but guests can use them for free. It is set in a beautiful wooded glen with camping pitches, chalets and self-catering rooms in some old stone buildings. There's also a restaurant with passable food, though most people self-cater. Camping R300, doubles R1100

Hebron B&B On the N7, 400m after the summit on Piekenierskloof Pass ☎ 022 921 2595 or ☎ 022 921 2581, ✪ hebron.co.za. A beautiful old farm with six en-suite rooms: three (one of which is self-catering) sharing a peaceful courtyard and three with a veranda looking out

over the valley. There's also a large garden with a spectacular swimming pool and a restaurant where breakfast and lunch are available (dinner needs to be arranged in advance) – all the food is made from fresh organic ingredients, most of it from the farm. Doubles R2010

★ **Petersfield Mountain Cottages** 4km from Citrusdal ☎ 022 921 3316, ✪ petersfieldfarm.co.za. On a working rooibos and citrus farm, with some of the best self-catering cottages you'll find anywhere; each secluded cottage sleeps 2–4 people and has its own private pool. For weekends, you'll need to book a year in advance, with a minimum stay of two nights; the weekday rate is about R300 cheaper. Cottages R1400

EATING

The Grapevine Coffee Shop 30 Voortrekker Rd, Citrusdal ☎ 022 921 2190. Visitors rarely venture into Citrusdal itself, but if you do, this popular, centrally located place is worth checking out for its good

egg breakfasts and light lunches – dishes such as smoked *snoek* and salad (R65) – as well as its coffee and great home-made cakes. Mon–Fri 8am–4pm, Sat 8am–1pm.

The Cederberg Wilderness Area

The main route into the Cederberg, and Algeria, the forest station that serves as a focal point for the area, heads east off the N7, 28km north of Citrusdal, and connects all the way towards Ceres in the east. The 710-square-kilometre **Cederberg Wilderness Area** features many designated trails, including the two main peaks, **Sneeuberg** (2027m) and **Tafelberg** (1969m), as well as the awesome rock formations of the huge **Wolfberg Arch** and **Cracks** in the southeast of the reserve, and a 30m-high freestanding pillar shaped like (and known as) the **Maltese Cross**, to its south.

ARRIVAL AND INFORMATION

THE CEDERBERG WILDERNESS AREA

By car The main route into the Cederberg is along Algeria Rd (clearly signposted). It's a rough dirt road, but fine in an ordinary car if you take it slowly. From Cape Town it is about 250km, so you should allow three and a half hours.

Information There is a R60 entry fee (gates open 7am–7pm) and you'll need permits to hike, which

you can book beforehand on ☎ 021 483 0190/0000 or obtain at the CapeNature Office at Algeria campsite (Mon–Fri 7.30am–4pm; ☎ 027 482 2403, ✪ capenature .co.za). An indispensable map, *Exploring the Cederberg* (✪ slingsbymaps.com), is available from hiking shops.

ACCOMMODATION

Algeria Campsite 18km east on Algeria Rd, signposted off the N7 ☎ 021 483 0190 or ☎ 021 483 0000, ✪ capenature.co.za. A pretty riverside site, with a gorgeous river pool and hikes leaving from the campsite itself into the surrounding mountains. It can be

crowded and noisy during school hols, but the kids will have a ball. There are also a couple of self-catering chalets, and isolated cottages a few kilometres away with paraffin lamps rather than electricity. Camping R220, chalets R580

2

Jamaka Organic Farm and Resort Signposted and accessed just before Algeria, on the Algeria Rd ☎ 027 482 2801/5, ⓦ jamaka.co.za. The campsite on this organic citrus and mango farm has a lovely setting, though for good hikes you will need to drive over to *Algeria Campsite*, and do the trails from there. If you want a roof over your head, note that the best of their twelve reasonably priced cottages is the stone one next to the river. Camping R180, cottages R520

Kromrivier Cederberg Park 50km south of Algeria ☎ 027 482 2807, ⓦ cederbergpark.com. Ten fully equipped chalets, sleeping four, plus two backpacker chalets with outside toilet and central hot shower block. There are also camping pitches near river

pools for swimming, plus a coffee shop on-site if you don't feel like cooking, though you'll need to pre-order dinner by 4pm on the day. They also offer horseriding. Camping R200, chalets R500

★ **Sanddrif** About 26km south of Algeria, along the same dirt road ☎ 027 482 2825, ⓦ sanddrif.com. Fully equipped chalets with one to three rooms, on a farm with river pools and good walks, as well as camping. *Sanddrif* also sells permits for the classic walks on its property – the Maltese Cross, Wolfberg Arch and Cracks – and offers tasting sessions of the wines made from grapes grown on the farm. There's a shop selling basics, and an observatory that is open on Saturday evenings for two hours of stargazing. There's a minimum stay of two nights at weekends. Camping R220, chalets R920

Koue Bokkeveld (Southeastern Cederberg)

The southeastern Cederberg mountain range, known as the **Koue Bokkeveld**, is remote and wild, with some wonderful places to stay. You'll need to be self-sufficient if you are self-catering, as there are no shops or cafés hereabouts, though all the places listed below have restaurants. The best way to approach this region is from Worcester on the N1: from here, take the R303 to Ceres, then turn right at Op de Berg to join the Algeria dirt road which heads north and eventually joins the N7.

ACCOMMODATION   **KOUE BOKKEVELD**

Cederberg Oasis On the R303, 70km from Op de Berg and 62km east of Algeria ☎ 027 482 2819, ⓦ cederbergoasis.co.za. Backpacker accommodation in basic rooms, doubles and dorms, plus camping on the lawn. There's a licensed restaurant, serving meals of gigantic proportions, though you'll need to prebook for dinner. The owner Gerrit will draw you a map and help you get permits so you can visit the nearby sandstone formations and rock art at Tanjieskraal and Stadsaal Caves, or any hiking trails you wish to undertake. Camping R150, doubles R340

★ **Kamma** 52km from Op de Berg, off the R303 ☎ 021 872 4343, ⓦ kaggakamma.co.za. A luxury lodge with some accommodation built into the rocks, plus thatched chalets with verandas looking out onto natural veld. There are walks, game drives, and a good restaurant and bar, and guests can opt for a stargazing tour – a high-powered telescope enables you to see the moons of Jupiter. The rock

art and rock formations on the property are magnificent – some of the best are close to the large swimming pool. One of the highlights is the sundowner game drive followed by a fireside dinner under the stars. There's an all-inclusive rate that includes meals and activities (R4140 per person), or you can opt for bed and breakfast. Camping R125, doubles R2900

★ **Mount Ceder** On the R303, 42km from Op de Berg ☎ 023 317 0113, ⓦ mountceder.co.za. A very comfortable mountain retreat with self-catering cottages, some with jacuzzis. Some of the cottages have mains electricity and sleep four, while others sleep two and are solar-powered. There are also three sought-after luxury camping pitches, each with ablutions and solar lighting. Set on an olive farm along a river with pools for swimming, it's surrounded by fierce, rugged mountains. There's also a restaurant and activities such as hiking, fishing and mountain biking. Camping R330, cottages R800

Clanwilliam

At the northern end of the Cederberg, **CLANWILLIAM** is an attractive and assured small town. It carries off with some aplomb its various roles as a base for the majestic Cederberg Wilderness Area: as a centre for spring flowers, a service centre for surrounding farms, and the place to head for if you want to see good **rock art** within easy striking distance of Cape Town. Established in the last years of the eighteenth century, Clanwilliam is one of the older settlements north of Cape Town and features a number of historic buildings.

CEDERBERG ROCK ART

The Cederberg has around 2500 known **rock-art sites**, estimated to be between one and eight thousand years old. They are the work of the first South Africans, hunter-gatherers known as San or **Bushmen**, the direct descendants of some of the earliest *Homo sapiens* who lived in the Western Cape 150,000 years ago.

One of the best ways to see the rock art is on a self-guided 4km walk from *Travellers Rest* farm (see p.210) along the Sevilla Trail, which takes in ten sites.

2

ARRIVAL AND INFORMATION   CLANWILLIAM

By bus The daily Intercape bus from Cape Town to Windhoek stops 7km away at a garage on the N7, though there's no way of getting from there into town.
Information The tourist office is on Main Rd (Mon–Fri 8.30am–5pm, Sat 8.30am–12.30pm; ☎027 482 2024, ⊚ clanwilliam.info), and can help with accommodation and maps.

ACCOMMODATION

Blommenberg Guest House 1 Graafwater Rd ☎027 482 1851, ⊚ blommenberg.co.za. Opposite the garage as you come into Clanwilliam, this guesthouse has good-value rooms with pine beds and fittings set around a pleasantly shady courtyard garden and swimming pool. Four family-sized rooms on the veranda can be used for self catering. R1090
Clanwilliam Living Landscape Project 18 Park St ☎027 482 1911. This is an acceptable place to stay, and the only backpacker accommodation in the centre of Clanwilliam, with dorms in a suburban house next door to a community project. It is mostly geared towards school and university groups on rock-art projects. R150
Ndedema Lodge 48 Park St ☎027 482 1314, ⊚ ndedemalodge.co.za. A romantic Victorian B&B with an upmarket feel, and a charming garden with a pool. Its six stylishly decorated and air-conditioned rooms are filled with antiques and come with cotton bed linen, plush towels and dressing gowns. R1300

EATING

Nancy's Tea Room 33 Main Rd ☎027 482 2661. The outdoor garden here is a peaceful place for breakfast or lunch, with toasted sandwiches, savoury mince and cheddar melt (R60) and good coffee all on offer. Slightly heavier lunch dishes include *bobotie*, one of the few meals that doesn't come with chips. Mon–Sat 8am–4pm.
Velskoendraai Farmers Market & Restaurant Twee Riviere Farm at the entrance to Clanwilliam ☎082 727 1751 or ☎027 482 2503, ⊚ velskoendraai.co.za. Home-made rooibos ice cream and *roostekoek* (sandwiches made on the coals) are good reason to stop here, as is the home-made bread, preserves and other goods for sale. Breakfasts are reasonable too (R70). Mon–Fri 8am–5pm, Sat 8am–2pm.
★Yellow Aloe 1 Park Rd ☎027 482 2018, ⊚ yellow aloe.co.za. Its setting on a veranda looking onto the garden and nursery makes this a charming place to enjoy a full bacon-and-egg breakfast (R75) or a light lunch. If you book in advance, they'll serve a romantic dinner beneath the trees (three courses R200). Daily 8am–3pm.

DRINKING

Netmar 4 Voortrekker St ☎027 482 1007, ⊚ rooibos teahouse.co.za. A great place to sample the delights of rooibos tea (see p.208), this teahouse sells more than 100 flavours and blends from the region as well as other rooibos products, such as food stuffs and cosmetics. They offer a tasting of up to seven varieties and serve cups of rooibos outside in a lovely garden setting. Mon–Fri 8am–5pm, Sat 8am–2pm, Sun 10am–4pm.

The Boskloof

About 1km east of Clanwilliam along the Pakhuis Pass road, a good dirt road heads south and drops into the **Boskloof**, through which the Jan Dissels River traces its course. Although less than 10km from the town, and 290km from Cape Town, the valley feels a very long way from anywhere and is a relaxed spot where you can spend time lolling about along the riverbank, swimming in its natural pools or just walking along the dirt road that twists through the mountains. From the valley you can hike up into the Cederberg Mountains on the **Krakadouw hiking**

2

ROOIBOS TEA

Few things in South Africa create such devotion or aversion as **rooibos** (literally, "red bush") **tea**. Still sown and harvested by hand on many farms, rooibos is a type of *fynbos* plant grown only in the mountainous regions around Clanwilliam and Nieuwoudtville. The caffeine-free, health tea brewed from its leaves is firmly entrenched alongside regular tea and coffee in South African homes, and now even comes as a delicious coffee substitute, known as Red Espresso. Spicy chai rooibos, slightly sweetened, is another firm favourite.

To see how the tea is grown and processed on a farm, take one of the **tours** offered by Elandsberg Eco Tours (☎027 482 2022, 🌐elandsberg.co.za; R175), which leave from their premises 20km west of Clanwilliam on the Lambert's Bay road. Alternatively, you can visit the country's main **rooibos tea processing factory** in Ou Kaapse Weg in Clanwilliam (☎027 482 2155), which shows videos of the manufacturing process (Mon–Fri at 10am, 11.30am, 2pm & 3.30pm) and sells rooibos tea and rooibos-inspired cosmetics.

---

trail, which starts at **Krakadouw Cottages**, where you can purchase permits. Hikes can last up to a week, though you can also do day or half-day hikes along a section of the trail.

ACCOMMODATION   THE BOSKLOOF

Boskloof Swemgat Boskloof Rd, 13km from Clanwilliam ☎027 100 3686, 🌐boskloofswemgat .co.za. Accommodation is in eight simple, self-catering cottages without a great deal of privacy but in an open, grassy area, right on the river. The appeal of this place is the excellent swimming in a clean river and the very reasonable prices. **R600**

Klein Boschkloof Chalets Boskloof Rd, 9km from Clanwilliam ☎027 482 2441 or ☎021 100 3597, 🌐kleinboschkloof.co.za. A collection of 250-year-old Cape Dutch farm buildings converted into guest chalets. All are finished to a high standard, with cooking gear, bed linen and towels provided. Breakfast and dinner are by prior arrangement. **R1000**

Northern Cederberg and the Pakhuis Pass

The **R364** northeast from Clanwilliam winds over the **Pakhuis Pass**, a drive worth taking for its lonely roadside scenery and inspiring views. This area, called **Rocklands**, is said to be one of the two best places in the world for **bouldering**, so expect to see plenty of lithe climbers going to and from the graded routes, particularly in the milder winter months. Although you are below the Cederberg massifs, the rocks, rivers, valleys and sense of space make this area very appealing, with the added attraction of providing access to the finest rock art in the Western Cape (see p.207).

ARRIVAL AND INFORMATION   NORTH CEDERBERG AND THE PAKHUIS PASS

By car All accommodation in this area is along the Pakhuis Pass (R364), a tarred road that peters out beyond Bushman's Kloof into a network of dirt roads leading to farms.
Information Bouldering permits (R60 per day)

must be purchased from *De Pakhuys* at Rocklands (see p.210), which acts as the informal centre of the region (☎027 482 1879, 🌐depakhuys.com; Mon–Fri 7am–5.30pm, Sat 9.30am–noon).

ACCOMMODATION

Alpha Excelsior Guest Farm and Winery ☎027 482 2700, 🌐alphaexcelsior.co.za. Two cottages, the nicest of which, *Weaver*, is nearest to the river and sleeps two. There are also three fully equipped retro caravans, and doubles inside the elegant Cape Dutch homestead and farmhouse. The farm has its own small winery, and its red wine and olive oil are for sale. Caravan **R350**, cottages and doubles **R700**

Bushmans Kloof ☎027 482 2627 or ☎021 437 9278, 🌐bushmanskloof.co.za. A luxury lodge, with a range of stylish rooms and a private villa, which has won many accolades. It is set in a wilderness area with game drives and rock art – there are more than 125 recorded sites on the property – and the rangers are trained in both wildlife guiding and rock-art interpretation. The rate includes all meals, game drives and guided rock-art trails. **R10,240**

2

OUDRIF

Oudrif is an exceptional retreat lodge in the Cederberg back country, 48km from Clanwilliam along rough dirt roads (booking essential; ☎027 482 2397, ⓦoudrif.co.za; R2200). It's set in inspiring countryside in the transitional zone between the foothills of the mountains and the dry Karoo, with redstone gorges and a wide valley incised by the Doring River. Although there are wonderful **guided walks** through *fynbos* to rock-art sites and paddling opportunities on the river, this is as much a place to chill out – the only rule of the co-owner and manager Bill Mitchell, and his wife Janine, is that there are no rules. The multi-talented Mitchell is also a qualified chef and does all the cooking at this full-board establishment.

Accommodation is in five straw-bale houses. The cream-coloured chalets have an uneven hewn quality that befits their isolation on the edge of the gorge that falls away to the Doring River. Each is stylishly equipped with retro furniture and has a double and a three-quarter bed; the power for lighting is provided by solar panels, and showers are heated.

De Pakhuys Rocklands ☎027 482 1879, ⓦdepakhuys .com. Garden cottages of varying sizes and camping facilities on a friendly rooibos farm. It's 26km from Clanwilliam in a stunning location, with marked hiking trails starting near the secluded campsite, and its own climbing area. The farm is mostly used by climbers, and it is where you purchase permits for bouldering. Camping R80, cottages R800

Travellers Rest ☎027 482 1824, ⓦtravellersrest .co.za. Twenty-five self-catering cottages in different locations on a farm, with plenty of walks and river pools for summer swimming. Meals can be pre-arranged and there is a farm stall that serves daytime meals. The main attraction is the 4km Sevilla bushman painting trail, starting beside the farm, which takes in nine sites and provides a good introduction to the subject. R500

Wuppertal and the Biedouw Valley

One of the best drives you can do in the Western Cape is along the mountainous R364 dirt road (pretty awful and steep in parts), which winds through remote valleys to reach historic **WUPPERTAL**. Set deep in the tunefully named Tra-tra Valley, the Moravian mission station is one of the oldest in the Western Cape and, with its tiny collection of thatched cottages, remains one of the most untouched settlements in South Africa. Run by the church elders but with an entirely coloured population, the mission is famous for making **velskoene** (literally "hide shoes"), the suede footwear commonly known as *vellies* and part of Afrikaner national dress. You can see the shoes being made and buy them at the little shop at De Werf – the centre that clusters around the church.

On the way to Wuppertal you can turn into the **Biedouw Valley**, which only has traffic during the spring, when the valley floor is carpeted with flowers.

ACCOMMODATION	WUPPERTAL AND THE BIEDOUW VALLEY

Enjo Nature Farm Biedouw Valley Rd ☎027 482 2869, ⓦsoulcountry.info. The best reason to visit the Biedouw Valley is to stay at this isolated 200-year-old farmhouse, run by a German couple who offer lovely self-catering chalets. There's also camping, though the campsite is not so appealing. The emphasis here is on enjoying nature, and in the hot summer you can swim at the farm dam. Its isolation makes this a place to spend a few days, rather than just overnight. Access is only on dirt roads. Dinners can be booked on request and the owner can arrange flights here. Camping R70, chalets R1180

The Garden Route

The **Garden Route**, a slender stretch of coastal plain between Mossel Bay and Storms River Mouth, has a legendary status as South Africa's paradise – reflected in local names such as **Garden of Eden** and **Wilderness**. This soft, green, forested swathe of nearly 200km is cut by rivers from the mountains to the north, tumbling down to its southern rocky shores and sandy beaches.

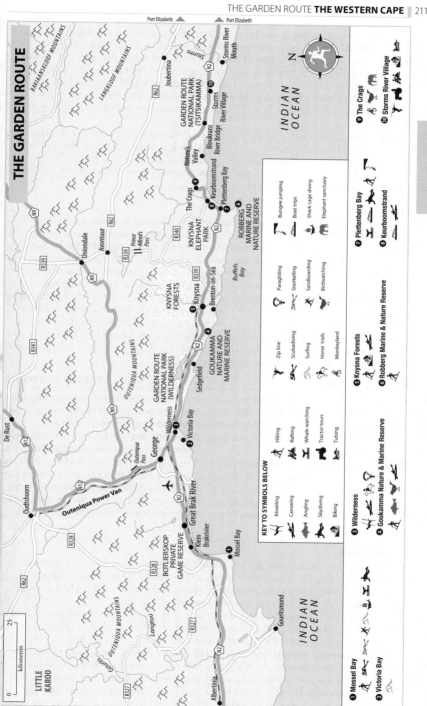

THE GARDEN ROUTE

KEY TO SYMBOLS BELOW

Abseiling	Hiking	Zip line	Paragliding	Bungee jumping
Canoeing	Rafting	Scubadiving	Snorkelling	Boat trips
Angling	Whale watching	Surfing	Sandboarding	Shark cage diving
Skydiving	Tractor tours	Horse trails	Birdwatching	Elephant sanctuary
Biking	Tubing	Monkeyland		

① Mossel Bay

② Victoria Bay

③ Wilderness

④ Goukamma Nature & Marine Reserve

⑤ Knysna Forests

⑥ Robberg Marine & Nature Reserve

⑦ Plettenberg Bay

⑧ Keurboomstrand

⑨ The Crags

⑩ Storms River Village

2

INDIAN OCEAN

LITTLE KAROO

0   25
kilometres

The Garden Route coast is dominated by three inlets, of which the closest to Cape Town is **Mossel Bay**, an industrial centre of some charm that marks the official start of the Garden Route. Next is **Knysna**, with a well-rooted urban character but no beach. A major draw here is the **Knysna forest**, covering some of the hilly country around Knysna, the awe-inspiring remnants of once vast ancient woodlands. Knysna's eastern neighbour, **Plettenberg Bay**, has good swimming beaches, while all the towns offer a plethora of outdoor activities, from hiking in forests to marine safaris or exploring deep river gorges on a tube.

Between the coastal towns are some ugly modern holiday developments, but also some wonderful empty beaches and tiny coves, such as **Victoria Bay** and **Nature's Valley**. Best of all is the **Tsitsikamma** section of the Garden Route National Park, which has it all – indigenous forest, dramatic coastline, the pumping **Storms River Mouth** and South Africa's flagship hike, the **Otter Trail**.

Brief history

Khoi herders who lived off the Garden Route's natural bounty considered the area a paradise, calling it Outeniqua ("the man laden with honey"). Their Eden was quickly destroyed in the eighteenth century with the arrival of Dutch **woodcutters**, who had exhausted the forests around Cape Town and set about doing the same in Outeniqua, killing or dispersing the Khoi and San in the process. Birds and animals also suffered from the encroachment of Europeans. In the 1850s, the Swedish naturalist Johan Victorin shot and feasted on the species he had come to study, some of which – including an endangered bird, the narina trogon – he noted were both "beautiful and good to eat".

Despite the dense appearance of the area, what you see today are only the remnants of one of Africa's great **forests**; much of the indigenous hardwoods have been replaced by exotic pine plantations, and the only milk and honey you'll find now is in the many shops servicing the Garden Route coastal resorts.

GETTING AROUND

THE GARDEN ROUTE

By air The airport at George, the largest town on the Garden Route, is served by daily scheduled flights from Johannesburg and Cape Town (1hr). CeMair also run direct flights to Plettenberg Bay's tiny airport from Johannesburg (2hr 30min) and Cape Town (1hr 15min).

By Baz Bus A Baz Bus (☎ 086 122 9287, ⊕ bazbus.com) service running between Cape Town and Port Elizabeth picks up passengers in Cape Town at 7.15–8.30am and in Port Elizabeth at 6.45–7.30am on Mon–Tues & Thurs–Sat. It covers the central districts of all the towns along the way

and will carry outdoor gear, such as surfboards or mountain bikes. Although the buses take standby passengers if space permits, you should book ahead to secure a seat.

By intercity bus Intercape, Greyhound and Translux intercity buses from Cape Town and Port Elizabeth stop at Mossel Bay, George, Wilderness, Sedgefield, Knysna and Storms River (the village, not the river mouth). They are better and cheaper than the Baz Bus for more direct journeys, though buses often don't go into the towns, letting passengers off at petrol stations on the highway instead.

Mossel Bay

MOSSEL BAY, a midsized town 397km east of Cape Town, gets a bad press, mainly because of the huge industrial facade it presents to the N2. Don't panic – the historic centre is a pleasant contrast, set on a hill overlooking the small working harbour and bay, with an interesting museum and safe swimming beaches.

Mossel Bay bears poignant historical significance as the place where indigenous Khoi cattle herders first encountered Europeans in a bloody confrontation. A group of Portuguese mariners under **Bartolomeu Dias** set sail from Portugal in August 1487 in search of a sea route to India, and months later rounded the Cape of Good Hope. In February 1488, they became the first Europeans to make landfall along the South African coast when they pulled in for water at an inlet they called Aguado de São Brás ("watering place of St Blaize"), now Mossel Bay. The Khoikhoi were organized into distinct groups, each under its own chief and each with territorial rights over pastures and water sources. The Portuguese, who were flouting local customs, saw it as "bad manners" when the Khoikhoi tried to drive them off the spring, so they retaliated with crossbow fire that left one of the herders dead.

Bartolomeu Dias Museum Complex

1 Market St • Maritime Museum Mon–Fri 9am–4.45pm, Sat & Sun 9am–3.45pm • R20; Dias caravel R20 extra • ⓦ diasmuseum.co.za

Mossel Bay's main urban attraction is the **Bartolomeu Dias Museum Complex**, housed in a collection of historic buildings within a couple of minutes' walk of each other and well integrated into the small town centre. The highlight is the **Maritime Museum**, a spiral gallery with displays on the history of European – principally Portuguese – seafaring, arranged around a full-size replica of Dias' original caravel. The ship was built in Portugal and sailed from Lisbon to Mossel Bay in 1987 to celebrate the five-hundredth anniversary of Dias' historic journey.

The **Post Office Tree**, just outside the Maritime Museum, purportedly may be the very milkwood under which sixteenth-century mariners left messages for passing ships in an old boot. You can post mail here in a large, boot-shaped letterbox and have it stamped with a special postmark. Of the remaining exhibitions, the **Shell Museum and Aquarium**, next to the Post Office Tree, is the only one worth taking time to visit. This is your chance to see some of the beautiful shells found off the South African coast, as well as specimens from around the world.

The Point and St Blaize Lighthouse

East of the harbour, the coast bulges south towards the **Point**, which has several restaurants and a popular bar/restaurant (see p.215) with a deck at the ocean's edge, from which you may see dolphins cruising past.

A couple of hundred metres to the south at the top of some cliffs, the **St Blaize Lighthouse**, built in 1864, is still in use as a beacon for ships. Below it, the **Cape St Blaize Cave** is both a marvellous lookout point and a significant archeological site. A boardwalk leads through the cave past three information panels describing the history of the interpretation of the cave, where in 1888 excavations uncovered stone tools and showed that people had been using the cave for close on 100,000 years. The path leading up to the cave continues onto the Cape St Blaize trail (see box, p.214).

ARRIVAL AND INFORMATION

MOSSEL BAY

By Baz Bus Only the daily Baz Bus comes right into town, dropping passengers off at *Mossel Bay Backpackers* and *Park House Lodge*.

By intercity bus Greyhound, Intercape, SA Roadlink and Translux buses stop at Shell Voorbaai Service Station on the N2, 7km from the centre, at the junction of the national highway and the road into town. (Voorbaai Truckport offers a centralized bus booking service ☎ 044 695 1172.)

Destinations Cape Town (3 daily; 6hr); George (1–2 daily; 45min); Knysna (1–2 daily; 2hr); Oudtshoorn (1–2 daily;

1hr 15min); Plettenberg Bay (1–2 daily; 2hr 30min); Port Elizabeth (1–2 daily; 6hr 30min).

By taxi Mossel Bay is small enough to negotiate on foot, but should you need transport, call 24/7 Taxi Services on ☎ 082 932 5809.

Information The tourist office is on the corner of Church and Market streets (Mon–Fri 8am–6pm, Sat & Sun 9am–4pm; ☎ 044 691 2202, ⓦ visitmosselbay.co.za) and has brochures and maps of the town. The website has comprehensive listings of accommodation, restaurants and activities.

ACCOMMODATION

Edward Charles Manor Hotel 1 Sixth Ave ☎ 044 691 2152, ⓦ edwardcharles.co.za. An upmarket two-storey guesthouse in a central location overlooking Santos Beach, with fifteen en-suite rooms, a swimming pool and a courtesy shuttle to take you to town, if you don't have your own car. R1150

Mossel Bay Backpackers 1 Marsh St ☎ 044 691 3182, ⓦ mosselbaybackpackers.co.za. Well-run lodge with

squeaky-clean rooms accommodating 65 people, just 300m from the sea. They also do adventure activity bookings, and there's a swimming pool, garden and football table. Dorms R150, doubles R550

Park House Lodge 121 High St ☎ 044 691 1937, ⓦ parkhouse.co.za. Top-notch budget accommodation in twenty rooms distributed across three buildings, one of which is a beautiful nineteenth-century sandstone manor house. Some rooms have private entrances leading onto the lush garden. The doubles with a shared bathroom are very affordable; en-suite rooms are a little more expensive (R780). Dorms R170, doubles R600

Protea Hotel Mossel Bay Bartholomeu Dias Museum Complex, Market St ☎044 691 3738, ⓦproteahotels.com/mosselbay. Opposite the tourist office, in an old – if rather over-restored – Cape Dutch manor house, this swish hotel (part of the Marriott chain) is in the town centre overlooking Santos Bay and the harbour. Breakfast is served at the nearby *Café Gannet*, Mossel Bay's nicest restaurant (see below). R2020

EATING

You don't come to Mossel Bay for the food, but there are a number of reasonable places to eat, some with superb sea views. The small Point Village shopping development at the north end of town has a couple of inexpensive to mid-priced family restaurants, opening daily from the morning until around 11pm.

Café Gannet Market St ☎044 691 1885 or ☎044 691 3738, ⓦoldposttree.co.za/café-gannet. Close to the Bartholomeu Dias Museum, Mossel Bay's smartest restaurant serves local fish, sushi and delicacies like wild Mossel Bay oysters (R25 per oyster) and their popular seafood casserole (R240) at reasonable prices. The stylish garden has glimpses across the harbour and is a good spot for sundowners. Daily 7.30am–10pm.

ACTIVITIES AROUND MOSSEL BAY

Mossel Bay is a springboard for popular **activities**, including skydiving, sandboarding and deep-sea fishing, all of which can be booked through the Garden Route Adventure Centre at *Mossel Bay Backpackers* (☎044 691 3182, ⓦgardenrouteadventures.co.za). It is worth noting that although fishing is available at Mossel Bay, you should question operators about which fish they target as some are known to catch threatened or endangered species.

DIVING AND SNORKELLING

These aren't tropical seas, so don't expect clear warm waters, but with visibility usually between 4m and 10m you stand a good chance of seeing octopus, squid, sea stars, soft corals, pyjama sharks and butterfly fish. There are several rewarding diving and snorkelling spots around Mossel Bay.

Electro Dive ☎082 561 1259, ⓦelectrodive.co.za. This outfit rents out gear and provides certification courses (R5000), guided snorkelling trips (R300) and shore- and boat-based dives to local reefs and wrecks (R240/400 including kit).

HIKING

You can check out the coast on the St Blaize hiking trail, an easy 15km walk (roughly 4hr each way; a map is available from the tourist office) along the southern shore of Mossel Bay. The route starts from the Cape St Blaize Cave, just below the lighthouse at the Point, and heads west as far as Dana Bay, taking in magnificent coastal views of cliffs, rocks, bays and coves.

SANDBOARDING

Mossel Bay is one of the best places in the country for sandboarding – the dunes are big, the sand is moist and fine and you pay roughly half what you would in Cape Town.

Billeon Surf Meeting Point Engen One-Stop Garage ☎082 971 1405, ⓦdragondune.com. This well-run outfit runs trips to the so-called "Dragon Dune", which, at 320m, is the longest runnable stretch of sand in the country. The activity is suitable for all levels, from beginner to extreme, and is very popular so book in advance (R400/person for a 2hr trip). From their meeting point, you are taken by 4WD to the dunes, and a shuttle service is offered from the hostels.

SKYDIVING

Skydive Mossel Bay Mossel Bay Airfield ☎044 695 1771, ⓦskydivemosselbay.com. For hardcore adrenaline junkies, Skydive Mossel Bay offers tandem skydives from 3000m (R3000) and skydiving training in both static line and accelerated free fall.

WHALE-WATCHING AND SEAL ISLAND CRUISES

The Romonza ☎044 690 3101, ⓦromonzaboat trips.co.za. Cruises around Seal Island (hourly 10am–3pm, adults R160), about 10km northwest of Santos Beach, to see the African penguin and seal colonies, can be taken on the *Romonza*, a medium-sized yacht that launches from the marina in the harbour. It's also the only registered boat in Mossel Bay allowed to run boat-based whale-watching cruises (2–3hr; adults R700). As elsewhere along this coast, the whale season is variable, with southern rights appearing from June till late October. If you're extremely lucky, you may also see a humpback whale.

Delfino's Restaurant Point Village ☎044 690 5247, ⓦ delfinos.co.za. A good place for pasta (R70), pizza, burgers and steaks, as well as decent coffee – all at reasonable prices. There are great views of the sea. Daily 7am–11pm.

★**Kaai4** Mossel Bay Harbour ☎044 691 0056, ⓦ kaai4 .co.za. Relaxed, open-air beach restaurant, with sprawling picnic tables in a stunning location on the beach, where you can watch your seafood braai on an open fire (R90). The menu is small, but the servings are large. Daily 10am–10pm (closed when raining).

King Fisher Point Village ☎044 690 6390, ⓦ thekingfisher.co.za. A relaxed joint that, as its name suggests, specializes in seafood, from humble fish and chips (R60) to local line fish. It also has a kids' menu. Its elevated position above *Delfino's* means it has excellent views. Daily 11.30am–11pm.

2

Along the R328

Heading inland towards **Oudtshoorn** (see p.244) from Mossel Bay on the **R328** takes you over the forested coastal mountains of **Robinson Pass** into the desiccated Little Karoo. The draw of this road is some great scenery, and it's a much prettier route to Oudtshoorn than travelling via George. Day visitors are welcome at **Botlierskop Private Game Reserve** (see below), with plenty of activities on offer that can be booked in advance.

ACCOMMODATION

Botlierskop Private Game Reserve 22km from Mossel Bay ☎044 696 6055, ⓦ botlierskop.co.za. While there is nothing wild about it, the tented accommodation has a real safari atmosphere, with decks and outdoor seating from which to admire the lovely views. You will usually see lions, and there's a good chance of spotting rhinos, elephants, giraffes and antelope. Their packages are professionally put together and include a number of activities for both day- and overnight-visitors, including game drives (R450; 3hr) and horse rides (R310; 1hr). Half-board per person, including a game drive R3100

Eight Bells Mountain Inn 35km from Mossel Bay ☎044 631 0000, ⓦ eightbells.co.za. Close to the top of the mountainous pass, this is a firm favourite with well-heeled families wanting a hotel-style holiday, with all sorts of activities laid on for children, including horseriding, swimming, tennis and walking. The atmosphere is friendly and it's superbly run. Out of school holidays, it remains a restful stop-off with lovely gardens and extensive grounds. R1500

★**Outeniqua Moon Percheron Stud & Guest Farm** 23km from Mossel Bay, just below the Robinson Pass ☎044 631 0093 or ☎082 564 9782, ⓦ outeniquamoon.co.za. Comfortable and classy self-catering or B&B accommodation in four colonial farm-style cottages on a working farm with beautiful views of the Outeniqua mountains. You can swim laps in the 25m ozone pool, explore the farm's 250 acres of forest, or spend some time with the huge Percheron draught horses, petting foals or taking a carriage ride. If you eat here, prepare to be spoilt with home-made bread and other farm delights. Prices are reasonable, and drop further outside of school holidays. Self-catering cottage R1500, half-board cottage R1980

George

There's little reason to visit **GEORGE**, unless you need what a big centre offers – airport, hospital and shops – and it does lie conveniently halfway between Cape Town and Port Elizabeth. A large inland town, surrounded by mountains, George is a 5km detour

THE OUTENIQUA POWER VAN

Sadly, South Africa's main-line railways are slowly dying. The Garden Route's train line once penetrated some of the region's most visually stunning back country, making the Cape Town–Port Elizabeth run one of the great railway journeys of the world. That ended when some of the tracks were washed away and never replaced.

Fortunately, you can still get a taster of the line on the **Outeniqua Power Van**, a single-cab diesel-powered train that trails into the Outeniqua Mountains just outside George. The train stops at a scenic site for a picnic before returning to the town. En route you pass through forest, negotiate passes and tunnels, and see waterfalls and *fynbos*. The train departs from the Outeniqua Transport Museum, 2 Mission Rd, George (Mon–Sat on demand, booking essential ☎082 490 5627; R140; 2.5hr). Bring your own picnic, sunglasses, a warm jacket and a hat.

northwest off the N2, and 9km from the nearest stretch of ocean at Victoria Bay. Sadly, all that's left of the forests and quaint character that moved Anthony Trollope, during a visit in 1877, to describe it as the "prettiest village on the face of the earth" are some historic buildings, of which the beautiful Dutch Reformed Church in Davidson Street is the most notable. Other than that, George's claim to recent fame (or notoriety) is that it was the parliamentary seat of former State President **P.W. Botha** (see box below), the last of South Africa's apartheid hardliners.

2 ARRIVAL AND INFORMATION   GEORGE

By car George is 531km from Cape Town (allow 6 hours for the journey) and 66km northeast of Mossel Bay.

By plane Kulula and SAA fly between Johannesburg and the small George airport, 10km west of town on the N2 (6 daily; 1hr 50min). SAA also flies here from Cape Town (2 daily; 50min).

By Baz Bus The Baz Bus drops off at *Outeniqua Backpackers* on Merriman St on its daily run between Cape Town and Port Elizabeth.

By intercity buses Intercape, Translux and Greyhound intercity buses pull in at George station, adjacent to the

railway museum, and at the Sasol garage station on the N2 east of town.

Destinations Cape Town (2 daily; 7hr); Johannesburg (daily; 16hr); Knysna (2 daily; 1hr 30min); Mossel Bay (6–7 daily; 45min); Oudtshoorn (daily; 1hr 10min); Plettenberg Bay (2 daily; 2hr); Port Elizabeth (2 daily; 5hr 30min); Johannesburg and Pretoria (1–2 daily; 16hr).

Information The George tourist office, at 124 York St (Mon–Fri 7.45am–4.30pm, Sat 9am–1pm; ☎ 044 801 9295, ⓦ visitgeorgetourism.org.za), can provide town maps and help with accommodation bookings.

ACCOMMODATION

10 Caledon Street 10 Caledon St ☎ 044 873 4983, ⓦ 10caledon.com. The pick of the mid-priced B&Bs, this spotless guesthouse is on a quiet street, within an easy walk of the city centre. There's a garden and the rooms have balconies with mountain views. The owners are great hosts and provide an excellent breakfast. R1200

Die Waenhuis 11 Caledon St ☎ 044 874 0034, ⓦ diewaenhuis.co.za. Charming mid-nineteenth-century house that has retained its period character. There are eleven spacious en-suite rooms, several decorated with

antiques, and a beautiful garden with a pool. English breakfasts are served in a sunlit dining room, which is warmed in winter by a wood-burning stove. R1300

Mount View Resort & Lifestyle Village York St ☎ 044 874 5205, ⓦ mountviewsa.co.za. Modern complex rather lacking in character, but providing great value in its one-, two- and three-bedroom en-suite chalets, rondavels and camping facilities. The gardens are well kept and pleasant, and there's a gym and indoor and outdoor swimming pools. Camping R380, rondavels R580, chalets R750

PRESIDENT BOTHA AND APARTHEID'S LAST STAND

Pieter Willem Botha was the last and most rabid of South Africa's apartheid enforcers. A National Party hack from the age of 20, Botha worked his way up through the ranks, becoming an MP in 1948 and subsequently **Minister of Defence**, a position he used in 1978 to unseat Prime Minister John Vorster. Botha set about streamlining apartheid, modifying his own role from that of a British-style prime minister, answerable to parliament, to one of an executive president taking vital decisions in the secrecy of a President's Council heavily weighted with army top brass.

Informed by the generals that apartheid couldn't be preserved purely through force, Botha embarked on his **Total Strategy**, reforming peripheral aspects of apartheid while fostering a black middle class as a buffer against the ANC. He also pumped vast sums into building an enormous military machine that crossed South Africa's borders to bully or crush neighbouring countries that harboured anti-apartheid activists. At home, security forces were free to murder, maim and torture **opponents of apartheid**.

Botha blustered on through the late 1980s, while his bloated military sucked the state coffers dry. Even National Party stalwarts realized that his policies were leading to ruin, and in 1989, when he suffered a stroke, the party was quick to replace him with **F.W. de Klerk**, who swiftly announced reforms.

Botha lived out his unrepentant retirement near George, steadfastly refusing to apologize for the political crimes committed by his administration. Curiously, when he died in 2006, he was given an uncritical, high-profile state funeral, broadcast on national television and attended by members of the government, including the then president, Thabo Mbeki.

Oakhurst Hotel Cnr Meade & Cathedral sts ☎044 874 7130, ⓦoakhursthotel.co.za. Charming, centrally located manor house with a country feel, green lawns, and a peaceful garden with pool. There's a lovely dining area and views of the Outeniqua Mountains, too. **R1000**

Outeniqua Travel Lodge 19 Montagu Rd ☎082 316 7720, ⓦouteniqualodge.co.za. Friendly hostel in a bright and airy suburban house with comfortable double rooms, some with mountain views. There's a swimming pool, and the lodge provides free airport pick-ups. **R430**

EATING

Fat Fish 124 York St ☎044 874 7803. This popular venue in the centre of town is a good choice for a well-priced meal, from meze for one (R85) to rump steaks of varying sizes (R145), and – as the name suggests – plenty of excellent fish choices. Daily 11.30am–10pm.
La Capannina 122 York St ☎044 874 5313, ⓦlacapanninageorge.co.za. Italian restaurant that in addition to excellent pizzas and pasta, has other tricks up its sleeve, such as beef fillet on a bed of polenta and some

distinctly un-Italian dishes like ostrich jambalaya with a hint of curry (R160). Mon–Sat noon–10pm.
The Old Town House Cnr York and Market sts ☎044 874 3663. There's a lovely ambience in this old townhouse, where the food is well cooked with attention to detail in an intimate setting. Despite the place's carnivorous inclination – they specialize in venison and beef – vegetarians are catered for and their baked pasta is delicious (R65). Mon–Fri noon–3pm & 6–10pm, Sat 6–10pm.

Victoria Bay

Some 9km south of George and 3km off the N2 lies the minuscule hamlet of **VICTORIA BAY**, on the edge of a small sandy beach wedged into a cove between cliffs, with a grassy sunbathing area, safe swimming and a tidal pool. During the December holidays and over weekends, the place packs out with day-trippers, and rates as one of the top **surfing** spots in South Africa. Because of the cliffs, there's only a single row of buildings along the beachfront, home to some of the most dreamily positioned guesthouses along the coast.

ARRIVAL AND DEPARTURE VICTORIA BAY

By car Arriving by car, you'll encounter a metal barrier as you drop down the hill to the bay, and you'll have to try and park in the car park, which is frequently full (especially in summer). If you're staying at one of the B&Bs, leave your

car at the barrier and collect the key from your lodgings to gain access to the private beach road.
By bus The daily Baz Bus provides the only public transport, dropping passengers at the *Victoria Bay Surf Lodge*.

ACCOMMODATION

Land's End Self-Catering The Point, Beach Rd ☎044 889 0123, ⓦvicbay.com. Spectacularly sited right on the shoreline, this place offers a variety of rooms, the price depending on views and facilities. You can bring your own food to cook, or go down to the beachside restaurant. **R1600**
Seabreeze Cabanas Along the main road into the settlement ☎044 889 0098, ⓦseabreezecabanas co.za. A variety of budget self-catering units, including two-storey holiday huts and wooden chalets, sleeping two,

four or eight people. The huts have no sea views, but it's an easy walk to the beach. **R900**
Surfari Victoria Bay Rd ☎044 889 0113, ⓦvicbay surfari.co.za. This is predominantly a surfers' lodge with home comforts including a DSTV, a self-catering kitchen and BBQ areas. The lodge offers surfboard and wetsuit rental as well as lessons on request for all levels at the local easy, right-hand point break. There's also a trampoline, pool table, table tennis and volleyball. Shuttles run to the beach and George. Dorms **R200**, doubles **R650**, family room **R900**

EATING

There are no food shops and only one restaurant at Victoria Bay itself, so it's best to bring your own supplies, or drive back to George. Mr Delivery (☎044 873 6677) will collect pre-ordered takeaways from George, as well as groceries bought online at Pick n Pay.

Vikki's @ The Beach ☎044 899 0212. Unmissable, as it's on the seafront with tables and umbrellas out in the sun. The food it serves is rather dull, but reasonably priced and includes burgers and chips (R70), fish and

chips, egg breakfasts, and pizzas, all served up in a delightful setting. It's a family-friendly establishment. but often closes when the weather is poor, or when there are no customers. Daily 9am–5pm.

2

Wilderness

East of Victoria Bay, across the Kaaimans River, the beach at **WILDERNESS** is so close to the N2 that you can pull over for a quick dip and barely interrupt your journey, though you'll struggle to find African wilderness among the sprawl of retirement homes, holiday houses and thousands of beds for rent in the vicinity. The beach, renowned for its long stretch of sand, is backed by tall dunes, blighted by holiday houses which have fantastic ocean views. Once in the water, stay close to the shoreline: the coast here is notorious for its unpredictable currents.

Despite being good for bird-spotting, the Wilderness section of the Garden Route National Park is disappointing, as it never feels far from the rumbling N2.

ARRIVAL AND INFORMATION   WILDERNESS

By bus Greyhound, Intercape and Translux buses running between Cape Town and Port Elizabeth stop at the Caltex Garage, on the corner of South St and the N2. The daily Baz Bus stops at Fairy Knowe Backpackers.
Destinations Cape Town (3–4 daily; 7hr 40min); Knysna (3–4 daily; 40min); Mossel Bay (3–4 daily; 1hr); Plettenberg Bay (3–4 daily; 1hr 10min); Port Elizabeth (3–4 daily; 4hr 30min); Sedgefield (3–4 daily; 20min);

Storms River Bridge (3–4 daily; 2hr).
Information The tourist office is in Milkwood Village Mall, Beacon Rd, off the N2 opposite the Caltex garage (Mon–Fri 7.45am–4.30pm, Sat 9am–1pm; ☎044 877 0045, ⓦgeorge.org.za).
Services Wilderness's tiny village centre, on the north side of the N2, has a petrol station and a few shops.

ACCOMMODATION

Fairy Knowe Backpackers 6km from the village, follow signs from the N2 east of Wilderness ☎044 877 1285, ⓦwildernessbackpackers.com. Built in 1897, this is the oldest home in the area. It's set in the quiet woodlands near the Touw River, though not near the sea, and features a wraparound balcony. Note that during peak season it gets busy and can be very noisy near the bar. The Baz Bus drops off here. Dorms R160, doubles R600
Island Lake Holiday Resort Lakes Rd, 2km from the Hoekwil/Island Lake turn-off on the N2 ☎044 877 1194, ⓦislandlake.co.za. Camping and self-catering rondavels that sleep four, located at one of the quietest and prettiest spots on the lakes. The rondavels are basic one-room affairs with kitchenettes equipped with hotplates, microwaves and utensils, but you share communal washing and toilet facilities. Camping R300, rondavels R750
Mes Amis Homestead Buxton Close, signposted off the N2 on the coastal side of the road, directly opposite

the national park turn-off ☎044 877 1928, ⓦmesamis .co.za. Nine double rooms, each of which has its own terrace, offering some of the best views in Wilderness, with a private path down to the beach. Rooms are elegantly furnished and there are luxurious touches such as bathrobes and espresso machines in each room. R1700
Wilderness Beach House Western Rd ☎044 877 0549, ⓦwildernessbeachhouse.com. Set on the hill, with views of the ocean from the hammocks on the terrace, this backpackers has very basic dorm rooms and doubles. There is a bar and a communal kitchen, and surf lessons and board rental are also available. Dorms R170, doubles R550
Wilderness Bushcamp Heights Rd, follow Waterside Rd west for 1600m up the hill ☎044 877 1168, ⓦboskamp.co.za. Six self-catering timber units with loft bedrooms, thatched roofs and ocean views. The camp, set on a hillside amid *fynbos* wilderness, is part of a conservation estate where you're free to roam around. R850

EATING

The Girls George Rd ☎044 877 1648, ⓦthegirls .co.za. Deservedly one of the most popular restaurants in the village, *The Girls* fuses classic French dishes, such as steak tartare, with North African and Middle Eastern influences. The prawns are fantastic, they do a mean steak (R165), and vegetarians get a decent look in. Tues–Sun 5.30–11pm.
Salinas Beach Restaurant Cnr N2 and Zundorf Lane ☎044 877 0001, ⓦsalinas.co.za. An easy stop-off on the N2 with a great view over the beach from the tables under umbrellas on the terrace. They're known for fresh fish brought in from Mossel Bay or

Knysna (R165), good cocktails and excellent cheesecake. Daily 11am–10pm.
★**Serendipity** Freesia Ave ☎044 877 0433, ⓦserendipitywilderness.com. This fine-dining restaurant is one of the country's top places to eat. Located on the banks of the Touw River Lagoon, come here for a fabulous dinner, with Asian, Mediterranean and strong South African influences, cooked by a husband-and-wife team. Vegetarians will be seriously tempted by twice-baked goat's cheese soufflé or aubergine and pumpkin roulade. A seasonal, ever-changing five-course set menu is on offer (R550). Mon–Sat 6.30pm–late.

Goukamma Nature Reserve

Daily 7.30am–4pm • R40, free entry for overnight visitors • ☎ 044 383 0042

An unassuming sanctuary of around 220 square kilometres, **Goukamma Nature Reserve** starts near Sedgefield and stretches east to Buffalo Bay (also known as Buffels Bay). The reserve's boundaries take in the freshwater **Groenvlei Lake** and approximately 18km of beach frontage, as well as some of the highest vegetated dunes in the country. The landscape is good for walking, as it's covered with coastal *fynbos* and dense thickets of milkwood, yellowwood and candlewood trees.

Because of the diversity of coastal and wetland habitats, over 220 different kinds of birds have been recorded in the reserve, including fish eagles, Knysna louries, kingfishers and very rare African black oystercatchers. Away from the water, you stand a small chance of spotting one of the area's mammals, including bushbuck, grysbok, mongoose, vervet monkeys, caracals and otters.

ARRIVAL AND DEPARTURE

GOUKAMMA NATURE RESERVE

By car Two roads off the N2 provide access to the reserve, though there are no public roads within the reserve itself. The main entrance is accessed from the Buffalo Bay side along Buffalo Bay Rd, and the reserve office is halfway down here. On the western side, a dirt road runs down to Platbank Beach, taking you past the tiny settlement of Lake Pleasant on the south bank of Groenvlei Lake, which consists of little more than a hotel and holiday resort.

ACCOMMODATION

There are two fully equipped bush camps on the Groenvlei side of the reserve and three thatched rondavels on the east side; all can be booked through CapeNature (☎ 021 483 0000, ⊕ capenature.co.za). Alternatively, the privately run *Teniqua Treetops* camp is just outside the park, but close enough to explore the area.

★**Teniqua Treetops** 23km northeast of Sedgefield ☎ 044 356 2868, ⊕ teniquatreetops.co.za. A retreat beneath the boughs of virgin forest between Sedgefield and Knysna, with 4km of woodland walks and a river with pools for swimming. Luxury tents are raised on timber decks, and one unit is wheelchair accessible. As well as being a chilled-out hideout, this is a great example of sustainable living in practice: no trees were felled to build *Teniqua*; recycled materials were used where possible; water is gravity fed; showers are solar-heated; and toilets use a dry composting system. R1800

Knysna

KNYSNA (pronounced "nize-na"), 102km east of Mossel Bay, stands at the hub of the Garden Route. Its lack of ocean beaches is compensated for by its hilly setting around the **Knysna lagoon**, its handsome **forests**, good opportunities for **adventure sports** and a pleasant **waterfront development**. If you're looking for somewhere quiet or rural, Knysna is not for you – it is busy yet sophisticated, with good restaurants and ever-burgeoning housing developments.

ACTIVITIES IN GOUKAMMA NATURE RESERVE

Apart from **angling** and **birdwatching**, the Goukamma offers a number of self-guided activities, including safe **swimming** in Groenvlei Lake. There are also several day-long **hiking** trails that enable you to explore the reserve's different habitats. A beach walk, which takes around four hours one way, traverses the 14km of crumbling cliffs and sands between the Platbank car park on the western side of the reserve and the Rowwehoek one on the eastern side. Alternatively, you can go from one end of the reserve to the other via a slightly longer inland trek across the dunes. There's also a shorter circular walk from the reserve office through a milkwood forest.

Alternatively, you can **canoe** on the Goukamma River on the eastern side of the reserve; a limited number of canoes can be rented from the reserve office during the week or at the gate over the weekend (single or double canoes R100 per day).

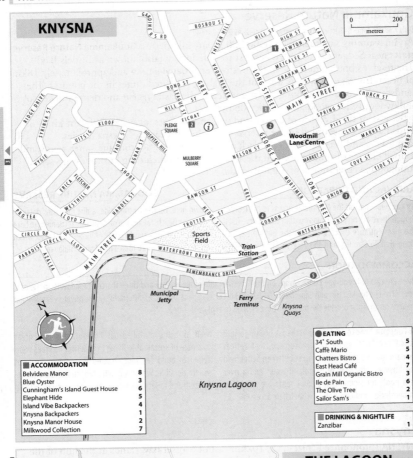

KNYSNA

ACCOMMODATION

Belvidere Manor	8
Blue Oyster	3
Cunningham's Island Guest House	6
Elephant Hide	5
Island Vibe Backpackers	4
Knysna Backpackers	1
Knysna Manor House	2
Milkwood Collection	7

EATING

34° South	5
Caffè Mario	5
Chatters Bistro	4
East Head Café	7
Grain Mill Organic Bistro	3
Ile de Pain	6
The Olive Tree	2
Sailor Sam's	1

DRINKING & NIGHTLIFE

Zanzibar	1

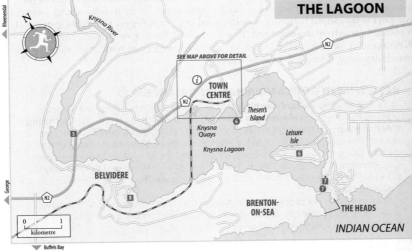

THE LAGOON

Knysna wraps around the lagoon, with its oldest part – the **town centre** – on the northern side. Here, a small historic core of Georgian and Victorian buildings gives the town a distinctive character that is enhanced by coffee shops, craft galleries, street traders and a modest nightlife. The lagoon's narrow mouth is guarded by a pair of steep rocky promontories called **The Heads**, the western side being a private nature reserve and the eastern one an exclusive residential area (confusingly, also called The Heads), along dramatic cliffs above the Indian Ocean. Although you can swim in the lagoon, there's no sea beach at Knysna – the closest one is 20km from town at Brenton-on-Sea.

2

Brief history

At the beginning of the nineteenth century, the only white settlements outside Cape Town were a handful of towns that would have considered themselves lucky to have even one horse. Knysna, an undeveloped backwater hidden in the forest, was no exception. The name comes from a Khoi word meaning "hard to reach", and this remained its defining characteristic well into the twentieth century. One important figure was not deterred by the distance – **George Rex**, a colonial administrator who placed himself beyond the pale of decent colonial society by taking a coloured mistress. Shunned by his peers in Britain, he headed for Knysna in the early 1800s in the hope of making a killing exporting hardwood from the lagoon.

By the time that Rex died in 1839, Knysna had become a major **timber centre**, attracting white labourers who felled trees with primitive tools for miserly payments, and looked set eventually to destroy the forest. The forest narrowly escaped devastation by far-sighted and effective conservation policies introduced in the 1880s.

By the turn of the twentieth century, Knysna was still remote, and its forests were inhabited by isolated and inbred communities made up of the impoverished descendants of the woodcutters. As late as 1914, if you travelled from Knysna to George you would have to open and close 58 gates along the 75km track. Fifteen years on, the passes in the region proved too much for **George Bernard Shaw**, who did some impromptu off-road driving and crashed into a bush, forcing Mrs Shaw to spend a couple of weeks in bed at Knysna's *Royal Hotel* with a broken leg.

Such a heavily forested area is susceptible to fire, and in June 2017 devastating fires swept through the town and the surrounding forests, destroying many houses and hotels, and leaving seven people dead.

Knysna Quays and Thesen's Island

About 500m south of Knysna Tourism, at the end of Grey Street

Knysna Quays, the town's waterfront complex and yacht basin, was built at the end of the 1990s; the elegant two-storey steel structure with timber boardwalks resembles a tiny version of Cape Town's V&A Waterfront. Here you'll find a mix of hotels, shops and a couple of good eating places, some with outdoor decks, from which you can watch yachts drift past. Further stylish shops and places to eat, at the edge of the lapping lagoon, can be found on **Thesen's Island**, reached by a causeway at the south end of Long Street.

Leisure Isle and Eastern Head

The main reasons to head for **Leisure Isle**, off the eastern suburbs, are the excellent swimming in the lagoon and the views out to sea through the gap between The Heads. The best bathing spots are along the southern shore of the island, particularly the western section along Bayswater Drive, though the swimming is only good around high tide in summer. Continuing south along George Rex Drive brings you to the web of roads winding through the small suburban areas of The Heads.

ARRIVAL AND INFORMATION

KNYSNA

By car Knysna is 491km and six hours' drive from Cape Town on the N2, which merges with Knysna's Main Street as it enters the town.

By bus The Baz Bus drops off at *Knysna Backpackers* (see below), while Intercape and Translux buses drop passengers at the old train station in Remembrance Avenue opposite Knysna waterfront; Greyhound buses stop at the Toyota Garage, 9 Main Rd.

Destinations Cape Town (4–5 daily; 7hr); Durban (daily; 17hr); George (4–5 daily; 1hr); Johannesburg (1–2 daily; 16hr); Mossel Bay (4–5 daily; 1hr 15min); Oudtshoorn (1–2 daily; 2hr); Plettenberg Bay (4–5 daily; 1hr 30min); Port Elizabeth (5–6 daily; 4hr 30min); Pretoria (1–2 daily; 17hr); and all Garden Route towns along the N2.

Information Knysna Tourism, 40 Main St (Mon–Fri 8am–5pm, Sat 8.30am–1pm; ☎044 382 5510, ⓦ visitknysna.co.za), provides maps and can book activities and accommodation around Knysna.

ACCOMMODATION

The best places to stay in Knysna are well away from the N2 main road, with views of the lagoon and The Heads. Out of town there are some excellent establishments as well as reasonably priced self-catering cottages right in the forest. For somewhere quieter on the lagoon, make for the western edge at Brenton-on-Sea.

TOWN CENTRE AND KNYSNA QUAYS

Island Vibe Backpackers 67 Main Rd ☎ 044 382 1728, ⓦ islandvibe.co.za; map p.220. Part of the popular *Island Vibe Backpackers* group that are situated along the Garden Route, this branch has a good location, swimming pool and a deck. The facilities are not plush but it is a good cheap option and excellent place to meet buddies to join up with for adventure activities. It is on the Baz Bus route. Dorms R140, doubles R550

Knysna Backpackers 42 Queen St ☎ 044 382 2554, ⓦ knysnabackpackers.co.za; map p.220. Spotless, well-organized hostel in a large, rambling and centrally located Victorian house that has been declared a National Monument. This tranquil establishment has five rooms rented as doubles (but able to sleep up to four people) and a dorm that sleeps eight. It's also on the Baz Bus route. Dorm R140, doubles R480

Knysna Manor House 19 Fichat St ☎ 044 382 5440, ⓦ knysnamanor.co.za; map p.220. A centrally located, hundred-year-old house with yellowwood floors and colonial furnishings. It is good value for money although a little dated in style. The twin, double and family rooms come with the use of a swimming pool and garden. R1100

LEISURE ISLE AND THE HEADS

Cunningham's Island Guest House 3 Kingsway, Leisure Isle ☎ 044 384 1319, ⓦ islandhouse.co.za; map p.220. Purpose-built two-storey, timber-and-glass guesthouse with eight suites, decked out in dazzling white relieved by a touch of blue and some ethnic colour (stripy cushions and African baskets). Each room has its own entrance leading to the garden, which has a swimming pool shaded by giant strelitzias. Stylish and comfortable, its only drawback is the lack of views. R1010

The Milkwood Collection The Heads ☎ 044 384 0745, ⓦ milkwood.co.za; map p.220. A portfolio of luxury self-catering accommodation, variously positioned and priced, on the lagoon at the foot of the Knysna Heads. The best of them, *Under Milkwood*, comprises 16 two-bedroom, self-catering chalets with direct access to the beach and terrific views of the mountains and water. R1459

WEST OF TOWN

Blue Oyster Cnr Rio & Stent sts ☎ 044 382 2265, ⓦ blueoyster.co.za; map p.220. Hospitable three-storey, vaguely Greek-themed B&B set on one of the hills that rise up behind Knysna, offering fabulous panoramas across the lagoon to The Heads. There are four comfortable rooms, of which the ones on the top floor have the best views. The guesthouse was affected by the 2017 fire but has been rebuilt. R1400

Elephant Hide Cherry Lane ☎ 044 382 0426, ⓦ elephant hide.co.za; map p.220. Overlooking the lagoon, 3km from the town centre, this peaceful guesthouse has seven rooms, each lavishly styled. The lagoon suites are a honeymooner's dream, each with a spa bath set with floor-to-ceiling windows overlooking the lagoon, a private balcony and a king-sized bed. The guesthouse has a spacious communal lounge and a fireplace for winter; there's a dreamy swimming pool and deck area to laze on in the summer. R2300

FOREST ENVIRONS

★ Forest Edge Cottages Rheenendal turn-off, 16km west of Knysna on the N2 ☎ 082 456 1338, ⓦ forestedge .co.za; map p.225. Ideal if you want to be close to the forest itself, these traditional two-bedroom woodcutters' cottages have verandas built in the vernacular tin-roofed style, and have been upgraded for extra comfort with good linen and fittings. The cottages are private and romantic. Forest walks and cycling trails start from the cottages, from where you can walk to rock pools and waterfalls. A minimum stay of two nights is required. R1025

BELVIDERE

Belvidere Manor Duthie Drive, Belvidere Estate ☎ 04 387 1055, ⓦ belvidere.co.za; map p.220. A collection o tin-roofed repro-Victorian cottages, nicely positioned on the water's edge. This is the only accommodation in this exclusive leafy area, with its lush gardens and replica Norman church, built in the 1850s. **R3040**

EATING

Knysna has a lot of good restaurants catering to a wide range of palates, though in summer and holiday periods you'll need to book ahead. There are also one or two excellent coffee shops in town, and no shortage of tempting delis, where you can make up a picnic to take into the surrounding forests, waterways and beaches.

34° South Knysna Quays ☏044 382 7331, ☜34south .biz; map p.220. A good deli, café, restaurant, bar and sushi joint with imported groceries, home-made food and an extensive menu that includes seafood in all its guises – from *peri-peri* calamari heads to a red Thai curry mussel pot (R145) and a variety of sushi. From here you can watch the drawbridge open to let yachts sail through. Daily 9.30am–10pm.

Caffè Mario Knysna Quays ☏044 382 7250; map p.220. An intimate Italian waterside restaurant with outdoor seating. The food is consistently good value; there's *vaninoteca* and *tramezzini* on its snack menu as well as great pizza (R90) and pasta. Daily 8am–10pm.

Chatters Bistro Corner of Gray and Gordon sts ☏044 382 0203, ☜chattersbistro.co.za; map p.220. Set within an enclosed garden, and with a roaring fire in winter and mighty wines on the drinks list, this is the place to go in Knysna for superb thin and crispy pizzas (with wheat and gluten-free bases available) and delicious pasta dishes (R80). Tues–Sun noon–9.30pm.

East Head Café 25 George Rex Drive ☏44 384 0933, ☜eastheadcafe.co.za; map p.220. Very popular café with an outdoor area, panoramic views of the Knysna Heads and a kids' playground. Try their simple, delicious seafood dishes (R95), classic wraps and salads, or a spirited milkshake as a cocktail. They don't take bookings and parking can be tricky. Daily 8am–3.30pm.

★**Grain Mill Organic Bistro** 3 Union St, Waterfront Drive ☏083 635 7634, map p.220. Fabulous restaurant, with sustainably grown food, freshly milled flour for its baked goods, and ethically reared meat and fish. The blackboard menu provides plenty of options for vegetarians – try the creamy vegan pumpkin soup (R60). Bring your own bottle. Mon–Sat 8.30am–3pm.

★**Ile de Pain** 10 The Boat Shed, Thesen Island ☏044 302 5705, ☜iledepain.co.za; map p.220. A trendy restaurant in an artisan bakery with stone floors and an open bakery, serving salads, baguettes and pastas. Try the crusty wood-fired bread with butter and preserves for breakfast or enjoy one of the delicious pastries with coffee (R80). Tues–Sat 8am–3pm.

The Olive Tree 12 Woodmill Lane Shopping Centre, Main Rd ☏044 382 5867; map p.220. This local favourite offers bistro dining, with fresh ingredients and Mediterranean-influenced and beautifully presented dishes. Vegetarians have a couple of options, including vegetarian pasta (R100). Mon–Sat 6–10pm.

★**Sailor Sam's** Main Rd, opposite the post office ☏044 382 6774; map p.220. A warm-hearted, old-fashioned chippy that offers incredible value, brilliant fish and chips and the cheapest oysters in town (R16 per oyster). Don't tell a soul, but the delicious shellfish aren't local; they're shipped in from South Africa's west coast. Mon–Sat 11am–8pm.

DRINKING AND NIGHTLIFE

Knysna has perked up over the past decade, but it still isn't somewhere you come if your main aim is to party. However, there are one or two clubs in town where you may catch some live music or DJs.

Zanzibar Main St ☏044 382 0386, ☜bit.ly /zanzibarknysna; map p.220. Knysna's longest-established nightclub occupies the premises of the Old Barnyard Theatre and blends everything from pop to commercial house and beyond. It has occasional live acts – mostly bands, but it's best to check out what's happening on Facebook. Expect to pay around R60 for a spirit and mixer drink. Daily 7pm–2am.

TOWNSHIP TOURS AND HOMESTAYS

Get a taste of Knysna's townships by joining one of the tours run by **Eco Afrika** (tours daily at 10am & 2pm; R400; booking essential; ☏082 558 9104, ☜eco-afrika-tours.co.za). You visit five areas where you are given some historical background and get a chance to walk around and chat to people. Lunch with a township family can be included for R60. Eco Afrika can also arrange **homestays** in a shantytown within the townships, where you stay with a family in a corrugated-iron shack (R300). The tour operator will drop you off and pick you up the next morning.

2

Emergencies General emergency number from landline ☎ 107, from mobile phone ☎ 112; Police ☎ 044 302 6600; National Sea Rescue ☎ 082 990 5956.

Hospital Life Knysna Private Hospital, Hunters Drive (☎ 044 384 1083), is well run and has a casualty department.

The Knysna forests

The best reason to come to Knysna is for its **forests**, shreds of a once magnificent woodland that was home to **Khoi** clans and harboured a thrilling variety of wildlife, including **herds of elephants**. The forests attracted European explorers and naturalists, and in their wake woodcutters, gold-diggers and businessmen such as George Rex (see p.221), all bent on making their fortunes here.

The French explorer Francois Le Vaillant was one of the first Europeans to shoot and kill an elephant in the forest. The explorer found the animal's feet so delicious that he pronounced: "Never can our modern epicures have such a dainty at their tables." Two hundred years later, all that's left of the Khoi people are some names of local places, while the legendary Knysna elephants have fared little better and are teetering on the brink of extinction.

Goudveld State Forest

Just over 30km northwest of Knysna • Daily sunrise–sunset • R100 • Follow the N2 west from Knysna towards George, turning right onto Rheenendal Rd just after the Knysna River, and continue for about 25km, following the Bibby's Koep signposts until the Goudveld sign

The beautiful **Goudveld State Forest** is a mixture of plantation and indigenous woodland. It takes its name from the gold boom (*goudveld* is Afrikaans for goldfields) that brought hundreds of prospectors to the mining town of **Millwood** in the 1880s. The boom was short-lived, and bust followed in 1890 after most of the mining companies went to the wall. Today, the old town is completely overgrown, apart from signs indicating where the old streets stood. The forest itself is still lovely, featuring tall, indigenous trees, a delightful valley with a stream, and plenty of swimming holes and picnic sites.

Hiking in the Goudveld

A number of clearly **waymarked hikes** traverse the Goudveld. The most rewarding (and easy going) is along **Jubilee Creek**, which traces the progress of a burbling brook for 3.5km through giant woodland to a gorgeous, deep rock pool – ideal for cooling off. Along the way you'll see miners' excavations scraped or blasted out of the hillside. Some of the old mine works have been restored, as have the original **reduction works** around the cocopan track, used to carry the ore from the mine to the works, which is still there after a century. Jubilee Creek is also an excellent place to encounter **Knysna louries**; keep an eye focused on the branches above for the crimson flash of their flight feathers as they forage for berries. You can pick up a **map** directing you to the creek from the entrance gate to the reserve; note that the waymarked trail is linear, so you return via the same route. There's a pleasant **picnic site** along the banks of the stream at the start of the walk.

> ## THE KNYSNA ELEPHANTS
>
> Traffic signs warning motorists about elephants, along the N2 between Knysna and Plettenberg Bay, are rather optimistic: such elephants have approached mythical status, although there is the occasional rare sighting by forestry workers. By 1860, the thousands that had formerly wandered the once vast forests were down to five hundred, and by 1920 (twelve years after they were protected by law), there were only twenty animals left – the current estimate is 0–3. Loss of habitat and consequent malnutrition, rather than full-scale hunting, seems to have been the principal cause of their decline. The only elephants you're guaranteed to see near Knysna are at the **Elephant Sanctuary** (see p.231) near Plettenberg Bay.

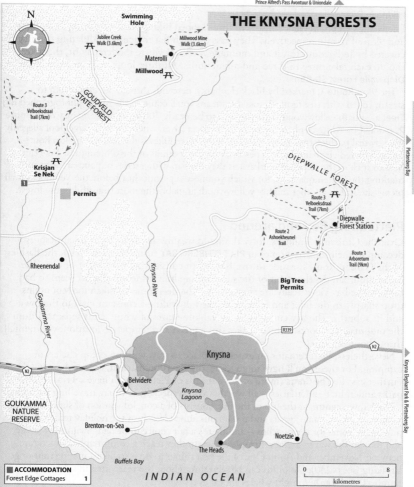

THE KNYSNA FORESTS

N

Swimming Hole

Jubilee Creek Walk (3.6km)

Millwood Mine Walk (3.6km)

Materolli

Millwood

GOUDVELD STATE FOREST

Route 3 Velboeksdraai Trail (7km)

Krisjan Se Nek

Permits

DIEPWALLE FOREST

Route 3 Velboeksdraai Trail (7km)

Diepwalle Forest Station

Route 2 Ashoekheunel Trail

Route 1 Arboretum Trail (9km)

Rheenendal

Knysna River

Goukamma River

Big Tree Permits

R339

N2

Knysna

Belvidere

Knysna Lagoon

GOUKAMMA NATURE RESERVE

Brenton-on-Sea

Noetzie

The Heads

Buffels Bay

INDIAN OCEAN

■ **ACCOMMODATION**
Forest Edge Cottages 1

0 ——— 8
kilometres

A more strenuous option is the circular **Woodcutter Walk**, though you can choose either the 3km or the 9km version. Starting at **Krisjan se Nek**, another picnic site not far past the Goudveld entrance gate, it meanders downhill through dense forest, passing through stands of tree ferns, and returns uphill to the starting point.

Diepwalle Forest

Around 20km northeast of Knysna • Daily 6am–6pm • R100 • Follow the N2 east towards Plettenberg Bay, turning left onto the R339 after 7km. Continue towards Avontuur and Uniondale for 17km until the signposted turn-off to the Diepwalle Forest Station

The **Diepwalle Forest** is the last haunt of Knysna's almost extinct elephant population. The only elephants you're guaranteed to see are on the painted markers indicating the three main hikes through these woodlands. However, if you're quiet and alert, you stand a chance of seeing vervet monkeys, bushbuck and blue duiker. Diepwalle ("deep walls") is one of the highlights of the Knysna area and is renowned for its impressive density of huge trees, especially **yellowwoods**.

Hiking in Diepwalle

Diepwalle's **Elephant Walk** consists of three looped hiking routes covering 7km, 8km and 9km of terrain respectively. They pass through flat to gently undulating country covered by indigenous forest and montane *fynbos*. If you're moderately fit, the hikes should each take three to three-and-a-half hours. All three loops start and end at the **Diepwalle Forest Station**.

The 9km **Route 1**, marked by black elephants, descends through an **arboretum** to a stream edged with tree ferns. Across the stream you'll come to the much-photographed **Big Tree**, a Goliath yellowwood that's thought to be nearly 700 years old. The easy 8km **Route 2**, marked by white elephants, crosses the Gouna River, where there's a large pool allegedly used by real pachyderms. Most difficult of the three hikes is the rewarding 7km **Route 3**, marked by red elephants, which passes along the foothills of the Outeniquas. Take care here to stick to the elephant markers, as they overlap with a series of painted footprints marking the Outeniqua Trail, for which you need a permit. Just before the Veldboeksdraai picnic site stands another mighty yellowwood, arguably the most beautiful in the forest.

Plettenberg Bay and around

Over the Christmas holidays, forty thousand wealthy residents from Johannesburg decamp to their holiday homes in **PLETTENBERG BAY** (usually called Plett), the flashiest of the Garden Route's seaside towns, but worth considering for a night or two. The banal suburban development of the surrounding hills somehow doesn't seem so bad because the bay views really are stupendous. The deep-blue **Tsitsikamma Mountains** drop sharply to the inlet and its large estuary, providing a constant vista to the town and its suburbs. The bay curves over several kilometres of white sands separated from the mountains by forest, which makes this a green and temperate location with rainfall throughout the year.

Nevertheless, Plett remains an expensive place to stay, with no cheap chalets or camping. For these you'll have to go to nearby **Keurboomstrand**, east of the bay. Further east lie **The Crags** (more or less suburbs of Plett), which have several wildlife parks and animal sanctuaries – all worth a visit, especially if you're travelling with kids.

Plett's town **centre**, at the top of the hill, consists of a conglomeration of supermarkets, swimwear shops, estate agents and restaurants aimed largely at the holiday trade. Visitors principally come for the **beaches** – and there's a fair choice to be had. Swimming is safe, and though the waters are never tropically warm they reach a comfortable temperature between November and April. One of the best things to do is to take a marine tour or go kayaking (see p.230). Dolphins can be seen throughout the year, often in substantial numbers, and southern right whales appear every winter.

Southeast of the town centre on a rocky promontory is **Beacon Island**, dominated by a 1970s hotel, an eyesore blighting a great location. Fortunately, development has been halted on the magnificent **Robberg Peninsula**, the great tongue of headland that contains the western edge of the bay. This is the place to go for the Garden Route's best short **hikes**, and should not be missed – it's enough of an attraction in itself to justify a stopover at Plett.

The beaches

Beacon Island Beach, or **Main Beach**, right at the central shore of the bay, is where the fishing boats and seacats anchor a little out to sea. The small waves here make for calm swimming, and this is an ideal family spot. To the east is **Lookout Beach**, which is also one of the nicest stretches of sand for bathing, or sun-lounging, with the added attraction of a marvellously located restaurant (see p.229), from which you can often catch sight of **dolphins** cruising into the bay. From here you can walk several kilometres down the beach towards Keurboomstrand and the **Keurbooms Lagoon**. Robberg Beach, towards the National Park at Robberg, offers fine long beach walks and swimming.

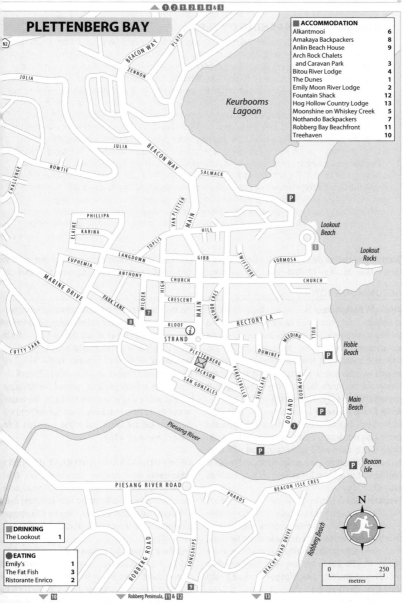

PLETTENBERG BAY

■ ACCOMMODATION	
Alkantmooi	6
Amakaya Backpackers	8
Anlin Beach House	9
Arch Rock Chalets and Caravan Park	3
Bitou River Lodge	4
The Dunes	1
Emily Moon River Lodge	2
Fountain Shack	12
Hog Hollow Country Lodge	13
Moonshine on Whiskey Creek	5
Nothando Backpackers	7
Robberg Bay Beachfront	11
Treehaven	10

■ DRINKING	
The Lookout	1

● EATING	
Emily's	1
The Fat Fish	3
Ristorante Enrico	2

ARRIVAL AND INFORMATION

PLETTENBERG BAY

By car Plettenberg Bay is 33km east of Knysna, 520km from Cape Town and 1140km from Johannesburg.

By Baz Bus The Baz Bus drops passengers off at accommodation in town.

By intercity bus Intercape, Greyhound and Translux intercity buses stop at the Shell Ultra City petrol station, just off the N2 in Marine Way, 2km from the town centre. As there's no transport around town, you'll need to arrange for your guesthouse to collect you.

Destinations Cape Town (2 daily; 9hr); George (2 daily; 2hr); Joburg (2 daily; 18hr); Knysna (2 daily; 1hr 30min); Mossel Bay (2 daily; 2hr 20min); Port Elizabeth (2 daily; 3hr 30min).

2

WHALING AND GNASHING OF TEETH

For conservationists, the monumental 1970s eyesore of *Beacon Island Hotel*, on a promontory on the southern side of the Piesang River mouth, may not be such a bad thing, since previously it was the site of a whale-processing factory established in 1806 – one of some half-dozen such plants erected along the Western Cape coast that year. Whaling continued at Plettenberg Bay until 1916. Southern right whales were the favoured species, yielding more oil and – **whalebone** – an essential component of Victorian corsets – than any other. In the nineteenth century, a southern right would net around three times as much as a humpback caught along the Western Cape coast, leading to a rapid decline in their population by the mid century. In 1913, Plettenberg Bay was the site of one of seventeen shore-based and about a dozen floating factories between West Africa and Mozambique, which that year between them processed a mammoth ten thousand whales.

Declining numbers meant that by 1918 all but four of the shore-based factories had closed owing to lack of prey. The remaining whalers now turned their attention to fin and blue whales. When the South African fin whale population became depleted by the mid-1960s to twenty percent of its former size, they turned to sei and sperm whales. When these populations declined, the frustrated whalers started hunting minke whales, which at 9m in length are too small to be a viable catch. In 1979 the South African government banned all whaling activity.

Tourist information The tourist office, Shop 35, Melville Corner, Main St (Mon–Fri 9am–5pm, Sat 9am–1pm; ☎ 044 533 4065, ⓦ plett-tourism.co.za), has maps of th town and may be able to help with booking accommodatio

ACCOMMODATION

Amakaya Backpackers 15 Park Lane ☎ 044 533 4010, ⓦ amakaya.co.za; map p.227. Located close to town and the beach, this place is well set up for backpackers – there are communal lounge areas, an outside fire pit and hammocks to while away your time. There's also an upstairs veranda with bar and swimming pool and views of the lagoon and mountains. Minimum stay of two nights at weekends. Dorms R170, doubles R480

Anlin Beach House 33 Roche Bonne Ave ☎ 044 533 3694, ⓦ anlinbeachhouse.co.za; map p.227. Stylish and comfortably kitted-out self-catering garden studios, a sea-facing double room and a larger family unit with three bedrooms and a kitchen, in a garden setting on the side of Plett nearest to Robberg Nature Reserve. Breakfast is an extra R85. R1800

Fountain Shack Robberg Nature Reserve ☎ 021 483 0190, ⓦ capenature.co.za/reserves/robberg-nature -reserve; map p.227. A remote bungalow sleeping eight; there is no electricity but it's a beautiful setting by the ocean. It is the only accommodation in the reserve with no vehicle access – it's a 2hr walk to get there. Linen, cooking facilities and cutlery are provided, so just bring your own food. R1400

Nothando Backpackers 5 Wilder St ☎ 044 533 0220, ⓦ nothando.com; map p.227. This top-notch child-friendly hostel, 5min from Plett's shops, is a suburban house with seven doubles, three dorms and a four-bedded family room. Breakfast and dinner are available for an extra R50/80. Dorms R180, doubles R550, family room R990

★ **Robberg Bay Beachfront** 2 Robberg Rd ☎ 082 809 3931, ⓦ robbergbay.com; map p.227. Poised above Robberg Beach, with the full sweep of the bay in front of you, this stupendously located and immaculate guesthous overflows with easy luxury and relaxation. All seven unit have unobstructed sea views and there is a path from th house straight onto the beach 700m away. R2800

Treehaven 45 Hanois Crescent ☎ 044 533 198! ⓦ treehavenholidays.co.za; map p.227. Tranquil an comfortable self-catering suite, part of the fascinatin home of artistic couple Carol and Feo Sachs. The house i surrounded by trees with a lack of sea but sheltered fror the wind, and the beach and Robberg are just a fev minutes' drive away. R900

KEURBOOMSTRAND AND EAST OF PLETT

Alkantmooi Keurboom Rd, Keurbooms River ☎ 04 535 9245, ⓦ alkantmooi.co.za; map p.227. Four moder one- or two-bedroom self-catering units in varying style with lagoon rather than sea views. There are fully equippe kitchens and braai or outdoor patio facilities. Good value fo money. R1400

Arch Rock Chalets & Caravan Park Arch Rock ☎ 04 535 9409, ⓦ archrock.co.za; map p.227. Seventeen self catering chalets, with one or two bedrooms, in the bes position at Keurbooms – right on the beach. Apart from th forest chalets and log cabins, which are set back amon trees (R800), the rest have sea views. Chalets R1200

Bitou River Lodge Bitou Valley Rd (the R340), abou 4km from the N2 ☎ 044 535 9577, ⓦ bitou.co.za; ma p.227. Great value in a lovely spot on the banks of the Bito River, this intimate establishment has five comfortable bu unfussy bedrooms that overlook a pretty garden with a lil pond. Rate includes use of canoes on the river. R1700

The Dunes Park Keurboomstrand Rd, leading off the N2 and running along the shore to Keurbooms ☎ 044 535 9606, ⓦ dunesresort.co.za; map p.227. Luxury hotel and resort, close to the sea, whose airy bedrooms are simple and stylish. Two-bedroom self-catering cottages built on top of high dunes provide great views. There's also a good, family-friendly restaurant. Doubles R990, cottages R1500

★ **Emily Moon River Lodge** Rietvlei Rd, off the N2 (turn off at Penny Pinchers) ☎ 044 533 2982, ⓦ emilymoon.co.za; map p.227. This place is not only filled with Batonga sculptures and Swazi crafts, parts of it are constructed out of artworks, such as the intricate Rajasthani arched screen that is the entrance to the magnificently sited restaurant. Each of its chalets jetties out of the hillside, offering views of the oxbowing Bitou, along which small game can occasionally be seen. There is a family suite that sleeps four. R3440

★ **Hog Hollow Country Lodge** Askop Rd, 18km east of Plettenberg Bay, turn south off the N2 at the signpost ☎ 044 534 8879, ⓦ hog-hollow.com; map p.227. A touch of luxury on a private reserve where each of the chalets, spiced up with African artefacts, has a bath or shower and its own wooden deck with vistas across the forest and Tsitsikamma Mountains. Superb food is also on offer. Hike for a couple of hours through forest to reach Keurbooms beach, or drive there in 15min. R3680

Moonshine on Whiskey Creek 14km east of Plettenberg Bay along the N2, signposted north of the N2 ☎ 044 534 8515 or ☎ 072 200 6656, ⓦ whiskeycreek .co.za; map p.227. Fully equipped bungalows, three wooden cabins and one creatively renovated labourer's cottage (R950), nestled in indigenous forest, with a children's play area. One of the best reasons to come here is the access to a secluded natural mountain pool and waterfall at the bottom of the nearby gorge. R1440

EATING

Restaurants come and go in Plett at a similar lick to the tides, but one or two long-standing establishments have managed to remain afloat. Locally caught fresh fish is the thing to look out for, and because the town is built on hills, many restaurants have terrific views.

★ **Emily's** Rietvlei Rd, off the N2 (turn off at Penny Pinchers) ☎ 044 533 2982, ⓦ emilymoon.co.za/dining -at-emilys; map p.227. One of the best restaurants in the area, offering classical French cuisine with an edge and great views of the Bitou Wetland. Everything is sustainable, fresh and appetizing. Vegetarians should try the superb lentil dhal (R90) or goats' cheese and beetroot salad (R75). Booking is essential, especially for a table on the deck. Mon 6.30–10pm, Tues–Sun noon–3pm & 6.30–10pm.

The Fat Fish Milkwood Centre, Central Beach ☎ 044 533 4740; map p.227. Cheerful restaurant with reasonably priced seafood including tapas-sized portions of oysters, tempura prawns or salmon, and with various meze platters to share (R85), as well as steaks and heavier dishes. There's a good selection of wines to help you wash it down. Daily 11.30am–4pm & 5.30–10pm.

Ristorante Enrico Main Beach, Keurboomstrand ☎ 044 535 9818, ⓦ enricorestaurant.co.za; map p.227. Easy-going restaurant with a holiday vibe situated right on the beach. The mid-priced Italian standards – thin-based pizzas, pasta and veal (R130) – can be eaten outside while enjoying the fresh sea breezes. Tues–Sun noon–9pm.

DRINKING

The Lookout Lookout Beach ☎ 044 533 1379, ⓦ lookout.co.za; map p.227. There are marvellous bay views at this bar-restaurant, with umbrellas and outdoor tables. The focus is on seafood, but there are appealing vegetarian options, and it's definitely the best place in town for cocktails (R60). Daily 9am–10pm.

WHALE-WATCHING VIEWPOINTS IN PLETTENBERG BAY

Elevated ocean panoramas give Plettenberg Bay some **outstanding viewpoints** for watching southern right whales between June and October. An especially good vantage point is the area between the wreck of the *Athene* at the southern end of Lookout Beach and the Keurbooms River. The Robberg Peninsula is also excellent, looming protectively over this whale nursery and giving a grandstand view of the bay. Other good viewpoints in town are from Beachy Head Road at Robberg Beach; Signal Hill in San Gonzales Street past the post office and police station; *Beacon Island Hotel* on Beacon Island; and the deck of the restaurant *The Lookout* (see above) on Lookout Beach. Outside Plett, the Kranshoek viewpoint and hiking trail offers wonderful whale-watching points along the route; to get there, head for Knysna, take the Harkerville turn-off, and continue for 7km .

2

Robberg Marine and Nature Reserve

Robberg Rd • Daily 8am–5pm; R40 • ⓦ capenature.co.za/reserves/robberg-nature-reserve

One of the Garden Route's nicest walks is the four-hour, 9km circular route around the spectacular rocky peninsula of **Robberg**, 8km southeast of Plett's town centre. Here you can completely escape Plett's development and experience the coast in its wildest state, with its enormous horizons and lovely vegetation. Much of the walk takes you along high cliffs, from where you can often look down on seals surfacing near the rocks, dolphins arching through the water and, in winter, whales further out in the bay. If you don't have time for the full circular walk, there is a shorter two-hour hike and a thirty-minute ramble – a map is provided at the entrance gate. There is one rustic cottage, *Fountain Shack*, to stay overnight (see p.228).

Keurboomstrand

Some 14km east of Plettenberg Bay by road, across the Keurbooms River, is the uncluttered resort of **KEURBOOMSTRAND** (Keurbooms for short), little more than a suburb of Plett, sharing the same bay but less safe for swimming. The best place to take the waves is at **Arch Rock**, in front of the caravan park, though **Picnic Rock beach** is also pretty good. A calm and attractive place, Keurbooms has few facilities; and if you're

---

ACTIVITIES AND TOURS AROUND PLETTENBERG BAY

BOAT TRIPS

Keurbooms River Ferries Signposted on the east side of the Keurbooms River Bridge ☎ 083 254 3551, ⓦ ferry.co.za. This company runs daily boat trips upriver (11am, 2pm, sunset; R180) with knowledgeable guides skilled at spotting rare birds – the indigenous forest comes right down to the water's edge. Booking required. Cape Nature entrance fee is R40 per person.

BUNGEE JUMPING

Bloukrans Bungy ☎ 042 281 1458, ⓦ faceadrenalin.com. The world's highest commercial bungee jump takes place off the 216m Bloukrans River Bridge and costs R9500 (excluding pictures or video) for the seven-second descent. You'll need to book at least 48hr in advance.

CANOEING

CapeNature On the east side of the Keurbooms River Bridge along the N2, on the road marked Keurbooms River Ferry. There's a kiosk where you can reserve a fairly basic craft – easily available, especially out of season (R135/day for a two-person canoe).

ROCK CLIMBING

GoVertical Mountaineering Adventures ☎ 082 731 4696, ⓦ govertical.co.za. Kloofing (also known as canyoning) is the most adventurous way of exploring the deep river gorges between Knysna and Plett. GoVertical can teach the basics of rock-climbing and take experienced climbers out; prices vary depending on the size of the group, and are provided when you enquire.

SKYDIVING

Skydive Plettenberg Bay ☎ 082 905 7440, ⓦ skydiveplett.com. If you fancy an adrenaline rush, you can go tandem skydiving (no experience required) with these guys, who charge R2300 for a 10,000ft jump, with the option of paying extra for a DVD or video of the event.

TOWNSHIP TOURS

Ocean Blue Central Beach ☎ 044 533 5083, ⓦ ocean adventures.co.za. Ocean Blue arranges relaxed tours into Plett's township with a guide who is a member of the host community. Trips cost R200 per person and the profits go into a development trust, which among other things pays teachers' salaries and funds a crèche.

WHALE- AND DOLPHIN-WATCHING

Dolphin Adventures Central Beach ☎ 083 590 3405, ⓦ dolphinadventures.co.za. Sea kayaking is one of the best ways to watch whales, and this outfit offers unforgettable trips with experienced and knowledgeable guides in two-person kayaks (2hr–2hr 30min, R300) or just rentals (2hr R150).

Ocean Blue Central Beach ☎ 044 533 4897 or ☎ 083 701 3583, ⓦ oceanadventures.co.za. A licensed outfit that offers sea-kayaking (R300) and boat-based whale-watching (R750) tours, from July to September (R750).

Ocean Safaris Shop 3, Hopwood St ☎ 044 533 4963, ⓦ oceansafaris.co.za. Tailor-made cruises from a licensed whale-watching company. Whale-watching by boat (R750) virtually guarantees sightings between July and September. Out of whale season it's still worth going out to see dolphins and seals (R450).

ntending to stay here you should stock up in Plett beforehand. One of Keurbooms'
ighlights is **canoeing** up the river (see box opposite).

The Crags

The Crags, 2km east of Keurboomstrand, comprises a collection of smallholdings along
he N2, a bottle store and a few other shops on the forest edge. The reason most
isitors pull in here is for the **Elephant Sanctuary**, **Monkeyland**, **Birds of Eden** and
ukani Wildlife Sanctuary. Collectively, the last three make up the South African Animal
anctuary Alliance (SAASA) and can be visited separately or on a combined ticket. To
each all four attractions from Keurbooms, look out for the BP petrol station, then take
he Monkeyland/Kurland turn-off and follow the Elephant Sanctuary/Monkeyland
igns for 2km.

Elephant Sanctuary

Monkeyland Rd, 19km east of Plettenberg Bay off the N2 • Daily 8am–5pm • Trunk-in-Hand programme daily at 7.30am • R580; elephant
rush-down R705 • ☎ 044 534 8145, ⓦ elephantsanctuary.co.za

The **Elephant Sanctuary** offers a chance of close encounters with its half-dozen
lephants, all of which were saved from culling in Botswana and Kruger National Park.
On the popular one-hour Trunk-in-Hand programme, which includes an informative
alk about elephant behaviour, you get to walk with an elephant, holding the tip of its
runk in your hand, and also to feed and interact with it. You can also help to brush
own the elephants – a thrilling experience.

Monkeyland

00m beyond the Elephant Sanctuary • Daily 8am–5pm • R230, combined ticket for two sanctuaries R360, combined ticket for all three
anctuaries R450 • ☎ 044 534 8906 or ☎ 082 979 5683, ⓦ monkeyland.co.za

Monkeyland brings together primates from several continents, all of them orphaned or
aved from a life as pets. None of the animals has been taken from the wild – and most
vouldn't have the skills to survive there. The monkeys are free to move around the
eserve, looking for food and interacting with each other. For your and the monkeys'
afety, you are not allowed to wander around alone. **Guides** take visitors on walking
safaris", during which you come across water holes, experience a living indigenous
orest and enjoy chance encounters with creatures such as ringtail lemurs from
Madagascar and squirrel monkeys from South America.

One of the sanctuary's highlights is crossing the long Indiana Jones-style **rope bridge**
panning a canyon to pass through the upper reaches of the forest canopy, where a
umber of species spend their days.

Birds of Eden

aily 8am–5pm • R230, combined ticket for two sanctuaries R360, combined ticket for all three sanctuaries R450 •
Ⓦ birdsofeden.co.za

Under the same management as Monkeyland and right next door, **Birds of Eden** is
. huge bird sanctuary. Great effort has been taken to place netting over a substantial
ract of forest with as little environmental impact as possible. As with Monkeyland,
nost of Birds of Eden's charges were already living in cages and are now free to
nove and fly around within the confines of the large enclosure (so large in fact that
ou can easily spend an hour slowly meandering along its winding, wheelchair-
riendly, wooden walkway).

Most of the birds are exotics, some impossibly brightly coloured (such as the
ncandescent scarlet ibis from South America and golden pheasant from China), but
ou'll also see a number of locals, such as the Knysna turaco and South Africa's national
ird, the blue crane. Watch out for the cheeky cockatoos that may alight on your
houlder and steal buttons from your shirt.

2

Jukani Wildlife Sanctuary

Daily 9am–5pm • R230, combined ticket for two sanctuaries R360, combined ticket for all three sanctuaries R450 • ⓦ jukani.co.za

Signposted off the N2 at the Crags, 7km west of Monkeyland, this is the place to see big cats. There are a couple of large enclosures, with African cats, as well as exotic jaguars, tigers and cougars. Other predators include hyenas, wild dogs, jackals and even some snakes. The animals have all been born in captivity and rescued, there is no breeding programme and, unlike some private reserves, the lions here are not used to supply the notorious lion hunting trade. As with Monkeyland, you are taken around on guided "safaris" by highly knowledgeable guides, each tour lasting around one and a half hours.

Tsitsikamma

The **Tsitsikamma section** of the Garden Route National Park, roughly midway between Plettenberg Bay and Port Elizabeth, is the highlight of any Garden Route trip, extending for 68km along a narrow belt of coast, with dramatic foamy surges of rocky coast, deep river gorges and ancient hardwood forests clinging to the edge of tangled, green cliffs. Don't pass up its main attraction, **Storms River Mouth**, the most dramatic estuary on this exhilarating piece of coast. Established in 1964, Tsitsikamma is also South Africa's oldest marine reserve, stretching 5.5km out to sea, with an **underwater trail** open to snorkellers and licensed scuba divers.

Tsitsikamma itself has two sections: **Nature's Valley** in the west and **Storms River Mouth** in the east. Each section can only be reached down a winding tarred road from the N2 (apart from hiking, there's no way of getting from one to the other through the park itself). Nature's Valley incorporates the most low-key settlement on the Garden Route, with a fabulous sandy beach stretching for 3km. South Africa's ultimate hike, the five-day **Otter Trail** (see box, p.234), connects the two sections of the park.

The nearest settlement to Storms River Mouth, some 14km to its north at the top of a steep winding road, is the confusingly named **Storms River Village**, which is outside the national park and some distance from any part of the river, but makes a convenient base for adventure activities in the vicinity and day-trips down to Storms River Mouth.

Nature's Valley

Nature's Valley, at the western end of the Tsitsikamma section of the Garden Route National Park, 29km east of Plettenberg Bay and two and a half hour's drive from Port Elizabeth (204km), extends inland into the rugged and hilly interior. It incorporates a settlement of wooden houses set on the stunningly beautiful Groot River Lagoon, with 20km of sandy beach and miles of indigenous forest to explore, which is highly sought-after among nature lovers. The strict legislation here (highly unusual in South Africa) means there are no crass holiday houses, housing developments, hotels or tour buses and only one small restaurant and village shop.

There are plenty of good **walks** at Nature's Valley, many starting from the national park campsite, 1km north of the village, where you can pick up maps and information about birds and trees. One of the loveliest places to head for is **Salt River Mouth**, 3km west of Nature's Valley, where you can swim and picnic – though you'll need to ford the river at low tide. This walk starts and ends at the café at Nature's Valley. Also recommended is the circular 6km **Kalanderkloof trail**, which begins at the national park campsite, ascends to a lookout point, and descends via a narrow river gorge graced with a profusion of huge Outeniqua yellowwood trees and Cape wild bananas.

ARRIVAL AND INFORMATION

By car Nature's Valley is 29km east of Plettenberg Bay, down the lovely winding Groot River pass.

By bus The Baz Bus drops off here at the *Wild Spirit Lodge*, 8km from the ocean.

Information Nature's Valley Trading Store, on the corner of Forest and St Michael sts (☏ 044 531 6835, ⓦ facebook /naturesvalleyrestaurant), is effectively the village centre and acts as an informal but excellent information bureau.

ACCOMMODATION

Accommodation in Nature's Valley is pretty limited, which contributes to its low-key charm, but you'll find some choice options on the road leading off the N2 into the village, just before the switchbacks begin, which all require driving down to the beach and lagoon.

Four Fields Farm Nature's Valley Rd, 3km from the N2 along the R102 and 8km from Nature's Valley ☏ 044 534 8708, ⓦ fourfields.iowners.net. A welcoming and charmingly unpretentious former dairy farm, less than 10min drive from the sea. The self-catering farmhouse has four bedrooms simply furnished with beautiful old pieces and with French doors leading to their own private decks, which in turn open onto a much-loved garden surrounded by fields. There is also a flat that sleeps four (R1200) and another which sleeps a couple (R660). R2400

Lily Pond Lodge 102 Nature's Valley Rd, 3km from the N2 along the R102 and 6km from Nature's Valley ☏ 044 534 8767, ⓦ lilypond.co.za. The most memorable accommodation in Nature's Valley and the most luxurious: the four en-suite rooms have sound systems and TVs and open onto private terraces, while the spacious luxury suites have their own lounge, under-floor heating and king-sized beds. There's a honeymoon suite with its own private garden, and a large, shared garden for all guests. R1980

★ **Nature's Valley Restcamp** 1km to the north of the village. Book through SANParks (☏ 044 531 6700, ⓦ sanparks.org/parks/garden_route/camps/natures _valley) or the camp supervisor on ☏ 044 531 6700. Campsites tucked into indigenous forest, plus basic two-person forest huts with communal ablution facilities. Camping R205, huts R510

Rocky Road Backpackers 1.5km from the N2 along the R102, 12km from Nature's Valley ☏ 072 270 2114, ⓦ rockyroadbackpackers.com. A tranquil backpacker retreat set on a large forested property. While the setting and landscaped gardens are the big draw, it also has an outdoor pizza oven, forest bathroom and a highly sociable Friday braai night. There is a range of sleeping options, the most appealing being the luxury tents with soft bedding and electric blankets. It's on the Baz Bus route. Camping R100, luxury tent R220, dorms R190, doubles R500

Tranquility Lodge 130 St Michael's Ave (next to the shop) ☏ 044 531 6663, ⓦ tranquilitylodge.co.za. If Nature's Valley has a centre, then this comfortable lodge, next to the village's only shop, is bang in the middle of it. A two-storey brick and timber building set in a garden that feels as if it's part of the encroaching forest, it is just 50m from the beach. Breakfast is served on an upstairs deck among the treetops. All rooms are en suite and there's also a larger honeymoon suite (R1800) with double shower, fireplace and private deck. R1500

★ **Wild Spirit Lodge and Backpackers** Nature's Valley Rd, 8km from Nature's Valley ☏ 044 534 8888, ⓦ wildspiritlodge.co.za. One of the best Garden Route lodges, with accommodation in bunk-free dorms in three, two-storey garden cottages, safari tents and a kitchen for self-catering. As the name suggests, this place has an alternative vibe: there's a yoga and meditation room, book exchange, live music and drumming nights and a big outdoor braai, or you can simply explore the surrounding forest or hang out in the tree house. It's on the Baz Bus route. Camping R90, bunk-free dorms R150, doubles R450

Storms River Mouth

55km east of Plettenberg Bay • Daily 7am–7.30pm • R200 • ☏ 042 281 1607

In contrast to the languid lagoon and long soft sands of Nature's Valley, **Storms River Mouth** presents the elemental face of the Garden Route, with the dark Storms River surging through a gorge to battle with the surf. Don't confuse this with **Storms River Village** just off the N2, which is nowhere near the sea, but right in the forest. Storms River Mouth lies 18km south of Storms River Bridge, on the N2. Most people stop at the bridge to gaze into the deep river gorge and fill up at the most beautifully located service station in the country. Even if your time is limited and you can't spend the night, it's worth detouring the 18km down to Storms River Mouth to gaze at the coastline.

Walking is the main activity at the Mouth, and at the visitors' office at the restcamp you can get maps of short, waymarked coastal trails that leave from here. Most rewarding is the 3km hike west from the restcamp along the start of the Otter Trail to a fantastic waterfall pool at the base of 5m-high falls. Less demanding is the kilometre-long boardwalk stroll from the restaurant to the suspension bridge to see the river mouth. On your way to the bridge, don't miss the dank *strandloper* (beachcomber) cave. Hunter-gatherers frequented this area between five thousand and two thousand years ago, living off seafood in wave-cut caves near the river mouth. A modest display

2

shows an excavated midden, with clear layers of little bones and shells. Swimming at the Mouth is restricted to a safe and pristine little sandy bay below the restaurant, with a changing hut, though conditions can be cold in summer if there are easterly winds and cold upwellings of deep water from the continental shelf.

ACCOMMODATION   STORMS RIVER MOUTH

Storms River Mouth Restcamp ☎042 281 1607, ⊛bit.ly/SANParksstormsriver. Sited on tended lawns, the restcamp is poised between a craggy shoreline of black rocks, pounded by foamy white surf, and steeply raking forested cliffs. It has a variety of accommodation options, none of which is outstanding, but all have sea views and the ever-present sound of the surging surf. Advance booking is essential (see p.65) and you may have to take whatever is available, as its location makes it understandably popular. Two units have disabled access. Camping R390, forest hut R755, chalet R1385

EATING

Tsitsikamma Restaurant The only place to eat at Storms River Mouth has such startling views that it can be forgiven for its mediocre fare of English breakfasts, toasted sandwiches, burgers, pastas and steak, and its indifferent service. There's a reasonable range of seafood dishes (R120), however, and you can get a drink outside on the wooden deck. Daily 8.30am–10pm.

GARDEN ROUTE LONG-DISTANCE WALKING TRAILS

Dolphin Trail This is the Garden Route's luxury, portered trail, with stays in comfortable accommodation. It's the only one suitable if you are holidaying solo without your own gear (the others trails are geared towards local groups of well-equipped hikers). The terrain through the Tsitsikamma National Park is breathtaking, covering the rugged coastal edge and the natural forest.

The trail starts at Storms River Mouth and ends at Sandrif River Mouth, covering a distance of 20km over three and a half days. The price (R5990 per person) includes food, accommodation and permits, a guide, a boat trip up the Storms River Gorge and a 4WD through the Storms River Pass: book through the Fernery ☎042 280 3588, ⊛dolphintrail.co.za.

Otter Trail The Otter Trail is South Africa's flagship hike; it is simply magnificent hiking along a pristine stretch of coastline and forest where there is no habitation or vehicle access. It is geared to locals in a group, but if you're desperate to do it and have been told it is full, keep checking the website for cancellations. You need to be fit for the steep sections, and an experienced hiker – you carry everything from hut to hut and have to be able to manage river crossings.

It starts at Storms River Mouth and ends at Nature's Valley (distance 42km; duration five days), and the maximum number of people on the trail is twelve; book through South African National Parks at least twelve months in advance (R1150 per person; ☎012 428 911, ⊛sanparks.org).

Tsitsikamma Trail Not to be confused with the Otter Trail, this is an inland hike through indigenous forest, long stretches of open *fynbos* and the Tsitsikamma mountain range. Five overnight huts accommodate 24 people. It is a strenuous hike, though porterage has now been introduced, which makes it a lot easier.

It starts at Nature's Valley and ends at Storms River Bridge (distance 60km; duration six days). Book through MTO Ecotourism (R200 per person per night; ☎042 281 1712, ⊛mtoecotourism.co.za).

Harkerville Coastal Trail Closer to the roads, this circular trail doesn't feel as remote as the Otter Trail but is a good second-best, taking in magnificent rocky coastline, indigenous forest and *fynbos*. There is plenty of rock scrambling and some traversing of exposed, narrow ledges above the sea, so do not attempt without experience of similar terrain, or a good degree of fitness. Because it is relatively short, it makes a good choice if you don't have a lot of time.

The trail starts and ends at Harkerville Forestry Station, signposted off the N2, 12km west of Plettenberg Bay (distance 26.5km; duration two days). Book at the SAN Parks office in Knysna (R260 per person; ☎044 302 5600, ✉reservations@sanparks.org).

Storms River Village

About a kilometre south of the national road, **STORMS RIVER VILLAGE** is a tranquil place crisscrossed by a handful of dirt roads and with about forty houses, enjoying mountain views. Its main attraction is as a centre for adventure activities, of which the **Canopy Tour** is the main draw. It also makes a lovely, forested and easily accessible place to overnight, if you're travelling from Cape Town (579km west) to Port Elizabeth (179km east).

2

The Armagh Fynbos Ave ☎042 281 1512, ⓦthearmagh.com. A hospitable and very comfortable guesthouse with excellent bathrooms and bed linen, in a beautiful garden that drifts off into the *fynbos*. The rooms include two budget rooms, four standard ones, a garden cottage and an ultra-luxurious and very private honeymoon room, all of which open onto the garden. There's a nice swimming pool and a decent restaurant. R1200

★ **At the Woods Guest House** 49 Formosa St, along the main drag into town ☎042 281 1446, ⓦatthewoods.co.za. Friendly, modern guesthouse that's the nicest place in town, with traditional reed ceilings and large, comfortable rooms with king-sized beds and French doors that open onto garden verandas, or, upstairs, onto private decks with mountain views. There's a very good café for meals and a nice communal lounge with a fireplace, where you can use the internet. R1190

Tsitsikamma Backpackers 54 Formosa St ☎042 281 1868, ⓦtsitsikammabackpackers.co.za. Well-run hostel, whose accommodation options include luxury tents set in a beautiful garden that claims environmentally friendly and fair-trade credentials. You can self-cater or order a reasonably priced breakfast or dinner, and there's a bar. They offer a shuttle service to local attractions and pick up guests for free from the Storms River Bridge. Dorms R180, luxury tent R500, doubles R600

Tsitsikamma Village Inn Darnell St, along the road into the village and left at the T-junction ☎042 281 1711, ⓦtsitsikammahotel.co.za. An old-fashioned and consistently well-run hotel in the village amid the trees and with a well-tended garden. It has 49 rooms in eleven cottage units, and has the advantage of a pub, microbrewery and restaurant on the premises. R1400

Tube 'n Axe Backpackers Cnr Darnell and Saffron sts ☎042 281 1757, ⓦtubenaxe.co.za. A wacky place that works hard to compete with the bright lights of Knysna and Plett by offering drumming nights, a pool table and bonfires. It's on the Baz route, and they will collect or drop off at the Storms River Bridge bus stop for mainline coaches, and also offer shuttles around the area. Camping R105, dorms R175, doubles R480

STORMS RIVER ACTIVITIES

BOAT TRIPS

SANParks ☎042 281 1607. SANParks runs trips for up to twelve people (R180 for 30min trip and conservation gate entry fee) about 1km up Storms River. Booking is at the Storms River Mouth restcamp, at the Untouched Adventures office, close to the boathouse, and just below the restcamp's restaurant.

TOURS

Woodcutters' Journey ☎042 281 1836, ⓦstormsriver.com. A relaxed jaunt organized by Storms River Adventures (teatime trip R300, lunch trip R400), headquartered next to the post office. The trip takes you through the forest to the river along the old Storms River Pass in a specially designed trailer, drawn by a tractor.

TUBING

Tube 'n Axe Backpackers ☎042 281 1757, ⓦtubenaxe.co.za. *Tube 'n Axe Backpackers* operates trips down the Storms River gorge, where you ride the river and its rapids buoyed up by a small inflatable (R595 half day, R995 full day).

ZIP LINE

Storms River Adventures ☎042 281 1836, ⓦstormsriver.com. The Storms River Adventures Canopy Tour (R750) through the treetops gives a bird's-eye view of the forest as you travel 30m above ground along a series of interconnected cables attached to the tallest trees. The system has been constructed in such a way that not a single nail has been hammered into any of the trees.

Tsitsikamma Falls Adventures ☎042 280 3770, ⓦtsitsikammaadventure.co.za. A faster, higher alternative to the Canopy Tour, geared more to adrenaline junkies, this zipline tour across the Kruis River (R380) crisscrosses an awesome ravine, zipping over three waterfalls. At times, it is 50m above the ground, and the longest slide measures 211m.

EATING

De Oude Martha Darnell St. *Tsitsikamma Village Inn's* decent hotel restaurant serves up unpretentious breakfasts, lunches and dinners (mains average R160), but the best thing about it is the cosy, panelled pub with a welcoming fireplace on damp winter nights. Daily 7am–9pm.

Rafters Fynbos Ave. *Rafters*, the restaurant of *The Armagh* guesthouse, has a dinner menu that emphasizes local South African cuisine, using garden greens in their salads, fish from Plettenberg Bay and locally sourced meat. Cape Malay sweet and mild curries (R130) are another speciality of the house. Daily 8am–9pm.

Tsitrus Café At the Woods Guest House, 49 Formosa St. A small, selective menu of soups and salads (R75), as well as pizza and cheesecake, makes this the best option for a light lunch. Daily 8am–8pm.

Route 62 and the Little Karoo

One of the most rewarding journeys in the Western Cape is the **mountain route** from Cape Town to Port Elizabeth, which runs largely along the R62, and thus is often referred to as **Route 62**. Less known than its coastal counterpart, the Garden Route (see p.210), this trip takes you through some of the most dramatic mountain passes in the country and crosses a frontier of *dorps* and drylands. This "back garden" of the Little Karoo is in many respects more rewarding than the Garden Route, being far less developed, with spectacular landscapes, quieter roads and some wonderful small towns to visit.

The most likeable of these towns are the historic spa town of Montagu, rural and arty Barrydale, and the port capital Calitzdorp. Oudtshoorn and the Cango Caves mark the convergence of the mountain and coastal roads; over the most dramatic of all passes in the Cape – the unpaved **Swartberg Pass**, 27km of spectacular switchbacks and zigzags through the Swartberg Mountains – is **Prince Albert**, a Karoo village whose spare beauty and remarkable light make it popular with artists.

From Prince Albert, the hinterland of the **Great Karoo** opens up, the semi-desert that covers one-third of South Africa's surface. The fruit farms of the **Little Karoo** spread out into treeless plains, vegetated with low, wiry scrub, and dotted with flat-topped hills. The best of the Karoo can be found in the **Karoo National Park**, while, in **Sutherland**, the clear, clean air provides some of the best stargazing opportunities in the world.

DRIVING THE MOUNTAINS OF THE LITTLE KAROO

The Little Karoo is hemmed in by a gauntlet of rugged mountains and steep-sided valleys (or *poorts*) that for centuries made this area virtually impassable for wheeled transport. In the nineteenth century, the British began to tackle the problem and dozens of passes were built through the Cape's mountains, 34 of which were engineered by the brilliant road-builder Andrew Geddes Bain and his son Thomas. In fact, whatever the Little Karoo lacks in museums and art galleries is amply compensated for by the towering drama of these Victorian masterpieces. Some of the best of these passes are listed below.

Cogman's Kloof Pass Between Ashton and Montagu. A 5km route that's at its most dramatic as it cuts through a rock face into the Montagu Valley.

Gamkaskloof Pass Also called Die Hel or The Hell (see box, p.250), reached from the summit of the Swartberg Pass. This is arguably the most awesome of all the passes, leading into a dramatic and lonely valley, all on gravel.

Meiringspoort A tarred road through a gorge in the Swartberg, which can be taken to reach Prince Albert. The road keeps crossing a light-brown river, while huge slabs of folded and zigzagging rock rise up on either side.

Prince Alfred's Pass On the R339, between the N2, just east of Knysna, and Avontuur on the R62. A dramatic dirt road twisting through mountains, past a few isolated apple farms.

Swartberg Pass Between Oudtshoorn and Prince Albert. Over-the-Swartberg counterpart of Meiringspoort, with 1:7 gradients on narrow untarred roads, characterized by precipitous hairpins.

2

Worcester

The best part of the journey from Cape Town to **WORCESTER**, 110km east, is the **Huguenot Toll Tunnel** on the N1, burrowing through high mountains that give onto a magnificent valley. A relatively large town for this part of the world, Worcester is an agricultural centre with a number of factories and smelly chicken farms. It's at the centre of a wine-making region, consisting mostly of cooperatives bulk-producing the plonk that makes up about a fifth of the national output.

J.M. Coetzee, South Africa's most internationally acclaimed writer, grew up here, though there's no museum, plaque or anything to celebrate his work. His fictionalized memoir *Boyhood*, set in 1950s Worcester, is unlikely to have endeared him to the locals. The main reason to stop here is to visit the peaceful botanical gardens.

Karoo Desert National Botanical Garden

108 Roux Rd, off the N1 • Daily 7am–7pm • R25 • Restaurant Mon–Sat 8.30am–9pm, Sun 8.30am–4pm • ☎ 023 347 0785, ⓦ sanbi.org/gardens/karoo-desert/overview

Entering Worcester from Cape Town, you'll see signs to the **Karoo Botanical Garden**, a sister reserve to Cape Town's Kirstenbosch, known for its show of indigenous spring flowers and succulents. The best time to visit the gardens is from late July to early September when purple, orange and yellow flowers bloom here in profusion. Three hiking trails meander through large wild areas, full of desert plants and prickly blooms, and in winter, snow caps the dramatic backdrop of the Hex River mountain range.

Worcester Museum

Just outside the centre of town at Kleinplasie – to get here, head east along High St and turn right onto the road to Robertson • Mon–Sat 8am–4.30pm • R20

The absorbing **Worcester Museum** depicts life on the Karoo frontier between 1690 and 1900, and is made up of about two dozen reconstructed buildings, with staff in old-style workshops engaged in crafts and home industries. Look out for the corbelled shepherd's hut, which represents a vernacular style unique to the Karoo, using domed stone roofs rather than beam-and-lintel construction – a response to the dearth of timber in the treeless expanse.

Robertson

ROBERTSON is the largest town in the attractive stretch of the Breede River Valley, known locally as the Robertson Valley. The acidity level of the soil is ideal for growing grapes – the valley is responsible for some ten percent of South Africa's vineyards. The best wines tend to be Chenin Blancs and Colombards, and some good Muscadels are made too. But the area is best known for providing cheap, drinkable wines – the reds in particular.

The Robertson Valley wine route is also notable for the bright flowers, such as scarlet cannas and roses, which grow in profusion alongside the roads and vineyards.

ARRIVAL AND INFORMATION
ROBERTSON

By car Some 160km from Cape Town, on the R60, Robertson is best approached via the N1. There are no organized coaches or shuttles.

Information The tourist office is on Voortrekker St (Mon–Fri 8am–5pm, Sat 9am–2pm, Sun 10am–2pm; ☎ 023 626 4437, ⓦ robertsontourism.co.za).

ACCOMMODATION

The Lemontree House 2 Church St ☎ 023 626 1384, ⓦ lemontreehouse.co.za. A Victorian house with comfortable rooms furnished in a tasteful cottagey style. The beautiful garden, with oak and pecan trees and a

salt-water pool, plus a cosy fireplace in winter, add to the feeling of peace and tranquillity. R800

Robertson Backpackers 4 Dordrecht Ave ☎ 023 62 1280, ⓦ robertsonbackpackers.co.za. This spaciou

WINERIES IN AND AROUND ROBERTSON

The Robertson Valley's **wine route** extends to McGregor in the south and to Bonnievale in the east, covering some forty or so wineries, all free to visit, and some offering free tastings. If you don't have time to meander, you can purchase wine from **La Verne Wine Boutique** (Mon–Thurs 9am–5.30pm, Fri 9am–6pm, Sat 9am–5pm, ⓦ lavernewines.co.za), situated in a converted railway cottage, next to the Robertson Art Gallery as you enter town from the west on the R60. It's an exceptionally well-stocked shop, with most of the local wine producers represented, where you can taste wine as well as buy by the case or the bottle.

Bon Courage Roughly 10km southeast of Robertson along the R317 ☎023 626 1384, ⓦ boncourage.co.za. Producer of some great sweet whites, especially Muscadel, with a tasting room in a beautiful old homestead along the Breede River. Tastings are free and its *Café Maude* serves breakfast and light lunches. Mon–Fri 8am–5pm, Sat 9am–3pm.

De Wetshof About 12km southeast of town along the R317 ☎023 615 1853, ⓦ dewetshof.com. Top-notch estate with photogenic mountain and vineyard views, producing several excellent whites, including its flagship Bateleur Chardonnay. Tastings are R70 per person, with 14 wines on offer, two of which are sparkling. Mon–Fri 8.30am–4.30pm, Sat 9.30am–1pm.

Graham Beck About 7km west of Robertson along the R60 ☎023 626 1214, ⓦ grahambeckwines .co.za. A modern, high-flying estate making an international splash, with orders from British supermarket giants for its vast range of reds and whites. R75 per person gets you five sparkling wine tastings in their splendidly modern tasting room. Mon–Fri 9am–5pm, Sat & Sun 10am–4pm.

Robertson Winery In town, just off the R60 ☎023 626 3059, ⓦ robertsonwinery.co.za. Producer of some good-value and highly drinkable Chardonnays and Colombards, sold cheaper here than in the shops and with free tasting. Mon–Fri 9am–5.30pm, Sat 9am–3pm, Sun 9am–1pm.

Springfield A few kilometres southeast of Robertson on the R317 ☎023 626 3661, ⓦ springfieldestate.com. Stellar estate that produces a range of really outstanding reds and whites, a number of which are among South Africa's frontrunners. Tastings are free, and though there isn't a restaurant, you can bring your own picnic and while away a few hours on the lawn overlooking the lake. Mon–Fri 8am–5pm, Sat 9am–3pm.

Van Loveren 15km northwest of Bonnievale along the R317 ☎023 615 1505, ⓦ www.vanloveren .co.za. Wine tasting in a lovely garden at a winery known for its hugely quaffable wines, including River Red, South Africa's classic plonk. Tasting gets you eight wines, paired with chocolate, cheese, nuts or meat, for R55 per person. There is also a restaurant, *Christina's Bistro*, which is open 10am–3pm. Mon–Fri 8am–5pm, Sat 9.30am–3.30pm, Sun 11am–2.30pm.

house is one of the best backpackers in the Western Cape, with a nice garden and a fireplace for chilly winter nights. There's a reasonably priced wine tour on offer (R400 per person), and a good river-rafting trip in the summer (R550). Camping R100, dorms R160, doubles R420

McGregor

MCGREGOR is an attractive place, with thatched, whitewashed cottages glaring in the summer daylight amid the low, rusty steel-wool scrub, vines and olive trees, and a quiet, relaxed atmosphere that has attracted a small population of spiritual seekers and artists. It makes a great weekend break from Cape Town, with a couple of decent restaurants, plenty of well-priced accommodation, and a beautiful retreat centre that offers reasonably priced massage. Spending the day wine tasting in the environs is another attraction, as long as it's not a Sunday when almost everything is closed.

McGregor gained modest prosperity in the nineteenth century by becoming a centre of the whipstock industry, supplying wagoners and transport riders with long bamboo sticks for goading oxen. There aren't too many ox-drawn wagons today, and tourism, though developing, is still quite limited. A great draw is to walk the **Boesmanskloof Traverse** (see box, p.181), which starts 14km from McGregor and crosses to Greyton on the other side of the mountain. From McGregor you can walk a section of the trail, hiking to the main waterfall and back to the trailhead – a beautiful three- to four-hour round hike through the river gorge (*kloof* in Afrikaans).

ARRIVAL AND INFORMATION
MCGREGOR

By car 180km from Cape Town and 15min to the south of Robertson, McGregor is at the end of a minor road signposted off the R60. Don't be tempted by an approach from the south which looks a handy back route – you'd need a 4WD for this. Allow 2hr 30min for the drive from Cape Town along the N1, turning onto the R62 at Worcester for Robertson.

Information The tourist office on Voortrekker St (Mon–Sat 9am–1pm & 2–4.30pm, Sun 9am–1pm; ☎ 023 625 1954, ⓦ tourismmcgregor.co.za) can book accommodation and issue permits for walking the whole Boesmanskloof Traverse or simply for the waterfall section (R40). They will also direct you to artists' studios in town, and to complementary health practitioners.

ACCOMMODATION

Green Gables Country Inn 7 Smith St ☎ 023 625 1626, ⓦ greengablesmcgregor.co.za. Country accommodation at the edge of the village, with a swimming pool, an English-style pub, and a restaurant that is open three nights a week. The decor is cosy, if slightly cluttered, and the service is warm and personal; rates are very reasonable for what you get. <u>R900</u>

McGregor Backpackers Bree St ☎ 083 206 8007, ⓦ mcgregorbackpackers.co.za. Comfortable, homely backpackers accommodating a maximum of 25 guests in a variety of room types catering for doubles or groups. All rooms are en suite except for two, and there's a laundry service on offer. <u>R500</u>

The Old Village Lodge Voortrekker St ☎ 023 625 1692, ⓦ oldvillagelodge.co.za. Upmarket B&B in a Victorian cottage on the main road, with a pretty garden, swimming pool and rooms furnished in an elegant and comfortable country style. <u>R1300</u>

Rhebokskraal Farm Cottages 2km south of town ☎ 082 896 0429, ⓦ rhebokskraalolives.co.za. Secluded cottages, each on a different part of this beautiful fruit, olive and grape farm, which is within easy reach of the restaurants in town. <u>R700</u>

★**Tanagra Guest Wine Farm** 4.5km northeast of McGregor, towards Robertson ☎ 023 625 1780, ⓦ tanagra-wines.co.za. Idyllic farm with three stylish, light and airy cottages, all with private verandas and mountain views. One cottage is totally set apart, with a private plunge pool, hammocks and a fireplace. There are also two apartments and a loft studio on offer, and all the accommodation is fully equipped for self-catering. Walking trails are on the farm itself or the adjoining Vrolijkheid Nature Reserve. <u>R900</u>

★**Temenos Country Retreat** On the corner of Bree and Voortrekker sts ☎ 023 625 1871, ⓦ temenos.org .za. Retreat centre with cottages dotted about beautiful gardens and walkways, a swimming pool, library and meditation spaces. Breakfast is included and it's safe and peaceful – an ideal place for solo women travellers. <u>R815</u>

Whipstock Farm 7km southwest of McGregor, towards Boesmanskloof ☎ 073 042 3919, ⓦ whipstock.co.za Farm accommodation in a Victorian house with five white-washed cottages. Meals are served communally in a large dining room with a fireplace. It's perfect for families who want a nature-based holiday; self-catering rates are also available. <u>R560</u>

EATING

Flora's Eating House & Gallery 54 Voortrekker St ☎ 082 070 9004. Great for fresh and interesting breakfasts and lunches. You can sit on the front or back porch to savour home-made food, such as a Turkish-style breakfast, spicy lentil soup, free-range chicken dishes, vegan salads (R75) or bockwurst with mash. Booking essential. Mon 6–9pm, Thurs–Sun 9am–3pm.

Green Gables Country Inn 7 Smith St ☎ 023 625 1626, ⓦ greengablesmcgregor.co.za. Alfresco dinners on the terrace overlooking vineyards and the village, with a cosy dining room warmed with a fireplace in winter, plus a "village pub". There are generally three well-cooked dishes on offer, such as chicken curry, fish and chips, and lamb shank (R115). Wed & Fri–Sun 6–10pm.

★**Karoux Restaurant** 42 Voortrekker St ☎ 023 625 1421. Award-winning gourmet food you wouldn't expect to find in a sleepy village, such as pan-roasted duck breast with cauliflower purée, wilted baby spinach, confit lamb croquettes and free-range chicken liver parfait with truffled blueberry vinaigrette (R140). Booking essential. Wed–Sat 7–10pm & Sun noon–3pm.

Tebaldi's at Temenos On the corner of Bree and Voortrekker sts ☎ 023 625 1871, ⓦ temenos.org.za Well-established but fading slightly alongside the upstart gourmet newcomers, but still reliable. Breakfasts and salad lunches served in a tranquil garden setting, or on the street-facing *stoep*. Tues & Sun 9.30am–3.30pm, Wed–Sat 9.30am–3.30pm & 7–9.30pm.

DRINKING

Bemind Wyne 45 Voortrekker St ☎ 083 380 1648, ⓦ bemindwyne.co.za. A chance to try McGregor wines in a very relaxed atmosphere where you can chat to the wine-maker, Ilse Schutte, who has been producing small quantities of Sauvignon Blanc, MCC Brut, Shiraz and Cinsault since 2015. The quality is excellent and the price of a bottle very reasonable (R90–170). Wed–Fri 10am–5pm & Sat 10am–2pm.

Montagu

As you approach **Montagu**, soaring mountains rise up in vast arches of twisted strata that display reds and ochres; in spring, the town, known for its fruit growing, is full of peach and apricot blossoms. Montagu is certainly very pleasing, with sufficient Victorian architecture to create an historic character, and worth a night at least.

The town was named in 1851 after **John Montagu**, the visionary British Secretary of the Cape, who realized that the colony would never develop without decent communications and was responsible for commissioning the first mountain passes connecting remote areas to Cape Town. The grateful farmers of Agter Cogman's Kloof (literally "behind Cogman's Kloof") leapt at the chance of giving their village a snappier name.

Montagu is best known for its **hot springs**, but serious **rock climbers** come for its cliff faces, which are regarded as among the country's most challenging. You can also explore the mountains on a couple of trails or, easiest of all, on a tractor ride onto one of the peaks. Montagu is also conveniently positioned for excursions along both the Robertson and Little Karoo **wine routes** (see p.239).

Montagu Springs Resort

About 3km northwest of town on the R318 · Daily 8am–11pm · R100 · ☎ 023 614 1050, ⓦ www.montagusprings.co.za

Montagu's main draw is the **Montagu Springs Resort**; several chlorinated open-air pools of different temperatures and a couple of jacuzzis are spectacularly situated at the foot of cliffs – an effect spoilt by the neon lights of a hotel complex and fast-food restaurant. It's a fabulous place to take kids, though at weekends it becomes a mass of splashing bodies. If you want a quiet time, go first thing in the morning or last thing at night. The temperatures in winter are not hot enough to be entirely comfortable, when you're better off heading to the springs at Caledon (see box, p.180) or Warmwaterberg (see box, p.243), which are much hotter and quieter.

ARRIVAL AND INFORMATION

MONTAGU

By car Montagu is 190km from Cape Town; take the N1 as far as Worcester and then head southeast on the R60. The journey from Worcester (roughly 60km) takes you through Robertson and Ashton.

By minibus Danie (☎ 072 750 3125) runs a reasonably priced on-demand shuttle service (R170) between Montagu and Cape Town, but you will need to be flexible about times of departure and arrival, as well as the number of stops.

Information The tourist office is at 24 Bath St (Mon–Fri 8am–6pm, Sat 9am–5pm, Sun 9.30am–2pm; ☎ 023 614 2471, ⓦ montagu-ashton.info).

ACCOMMODATION

★ **Aasvoelkrans** 1 Van Riebeeck St ☎ 023 614 1228, ⓦ aasvoelkrans.co.za. Set in a pretty part of town, these four exceptionally imaginative garden rooms are housed in a guesthouse situated on a farm, with Arab horses grazing in the fields. There is also a two-bedroomed self-catering cottage suitable for a family or larger group. Cottage R900, doubles R1000

De Bos Guest Farm 8 Brown St ☎ 023 614 2532, ⓦ debos.co.za. Lovely shady camping pitches, dorms, basic en-suite doubles and family bungalows on a farm at the western edge of town, close to the spectacular twisted mountain slopes. There are hikes on the doorstep, and it's also popular with rock climbers who bring their own kit to tackle climbs in the area. Camping R80, dorms R130, doubles R900

Montagu Rose Guest House 19 Kohler St ☎ 023 614 2681, ⓦ montagurose.co.za. A well-run guesthouse in a modern home, decorated with plenty of paintings and knick-knacks. All the rooms have baths and mountain views, one is wheelchair friendly, and there is a family room for four. R800

2

MONTAGU ACTIVITIES

Montagu's tourist office (see p.241) can provide maps for three **hikes** that begin from the Old Mill at the north end of Tanner Street. Two are full-day hikes, while the shortest is the **Lover's Walk**, a stroll of just over 2km that follows the Keisie River through Bath Kloof (or Badkloof) to the hot springs.

The less energetic may prefer a recommended three-hour **tractor ride** (Wed & Sat at 10am & 2pm; R110; ☎ 023 614 3012) up the **Langeberg Mountains**. The tractor leaves from Protea Farm, which is 29km from Montagu along the R318 Koo/Touws River road. Book in advance and remember to take warm clothes in the cooler months.

Montagu Springs Signposted off the R62, west of town ☎ 023 614 1050, ⊚ montagusprings.co.za. Large resort with fully equipped self-catering chalets sleeping four – some more luxurious than others. It is especially suitable for families, and children will love the pools and playing areas. Prices go down by roughly a third during the week. R1300

Squirrel's Corner Corner of Bloem and Jouberts sts ☎ 023 614 1081, ⊚ squirrelscorner.co.za. A reasonably priced B&B situated two blocks from the main road, with four comfortable, spotless en-suite rooms in the main house, as well as an African-themed garden suite. You are greeted with a glass of Montagu muscadel on arrival. R970

EATING

The farm stalls as you drive through Montagu on the R62 are worth stopping at for nibbles and local produce, and there are several appealing **cafés** to choose from on Long Street. In summer, bags of peaches and apricots are often sold from backyards or along the roadside for next to nothing. On Saturday mornings, don't miss the local **farmers' market** at the church, where you can get olives and olive oil, bread, cheese, almonds and dried fruit from the surrounding farms. All **restaurants** need to be booked ahead for dinner.

Die Stal 8km out of town on the R318 ☎ 082 324 4318. A pleasant café/restaurant on a farm where you can sit on the porch and view the surrounding orchards and farmlands. It serves breakfast, lunches and teas – a hearty favourite is lamb rump (R130), while vegetarians may opt for the ploughman's platter (R85). Tues–Sun 9am–5pm.

Ma Cuisine Mimosa Lodge, 19 Church St ☎ 023 614 235, ⊚ mimosa.co.za/index.php/dining. Reserve a candle-lit table for a memorable dinner along the R62, in a posh guesthouse. Expect to dine on South African dishes with a French influence, such as Karoo lamb with muscadel and thyme jus. Vegetarians are also catered for, with good and fresh ingredients. There's a four-course set menu for R500, which costs R670 with wine. Daily 6–9pm.

Mystic Tin 38 Bath St ☎ 082 572 0738, ⊚ themysticín .co.za. Tablecloths, candlelight and a winter fireplace create a cosy atmosphere to enjoy South African specialities done with flair. The ostrich fillet is worth a try (R110) and there are some appealing vegetarian options, all accompanied by hand-crafted beers brewed in their Karoo microbrewery. Mon–Sat 5–9.30pm.

Simply Delicious Restaurant Four Oaks, 46 Long St ☎ 023 614 3483, ⊚ four-oaks.co.za. A good choice for a light lunch or dinner, set in a handsome 1860 thatched house with a shady courtyard. Dishes include steak with seasonal vegetables (R125) and various wraps and salads. Summer daily 12.30–2.30pm & 7–9pm; winter Mon–Sat 12.30–2.30pm & 6.30–9pm.

Barrydale and around

BARRYDALE, 240km from Cape Town, is perfect for a couple of days of doing very little other than experiencing small-town life in the Little Karoo, visiting the hot springs at **Warmwaterberg** (see box opposite), picnicking along the Tradouw Pass and wine tasting. The village has a couple of excellent restaurants, some good, reasonably priced accommodation and a number of craft outlets. The drive here, a 60km journey from Montagu, offers spectacular mountain scenery, as does the route from Swellendam via the Tradouw Pass. There's a distinct rural feel about the place: a large vineyard is just off the main road, farm animals are kept on large plots of land behind dry-stone walling, and you'll find fig, peach and quince trees thriving in the dryness.

Its arid beauty has attracted its fair share of artists, and every year, on the weekend closest to the December 16 public holiday, the Handspring Puppet Company – famous for their work on the play *War Horse* – have an open-air show at the local school.

Sanbona Wildlife Reserve

20km west of Barrydale off the R62 • R16,500 per person per night at a lodge including meals and two game drives • ☎ 021 010 0028, ⓦ sanbona.com

An amalgamation of 21 farms that together create a massive wilderness area, **Sanbona Wildlife Reserve** is set in gorgeous landscape – rocky outcrops, mountains and semi-desert vegetation with three luxurious all-inclusive lodges, and a camping option. Of the lodges, *Dwyka Tented Lodge* is closer to where most of the game is to be found and has the most spectacular setting. However, the option that gets you closest to nature is the *Explorer Camp* – situated by a riverbed and with guides to help you get the most from the two-day wilderness trails (R4620 per person, limited to those aged 16–60). Although the game is sparser here than in the major parks such as Kruger, it is the only place in the Western Cape with free-roaming lions and cheetahs, and there's also a herd of elephants. A two-night stay is recommended and day visitors are not allowed – check for specials and cheaper winter rates.

ARRIVAL AND INFORMATION

By car Allow 3–3hr 30min for the journey from Cape Town, either taking the N1 and R62, via Montagu, or the N2, and cutting inland on the R324 just east of Swellendam for the lovely drive through Suurbraak and the Tradouw Pass. Both routes are equally recommended.

Information There's a tiny visitor information centre

BARRYDALE

(Mon–Fri 9am–5pm, Sat & Sun 9am–2pm; ☎ 028 572 1572, ⓦ barrydale@swellendamtourism.co.za) on the R62, in the strip of shops and restaurants, closest to *Diesel* and *Cream Diner*. They can also help with finding accommodation. The supermarket on the main drag, Van Riebeeck St, houses an ATM and post office.

ACCOMMODATION

InKaroo Cottage 2 Bain St near the cemetery ☎ 028 572 1344. Beautifully restored and furnished in a contemporary style, this self-catering Karoo farmhouse cottage has two bedrooms sleeping 4 people. There are dry-stone walls and seating at the back of the house under vines, with sunset views onto the mountains. The nearest shops are 5min away. __R800__

★ **Tradouw Guest House** 46 Van Riebeeck St ☎ 028 572 1434, ⓦ tradouwguesthouse.co.za. One of the best accommodation options along the R62, the friendly *Tradouw Guest House* has six simple, homely rooms, four of which open onto a courtyard shaded by vines where you can have breakfast, while two are accessed from the appealing large garden. There's a roaring fire in the lounge in winter. __R700__

EATING

There's a number of places to eat strung along the R62 – many of which are only open during the day. However, you will always find at least one restaurant open in the evening, but it's advisable to book in advance.

Barrydale Cellar 1 Van Riebeeck St ☎ 028 572 1012. With a lovely setting open to the river, it's the hand-crafted

brandy, beer and ale tastings (two tastings for free, thereafter R30 per person) that are the main attraction

WARMWATERBERG SPA

Thirty kilometres east of Barrydale (just beyond *Ronnie's Sex Shop*, a pub and well-known landmark in the middle of nowhere) is **Warmwaterberg Spa** (☎ 028 572 1609, ⓦ warmwaterbergspa.co.za), a Karoo farm blessed with natural hot water siphoned into two outdoor, unchlorinated hot pools and surrounded by lush green lawns and lofty palms. Primarily aimed at South Africans, it gets rather crowded and noisy during school holidays and over weekends. The best time of day to enjoy the baths is after dark, when the steam rises into the cold, starry Karoo sky. The farm is attractively set, with mountain vistas to gaze at from the baths and fantastic birdlife drawn by this oasis amid the desert landscape.

Accommodation is in wooden cabins or rooms in the main farmhouse, each of which has an indoor spa bath (R750). All are self-catering and pretty basic, but reasonably priced. There are also some camp pitches available (R380 for two), a bar, and a restaurant serving dinners and breakfasts. Rates are lowered on weekdays and during the school term. If you are driving past, and want to have a swim, day visitors pay R50 at the reception.

here. But there's also a restaurant, offering delectable pizzas at lunchtime. Mon–Fri 9am–5pm, Sat 9am–3pm.
Clarke of the Karoo Mud Gallery, on R62 ☎ 028 572 1017, ⊛ clarkeofthekaroo.co.za. A great option for hearty country food, with a starter on the house, the Karoo lamb burgers or curry and roti are particularly recommended. Seating is in a pleasant dry-stone walled courtyard. Dinner is provided four nights of the week (R130 for two courses). Sun–Tues 8am–4pm, Wed–Sat 8am–8pm.
Diesel and Creme Vintage Diner, on R62 ☎ 028 572 1008. The most popular stop along the R62, this place is always packed. The interior is retro style, having been done up with junk to create the romance of the USA's Route 66. Their milkshakes are great, and burgers the order of the day (R70). Daily 8am–5pm.
★ **Mez Karoo Kitchen** Van Riebeeck St ☎ 082 077 5980. Outstanding and reasonably priced Mediterranean food and wine, with light tapas meals and the house Greek lamb speciality (R140), served at the chef's spacious home. Equally memorable are the bright pink rose-water ice cream served with pistachios and fresh mint, and the honey and rose ice cream. Sitting in the garden on a summer's evening is a particular delight. Book ahead and check the hours, which can vary. Tues, Thurs–Sat 6–10pm, Sun 11am–2pm; closed in winter.

SHOPPING

Barrydale has a couple of wine outlets that are worth a visit for tasting and buying, and there are a couple of browsable craft shops along the R62.

Magpie Studio 27 Van Riebeeck St ☎ 028 572 1997, ⊛ magpieartcollective.com. An imaginative craft shop that produces colourful furniture, light fittings and chandeliers from recycled materials – Michelle Obama even ordered one for the White House. Tues–Fri 10am–5pm, Sun 9am–1pm.

Oudtshoorn

OUDTSHOORN, 420km from Cape Town and an arid, mountainous 180km from Barrydale, styles itself as the ostrich capital of the world; the town's environs are indeed crammed with ostrich farms, several of which you can visit, and the local souvenir shops keep busy dreaming up 1001 tacky ways to recycle ostrich parts as comestibles and souvenirs. You'll see flocks of them on farms and along the roadsides all over the region, standing in the sun, or pecking at the ground. Most people stop in Oudtshoorn to visit the nearby Cango Caves (see p.246), while the town's main visual interest lies in its grand Victorian and Edwardian sandstone buildings.

Brief history

Oudtshoorn started out as a small village named after Geesje Ernestina Johanna van Oudtshoorn, wife of the first civil commissioner for the nearby town of George. By the 1860s **ostriches**, which live in the wild in Africa, were being raised in the ideal conditions of the Oudtshoorn Valley. The Victorian fashion for large feathers, mostly for decorating hats, had turned the ostriches into a source of serious wealth, and by the 1880s hundreds of thousands of kilos of feathers were being exported. Despite this economic boom, the labourers – mostly coloured descendants of the Outeniqua and Attaqua Khoikhoi and trekboers – received derisory wages supplemented by rations of food, wine, spirits and tobacco. In the early twentieth century, the most successful farmers and traders built themselves feather palaces, ostentatious sandstone Edwardian buildings that have become the defining feature of Oudtshoorn.

C. P. Nel Museum

Corner of Baron Van Reede St and Voortrekker Rd · Mon–Fri 8am–5pm, Sat 9am–1pm · R15 · ☎ 044 272 7306, ⊛ cpnelmuseum.co.za

The **C.P. Nel Museum** is a good place to start your explorations. A handsome sandstone building, with an imposing central tower, it was built in 1906 as a boys' school, but now houses an eccentric collection of items, many of which relate to ostriches. A local synagogue, built during the boom years when many Jewish immigrants were involved in the feather trade, has been reconstructed within the museum.

Le Roux Town House

Corner of Loop and High streets · Mon–Fri 9am–5pm · R15 · ☎ 044 272 3676

Le Roux Town House is a perfectly preserved family townhouse, and the only one of the much vaunted "feather palaces" that is open to the public. Built for ostrich farmer John le Roux and completed in 1910, it was designed by local architect Charles Bullock in a typically eclectic style, with Art Nouveau elements and some delicate exterior ironwork on the verandas. The beautiful furnishings were all imported from Europe between 1910 and 1920, and there is plenty to look at and admire.

ARRIVAL AND DEPARTURE

By car Allow 6hr from Cape Town for the 420km journey along the R62. Alternatively, take the N2 to George along the Garden Route and cut inland to Oudtshoorn on the N12.

By bus Intercity buses pull in at Queens Mall, off Voortrekker St, across the river from the main road, Baron Van Reede St. Intercape (ⓦ intercape.co.za) has a daily service from Cape Town at 4.30pm, which takes nine hours, arriving at 1.30am. The service to Cape Town leaves at 10.30pm and arrives at 6.30am. Greyhound does not travel via Oudtshoorn.

By minibus There are two local transport companies that offer door-to-door services, on demand, from Oudtshoorn to Cape Town along the R62 (R300). The journey takes most of the day, as about fifteen people need to be collected and dropped off at their destinations. Hilton de Villiers is at Divvies Transport (☎ 082 841 0107 or ☎ 078 209 3866) and Gysman Transport is at Leeu Rd (☎ 044 272 0516 or ☎ 083 946 8862).

INFORMATION AND ACTIVITIES

Information The tourist office at 80 Voortrekker Rd, near the library (Mon–Fri 8.30am–5pm, Sat 9.30am–12.30pm; ☎ 044 279 2532, ⓦ oudtshoorn.com), is a good source of information about the caves and ostrich farms.

Cycling *Backpacker's Paradise* (see below) rents out bikes and arranges adventurous cycling trips down the Swartberg Pass, with motor vehicle back-up.

Ostrich tours A number of show farms offer tours. Best of the bunch is Cango Ostrich Farm on the main road between Oudtshoorn and the Cango Caves, in the Schoemanshoek Valley, which runs tours every twenty minutes (45min; R100; ☎ 044 272 4623, ⓦ cangoostrich.co.za). Wine tasting, a restaurant and a gift shop are also on offer.

ACCOMMODATION

Oudtshoorn has a number of large **hotels** catering mainly to tour buses, plus plenty of good-quality **B&Bs** and **guesthouses**, a centrally located **campsite** with chalets, and one of the country's best-run **backpacker lodges**. Some of the nicest places to stay are in the attractive countryside en route to the Cango Caves. Rates fall dramatically during the winter months following the week-long **Klein Karoo Nasionale Kunstefees** (KKNK; ⓦ absaknk.co.za), a major arts festival (mostly in Afrikaans), and after the street party that takes place in the April Easter holidays.

Backpacker's Paradise 148 Baron van Reede St ☎ 044 272 3436, ⓦ backpackersparadise.net. A well-run two-storey hostel along the main drag, with en-suite doubles and family rooms as well as dorms. There are nightly ostrich, veg-friendly, braais, and a daily shuttle from the Baz Bus drop-off in George to the hostel. The on-site adventure centre organizes cycle trips in the Swartberg Pass and there's a daily shuttle to the caves, ostrich farm and wildlife ranch, as well as horseriding. Camping R100, dorms R160, doubles R520

Buffelsdrift Game Lodge 7km from town on the road to the caves ☎ 044 272 0106, ⓦ buffelsdrift.com. The area's top stay is in luxurious en-suite safari tents overlooking a large dam where hippo can be seen. Breakfast – served in the grand thatched dining space – is included, and game drives or horseback rides to view rhino, buffalo, elephant, giraffe and various antelope can be added to a package, or paid for separately. R2500

★ **De Oue Werf** Signposted off the R328 to Cango Caves, 12km north of Oudtshoorn ☎ 044 272 8712, ⓦ ouewerf.co.za. Luxurious and well-priced garden rooms on a working farm, run by the very welcoming sixth generation of the family. Green lawns run down to a dam, which has a swinging slide and raft to play on, and lots of birdlife. A great option if you're visiting the caves and want to stay in the country. R1300

Gum Tree Lodge 139 Church St ☎ 044 279 2528, ⓦ gumtreelodge.co.za. Five rooms in a peaceful B&B, as well as a two-roomed self-catering cottage sleeping four, conveniently located a few minutes' walk from the centre, fronting onto a river with good birdlife. There's a pool and deck, a well-stocked pub, and the rooms have modern bathrooms, a/c and TV. Doubles R1150, cottage R1800

Kleinplaas Holiday Resort 171 Baron van Reede St ☎ 044 272 5811, ⓦ kleinplaas.co.za. Well-run, shady sites for camping and fully equipped self-catering chalets, conveniently close to town, plus a swimming pool and launderette. The owners know the town well and will show you the ropes, and can provide breakfast for a little extra. Camping R320, chalet R1300

Lodge 96 96 Langenhoven Rd ☎ 044 272 2996, ⓦ lodge96.co.za. Simple, neat house with clean rooms and pine furniture. There's one dorm and one family room, with a garden for a few tents, plus a pool, laundry service and a good kitchen for self-catering. An ideal option if you are on a budget and don't want a noisy hostel scene; they can also organize activities in the area. Camping R100, dorm R160, doubles R550

EATING

Oudtshoorn has plenty of places to eat, mostly strung out along Baron van Reede Street and catering to the tourist trade – with the obligatory ostrich nearly always on the menu.

Bello Cibo 145 Baron van Reede St ☎ 044 272 3245. Relaxed and reasonably priced Italian place with indoor and outdoor seating, making it a good choice if you're with children. Besides pizza and pasta, there are some creative ostrich (R90) dishes. Booking advisable. Mon–Sat 5–10pm.

Buffelsdrift Game Lodge 7km out of town towards Cango Caves ☎ 044 272 0106. Have a great breakfast or lunch on a wooden deck overlooking the water hole, and do a spot of game viewing at the same time. It is open to non-guests for meals, and you could combine it with an elephant encounter or other game activity. Breakfast buffets with some local specialities such as *roesterkoek* – delicious sandwiches roasted on the coals (R90). Daily 10am–10pm.

Café Brule Queen's Hotel, 5 Baron van Reede St ☎ 044 279 2412, ⓦ queenshotel.co.za. The nicest café in town, set in the restored *Queen's Hotel* which has a rather grand, colonial ambience. The menu includes generous cooked breakfasts and ostrich burgers (R70) for lunch; it's also a great spot to sip a cappuccino overlooking the main street. They make their own pastries and breads too, and their deli counter is good for picnic supplies. Daily 7am–5pm.

Cango Caves

30km from Oudtshoorn • Daily 9am–4pm • R100 • ☎ 044 272 7410, ⓦ cangocaves.co.za • From Oudtshoorn, head north for 30km along the signposted, scenic R328, which continues on to Prince Albert via the majestic Swartberg Pass

The **Cango Caves** number among South Africa's most popular attractions, drawing a quarter of a million visitors each year to gasp at their fantastic cavernous spaces, dripping rocks and rising columns of calcite. In the two centuries since they became known to the public, the caves had been seriously battered by human intervention, but they still provide a stunning landscape inside the Swartberg foothills. Don't go expecting a serene and contemplative experience, though: the only way of visiting the caves is on a **guided tour** with a commentary.

The tours are every hour and must be booked in advance. The one-hour Standard Tour (R100, on the hour) gets you through the first six chambers, but far more interesting is the ninety-minute Adventure Tour (R150, on the half-hour) which takes you into the deepest sections accessible to the public, where the openings become smaller and smaller. Squeezing through tight openings with names like Lumbago Walk, Devil's Chimney and The Letterbox is not recommended if you are claustrophobic.

Brief history

San hunter-gatherers sheltered in the entrance caves for millennia before white settlers arrived, but it's unlikely that they ever made it to the lightless underground chambers. **Jacobus van Zyl**, a Karoo farmer, was probably the first person to penetrate beneath the surface, when he slid down on a rope into the darkness in July 1780, armed with a lamp. Over the next couple of centuries the caves were explored and pillaged by a growing number of visitors, some of whom were photographed cheerfully carting off wagonloads of limestone columns.

In the 1960s and 1970s the caves were made accessible to mass visitors when a **tourist complex** was built, the rock-strewn floor was evened out with concrete, ladders and walkways were installed, and the caverns were subsequently turned into a kitsch extravaganza with coloured lights, piped music and an indecipherable commentary that drew hundreds of thousands of visitors each year. Under the premiership of

Dr Hendrik Verwoerd, the arch-ideologue of racial segregation, a separate "non-whites" entrance was hacked through one wall, resulting in a disastrous through-draught that began dehydrating the caves. Fortunately, the worst excesses have now ended; concerts are no longer allowed inside the chambers, and the coloured lights have long been removed.

Calitzdorp

The up-and-coming small Karoo village of **CALITZDORP** hangs in a torpor of midday stillness, with its attractive, unpretentious Victorian streets and handful of wineries. Its picturesque qualities have made it another spot favoured by artists. Only 50km from Oudtshoorn, but smaller, cheaper and more appealing, it makes a good alternative base from which to explore the area.

Queen Street is home to a handful of charming guesthouses, quirky cafés and galleries, all of which are en route to the three key wineries, a few hundred metres from the centre, and clearly signposted off the R62. South Africa's finest ports are produced here, and it's also a good place to purchase olives – there are groves and groves of olive trees nearby.

ARRIVAL AND INFORMATION

CALITZDORP

By car Calitzdorp is 370km from Cape Town, 50km west of Oudtshoorn on the R62. If you're driving from Cape Town, allow for a 5hr drive with a lunch stop; this would be a good halfway, overnight stop along the R62 if you are travelling between Cape Town and Port Elizabeth.

Information The tourist office is at the Shell garage on Voortrekker St (Mon–Fri 9am–5pm, Sat 8am–1pm; ☎ 044 213 3775, ⓦ calitzdorp.org.za).

ACCOMMODATION

Calitzdorp Country House Besemkop, Calitz St ☎ 044 213 3760. A luxurious and friendly guesthouse, with five rooms, a swimming pool and dam. Each unit has its own patio looking out onto vines and the Swartberg beyond, and is furnished with antiques. Best of all is the food, with delicious dinners (R300) that can be booked in advance. R1800

Port-Wine Guest House Cnr Queen and Station sts ☎ 044 213 3131, ⓦ portwine.net. The smartest and most comfortable guesthouse in town, in a renovated early nineteenth-century homestead with local paintings on the walls, and a veranda overlooking the Boplaas wine estate. There is a pool and rose garden at the back. R900

Welgevonden Guesthouse St Helena Rd ☎ 044 213 3642, ⓦ welgevondenguesthouse.co.za. A comfortable country-style guesthouse, on a smallholding adjacent to Boplaas wine estate, 300m from the main road. The four en-suite bedrooms, set in an 1880 outbuilding, are furnished with brass or wooden bedsteads, patchwork quilts and wooden furniture. R700

The Groenfontein Valley

A circuitous minor route diverts off the R62, just east of Calitzdorp, and drops into the highly scenic **Groenfontein Valley**. The narrow dirt road twists through the Swartberg foothills, past whitewashed Karoo cottages and farms and across brooks, eventually

SOUTH AFRICAN PORT

Some of South Africa's best **ports** are produced at Calitzdorp's wineries, signposted down side roads, a few hundred metres from the centre of town. The most highly recommended is **Die Krans Estate** (Mon–Fri 9am–5pm, Sat 9am–3pm; free; ☎ 044 213 3314, ⓦ dekrans .co.za), where you can sample the wines and ports – its vintage reserve port is reckoned to be among the country's top three – and stretch your legs on a thirty-minute vineyard walk in lovely countryside. **Boplaas Estate** (Mon–Fri 9am–5pm, Sat 9am–3pm; free tasting; ☎ 044 213 3326, ⓦ boplaas.co.za) also produces some fine, award-winning ports and is worth a visit to see its massive reed-ceiling tasting room, which looks like a cantina that fell off the set of a spaghetti western.

joining the R328 to Oudtshoorn. Winding through these back roads is also an option to reach the Cango Caves (see p.246) and Prince Albert (see below), and is one of the best drives you'll ever do in South Africa. Many of the roads are unsealed but are perfectly navigable in an ordinary car if taken slowly.

2

ACCOMMODATION
THE GROENFONTEIN VALLEY

Kruis Rivier Guest Farm 17km off the R62 (signposted turn-off 14km east of Calitzdorp) ☎044 213 3788, ⓦkruisrivier.co.za. Homely, simply furnished cottages beneath the mountains, surrounded by lovely streams and waterfalls. It makes an excellent base for hiking, and the owners will do breakfast on request and provide braai packs, home-made bread and wood. Camping R300, doubles R500
Red Stone Hills 6km off the R62 (signposted turn-off 14km east of Calitzdorp) ☎044 213 3783, ⓦredstone .co.za. Eight lovely, period-furnished cottages on a working farm in a landscape full of red rock formations. Besides walking and cycling trails, there's birdwatching and

the four horses on the farm can be ridden. Breakfast and dinner provided on request. R690
★**The Retreat at Groenfontein** 20km northeast of Calitzdorp and 59km northwest of Oudtshoorn ☎044 213 3880, ⓦgroenfontein.com. This isolated Victorian colonial farmstead borders the 2300-square-kilometre Swartberg Nature Reserve, an outstandingly beautiful area of gorges, rivers and dirt tracks. Accommodation is in comfortable en-suite rooms, each with its own fireplace, and rates include full board, with vegetarians well catered for – the hospitable and helpful owners turn every evening into a fine dinner party. R1520

Prince Albert and around

Isolation has left intact the traditional rural architecture of **PRINCE ALBERT**, an attractive little town 70km north of Oudtshoorn. Reached across the loops and razorbacks of the Swartberg Pass, this is one of the most dramatic drives and entries to a town imaginable. Although firmly in the thirstlands of the South African interior, on the cusp between the Little and Great Karoo, Prince Albert is all the more striking for its perennial spring, whose water trickles down furrows along its streets – a gift that propagates fruit trees and gardens. It is undoubtedly one of the best small towns outside Cape Town to spend a couple of days, with great guesthouses, restaurants and craft shopping, plus the spectacular landscapes.

Many come to Prince Albert for the drives themselves, through its two southerly gateways – the aforementioned **Swartberg Pass** on the R328 and **Meiringspoort** on the N12. Once you are in the town it is small enough to explore on foot, and you'll find everything you want on the main road.

The essence of the town is in the fleeting impressions that give the flavour of a Karoo *dorp* like nowhere else: the silver steeple of the Dutch Reformed church puncturing a deep-blue sky with a mountainous backdrop, and residents sauntering along or progressing slowly down the main street on squeaky bikes.

ARRIVAL AND DEPARTURE
PRINCE ALBERT

By car From Cape Town allow 5–6hr for the 420km trip. The fastest and least scenic route is along the N1, past Laingsburg, and involves no mountain passes; turn off onto the Prince Albert Road. The most scenic is along the R62 to Calitzdorp or Oudtshoorn, then along the R328 over Swartberg. The pass is unpaved, with switchbacks, but fine in an ordinary car, if you go slowly. For a gentler experience, approach the town via Meiringspoort from De Rust, a paved road that goes past rivers and valleys with spectacular rock formations and places to picnic. If you get a puncture or other car trouble, contact Benny (☎073 455 1174). Petrol is available in Prince Albert at the Agri Co-op, 99 Church

Street, which is closed on Saturdays from 11am and all day on Sundays.
By train There is one train per day, three times per week, between Cape Town and Johannesburg (Wed, Fri & Sun; ☎086 000 8888), stopping at Prince Albert Road station, 45km from the hamlet. Trains are often late and the station has absolutely no facilities. From Cape Town the journey is some seven and a half hours. From Johannesburg it's an overnight trip of approximately nineteen hours. Arrange to be collected by your guesthouse, or book a taxi in advance through Billy van Rooyen (☎072 337 3149; R450 for two people).

FROM TOP LEFT SUSPENSION BRIDGE, STORMS RIVER MOUTH (P.233); CANOPY TOUR, STORMS RIVER ADVENTURES (P.236), WOLFBERG ARCH, CEDERBERG WILDERNESS AREA (P.205) >

By bus Greyhound buses (☎083 915 9000, ⓦgreyhound .co.za) stop daily at the *North and South Hotel* in Prince Albert Road station, on the N1, on its route from Cape Town to Johannesburg, but you will need to arrange to be picked up (see p.248) for the 45km journey to Prince Albert. Allow 7–8 hours by bus from Cape Town.

INFORMATION AND ACTIVITIES

Information The tourist office on Church St (Mon–Fri 9am–5pm, Sat 9am–noon; ☎023 541 1366, ⓦprincealbert .org.za) has maps showing accommodation, restaurants and craft shops, and can point you to other activities in the area, such as olive oil tasting or visiting the largest fig farm in South Africa. The website has the dates of the Olive Festival in April, as well as details of photography courses.
Bank There is limited use of credit cards in town, and no foreign exchange, but there is an Absa bank with an ATM at 29 Church St.
Hiking permits *Lazy Lizard* (daily 7.30am–5pm; ☎023 541 1379) in Church St sells Cape Nature hiking permits for exploring the Swartberg.
Theatre The Showroom, 41 Church St (☎023 541 1563, ⓦshowroomtheatre.co.za), is an Art Deco-styled, multipurpose venue that is something of a cultural oasis in the heart of the Karoo. The website provides the dates of performances, which include theatre, music and cinema, and tickets can be purchased online. The venue also hosts the annual Indie Karoo Film Festival (ⓦindiekaroofilmfestival.com), showcasing the best of South Africa's up-and-coming cinematic talent.
Stargazing tours The Karoo sky is heaven for astronomers due to the lack of light pollution, and you get some of the southern hemisphere's sharpest views of the firmament from here. One of the most exciting things you can do here is explore the night skies with local astronomers Hans and Tilanie Daehne (new moon only; R350 for a lecture and viewing; ☎072 732 2950, ⓦastrotours.co.za). Book well in advance.

ACCOMMODATION

Dennehof Guest House Off Christina de Wit St, on the outskirts of town ☎023 541 1227, ⓦdennehof .co.za. Stay in one of seven rooms in this 1835 homestead (a National Monument); there is also a self-catering option. Hiking trips are offered, as well as mountain bike trips where you're driven up the Swartberg and descend the terrifying 18km on two wheels (R400). Renting a bike for a day around town is another, more sedate, option (R200). **R1300**
Karoo Lodge 66 Church St ☎023 541 1467 or ☎082 692 7736, ⓦkaroolodge.com. You'll find reasonably priced, spacious accommodation at this B&B, run by a hospitable couple. Each of the suites, complete with pure cotton sheets and goose down duvets, leads onto the pool and the garden, which is filled with crimson bougainvillea. **R1030**
Karoo View Margrieta Prinsloo Rd ☎023 541 1929, ⓦkarooview.co.za. Upmarket, comfortable self-catering in four modern Karoo-style cottages on the edge of town with views of the Swartberg and surrounding countryside, but close enough to walk into town. In addition, there's Karoo View House, which has three en-suite bedrooms, and the Stoep Suite, which sleeps two or three. A light breakfast is provided, as is firewood for braais. **R1090**

GO TO HELL

Prince Albert is one of the best places to begin a trip into **Die Hel** (also known as Hell, The Hell or Gamkaskloof), a valley that's part of the Swartberg Nature Reserve, and not on the way to anywhere. The attraction of the place is the silence, isolation and birdlife. A deep cleft between the towering Swartberg Mountains, with the Gamka River running through it, the valley only opened to road transport in 1962, and still has no electricity supply, petrol, ATMs, mobile phone reception or shops.

Although it doesn't look far on the map, you'll need to allow two-and-a-half hours from Prince Albert to make the spectacular but tortuous **drive** into the valley along a dirt road. A 4WD isn't needed, but you should definitely not attempt the drive in the killing heat of December or January without air conditioning.

There's **accommodation** at *Fontein Guest Farm* (☎023 541 1107, ⓦgamkaskloof.co.za), which is run by one of the area's original farming families. There are four different houses (R350 per person) and sites for camping (R200 per site). Meals and picnic baskets can be made on request, dinner booked beforehand, and the farm's restaurant is always open for breakfast (7–10am). Another option is on the Nature Reserve itself (☎021 483 0190, ⓦbit.ly /swartbergnature), which has well-kept camping sites (from R150) and restored historical cottages (R640 per cottage).

Mai's Guest House 81 Church St ☎023 541 1188, ⓦmaisbandb.co.za. Expect a comfortable stay in this restored nineteenth-century house – all the rooms have a/c and there's a pool (and lots of cats). A fabulous breakfast is served under the vines by the enthusiastic Irish owner. R1000

★**Onse Rus** 47 Church St ☎023 541 1380, ⓦonserus .co.za. Five cool, thatched B&B rooms attached to a restored Cape Dutch house, with welcoming and knowledgeable owners who serve you tea and cake on arrival. Day visits can be arranged to the owners' nearby farm and labyrinth. R1040

EATING

★**Gallery Café** 57 Church St ☎023 541 1197, ⓦprincealbertgallery.co.za/gallery-cafe. Imaginative dishes created by passionate chef Brent Phillips-White in a relaxed ambience above the *Prince Albert Gallery*. There are delightful starters, the meat dishes include game (R160), but vegetarians and vegans are well catered for. For dessert, check out the home-made ice creams. Daily 6–9.30pm.

Lazy Lizard 9 Church St ☎023 541 1379, ⓦlazylizardprincealbert.co.za. This is the best place in Prince Albert to come for a light lunch or a coffee. A former

bus station built in 1903, there's a veranda where you can sit and enjoy a tasty salad, quiche (R60) or sandwich while using the internet. Daily 7.30am–5pm.

★**Simply Saffron** 10 Church St ☎023 541 1040 or ☎082 873 9985. A healing centre which produces delicious dinners two nights a week. Meals are served by the owners in their own dining room, using vegetables from their kitchen garden or local ingredients, cooked with great flair. The three-course set menus offer a choice of two dishes, with plenty of options for vegetarians (R190). Bring your own wine and book well in advance. Fri & Sat 6–9pm.

SHOPPING

Prince Albert is known for its **mohair products**: magnificent blankets, rugs and mats, socks, scarves and other garments. *Prince Albert Gallery* on Church Street is a good place to start if you are looking for artworks, though there are a number of smaller shops nearby. Like most small towns, there is a modest Saturday morning **market** for locals, next to the Fransie Pienaar Museum, selling a range of home-made and home-grown produce. Prince Albert is well known for its figs and olives – you'll find the dried varieties everywhere, and delicious fresh figs in the summer, especially in February. The local olive oil is outstanding.

Gay's Guernsey Dairy Christina de Wit St ☎023 541 1274, ⓦgaysguernseydairy.com. Award-winning home-made cheeses which you can taste before buying, as well as yoghurts and cream. If you're travelling with children, take them to watch the milking at sunrise, and walk around the farm. Mon–Fri 7–9am, 10am–noon & 4–6pm, Sat & Sun 7–10am & 4.30–6pm.

Karoo Looms 55 Church St ☎023 541 1363, ⓦkarooweavery.co.za. The best place in Prince Albert for mohair carpets and rugs with bright, funky designs. Also look out for cotton bathmats off the looms. Mon–Fri 9am–5pm, Sat 9am–1pm.

Prince Albert Gallery 57 Church St ☎023 541, ⓦprincealbertgallery.co.za. The town's beauty has attracted a number of artists over the years, and this excellent gallery, located in an airy Victorian building, sells their work. Come here to buy paintings, sculpture, affordable beadwork, jewellery, ceramics and etchings

by local artists. Mon–Fri 9am–5pm, Sat 9am–1pm, Sun 10am–1pm.

The Watershed 19 Church St ☎082 938 2531, ⓦwatershedprincealbert.co.za. The town's top gallery, in a restored Victorian house, sells prints by legendary photographer Jürgen Schadeberg, most famous for his iconic anti-apartheid images of the 1950s and 60s. There is also retro furniture, and textiles and prints by local Karoo artists. The website has a catalogue and they ship goods abroad. Daily 10am–4pm.

Weltevrede Fig Farm Signposted from the town's cemetery, on the south side of Church St ☎023 541 1229, ⓦfigfarm.co.za. Visitable during fig season only (end of Jan–end of April), the farm is an awe-inspiring 25km drive, mostly on gravel, situated in the foothills of the Swartberg. As well as tours of the premises, there are plenty of fig products to purchase. Mon–Fri 10am–noon & 2–4pm, Sat 10am–noon.

Matjiesfontein

One of the quirkier manifestations of Victorian colonialism lies 250km northeast of Cape Town at the historic village of **MATJIESFONTEIN** (pronounced "Mikey's-fontayn"). Little more than two dusty streets beside a train track, the village resembles a film set rather than a Karoo *dorp*: every building, including the grand train station, is a classic period piece, with tin roofs, pastel walls, well-tended gardens and Victorian frills.

At the eastern end of the main street is the centrepiece, the *Lord Milner*, a grand hotel named after the controversial Victorian governor of the Cape, which is decked out with turrets and balconies and fountains by the entrance. If you're passing by, make sure you stop at least for a look around.

The origins of this curious place lie in the tale of a young Scottish entrepreneur, **James Douglas Logan**, who came to Cape Town to work on the railways. His rapid promotion to district superintendent of the line between Hex River and Prince Albert brought him to the Karoo, where he started growing fruit trees, eventually making a fortune in catering. He built Matjiesfontein as a health resort – making much play of the clean Karoo air – and it became a gathering point for the wealthy and influential in the early years of the twentieth century. Today the village survives as a treasured relic.

ACCOMMODATION   MATJIESFONTEIN

Lord Milner Hotel ☎ 023 561 3011, ⓦ matjiesfontein .com. Inside the *Lord Milner*, there are huge portraits on the wall, grand staircases, polished brass fittings and – perhaps taking the Victorian Imperialist theme a touch too far – red-jacketed porters and waitresses dressed in black and white. There's also a dimly lit dining room and an aged and creaking bar, and thankfully not much has been modernized. R1740

Sutherland

Remote **SUTHERLAND**, fearfully known to South Africans as the coldest spot in the country and featured on every weather report, is actually most notable for its clear, unpolluted skies, and for being one of the handful of places in the world where scientists can study Deep Space. You can visit the Observatory here, which is actually a hilltop covered with huge silver domes, housing massive telescopes where experts from all over the world spend freezing nights, extending the world's knowledge of the cosmos. The largest telescope here is **SALT** (the **South African Large Telescope**), the largest optical telescope in the southern hemisphere.

The tiny settlement has seen a rapid increase of visitors in the past few years, and there are now a couple of dozen guesthouses and cottages and several restaurants.

Observatory

18km east of Sutherland • Tours Mon–Sat at 10.30am & 2.30pm • R60 • Night tours Mon, Wed, Fri & Sat ; the time depends on the season • R80 • Book tours in advance; punctuality essential • Sat 9am–3pm, shorter tours leave on the hour which do not need advance booking • R40 • ☎ 023 571 2436, ⓦ salt.ac.za/about/tours

Day-time tours of the Observatory start from the informative visitors' centre and take you to see the massive **SALT** – an extremely valuable machine behind protective glass, which is powerful enough, with its 91 hexagonal mirrors, to be able to see just one candle were it placed on the moon. Only scientists at the Observatory actually get to look through SALT, though the night tours provide smaller telescopes for visitors and an interesting talk on the stars.

AMATEUR STARGAZING

Besides the Observatory, there's the chance for more stargazing in the town itself at *Sterland Boedery* (☎ 023 571 1481 or ☎ 082 556 9589, ⓦ sutherlandinfo.co.za), 1km before you reach Sutherland on the R345 from Matjiesfontein. Every night, local amateur astronomer Jurg Wagener sets up six 11-inch telescopes and gives a fascinating stargazing talk. It is a nice addition to an Observatory visit, and much more informal. Tours (R100) take place every night from 6–8pm and must be booked in advance. Start times can vary according to the season, so you should always ring first to check, and it's important to wrap up warmly as the evenings can get very cold.

ACCOMMODATION

SUTHERLAND

Kambrokind B&B 19 Piet Retief St ☎ 023 571 140. Run by Juanita Hutchings (the daughter of local astronomer Jurg Wagener) and her husband, this well-established Karoo stone house has six comfortable and warm en-suite rooms. There are also two communal lounges with roaring log fires. R1000

EATING

White House Restaurant 17 Piet Retief St ☎ 023 571 1444. Predictable offerings of karoo lamb chops, burgers, pasta and soups, at a popular, central spot. You can also catch a game of rugby on the screen at the *Mars Bar*. Book an early dinner before the stargazing activities in the evening. Mon–Sat 8am–6pm, Sun 8am–5pm.

Karoo National Park

The entrance gate is 2km south of Beaufort West, with the reception by the Rest Camp, 10km into the park • R176 • Gate summer daily 5am–7pm, winter 7am–6pm • Reception daily 7am–7pm • ☎ 023 415 2828, ⓦ sanparks.org/parks/karoo

Karoo National Park's attraction is in its mountainous, spare landscape and the serene atmosphere – and it scores highly as a place to break the long drive between Johannesburg and Cape Town. There's an environmental **education centre** near the main restcamp, along with three **trails**: an 11km day-walk; a short but informative tree trail; and an imaginative fossil trail (designed to accommodate wheelchairs and incorporating Braille boards), which tells the fascinating 250-million-year geological history of the area and shows fossils of the unusual animals that lived when the Karoo was a vast inland sea. While there are some **black rhino**, big game is limited, although there are some impressive raptors, including the **black eagle**.

ACCOMMODATION

KAROO NATIONAL PARK

★ **Main Rest Camp** 10km into park ☎ 023 415 2828, ⓦ sanparks.org/parks/karoo. Thirty fully equipped chalets and cottages strung out on either side of the main complex, all with lovely outlooks onto the Karoo landscape. There's a pool nearby, a shop selling basic foodstuffs and a restaurant (daily breakfast is included in the rate, but you need to book dinner in advance). The campsite is hidden away over a rise. Camping R260, doubles R1300

★ **Matoppo Inn** On the corner of Bird and Meintjies sts, Beaufort West ☎ 023 415 1055, ⓦ matoppo inn.co.za. Elegant rooms with brass beds and antique furniture, as well as standard rooms with more modern furnishings, in the town's old *drostdy*, or magistrate's house. The gardens are beautiful – a green oasis in the desert-like Karoo – and there's a pool, good food all day, and a tranquil atmosphere. R1400

The Northern Cape

RICHTERSVELD TRANSFRONTIER PARK

The Northern Cape

The vast Northern Cape, the largest, most dispersed and sparsely populated of South Africa's provinces, is not an easy region for a visitor to tackle. From the lonely Atlantic coast to the provincial capital Kimberley, right by the border with the Free State, it covers over one-third of the nation's landmass, an area dominated by heat, aridity, empty spaces and huge travelling distances. But under great cloudless skies, it's the miracles of the desert that provide the province's main attraction – improbable swathes of flowers that transform the landscape into riots of colour, and wild animals roaming the dunes and golden grasses.

3

The most significant of these surprises is the **Orange** (or Gariep) **River**, flowing from the Lesotho Highlands to the Atlantic where it marks South Africa's border with Namibia. The river separates the **Kalahari** and the **Great Karoo** – the two sparsely populated semi-desert ecosystems that fill the interior of the Northern Cape. On its banks, the isolated northern centre of **Upington** is the main town in the Kalahari region, the gateway to the magnificent **Kgalagadi Transfrontier Park** and the smaller **Augrabies Falls National Park**.

In **Namaqualand**, on the western side of the province, the brief winter rains produce a truly glorious metamorphosis when in August and September the land is carpeted by a magnificent display of wild flowers. A similar display of blossoming succulents can be seen at the little-visited **Ai-Ais Richtersveld Transfrontier Park**, a mountain desert tucked around a loop in the Orange River either side of the Namibian border.

Despite these impressive natural attractions, most of the traffic to the Northern Cape is in its southeastern corner, through which the two main roads between Johannesburg and Cape Town, the **N1** and the **N12**, pass. However, given the uninspiring nature of this area, it isn't covered in this book. A less obvious way to get from Johannesburg to Cape Town involves taking the **N14** through Upington, passing the atmospheric old mission station at **Kuruman**, then driving on to **Springbok** and following the scenic **N7** down the coast. This route is around 400km longer than the N1 or N12, but, while the N14 has more than its fair share of long, empty landscapes, the sights along the way are more interesting.

Getting around by **public transport** can be a pain. While the main towns of Kimberley, Springbok and Upington lie on Intercape's bus routes (with connections to Windhoek in Namibia), many services arrive and depart at night and thus miss the scenery. Minibus taxis cover most destinations several times a day during the week, but are much reduced or nonexistent at weekends. Taxis don't serve the national parks (take an organized tour instead). Details of the most useful routes are given in the text.

AUGRABIES FALLS

Highlights

❶ **The Big Hole** The vast hand-dug crater that dominates Kimberley is an awesome testament to South Africa's pioneer diamond hunters. **See p.262**

❷ **Kgalagadi Transfrontier Park** Discover lion, gemsbok and meerkat among the parched red sand dunes of the Kalahari. **See p.277**

❸ **Augrabies Falls** Marvel at South Africa's most powerful waterfall, where the Orange River thunders into an echoing gorge carved out of the desert. **See p.280**

❹ **Driving down the N7** The province's most scenic drive stretches south from Springbok

through rocky mountains and peaceful *dorps*. **See p.283**

❺ **Namaqualand flowers** In August and September the veld bursts into colour with a superb natural floral display, and boasts a fascinating variety of unusual succulents year-round. **See p.285**

❻ **Ai-Ais Richtersveld Transfrontier Park** South Africa's only mountain desert, a hot, dry and forbidding place that can only be explored by 4WD or by drifting down the Orange River in an inflatable canoe. **See p.291**

HIGHLIGHTS ARE MARKED ON THE MAP ON P.258

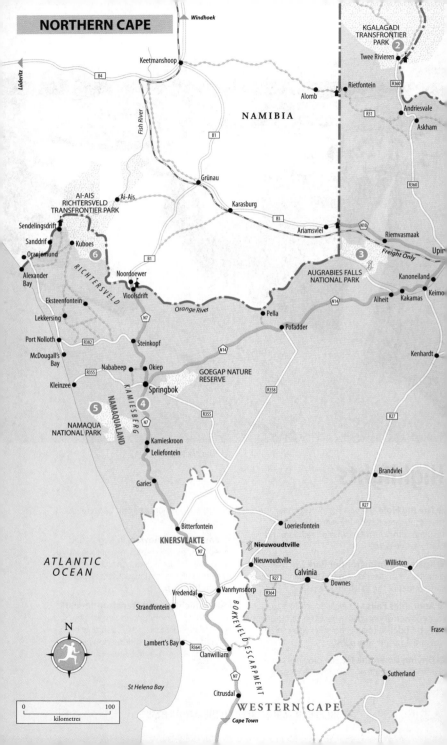

BOTSWANA

NORTHWEST

Mafikeng

R49

Pretoria & Jo'burg

Van Zylsrus

Sonstraal

R31

Hotazel

KALAHARI

Kuruman

Vryburg

N14

R49

Johannesburg

Sishen

Olifantshoek

N14

Danielskuil

Wonderwerk Cave

Jan Kempdorp

Christiana

Warrenton

R31

WITSAND KALAHARI NATURE RESERVE

Barkly West

Wildebeest Kuil

① Kimberley

Modderrivier

Magersfontein

R64

...rshoop

N10

N8

Griquatown

R313

Orange River

Vaal River

MOKALA NATIONAL PARK

Belmont

N8

BLOEMFONTEIN

Johannesburg

...33

Marydale

Prieska

Hopetown

N12

Orange River

FREE STATE

N6

East London

R357

N10

Van Wyksvlei

Britstown

R48

De Aar

N10

Hanover

N1

N9

Colesberg

Trompsburg

R26

Philippolis

Carnarvon

Victoria West

Richmond

Middelburg

EASTERN CAPE

R63

GREAT KAROO

Three Sisters

R63

S N E E B E R G

KAROO NATIONAL PARK

N12

Beaufort West

N9

Graaff-Reinet

Leeu-Gamka

N12

Port Elizabeth

HIGHLIGHTS

① The Big Hole

② Kgalagadi Transfrontier Park

③ Augrabies Falls

④ Driving down the N7

⑤ Namaqualand flowers

⑥ Ai-Ais Richtersveld Transfrontier Park

DIAMONDS ARE FOREVER

Diamonds originate as carbon particles in the Earth's mantle, which are subjected to such high pressure and temperature that they crystallize to form diamonds. Millions of years ago the molten rock, or magma, in the mantle burst through weak points in the Earth's crust as volcanoes, and it is in the pipe of cooled magma – called **kimberlite**, after Kimberley – that diamonds are found. Finding kimberlite, however, isn't necessarily a licence to print money – in every one hundred tonnes there will be about twenty carats (4g) of diamonds.

The word "carat" derives from the carob bean – dried beans were used as a measure of weight. (Carat has a different meaning in the context of gold, where it is a measure of purity.) De Beers estimates that fifty million pieces of diamond jewellery are bought each year – which represents a lot of marriage proposals.

Brief history

The history of the Northern Cape area is intimately linked to the **San**, South Africa's first people, whose hunter-gatherer lifestyle and remarkable adaptations to desert life exert a powerful fascination. Although no genuine vestiges of the San way of life can be found in South Africa (only tiny pockets remain in the Namibian and Botswanan sections of the Kalahari desert), their heritage is most visible in the countless examples of **rock art** across the province, and, to a lesser extent, in their ancient legends and place names. The movement of Africans from the north and east, and Europeans from the southwest, drove the San from their hunting grounds and eventually led to their extinction; yet for both sets of newcomers, the semi-desert of the Karoo and the Kalahari at first appeared to offer little more than hopelessness and heartbreaking horizons.

What it did provide – wealth under the dusty ground – the Europeans pursued without restraint, beginning in 1685, soon after the Dutch first established their settlement in the Cape, with an expedition into Namaqualand to mine for copper led by **Governor Simon van der Stel**. The other Europeans who made an early impression on the province were **trekboers**, Dutch burghers freed from the employment of the Dutch East India Company in the Cape who wanted to find new lands to farm away from the authoritarian company rule, and **missionaries**, who established a framework of settlement and communication used by all who came after.

Within a few years of the discovery of **diamonds** in the area, a settlement of unprecedented size had grown up around Kimberley. The town soon boasted more trappings of civilization than most of the southern hemisphere, with public libraries, electric streetlights and tramways, as well as South Africa's first urban "location" for Africans and coloured people. The British authorities in the Cape were quick to annexe the new diamond fields – a move which didn't endear them to either the Orange Free State or the mainly coloured **Griqua** people, who both claimed this ill-defined region. It was no surprise, therefore, that at the outbreak of the **Anglo-Boer War** in 1899, rich and strategic Kimberley was one of the first towns besieged by the Boer armies. Many reminders of the war can still be seen in the area.

Kimberley

Although it's a provincial capital and the historic centre of production of one of the world's most valuable materials, **KIMBERLEY** itself is neither large nor glamorous. During the diamond rush, it was the fastest-growing city in the southern hemisphere and Cecil Rhodes held in his grip not only the fabulously wealthy diamond industry, but the heart and mind of the British empire; yet status and sophistication have been draining from Kimberley ever since. Even the all-controlling De Beers Group (sometimes called the "grandfather" of Kimberley for the number of people it has

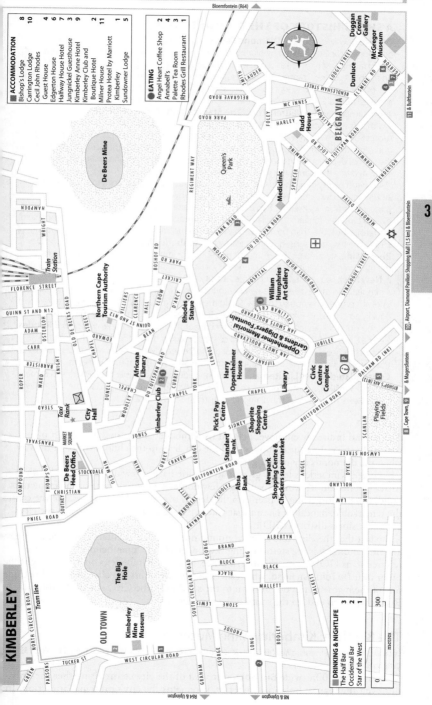

KIMBERLEY

■ ACCOMMODATION
Bishop's Lodge	8
Carrington Lodge	10
Cecil John Rhodes Guest House	4
Edgerton House	6
Halfway House Hotel	7
Jungnickel Guesthouse	3
Kimberley Anne Hotel	9
Kimberley Club and Boutique Hotel	2
Milner House	11
Protea Hotel by Marriott Kimberley	1
Sundowner Lodge	5

● EATING
Angel Heart Coffee Shop	2
Annabell's	4
Palette Tea Room	3
Rhodes Grill Restaurant	1

■ DRINKING & NIGHTLIFE
The Half Bar	3
Occidental Bar	2
Star of the West	1

3

A SHORT HISTORY OF THE DIAMOND FIELDS

The area now known as the **Diamond Fields** was once unpromising farmland, marked by occasional *koppies* inhabited by pioneer farmers and the Griquas, an independent people of mixed race. In 1866 this changed forever, when a 15-year-old boy noticed a shiny white pebble on the banks of the Orange River near Hopetown, about 120km southwest of Kimberley. Just as word of that discovery was spreading, another Hopetown resident, Schalk van Niekerk, acquired from a Griqua shepherd a massive 83.5-carat diamond. These two stones became known, respectively, as "**Eureka**" and "**The Star of South Africa**"; the latter was described – with some justification – by the British Colonial Secretary as the "rock on which the future success of South Africa will be built". Certainly in the short term, the discoveries provoked wild optimism: thousands of prospectors made the gruelling trek across the Karoo to sift through the alluvial deposits along the banks of the Orange and Vaal rivers, and by 1873 there were an estimated fifty thousand people living in the area.

Although plenty of diamonds were found in the rivers, **prospectors** also began scratching around in the dry land between them, encouraged by tales of diamonds found in farmhouse bricks made from local earth. Two of the most promising "dry diggings" were on a farm owned by two brothers, Johannes Nicolas and Diederick Arnoldus de Beer. In 1871 the brothers sold the farm, which they had bought a few years previously for £50, to prospectors for the sum of £6300. The two sites subsequently became the **Kimberley Mine**, or Big Hole, and the **De Beers Mine**, situated on either side of the centre of Kimberley. The Big Hole was the focus of the most frenetic mining activity of the early years, and the shantytown that grew up around it, **New Rush**, was the origin of the present city.

Kimberley in those days was a heady, rugged place to live, with little authority or structure, but with prizes rich enough to attract bold men with big ideas. Of these, two very different, if equally ambitious, men rose to prominence in the new settlement. **Barney Barnato**, a flamboyant Cockney, established his power base at the Kimberley Mine, while **Cecil Rhodes** (see box, p.264), a parson's son who had come out to join his brother in South Africa to improve his health, gradually took control of the De Beers Mine. The power struggle between the two men was intense, culminating in the formation in 1888 of the **De Beers Consolidated Mines Limited**, an agreement involving the transfer from Rhodes to Barnato of over £5 million, an astronomical sum in those days. This consolidation laid the foundation for De Beers' monopoly of the diamond industry in South Africa.

directly and indirectly employed) closed its Kimberley mines in 2005 as part of a process to streamline the company, and the city lives in the chilly shadow of the day when the diamonds dry up altogether.

However, Kimberley's legacy gives it an historic flavour few other cities in South Africa can match. It's worth spending a few hours seeking out some of the many old buildings, not forgetting to peer into the depths of the Big Hole just west of the centre, the remarkable, hand-dug chasm that takes up almost as much land area as the city's central business district (CBD).

The fact that the Big Hole is underground doesn't make orientation immediately easy; a useful landmark is the stern-looking skyscraper, **Harry Oppenheimer House** (often referred to as HOH), near the tourist office. Many of Kimberley's other main sights lie on or near **Du Toitspan Road**, which slices diagonally across the city centre and becomes one of the main arteries out of town to the southeast. The CBD sits at Du Toitspan Road's northern end, to the south of Lennox Street.

The Big Hole: Kimberley Mine Museum

On the western side of the hole along West Circular Rd · **Museum** Daily 8am–5pm, last entry 4pm · R100 · **Tram** · R10 · ☏ 053 839 4600 · ⓦ thebighole.co.za

Although the 500m-wide **Big Hole**, just west of the city centre, is neither the only nor even the biggest hole in Kimberley, it remains the city's principal attraction. In

1871, with diamonds known to be in the area (see box opposite), a group of workers known as the Red Cap Party were scratching around at the base of **Colesberg koppie**, a small hill on the De Beers brothers' farm. The story goes that they sent one of their cooks to the top of the hill as a punishment for being drunk, telling him not to return until he'd found a diamond. The unnamed servant duly came back with a peace offering, and within two years there were over fifty thousand people in the area frantically turning Colesberg *koppie* inside out. In its heyday, tens of thousands of miners swarmed over the mine to work their 10-square-metre claim, and a network of ropes and pipes crisscrossed the surface; each day saw lives lost and fortunes either discovered or squandered. Once the mining could go no further from the surface, a shaft was dug to allow further excavations beneath it to a depth of over 800m. Incredibly, the hole was dug to a depth of 240m entirely by pick and shovel, and remains one of the largest manmade excavations in the world. By 1914, when De Beers closed the mine, some 22.6 million tonnes of earth had been removed, yielding over 13.6 million carats (2722kg) of diamonds.

The only official way to see the Big Hole is from inside **The Big Hole: Kimberley Mine Museum**, which gives a comprehensive insight into Kimberley's main claim to fame. A delightfully rickety, open-sided tram runs from the entrance in the Old Town halfway around the Big Hole before returning; approximately a 15-minute trip. The Big Hole itself is viewed from a suspended platform, from which you can peer down into nothingness. An informative film puts it all into context, as do other displays, from a re-creation of a nineteenth-century mineshaft to a vault full of real diamonds.

The Old Town

West Circular Rd • Daily 8am–5pm • Free

This impressive collection of **historic buildings**, many originating from the days of Rhodes and Barnato, is scattered around the entrance to the Mine Museum and can be wandered through without paying the museum entry fee. The old shops, churches, pub, banks and sundry other period institutions were moved here from the city centre when development and demolition threatened; now there's enough here to create a fairly complete settlement, and most of the fixtures, fittings and artefacts are genuine.

Market Square and around

At the heart of the city centre is **Market Square**, dominated by the cream and white, classical City Hall, designed by the Scottish architect F.C. Rogers and completed in 1899. During the early diamond days, the square was the hub of buying and selling, and still today around the square, the sense of movement and commerce is perpetuated by a large taxi rank and an assortment of scruffy but colourful stalls and traders. One block west of Market Square, at **36 Stockdale Street**, lies the head office of De Beers, a dignified but unremarkable old building (not open to the public) rather swallowed up by the city around it.

Africana Library

63–65 Du Toitspan Rd • Mon–Fri 8am–12.45pm & 1.30–4.30pm • ☎ 053 830 6247, ⓦ africanalibrary.co.za

The small but engrossing **Africana Library**, across the road from the Kimberley Club, specializes in historical material relevant to Kimberley and the Northern Cape including records by early European travellers and documentation and photos of the Anglo-Boer War (1899–1902). Opened in 1887 as the Kimberley Public Library, it retains many original features, and one of the librarians will show you around if you ask nicely.

The CBD

At the junction of Du Toitspan Road and Lennox Street stands a statue of **Cecil Rhodes**, who sits astride a horse while clutching a map of Africa and gazing into the distance. The **CBD** area begins across Lennox Street, where the **Oppenheimer Memorial Gardens** contain a bust of mining magnate Sir Ernest Oppenheimer and the Diggers' Fountain; the latter depicts five miners holding aloft a massive sieve, and looks particularly impressive when floodlit after dusk. The tall building overlooking the gardens is **Harry Oppenheimer House** (HOH), the offices of De Beers' DTC (Diamond Trading Company; not open to the public), on the upper floors of which all of the company's South African-mined diamonds are assessed for caratage, colour, clarity and shape. To enable this to take place in the best natural light, the building faces south, with special windows to eliminate glare; there are no windows on the other faces other than small ones along the stairwell.

William Humphreys Art Gallery

1 Cullinan Crescent, on the opposite side of the gardens to HOH • Mon–Fri 8am–4.45pm, Sat 9am–4.45pm, Sun 9–11.45am • R5 • ☎ 053 831 1724, ⓦ whag.co.za

Part of the Civic Centre complex, the **William Humphreys Art Gallery** is one of South Africa's few top-notch art galleries and is an unexpected gem. Although dominated by European Old Masters when it opened in 1952, the collection has moved with the times and now houses an impressively well-balanced representation of South African art, including both traditional and contemporary work and some excellent modern sculpture. The gallery was one of the first places in the world to display **San rock paintings** as works of art rather than anthropological museum pieces. At the back of the gallery is a very pleasant **tea room** (see p.267).

The Kimberley Club

72 Du Toitspan Rd • ☎ 053 832 4224, ⓦ kimberleyclub.co.za

Not far southwest of Market Square is the two-storey **Kimberley Club**, founded in 1881 by the new settlement's movers and shakers. The club was modelled on London's gentlemen's clubs, but its colourful, enterprising members made the place dynamic rather than stuffy. Today it is a smart hotel (see p.267), and retains its original fixtures

CECIL JOHN RHODES

When **Cecil Rhodes** first arrived in the Kimberley Diamond Fields he was a sickly 18-year-old, sent out to join his brother Herbert for the sake of his health. Soon making money buying up claims, he returned to Britain to attend Oxford University, where his illnesses returned and he was given six months to live. He came back out to South Africa, where he was able to improve both his health and his business standing, allowing him to return to Oxford and graduate in 1881. By that point he had already founded the **De Beers Mining Company** and been elected an MP in the **Cape Parliament**.

Within a decade, Rhodes controlled ninety percent of the world's diamond production and was champing at the bit to expand his mining interests north into Africa, with the British empire in tow. With much cajoling, bullying, brinkmanship and obfuscation in his dealings with imperial governments and African chiefs alike, Rhodes brought the regions north of the Limpopo under the control of his **British South African Company** (BSAC). This territory – now Zimbabwe and Zambia – became known as **Rhodesia** in 1895, the same year as a Rhodes-backed invasion of the Transvaal Republic, the **Jameson Raid**, failed humiliatingly. Rhodes was forced to resign as prime minister of the Cape Colony, a post he had assumed in 1890 at the age of 37, while the Boers and the British slid towards war. He spent the first part of the war in besieged Kimberley, trying to organize the defences and bickering publicly with the British commander. A year after the end of the war, Rhodes died at Muizenberg near Cape Town, aged only 49 and unmarried; he was buried in the Matopos Hills near Bulawayo in Zimbabwe.

and fittings such as the leather armchairs in the smoking lounge and marble in the hallway, and there are plenty of fine antiques. It's possible to look around or eat at the restaurant (see p.267), though you'll get a much less chilly welcome if you introduce yourself at the reception and respect the club's dress code, which includes no T-shirts or shorts in the dining room and bar.

Belgravia

Du Toitspan Rd

Belgravia, the residential suburb where most of Kimberley's wealthy families lived during the boom years, lies about 1km southeast of the CBD. The focus of the area is at the junction of Du Toitspan and Egerton roads, where you'll find the historic **Halfway House Hotel** (see p.267). Dating to 1872 and also known as "the Half", it takes its name from its location halfway between the De Beers and Bultfontein mines, and gained fame as a drive-in (or, in those days, ride-in) pub, a custom started by Cecil Rhodes who liked a tipple while in the saddle. You can't drive up nowadays (it's illegal), and unfortunately a fire destroyed half of the original bar and memorabilia in 1990, but it still retains an historic atmosphere, with paintings and photographs giving a glimpse into its heyday.

McGregor Museum

Atlas Rd • Mon–Sat 9am–5pm • R25 • ☎ 053 839 2717, ⓦ museumsnc.co.za

The fabulous **McGregor Museum**, named after an early mayor of Kimberley, is housed in a magnificent Victorian mansion. The highlight here is the extensive and imaginative Ancestors Display, which draws on archeological evidence to piece together an absorbing and – unusual still in South Africa – well-balanced exhibition on the various ancestral roots of today's inhabitants of the Northern Cape, going right back to evidence of the earliest hominids millions of years ago. There's also an evocative section on the siege of Kimberley; during the siege, Cecil Rhodes stayed in two of the ground-floor rooms here, which have been furnished in the style of the day.

Duggan-Cronin Gallery

Egerton Rd • Mon–Fri 9am–5pm • Donation • ☎ 053 839 2700

The **Duggan-Cronin Gallery**, adjacent to the McGregor Museum, includes over eight thousand photographs portraying the indigenous people of Southern Africa and recording their culture. The majority were taken by Alfred Duggan-Cronin, an Irishman from County Cork and a mine compound guard for De Beers. He bought a box camera in 1904, and his first subjects were miners. Intrigued by where they came from, he travelled all over Southern Africa between the two world wars photographing faces and traditional lives – picking up the nickname Thandabantu; "someone who loves people" in the language of the Matabele.

Lodge Road houses

Lodge Rd • Arrange a guide from the McGregor Museum to visit Rudd House and Dunluce • R30 • Mon–Fri only

A trio of elegantly restored Belgravia houses, all on Lodge Road, evokes the atmosphere of old Kimberley and gives a sense of the kind of wealth the city once attracted: **Rudd House** at no. 5 was the mansion of Charles Dunnell Rudd, a mining magnate and partner of Rhodes; no. 7, built in 1907 and the birthplace of Harry Oppenheimer one year later, was the family's last Kimberley home before they moved to Johannesburg in 1915; and **Dunluce** at no. 10 is an elegant late-Victorian house built for the diamond baron Gustav Bonas. Originally called Lillianville, its main occupants were the family of John Orr, the department store magnate and mayor of Kimberley who bought and renamed the house in 1907. Many of the original furnishings and fittings have remained *in situ*.

3

ARRIVAL AND DEPARTURE

By plane Kimberley Airport (☎053 830 7106, ⊛airports .co.za) lies 7km to the south of the city, along the N8 to Bloemfontein. South African Airways (☎053 838 3337, ⊛flysaa.com), based at the airport, operates flights to Johannesburg and Cape Town. There's no regular transport into town, so phone for a taxi (see below). Most of the major car rental agencies are based at the airport, including Avis (☎053 851 1082, ⊛avis.co.za), First Car Rental (☎053 851 1476, ⊛firstcarrental.co.za), and Hertz (☎053 830 2200).

Destinations: Cape Town (2 daily except Sat; 1hr 35min); Johannesburg (4–5 daily; 1hr 10min).

By bus Intercity buses stop outside the Sol Plaatje Tourist Information Centre (see below), which is handy when arriving on overnight services from Cape Town, but to be avoided on daytime departures from Cape Town or Joburg, which arrive at night when the place is deserted. You can either arrange for a hotel to pick you up, ask to be dropped off at one of the hotels along the N12 (Bishops Avenue) just south of the centre, or alight at the Shell Ultra City service station 6km north of town on the N12, which is a much safer place to call a taxi. Citiliner, City to City, Intercape, Greyhound and Translux all have services to Joburg and Cape Town via Bloemfontein, and Intercape has a service to Upington via Kuruman. Information and tickets are available at the Tickets 4 Africa bureau inside the Sol Plaatje

Tourist Information Centre (Mon–Fri 8am–7.30pm, Sa 8am–12.30pm; ☎053 832 6040). Alternatively, book a either the Shoprite or Checkers supermarkets o Bultfontein Rd north of the tourist office.

Destinations: Bloemfontein (daily; 2hr 15min); Cape Tow (daily; 11hr 30min); Johannesburg (daily; 5hr 45min–7h 10min); Kuruman (3hr 20min); Upington (daily; 7hr 25min)

By train The train station (☎053 838 2709 ⊛shosholozameyl.co.za) is on Florence St on th northeastern edge of town. As services arrive and depar after dark, always get a taxi to and from you accommodation; they can be found outside the station.

Destinations: Cape Town (4 weekly; 17hr 40min) Johannesburg (4 weekly; 7hr 40min).

By minibus taxi Minibus taxis operate from Pniel Rd (th northern extension of Bultfontein Rd), 1.5km from th tourist office. To be sure of a ride in daylight, arrive a 6.30am (7am winter); most destinations also have earl afternoon departures, but on these you risk being droppe off at night. Services on all routes are reduced on Saturday and often nonexistent on Sunday. Frequencies given belo refer to weekdays. Except to Barkly West (for which you pa on board), fares are paid at an office on Pniel Rd beside th long-distance rank.

Destinations: Barkly West (hourly; 30min); Kuruman (1–2 daily; 2hr 30min); Upington (3–4 daily; 5hr).

INFORMATION

Tourist offices The Sol Plaatje Tourist Information Centre is at 121 Bultfontein Rd, part of the Civic Centre complex (Mon–Fri 8am–5pm; ☎053 830 6779/6271, ⊛solplaatje.org.za). The staff can provide city plans, lists of places to stay, and gives out maps for a self-guided walking tour of Kimberley – the Belgravia Historic Walk, which starts and ends at the McGregor

Museum where maps are also available. They als maintain a list of accredited guides for local tours. Th office for the Northern Cape Tourism Authority is at 1! Villiers St, off Quinn St (Mon–Fri 8am–4pm; ☎053 832 2657, ⊛experiencenortherncape.com), which car provide more information about the province particularly wildlife parks and reserves.

GETTING AROUND

On foot Central Kimberley is fairly walkable, but always take taxis at night; note that around town, many street names are written on the kerbide rather than on signs.

By taxi The main taxi rank is in Market Square behind the City Hall; alternatively, contact Rikki's Taxis (☎053 842 1764, ⊛rikkistaxis.co.za).

ACCOMMODATION

The bulk of the town's hotels, guesthouses and B&Bs lie in the southern suburbs, most within a kilometre or two of the centre. The most atmospheric places – those occupying historic buildings – are clustered in and around the upmarket Belgravia suburb.

Bishop's Lodge 9 Bishops Ave ☎053 831 7876, ⊛bishopslodge.co.za; map p.261. Close to the tourist office, this quiet, modern affair offers spotless twins and doubles, keenly priced self-catering apartments, and a suite with wheelchair access. There's a swimming pool, but no meals except breakfast (extra). Rooms R930, apartments R1150

Carrington Lodge 60 Carrington Rd, at the corner with Oliver Rd ☎053 831 6448, ⊛carringtonlodge.co.za; map p.261. Friendly guesthouse on the edge of Belgravia with sixteen stylish rooms, a colonial-style wrap-around veranda, pleasant garden with a pool and braai area, and a bar with a pool table. Rates include breakfast in the restaurant, where dinners are also available on request. R1400

Cecil John Rhodes Guest House 138 Du Toitspan Rd ☏ 053 830 2500, ⓦ ceciljohnrhodes.co.za; map p.261. The most central of the historic guesthouses, built in 1895, with eight airy and elegantly furnished B&B rooms with all mod cons, plus a shady tea garden facing the road (Mon–Fri 9am–5pm). Dinner on request. R900

Edgerton House 5 Egerton Rd ☏ 053 831 1150, ⓦ edgertonhouse.co.za; map p.261. Opposite the McGregor Museum, this Belgravia option has thirteen slightly dated but perfectly comfortable rooms in an attractive Edwardian house built in 1901.There's a pool and tea garden and rates include breakfast. Reception is at the *Halfway House Hotel* (see below). R750

Halfway House Hotel 229 Du Toitspan Rd, at the corner with Egerton Rd ☏ 053 831 6324, ⓦ halfwayhousehotel.co.za; map p.261. Seven large and airy en-suite rooms around a paved beer garden behind the historic boozer. One has a claw-foot bathtub, and all have large beds and period furnishings. A decent buffet breakfast (extra) is taken at *Annabell's* restaurant (see below). R795

Jungnickel Guesthouse 12 Park Rd ☏ 053 832 5630, ⓦ jungnickel.co.za; map p.261. Opposite Queen's Park in Belgravia, the *Jungnickel's* delightful B&B rooms are either in the main Victorian house dating to 1885, or at two other equally pleasant houses on Park Rd that share a swimming pool and braai area. Excellent cooked breakfasts are included, and packed lunches and suppers can be arranged with the on-site chef. R895

★**Kimberley Anne Hotel** 60 Mac Dougall St, Royldene ☏ 053 492 0004, ⓦ kimberleyanne.co.za; map p.261. This smart, stone and glass, architecturally interesting hotel is in the southern suburbs, 4km from the CBD with easy access to the N12, although a car is useful to get to the sights. With lovely contemporary interiors, the rooms are the most luxurious in town but still well priced. There's a swimming pool, and a restaurant for excellent breakfasts (included) and dinners. R1250

The Kimberley Club and Boutique Hotel 72 Du Toitspan Rd ☏ 053 832 4224, ⓦ kimberleyclub.co.za; map p.261. This local landmark, founded in 1881, offers 17 spacious rooms decorated in colonial style, some with balconies and claw-foot baths. Best of all, staying gives you access to the historic members' bar. Book ahead for weekdays; rates include breakfast. R1230

Milner House 31 Milner St ☏ 053 831 6405, ⓦ milnerhouse.co.za; map p.261. Another Belgravia guesthouse, this one more modest and down to earth than the others, with comfortable rooms decorated in refreshing whites, and a swimming pool set in a shady garden. Breakfast, included in the rates, is taken on the patio on sunny days. R800

Protea Hotel by Marriott Kimberley West Circular Rd ☏ 053 802 8200, ⓦ marriott.com; map p.261. Perched on the edge of the Big Hole, Kimberley's *Protea* is of excellent quality and furnished with all the mod cons. Some effort has been made to make the place look suitably antique, with brick walls and a pool shaped like a cattle trough. Breakfasts are a little pricey, though (R130–195). R1760

Sundowner Lodge 1 Bishops Ave ☏ 053 831 1145, ⓦ sundownerlodgekby.co.za; map p.261. Within shouting distance of the tourist office, this friendly family-run place has a vaguely colonial feel and leafy peaceful gardens, and offers modestly furnished but huge rooms in rows of chalets with verandas. Breakfast included and evening meals on request. R660

EATING

Kimberley has no shortage of chain restaurants and takeaways, and some of these can be found at the city's largest mall: Diamond Pavilion Shopping Mall off the N8 on Kimberley's southern approach.

Angel Heart Coffee Shop 53 Long St ☏ 053 831 5577; map p.261. About 800m south of the entrance to The Big Hole, this bright and friendly café offers speciality coffees, cooked breakfasts, inventive salads or filled croissants for lunch (from R39) and teatime cakes – check out their excellent lemon meringue pie. It also sells locally made crafts including paintings, ceramics and glassware. Mon–Fri 7.30am–4pm, Sat 8am–2pm.

Annabell's Halfway House Hotel, 229 Du Toitspan Rd ☏ 053 831 6324; map p.261. Offers a similar range of pub food to *The Half Bar* next door, but served at padded leather booths in a more elegant atmosphere, with a few pizzas and pasta dishes thrown in (around R85). Also on the property is a branch of the popular seafood chain restaurant *Ocean Basket*. Mon–Sat 6–11pm.

Palette Tea Room William Humphreys Art Gallery, 1 Cullinan Crescent ☏ 072 143 5829; map p.261. Modest little tea room at the back of the gallery serving healthy food like fruit shakes, teas and fresh salads – a nice change from the meaty offerings you find elsewhere. Mon–Fri 8am–4.30pm, Sat 10am–2pm.

Rhodes Grill Restaurant The Kimberley Club, 72 Du Toitspan Rd ☏ 053 832 4224, ⓦ kimberleyclub.co.za; map p.261. One of the town's most sophisticated restaurants, serving a mix of local and international dishes – everything from springbok steak to Thai curry (R70–140), along with a hefty wine list. The *Vitello Café* is a more informal spot for light meals on the front porch of the club. Restaurant daily 6.30–10am, noon–2.30pm & 6–9.30pm; café daily 11am–6pm.

3

DRINKING AND NIGHTLIFE

There's little in the way of nightlife in Kimberley, but there are some atmospheric and historic pubs for a late-night drink. The restaurant and bar at the Flamingo Casino complex just out of town on Phakamile Mabije Rd (☎053 830 2600, ⓦsuninternational.com) both stay open until the early hours, while the casino itself is 24hr.

The Half Bar Halfway House Hotel, 229 Du Toitspan Rd ☎053 831 6324; map p.261. Cecil Rhodes' old refreshment stop is still a favourite for its unpretentious atmosphere, and there's a beer garden out the back that shares tables with the *Ocean Basket* seafood restaurant. Also serves good, cheap British pub food (mains from R60). Mon–Sat 11am–11pm.

★**Occidental Bar** At the Big Hole: Kimberley Mine Museum, West Circular Rd ☎053 831 1296; map p.261. Unlike the other museum buildings in the Old Town, this is a fully functioning bar and restaurant and is known locally as "The Ox" – you can access it without paying museum

entry. There's craft beer on tap, often live music including jazz at Sunday lunchtime, and varied and tasty pub fare like steaks, pork belly or Karoo lamb chops, plus vegetarian choices (mains R70–140). Mon–Thurs noon–10pm, Fri–Sat noon–midnight, Sun noon–3pm.

Star of the West West Circular Rd, cnr North Circular Rd ☎053 832 6463; map p.261. Kimberley's oldest pub (1870) remains a defiantly local dive, complete with eccentric locals propping up the bar. It also receives its fair share of tourists, who enjoy drinking a beer or eating a decent, cheap pub meal in the beer garden (mains from R50). Daily 10am–midnight.

DIRECTORY

Banks Standard Bank, corner of Bultfontein Rd and Long St, and Absa, opposite Standard on Bultfontein Rd, have foreign exchange facilities.
Hospitals The best-equipped is the 24hr Mediclinic, 177 Du Toitspan Rd (☎053 838 1111, emergencies ☎053 838 0573, ⓦmediclinic.co.za).
Pharmacies Clicks Pharmacy, in the Shoprite Shopping

Centre, Bultfontein Rd (☎053 831 2342; Mon–Fri 8am–6pm, Sat 8am–5pm, Sun 9am–2pm); Kimberley Apteek, 16 Market St (☎053 831 3035; Mon–Fri 8am–5.30pm, Sat 8am–1.30pm).
Post office The main post office is on the eastern side of Market Square (☎053 831 5100, Mon–Fri 8am–5pm, Sat 8am–1pm).

Around Kimberley

A few interesting places lie near the R31, which runs from Kimberley to Kuruman: there is some fascinating San rock art at **Wildebeest Kuil**, while the area around Barkly West was where some of the first **diamond camps** sprang up in the 1860s. South of Kimberley along the N12, the mostly unremarkable landscape around Magersfontein was the setting for one of the most dramatic campaigns of the **Anglo-Boer War**, while one of South Africa's newest parks, **Mokala National Park**, is the nearest place to Kimberley to see wildlife in a natural bush environment.

Wildebeest Kuil

Around 15km from Kimberley along the R31 to Barkly West • Mon–Fri 9am–4pm, Sat & Sun by appointment • R35 • ☎053 833 7069 or ☎082 222 4777, ⓦwildebeestkuil.itgo.com • Coming from Kimberley, you can catch one of the frequent minibus taxis to Barkly West and ask to be dropped at the signposted turning – the site is close by

Wildebeest Kuil is a small *koppie* of ancient andesite rock. This is an important rock-art site, unusual in that the images are engraved (rather than painted) and are found on loosely scattered rocks and small boulders, rather than cave walls or overhangs. Dating from the Late Stone Age, there are around 400 images, many depicting animals including elephants, buffalo and antelope. It has been suggested that the imagery may relate to shamanistic visions. A number of boardwalks have been built to allow access without disturbing the engravings. Under South Africa's programme of land restitution, ownership of the site has been given to the local !Xun and Khwe San communities, and trained guides (included in the price) are on hand to show you around. The visitor centre at the base of the *koppie* provides an introductory display and shows a video, and there are some San crafts for sale.

FROM TOP MOSU LODGE, MOKALA NATIONAL PARK (P.271); ORANGE RIVER, NEAR UPINGTON (P.272) >

Magersfontein

32km south of Kimberley via the airport road and after the airport follow the gravel road to Modderrivier, or take the longer but quicker 47km route via the N12 and Modderrivier • Daily 8am–5pm • R20 • Contact McGregor Museum ☎ 053 839 2722, ⓦ museumsnc.co.za

The Anglo-Boer War battlefield at **Magersfontein** provides a poignant reminder of the area's blood-spattered past. This is where Boer forces put trench warfare into effect against British troops, with devastating results (see box below). Signs at the battlefield point the way to the **visitors' centre** and its small **museum**, which has some vivid exhibits, including an audiovisual re-creation of the battle. You can also hike up to various monuments situated on the western end of the line of hills. Out on the battlefield itself – now open veld with springbok grazing and the occasional car throwing up a plume of dust along the dirt road – the lines of **trenches** and other memorials can still be seen, including a pair of granite crosses marking the graves of Scandinavian soldiers who fought on the Boer side.

3 Mokala National Park

Daily May–Aug 6am–5.30pm, Sept–April 6am–7pm • R160 • ☎ 053 204 8000, ⓦ sanparks.org/parks/mokala

Opened in 2007, Mokala became the new home for animals relocated from the former Vaalbos National Park, which was closed after a successful land claim by local people. Mokala is a Setswana name for the gnarly camelthorn tree (*Acacia erioloba*), which dominates the hilly, sandy landscape, and the park covers 48,000 acres in the transition zone between the Karoo and Kalahari biomes. As such there is a good variety of plains game including both black and white rhino, buffalo, tsessebe, roan, eland, sable, giraffe, zebra, and blue and black wildebeest. There are no large cats or other predators, but Mokala's dolerite outcrops and riverine vegetation attract a prolific number of raptors – you'll see plenty of pale chanting goshawks, martial eagles, and lappet-faced, white-backed and Cape vultures. At night, with the Kalahari sky full of stars, keep an eye open for Cape

---

THE KIMBERLEY CAMPAIGN

At the outbreak of the **Anglo-Boer War**, the Boer forces identified diamond-rich Kimberley as an important strategic base and quickly besieged the city, trapping its residents, including Cecil Rhodes, inside. In response, the British deployed an army under **Lord Methuen** to relieve the city. The size of the army and lack of knowledge of the terrain compelled them to advance from the coast along the line of the railway so that a supply of troops, water, food and equipment could be ensured.

Methuen first encountered Boer forces at Belmont; this was followed by further battles at Graspan and the Modder River, from which the Boers made a tactical withdrawal to Magersfontein, a range of hills 30km south of Kimberley. Here the Boer generals, under the leadership of General Cronjé and the tactical direction of **Koos de la Rey**, decided to dig a line of trenches along the bottom of the *koppie* rather than defend the top of the ridge of hills, as was their usual tactic.

In the early hours of December 11, 1899, the British advanced on Magersfontein, fully expecting the enemy to be lined along the ridge. The British were led by the **Highland Regiment**, fresh from campaigns in North Africa and India, and considered the elite of the British army. Just before dawn, as they fanned out into attack formation, four thousand Boers in the trenches just a few hundred metres away opened fire. The use of trenches was, at that point, a rare tactic in modern warfare, and the element of surprise caused devastation in the ranks. Those not killed or wounded in the first volleys were pinned down by snipers for the rest of the day, unable to move in the coverless veld and suffering appallingly under the hot sun. The next day the British withdrew to the Modder River, and the relief of Kimberley was delayed for two months. The defeat was one in a series of three the British suffered within what became known as "Black Week", news of which sent shock waves through the British public, who had been expecting their forces to overrun the "crude farmers" before Christmas.

eagle owls in the camelthorns. Within the park a gravel road (26km) links Lilydale and Mosu and there are several game-viewing circuits. A normal car is sufficient except after heavy rain when a 4WD may be necessary.

ARRIVAL AND INFORMATION
MOKALA NATIONAL PARK

By car The park lies roughly 70km southwest of Kimberley. There are two entrances off the N12 towards Cape Town; the first turn-off is 37km from Kimberley and leads 16km to *Lilydale Rest Camp*; the second turn-off is 57km from Kimberley at the Heuningneskloof Crossing and goes 21km to the main reception and *Mosu Lodge*. The closest fuel station is at Modderrivier on the N12, 36km south of Kimberley.

Information Both *Lilydale* and *Mosu* are 6km from the park entrance gates. There are no shops, but there is a restaurant at *Mosu Lodge* (daily 8–10am, noon–2pm & 6–9pm). Guided morning, sunset and night drives can be arranged at Mosu (R240).

ACCOMMODATION

Reservations for all accommodation should be made through South African National Parks in Pretoria (☎012 428 9111, ⓦsanparks.org). For late bookings (under 48 hours) and camping contact the park direct (☎053 204 8000). Wheelchairs are accommodated in all the camps.

3

Lilydale Rest Camp The more rustic option in the park, with twelve self-catering thatched chalets, some with mattresses in the loft for children, and a shared swimming pool, in a picturesque location on the Riet River in the north of the park, which will particularly appeal to birders. R790
Mosu Lodge Comfortable, smart and well designed, Mokala's main camp has low stone and thatched bungalows; some are family-sized with kitchens, while others are two-person units with fridge and kettle, and facilities include a pool, communal lounge with fireplace, and a restaurant and bar. R750
Motswedi Camp Site About 10km from *Mosu* in the south of the park, *Motswedi* offers attractive camping sites, arranged in a half-moon around a water hole and each with its own ablution and cooking facilities. You can eat at the *Mosu* restaurant but must pre-book dinner. Camping R400

The Kalahari

While the Northern Cape has no shortage of dry, endless expanses, the most emotive by far is the **Kalahari**. The very name holds a resonance of sun-bleached, faraway spaces and the unknown vastness of the African interior, both harsh and magical. The name derives from the word *kgalagadi* (saltpans, or thirsty land), and describes the semi-desert stretching north from the Orange River to the Okavango Delta in northern Botswana, west into Namibia and east until the bushveld begins to dominate in the catchment areas of the Vaal and Limpopo rivers.

The Kalahari in the Northern Cape is characterized by surprisingly high, thinly vegetated red or orange sand dunes, scored with dry riverbeds and large, shimmering

KALAHARI TOURS

To save yourself driving the vast distances of the Kalahari region – and to take advantage of specialized knowledge of the area's distinctive flora, fauna, landscapes and climate – it's worth considering joining a **guided tour**. The following is a list of reliable, knowledgeable and well-organized tour operators offering a range of Kalahari-based tours, which incorporate a visit to **Augrabies Falls** and the **Kgalagadi Transfrontier Park**, although customized itineraries are also available. Prices start at around R5000–7500 per person for a three-night camping safari depending on numbers and what's included. These operators can also organize tours to the Ai-Ais Richtersveld Transfrontier Park (see p.291).

Kalahari Outventures Augrabies Village ☎082 476 8213, ⓦkalahari-adventures.co.za.
Kalahari Safaris Upington ☎087 233 5067, ⓦkalaharisafaris.co.za.

Kalahari Tours & Travel Upington ☎054 338 0375, ⓦkalahari-tours.co.za.
Tata Ma Tata Tours Upington ☎082 535 8830, ⓦtatamatata.co.za.

saltpans. Although this is, strictly speaking, semi-desert, daytime temperatures are searingly hot in summer and nights are numbingly cold in winter. North of the Orange, South Africa's longest river, the land is populated by tough, hard-working farmers and communities largely descended from the indigenous San hunter-gatherers and nomadic Khoi herders. For many land-users, there is an increasing realization that **eco-tourism** may be the only viable option on huge areas where stock farming and hunting provide at best a marginal living.

Upington, the main town in the area, stands on the northern bank of the Orange at the heart of an irrigated corridor of intensive wheat, cotton and, most prominently, grape farms. At the far end of the farming belt, about an hour's drive west, the Orange picks up speed, frothing and tumbling into a huge granite gorge at **Augrabies Falls**, the focus of one of the area's two national parks. The other is the undoubted highlight of this area, the **Kgalagadi Transfrontier Park**. A vast desert sanctuary rich in game and boasting a magnificent landscape of red dunes and hardy vegetation, it's well worth the long trek to get there.

Upington

As an inevitable focus of trips to Kgalagadi and Augrabies, as well as those to and from Namaqualand and Namibia, **UPINGTON**, just over 400km west of Kimberley, is a good place to stop for supplies, organize a park tour or onward accommodation, or simply draw breath. Situated on the banks of the Orange River (also called the Gariep River), central Upington is compact and easy to get around, with most of the activity on the three main streets running parallel to the riverbank. It can be a mellow spot, with plenty of greenery softening the arid landscape that surrounds it – a result of the irrigation that allows Upington to be surrounded by vineyards. However, the savage summer temperatures mean you probably won't want to linger too long.

Kalahari Oranje Museum

4 Schröder St • Mon–Fri 9am–12.30pm & 2–5pm, Sat 9am–noon • Free • ☎ 054 332 6064

The **Kalahari Oranje Museum** is housed in a church and mission station that was erected by the Reverend Schröder in 1875 – Upington was founded in 1884, nine years after Schröder started his mission. The domestic items and historic photographs on display offer a good insight into the resourcefulness and hardships of the first settlers in the largely inhospitable expanses of semi-desert that covers most of the Northern Cape. Outside is a life-sized bronze statue of a donkey working a horse mill; it symbolizes the contribution made by donkeys during the irrigation of the lower Orange River Valley in the 1920s and 1930s.

The Orange River

Sakkie se Arkie cruise Sept–April daily 5.30pm, by prior arrangement in winter if the river is sufficiently high • R100 • ☎ 082 564 5447 or ☎ 082 575 7285, ⓦ arkie.co.za

Upington's obvious highlight is the **Orange River**, but unless you're staying at one of the riverside guesthouses (see p.274), it tends to be hidden from view. The terrace behind *O'Hagan's* on Schröder Street (see p.275) is a good place to admire the river and its swans. Better still, take a one-and-a-half-hour sunset cruise with Sakkie se Arkie on its two-tier barge; it departs from the riverbank at the east end of Park Street.

The vineyards

Upington's **vineyards** produce mostly table grapes, raisins and sultanas (important export crops for the region), though some wine is also made. Wine tasting is offered at the smart Orange River Cellars Wine Tasting Centre (Mon–Fri 10am–6pm, Sat 10am–3pm; ☎ 054 495 0040, ⓦ orangeriverwines.com) at 138 Schröder Street or the

N14, about 3km from the centre as it heads northeast out of town. Tastings of five (R25) or seven (R35) white, red and dessert wines are accompanied by platters of olives, biltong or cheese, and bottles are for sale.

ARRIVAL AND DEPARTURE
UPINGTON

By plane Upington Airport is 7km north of town off the N10 towards the Kgalagadi Transfrontier Park (☎054 337 7900, ⓦairports.co.za). South African Airways (☎054 332 2161, ⓦflysaa.com), based at the airport, flies from here to Cape Town and Johannesburg. There is no public transport from the airport but taxis meet the flights; getting to the airport, pre-book a taxi with Eben Oranje Taxis (☎054 339 0576). Most of the major car rental agencies are based at the airport, including Avis (☎054 332 4746/7, ⓦavis.co.za),

First Car Rental (☎051 430 0390, ⓦfirstcarrental.co.za) and Europcar (☎054 332 2383, ⓦeuropcar.com).
Destinations: Cape Town (daily except Sat; 1hr 20min); Johannesburg (2–3 daily; 1hr 30min).
By bus The only major bus company operating from Upington is Intercape (☎054 332 6091, ⓦintercape.co.za); buses arrive at and depart from their office on Lutz St. If you're likely to arrive at night, it's best to get your accommodation to pick you up or arrange for a taxi to meet you off the bus.

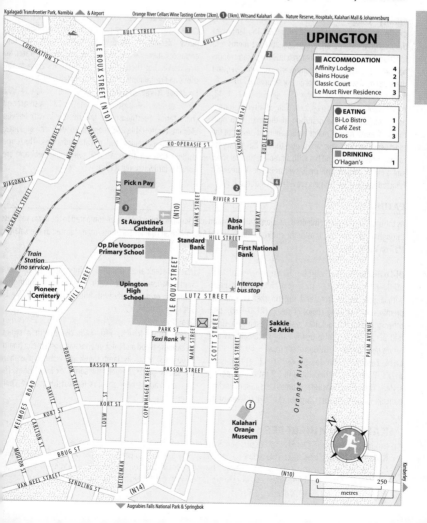

Destinations: Bloemfontein (daily; 9hr 15min); Cape Town (daily; 13hr 25min); Johannesburg (daily; 11hr 30min); Kimberley (daily; 6hr 45min); Kuruman (daily; 3hr 25min); Springbok (daily; 4hr 15min); Windhoek, Namibia (daily; 13hr 15min).

By minibus taxi Minibus taxis use the rank on Park St, between Le Roux and Mark sts. There are regular services throughout the day (fewer on Sun) to Kimberley, Kuruman and Springbok.

Tourist information Tourist information can be found at the Kalahari Oranje Museum (see p.272; Mon–Fri 9am–12.30pm & 2–5pm, Sat 9am–noon; ☎054 332 6064), which provides maps and brochures, an accommodation list and details of local tours. For regional information, including details of Augrabies and Kgalagadi, there are a number of helpful websites including ⓦupington.co.za and ⓦgreenkalahari.co.za.

ACCOMMODATION

Upington is often used as a staging post on the way to or from the Kgalagadi Transfrontier Park (265km). Reservations are advisable at all times to ensure that someone is there when you arrive, especially if you leave the park late.

Affinity Lodge 4 Budler St ☎054 331 2101, ⓦaffinityguesthouse.co.za; map p.273. The largest of the riverfront choices, offering reasonable a/c rooms in a functional whitewashed two-storey building. Many rooms have access to a common balcony overlooking the river, and there's a small swimming pool and braai area. R720

Bains House 80 Schröder St ☎054 332 1333, ⓦbainshouse.com; map p.273. Named after its former owner Major Bain, the grandson of the man who built many of South Africa's major mountain road passes in the nineteenth century, this smart guesthouse has six stylish rooms, a cosy lounge and bar with a fireplace and veranda, and a pretty garden with small swimming pool. Breakfast is included and good suppers provided on request. R680

Classic Court 26 Josling St ☎054 332 6142; ⓦclassiccourt.co.za; map p.273. Reliable B&B with nicely decorated, good-value rooms with separate entrances; there's also a kitchen if you want to self-cater. No river views, but there is a tiny pool and it's close to the shops and restaurants in the Kalahari Mall. R900

Le Must River Residence 14 Budler St ☎054 332 3971, ⓦlemustupington.com; map p.273. A smart and characterful guesthouse on the riverbank with eleven elegant, comfortable B&B rooms decorated with antiques, some with balconies and private entrances. The large gardens have an attractive oval swimming pool and are good for birdwatching. R1700

EATING

As the only large town for hundreds of kilometres, Upington may seem like culinary heaven compared to the *dorps* you pass through to get here, but mostly the choice is still the usual South African chain restaurants, many located in the Kalahari Mall on Van Reebek St.

Bi-Lo Bistro 9 Green Point Rd, 3km northwest of town off the N14 ☎054 338 0616; map p.273. A curious set-up with a pub, liquor store and supermarket also on the premises. There's a big choice of steaks (R120–180), plus other grilled food, vegetarian pastas and even sushi (from R40 per portion); it also opens early for breakfasts and serves good coffee. Daily 8am–10pm.

Café Zest 49 Schröder St ☎054 332 1413; map p.273. Pleasant café decorated in a light contemporary style. The food includes breakfasts, sandwiches, pancakes, cakes and tarts, and lunches like chicken pasta

(R50) or steak and sides (R95). Dinner specials take on South African flavour, with the likes of Springbok carpaccio or pork belly with biltong pear salad. Mon–Sat 9am–10pm.

Dros Pick n Pay Centre, Hill St ☎054 331 3331; map p.273. Family-friendly restaurant chain with a typical steakhouse wood and brick interior and a grill menu (mains R100–165) of steaks, lamb shank and eisbein, plus there are salads, pizzas, burgers and some Tex-Mex dishes. The bar has draught beer and TVs for watching sport. Daily 9am–11pm.

KALAHARI KUIERFEES

In late September, *Die Eiland Resort*, across the river from Upington, plays host to the **Kalahari Kuierfees** (last Thursday to Saturday; ⓦkalahari-kuierfees.co.za). A chance for the local Afrikaner community to come together to celebrate their culture, language and food, the event combines flea markets and craft stalls with a triathlon, arts, live Afrikaner music and dance.

DRINKING

O'Hagan's 20 Schröder St ☎ 054 331 2005; map p.273. With a lovely terrace at the back overlooking the river, this Irish-themed pub has Guinness and other beers on tap. The meat-heavy menu offers ostrich and springbok, but there's also a choice of lighter pastas and vegetarian meals (mains R70–150). Mon–Sat 8am–midnight, Sun 9am–11pm.

Kuruman

The Eye Daily sunrise–sunset • R11

Around 265km east of Upington, lying near the border between the Northern Cape and North West Province, the historic settlement of **KURUMAN** is an important landmark along the main N14 route to and from Gauteng. The settlement grew up around **The Eye** ("Die Oog" in Afrikaans), a natural spring which, since time immemorial and through drought and flood, has consistently delivered twenty million litres a day of crystal-clear water. The Eye was the focal point for a rather unsettled Tswana clan called the **Batlhaping**, whose chief, Mothibi, first invited missionaries to live among his people in the early nineteenth century. It was a decision that led to the building of the famous **Mission Station** by Robert Moffat, and the establishment of Kuruman as the "Gateway to the Interior" of darkest Africa.

These days, Kuruman's centre is pretty scruffy, dominated by cut-price chain stores, faceless supermarkets and litter-strewn minibus-taxi ranks. You can visit **The Eye**, next to the tourist office, though there isn't much to look at: a moss-covered slab of rock dribbling water and a lily-covered pond surrounded by a high green fence, although there are pleasant picnic benches under the willow trees. More interesting is the Moffat Mission Station, some 5km north of town (see below).

Moffat Mission Station

About 5km north of town, on Moffat Lane, follow the sign on the R31 • Daily 8am–5pm • R10; if no one is there drop fee into the "trust box" • ☎ 053 712 1352

Kuruman's main attraction is **Moffat Mission Station**, where a large, often gruff, energetic Scot, Robert Moffat, and his demure but equally determined wife, Mary, established a mission (see box below) where they lived for fifty years. During this time they produced and printed the first Tswana Bible, and saw their eldest daughter, also called Mary, married to the missionary/explorer David Livingstone. Charmingly overgrown and shaded by tall acacia and camelthorn trees, the atmospheric old village looks much as it did in the nineteenth century. It includes the Moffat homestead, with the original printing press on display, along with a collection of furniture, portraits and

---

THE MOFFATS AND THEIR MISSION

Robert and Mary Moffat, envoys of the London Missionary Society, were married at St George's Church (now Cathedral) in Cape Town in 1819 and arrived in the Northern Cape region in 1820. They initially established a station in Namaqualand, then at New Lattakoo, about 14km from Kuruman, and then in 1825 established their mission at Kuruman – as a former market gardener, Moffat soon saw the advantages of irrigation from the flow of The Eye.

Moffat didn't clock up too many converts – by the time he had built his eight-hundred-seater "Cathedral of the Kalahari" in 1838, he had just nine – but the challenge of preaching and establishing a school inspired him not only to learn the local language, which he did by living for a period in a remote Tswana village, but also to attempt the daunting task of **translating the Bible** into Tswana, which he then published on an imported iron printing press. The mission at Kuruman, meanwhile, carried on until the passing of the Group Areas Act of 1950, which brought about the end of the school and the church as a functioning place of (multiracial) worship.

3

a wagon used by the missionaries. In front of the homestead is the furrow that Robert dug to bring water from The Eye.

Witsand Kalahari Nature Reserve

Halfway between Kuruman and Upington, reached by heading south off the N14 from Olifantshoek • Daily 8am–6pm • R60, picnic/braai sites R100 • ☏ 083 234 7573, ⟨w⟩ witsandkalahari.co.za • For organized trips, contact Kalahari Safaris in Upington (see box, p.271)

The **Witsand Nature Reserve** is famous for its pristine white "roaring" dunes: in summer a curious rumbling sound occurs when the dunes, 9km in extent, are disturbed, possibly by ground water. While the reserve isn't exactly teeming with wildlife, it does have an abundance of desert bird species, and with patience you may also be rewarded by springbok, duikers and ground squirrels. It's also possible to stay here (see below).

ARRIVAL AND INFORMATION
KURUMAN

By bus The daily Intercape bus stops at the Kalahari Tourism Centre on Main St (below) (reservations ☏ 021 380 4400, ⟨w⟩ intercape.co.za); Arrange in advance for your accommodation owners to pick you up.
Destinations: Johannesburg (daily; 7hr 40min); Upington (daily; 3hr 25min).

By minibus taxi Minibus taxis are the only option to get to Kimberley (2–3 daily; 2hr); they stop at the rank on Voortrekker St, just south of Main St. Minibus taxis for

Upington (1–2 daily; 2hr 45min) leave from the sprawling taxi rank on Tsening Rd north of Main St – note, however, that services on all routes are reduced on Saturday and often nonexistent on Sunday.

Tourist information The Kalahari Tourism Centre is on Main St on the corner of Livingstone St just west of The Eye (Mon–Fri 9.30am–1pm & 2–4pm; ☏ 053 712 1001, ⟨w⟩ visitkuruman.co.za).

ACCOMMODATION

Die Mynhuis Guesthouse 10 Botha St ☏ 053 712 2546, ⟨w⟩ diemynhuis.co.za. Six rooms surrounding a garden, each with its own entrance and with the decor themed to the mine after which it is named. There are also two larger family suites, and meals are available on request. **R800**

Oude Werf Lodge 12 Winkel St ☏ 053 712 0117, ⟨w⟩ oudewerf-lodge.co.za. Modern lodge about 1.5km north of the centre offering budget and double rooms with bushman-themed decor and motel-style parking outside. There's a swimming pool, breakfast is included and the friendly pub-restaurant is popular with locals. **R760**

Red Sands Country Lodge In the Kuruman Hills, 15km along the N14 towards Upington ☏ 053 712 0033, ⟨w⟩ redsands.co.za. A pleasant option outside weekends and school holidays (when it gets very busy).

Besides good camping facilities (with some private sites having their own bathrooms; R150), there are characterful thatched stone rondavels and comfy self-catering chalets sleeping up to four. There's also a good German/South African restaurant for breakfast and dinner and a generous buffet lunch on Sunday, and the swimming pool has its own bar. Camping **R95**, rondavels and chalets **R1090**

Witsand Kalahari Nature Reserve Off the N14 between Kuruman and Upington ☏ 083 234 7573, ⟨w⟩ witsandkalahari.co.za. There are some superb self-catering a/c chalets, each sleeping up to six, and a campsite. The kiosk on-site stocks some dried and tinned food, alongside non-alcoholic drinks; bring everything else with you. Dune boards and bikes can be rented and there are numerous hiking trails. Camping **R110** chalets **R1340**

EATING

Eating out is limited in Kuruman, though there are branches of Spur (a franchise steakhouse), Wimpy and KFC on Main Street, and the Spar and Pick n Pay supermarkets, both of which are also on Main Street, have takeaway counters.

Cappello 22 Main St ☏ 053 712 3956. One of the better South African chain restaurants, with a fairly long menu and a decent choice of wine and beers on tap. Light meals include sticky chicken wings and burgers, or if you're really

hungry go for the large T-bone steaks or lamb shank (R45–130). The bar may stay open late if there is the demand. Daily 9am–10.30pm.

DIRECTORY

Hospital On Main St, 1km east of the tourist office (☏ 053 712 8100).

Post office On Church St, two blocks north and one block west of the tourist office.

Tswalu Kalahari Reserve

On the R31, 100km northwest of Kuruman · ☎ 053 781 9311, reservations ☎ 011 274 2299, ⓦ tswalu.com

The upmarket Tswalu Kalahari Reserve centres on an impeccably stylish game lodge not far from the tiny settlement of Sonstraal, northwest of Kuruman. Tucked under the 1500m Korannaberg Mountains, this is the largest privately owned game reserve in South Africa. Some R50 million was spent bringing over nine thousand head of game to this desert setting, including some highly endangered desert black rhino, sable, roan antelope and cheetah. The reserve is only accessible to overnight guests, and the price for accommodation (from R26,000 per couple) includes game drives, horseriding and full board.

Wonderwerk (Miracle) Cave

Along the R31 towards Danielskuil, 43km south of Kuruman · Mon–Fri 8am–5pm · R25 · ☎ 082 222 4777

This intriguing limestone **cave**, burrowing 139m into the hillside, is thought to be one of the longest-inhabited caves on Earth. A major archeological site, it has yielded important evidence of human occupation in various eras dating back over 800,000 years, including fossils, animal teeth, San rock paintings and engraved stones. A number of these are on display in the McGregor Museum in Kimberley. There is a small visitors' centre on the site and the cave is accessed via a walkway that is wheelchair-friendly. Occasionally you will find archeologists working in the cave, but if there's no one around, you'll have to ask at the farm for the gate to be unlocked.

Kgalagadi Transfrontier Park

Opening hours vary from month to month, roughly sunrise–sunset · R328 · ☎ 054 561 2000, ⓦ sanparks.org/parks/kgalagadi

Africa's first official transfrontier park, named **KGALAGADI TRANSFRONTIER PARK** after the ancient San name for the Kalahari (it's pronounced "kha-la-khadi", the kh as in the Scottish "loch"), is the result of the formalization of a long-standing joint management arrangement between South Africa's Kalahari-Gemsbok National Park and Botswana's neighbouring Gemsbok National Park. The local **Mier** and **San** communities have agreed that their land be jointly managed by themselves and South African National Parks, so that the land remains part of the wildlife sanctuary. The park is run as a single ecological unit and gate receipts are shared, although the tourist facilities in South Africa and Botswana are still run autonomously.

KGALAGADI WILDLIFE

The open landscape of the Kgalagadi Transfrontier Park offers almost unobstructed game viewing and it is especially renowned for predator watching, with excellent chances of seeing cheetah, leopard, brown and spotted hyena and the black-maned Kalahari lion. These commonly have much darker manes than those found in the bushveld, and studies have shown their behavioural and eating patterns to be distinctively well adapted to the semi-desert conditions here. The park is also known for the seasonal movement of large herbivores such as blue wildebeest, springbok, eland and red hartebeest, but the star of the Kgalagadi show is the gemsbok, a beautiful, large, lolloping antelope with classically straight, V-shaped horns, which is frequently spotted galloping across the plains and dunes. Birdwatchers will be well rewarded with some extravagant **birdlife** including vultures, eagles, the dramatic bateleur (an eagle which takes its name from the French word for an acrobatic tumbler), bustards and ostrich. There's also a good chance you'll see family groups of **meerkat**, a relative of the mongoose and squirrel, striking their characteristic pose of standing tall on their hind legs while looking round nervously for signs of danger.

3

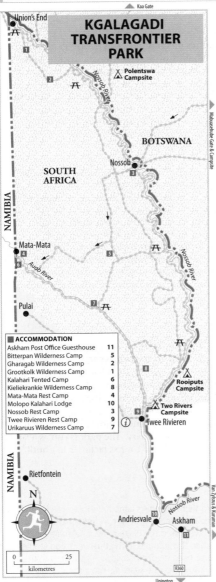

KGALAGADI TRANSFRONTIER PARK

Kaa Gate

Union's End

Polentswa Campsite

Nossob River

BOTSWANA

Nossob

SOUTH AFRICA

NAMIBIA

Mabuasehube Gate & Campsite

Mata-Mata

Auob River

Pulai

Nossob River

Rooiputs Campsite

Two Rivers Campsite

Twee Rivieren

NAMIBIA

Rietfontein

N

Andriesvale   Askham

Nossob River

Van Zylsrus & Kuruman

R360

Upington

0   25
kilometres

■ ACCOMMODATION
Askham Post Office Guesthouse   11
Bitterpan Wilderness Camp   5
Gharagab Wilderness Camp   2
Grootkolk Wilderness Camp   1
Kalahari Tented Camp   6
Kieliekrankie Wilderness Camp   8
Mata-Mata Rest Camp   4
Molopo Kalahari Lodge   10
Nossob Rest Camp   3
Twee Rivieren Rest Camp   9
Urikaruus Wilderness Camp   7

Kgalagadi covers an area of over 37,000 square kilometres – nearly twice the size of Kruger National Park – and although the South African side is by far the smaller section, it still encompasses a vast 9500 square kilometres. Be prepared to clock up some serious mileage here; the game drive between the park entrance at **Twee Rivieren** and the **Mata-Mata restcamp** on the western edge of the reserve takes about two-and-a-half hours. The park is bounded on its western side by the Namibian border, and to the south by the dry Auob River and a strip of land running parallel to this. The national boundary with **Botswana** follows the dry Nossob river bed, as does one of the few roads in the park. No fences exist along this line, allowing game undisturbed access to the ancient migration routes so necessary for survival in the desert. The main roads follow the river beds, and this is where the game – and their predators – are most likely to be. Water flows very rarely in the two rivers, but frequent boreholes have been drilled to provide water for the game. Larger trees such as camelthorn and witgat (shepherd's tree) offer a degree of shade and nutrition, and desert-adapted plants, including types of melon and cucumber, are a source of moisture for the animals.

Much of the park is dominated by **red sand dunes**, which, when seen from the air, lie strung out in long, wave-like bands. From a car, the perspective is different, as you are in the valley of the river bed, but this doesn't prevent the path from offering one of the finest **game-viewing** experiences in South Africa – not only for the animals, but for the setting, with its broad landscapes, the crisp light of morning and the huge open skies. The clear viewing and wonderful light are ideal for **photography**, as shown by the exhibition at the visitor centre at *Twee Rivieren Rest Camp*.

While many visitors only encounter the South African section, where most of the established tourist facilities are found, three-quarters of the park lies within Botswana territory. If you are in a 4WD, the option is to go over from *Twee Rivieren* – Botswana park fees are P20, plus P4 per vehicle (the Botswana Pula is worth about R1.30). Immigration and customs facilities allow travellers to enter the park in one country and

---

WHEN TO VISIT THE KGALAGADI TRANSFRONTIER PARK

In a place where ground temperatures in the **summer** can reach a scorching 70°C, **timing your visit** is everything. The best period to be in the park is **between March and May**, when there is still some greenery left from the summer rain and the sun is not so intense. **Winter** can be very cold at night, while **spring**, though dry, is a pleasant time before the searing heat of summer.

---

depart in the other. You can also enter for a few days and stay at one of the campsites without having to go through border procedures, just as long as you return to South Africa through *Twee Rivieren*.

ARRIVAL AND DEPARTURE

By car Coming from Gauteng, the shorter but slower approach to the park is by taking the R31 off the N14 at Kuruman, which is surfaced only as far as Hotazel – the remainder is a long, bleak dirt road which should only be tackled in a sturdy vehicle, as beyond Vanzylsrus it is badly corrugated. Alternatively, you can drive further along the N14 to Upington and turn onto the R360, which is surfaced along the 265km to the park entrance at *Twee Rivieren*. You can also access the park from Namibia through the Mata-Mata Gate and from Botswana through the Two Rivers, Mabuasehube and Kaa gates. Visitors wanting to exit the park via a different country from the one they entered from should note that all immigration controls must be done at *Twee Rivieren* and that a two-night stay in the park is compulsory. Whichever way you get there, the journey is a

KGALAGADI TRANSFRONTIER PARK

hot and weary one, but you'll see plenty of the classic red dunes of the Kalahari on the way. Fuel is available at Andriesvale and Askham on the R360 before *Twee Rivieren*, and at *Twee Rivieren*, *Nossob* and *Mata-Mata* camps, but note it is more expensive within the park than at the filling stations outside.

By plane and tour The two alternatives to making the long drive to Kgalagadi from Gauteng or the Cape are to go on a package tour (see box, p.271), or to fly to Upington Airport from where you can pick up a rental car (see p.273); there are also companies in Upington that rent out 4WDs with camping equipment, which can be an affordable way to explore the park; try Desert 4x4 Rental (☎ 082 334 2243, ⓦ desert4x4.co.za) or Kalahari 4x4 Hire (☎ 054 332 3099/8, ⓦ kalahari4x4hire.co.za).

INFORMATION AND ACTIVITIES

Tourist information *Twee Rivieren* is the largest restcamp and administrative headquarters and has the main reception, plus a shop, fuel, an ATM, immigration facilities, restaurant and swimming pool. It is the only restcamp with cell-phone reception. The visitors' centre (☎ 054 561 2000) has exhibitions and slide shows that are worth checking out.

Activities The focus in Kgalagadi Transfrontier Park is on self-guided game drives, but night and day game drives and day walks can be booked on arrival at *Twee Rivieren*, *Mata-Mata* and *Nossob* restcamps. Look out for details posted at the restcamp offices about what's happening on any given day. Rates are R240–400 per person depending on numbers and duration.

GETTING AROUND

By car The park roads are gravel. While you can travel in a normal car, bear in mind that the higher the clearance the better – a car packed with four adults might struggle. It's also a good idea to reduce the pressure in your tyres by about half a bar before setting off and to play the steering to maintain traction. You might find it's often easier to drive either side of the

"road" along tracks left by other drivers. If you're in a rental car, check the small print as it may exclude cover for damaged wheels, undercarriage and paintwork. In the event of a breakdown you just have to sit it out until someone else passes; a park vehicle patrols most roads each day. Entry to the Botswana side of Kgalagadi is only allowed by 4WD.

ACCOMMODATION

INSIDE THE PARK

It's vital to book park accommodation, even for campsites, as early as you can through South African National Parks in Pretoria (☎ 012 428 9111, ⓦ sanparks.org). The park has a choice of cottages and camping in two broad types of site: fenced restcamps at *Twee*

Rivieren, *Mata-Mata* and *Nossob*, which have electricity (even in the campsites) and creature comforts such as kitchens, fans or air conditioning, braai areas and shops, with some of the units wheelchair accessible; and six far more basic and remote unfenced wilderness camps, for which you need to be completely self-sufficient. It's worth staying at least a night at a park restcamp away from *Twee Rivieren* to taste the raw flavour of the desert. If time is limited, an excursion to *Mata-Mata* makes sense, but *Nossob*, although further off, is better for atmosphere and game viewing: as well as hearing the lions roaring at night, you'll probably have your best chance of seeing them in this area. The roads to *Nossob* and *Mata-Mata* follow river beds, and so are good for spotting game. On the Botswana side, facilities are limited but include campsites run by the Botswana Department of Wildlife and National Parks at *Mabuasehube*, *Two Rivers*, *Rooiputs* and *Polentswa*; visitors need to be completely self-sufficient. For reservations, contact the Botswana Department of Wildlife and National Parks office in Gaborone (☎09 267 318 0774, ✉dwnp@gov.bw). There are also several campsites in the north and east of the Botswana section run by private operators.

Bitterpan Wilderness Camp Map p.278. A peaceful spot near the centre of the park on a 4WD trail between *Nossob* and *Mata-Mata* (4WD access only), with four reed cabins perched on the edge of a saltpan. R1745

Gharagab Wilderness Camp Map p.278. Four log cabins in an unfenced area in the far north, a 4hr drive from *Nossob* (access by 4WD), with elevated views onto a landscape of dunes and thornveld savanna. R1745

Grootkolk Wilderness Camp Map p.278. This unfenced desert camp near Union's End at the very northern tip of the South African section is in prime predator country; its four chalets come fully equipped with cooking supplies, linen and fans, and they're usually solidly booked months in advance. R1745

★Kalahari Tented Camp Map p.278. Guarded by an armed guide, this unfenced site has comfortable, fully equipped, self-catering tents built of sandbags and canvas (including one luxurious "honeymoon tent"), all decorated in desert tones with views over the Auob River. R1600

Kieliekrankie Wilderness Camp Map p.278. This is the closest wilderness camp to *Twee Rivieren* (41km), and is accessible to ordinary vehicles; it offers four unfenced cabins sunk into a red sand dune, providing lovely panoramic views of the desert. R1745

Mata-Mata Rest Camp Map p.278. This fenced restcamp is 120km northwest of *Twee Rivieren* on the Namibian border at the end of the road that follows the course of the Auob River. There are fully equipped family cottages (sleeping six), comfortable two-person chalets and a campsite. Other amenities include a water hole lit up at night and a shop. Camping R305, chalets R1015

Nossob Rest Camp Map p.278. On the Botswana border, 160km north of *Twee Rivieren* along the Nossob River Rd, this is the most remote of the three fenced restcamps, and a 4WD is advisable. It has fifteen simple chalets, better family-size guesthouses (sleeping four), a cottage and campsites (the premium one has sites with their own bathrooms and kitchens; R600 for two people). There's also a supply shop, fuel, plus a predator information centre (the place is famed for nocturnal visits by lions). Camping R305, chalets R1065

Twee Rivieren Rest Camp Map p.278. The most developed of the three fenced restcamps, right by the entrance, offering over thirty pleasant self-catering chalets with thatched roofs and nice patio areas, a sizeable campsite (with or without electricity), a mediocre restaurant, a pool, fuel, and a shop selling souvenirs and simple foodstuffs. Camping R265, chalets R1120

Urikaruus Wilderness Camp Map p.278. Roughly halfway between *Twee Rivieren* and *Mata-Mata*, with an attractive setting among camelthorn trees overlooking the Auob River; the four two-person cabins, all equipped with solar power and kitchen supplies, are built on stilts and connected by a plank walkway. R1745

OUTSIDE THE PARK

On the approach road to Kgalagadi there are a couple of places to stay. However, with morning being the best time for game viewing, staying en route to the park isn't really an option if you're on a tight schedule.

Askham Post Office Guesthouse 52 Kameeldoring Ave, Askham, 72km from Twee Rivieren ☎054 511 0025 or ☎082 494 4520, ✉askhamk@mweb.co.za; map p.278. This B&B offers three spacious and neat en-suite rooms and a self-catering flat for four on the site of the old post office. There's also a small coffee shop and craft shop; overnight guests can pre-order evening meals. R600

Molopo Kalahari Lodge 55km from Twee Rivieren, in Andriesvale ☎054 511 0008, ⓦmolopolodge .co.za; map p.278. A smart, well-run place with over fifty comfortable chalets around a pool, as well as luxury bush tents, campsites, a bar and a decent restaurant. It also has a filling station and a small shop selling drinks, ice and meat for braais, and you can stop for coffee when driving towards the park. All rates (even camping) include a simple tea/coffee and toast breakfast. Camping R300, chalets R600

Augrabies Falls National Park

Daily 7am–6.30pm • R192 • ☎054 452 9200, ⓦ sanparks.org/parks/augrabies

One of the undoubted highlights of any trip to the Northern Cape is **AUGRABIES FALLS NATIONAL PARK**, 120km west of Upington. Roaring out of the barren semi-desert, sending great plumes of spray up above the brown horizon, the falls – still known by their Khoikhoi name, *Aukoerabis*, "the place of great noise" – are the most spectacular moment in the two-thousand-kilometre progress of the Orange River. At peak flow, the huge volume of water plunging through the narrow channel actually compares with the more docile periods at Victoria Falls and Niagara, although Augrabies lacks both the height and the soul-wrenching grandeur of its larger rivals. But in its eerie desert setting under an azure evening sky, the falls provide a moving and absorbing experience. The sides of the canyon are shaped like a smooth parabola, and there are many tales of curious visitors venturing too far to peer at the falls and sliding helplessly into the seething maelstrom below. Despite the odd miraculous survival, several dozen people have died here since the national park was created in 1966.

Visiting the park

The **falls** are viewed from behind a large fence, while a boardwalk allows wheelchair access to the viewpoint. To see more of the **gorge**, walk the short distance to **Arrow Point** or drive on the link roads round to Ararat or Echo Corner. The atmosphere is at its best near **sunset**, when the sun shines straight into the west-facing part of the gorge.

The fairly inhospitable **northern section** of the park covers 184 square kilometres on both sides of the river. The land is dry and harsh, with sparse plants typical of arid areas, such as kokerboom (quiver tree), camelthorn and Namaqua fig. The landscape is punctuated by various striking rock formations, notably **Moon Rock**, a huge dome of smooth, flaking granite rising out of the flat plains. If you drive on the (unsurfaced) roads in the park you'll probably spot some of the resident fauna – including eland, klipspringer and springbok – while you're likely to see dassie, mongoose and lizards around the falls and the camp.

The **best time to visit** Augrabies is from March to May, when the temperatures are slightly cooler and the river is at its maximum flow after summer rainfall up in the Lesotho catchment areas. With your own transport, the falls are easily visited as a day-trip from Upington, although there's plenty of reasonable accommodation both in the park itself and nearby.

Keimoes and Kakamas

The route to Augrabies from Upington is west along the N14 via Keimoes and Kakamas, and follows the Orange River and its rich fringe of vineyards, orchards and alfalfa fields. An interesting place to break your drive, 30km from Upington, is the **Bezalel Wine & Brandy Estate** (Mon–Fri 8.30am–5pm, Sat Mon–Fri 8.30am–1pm, tastings R15, ☎054 491 1325, ⊛bezalel.co.za). Several alcohol-based products are made here, including a pot-stilled brandy, chocolate and coffee liqueurs and traditional mampoer and witblits spirits, all of which can be bought at the estate's tasting room. The shop/café sells locally made jams, rusks and biscuits, and you can get a cup of coffee and sit on the *stoep*. Phone ahead if you'd like a free cellar tour.

Forty kilometres from Upington, **Keimoes** is a pretty village with an 1889 Dutch Reformed Mission Church and an old restored waterwheel that pumps water from the Orange River to farms in the area. It marks the junction with the R27, which first crosses over the Orange River on a scenic bridge 2km south of the village and then heads to Calvinia and Vanrhynsdorp and ultimately the N7 to Cape Town. This road is fairly desolate but is very scenic and in good condition and is a quicker route to and from the south than via Springbok.

KAKAMAS is the last town before Augrabies Falls National Park and a handy base if you're driving. Eighty kilometres southwest of Upington, the settlement was founded in 1897 by the Dutch Reformed Church as a colony for livestock farmers rendered destitute by a prolonged drought; each farmer contributed manpower for a system of

ACTIVITIES AT AUGRABIES FALLS

The circular **Dassie nature trail** is an easy 5km hike out from the main restcamp along the river and to Moon Rock; reception can provide maps. More challenging is the three-day **Klipspringer trail** (April 1 to Sept 30; R280), which involves two overnight stops at simple huts; advance booking is essential. **Night game drives** can also be booked at reception (R260), and there's a 94km **self-drive route** (4WD only) in the park's northwestern section for viewing plains game that takes about six hours to complete.

Perhaps more instantly gratifying is the "**Augrabies Rush**", a half-day trip on small rafts down 9km of increasingly swift river immediately above the falls. This is by Kalahari Outventures (see box, p.271; R450 per person with a minimum of four), which also runs an overnight rafting trip (R1795), and the four-day Augrabies Canoe Trail (R4495) that takes you deep into the empty country upriver of the falls with simple camps set up on the riverbank.

3

irrigation canals and tunnels, and was rewarded with a plot of irrigated land. Considered primitive by the experts of the day, their handiwork continues to funnel water to the land today, and a number of functioning waterwheels can still be spotted around the town.

ARRIVAL AND INFORMATION

By car The signposted turn-off to the park is at Alheit on the N14, 10km west of Kakamas. From here, it is 39km to the park along the R359. There is no public transport, but most of the Kalahari tours in the Northern Cape (see box, p.271) include a visit to the falls.

AUGRABIES FALLS NATIONAL PARK

Information The park's reception, just up the road from the entrance gate (daily 7am–7pm), has a shop, a self-service snack bar and a restaurant with views towards the gorge.

ACCOMMODATION

The park accommodation is perfectly adequate, but there are other good choices within 10–20 kilometres. Given that the falls are the main attraction, there's little need to be there at the crack of dawn for game viewing.

Augrabies Falls Backpackers Augrabies village, 11km before the park gate ☏072 515 6079, ✉ augrabiesbackpackers@gmail.com. Rustic, laidback country house 2km down a dirt road (follow the signs from the main road to the falls). The six rooms are simple, only one is en suite, others share bathrooms, but the owner is full of tips on local activities. There's a kitchen, outdoor bar and braai facilities, and you can swim in a dam on the property. Dorms **R195**, doubles **R440**

Augrabies Falls Lodge & Camp 3km before the gate ☏054 451 7203, ⊛ augfallslodge.co.za. This revamped lodge, close to the falls, offers a/c double rooms and self-catering chalets set among palm trees, and with a swimming pool. There's also a campsite and each site has its own bathroom, and there's a decent bar and restaurant. Camping **R250**, doubles **R620**

The Falls Guest House On the R359, 2km before the gate ☏082 928 7938, ⊛ thefallsaugrabies.com. One of the more upmarket options in the area, this renovated farmhouse has four big, cool rooms and one family cottage, with nice furnishings and a generous veranda overlooking rows of vines. English breakfast is included and dinners or braais can be arranged. **R1015**

Ikaia River Lodge Off the R27 on the south side of the bridge over the Orange River, 2km from Keimoe ☏082 337 7575, ⊛ ikaia.co.za. Superbly sited on the banks of the Orange, this tranquil spot has spectacular views and is a great spot for viewing fish eagles, goliath herons and other birds. There are comfortable rooms, self-catering chalets, and four camping sites with private bathrooms. The restaurant serves breakfast (R80) and has a short but adequate menu for dinner. Camping **R300**, rooms and chalets **R750**

Kalahari Gateway Hotel 19 Voortrekker St, Kakamas ☏054 431 0838, ⊛ kalaharigateway.co.za. Large and a bit tired-looking, with the stuffy atmosphere of a conference venue, but the rooms are adequate enough. There's also a swimming pool, two bars and a restaurant, as well as a few self-catering apartments. **R970**

National Park Chalets At the park reception, reservations through SANParks in Pretoria ☏012 428 9111, ⊛ sanparks.org; for camping and late bookings contact reception directly ☏054 452 9200. A large camp with a number of comfortable brick chalets and family cottages (three of which are wheelchair accessible), all located within walking distance of the falls and with access to three swimming pools. There is also a campsite. You can either self-cater (the nearest supermarket is in Kakamas) or eat at the restaurant. Camping R250, chalets R1095

Vergelegen Guesthouse & Restaurant On the N14 about 3km east of Kakamas ☎ 054 431 0976, ⓦ augrabiesfalls.co.za. Located on a farm by the main road, this is one of the most attractive guesthouses in the region with sixteen neat rooms, two of which are self-catering, and a swimming pool. The restaurant is excellent, with a menu of interesting local dishes like lamb shank, biltong soup and springbok carpaccio. Rates include breakfast. R980

Namaqualand

NAMAQUALAND is another Northern Cape region whose name conjures up images of desolation and magic. Also known as Namakwaland (the Afrikaans spelling), this is the land of Khoikhoi herders called the **Nama** – the Little Nama, who lived south of the Orange River, and the Great Nama who lived north of the river in what is now Namibia. Sparsely populated, the region stretches south from the Orange to the empty **Knersvlakte** plains around Vanrhynsdorp, and from the **Atlantic coast** to the edge of the **Great Karoo**. Above all, Namaqualand is synonymous with the incredible annual display of brightly coloured **wild flowers** that carpet the landscape in August and September, one of South Africa's most compelling spectacles. Even outside flower season, swathes of orange, purple and white daisies emerge, and there is a tenacious beauty about this dry, empty landscape of mountain deserts, mineral-bearing granite hills and drought-defiant succulents.

The **N7** highway between Namibia and Cape Town cuts across Namaqualand, offering one of the most scenic drives in the country. At its northern end, at the junction with the dusty **N14** from Upington and the Kalahari, lies the region's capital, **Springbok**. This is the best base for flowers – the nearby **Namaqua National Park** provides reliable displays even in years of low rainfall, when displays elsewhere may be muted – and for visiting the Province's remote northwestern corner: the **Diamond Coast**, stretching from Port Nolloth to the Namibian border. The harsh but spectacular **Ai-Ais Richtersveld Transfrontier Park** stretches inland, bisected by the Orange River – canoeing on which ranks high among the region's attractions.

Springbok

The semi-arid expanse of northern Namaqualand is where the Karoo merges into the Kalahari, and both meet the ocean. If it weren't for the discovery of copper in the 1600s, and more recently of alluvial and offshore diamonds washed down from the Kimberley area by the Orange River, the region might well not have acquired any towns at all. Fresh water is scarce, and its presence here ensured the survival of SPRINGBOK, the region's capital, after its copper mines were exhausted.

Attractively hemmed in by hills, Springbok is the main commercial and administrative centre of Namaqualand, and an important staging post at the junction of the N7 and N14 highways. Lying 381km southwest of Upington, and 119km south of the border with Namibia at Vioolsdrift, it makes a pleasant base for visiting northern Namaqualand's flower fields in August and September (see box, p.285) or a springboard for visiting the coast, and it's a good place to arrange trips to the Ai-Ais Richtersveld Transfrontier Park (see p.291).

Springbok's main action is centred on the mound of granite boulders next to the taxi rank in the town centre. Called **Klipkoppie** ("rocky hill"), this was the site of a British fort blown up by General Jan Smuts' Boer commandos during the Anglo-Boer War. A few hundred metres up from Klipkoppie, at the back of town, a gash in the hillside marks the **Blue Mine**, the first commercial copper mine in South Africa,

3

sunk in 1852. Recent activity here has been in search of gemstones – previously ignored in the frantic hunt for copper ore – and zinc. A short trail wends up to a good **viewpoint** over town. You'll find a good selection of gemstones for sale at *Springbok Lodge*, together with an excellent display of mineralogical specimens from all over the globe.

Goegap Nature Reserve

Entrance on the R355, 15km east of Springbok • Daily 8am–6pm during flower season, otherwise 8am–4pm • R30 • ☎ 027 718 9906

An easy excursion from Springbok to the east of the N7, the **Goegap Nature Reserve** proclaims itself to be "Namaqualand in miniature". With close to six hundred indigenous flower species, it is a popular destination during flower season, and a garden showcasing some of the unusual, alien-like succulents endemic to the area makes it a good place to visit year-round. The reserve is also home to a number of animal species, including the Namaqualand sandgrouse, the bat-eared fox and the aardwolf. There is a 17km loop on a gravel road from the gate that you can self-drive, or you can explore on foot on one of the short trails.

ARRIVAL AND DEPARTURE   SPRINGBOK

By car Coming from Upington, the N14 eventually becomes Voortrekker St, the town's main drag, and veers south at the taxi rank to rejoin the N7 for Cape Town.
By bus Intercape buses pick up and drop off next to the Engen Garage on Voortrekker St (reservations ☎ 021 380 4400, ⓦ intercape.co.za, or buy tickets at Shoprite supermarket, 200m back towards town).

Destinations: Cape Town (daily; 9hr); Upington (daily; 4hr 40min); Windhoek, Namibia (daily; 14hr 15min).
By minibus taxi Most minibuses leave from the taxi rank at Klipkoppie, and run to Cape Town (6–8hr) at around 11am every day except Saturdays and go via the other towns on the N7.

INFORMATION

Tourist information The helpful Namakwa Tourism office (Mon–Fri 8am–4.45pm, during flower season Sat & Sun 8.30am–4pm; ☎ 027 712 8034/5, ⓦ namakwa-dm .gov.za) is at 40 Voortrekker St, 700m south of the taxi rank. They operate the Namakwa Flower Line during spring (daily 8am–8pm, ☎ 079 294 7260) for pre-recorded information about flower "sightings" and related

information. Another source of local wisdom is the *Springbok Lodge & Restaurant* at 37 Voortrekker St on the corner of Kerk St. A hub for travellers and locals, the shop in the main reception (daily 7am–10pm) sells souvenirs and an excellent selection of books, including plenty of titles on Namaqualand and its flowers, the history of copper mining and the Nama, the Richtersveld and rock art.

ACCOMMODATION

There's no shortage of rooms in Springbok, but you're still advised to book ahead in flower season (usually Aug–Sept) when room rates may be slightly higher.

★**Annie's Cottage** 4 King St, signposted from Klipkoppie ☎ 027 712 1451, ⓦ anniescottage.co.za. Extremely stylish, comfortable and colourful B&B rooms in a restored colonial house decorated with local artwork, with a swimming pool under jacaranda trees. There are hiking trails nearby, and the gregarious owner is a good source of information about where to see the best flowers. R1010
Elkoweru Guest House 1 King St ☎ 027 718 1202, ⓦ elkoweru.co.za. A modern two-storey guesthouse in vaguely Mediterranean style with a range of a/c rooms – from very small budget rooms (from R500) to larger doubles and family self-catering flats. Each has tea and coffee stations, breakfast included and dinner on request. R820

Mountain View Guest House 2 Overberg Ave (turn-off is 100m south of the tourist office, from where it's another 1km along Overberg Ave) ☎ 027 712 1438, ⓦ mountview.co.za. Ten colourful but tasteful African-themed rooms (two self-catering) in this stylish guesthouse, pleasantly situated on the fringe of the town, right by a short trail with views over Springbok. R1000
Naries Namakwa Retreat 27km west of town along the Kleinzee Rd (R355) ☎ 027 712 2462, ⓦ naries.co.za. A homely, comfortable place to stay, with stylish rooms in an atmospheric Cape Dutch farmhouse, plus a self-catering cottage and three luxurious dome-shaped suites nestled among the boulders nearby. No under-12s allowed in the main farmhouse or the suites. The candlelight dinners are a

big draw, and hiking and horseriding can be arranged. Rates are for half board. R2430

Springbok Caravan Park 2km southeast of town along the R355 ☎ 027 718 1584, ⓦ springbokcaravan park.co.za. Convenient for the N7, the park is well maintained and attractively surrounded by quiver trees; along with tent sites, it offers two-bed rondavels sharing kitchen and bathrooms with campers, self-catering chalets

and a swimming pool. Camping R220, rondavels R370

Springbok Lodge 37 Voortrekker St, entrance on Kerk St ☎ 027 712 1321, ⓦ springboklodge.com. Simple but characterful and good value, offering 48 rooms with or without kitchens, all in distinctive white and yellow buildings within walking distance of the reception office/curio shop. The reliable restaurant offers the usual range of fish and chips, burgers and pizzas. R620

EATING

Herb Garden Voortrekker St, corner of Kruis Rd ☎ 027 712 1247, ⓦ herb-garden.co.za. On the same property as a plant nursery, an airy coffee shop by day offering build-your-own breakfasts (from R30), pizzas, sandwiches and desserts like malva pudding (R35), with more sophisticated meals in the evening such as lamb chops or steaks (from R110). Mon–Sat 8am–9.30pm, Sun 8am–3pm.

Springbok Lodge Restaurant 37 Voortrekker St, entrance on Kerk St ☎ 027 712 1321. Vaguely reminiscent of an American diner from the 1950s, serving a large selection

of steak, fish and burger meals, plus local favourites like Karoo lamb and beef *bobotie* (mains R50–100). Or you could just stop for a coffee, milkshake or a big serving of "slap-chips" (fries). Mon–Sat 7am–10pm, Sun 8am–10pm.

Tauren Steak Ranch 2 Hospital St, just north of the taxi rank ☎ 027 712 2717. Attractive African-style decor, serving steaks dished up in a number of adventurous ways – topped with snails, for instance, or flambéed in brandy (mains around R100). Mon–Fri 11.30am–10pm, 6–11pm on Sun in flower season.

3

VIEWING THE FLOWERS OF NAMAQUALAND

The seeds of the spectacular **flowers of Namaqualand** – daisies, aloes, gladioli and lilies – lie dormant under the soil through the droughts of summer, waiting for the rain that sometimes takes years to materialize. About four thousand floral species are found in the area, a quarter of which are found nowhere else on Earth. Although it's difficult to predict where the best displays will occur, for more or less guaranteed flowers you can head for the Skilpad section of **Namaqua National Park** (see p.286) or to the **Ai-Ais Richtersveld Transfrontier Park** (see p.291), with its ocean-mist-fed succulents.

One indication of where the displays will occur is **winter rainfall**; flowers follow the rain, so early in the season they will be out near the coast, moving steadily inland.

PRACTICALITIES

Viewing flowers in Namaqualand involves a lot of driving, simply because the distances are so great. Book **accommodation** well in advance, either on a farm (ideal if you don't have your own transport, as you can walk around the farm's own flower fields) or in a town like Springbok. Note that accommodation rates can increase substantially during flower season. The following tactics are worth keeping in mind:

- Plan your route before heading out – your hosts may have inside information about the best spots on a particular day.
- Flowers open only in sunshine in a minimum temperature of 18°C, and do not open on rainy or overcast days. Because they turn to face the sun, it's best to drive westwards in the morning and eastwards in the afternoon.
- The flowers only open up from around 11am to 3pm, so you have time for a good breakfast.
- Take lots of pictures, but don't pick the flowers.

FLOWER TOUR OPERATORS

Several tour operators offer three- to five-day tours from Cape Town to Namaqualand during flower season and can make arrangements to pick up locally, and some also stop at selected fishing villages on the West Coast. Expect to pay around R7000 per person for a three-night/four-day tour from Cape Town staying in B&B accommodation, but not including dinners.

Namaqualand Flower Tours Stellenbosch ☎ 082 443 6480, ⓦ flower-tours.co.za.

Namaqua Tours Based at Namaqualand Lodge (see p.287) ☎ 027 219 1377, ⓦ namaquatours.com.

3

DRINKING

Pot & Barrel Pub and Restaurant 39 Voortrekker St, just south of Springbok Lodge ☎ 027 718 1475. A no-frills pub and the best place for a drink, and often the venue for local Afrikaans live music. Food includes mainly meaty dishe like pork chops or lamb curry, and pizzas (mains R50–100) Mon–Sat 8am–2am, Sun 11am–2pm, 5–10pm.

Namaqua National Park

21km northwest of Kamieskroon • Daily 8am–5pm • R80 • ☎ 027 672 1948, ⓦ sanparks.org/parks/namaqua

A place well worth visiting in flower season, even if you're just passing through on the highway, is the Skilpad section of the southern half of **Namaqua National Park**. It is accessed by signposted gravel road from the village of **KAMIESKROON**, 70km south of Springbok – itself a useful stop on the N7 for its filling station, small shops and a hotel (see below). Once in the park, the floral displays here, featuring great swathes of orange, tend to be more reliable than elsewhere, even in years with low rainfall. Butterfly fanatics and twitchers should be in for a treat too, and there are small antelope to be seen, including klipspringer, steenbok and duiker. There's a circular 5km drive around the reserve, two short walking trails and a scenic picnic site.

ACCOMMODATION   NAMAQUA NATIONAL PARK

Kamieskroon Hotel To the right as you come off the N7 at Kamieskroon ☎ 027 672 1614, ⓦ kamieskroon hotel.com. A good option on the way to the park or as a stopover on the N7, with comfortable rooms, some of them with self-catering facilities, and a caravan and camping park. The restaurant offers generous farm-style breakfasts (R95) and dinners on request, there's a swimming pool and the owners run photographic tours during flower season. Camping R200, doubles R680

Skilpad Rest Camp In the Skilpad section of the park, reservations through South African National Parks in Pretoria ☎ 012 428 9111, ⓦ sanparks.org; for camping and late bookings, contact reception directly ☎ 027 672 1948. Four three-bed chalets set in the park's rock hills, all comfortably equipped with fireplaces, cooking equipment and enclosed verandas. You can also camp here but there is no electricity or showers and only simple toilets. Bring all supplies including firewood. During flower season (August and September) SANParks operates two "flower camps" in the reserve, with accommodation in dome tents and all meals provided (from R1650 per person). Camping R145, chalets R870

Vanrhynsdorp

Travelling south from Kamieskroon, the mountains gradually give way to the bleaker landscape of the pebble-strewn **Knersvlakte** – the "plains of the gnashing teeth", referring to the sound made by the wooden wagons toiling across the harsh terrain. The small agricultural town of **VANRHYNSDORP**, 196km from Kamieskroon, is the most southerly of the Namaqualand towns. Although it's officially in the Western Cape, this is the gateway to the region if you're coming from Cape Town, 307km to the south. It also marks the crossroads between the N7 and the R27, which connects via the glorious **Bokkeveld Escarpment** with Calvinia and ultimately Upington, on the northern fringe of the Great Karoo. Set in the lee of the spectacular flat-topped Maskam Mountain, Vanrhynsdorp is pretty much deserted out of flower season.

Museums and historical sites

Vanrhynsdorp, dominated by the tall spire of its church, offers a surprising number of local museums and historical sites for a town of its size. The **Van Rhijn Museum** on Van Riebeeck Street (Mon–Fri 9am–6pm, Sat & Sun 9am–1pm; free) is diverting enough, featuring a collection of old military pieces and domestic paraphernalia from early Boer homesteaders. Also in town is the quirky **Latsky Radio Museum**, behind the church at 4 Church St (Mon–Sat 9am–noon & 2–5pm during flower season, on request the rest of the year; free; ☎ 027 219 1032), nurturing a collection of some two hundred valve radios dating back to the 1920s. Venture about 500m out of town along Troe Troe Street and you'll find the town's dusty little **cemetery**, which contains the touchingly derelict graves of a number of casualties of the Anglo-Boer War – some marked by nothing more than piles of stones.

Kokerboom Kwekery

4 Voortrekker St, five blocks east of the church • Mon–Fri 8am–5pm, daily Aug–Sept • R10 during flower season, free the rest of the year • 📞 027 219 1119, 🌐 kokerboom.co.za

Worth a look in or out of the flower season, this **nursery** specializes in succulents, displaying dozens of the more unusual varieties. Around a third of the world's succulent species grow in this area, many of them endemic. There's also a small café and shop.

ARRIVAL AND INFORMATION   VANRHYNSDORP

Most buses and taxis running to and from Cape Town, Springbok or Upington stop at either the Shell or Caltex garages at the start of Van Riebeeck St after turning off the N7 highway.

By bus Intercape buses (reservations 📞 021 380 4400, 🌐 intercape.co.za) run daily to Cape Town (5hr 35min), Springbok (3hr 5min), Upington (8hr 15min), and Windhoek (17hr 10min). Be aware that some pass through Vanrhynsdorp in the middle of the night.

By minibus taxi Minibus taxis to Cape Town and Springbok usually depart Vanrhynsdorp in the early afternoon as they pass through town on the N7. Note that there are few taxis in either direction at the weekends.

Tourist information The tourist office is in the museum on Van Riebeeck St (Aug & Sept Mon–Fri 8am–5pm, Sat 9am–1pm; Oct–July Mon–Fri 8am–5pm; 📞 027 219 1552, 🌐 namaquawestcoast.com).

ACCOMMODATION

Letsatsi Lodge Off the R27 on the western side of the N7, 2km from the centre of Vanrhynsdorp 📞 027 219 2828, 🌐 ncfamouslodges.co.za. Newly built attractive stone lodge designed for stopover guests along the N7, with smart double and family rooms, some with braai areas and outside showers, and self-catering chalets in gardens of aloes and succulents with a swimming pool. Buffet breakfast (R95), and the *Red Ox Steakhouse* is open for passing trade. **R1100**

Namaqualand Lodge 22 Voortrekker St, next to the church 📞 027 219 1633 or 📞 082 896 6444, 🌐 namaqualodge.co.za. A family-run lodge that has been in operation for over a century, with quirky, old-fashioned charm (think taxidermied wildlife and the country's largest collection of neckties). There's a swimming pool, and a

restaurant, *Mikie's*, next door. They also run flower tours from Vanrhynsdorp or Cape Town (see p.285). **R550**

Van Rhyn Guest House Van Riebeeck St 📞 027 219 1429, 🌐 vanrhyngh.co.za. Calm, welcoming and artsy, with nine rooms in the Victorian-style house or in converted outhouses, which have high ceilings and remain cool even during the summer heat. Breakfast included, and excellent dinners are provided by prior arrangement. **R600**

Vanrhynsdorp Caravan Park 800m along Troe Troe St (which becomes Gifberg Rd) 📞 027 219 1287, 🌐 vanrhynsdorpcaravanpark.co.za. Reasonably quiet out of season, with a cheap campsite and basic chalets with kitchenettes and braais; pay a little extra for a/c and DSTV. There's also a licensed restaurant. Camping **R170**, chalets **R500**

EATING

Aside from the options below, there are reasonable restaurants at both the Shell and Caltex garages catering mainly to passing motorists on the N7.

Mikie's Restaurant & Grill Namaqualand Lodge, 22 Voortrekker St 📞 027 219 1633. An unexciting place that is, nonetheless, one of the few proper restaurants in the town centre. *Mikie's* offers a fairly standard menu of steaks, burgers and other meat-based offerings from around R70. The bar has pool tables and TVs showing sport. Mon–Sat 8am–10pm.

Red Ox Steakhouse Letsatsi Lodge, off the R27 on the western side of the N7 📞 027 219 2828. Stylish modern restaurant offering steaks and other grills, with the option of choosing your own cut of

meat (from R120), plus seafood and vegetarian choices and a good selection of Cape wines. Morning or afternoon tea and coffee are also available. Daily 6.30am–10pm.

ZAR (Zuid Afrikaanse Restaurant) Vanrhynsdorp Caravan Park, 800m along Troe Troe St 📞 027 219 1287. The best restaurant in town (mains R60–120), where well-prepared steaks are served with snails, mussels and other interesting combinations, all in surprisingly refined surroundings. Mon–Thurs 6am–10pm, Fri–Sat 6am–11pm.

3

Nieuwoudtville

Heading east from Vanrhynsdorp on the R27, you have a very clear impression of the sudden elevation of the land from the plains up to the **Bokkeveld Escarpment**, which the road tackles by way of Van Rhyn's Pass, complete with a couple of neck-achingly tight hairpins near the top. There's an excellent viewpoint overlooking the plains, signposted soon after you reach the plateau.

Eight kilometres on from the top of Van Rhyn's Pass, just over 50km from Vanrhynsdorp, the R27 passes just to the north of the picturesque *dorp* of **NIEUWOUDTVILLE** ("Knee-voet-vil"), with an attractive collection of tin-roofed, honey-coloured sandstone buildings and the sombre ruins of early settler homesteads on the outskirts. The area around Nieuwoudtville receives unusually high rainfall thanks to its location at the edge of the escarpment, and consequently boasts over three hundred different floral species; flowering starts after the first rains in April or May, and peaks in August and September. But even if you're here out of flower season, you're likely to find something in bloom any time between March and October and be privy to some fantastic scenery.

About 7km north of Nieuwoudtville on the R357 towards Loeriesfontein, the Willems and Grass rivers combine to form the Doring (thorn) River, which tumbles over 100m into the Maaierskloof as the Nieuwoudtville Waterfall. The flow of water during the spring months – fed by rains across the Bokkeveld Escarpment – provides a fine spectacle, and large raptors such as martial and Verreaux's eagles can sometimes be spotted soaring around the tall cliffs. The waterfall is a short walk from the parking area alongside the R357.

Hantam National Botanic Garden

Oorlogskloof Rd • During flower season (usually Aug–Oct) daily 8am–5pm • R18 • Rest of year Mon–Fri 7.30am–4.30pm • R20 • ☎ 027 218 1200, ⓦ sanbi.org/gardens/hantam

One of the best places in the country for seeing wild flowers is the **Hantam National Botanic Garden**, formerly the farm Glenlyon. David Attenborough and the BBC Natural History Unit visited here twice in the 1990s to film the garden's extraordinary flora for the documentary series *The Private Life of Plants*. While spring is obviously the best time to visit, you'll also find a number of early-blooming flowers in winter, and autumn features brilliant displays of pink candelabra lilies (*hantam* is Khoi for "where the red bulbs grow") and yellow crossyne. More than 150 bird species have been recorded, including the secretary bird, the endangered blue crane and the rare black harrier.

QUIVER TREES

Also known locally as the kokerboom, the characteristic **quiver tree** (*Aloe dichotoma*) is broadly distributed throughout the Northern Cape and Namibia. Because it can store water in its trunk, it is known to live up to 400 years and is perfectly adapted to the region's arid conditions. Discovered in 1685, during Governor Simon van der Stel's expedition to Namaqualand in search of copper, it is not actually a tree but an aloe, with greyish-green leaves and bright yellow flowers. Plants can grow as high as 9m and their smooth trunks can be up to 1m in diameter at ground level. Quiver trees are often encountered growing at the most precarious positions, such as on the edges of canyons where the rocks anchor the plants' spread-root system. The name comes from the San practice of making quivers for their poison arrows from the dried-out hollow branches. The best time to photograph these sculptural trees is when they produce flowers, usually from May to July. The largest quiver tree "forest" in South Africa is situated on Gannabos Farm (☎ 027 218 1249 or ☎ 087 150 8101, ⓦ gannabos .co.za), 35km north of Nieuwoudtville, off the R357 towards Loeriesfontein. There's no charge to visit the forest, and if you want to stay to photograph the trees at dawn or dusk, there are a couple of farm cottages to rent.

ARRIVAL AND INFORMATION

By minibus taxi Public transport to Nieuwoudtville is limited to occasional minibus taxis to and from Vanrhynsdorp (45min), which drop off and pick up on Kerk St, 700m east of the tourist office.

Tourist information The tourist office operates out of the church hall on Kerk St (mid-July to Sept Mon–Sat 9am–5pm, Sun 9am–2pm; Oct to mid-July Mon, Wed & Fri 9am–2pm; ☎ 027 218 1336, ⓦ nieuwoudtville.com).

Flower routes The tourist office can provide maps and information about local seasonal flower routes. These include the 7km Matjiesfontein route that crisscrosses the fields of the farm of the same name 14km south of Nieuwoudtville, and the Rondekop/Naressie Route, a 42km circular drive from Nieuwoudtville through an area displaying vast numbers of daisies and vygies.

ACCOMMODATION

Papkuilsfontein Guest Farm 23km south of town off the dirt road to Clanwilliam ☎ 027 218 1246, ⓦ papkuilsfontein.com. Six lovingly restored white-washed, self-catering cottages spread around the farm – some date back to the 1800s and are hugely atmospheric. Tasty home-cooked light lunches, cakes and coffee are available at the farm restaurant, *Die Waenhuis* (daily 10am–4pm), with dinners by prior arrangement. Activities include hiking, birding, and swimming in the farm dams. **R1000**

Van Zijl Guesthouses and Caravan Park 1 Neethling St ☎ 027 218 1535, ⓦ nieuwoudtville .co.za. A collection of six attractive self-catering houses, sleeping two to six, clustered around the *Smidswinkel Restaurant*. Most are in restored traditional sandstone buildings, complete with fireplaces and cosy old furniture. The pleasant caravan park and campsite is on Kerk St. All the pitches have electricity and hot-water showers and there's a large thatched braai area. Camping **R180**, doubles **R680**

EATING

Smidswinkel Restaurant 1 Neethling St ☎ 027 218 1535. For somewhere to eat, you can't do better than this excellent restaurant at the *Van Zijl Guesthouses*; the leg of lamb is famously good, especially when washed down with

the local wine. For less common Afrikaner specialities like baked sheep's heads and stuffed heart, give them a day's notice. Main courses average around R100, and light meals and teas are served in the garden. Daily 7am–10pm.

Calvinia

Despite its stern-sounding name, bestowed by an early dominee (clergyman), CALVINIA, 70km east of Nieuwoudtville, has quite an appealing setting beneath the impressive Hantam Mountains. The town acts as a service centre for the western part of the **Great Karoo**, but it isn't a place where you'll want to spend a lot of time, unless you're here for the flowers in the surrounding area. It does however provide a stopover on the good, very scenic and quiet R27 towards Upington; it's 370km from Calvinia to Keimoes on the N14.

INFORMATION

Tourist office Located on 44 Church St (Mon–Fri 8am–1pm & 2–5pm, Sat 8am–noon; ☎ 027 341 1100/1043), in an old synagogue built in the 1920s, with a

few farm tools and early photographs on display, this is the place to get details of flower routes and the various hiking and 4WD trails in the Hantam district.

ACCOMMODATION AND EATING

Carmel Villa 19 Pastorie St, ☎ 027 341 1446, ⓦ carmel calvinia.co.za. This charming guesthouse, in a recently restored Edwardian villa, has three large B&B rooms and two self-catering garden chalets. There's a splash pool, and is strolling distance to restaurants in town. **R720**

Die Blou Nartjie 35 Water St ☎ 027 341 1263, ⓦ nartjie.co.za. A smart guesthouse with ten B&B rooms with private entrances in a garden with a small swimming pool and relaxing braai area. The excellent restaurant and bar (Mon–Sat 6.30–9pm) is in another converted old

synagogue; it's the focal point for the town and is well known for its Karoo lamb dishes. **R710**

Hantam Huis 42–44 Hope St ☎ 027 341 1606, ⓦ calvinia.co.za. An atmospheric collection of restored old homes, turned into guesthouses and filled with beautiful antique furniture. Self-catering is available, but there is also a restaurant serving traditional Afrikaner food, fresh bread, cakes and coffee. It's worth stopping at the reception to investigate the craft shop and the interesting jumble of collectibles on display. **R790**

The west coast and the Richtersveld

North from St Helena Bay, the hook of land 100km north of Cape Town, the long, lonely **west coast** of South Africa has two simple components: the cold, grey Atlantic Ocean, and the dominant sandveld vegetation, which is hardy but infertile. There isn't much more on offer. Between the mouth of the Olifants River near Vanrhynsdorp and the Orange River over 400km to the north, the only settlement of any size or significance is **Port Nolloth**, but there are good sealed roads connecting the N7 highway to the coast.

When Namaqualand's first **diamonds** were discovered in 1925, it confirmed that the stones could be carried the length of the Orange, washed out into the ocean and then dispersed by currents and longshore drift. Although the first prospecting was carried out along the course of the Orange and in the coastal dunes, it's the diamonds lying offshore on the seabed that are now more eagerly chased, mostly by boats operating with huge underwater "vacuum cleaners" and divers working in often dangerous conditions. Whereas much of Namaqualand's coast remains off limits thanks to the presence of diamonds, the "**Diamond Coast**" from Port Nolloth to Alexander Bay, the mouth of the Orange River, can be visited. Springbok serves as a good access point.

During **flower season**, the rains fall first on the coastal areas, and you can often see displays beginning about 20km inland, making the few roads down to the coast from the N7 worthwhile detours. The tarred R355 through the **Spektakel Pass** between Springbok and Kleinzee is one of the most spectacular drives in Namaqualand, and the **Anenous Pass** on the tarred R382 between Steinkopf and Port Nolloth is also impressive. It's along this road that you'll see wandering herds of goats belonging to the pastoral **Nama** people living in the area, as well as the peaks and valleys of the **Ai-Ais Richtersveld Transfrontier Park**, the protected mountain desert occupying the area immediately south of the Orange River.

Port Nolloth

PORT NOLLOTH, 136km northwest of Springbok, is an odd but delightful place. In the hazy sunshine the horizons are never quite in focus, while the heavy morning mists shroud the town in a quiet eeriness. Populated by a mix of fishermen and diamond-boat owners, Port Nolloth is also a place with a whiff of mystery and excitement, and tales are thick about "IDB" (illegal diamond buying). Attractions are limited and the Atlantic too cold for swimming, but a stroll to the **harbour** is always interesting. There are no tours on the diamond boats, but the guesthouses at McDougall's Bay, around 5km to the south, provide canoes and small boats for their guests.

ARRIVAL AND DEPARTURE

PORT NOLLOTH

By minibus taxi The only public transport for Port Nolloth is the sporadic minibus taxi service that runs Mon–Sat between Sanddrif on the Namibian border and Springbok (enquire at the taxi rank in Springbok the day before). In Port Nolloth the stop is next to the Port Nolloth Pharmacy on Main Rd (which runs parallel with Beach St). Ask the drivers about departures for the return trip.

ACCOMMODATION

Bedrock Lodge 2 Beach Rd, Port Nolloth ☎027 851 8865, ⓦ bedrocklodge.co.za. A great place to stay, and a good source of local information, is this stylish, laidback old beach house complete with period furniture. You can stay either in B&B rooms in the main house or in one of the six cottages (three self-catering) of various sizes, all with sea views, and a swimming pool. R850

McDougall's Beach House Accommodation Voetbay St, McDougall's Bay ☎082 535 9411 ☎027 851 8064, ⓦ beachhouseportnolloth.co.za. A collection of modern self-catering houses around

McDougall's Bay; all are fairly simple but most come with sea views and are good value for groups and families. Check in at reception (where you can also get wood for the braais) and they'll drive you to your accommodation. R725

Port Indigo On Kamp St, McDougall's Bay ☎ 027 851 8012, ⓦ portindigo.co.za. One en-suite double in a B&B, plus a scattering of self-catering beachfront houses, of varying quality, with one to four bedrooms each. Can help to arrange local tours. Doubles R500, self-catering R1080

EATING

Anita's Tavern Next to First National Bank, Coastal Rd ☎ 084 726 7090. This cosy pub is the best place in town to eat, serving good fish, mussels and calamari, plus meat and pasta dishes (mains from R70), in a rustic beachside fisherman's hut decorated with nautical bric-a-brac. No credit cards, but an ATM is next door. Daily 10am–11pm.

Vespetti 2099 Coastal Rd ☎ 027 851 7843. This friendly set-up, with a Vespa scooter theme (the owners are fans), is well located right on the beachfront, offering an Italian-inspired menu of pizza and pasta (R50–90) and some pricier seafood dishes. Takeaways available. Mon–Fri 10am–9pm, Sun 10am–3pm.

Alexander Bay

The westernmost point of South Africa is **ALEXANDER BAY**, 84km north of Port Nolloth at the mouth of the Orange River, within a stone's throw of Namibia. It is named after Sir James Edward Alexander who began exporting copper in the 1860s, but the little town really came to life in 1926 when the first diamonds were discovered. The largest stone ever found here was the Merensky Diamond in 1944, which weighed in at a cool 211.5 carats. Alluvial **diamonds** are still the town's *raison d'être*, with the **Alexkor** mining company controlling most commercial activity in and around town. For the tour of the diamond area, which takes place on Thursday at 8am, contact Alexkor (☎ 027 831 8300, ⓦ alexkor.co.za). You need to book at least a week in advance and supply copies of your passport (the price depends on the size of the group; generally around R200 per person).

3

ARRIVAL AND DEPARTURE   ALEXANDER BAY

Note that there is no border crossing to Oranjemund on the Namibian coast; the border posts to Namibia are at Vioolsdrift on the N7 or the vehicle pontoon over the Orange River at Sendelingsdrift in the Ai-Ais Richtersveld Transfrontier Park (see below).

By minibus taxi The only public transport for Alexander Bay is the sporadic minibus taxis that run Mon–Sat between Sanddrif on the Namibian border and Springbok (enquire at the taxi rank in Springbok the day before). In Alexander Bay they stop near Pep Stores on Oranje St – ask the drivers about departures for the return trip.

Ai-Ais Richtersveld Transfrontier Park

Daily May–September 7am–6pm, Oct–April 7am–7pm, reception 8am–4pm • R230 • ☎ 027 831 1506, ⓦ sanparks.org

The **AI-AIS RICHTERSVELD TRANSFRONTIER PARK** in northwestern Namaqualand – commonly known as **the Richtersveld** – covers an area roughly bounded by the Orange River to the north, the N7 to the east, and the R382 to Port Nolloth to the south. The starkly beautiful park was formed in 2003 by the merger of South Africa's Richtersveld National Park (by which name the new park is still often known in South Africa) and Namibia's former Ai-Ais Hot Springs Game Park. Tucked along either side of a loop in the Orange, the landscape is fierce and rugged; names such as Hellskloof, Skeleton Gorge, Devil's Tooth and Gorgon's Head indicate the austerity of the inhospitable brown mountainscape, tempered only by a broad range of hardy succulents, mighty rock formations, the magnificence of the light cast at dawn and dusk, and the glittering canopy of stars at night. Annual rainfall in parts of the park is under 50mm, making this the only true desert – and mountain desert at that – in South Africa. In summer the daytime heat can be unbearable, with temperatures over 50°C recorded, while on winter nights the temperature drops below freezing.

3

ACTIVITIES IN THE RICHTERSVELD

Between April and September it's possible to take **guided hikes** along three designated trails in the park, although note that these trails are pretty tough going and should only be attempted by experienced wilderness hikers. They are: the Vensterval Trail (four days, three nights), the Lelieshoek–Oemsberg Trail (three days, two nights) and the Kodaspiek Trail (two days, one night). Most overnights on the trails are in the Hiking Trails Base Camp in the Ganakouriep Valley within the park, which has bunks, gas stoves, fridges and hot showers. For more information and reservations contact South African National Parks in Pretoria (☎ 012 428 9111, ⊛ sanparks.org).

Several companies on both the South African and Namibian side of the Orange River offer multiday **canoeing trips**; two-person inflatable rafts or fibreglass canoes are used and nights are spent camping under the stars on the riverbanks. These trips are a gentle and relaxing jaunt and are not too physically challenging; children over the age of 6 can join. Expect to pay from R450 for a day-trip to R2750 per person for a three-night/four-day trip. A recommended South African canoeing company is **Bushwhacked Outdoor Adventure** (☎ 027 761 8953, ⊛ bushwhacked.co.za), based at the riverside Fiddler's Creek campsite, 12km along the south bank of the river from Vioolsdrif. You can camp here (R85) or there are pre-erected dome tents under reed shelters (R300 for two), a bar, and all meals are available. Transfer from the border can be arranged for R300 for up to four people. A similar set-up is offered by Cape Town-based **Umkulu Adventures** (☎ 082 082 6715, ⊛ umkuluadventures.com), based at Growcery Camp on the river 22km from the border, which has budget huts (R350), camping (R120), and again all meals and border transfers are available.

The **best time to visit** is August and September, when the area's succulents – representing almost one-third of South Africa's species – burst into flower. There's little fauna in the park other than lizards and klipspringer, springbok and zebra concentrated in the denser vegetation around the Orange River, although leopards are present, if characteristically shy, and there are more than 200 species of birds including raptors like Verreaux's and martial eagles.

ARRIVAL AND DEPARTURE   AI-AIS RICHTERSVELD TRANSFRONTIER PARK

Given its remoteness, this is not the place for a day visit, and there's no public transport. Unless you're a skilled driver, the best way of seeing the park is as part of a tour, (see box, p.271).

By car The most direct route to the park is to drive north from Springbok on the N7 to Steinkopf (49km). From here, follow the R382 via the Annenous Pass to Port Nolloth and then Alexander Bay, from where the park is signposted. It is 93km on a gravel road from Alexander Bay to the park office at Sendelingsdrift, and you need to be at the park office before 4pm. Those coming from Namibia can take the road from the Vioolsdrift border on the N7, via Kotzehoop,

Eksteenfontein, and then take the Sendelingsdrift pontoon (daily 8am–4pm) across the Orange River, which marks the boundary between South Africa and its neighbour (with immigration facilities). In high-water season from December to April, you should phone the park in advance to find out if it is operating. Note that ordinary cars are not allowed inside the park (see below), and you must arrive before 4pm to reach campsites before dark.

GETTING AROUND

By car Ordinary cars are not allowed inside the park; the only way to explore is in a 4WD or a pick-up with a high enough clearance to handle the sandy river beds and rough mountain passes between the designated campsites. Pay particular attention along the track linking the Richtersberg

and De Hoop campsites, which is covered with thick sand and treacherously jagged rocks. It is recommended that you travel in a group of two vehicles; single vehicles must sign an agreement to report back to park headquarters on departure. No driving is allowed at night.

ACCOMMODATION

It's advisable to prebook accommodation; reservations should be made through South African National Parks in Pretoria (☎ 012 428 9111, ⊛ sanparks.org). For camping and late bookings, contact reception directly (☎ 027 83

1506). There is no shop or restaurant in the park, but fuel is available at the park headquarters at Sendelingsdrift (daily 8am–4pm), 93km from Alexander Bay. The nearest shops are at Alexander Bay, but there is far greater choice in the large supermarkets in Springbok.

Campsites Spread throughout the park at Kokerboomkloof, Potjiespram, Richtersberg and De Hoop. These are four very basic wilderness campsites; all have cold showers except for *Kokerboomkloof*, which doesn't have any showers. You will need to bring all drinking water, and jerry cans should be filled at Sendelingsdrift. R265

Sendelingsdrift Rest Camp By the gate at Sendelingsdrift. Ten decent chalets sleeping between two and four people, each equipped with a/c, fridges and stoves. There are views over the Orange River from the front porches, and a swimming pool as well as a campsite. Camping R265, chalets R960

Ganakouriep Wilderness Camp Set among dramatic boulders in the south of the park. There are four picturesque, two-person reed cabins that come with cooking facilities and showers, but you should bring your own drinking water. There is a resident caretaker on-site. R960

Tatasberg Wilderness Camp Overlooking the Orange River. With views across to the mountains on the Namibian side, this is a similar set-up to Gannakouriep, with four, two-person reed cabins and an on-site caretaker. R960

3

The Eastern Cape

VIEW ACROSS THE KAROO

The Eastern Cape

Sandwiched between the Western Cape and KwaZulu-Natal (South Africa's two most popular coastal provinces), the Eastern Cape tends to be bypassed by visitors – and for all the wrong reasons. The relative neglect it has suffered as a tourist destination and at the hands of the government is precisely where its charm lies. You can still find traditional African villages here, and the region's 1000km of undeveloped coastline alone justifies a visit, sweeping back inland in immense undulations of vegetated dunefields. For anyone wanting to get off the beaten track, the province is one of the most rewarding regions in South Africa.

Port Elizabeth is the province's commercial centre, principally used to start or end a trip along the Garden Route, though it's a useful springboard for launching out into the rest of South Africa – the city is the transport hub of the Eastern Cape. **Jeffrey's Bay**, 75km to the west, has a fabled reputation among surfers for its perfect waves. Around an hour's drive inland are some of the province's most significant game reserves, among them **Addo Elephant National Park**, a Big Five reserve where sightings of elephants are virtually guaranteed. Addo and the private reserves nearby are among the few game reserves in South Africa that are malaria-free throughout the year. The hinterland to the north takes in areas appropriated by English immigrants shipped out in the 1820s as ballast for a new British colony. Here, **Grahamstown** glories in its twin roles as the spiritual home of English-speaking South Africa and host to Africa's biggest arts festival.

The northwest is dominated by the sparse beauty of the **Karoo**, the thorny semi-desert stretching across much of central South Africa. The rugged **Mountain Zebra National Park**, 200km north of Port Elizabeth, is a stirring landscape of flat-topped mountains and arid plains stretching for hundreds of kilometres. A short step to the west, **Graaff-Reinet** is the quintessential eighteenth-century Cape Dutch Karoo town.

The eastern part of the province, largely the former Transkei (and often still called that) is by far the least developed, with rural Xhosa villages predominating. **East London**, the province's only other centre of any size, serves well as a springboard for heading into the Transkei, where the principal interest derives from political and cultural connections. **Steve Biko** was born here, and you can visit his grave in **King William's Town** to the west. Further west is **Fort Hare University**, which educated many contemporary African leaders. The only established resorts in this section are in the **Amatola Mountains**, notably Hogsback, where indigenous forests and mossy coolness provide relief from the dry scrublands below.

DANCERS AT THE GRAHAMSTOWN FESTIVAL

Highlights

❶ Port Elizabeth township tour Accessible tours to areas which were the stomping ground of several significant black South Africans and the site of anti-apartheid resistance. **See p.304**

❷ Addo Elephant National Park See elephants and the rest of the Big Five in the best game reserve in the malaria-free, southern half of the country. **See p.308**

❸ Grahamstown Festival Africa's largest arts festival wakes up this pretty colonial university town. **See p.320**

❹ The Tuishuise The historic frontier town of Cradock offers accommodation in a street of

beautifully restored and furnished Victorian houses. **See p.323**

❺ Karoo farmstays Experience the sharp light and panoramic landscape of the Karoo semi-desert that sweeps across South Africa's interior. **See p.328**

❻ Bulungula Backpacker Lodge In a remote Wild Coast village, this brilliant base offers a vivid experience of Xhosa life and culture. **See p.344**

❼ Qunu, Nelson Mandela's birthplace Follow in the footsteps of South Africa's greatest hero to the village where he was born and was buried in 2013, just outside Mthatha. **See p.346**

HIGHLIGHTS ARE MARKED ON THE MAP ON P.298

Tucked into the northeastern corner of the province, the **Eastern Cape Highlands** make a steep ascent out of the Karoo and offer trout-fishing and ancient San rock art. The focus of the area is the remote, lovely village of **Rhodes**. Further east, the **Wild Coast region** remains one of the least developed and most exciting regions in the country. The poorest part of the poorest province, the region is blessed with fabulously beautiful subtropical coast. Green hills roll down to the best beaches in the country, largely deserted, except for the long-horned Nguni cattle that laze on the sand. All the

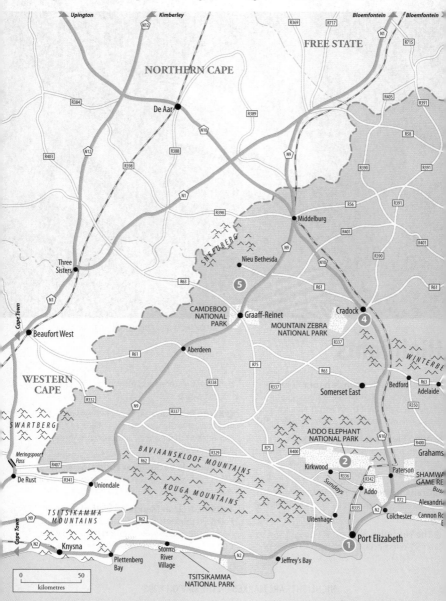

way to the KwaZulu-Natal border, dirt roads trundle down to the coast from the N2 to remote and indolent hillside resorts, each one dominated by a family hotel. The Transkei also has some of the best backpacker lodges in the land, particularly if you are looking for an African community experience and wild beaches. **Port St Johns** is the biggest and best-known destination, followed by Coffee Bay, both of which are blessed with tarred roads. In the rugged, goat-chewed landscape inland, Xhosa-speakers live in mud-and-tin homesteads, scraping a living herding stock and growing crops. Most

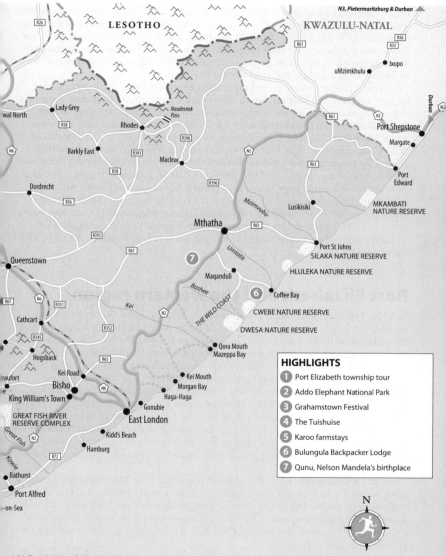

HIGHLIGHTS

1. Port Elizabeth township tour
2. Addo Elephant National Park
3. Grahamstown Festival
4. The Tuishuise
5. Karoo farmstays
6. Bulungula Backpacker Lodge
7. Qunu, Nelson Mandela's birthplace

EASTERN CAPE

visitors pass as quickly as possible through **Mthatha** (formerly Umtata), the ugly former capital of the Transkei – but if you're following in the footsteps of Nelson Mandela, the **Nelson Mandela Museum** in the centre of Mthatha, and **Qunu**, his birthplace and grave site, southwest of the town, are obvious ports of call, though underplayed and currently rather disappointing.

Brief history

The Eastern Cape was carved up into black and white territories under apartheid in a more consolidated way than anywhere else in the country. The stark contrasts between wealth and poverty were forged in the nineteenth century when the British drew the Cape colonial frontier along the **Great Fish River**, a thousand kilometres east of Cape Town, and fought nine separate campaigns (known as the **Frontier Wars**) to keep the **Xhosa** at bay on its east bank. In the 1820s, the British shipped in thousands of settlers to bolster white numbers and reinforce the line.

Even for a country where everything is suffused with politics, the Eastern Cape's identity is excessively **political**. South Africa's black trade unions have deep roots in its soil, which also produced many anti-apartheid African leaders, including former **Nelson Mandela**, his presidential successor **Thabo Mbeki**, and Black Consciousness leader **Steve Biko**, killed by Port Elizabeth security police in 1977. The Transkei or Wild Coast region, wedged between the Kei and KwaZulu-Natal, was the testing ground for grand apartheid when it became the prototype in 1963 for the Bantustan system of racial segregation. In 1976 the South African government gave it notional "independence", in the hope that several million Xhosa-speaking South Africans, surplus to industry's needs, could be dumped in the territory and thereby become foreigners in "white South Africa". When the Transkei was reincorporated into South Africa in 1994 it became part of the new Eastern Cape, a province struggling for economic survival under the weight of its apartheid-era legacy and the added burden of widespread corruption.

Port Elizabeth and the western region

In 1820, **Port Elizabeth** was the arrival point for four thousand British settlers, who doubled the English-speaking population of South Africa and have left their trace on the architecture in the town centre. The smokestacks along the N2 bear testimony to the fact that it was the industrial centre of the Eastern Cape and thrived on cheap African labour, which accounts for its deep-rooted trade unionism and strong tradition of African nationalism. The port's industrial feel, however, is mitigated by some outstanding **city beaches** along Nelson Mandela Bay, beautiful **coastal walks** a few kilometres from town, and a small **historical centre** with some excellent places to eat.

However, the main reason most people wash up here is to start or finish a tour of the **Garden Route** – or head further up the highway to **Addo Elephant National Park** (see p.308), the most significant game reserve in the southern half of the country. Also within easy striking distance are several other smaller, and utterly luxurious, **private game reserves**.

East of Port Elizabeth, a handful of **resorts** punctuate the **R72 East London coast road**, where the roaring surf meets enormously wide sandy beaches, backed by mountainous dunes. The inland route to East London deviates from the coast and passes through **Grahamstown**, a handsome if somewhat run-down university town that hosts the National Arts Festival every July, and offers good wildlife viewing on private farms and reserves.

A couple of hundred kilometres north of Port Elizabeth, an area of flat-topped hills and treeless plains opens out to the **Karoo**, the semi-desert that extends across a third of South Africa. The oldest and best known of the settlements here is the picture-postcard

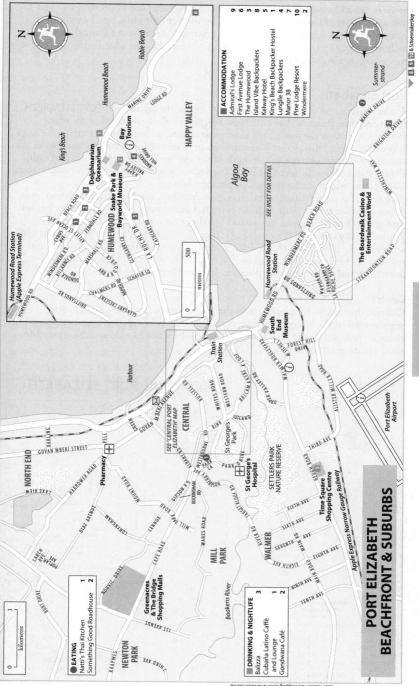

PORT ELIZABETH
BEACHFRONT & SUBURBS

ACCOMMODATION
Admiral's Lodge 9
First Avenue Lodge 6
The Humewood 3
Island Vibe Backpackers 8
Kelway Hotel 5
King's Beach Backpacker Hostel 1
Lungile Backpackers 4
Manor 38 7
Pine Lodge Resort 10
Windermere 2

EATING
Natti's Thai Kitchen 1
Something Good Roadhouse 2

DRINKING & NIGHTLIFE
Balizza 3
Cubaña Latino Caffè and Lounge 1
Gondwana Café 2

town of **Graaff-Reinet**, a solid fixture on bus tours. Just a few kilometres away are the awesome **Valley of Desolation** and the village of **Nieu Bethesda**, best known for its eccentric Owl House museum. Nearly as pretty as Graaff-Reinet (though not as architecturally rich), the town of **Cradock**, to its east, has the added attraction of the rugged **Mountain Zebra National Park**.

Port Elizabeth

At the western end of Nelson Mandela Bay (formerly Algoa Bay), **PORT ELIZABETH**, commonly known as **PE**, has long been a popular holiday destination for white families. Although the town itself is no great beauty, its beachfront stretches for several kilometres along Humewood Road, and boasts some of the safest **city beaches** in the country, while the beaches to the south of the city have some great walks and trails. Don't be put off by the fact that PE is known as the windy city – it's no more so than Cape Town, which is also afflicted by summer winds.

As a city, PE is pretty functional, though it has some terrific accommodation and reasonable restaurants. Although the town has been ravaged by industrialization and thoughtless modernization, one or two buildings do stand out in an otherwise featureless **city centre**, and a couple of classically pretty rows of Victorian terraces still remain in the suburb of **Central**, sliding into a revamped street of trendy cafés and restaurants. Holidaymakers head for the beachfront suburbs of **Humewood** and **Summerstrand** where there are places to stay plus bars and restaurants.

Central

Central, the area on the slopes above the actual town centre, has seen pleasing regeneration in the last couple of years with a number of creative businesses choosing to locate here, and some grand old hotels set to be restored – there's also a number of good places to eat in Richmond Hill.

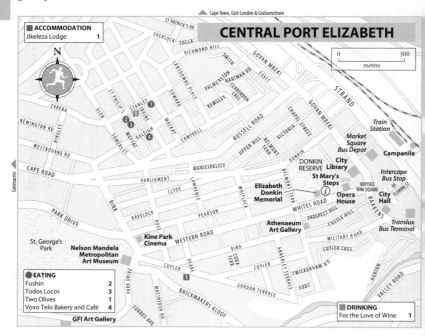

ART ROUTE 67

Commemorating Nelson Mandela's period of 67 years fighting for democracy, **Art Route 67** is a walk round central Port Elizabeth, which takes in a series of works of art by artists from the Eastern Cape. The artworks come in all sizes – from small tile mosaics, to vinyl street stickers, beadworks, 30m-wall murals, metal installations, and two-tonne sculptures that tower up to 6m high.

A good place to start is at the 52m-high **Campanile Memorial** on Strand Street, Central (Tues–Sun 9am–12.30pm, 1–2pm; free), from the top of which are great views of the harbour and its surroundings. From the bottom of the campanile, the route follows markers up the steps to Vuyisile Square, then continues up the staircase at St Mary's Terrace before meandering through the Donkin Reserve to the top of the hill.

Running parallel to the freeway as it sweeps into town is Port Elizabeth's main street, **Govan Mbeki Avenue**, renamed in honour of the veteran ANC activist who died in 2001. The symbolic heart of town is the **City Hall**, standing in **Market Square**, a large public space surrounded by some striking mid-Victorian buildings. Just north of the square is the dramatic **Campanile Memorial**, a tall bell tower built in 1920 to commemorate the centenary of the first British settlers. One block further east is the former Sanlam Building where the young activist Steve Biko (see p.333) was brutally tortured, later dying from his injuries after being transported to Pretoria. Derelict and dismal, the building can't be visited, though there are plans to restore it as a political monument.

A steep walk uphill from the Campanile takes you to the **Donkin Reserve**, an open space topped by a lighthouse (built in 1861) and a pyramid – a memorial to Elizabeth Donkin, the deceased wife of the colony's acting governor, Sir Rufane Donkin, who named the settlement after her. The walk is also rich in anti-apartheid history, with information plaques relating to Nelson Mandela, and several sculptures, including a line of steel figures of voters in the 1994 election. There are great views of the harbour, beaches and bay from the Reserve.

Nelson Mandela Metropolitan Art Museum

1 Park Drive • Mon & Wed–Fri 9am–5pm, Tues 2–5pm • Free • ⓦ artmuseum.co.za

Situated in two buildings framing the entrance to St George's Park, the **Nelson Mandela Metropolitan Art Museum** has a good collection, ranging from 1800 to the present, with much of it relating to Port Elizabeth and the Eastern Cape. There's usually a good selection of contemporary South African works on display, temporary exhibitions are also staged, and there's a small shop selling postcards and local arts and crafts. The Eastern Cape art section is the one to aim for: as well as painting and sculpture – including work by the celebrated Port Elizabeth painter George Pemba – it has some outstanding Nguni beadwork. There are also some minor European and Asian works. Unfortunately, limited space means that only a small part of the collection can be shown at any one time, and insufficient funding means the museum is closed at weekends.

South End Museum

Corner of Humewood Rd and Walmer Boulevard • Mon–Fri 9am–4pm, Sat & Sun 10am–3pm • Free • ⓦ southendmuseum.co.za

Based in the old Seamen's Institute, the **South End Museum** recalls the bygone days of the South End, a vibrant multicultural neighbourhood which grew up because of PE's then booming harbour. As a result of the Group Areas Act it was razed street by street in the 1960s, save for a handful of churches and mosques. Today, the area is full of pricey townhouses.

The beachfront

Port Elizabeth's sandy **beaches** are its main attraction. The protection provided by Nelson Mandela Bay makes them safe for swimming (that said, it's best to do so between the lifeguard beacons), and clean enough to make **beachcombing** a pleasure.

The beachfront strip, divided from the harbour by a large wall, starts about 2km south of the city centre. The first of the beaches is **King's Beach**, somewhat marred by a jumble of coal heaps and oil tanks behind it. To the southeast lies **Humewood Beach**, across the road from which is the Bayworld complex, housing the **Bayworld Museum and Snake Park** (daily 9am–4.30pm; R40; ⊚www.bayworld.co.za). **Brookes on the Bay** and **Dolphin's Leap** are nearby complexes of restaurants, pubs and clubs with great views. Beyond, to the south, **Hobie Beach** and **Summerstrand** are good for walking and sunbathing. Summerstrand's **Boardwalk Casino Complex** (⊚suninternational.com /boardwalk) houses a hotel, convention centre, casino, places to eat and shop, and a cinema, plus adventure golf and ten-pin bowling. Popular and busy in the summer, it's safe at night and a good day out for the kids.

Schoenmakerskop and Sardinia Bay

Port Elizabeth's most beautiful coastline lies to the south of the city. From Summerstrand, Marine Drive continues 15km down the coast as far as the quiet seaside suburb of **Schoenmakerskop** (Schoenies to the locals), along an impressive coastline that alternates between rocky shores and sandy beaches, with the odd café along the way. From Schoenies you can walk the 8km **Sacramento Trail**, a shoreline path that leads to the huge dunes of **Sardinia Bay**, the wildest and most dramatic stretch of coast in the area. To get to Sardinia Bay by road, turn right at the Schoenmakerskop intersection and follow the road until Sardinia Bay is signed, on the left. Always walk with others for safety.

4

ARRIVAL AND DEPARTURE PORT ELIZABETH

By plane Port Elizabeth's airport is conveniently situated on the edge of Walmer suburb, 4km south of the city centre, and is served by Safair (☎087 135 1351, ⊚safair .co.za), Kulula (☎0861 585 852, ⊚kulula.com), SAA (☎041 507 1111, ⊚flysaa.com) and Mango (☎086 100 1234, ⊚flymango.com). There's a taxi rank outside the airport as well as the major car rental companies.
Destinations Cape Town (3 daily; 1hr 15min); Durban (3 daily; 1hr 15min); Joburg (6–7 daily; 1hr 35min).
By train The train station (☎041 507 2662) is centrally located on the Strand. The Shosholoza Meyl train (⊚www.shosholozameyl.co.za) connects Joburg to PE (Wed, Fri & Sun; 20hr 35min). You will need to arrange to

be met by your hotel or a taxi (see p.306) beforehand, as this downtown area is prone to crime.
By bus Greyhound, Intercape and Translux buses stop at Greenacres shopping mall in Newton Park suburb, 3km from the centre. There are waiting taxis during business hours (see p.306), but it's best to arrange to be met here by your accommodation. Leaving PE, buses stop at every major town along the Garden Route to Cape Town, and also head east to Mthatha and Durban.
Destinations Cape Town (6–7 daily; 12hr); Durban (daily; 12hr 30min); Joburg (daily; 14hr 30min); Knysna (daily; 5hr); Mthatha (daily; 8hr 50min).

INFORMATION

Tourist information Nelson Mandela Bay Tourism (⊚nmbt.co.za) has several offices including: Port Elizabeth Airport Arrivals Hall (Mon–Fri 7am–7pm, Sat 7am–6pm, Sun 8am–6pm; ☎041 581 0456); Shop 48 at the

Boardwalk, Marine Drive, Summerstrand (Mon–Fri 8am–7pm, Sat & Sun 10am–7pm; ☎041 583 2030); and Donkin Reserve Lighthouse Building, Belmont Terrace, Central (Mon–Fri 8.30am–4pm; ☎041 582 2575).

TOURS AND ACTIVITIES

Guided tours It's possible to explore the various historical landmarks of Central on foot, but the best way to see Port Elizabeth is on one of the excellent bus tours, which shed light on a city shaped by layers of political history. Calabash Tours (☎041 585 6162, ⊚calabashtours.co.za) operates "Real City Tours" by day and *shebeen* tours by night, as well as day-trips to Addo.
Horseriding Heavenly Stables, 431 Sardinia Bay Rd

(☎081 890 7080, ⊚heavenlystables.co.za; R450), offers riding on quiet, well-behaved horses, for both beginners and experienced riders. The rides go through coast dune forest and end up on the beach at Sardinia Bay.
Sea cruises Raggy Charters (☎073 152 2277, ⊚raggycharters.co.za) runs sea cruises (R1400) from the Algoa Yacht Club in PE harbour to spot humpback and southern right whales (July–Nov) and dolphins

(year-round), and to the massive penguin colony at St Croix Island.

Watersports Although the ocean around PE is not tropically clear and warm, the diving is good, especially for soft corals, and there is the chance of diving with ragged tooth sharks. Pro Dive, 189 Main Rd, Walmer (☎041 581 1144, ⊛prodive.co.za), offers diving and dive courses, snorkelling, kiteboarding, stand-up paddling and kayaking.

GETTING AROUND

By car Renting a car from the airport is your best option (see p.304) for navigating PE and for reaching the premier destination of Addo. If you don't want to drive yourself, there are several companies which offer day-trips to Addo (see p.308).

Taxis PE's minibus taxis run regularly from town to the beachfront, but are the least recommended way to travel in terms of safety. There are some metered taxis about, but it's better to arrange transport beforehand; try King Cab (☎041 368 5559) or Uber.

ACCOMMODATION

The obvious place to stay is on the beachfront at Summerstrand or Humewood. During the December and January peak holiday period, prices are highest. Away from the beachfront, the salubrious suburb of Walmer is close to the airport and shopping hubs, with some decent B&Bs, while the suburb of Central is the oldest part of PE with Victorian houses, some good restaurants, and a short distance down the hill to the beachfront.

Admiral's Lodge 47 Admiralty Way, Summerstrand ☎041 583 1894 or ☎083 455 2072, ⊛admirals lodge.co.za; map p.301. Spacious and stylish rooms at a good B&B situated at the far end of Summerstrand, roughly 7km from the centre; airport transfers are available. There's a braai area, communal lounge, pool and a trampoline for the kids. R1090

First Avenue Lodge 3 First Ave, Summerstrand ☎041 583 5173, ⊛firstavenuelodge.co.za; map p.301. Sixteen en-suite rooms, with their own entrances, offered on a B&B or self-catering basis. It's a popular and pleasant establishment close to the beach with a lawn pool and chill-out area. B&B R1200

The Humewood 33 Beach Rd, Humewood ☎041 585 8961, ⊛humewoodhotel.co.za; map p.301. An old-fashioned hotel, with large rooms featuring wicker furniture and floral prints. The service is excellent and there's a good bar, restaurant and sun deck; babysitting can also be arranged. Airport transfers and laundry facilities are available. R1120

★Island Vibe Backpackers 4 Jenvey Rd, Summerstrand ☎041 583 1256, ⊛islandvibe.co.za; map p.301. Ideal for backpackers seeking more creature comforts without sacrificing the social backpacker atmosphere. It's in a beautiful setting, a few minutes from the beach and restaurant strip, with 4-bed rooms with wooden bunks, a swimming pool, jacuzzi, pool and soccer tables. Dorms R180, doubles R650

Jikeleza Lodge 44 Cuyler St, Central ☎041 586 3721, ⊛highwinds.co.za; map p.302. This friendly backpacker place has dorms, doubles and a family room. Its adventure centre, High Winds, can sort out tours around Addo, as well as recommended combo tours to Addo and Schotia for the evening or night. Dorms R140, doubles R360

Kelway Hotel Brookes Hill Drive, Humewood ☎041 584 0638, ⊛thekelway.co.za; map p.301. Stylish hotel kitted out with timber panelling, seagrass chairs and handcrafted wooden tables. The lovely pool area has a natural rock wall, wooden decking with sunbeds, and overlooks the sea. Standard, luxury and family rooms are available. R1180

King's Beach Backpacker Hostel 41 Windermere Rd, Humewood ☎041 585 8113; map p.301. Spotless, if slightly outdated, hostel, a block away from the beach, with camping facilities, dorms and double rooms, plus an outside bar and braai area. Although mainly self-catering, it lays on tea, coffee, bread and jams in the morning. The travel desk can book township and game park tours among others. Camping R100, dorms R160, doubles R500

Lungile Backpackers 12 La Roche Drive, Summerstrand ☎041 582 2042, ⊛lungilebackpackers .co.za; map p.301. Large and popular beachfront hostel with a sociable party vibe, situated in the heart of PE's beachfront nightlife strip. Perched on a hill, it has facilities for camping and a large lawn to relax on, twin rooms, a swimming pool, plus dorms inside the main house. Camping R100, dorms R160, doubles R500

Manor 38 38 Brighton Drive, Summerstrand ☎083 270 7771, ⊛manorcollection.co.za; map p.301. Modern, sparklingly clean boutique hotel in an excellent location close to Summerstrand and the Boardwalk. There's a lovely pool area with sunbeds, and two communal lounge areas plus off-street parking. R1320

Pine Lodge Resort Off Marine Drive, Humewood ☎041 583 4004, ⊛pinelodge.co.za; map p.301. Right on the beach near the historic lighthouse and next to Cape Recife Nature Reserve, where you can spot owls, mongooses and antelope. The excellent-value accommodation consists of log cabins, some with full kitchens, sleeping from four to eight people. There's a popular bar and restaurant, and the lodge also houses swimming pool, a modest spa for beauty treatments and games room. R1075

Windermere 35 Humewood Rd, Humewood ☏ 041 582 2245, ⓦ thewindermere.co.za; map p.301. Stylish hotel with ten large, nicely decorated bedrooms and friendly staff. Facilities include a plunge pool, bar, laundry, secure parking, and discounts with Humewood Golf Course. The sea-view rooms cost no more than those without, so ask for one with a view. **R1990**

EATING

The Richmond Hill precinct is a great area for trendy alfresco cafés and restaurants, open during the day as well as in the evening, while having a meal or drink along the beachfront is another obvious choice – wander about and see what takes your fancy.

Fushin Stanley on Bain, 15 Stanley St, Richmond Hill ☏ 041 811 7874, ⓦ fushin.co.za; map p.302. This is the place to head for the best sushi in town (R60–160), either sitting at the long counter or outside at the pavement seating. The restaurant also serves salads and Eastern-influenced tapas-style small dishes. Mon–Sat 10am–10pm, Sun 11am–9pm.

Natti's Thai Kitchen 5 Park Lane, Central ☏ 041 373 2763; map p.301. Reliable restaurant, which has been going for years, serving reasonably priced, authentic Thai cuisine in a relaxed atmosphere, with a BYO alcohol policy; mains average R90. Mon–Sat 6.30–10pm.

★ **Something Good Roadhouse** Marine Drive, Summerstrand ☏ 041 583 6986; map p.301. A stripped-down surfer bar on the beachfront, where you can get breakfast (until 11am; R70), pizzas, burgers, foot-long sandwiches and other classic roadhouse meals. Sit out on the deck, which is humming with people and has a beautiful view of the sea. Daily 7am–11pm.

Todos Locos 32 Bain St, Richmond Hill ☏ 041 582 2914; map p.302. Excellent Spanish restaurant whose welcoming Spanish owner, Ana, cooks up a storm. There are blackboard specials, tapas and old favourites, such as seafood paella (R80), sangria and Spanish omelette. Tues–Sat noon–3pm & 6–10pm.

★ **Two Olives** 1a Stanley St, Richmond Hill ☏ 041 585 0371, ⓦ twoolives.co.za; map p.302. Located on a first-floor wraparound balcony, this is one of the best of the popular Richmond Hill restaurants and a great evening out. The style is Mediterranean – delicious, generously sized and varied tapas (R60) are served with Cape wines, and there are plenty of options for vegetarians and seafood lovers. The steaks and pizzas are also recommended. Mon–Sat 11.30am–10.30pm, Sun noon–10pm.

Vovo Telo Bakery and Café 16 Raleigh St, Richmond Hill ☏ 041 585 5606, ⓦ vovotelo.co.za; map p.302. This is an ideal place for breakfast and lunch, with freshly baked Italian and French breads and pastries (R40), real coffee and veranda seating. Mon–Sat 7am–3pm.

DRINKING AND NIGHTLIFE

Balizza Times Square Shopping Centre, cnr Heugh Rd & 5th Ave, Walmer; map p.301. This sprawling nightclub complex houses two bars, three lounges and two dancefloors. The DJs mix recent house anthems and old school tunes, and there's a range of cocktails and shooters to enjoy (cocktails from R56). Daily 11am–2am.

Cubaña Latino Caffè and Lounge 49 Beach Rd, Humewood ☏ 041 582 5282; map p.301. A café during the day, at night it morphs into a cigar lounge offering a sizeable cocktail menu (from R60) and Mexican-inspired food. The outside deck has a sea view and at weekends there's Cuban music and DJs. Smart-casual dress code in the evenings (no trainers or shorts). Mon–Wed & Sun 8am–midnight, Thurs 8am–2am, Fri & Sat 8am–4am.

For the Love of Wine 1st Floor, 20 Stanley St, Richmond Hill ☏ 072 566 2692, ⓦ ftlow.co.za; map p.302. This smart, compact bar is situated on the first floor with a wraparound balcony that overlooks Stanley St. Despite being PE's only decent wine bar, it is not overpriced and the selection is broad, either to drink there (from R45) or take home from their shop which stocks interesting boutique wines. Tues–Sat noon–10pm.

Gondwana Café 2 Dolphin's Leap, Humewood ☏ 041 585 0990; map p.301. An enjoyably relaxed venue with decent cocktails, live music on Sunday nights and DJs on every other night (beer from R26). It's worth checking out beforehand what is happening on any particular evening. Daily 4pm–4am.

DIRECTORY

Cinema The Nu Metro Cinema has branches at the Walmer Park Shopping Centre and at the Boardwalk Complex.

Banks and exchange American Express Foreign exchange, Boardwalk Casino Complex (Mon–Fri 9am–8pm, Sat & Sun 10am–4pm; ☏ 041 583 2025). ATMs can be found at every shopping mall.

Hospital St George's (private), 40 Park Drive, Settlers Park (☏ 041 392 6111).

Pharmacy Mount Road Pharmacy, 559 Govan Mbeki Ave (daily 8.15am–11pm; ☏ 041 484 3838).

Post office 259 Govan Mbeki Ave (Mon–Fri 8am–5pm & Sat 8.30am–1pm; ☏ 041 508 4039).

4

Addo Elephant National Park

73km northeast of Port Elizabeth • Daily 7am–7pm • R248 • ⓦ addoelephantpark.com

A Big Five reserve, **Addo Elephant National Park** should be your first choice for an excursion from Port Elizabeth, for one day or for several. You can also stay at one of the nearby **private reserves** – especially if you want to be pampered. There are three on the N2 highway between PE and Grahamstown alone – **Shamwari**, **Amakhala** and **Lalibela** – while **Schotia**, 1km off the N10/N2 interchange, has exciting night drives and is the least upmarket. One big attraction of Addo and these private reserves is that, unlike the country's other major game parks, they are **malaria-free**. Beyond Addo, in the Grahamstown area, you'll also find good game watching (see box, p.321), but nowhere has as many elephants as Addo.

Addo is also the only national park in the country with a coastline, though the area lies to the south, and has a separate entrance. **Elephants** remain the park's most obvious attraction, but with the reintroduction of a small number of **lions**, as well as the presence of the rest of the Big Five – **buffalo**, **hippos** and **leopards** – it has become a game reserve to be reckoned with. Spotted **hyenas** have also been introduced as part of a programme to re-establish predators in the local ecosystem. Other species to look out for include cheetah, black rhino, eland, kudu, warthog, ostrich and red hartebeest.

Wildlife watching

Daytime game drives at sunrise, 9am, noon & 3pm; R370 • Sundowner game drive (including drinks & snacks) R470 • Night game drive R370 • Advance bookings essential on ☎ 042 233 8657 • ⓦ sanparks.co.za/parks/addo/tourism/activities

The Addo bush is thick, dry and prickly, making it sometimes hard to spot the 600 or so elephants and other game; when you do, though, it's often thrillingly close up. The best strategy is to ask staff at the park reception where animals have last been seen, or to head for the **water hole** in front of the restaurant and scan the bush for large grey backs quietly moving about. It's also worth taking a **guided game drive**

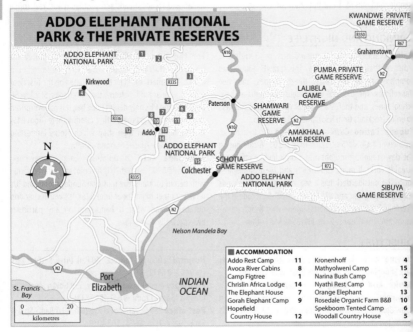

ADDO ELEPHANT NATIONAL PARK & THE PRIVATE RESERVES

◼ ACCOMMODATION			
Addo Rest Camp	11	Kronenhoff	4
Avoca River Cabins	8	Mathyolweni Camp	15
Camp Figtree	1	Narina Bush Camp	2
Chrislin Africa Lodge	14	Nyathi Rest Camp	3
The Elephant House	7	Orange Elephant	13
Gorah Elephant Camp	9	Rosedale Organic Farm B&B	10
Hopefield		Spekboom Tented Camp	6
Country House	12	Woodall Country House	5

HORSERIDING IN ADDO

A number of escorted **horse rides** are on offer in Addo, at extremely low prices. Experienced riders – you need to be able to gallop in case of danger – head into the Nyathi area, setting out at 8.30am or 2pm (R510). Novices as well as experienced riders can ride in the beautiful Zuurberg section, 21km beyond *Main Camp*, where there is not much game, but ample mountain and river valley scenery to make up for it (you'll need a head for heights on the longer trails). There are one-hour rides for novices (three daily; R220), and longer excursions for more experienced riders (three or five hours, starting at 9am; R330). There is also a ride that overnights at *Narina Bush Camp* (R600). Advance booking by phone is required for all rides (☏042 233 8657).

with a knowledgeable national parks driver in an open vehicle that is higher than a normal sedan to improve viewing opportunities.

ARRIVAL AND DEPARTURE

By car Addo's southern gate lies about 5km from *Matyholweni Camp* and is accessed off the N2 at the village of Colchester, 43km northeast of Port Elizabeth. From here, you can take a slow, scenic drive north through the park to *Main Camp*, Addo's older and more established base – a journey of at least an hour along untarred, but good condition, roads. Alternatively, to reach most of the accommodation outside

ADDO ELEPHANT NATIONAL PARK

the park, follow the R335 along the park's western flank – from Port Elizabeth take the N2 east towards Grahamstown for 5km, branching off at the Addo/Motherwell/Markman signpost onto the R335 through Addo village. To get to the Zuurberg section, including *Narina Bush Camp* and the Zuurberg horse trails, turn off 1km before you reach *Main Camp*, and travel for 21km along a good gravel road.

INFORMATION AND TOURS

Eating The restaurant at *Main Camp* is open for three meals a day (daily 7.30am–10pm), while the shop is well stocked with food and drink.

Guided tours Tours can be booked in advance at *Main Camp* or on the park's website. Two-hour guided game drives leave throughout the day and cost R370 per person for daytime drives, R470 per person for sunset trips (including snacks and drinks), and R370 per person for night drives. The vehicles used are higher off the ground than a normal sedan to improve viewing opportunities. In PE, Calabash Tours (see p.304) run day-trips at Addo, as do most of the backpacker hostels. You can also hire the exclusive services of a hop-on guide (R210) who joins you in your own car for two hours and directs you to the best places to find game.

Maps Park maps indicate the location of picnic and braai sites and are available at Main Camp reception. *Main Camp* also has a bird hide and a museum showing wildlife films more or less continuously.

ACCOMMODATION

INSIDE THE PARK

Bear in mind that reservations are essential in high season. This can be done through SANParks (☏012 428 9111, ☏addoelephantpark.com) or directly with Addo if it's less than 72 hours in advance (☏042 233 8600). You are likely to have to take whatever is available, as it's a highly popular destination. There are few villages in the area, so stock up on self-catering supplies in PE or Colchester.

Addo Rest Camp map opposite. Also known as *Main Camp*, this is the oldest and largest of the National Parks camps. In addition to camping facilities, there are forest cabins that sleep two people and share cooking facilities in communal kitchens, and more luxurious two-person chalets with their own kitchenettes. Some units sleep up to four people (minimum charge is for two occupants). The cheapest accommodation is in well-designed, spacious safari tents, perfect during the summer months, with decks right next to the perimeter fence. Camping R330, safari tent R830, forest cabin R1010, chalet R1160

Mathyolweni Rest Camp map opposite. Accommodation is in a dozen fully equipped self-catering chalets that sleep two people, and have showers and viewing decks. The chalets are set in a secluded valley surrounded by thicket that supports a wealth of birdlife. R1300

Narina Bush Camp map opposite. A small, very attractive bush camp in the mountainous Zuurberg area; the four safari tents each sleep four people and there are shared washing and cooking facilities. There is no restaurant, so bring your own provisions. R1410

Nyathi Rest Camp map opposite. Close to the foot of the Zuurberg Mountains and boasting spectacular views, this is the latest Addo camp and one of the most luxurious, with individual plunge pools and a braai area. There are eleven self-catering, domed cottages on offer – eight 2-bed, one 4-bed and two 6-bed units. R1650

★ Spekboom Tented Camp map opposite. The most rustic of the National Parks accommodation, consisting of five fixed tents on decks with twin beds. Each tent is

4

equipped with camp chairs, a table and solar light, with communal showers and toilets within a short walking distance. There is no electricity, so you'll need to bring a torch; barbecue facilities and a communal gas fridge and stove plates are available. R1010

OUTSIDE THE PARK

Outside the park, but within easy striking distance, you'll find an abundance of B&Bs and guesthouses, especially among the citrus groves of the Sundays River Valley. Many offer day and night drives in the game reserve.

Avoca River Cabins 13km northwest of Addo village on the R336 ☎ 082 677 9920, ⊛ avocarivercabins.co.za; map p.308. Reasonably priced B&B and self-catering accommodation on a farm in the Sundays River Valley. The self-catering accommodation ranges from budget cabins (sleeping four/five) to more comfortable thatched huts (some on the banks of the river). There is a swimming pool, some pleasant walks to be had on the citrus farm, plus a treetop course for kids, and canoes are available to rent. Four-sleeper cabin R700

★ **Camp Figtree** 30 km northwest of Addo village on the R335 ☎ 082 611 3603, ⊛ campfigtree.co.za; map p.308. Luxury mountain lodge, built on the Zuurberg slopes with glorious views, and built to satisfy every dream of romantic Africa. The rates include excellent food, and the packages on offer include a three-hour game drive into the park. It scores high on hilly scenery and total relaxation, though it is not near enough to nip in and out of the main part of the park, and the drive there involves 15km on gravel road, as you twist up the mountain. R3692

Chrislin Africa Lodge 12km south of Addo main gate, off the R336 ☎ 042 233 0022 or ☎ 082 783 3553, ⊛ chrislin.co.za; map p.308. This quirky B&B offers accommodation in thatched huts that have been built using traditional Xhosa construction techniques. There's also a lovely *lapa* (courtyard) and pool, and they serve up hearty country breakfasts, as well as dinners, though these are on request. R1440

★ **The Elephant House** 5km north of Addo village on the R335 ☎ 042 233 2462 or ☎ 083 799 5671, ⊛ elephanthouse.co.za; map p.308. Just minutes from Addo, this stunning thatched lodge, filled with Persian rugs and antique furniture, perfectly balances luxury with a supremely relaxed atmosphere. The eight bedrooms and six garden cottages (ideal for families, and half the price) open onto a lawned courtyard. Candlelit dinners are available, as are game drives (R1000/person) into Addo and the surrounding reserves. Main house R3700, stable cottage R1450

Gorah Elephant Camp 9km west along the Addo Heights Rd leading from the N10 to Addo village ☎ 044 501 1111, ⊛ gorah.hunterhotels.com; map p.308. Ultra-luxurious outfit based around a Victorian homestead, with a landscaped pool and decked out with the appropriate paraphernalia including mounted antelope skulls above the fireplace. Meals are included in the price, as are game drives. R17,543

Hopefield Country House 20km southwest of Addo main gate ☎ 042 234 0333, ⊛ hopefield.co.za; map p.308. An atmospheric 1930s farmhouse set in beautiful English-style gardens on a citrus farm. The nine bedrooms are imaginatively furnished with period pieces in a style the owners – a pair of classical musicians who sometimes organize concerts for guests – describe as "farmhouse eclectic". R1300

Kronenhoff Guest House On the R336 as you enter Kirkwood ☎ 042 230 1448, ⊛ kronenhoff.co.za; map p.308. Situated in a small farming town, this is a hospitable, high-ceilinged Cape Dutch-style home, with five spacious suites, polished wooden floors, large leather sofas and a reasonable restaurant. In summer the scent of orange blossom carries from the surrounding citrus groves. R1300

Orange Elephant On the R335, 8km from the National Park gate ☎ 042 233 0023, ⊛ addobackpackers.com; map p.308. Budget accommodation at a comfortable hostel, whose management will help you organize outings into the surrounding game reserves – an Addo full-day tour including a braai in the park, with an excellent guide, costs R1200. The lively bar is well known for its large portions of pub grub. Dorms R130, doubles R400

★ **Rosedale Organic Farm B&B** On the R335, 1km north of Addo village ☎ 042 2330404, ⊛ rosedalebnb .co.za; map p.308. Very reasonably priced accommodation in eight cottages on a certified organic farm that exports citrus fruits to the EU. Hosts Keith and Nondumiso Finnemore are seriously committed to sustainable farming and tourism – water for the cottages is solar-heated, and you can enjoy organic oranges and juice at breakfast. Keith offers a free one-hour walking tour of the farm to guests. There is also a kitchen available for guests who prefer to self-cater. R950

Woodall Country House About 7km west of Addo main gate ☎ 042 233 0128, ⊛ woodall-addo.co.za; map p.308. Excellent luxury guesthouse on a working citrus farm with eleven self-contained suites and rooms. There's a swimming pool, gymnasium, spa and sauna (massages are available and there's a resident beautician). A lovely sundowner deck overlooks a small lake full of swans and other waterfowl. Renowned for its outstanding country cuisine, its restaurant offers three- to six-course dinners. R3250

The private game reserves

Although driving yourself through Addo can be extremely rewarding, nothing beats getting into the wild in an open vehicle with a trained guide – something the **private** reserves excel at. If you're strapped for cash or pushed for time, a good option is one of the day or half-day safaris that start at R950 per person offered by **Schotia** and **Amakhala**. If you want the works – game drives, outstanding food, uncompromising luxury and excellent accommodation – you'll find it at top-ranking **Shamwari**, with prices over R5500 per person a day.

ACCOMMODATION	PRIVATE GAME RESERVES

Amakhala Game Reserve 67km north of Port Elizabeth on the N2 ☎ 041 502 9400 or ☎ 082 659 1796, ⊛ amakhala.co.za. A fantastic, family-friendly reserve stocked with the Big Five as well as cheetah, giraffe, zebra, wildebeest and antelopes. The Bushman's River meanders through the reserve, allowing for canoe safaris and riverboat sundowner cruises. Safaris for day visitors include a 3hr game drive with lunch (R950; book ahead). The accommodation includes fabulous farmhouse lodges and a camp with beds fashioned from restored ox wagons – all with fabulous views. R9660

Lalibela Game Reserve 90km northeast of Port Elizabeth on the N2 to Grahamstown ☎ 041 581 8170, ⊛ lalibela.co.za. An excellent mid-range choice that is home to diverse flora and fauna and the Big Five. Safaris are included in the accommodation rate, along with all meals and drinks – you can dine on terrific contemporary Eastern Cape cuisine – and they also offer an African drumming and dancing session for large groups. There are three fabulous lodges with private viewing decks, swimming pools and *bomas* to choose from. R9900

Schotia Game Reserve On the eastern flank of Addo ☎ 042 235 1436, ⊛ schotiasafaris.co.za. Schotia is the smallest and the busiest of the private reserves, on account of the excellent value it offers. Although not quite a Big Five reserve, it's really only missing the elephants, which they make up for by driving you through Addo itself. Full-day visitors can be collected from Port Elizabeth or anywhere in the Addo vicinity; full-day safaris (R2500/person) involve a game drive through Addo and an evening game drive with lunch and dinner, or you can just opt for the afternoon game drive (R1500/person). An overnight stay in one of three bush lodges or eight double rooms is the cheapest of the private reserves; rates include game drives into Addo. R4000

Shamwari Game Reserve 65km north of Port Elizabeth on the N2 ☎ 042 203 1111, ⊛ shamwari.com. The largest and best known of the private reserves, Shamwari has cultivated a jetsetter fan base, hosting such celebrities as Tiger Woods and John Travolta. Voted the World's Leading Eco-lodge in 2013 at the World Travel Awards, it deserves its accolades for the diverse landscapes, requisite animals and high standards of game-viewing. Accommodation is in the colonial-style, family-friendly *Long Lee Manor* or in attractive lodges and tented camps, furnished with every conceivable comfort. R5434

Alexandria State Forest

Alexandria Hiking Trail reservation • R190 • ☎ 041 468 0916

A 50km tract of Eastern Cape beachfront, and the most deserted section of the coast, is protected by the **Alexandria State Forest**. Part of the **Woody Cape** section of the Addo Elephant National Park, it can be walked on the circular two-day **Alexandria Hiking Trail**, one of South Africa's finest coastal hikes, which winds through indigenous forest and crosses a landscape of great hulking sand dunes to the ocean.

The 35km trail starts at the Woody Cape office, 8km from the R72 (and not served by public transport), where you collect permits. If you're heading east, the signposted turn-off is on the right, just before you reach Alexandria, 86km from Port Elizabeth. If you are picnicking rather than hiking, you can visit the forest and walk the 7km Tree Dassie Trail from the Woody Cape offices.

Jeffrey's Bay

Some 75km west of Port Elizabeth, off the N2, **JEFFREY'S BAY** (known locally as J Bay) is jammed during the holiday seasons, when thousands of visitors throng the beaches, surf shops and fast-food outlets, giving the place a tacky seaside resort feel.

Despite its unappealing suburbs and retirement homes, J Bay is said by some to be one of the world's top three **surfing** spots. If you've come to surf, head for the break at **Super Tubes**, east of the main bathing beach, which produces an impressive and consistent swirling tube of white water, attracting surfers from all over the world throughout the year. Riding inside the vortex of a wave is considered the ultimate experience by surf buffs, but should only be attempted if you're an expert. Other key spots are at Kitchen Windows, Magna Tubes, the Point and Albatross. Surfing gear, including wet suits, can be rented from the multitude of surfing shops along Da Gama Road, and all the international surfing clothing brands have factory shop outlets in town boasting massive reductions.

Dolphins regularly ride the waves here, and **whales** can sometimes be seen between June and October. The main **bathing areas** are Main Beach (in town) and Kabeljous-on-Sea (a few kilometres north), with seashells to be found between Main and Surfer's Point.

For a drink or meal on the beach, the Marina Martinique is the place to head for. You'll also find boat cruises here, as well as activities suitable for kids.

ARRIVAL AND INFORMATION   JEFFREY'S BAY

By bus The Baz Bus stops at Jeffrey's Bay on its daily trek between Cape Town and Port Elizabeth, as do Greyhound and Intercape buses.

Tourist information In the Shell Museum Complex on the corner of Da Gama Rd and Drommedaris St (Mon–Fri 9am–5pm, Sat 9am–2pm; ☎ 042 293 2923, ⓦ jeffreysbaytourism.org).

ACCOMMODATION

With lots of hostels to choose from, J Bay is definitely backpacker territory, but there are also numerous good B&Bs and some self-catering places in town. It's essential to book accommodation in advance in December, January, at Easter, and during the Billabong world-championship surfing competition, usually in July. Off-season, things are very quiet.

A1 Kynaston 23 & 27 Chestnut Ave ☎ 084 900 3006/8, ⓦ a1kynaston.co.za. A friendly establishment offering B&B rooms as well as a comfortable, well-equipped, self-catering flat, in a suburban area, not too far from either the beach or town centre. Prices are a little cheaper for self-catering, and vary with each room. R950

African Perfection B&B Pepper St ☎ 042 293 1401, ⓦ africanperfection.co.za. Three places are available: a B&B offering good-value luxury en-suite rooms with private balconies overlooking Supertubes Beach; a property across the road with similar prices, but including a kitchen for self-catering; and the cheaper *Aloe Again*, which is just self-catering. Self-catering R650, B&B R1300

African Ubuntu Backpackers 8 Cherry St, Wavecrest ☎ 042 296 0376. Only 100m from the beach, with good views, a lush garden dotted with hammocks, movie nights and Friday-night parties with fish braais. Camping R110, dorms R140, doubles R350

Cristal Cove 49 Flame Crescent, opposite the Spar Shopping Centre on Da Gama Rd ☎ 042 293 2101, ⓦ cristalcove.co.za. Just steps away from the beach, this backpacker joint has dorms and doubles, as well as spacious, self-contained flats that are excellent value for money. There is also a cosy pub. Dorms R130, doubles R350, seaview en-suites R600

Island Vibe 10 Dageraad St ☎ 042 293 1625 ⓦ islandvibe.co.za. Backpacker lodge built on a dune with a wooden walkway onto the beach and plenty of activities on offer. Accommodation includes camping dorms and doubles, with spectacular views. There's

---

BEACH RIDING: J BAY TO PORT ALFRED

Eastern Cape beaches are the best in the country for **horseriding**, while the Wild Coast beaches are even more deserted. There is no vehicle access, so riding (or hiking) is the best way to explore them.

Papiesfontein Farm 65km west of Port Elizabeth, close to Jeffrey's Bay ☎ 079 299 8080, ⓦ horsetrails.co.za. Here, good horses take you on a 13km route that combines bush, river and beach and is suitable for intermediate and advanced riders (R400 for 2 hours). There is also a less arduous ride suitable for beginners. Papiesfontein is clearly marked on the R102 turn-off, after you take the Jeffrey's Bay exit from the N2.

Three Sisters Horse trails 14km east of Port Alfred, on the R72 ☎ 082 645 6345, ⓦ threesisters horsetrails.co.za. Two-hour beach rides for beginners or experienced riders which take you from a farm, through coastal dune bush, cantering along a beautiful deserted beach, and back past Riet River which teems with bird life (R450). An overnight trail is also on offer, which combines riding and a night in a charming tree house. (R1500 per person).

ounge, bar, pool table and self-catering facilities. Camping **R100**, dorms **R150**, doubles **R500**

Super Tubes Guest House 12 Pepper St ☏ 042 293 2957, ⓦ supertubesguesthouse.co.za. A beach house whose modest en-suite rooms, with old wooden bedsteads, open onto a patio or garden, while the luxury en-suite rooms (R2100) come with a sea view, balcony and DSTV. The Super Tubes beach is practically on the doorstep. **R1380**

EATING

Die Walskipper Marina Martinique ☏ 042 292 0005, ⓦ walskipper.co.za. Eat on the beach (the dining area has benches and tables in the sand) and drink out of a tin cup at this weather-beaten wooden shack in Marina Martinique Harbour. Main courses – including seafood (R195) – are cooked on an outside fire, and there are delicious homemade breads, pâtés and jams. Tues–Sat noon–8pm, Sun noon–3pm.

The Greek Restaurant & Wine Bar Cnr Da Gama Rd & Beverland St ☏ 083 287 6406. A Mediterranean restaurant near the beach with ocean views and Greek music, serving Greek-inspired food baked in a clay oven or grilled over open coals – try the kilo of tiger prawns (R350 for two). Vegetarians will find meze and other offerings. Daily 11am–10pm.

Infood Bakery & Deli Restaurant Cnr Schelde & Jefferies sts ☏ 042 293 1880, ⓦ infood.co.za. Light and airy café known for its great coffee and artisanal breads, as well as light lunches. The salads are fresh, the service good and it opens early for breakfast – ideal after a morning swim. Mon–Sat 7am–5pm.

J Bay Bru 10 Da Gama Rd ☏ 042 940 0165, ⓦ jbaybruco .co.za. Fun eating place with plenty of healthy options plus wraps, toasties and pizzas. Friday nights have live music and Tuesdays are their pasta and movie evenings (R70). Mon–Sat 8am–11pm, Sun 8am–5pm.

DRINKING

Kitchen Windows 80 Ferreira St ☏ 042 293 4230, ⓦ kitchenwindows.co.za. Situated at Main Beach with a great view of the sea, this is the perfect place for sundowners and cocktails, as well as seafood lunches and dinners. The wine list is considerable, and you can rifle the cellar for a bottle of your choice. There are also excellent South African brandies and craft beers, and sparkling wine by the glass (R45). A shuttle can be organized to get you safely home. Mon–Sat 11am–10pm, Sun 11am–3pm.

Kenton-on-Sea

Some 115km east of Port Elizabeth and 56km from Grahamstown, the resort of **KENTON-ON-SEA** lies along two river valleys, perfect for a short beach holiday. A conglomeration of holiday houses served by a few shops and places to eat, Kenton is a good choice if you want to be somewhere undemanding and very beautiful – there's little to do except enjoy the sandy beaches, rocky coves and dunes. While you can swim in the rivers, avoid getting close to the entrance to the sea, as strong **riptides** occur and drowning is a real risk.

INFORMATION

Tourist information Signposted on the main road, the tourist office (Mon–Fri 9.30am–5pm, Sat 9.30am–1pm; ☏ 046 648 2411, ⓦ kenton.co.za) also coordinates various interesting community projects run by Xhosa women.

ACCOMMODATION

Dunwerkin 5 Park Rd ☏ 046 648 1173, ⓦ dunwerkin .co.za. In a fine location, and just a 2min walk from the beach, this affordable self-catering option can accommodate either one or two families in a spanking-new four-bedroomed house, or a couple (or a single person) in a small flat. **R650**

★ Oribi Haven Kasouga Farm, 9km from Kenton, on a gravel road off the R72 (turn right at the first cattle grid) ☏ 084 477 1166, ⓦ oribihaven.co.za. Kasouga Farm sits on a hillside overlooking one of the finest and least-known beaches in the country. The farm, which has been declared a Natural Heritage Site for its large population of Oribi antelope, has two well-equipped and spacious two-bedroom cottages, which can be taken on a B&B or self-catering basis. Farm game drives can be arranged, as can sundowners on the beach, and there is the use of sandboards for the dunes. **R700**

The Oysterbox Beach House ☏ 046 648 3466, ⓦ theoysterboxbeachhouse.co.za. Six luxury beachside properties of varying sizes, within an easy walk of the sea and lagoon. They are all furnished in an appealing contemporary beach-house style, with great views and

4

SUNSHINE COAST CANOEING

The **Bushman's River Trail** is a two- to five-hour paddle, which heads 15km upriver through countryside lined with cycads and euphorbias. To explore the Bushman's River, you can rent **canoes** from Kenton Marina (daily 8am–4pm; ☎046 648 1223; R260 for 8hr), signposted off the R72, 300m up the R343 to Grahamstown.

The **Kowie Canoe Trail**, a 21km paddle up the Kowie River from Port Alfred, is one of the few self-guided canoeing and hiking trails in South Africa. Much of its charm comes from the chattering birdlife and the landscape – hills of dense, dry bush that slope down to the river. On the trip, you stay overnight in a hut in the **Horseshoe Bend Nature Reserve**, from where you can explore the forest on foot, and climb the steep escarpment to get an impressive view over the horseshoe. It's a popular excursion, so it's advisable to book in advance (☎046 624 2230 or ☎082 491 0590, ⊛kowiecanoetrail.co.za; R200 per person).

terraces. Two of the houses can be rented on a self-catering basis from R1995. Doubles R2500

River Roost Grahamstown Rd, 1km inland from Kenton on the R343 ☎046 648 2850, ⊛riverroost .co.za. On a hill above the Bushman's River with panoramic views and jetty access to the river, *River Roost* provides luxury self-catering (R3500 for a cottage) or B&B in a French Provencal-style main house with farmhouse kitchen, reading room and rock swimming pool. It is just a few minutes' drive from the beach. R1400

Woodlands Cottages & Backpackers 2km from th town centre along the R343 to Grahamstown ☎04 648 2867 or ☎082 808 5976, ⊛woodlandscottage .co.za. A charming, large property with acres of garden an bush leading down to the Bushman's River, with cottage dotted along pathways cut through the vegetation Backpacker accommodation ranges from family rooms t cosy 8-bed dorms. They also have a bush bistro, *The Goo Shed*, a firm favourite with locals and rumoured to have th best pizzas, steaks and calamari in the area (R110). Dorm R175, couples, R350

EATING

Homewoods 1 Eastbourne Rd ☎046 648 2700. The closest spot to the beach, this restaurant and pub at the mouth of the Kariega River has grand views, though the food is fairly run-of-the-mill burgers, fish and chips, sandwiches and steaks (R130). Tues–Fri 11am–3pm & 6–9pm, Sat 10am–4pm & 6pm till late, Sun 9am–4pm.

The House Kitchen Restaurant 42 Kenton Rd ☎046 648 1786, ⊛housequarters.co.za/the-house -kitchen. A café with sea and river views, that offers Mediterranean-style food with gluten-free options (R140)

and good breakfasts with real coffee. There is a spa belo and a shop to browse in while you wait. Mon–Fr 8am–5pm (closed Tues lunch), Tues–Fri 6.30–9pm, Sa 8am–9pm, Sun 8am–3pm.

Stanleys Restaurant Just outside Kenton on the R34 Grahamstown Road ☎082 774 9326. A relaxed plac that serves the best food in Kenton – succulent steak (R120) and fresh seafood can be eaten outside with view of subtropical gardens and the Kariega River. Bookin required. Mon 5–9.30pm, Tues–Sat 11am till late, Su 11.30am–3.30pm.

DRINKING

Sandbar Floating Restaurant River Bend, Bushman's River ☎046 648 2450. Moored on the river, this houseboat restaurant/pub is a great place for sundowners (beer R30).

It also serves pub-style meals such as burgers or fish an chips. The river setting is amazing, but don't expect fas service. Booking essential. Daily 11am till late.

Port Alfred

Of all the settlements between Port Elizabeth and East London – a largely undevelope stretch of coast with substantial dunes and exhilarating surf – only **PORT ALFRED**, midway between the two, can make any claims to a town life outside the holiday season, when for a few weeks the small centre is transformed into a hectic bustle. Like many other places along the coast, it is developing apace, with housing developments sprouting along its once lonely beaches. Besides beach walking and swimming, it's an excellent place to do some **canoeing**, **diving**, waterskiing, abseiling, deep-sea fishing and horseriding.

Nicknamed "Kowie" by locals, after the river, Port Alfred was named in honour of the second son of Queen Victoria, although he never actually made it here, since he chose to go on an elephant hunt instead. Port Alfred's attractions are firmly rooted in its beaches and the Kowie River; the town itself has little else to offer. The landmark *Halyards Hotel* and *Spur* restaurant are at the Marina, a development which gobbled up a beautiful lagoon for boats and smart homes on the water; far more authentic, however, is the river frontage on Wharf Street, next to the old bridge, which has been revamped and the row of Victorian buildings spruced up.

The beaches

West Beach, where the river is sucked out to sea and the breakers pound in, is a good place to start exploring Port Alfred. From the stone pier you can watch the surfers and see fishing boats make dramatic entries into the river from the open ocean. Fifteen minutes'

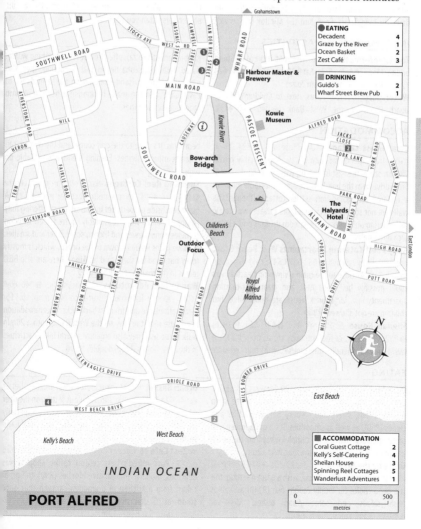

EATING

Decadent	4
Graze by the River	1
Ocean Basket	2
Zest Café	3

DRINKING

Guido's	2
Wharf Street Brew Pub	1

ACCOMMODATION

Coral Guest Cottage	2
Kelly's Self-Catering	4
Sheilan House	3
Spinning Reel Cottages	5
Wanderlust Adventures	1

PORT ALFRED

0   500
metres

walk west along the beach lies **Kelly's Beach**, by far the most popular stretch, where you can swim safely in a gentle bay. **East Beach**, reached from the signposted road next to *Halyards Hotel*, is the best beach for walking, with a backdrop of hilly dunes popular for sandboarding, stretching to the horizon. For toddlers, the safest and most popular spot is **Children's Beach**, a stretch of sand close to the town centre along a shallow section of river, reached from Beach Road, a few hundred metres from the arched bridge.

ARRIVAL AND DEPARTURE — PORT ALFRED

By bus The reasonably priced SA Connection minibus (T 043 722 0284 or T 086 110 2426, W saconnection.co.za) calls in at Beavers shop at the R72 petrol station on the west bank of town, on its way between Port Elizabeth and East London (Mon, Wed, Fri, Sat & Sun), and between Cape Town and East London on the same days. On Tues, Thurs, Fri & Sun the Minilux bus service (T 043 741 3107), connecting Port Elizabeth to East London via Grahamstown, pulls into the *Halyards Hotel* off the main coastal road on the east side of the Kowie River. Otherwise, Wayne's Transport (T 046 624 2358 or T 084 644 6060) offers a shuttle service from Port Elizabeth's airport, with times and drop-offs to suit passengers when you book.

INFORMATION AND ACTIVITIES

Tourist information On the riverfront at the Main Street bridge (Mon–Fri 8am–5pm, Sat 8.30am–noon; T 046 624 1235, W sunshinecoasttourism.co.za).

Watersports Outdoor Focus, next to Children's Beach, Beach Road, on the West Bank (T 046 624 4432, W outdoorfocus.co.za), offers courses in everything water-based, including scuba diving and skippering. They also rent out boards for sand-boarding on the sand dunes of East Beach, and can make bookings for horse trails and other outdoor activities.

4

ACCOMMODATION

Coral Guest Cottage Jack's Close T 046 624 2849, W coralcottages.co.za; map p.315. A reasonably priced B&B on one of the East Bank hills, with a luxuriant garden, 5min drive from the beach. There are comfortable rooms in a restored corrugated-iron settler cottage (though the walls are not soundproof) and a more private two-storey, self-catering unit with a big bedroom upstairs and a living area downstairs. R750

Kelly's Self-Catering Apartments West Beach Drive, opposite Kelly's Beach T 082 657 0345, W kellys.co.za; map p.315. As close to the main swimming beach as you could possibly be, these neat and clean self-catering apartments in a large brick house are good value, but children are not allowed. R800

Sheilan House 27 Prince's Ave T 046 624 4076 or T 082 894 1851, W sheilanhouse.co.za; map p.315. A well-run and friendly guesthouse with four en-suite bedrooms. It's close to the golf course and the owners can organize other activities. Evening meals are available on request. R1000

Spinning Reel Cottages 4km from the town centre T 046 624 4281, W spinningreel.co.za; map p.315. A quiet beachside property set in coastal forest, offering fully equipped and very reasonably priced self-catering cottages, some newer and bigger, some older and smaller. All have paths leading down to the beach, which is mostly rocky but good for shells and walking. There are also B&B rooms in the main house. B&B R800

Wanderlust Adventures 11 Stocks Ave T 046 624 1659, W wanderlustadventures.co.za; map p.315. Clean, affordable and friendly backpacker accommodation in a house near the river on the West Bank, with a 20min walk to the sea. They also organize several hiking activities in the area. Dorms R200, doubles R600

EATING

Decadent Postmasters Village, 20 Stewart Rd T 046 624 8282; map p.315. Cheerful daytime coffee shop serving salads, sweet and savoury Belgian waffles and crepes (R60), as well as smoothies. It's a quiet, green and pretty spot located in a small complex away from the beach and town. Mon–Fri 9am–4pm, Sat 9am–2pm.

Graze by the River 38 Van der Riet St T 046 624 8095; map p.315. Located in a house, with a garden setting, this is a good choice for locally caught fish (R140) as well as fresh salads and some Asian dishes. Mon–Sat 8.30am–5pm, Sun 9.30am–4pm.

Ocean Basket In Port Frances House on Van der Riet St T 046 624 1727; map p.315. Fabulous setting on the river where you can eat either outside or in; it's especially reliable for fish and chips (R60), but also serves sushi and seafood platters. Daily 11.30am–9pm.

★ **Zest Cafe** 48 Van der Riet St T 046 624 5783; map p.315. Port Alfred's best central coffee shop serves delicious, modern, imaginative lunches (R90) and great cakes, from a kitchen in a wooden canteen that once stood at Grahamstown's railway station. Mon–Fri 8am–5pm, Sat 8am–3pm.

DRINKING

Guido's West Beach ☎ 046 624 5264; map p.315. Open since 1985, *Guido's* is Port Alfred's only place right on the sea front. There are stunning views, and you can drink on the deck while looking out at the river mouth and East Beach. Great for sundowners, but the service can be slow and the pizzas are disappointing. Daily 11am–9pm.

Wharf Street Brew Pub 18 Wharf St ☎ 046 624 4947; map p.315. This microbrewery, in a row of restored historical buildings on the river front, offers some great craft beers (R90), and the food is equally good (the owner is a chef). Scores high on ambience, with walls lined with interesting historic photos. Tues–Sat noon–10pm, Sun noon–4pm.

Grahamstown

Just over 50km inland from Port Alfred, **GRAHAMSTOWN** projects an image of a cultured, historic town, quintessentially English, with reminders of its colonial past in evidence in the well-preserved architecture.

Dominated by its cathedral, prestigious private boarding schools and one of South Africa's best universities, this is a pleasant place to wander through, with colonial **Georgian** and **Victorian buildings** lining the streets, and pretty suburban gardens – though in recent years it has begun to look a little run-down. Every July, the town hosts an **arts festival**, the largest of its kind in Africa and one of the biggest worldwide (see box, p.320).

As elsewhere in South Africa, there are reminders of conquest and dispossession. Climb up Gunfire Hill, where the fortress-like 1820 **Settlers Monument** celebrates the achievement of South Africa's English-speaking immigrants, and you'll see

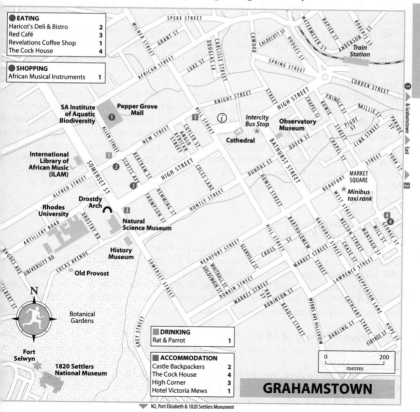

GRAHAMSTOWN

EATING
Haricot's Deli & Bistro	2
Red Café	3
Revelations Coffee Shop	1
The Cock House	4

SHOPPING
| African Musical Instruments | 1 |

DRINKING
| Rat & Parrot | 1 |

ACCOMMODATION
Castle Backpackers	2
The Cock House	4
High Corner	3
Hotel Victoria Mews	1

N2, Port Elizabeth & 1820 Settlers Monument

Makanaskop, the hill from which the **Xhosa** made their last stand against the British invaders. Their descendants live in desperately poor ghettos here, in a town almost devoid of industry, which more recently has had problems providing enough clean drinking water for its citizens.

Despite this, Grahamstown makes a good stopover, and is the perfect base for excursions: a number of **historic villages** are within easy reach, some **game parks** are convenient for a day or weekend visit and, best of all, kilometres of **coast** are just 45 minutes' drive away.

Brief history

Grahamstown's sedate prettiness belies its beginnings as a **military outpost** in 1811. **Colonel John Graham** made his – and the town's – name here, driving the Xhosa out of the Zuurveld, an area between the Bushman's and Fish rivers. The Fish River, 60km east of Grahamstown, marked the eastern boundary of the frontier, with Grahamstown as the capital. The ruthless expulsion of the Xhosa sparked off a series of nineteenth-century **Frontier Wars**.

The British decided to reinforce the frontier with a human barrier. With the promise of free land, they lured the dispossessed from a depressed Britain to occupy the lands west of the Fish River. In the migration mythology of English-speaking white people, these much-celebrated **1820 Settlers** came to take on a larger-than-life status as ancestors to whom many trace back their origins. However, far from discovering the hoped-for paradise, the ill-equipped settlers found themselves in a nightmare. The plots given to them were subject to drought, flood and disease, and the threat of Xhosa attack was never far away.

Not surprisingly, many settlers abandoned their lands and headed to Grahamstown in the early 1820s. This brought prosperity and growth to the town, which enjoyed a boom in the 1840s, when it developed into the emporium of the frontier.

High Street

High Street is Grahamstown's modest shopping axis, with terraces of nineteenth-century buildings lending it a graceful air. Running from the station at its seedier east end, High Street continues past the cathedral at the junction of Hill Street, terminating at the 150-year-old **Drostdy Arch**, the whitewashed entrance gate to prestigious Rhodes University, named after Cecil John Rhodes (see box, p.264). At the centre of the street is the Anglican **Cathedral of St Michael and St George**, opened in 1830 but subsequently rebuilt several times. **Pepper Grove Mall**, five minutes' walk north, with entrances in African and Allen streets, is a good retail option, dominated by a large Pick n Pay supermarket.

Natural Science Museum

Somerset St • Mon–Fri 9am–4.30pm • R20

If you've time for only one museum, head for the **Natural Science Museum**, just south of the university entrance. The display of Eastern Cape fauna and flora from 250 million years ago is excellent, with intriguing plant fossils and the bones of dinosaurs that once roamed these parts. The **History Museum** next door houses a dusty collection of 1820 settler memorabilia, nineteenth-century paintings and antique firearms, as well as Xhosa beadwork and traditional dress.

International Library of African Music

Near the corner of Somerset and Prince Alfred streets • Mon–Fri 8.30am–12.45pm & 2.15–4.45pm • Free but donations welcomed • ☎ 046 603 8557, ⦿ ilam.ru.ac.za

Beyond the Drostdy Arch, tucked behind some buildings, is the **International Library of African Music (ILAM)**. This is an absolute treasure trove of traditional African music recordings and rare musical instruments from eighteen sub-Saharan countries.

SA Institute of Aquatic Biodiversity

Somerset St • Mon–Fri 8.30am–1pm & 2–5pm • Free • ⓦ saiab.ac.za

The **SA Institute of Aquatic Biodiversity** was originally named after J.L.B. Smith, the Rhodes University scientist who shot to fame in 1939 after identifying the coelacanth, a "missing link" fish, caught off the East London coast and thought to have become extinct fifty million years ago. In the foyer are two huge stuffed specimens, with fins that look like budding arms and legs. The museum is worth a visit to see the coelacanths alone.

Observatory Museum

Bathurst St • Mon–Fri 9am–1pm & 2–5pm; Sat 9.30am–1pm • Donation

The **Observatory Museum** is set in a restored building that was once the home and shop of a notable watchmaker and jeweller during the mid-1850s. The thing you should not miss is the rooftop Victorian **camera obscura**, which projects magnified images of the streets below onto a wall. It's best seen on a bright day, when the reflections are particularly crisp and clear.

ARRIVAL AND INFORMATION
GRAHAMSTOWN

By bus Grahamstown is on the N2, 127km inland from Port Elizabeth, and roughly twelve hours by bus from Cape Town, Johannesburg and Durban. Translux, Intercape, City to City and Greyhound buses stop outside the *Frontier Country Hotel* on the corner of Bathurst and High streets; all (with the exception of Greyhound) can be booked through the tourist office (see below), or directly with each bus company. The Minilux minibus (☎ 043 741 3107) stops at the Wimpy in Pepper Grove Mall, with connections to Port Elizabeth, Port Elizabeth airport and Port Alfred (Tues & Thurs) and East London (Tues, Thurs, Fri & Sun).

Tourist information 63 High St, next to City Hall (Mon–Fri 8.30am–5pm, Sat 9am–noon; ☎ 046 622 3241, ⓦ grahamstown.co.za).

GETTING AROUND

By taxi Grahamstown is easily explored on foot, but if you want a taxi, use the reliable JC Shuttles (☎ 083 590 2169).

ACCOMMODATION

There's a good selection of hotels in Grahamstown, but the choicest places to stay are in the town's historic houses. The only time you may have difficulty finding accommodation is during the festival in July, when you'd be well advised to book as early as March – the tourist office can help find accommodation during this period.

Castle Backpackers Belmont Valley Drive ☎ 082 813 1611; map p.317. This comfortable and eco-friendly establishment, with dorms and doubles, is located on a smallholding just outside town. As well as catering for the backpacker scene it's also popular with people using the nearby golf course and with parents visiting their student kids. There are a couple of communal kitchens for self-catering. Dorms R150, doubles R550

The Cock House 10 Market St ☎ 046 636 1295, ⓦ cockhouse.co.za; map p.317. Plush rooms in a handsome Victorian house with the excellent *Norden's* restaurant, though it's not in the best location, being well away from the university and centre. It once belonged to the famous South African writer André Brink, who had an eye for beautiful homes. R1120

★**High Corner** 122 High St ☎ 046 622 8284, ⓦ highcorner.co.za; map p.317. A beautiful historical home in a great location across the road from the university, with six rooms furnished with Cape antiques and original art. Formerly the home of notable South African writer and academic Guy Butler who was also an excellent carpenter, so you will find some beautiful yellowwood inside. Two comfortably furnished self-catering cottages are also available. Cottages R960, doubles R1180

TOWNSHIP TOURS

Recommended guide Otto Ntsheve will take you in your own car on a **township tour** (☎ 082 214 4242; 2hr 30min–3hr; R380). Tours visit the Umthathi self-help project, which teaches skills such as vegetable growing, and the Egazini Outreach Project, an arts and crafts initiative in Joza township. A traditional Xhosa lunch is available on request (R100).

THE GRAHAMSTOWN FESTIVAL

For ten days every July, Grahamstown's population doubles, with visitors descending for the annual National Arts Festival – usually called the **Grahamstown Festival**. At this time, seemingly every home is transformed into a B&B and the streets are alive with colourful food stalls. Church halls, parks and sports fields become flea markets and several hundred shows are staged, spanning every conceivable type of performance.

This is the largest arts festival in Africa, with its own fringe festival, plus free art exhibitions at the museums and other smaller venues. The hub of the event is the 1820 Settlers Monument, which hosts drama, dance and operatic productions in its theatres, as well as art exhibitions and free early-evening concerts. While work by African performers and artists is well represented, and is perhaps the more interesting aspect of the festival, the festival-goers and performers are still predominantly white.

The **programme** – spanning jazz, classical music, drama, dance, cabaret, opera, visual arts, crafts, films and a book fair – is bulky, but essential, and it's worth planning your time carefully to avoid walking aimlessly around the potentially cold July streets, though there is a festival shuttle bus between venues. For more **information and bookings**, contact the National Arts Festival (☎046 603 1103, ⍈nationalartsfestival.co.za).

Hotel Victoria 8 New St ☎046 622 7261/7208, ⍈hotelvictoria.co.za; map p.317. Built in 1849, this centrally located hotel has fifteen en-suite rooms, a garden, secluded swimming pool and secure off-stree parking. Its Italian restaurant, *Gino's* (open noon–11pr daily), serves excellent pizzas (R90). **R1150**

4

EATING

★**Haricot's Deli & Bistro** 34 New St ☎046 622 2150, ⍈haricots.co.za; map p.317. French, European and Mediterranean food in a tranquil, secluded spot, with contemporary decor and a central location – the muesli and croissant breakfasts (R60) are great, as are the local meat dishes, such as lamb cutlets with salsa (R120). Mon–Sat 9am–9.30pm.

Red Café 127 High St ☎046 622 8384, ⍈bit.ly /redcafegrahamstown; map p.317. Popular with students and hipsters, this centrally located spot close to campus offers cheap breakfasts (R50), wraps and sandwiches during the day, a bistro-style menu in th evening, and Sunday lunches. Mon–Fri 7am–9pm, Sa 9am–2pm & 5–9pm, Sun 10am–3pm.

Revelations Coffee Shop Pepper Grove Mall, African S ☎046 636 2433, ⍈revelationscoffeeshop.co.za; ma p.317. The pick of the restaurants in this tiny mall, wit outdoor seating and an extensive menu including breakfa fry-ups and specials such as butternut and orange soup, plu an array of budget lunches (R50). It's good for plain suppe too, served on just three nights of the week. Mon–Sa 7am–5pm, Wed, Fri & Sat 7am–9pm, Sun 9am–4pm.

DRINKING

Rat & Parrot 59 New St ☎046 622 5002; map p.317. Close to the university, this long-established gastro-pub is the best place to take advantage of some exceedingly cheap wine (R20) and hang out with students till the earl hours. The vibe is definitely better than the food, howeve Mon–Sat 11am–midnight, Sun 11am–10pm.

SHOPPING

★**African Musical Instruments** Cnr Cloncore & Jarvis sts ☎046 622 6252, ⍈kalimba.co.za ; map p.317. The place to buy fine-quality, handmade African musical instruments. It is best known for its range of percussion instruments, particularly *kalimbas*, which are all made a their small factory using the highest-quality woods. Mon– Fri 8am–4.30pm.

Bathurst

A significant centre in the nineteenth century, **BATHURST**, 45km south of Grahamstown, i today little more than a picturesque straggle of smallholdings, gardens and craft shops, anchored around the Victorian landmark of the *Pig and Whistle*, a pub. Some of the **craft shops** are good for ceramics, beadwork, paintings, woollen products and creams made from beeswax and herbs produced in the village, and there's a small outdoor **Farmers'**

Market on Main Road on Sundays (9am–noon), where you can buy fantastic local breads, produce and herbal ointments, and sit under the coral trees having a pancake or fry-up.

ARRIVAL AND INFORMATION

BATHURST

By bus The Minilux bus between Grahamstown and Port Alfred stops at the *Pig and Whistle* (see p.322) on Tues, Thurs, Fri & Sun.

Tourist information The *Pig and Whistle* (see p.322) will let you see maps of historical sites from their

private collection. Port Alfred Tourist Information Office provides maps and brochures of the Bathurst area (Mon–Fri 8am–5pm, Sat 8.30am–noon; ☎ 046 624 1235, ⓦ sunshinecoasttourism.co.za).

ACCOMMODATION

★**Kingston Farm** On the R67 between Port Alfred and Grahamstown ☎ 046 625 0129, ⓦ kingstonfarm.co.za. An Appaloosa stud farm offering accommodation in three comfortable self-catering apartments in a large Edwardian main house. It's also a great choice for dinner, whether you are staying or not. Book in advance. **R1000**

Morley House On the R67 ☎ 078 353 6181, ⓦ morley house.com. Picturesque settler house and tea garden, with one of the oldest stone houses in the region set up for self-catering groups (R1200). If you're a couple, or on your own, there's either the thatched rondavel (R800) or a safari-style tent – both come with an excellent breakfast. **R600**

EATING

Lara's Eatery & Deli York Rd ☎ 071 370 1019. Very rustic café in a beautiful garden serving a range of fusion food. The salads, brimming with fresh local produce, are especially popular (R75). Mon & Wed 9am–3pm, Wed–Sat 9am–3pm & 6.30–10pm, Sun 9am–3pm.

Pickwick's Oven Cnr of York & Trappes sts ☎ 046 625 0350. A cosy café-restaurant offering pasta, salads and pizza cooked in a wood oven (R80), plus coffee and cake, with an adjoining bar next door. There's a garden for summer meals and a fireplace in winter. Tues–Sat 11am–9pm, Sun 11am–4pm.

4

EASTERN CAPE GAME RESERVES

The Eastern Cape is fast developing as a region for game viewing, with several fine reserves in the Grahamstown area, many of which offer day-trips as well as overnight excursions.

Great Fish River Reserve Complex On the R67, 34km north of Grahamstown; office daily 8am–4.30pm; day visitors R20 ☎ 087 286 6545, ⓦ visiteasterncape.co.za. This is an amalgamation of three separate reserves covering 430 square kilometres situated along the banks of the Fish and Kat rivers, and accessed by rough dirt roads. Although there is plenty of game, it is difficult to see, so if you want to tick off the Big Five, this reserve is not for you. In the southwestern section, closest to Grahamstown, there's accommodation in chalets for up to four people at *Mvubu*. **R2190**

★**Kwandwe Private Game Reserve** On the R67, 41km north of Grahamstown and 160km from Port Elizabeth ☎ 046 603 3400, ⓦ kwandwe.com. The Eastern Cape's top wildlife destination, with 30km of Fish River frontage plus the Big Five. As well as game drives, Kwandwe offers guided river walks, canoeing on the Great Fish and rhino tracking, plus cultural tours that explore the social and archeological history of the area. The accommodation ranges from a luxury lodge with nine suites and thatched roofs, wooden walkways and French windows with panoramic views, to a funky boutique-hotel-in-the-bush ingeniously designed with glass walls

that allow you to lie on your bed and feel you're totally alone in the middle of the wilderness. **R23,700**

Pumba Private Game Reserve 22km west of Grahamstown off the N2 ☎ 041 502 3050, ⓦ pumbagamereserve.co.za. A good bet if you want to see lions and other game at close quarters, delivered to you on daily game drives. You can be collected from your accommodation in Grahamstown and the early morning drive includes breakfast at the camp, while the 4pm game drive includes dinner (both R1060 per person). Drives are on a ten-seater Land Rover, with no children under 8 permitted. The full overnight safari experience includes luxury accommodation, meals, drives and drinks. **R13,880**

Sibuya Game Reserve Access only by boat ☎ 046 648 1040, ⓦ sibuya.co.za. At the cheaper end of the scale, as it doesn't have lions, though you can still see zebra, giraffe, buffalo and rhinos on its recommended day tours where guests are collected by boat from Kenton-on-Sea for a meander up the Kariega River, with a river cruise, game drive and lunch (R1379). If you stay overnight in the luxuriously tented camps, the rate includes all meals and game activities, as well as canoeing and walking. **R9038**

DRINKING

Pig and Whistle Inn On the R67 at the Grahamstown & Port Alfred crossroads ☎ 046 625 0673, ⓦ pigandwhistle.co.za. A colonial Victorian village inn and one of the most historical pubs in South Africa, which still functions as the effective centre of Bathurst (and still allows smoking); sit on the veranda with a beer (R30) and watch the world go by. The restaurant offers traditional pub food – steak and chips, or toasted sandwiches. Daily 11am–11pm.

The Eastern Cape Karoo

Between Grahamstown and the towns of Cradock and Graaff-Reinet (the Eastern Cape's two most-visited Karoo towns) is **sheep-farming country**, with the occasional *dorp* rising against the horizon, offering the experience of an archetypal one-horse outpost. The roads through this vast emptiness are quiet, passing dun-coloured sheep, angora goats and the occasional springbok grazing on brown stubble, plus groups of charcoal-and-grey ostriches in the veld. Some of South Africa's most magnificent farm stays are here, with a distinct outback feel (see below).

Cradock, 240km north of Port Elizabeth, lies in the **Karoo** proper, and makes a great stopover on the Port Elizabeth to Johannesburg run, because of its excellent accommodation and its proximity to the beautiful **Mountain Zebra National Park**. Some 100km due west of Cradock, **Graaff-Reinet**, surrounded by the **Camdeboo National Park**, is one of the oldest towns in South Africa, with much of its historical centre intact. For more of a sense of the Karoo's dry timelessness, head to **Nieu Bethesda**, 50km to the north of town.

4

ACCOMMODATION   THE EASTERN CAPE KAROO

★ **Cavers Country Guest House** Just outside Bedford, an hour north of Grahamstown ☎ 046 685 0619, ⓦ cavers.co.za. One of the best working farm stays in the region this grand 1850 refurbished two-storey stone manor house has stunning gardens, watered by mountain springs, and a breathtaking mountain backdrop. The friendly owners cook delicious dinners. R1400

Cradock

As you enter **CRADOCK**, you will see Xhosa hawkers selling intricately crafted wire model windmills – the silvery windmills on the surrounding sheep farms having become the unofficial symbol of the town. The town itself has some handsome colonial architecture, with the main street dominated by the 1868 **Dutch Reformed Church**, based on London's St Martin's-in-the-Fields. In March the annual **Karoo Food Festival** takes place here, where you can taste specialities of the region.

But poverty has overshadowed Cradock since the Frontier Wars of the nineteenth century and the subjugation of the Xhosa people. Against this history of conquest the town has provided fertile grounds for **resistance**: ANC members in the vicinity almost single-handedly kept the organization alive during the 1930s. In 1985, Cradock hit the headlines when anti-apartheid activist **Matthew Goniwe** and three colleagues were murdered. It was only in 1997, during the **Truth and Reconciliation Commission** hearings, that five Port Elizabeth security policemen were named as the perpetrators. There is a modest **memorial** to the Cradock Four in the run-down municipal park on the banks of the Fish River, off the Middelburg Road, and an unfinished and neglected monument created with four huge slabs of rock, on a hill close to the township where Goniwe lived, clearly visible as you enter town from Port Elizabeth.

Schreiner House Museum

9 Cross St • Mon–Fri 8.30am–4.30pm, weekends by appointment • Donation • ☎ 048 881 5251

Schreiner House is dedicated to the writer Olive Schreiner, best known for her ground-breaking novel *The Story of an African Farm* (1883). It was remarkable enough for a woman from the conservative backwoods of nineteenth-century Eastern Cape to write a

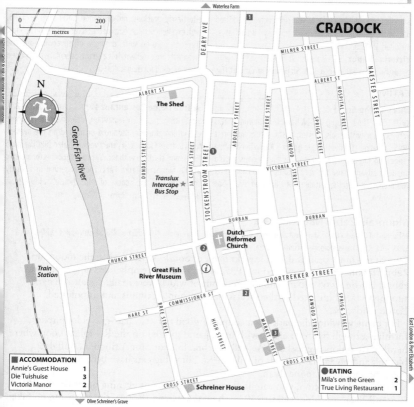

CRADOCK

ACCOMMODATION
Annie's Guest House	1
Die Tuishuise	3
Victoria Manor	2

EATING
Mila's on the Green	2
True Living Restaurant	1

novel, but even more amazing that she espoused such radical ideas as universal franchise for men and women irrespective of race. Schreiner died in 1921 and is buried near Cradock on the Buffelskop Peak, with her one-day-old daughter and favourite dog. Her **burial site** has become something of a place of pilgrimage, and details of how to get there are available from Schreiner House – it is a long hike up. The house also has a small bookshop selling works by Schreiner and other South African writers, and each July it plays host to the **Schreiner Karoo Writers' Festival** (ⓦkaroowritersfestival.weebly.com).

ARRIVAL AND INFORMATION

CRADOCK

By bus Translux and Intercape buses from Port Elizabeth and Johannesburg pull in daily at Shoprite Checkers on Voortrekker St.

By train Cradock is a daily stop on the Port Elizabeth–Johannesburg rail line; the station is on the west bank of the Great Fish River.

Information Cradock Tourist Office, JA Calata St (ⓣ048 881 1137, ⓦcradockmiddelburg.co.za), is understaffed and not very reliable. Check out the website for basic local information, along with ⓦcradock-info.co.za for basics.

ACCOMMODATION

Annie's Guest House 112 Adderley St ⓣ048 881 5241, ⓦanniesguesthouse.co.za; map above. Reliable, clean and well-run B&B guesthouse in a Victorian house with 12 brightly coloured rooms, a swimming pool and a garden. Transportation is provided to and from the bus stop, if you need it. R1200

★**Die Tuishuise** Market St ⓣ048 881 1322, ⓦtuishuise.co.za; map above. Staying in this street of comfortable and stylish one- to four-bedroomed Victorian houses, with their candy-striped veranda roofs, gives an authentic sense of colonial domestic life in the 1850s. Prices are very reasonable, given that you get what amounts to a mini-museum to yourself, each house kitted out with antique furniture and crockery. Breakfast is included. R1120

Victoria Manor 36 Market St ☎048 881 1650, ⓦtuishuise.co.za; map p.323. Step back in time at this effortlessly gracious, old-fashioned hotel built in 1848, with excellent service, bags of character and period fittings. The rooms are en suite, dining is off silverware and the breakfasts are excellent. It is also the only place that's open every evening for dinner. R950

EATING

Mila's on the Green Cradock Golf Club, Hofmeyer Rd ☎073 924 1563; map p.323. A homely restaurant that is very popular with locals, serving pasta, steaks and grills (R95). Local meat is the thing to go for – Karoo lamb is free range and organic here. Vegetarians and vegans should phone in advance, and the very accomplished chef Pieter will prepare something suitable. Fully licensed. Wed–Sat 6.30–9pm.

★**True Living Restaurant** 44 J A Calata St ☎048 881 3288; map p.323. A restaurant, deli and bakery where everything is made, produced or hunted on the owners' farm outside Cradock. Try their venison salad (R80) or lamb livers, and stock up with locally grown goodies for a picnic at the Mountain Zebra Park. Food is served in a shady courtyard at the back of the house. Mon–Thurs 8am–5pm, Fri 8am–9pm, Sat 8am–1pm.

Mountain Zebra National Park

26km west of Cradock • Daily: April–Sept 7am–6pm; Oct–March 7am–7pm • Adults R176, children R88, SA citizens R44 • ☎048 801 5700/5701, ⓦsanparks.org/parks/mountain_zebra

One of the most beautiful, but least known, of South Africa's parks, the **Mountain Zebra National Park** was created in 1937, when there were only five Cape **mountain zebras** left on its 65 square kilometres – four of which were male. Today, the park supports several hundred in the spectacular, dry, mountainous and unpolluted Karoo landscape.

For **game viewing**, the park has a couple of good part-tar, part-gravel loop roads forming a rough figure of eight, with most game spotted on the Rooiplaat Loop where herds graze on open grassland. As well as zebra, look out for springbok, buffalo, blesbok and several large herds of wildebeest. Some big cats have been introduced, but you'll be very lucky to see them.

At the park reception, you can book morning, sunset or evening **game drives** (R212, sunset R282), morning **walks** (R303), **cheetah tracking** (R364), the Saltpeterkop **hike** for a magnificent view over the park (3hr; R359), or visits to San cave paintings (R202). You can also do your own **bush walk** on two trails which start from the swimming pool and are within a fenced-off area.

ARRIVAL AND SERVICES — MOUNTAIN ZEBRA NATIONAL PARK

By car To reach the park, which is 26km from town, head north out of Cradock on the N10 Middelburg Rd. Signposts direct you to the main gate of the reserve, from where it is approximately 12km to the accommodation, game viewing all the way. From Port Elizabeth, it is 256km on the N10.

Services A small shop at reception sells basics, souvenirs, alcohol and soft drinks, but if you're staying for a few days you should stock up in Cradock. There's a reasonable licensed à la carte restaurant (daily 7.30am–9pm), a post office, a filling station and a swimming pool.

ACCOMMODATION

Park accommodation ☎012 428 9111 or ☎082 233 9111, ⓦsanparks.org/parks/mountain_zebra. Choose from either comfy two-bedroom cottages with outstanding mountain views and their own kitchens and bathrooms, or lovely camp sites. All accommodation must be confirmed with reception by 6pm the day before you arrive. Camping R295, cottages R1000

Graaff-Reinet

GRAAFF-REINET is a beautiful town and one of the few places in the Eastern Cape where you'd want to wander freely day and night, taking in historical buildings and the occasional museum, or having a meal and a drink. The town centres around the imposing 1886 **Dutch Reformed Church** on Church Street, the main thoroughfare, from which little roads fan out, lined with whitewashed Cape Dutch, Georgian and

Victorian buildings. The dry mountains surrounding the town are part of the **Camdeboo National Park** whose main attraction is the impressive **Valley of Desolation**. This is a favourite stop on the road between Johannesburg and the coast, with some excellent guesthouses and a couple of decent restaurants. The town deserves at least a couple of days' stay to take in all the historical sites, fossil collections, rock art and nature reserves.

Brief history

By the late eighteenth century, Dutch burghers had extended the Cape frontier northwards into the Sneeuberg Mountains, traditionally the stomping ground of Khoi pastoralists and San hunter-gatherers. The settlers raided Khoi cattle and attacked groups of San, killing the men and abducting women and children to use as farm and domestic labourers. Friction escalated when the Khoi and San retaliated, and, in 1786, the Cape authorities sent out a *landdrost* (magistrate) to establish Graaff-Reinet, administer the surrounding area and pacify the frontier.

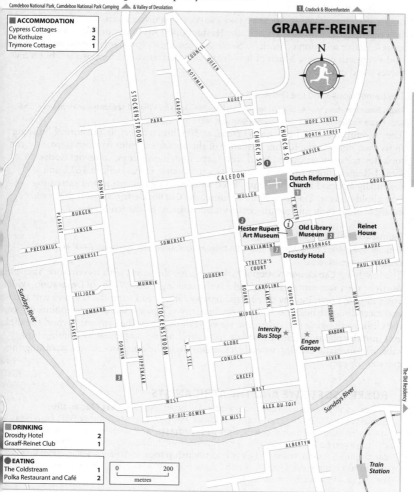

GRAAFF-REINET

Camdeboo National Park, Camdeboo National Park Camping   & Valley of Desolation

Cradock & Bloemfontein

■ ACCOMMODATION

Cypress Cottages	3
De Kothuize	2
Trymore Cottage	1

Dutch Reformed Church

Hester Rupert Art Museum

Old Library Museum

Reinet House

Drostdy Hotel

Intercity Bus Stop

Engen Garage

The Old Residency

■ DRINKING

Drosdty Hotel	2
Graaff-Reinet Club	1

● EATING

The Coldstream	1
Polka Restaurant and Café	2

0   200
metres

Train Station

Port Elizabeth

4

Colonial control over the district was slowly consolidated, with vast tracts turned over to grazing sheep. The **wool boom** of the 1850s brought prosperity to the town and established a pattern of farming and land ownership which continues to this day. Today, Graaff-Reinet has a large population of Afrikaans-speaking coloured people, mostly living on the south side of town, some of slave origin, others the descendants of indigenous Khoi and San.

Old Library Museum

Church St • Mon–Thurs 8am–4.30pm, Fri 8am–4pm, Sat & Sun 9am–1pm • R30 • Ⓦ graaffreinetmuseums.co.za

The most spectacular attraction at the **Old Library Museum**, one block south of the Dutch Reformed church, is the compelling collection of **fossil skulls** and skeletons of reptiles that populated the prehistoric Karoo, some 230 million years ago. There is also a slavery exhibition, a display on Africanist Robert Sobukwe (see below) and a fine collection of old books on Africa.

Hester Rupert Art Museum

Church St • Mon–Fri 9am–12.30pm & 2–5pm, Sat & Sun 9am–noon • R30 • Ⓦ rupertartmuseum.co.za

In a restored 1821 mission church, the **Hester Rupert Art Museum** features a representative selection of work by South African artists (primarily white) active in the mid-twentieth century. Much of it is dreary and derivative of European art, but a few pieces stand out.

The Reinet House and the Old Residency

Reinet House Mon–Thurs 8am–4.30pm, Fri 8am–4pm, Sat & Sun 9am–1pm • R20 • **The Old Residency** Mon–Thurs 8am–1pm & 1.45–4.30pm, Fri 8am–1pm & 1.30–4pm, Sat & Sun 9am–noon • R30

The graceful, whitewashed *Drostdy Hotel*, at 30 Church Street, is a historical building in its own right, as the former residence of the *landdrost*. From its front steps, you can look down Parsonage Street, lined with Cape Dutch buildings, to **Reinet House**, Graaff-Reinet's finest museum. Formerly a parsonage, it was built in 1812 and is essentially a period house museum, filled with covetable furniture and intriguing household objects. Opposite Reinet House, the **Old Residency** is a well-preserved example of an early nineteenth-century Cape Dutch, H-shaped house.

Camdeboo National Park

5km north of Graaff-Reinet, off the Marraysburg Rd • R100 • Daily 6am–7pm (winter), 6am–8pm (summer) • ☎ 049 892 3453, Ⓦ sanparks.org/parks/camdeboo

The low-lying **Camdeboo National Park** surrounds the town, with its entrance 5km north of the town centre. Its highlight is the strikingly deep **Valley of Desolation**, which you can gaze down into by driving the narrow tarred road from the reserve's entrance and ascending the bush-flecked mountainside; you'll pass a series of viewpoints up to the cliffs overlooking the valley. The views from the lip of the canyon, beyond the rock and into the plains of Camdeboo, are truly thrilling, accompanied by echoing bird calls; it's especially exciting when black eagles circle the dolomite towers, scanning the crevices for prey.

ROBERT SOBUKWE AND THE AFRICANISTS

One of Graaff-Reinet's most brilliant but often-forgotten sons is **Robert Managaliso Sobukwe** (1923–78), the charismatic founder of the Pan Africanist Congress (PAC). He is best known for launching the nationwide **anti-pass protests**, which ended in the Sharpeville massacre and his imprisonment, in solitary confinement, on Robben Island for nine years. You can visit the Sobukwe home and grave on a **township tour**, and there are plans afoot for a museum commemorating his life. Karoo Connections (☎ 049 892 3978; Ⓦ karooconnections .co.za) provides a reliable township tour.

There are a couple of good walks: the looped **Crag Lizard Walk** (45min) along the canyon lip, well marked with a lizard emblem; and the **Eerstefontein Day Walk**, which starts and ends at Spandaukop gate, with route options of 5km, 11km and 14km. The park has six designated picnic areas.

ARRIVAL AND DEPARTURE   GRAAFF-REINET

By bus Translux buses between Johannesburg and Port Elizabeth, and Intercape buses connecting Joburg with the Garden Route towns, pull in daily at the Engen garage on Church St. For bus tickets and timetables, check at the tourist office (see below) or the bus company websites.

INFORMATION AND TOURS

Tourist information The tourist office at 13 Church St (Mon–Fri 8am–5pm, Sat 9am–noon; ☎ 049 892 4248, ☑ graafreinet.co.za) provides maps and accommodation lists.

Guided tours Karoo Connections (☎ 049 892 3978, ☑ karooconnections.co.za) runs a series of recommended and reasonably priced tours, including visits to historical sites in Graaff-Reinet, the nearby national parks, Nieu Bethesda, and Bushman rock art and Gondwanaland fossil sites.

ACCOMMODATION

Cypress Cottages 76 Donkin St ☎ 049 892 3965 or ☎ 083 456 1795, ☑ cypresscottage.co.za; map p.325. Two restored Karoo cottages each with three double en-suite rooms and a communal lounge and dining room. In addition, there four self-catering units, *River Bend*, also housed in renovated historical cottages. All the cottages are tastefully furnished with antiques and natural fabrics, and there is a swimming pool. B&B R1300

De Kothuize 6 Parsonage St ☎ 082 339 1680, ☑ dekothuize.co.za; map p.325. *De Kothuize* comprises eight beautifully restored Karoo cottages – most of them National Monuments – in three of the oldest streets in the centre of town. Five are on Parsonage St, two on Cradock St and one on Middle St. All are self-catering, comfortably furnished with a/c, and an easy walk from the museums and restaurants. R1000

★**Trymore Cottage,** Wellwood Farm, 31km north of town, on the road to Nieu Bethesda ☎ 049 840 0302, ☑ wellwood.co.za; map p.325. A self-catering, comfortable, four-bedroom house on a beautiful, long-established Karoo farm. Braai packs are available and evening dinners can be arranged, with Karoo lamb or venison on the menu. An added bonus is the outstanding collection of Karoo reptile fossils, which is available to guests to look at. R1400

CAMPING

Camdeboo National Park Book in advance through the National Park's office in Port Elizabeth ☎ 041 583 2030. The park's two overnight camps are both equipped with communal kitchens and showers/toilets, the Nqweba campsite (15 places) and the Lakeside Tented Camp, with four rustic furnished tents. Nqweba R225, Lakeside R650

EATING

The Coldstream 3 Church Square ☎ 049 891 1181; map p.325. In a wing of the former colonial Graaff-Reinet Club, with veranda seating overlooking the garden, this restaurant serves Karoo lamb chops (R130), a considerable variety of local meats, plus generous snack platters. Mon–Sat 9am–9pm.

Polka Restaurant, Café, Bakery & Deli 52 Somerset St ☎ 087 550 1363; map p.325. A cottage restaurant on a quiet, leafy side street serving well-presented and delicious Karoo cuisine, such as lamb shanks (R130) and *bobotie* with unusual touches. Mon–Sat 7.30am–9pm.

DRINKING

Drosdty Hotel 30 Church St ☎ 049 892 2161; map p.325. As well as a good indoor restaurant, the town's premier – and very upmarket – historical building has the best garden setting for a tranquil drink, coffee or light lunch. If it's too cold outside, the indoor bar is a snug place to sip your gin and tonic (R40). Daily 11am–11pm.

The Graaff-Reinet Club 3 Church Square ☎ 049 892 4248; map p.325. Founded in 1875, this is a great place to experience some Anglo-Boer War atmosphere over a whisky (R60), with historic photos, a large firearm collection, caricatures of former members, and seven bullet holes in the bar counter. Daily 11am–10pm.

Nieu Bethesda

Off the beaten track, in the mountains north of Graaff-Reinet, **NIEU BETHESDA** (☑ nieubethesda.info) is dry and dusty, especially in midsummer when it boils with harsh, bright light. There are no streetlamps, and on winter nights temperatures plummet to zero, though the whitewashed **village** has plenty of charm, with a village shop and butcher on the main road. Once an archetypal conservative Karoo *dorp*, it ha reinvented itself as a tiny artists' colony, attracting a growing number of visitors.

Bethesda Arts Centre

Muller St, opposite the police station • ☎ 073 028 8887, ⓦ bethesdafoundation.org • **Tower Restaurant** daily 8.30am–8pm

The non-profit **Bethesda Arts Centre** has provided opportunities for craft workers, artists and performers to get trained and to sell their work; it now houses an art gallery, working studios and an open-air theatre. It's worth dropping in to check what's on, or you can get curry and rice (R90) and other light food at the quaint Tower restaurant.

The Owl House

River St • Daily April–Sept 9am–5pm; Oct–March 8am–5pm • R60 • R85 Owl House & Fossil Museum • ☎ 049 841 1733, ⓦ theowlhouse.co.za

Most people who come to Nieu Bethesda visit the **Owl House**, the former home of Helen Martins, a reclusive artist who expressed her disturbing and fascinating inner world through her work. Every corner of the house and garden has been transformed to reflect her vision. The interior walls glitter with crushed glass, owls with large eyes gaze from the tin-roofed veranda, while at the back of the house, trapped by a stone wall and high chicken wire, are hundreds of glass and cement sculptures: camels, lambs, sphinxes and human figures. Adjoining her house is the Fossil Museum and Art Gallery, worth a look, unless you've already seen the region's substantial fossil collectior in Graaff-Reinet.

4

ARRIVAL AND DEPARTURE

By car Nieu Bethesda is 23km off the N9 between Graaff-Reinet and Middelburg, on a newly tarred road with only 5km of dirt road, some 60km from Graaff-Reinet and 308km from Port Elizabeth. There's no ATM or petrol in Nieu Bethesda, so it's a good idea to fill up in Graaff-Reine There are also no facilities for credit cards, so make sure yo take enough cash with you.

ACCOMMODATION

Doornberg Farm 9km north of Nieu Bethesda ☎ 049 841 1401, ⓦ nieubethesda.co.za. For those wanting to stay on a working farm, the friendly *Doornberg Farm* is set up for B&B and self-catering. There are five places to choose from, the nicest of which is *Die Vleihuisie*, a little cottage 4km away from the farmstead. **R750**

★**Ganora Farm** Off the N9, 7km east of Nieu Bethesda ☎ 049 841 1302 or ☎ 082 698 0029, ⓦ ganora.co.za. A working farm with B&B accommodation, plus self-catering cottages sleeping six (R1400). The owners offer a variety of activities, including visits to Bushman rock paintings, a medicinal plant excursion and access to their fossil collection. There's also a swimming pool and hiking and cycling trails. Dinner can be ordered in advance (R160). B&B **R970**

Ibis Guest House Martin St ☎ 072 110 6254 ⓦ theibislounge.co.za. Three comfortable en-suit rooms, decorated in a contemporary, funky way with welcome swimming pool, and the convenience of a goo restaurant on the premises. The owners are ver welcoming, but don't allow children under 12 years ol **R1300**

Owl House Backpackers Lodge Martin St ☎ 049 84 1642 or ☎ 072 742 7113, ⓦ owlhouse.info. Nie Bethesda's only backpacker lodge is friendly, laidback an well organized with dorm beds, en-suite rooms (B&B c self-catering) and two self-contained cottages. Wit sufficient notice, you can be picked up from Graaff-Reine for R200. Camping **R85**, dorms **R150**, doubles **R550**

EATING

Auntie Evelyne se Plek 4 Kloof St (just on the top of the rise on entering Pienaarsig) ☎ 083 873 5526. Auntie Evelyne lives in Pienaarsig (the township area) and serves traditional township food in her home. In summer, meals are served on her *stoep*; in winter you sit in a painted tin shack, warmed by a heater and an oudoor stove. The menu varies and could include traditional *bredies*, samp-and-beans (R70), *roosterkoek* and *lekker poedin* Advance booking essential; phone for opening hours.

Ibis Lounge Martin St ☎ 072 110 6254, ⓦ theib lounge.co.za. A comfortable place to relax and enjoy wide range of speciality coffees. You can sit outdoors in th shade of the big *stoep* or inside on leather couches, warme by fireplaces in winter. Sample the home-made pies an

bread, their garden veg in season or the excellent slow-roast Karoo lamb (R90) for Sunday lunch. Daily 8am–8pm.
Two Goats Deli & The Brewery Pienaar St ☎049 841 1602. A good choice for an unhurried lunch, consisting of a

platter of home-made cheese, bread, olives and salami (R75), accompanied by a choice of three beers brewed on the premises – Karoo, Honey and Roasted Ale (R15). Daily 9am–5pm.

East London and the central region

Between Port Alfred and East London lies some of the Eastern Cape's least-developed **coastline**, although there are the usual enclaves of white South African holiday homes. **East London**, the largest city in the central region of the province, though dowdy and eminently missable, has some excellent beaches for surfing and swimming and good transport links to Johannesburg and along the coast. Inland, **Fort Hare University** near Alice has educated political leaders across the subcontinent, including Nelson Mandela, and boasts the country's finest collection of contemporary black South African art.

Sweeping up from Fort Hare's valley, the misty, wooded **Amatola Mountains** yield to the dramatic landscapes of the **Eastern Cape Drakensberg**, which offer hiking, trout fishing and remote landscapes. Before white settlers (or even the Xhosa) arrived, these towering formations were dominated by **San hunter-gatherers**, who decorated the rock faces with thousands of ritual **paintings**, many of which remain surprisingly vivid.

East London

EAST LONDON, the second-largest city in the Eastern Cape, is the obvious jumping-off point for exploring the Transkei. **Nahoon Beach** is a great **surfing spot**, and the town has a dedicated and lively surfing scene. It's also gradually becoming a place for black holidaymakers – a post-apartheid phenomenon. The beaches to the east of town are

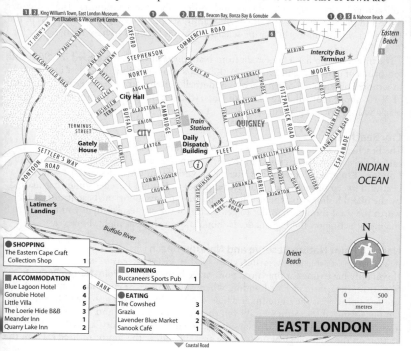

EAST LONDON

very beautiful, with long stretches of sand, high dunes, estuaries and luxuriant vegetation, and good swimming.

The drab city centre is dominated by **Oxford Street**, parallel to Station Street and the train station. Although a major traffic thoroughfare, it is largely deserted at night, when you shouldn't wander around alone. Apart from a couple of handsome buildings, East London's Victorian heart has progressively been demolished, though its principal landmark, the splendid terracotta and lace-white **City Hall**, opened in 1899, remains. Over the road is a rather lifeless statue of martyred Black Consciousness leader **Steve Biko** (see box, p.333).

Away from the holiday strip, East London is dominated by an industrial centre served by **Mdantsane**, a huge African township 20km from the city towards King William's Town.

Brief history

Before the British, and even the Xhosa, the area was home to the **Khoikhoi** people, who called it Place of the Buffaloes. The Buffalo River once teemed with game, but the animals were gradually killed off with the arrival of British hunters. East London began life as a permanent British settlement during the nineteenth-century **Frontier Wars**, when it was used as a beachhead to land military supplies needed to push back the Xhosa. Taken by its strategic possibilities as a port, the British governor Sir Harry Smith optimistically called it **London** in 1848. Later it was changed to East London, because the port was on the east side of the Buffalo River. There's also a tiny Hamburg and Berlin, both not far from East London – tattered remnants of German settlers who left little legacy besides their city names.

East London Museum

Upper Oxford St • Mon- Fri 9am–4pm • R15 • ☎ 043 743 0686

A few kilometres north of the city centre, the **East London Museum** has a stunning collection of South Nguni beadwork and contemporary wire sculpture. The museum's pride and joy, however, is its stuffed coelacanth (see p.319), caught off the coast in the 1950s – a wonder in world marine science, as it was believed to have been extinct for 70 million years.

The museum also has a large rock from Nahoon's Bat Cave, discovered in 1964, with footprints of a human child from 124,000 years ago – possibly the oldest in the world. In a more contemporary vein, there is a football diorama from the Soccer World Cup of 2010, about football in the Eastern Cape (though this is one of the few areas where black South Africans play rugby).

City Beaches

The beaches to make for (and stay close to) are Nahoon and Bonza Bay, both to the east of the centre. Those closest to the city centre are rather less appealing. East London's **Esplanade** loops from Orient Pier, with its industrial feel, into a wide and beautiful sweep of rocks, beach and sand dunes to Eastern Beach – somewhat marred by the bland holiday apartments, hotels and restaurants along the beachfront. It is worth the walk though, in order to get a sense of the city, especially if you happen to be staying or eating on the Esplanade. It should not be done at night, however.

Nahoon Point Nature Reserve and Nahoon Beach

Visitor's Centre signposted off Epson Rd, Nahoon • Daily 8.30am–4pm • Free • Reef Café Tues–Sun 9am–4pm

If you only have time for one attraction, make it the **Nahoon Point Nature Reserve**, 5km from the centre of East London, where you can see the coastline from a good vantage point, visit the museum and have a coffee. In a building shaped like the area's famous fossilized footprint (see above), the Coastal Education and Visitors' Centre has a worthwhile museum with displays on the town's surfing history, as well as an excellent section on the archeological finds of the area (including the footprint itself). From the

Museum car park, you can stroll on wooden walkways along the coast, or go on longer hikes, to take in the best of the city's coastline.

Superb for swimming and surfing, **Nahoon Beach**, to the east of Nahoon Point, is a long stretch of sand, backed by dunes, with some of the best waves in the country.

Bonza Bay and Gonubie Beach

East of the Nahoon River, 10km from the town centre, the coast curves into **Bonza Bay**, with kilometres of beach walks and a lazy lagoon at the mouth of the Quinera River. Further on, **Gonubie Beach**, 18km northeast of the centre, at the Gonubie River Mouth, is still close enough to be considered part of East London, with some good accommodation, a beautiful beach and walks.

ARRIVAL AND DEPARTURE   EAST LONDON

By plane East London's small airport (☎ 043 706 0306), a few kilometres west of the centre on the R72, connects the city to all major centres. Imonti Tours (☎ 043 741 3884 or ☎ 083 487 8975) also makes transfers from the airport to the city centre, as does Dean's Taxi Services (☎ 073 194 6367).

By bus All three of the intercity buses – Translux (☎ 086 158 9282, ⌨ translux.co.za), Intercape (☎ 086 128 7287, ⌨ intercape.co.za) and Greyhound (☎ 083 915 9000, ⌨ greyhound.co.za) – offer a frequent, comprehensive and inexpensive service connecting East London to major cities. The buses drop off at the Intercity Bus Terminal at Windmill Park on Moore St, close to the beach. The Minilux minibus (☎ 043 741 3107), which connects Grahamstown with the airport at Port Elizabeth daily, goes on to Port Alfred on Tues and Thurs, and East London on Mon, Tues, Thurs & Fri.

By train The train station (☎ 086 000 8888) is on the eastern edge of East London's small business and shopping district. Metered taxis outside the station will get you to your accommodation.

GETTING AROUND

By car Like most South African cities, central East London is gridded. With uncongested roads and easy parking, it's far more geared to driving than walking.

By taxi Dean's Taxi Services (☎ 073 194 6367 or ☎ 079 293 5132) provides a day and night service, and reasonably priced transport to the airport.

INFORMATION AND TOURS

Tourist information Tourist information can be obtained at the airport (Mon–Fri 8am–4.30pm; ☎ 043 736 3019) or in town at the Firestation, 2nd Floor, Fleet St (☎ 043 736 2019, ⌨ bctourism.co.za).

Guided tours Imonti (☎ 043 741 3884 or ☎ 083 487 8975, ⌨ imontitours.co.za) runs excellent and well-organized township and city tours (half-day from R350), as well as full-day tours to Mthatha and Qunu for the Nelson Mandela sights. This is probably the easiest way to get to see where Mandela spent his early years, with a stopover for lunch at the Country Club in Mthatha (R850).

ACCOMMODATION

East London's beachfront sports graceless blocks of holiday apartments and functional hotels, redeemed by their fabulous views of the Indian Ocean. For a less urban feel, head for the suburbs of Nahoon Mouth at the end of Beach Rd, Beacon Bay, Bonza Bay or Gonubie, close to the river and sea and reached via the N2 east of the city; without your own transport, you'll need to take a taxi or arrange to be picked up.

BEACHFRONT AND NORTHERN SUBURBS

Blue Lagoon Blue Bend Place, Beacon Bay ☎ 043 748 3821, ⌨ bluelagoonhotel.co.za; map p.329. Very pleasant accommodation surrounded by palm trees and close to the beach. Rooms are quiet and spacious, with balconies looking onto the river. R1800

Gonubie Hotel 141 Main Rd, Gonubie ☎ 043 740 4010, ⌨ gonubiehotel.co.za; map p.329. Located on the beachfront of Gonubie, this family-run hotel is comfortable, has magnificent views over the bay, and is a short walk to the swimming beach. You can choose between B&B rooms in the hotel proper or the Bayview self-catering apartments; there's also a restaurant and two bars. Hotel R875, self-catering apartments R1200

Little Villa 6 Claremont Rd, Nahoon ☎ 043 735 1128 or ☎ 082 673 2083, ⌨ littlevillabnb.com; map p.329. Quaint, homely, beautifully furnished B&B accommodation for couples, in a double-storey cottage with kitchenette, or a garden room with a pleasant patio. Cottage R1800, garden room R695

The Loerie Hide B&B 2B Sheerness Rd, off Beach Rd, Nahoon ☎ 043 735 3206, ⌨ loeriehide.co.za;

4

map p.329. Seven en-suite rooms at variable rates and a rondavel in the vicinity of Nahoon Beach; all are located at the bottom of a garden that gives way to indigenous bushland. Rondavel R1000, doubles R1300

Meander Inn 8 Clarendon Rd, Selborne ☎ 043 726 2310, ⊚ meanderinn.co.za; map p.329. Ten spacious, tastefully furnished rooms with white linen and ceiling fans, five of which are in the luxurious main house, with the rest in the garden and annexe. There's a swimming pool, patio and bar, and airport transfers can be provided. R1550

Quarry Lake Inn Quartzite Drive, off Pearce St, The Quarry ☎ 043 707 5400, ⊚ quarrylakeinn.co.za; map p.329. Spacious, well-appointed rooms in a lovely setting on the edge of a flooded disused quarry that has become home to abundant vegetation and birdlife. R1836

EATING

The Cowshed 54 Beach Rd Shopping Centre, Nahoon ☎ 043 735 1513; map p.329. Strangely named restaurant where, unsurprisingly, steaks are the thing (R170), with lamb shank and pork belly also on offer as well as vegetarian options. There's also a next-door bar, *The Milk Shed*. Mon–Sat 6–10pm.

Grazia Upper Esplanade, Beach Front Rd ☎ 043 722 2009, ⊚ graziafinefood.co.za; map p.329. A light and airy restaurant at the beachfront, with sea views, serving Italian-style food. The *linguine alla marinara* and layered vegetable gnocchi (R140) are recommended. Daily noon–10pm.

Lavender Blue Market & Coffee Shop Ocean Way Drive, Beacon Bay ☎ 043 732 1172; map p.329. The farmers' market sells great local produce on Saturdays, and during the week you can get good coffee and salads – eating either indoors or in the garden. It's a great choice for breakfast, and if you don't feel like muffins, check out the Hot Chick or the peri-peri chicken livers (R60). Daily 8am–3.30pm.

Sanook Café 11 Chamberlain Rd, Berea ☎ 043 721 3215; map p.329. If you've only one night in town, you could confidently choose *Sanook* as the place to eat. The thin-crust, wood-fired pizzas are recommended, as are the daily specials, such as beef fillet topped with oregano butter and marinated cherry tomatoes (R135). There is also a branch, *Sanook Eatery*, in Bonza Bay Rd, Beacon Bay. Mon–Sat 9am–10pm.

DRINKING

Buccaneers Sports Pub and Grill Eastern Beach, ☎ 043 743 5171, ⊚ buccaneers.co.za; map p.329. A lively bar (beer R20) that buzzes till the early hours, with occasional live music, usually on Sunday afternoons. During the day, you can watch the rodeo riders of the surf from wooden tables and benches. Pub fare includes fish and chips, and burgers (R70), with a couple of options for kids. Daily 10am–2am.

SHOPPING

For shopping head to **Devereux Avenue**, 5km north of the city centre, in the salubrious suburbs of Vincent and Stirling. Here, you'll find the **Vincent Park Centre** (⊚ vincentpark.co.za), a popular shopping mall with restaurants. **Hemingway Mall** (⊚ hemingwaymall.co.za) is a little further north, just off the N2. **The Eastern Cape Craft Collection Shop** (☎ 043 735 1306; map p.329), at the Nahoon Shopping Centre on Old Transkei Rd, is the city's best curio outlet, stocking authentic Xhosa crafts: beautifully beaded bags, wire crafts, jewellery, woven goods and ceramics.

The Amatola Mountains

Most visitors drive quickly through the scrubby, dry, impoverished area between East London and the **Amatola Mountains** proper, to reach the cool forests and holiday lands at **Hogsback**. However, it's worth deviating en route, to see the fine collection of African art at **Fort Hare University**, on the edge of the little run-down town of Alice.

Hogsback

Made sweeter by the contrast with the dry valleys below, the village of **HOGSBACK** in the Amatola Mountains, 32km north of Alice and 145km from East London, offers cool relief after hauling through prickly, overgrazed country. The name "Hogsback" applies to the area as much as to the village, and comes from the high rocky ridge (actually three peaks) resembling a bushpig's spine, which runs above the settlement.

Hogsback represents a corner of England, a fantasy fed by mists, pine plantations and exotic trees such as oak, walnut and azaleas, and occasional snowfalls. It's a great place to spend a relaxing couple of days, with plenty of walks and good air among the flowers, grasslands and forests, and there are many places to stay. The real attraction is

STEVE BIKO AND BLACK CONSCIOUSNESS

Steve Biko's brutal interrogation and death while in police custody triggered international outrage and turned opinion further against the apartheid regime.

Steven Bantu Biko was born in 1946 in King William's Town. His political ascent was swift, due to his eloquence, charisma and focused vision. While still a medical student at Natal University during the late 1960s, he was elected president of the exclusively black **South African Students' Organization** (SASO) and started publishing articles in their journal, fiercely attacking white liberalism, which SASO saw as patronizing and counter-revolutionary. In an atmosphere of repression, Biko's brand of **Black Consciousness** immediately caught on. He called for black Africans to take destiny into their own hands, to unify and rid themselves of the "shackles that bind them to perpetual servitude". From 1973 onwards, Biko suffered banning, detention and other harassment at the hands of the state. In 1974, he defended himself in court, presenting his case so brilliantly that his international profile soared.

Barred from leaving King William's Town, Biko continued working and writing, frequently escaping his confinement. In August 1977 he was detained and taken to Port Elizabeth where he was interrogated and tortured. A month later he died from a brain haemorrhage after a beating by security police. No one was held accountable.

He is buried in the **Steve Biko Garden of Remembrance** in King William's Town, now part of a heritage site that includes several other Biko-related mounuments, such as his mother's Ginsberg home, Biko's office in King William's Town and the Steve Biko Bridge over the Buffalo River.

You can organize a guided tour of the memorial sights at the **Steve Biko Centre** and museum, 1 Zotshie St, Ginsberg, King William's Town (☎ 043 605 6700, ⊛ sbf.org.za; Mon–Fri 8.30am–4.30pm & Sat 9am–1pm; R25). The Centre is easy to find, signposted off the main road as you head west towards Alice and Fort Beaufort.

4

the **Afro-montane cloud forest**, dense with yellowwood, stinkwood and Cape chestnut, filled with bird calls and waterfalls, and populated by the odd troop of **samango monkeys**, colourful turacos and endangered Cape parrots. Note that Hogsback can be wet and cold, even in summer, so bring a warm pullover, sturdy shoes and rain gear.

The hamlet itself is strung out along 3km of tarred road, with gravel and fairly rough lanes branching out on either side to hotels and cottages. The closest thing to a **centre** is the small conglomeration of a general store, post office and filling station. Hogsback has its own **indigenous craft** found nowhere else in the country: prepare to be pestered by hawkers selling the characteristic, and rather lovely, unfired clay horses and hogs with white markings.

The trails

Hogsback is prime **rambling** country, with short, relatively easy trails indicated by hogs painted onto trees. For a rewarding taste of indigenous forest, head to the Arboretum and up the path towards **Tor Doone**, which overlooks the settlement, and is the easiest summit to climb – but still steep. Alternatively, following the path to Tor Doone and then turning right onto the contour path will take you on a one-hour circular walk back to the Arboretum. One of the most rewarding waterfall trails is the one-hour steep downhill walk to the lovely **Madonna and Child Waterfall**. Walks are detailed in inexpensive **guidebooks** available at the information centre.

One of South Africa's best mountain walks, the 105km, backpacking **Amatola Trail** takes in numerous waterfalls and rivers as well as grasslands, plateaus and the Hogs themselves – it's a tough hike, however, and best done in an experienced hiking group or through a tour organization (see p.334).

ARRIVAL AND DEPARTURE

HOGSBACK

By shuttle The backpackers' hostel *Away With The Fairies* (see p.334) operates a shuttle between Hogsback and East London (R160), and Hogsback and Chintsa (R190), on Tues, Wed, Fri and Sun. It will also collect passengers off the Port Elizabeth–Durban Baz Bus at *The Sugarshack* backpackers' hostel in East London.

FORT HARE UNIVERSITY

Despite decades of deliberate neglect, and its relegation after 1959 to a "tribal" university under apartheid, **Fort Hare**, 2km east of Alice on the R63, is assured a place in South African history. Established in 1916 as a multiracial college by missionaries, it became the first institution in South Africa to deliver tertiary education to black people, and was attended by many prominent African leaders. The most famous former student is Nelson Mandela (see box, p.346), making this a point of interest, if you're following his footsteps.

The university's **De Beers Art Gallery** (Mon–Fri 8am–4.30pm; free) is a treasury of contemporary black Southern African art, and one of the most significant and least publicized collections anywhere. The gallery also houses Fort Hare's **ethnographic collection** – a major museum of traditional crafts and artefacts, with many rare and valuable pieces. **Tours** of the university, its art gallery and the ANC archives are run during the week (Mon–Thurs 8am–4.30pm, Fri 8am–3.30pm; ☎ 040 602 2277, ⓦ ufh.ac.za; book in advance).

INFORMATION AND ACTIVITIES

Tourist information The tourist office on Main Rd (Mon–Sat 9am–3pm, Sun 9am–1pm; ☎ 045 962 1245, ⓦ hogsback.com) can book accommodation, much of which is self-catering. You will need to stock up in a bigger centre before you come, as the village shop has limited stock, particularly of fresh produce. Also bring cash, as the one ATM is often out of order, and though there's a petrol pump, you may be safer filling up at somewhere larger.

Hiking trails Amatola Trails (☎ 043 642 2571, ⓦ amatola trails.co.za) offers a spectacular but challenging 6-day, 5-night trail (R1200 per person), covering 106km of sensational scenery – one of the best hikes in the whole country. There's also a 2-day, 1-night trail of around 37km

(R360 per person), which begins and ends at the *Away With The Fairies* hostel. The price covers hiking permits, overnight accommodation, and liaising with Rangers in the event of an emergency.

Horseriding trails *Lowestoffe Country Lodge* (☎ 045 843 1716 or ☎ 083 654 5935) offers trails (R350) through a wide valley and up mountain slopes for beginners and experienced riders alike. They can also do all-day or overnight trails. For forest rides at Hogsback, contact Shane at *Terra-Khaya Backpackers* (☎ 082 897 7503); he's a superb natural horseman who will take you on one of the best rides you can do anywhere (R350). The full-day rides exploring the area and the overnight trails are recommended.

ACCOMMODATION

Away With The Fairies Hydrangea Lane; down the first turning on your right and signposted as you drive into Hogsback ☎ 045 962 1031, ⓦ awaywiththefairies.co.za. This sociable hostel, in a large converted house, has small dorms sleeping five to eight, plus twin and double rooms, some en suite and one with its own fireplace. One of the nicest features is the bathtub set on the edge of a cliff. It's central and ideally situated for the start of many Hogsback hikes and mountain bike trails. They also operate a useful shuttle service to and from Chintsa and East London. Camping R70, dorms R120, doubles R340

★ **Back O' The Moon Holiday Cottage** Trewennan Lane ☎ 045 962 1017, ⓦ backofthemoon.hogsback .co.za. An ideal, old-world thatched home, spotlessly kept, with a sunny veranda and a magnificent six-acre garden. There are three comfortable bedrooms with good, warm bedding, a lounge with fireplace and DSTV, and a nicely equipped kitchen for self-catering. R750

The Edge Signposted off Main Rd ☎ 045 962 1159, ⓦ theedge-hogsback.co.za. The best of the self-catering accommodation, with twenty comfortable and stylishly

furnished cottages, and ten B&B rooms, situated a few kilometres from the centre of the village, along a rough dirt road. There are superb valley and forest views, hikes, a labyrinth for contemplation, and a good restaurant and bar on site. Booking is essential for the cottages; the price depends on the location – the best are right on the lip of the gorge. B&B R900, cottages R800

Lowestoffe Country Lodge Off Cathcart Rd ☎ 045 843 1716 or ☎ 083 654 5935, ⓦ lowestoffecountry lodge.co.za. Three fairly modern self-catering cottages on a farm where you can ride horses or fish for trout. The farm is 24km out on the unpaved road to Cathcart, so its draw is the dramatic and lonely mountain scenery on a working farm with friendly owners. There are dams and mountain pools for swimming, and you may not feel like going anywhere else. R900

★ **Terra-Khaya** Off Plaatjieskraal Rd ☎ 082 897 7503, ⓦ terrakhaya.co.za. Tucked into the backwoods is a wonderful and well-run backpackers on a permaculture eco-farm. With a lovely communal lounge and kitchen area, where you can get delicious meals cooked on an Aga, this is a place to chill around the outdoor fire, enjoy the lovel views from the sunny veranda, or go horseriding with Shane (see opposite). Phone for directions; it's a few kilometres off Main Rd, with a slightly hairy – but

signposted – final track to the lodge. Aim to arrive in daylight. Camping R85, dorms R135, doubles R325

EATING

Butterfly's Bistro Main Rd, next to the tourist office ☎ 045 962 1326. Well regarded for its wood-fired pizzas (R90), pastas and salads, with the odd deli item for sale if you are picnicking. On Saturday mornings there's a tiny farmers' market under the oak tree, where you can buy breads, preserves, ready-made vegetarian meals and locally smoked trout. Daily 9am–5pm.

The Edge Signposted off Main Rd ☎ 045 962 1159, ⊛ theedge-hogsback.co.za. The best place in town for lunch or dinner, with great views onto the escarpment. The slow-cooked crispy duck is recommended (R135), and there are one or two appealing vegetarian options. You can combine a meal with a walk in the magnificent surroundings or along the elaborate labyrinth. Daily 8am–8pm.

DRINKING

Happy Hogs Restaurant & Bar Main Rd ☎ 082 872 7705, ⊛ happyhogs.co.za. The pick of the establishments strung along Main Road, *Happy Hogs* is good for an evening

meal or a drink, and somewhere you could pleasantly sink a few beers (R25) and chat to the locals. Daily 10am–2.30pm & 6–9pm.

The Eastern Cape Highlands

The **Eastern Cape Highlands** is the most southerly section of Southern Africa's highest and most extensive mountain chain, the Drakensberg, which stretches east across Lesotho and up the west flank of KwaZulu-Natal into Mpumalanga. It is one of the remotest destinations in the whole country, far from any major towns, but the landscape is overwhelmingly grand. The obvious goal of this world of **San rock paintings**, sandstone **caves** and craggy sheep farms is **Rhodes**, one of the country's best-preserved and prettiest Victorian villages. Since there is no national park here, all activities are arranged through private farms.

Rhodes and around

RHODES is almost too good to be true – a remote and beautiful village girdled by mountains. Few people actually live here: like other villages in this region, Rhodes was progressively deserted as residents gravitated to the cities to make a living, leaving its Victorian tin-roofed architecture stuck in a pleasing time warp. Today, its main function is as a low-key holiday place for people who appreciate its isolation, wood stoves and restored cottages. Although electricity reached the village a few years ago, paraffin lamps and candles are still used. Given that Rhodes is very remote and not on the way to anywhere (it doesn't even appear on some maps), it is a place to dwell for a few days, rather than an overnight stop. While nights are cool even in summer, in winter they are freezing, and there's no central heating, so pack warm clothes.

The village itself is not much more than a few crisscrossing gravel roads lined with pine trees. At its heart is the *Rhodes Hotel* (currently closed). There is no shop, garage or banking facilities.

Rock-art sites

Book at Rhodes Info Centre ☎ 045 971 9003

Rhodes is a good base for exploring millennia-old **San rock paintings**, the majority of which are on surrounding private farms which can be visited with the farmers' permission. Rhodes locals can direct you to nearby farms with their own paintings, but the best option is to book a visit through the Rhodes Info Centre.

Closest to Rhodes, **Martindell** Farm, 14km west of the village, is definitely worth a visit, not just for the paintings, which are some of the best preserved in the province, but for the lovely, lonely valley you drive through to get there. Nearby Buttermead is another good site for rock paintings, and there are fine examples at Chamisso (halfway between Rhodes and Maclear) and Craigmore (west of Maclear), though these last two are more difficult to access.

Rock art had an essentially religious purpose, usually recording experiences of trance states (see p.10); shamans' visions often included powerful animals like the eland, which you can see depicted at Martindell.

ARRIVAL AND INFORMATION   RHODES

By car There's no public transport in or out of the village, so you'll have to drive. Rhodes is reached from Barkly East, which itself is 130km from Aliwal North on the N6. The 60km journey to Rhodes from Barkly East is along rough dirt roads, with some sheer unfenced drops, and takes a good ninety minutes. There is no garage in Rhodes so be

sure to fill up in Barkly East and check the weather forecast.
Tourist information The Rhodes Information Centre, at 166 Muller St (Mon–Sat 8.30am–5pm, Sun 10am–2pm; ☎045 971 9003, ⓦrhodesinfo.co.za), can book accommodation and activities – the area is particularly renowned for its trout fishing.

ACCOMMODATION

Gateshead Lodges ☎045 974 9303, ⓦgateshead .co.za. A pair of excellent cottages and a sandstone farmhouse in remote and rugged territory, all within a large radius of Rhodes and Barkly East – the roads are rough, however, and you'll need a vehicle with good clearance to reach some of the cottages. The owners, Basie and Carien Vosloo, organize trout fishing and horse-riding. **R600**
Rubicon Flats Old School House, signposted off Main Rd ☎083 659 3271, ⓦrubiconflats.co.za. The best-value, and the warmest, place in town, this handsome old

schoolhouse, designed by Sir Herbert Baker (see box, p.460), has been converted into self-catering rooms, each with an anthracite burner; there are also simple dorms. Good Afrikaans farm-style meals can be provided if you are staying here (3-course meal R150). **R600**
Walkerbouts Inn Signposted off the main road ☎045 974 9290, ⓦwalkerbouts.co.za. A relaxed house with six en-suite guest rooms. The friendly owner, Dave Walker, knows a good deal about the area and organizes a range of activities – including fishing, birdwatching and hiking. **R330**

EATING

Walkerbouts Walkerbouts Inn, signposted off the main road ☎045 974 9290. The best choice in town for food, offering home-cooked meals. Breakfast (R95),

pizzas for lunch and a 3-course set menu for dinner (R195). Booking essential; phone for opening times.

Naude's Nek

The most exhilarating drive out of Rhodes is on the R396 along **Naude's Nek**, the highest mountain-pass road in South Africa, connecting Rhodes with **Maclear** to the south, in a series of snaking hairpin bends and huge views. If you're chiefly looking for scenery, it's not essential to do the whole route to Maclear. Be sure to park your car facing into the wind to ensure the doors don't fly off, as the wind gets very strong up here. There is no mobile reception, so be prepared for emergencies (food, water and sleeping bags) as few cars pass this way.

While it's only 30km from Rhodes, the journey can take a couple of hours to the Nek because so many changing vistas en route demand stops. You'll need a car with high clearance (and a 4WD in winter) as the road is harsh and impassable after snow.

ACCOMMODATION   NAUDE'S NEK

Tenahead Lodge and Spa 33km from Rhodes, on the R396 ☎086 174 8374, ⓦbit.ly/tenaheadlodge. Situated in a remote and spectacular position at the top of the pass, this luxurious 5-star hotel has seven en-suite rooms, all with fireplaces and DSTV, and all the amenities a resort could offer. There are no refunds if you fail to arrive because of bad weather. **R5990**

Woodcliffe Country House 16km before Maclear ☎045 932 1550, ⓦwoodcliffe.co.za. Self-catering accommodation on a farm well below Naude's Nek in the beautiful foothills of the Drakensberg. Rooms in the farmhouse are available, or there's a three-bed cottage and flat. Meals are on request, and guides (when available) offer guided rock art and orchid trails. **R660**

The Wild Coast region

The **Wild Coast region** is aptly named: this is one of South Africa's most unspoilt areas, a vast stretch of undulating hills, lush forest and spectacular beaches skirting a section of the Indian Ocean. Its undeveloped sandy beaches stretch for hundreds of kilometres, punctuated by rivers and several wonderful, reasonably priced hotels geared to family holidays, and brilliant backpacker lodges. The wildness goes beyond the landscape, for this is the former **Transkei** homeland, a desperately poor region that was disenfranchised during apartheid, and is still one of the poorest regions of the country, with dismal infrastructure and many inhabitants having migrated to work in Cape Town.

The Wild Coast region's inhabitants are predominantly Xhosa, and those in rural areas live mostly in traditional rondavels dotting the landscape for as far as the eye can see. The **N2** highway runs through the middle of the region, passing through the old Transkei capital of **Mthatha** and a host of scruffy, busy little towns along the way. To the south of the highway, the **coastal region** stretches from just north of East London to the mouth of the **Mtamvuna River**. With its succession of great beaches, hidden reefs, patches of subtropical forest, rural Xhosa settlements and the attractive little towns of **Coffee Bay** and **Port St Johns** (both popular with backpackers), this region offers the most deserted and undeveloped beaches in the country.

The Wild Coast, unlike the Western Cape Garden Route, is not a stretch that you can easily tour by car. There's no coastal road, and no direct route between one seaside resort and the next. Yet in this **remoteness** lies the region's charm. Resorts are isolated down long, winding, potholed and corrugated gravel roads off the N2, which sticks to the high inland plateau. Choose one or two places to stay, and stay put for a relaxing few days. Most places along this stretch of coast are known simply by the name of the hotel that dominates the settlement, though you will also see the Xhosa name of the river mouth, on which each hotel is situated, on many maps.

If you are exploring the Wild Coast, make sure you have a good map, as the roads are confusing, and the connections between places mysterious without one.

4

RIDING AND HIKING ALONG THE WILD COAST

Since there's no coastal road, the only way to explore stretches of the Wild Coast is **on foot** or **horseback**.

WILD COAST HIKING TRAILS

Strandloper Coastal Hiking Trail (☎ 043 841 1046, ⓦ strandlopertrails.org.za). Three-night, 58km hiking trail between Kei Mouth and Gonubie (R650 per person). Varied terrain, well-planned stages, small coastal villages and friendly pubs en route make this a popular hike, suited to family groups. Overnight accommodation is provided in comfortable twelve-bunk self-catering cabins.

Wild Coast Holiday Reservations (☎ 043 743 6181, ⓦ wildcoastholidays.co.za). Offers portered packages including transfers from East London, hotel accommodation and all meals, on three trails: the 55km Wild Coast Hotel Meander along pristine, wild coast from the Kob Inn to Morgan Bay (five nights, R9290); the 56km Wild Coast Amble starting north of Kei River and ending in Chintsa, covering terrain of moderate difficulty (four nights R8685); and the Wild Coast Pondo Walk – five nights based at the *Mboyti River Lodge*, near Lusikisiki, including two coastal walks and two inland trails, ranging from 13km to 26km a day (R885 per day).

★ **Wild Coast Horseback Adventures** (☎ 043 831 1087 or ☎ 082 56 0972, ⓦ wildcoasthorseback adventures.com). Reputable establishment based at Sunray Farm near Kei Mouth, with fit horses and riding on some of the best and most unspoiled beaches in the country – sweeping sandy bays, warm lagoons, river crossings, inland riding through traditional rural settlements, indigenous forest, rolling grasslands and green hills. Trips are reasonably priced too, and there are several options available, including a horseback safari. Kei River rides range from two-night trails (R2070) to multi-day trips along the coast, overnighting at hotels – it's hard to imagine better beach riding anywhere else in the world.

THE WILD COAST

Chintsa

Of the smattering of resorts between East London and the Kei River, one of the best is at **CHINTSA**, where endless sandy beaches back up into forested dunes, sliced through by lagoons and rivers. Chintsa is actually two places divided by a river: **CHINTSA EAST**, 45km from East London, is an upmarket holiday village of some two hundred houses, while **CHINTSA WEST** is famous for its beautiful tidal pool.

Haga-Haga

Just northeast of Chintsa, **HAGA-HAGA** is dominated by the box-like but perfectly positioned *Haga-Haga Resort* (see p.343). To reach a sandy beach from the hotel, take the 2km path to Pullens Bay, which is ideal for swimming among the breakers. A 4km walk takes you to Bead Beach, where vendors sell beads made from carnelian, and bits of pottery.

Morgan Bay

MORGAN BAY, 90km from East London, lies magnificently in an estuary at the confluence of two rivers carving their passage through forested dunes. A hike from the *Morgan Bay Hotel*, one of the best resorts along the Wild Coast (see p.343), leads over some grassy knolls to the 50m Morbay Cliffs, an excellent vantage point for spotting dolphins and, in season, whales. The bay is pounded by massive breakers, but the estuary provides a safe and tranquil place for toddlers to paddle.

Kei Mouth and Trennery's (Qholorha Mouth)

Pontoon daily: summer 6am–6pm; winter 7am–5.30pm

From Morgan Bay, it's a short drive to the village of **KEI MOUTH**, though there's no particular point in dallying here. To get to beautiful **TRENNERY'S**, only 6km along the beach as the crow flies, but considerably longer by road, cross the Kei River on a pontoon (which can take your car, horse or cattle); after disembarking, continue driving for another 17km to *Trennery's Hotel* – signposted (see p.343). From the hotel, it's a steep walk through luxuriant vegetation to the spectacular beach, where canoes and rowing boats are available.

Trevor's Trail

Daily 9am • ☎ 073 575 7223, or book through your hotel • R155

A recommended excursion from Trennery's is **Trevor's Trail**, a three-hour bush walk and boating trip to "The Gates" – the short corridor of rock face towering above the Qholorha River; it's run by local resident Trevor Wigley, who also runs a number of other trails that include a visit to a local **traditional healer**.

Wavecrest (Nxaxo Mouth)

Wavecrest, just north of Trennery's (though not drivable from there), is a tranquil location where mangrove swamps teem with wildlife. It's an ideal place for hiking, shoreline fishing and general relaxation, as well as the more strenuous **activities** – canoeing, waterskiing and deep-sea fishing. All of this can be arranged through the resort's only **accommodation**, the *Wavecrest* (see p.343).

Mazeppa Bay

One of two good fishing and general chill-out spots on the Wild Coast (the other being by *Kob Inn*), **MAZEPPA BAY** lies northeast of *Wavecrest* – a lovely spot surrounded by dunes and coastal forest. Swimming in the bay is safe, and the surfing is legendary.

Kob Inn (Qora Mouth)

Just northeast of Mazeppa, **KOB INN** is situated right on the sea front at the **Qora River Mouth**. Apart from the hotel (see p.344), there is nothing else at the settlement. A small ferry traverses the river mouth and takes you to some good hiking trails along the coast, through grassland and into nearby forest patches.

THE GREAT CATTLE KILLING

The 1850s were a low point for the **Xhosa** nation: most of their land had been seized by the British, drought had withered their crops, and cattle-sickness had decimated their precious herds. In 1856, a young woman called **Nongqawuse**, whose uncle Mhlakaza was a prophet, claimed to have seen and heard ancestral spirits in a pool on the Gxara River. The spirits told her the Xhosa must kill all their remaining cattle and destroy their remaining crops; if they did this, new cattle and crops would arise, along with new people who would drive the white people into the sea.

As news of her **prophecy** spread, opinion was sharply divided among the Xhosa – those whose herds had been badly affected by cattle-sickness were most inclined to believe her. A turning point came when the Gcaleka paramount chief Sarili became convinced she was telling the truth and ordered his subjects to start the cull. Thousands of cattle were killed, but when the "new people" failed to materialize, the unbelievers who had not killed their herds were blamed. By February 1857, the next date for the appearance of the new people, over 200,000 cattle had been slaughtered. When the new people failed once more to materialize, it was too late for many Xhosa. By July there was **widespread starvation**; 30,000 of an estimated population of 90,000 died of hunger.

The British administration saw the famine as a perfect way to force the destitute Xhosa into working on white settlers' farms. To speed up the process, the Cape governor Sir George Grey closed down the feeding stations established by missionaries and laid the blame for the disaster on the Xhosa chiefs, imprisoning many of them on Robben Island.

Bulungula (Nqileni)

Idyllically located at the mouth of the Bulungula River, the spread-out village of **NQILENI**, focused around *Bulungula Lodge* (see p.344), gives you the opportunity to experience rural Transkei life. The river winds its way to the sea through rolling green hills dotted with rondavels, maize fields and livestock, ending at a tranquil river mouth. Here, the coastline is carpeted in dense forest stretching into kilometres of soft, white beach.

Coffee Bay and around

The densely populated, gentle hills of **COFFEE BAY**, known to the Xhosa as Tshontini after a dense wood that grows there, mark the traditional boundary between the Bomvana and Pondo clans of the Xhosa nation. Coffee Bay, with its laidback, relaxed atmosphere, draws a growing number of visitors – yet retains its feeling of idyllic obscurity.

The **landscape** consists of dramatic high cliffs dropping to sandy beaches speckled with black pebbles, which contrasts with the grasslands, forested sand dunes and

---

SOME XHOSA TRADITIONS

The Wild Coast is largely populated by **rural Xhosa** who still follow traditional practices and customs that have faded in more urban areas. Many people, for example, believe that the sea is inhabited by a strange people, who do not always welcome visitors. This explains the relative scarcity of the activities you would normally find thriving among seashore-dwelling people, such as fishing and diving.

Initiation for teenage boys and young men is still common, and sadly every year there are a number of deaths from infections associated with circumcision. The main circumcision period is the December holidays, when you may see white-daubed young men by the roadside, or men with ochre faces sporting English-styled tweed caps. Young men usually leave their homes to stay in "circumcision lodges", dress in distinctive white paint and costumes and learn the customs of their clan. At the circumcision ceremony the men are expected to make no sound while their foreskin is cut off (with no anaesthetic). After the ceremony, they wash off the paint and wrap themselves in new blankets, and all their former possessions are burned. There follows a feast to celebrate the beginning of manhood and the start of a year-long intermediary period during which they wear ochre-coloured clay on their faces. After this, they are considered men.

Like other African peoples, although they believe in one God, **uThixo**, or uNhkulukhulu (the great one), many Xhosa also believe that their **ancestors** play an active role in their lives. However, the ancestors' messages are often too obscure to be understood without the aid of specialists, or *amagqira*.

The Xhosa are patriarchal by tradition, with women's subordinate status symbolized by *lobola*, the **dowry** payment in cattle and cash that a prospective husband must make to her parents. If the woman is not a virgin, the man pays less. Married Xhosa women have the same right as men to smoke tobacco in **pipes**, and can sometimes still be seen doing so, the pipes' long stems designed to prevent ash falling on babies suckling at their breasts.

The Xhosa did not wear **cloth** until it was introduced by Europeans, when it was quickly adopted. Today, what is now seen as traditional Xhosa cloth is almost always worn by women, mostly in the form of long skirts, beautifully embroidered with horizontal black stripes. The breasts of unmarried women were traditionally uncovered, while those of married women were usually covered with beads or matching cloth. These days, women wear T-shirts, though almost all still cover their heads with scarves and dress modestly in rural areas. In the cities, however, young Xhosa women wear jeans and make-up. For Xhosa who had to leave the Eastern Cape, there is still a powerful connection to their place of origin. Xhosas dying in Cape Town, for example, will still be buried in the Eastern Cape with their family and ancestors. Every Friday night scores of minibuses leave Cape Town transporting mourners and corpses to Saturday **funerals** in the Eastern Cape, a journey of 12–17 hours. Funerals are the most important ritual of all for Xhosa families – and their single greatest expense.

FROM TOP DIE TUISHUISE, CRADOCK (P.323); XHOSA WOMAN, COFFEE BAY (ABOVE) >

lagoons further south. The **huts** around here are also very distinctive: many are thatched with a topknot made from a tyre, coloured glass or even an aloe plant – said to discourage owls, harbingers of ill-omen, from roosting on roofs. The main attraction, however, is the **coastal hikes** – the walk to Hole in the Wall is outstanding, as is the stunning two-day coastal route to Bulungula, overnighting in *Wild Lubanzi Backpackers* (see p.344): *Coffee Shack* (see p.344) and *Bulungula Lodge* (see p.344) can both arrange guides (R400 per day) and free luggage transfer.

Village visits

An excellent community-run **village tour** can be organized through the impressive ANC Women's League veteran, Betty Madlalisa (R85, ☎083 339 0454). Apart from visiting homesteads, the outing takes in the Masizame Women's Project (daily 8am–5pm), housed in a colourful building opposite the Bayview Store, 5km out of Coffee Bay on the Mthatha Road. The project is one of the very few outlets in South Africa where you can buy traditional Xhosa craftwork, including beaded bags and belts, traditional clothing, baskets, mats and blankets. With advance notice, they also offer Xhosa meals (R65) washed down with traditional beer.

Hole In The Wall

The settlement of **HOLE IN THE WALL**, 9km northwest of Coffee Bay, has grown up on the shoreline near the large cliff that juts out of the sea, from which it gets its name. The cliff has a tunnel at its base through which huge waves pound during heavy seas, making a great crashing sound. As well as good fishing, safe swimming and snorkelling, there are several spectacular hikes.

4

ARRIVAL AND DEPARTURE   **THE WILD COAST**

TRANSPORT

By car Phone your resort in advance for up-to-date directions, as roads and conditions change, and make sure you fill up with petrol before leaving the N2. Although some of the Wild Coast roads are being surfaced as part of an upgrading programme, most remain untarred and, while generally passable in an ordinary car, it's best to carry a tool kit, a spare tyre and take the roads slowly. Many roads are very rough and full of potholes. Watch out for livestock on all Wild Coast roads, including the N2, and avoid driving in rainy weather and at night. Do not park overnight anywhere that does not have security.

By bus The Baz Bus stops in Chintsa West and Mthatha; you can arrange to be met by hostels in Port St Johns and Coffee Bay, or in Butterworth for Mazeppa. Greyhound and other services ply the N2 between Durban and East London, stopping at Mthatha. Minibus taxis cover all routes, and you should be able to get from Mthatha quite easily to Coffee Bay or Port St Johns.

By plane If you are flying into East London and making for a specific resort, there are several shuttle services, including the East Coast Shuttle Service (☎043 740 3060 or ☎083 282 8790), which will quote a price when you book, depending on how many people are travelling.

DIRECTIONS

Chintsa Chintsa East can be reached on a tarred road: turn off the N2 at the East Coast Resorts Rd (30km out of East London) then, after 8km, turn left at the sign to Cefane Mouth, from where the village is 7km away. Chintsa West is on the Baz Bus Route, which drops off at *Buccaneer's Backpackers* (see p.343).

Haga Haga Signposted off the N2, Haga Haga is 72km from East London, 27km of which is along a dirt road and 210km from Mthatha.

Wavecrest (Nxaxo Mouth) To get to *Wavecrest*, follow the 34km of tarred road to Centani from the N2 at Butterworth. At Centani, take the signposted road (to the

---

THE EASTERN CAPE'S COASTAL NATURE RESERVES

The Eastern Cape has some undeveloped and gorgeous **coastal reserves**: Dwesa, Hluleka and Mkhambathi. All accommodation in the reserves is self-catering, and there are no shops or facilities, so you need to be fully self-sufficient and stock up before you leave the N2. The reserves are accessible in a rugged vehicle on slow, dirt roads and suitable for a stay of a few days, though they have a reputation of being poorly run. Accommodation can be booked with the Eastern Cape Parks Board (☎043 705 4400, ⊕visiteasterncape.co.za).

left) to Nxaxo for 8km, then the dirt road for 24km to *Wavecrest* (on the right).

Mazeppa Bay To reach the bay, follow the 34km of tarred road to Centani from the N2 at Butterworth, then take the signposted road another 45km to Mazeppa.

Kob Inn (Qora Mouth) To get to *Kob Inn* from the N2, take the signposted dirt road heading east for 34km from Idutywa.

Bulungula (Nquileni) The turn-off to Bulungula is 50km along the road to Coffee Bay from the N2: you will get detailed directions when booking at *Bulungula Lodge* (see p.344), and you should aim to arrive before nightfall. The Lodge also runs a shuttle service (R90) from the Shell Ultra City in Mthatha (arrange this when booking) on Tues, Thurs, Fri & Sun. If you are coming from Coffee Bay, they will collect you from the Bulungula/Coffee Bay turn-off (called Lutubeni) so you don't need to go all the way back to Mthatha.

Mdumbi Follow the N2 to Mthatha, then take Coffee Bay road for 70km before turning left onto Umdumbi gravel road and following Mdumbi Backpacker signs for 23km.

The Mdumbi shuttle pickup from Coffee Bay costs R50.

Freedom "O" Clock Once booking has been confirmed, detailed GPS coordinates will be sent to you. Pickups can be made from Mthatha.

Lubanzi Village In the Zithulele Mission Hospital area, off the road to Coffee Bay, Lubanzi Village is a 2hr drive from the N2 – check directions with *Wild Lubanzi Backpackers*. There's also a Lubanzi shuttle (R15 per person) from Zithulele Hospital; book with *Lubanzi Backpackers* the day before.

Coffee Bay A tarred road leaves the N2 14km south of Mthatha's Shell Ultra City for Coffee Bay.

Hole In The Wall A 9km gravel road links Coffee Bay with Hole In The Wall – a scenic drive through traditional villages and along cliffs with sea views .

Lambazi Bay Follow the concrete road off the R61 (1km south of Lusikisiki), and then continue for some 40km on gravel roads toward Port Grosvenor. Follow the Drifters signs to Lambazi Bay.

INFORMATION

Services Apart from Port St Johns, none of the places on the coast has a bank or ATM, so be sure to get enough money from East London or Mthatha. Petrol is available in Coffee Bay and Port St Johns.

4

ACCOMMODATION

The **hotels** on the Wild Coast are typically run along old-fashioned, colonial lines, with set meals, tea times and a well-patronized pub. Most offer full board – apart from in Chintsa, Port St Johns and Mthatha, there are no restaurants besides those provided by the accommodation establishments. If you're travelling with children, you will find many hotels have experienced Xhosa nannies who can be employed for a day or for short stretches while you take a break. There are a number of brilliant backpacker lodges along the coast, and plenty of campsites, but **camping** in rural areas is not advisable, even if a beach looks idyllic and is deserted – theft is common. It's wise to **book in advance**: the well-informed Wild Coast Holiday Reservations (☎ 043 743 6181, ⓦ wildcoastholidays.com), based in East London, can arrange accommodation and organize **activities** in the region.

CHINTSA

Buccaneer's Backpackers Chintsa West ☎043 734 3012, ⓦcintsa.com; map p.338. One of South Africa's most popular hostels, *Buccaneer's* has built its reputation on the excellence of its ten cottages of varying sizes, with fantastic sea and lagoon views, unspoilt beaches, and the plethora of activities they lay on. You can self-cater, or eat inexpensive breakfasts and dinners in the café and pub. It also lays on trips to a local African school and township. Dorms R170, doubles R430

Crawford's Lodge & Cabins 42 Steenbras Drive, Chintsa East ☎043 738 5000, ⓦcrawfordsbeachlodge .co.za; map p.338. Just a few minutes' walk from the beach, *Crawford's* offers guesthouse B&B accommodation; for a room with a spectacular view, expect to pay R2542. R1642

HAGA-HAGA

Haga-Haga ☎043 841 1670 or ☎082 659 8881, ⓦhagahagahotel.co.za; map p.338. This pleasant hotel offers full board in hotel rooms, and self-catering in eight chalets sleeping two or four. The en-suite rooms have

balconies. A tidal swimming pool is sculpted into the rocky shoreline in front of the hotel. One of its advantages is being only 70km from East London with a mere 13km of dirt road. Chalets R1700, doubles R1820

MORGAN BAY

★**Morgan Bay Hotel** 41 Beach Rd, Morgan Bay ☎043 841 1062, ⓦmorganbayhotel.co.za; map p.338. This friendly, well-run place overlooks a gorgeous beach and is one of the best hotels along the Wild Coast, particularly for family holidays. It offers good food and fresh, airy rooms; a caravan park is also available. Rates include breakfast and dinner. Another draw is that it's only 76km from East London, all on tar roads. Camping R265, doubles R2030

TRENNERY'S (QHOLORHA MOUTH)

★**Trennery's** ☎047 498 0025/95 or ☎082 908 3134, ⓦtrennerys.co.za; map p.338. Founded in 1928, *Trennery's* has an old-fashioned feel but remains a firm favourite for family holidays. Uniformed nannies accompany children at the pool, and in the separate children's dining room, and it is a short hop through forest to the magnificent beach, with various activities laid on. The well-kept gardens and flowering trees may obscure the sea views, but they act as a welcome shelter from the wind. The hotel's spacious rooms and thatched chalets are en suite, there are ten sites for camping, while the English-style food is wholesome and well cooked. Camping per site R450, full board R1780

WAVECREST (NXAXO MOUTH)

★Wavecrest ☎047 498 0022, ⓦwavecrest.co.za; map p.338. A cluster of pleasant thatched bungalows and family rooms at arguably the most beautifully positioned of the Wild Coast hotels, right on the edge of a mangrove-lined estuary. You can take a canoe and go birdwatching on the estuary, or cross it to explore the forests backing a sandy beach that stretches as far as you can see. The view from the bar and outside deck takes this all in, and when you've finished gazing at the vista, you can have a massage at their modest spa. Full board R1500

MAZEPPA BAY

Mazeppa Bay Hotel ☎047 498 0033, ⓦmazeppa bayhotel.co.za; map p.338. This charming hotel offers full board in comfortable cabanas or family rooms, 39 steps up from the beach. Units are thatched and surrounded by palms and tropical plants. It has the added attraction of its own island (reached along a bridge), and there's excellent game fishing and surfing. R1930

KOB INN (QORA MOUTH)

Kob Inn ☎083 452 0876, ⓦkobinn.co.za; map p.338. The popular *Kob Inn* has sea-facing rooms and a bar right on the rocky shore, close to the wide Mbashe River. The thatched bungalows are comfortable and spacious, and the restaurant is renowned for its seafood banquets. It has a tidal swimming pool built into the rocks. Staff can arrange a boat and fishing tackle, or equip you for canoeing, waterskiing and boardsailing. There is also a tennis court and trampoline, and satellite TV. Full board R1840

BULUNGULA (NQILENI)

★Bulungula Lodge ☎047 577 8900 or ☎083 391 5255, ⓦbulungula.com; map p.338. Situated on the estuary of the river, this eco-lodge offers ten brightly painted rondavels (sleeping 2–6), luxury safari tents (double or twin beds, with electric lights) on wooden platforms in the forest, and camping with shared ablutions. *Bulungula* is a joint venture between the community and seasoned traveller Dave Martin. If you're looking for relaxation and an authentic cultural experience, you'll be hard pressed to find a better place to stay. Booking essential. Camping R100, doubles R450, dorms R190, luxury tents R420

MBOLOMPO

Mbolompo Homestay Near Zithulele Mission Hospital ☎083 542 5561, ⓦmbolompohomestay.weebly.com; map p.338. Stay in a Xhosa village in an indigenous forest overlooking the Mncwasa River mouth. Accommodation is in a thatched mud hut with clean linen, showers and compost toilets. Evening meals are available on request (R50) and activities include tubing on the river, cliff jumping, fishing, birdwatching and volunteering in local projects. Dorms R120

MDUMBI

★Mdumbi Backpackers ☎083 461 1834, ⓦmdumbi .co.za; map p.338. A community-driven, eco-tourism initiative, Mdumbi provides rondavel accommodation, camping facilities and a café serving good home-made food. There's a nearby shebeen, or unlicensed bar, for drinks. With panoramic views and just a short walk to the beach, this is a great choice for backpackers wishing to experience rural Xhosa life. Camping R80, dorms R155, doubles R330

Freedom "o" Clock Backpackers ☎082 795 3944 or ☎071 192 6031, ⓦfreedomoclock.co.za; map p.338. Situated in a small Pondo village on the beautiful Mdumbi River mouth, this laidback place offers great surfing and a whole lot of nature. Basic, rustic, self-catering accommodation and camping with communal ablutions. Catering can be requested when you book (dinner R75, breakfast R45). Camping R80, doubles R350

★LUBANZI VILLAGE

Wild Lubanzi Backpackers ☎078 530 8997, ⓦwildlubanzi.co.za; map p.338. Beautifully hand-crafted buildings using solar power, in a breathtaking setting of hill and sea and beach, with a friendly community vibe. Home-cooked meals from the veggie garden (dinner R75). Internet available. Dorms R150, doubles R350

COFFEE BAY

Friends Wild Coast Backpackers Main St ☎073 077 1735, ⓦfriendswildcoast.com; map p.338. On the forested edge of the Bomvu River, *Friends* hosts drumming sessions around an evening fire and offers yoga, massage and surfing lessons, as well as tours to the nearby village. All meals, including home-made bread and cakes, are available from the *Sea View Café*, while the *Paradise Bar* is the place to drink. Camping R50, dorms R150, doubles R450

Coffee Shack ☎047 575 2048 or ☎083 656 4350, ⓦcoffeeshack.co.za; map p.338. Well located on the Bomvu River, *Coffee Shack* is the liveliest of Coffee Bay's backpacker lodges, with dorms, double rooms and camping. It has a restaurant, where a two-course dinner costs R55. Its shuttle bus plies the route between Mthatha and Coffee Bay, meeting the Baz Bus on request. Camping R90, dorms R150, doubles R400

Ocean View Hotel ☎047 575 2005/6, ⊛oceanview
.co.za; map p.338. The smartest accommodation in Coffee
Bay, situated right by the sandy beach. It's a friendly place,
with bright rooms, terraced gardens, a pool area, and a
trampoline and playground. The restaurant and bar serves
English-styled food. Full board R2100

White Clay ☎083 262 5239 or ☎083 979 4499,
⊛whiteclayresort.co.za; map p.338. One bay west of
Coffee Bay, and set on a cliff high above the water, *White Clay*
has en-suite double rooms, 12 self-catering chalets, and
camping facilities. No one else lives on this bay, so you have it
all to yourself, and the location couldn't be better: there are

stunning views, whales can sometimes be seen between
August and November, and dolphins all year round. They also
have a fully licensed restaurant serving seafood specialities.
Camping R160, doubles full board R1590

LAMBAZI BAY

Drifters Greenfire Lodge Lambazi Bay ☎011 888
1160, ⊛drifters.co.za; map p.338. On an untouched and
dramatic stretch of coastline, the lodge is hidden in a grove
of coastal milkwood trees, less than 100m from the beach.
The en-suite rooms are in 12 pondo-style thatched huts
with a central restaurant and bar. Full board R1950

EATING

All of the resorts have their own restaurants, with meals often included in their rates. If you're self-catering, it's best to pick
up supplies in a city, before heading to your accommodation. Otherwise, absolute basics can be purchased at trading stores
along the main roads, but you should not rely on this.

Mthatha and around

Straddling the Mthatha River and the N2 highway 235km from East London, the
fractious, shambolic town of **MTHATHA** (formerly Umtata) is the erstwhile capital of the
Transkei, and the Wild Coast region's largest town. It's an ugly town, its crowded and
litter-strewn streets lined with nondescript 1970s office buildings, with the odd older
architectural gem, albeit dilapidated. However, the Mthatha outskirts are useful for
stocking up and drawing money, all of which can be done at the Spar Centre or Shell
Ultra City on the edge of town. The only reason to venture into the centre is to visit
the **Nelson Mandela Museum**.

4

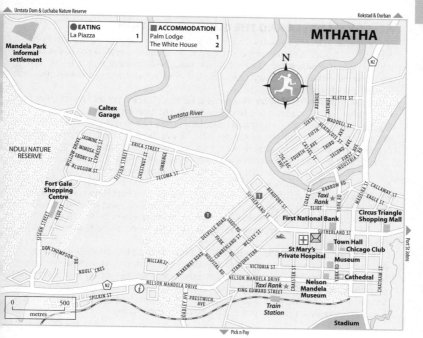

Nelson Mandela Museum

Corner of Owen St and Nelson Mandela Drive • Daily 9am–4pm • Free • ☎ 047 532 5110, ⓦ mandelamuseum.org.za

The **Nelson Mandela Museum** is housed in the old **parliament**, or *bungha*, built in 1927. Refurbished in 2014, the museum's most interesting display traces Mandela's life with photos and other visual material. The museum coordinates guided **trips** to **Qunu** and **Mveso**, where he spent his early years, though you may be better off doing this as a planned day-trip from East London with Imonti Tours (see p.331).

Qunu and the Nelson Mandela Youth and Heritage Centre

500m from the N2, 30km west of Mthatha • Dailhy 9am–4pm • Free • Tours by arrangement • ☎ 047 532 5110, ⓦ mandelamuseum.org.za

Some 30km from Mthatha, on the East London side, are the scattered dwellings of **Qunu**, where Mandela grew up. The N2 thunders through it, but his large and rather plain mansion, which you may photograph but not enter, is clearly visible on the roadside. Signs from the N2 direct you to the **Nelson Mandela Youth and Heritage Centre**, where you can look around the craft centre, and arrange a free guide to accompany you in your car to visit the remains of Mandela's primary school and the rock he used to slide down with friends. Mandela's grave can be seen in the distance, but it's situated on private land and currently inaccessible, although there are plans to create a visitor site.

ARRIVAL AND DEPARTURE

MTHATHA AND AROUND

By plane The small Mthatha airport (☎ 047 536 0121) lies 10km west of town on the Queenstown Rd, with expensive daily flights on SA Airlink (☎ 047 536 0023) to Joburg. There is no public transport from the airport, but you can rent a car here from Avis or Budget.

By bus Greyhound and Translux buses pull in at Shell Ultra City, 6km from the centre, on the N2, which is also served by the Baz Bus, and is the connecting point for backpackers to take organized shuttles to Port St Johns. There's an ATM here, and the new Mthatha Visitors Information Centre. Minibuses can take you into town.

NELSON MANDELA AND THE QUNU CONNECTION

Nelson Rolihlahla Mandela was born in the village of **Mveso**, close to Qunu (see above), on July 18, 1918. His father was a member of the Xhosa royal house – he was also chief of Mveso, until he crossed swords with the local white magistrate over a minor dispute. After his sacking, the family moved to a small kraal in Qunu, which Mandela remembers as consisting of several hundred poor households.

Mandela is often called **Madiba** – the name of his family's subclan of the Thembu clan. The name Nelson was given to him by a schoolteacher, and Rolihlahla means, colloquially, "troublemaker". Mandela has said that at home he was never allowed to ask any questions, but was expected to learn by observation. Later in life, he was shocked to visit the homes of white people and hear children firing questions at their parents and expecting replies.

Shortly after his father died, Mandela was summoned from Qunu to the royal palace at Mqhakeweni, where he sat in on disputes in court and learned more about Xhosa culture. At 16 he was initiated into manhood before enrolling in Clarkebury, a college for the Thembu elite, then Healdtown at Fort Beaufort, and finally the celebrated **Fort Hare** in Alice (see box, p.334), which has educated generations of African leaders. Mandela was expelled from Fort Hare after clashing with the authorities, and returned to Mqhakeweni. In 1941, faced with the prospect of an arranged marriage, he ran away to Johannesburg where he immersed himself in politics.

It was only on his release from prison in 1990 (at the age of 72) that Mandela was able to return to Qunu, visiting first the grave of his mother, who had died in his absence. He noted that the place seemed poorer than he remembered it, and that the children were now singing songs about AK47s and the armed struggle. However, he was relieved to find that none of the old spirit and warmth had left the community, and he arranged for a large home to be built there. Following his death in December 2013, he was buried in Qunu.

INFORMATION

Tourist information The Mthatha Visitors Information Centre is at Shell Ultra City.
Self-catering supplies You can pick up groceries at the Spar Centre (daily 7am–9pm), 2.5km from town on the N2

(next to the *Wimpy* restaurant), or Pick n Pay (Mon–Fri 8.30am–7pm, Sat & Sun 9am–4pm) at the Southernwood Shopping Centre on Errol Spring Avenue.

ACCOMMODATION

MTHATHA

Palm Lodge 19 Blakeway Rd ☎ 072 707 9847, ⊛ palm lodgemthatha.co.za; map p.345. Near the golf course, the ten en-suite rooms here have their own entrance, plus a swimming pool, garden and braai area. Dinner available on request. R930

The White House 5 Mhlobo St, South Ridge Park ☎ 047 537 0580 or ☎ 083 458 9810, ⊜ whitehouse .@indepco.co.za; map p.345. Twenty-five rooms, eight en suite, in two adjoining suburban houses in a quiet area just off the N2, opposite the Shell Ultra City. An evening meal can be provided if booked beforehand. R1100

EATING

MTHATHA

Most guesthouses in town have their own restaurants, so you're unlikely to need to head out for food. The town has a thriving nightlife, with plenty of bars and *shebeens*, but exploring it without a local escort is risky and not recommended.

La Piazza Restaurant Country Club, Delville Rd ☎ 047 531 0795; map p.345. The *La Piazza Restaurant* in the Country Club is open to the public and has a thatch-covered deck overlooking the golf course. It is definitely the best place in town to have lunch, dinner or a drink (mains R160). Mon–Fri 11am–late, Sat 12.30–10pm.

Port St Johns

4

The 90km drive on the R61 to **PORT ST JOHNS** from Mthatha is one of the best and scariest journeys on the Wild Coast – just don't look down the sheer drops at the cars which never made it, and make sure you tackle the drive by day. After passing tiny **Libode**, with its small hotel and restaurant, you start the dramatic descent to the coast, past craggy ravines and epic vistas of forest and rondavel-spotted grassland. The road runs alongside the Mzimvubu River for the last few kilometres, giving you a perfect view of the Gates of St John, before reaching the town square and taxi rank. The big surprise, coming from the sparse hillsides around Mthatha, is how dramatic, hilly, lush and steamy it all is.

Initially the town is quite confusing – it meanders into three distinct localities, some kilometres apart. **First Beach**, where the river meets the sea, is along the main road from the post office and offers good fishing, but is unsafe for swimming. Close by is the rather run-down town centre, where you'll find shops and minibus taxis. **Second Beach**, 5km west along a tarred road off a right turn past the post office, is a fabulous swimming beach with a lagoon, and a couple of nice places to stay nearby. The area along the river around the **Pondoland Bridge** also has some accommodation that is popular with anglers.

Port St Johns is a favoured destination for backpackers, drawn by its stunning location at the mouth of the Mzimvubu River, dominated by Mount Thesiger on the west bank and Mount Sullivan on the east. A further attraction for some visitors is the strong, good quality **cannabis** grown in the area, and the town's famously laidback atmosphere may tempt you to stay longer than you intended. Port St Johns also has good **fishing** and **swimming beaches**, a wider choice of accommodation than anywhere else on the Wild Coast, and a good tarred road all the way into town. If you are looking for a stop-off along the Wild Coast, note that Port St Johns is much better than Mthatha, though it's a 90km drive from the N2.

The Gates of St John

Both the mountains of the **Gates of St John** merit a stiff climb to the top, from where you get a superb view of the lush surrounding landscape. To get here by car, drive up to the aircraft landing strip at the top of Mount Thesiger. Look out for the birds of prey, making use of the updraughts.

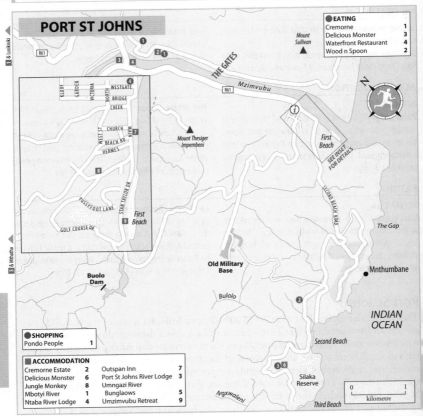

PORT ST JOHNS

EATING
Cremorne	1
Delicious Monster	3
Waterfront Restaurant	4
Wood n Spoon	2

SHOPPING
Pondo People	1

ACCOMMODATION
Cremorne Estate	2	Outspan Inn	7
Delicious Monster	6	Port St Johns River Lodge	3
Jungle Monkey	8	Umngazi River	
Mbotyi River	1	Bunglaows	5
Ntaba River Lodge	4	Umzimvubu Retreat	9

ARRIVAL AND DEPARTURE

By bus and minibus taxi The Baz Bus drops off at Shell Garage, from where you can catch a shuttle bus to *Jungle Monkey* hostel (pre-book on ☎047 564 1517); they will phone your accommodation to pick you up from there. If you're travelling from KwaZulu-Natal to Port St Johns by public transport, an alternative route is by minibus taxi via Port Edward, Bizana and Lusikisiki on the R61. This is also the route to take from Durban.

INFORMATION AND TOURS

Tourist information The tourist office is in an obvious building at the roundabout as you enter town (daily 8am–4.30pm; ☎047 564 1187, ⓦportstjohns.org.za /tourism.htm); it provides maps and information about local Xhosa homestays.

Guided tours Jimmy Gila and his brother (☎082 507 2256, ⓦwildcoasthikes.com) run brilliant hiking tours in the area, with overnight accommodation in huts or in Xhosa villages. Guides cost R350 per day, accommodation R300 per night (including meals), and the river crossing R80.

ACCOMMODATION

Cremorne Estate 5km from the centre on the Mzimvubu River, signposted from the Pondoland Bridge ☎047 564 1110 or ☎076 430 2194, ⓦcremorne .co.za; map above. One of Port St Johns' few upmarket places, offering self-catering timber cottages on stilts set on tidy lawns running down to the Mzimvubu River, with views of Mount Thesiger's red-slabbed cliffs. The cottages have two en-suite bedrooms, making them very affordable for a party of three or four. A row of small B&B doubles shares the view; cheaper still are some tiny cabins equipped with double bunks. There's a very good restaurant, bar, and a relaxing swimming pool area. **R1280**

Delicious Monster Near Second Beach ☎083 997 9856, ⓦdeliciousmonsterpsj.co.za; map above. Homely commodation in a thatched hut or a loft room, on the premises of the small, friendly restaurant of the same name where you can get all your food. **R600**

Jungle Monkey Berea Rd, second right off the main road after the post office ☎047 564 1517, wjungle monkey.co.za; map opposite. Hostel in a converted house near the centre, with camping, dorms and doubles in log cabins surrounded by forest. Accommodation is self-catering, though there's a restaurant, bar and live music at weekends. The owners can arrange guided trips into the villages and overnight visits to a traditional healer, as well as drive you to the Silaka Nature Reserve. The Baz Bus stops in Mthatha and they will pick you up from there. Camping R80, dorms **R120**, doubles **R450**

★ **Mbotyi River Lodge** Just north of Port St Johns; signposted off the R61, just before Lusikisiki; follow km of cement road to the end, and then turn right at Mbotyi sign and follow the dust road for 19km ☎082 74 1064 or ☎039 253 7200, wmbotyi.co.za; map opposite. At the mouth of the Mbotyi River in complete wilderness, surrounded by green rolling hills, estuarine wetlands, golden beaches, forests and sheer cliffs. Accommodation is in wooden bungalows with balconies overlooking the tranquil lagoon, and there is also a pub. Activities such as horseriding, canoe trips, mountain bikes, fishing, trails and game viewing can be organized. They can also book pitches (R95) at a nearby campsite, run by Mbotyi Campsite Trust, a joint venture with the local community, which also has three pondo huts sleeping six (R700), electricity, water and 24hr security. Full board **R1400**

taba River Lodge On the banks of the Mzimvubu River, signposted on the R61 from Mthatha, just before you reach Port St Johns ☎047 564 1707,

wintabariverlodge.co.za; map opposite. A collection of chalets, with a restaurant where you can enjoy *idombolo* (steamed bread). The friendly service is impeccable and there's plenty of activities on offer. B&B **R1600**

Outspan Inn In the centre, past the town hall on the road to First Beach ☎047 564 1057, woutspaninn .co.za; map opposite. Two-storey ochre B&B with en-suite rooms set in an appealing large garden. Some rooms have unusually high beds that give a view of nearby First Beach. The pub and restaurant are open daily and there's a swimming pool. **R850**

Port St Johns River Lodge Mthatha Tar Rd ☎047 564 0005, wportstjohnsriverlodge.co.za; map opposite. Wooden self-catering cottages on the riverside (R800) or B&B en-suite rooms in the lodge. There's also a swimming pool, a bar and a restaurant. **R1000**

Umngazi River Bungalows Umngazi river mouth, west of Port St Johns ☎047 564 1115, wumngazi .co.za; map opposite. Unsurpassed as a Wild Coast holiday resort, *Umngazi* delivers superb beachside family holidays, though it is more expensive than the other family hotels further south. It's frequently fully booked, especially during school holidays, so reserve as far in advance as possible. It's signposted off the R61, about 10km before you reach Port St Johns from Mthatha. Full board **R2770**

Umzimvubu Retreat Guest House Follow the road to First Beach; the entrance is clearly marked after the tar road ends ☎047 564 1741, wumzimvuburetreat.co.za; map opposite. Smart, yet homely, owner-run guesthouse set in a vast natural garden with scenic views. All rooms are en suite, and there is self-catering available, as well as accommodation for families. Book in advance for dinner at the restaurant (R150). **R1100**

EATING

If you're self-catering, you can often buy local fruit by the roadside, and sometimes fresh fish and seafood can be bought from hawkers. In the centre, Boxer Supermarket has most of the foodstuffs you'll need.

remorne Mzimvubu River; follow the signs from the Pondoland Bridge ☎047 564 1110; map opposite. The poshest place to eat, serving very good fish, steaks (R100) and puddings, plus there's a pizza oven (pizzas only Wed, Fri and Sat) and a well-stocked pub. Daily 6–10pm.

elicious Monster Near Second Beach ☎083 997 9856, wdeliciousmonsterpsj.co.za; map opposite. A licensed garden restaurant, where you can get breakfast and dinner of seafood, *schwarmas* and delicious vegetarian fare, cooked with fresh herbs from the garden, as well as home-baked goodies for tea (R60). Mon–Sat 9–10am & 6–9pm.

Wood n Spoon Second Beach ☎083 532 8869; map opposite. Fantastic little local eatery with food cooked in a campervan kitchen: great breakfasts, traditional African dishes, burgers, curry and sandwiches (R85). There's rustic outside seating from where you can watch cows wandering across the beach. Thurs–Tues 10.30am–9pm.

Waterfront Restaurant The Knoll ☎047 564 1234; map opposite. Traditional South African cuisine under the attractive thatched lapa, or outside on a wooden deck overlooking the Umzimbuvu River. Their large T-bone steaks (R110) are a good bet. Mon–Sat 11am–9pm.

SHOPPING

ondo People On the east side of the Mzimvubu River across the Pondoland Bridge ☎047 564 1274; map opposite. Easily the best craft shop on the Wild Coast,

Pondo People sells beautiful beaded clothing, aiming to retain the tradition of beadwork in the Transkei. Mon–Fri 8.30am–4.30pm, Sat 8.30am–1pm.

KwaZulu-Natal

SHAKALAND

5

KwaZulu-Natal

KwaZulu-Natal, South Africa's most typically African province, has everything the continent is known for – beaches, wildlife, mountains and accessible ethnic culture. South Africans are well acquainted with KwaZulu-Natal's attractions; it's the leading province for domestic tourism, although foreign visitors haven't quite cottoned on to the incredible amount packed into this compact and beautiful region. The city of Durban is the industrial hub of the province and the country's principal harbour. British in origin, it has a heady mixture of cultural flavours deriving from its Zulu, Indian and white communities. You'll find palm trees fanning Victorian buildings, squatters living precariously under truncated flyovers, high-rise offices towering over temples and curry houses, overdeveloped beachfronts, and everywhere an irrepressible fecundity.

To the north and south of Durban lie Africa's most developed beaches, known as the **North and South coasts**. Stretching along the shore from the Eastern Cape border in the south to the Tugela River in the north, this 250km ribbon of holiday homes is South Africa's busiest coastal strip. However, north of the Tugela River you'll find some of the most pristine shores in the country. Here, along the **Elephant Coast**, a patchwork of wetlands, freshwater lakes, wilderness and Zulu villages meets the sea at a virtually seamless stretch of sand that begins at the St Lucia Estuary and slips across the Mozambique border at Kosi Bay. Apart from **Lake St Lucia**, which is fairly developed in a low-key fashion, the Elephant Coast is one of the most isolated regions in the country, rewarding visitors with South Africa's best snorkelling and scuba diving along the coral reefs off **Sodwana Bay**.

KwaZulu-Natal's marine life is matched on land by its **game reserves**, which are easily the best place on the continent to see both black and white rhinos. Concentrated in the north, the reserves tend to be compact and feature some of the most stylish game-lodge accommodation in the country. Most famous and largest of the reserves is the **Hluhluwe-iMfolozi Park**, visited by a respectable cross section of wildlife that includes all of the Big Five.

Since the nineteenth century, when missionaries were homing in on the region, the **Zulus** have captured the popular imagination of the West and remain one

HAWKSBILL TURTLE, SODWANA BAY

Highlights

❶ Indian curries The tangy food of KwaZulu-Natal's second-largest ethnic group can be experienced in the heart of Durban. **See p.372**

❷ uKhahlamba-Drakensberg Towering peaks and ancient San (Bushman) rock paintings in one of KwaZulu-Natal's two World Heritage sites. **See p.388**

❸ Hluhluwe-iMfolozi Park KwaZulu-Natal's most outstanding game park, and one of the best places in the world to see both black and white rhinos. **See p.401**

❹ Lake St Lucia Highlight of the iSimangaliso Wetland Park, a World Heritage Site reserve that is home to five ecosystems, full of marine life and wildlife. **See p.404**

❺ Sodwana Bay Swim with ragged-tooth sharks, sea turtles and bright tropical fish at South Africa's premier diving and snorkelling destination. **See p.410**

❻ Eshowe's authentic Zulu culture Be a guest at a traditional Zulu wedding or coming-of-age ceremony, or inspect Zulu baskets at the Vukani Zulu Cultural Museum. **See p.419**

❼ Battlefield tours Experience the drama of the Anglo-Zulu wars with world-renowned storytellers and guides. **See p.424**

HIGHLIGHTS ARE MARKED ON THE MAP ON P.354

5

of the province's major draws for tourists. You'll find constant reminders of the old Zulu kingdom and its founder Shaka, including an excellent reconstruction of the beehive-hutted capital at **Ondini** and the more touristy **Shakaland** near **Eshowe**. The interior north of the Tugela River was the heartland of the Zulu kingdom and witnessed gruesome battles between Boers and Zulus, British and Zulus, and finally Boers and British. Today, the area can be explored through **Battlefield tours**, a memorable way of taking in some of South Africa's most turbulent history.

From the Midlands, South Africa's highest peaks sweep west into the soaring **uKhahlamba-Drakensberg** range, protected by a chain of wildlife reserves. The area's restcamps are ideal bases for walks in the mountains or ambitious hikes; with relatively

HIGHLIGHTS

1. Indian curries
2. uKhahlamba-Drakensberg
3. Hluhluwe-iMfolozi Park
4. Lake St Lucia
5. Sodwana Bay
6. Eshowe's authentic Zulu culture
7. Battlefield tours

KWAZULU-NATAL

EZEMVELO KZN WILDLIFE

Most of the public game parks and wilderness areas in KwaZulu-Natal fall under the auspices of **Ezemvelo KwaZulu-Natal Wildlife**, also known as **KZN Wildlife** (☎033 845 1000, ⊕kznwildlife.com). **Accommodation** in these areas is best booked in advance through them.

little effort, you can experience crystal rivers tumbling into marbled rock pools, awe-inspiring peaks and rock faces enriched by ancient San paintings.

KwaZulu-Natal experiences considerable variations in **climate**, from the occasional heavy winter snowstorms of the uKhahlamba-Drakensberg to the mellow, sunny days and pleasant sea temperatures along the **subtropical coastline**, which offers a temperate climate year-round. This makes the region a popular winter getaway, but in midsummer the low-lying areas, including Durban, the coastal belt and the game reserves, can be uncomfortably humid.

Brief history

Despite their defeats in battles with the Boers and the British during the nineteenth century, the Zulus have remained an active force in South African politics and are particularly strong in KwaZulu-Natal. The **Inkatha Freedom Party** (IFP), formed in 1975 by former ANC Youth League member **Mangosuthu Buthelezi**, has long been associated with Zulu nationalism and draws most of its support from Zulu-speaking people. The IFP and ANC were originally allies in the fight against apartheid, but the IFP's ardent nationalism soon proved to be a major hassle for the ANC, who responded with attacks on opposing IFP members. A bitter and violent conflict between the two parties ensued during the 1980s and 1990s, which claimed up to twenty thousand lives. The political rivalry continues, but it is the ANC which has now gained the upper hand in KwaZulu-Natal. South Africa's president, **Jacob Zuma**, a Zulu from KwaZulu-Natal, has played an important role in trying to end the violence between the ANC and IFP. He often makes speeches in Zulu, and enjoys strong support among his people despite his controversial political career.

Durban

Until the 1970s, **DURBAN** – South Africa's third-largest city and the continent's largest port – was white South Africa's quintessential seaside playground, thanks to its tropical colours and itinerant population of surfers, hedonists and holidaying Jo'burg families. Then, in the 1980s, the collapse of apartheid saw a growing stream of black Africans flood in from rural KwaZulu-Natal, and shantytowns and cardboard hovels revealed the reality of one of the most unmistakably **African conurbations** in the country. The city's second-largest group is its **Indian population**, whose mosques, bazaars and temples are juxtaposed with the Victorian buildings of the colonial centre.

Although the **beachfront** pulls thousands of Jo'burgers down to "Durbs" every year, the city's main interest lies in its gritty urbanity, a seemingly endless struggle to reconcile competing cultures. Durban also provides a logical springboard for visiting the surrounding region. The city is well connected to the rest of South Africa and, thanks to King Shaka International Airport, to a handful of international destinations as well.

There's enough here to keep you busy for a few days. The pulsing warren of bazaars, alleyways and mosques that makes up the Indian area around Dr Yusuf Dadoo Street is ripe for exploration, and Durban's bustling **harbour** area is always photogenic. Swanky **northern suburbs** such as the **Berea**, a desirable residential district perched on a cooler ridge, are replete with luxuriant gardens and packed with fashionable cafés, restaurants and bars.

5

Durban's **city centre** grew around the arrival point of the first white settlers, and the remains of the historical heart are concentrated around **Francis Farewell Square**. Durban's expansive **beachfront** on the eastern edge of the centre is lined with high-rise hotels and tacky family entertainment, although its broad promenade is a wonderful place for a stroll.

Much further afield lie dormitory towns for black communities who commute to work, including the apartheid **ghettos** of KwaMashu and Inanda to the northwest. **Cato Manor**, the closest township to the city, provides an easily accessible vignette of South Africa's growing urban contradictions.

Brief history

Less than two hundred years ago Durban was known to Europeans as **Port Natal**, a lagoon thick with mangroves, eyed by white adventurers who saw business opportunities in its ivory and hides. In 1824 a British party led by **Francis Farewell** persuaded the Zulu king, **Shaka**, to give them land. Not long after, the British renamed

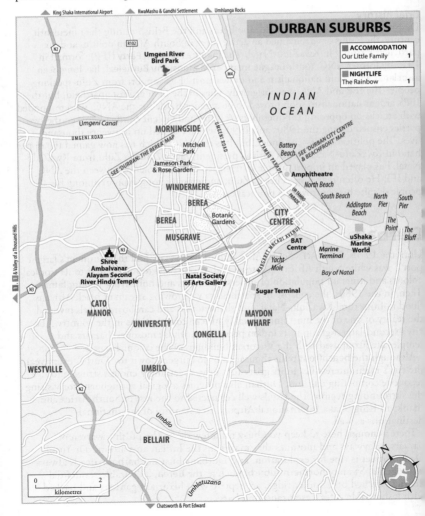

the settlement **Durban** after Sir Benjamin D'Urban, governor of the Cape Colony, whose support, they believed, might not go amiss later.

Britain's tenuous toehold looked threatened in 1839, when **Boers** trundled over the uKhahlamba-Drakensberg in their ox wagons and declared their Republic of Natalia nearby. The following year, a large force of now-hostile Zulus razed the settlement, forcing the British residents to take refuge at sea in the brig *Comet*. Capitalizing on the situation, a group of Boers annexed Durban, later laying siege to a British detachment. This provided the cue for a much-celebrated piece of Victorian melodrama when teenager **Dick King** heroically rode the 1000km from Durban to Grahamstown in ten days to alert the garrison there, which dispatched a rescue detachment to relieve Durban.

Industrialization and apartheid

While Cape Town was becoming a cosmopolitan centre by the 1840s, Durban's population of barely one thousand lived a basic existence in a near wilderness roamed by lions, leopards and elephants. Things changed after Britain formally annexed the **Colony of Natal** in 1843; within ten years, a large-scale immigration of settlers from the mother country had begun. The second half of the nineteenth century was marked by considerable industrial development and the arrival of other groups. Indentured **Indian labourers** came to work in the KwaZulu-Natal cane fields, planting the seeds for South Africa's lucrative **sugar industry** and the city's now substantial Indian community; and **Zulus** headed south after their conquest by the British, in 1879, to enter Durban's expanding economy. In 1895, the completion of the railway connecting Johannesburg and Durban accelerated the influx of migrant labour. This link to South Africa's industrial heartland, and the opening of Durban's harbour mouth to large ships in 1904, ensured the city's eventual pre-eminence as South Africa's principal harbour. In 1922, in the face of growing Indian and black African populations, Durban's strongly English city council introduced **legislation** controlling the sale of land in the city to non-whites, predating Afrikaner-led apartheid by 26 years.

With the strict enforcement of **apartheid** in the 1950s, Durban saw a decade of ANC-led **protests**. When the party was banned in 1960 and formed its armed wing, the ANC made plans for a nationwide **bombing campaign** that began with an explosion in Durban on December 15, 1961. Durban scored another first in 1973 when workers in the city precipitated a wildcat strike, despite a total ban on black industrial action. This heralded the rebirth of South Africa's **trade unions** and reawakened anti-apartheid activity, ushering in the final phase of the country's road to democracy.

The centre

Standing at the heart of colonial Durban, **Francis Farewell Square** is hemmed in by the centre's two main thoroughfares, Dr Pixley Kaseme (formerly West) Street and Anton Lembede (formerly Smith) Street. The square is a palm-fringed garden overlooked by some fine old buildings, the focal point being the **Cenotaph**, a marvellous Art Deco monument to the fallen of World War I. It marks the site where the British adventurers Francis Farewell and Henry Fynn set up Durban's first white encampment to trade ivory with the Zulus. North of here at 160 Monty Naicker Road are the remnants of the **Natal Great Railway Station**, built in 1894 and recycled a century later as shops and offices. The city centre's main shopping centre, Workshop Mall, is just across the road on the corner of Dr A B Xuma and Samora Machel streets.

City Hall

City Hall Dr Pixley Kaseme St • **Natural Science Museum** Mon–Sat 8.30am–4pm, Sun 11am–4pm • Free • ☎ 031 311 2256 • **Durban Art Gallery** Mon–Sat 8.30am–4pm, Sun 11am–4pm • Free • ☎ 031 311 2264

The imposing neo-Baroque **City Hall** is the monumental centrepiece of the city centre. Erected in 1910, it now houses the **Natural Science Museum** on its first floor,

5

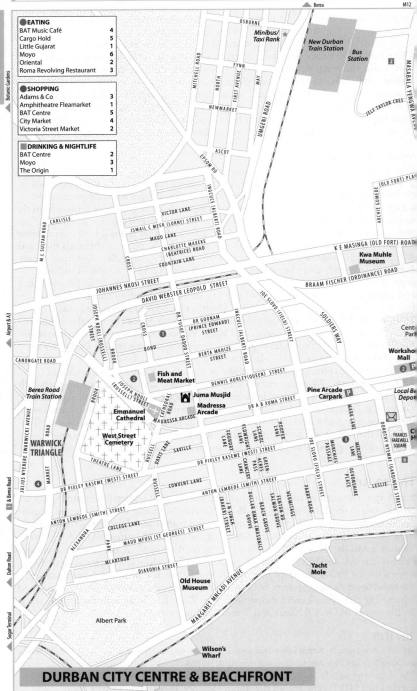

● EATING
BAT Music Café	4
Cargo Hold	5
Little Gujarat	1
Moyo	6
Oriental	2
Roma Revolving Restaurant	3

● SHOPPING
Adams & Co	3
Amphitheatre Fleamarket	1
BAT Centre	5
City Market	4
Victoria Street Market	2

■ DRINKING & NIGHTLIFE
BAT Centre	2
Moyo	3
The Origin	1

Botanic Gardens

Airport & A3

& Berea Road

Dalton Road

Sugar Terminal

DURBAN CITY CENTRE & BEACHFRONT

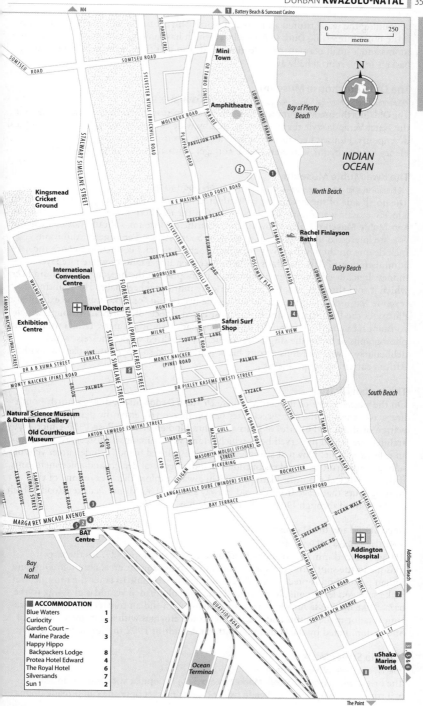

M4

SOMTSEU ROAD
SOMTSEU ROAD

SOL HARRIS CRES

SYLVESTER NTULI (BRICKHILL) ROAD

OR TAMBO (SNELL) PARADE

LOWER MARINE PARADE

Mini Town

Amphitheatre

MOLYNEUX ROAD

PLAYFAIR ROAD

PAVILION TERR.

Bay of Plenty Beach

INDIAN OCEAN

STALWART SIMELANE STREET

Kingsmead Cricket Ground

K E MASINGA (OLD FORT) ROAD

North Beach

GRESHAM PLACE

SYLVESTER NTULI (BRICKHILL) ROAD

BAUMANN ROAD

BOSCOMBE PLACE

OR TAMBO (MARINE) PARADE

Rachel Finlayson Baths

NORTH LANE

MORRISON

Dairy Beach

WEST LANE

International Convention Centre

FLORENCE NZAMA (PRINCE ALFRED) STREET

HUNTER

EAST LANE

JOHN MILNE ROAD

MILNE

SOUTH LANE

Travel Doctor

Exhibition Centre

WALNUT ROAD

SAMORA MACHEL (ALIWAL) STREET

Safari Surf Shop

SEA VIEW

LOWER MARINE PARADE

3

4

PINE TERRACE

DR A B XUMA STREET

MONTY NAICKER (PINE) ROAD

MONTY NAICKER (PINE) ROAD

PALMER

STALWART SIMELANE STREET

5

DR PIXLEY KASEME (WEST) STREET

PALMER

South Beach

UNION

PECK RD

TYZACK

GILLESPIE

MAHATMA GANDHI ROAD

OR TAMBO (MARINE) PARADE

Natural Science Museum & Durban Art Gallery

Old Courthouse Museum

ANTON LEMBEDE (SMITH) STREET

TIMBER

ROY RD

MAZEPPA

GULL

MASOBIYA MDLULI (FISHER) STREET

ROCHESTER

CATO SQ

CREEK

CATO

GILLIGAN

PICKERING

RUTHERFORD

ERSKINE TERRACE

SAMORA MACHEL (ALIWAL) STREET

ALBANY GROVE

MONA ROAD

JONSSON LANE

MILLS LANE

DR LANGALIBALELE DUBE (WINDER) STREET

BAY TERRACE

3

MAHATMA GANDHI ROAD

SHEARER RD

OCEAN WALK

MARGARET MNCADI AVENUE

9 2 4

BAT Centre

Bay of Natal

MASONIC RD

Addington Hospital

HOSPITAL ROAD

PRINCE

Addington Beach

7

QUAYSIDE ROAD

SOUTH BEACH AVENUE

BELL ST

3, 5 & 6

Ocean Terminal

uShaka Marine World

8

0 ——— 250
metres

N

■ ACCOMMODATION	
Blue Waters	1
Curiosity	5
Garden Court – Marine Parade	3
Happy Hippo Backpackers Lodge	8
Protea Hotel Edward	4
The Royal Hotel	6
Silversands	7
Sun 1	2

5

containing the usual stuffed animals and worth only a brief look. On the second floor is the more interesting **Durban Art Gallery**, which has rotating exhibitions in its main rooms and a small permanent collection of African paintings, prints, carvings and baskets in the central hallway.

The Old Courthouse Museum

99 Samora Machel St • Mon–Sat 8.30am–4pm, Sun 11am–4pm • Free • ☎ 031 311 2226

The **Old Courthouse Museum** was Durban's first two-storey building, erected in 1866 in the Natal Veranda style that is characterized by wide eaves to throw off heavy subtropical downpours. Housed here in a somewhat austere atmosphere is a reconstruction of Henry Francis Fynn's wattle-and-daub cottage, Durban's first European structure.

The Kwa Muhle Museum

130 Braam Fischer Rd • Mon–Sat 8.30am–4pm, Sun 11am–4pm • Free • ☎ 031 311 2237

The north side of the city centre is dominated by **Central Park**, a large green space with a lovely mosaic water fountain as its focus. On the northern perimeter of the park, the **Kwa Muhle Museum** – also known as the Apartheid Museum – should not be missed if you are interested in understanding modern South Africa. Permanent exhibitions include one on the Durban System, which enabled the city council to finance the administration of African affairs without ever spending a rand of white ratepayers' money. It achieved this by granting itself a monopoly on the brewing of sorghum beer, which it sold through vast, black African-only municipal beer halls. The resulting revenue was used to ensure that black people lived in an "orderly" way. The exhibit also illustrates the Pass System, one of the most hated aspects of apartheid, through which constant tabs could be kept on the black population in urban areas. Look out, too, for photographs of life in the single-sex, artificially tribalized worker hostels, which deliberately sowed divisions among black workers, and so played their part in South Africa's current social problems.

The Indian District

On the western edge of the centre, where **Dr Yusuf Dadoo Street** draws a north–south line across the city, the pace accelerates perceptibly as you enter the densely packed warren of shops and eateries of Durban's central **Indian district**. Post-1910 Union-style architecture is well preserved here, which, along with minarets and steeples, makes for an eclectic skyline. Down at street level, the rich cultural blend includes street vendors selling herbs, fruit and trinkets outside the Indian general dealers and spice merchants. If the crowds feel too intimidating, you can always explore this area on one of the **walking tours** that leave from the old railway station, 160 Monty Naicker Road, which can be booked through Durban Tourism (see box, p.370).

Juma Musjid and the Madressa Arcade

Corner of Dr Yusuf Dadoo and Dennis Hurley streets

The gilt-domed minarets of **Juma Musjid** were completed in 1927. It's the largest mosque in the southern hemisphere and a focal point for the area, although Durban's Indian population is predominantly Hindu. You're welcome to enter the mosque, but make sure you leave your shoes at the door. The colonnaded verandas give way to the bazaar-like **Madressa Arcade** next door, heaving with Indian traders peddling kerosene lamps, tailor-made outfits and beads. The arcade emerges with a start into Cathedral Street, dominated by the **Emmanuel Cathedral**, built in 1902 in Gothic Revival style.

Victoria Street Market

Corner of Dennis Hurley and Joseph Nduli streets

The bright-pink **Victoria Street Market** (see p.374) is popular with tourists in search of a trinket or two, while the hectic fish and meat market opposite can provide drama, particularly on Sunday mornings when the stallholders compete to sell their stocks before the afternoon close-down. Both can be explored independently, but a guided tour with a company like Markets of Warwick (see box, p.370) can be even more rewarding.

Joseph Nduli Street and the West Street Cemetery

To the west of the Victoria Street Market, African hawkers gather on **Joseph Nduli Street** (formerly Russell St), where they do a brisk trade in *umuthi* (traditional herbal medicines). West of here and jammed between the railway tracks and the N3, **West Street Cemetery** is zoned according to religion. Many of the city's colonial big names are buried here, such as Durban's first mayor, George Cato, and the Victorian documentary painter, Thomas Baines. In the Muslim section some tombstones are inscribed "*hagee*" or "*hafez*", the former indicating someone who has been to Mecca and the latter an individual who managed to memorize the entire Koran.

Warwick Triangle

In a scene reminiscent of *Bladerunner*, west of Dr Yusuf Dadoo Street, concrete freeways run over chaotic roads and minibus taxi ranks; here you'll find Durban's real urban heart of hawkers, shacks and *shebeens*. You'll need to be bold to explore the **Warwick Triangle**, which lies between King Dinizulu Road, Brook Street and Canongate Road – walk with confidence, wear nothing easily snatched, and you should be fine.

The gateway to the triangle is across Brook Street – known until 1988 as Slaughterhouse Road because butchers slaughtered livestock here – through the hectic Berea station concourse full of pumping music and hawkers, and over the Market Road footbridge, where you'll come to the main **city market** (see p.374) between Julius Nyerere Avenue and Market Road.

The harbour area

Margaret Mncadi Avenue (formerly Victoria Embankment), or the Esplanade, runs the length of Durban's harbour, the lifeblood of the city's economic power. Durban is one of the few cities in the world with a busy port a mere block from the city centre, edged by a narrow strip of park too seedy to make for a very pleasant stroll. But you'll find a lively cultural scene at the **BAT Centre** at the eastern end, which is a good spot from which to watch the sun glinting off the sparkling water and take in the mix of yachts and cargo ships chugging past.

The Sugar Terminal

51 Maydon Wharf Rd • Tours Mon–Thurs 8.30am, 10am, 11.30am & 2pm • R16 • Book at the SA Sugar Association Tour Centre, or by phone • ☎ 031 365 8100

At the western edge of the harbour, where Margaret Mncadi Avenue joins Maydon Wharf Road, is a photogenic complex of functional industrial architecture, most notable of which are the three dramatic sugar silos at the **Sugar Terminal**. The terminal, whose design has been patented and used internationally, has become something of a tourist attraction; a tour gives you one hour of sugary history and access to half a million tonnes of sugar.

Old House Museum

31 Diakonia St • Mon–Fri 8.30am–4pm, Sun 11am–4pm • Free • ☎ 031 311 2261

Margaret Mncadi Avenue and the streets around it were prime residential areas during the city's early development in the nineteenth century, and here you'll find a reminder of the city's colonial heritage at the **Old House Museum**, one block north of Margaret Mncadi Avenue. Once the home of Sir John Robinson, who became Natal's first prime minister in 1893, the two rooms of this renovated settler house are crammed full of period furniture and numerous ticking clocks.

5

Yacht Mole and the BAT

BAT Office Mon–Fri 8am–4pm, Sat 8am–2pm • ☎ 031 332 0451, ⓦ batcentre.co.za

On the waterfront you'll find the **Yacht Mole**, a slender breakwater jutting into the bay and home to the Point and Royal Natal Yacht clubs. This is also the access point for the **BAT (Bartle Arts Trust) Centre**, an industrial-chic arts development and community venue boasting a concert hall, practical visual art workshops, classes and exhibition galleries (see p.374). The *BAT Music Café* restaurant upstairs (see p.372) provides a magnificent lookout for watching the passing harbour scene.

Ocean Terminal Building

The **Ocean Terminal Building**, which harks back to the romantic days of sea travel, is one of Durban's architectural masterpieces. Although you can't enter the building, the view from outside it at night, looking back onto the city, is spectacular. To get here, head east on Margaret Mncadi Avenue towards the Stalwart Simelane Street intersection, enter the Harbour at Port Entrance no. 3 and follow the signs.

The beachfront

Durban's **beachfront**, a high-energy holiday strip just east of the centre, is South Africa's most developed seaside; however, it's of limited appeal unless you enjoy unabashed kitsch and garish amusement parks. This 6km stretch was traditionally called the **Golden Mile**, though the prevalence of crime along the beachfront earned it the moniker of Mugger's Mile. However, in the build-up to the 2010 football World Cup, concerted efforts were made to clean up the beachfront, including increased police presence and new CCTV cameras. These measures have improved security, although you should still exercise caution and use common sense – for example, never leave valuables unattended on the beach – and avoid walking along the beachfront at night.

uShaka Marine World

Just south of Addington Beach • Wet 'n Wild Wed–Fri 10am–5pm, Sat & Sun 9am–5pm; Sea World daily 9am–5pm • R168 to visit Sea World, R175 for Wet 'n Wild, or R209 for both • ☎ 031 328 8000, ⓦ ushakamarineworld.co.za

The big draw of Addington Beach – and the only really worthwhile attraction along the beachfront – is **uShaka Marine World**. This impressive water adventure wonderland is a tropical theme park, complete with palm trees, fake rock formations and thatched bomas. The most appealing section is **uShaka Sea World**, its design centred on a superb mock-up of a wrecked 1920s cargo ship. The main entrance leads you down to the darkened hull with its battered engine room, ropes and sloping floors. Its walls serve as windows into the "ocean" (a series of large tanks), where turtles, stingrays, octopus, sharks and a host of other marine life can be seen. The complex also includes a penguin rookery, a dolphin stadium and a seal pool, where shows (seven a day) feature these creatures, as well as **uShaka Wet 'n Wild**, a series of pools and water slides, including The Drop Zone, the highest water slide in the southern hemisphere. The **uShaka Village Walk** is home to plenty of restaurants, making it a great (and safe) night-time venue.

South Beach

Just north of uShaka Marine World lies **South Beach**, arguably South Africa's busiest beach, which heralds the start of the beachfront tourist tack. On weekends and holidays the paved promenade swarms with surfers, skateboarders and hawkers. Further along OR Tambo Parade, you'll find paddling pools, stepping stones, an aerial cableway and amusement rides.

Dairy Beach and the Rachel Finlayson Baths

OR Tambo Parade • **Rachel Finlayson Baths** Oct–April Mon–Fri 5.30am–6pm, Sat & Sun 6am–6pm; May–Sept daily 6am–5pm • R9

Dairy Beach is so-called because of the milking factory that once stood here. It's now regarded as one of the country's best surfing beaches, and it's home to the saltwater **Rachel Finlayson Baths**, a good spot for sheltered swimming and sunbathing; the baths were undergoing renovation at the time of writing in preparation for the 2022 Commonwealth Games, and it was unclear when they would reopen.

North Beach and the Bay of Plenty

Both **North Beach** and the adjacent **Bay of Plenty** host regular international and local professional surfing contests (see p.369). Between OR Tambo Parade and the pedestrian walkway at the Bay of Plenty is the attractively landscaped **Amphitheatre**; a long-running flea market crops up every Sunday just south of here (see p.374).

Mini Town

41 OR Tambo Parade • Daily 9.30am–4.30pm • Adults R25, children R20 • ☎ 031 337 7892

Near the corner of OR Tambo Parade and KE Masinga Road, **Mini Town** is a scale replica of Durban's landmarks and great fun for kids; walkways lead you past hotels, beaches and the airport, giving you a bird's-eye view of the city.

Battery Beach and the Suncoast Casino

A kilometre north of the centre along Marine Parade, past **Battery Beach** (a good place for swimming), is the massive **Suncoast Casino**, a mock Art Deco entertainment complex with restaurants, gambling tables, eight cinemas and a pristine private beach.

The Berea

High on a ridge overlooking the city centre, the **Berea** is Durban's oldest and most desirable residential district, where mansions and apartment blocks enjoy airy views of the harbour and the sea. Its palmy avenues provide an alternative to the torrid city centre and beachfront for accommodation, eating and entertainment. The term Berea actually refers to two different localities: the residential area immediately north and west of the city centre is called the Berea, though within this is a suburb known as the Berea, as well as suburbs such as Morningside and Musgrave.

KwaZulu-Natal Society of Arts Gallery

66 Bulwer Rd • Tues–Fri 9am–5pm, Sat 9am–4pm, Sun 10am–3pm • Free • ☎ 031 277 1705, ⦿ kznsagallery.co.za

The **KwaZulu-Natal Society of Arts Gallery**, or NSA, provides a breezy venue for taking in a broad spectrum of rotating exhibitions by local artists. Designed for the local climate, the 1990s building is a mass of interlinked spaces divided by a timber screen that forms a veranda. There's a good arts and crafts shop (see p.374) and a relaxing coffee shop.

Botanic Gardens

John Zikhali Rd, enter on St Thomas Rd • Daily: gardens 7.30am–5.15pm, orchid house 9am–5pm • Free • ☎ 031 309 9240, ⦿ durbanbotanicgardens.org.za

Northwest of the centre, Durban's **Botanic Gardens**, established in 1849, are famous for their cycad collection, which includes *Encephalartos woodii*, one of the rarest specimens in the world. The gardens also boast cool paths, excellent picnic spots, a lovely teahouse and a magnificent array of orchids.

Muckleneuk and Campbell Collections

20 Gladys Mazibuco Rd, corner of Steven Dlamini Rd • **Campbell Collections** Mon, Tues & Fri 9am–3pm • Tours by appointment R20 • ☎ 031 260 1720 • **Killie Campbell Africana Library and Museum** Mon–Fri 8.30am–4.30pm, Sat 9am–noon • Free • **Mashu Museum of Ethnology** Mon–Fri 8.30am–4.30pm • Free • ⦿ campbell.ukzn.ac.za

The Cape Dutch-revival former homestead of sugar baron Sir Marshal Campbell, **Muckleneuk** houses one of the finest private collections of Africana in the country, including material relating to KwaZulu-Natal's ethnic heritage. The **Campbell**

5

DURBAN: THE BEREA

ACCOMMODATION
Audacia Manor	2
The Benjamin	6
The Concierge	8
The Elephant House	3
Essenwood House	4
Gibela Lodge	7
Goble Palms	1
Nomad's Backpackers	9
Tekweni Backpackers	5

DRINKING & NIGHTLIFE
Club Altitude	3
Dropkick Murphy's	1
Sidebar	2
Skyybar	3

Asherville
Sports Field

ALPINE ROAD

EARL HAIG ROAD

EARL HAIG ROAD

FERNDALE RD

NIMMO RD

MOUNTAIN VIEW RD

HOPECRAIG AVE

PETER MOKABA (NORTH RIDGE) ROAD

BEMERSYDE RD

Jameson Park
& Rose Garden

MONTPELIER ROAD

FLORIDA RD

SPRINGFIELD ROAD

WOODLEY CRES

MONTPE

FELIX DLAMINI (BRICKFIELD) ROAD

EAST STREET

ESSENWOOD

Muckleneuk &
Campbell Collections

CURRIE ROAD

HADEN ROAD

SOUTH ROAD

MCCORD ROAD

PALM GROVE

HIGH ROAD

JESMOND GR

JULIA ROAD

PETER MOKABA (RIDGE) ROAD

VAUSE ROAD

OVERPORT DRIVE

STEVEN DLAMINI (ESSENWOOD) ROAD

MUSGRAVE ROAD

GLADYS MAZBUKO ROAD
(MARIOTT GARDENS)

NORFOLK ROAD

RORVIK ROAD

PROBLEM MKHIZE (COWEY) ROAD

ESSELMONT AVE

St Thomas
Cemetery

KENILWORTH ROAD

ST THOMAS ROAD

Berea
Park

BEREA PARK ROAD

JOHN ZIKHALI (SYDENHAM) ROAD

LAWRENCE ROAD

CALDWELL DR

CLIVE ROAD

RAPIER ROAD

MADRAS ROAD

KENMOOR ROAD

AVONDALE ROAD

MUSGRAVE

WINDMILL ROAD

ST THOMAS ROAD

CURRIE ROAD

SILVERTON ROAD

PETER MOKABA (RIDGE) ROAD

VAUSE ROAD

ST THOMAS AVENUE

CLYDE AVE

HURST GR

CLIFTON PL

GRANTS GR

EVERED POOLE PL

PROBLEM MKHIZE
(EDITH BENSON) ROAD

Botanic
Gardens

ST THOMAS RD

WINTERTON WK

JOHN ZIKHALI (SYDENHAM) ROAD

Mazisi Kunene Road & Life Entabeni Hospital

BELLEVUE ROAD

SILVERTON ROAD

STEVEN DLAMINI (ESSENWOOD) ROAD

Musgrave
Centre

MUSGRAVE ROAD

MUSGRAVE AVE

CURRIE ROAD

BOTANIC GARDENS ROAD

M L SULTAN / FEN

N

WESTERN FREEWAY

0 — 500
metres

Club Altitude, Skyybar & KwaZulu-Natal Society of Arts Gallery

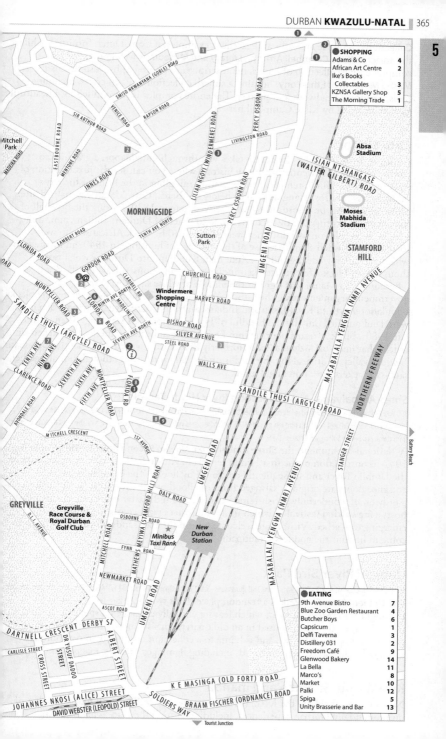

● **SHOPPING**

Adams & Co	4
African Art Centre	2
Ike's Books Collectables	3
KZNSA Gallery Shop	5
The Morning Trade	1

SMISO NXWANYANA (GOBLE) ROAD

SIR ARTHUR ROAD

VENICE ROAD

RAPSON ROAD

EASTBOURNE ROAD

MENTONE ROAD

MADEIRA ROAD

Mitchell Park

PERCY OSBORN ROAD

LILIAN NGOYI (WINDERMERE) ROAD

LIVINGSTON ROAD

Absa Stadium

ISIAH NTSHANGASE (WALTER GILBERT) ROAD

INNES ROAD

MORNINGSIDE

LAMBERT ROAD

TENTH AVE NORTH

Sutton Park

UMGENI ROAD

Moses Mabhida Stadium

STAMFORD HILL

FLORIDA ROAD

GORDON ROAD

CLAMBELL RD

CHURCHILL ROAD

MONTPELIER ROAD

NINTH AVE NORTH

FLORIDA ROAD

MADELINE RD

HARVEY ROAD

Windermere Shopping Centre

SANDILE THUSI (ARGYLE) ROAD

SEVENTH AVE NORTH

BISHOP ROAD

SILVER AVENUE

STEEL ROAD

MASABALALA YENGWA (NMR) AVENUE

NORTHERN FREEWAY

TENTH AVE

NINTH AVE

SEVENTH AVE

SIXTH AVE

WALLS AVE

CLARENCE ROAD

AVONDALE ROAD

FIFTH AVE

MONTPELIER ROAD

FLORIDA RD

SANDILE THUSI (ARGYLE) ROAD

STANGER STREET

Battery Beach

MITCHELL CRESCENT

1ST AVENUE

UMGENI ROAD

DALY ROAD

GREYVILLE

D.L.I. AVENUE

Greyville Race Course & Royal Durban Golf Club

MITCHELL ROAD

STAMFORD HILL ROAD

OSBORNE ROAD

MATHEWS MEYIWA ROAD

★ Minibus Taxi Rank

New Durban Station

MASABALALA YENGWA (NMR) AVENUE

FYNN ROAD

NEWMARKET ROAD

ASCOT ROAD

UMGENI ROAD

DARTNELL CRESCENT DERBY ST

DR VUSI DADOO STREET

ALBERT STREET

CARLISLE STREET

CROSS STREET

K E MASINGA (OLD FORT) ROAD

JOHANNES NKOSI (ALICE) STREET

DAVID WEBSTER (LEOPOLD) STREET

SOLDIERS WAY

BRAAM FISCHER (ORDNANCE) ROAD

Tourist Junction

● **EATING**

9th Avenue Bistro	7
Blue Zoo Garden Restaurant	4
Butcher Boys	6
Capsicum	1
Delfi Taverna	3
Distillery 031	2
Freedom Café	9
Glenwood Bakery	14
La Bella	11
Marco's	8
Market	10
Palki	12
Spiga	5
Unity Brasserie and Bar	13

5

Collections comprise artworks and excellent examples of Cape Dutch furniture, while the adjacent **Killie Campbell Africana Library and Museum** is well known for its comprehensive collection of books, manuscripts and photographs. Also here is the **Mashu Museum of Ethnology**, housing a superb collection of Zulu crafts, including tools, weapons, beadwork and pottery. The entire complex is surrounded by a beautiful garden designed by Killie Campbell herself.

Cato Manor

A short drive west of the city centre takes you through **Cato Manor**, a graphic cross section of Durban's twentieth-century history, where you can see the juxtaposition of squatter camps, Hindu temples and vegetation mingling in the heart of the city's middle-class suburbs. Lying in a valley below the Berea, Cato Manor was named after Durban's first mayor, **George Cato**, who arrived here in 1839. During the first half of the twentieth century the district was home to much of Durban's Indian community, who built temples on its hills. They were later joined by black Africans, who were forced into crowded slums because of the shortage of housing. In 1949, an incident in which an Indian trader assaulted a Zulu man flared up into Durban's worst **riot**; thousands of black Africans attacked Indian stores and houses, leaving 142 dead.

Because Cato Manor was right in the middle of white suburbs, the apartheid government began enforcing the Group Areas Act here in the 1960s, moving the black population north to KwaMashu and Indians south to Chatsworth, leaving a derelict wasteland guarded only by the handful of Hindu temples left standing. Then, in the late 1980s, black Africans pouring into Durban began building the closely packed tin shacks that line **Vusi Mzimela Road** (formerly Bellair Rd), winding its way through Cato Manor's valley. A drive along the road is undeniably interesting, though not altogether safe – carjackers are a potential hazard.

Shree Ambalvanar Alayam Second River Hindu Temple

890 Vusi Mzimela Rd · Can be visited safely on a tour (see box, p.370) · Leave the city centre on the M13, take the Felix Dlamini Rd (formerly Brickfield Rd) exit and then turn left into the M10, which becomes Vusi Mzimela Rd; the temple is on the right if you're coming from town, just before Solomon Mahlangu Drive

A National Monument, the **Shree Ambalvanar Alayam Second River Hindu Temple** is a 1947 reconstruction of the first Hindu temple in Africa, built in 1875 on the banks of the Umbilo River and subsequently destroyed by floods. The beautifully carved entrance doors are originals salvaged from the flood, while the facade is adorned with a pantheon of wonderfully garish Hindu deities. Around Easter every year the temple hosts a **firewalking festival** in which unshod devotees walk across red-hot coals, emerging unscathed. Visitors are welcome to join the thousands of worshippers who come to honour the goddess Draudpadi.

Umgeni River Bird Park

490 Riverside Rd, Durban North · Daily 9am–5pm; bird shows Tues–Sun 11am & 2pm · R52 · ☎ 031 579 4601, ⓦ umgeniriverbirdpark.co.za

The **Umgeni River Bird Park** is a tranquil place that's worth a visit for its fantastic free-flight bird shows, some of which feature critically endangered species such as the wattled crane. The park, housed in an old quarry, consists mostly of walk-through aviaries and open paddocks, and is home to a collection of more than two hundred species of indigenous and exotic birds including flamingos, finches, magpies and macaws.

KwaMashu, Shembe and Inanda

North of the city along the R102 (which becomes the M25), you'll find a number of quintessentially Durban experiences, including visiting the place where Gandhi dreamed up passive resistance and witnessing the epic religious ceremonies of the Zulu–Christian Shembe sect. A word of **warning**: driving through some of the areas covered here carries a certain risk; you're advised to go with someone familiar with the area or on an organized tour (see box, p.370).

KwaMashu

Driving north along the M25 towards Inanda, you'll pass the black township of **KwaMashu** on the left, established in the late 1950s to house residents of Cato Manor who had been forcibly resettled. It displays all the unimaginative planning typical of such low-cost housing schemes. The area is a sea of hills, vegetation and colour, which makes it tempting to romanticize the locality's poverty.

The Gandhi Settlement

Mon–Fri 8am–4pm, Sat 9am–2pm • Donation • ☎ 031 373 5486

A well-signposted turn off the M25 takes you to the **Gandhi Settlement**, also known as the Phoenix Settlement. On the eastern edge of the vast Inanda squatter camp, it's the site of a self-help scheme established by Mohandas Gandhi soon after his arrival in Durban in 1903. It was from here that Gandhi began to forge his philosophy of passive resistance; in a sad irony, violence brought it to ruin in 1985 when squatters from the adjacent camp looted and razed the settlement. With the help of the Indian Government, it was rebuilt in time for its centenary celebration. A bronze bust of Gandhi now stands near the entrance to his house, **Sarvodaya** ("a place for the upliftment for all"), which is now a **museum** focusing on his time in South Africa and on Indian resistance to segregation.

Shembe

At **Ekuphakameni** ("the elated place"), west of the Gandhi Settlement along the M25, two "stars" laid in stone in the hilly landscape mark the spots where meteorites from the 1906 appearance of Halley's Comet struck the earth. From here, you can continue to the Inanda police station at the top of the hill, then turn left into the valley and cross the Umhlanga River bridge. At the next intersection, take the dirt road to the left, past the sports field, and turn left again to view the **Shembe settlement** at Ebuhleni, established by the Holy Church of Nazareth as a refuge for black people dispossessed by the Land Act of 1913. According to the founding history of the Church, its prophet Isaya Shembe was "called" in 1910 to a mountaintop outside Durban, where he vowed before God to bring the Gospel to the Zulus. The Church's membership of tens of thousands was drawn initially from rural people who were eager to embrace Christianity, but were unwilling to give up traditional customs. The resulting religion was a rich synthesis that rejected drinking, smoking and cults, while encouraging a work ethic centred around crafts.

Every July devotees of the Holy Church of Nazareth gather in Ebuhleni for a month of worship. On these occasions, the men and women live on different sides of the village, and unmarried women live in a separate enclosure. At the entrance gates, rows of tables display holographic images of Isaya Shembe and key rings with religious icons.

Leaving Ebuhleni, ignore the dirt road turn-off and head straight on to reach the Inanda Dam. The deep gorge to your left is the **Inanda Falls**, where the Shembe have baptismal ceremonies, which visitors are welcome to attend.

ARRIVAL AND DEPARTURE

DURBAN

BY PLANE

King Shaka International Airport Durban's international airport (☎ 032 436 6585) is located 35km north of the city in the village of La Mercy. A shuttle service to the city centre runs every 45min (daily 5am–8pm; R80; ☎ 031 465 1660) and will drop you at your accommodation. A metered taxi to the city should cost no more than R450. Several car-rental companies are based here (see p.369), and there are Absa and Nedbank ATMs in the arrivals terminal. The following airlines are based at the airport: Air Mauritius (☎ 032 436 0007); British Airways (☎ 011 441 8600); Emirates (☎ 086 160 6606); Fly Safair (☎ 087 135 1351); Kulula (☎ 086 158 5852); Mango (☎ 086 116 2646); Skywise (☎ 086 191 1435); and South African Airways (☎ 086 160 6606).

5

Destinations Bloemfontein (daily; 1hr 5min); Cape Town (11 daily; 2hr 15min); Dubai (daily; 8hr 20min); East London (daily; 1hr 15min); Gaborone (daily; 1hr 20min); George (daily; 1hr 50min); Johannesburg (frequent; 1hr 10min); Lanseria (6 daily; 1hr 10min); Maputo (daily; 1hr 16min); Mauritius (daily; 3hr 50min); Nelspruit (2 daily; 1hr 20min); Port Elizabeth (4 daily; 1hr 20min).

BY TRAIN
New Durban Station The Trans-Natal service from Johannesburg arrives at the grim main train station off Masabalala Yengwa Avenue, just north of the main commercial centre. The best option from here is to take a metered taxi from the rank in front of the bus station that occupies the ground level of the station complex; a ride to the beachfront or Florida Rd costs R50–60.
Destinations Johannesburg (3 weekly; 14hr 20min); Pietermaritzburg (3 weekly; 2hr 30min).

BY BUS
Intercity buses Intercape (☎ 021 380 4400), Greyhound (☎ 031 334 9702), Translux (☎ 031 361 7670) and other intercity buses arrive at and depart from the bus station attached to the New Durban station complex. The Margate

Mini Coach (☎ 039 312 1406, ⓦ margatecoach.co.za) from the South Coast pulls in here, as well as outside domestic departures at King Shaka International Airport.
Destinations Ballito (daily; 45min); Bloemfontein (4 daily; 9hr); Cape Town (4 daily; 22hr); East London (2 daily; 10hr); Grahamstown (3 daily; 12hr); Harrismith (9 daily; 4hr 30min); Jeffrey's Bay (3 daily; 15hr 45min); Johannesburg (21 daily; 10hr); Knysna (4 daily; 18hr 30min); Ladysmith (3 daily; 3hr); Margate (4 daily; 2hr); Melmoth (daily; 4hr); Mossel Bay (5 daily; 19hr 40min); Pietermaritzburg (18 daily; 2hr 15min); Plettenberg Bay (4 daily; 16hr 30min); Port Elizabeth (3 daily; 14hr 30min); Port Shepstone (7 daily; 1hr 30min); Pretoria (12 daily; 9hr 30min); Richards Bay (daily; 2hr 30min); Sedgefield (5 daily; 19hr); Umtata (5 daily; 6hr); Vryheid (daily; 6hr).
Baz Bus (☎ 086 122 9287, ⓦ bazbus.com). Stops four times a week at most of the Durban backpacker hostels, as part of its regular route (see p.49).
Destinations Amphitheatre (5hr); Chintsa (10hr); Coffee Bay (7hr); East London (11hr); Johannesburg (10hr); Kokstad (4hr); Mthatha (7hr); Pietermaritzburg (2hr); Port Alfred (11hr); Port Elizabeth (15hr); Port Shepstone (3hr); Pretoria (11hr); Umtentweni (3hr); Umzumbe (2hr); Warner Beach (1hr).

INFORMATION
Tourist information Durban Tourism (the city's tourist bureau) is based at 90 Florida Rd, the Berea (daily 8am–5pm; ☎ 031 322 4164, ⓦ www.durbanexperience.co.za). There are several other well-equipped tourist offices at uShaka Marine World on the beachfront (Mon–Thurs & Sun 9am–6pm, Fri & Sat 9am–7pm; ☎ 031 337 8099), on Marine Parade on North

Beach (daily 8am–4.30pm; ☎ 031 322 4205) and in the arrivals terminal at King Shaka International Airport (daily 6.30am–9pm; ☎ 031 322 6046). Apart from the Florida Rd office, all share space with the province's excellent tourist bureau Tourism KwaZulu-Natal (ⓦ zulu.org.za), which can provide information on excursions further afield.

OUTDOOR ACTIVITIES AND SPECTATOR SPORTS
Birdwatching A popular activity in the green fringes of the city, birdwatching is aided by the Durban Metropolitan Open Space System (DMOSS), a project linking all the city parks via narrow green corridors. Promising spots include the Manor Gardens area; the Botanic Gardens; the Berea; Burman Bush, to the north of the city; Pigeon Valley, below the University of KwaZulu-Natal; the Umgeni River Mouth; Virginia Bush, on the road to Umhlanga Rocks; and the

Hawaan Forest in Umhlanga, where the spotted thrush and green coucal have been seen.
Golf Enclosed within the tracks of the Greyville Race Course (see opposite), the Royal Durban Golf Club (R275 for eighteen holes; ☎ 031 309 1373, ⓦ royal durban.co.za) is notable for its unusual setting, while the Durban Country Club on Isiah Ntshangase Rd (R385 for eighteen holes; ☎ 031 313 1777, ⓦ dcclub.co.za)

DURBAN'S NEW STREET NAMES
Many of Durban's main thoroughfares have been renamed to better reflect the cultural balance in the new South Africa. Well-known Durban streets, such as Point Road and West Street, now bear the names of famous and not-so-famous people who have contributed in one way or another to the democratization of South African society. However, some Durbanites question the merits of naming streets after foreigners such as Che Guevara and Samora Machel, and the changes have been challenged in court. Despite this, most of the proposed changes have been made and are reflected on street signs around the city. In practice, longtime Durban residents still commonly use the old names, so on the maps in this Guide, we have given the new name followed by the old name in brackets.

EXTREME SPORTS AT MOSES MABHIDA STADIUM

Durban's newest architectural landmark, the **Moses Mabhida Stadium**, may have been designed with the 2010 football World Cup in mind, but city authorities seem determined to keep it from gathering dust. There are a number of activities on offer at the stadium, including mounting the striking 106m central arch by **cable car** for a 360-degree view of the city (daily 9am–5pm; R60), or strapping on safety equipment and scaling the arch on foot (Sat & Sun 10am, 1pm & 3pm; R90). Adrenaline junkies can also try the **Big Rush Big Swing**, billed as the world's tallest swing, which sends you plunging off one side of the stadium to swoop across in a 220m arc (Mon–Fri 9.30am–6pm, Sat & Sun 8am–6pm; R695; ⓦbigrush.co.za). For more information check ⓦmmstadium.com.

is considered by many to be the finest course in South Africa.

Scuba diving Pleasurable in KwaZulu-Natal's subtropical waters, but somewhat limited immediately around Durban. The best diving sites are Vetches Pier at the southern tip of the beachfront, and Blood Reef at the tip of the Bluff (opposite the Point). Scuba-diving courses can be arranged through Underwater World, 251 Mahatma Gandhi Rd (ⓣ031 332 5820, ⓦunderwaterworld.co.za); a full six-day internationally recognized PADI course costs R3250, including use of the gear you'll need.

Surfing Given Durban's seafront location, surfing is extremely popular, and night surfing competitions draw enormous crowds. The favourite spot for surfers is North Beach, while a good place to pick up gear is the Safari Surf Shop, 6 Milne St (ⓣ031 337 4230, ⓦsafarisurf .com), where Spider Murphy, South Africa's top board-shaper, will custom-build a world-class board for much less than a comparable order would cost in Europe or North America. Ocean Ventures at uShaka Marine World (ⓣ086 100 1138, ⓦoceanventures.co.za) offers surfing lessons with experienced instructors (R200/hr, plus R120 for board rental).

Swimming Durban's largest pool is the heated King's Park Olympic Swimming Pool on Masabalala Yengwa Ave, between Sandile Thusi and Battery Beach roads in Stamford Hill (ⓣ031 312 0404; R14). The seawater Rachel Finlayson Baths on OR Tambo Parade are handy if you're staying near the beachfront, though they were under renovation at the time of writing (R9).

Cricket The Kingsmead Cricket Ground in the centre (ⓣ031 335 4200) is the principal venue for local and international cricket matches and is home to the provincial cricket team, the Sunfoil Dolphins.

Horseracing The horseracing season runs from May to August and centres around the Greyville Race Course, Avondale Rd, Greyville (ⓣ031 314 1651). The annual Vodacom Durban July (ⓦdurbanjuly.info), which, as the name suggests, takes place during July, is South Africa's premier horseracing event, drawing bets from across the country.

Rugby You'll have plenty of opportunity to watch rugby in season at Kings Park Stadium, Isiah Ntshangase Rd, Stamford Hill (ⓣ031 308 8400), home to the local Sharks. The spectacular Moses Mabhida Stadium (ⓣ031 029 933) is just next door (see above).

GETTING AROUND

By car The easiest way to explore Durban is by car. The city's freeways are well signposted, and getting around is straightforward. There are several car rental companies in Durban, including Avis/Budget (ⓣ032 436 7800), Europcar (ⓣ032 436 9500), Hertz (ⓣ032 436 0300) and Tempest (ⓣ032 436 9800); all are based at the airport, while Avis/ Budget also has a downtown office at the *Royal Hotel* (ⓣ031 310 9700), Europcar has an office at 50 Florence Nzama St (ⓣ031 337 3731), Hertz has an office in the Durban *Hilton* at 12–14 Walnut Rd (ⓣ031 561 1582), and Tempest has an office at 47 Victoria Embankment (ⓣ031 368 5231). The most convenient and central car parks are those at Pine Arcade, at the west end of Monty Naicker Rd, and in the Workshop Mall.

By bus Durban's most useful urban transport is the cheap and regular bus system operated by Mynah, which covers the central districts, including the city centre, the beachfront, the Berea and Florida Rd. If you want to get to the more far-flung

suburbs, the Aqualine buses are quite functional, although slightly worse for wear. For information about times and routes for all of these companies call ⓣ031 309 3250, or go to the bus depot on Monty Naicker Rd, which is adjacent to the Workshop Mall and is the starting point for most local bus services (you can also pick up bus schedules from the tourist office at uShaka Marine World). One useful route is Mynah's Musgrave/Mitchell Park Circle buses, which either go along Florida Rd (on the Mitchell Park Circle bus) or Musgrave Rd (on the Musgrave Rd bus). For travel within the city centre, the Durban People Mover operates modern buses along three routes linking the beachfront (from the Moses Mabhida Stadium to uShaka Marine World) with the centre as far west as the botanic gardens. A ride on the People Mover costs R5.50, while a card worth ten trips on a Mynah bus costs R28.

By minibus Minibuses cover the entire city, and run with

5

DURBAN TOURS AND HARBOUR RIDES

One of the safest and easiest ways to get under the skin of ethnic Durban is to take a **guided tour**. Standard three-hour tours cost around R450 per person (R1100 for a full day).

Curiocity 61 Monty Naicker Rd, 1st floor, Ambassador House ☎ 031 266 0025, ⓦ curiocityhostels.com. Both day and night bicycle tours of Durban leave from this backpackers on Monty Naicker Rd (see below), wheeling through the Berea, along the beachfront and invariably stopping by a pub. Tours leave daily, as long as there are two or more participants (R200).

Isle of Capri Cruises ☎ 031 305 3099, ⓦ isleof capri.co.za. Harbour trips leave daily on the hour (10am–4pm) from Wilson's Wharf (R150).

Markets of Warwick ☎ 031 309 3880, ⓦ marketsof warwick.co.za. A variety of fascinating walking tours that take in the multitude of markets around the Warwick Triangle, including the early morning market, the bead market, the bovine head market (where you can sample this Zulu delicacy) and many others.

Street Scene Tours ☎ 031 321 5079, ⓦ streetscene tours.co.za. One-day and overnight township and Durban tours with an emphasis on the "local" experience, which can include anything from playing football with township kids to trawling through hip vintage clothing stores or trying your hand at brewing your own beer.

Tekweni Eco Tours ☎ 082 303 9112, ⓦ tekwenieco tours.co.za. Durban city tours and visits to Zulu villages in the Valley of a Thousand Hills, for a Zulu meal and beer, traditional dancing and an encounter with a traditional healer.

Walkabout Tours Book through Durban Tourism (see p.368). A good way to explore Durban's Indian areas is by joining one of the walking tours organized by the tourist office (R100 per person).

---

greater frequency than the buses. You can catch a minibus in the city centre going to Florida Rd from Field St, between Anton Lembele and Dr Pixley Kaseme sts.

By taxi Reputable taxi companies in central Durban include Eagle Taxis (☎ 031 337 8333), East Coast Cabs (☎ 082 632 7410), Mozzies (☎ 031 303 5787) and Zippy (☎ 031 202 7067).

By bike Cycling is safe along the beachfront, but hazardous on any major road and not recommended on your own; Curiocity hostel (see below) runs guided cycling tours.

ACCOMMODATION

Durban's high-rise **accommodation** is concentrated along the beachfront and in the city centre, both convenient locations but less salubrious at night – take taxis to your doorstep after dark. A popular alternative is the Berea residential area west and north of the centre, which boasts the best backpacker hostels, as well as guesthouses and B&Bs in beautifully renovated old homes. Durban also has a selection of **township homestays** where you can experience the warmth of urban Zulu hospitality. Durban Tourism (see p.368) can arrange your accommodation and transport into the townships.

CITY CENTRE

Curiocity 61 Monty Naicker Rd, 1st floor, Ambassador House ☎ 031 266 0025, ⓦ curiocityhostels.com; map p.358. Lively backpackers in an old Durban building close to the beach, whose spacious rooms have a sleek, minimalist aesthetic and whose open-air courtyard hosts weekly movie nights, yoga, salsa classes and other activities. There are bicycles and surfboards available (both R60/hr), plus a bar, a chill lounge and even a small library. Dorms R209, doubles R690

The Royal Hotel 267 Anton Lembede St ☎ 031 333 6000, ⓦ theroyal.co.za; map p.358. Once Durban's finest establishment, the Royal Hotel now feels rather musty and dated, and has long since been outshone by its luxurious competitors on the waterfront. But it's smack in the centre, and fairly good value. R952

Sun 1 Directly opposite the bus station, near the corner of Masabalala Yengwa Ave and Jeff Taylor Crescent ☎ 031 301 1551, ⓦ tsogosun.com; map p.358. No-frills chain hotel that's tremendously convenient if you arrive late at night by train or bus. Rooms sleep up to three people. R522

BEACHFRONT

Blue Waters 175 OR Tambo Parade ☎ 031 327 7000, ⓦ bluewatershotel.co.za; map p.358. A delightful 1950s Durban landmark in a period building with a tiled facade, now a high-end hotel opposite Battery Beach with great views onto the oceanfront. There's also a pleasant café on the wooden deck out front, good for watching the beach-going crowds. R1094

Garden Court – Marine Parade 167 OR Tambo Parade ☎ 031 337 2231, ⓦ tsogosun.com; map p.358. All rooms in this modern hotel face the sea, and the view from the thirtieth-floor swimming pool is fabulous. A cool through-breeze offers respite against the summer heat, and a back entrance across from Victoria Park provides handy access to the city centre. R1405

Happy Hippo Backpackers Lodge 222 Mahatma Gandhi Rd ☎031 368 7181, ⓦhappyhippodurban.co.za; map p.358. Extremely spacious hostel a stone's throw from uShaka Marine World and the beach, in a renovated old factory with a decidedly industrial feel. The nice rooftop bar makes it popular with a younger crowd in the mood for a party. Dorms R185, doubles R520

Protea Hotel Edward OR Tambo Parade, ☎031 337 3681, ⓦprotea.marriott.com; map p.358. Crystal chandeliers, a colonial-style ambience, sea-view balconies and a ladies' bar leading onto a cool veranda make this Art Deco mansion the *grande dame* of the beachfront. R1330

Silversands 16 Erskine Terrace, near the Addington Hospital ☎031 332 1140; map p.358. These clean, comfortable and spacious self-catering apartments sleeping four to eight people are among the best value on the beach, especially for families. R1140

THE BEREA

Audacia Manor 11 Sir Arthur Rd ☎031 303 9520, ⓦmarriott.com; map p.364. Luxurious guesthouse in a restored colonial mansion. The restaurant and bar on the veranda boast gorgeous sea views, and some of the rooms feature outdoor showers and jacuzzi baths. R2303

The Benjamin 141 Florida Rd ☎031 303 4233, ⓦbenjamin.co.za; map p.364. A boutique hotel in an elegant old house that attracts corporate guests, although its location makes it perfect for tourists as well. There's a pool and safe parking, and rooms can be cheaper at weekends; the ones facing the courtyard tend to be quieter. R1655

The Concierge 37–43 St Mary's Ave, Greyville ☎031 309 4453, ⓦthe-concierge.co.za; map p.364. Sharing a lot with *Freedom Café* (see p.372), these twelve rooms in four 1920s-era cottages are all uniquely decorated with an eye towards modern design, and wonderfully located in the heart of the Berea's bar and restaurant scene. R1200

★The Elephant House 745 Peter Mokaba Rd ☎031 208 9580 or ☎082 4522 574, ⓔelephanthouse @mweb.co.za; map p.364. With the feel of staying in someone's home, this is one of the best B&Bs in South Africa. The home in question is the oldest in Durban, built in 1847 as a hunting lodge and oozing with character. The

extremely kind and generous hosts are great storytellers and love showing travellers around. Highly recommended and excellent value for money, especially for single travellers, as it is priced per person (R500). R1000

Essenwood House 630 Steven Dlamini Rd ☎031 207 4547, ⓦessenwoodhouse.co.za; map p.364. This grand house with a sumptuous garden has seven large, comfortable rooms (the upstairs ones have sea views), an attractive pool and a good-natured host. R1150

Gibela Lodge 119 Ninth Ave, Morningside ☎031 303 6291, ⓦgibelabackpackers.co.za; map p.364. Quiet hostel with a restful atmosphere, tastefully decorated rooms and single-sex dorms; there's even a small pool. The owner has tremendous knowledge of Durban and the rest of the province. There's a strict no-smoking policy and no check-in after 8pm. Rates include a good breakfast. Dorms R300, doubles R825

Goble Palms 120 Smiso Nkwanyana Rd ☎031 312 2598, ⓦgoblepalms.co.za; map p.364. This house, built in 1900, features a sunny patio with sea views, a pool and an intimate on-site English-style pub, as well as pretty, peaceful rooms. R1190

Nomad's Backpackers 70 Steven Dlamini Rd ☎031 202 9709, ⓦnomadsbp.com; map p.364. This chilled-out hostel is good for conversations at the bar or around the pool. The dorms are tidy and nicely decorated, though the lounge is a bit dark and some of the bunks are triples. Meals available on request. Dorms R180, doubles R475

Tekweni Backpackers 169 Ninth Ave ☎031 303 1433, ⓦtekwenibackpackers.co.za; map p.364. This large hostel near Florida Rd features plenty of communal areas, a pool and a bar. Braais and other social gatherings cater to a young, energetic clientele. Weekly accommodation is also available. Dorms R180, doubles R600

WESTVILLE

Our Little Family 35 Menston Rd ☎083 777 1245, ⓦourlittlefamily.co.za; map p.356. A family home in an old farmhouse stocked with historical maps and fascinating military antiques from the Boer wars, offering seven homely rooms of varying sizes. Most are self-catering and there are several braai areas, though the friendly hosts also prepare meals on request. Ten minutes from town by car. R860

EATING

Although all types of cooking are found here, **Indian food** is what the city excels at – hardly surprising for a place with one of the largest Indian populations outside Asia. The Indian takeaways are good places to try bunny chow – Durban's big contribution to the national fast-food scene – and *rotis* (Indian bread) stuffed with curries. **Shisanyama** outlets at the African markets and around the taxi ranks offer hunks of meat cooked over an open fire. Downtown Durban has been largely colonized by South Africa's ubiquitous chain eateries, though there are still a few good sit-down options. For more refined dining, the Berea has the city's best and most diverse range of restaurants.

BEACHFRONT

Cargo Hold uShaka Marine World ☎031 328 8065,

ⓦushakamarineworld.co.za; map p.358. A rather staid international menu – half of which consists of fish dishes

5

like prawns and kingklip (R165) – although eating in front of the giant fish tank is a thrill (these tables should be reserved well in advance). Note that the dress code for dinner is smart casual, which means no sandals. Mon–Sat noon–3pm & 6–9pm, Sun noon–5pm.

Moyo uShaka Marine World ☎031 332 0606, ⓦmoyo.co.za; map p.358. A large, breezy dining room overlooking the sea where you can order a range of African specialities, from Moroccan *tajines* to Mozambique peri-peri prawns and Senegalese line fish with coconut, mango and peanuts (R155). Light meals and drinks are available at the end of the pier opposite the restaurant – a good idea at sunset. Daily 8am–11pm.

THE HARBOUR AREA

BAT Music Café BAT Centre, Margaret Mncadi Ave ☎031 332 0451, ⓦbatcentre.co.za; map p.358. This lively venue dishes up African fusion food like samp and beans, and ox tripe with steamed Zulu bread, as well as burgers (R45). Regular jazz on Sundays and a great terrace overlooking the harbour add to the appeal. A good place to meet the locals. Daily 10am–late.

Roma Revolving Restaurant John Ross House, Margaret Mncadi Ave ☎031 337 6707, ⓦroma.co.za; map p.358. No visitor to Durban should miss the view from the *Roma* as it revolves above the city. The international menu includes tasty mussel starters (R69) and hit-and-miss Italian specialities, plus an excellent dessert trolley. You pay for the view as much as for the food; reservations required. Mon–Thurs 6–10.30pm, Fri & Sat noon–2.30pm & 6–10.30pm.

THE BEREA

★**9th Avenue Bistro** Shop 2, Avonmore Centre, Ninth Ave Morningside ☎031 312 9134, ⓦ9thavenuebistro.co.za; map p.364. One of the most highly regarded restaurants in Durban, serving refined French-inspired dishes such as free-range duck with crumbled ginger (R195). Mon & Sat 6–9.30pm, Tues–Fri noon–2.30pm & 6–9.30pm.

Blue Zoo Garden Restaurant 6 Nimmo Rd, Morningside ☎031 303 2265, ⓦbluezoo.co.za; map p.364. The food

here – which includes lamb shank in a port wine sauce (R140), steaks and a salad with mango-chilli dressing – is fairly average, but the beautiful garden setting of this Mitchell Park restaurant is hard to beat. Daily 8am–4.30pm.

Butcher Boys 170 Florida Rd ☎031 312 8248, ⓦbutcherboysgrill.co.za; map p.364. This grill house is known for its steaks, but it also offers a wide range of other meats such as lamb shank (R196), roasted marrow bones and cuts of game meat when available. Mon–Thurs noon–2.30pm & 6–10pm, Fri & Sat noon–3pm & 6–10.30pm, Sun noon–3pm & 6–9.30pm.

Delfi Taverna 386 Lilian Ngoyi Rd, Morningside ☎031 312 7032; map p.364. This cosy restaurant boasts excellent, authentic Greek dishes such as *kleftiko* (lamb shank) and *moussaka* (R95), and has a wonderfully congenial atmosphere created by plenty of regular customers. Mon & Wed–Sun noon–3pm & 6pm–late.

★**Distillery 031** 43 Station Drive ☎079 185 9353, ⓦdistillery031.com; map p.364. Located in an old Levi's factory, this classy craft distillery produces its own gin, vodka, absinthe and tonic, and prides itself on its classic cocktails (from R40) featuring home-made ingredients. It's also a great place for a meal, with a creative menu featuring dishes like a Korean fried chicken burger (R95), "truffled biltong mac 'n chini", and chocolate mousse with pop rocks. Wed–Fri 5pm–late, Sat noon–late, Sun 10am–4pm.

Freedom Café 37–43 St Mary's Ave, Greyville ☎031 309 4453, ⓦtastefreedom.co.za; map p.364. An artsy café with a decidedly hipster vibe, located in and around a creatively converted shipping container under a spreading tree, where you can sip your milkshake out of a jam jar and nibble on home-made baked goodies. The food, which ranges from quinoa tabbouleh (R95) to pulled pork sandwiches, is wonderful, and it's a good place for breakfast. Tues–Sun 7am–4pm.

★**Glenwood Bakery** 398 Esther Roberts Rd, Glenwood ☎031 205 0217, ⓦglenwoodbakery.co.za; map p.364. Durban's best-known producers of delicious artisanal breads like baguettes and ciabattas, all of which tend to sell out quickly (try the focaccia with roasted aubergine and olives, at R20 a slice). Also a great place for

---

EATING INDIAN IN DURBAN

Inexpensive Indian **takeaways** – all open very early and many shut by 5pm – abound in Durban.

Capsicum Beneath the Britannia Hotel, 1299 Umgeni Rd, the Berea ☎031 303 2266; map p.364. *Capsicum* in the Berea offers some of the most traditional South African Indian food around, including trotter bunny chow (R59), crab curry and tripe. Mon, Tues & Sun 7am–8.30pm, Wed–Sat 7am–9.30pm.

Little Gujarat 107 Dr Goonam St ☎031 306 2272; map p.358. A simple local eatery that has long been

noted for its excellent (and cheap) vegetarian food such as potato or paneer curries (around R20 for a large), pakoras and bhajis. Mon–Fri 6am–4pm, Sat 6am–3pm, Sun 7am–2pm.

Oriental Workshop Mall ☎031 304 5110; map p.358. This takeaway serves up a hotchpotch of fare – delicious Indian-style *shawarmas*, bunny chows (R50) and curries. Mon–Thurs 8am–9pm, Fri–Sun 8am–10pm.

brunch, with a menu that changes daily. Mon–Fri 6am–3.30pm, Sat & Sun 6am–1pm.

La Bella Corner of Steven Dlamini and St Thomas roads ☎031 201 9176, ⓦlabellacafe.co.za; map p.364. Housed in a former power station, with outdoor seating that's good for a coffee or a stone oven-cooked pizza with imaginative toppings such as banana and avocado (R98). There's also a pub at the back, and weekly Sunday roasts. Daily 7am–9.30pm.

Marco's 45 Lilian Ngoyi Rd ☎031 303 3078; map p.364. This colourful and authentic little Italian restaurant prides itself on its home-made pastas, wood-fired pizzas and wonderful gnocchi (from R80), and is very popular with the locals. Its sister restaurant, *Mama Luciana's*, is in the same building with an entrance on Florida Rd. Daily noon–10.30pm.

Market 40 Gladys Mazibuko Rd ☎031 309 8581, ⓦmarketrestaurant.co.za; map p.364. With its shady courtyard sheltered from the street and sparkling with candles in the evening, this trendy bistro is the perfect spot to enjoy luxurious breakfasts, or a fresh and wholesome meal such as roasted vegetable couscous salad or a sesame

lentil burger (R95). Mon 7.30am–4pm, Tues–Sat 7.30am–9.30pm, Sun 8.30am–3.30pm.

★**Palki** 225 Musgrave Rd, Musgrave ☎031 201 0019, ⓦpalki.co.za; map p.364. The South African representative of a chain of restaurants based in the East, this restaurant is well known in Durban for its mouthwatering, authentic dishes mainly from South India, including *pooris* and *dosas* (from R62), and its curries are among the best in town. Vegetarians are well catered for. Daily 11am–3pm & 6–10pm.

Spiga 200 Florida Rd, Morningside ☎031 303 9511, ⓦspiga.co.za; map p.364. Justifiably popular Italian restaurant serving several types of pasta dishes (around R90) and pizza, with outside tables on Florida Rd giving the place a European feel. The friendly and efficient service adds to the appeal. Sun–Wed 7am–10pm, Thurs–Sat 7am–midnight.

Unity Brasserie and Bar Corner of Silverton and Vause roads ☎031 201 3470, ⓦunitybar.co.za; map p.364. A buzzing gastro-pub dishing up hearty yet sophisticated dishes such as bone marrow on toast or aged sirloin steak (R135); it also offers microbrews on tap. Mon–Sat noon–late.

DRINKING AND NIGHTLIFE

Durban has a healthy nightlife scene, with a decent number of bars and clubs. Many are concentrated around Florida Rd in the Berea, although university students often prefer going out in the industrial area.

Dropkick Murphy's 219 Florida Rd ☎031 825 1858, ⓦdropkickmurphys.co.za; map p.364. A friendly pub that's perennially packed with beer-lovers attracted by the healthy range of craft brews on offer, many made in and around Durban (R39/pint). There's food as well, including Guinness-and-beef pie (R99), but it's the beer that's the star of the show. Mon–Thurs noon–midnight, Fri–Sun noon–2am.

The Origin 9 Clark Rd ☎031 201 9959, ⓦtheorigin .co.za; map p.358. A long-time favourite on Durban's hard-core clubbing scene, this nightclub in an industrial area near the university attracts serious dancers with its multiple dancefloors and DJs spinning different genres on each. The area can be unsafe at night, so take a taxi.

Entrance usually around R70. Sat 8.30pm–late, sometimes open Fri as well.

Sidebar 200 Florida Rd ☎031 303 9511; map p.364. Squeezed in alongside *Spiga*, this minimalist yet cosy brick-walled bar is popular for its craft beers and intimate little garden courtyard. There isn't much space, so it's a good spot to rub shoulders – literally – with the locals. Tues–Thurs 4–11pm, Fri & Sat 11am–1.30am, Sun 11am–11pm.

Skyybar 25 Silver Ave, Morningside ☎031 313 7424; map p.364. This flashy club has a fabulous outdoor deck with views of the city, an emphasis on house music and a largely middle-class black clientele. Entrance usually around R70. Fri & Sat 9pm–4am.

ENTERTAINMENT

Durban is a good place to catch live music. For entertainment and nightlife listings, the *Mercury* is the better of Durban's two English-language dailies. *Durban Africa* also publishes a monthly events brochure, available from tourist offices.

LIVE MUSIC

You'll find plenty of live indie music on offer in Durban. More interesting, but less accessible, are some of the Zulu forms such as *iscathamiya* and *maskanda*. On the jazz scene, the city's most indigenous offering is a spicy combination of American mixed with township jazz and Zulu music. As for classical music, the best place to hear concerts by the **KwaZulu-Natal Philharmonic** (☎031 369 9438, ⓦkznphil.org.za) is at a sundowner concert held in the Botanic Gardens (see p.363).

BAT Centre Next to the harbour at 42 Maritime Place ☎031 332 0451, ⓦbatcentre.co.za; map p.364. This cultural centre is your best bet for live concerts and its café (see opposite) has jazz sundowners on Sundays.

Moyo uShaka Marine World ☎031 332 0606, ⓦmoyo .co.za; map p.358. Live African music and drumming on Friday and Saturday evenings at this seaside restaurant (see opposite).

The Rainbow 23 Stanfield Lane in Pinetown, northwest of Durban ☎031 702 9161, ⓦtherainbow.co.za;

5

LGBT DURBAN

Durban's **LGBT scene** is fairly well developed, although nothing like what you'll find in Cape Town. Among the smattering of gay or gay-friendly clubs, *Club Altitude*, 25 Silver Ave, Morningside (ⓦclubaltitude.co.za; map p.364), is one popular meeting place; it shares a building with *Skyybar* (see p.373), though there's no sign outside.

map p.356. A long-established restaurant offering monthly Sunday-lunchtime performances ranging from Afro-fusion to jazz, and more regular weekday sessions by up-and-coming bands.

THEATRE AND CINEMA

There are multiscreen complexes at the Musgrave Centre, the Workshop Mall in the city centre and the Suncoast Casino on the beachfront. The only place to see art-house movies is at Gateway Mall in Umhlanga Rocks.

Elizabeth Sneddon Theatre University of KwaZulu-Natal, Mazisi Kunene Rd ☎031 260 2296, ⓦsneddontheatre.co.za. A modern venue for university and visiting productions.

Playhouse Drama Theatre 231 Anton Lembede St ☎031 369 9555, ⓦplayhousecompany.com. A mock-Tudor building (built as a cinema in the 1920s) that tends to host middle-of-the-road productions, but also sees performances by the resident progressive Playhouse Dance Company.

SHOPPING

As one of South Africa's major cities, Durban is a good place to pick up general supplies and local books. But it's for **crafts and curios** that it scores particularly highly, with a dazzling range of handmade Zulu goods (see box opposite). The best places to browse for crafts are in the downtown markets, the weekend flea markets and the specialist shops around the city. Durban is littered with shopping malls of varying sizes, the two largest being the central Workshop Mall (see p.357) and the more upmarket Musgrave Centre in Musgrave.

BOOKS

Adams & Co Shop 223 Musgrave Centre, Musgrave ☎031 319 4450, ⓦadamsbooks.co.za; map p.364. Durban's oldest bookshop has an excellent selection of books on the history of Durban and KwaZulu-Natal. There's another branch in the city centre at 341 Dr Pixley Kaseme St (map p.358). Mon–Sat 9am–6pm, Sun 9am–5pm.

★**Ike's Books & Collectables** 48a Florida Rd, Morningside ☎031 303 9214, ⓦikesbooks.com; map p.364. A fascinating secondhand bookshop with an interesting range of items covering KwaZulu-Natal's history. Speciality areas include Africana and the Anglo-Boer War, travel and exploration, and South African politics. Mon–Fri 10am–4pm, Sat 9am–2pm.

CRAFTS AND CURIOS

African Art Centre 94 Florida Rd, Morningside ☎031 312 3804, ⓦafriart.org.za; map p.364. A gallery and shop where many rural artists sell their work, well worth visiting for its traditional and modern Zulu and Xhosa beadwork, beaded dolls, wire sculptures, woodcuts and tapestries. Mon–Fri 8.30am–5pm, Sat 9am–3pm.

BAT Centre Off Margaret Mncadi Ave, city centre ☎031 332 0451, ⓦbatcentre.co.za; map p.358. A group of several shops selling Zulu and other African crafts, with clothing and jewellery well represented. Mon–Fri 8.30am–4pm, Sat 9am–2pm.

KZNSA Gallery Shop KZNSA Gallery, Bulwer Rd, Berea ☎031 277 1700, ⓦkznsagallery.co.za; map p.364. This menagerie of contemporary hand-crafted goods includes a wonderful selection of functional art, including pewter cutlery, etchings and paintings. Tues–Fri 9am–5pm, Sat 9am–4pm, Sun 10am–3pm.

MARKETS

Amphitheatre Fleamarket OR Tambo Parade, beachfront, south of the Amphitheatre; map p.358. Crafts and beadwork sold by both local traders and by merchants from as far afield as Zimbabwe, Malawi and Kenya. Sun 8am–5pm.

City Market Between Julius Nyerere Ave and Market Rd, Warwick Triangle; map p.358. The cheapest fruit and veg in town, from aubergines and jackfruit to betel nut for red-stained lips and a two-minute rush. Daily dawn–dusk.

The Morning Trade 15 Station Dr, Morningside ⓦthemorningtrade.co.za; map p.364. Part of the creative urban renewal around Durban's old "denim district", this weekly food market is the place to sample artisanal breads, organic hot chocolates, excellent coffee and gourmet burgers. Sun 8am–1pm.

Victoria Street Market Corner of Dennis Hurley and Joseph Nduli sts, city centre; map p.358. Traders here sell all manner of stuff, from curios and jewellery to spices with labels like "mother-in-law exterminator". Touristy, but fun nonetheless. Daily dawn–dusk.

ZULU CRAFTS AND CURIOS

Durban's huge range of galleries, craft shops and markets makes it one of the best places in the country to pick up **Zulu crafts**. Traditional works include functional items such as woven beer strainers and grass brooms, and basketry that can be extremely beautiful. Also traditional are beadwork, pottery and Zulu regalia, of which *assegais* (spears), shields, leather kilts and drums are a few examples.

The availability of cheap plastic crockery and enamelware has significantly eroded the production of traditional ceramics and woven containers for domestic use. Even so, the effects of urbanization have led to the use of new materials, or new ways of using old materials. Nowadays you'll find beautifully decorated black-and-white sandals made from recycled rubber tyres, wildly colourful baskets woven from telephone wire, and *sjamboks* (whips) decorated with bright insulation tape. On the more frivolous side, industrial materials have been married with rural life; attractive tin boxes made from flattened oil cans and chickens constructed from sheet plastic are just some of the results.

DIRECTORY

Consulates Canada, 81 Richefond Circle, Umhlanga (☎031 536 8214); Lesotho, West Guard House, corner of Dr Pixley Kaseme and Dorothy Nyembe sts, city centre (☎031 307 2168); US, Old Mutual Centre, 31st floor, 303 Dr Pixley Kaseme St, city centre (☎031 305 7600).

Currency exchange The First National Bank bureau de change, 359 Dr Pixley Kaseme St, city centre (Mon–Fri 9am–3.30pm, Sat 8.30am–12.30pm); American Express, Musgrave Centre, Musgrave (Mon–Fri 8.30am–4.30pm, Sat 8.30am–noon; ☎031 202 8733).

Emergencies Fire and ambulance ☎031 361 0000; police ☎10111.

Hospitals and medical centres The main state hospital is the Addington, Erskine Terrace, South Beach ☎031 327 2000), which offers a 24hr emergency ward. A better alternative is Life Entabeni private hospital, 148 Mazisi Kunene Rd, Berea (☎031 204 1300), which has a casualty unit and can also treat minor conditions, but you'll have to pay a deposit on admission. Travel Doctor, 45 Braam Fischer Rd, International Convention Centre, city centre (☎031 360 1122, ⊛durbantraveldoctor .co.za), is a clinic offering travel information, as well as advice on malaria and the necessary jabs for visiting other African countries.

Internet City Zen, 161 Garden Rd, Berea (daily 8am–10pm).

Pharmacies Sparkport, corner of Anton Lembede and Dr Yusuf Dadoo sts (Mon–Sat 7.30am–8.30pm, Sun 9am–5pm; ☎031 304 9767).

Post The main post office, on the corner of Dorothy Nyembe and Dr Pixley Kaseme sts, has a poste restante and enquiry desk (Mon–Fri 8am–5pm, Sat 8am–1pm).

The South Coast

The **South Coast**, the 160km seaboard stretching from Durban to Port Edward on the Eastern Cape border, is a ribbon of seaside suburbs linked for most of its length by the **N2** and **R102** roads, running side by side. In the winter months it's much warmer and sunnier along this stretch than on any of the beaches between here and Cape Town. Away from the sea, the land is hilly and green, dotted with sugar-cane fields, banana plantations and palm and pecan-nut trees. Note that many beaches shelve steeply into the powerful surf, so only swim where it's indicated as safe.

Margate, 133km from Durban, is the area's transport and holiday hub, with plenty of resorts lying to the east and west of it. The highlight of the South Coast, however, lies just inland, where **Oribi Gorge Nature Reserve** has lovely forest hikes, breathtaking views and good-value accommodation.

ARRIVAL AND DEPARTURE
THE SOUTH COAST

By car Driving from Durban, head for the N2, which runs south from the city as far as Port Shepstone before heading inland to Kokstad. From Port Shepstone to Southbroom, the South Coast Toll Rd is even faster and less congested.

By bus Margate Mini Coach (☎039 312 1406) has two to four daily bus services departing from King Shaka International Airport (domestic arrivals) and calling at the Durban bus station (Greyhound terminal), Amanzimtoti (prebooked only),

5

Scottburgh (prebooked only), Hibberdene, Port Shepstone (Shell Garage), Margate (Maroela Flats on Marine Parade), Sam Lameer (prebooked only), Port Edward (prebooked only) and Wild Coast Sun Casino (prebooked only). The Baz Bus between Durban and Port Elizabeth calls at Umzumbe, Umtentweni and Port Shepstone four days a week.

Aliwal Shoal

The resorts that line the first 50km of coastline south of Durban – places such as **Amanzimtoti**, 27km down – feel more like beachside suburbs than towns in their own right. For diving enthusiasts, however, the faded town of **UMKOMAAS**, 20km further down the coast from Amanzimtoti, is the perfect point to set out for **Aliwal Shoal**, a scattered reef quite close to the shore and one of Southern Africa's top **dive sites**. Rewards for experienced divers include sightings of ragged-tooth and tiger sharks, and the chance to go wreck-diving to three stunning sites. The ideal time to dive is between June and October, when visibility is at its best.

ARRIVAL AND ACTIVITIES
ALIWAL SHOAL

By minibus taxi The Margate Mini Coach doesn't stop at Umkomaas; if you're coming by public transport, your best option is to catch a minibus from Durban heading south and have them drop you off en route.

Diving Various dive centres organize trips to Aliwal Shoal (around R420), as well as PADI-certified four-day Open Water diving courses (around R4750); prices include equipment rental. Try Meridian Dive Centre (☎082 894 1625, ⓦmeridiandive.com) or Aliwal Dive Centre (☎039 973 2233, ⓦaliwalshoal.co.za).

ACCOMMODATION

Agulhas House 30 Barrow St, Umkomaas ☎039 973 1640, ⓦagulhashouse.com. Centrally located B&B in a renovated doctor's clinic, whose simple en-suite rooms, with fridges and private entrances, are set around an attractive swimming pool. They can also arrange dive packages. Full board **R1450**

Aliwal Dive Centre and Lodge 2 Moodie St, Umkomaas ☎039 973 2233, ⓦaliwalshoal.co.za. Just above the dive centre are double rooms and backpacker accommodation, which is handy for anyone planning to dive. Rooms come with balconies, some sea-facing, and there's a pool. Dorms **R252**, doubles **R920**

Oribi Gorge Nature Reserve

Daily: Oct–March 5am–7pm; April–Sept 6am–6pm • R10 • ☎072 042 9390, ⓦkznwildlife.com

A highly scenic area traversed by the fast-flowing Umzimkulu and Umzimkulwana rivers, with cliffs rising from vast chasms and forest, the **Oribi Gorge Nature Reserve**, 27km from Port Shepstone and signposted off the N2, is the South Coast's most compelling attraction. There are numerous idyllic picnic spots on the riverbanks (though avoid swimming here, as bilharzia parasites are present in the water), and waymarked **hikes** ranging from thirty-minute to day-long excursions lead through the forest or to dizzying lookout points. A fine one-hour **walk** starts from the Umzimkulu car park, crosses the river and heads immediately up some steps into the forest. You'll only see the river when it opens out dramatically to reveal **Samango Falls** and a perfect

---

THE SARDINE RUN

Around June or July, the South Coast is witness to the extraordinary annual migration of millions of **sardines** moving northwards along the coast in massive shoals. They leave their feeding ground off the Southern Cape coast and move up towards Mozambique, followed by about 23,000 dolphins, 100,000 Cape gannets and thousands of sharks and game fish, attracting fishermen from all over the province to join in the jamboree. The shoals appear as dark patches of turbulence in the water, and when they are cornered and driven ashore by game fish, hundreds of people rush into the water either to scoop them out with their hands or to net them. For updates on shoal coordinates and other information of use for sardine-spotting, call the Sardine Hotline on ☎083 913 9495 or visit ⓦshark.co.za.

little rock-bounded sandy beach. **Wildlife** in the reserve includes bushbuck, common reedbuck and blue and grey duiker, but not oribi, which have left for the succulent shoots of the surrounding sugar-cane plantations. More difficult to see are the shy samango monkeys hiding in the high canopy of the forest, and leopards.

ARRIVAL AND DEPARTURE | ORIBI GORGE NATURE RESERVE

By car and minibus taxi There's no public transport running to Oribi Gorge; if you don't have your own vehicle, you'll have to catch a minibus to Port Shepstone then hire a private taxi for the last 27km. If you're driving, the nature reserve is clearly signposted off the N2 about 3km south of Port Shepstone.

INFORMATION AND ACTIVITIES

Tourist information KNZ Wildlife has an office at the main gate (daily 8am–12.30pm & 2–4pm; ☎ 072 042 9390).

Activities There are a few adventure activities on offer in the reserve, all run by Wild 5 (☎ 082 566 7424, ⌨ wild5adventures.co.za), which operates from the *Oribi Gorge Hotel* (see below). There's an abseil (R400) with a tough half-hour walk out of the gorge afterwards; a gorge swing that requires you to leap off the top of the Lehrs Falls (R550); a gorge slide (R250), erected 160m above the gorge floor; and rafting trips down the Umzimkulu River (R550). There are also a number of guided hikes available in the reserve (R20).

ACCOMMODATION

KZN Wildlife huts ☎ 072 042 9390; book through KZN Wildlife ☎ 033 845 1000, ⌨ kznwildlife.com. The spectacularly situated KZN Wildlife huts sleep two to eight people, and you can also camp. The restcamp is at the head of the Umzimkulwana Gorge, peering into the chasm of Oribi Gorge itself. All crockery, cutlery and bedding is provided. Camping R90, huts R420

Oribi Gorge Hotel Some 16km from the restcamp, off the Oribi Flats Rd ☎ 039 687 0253, ⌨ oribi gorgehotel.co.za. This colonial-style hotel, dating back to the 1890s, has spectacular views, including of the famous overhanging rock, and offers spacious rooms, meals to suit most budgets and a pleasant outdoor tea area. R1190

The Hibiscus Coast

The 44km of coast from Port Shepstone to Port Edward has been dubbed the **Hibiscus Coast** because of its luscious, bright gardens, luxury suburbs, beachside developments and attractive caravan parks. It's also known as the **Golf Coast**: there are nine top courses on this short stretch of coastline, and many people come specifically to play. Although the whole area is built up, particularly around Margate, the Hibiscus Coast gets nicer the further south you go.

Margate and Ramsgate

Some 14km south of Port Shepstone, the brash holiday town of **MARGATE**, with its high-rise apartments, fast-food outlets and ice-cream parlours, offers little in the way of undiscovered coves or hidden beaches, but it's the liveliest town on the South Coast. Adjoining Margate to the south, **RAMSGATE** is quieter and slightly more refined – as evidenced by the Gaze Gallery (daily 8am–5pm; free; ☎ 039 314 4011), attached to the restaurant *Waffle House* (see p.378), just across the lagoon coming from Margate, which displays some reputable work by local artists.

Southbroom and Port Edward

Some 7km beyond Margate, **SOUTHBROOM** is known disparagingly as "Houghton-by-Sea" after one of Johannesburg's wealthiest suburbs, which is said to relocate here en masse in December. The town is predominantly a sumptuous development of large holiday houses set in expansive gardens and centred on the pretty **Southbroom Golf Course** (R395 for eighteen holes; ☎ 039 316 6026, ⌨ southbroomgolfclub.co.za). Huge dunes covered by lush vegetation sweep down to the sea, and there are good long walks along the shore. The best place for swimming is **Marina Beach**, 3km south of Southbroom Beach.

5

Heading on for another 10km or so brings you to **PORT EDWARD**, which marks the border with the Eastern Cape. The town has some nice sandy beaches, but its main interest lies in its proximity to the Umtamvuna Nature Reserve (see p.380).

ARRIVAL AND INFORMATION

By bus and minibus taxi The Margate Mini Coach (see p.368) runs between Durban and Margate two to four times a day (1hr 30min), and minibus taxis connect Margate to Port Shepstone, Ramsgate, Southbroom and Port Edward. The only public transport heading west from Port Edward is the minibus taxis, which form a lively rank on the R61 just outside town, collecting passengers for the Eastern Cape.

Tourist information The tourist office on the beachfront at Margate (Mon–Fri 8am–5pm, Sat 8am–1pm, Sun 9am–1pm; ☎ 039 312 2322, ⓦ tourismsouthcoast.co.za) can provide details of accommodation plus general information for the whole South Coast area.

ACCOMMODATION

UMTENTWENI

The Spot Backpackers 23 Ambleside Rd, Umtentweni, 4km north of Port Shepstone ☎ 039 695 1318, ⓦ spotbackpackers.com. This collection of basic but comfortable dorms and cottages is right on the beach, which makes it a magnet for surfers. It's also on the Baz Bus route. Dorms R180, doubles R450

RAMSGATE

Beachcomber Bay 75 Marine Drive, Ramsgate ☎ 039 317 4473, ⓦ beachcomberbay.co.za. With splendid views of the seafront and private access to the beach, this comfortable, easy-going guesthouse has six rooms, a jacuzzi and sauna, and is very close to Margate's restaurants and bars. R950

BillsBest Corner of Marine Dr and Penshurst Rd, Ramsgate ☎ 039 314 4837, ⓦ billsbest.co.za. This outfit offers a range of well-maintained and regularly serviced cabanas and self-catering units sleeping two to six people, all close to the beach and with good security. R255

SOUTHBROOM

Bushbuck Lodge 720 Tavistock Rd ☎ 039 316 6399, ⓦ bushbuck-lodge.co.za. On the northern edge of town and surrounded by lush tropical forest visited by wildlife, this Polish-run lodge offers a good-value collection of simply furnished self-catering cottages sleeping four or five. There's a pool in the garden, and braai facilities. R500

Coral Tree Colony 593 Mandy Rd ☎ 039 316 6676, ⓦ thecoraltree.com. Six rooms are housed in a pretty stately house with a wraparound veranda, spreading flame trees and wicker furniture. It's just on the edge of the golf course, and the friendly proprietor is full of information about the area. R1550

PORT EDWARD

Ku-boboyi River Lodge Old Main Rd, Leisure Bay, Port Edward ☎ 072 222 7760, ⓦ kuboboyi.co.za. This attractive backpacker hostel, on a hilltop with sweeping views of the ocean, has a relaxing atmosphere and a pool, making the double, triple and family rooms (which sleep up to six) great value. Meals are also available. Doubles R350

EATING AND DRINKING

MARGATE

Larry's Corner of O'Connor and Panorama Parade across from the tourist office, Margate ☎ 039 317 2277, ⓦ larrys.co.za. This quirky little diner on the beach is something of a local institution, and has been serving up reliably good seaside fare like burgers (R65) and seafood baskets for decades. Its patio is a good place to watch the parade of holidaymakers drift by. Daily 10am–late.

RAMSGATE

Flavours The Bistro Village, 1303 Marine Drive, Ramsgate ☎ 039 314 4370. One of the area's most highly regarded restaurants, serving good prawns, steaks and Moroccan lamb (R140). Tues–Sat noon–2pm & 6–9pm, Sun noon–2pm.

★**Pistols Saloon** Old Main Rd, Ramsgate ☎ 039 316 8463, ⓦ pistolssaloon.co.za. A lively, slightly surreal cowboy-themed bar on the southern edge of Ramsgate (R25 for a pint of beer), where the resident donkey is paraded in front of drinkers and there's live music on Friday nights. Daily 10am–midnight.

Waffle House Marine Drive, Ramsgate ☎ 039 317 9424, ⓦ wafflehouse.co.za. The best waffles in the province, with elaborate toppings such as lemon meringue or hummus and avocado (R82), and chicken à la king. Enjoy them on a lovely wooden deck nestled in the reeds overlooking a lagoon. Daily 8am–5pm.

SOUTHBROOM

Trattoria La Terrazza Outlook Rd, Southbroom ☎ 039 316 6162, ⓦ trattoria.co.za. Solid Italian food such as linguine with zucchini and artichoke (R92) served in a lovely setting next to a lagoon where, at around sunset, thousands of swallows come home to roost. Tues–Thurs 6.30–10pm, Fri & Sat 12.30–2.30pm & 6.30–10pm, Sun 12.30–2.30pm.

5

Umtamvuna Nature Reserve

About 8km north of Port Edward, signposted off the R61 to Izingolweni • Daily 6am–6pm • R15 • ☎ 039 311 2383

You'll find some of the best nature walks in the whole of KwaZulu-Natal at the **Umtamvuna Nature Reserve**. Extending 19km upstream along the tropical Umtamvuna River and the forested cliffs rising above it, the reserve is well known for its spring flowers, as well as the sunbirds and sugar birds that feed on the nectar. It's home to three hundred species of birds, including a famous colony of rare **Cape vultures**, though to see where they nest you'll have to be prepared for a whole day's walk. Waymarked paths are dotted throughout the reserve.

| ACCOMMODATION | UMTAMVUNA NATURE RESERVE |

Umtamvuna River Lodge Holiday Rd, inside the reserve ☎ 039 311 3583, ⓦ theriverlodge.co.za. Eight rooms in tranquil, lushly forested surroundings on the banks of the river, all restful and tastefully decorated. Wakeboarding is also available, and there's a restaurant on-site with a wonderful view over the river. **R1290**

Vuna Valley Ventures 9/10 Michelle Rd, 50m from the entrance to the reserve ☎ 083 503 5056. This family-friendly budget guesthouse is handily located for forays into the reserve, with attractive rooms that can sleep between two and four people, plus self-catering chalets sleeping six to ten. **R550**

The North Coast

KwaZulu-Natal's **North Coast**, the 80km stretch along the coast north of Durban from Umhlanga Rocks to the mouth of the Tugela River, is also known as the **Dolphin Coast**. The combination of a narrow continental shelf and warm, shallow waters creates ideal conditions for bottlenose dolphins, which come here to feed all year round.

Less tacky and developed than the South Coast, the North Coast attracts an upmarket breed of holidaymaker, especially to the main resort of **Umhlanga Rocks**, which is within easy striking distance of Durban. While the Dolphin Coast is still pretty much dominated by the white population, the inland towns of **Tongaat** and **KwaDukuza**, linked by the old **R102** road, have substantial Zulu and Indian populations, with Indian temples at Tongaat and the Shaka memorial at KwaDukuza. Also on the R102 is the grave of one of the ANC's best-loved leaders, Albert Luthuli, at **Groutville**.

Umhlanga Rocks

With a permanent population of around a hundred thousand, the swish resort of **UMHLANGA ROCKS**, 17km from the centre of Durban, merges with the suburb of Durban North. The town makes a good day-trip from the city, with a pleasant, sandy beach dominated by a red-and-white lighthouse. The shopping area along Chartwell Drive has a collection of smart, well-stocked malls, while a couple of kilometres up the hill on Umhlanga Ridge, the monster **Gateway Theatre of Shopping** has four hundred shops, 27 cinemas, a wave pool and an indoor climbing rock.

KwaZulu-Natal Sharks Board

1a Herrwood Drive, signposted off the N2 • **Shark dissection** Tues, Wed & Thurs 9am & 2pm • R50 • ☎ 031 566 0400 • **Boat trips** Mon–Fri at 6.30am; advance booking required • R350 • ☎ 082 403 9206 • ⓦ shark.co.za

A couple of kilometres north of Umhlanga's centre, the **KwaZulu-Natal Sharks Board** shows a multiscreen audiovisual presentation about sharks and conducts dissections of recently caught sharks, which disabuses any notion of these creatures as the hooligans of the oceans. It also plugs the board's work in maintaining the province's **shark nets**; although these nets protect swimmers all along the coast, they are controversial, as not just sharks but also endangered turtles and dolphins die in them, thus affecting the balance of the inshore ecosystem. The Sharks Board is investigating an electronic shark barrier that might improve the situation, while still ensuring safe swimming; it's urrently being tested in Cape Town. They also run dolphin- and whale-sighting **boat rips** from Wilson's Wharf in Durban, which include an inspection of the shark nets.

ARRIVAL AND INFORMATION — UMHLANGA ROCKS

y road To get to Umhlanga from Durban, follow the M4 each Highway straight into the centre of town, or branch ff onto the M41 to reach Gateway.

y taxi and minibus taxi The Umhlanga Explorer huttle Service (☎ 031 561 1846) operates a fleet of private axis that run between Durban and Umhlanga on request

(R250). Otherwise, minibus taxis make the trip to Gateway Mall from the taxi rank on Johannes Nkosi St.
Tourist information 1A Chartwell Drive (Mon–Fri 8.30am–5pm, Sat 9am–1pm; ☎ 031 561 4257, ⓦ umhlangatourism.co.za).

ACCOMMODATION

nchor's Rest 14 Stanley Grace Crescent ☎ 031 561 380, ⓦ anchorsrest.co.za. Centrally located and elegant Mediterranean-style guesthouse with spacious and well-ecorated suites (some self-catering), all with a private ntrance and patio. There's also an expansive veranda verlooking the pool. R1150

everly Hills Hotel Lighthouse Rd ☎ 031 561 2211, ⓦ tsogosun.com. The oldest of Umhlanga's luxury eachfront hotels is still a very comfortable choice, ccupying a prime location in the centre of town. All rooms ave sea views, as does the restaurant – a good spot for a undowner. R5265

Honeypot 11 Hilken Drive ☎ 031 561 3795, ⓦ honeypotguesthouse.com. An attractive B&B in a residential area, with six cosy garden rooms all with private patios and outdoor fireplaces. There is also a self-catering flat that sleeps four, and a small pool. R1000

The Oyster Box 2 Lighthouse Rd ☎ 031 514 5000, ⓦ oysterboxhotel.com. Beautifully restored in the style of the 1950s hotel that once stood on the site, the *Oyster Box* takes the prize for the swishest rooms in town. With its palm-shaded atrium, luxury spa, classy restaurants and high teas served overlooking Umhlanga's lighthouse, this is definitely the place to see and be seen. R6896

EATING

atch 14 Chartwell Dr ☎ 031 561 2303. A solid option for ood seafood, including fresh oysters you can choose out of tank (R18 each), sushi and a variety of appealing combo atters (from R140). Wash it all down with fishbowl ocktails. Daily noon–10pm.

e Maurice 9 McCausland Crescent ☎ 031 561 7609 ⓦ ilemauricerestaurant.co.za. A gastronomic Franco-Mauritian restaurant run by a Mauritian chef with a certain ropical flair, where you can expect rabbit cooked in red

wine and octopus curry (R185) on the menu. Tues–Sun noon–2.30pm & 6.30–9.30pm.
Little Havana 16 Chartwell Drive ☎ 031 561 7589, ⓦ littlehavana.co.za. Umhlanga's best steakhouse is an elegant affair, specializing in juicy grain-fed and free-range slices of beef (from R150) alongside sophisticated starters like roasted marrow bones and three flavours of snails. Daily noon–3pm & 6–10pm.

Tongaat

TONGAAT lies a few kilometres inland of Umhlanga Rocks across the N2 highway, a barrier between the coastal resorts and the workings of KwaZulu-Natal's sugar industry. The town, fronted by neglected imitation Cape Dutch cottages, has long associations with South Africa's Indian community and boasts a handful of temples. The most distinguished of these, and a National Monument, is the small, whitewashed **Shri Jugganath Puri Temple**, built at the turn of the last century by the Sanskrit scholar Pandit Shrikishan Maharaj and dedicated to Vishnu. To get to the temple from the R102, turn west into Ganie Street, then left into Plane Street and left again into Catherine Street; the temple is at the junction of Catherine and Plane.

Ballito

There's nothing very African about **BALLITO**, a Mediterranean-style resort a further 0km up the coast from Tongaat, with a splurge of time-shares, high-rise holiday partments and shopping malls by the sea. It's a pleasant enough place nevertheless, with a beach offering safe swimming and full-time lifeguards.

5

ARRIVAL AND DEPARTURE

BALLITO

By bus and minibus taxi One of the Greyhound bus routes between Durban and Johannesburg passes through Ballito (daily; 45min to Durban, 11hr 45min to Johannesburg). Otherwise, a number of minibus taxi trundle up the coast from Durban.

ACCOMMODATION

Dolphin Holiday Resort 5min walk from the beach on the corner of Compensation Beach Rd and Hillary Drive ☎ 032 946 2187, ⓦ dolphinholidayresort.co.za. A good budget option, consisting of a well-shaded caravan park (where you can also pitch a tent) and a collection of self-catering cottages, log cabins and rondavels. Caravans **R495**, cottages **R940**

Zimbali Lodge 1km south of Ballito ☎ 032 538 500 ⓦ fairmont.com/zimbali-lodge. The fanciest place t stay, with luxury suites set in subtropical coastal forest i the heart of the wetlands. Even if you aren't staying consider stopping for a meal or a sundowner in the ba raised on stilts overlooking the golf course, which reward you with soaring views across the Indian Ocean. **R1800**

KwaDukuza and around

Head inland from Ballito and follow the R102 north for around 30km • KwaDukuza Interpretative Centre Mon–Fri 8am–4pm, Sat & Sun 9am–4pm • R10 • ☎ 032 552 7210

KWADUKUZA (still widely known by its pre-1994 election name, **Stanger**) has a special place in the cosmology of Zulu nationalists. This was the site of King Shaka's last kraal (the round formation of huts where the king lived), and it was the place where he was treacherously stabbed to death in 1828 by his half-brother Dingane, who succeeded him. The warrior-king is said to have been buried upright in a grain pit, and is commemorated by a small park and memorial on King Shaka Street in the centre of town. Near the memorial is a rock with a groove worn into it – supposedly where Shaka sharpened his spears. At the rear of the park, the **KwaDukuza Interpretative Centre** has a small display on Shaka and a very good fifteen-minute audiovisual display. The park is also the venue of annual **King Shaka Day** celebrations (see box, p.419) on September 24, which is also the Heritage Day public holiday.

Groutville

8km southwest of KwaDukuza on the R102, just across a bridge over the Mvoti River

Tiny **GROUTVILLE** is remarkable mainly for the grave of **Albert Luthuli**, one of South Africa's greatest political leaders. A teacher and chief of the Zulus in Groutville, Luthuli became President General of the ANC in 1952. Advocating a non-violent struggle against apartheid, he was awarded the Nobel Peace Prize in 1960, which at home earned him a succession of banning orders restricting him to the KwaDukuza area. He died under mysterious circumstances in 1967 in KwaDukuza, apparently knocked down by a train. Luthuli is buried next to a whitewashed, nineteenth-century corrugated-iron mission church. His life is recounted in the moving autobiography *Let My People Go*.

ARRIVAL AND DEPARTURE

KWADUKUZA AND AROUND

By bus and minibus taxi One of the Greyhound bus routes between Durban and Johannesburg passes through KwaDukuza (daily; 1hr to Durban, 11hr 30min t Johannesburg). Otherwise, catch a minibus from Durban.

ACCOMMODATION

The best place to stay close to KwaDukuza is Blythdale, the closest stretch of sand, where a ban on high-rise constructio has preserved the deserted appearance of its endless beach.

Mini Villas 52 Umvoti Drive ☎ 032 551 1277, ⓦ minivillas.co.za. Simply decorated but well-equipped self-catering villas sleeping four to six people, some giving out onto a garden, with a nearby path leading down to the beach. **R630**

Palm Dune Beach Lodge 9 Umvoti Drive ☎ 032 55 1588, ⓦ palmdune.co.za. An upmarket resort where yo can opt for a classy one-, two-, or three-bedroom chale and partake of a wide range of activities, from jetskiing t beach volleyball. **R2178**

Harold Johnson Nature Reserve

Signposted 24km north of KwaDukuza off the N2 – take the Zinkwazi turn-off and turn left at Darnall • Daily: April–Sept 6am–6pm; Oct–March 5am–7pm • R30 • Camping R180/2 people • ☎ 032 486 1574 , ⓦ kznwildlife.com

Abutting the Tugela River is KZN Wildlife's **Harold Johnson Nature Reserve**. With its well-preserved coastal bush, steep cliffs and gullies, this is a fine place to come for a day's visit or to camp overnight – there are no shops or facilities, so be sure to stock up before arrival. The reserve has several hiking **trails** that take you past various historical sites, most of them connected to the Anglo-Zulu War of 1879. These include the **Ultimatum Tree**: the wild fig tree where the British issued their ultimatum to King Cetshwayo in 1878, part of which required the Zulus to demobilize their standing army.

Valley of a Thousand Hills

The evocatively named **Valley of a Thousand Hills** makes for a picturesque drive along the edge of densely folded hills where Zulu people still live in traditional homesteads, and which visitors rarely venture into. However, the area is only worth a special trip if you're not exploring the KwaZulu-Natal interior, where scenes like this occur in abundance. While the valley, 45km from Durban, is best suited to touring in your own car (take the N3 from Durban, following the Pinetown signs), there are also **daily tours** from Durban offered by Tekweni Eco Tours (see box, p.370) that take in the highlights. The trip to the valley and back can be done in half a day, but there are sufficient attractions along the route to extend it to a full day's outing.

Vintage train trip

Second and last Sunday of the month; check the website for occasional extra trips • Departures 8.30am & 12.30pm from the Kloof Station, Stockers Arms, Old Main Rd • R240 • ☎ 082 353 6003, ⓦ umgenisteamrailway.co.za

If you're in Durban on the second or last Sunday of the month, consider taking a **vintage train trip** with Umgeni Steam Railways, which boasts one of the largest collections of historic locomotives and coaches in the southern hemisphere. From Kloof, the trains chug for 45 minutes along the edge of the Valley of a Thousand Hills, terminating at Inchanga Station and its crafts market.

Phezulu Safari Park

Old Main Rd • Daily 8am–4.30pm • Reptile park R55 • Zulu dancing daily at 10am, 11.30am, 2pm & 3.30pm; R120 • ☎ 031 777 1205, ⓦ phezulusafaripark.co.za

Just south of the valley is **Phezulu Safari Park**, which brings you close to deadly serpents – tucked away in cramped little glass boxes – plus crocodiles and other penned animals. There's also a reconstruction of a pre-colonial Zulu village, where you can watch tourist-geared – but nonetheless spirited – displays of **Zulu dancing** set against the dramatic horizon of the valley.

Pietermaritzburg

Although **PIETERMARITZBURG** (often called Maritzburg), the provincial capital of KwaZulu-Natal, sells itself as the best-preserved Victorian city in South Africa, with strong British connections, little of its colonial heritage remains. It's actually a very South African city, with Zulus forming the largest community, followed by Indians, with those of British extraction a minority – albeit a high-profile one. This multiculturalism, together with a substantial student population, adds up to a fairly lively city that's also relatively safe and small enough to explore on foot, with most

5

places of interest within easy walking distance of the centre's heart. Only 80km inland from Durban along the fast N3 freeway, Pietermaritzburg is an easy day's outing from the coast; it can be combined with visits to the Valley of a Thousand Hills (see p.383) along the Old Main Road (R103), or used as an overnight stop en route to the uKhahlamba-Drakensberg (see p.388) or the battlefields around Ladysmith (see p.426).

Brief history

Pietermaritzburg's Afrikaner origins are reflected in its name; after slaughtering three thousand Zulus at the Battle of Blood River, the Voortrekkers established the fledgling Republic of Natalia in 1839, naming their capital in honour of the Boer leaders **Piet Retief** and **Gerrit Maritz**. The republic's independence was short-lived: Britain annexed it only four years later, and by the closing decade of the nineteenth century Maritzburg was the most important centre in the colony of Natal, with a population of nearly ten thousand (more than Durban at that time). Indians arrived at the turn of the twentieth century, mostly as indentured labourers, but also as traders. Among their number was a young, little-known lawyer called Mohandas Gandhi, who went on to change the history of India. He later traced the embryo of his devastatingly successful tactic of passive resistance to an incident in 1893, when as a non-white passenger he was thrown out of a first-class train compartment at Pietermaritzburg station.

Tatham Art Gallery

Corner of Chief Albert Luthuli and Langalibalele sts • Tues–Sun 9am–5pm • Free • ☏ 033 392 2801, ⌨ tatham.org.za

Across from the imposing **City Hall**, a late Victorian red-brick building with an impressive 15m clock tower, you'll find the **Tatham Art Gallery**, another fine brick edifice, which was previously the Supreme Court of the Colony of Natal. This is the highlight of the city's attractions, housing one of the country's best collections of art. Pieces by South Africans such as Zwelethu Mthethwa and Sam Nhlengethwa are exhibited alongside those by Marc Chagall, Georges Braque and Henri Matisse. A good way to enjoy the art is by attending the free **classical music concerts** that often take place at the gallery on Wednesday afternoons.

Old Natal Parliament Building, First National Bank and the Lanes

South of the Tatham on Langalibalele Street stands a series of attractive period buildings, including the typically imperial **Old Natal Parliament Building** and the **First National Bank**, which dates from 1903 and had its facade chosen from an Edwardian catalogue and shipped out from England. Across from the First National Bank building is the pedestrianized warren of alleyways known as **the Lanes**, which was the financial

---

ALAN PATON

Writer, teacher and politician **Alan Paton** was born in Pietermaritzburg in 1903. His visionary first novel, *Cry, the Beloved Country*, focused international attention on the plight of black South Africans and sold millions of copies worldwide. The book was published in 1948 – the same year the National Party assumed power and began to establish apartheid – and Paton subsequently entered politics to become a founder-member of the non-racial and fiercely anti-apartheid Liberal Party. He was president of the party from 1960 until 1968, when it was forced to disband by repressive legislation forbidding multiracial political organizations.

Paton died in Durban in 1988, having published a number of works, including two biographies and his autobiography. The following year, the **Alan Paton Centre** was established at the University of KwaZulu-Natal's archives building on Milner Rd, Scottsville (Mon–Fri 8.30am–1pm, or 2–4.30pm by appointment; ☏ 033 260 5926, ⌨ paton.ukzn.ac.za), where you can see a re-creation of Paton's study, as well as personal memorabilia and documents.

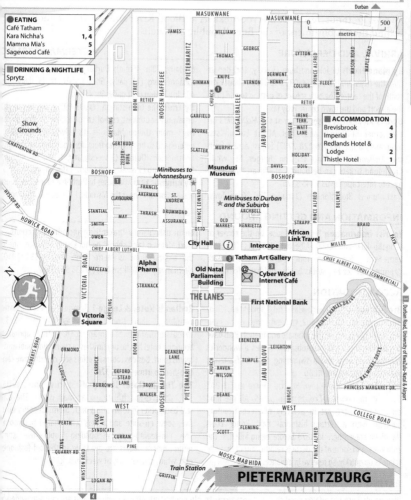

EATING

Café Tatham	3
Kara Nichha's	1, 4
Mamma Mia's	5
Sagewood Café	2

DRINKING & NIGHTLIFE

Sprytz	1

ACCOMMODATION

Brevisbrook	4
Imperial	3
Redlands Hotel & Lodge	2
Thistle Hotel	1

PIETERMARITZBURG

ub of Natal from 1888 to 1931 and housed four separate stock exchanges. This area is njoyable to explore during the day, but it's notorious for pickpockets, so stay alert and on't come here after dark.

Msunduzi Museum

ngalibalele St • Mon–Fri 9am–4pm, Sat 9am–1pm • R8 • ☎ 033 394 6834, ⓦ voortrekkermuseum.co.za

he best of the town's museums is the **Msunduzi Museum**, which centres on the riginal Church of the Vow, built in 1838 by Boers in honour of their victory ver the Zulus three years earlier at the Battle of Blood River. The church was their part f a bargain allegedly struck with God (see p.425). The museum connects with the Voortrekker roots of Pietermaritzburg and is worth a visit to gain some insight into life n a trek. The most interesting items are the home-made children's toys and beautifully mbroidered *kappies* (hats) which the women used to shield themselves from the sun. cross the lovely courtyard garden is a reconstruction of the 1846 thatched house of

5

Andries Pretorius, leader of the Voortrekkers at Blood River and the driving force behind the establishment of the Boer Republic of Natalia.

ARRIVAL AND DEPARTURE

By plane Flights to Johannesburg (3 daily; 1hr) depart from the city's Oribi Airport (☎033 392 3100), about 6km south of the centre. The only means of getting to and from the airport and the town centre is by taxi.

By bus All intercity buses pull in at the *McDonald's* on the corner of Burger and Chief Albert Luthuli sts. Intercape's office (☎086 128 7287) is just across from the *McDonald's* parking lot, on Burger St, while Greyhound tickets can be bought at African Link Travel next to Intercape (☎033 345 3175).

Destinations Bloemfontein (3 daily; 9hr); Cape Town (2 daily; 20hr 45min); Durban (12 daily; 1hr 20min); Johannesburg (11 daily; 6hr); Ladysmith (3 daily; 1hr 45min); Pretoria (11 daily; 6hr 45min).

By train The train station (☎033 897 2350) lies at the unsavoury southwest end of Langalibalele St, one of the city's main thoroughfares – it's advisable to arrange beforehand to be collected from here, particularly at night. Destinations Durban (3 weekly at 6.32am; 2hr 40min); Johannesburg (3 weekly at 9.53pm; 11hr 40min).

By minibus taxi Minibuses to Durban and Johannesburg leave from ranks near the Msunduzi Museum in the centre.

INFORMATION AND GETTING AROUND

Tourist information Publicity House, on the corner of Langalibalele and Chief Albert Luthuli sts (Mon–Fri 8am–5pm, Sat 8am–1pm; ☎033 345 1348, ⊚pmbtourism.co.za), stocks books, and has information on the uKhahlamba-Drakensberg and other attractions.

Taxi Metered taxis should be booked in advance; one of the biggest firms is Metro Taxis (☎033 397 1910), alternatively, try Wilkens Taxi (☎033 391 4462).

ACCOMMODATION

Brevisbrook 28 Waverleydale Rd, Boughton, 5km from centre ☎033 344 1402, ⊚brevisbrook.co.za; map p.385. All five rooms in this intimate and friendly B&B have private entrances and bathtubs, and there's a wonderful woodsy braai area and a swimming pool. Self-catering option is available, too. **R880**

Imperial 224 Jabu Ndlovu St, city centre ☎033 342 6551, ⊚imperialhotel.co.za; map p.385. All the mod cons you'd expect, set in a lovely nineteenth-century building with a certain historical flair; Prince Louis Napoleon stayed here in 1879 before being killed in the Zulu Wars, and some of the decor is reminiscent of that era. It books up quickly, so reserve in advance. **R1110**

Redlands Hotel & Lodge 1 George MacFarlane Lane Wembley, 3km from centre ☎033 394 3333, ⊚redlandshotel.co.za; map p.385. This upmarket boutique hotel has luxury finishes, a swimming pool and tennis court. Besides rooms, it offers self-catering one- and two-bed apartments. **R1920**

The Thistle Hotel 30 Boshoff St, city centre ☎033 342 4204, ⊚hotelthistle.co.za; map p.385. The only real backpacker in town offers basic rooms sleeping up to five, some en-suite and others with shared bathrooms. The nineteenth-century building could use some refurbishment. Meals are available in the old-fashioned pub, which can get busy at weekends. **R280**

EATING

Pietermaritzburg has a fairly good choice of **restaurants**, although South Africa's chain eateries are much in evidence. Around Boshoff St, at the heart of the city's Indian quarter, you'll find a concentration of shops selling cheap spicy snacks like *rotis* and bunny chows.

Café Tatham Tatham Art Gallery, Chief Albert Luthuli St ☎033 342 8327, ⊚tatham.org.za; map p.385. A colourful little coffee shop that's the best place in town for light lunches, with sandwiches, soups and specials such as oxtail (R99) or cold beetroot soup. Tues–Fri 9am–4.30pm, Sat 9am–3pm.

★Kara Nichha's 470 Church St ☎033 394 4195; map p.385. An excellent, very cheap vegetarian Indian takeaway (curries for R9.50), particularly good for filled *rotis* and Indian sweets. There's another branch at 151 Victoria Rd (☎033 345 0228). Mon–Fri 7.15am–5.15pm, Sat 7.15am–3pm.

Mamma Mia 101 Roberts Rd, Wembley ☎033 345 4130; map p.385. A decent Italian restaurant offering the usual classics along with some more unusual dishes, such a roast lamb pizza with mint chutney (R100). Daily 1–10pm.

Sagewood Café Blackwood's Home of Gardening, Chatterton Rd ☎063 483 1950, ⊚sagewoodcafe.co.za; map p.385. Occupying a tranquil, shaded spot overlooking the river, this popular lunch spot features rustic decor and focus on seasonal ingredients. Hearty breakfasts include waffles (R65), and vegans are well catered for, with dishes like broccoli and cashew curry (R110); walk through the garden centre to find it. Mon–Sat 8am–4pm, Sun 8am–3pm.

5

DRINKING AND NIGHTLIFE

Pietermaritzburg's nightclub scene has been in decline for years, though there are still a handful of decent **pubs** to be found; the university quarter across the river in Scottsville can be fun for a night out.

Sprytz 40 Alan Paton Ave, Scottsville ☎ 033 342 3206, Ⓦ sprytz.co.za; map p.385. Upscale cocktail bar that draws a well-heeled, mostly black clientele. Cocktails on offer range from the classic to the more creative, and cost around R40. Tues–Thurs noon–11pm, Fri & Sat noon–2am, Sun 2pm–midnight.

DIRECTORY

Emergencies AA ☎ 083 84322.
Hospital Pietermaritzburg Mediclinic, 90 Payn St (☎ 033 845 3700).
Internet access Cyber World Internet Café, 258 Langalibalele St (Mon–Sat 7.30am–6pm, Sun 10am–4pm; ☎ 074 712 5450).
Pharmacy Alpha Pharm, 62 Chief Albert Luthuli St (Mon–Fri 8am–5pm, Sat 8.30am–12.30pm; ☎ 033 342 4218).

The Midlands

For most travellers, the verdant farmland that makes up the **Midlands** is picture-postcard terrain, to be whizzed through on the two-hour journey from Durban or Pietermaritzburg to the uKhahlamba-Drakensberg. There's little reason to dally here, unless you fancy taking in the region's quaint, English-style country inns, tea shops and craft shops, several of which are on the so-called **Midlands Meander**, a route that weaves its way around the N3 on back roads between Pietermaritzburg and the **Mooi River** 60km to the northwest.

As you head north out of Pietermaritzburg on the N3 through the Midlands, you're roughly tracing the last journey of **Nelson Mandela** as a free man before his arrest in 1962. On the run from the police, Mandela had been continuing his political activities, often travelling in disguise – a practice that earned him the nickname of the "Black Pimpernel". **Howick**, 18km northwest of Pietermaritzburg, is recorded as the place where his historic detention began; the actual spot is on the R103, 2km north of a side road heading to the Tweedie junction. On this occasion, he was masquerading as the chauffeur of a white friend, when their car was stopped on the old Howick road, apparently because of a tip-off. A memorial unveiled by Mandela himself in 1996 marks the unassuming spot.

INFORMATION   THE MIDLANDS

A free **map** outlining the attractions on the Midlands Meander is available from most tourist offices in the vicinity, while the KZN Wildlife and the Midlands Meander Association (☎ 033 330 8195, Ⓦ midlandsmeander.co.za) can provide lists of self-catering accommodation in the area and make bookings on your behalf.

ACCOMMODATION

Granny Mouse Country House Old Main Rd, Balgowan, 28km northwest of Howick on the R103 ☎ 033 234 4071, Ⓦ grannymouse.co.za. Stylishly renovated and offering rooms in thatched cottages decorated with rich-textured fabrics. There's a health spa, a restaurant and loads of small lounges with large comfortable chairs to relax in. R2475
Loxley House South off the Lonteni/Sani Pass Rd in the

HANG TIGHT

The Midlands offers a couple of **adventure activities** for those itching to take to the skies. Bulwer, southwest of Pietermaritzburg, is one of the country's premier paragliding destinations, and Wild Sky Paragliding (☎ 082 395 3298, Ⓦ wildsky.co.za) can provide two-day basic courses for R2900, or tandem flights for R950. Meanwhile north of Howick, at the Karkloof Nature Reserve, you can undertake a **canopy tour** with Karkloof Canopy Tours (☎ 033 330 3415, Ⓦ karkloofcanopytour.co.za; R595 including lunch), where you're strapped into a harness and glide along steel cables between platforms erected high above the forest floor.

5

hamlet of Nottingham Rd, 30km northwest of Howick on the R103 ☎ 033 266 6362, ⓦ loxleyhouse.com. Comfortable rooms in a small B&B with its own restaurant; electric blankets on request for chilly winter nights. R1590

Rawdon's Old Main Rd, Nottingham Rd ☎ 033 266 6044, ⓦ www.rawdons.co.za. Set in a gracious thatch-roofed country estate looking on to its own trout lake, with welcoming log fires for cool misty days and airy verandas for hot summers. It also has an atmospheric pub with its own on-site brewery. R1900

The uKhahlamba-Drakensberg

Hugging the border with Lesotho, South Africa's premier mountain wilderness is officially known as the uKhahlamba-Drakensberg **Park**. The tallest range in Southern Africa, the "Dragon Mountains" (or, in Zulu, the "barrier of spears") reach their highest peaks along the border with Lesotho. The range is actually an escarpment separating a high interior plateau from the coastal lowlands of KwaZulu-Natal. Although this is a continuation of the same escarpment that divides the Mpumalanga highveld from the game-rich lowveld of the Kruger National Park and continues into the northern section of the Eastern Cape, when people talk of the Berg, they invariably mean the range in KwaZulu-Natal.

For elating scenery – massive spires, rock buttresses, wide grasslands, glorious waterfalls, rivers, pools and fern-carpeted forests – the uKhahlamba-Drakensberg is unrivalled. Wild and unpopulated, it's a paradise for **hiking**. One of the richest **San rock-art** repositories in the world, the uKhahlamba-Drakensberg is also a World Heritage Site, with more than six hundred recorded sites hidden all over the mountains featuring over 22,000 individual paintings by the original inhabitants of the area; three easily accessible ones are at **Giant's Castle**, **Injisuthi** and **Kamberg**.

The park is hemmed in by rural African areas – former "homeland" territory, unsignposted and unnamed on many maps, but interesting to drive through for a slice of traditional **Zulu life** complete with beehive-shaped huts. Visitors to the uKhahlamba-Drakensberg can **stay** either in the self-catering and camping options provided by KZN Wildlife, or in hotels or backpacker hostels outside the park (the most feasible option if you don't have your own transport). As for the **weather**, summers are warm but wet; expect both dramatic thunderstorms and misty days that block out the views. Winters tend to be dry, sunny and chilly, with freezing nights and, on the high peaks, occasional snow. The best times for hiking are spring and autumn. As the weather can change rapidly at any time of year, always take sufficient clothing and food.

ARRIVAL AND DEPARTURE   THE UKHAHLAMBA-DRAKENSBERG

By car You can reach the Southern Drakensberg using the R626 or R612/R617, which put you within striking distance of Sani Pass. For Central and Northern Drakensberg, most roads to the mountains branch off westwards from the N3 between Pietermaritzburg and the Ladysmith area, and come to a halt at various KZN Wildlife camps. With no connecting road through the uKhahlamba-Drakensberg, it's not possible to drive from one end to the other.

By bus Public transport serving the uKhahlamba-Drakensberg is limited. Many hotels offer transfers from the bus terminals in Estcourt, a commercial centre 88km north of Pietermaritzburg on the N3, or Ladysmith. Underberg Express shuttle service (see p.392) runs daily between Durban and *Sani Lodge* (see p.393), while the Baz Bus Durban–Joburg service goes via *Amphitheatre Backpackers* (see p.398) for the Northern Drakensberg.

The Southern Drakensberg

While the southern section of the uKhahlamba-Drakensberg lacks some of the drama and varied landscape found further north, it does have an outstanding highlight: the **Sani Pass** into Lesotho, a precipitous series of hairpins that twist to the top of the escarpment, the highest point in Southern Africa reachable on four wheels. It is easily one of the most beautiful drives in the country, offering breathtaking views from the top on clear days. The area offers lots of good hiking as well, and several local operators organize pony trekking in the mountains just across the border.

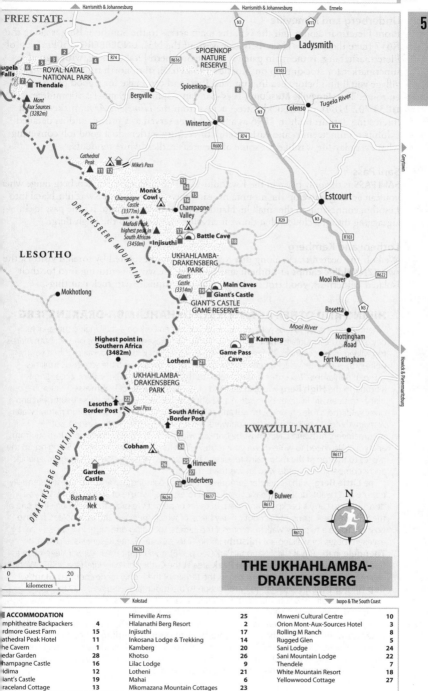

THE UKHAHLAMBA-
DRAKENSBERG

5

Underberg and Himeville

From Pietermaritzburg and the N3, the main access to the Southern Berg is along the R617 (take the Bulwer/Underberg exit west off the N3). **UNDERBERG**, 150km west of Pietermaritzburg, is the main gateway to the Southern Drakensberg, with a good supermarket for stocking up on supplies. **HIMEVILLE**, 4km north from here, is the last village you'll find before heading up Sani Pass, and can make for a good place to stay en route. The **Himeville Museum** (Tues–Sat 9am–3pm, Sun 9am–12.30pm; free; ☎033 702 1184), on Arbuckle Street across from the *Himeville Arms*, makes for an interesting detour; built in 1896 as a fort, it later served as a prison, and its detailed exhibits on nineteenth- and early twentieth-century settlers do a good job conveying what everyday life was like for some of the area's earliest white residents.

Sani Pass

SANI PASS is the only place in the KwaZulu-Natal uKhahlamba-Drakensberg range where you can actually drive up the mountains using the only road from KwaZulu-Natal into Lesotho, connecting to the small highland outpost of **Mokhotlong**. It's the pass itself, zigzagging into the clouds, that draws increasing numbers into the High Berg.

Lotheni and Kamberg

Well off the beaten track, along dirt roads and seldom explored by foreign visitors, the two **KZN Wildlife camps** at Lotheni and Kamberg are worth venturing into for their isolated wilderness, good trout fishing and some exquisite San rock paintings.

HIKING AND OTHER ACTIVITIES IN UKHAHLAMBA-DRAKENSBERG

Whether you choose to take your time on easy walks or embark on a challenging three- or four-day trip into the mountains, **hiking** in the uKhahlamba-Drakensberg remains one of South Africa's top wilderness experiences. The marvel of setting out on foot in these mountains is that you're unlikely to encounter vehicles, settlements, or even other people, and the scenery is sublime.

The uKhahlamba-Drakensberg is divided into the High Berg and Little Berg, according to altitude. In the **High Berg** you're in the land of spires and great rock buttresses, where the only places to sleep are in caves or, in some areas, huts. You'll need to be totally self-sufficient and obey wilderness rules, taking a trowel and toilet paper with you and not fouling natural water with anything – which means carrying water away from the streams to wash in. Both mountaineers' huts and caves must be booked with the KZN Wildlife office you start out from, and you'll also need to write down your route details in the mountain register. Slogging up the passes to the top of the mountains requires a high degree of fitness, some hiking experience and a companion or guide who knows the terrain.

The **Little Berg**, with its gentler summits, rivers, rock paintings, valleys and forests, is equally remote and beautiful. It's also easier (and safer) to explore if you're of average fitness. If you don't want to carry a backpack and sleep in caves or huts, it's feasible to base yourself at one of the KZN Wildlife camps and set out on day hikes, of which there are endless choices. It's also possible to do a two-day walk from one of the camps, spending one night in a cave. Two excellent bases for walking are **Injisuthi** in the Giant's Castle Game Reserve (see p.394), or **Thendele** in the Royal Natal National Park (see p.398). If you want the luxury of sleeping in a hotel, base yourself in the **Cathedral Peak** area at the *Cathedral Peak Hotel* (see p.397). With extensive grasslands, the Southern Berg is the terrain of the highly recommended **Giant's Cup Hiking Trail**, an exhilarating introduction to the mountains (see box, p.392).

KZN Wildlife offices sell books on uKhahlamba-Drakensberg walks, as well as trail maps they produce themselves (1:50,000). If you don't feel confident tackling the terrain, or are alone, note that Drakensberg Adventures, based at *Sani Lodge* (see p.393), offers a range of **guided hikes** across the uKhahlamba-Drakensberg and into Lesotho. **Angling** at Cobham, Garden Castle or Giant's Castle costs R70 per day by permit only from KZN Wildlife, with a bag limit of ten trout per day. At Lotheni and Kamberg the permit costs R70 and R120 respectively, with a bag limit of ten trout. You'll need to bring all your own gear.

RIGHT TRADITIONAL HUT LOOKING TOWARD CATHEDRAL PEAK (P.396)

In a valley in the foothills of the Berg and accessible by car either via Nottingham Road to the northeast or from Himeville to the southeast, **LOTHENI** is tranquil and beautiful, with waterfalls, grasslands and the lure of fishing in the Lotheni River, which flows through the reserve and is stocked with brown trout.

Apart from the superb fishing, the best reason to visit **KAMBERG**, 42km west of **Rosetta**, is for the rock art. At **Game Pass Cave** (one of three caves in the uKhahlamba-Drakensberg open to the public, also known as Shelter Cave), images of stylized figures in trance states and large, polychrome eland dance across the wall. These can only be visited with a guide (arrange in advance), and the walk there and back takes around three hours, following a contoured path through the grasslands. Alternatively, you can join one of the guided tours departing daily from Kamberg restcamp at 9am (R75), which also has its own rock-art centre that's worth a visit. There are other less distinct paintings near the waterfall that you can visit at will. **Walks** from Kamberg are undemanding and very scenic, and include a 4km trail with handrails for wheelchair-users and the visually impaired.

ARRIVAL AND INFORMATION — THE SOUTHERN DRAKENSBERG

By bus and minibus For all its isolation, Sani Pass is fairly straightforward to get to. Underberg Express (T 079 696 7108) operates a shuttle service between Durban airport, Durban centre, Pietermaritzburg, Howick, Bulwer, Himeville and *Sani Lodge* (see opposite), from where you can catch a minibus taxi. The fare from Durban's King Shaka airport to *Sani Lodge* is R650/person and the journey takes around 3hr 30min. At least two minibus taxis run Mon–Sat between Underberg and the ruins of Good Hope trading post (also known as Ha Makhakhe) near *Sani Lodge*, where they are met by Basotho minibuses heading over the pass and on to Mokhotlong in Lesotho. *Sani Mountain Lodge* (see opposite) also runs a shuttle service between Sani Pass and Underberg, leaving the pass at 9.30am and 1.30pm and making the trip back up at 11am and 3pm; it costs R350/person, and must be booked in advance.

By car If you intend to drive up to Sani Pass, it's recommended to use a 4WD vehicle, and you'll need your passport. The South African and Lesotho border posts are both open daily from 6am to 6pm.

Tourist information The best place to get information about the region is in the centre of Underberg, at Southern Drakensberg Tourism (Mon–Fri 7.45am–4.15pm, Sat & Sun 9am–1pm; T 033 701 1471, W drakensberg.org).

TOURS AND SERVICES

SANI PASS

Tours Roof of Africa Tours in Himeville (T 073 696 6782, W roofofafricatours.co.za) runs tours up the pass and into Lesotho, including a visit to a Basotho village; it also organizes trips to local cheese and wine farms, where you can view the production process and taste the end product. In addition, it offers walking tours (3–7hr) to visit the region's historic San rock paintings.

GIANT'S CUP HIKING TRAIL

The 60km, five-day **Giant's Cup Hiking Trail** (R100 per person per night, includes entrance fee to the reserve), part of which traverses a depression that lends the trail its name, is the only laid-out trail in the uKhahlamba-Drakensberg. It starts at the Sani Pass road, then leads through the foothills of the Southern Drakensberg and winds past eroded sandstone formations, overhangs with San paintings, grassy plains and beautiful valleys with river pools to swim in. No single day's hike is longer than 14km and, although there are some steep sections, it is not a difficult trail – you need to be fit to enjoy it, but not an athlete.

The **mountain huts** at the five overnight stops have running water, toilets, tables and benches, and bunks with mattresses. It's essential to bring a camping stove, food and a sleeping bag. The trail can be shortened by missing the first day and starting out at Pholela Hut, an old farmhouse where you spend the night, then terminating one day earlier at Swiman Hut close to the KZN Wildlife office at Garden Castle. You can also lengthen the trail by spending an extra night at Bushmen's Nek Hut, in an area with numerous caves and rock-art sites.

The trail is restricted to thirty people per day and tends to get booked out during holiday periods; **bookings** should be made through KZN Wildlife (W kznwildlife.com), where you can also get a map and a trail booklet.

LOTHENI AND KAMBERG

Access and supplies The rest camps at Lotheni (☎033 702 0540) and Kamberg (☎033 267 7251) are open daily April–Sept 6am–6pm and Oct–March 5am–7pm. In Lotheni, there's a trading store about 10km before you reach the restcamp. At Kamberg, however, the nearest major supplies are at Rosetta, so it's best to bring all your own food and drink.

ACCOMMODATION

NIMEVILLE

Nimeville Arms Arbuckle St ☎033 702 1305, ⊛himeville otel.co.za; map p.389. A decent country inn that makes a good stopover before the final haul to the mountains. Operating since 1904, it offers basic but comfortable rooms, and also has a block of dorm accommodation for backpackers. Meals are available, and the cosy old-fashioned bar has a fireplace. Dorms **R220**, doubles **R790**

Yellowwood Cottage 8 Mackenzie St ☎033 702 1065, ⊛rays@tiscali.co.za; map p.389. One of the nicest B&Bs in the area, with friendly and helpful hosts, and a spectacular garden boasting wonderful Berg views. There are four en-suite rooms with electric blankets for cold nights, and a fully equipped kitchenette. **R700**

UNDERBERG

Cedar Garden 1 Polo Way ☎033 701 1153 or ☎083 548 4111, ⊛cedargarden.co.za; map p.389. A stately old house with elegant light-filled rooms, some in the main house and others in a four-person self-catering cottage or separate self-catering house. The best rooms overlook the gardens, and there's a fireplace in the cosy lounge. **R900**

SANI PASS

Most accommodation is at the foot of the mountains, just before the pass hairpins its way up to the top.

Khotso Drakensberg Gardens Rd, 9km northwest of Underberg ☎082 412 5540, ⊛khotso.co.za; map p.389. Specializing in horse trekking, this friendly place offers accommodation in rooms, rondavels and dorms, as well as camping on the leafy grounds. Horseriding excursions range from short sunset rides to multi-day trips to nearby Lesotho (R680 per person for a full day); meals available if booked in advance. Camping **R120**, dorms **R160**, doubles **R500**, rondavels **R800**

Mkomazana Mountain Cottages 25km northwest of Underberg along the Sani Pass Rd ☎082 521 6343, ⊛mkomazana.co.za; map p.389. Five self-catering cottages, sleeping two to six people, on the site of an old trading post near the start of Giant's Cup Hiking Trail. Less ambitious walks into the mountains begin right on the property, which has its own river and waterfall, and a private dam with trout. **R850**

★ **Sani Lodge** 19km northwest of Underberg along the Sani Pass Rd ☎033 702 0330, ⊛sanilodge.co.za; map p.389. There are dorms, doubles and self-catering cottages at this popular backpacker hostel, some in picturesque thatched rondavels. The view from the veranda is stunning, and delicious home-made goodies are available at the café next door. It's a good base for walking to waterfalls and rock paintings – packed lunches can be supplied – and there are also tours up Sani Pass, guided hikes and 4WD excursions on offer. Camping **R90**, dorms **R165**, doubles **R460**

Sani Mountain Lodge At the top of Sani Pass, just inside Lesotho ☎078 634 7496, ⊛sanimountain.co.za; map p.389. The cliff-edge setting at this lodge is certainly hard to beat, with awesome views into KwaZulu-Natal. There's a pub with hearty food on offer, while in the evenings you can sit on the balcony and watch the sun set over the mountaintops. Rooms sleeping up to six are in attractive rondavels with fireplaces, and there's camping and backpacker accommodation available. Guided hikes and horseriding (R140/hr) can be arranged. Camping **R105**, dorms **R275**, doubles **R589**

LOTHENI AND KAMBERG

Kamberg In the foothills of the Drakensberg, between Lotheni and Giant's Castle; book through KZN Wildlife ☎033 845 1000, ⊛kznwildlife.com; map p.389. The restcamp here consists of chalets sleeping two to six; there's a communal kitchen but no campsite. Trout fishing is possible nearby, as well as a number of scenic walks in the area. **R780**

Lotheni In a remote area of the park north of Sani Pass; book through KZN Wildlife ☎033 845 1000, ⊛kznwildlife.com; map p.389. A small campsite plus fourteen comfortable self-catering chalets with three to six beds, all with well-equipped kitchens. Also on-site is *Simes Cottage* (R2800), a stone farmhouse with a majestic outlook, its own trout lake and grounds traversed by bushbuck and eland. The cottage sleeps ten, and you have to rent the whole thing and bring all your supplies. Camping **R180**, chalets **R560**

The Central Drakensberg

The **Central Drakensberg** incorporates four distinct areas, all clearly signposted from the N3. **Giant's Castle**, the site of a beautiful game reserve, is where you'll find the popular vulture hide and access to important San rock paintings. More San art is at **Injisuthi** to the north, principally a hiking destination and the place to head for if you're after complete wilderness. Far more accessible and tourist-trammelled is **Champagne Valley**, which offers a healthy number of hotels with ample sporting facilities, while to the north, the hotel at **Cathedral Peak** is the best place to base yourself for some serious walking.

Giant's Castle Game Reserve

Daily: April–Sept 6am–10pm; Oct–March 5am–10pm • R40 • ☎ 036 353 3718

Giant's Castle Game Reserve was created to protect the dwindling numbers of **eland**, which were numerous in the uKhahlamba-Drakensberg before the arrival of colonialists. Antelope of the montane zone are also found here – oribi, grey rhebok, mountain reedbuck and bushbuck – as well as four dozen other mammal species and around 160 bird species. The reserve is bordered to the west by three of the four highes peaks in South Africa: Mafadi (the highest at 3450m), Popple Peak (3325m) and the bulky ramparts of Giant's Castle itself (3314m). This is not a traditional game park – there are no roads inside the reserve apart from access routes, which terminate at the two main KZN Wildlife accommodation areas, **Giant's Castle** and **Injisuthi**; the only way to see the wildlife here is by hiking through the terrain.

The vulture hide

May–Sept • R840 for up to three people • Book as much as a year in advance through KZN Wildlife • ☎ 033 845 1000, ⓦ kznwildlife.com

One of the big attractions at the Giant's Head peak is the thrilling **vulture hide** where you may see the rare bearded vulture, or lammergeier, a giant, black and golden bird with massive wings and a diamond-shaped tail. A scavenger, the lammergeier is an evolutionary link between eagles and vultures and was thought extinct in Southern Africa until only a couple of decades ago. The bird is found only in mountainous areas such as the Himalayan foothills, and in South Africa only in the uKhahlamba-Drakensberg and Maloti mountains. In the locality you may also spot Cape vulture, black eagle, jackal buzzard and lanner falcon, attracted by the carcasses of animals put out by rangers during the winter.

Main Caves

Daily 9am–3pm • Guided walks from Giant's Castle Camp R45

Giant's Castle has one of the three major **rock-art sites** open to the public in the uKhahlamba-Drakensberg, with more than five hundred paintings at **Main Caves**, about a half-hour's easy walk up the Bushman's River Valley.

EN ROUTE TO THE BERG

The tiny hamlet of **WINTERTON**, some 90km north of Pietermaritzburg along the R74 as it deviates west off the N3, offers some pleasant **places to stay** if you're looking for a stopover on the way to the Central Drakensberg. This is also a good place for **whitewater rafting**. The Tugela River east of the Drakensberg can be accessed from Winterton on trips (Dec–April) run by Four Rivers Rafting and Adventures (☎ 036 468 1693, ⓦ fourriversadventures.co.za); one-day forays into the river gorge cost R670/person, with multi-day trips available on request.

ACCOMMODATION IN WINTERTON

Lilac Lodge 8 Springfield Rd, the main drag as you drive into town ☎ 036 488 1025; map p.389. Accommodation is in small cottages and it has its own coffee and arts and crafts shop. Priced per person at R350, so a good option for single travellers. R700

Rolling M Ranch ☎ 082 736 4576, ⓦ rollingmranch .co.za; map p.389. A working farm outside town on the banks of the Tugela River – to get there, head 2km north from Winterton on the R600, then turn right at the signposted Skietdrift road; the camp is around 15km down this route and has self-catering cabins and cottages sleeping four to ten, as well as a bush camp. Since the farm is on the Battlefields route, there are trails from here to Spioenkop and Buller's Cross monuments. R1000

THE SAN AND THEIR ROCK PAINTINGS

Southern Africa's earliest inhabitants and the most direct descendants of the late Stone Age, the **San**, or Bushmen, lived in the caves and shelters of the uKhahlamba-Drakensberg for thousands of years before the arrival of the Nguni people and later the white farmers. Many liberal writers use the word "Bushmen" in a strictly non-pejorative sense to describe these early hunter-gatherers – though the word was originally deeply insulting. Several historians and anthropologists use "San", but as this refers to a language group and not a culture, it isn't strictly accurate. Since there is no agreed term, you'll find both words used in this book.

The San hunted and gathered on the subcontinent for a considerable period – paintings in Namibia date back 25,000 years. In the last two thousand years, the southward migration of Bantu-speaking farmers forced change upon the San, but there is evidence that the two groups lived side by side. However, tensions arose when the white settlers began to annex lands for hunting and farming. As the San started to take cattle from farmers, whites felt justified in hunting them in genocidal campaigns until they were wiped off the South African map.

San artists were also **shamans**, and their paintings of hunting, dancing and animals mostly depict religious beliefs rather than realistic narratives of everyday life. It's difficult to accurately **date** the paintings, but the oldest are likely to be at least eight hundred years old (although Bushmen lived in the area for thousands of years before that) and the most recent are believed to have been painted towards the end of the nineteenth century. The **medicine** or **trance dance** – journeying into the spiritual world to harness healing power – was the Bushmen's most important religious ritual and is depicted in much of their art. Look out for the postures the shamans adopted during the dance, including arms outstretched behind them, bending forward, kneeling, or pointing fingers. Dots along the spine depict the sensation of energy boiling upwards, while lines on faces or coming out of the nose usually refer to trance-induced nosebleeds. Other feelings experienced in trance, such as elongation, attenuation or the sensation of flight, are expressed by feathers or streamers. The depictions of horses, cattle and white settlers mark the end of the traditional way of life for the uKhahlamba-Drakensberg Bushmen, and it is possible that the settlers were painted by shamans to try to ward off their all-too-real bullets.

You'll also see the spiral-horned **eland** depicted in every cave – not because these antelope were prolific, but because they were considered to have spiritual power. Sometimes the elands are painted in layers to increase their spiritual potency. In the caves, you can see depictions of human-like figures transforming into their power animal. Besides antelope, other animals associated with trance are honeybees, felines, snakes, elephants and rhinos.

Paintings weather and fade, and many have been vandalized. People dabbing water on them to make them clearer, or touching them, has also caused them to disappear – so never be tempted. One of the best introductions to rock art is the slim **booklet** by David Lewis-Williams, *Rock Paintings of the Natal Drakensberg*, available from most decent bookshops in the area.

Injisuthi

April–Sept 6am–6pm, Oct–March 5am–7pm • R40 • Guided visits to the San paintings (R75 per person, min 4 people; 5hr) set out from Injisuthi camp at 8.30am; book through KZN Wildlife (see box, p.355) • ☎ 036 431 9000 • To get to the camp, take the indicated turning off the R615, then follow the dirt road for 30km

In the northern section of the Giant's Castle Game Reserve, some 50km from both Winterton and Estcourt, **INJISUTHI** is a hiker's dream. You can walk straight out into the mountains, swim in the rivers or take in rock art. One of the best day walks, albeit a tough one, is up Van Heyningen's Pass to the viewpoint – the friendly staff at the main camp can direct you. There are ten different day hikes at Injisuthi, lasting from one to ten hours.

If you have even a passing interest in rock art, don't miss the paintings at **Battle Cave**, named for a series of paintings that apparently depict an armed conflict between two groups of Bushmen. San art authority David Lewis-Williams has argued that these paintings are unlikely to depict a conflict over territory because there is no evidence that such conflicts took place in a society that was very loosely organized and non-territorial. Instead, he claims, the paintings are about the San spiritual experience and shamanic trance, the battles taking place in the spiritual realm where marauding evil shamans shoot arrows of "sickness", while good shamans attempt to fight them off. There are more than 750 beautifully painted people and animals in this extensive cave, though many are faded. The paintings are fenced off, and can be visited only on a guided walk with a KZN Wildlife guide.

Champagne Castle

Champagne Castle, the second-highest peak in South Africa, provides the most popular view in the uKhahlamba-Drakensberg, with scores of resorts in the valley cashing in on the soaring backdrop. The name, so the story goes, derives from an incident in 1861, when a Major Grantham made the first recorded ascent of the peak accompanied by his batman, who inadvertently dropped the bottle of bubbly and christened the mountainside.

Champagne Valley

Monk's Cowl daily 6am–6pm • R40 • Overnight hiking R70 • ☎ 036 468 1103

Champagne Valley is an easy 32km from Winterton, and has shops, restaurants and facilities absent in other parts of the uKhahlamba-Drakensberg. This over-civilized but extremely pretty area, which lies outside the KZN Wildlife reserve, is best avoided if you want to **hike** from your doorstep – you'll have to drive west along the R600 to Monk's Cowl, from where plenty of hikes into the mountains begin.

Ardmore Ceramic Art Studio

Signposted 20km from Winterton off the R600 • Daily 8am–4.30pm • ☎ 033 940 0034, ⓦ ardmoreceramics.co.za

The **Ardmore Ceramic Art Studio** is one of the area's highlights, started in the 1980s by fine-arts graduate **Fée Halsted-Berning** with trainee **Bonnie Ntshalintshali**, a young Zulu girl suffering from polio. By 1990 they had collected a clutch of awards for their distinctive ceramic works, and the studio now has around forty people creating beautiful sculpture and crockery with wildly colourful and often impossibly irrational motifs, which have included rhinos dressed as preachers administering the sacrament to a congregation of wild animals. Bonnie died of AIDS in 1999, as have at least eight other artists at the studio, but the distinctive style she pioneered has been continued here and the works are well worth seeing and buying. There's also a less pricey local **curio shop** on the premises, selling works by other local artists.

Cathedral Peak

North of Monk's Cowl and the Champagne Valley resorts are the Mlambonja River Valley and **Cathedral Peak**, a freestanding pinnacle sticking out of the 5km-long basalt Cathedral Ridge. The peak looks nothing like a cathedral (its Zulu name, *Mponjwane*, means "the horn on a heifer's head").

Hiking trails

A number of **hiking trails** start right from the *Cathedral Peak Hotel* (see opposite), which can provide maps and books. One of the most popular day walks is to the beautiful **Rainbow Gorge**, an 11km round trip (4–5hr) following the Ndumeni River, with pools, rapids and falls to detain you. The hike can be wet, so wear proper walking boots. The hotel also runs nine-hour guided trips up to Cathedral Peak, which include plenty of time at the top to revel in the views. It's a very steep climb, and the final section beyond Orange Peel Gap should only be tackled by experienced climbers.

Mike's Pass

4WD leaves the park gate at 9am, noon and 4pm • R60 (min 4 people)

Ten kilometres up a twisting forestry road is **Mike's Pass**, from where, on a clear day, you'll get outstanding views of the entire region. There's a scale model on top to help identify the peaks. At the time of writing the pass was closed to private vehicles because of soil erosion, but a 4WD is available to ferry visitors to the top.

ARRIVAL AND INFORMATION

By car The roads into the Central Drakensberg are good the whole way. For Champagne Valley look for the Estcort North turn-off from the N3; to reach Cathedral Peak from Winterton, follow the signs for "Central Berg", then the signs for "Cathedral Peak".

Information and services The reserve's only filling

THE CENTRAL DRAKENSBERG

station is at the main entrance to Giant's Castle; you'll find the park's reception office and a shop 7km further on (daily 8am–4.30pm; ☎036 353 3718). The Cathedral Peak reception office is 1.5km from the park entrance (daily 7am–7pm; ☎036 488 8000).

ACCOMMODATION

GIANT'S CASTLE

Giant's Castle Camp Book through KZN Wildlife ☎033 845 1000, ⓦkznwildlife.com; map p.389. Comfortable self-contained chalets, some with wonderful picture windows looking out to the peaks. For food, there's the pleasant buffet-style restaurant *Izimbali* (daily 7.30am–9pm). You can buy frozen meat for braais and some tinned food at the reception, but stock up on other supplies beforehand. There are fabulous hiking trails from the camp, and the eight-person Bannerman's Hut (R70/person) is one of the Berg's best-located hiking huts. R945

White Mountain Resort Along the road to Giant's Castle hutted camp, 34km from Estcourt and 32km from the reserve ☎036 353 3437, ⓦwhitemountain .co.za; map p.389. If the KZN Wildlife accommodation is full, try this hotel, the only one that gives access to the reserve, offering full board as well as self-catering cottages. It's located in the foothills and close to Zulu villages and farmlands, so while the area is pretty, it's neither grand nor remote. Camping for two people R270, doubles R770

INJISUTHI

Injisuthi Camp Book through KZN Wildlife ☎033 845 1000, ⓦkznwildlife.com; map p.389. Accommodation here includes comfortable self-catering chalets, safari tents and campsites. However, most people come with the express purpose of taking to the hills and camping in one of the designated caves, which have absolutely no facilities and must be booked at reception. Camping R95, safari tents R360

CHAMPAGNE VALLEY

Ardmore Guest Farm Signposted off the R600, midway between Winterton and Monk's Cowl ☎087 997 1194, ⓦardmore.co.za; map p.389. A thoroughly hospitable farmstay with accommodation in en-suite rondavels or cottages, some with their own fireplaces. Guests eat together from hand-crafted crockery made on the farm. Staff can arrange horse trails into Spioenkop Game Reserve through the battlefields. R590

Champagne Castle Along the R600 ☎036 468 1063, ⓦchampagnecastle.co.za; map p.389. This old-fashioned hotel, the closest accommodation to the hiking trails beginning at Monk's Cowl, has comfortable en-suite rooms and self-catering chalets sleeping six and set in lovely gardens with a swimming pool. Activities, such as horseriding and fishing, are available. Full board R2040

Graceland Cottage Signposted off the R600 ☎036 468 1011, ⓦgracelandsa.com; map p.389. A four-bedroom self-catering cottage with TV and fireplace as well as a smaller, two-bedroom cottage perched right on the edge of a mountain with spectacular views. For larger groups there is also a thirteen-bed house with its own pool. R1800

Inkosana Lodge and Trekking Along the R600, midway between Winterton and Monk's Cowl ☎036 468 1202, ⓦinkosana.co.za; map p.389. Backpacker accommodation in unpretentious thatched rondavels and a dorm, with beautiful indigenous gardens and a retreat-centre feel. Breakfasts and dinners also available. Dorms R225, doubles R650

CATHEDRAL PEAK

★**Cathedral Peak Hotel** 44km from both Winterton and Bergville ☎036 488 1888, ⓦcathedralpeak.co.za; map p.389. The only hotel in the Cathedral Peak area and the closest in the uKhahlamba-Drakensberg to the mountains – also within the KZN Wildlife protected area, it's an excellent place to stay. The views are perfect and the rooms in thatched two-storey wings are comfortably furnished with pine and country-style fabrics. Half board R3200

Didima At the top of Mike's Pass; book through KZN Wildlife ☎033 845 1000, ⓦkznwildlife.com; map p.389. Self-catering two- to six-bed chalets with satellite TV and fireplaces, as well as campsites. You'll also find a restaurant, a bar and a shop with basic food supplies, as well as the Didima San Art Centre (R60, including park entry fee), which has displays on San rock art and shows a short film. Chalet rates include breakfast. Camping R200, chalets R1120

The Northern Drakensberg

The dramatically beautiful **Northern Drakensberg** consists mainly of the **Royal Natal National Park** with a few resorts scattered around the fringes. The Tugela River and its bouldered gorge offer some of the most awe-inspiring scenery in the area, its most

5

striking geographical feature being the **Amphitheatre**, the crescent-shaped 5km rock wall over which the Tugela plunges. With a complete cross section of accommodation, the Northern Berg is a very desirable area to visit. The best place to get a real feel for these pristine mountains and valleys is **Thendele**, the main KZN Wildlife camp (see below).

Royal Natal National Park

Daily: Oct–March 5am–7pm; April–Sept 6am–6pm • R40 • ☎ 036 438 6310

The Royal Natal National Park, 46km west of Bergville, is famed for its views of the Amphitheatre, which probably appear on more posters and postcards than any other single feature of the uKhahlamba-Drakensberg. Almost everyone does the **Tugela Gorge walk**, a fabulous six-hour round trip from Thendele, which gives close-up views of the Amphitheatre and the **Tugela Falls** plummeting over the 947m rock wall.

Established in 1916, the park only earned its royal sobriquet in 1947 when the Windsors paid a visit. It sits at the northern end of the uKhahlamba-Drakensberg, tucked between Lesotho to the west and Free State province to the north. The three defining peaks are the Sentinel (3165m), the Eastern Buttress (3048m) and the Mont Aux Sources (3282m), which is also where five rivers rise – hence its name, bestowed by French missionaries in 1878.

ARRIVAL AND INFORMATION

By transfer Several of the resorts offer transfers from Bergville or the N3 if you book ahead, but they tend to be expensive.

By car Routes to the park are surfaced all the way. Coming from the south along the N3, take the Winterton/Berg resorts turn-off and follow the signposts through Bergville to the park entrance, 46km away.

THE NORTHERN DRAKENSBERG

Tourist information The Drakensberg Tourism Association (☎ 036 448 1557, �🖰 drakensberg.org.za) has information about the area and helps with booking accommodation, either by phone or email (there is no actual tourist office).

Supplies For supplies head to Bergville, the last place to stock up before heading into the park.

ACCOMMODATION

INSIDE THE PARK

KZN Wildlife (🖰 kznwildlife.com) offers some very reasonable campsites within the park, as well as some exceptional chalets. Book both through their usual reservation system (see box, p.355).

Mahai Campsite Along the river adjacent to the national park ☎ 036 438 6310; map p.389. With facilities for up to four hundred campers, *Mahai* attracts hordes of South Africans over school holidays and weekends. From here you can head straight into the mountains for some of the best walks in the Berg. Minimum charge for three. Three people R330

Rugged Glen Campsite Signposted 4km from Mahai ☎ 036 438 6310; map p.389. A smaller and quieter campsite than *Mahai*, though often only open during school holidays. The views and walks here aren't as good, but there is horseriding available (R200/hr), and the *Orion Mont-Aux-Sources Hotel* is an easy walk away – handy if you want a substantial meal. Minimum charge for two. Two people R220

★**Thendele Hutted Camp** At the end of the road into the Royal Natal National Park ☎ 036 438 6411; map p.389. This is one of the most sought-after places to stay in the0 whole of South Africa, with splendid views of the Amphitheatre and excellent walks right from your front door. Accommodation is in comfortable two- and four-bed chalets, the cheapest of which have hotplates, fridges, kettles, toasters and utensils. If you opt for the more luxurious cottages or lodge, chefs are on hand to cook, though you need to bring the ingredients. There's also a good curio and supply shop. R800

OUTSIDE THE PARK

Amphitheatre Backpackers On the R74, 21km west of Bergville ☎ 082 855 9767, �🖰 amphibackpackers .co.za; map p.389. On the Baz Bus route, this place is convenient for those without their own transport who want to explore the Northern Drakensberg. Accommodation is in en-suite dorms or safari tents with beds, though standard private rooms are also on offer. There's a bar and restaurant, and organized hiking trips, horseriding and mountain biking are available. Camping R95, dorms R200, safari tents/person R215, doubles R400

The Cavern Off the R74, about 20km from the Royal Natal National Park ☎ 036 438 6270, �🖰 cavern.co.za; map p.389. This is the most tucked-away of the hotels, family-run and with an old-fashioned feel. The rooms are adequate, though suites come with fireplaces, and there's also a swimming pool, horseriding and trout fishing. Full board R2400

Hlalanathi Berg Resort About 10km from the Royal Natal National Park ☎036 438 6308, ⓦhlalanathi .co.za; map p.389. A family resort with camping and self-catering thatched chalets sleeping two to six people. There's a swimming pool and trampolines, and a sit-down and takeaway restaurant serving cheap burgers, sandwiches and more substantial meals. Camping R120, doubles R850

Mnweni Cultural Centre In the Mnweni Valley 30km west of Bergville along the Woodstock Dam/Rookdale roads ☎072 712 2401; map p.389. Owned by the AmaNgwane and AmaZzizi communities, accommodation in this breathtaking valley is in simple four-bed thatched rondavels with shared ablutions and kitchen facilities. Aside from hiking in the mountains (R50 per night), there are craft stalls, horseriding and some San rock paintings, while overnight stays in traditional homesteads can also be arranged. Meals available with advance notice. Camping R90, chalets/person R250

Orion Mont-Aux-Sources Hotel About 4km from the Royal Natal National Park ☎087 353 7676, ⓦorionhotels.co.za; map p.389. A smart but fairly impersonal hotel with views of the Amphitheatre, as well as sports facilities that include tennis courts and horseriding. R1299

The Elephant Coast and Zululand game reserves

In startling contrast to the intensively developed 250km ribbon of coastline running north and south of Durban, the north of the Dolphin Coast drifts off into some of the wildest and most breathtaking sea frontage in South Africa – an area known as the **Elephant Coast**.

If you've travelled along the Garden Route and wondered where stereotypical Africa was, the answer is in the northern reaches of the Elephant Coast hemmed in by Swaziland and Mozambique – traditionally known as **Maputaland** – with its tight patchwork of wilderness and **ancestral African lands**, where **traditional life** continues. Once remote and so only the domain of hardy South African off-road drivers, today St Lucia, Sodwana Bay and KwaNgwanase can be reached via good tarred roads from the N2. Access is improving all the time, though you'll still need a 4WD vehicle to visit some of the idyllic spots along the Elephant Coast's 200km of virtually uninterrupted beachfront.

Further south, less than three hours' drive north on the N2 from Durban, is the big game country of **Hluhluwe-iMfolozi**, which rivals even Kruger National Park for beautiful wilderness. Turn right instead of left at the Mtubatuba junction and you'll hit the southernmost extent of South Africa's most satisfyingly "tropical" coast. It's protected all the way up to Mozambique by the country's third-largest protected area, the **iSimangaliso Wetland Park** (which includes Lake St Lucia, Cape Vidal, Western Shores, False Bay, Mkhuze Game Reserve, Sodwana Bay, Lake Sibaya and Kosi Bay). This 3320-square-kilometre UNESCO World Heritage Site is a patchwork of wetland reserves, coastal forests and marine sanctuaries, and activities include outstanding scuba diving and fishing as well as the opportunity to see some of South Africa's largest concentrations of hippos, crocodiles and sea turtles. Note that the far reaches of the northern KwaZulu-Natal coastal region are considered an intermediate **malarial risk region** between October and May (see p.71).

Mtubatuba and Hluhluwe Village

Travelling north on the N2 from Durban and the large industrial port of **Richards Bay**, you'll pass a few predominantly African villages that make adequate bases for exploring the Hluhluwe-iMfolozi Park.

Mtubatuba

Around 50km north of Richards Bay, **MTUBATUBA** (often shortened to Mtuba) is situated where the R618 intersects the N2, just twenty minutes from both the southern section of the Hluhluwe-iMfolozi Park and St Lucia. The town features lots of herbalists, traditional healers and a Zulu market, and is also a thriving centre for the local sugar-cane industry.

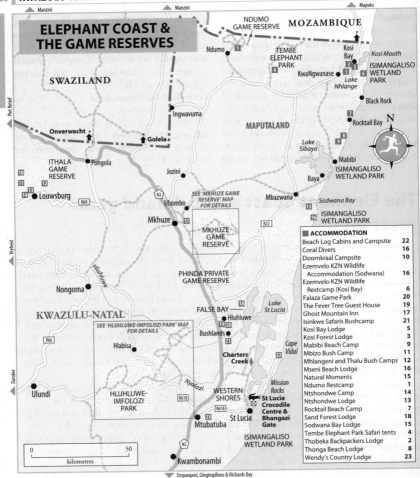

ELEPHANT COAST & THE GAME RESERVES

■ **ACCOMMODATION**

Beach Log Cabins and Campsite	22
Coral Divers	16
Doornkraal Campsite	10
Ezemvelo KZN Wildlife	
Accommodation (Sodwana)	16
Ezemvelo KZN Wildlife	
Restcamp (Kosi Bay)	6
Falaza Game Park	20
The Fever Tree Guest House	19
Ghost Mountain Inn	17
Isinkwe Safaris Bushcamp	21
Kosi Bay Lodge	5
Kosi Forest Lodge	3
Mabibi Beach Camp	9
Mbizo Bush Camp	11
Mhlangeni and Thalu Bush Camps	12
Mseni Beach Lodge	16
Natural Moments	15
Ndumo Restcamp	1
Ntshondwe Camp	14
Ntshondwe Lodge	13
Rocktail Beach Camp	7
Sand Forest Lodge	18
Sodwana Bay Lodge	15
Tembe Elephant Park Safari tents	4
Thobeka Backpackers Lodge	2
Thonga Beach Lodge	8
Wendy's Country Lodge	23

Empangeni, Gingindlovu & Richards Bay

Hluhluwe

Just off the N2, about 20km north of Mtubatuba, is the straggling village of **HLUHLUWE** (pronounced "shla-shloo-wee"), which is short on charm but nonetheless handy for accessing the northern section of the Hluhluwe-iMfolozi Park. Five minutes' drive from Hluhluwe on Ngweni Road, **Ilala Weavers** (Mon–Fri 8am–4.30pm, Sat & Sun 9am–4pm; ☎081 400 0947, ⓦilala.co.za) is a hub of community projects selling well-priced traditional **crafts** in a cheerful atmosphere: there's also a restaurant (see opposite).

ARRIVAL AND INFORMATION

By bus Greyhound buses from Durban (daily; 2hr 20min), Johannesburg (daily; 9hr 45min) and Pretoria (daily; 11hr 45min) stop in Richards Bay, from where you can catch regular minibuses on to Hluhluwe and Mtubatuba.
By plane There is an airport at Richards Bay, from which four flights a day leave for Johannesburg (1hr 15min).

MTUBATUBA AND HLUHLUWE VILLAGE

Tourist office The friendly Elephant Coast Tourism Association information office is based at the Engen petrol station on Main St in Hluhluwe (daily 8am–4.30pm; ☎035 562 0966, ⓦvisitelephantcoast .co.za), providing details of numerous lodges and game farms in the vicinity.

ACCOMMODATION

MTUBATUBA

Wendy's Country Lodge 3 Riverview Drive ☎ 035 550 0407 or ☎ 083 628 1601, ⓦ wendybnb.co.za; map opposite. Eight luxurious rooms in a house with a vaguely colonial atmosphere set in tropical gardens in a suburb of Mtubatuba, plus a cottage that sleeps six. There's also a swimming pool and a restaurant on-site. Rates include breakfast. R1200

HLUHLUWE

The Fever Tree Guest House In the residential area 300m south of the Engen petrol station ☎ 035 562 3194

or ☎ 083 744 5261, ⓦ thefevertree.co.za; map opposite. Comfy, en-suite rooms with kitchenettes opening onto an indigenous garden with a splash-pool, and there's a communal lounge/dining area. The guesthouse can arrange trips into Hluhluwe-iMfolozi Park. R880

Isinkwe Safaris Bushcamp 15km south of Hluhluwe ☎ 083 338 3494, ⓦ isinkwe.co.za; map opposite. A well-run rustic hostel offering camping, dorms and a number of small chalets, some en suite. It serves reasonably priced meals (or you can self-cater), and arranges tours to Hluhluwe-iMfolozi Park and St Lucia. Camping R140, dorms R200, doubles R600

EATING AND DRINKING

Fig Tree Cafe & Deli At Ilala Weavers, 5min drive from Hluhluwe on Ngweni Rd ☎ 082 045 1647. Serves decent breakfasts and lunches, including salads

and seafood dishes such as Thai fishcakes (R52), on a shaded terrace. Mon–Fri 8am–4.30pm, Sat & Sun 9am–4pm.

Hluhluwe-iMfolozi Park

Daily: June–Oct 6am–5pm; Nov–May 5am–6pm • R210 • ☎ 035 562 0848

Hluhluwe-iMfolozi is KwaZulu-Natal's most outstanding game reserve, considered by some to be even better than Kruger. While it certainly can't match Kruger's sheer scale (Hluhluwe is a twentieth of the size) or its teeming game populations, its relatively compact 960 square kilometres have a wilder feel. This has something to do with the fact that, apart from **Hilltop**, an elegant hotel-style restcamp in the northern half of the park, none of the other restcamps is fenced off, and wild animals are free to wander through. The vegetation, with subtropical forest in places, adds to the sense of adventure. The park also offers the best hiking wilderness **trails** in the country.

The park used to be two distinct entities – hence its tongue-twisting double-barrelled name (pronounced something like "shla-shloo-wee-oom-fa-low-zee") – and the two sections retain their separate characters, reinforced by a public road slicing between them. The southern **iMfolozi section** takes its name from a corruption of *mfulawozi*, a Zulu word that refers to the fibrous bushes that grow along its rivers. The topography here is characterized by wide, deep valleys incised by the Black and White Mfolozi rivers, with altitudes varying between 60m and 650m above sea level. Luxuriant riverine vegetation gives way in drier areas to a variety of woodland, savanna, thickets and grassy plains. The notable feature of the northern **Hluhluwe section** is the river of the same name, a slender, slithering waterway, punctuated by elongated pools. The Hluhluwe rises in the mountains north of the park and passes along sandbanks, rock beds and steep cliffs in the game reserve before seeping away into Lake St Lucia to the east. The higher ground is covered by veld and dense thicket, while the well-watered ridges support the softer cover of ferns, lichens, mosses and orchids.

Brief history

Despite Hluhluwe-iMfolozi being the oldest proclaimed national park in Africa (it was created in 1895), its future as a game refuge has hung by a thread several times in the last two hundred years. In the nineteenth century, iMfolozi was the private hunting preserve of the **Zulu** king, Shaka. During Shaka's reign between 1818 and 1828 the area saw the most sustained campaign of hunting in Zulu history, but this was nothing compared to the destruction caused by white farmers between 1929 and 1950, when a crusade of game **extermination** was launched to wipe out **nagama** disease, resulting in the slaughter of one hundred thousand head of game from sixteen species; rhinos alone were spared.

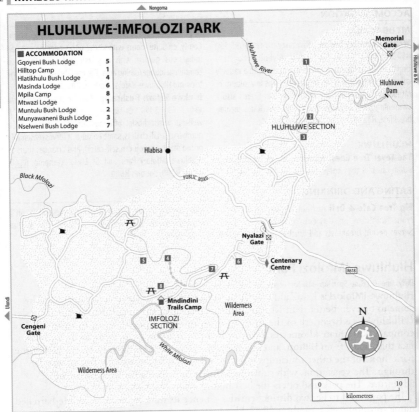

HLUHLUWE-IMFOLOZI PARK

ACCOMMODATION	
Gqoyeni Bush Lodge	5
Hilltop Camp	1
Hlatikhulu Bush Lodge	4
Masinda Lodge	6
Mpila Camp	8
Mtwazi Lodge	1
Muntulu Bush Lodge	2
Munyawaneni Bush Lodge	3
Nselweni Bush Lodge	7

It was only in 1952, when the park was handed over to the newly formed organization now known as **Ezemvelo KZN Wildlife**, that the slow process of resuscitating the threadbare game reserve began. It became the home of Operation Rhino, which was responsible for saving the white rhino from the brink of extinction. Breeding efforts increased the numbers from twenty animals at the start of the twentieth century to over 2500 by the late 2000s and rhino were even farmed out to repopulate other parts of Africa. However, sadly the success of this programme has in recent years been severely compromised by the rampant rhino poaching within the park – as well as in other South African parks such as Kruger – and today the number of white rhino is thought to be fewer than 1600.

ARRIVAL AND INFORMATION

Day-trips and tours There is no public transport to Hluhluwe-iMfolozi. If you don't have your own car, you can take a day-trip offered by any of the accommodation within an hour's drive of the park, or a tour operated by one of the Durban firms (see box, p.370).

By car Access to the park is via three gates. Just north of Mtubatuba, the R618 to Hlabisa and Nongoma reaches Nyalazi Gate after 27km, providing access to the southern section of the park. Further north, on the N2, an

HLUHLUWE-IMFOLOZI PARK

unclassified but signposted and tarred road near the turning for Hluhluwe village takes you 14km to Memorial Gate into the northernmost section of the park. A third gate, Cengeni, is accessible along a 30km tarred road from Ulundi to the west.

Information Maps and information, including details of game drives and guided walks, are available at the receptions of *Hilltop* and *Mpila* camps.

ACCOMMODATION

Accommodation is available in both the iMfolozi and Hluhluwe sections of the park, with iMfolozi being the less developed of the two. There are no fences around the iMfolozi camps, so take care when walking around, particularly at night. Hluhluwe's *Hilltop* camp has a pleasant **restaurant**, the *Mpunyane*, and a bar lounge, the *Usavolo*. Some of the bush lodges include the services of a cook to prepare your meals, although you'll have to provide the ingredients. *Hilltop* and *Mpila* camps also have small stores selling very basic supplies, but it's best to stock up before you enter the park; Hluhluwe village and Mtubatuba have well-stocked **supermarkets**. There are no campsites within the park, but there is a tented safari camp at Mpila with pre-erected tents. In iMfolozi you'll find the **Centenary Centre** (daily 9am–4.30pm), with a small takeaway restaurant, a craft centre, a rhino museum and information centre, and *bomas* that house animals brought from other parks to be introduced here. **Bookings** are made through KZN Wildlife (☎ 033 845 1000, ⦿ kznwildlife.com).

HLUHLUWE SECTION

★ **Hilltop Camp** ⦿ hilltopcamp.co.za; map opposite. Probably the best publicly run safari camp in South Africa, set high on the edge of a slope with sweeping views across the park's hills and valleys. The camp has modern, comfortable and varied accommodation: budget two-bed rondavels that share communal ablutions and kitchen facilities; self-catering en-suite chalets sleeping two to four, with kitchenettes; and two-person en-suite chalets without kitchens. There is also a restaurant and a shop. The camp is surrounded by an electric fence, which keeps out most animals, though nyala, zebra and other herbivores still graze around the chalets. R920

Mtwazi Lodge Near Hilltop; map opposite. Four luxurious en-suite rooms in the original home of the warden, set in a secluded garden. A chef is available to prepare meals. Minimum charge for six people. R5200

Muntulu and Munyawaneni bush lodges Map opposite. Four bedrooms with verandas at each of two upmarket lodges overlooking the Hluhluwe River. A cook is on hand to cater and a field ranger is available to take guests on walks. Minimum charge for six people. R5000

IMFOLOZI SECTION

Gqoyeni and Hlatikhulu bush lodges Map opposite. Both of these lodges have four two-bed units elevated

---

GAME VIEWING AND ACTIVITIES IN HLUHLUWE-IMFOLOZI

Despite its compact size, Hluhluwe-iMfolozi is home to 84 mammal species and close to 400 varieties of birds. The Big Five are all here, and it's no exaggeration to say that this is the best place in the world to see **rhino**, both black and white, despite the ongoing problems with poaching. About 160 elephants were introduced between 1985 and 1991 from Kruger, and that population today nears a thousand, which is fast approaching its ecological carrying capacity for a park of its size. Extinct in iMfolozi until 1958, **lions** have been reintroduced, and today they number around eighty, although they're not easy to see. Other **predators** present are cheetah, spotted hyena and wild dog. **Herbivores** include blue wildebeest, buffalo, giraffe, impala, kudu, nyala and zebra, although there are few hippo as the water in the rivers is too fast-moving most of the time. When it comes to **birds**, there are over a dozen species of **eagle**, as well as other **raptors** including hawks, goshawks and honey buzzards. Other larger birds include ground hornbills, vultures, owls and herons. **Reptile** species number in the sixties and include several types of venomous snake, none of which you're likely to see, but along the Hluhluwe River, keep an eye open for crocodiles and monitor lizards.

Apart from **self-driving** around the park, there are also **self-guided walks** near several of the restcamps, and both two-and-a-half-hour **game drives** (R330) and three-hour **game walks** (R290) each morning and evening from *Hilltop* and *Mpila* camps. In the morning, these depart at 5am (Oct–March) and 6am (April–Sept) so you must get to the park the previous night. The **wilderness trails** all start at *Mpila* camp in iMfolozi, and the reserve remains the best place in South Africa for these (all are available early Feb to mid-Dec). The three-night **base camp trail** (R4185) involves day walks in the Wilderness Area, with nights spent at the *Mndindini Trails* camp not far from *Mpila*; the three-night **primitive trail** (R2575) requires you to carry your own gear and sleep under the stars, wherever the ranger chooses, while the two-night **short wilderness trail** (R2520) starts from *Mpila*, and luggage and camping equipment is carried to a bush camp by donkeys. Both the primitive and the short wilderness trails can be extended by one night if you choose. You'll be accompanied by an armed ranger; all gear – including bedding, backpacks and food – is included in the price. They must be booked through KZN Wildlife well in advance as they are limited to a maximum of eight people.

5

above the Black Mfolozi River and are linked to the living area by wooden walkways. Their field ranger can conduct walks in the area, and there's a chef to cook meals. Minimum charge for six people. Gqoyeni R5700, Hlatikhulu R4500

Masinda Lodge Map p.402. Near Nyalazi Gate, this renovated upmarket lodge has three en-suite bedrooms decorated with Zulu art, plus the services of a cook. Minimum charge for six people. R3800

Mpila Camp Map p.402. This camp has excellent views of the surrounding wilderness from twelve one-roomed huts with two beds each, en-suite bathrooms and kitchenettes;

two self-contained three-bedroom cottages for seven people (minimum charge for five); and six self-catering chalets for five people (minimum charge for four). There's also a safari camp with twelve tents that sleep two people and two tents that sleep four. R1000

Nselweni Bush Lodge Map p.402. Located on the banks of the Black Mfolozi River, this lodge boasts wonderful views of the river and the bushveld. Its eight two-bed chalets are self-catering and share a comfortable lounge and a picturesque elevated veranda. Minimum charge for two people. R1360

Lake St Lucia

The most striking feature of the **iSimangaliso Wetland Park** is the 360-square-kilometre **Lake St Lucia**, South Africa's largest inland body of water, formed 25,000 years ago when the oceans receded. The lake is flanked by mountainous **dunes** covered by forest and grassland, whose peaks soar to an astonishing 200m above the beach to form a slender rampart against the Indian Ocean. Aside from the lake and dune ecosystems, the reserve protects a **marine zone** of warm tropical seas, coral reefs and endless sandy beaches; the **papyrus and reed wetland** of the Mkhuze swamps, on the north of the lake; and, on the western shore, dry **savanna** and **thornveld**. Any one of these would justify conservation, but their confluence around the lake makes this a world-class wilderness. The real prize of the area is **Cape Vidal** inside the wetland park, though the limited accommodation there may necessitate your making a day-trip from St Lucia town.

St Lucia

Once a rough and remote anglers' hangout, **ST LUCIA**, which lies at the mouth of the **St Lucia estuary** in the extreme south of the park, is in the process of reinventing itself as a well-organized eco-destination. The town's best feature is the **estuary**, the mouth of which was named Santa Lucia by Portuguese explorers when they reached it in 1576. During the second half of the eighteenth century, landlocked Boers made attempts to claim the estuary as a port, but were pipped at the post by the British, who sent HMS *Goshawk* in 1884 to annex the whole area, which then developed as a fishing resort. The estuary is hidden behind the buildings along the main drag, easy to miss if you drive quickly through.

The town of St Lucia lies 32km east of Mtubatuba, and can become pretty hectic in midsummer when **angling** fanatics descend for the school holidays. There's not much to do in St Lucia itself, but it does provide an excellent base for a number of activities (see box, p.406) and has a good choice of accommodation. Facilities in St Lucia include filling stations, a supermarket, self-service laundries, banks and ATMs.

St Lucia Crocodile Centre

Beside the Bhangazi Gate to Cape Vidal about 2km north of town • Daily 9am–4pm • R60 • Crocodile feeding Sat 3pm • ☎ 035 590 1386

This isn't another of the exploitative wildlife freak shows common throughout South Africa, but a serious educative spin-off from KZN Wildlife's crocodile conservation campaign. Until the end of the 1960s, "flat dogs" or "travelling handbags" were regarded as pests, and a hunting free-for-all saw them facing extinction in the area. Just in time, it was realized that crocs have an important role in the ecological cycle, and KZN Wildlife began a successful **breeding programme**, returning the crocs to the wild to bolster their numbers. The Crocodile Centre aims to rehabilitate the reputation of these maligned creatures, with informative displays and an astonishing cross section of species lounging around enclosed pools (only the Nile crocodile occurs in the wild in South Africa).

ARRIVAL AND INFORMATION

By minibus taxi Minibus taxis to Mtubatuba leave from the Dolphin Centre on the corner of McKenzie St and the R618 as you enter the village.

Tourist information The most helpful place is Advantage Tours & Charters at the Dolphin Centre on the corner of McKenzie St and the R618 as you enter the village

(Mon–Fri 8am–5pm, Sat 8am–2pm, Sun 8am–noon; ☎ 035 590 1259 ⓦ advantagetours.co.za), who can advise on accommodation and activities.

KZN Wildlife Has an office at the south end of Pelican Rd (daily 8.30am–4.30pm; ☎ 035 590 1340, ⓦ kznwildlife .com), two blocks east of and parallel to McKenzie St.

ACCOMMODATION

Elephant Lake Hotel 3 Mullet St ☎ 035 590 1001, ⓦ elephantlake.co.za. St Lucia's only hotel, complete with a pool and a restaurant with fantastic deck for evening drinks and views of the estuary. Also runs a second property, *Elephant Lake Inn*, at 41 Flamingo St. Rates include breakfast. R900

iGwalaGwala Guest House 91 Pelican St ☎ 035 590 1069, ⓦ igwalagwala.com. The spacious en-suite rooms here are simply but elegantly decorated, and the gracious hosts make you feel right at home. Some rooms open directly onto the quiet, leafy garden and swimming pool. R880

Jo-a-Lize Lodge 6 McKenzie St ☎ 035 590 1224, ✉ info@joalizelodge.com. One of the cheaper places in town, offering a variety of accommodation ranging from self-contained, self-catering flats to en-suite B&B units set around a pool. Rates include breakfast. R650

Marlin Lodge B&B 62 Garrick Ave ☎ 035 590 1929, ✉ info@marlinlodgestlucia.co.za. A friendly and convivial guesthouse whose light-filled rooms open onto a communal patio and pool, where guests gather to braai and socialize. Some rooms accommodate families. Rates include breakfast. R990

Monzi Safaris Backpackers 81 McKenzie St ☎ 035 590 1697, ⓦ monzisafaris.com/backpackers. Well-managed hostel on the main road with a well-stocked kitchen, comfortable outside lounge and

bar, and pool with sunbeds. Instead of dorms, there are pre-erected twin/double dome tents on wooden decks with proper camp beds and linen, plus a handful of double rooms at the back. Twin tent R440, doubles R520

★ **St Lucia Wetlands Guest House** 20 Kingfisher St ☎ 035 590 1098, ⓦ stluciawetlands.com. Six large rooms fitted out with elegant wooden furnishings, and there's a pool and a classy bar for guests. Exceptional service and the friendly atmosphere created by congenial hosts make this one of the best places to stay in St Lucia. Rates include breakfast. R1300

Sunset Lodge 154 McKenzie St ☎ 035 590 1197, ⓦ sunsetstlucia.co.za. Attractive, well-appointed self-catering log cabins sleeping two, four or five, with balconies and views of the estuary. Hippos occasionally feed on the lawn in front of the wooden pool deck. Good value, and great for families. R895

CAMPSITE

Sugarloaf Campsite Sugar Loaf Rd, south of town; book through KZN Wildlife ☎ 033 845 1000, or at the St Lucia office ☎ 035 590 1340, ⓦ kznwildlife.com. A sizeable campsite on the best site in St Lucia, right on the banks of the estuary, with an on-site swimming pool and plenty of fishing and birdwatching opportunities nearby. Two people R220

EATING AND DRINKING

Braza 73 McKenzie St ☎ 035 590 1242. Portuguese specialities like *espetada* (beef skewers with peppers) and *chouriço* (pork sausage), plus plenty of grilled meat, including a "Portuguese steak" topped with a fried egg (R120). Daily 11am–10pm.

Fisherman's 61 McKenzie St ☎ 035 590 1257. A good place for fresh seafood, this rough-and-ready local hangout is covered with fishing memorabilia. The owner himself is a fisherman, and serves up good prawns and seafood baskets (R85). At night it turns into one of the few bars in town. Daily 8am–midnight.

Ocean Basket Georgiou Centre ☎ 035 590 1241. It may be a chain, but good food and fast service make this one of the best places to eat in St Lucia. Big seafood platters and grilled fish served up in the pan (from R80) are the specialities of the house, and there's a pleasant balcony. Daily 10am–10pm.

Reef and Dune 51 McKenzie St ☎ 035 590 1048. A casual, family-friendly eatery decked out with picnic tables and a wrap-around deck. It serves the usual seafood, along with tasty grills like steak, ribs and eisbein from around R90. Daily 11.30am–11pm.

St Lucia Ski-Boat Club The end of Sugar Loaf Rd ☎ 035 590 1376. This pub and grill has a nice patio with pleasant views of the estuary (and hippos), making it a great place for sundowners. The food is mainly pub fare like burgers and fish and chips (R50). Daily noon–8.30pm.

Thyme Square 52 McKenzie St ☎ 035 590 1692. It may be decorated like Barbie's dream house, but this civilized little café is a relaxing place to indulge in tea and waffles with cream (R30), or a light and healthy lunch. Mon–Sat 9am–5pm, Sun 9am–4pm.

5

ACTIVITIES AROUND ST LUCIA

Small as it is, St Lucia is the biggest settlement around the iSimangaliso Wetland Park, and the best place to **organize activities**. If you're using St Lucia as a base from which to visit the Hluhluwe-iMfolozi Park, you can go on informative half- and full-day game drives (from R850) conducted by St Lucia-based Maputaland Tours (☎035 590 1041 or ☎082 899 7478, ⓦmaputaland.com), which also organizes other tours in and around St Lucia.

BIKING

A knowledgeable Zulu guide can lead you on a two- to three-hour gentle **cycle** through the southern part of the estuary, along the beach and around town; the guide will teach you about flora and fauna and the use of plants in Zulu culture and medicine along the way. Book through Shaka Barker Tours (R295 including bike rental; ☎035 590 1162, ⓦshakabarker.co.za).

FISHING

Deep-sea fishing trips, with a skipper, guide, experienced fisherman, bait and tackle supplied, are available for novices and seasoned anglers. Either tag and release your game fish or take it home to cook. Advantage Tours & Charters (☎035 590 1259, ⓦadvantagetours.co.za) runs six-hour trips from R1000 per person depending on numbers. Bring your own lunch and refreshments. Also enquire about charter boats at the St Lucia Ski-Boat Club.

HORSERIDING

Bhangazi Horse Safaris (☎083 792 7899, ⓦhorsesafari.co.za) offers **rides** through bushland, forests and lakes where you can view wildlife, or along the beach (R380/hr).

LAKE CRUISES

It's well worth going on a **lake cruise**, which gives you a good chance of seeing crocodiles and hippos, as well as pelicans, fish eagles, kingfishers and storks. Two-hour cruises are offered by most operators in town, the cheapest being the *Santa Lucia*, an 80-seater boat with a viewing deck and a bar operated by KZN Wildlife (R180; ☎035 590 1340). Shaka Barker Tours (R275) and Heritage Tours & Safaris (R240; ☎035 590 1555, ⓦheritagetoursandsafaris.com) go out in smaller boats and provide a more personalized experience with guides providing information about the wildlife and birds; refreshments are included.

WETLAND WILDLIFE TOURS

An outstanding range of **tours in the wetland** is operated by Shaka Barker Tours (see above), including the full-day St Lucia World Heritage Tour (R750) to the Eastern Shores and Cape Vidal, and the interesting and unusual Night Drive (R525; 3hr), which goes out in search of jackals, leopards, nightjars, owls and the sixteen chameleon species of the St Lucia region (a staggering fourteen of which are endemic). Also recommended is the one-night, two-day Turtle Tour (Nov–March; R4250) further up the coast to see leatherback and loggerhead turtles nesting, egg-laying and hatching, and walks led by local guides to the pans, grasslands and wetlands to learn about the ecology (R250; 3hr).

WHALE-WATCHING

Humpback and southern right whales cruise along the wetland's shore, and in season (June–Nov) you can join a **whale-watching boat trip** to look for them. Book through Advantage Tours & Charters (R990; 2hr); the trips leave from the Advantage office on McKenzie St. There's no jetty down at the beach and launching the boat into the waves is an adventure in itself – if the ocean is choppy, expect to get soaked.

Eastern Shores and Cape Vidal

Daily: April–Oct 6am–6pm; Nov–March 5am–7pm • R40, plus R50 per vehicle • ☎035 590 9012 • No public transport

Cape Vidal, a popular fishing spot within the iSimangaliso Wetland Park, is reached via a tarred road that heads north from St Lucia for 33km between the lake and the Indian Ocean (the extension of McKenzie Street goes to the Bhangazi Gate next to the St Lucia Crocodile Centre). En route you'll pass through the **Eastern Shores** area of grassland and wetlands populated by small game, birdlife and the occasional elephant and leopard, and several loop roads lead to game-viewing and scenic lookout points.

At the end of the road, a beautiful white-sand beach is right next to the KZN Wildlife accommodation. An offshore reef shelters the coast from the high seas, making it safe for **swimming** and providing good opportunities for **snorkelling** – you'll see hard and soft corals, colourful fish and tiny **rock pools** full of snails, crabs, sea cucumbers, anemones and urchins – while burly anglers use the rocks for casting their lines.

Whale-watching

Cape Vidal is an excellent place for shore sightings of **humpback whales**, which, in winter, breed off Mozambique not far to the north. In October they move south, drifting on the warm Agulhas current with their calves. If you're lucky you may see these and other whales from the dunes; a **whale-watching tower**, reached through the dune forest south of the restcamp, provides an even higher viewpoint. Eighteen-metre plankton-feeding whale sharks, the largest and gentlest of the sharks, have been sighted off this coast in schools of up to seventy at a time, and manta rays and dolphins are also common.

ACCOMMODATION — EASTERN SHORES AND CAPE VIDAL

Beach Log Cabins and Campsite Book through KZN Wildlife ☎ 033 845 1000, or at the St Lucia office ☎ 035 590 1340, ⓦ kznwildlife.com; map p.400. A collection of five- and eight-bed Swiss-style log cabins, all en suite and provided with linen and cooking utensils. Minimum charge for three and four people, respectively. There is space for fifty tents in the dune forest near the beach, with ablution facilities and power points. Bookings for the campsite in particular are vital during school holidays and over long weekends; there's a minimum charge for four and maximum per site is six. A small store sells basic supplies, bait, firewood and fuel. Three-person cabins R1575, camping for four R540

Western Shores

Daily: April–Oct 6am–6pm; Nov–March 5am–7pm • R40, plus R50 per vehicle • ☎ 035 550 9000

Accessible with your own transport or on a tour, the **Western Shores** section of Lake St Lucia has been transformed in recent years thanks to the managing authority of the iSimangaliso Wetland Park. Much of the area was formerly forestry plantation (mostly pine trees), but since 2007, and over a six-year period, alien trees were removed, allowing the indigenous vegetation to flourish. A 250-square-kilometre park was opened in 2013, which has been restocked with historically occurring game. It's now home to elephant, cheetah, buffalo, serval, tsessebe, giraffe, nyala, white and black rhino, zebra, red and grey duiker and wildebeest. Meanwhile, leopard has always been resident, and hippo, crocodile and a good variety of waterfowl can be seen in the numerous pans and wetlands. Game-viewing tracks include the uMphathe loop and uMdoni loop, which have several lookout points, while a boardwalk overlooks Lake St Lucia's narrows and has views as far as Cape Vidal in the north. About 5km northeast of Nhlozi Gate in the northeast of the park is **Charters Creek**, which is set on a wooded bluff looking eastward over Lake St Lucia and is a favourite spot to see both forest and aquatic birds.

ARRIVAL AND INFORMATION — WESTERN SHORES

By car Access is via Dukuduku Gate on the R618 just before St Lucia, or Nhlozi Gate off the N2, 20km north of Mtubatuba and 32km south of Hluhluwe. It's feasible to enter one gate and exit the other, which takes about 1hr 30min with stops. There is no accommodation, but Dukuduku Gate is only 3km from St Lucia. Many of the tour operators there offer 3hr safaris in open-top vehicles from R450; try Heritage Tours & Safaris (☎ 035 590 1555, ⓦ heritagetoursandsafaris.com) or Jabisa Tours (☎ 035 590 1635, ⓦ jabisatours.co.za).

False Bay

Daily 6am–6pm • R34 • ☎ 035 562 0425

False Bay perches on the western shore of a small, lozenge-shaped waterway connected to the top end of Lake St Lucia by a narrow, steep-sided channel known colourfully as "Hell's Gates". Two self-guided hikes, the 8km **Dugandlovu Trail** and the 10km circular **Mpophomeni Trail**, are clearly waymarked. They pass through a mixed terrain of woodland,

5

open savannah, shoreline, and one of the richest remaining pockets of sand forest left in South Africa. They offer the opportunity of seeing birds and a decent variety of antelope like nyala and suni and other small mammals such as mongooses and warthogs. There are picnic sites and a viewing platform at Lister Point overlooking the lake.

ARRIVAL AND ACCOMMODATION   FALSE BAY

By car You reach False Bay via Hluhluwe (see p.400); continue east through the village to a T-junction at the end of the road and follow the signposts for 15km to the False Bay Gate.
Falaza Game Park ☎ 035 562 2319, ⓦ falaza.co.za; map p.400. For a touch of luxury, head for this slick tented accommodation in a small reserve, which also boasts a restaurant, swimming pool and reasonably priced spa.

Activities can be arranged, such as guided walks around False Bay or game drives into Hluhluwe-iMfolozi Park. R2100
Sand Forest Lodge ☎ 082 417 6484 or ☎ 083 627 7080, ⓦ sandforest.co.za; map p.400. A collection of campsites and self-catering cottages, located on a small reserve with antelope, zebra and wildebeest. Meals are available on request. Camping R120, cottages R700

Mkhuze Game Reserve

Daily: April–Oct 6am–6pm; Nov–March 5am–7pm • R40, plus R50 per vehicle • ☎ 035 573 9004

Reached across the Lebombo Mountains, 28km east of **Mkhuze** village on the N2, **Mkhuze Game Reserve** is notable for its varied and beautiful countryside and rich birdlife, although it is also home to the Big Five. The reserve is a major part of the iSimangaliso Wetland Park, connected to the coastal plain by a slender corridor through which the Mkhuze River flows before emptying into Lake St Lucia. It marks the final haul of the coastal plain stretching down the east of the continent from Kenya. The

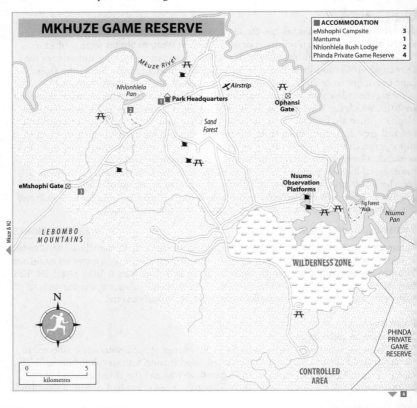

MKHUZE GAME RESERVE

ACCOMMODATION	
eMshophi Campsite	3
Mantuma	1
Nhlonhela Bush Lodge	2
Phinda Private Game Reserve	4

landscape varies from the **Muzi Pans**, wetlands consisting of seasonal flood plains floating with waterlilies, reed beds and swamps, to savanna. Elsewhere you'll come across stands of acacias, and in the south across the Mkhuze River you can wander through the cathedral-like fig forest that echoes to the shriek of trumpeter hornbills.

ARRIVAL AND INFORMATION   MKHUZE GAME RESERVE

By car If you're driving, the easiest way to get to the reserve is to leave the N2 at Mkhuze village and follow the signs along a good dirt road to eMshophi Gate. An alternative route to the same gate, which leaves the N2 further south, 35km north of Hluhluwe, involves a lot more driving on dirt and doesn't knock much off the distance. From Sodwana Bay and the northeast, travel south on the R22 and turn right down the D820 for 14km to the Ophansi Gate.

On a tour There's no public transport into Mkhuze, and if you don't have your own vehicle you'll need to join one of the daytime or night-time excursions into the park from Mkhuze village.

Information The park reception office at Mantuma, 9km from the entrance gate, provides a clear map showing all routes and distances and giving general information about the park. You can buy fuel at the entrance gate, and there's a shop selling basic supplies and books at reception, but you should stock up on provisions in Mkhuze village before heading out.

ACCOMMODATION

Ghost Mountain Inn On Fish Eagle Rd in Mkhuze village, signposted off the N2 ☎ 035 573 1025, 🌐 ghostmountaininn.co.za; map p.400. An attractive hotel with a broad range of rooms and good facilities, great for a drink or meal and a dunk in their pool even if you aren't staying. They organize 4hr game drives to Mkhuze (R800 per person for two people; R590 per person/four people), as well as a number of other options in the reserve, including bird walks and night drives, plus guided hikes up Ghost Mountain, which overlooks Mkhuze (3–4hr; R195). <u>R1970</u>

Mantuma 9km into the park in the northern section; book through KZN Wildlife ☎ 033 845 1000, 🌐 kzn wildlife.com; map opposite. The reserve's main restcamp and reception has a range of accommodation, the cheapest being two-bed rest huts with shared bathrooms and a kitchen. There are also larger chalets

GAME VIEWING AND ACTIVITIES IN MKHUZE

Some 84km of roads traverse Mkhuze, but one of the best ways to see game is to stay put and wait for the animals to come to you. Several **hides** have been erected at artificial watering holes and on the edge of pans, which attract plenty of animals, particularly in the drier months.

Mkhuze is among the top spots for **birdwatching** in the country, with an impressive 420 species on record. Some of the prizes include Pels fishing owl and Rudd's apalis, a small, insect-eating bird with a very restricted distribution. Even if you know nothing about birds, you're likely to appreciate one of Africa's most colourful here – the lilac-breasted roller. The two hides at **Nsumo Pan**, in the southern section of the park, overlook a beautiful natural waterway, and are superbly placed for observing **waterfowl**. Between July and September, if conditions are right, you can see up to five hundred birds on the water at one time, among them flocks of pelicans and flamingos, kingfishers, fish eagles, and many other species.

The other draw of Mkhuze is that it is now a Big Five reserve after the introduction of **lions**; they were relocated from Tembe Elephant Park in 2013 and Tswalu Kalahari Reserve in 2016, and to date several litters have been born. **Elephants** are easily seen, black and white **rhinos** are present, although not in the great numbers seen in Hluhluwe-iMfolozi Park, while cheetah and leopard are sometimes glimpsed. You also stand a very good chance of seeing several types of **antelope**, including nyala, impala, eland and kudu, and **primates** such as baboons and vervet monkeys can generally be seen rustling around in the trees and making a nuisance of themselves on the ground.

KZN Wildlife offers a number of activities, including recommended **night drives** from Mantuma (R250). During the day, you can explore Mkhuze on foot with a field ranger on two-hour **walks** (R150) that concentrate on either game or birds. Also good for birding is the two-hour guided **Mkhuze Fig Forest Walk** (R250) – this is another highlight of the reserve and includes a game drive to and from the start. Sycamore fig forest is one of the rarest types of woodland in South Africa, and the stands of massive trees along the banks of the Mkhuze River are upwards of 400 years old.

that sleep two, four or six. The most enticing units, however, are the large two- or four-person safari tents, each with its own ablutions. **R800**

Nhlonhlela Bush Lodge Overlooking Nhlonhlela Pan between Mantuma and eMshophi Gate; book through KZN Wildlife ☎ 035 573 9004, ⊛ kznwildlife.com; map p.408. Four two-bed rooms connected by wooden walkways to a communal kitchen and living area. There's a cook (you bring the ingredients) and a field ranger included in the price. Minimum charge for six. Six people **R3400**

Phinda Private Game Reserve Book through &Beyond Africa ☎ 011 809 4300, ⊛ andbeyond.com; map p.408. Considered the best private game reserve in KwaZulu-Natal and covering 170 square kilometres at Mkhuze's southern end, *Phinda* offers good chances of seeing lion, cheetah and both species of rhino.

Accommodation is at five opulent lodges in a variety of original styles, from stilted Afro-Japanese timber houses to intimate chalets chiselled into the rock. All provide hospitality of the highest standard, and game drives and walks are accompanied by well-informed expert guides who are as good as any you'll find in South Africa. Rates include all meals and game activities. **R12,000**

CAMPSITE

eMshophi Campsite 1km beyond eMshophi Gate; book through KZN Wildlife ☎ 033 845 1000, or direct ☎ 035 573 9004, ⊛ kznwildlife.com; map p.408. A simple, fairly large campsite handily located near the reserve's main entrance, with hot showers and a swimming pool; minimum charge for three in high season (namely Christmas and Easter). **R85**

Maputaland

Known as **Maputaland**, the extreme northeast section of the Elephant Coast is the remotest tract of South Africa and is bordered by the Indian Ocean to the east and the low-lying Lebombo Mountains to the west. A humid, subtropical and green wilderness area of lakes, estuaries, coastal forests, dune fields and beaches, much of it falls within the iSimangaliso Wetland Park. Once only accessible along dirt roads that worked their tortuous way to the coast, the region has opened up considerably thanks the tarring of the **R22** road that strikes north from **Hluhluwe** village for some 185km, passing **Sodwana Bay** and **Kosi Bay** before continuing on into Mozambique. This road also provides access to the **Ndumo Game Reserve** and **Tembe Elephant Park**, both reserves reaching down from the Mozambique border. Another tarred road, 11km north of **Mkhuze** village, snakes north via Jozini and then east for 133km, passing these two parks and eventually connecting with the R22 about 40km south of Kosi Bay – this is the normal route to Maputaland for those coming from Gauteng. Note that a 4WD, or at least a vehicle with high clearance, is required to get into some of the coastal reserves in the iSimangaliso Wetland Park.

Sodwana Bay

Around 80km northeast of Hluhluwe village · Daily 24hr · R35, plus R50 per vehicle · ☎ 035 571 0051/2

A tiny scoop in the Zululand Coast, **SODWANA BAY** is the only breach in an almost flawless strand extending 170km from St Lucia to Kosi Bay. It's the fortuitous convergence of the bay (which makes it easy to launch boats) with the world's southernmost coral reefs that makes Sodwana the most popular base in the country for **scuba diving** and the most popular KZN Wildlife resort. Because the continental shelf comes extremely close to shore (near-vertical drops are less than 1km away), it offers very deep waters, much loved by anglers who gather here for some of South Africa's best deep-sea **game fishing**, mostly tag and release. The abundance of game fish also makes for some of the best surf fly-fishing in the country.

When there's no one around, Sodwana Bay is paradise, with tepid waters, terrific sandy beaches, relaxed diving and snorkelling, and plenty of accommodation. Over weekends and during school holidays, however, fashion-conscious Joburgers tear down in their 4WDs, while anglers from Gauteng, Free State and Mpumalanga come here and drink themselves into a stupor. A gentler presence is the leatherback and loggerhead **turtles**, which have been making their way onto Sodwana's beaches for the last 60,000 years, and come from as far afield as Kenya and Cape Agulhas. Nesting season is usually from November to the end of February, and the hatching season is from the middle of January to the end of April each year. Meanwhile, pods of bottlenose dolphins routinely patrol up and down the coast, and, between June and November, southern right and humpback whales may be spotted beyond the breakers.

ARRIVAL, INFORMATION AND TOURS
SODWANA BAY

By minibus taxi Minibus taxis run to Sodwana Bay from Mbazwana (16km). If you haven't got your own vehicle, you'll have to either hitchhike your way around as the place is so spread out, or Off-Road Adventures in the village (☎063 870 7985, ⓦoffroadfun.co.za) runs minibus shuttles between Mbazwana, Sodwana Bay and the beaches (R30 per ride; minimum four people). They will also quote for transfers from Hluhluwe and Richards Bay.

Tourist facilities The park entry gate (24hr), and Ezemvelo KZN Wildlife office (Mon–Thurs 8am–4.30pm, Fri & Sat 7am–4.30pm, Sun 7am–3pm; ☎035 571

0051/2), are up the hill past the town. A small supermarket is across the road from the office, and fuel is available at the gate.

Guided Tours During the turtle nesting season from mid-November to the end of April, you can join a fascinating guided 4hr after-dark tour (R800) with Ufudu Turtle Tours (☎082 391 1503, ⓦufuduturtletours.co.za), the only operator permitted to conduct turtle tours in the Sodwana Bay area. Pre-booking is essential as spaces are limited to one vehicle per night and demand is very high. The excursion includes hot and soft drinks and a light dinner.

ACCOMMODATION

Some of the accommodation at Sodwana Bay lies inside the Ezemvelo KZN Wildlife property along the beach. If you're staying inside the property at the privately run *Coral Divers* or *Mseni*, you must pay an additional R95 daily fee to Ezemvelo KZN Wildlife. *Mseni* includes the fee in its rate; to stay at *Coral Divers*, pay the fee at the Ezemvelo KZN Wildlife office.

Coral Divers Sodwana Main Rd ☎035 571 0290, ⓦcoraldivers.co.za; map p.400. The largest dive outfit at Sodwana Bay is a basic but friendly divers' haunt with two-bed safari tents and two-bed cabins with or without their own bathrooms (those without use the KZN Wildlife ablutions); note that at least one person in each room must be planning to dive. You can self-cater or pay for half board, and takeaways are available throughout the day. Free transport to and from the beach to coincide with dives and meal times. Self-catering R390

Ezemvelo KZN Wildlife accommodation Spread along behind the beach south of the gate ☎035 571 0051, ⓦkznwildlife.com; map p.400. Twenty fully equipped log

cabins with either four or six beds, with minimum charges for three and four people, respectively. There are also a staggering 380 campsites here (minimum charge for four), and the seasonal population explosion allegedly makes Sodwana Bay the largest campsite in South Africa. Camping for four people R520, cabin for three people R1500

Mseni Beach Lodge Right on the water's edge, south of the village ☎033 345 6531 or ☎087 803 5878, ⓦmseni.co.za; map p.400. The only establishment with direct access to the beach, this comfortable lodge offers en-suite B&B log cabins or self-catering units sleeping two to eight people spread out amid thick coastal forest. There's a restaurant, bar and swimming pool. R870

DIVING AND SNORKELLING IN SODWANA BAY

Unless you're a keen angler, the principal reason to come to Sodwana Bay is for the diving off the **coral reefs** that thrive here in the warm waters carried down the coast by the Agulhas current. The sea is clear, silt-free and perfect for spotting some of the 1200 varieties of **fish** that inhabit the waters off northern KwaZulu-Natal, making it second only to the Great Barrier Reef in its richness.

The closest reef to the bay, and consequently the most visited, is **Two Mile Reef**, 2km long and 900m wide, offering excellent dives. Among the others is **Five Mile Reef**, which is further north and known for its miniature staghorn corals, while beyond that, **Seven Mile Reef** is inhabited by large anemone communities and offers protection to turtles and rays, which may be found resting here.

There's excellent **snorkelling** at Jesser Point, a tiny promontory at the southern end of the bay. Just off here is **Quarter Mile Reef**, which attracts a wide variety of fish, including moray eels and rays. Low tide is the best time to venture out. You can buy competitively priced snorkels and masks (or rent them for R30 per day) from the *Sodwana Bay Lodge Scuba Centre* (☎035 571 0117, ⓦsodwanadiving.co.za). Here you'll also find a **dive operation** offering various diving courses, diving packages and scuba equipment rental. There are also several other dive operators providing similar services.

5

Natural Moments Next to Sodwana Bay Lodge, Sodwana Main Rd ☎ 083 236 1756, ⊛ divesodwana .com; map p.400. A friendly and somewhat bohemian backpackers and dive school offering rustic but cosy cabins, most priced as dorms and some en suite, along with a couple of family units and a big communal kitchen. During the summer there's a good pizza joint out front, and campsites across the road. Camping R95, dorms R170, doubles R460

Sodwana Bay Lodge Sodwana Main Rd, in the village ☎ 035 571 9101 or ☎ 035 571 9113, ⊛ sodwanabay lodge.co.za; map p.400. Simple yet comfortable reed and thatched en-suite, two-bed B&B chalets. The *Leatherbacks Seafood and Grill* and a poolside bar with sun deck attracts visitors and locals. Meal packages available. R990

EATING

Most of the lodges have bars and restaurants that are open to all, and these are the best places to join in with the post-diving camaraderie.

The Lighthouse Sodwana Main Rd ☎ 083 471 0868. The classiest restaurant Sodwana has to offer, with pasta, seafood and good thin-crust pizzas (around R70) served on a pleasant patio strewn with fairy lights. Winter Thurs–Sun 8.30am–9pm; summer daily 8am–10pm.

Twisted Sisters Sodwana Main Rd ☎ 083 937 0780. A rustic shack with a tin roof and colourful art on the walls creates a bohemian feel, while the tapas and Mediterranean-style menu is chalked up on a blackboard and might feature mussels in white wine sauce (R125) or Portuguese chicken with slaw (R80). Tues–Sun noon–9pm.

Lake Sibaya

Lake Sibaya, South Africa's largest natural freshwater lake, covers 77 square kilometres and is fringed by white sandy beaches disappearing into dense forest. On a windless day, the lake, 10km due north of Sodwana Bay, appears glassy, azure and flat; the waters are so transparent that when KZN Wildlife take a hippo census they just fly over and count the dark blobs clearly visible from the air. From the margins, timid crocodiles cut the lake surface, exchanging the warmth of the sun for the safety of the water. This is not an unpopulated wilderness: the lake fringes are dotted with traditional African lands and villages. There's an exceptionally easy-going 3km **circular walk** that starts from the viewing platform behind KZN Wildlife's now closed *Baya Camp*, or you can drive it too. **Birdwatching** can be rewarding (there are two hides), with close on three hundred species present. Needless to say, with crocs and hippos lolling about, swimming in the lake is most unwise.

ARRIVAL AND DEPARTURE   LAKE SIBAYA

By car Approaching from the south on the R22, just north of Mbazwana turn right onto a dirt track. Next look for the fork and follow the D1848 road left to the lake. From the north, follow directions to Mabibi via the Coastal Forest turn-off (below), and once there drive south to the lake. Both routes are sandy and a 4WD is essential.

Mabibi

Daily 6am–6pm • R22, plus R20 per vehicle • ☎ 035 592 0235

Part of the iSimangaliso Wetland Park's Coastal Forest section, **MABIBI** is probably one of the most peaceful spots to camp in South Africa, where you can pitch your tent in luxuriant subtropical forest and follow a boardwalk down the duneside to the **sea** – a walk that takes about ten minutes. Outside school holidays, there's a fair chance of having a perfect tropical beach all to yourself, and you won't get the frenetic activity of outboard motors and 4WD vehicles found further south. The coast here offers **surf angling** and **snorkelling** matching that at Sodwana Bay, with rich tropical marine life thriving on the coral reefs offshore. A number of mammals live in the forest, but most of them – bushbabies, large-spotted genets and porcupines – only come out after dark.

ARRIVAL AND DEPARTURE   MABIBI

By car On the R22, 18km north of Mbazwana, turn right at the Coastal Forest turn-off and it's 24km to the gate. Soon untarred, this becomes a sandy track and is strictly 4WD. If you are in a regular car, you can park at the Coastal Cashews office (just under 5km from the R22) and arrange a transfer to the *Thonga Beach Lodge* and *Rocktail Beach Camp* (see opposite).

ACCOMMODATION

Mabibi Beach Camp ☎ 035 474 1504, ⓦ mabibi campsite.co.za; map p.400. Three remote and idyllic two-person chalets and eight camping pitches situated in subtropical forest, perched on a plateau on top of the dunes and sheltered from the wind. A boardwalk leads down to the sea. Camping **R134**, chalets **R728**

Thonga Beach Lodge ☎ 035 474 1473, ⓦ thonga beachlodge.co.za; map p.400. This luxury Robinson Crusoe-style lodge offers stunning thatched suites secluded in the coastal dune forest, along with a spa, dive operation, turtle-tracking tours, kayaking and sundowners at Lake Sibaya. Full board **R10,580**

Rocktail Bay

South Africa's most sublime beach-stay lies about 20km north of Mabibi along the coast at **ROCKTAIL BAY**, a stretch of sand and sea that's restricted to guests who are prepared to pay for the privilege. Few parts of the South African coastline are as unspoilt as the beaches around here. There's excellent **scuba diving** offshore, and a dive centre at Rocktail Beach Camp – one of the highlights is diving with pregnant ragged-tooth sharks as they migrate north up the KwaZulu-Natal coast from around late September to May. The **birdwatching** here is excellent; among a number of rare species are the green coucal, grey waxbill, Natal robin and – particularly prized – palmnut vulture.

Rocktail Bay is another great spot for viewing loggerhead and leatherback **turtles**, and **surf fishing** for kingfish, barracuda, blacktail and the like is another possibility.

ACCOMMODATION   ROCKTAIL BAY

Rocktail Beach Camp Book through Wilderness Safaris ☎ 011 807 1800, ⓦ wilderness-safaris.com; map p.400. The comfortable *Rocktail Beach Camp* is the ideal way to get away from it all. There are seventeen luxurious yet rustic en-suite rooms a short walk from the beach, each decorated with natural materials and

enjoying sweeping views of the coastal forest. Activities include turtle-watching, forest walks and diving, and there is a children's programme of things to do. Vehicles are left at the Coastal Cashews office (see opposite) and guests get ferried in by 4WD (included in the rate). Full board **R6270**

Kosi Bay

Kosi Mouth, 7km north of KwaNgwanase • Daily 6am–6pm • R43, plus R43 per vehicle • ☎ 035 592 0236

At the northernmost reaches of the KwaZulu-Natal coast, **KOSI BAY** is just before the Farazela Border between South Africa and Mozambique and at the centre of an enthralling area of waterways fringed by forest. Despite the name, this is not a bay at all, but a system of four lakes connected by narrow reed channels, which eventually empty into the sea at Kosi Mouth.

One of the most striking images of Kosi Bay is of mazes of reed fences in the estuary and other parts of the lake system. These are **fish traps**, or kraals, built by local Tonga people, a sustainable practice that has been going on for hundreds of years. The traps are passed down from father to son, and capture only a small fraction of the fish that pass through, with trap numbers strictly controlled. To see the fish traps – and the beach – you'll need to travel to **Kosi Mouth**, a hard-going twenty-minute drive for which you'll need 4WD. The Umdoni day-visitor area at the *Ezemvelo KZN Wildlife Restcamp* is shaded and has braai facilities.

ACCOMMODATION   KOSI BAY

Ezemvelo KZN Wildlife Restcamp On the western shore of Lake Nhlange; book through KZN Wildlife ☎ 033 845 1000, or camp reception ☎ 035 592 0236, ⓦ kznwildlife.com; map p.400. Two-bed, five-bed (minimum charge for four people) and six-bed cabins, and a small campsite with hot showers; some sites have power points and lake views. Drinks are available from reception. Access is strictly 4WD. Camping **R115**, cabins **R780**

Kosi Bay Lodge 2km before the reserve gate ☎ 083 262 4865, ⓦ kosibaylodge.co.za; map p.400. Popular as a place to stay overnight on the way to Mozambique but great as a base to explore the area too, and regular cars can reach here. There are two-, four- and six-bed rustic thatch-and-reed chalets on stilts, with kitchens, plus safari tents with shared bathrooms, a restaurant/pub and pool with sun deck. Self-catering or full board and plenty of

5

excursions including boat rides on Lake Nhlange are available. Safari tent R520, chalets R660

★**Kosi Forest Lodge** Inside the reserve ☎035 474 1473, ⓦisibindiafrica.co.za; map p.400. Arguably the most dreamy place to stay in KwaZulu-Natal, featuring eight reed-and-thatch suites in a remote landscape of palms, lakes, sand forest and bleached white beaches. There's limited electricity, and if you don't have your own 4WD you'll be collected from KwaNgwanase. Activities include game drives, guided canoeing trips, reef snorkelling and forest walks; there's a good chance you'll see hippos, crocodiles and turtles. Full board R4340

★**Thobeka Backpackers Lodge** 4km north of KwaNgwanase ☎035 592 9728 or ☎072 446 1525, ⓦkosi.co.za; map p.400. A delightfully rustic, friendly backpackers hidden away in the forest, with bush camp style rooms connected by wooded boardwalks, family cottages, dorms and camping, plus a self-catering kitchen, bar and pool. Owners Pieter and Maryna go out of their way to organize a variety of activities, including snorkelling tours into Mozambique, trips to a colourful border market and even courses in bush cooking. Camping R180, dorm R250, doubles R650

Tembe Elephant Park

Daily: April–Sept 6am–6pm; Oct–March 5am–7pm • R30, plus R35 per vehicle • ☎082 651 2868, ⓦtembe.co.za

The easy-going and remote **Tembe Elephant Park**, on the border with Mozambique, is co-managed by KZN Wildlife and the local Tembe community. Access is limited to those staying in the delightful tented camp, the only accommodation in the park, plus ten private 4WD vehicles per day, which are permitted – but only by pre-arrangement, as a guide accompanies each car. Tembe has a variety of interesting habitats, including sand forests, pans, wetlands and savannas that support more than 200 elephants that are well known for their large tusks and exceptional size; sightings are almost guaranteed. The park also contains the other Big Five species and there's a good chance of seeing white rhino and buffalo, even leopard during daylight hours, as well as nyala, impala and suni antelope and more than 340 species of bird.

ARRIVAL AND ACCOMMODATION

TEMBE ELEPHANT PARK

By car Tembe is on the D1837, 38km west of KwaNgwanase and 15km east of the turn-off to Ndumo. If staying overnight, you leave your car at the gate and are transferred to the park's own vehicle. A 4WD is required for driving yourself.

Tembe Elephant Park Safari tents ☎082 651 2868, ⓦtembe.co.za; map p.400. Accommodation at Tembe is in comfortable en-suite safari tents built on raised wooden platforms. The price includes all meals and game drives conducted by knowledgeable guides from the local community, with traditional Tembe dancers coming to perform in the evenings at the boma restaurant and bar. Guests pay an additional R50 per night community levy to the Tembe community. R3200

Ndumo Game Reserve

Daily: April–Sept 6am–6pm; Oct–March 5am–7pm • R60, plus R50 per vehicle • ☎035 591 0058

One of the most beautiful of the KwaZulu-Natal reserves, **Ndumo** looks across the flood plain into Mozambique to the north and up to the Lebombo Mountains in the south. Its northern extent hugs the **Usutu River**, which rises in Swaziland and defines South Africa's border with Mozambique.

No great volume of animals inhabits the reserve (nyala, hippo and both species of rhino are among the 62 mammal species here), and they may be more difficult to see than elsewhere. For twitchers, however, Ndumo ranks among the country's top **bird-watching** spots. The staggering 430 different varieties recorded here include the African broadbill, Pels fishing owl and the southern banded snake eagle.

It's possible to **drive** around some areas: one of the highlights is the trip to **Redcliffs**, where there's a picnic site with a vantage point offering soaring views across the Usutu River into both Swaziland and Mozambique.

ARRIVAL AND TOURS

NDUMO GAME RESERVE

By car The turn-off to the reserve is on the D1837 15km west of Tembe and 56km north of Jozini. A rough gravel track then goes 16km to the gate.

Tours A great way to explore the reserve is on the KZN

5

Wildlife morning and evening game drives (R250) to the lovely Inyamiti pan, which is inhabited by hippos, crocodiles and an array of waterfowl; guided walks are also available (R150).

ACCOMMODATION

Ndumo Restcamp Book through KZN Wildlife ☎ 033 845 1000, or camp reception ☎ 035 591 0058, ⓦ kznwildlife.com; map p.400. There are a number of campsites and seven well-maintained, two-bed huts perched on a hill, each with a fridge and shared ablutions. A shop near the entrance gate sells basic supplies, but you're better off stocking up en route. Camping R130, huts R800

Ithala Game Reserve

Daily: March–Oct 6am–6pm; Nov–Feb 5am–7pm • R120 • ☎ 034 983 2540

West of Maputaland and close to the Swaziland border, the small **Ithala Game Reserve** is little known, despite being one of the country's most uncrowded and spectacularly scenic places to watch wildlife. Ithala is largely mountainous and the terrain is extremely varied, with numerous cliffs and rock faces contained within a protective basin.

Like the rest of the KwaZulu-Natal game reserves, Ithala is excellent for white **rhino** and there's plenty of **plains game**, including zebra and giraffe. Of the **predators**, you could, if you're very lucky, encounter brown hyena, cheetah and leopard. If want to see the Big Five, however, Ithala is not for you – there are no lions, though the other four make periodic appearances. The best idea is to forget the mammal checklist and take a slow drive around the mountains into the valleys and along the watercourses. One of the most rewarding **drives** is along Ngubhu Loop, with a detour to Ngubhu picnic site.

ARRIVAL, INFORMATION AND TOURS ITHALA GAME RESERVE

By car There's no public transport to the park or near it, so driving is the only option. The entrance gate is just off the R69 near the village of Louwsburg, 70km east of Vryheid and 74km southwest of Pongola on the N2.

Information The camp's reception can provide information and maps, and fuel is available.

Tours There are some self-guided trails into the wooded mountainside above *Ntshondwe Camp*, which give the chance to stretch your legs if you've spent a morning driving around. Day and night drives (R250) and game walks with snacks and drinks (R250) can be organized.

ACCOMMODATION AND EATING

Ithala is a little out of the way, so ensure you pre-book accommodation, all through KZN Wildlife (☎ 033 845 1000, ⓦ kznwildlife.com); otherwise try camp reception in quiet times or for cancellations (☎ 035 591 0058). If you want to self-cater, you'll need to bring supplies – the camp shop specializes in beer and frozen meat and hasn't much by way of fresh food. Louwsburg has a very small general store that's a little better.

Doornkraal Campsite Map p.400. Ithala's basic but secluded campsite lies in the west of the reserve near *Mbizo Bush Camp* and is unfenced so animals wander through. It has flushing toilets and hot bush showers in reed huts, braai pits and a communal dining area, but only accommodates twenty people in total so reservations are advised. R150

Mbizo Bush Camp Map p.400. For a pared-down bush experience, you can't beat this marvellous bush camp with space for just eight people, shaded by thorn trees and ilala palms, on the banks of the Mbizo River where you can swim. There's a braai and campfire area and hot showers. Minimum charge for five people. R2450

Mhlangeni and Thalu Bush Camps Map p.400. A wonderful choice for something a bit wilder, these camps enjoy beautiful secluded settings and have four (minimum charge for three) or ten (minimum charge for seven) beds respectively. Both are staffed by an attendant and you can arrange a ranger to take you on walks. *Thalu* (three people R1470, *Mhlangeni* (seven people) R3430

★Ntshondwe Camp Map p.400. This is one of the best game-reserve restcamps in South Africa, offering comfortable two-, four- and six-bed self-catering chalets with fully equipped kitchens, lounge areas and verandas, as well as two-bed, non-self-catering units. Each chalet is surrounded by indigenous bush through which paved walkways weave their way around granite rocks and trees to the main reception area and swimming pool. The camp's restaurant (daily 7.30–9.30am & 6.30–9pm) serves surprisingly varied range of food from *escargot* to steaks – though meat-free meals aren't always on the menu – an takeaways can be eaten in your chalet. There's also a cosy bar whose sun deck looks out over the watering hole and across the valleys. R1020

Ntshondwe Lodge Map p.400. Next to the restcamp, yet

completely secluded, this luxury lodge has three beautifully decorated rooms and a small plunge pool overlooking the reserve; there's a minimum charge for five people. A cook is on hand to prepare food you bring. R3200

Central Zululand and the Battlefields

Central Zululand – the Zulu heartland – radiates out from the unlovely modern town of **Ulundi**, some 30km west of the Hluhluwe-iMfolozi Park. At the height of its influence in the 1820s and 1830s, under King Shaka, the core of the Zulu state lay between the **Black Mfolozi River** in the north and the **Tugela River** in the south, which discharges into the Indian Ocean roughly 100km north of Durban.

Contained in a relatively small area to the west of the heartland is a series of nineteenth-century **battlefield sites**, where Zulus and Boers, then Zulus and the British, and finally Boers and Brits came to blows. Don't attempt to visit this area on your own: all you'll see is empty veld with a few memorials. It's far better to join a tour with one of the several excellent guides who make it their business to bring the region's dramatic history to life (see box, p.424).

Don't expect to see "tribal" people who conform to the Zulu myth outside theme parks like Shakaland, near Eshowe (see box, p.421). Traditional dress and the **traditional lifestyle** are largely a nineteenth-century phenomenon, deliberately smashed by the British a century ago when they imposed a poll tax that had to be paid in cash – thus ending Zulu self-sufficiency, generating urbanization and forcing the Africans into the modern industrial economy, where they were needed as workers.

You will find beautiful Zulu crafts in this part of the country, the best examples being in museums such as the little-known but outstanding **Vukani Zulu Cultural Museum** in Eshowe (see p.420). Also worth checking out is the reconstructed royal enclosure of Cetshwayo, the last king of the independent Zulu, at **Ondini**, near Ulundi.

Brief history

The truth behind the Zulus is difficult to separate from the mythology, which was fed by the Zulus themselves as well as white settlers. Accounts of the Zulu kingdom in the 1820s rely heavily on the diaries of the two adventurers, **Henry Fynn** and **Nathaniel Isaacs**, who portrayed King Shaka as a mercurial and bloodthirsty tyrant who killed his subjects willy-nilly for a bit of fun. In a letter from Isaacs to Fynn, uncovered in the 1940s, Isaacs encourages his friend to depict the Zulu kings as "bloodthirsty as you can, and describe frivolous crimes people lose their lives for. It all tends to swell up the work and make it interesting."

A current debate divides historians about the real extent of the **Zulu empire** during the nineteenth century. What we do know is that in the 1820s Shaka consolidated a state that was one of the most powerful political forces on the subcontinent, and that internal dissent to his rule culminated in his assassination by his half-brothers **Dingane and Mhlangana** in 1828.

In the 1830s, pressure from white settlers exacerbated internal tensions among the Zulus, which reached a climax when a relatively small party of Boers defeated Dingane's army at **Blood River**. This led to a split in the Zulu state, with one half following **King Mpande**, and collapse threatened when Mpande's sons Mbuyazi and Cetshwayo led opposing forces in a pitched battle for succession. **Cetshwayo** emerged victorious and successfully set about rebuilding the state, but too late. Seeing a powerful Zulu state as a threat to a confederated South Africa under British control, the British high commissioner, Sir Bartle Frere, delivered a Hobson's choice of an **ultimatum** on the banks of the Tugela River, demanding that Cetshwayo should dismantle his polity or face invasion.

5

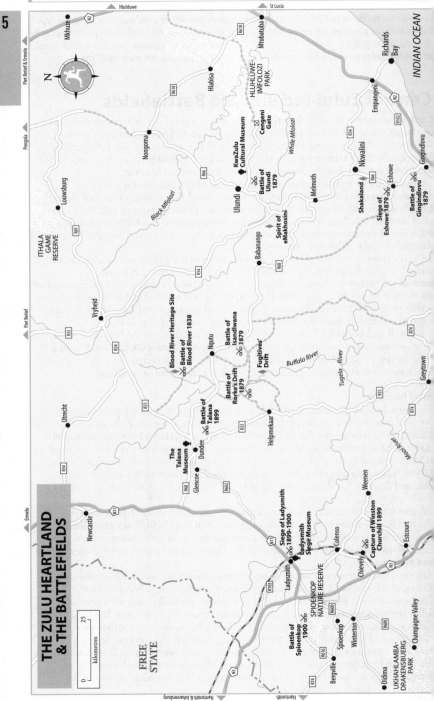

In January 1879, the British army crossed the Tugela and suffered a humiliating disaster at **Isandlwana** – the British army's worst defeat ever at the hands of native armies – only for the tide to turn that same evening when just over a hundred British soldiers repulsed a force of between three and four thousand Zulus at **Rorke's Drift**. By the end of July, Zulu independence had been snuffed, when the British lured the reluctant (and effectively already broken) Zulus, now eager for peace, into battle at **Ulundi**. The British set alight Cetshwayo's capital at **Ondini** – a fire that blazed for four days – and the king was taken prisoner and held in the Castle in Cape Town.

Eshowe

The name **ESHOWE** has an onomatopoeic Zulu derivation, evoking the sound of the wind blowing through the trees. Though visitors generally give the town a miss on the way to the more obvious drama of Ondini and the Battlefields, the place offers a gentle introduction to the Zulu heartland and deserves more than just a passing glance. Apart from its attractive setting, interlacing with the **Dlinza Forest**, the town is home to one of the world's finest collections of Zulu crafts and has a tour operator offering excellent excursions that take you out to experience some authentic Zulu culture and other aspects of life in Zululand that you would otherwise most likely miss.

ZULU FESTIVALS

In September and October KwaZulu-Natal is host to three significant Zulu **festivals** and it's possible to witness these on excursions with Eshowe-based Zululand Eco-Adventures (see p.421). If you're not around in September or October, Zululand Eco-Adventures can arrange for you to attend several lower-key Zulu ceremonies that give an authentic, non-touristy insight into various aspects of Zulu life. These range from *sangoma* healing ceremonies (Wed & Sun), to Zulu weddings (Sat & Sun), coming-of-age ceremonies (Sat & Sun) and a visit to a Zulu village (daily).

THE ROYAL REED DANCE

In the second week of September, the Zulu king hosts a four-day celebration at his royal residence at **Nongoma**. The event is both a rite of passage to womanhood for the young maidens of the Zulu nation, and a chance for them to show off their singing and dancing talents. The festival, known as **Umkhosi woMhlanga** in Zulu, takes its name from the riverbed reeds that play a significant role in Zulu life. Young women carry the reed sticks, which symbolize the power of nature, to the king. According to Zulu mythology, only virgins should take part, and if a woman participant is not a virgin, this will be revealed by her reed stick breaking. A second Reed Dance takes place in the last week of September at the king's other residence in Ingwavuma.

KING SHAKA DAY

In honour of King Shaka, a celebration is held yearly on September 24 in **KwaDukuza** (see p.382), Shaka's original homestead and the place where he was murdered in 1828 by his brothers Dingane and Mhlangana. It was Shaka who brought together smaller tribes and formed them into the greatest warrior nation in Southern Africa. Today, the celebration is attended by a who's who of South African Zulu society; there are speeches by the likes of Inkatha Freedom Party leader Chief Mangosuthu Buthelezi, along with music and fantastic displays of warrior dancing, the men decked out in full ceremonial gear and armed with traditional weapons.

SHEMBE FESTIVAL

Held in mid- to late October in **Judea**, near Eshowe, the Shembe Festival is the culmination of weeks of endless rituals, dancing and prayers held throughout KwaZulu-Natal. Some thirty thousand members of the Shembe Church (see p.367) return here every year to meet their leader and celebrate their religion with prayer, dances and displays of drumming.

5

Fort Nongqayi Museum Village

Nongqayi Rd • Mon–Fri 7.30am–4pm, Sat & Sun 9am–4pm • R35 • ☎ 035 474 2281, ⓦ eshowemuseums.org.za

At the southwestern end of town, picturesque **Fort Nongqayi** was built in 1883 to house the barefoot Zululand Native Police Force, but has since been turned into the largest historical complex in the area. Its shady grounds are home to several worthwhile museums and replicas of historical buildings, as well as a good restaurant, and make a pleasant place to spend an afternoon. The three museums are all included in the Fort admission fee, while entry to the Phoenix Gallery is free.

Vukani Zulu Cultural Museum

Containing more than three thousand examples of traditional Zulu arts and crafts, the brilliant **Vukani Zulu Cultural Museum** is housed in a purpose-built structure in the grounds of Fort Nongqayi. Guided tours take you through the huge range of **baskets** (a craft at which Zulu culture excels), each made for a specific purpose, the finest of which are the ones by **Reuben Ndwandwe** (1943–2007), arguably the greatest Zulu basket weaver. There are also carvings, beadwork, tapestries and some outstanding ceramics, including works by **Nesta Nala** (1940–2005), one of the leading proponents of the form. The benchmark examples here allow you to form an idea of the quality of basketry and crafts you'll see for sale as you work your way around Zululand. The museum itself sells baskets and pottery by local artists, which far surpass what's on offer at the on-site crafts shop.

The museum also houses the very touching **Phoenix Gallery** (free), where drawings and paintings by the male (overwhelmingly black) inmates of Eshowe prison exhibit the stark and sometimes shocking expressions of the prisoners' alienation and anger.

Zululand Historical Museum

With a collection that's eccentric and informative by turns, but never dull, the **Zululand Historical Museum** is the place to see furniture belonging to **John Dunn**, the only white man to become a Zulu chief; incidentally, he also took 49 wives, so becoming the progenitor of Eshowe's coloured community, many of whom still carry his last name. The museum also exhibits Zulu household artefacts and has displays on Zulu history.

Zululand Missionary Museum

Housed in a replica of Fort Nongqayi's chapel, the **Zululand Missionary Museum** contains exhibits relating to the Norwegian missionaries who came to this part of South Africa in the nineteenth century. There's also a working **paper mill** nearby, where you can see boxes, photo frames, notepads and the like being made from sugar-cane fibre and even elephant dung.

Dlinza Forest Aerial Boardwalk

Off Kangela St on the southwestern side of Eshowe (accessed from Fort Nongqayi Museum Village) • Daily: May–Aug 7am–5pm; Sept–April 6am–5pm • R30 • ☎ 035 474 4029

A must for birdwatchers, **Dlinza Forest** is also a great place for picnics or strolling along the impressive **Dlinza Forest Aerial Boardwalk**. Wheelchair-friendly, the boardwalk spans 125m and is raised 10m into the air just beneath the forest canopy, giving visitors a chance to experience a section of the woodland normally restricted to birds. The boardwalk leads to a 20m-high stainless-steel **observation tower**, offering stunning panoramas across the treetops to the Indian Ocean shimmering in the distance. A **visitors' centre** at the foot of the boardwalk provides information about forest ecology. Among the birds you might see here are black sparrowhawks, crowned eagles and spotted ground thrushes, while eighty species of butterfly have also been recorded in the forest. From the visitors' centre, the 1.3km iMpunzi Trail and the 1.8km uNkonka Trail go deeper into the forest through milkwood, giant ironwood, wild plum and other trees which are labelled and give a description of their uses in traditional medicine.

ARRIVAL AND TOURS

By minibus taxi Regular minibus taxis run from Eshowe to Durban and Empangeni.

★**Zululand Eco-Adventures** Based at the George Hotel ☎ 035 474 2298, ⓦ zululandeco-adventures.com. Tour company that takes an active role in the local community and runs tours that give an authentic experience of local Zulu life. They can take you to rural Zulu communities where you can attend a variety of Zulu ceremonies (see box, p.419), and spend unhurried visits to villages, markets and *shebeens* without feeling as if you're in a theme park.

ACCOMMODATION

★**Chase Guest House** About 1.5km along John Ross Highway from KFC on Main St ☎ 035 474 5491, ⓦ thechase.co.za. This lovely, peaceful farm has two large en-suite rooms and endless views of the surrounding sugar-cane fields. In the grounds there are also two smart self-contained units sleeping two, with the option of B&B or self-catering. A pool, tennis court and very charming hosts add to the appeal. R900

The George Hotel 36 Main St ☎ 035 474 4919, ⓦ thegeorge.co.za. Something of a focal point for the town, this busy hotel in a historic 1906 building is steeped in local history. It offers renovated en-suite rooms, many with their original wooden floors, and an on-site tour operator. R800

Sugar Hill Manor Guesthouse 36 Pearson Ave ☎ 035 474 2894, ⓦ eshowe.com. Under the same management as *The George Hotel*, this beautiful Victorian home boasts a veranda with views of the rolling hills of Zululand, a large garden and very comfortable rooms, all with their own entrances. Rates include breakfast. R750

Thornley's Guest House 17 Mansel Terrace ☎ 035 474 4179, ⓦ thornleysguesthouse.co.za. Six light and airy rooms in an old family home (one is a budget room sleeping four) run by an energetic young couple always happy to braai with guests in the garden or engage in good conversation at the little on-site bar, and there's a small pool. Rates include breakfast. R900

EATING AND DRINKING

Adam's Outpost In Fort Nongqayi Museum Village ☎ 035 474 1787. In a converted settler house, *Adams' Outpost* dishes up healthy salads, home-made bread and good curries (R70), plus a very popular Sunday lunch buffet (R145; reservations required). Mon–Fri 8.30am–4pm, Sun 9am–3pm.

Pablo Esco Bar The George Hotel. It's only open twice a week, but if you're in town on the right night head to the bar at *The George Hotel* where you'll get to taste a beer or two brewed at the on-site Zululand Brewery (home of the famous Zulu Blond), and catch the sunset from the deck overlooking the Dlinza Forest. Wed & Fri 4–9.30pm.

Prawn Shak 30km east of Eshowe at Amatikulu ☎ 084 737 6493. At weekends Eshowe locals (and people from Durban) head to this rambling wooden beach house that prides itself on its heady mixture of prawns and tequila, though that's just part of the seven-course menu – expect baked camembert and "Zulu sushi" as well. The set menu is R210, and there is no à-la-carte option. Also operates *Dokodweni Beach Camp* next door (☎ 071 205 9626, ⓦ shak.co.za), which has bungalows (R650), wooden chalets (R250) and a campsite (R50). Payment is by debit or credit card only. Sat & Sun 11.30am–5pm.

SHAKALAND

Shakaland, 14km north of Eshowe off the R68 at Norman Hurst Farm, Nkwalini (☎ 035 460 0912, ⓦ aha.co.za/shakaland), was built in 1984 as the set for the wildly romanticized TV series *Shaka Zulu*. This reconstruction of a nineteenth-century Zulu kraal has a bit of a "theme park" feel about it and is not especially representative of how people live today. However, it just about manages to remain on the acceptable side of exploiting ethnic culture, and offers the chance to sample Zulu food. **Tours** for day visitors (daily 11am & noon; 3hr; R560) include an audiovisual presentation about the origin of the Zulus, a guided walk around the huts, an explanation of traditional social organization, spear-making, a beer-drinking ceremony and a buffet lunch with traditional food. The highlight, however, is probably one of the best choreographed Zulu **dancing** shows in the country, with the dramatic landscape of the valleys that figure in the creation mythology of the Zulu nation as the backdrop – it's worth putting up with all the other stuff just to see it.

There is traditional-style **accommodation** at Shakaland in comfortable beehive huts (R2220), with untraditional luxuries such as electricity, TV and en-suite bathrooms. For overnight visitors, the tour starts at 4pm and the dancing is for an hour after dinner when flaming torches add to the atmosphere.

5

Quarters At the George Hotel ☎ 035 474 4919. One of Eshowe's best restaurants whose short but tasty selection of dishes includes German specialities like eisbein or schnitzel (R80) along with the usual steaks, chops and curries and a couple of vegetarian choices. There is also a coffee shop or the veranda for drinks and light meals. Restaurant: Mon–Fri 7–10am, noon–2pm & 6–9pm, Sat & Sun 8–10am & 6–8pm; coffee shop: Mon–Fri 7am–3pm.

Ulundi

The former capital of the KwaZulu Bantustan, **ULUNDI** lies at the centre of the **eMakhosini Valley** (Valley of the Kings). The latter holds a semi-mythical status among Zulu nationalists as the birthplace of the Zulu state and the area where several of its founding fathers lived and are now buried. A memorial to them was erected in 2003, the **Spirit of eMakhosini**, on a hill 3km up the R34, beyond the junction with the R66 for Ulundi. The circular memorial is surrounded by seven large aluminium horns representing the kings that came before Shaka, while in the centre is an impressive 600-litre bronze traditional beer pot.

The **Battle of Ulundi Memorial**, just outside town on the tarred road to the Cengeni Gate of the Hluhluwe-iMfolozi Park, is the poignant spot marking the final defeat of the Zulus. An understated small stone structure with a silver dome houses a series of plaques listing all the regiments on both sides involved in the last stand of the Zulus on July 4, 1879. The rectangular park around the memorial marks the site of the hollow square formation adopted by the British infantry and supported to devastating effect by seven- and nine-pounder guns.

KwaZulu Cultural Museum

A few kilometres from Ulundi on the road to the Cengeni Gate of Hluhluwe-iMfolozi Park • Mon–Fri 8am–4pm, Sat & Sun 9am–4pm • R35 • ☎ 083 661 7942, ⓦ zulu-museum.co.za

By far the most interesting sight here is the **KwaZulu Cultural Museum**, which houses the reconstruction of the royal residence of **King Cetshwayo**. After the decisive Battle of Ulundi, the royal residence at Ondini was razed and Cetshwayo was captured. Puzzled by Britain's actions, Cetshwayo wrote to the British governor in 1881 from his exile at the Castle in Cape Town: "I have done you no wrong, therefore you must have some other object in view in invading my land." The *isigodlo*, or **royal enclosure**, has been partially reconstructed with traditional Zulu beehive huts, while the museum has a model showing the full original arrangement, and an impressive bead collection.

ARRIVAL AND DEPARTURE

ULUND

By minibus taxi Ulundi is some 90km north of Eshowe on the R66, and is linked by minibus taxis, sometimes requiring a change at Melmoth. Another route is from Vryheid (106km to the north), and by car west from Ulund you can reach the Cengeni Gate of Hluhluwe-iMfolozi Par in about 45min on a newly tarred road.

ACCOMMODATION

uMuzi Bushcamp ☎ 035 870 2500, ⓦ umuzibushcamp .co.za. Stay in a Zulu hut, ranging from beehives to rondavels or more modern concrete huts, most en suite. All the huts are located in a traditional *umuzi* (homestead) with a central fire for night-time gatherings. The camp offer tours to eMakhosini Valley, the surrounding battlefields an Hluhluwe-iMfolozi Park; rates include entrance to th KwaZulu Cultural Museum. Half board **R940**

The Battlefields

Most of the major KwaZulu-Natal Battlefields lie in the northwestern corner of the province, where the Boers first came out of the mountains from the northeast into Zulu territory and inflicted a severe defeat on the Zulus at **Blood River** in 1838, 13km southeast of the tiny town of Utrecht. Some four decades later, the British spoiled for war and marched north to fight a series of battles against the Zulus, the most notable being at **Isandlwana** and **Rorke's Drift** southeast of Dundee.

Twenty years on, Britain again provoked war, this time against the **Boers** of the South African Republic and the Orange Free State to the north and west. In the early stages of the Second Anglo-Boer War (also known as the South African War) the huge, lumbering British machine proved no match for the mobile Boers. At **Ladysmith**, the British endured months of an embarrassing siege, while nearby, at **Spioenkop**, bungling British leadership snatched defeat from the jaws of victory. Although the empire successfully struck back, it took three years to subdue the South African Republic and the Orange Free State, two of the smallest states in the world, after committing half a million troops to the field in an operation that proved to be the costliest campaign since the Napoleonic Wars nearly a century earlier.

With more than eighty battlefield sites and monuments, some no more than cairns in fields reached by isolated gravel roads, it can be hard to know where to start. The best advice is to choose an era, war or campaign to focus on, and plan the sites you visit accordingly, whether using the services of a specialist guide (see box, p.424) or guiding yourself.

Isandlwana and Rorke's Drift

If you're only planning to take in one battlefield site, then **Isandlwana** should be it, though you really should take in **Rorke's Drift** as well, which you can combine in one day; both sites are eerily beautiful. Access by road is from the N2 on the coast via Eshowe and Ulundi, or from the N3 from either Gauteng or Pietermaritzburg and cutting east via Ladysmith.

Isandlwana Battlefield

Off the R68 just over 130km northwest of Eshowe and 70km southeast of Dundee • Mon–Fri 8am–4pm, Sat & Sun 9am–4pm • R35 • 034 271 8165

On January 22, 1879, the British suffered the greatest defeat in their colonial history when virtually an entire force of 1200 men was obliterated at Isandlwana by warriors armed with spears. One month earlier a British ultimatum, which included the disbanding of the Zulu army, had been refused. The British response was to send an invasion force of three columns, which was resisted by around 20,000 Zulus. On January 21, 1879, Zulu troops encamped 6km from Isandlwana Hill, where one of the British columns had set up camp. Unaware of the Zulus over the brow, the British commander took a large detachment to support another British force, leaving the men at Isandlwana undefended and unfortified.

Meanwhile, a British scouting party rode to the brow of a hill and was stunned to find the valley filled with some 25,000 Zulu warriors sitting in utter silence. Because of a superstition surrounding the phase of the moon, the Zulus were waiting for a more propitious moment to attack. On being discovered, they rose up and converged on the British encampment using the classic Zulu "horns of the bull" formation to outflank the unprotected British, whom they completely overran.

Dominated by an eerie hill, the **Isandlwana Battlefield** remains relatively unspoilt and unchanged apart from the white-cairn graves of those who fell. Modern additions to the site are a small **interpretation centre** that houses artefacts and mementos, and the **Memorial to the Zulu Warriors**, a circular bronze statue of an *isuqu*, the necklace of valour.

Rorke's Drift

15km west of Isandlwana on the D30 • Mon–Fri 8am–4pm, Sat & Sun 9am–4pm • Field Museum and interpretation centre R35; Craft centre free • 034 642 1687

The same evening as the Isandlwana battle, tattered British honour was restored when a group of British veterans successfully defended the field hospital at **Rorke's Drift**, just across the Buffalo River from the site of the earlier disaster, against four advancing Zulu regiments. Despite Cetshwayo's express orders not to attack Rorke's Drift, three to four thousand hot-headed young Zulu men were so fired up by the Isandlwana victory that

5

they launched the assault. For twelve hours spanning January 22 and 23, 1879, just over a hundred British soldiers (many of whom were ill) repulsed repeated attacks by the Zulus and so earned eleven Victoria Crosses – the largest number ever awarded in one battle.

Rorke's Drift is the most rewarding Battlefield to visit on your own, thanks to its excellent **museum**, and while you're here, it's also worth taking in the **ELC Art & Craft Centre Rorke's Drift** (ⓦcentre-rorkesdrift.com), known for its hand-printed fabrics and tapestries depicting rural scenes.

ACCOMMODATION   ISANDLWANA AND RORKE'S DRIFT

★**Fugitives' Drift Lodge** 9km north of Rorke's Drift along the D31 dirt road ☎034 642 1843, ⓦfugitives -drift-lodge.com. The ultimate Battlefields place to stay, this luxury lodge, located on a huge game farm, overlooks the drift where the few British survivors of Isandlwana fled across the Buffalo River. The colonial-style rooms are in individual cottages that open onto lawns, and there is also an annexe that sleeps four. Guests eat together in a dining room, among the world's largest Zulu battlefield memorabilia collection. Rates are full board. Doubles R8500, annexes R6000

Isandlwana Lodge Off the R68 just over 130km north-west of Eshowe and 70km southeast of Dundee ☎034 271 8301, ⓦisandlwana.co.za. Superbly located on the battlefield itself, the twelve-room stone-and-thatch lodge is spectacularly carved into a rocky escarpment overlooking the

sweeping plains and Isandlwana Hill. Facilities include a swimming pool and library, while Isandlwana and Rorke's Drift tours and authentic cultural Zulu village visits can be arranged, and an 8km hiking trail goes to the Buffalo River. No children under 7; rates include all meals. R7200

Penny Farthing Country House Along the R33 south of Rorke's Drift and 30km south of Dundee ☎034 642 1925, ⓦpennyf.co.za. Near the minuscule settlement of Helpmekaar, *Penny Farthing* is a historic pioneer farm still furnished with original objects and generations of hunting trophies, set in an area of big open grasslands and hills crisscrossed with hiking trails. The host Foy Vermaak is a Battlefields guide (see box below) who enjoys fireside chats on the subject, and has a personal collection of memorabilia. Rates include breakfast and dinner. R1460

BATTLEFIELD GUIDES

Visiting the **Battlefields** with a qualified guide will enhance the experience. The guides below specialize in different battle sites, usually those closest to their base. Most guides have negotiable fees, which vary depending on the size of the group, and some require you to have your own transport. If you prefer to explore the battlefields on your own, the late David Rattray's excellent set of CDs *The Day of the Dead Moon*, covering Rorke's Drift and Isandlwana, makes for good company; it's available directly from *Fugitive's Drift Lodge* (see above).

RECOMMENDED GUIDES

Elisabeth Durham ☎034 212 1014, ⓦcheznousbb .com. Informative half- and full-day tours in English and French of Rorke's Drift, Isandlwana and the route followed by the French Prince Imperial, who fell at Nqutu (R1300–1800; more if you don't have your own vehicle).
Fugitive's Drift Lodge ☎034 642 1843, ⓦfugitives-drift-lodge.com. David Rattray, the doyen of battlefield guides, was based at this lodge (see above) near Rorke's Drift until his untimely murder during a botched robbery. The baton has now been passed to the lodge's other excellent guides, Rob Caskie, Joseph Ndima and George Irwin, who, like Rattray, are great storytellers. Their half-day Isandlwana (departs at 7.30am) and Rorke's Drift (departs at 3pm in winter and 3.15pm in summer) tours cost R885–1120 per person for both battlefields, depending on the season.
Ron Gold, KwaZulu-Natal Tours ☎033 263 1908 or ☎083 556 4068, ⓦkwazulu-natal-tours.com. Gold specializes in the battles of Spioenkop, Willow

Grange and Colenso, and the site of Churchill's arrest, offering both half- and full-day tours (R1800–2800).
Evan Jones ☎034 212 4040 or ☎082 807 8598, ⓦbattleguide.co.za. Extensive full-day tours of all the Battlefields (from R1800 for two people) by a guide with a vast repository of knowledge, who breathes life into the battles.
Pat Rundgren ☎034 212 4560 or ☎072 803 2885, ✉gunners@trustnet.co.za. A large, burly man of Scandinavian/Irish descent, Pat, a military specialist, provides an alternative perspective on the battles around the Dundee area. Tours cost R450 per person per day, including transport.
Foy Vermaak ☎034 642 1925, ⓦwww.pennyf.co.za. Based at *Penny Farthing Country House* close to Isandlwana and Rorke's Drift, in which Foy Vermaak specializes; he also covers Helpmekaar and Fugitive's Drift. Tour rates are R1100 per day for up to six people, using your own vehicle.

Dundee

Some 32km west of the Rorke's Drift turn-off, along the R68, **DUNDEE** has little to offer except shops, supermarkets and pharmacies, but does serve as a good base for exploring the surrounding areas. Those with some time to kill in town could pick up Dundee Tourism's brochure, which includes a historical walking tour of the buildings dating back to Dundee's early days as a coal-fuelled boom town.

The Talana Museum and Kwakunje Cultural Village

1km outside Dundee on the R33 to Vryheid • Mon–Fri 8am–4.30pm, Sat & Sun 9am–4.30pm • R30.20 • ☎ 034 212 2654, ⊛ talana.co.za

Under shady blue gums, the excellent **Talana Museum** consists of ten historic whitewashed buildings from the time of the 1899 Battle of Talana Hill, the first engagement of the Anglo-Boer War. The most interesting of these is **Talana House**, which gives information about northern KwaZulu-Natal conflicts including the Anglo-Zulu, Zulu-Boer and Anglo-Boer wars. The displays include weapons and uniforms, but most evocative are the photographs that reveal fascinating personal details, such as showing the POW camps to which Boers were exiled in far-flung parts of the British Empire, including St Helena and the Far East. Often-neglected aspects of the Anglo-Boer War, including the roles of Africans and Indians, also get some coverage. In a photograph of Indian stretcher-bearers you may be able to spot the youthful Mohandas Gandhi, who carried wounded British soldiers off the Spioenkop and Colenso Battlefields. The museum curator can arrange guided tours of the museum and surrounding Battlefields.

On the same site, **Kwakunje Cultural Village** (*kwakunje* means "it was like this") is a model village where guides demonstrate and explain Zulu traditions and the way they've changed over the years. Zulu meals and dancing can also be arranged, if you call in advance.

ARRIVAL AND INFORMATION   DUNDEE

By minibus taxi The only public transport to Dundee is by minibus taxi, many of which, when coming from the east, require you to change in Vryheid. There are also direct routes to Ladysmith.

Tourist information Dundee Tourism, just off Victoria St in Civic Gardens (Mon–Fri 9am–5pm; ☎ 034 212 2121, ⊛ www.tourdundee.co.za), can recommend local tour guides, and provide information about the various re-enactments staged from time to time to coincide with the anniversaries of famous battles.

ACCOMMODATION AND EATING

Bergview Guest House 74 Browning St ☎ 034 218 3203, ⊛ bergviewguesthouse.co.za. Twin and double en-suite guest rooms in a modern brick house; nothing fancy but neat and tidy, and the owners can advise on Battlefields and tour guides in the Dundee area. Breakfast included and dinner provided on request. **R700**

Chez Nous 39 Tatham St ☎ 034 212 1014, ⊛ cheznousbb.com. You can stay on a B&B or self-catering basis at *Chez Nous*, run by gregarious French hostess Isabeth Durham, who cooks delicious three-course dinners on request, and also leads tours of the Battlefields (see box opposite). Accommodation is in spacious doubles or cottages sleeping up to six. **R900**

Lennox Guest House 3km east of town on the R68 ☎ 034 218 2201, ⊛ lennox.co.za. Advance booking is essential at this comfortable guest house which has both en-suite rooms and self-catering units. It's run by former rugby Springbok Dirk Froneman and his wife, Salome, who cooks good dinners on request. Breakfast included. **R1738**

Royal Country Inn 61 Victoria St ☎ 034 212 2147, ⊛ royalcountryinn.com. A short and simple menu of well-prepared Old World dishes such as oxtail soup (R90), steaks and apple tart, served in the subdued colonial elegance of Dundee's historic hotel, built in 1886. The separate *Garrulous Griffin* pub is named after the 24th Welsh Regiment who fought at Rorke's Drift. Daily 7am–9am, noon–2pm, 6–8pm.

Blood River Heritage Site

4km north of Nqutu on the R33, 43km east of Dundee • Daily 8am–4.30pm • R40, plus R25 per vehicle • ☎ 034 632 1695, ⊛ bloedrivier.org.za

The **battle of Blood River** takes its name from reports that the Ncome River turned red with blood when, on December 16, 1838, Andries Pretorius' band of 470 Voortrekkers barricaded themselves behind their wagons and defeated an army of 10,000 to 15,000 Zulu soldiers commanded by King Dingane. The resulting Zulu casualties numbered in the thousands, according to official counts, while the Voortrekkers suffered nothing

5

more than injuries. Although the event has become a defining moment for Afrikaner nationalists, some historians argue that the number of Zulu dead was most likely inflated by the victors.

Today you can't fail to be impressed by the Boer's **Bronze Wagon Laager**. Of all the Afrikaner quasi-religious monuments across the country, this definitely takes the biscuit, comprising a replica of 64 life-size bronze wagons on the site of the battle. During the apartheid years, the date of the battle, December 16, was celebrated by Afrikaners as the **Day of the Vow**, a public holiday honouring a supposed covenant made by the Boers with God himself that if he granted them victory, they would hold the day sacred. A pyramid-shaped beacon was erected during the Voortrekker Centenary in 1938 and is known as the **Covenant Renewal Beacon**. Few Afrikaners visit the monument today, and under the new government the public holiday has been recycled as the **Day of Reconciliation**, with Blood River also referred to by its Zulu name, Ncome.

The **Ncome Monument and Museum Complex** at the site presents a more balanced perspective on events and does a good job presenting the Zulu side of the conflict, with its horn-shaped design inspired by the Zulu martial formation. Exhibits include a display about battle strategy, and a reed garden relating the importance of river reeds in Zulu life. The video shown gives a good sense of the battle as it unfolded, making Blood River one of the easier sites to take in without the help of a guide. There's a gift shop, restaurant and campsite.

Ladysmith

LADYSMITH, 61km south of Dundee on the N11, owes its modest fame to one of the worst sieges in British military history over a century ago – the best reason to linger is to learn about the Anglo-Boer War at the Ladysmith Siege Museum – and, more recently, to **Ladysmith Black Mambazo**, the local vocal group that helped Paul Simon revive a flagging career in the mid-1980s. It's easy to walk around Ladysmith's small centre; **Murchison Street** is the main artery, where you'll find banks, the post office and shops.

Ladysmith Siege Museum

151 Murchison St • Mon–Fri 8am–4pm, Sat 9am–noon • R15 • ☎ 036 637 2992

The **Ladysmith Siege Museum** is the obvious starting point for any tour of the Anglo-Boer Battlefields. The siege began on November 2, 1899, and lasted 118 days, with twelve thousand British troops suffering the indignity of being pinned down by undisciplined farmers. This compelling little museum tells the story of the war through text and photographs, conveying the appalling conditions during the siege as well as key points in a war that helped shape twentieth-century South Africa, paving the way for its unification. The museum is also a good place to browse books about the war, written from both the British and Boer points of view.

ARRIVAL, INFORMATION AND TOURS   LADYSMITH

By bus Greyhound Johannesburg–Durban buses pull in at the Caltex Service Station on Murchison St.

By train The train station (☎ 036 271 2020) is 500m east of the town hall on Lyell St, though night-time arrival and departure times make the train an unrealistic option.

Tourist information At the Ladysmith Siege Museum (Mon–Fri 8am–4pm, Sat 9am–noon; ☎ 036 637 2992).

Guided Tours Local guide Liz Spiret (☎ 036 637 7702 o ☎ 072 262 9669, ✉ lizs@telkomsa.net) charges R995 for battlefields tour for up to four people (you'll need your own transport).

ACCOMMODATION AND EATING

Budleigh Guest House 12 Berea Rd ☎ 036 635 7700 or ☎ 084 512 2756, ✉ slabb12@telkomsa.net. Rooms in this elegant house are pleasantly decorated, featuring wooden floors and a subtle African feel. There's also a pool, a sunny patio and a lovely garden. Rates include breakfast. <u>R850</u>

Buller's Rest Lodge 59/61 Cove Crescent ☎ 036 63 6154, ⊛ bullersrestlodge.co.za. A smart thatche complex with country-style furnishings, a large woode deck and a small pool. The on-site pub display battlefield artefacts. Breakfast included, packed lunche rovided on request, and dinners available (Mon–Thurs & Sun). R1010

Hunters' Lodge 6 Hunter Rd ☎036 637 2359, ✉ hunterslodge@futurenet.co.za. This lovely old home is located in a peaceful neighbourhood and has fifteen en-suite rooms surrounding a well-manicured garden with swimming pool. Breakfast included and dinners available on request (Mon–Thurs). R1100

Royal Hotel 140 Murchison St ☎036 637 2176, ⊕royal hotel.co.za. In the heart of town, this is the hotel that harboured the upper classes during the siege – and was regularly shelled by the Boers. Now a mid-range establishment catering mainly to travelling reps, it's full during the week, which makes booking essential at any time of year. It can be noisy due to traffic. Breakfast included. R1325

Tipsy Trooper at the Royal Hotel 140 Murchison St ☎036 637 2176. This restaurant was patronized in former times by the more privileged of the besieged, including Frank Rhodes (brother of the more famous Cecil). It is still the best place to eat in town, though the food – mostly pub fare and steaks (around R85) – is not particularly sophisticated. Mon–Sat 6.30am–9pm, Sun 7am–10pm.

Spioenkop

Spioenkop Battlefield Off the R616 between Ladysmith and Bergville • Daily 9am–4pm • R35 • ☎036 637 2992 • **Spioenkop Nature Reserve** On the R600 35km west of Ladysmith and 14km north of Winterton • Daily: April–Sept 6am–6pm; Oct–March 7am–7pm • R100 • ☎036 488 1578

Spioenkop Battlefield overlooks the Spioenkop Dam and is clearly visible from the Spioenkop Nature Reserve, though its access point is off the road to Bergville. The bloodiest of all the Anglo-Boer War battles, Spioenkop took more British lives than any other and taught the British command that wars fought by means of set-piece battles were no longer viable. After this, the guerrilla-style tactics of modern warfare were increasingly adopted.

Some 1700 British troops took the hill under cover of a mist without firing a shot, but were able to dig only shallow trenches because the surface was so hard. When the mist lifted they discovered that they had misjudged the crest of the hill, but their real failure was one of flawed command and desperately poor intelligence. Had the British reconnoitred properly, they might have discovered that they were facing a motley collection of fewer than five hundred Boers with only seven pieces of artillery, and they could have called in their sixteen hundred reserves to relieve them. Despite holding lower ground, the Boers were able to keep the British, crammed eight men per metre into their trenches, pinned down for an entire sweltering midsummer day. Around six hundred British troops perished and were buried where they fell on the so-called "acre of massacre".

Meanwhile, the Boers, who were aware of the British reinforcements at the base of the hill, had gradually been drifting off, and, by the end of the day, unbeknownst to the British, there were only 350 Boers left. In the evening the British withdrew, leaving the hill to the enemy.

Today you can stand at the summit of the rocky hill and look out over the desolate battlefield, where small plaques mark out the positions of the two sides. A mass grave marks the final resting place of hundreds of fallen British troops.

The 60-square-kilometre **Spioenkop Nature Reserve** itself is located below the hills around the dam on the Tugela River and is managed by KZN Wildlife. It is popular for angling and boating and there are marked hiking trails and stables for horseriding (R150/1hr 30min) to see giraffe, wildebeest, small buck and the birds attracted to the shores. The Spioenkop Battlefield can also be reached by a steep but short walk from the campsite.

ACCOMMODATION   SPIOENKOP

Zemvelo KZN Wildlife Ipika Tented Camp Spioenkop Nature Reserve ☎036 488 1578, ⊕kznwildlife.com. This simple bush camp consists of just one four-bed safari tent on the slopes of Spioenkop Mountain, with kitchen and ablution block but no electricity, plus thirty camping pitches next to the lakeshore with power points and slipways for people from Gauteng bringing their own boats. Camping 90, safari tent (minimum charge three people) R730

Three Trees at Spioenkop (also known as Three Tree Hill Lodge) Adjoining the reserve, access road is off the R616 ☎036 448 1171, ⊕threetreehill.co.za. Tours of the battlefield and outdoor activities, including wildlife-spotting, mountain-biking, hiking and horseriding, can be arranged at this colonially stylish lodge. Each of the six suites has its own veranda overlooking the valley, and there's a separate cottage for families. Full board R5400

Free State

SOTHO MAN, BASOTHO CULTURAL VILLAGE

Free State

The Maloti Drakensberg Route, one of South Africa's most scenic drives, skirts the mountainous eastern flank of the Free State, the traditional heartland of conservative Afrikanerdom, which lies landlocked at the centre of the country. If you're driving from Johannesburg to Eastern or Western Cape, the Eastern Highlands, which sweep up to the subcontinent's highest peaks in Lesotho, are worth the detour. Bloemfontein, the capital, is only worth visiting if you are passing through, but once there you'll find very good guesthouses, restaurants and museums. Closer to Johannesburg, the riverside town of Parys is a pleasant rural escape that long ago was ground zero for a massive meteorite impact.

The highlight of the Eastern Highlands is the **Golden Gate Highlands National Park**, designated as such for the beauty of the Maloti Mountains, with their stripy red sandstone outcrops. Southeast of Golden Gate you can drive to the Sentinel car park – access point for hikes up to the highest plateaus of the Drakensberg – via the interesting **Basotho Cultural Village**. West of Golden Gate is **Clarens**, by far the nicest of the string of towns along the Lesotho border. In the rest of the province, flat farmlands roll away into kilometres of bright-yellow sunflowers and mauve- and pink-petalled cosmos, with maize and wheat fields glowing under immense blue skies.

Brief history

Britain took over from the Netherlands as the colonial power at the Cape of Good Hope in 1806. Subsequently, a number of its Dutch-speaking inhabitants (variously named Trekboers, Boers and Voortrekkers) trekked inland, first in small numbers, then, after 1834, in groups of hundreds. For nearly 150 years, the only free people in the "Free State" were these white settlers, who in 1854 were granted independence from Britain in a territory between the Orange and Vaal rivers, where they created a Boer Republic called the **Orange Free State** (the "Orange" part of the name came from the royal Dutch House of Orange). The system of government in the republic, inspired by the US Constitution, was highly democratic – if you were white and male. Women couldn't vote, while Africans had no rights at all, and were even forbidden from owning land. In 1912 the ANC was formed in the Bloemfontein township of Batho, while the Nationalist Party was founded two years later in Bloemfontein itself. In 1914, the Orange Free State became a bastion of apartheid, being the only province to ban anyone of Asian descent from remaining within its borders for longer than 24 hours. Africans fared little better; in 1970, under the grand apartheid scheme, a tiny barren enclave wedged between Lesotho, KwaZulu-Natal and the Free State became QwaQwa, a "homeland" for Southern Sotho people – a result of forced clearances from white-designated areas. The Bantustans have since been reincorporated into South Africa and, after an ANC landslide in Free State province in the 1994 elections, the "Orange" part of the name, with its Dutch Calvinist associations, was dropped.

OLIEWENHUIS ART MUSEUM, BLOEMFONTEIN

Highlights

1 Oliewenhuis Art Museum Admire South Africa's historical and contemporary artists at this delightful gallery with an excellent restaurant and magnificent gardens dotted with sculptures. **See p.435**

2 Maloti Drakensberg Route A scenic drive skirting the Lesotho border, past massive rock formations, cherry orchards and sandstone farming towns, including the delightful town of Clarens. **See p.437**

3 Drakensberg Escarpment Catch some of South Africa's most spectacular mountain views by climbing to the highest point on the escarpment via chain ladders. **See p.437**

4 Basotho vernacular architecture See the decorative adobe huts typical of the Eastern Free State and Lesotho at the Basotho Cultural Village, and spend the night in a comfortable rondavel. **See p.437**

5 Golden Gate Highlands National Park Hike or drive through this stunning reserve, dominated by the beautiful Maloti Mountains with their stripy red sandstone outcrops. **See p.438**

6 Parys Tour the remnants of the massive impact dome made by a meteorite two billion years ago, or simply relax in the town centre, shop for antiques, eat *vetkoek* and paddle down the Vaal River. **See p.442**

HIGHLIGHTS ARE MARKED ON THE MAP ON P.432

Bloemfontein

BLOEMFONTEIN, part of the Mangaung Metropolitan Municipality since 2011 is located at the crossroads of South Africa, which means that many travellers break their journey across the country here. Despite its reputation as the hick capital of South Africa, Bloem (or "flower", as it is lovingly called) is actually quite agreeable, and there's enough diversion for a day or two. The city's surprisingly fine **Oliewenhuis Art Museum** is set in beautiful gardens, while the unmistakably provincial **President Brand Street** is lined with handsome sandstone public buildings paying a pick 'n' mix homage to Mediterranean, British, Renaissance and Classical influences. Bloem is also the seat of the provincial parliament and South Africa's Court of Appeal.

As an overnight stop, the city offers good accommodation at reasonable prices, upmarket shopping centres and a couple of nightlife opportunities. In common with other South African cities, the white population has deserted the city centre. Instead, the suburbs just northwest of the city centre have become the place to shop and hang out. The **Loch Logan Waterfront Mall** beside the stadium and Westdene's four-storey **Mimosa Mall** in nearby Kellner Street provide coffee shops, chain restaurants, banks, bookshops and more.

If you're around in October, try to catch the ten-day Manguang African Cultural Festival (⬤macufe.co.za), which fills the city with storytelling, poetry, art, music and dance, which attracts people from all over the country, and is rounded off on the last day by the Sparta Macufe Cup soccer tournament.

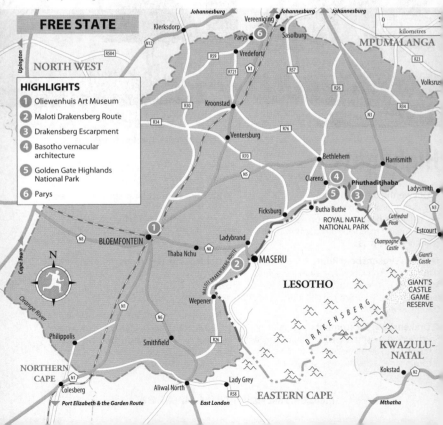

FREE STATE

HIGHLIGHTS

1. Oliewenhuis Art Museum
2. Maloti Drakensberg Route
3. Drakensberg Escarpment
4. Basotho vernacular architecture
5. Golden Gate Highlands National Park
6. Parys

President Brand Street

For a rewarding stroll past some of Bloemfontein's most distinguished buildings, head down **President Brand Street**, starting at the City Hall at the north end on the corner of Charles Street. Built in 1934, the building was designed in the "new tradition style" by Gordon Leith, a former employee of Sir Herbert Baker, and features large animal skulls above the windows. Sadly, in June 2017 it was completely gutted by fire, possibly deliberately. The municipal authorities have promised to restore it.

South of the City Hall stands the Supreme Court of Appeal of South Africa, built in 1929, which hears appeals of all decisions except those relating to the constitution. Staring at it from across the road is the Fourth Raadsaal, an imposing sandstone and red-brick parliament building of the independent Orange Free State republic that was completed in 1893 (it now houses the Free State Provincial Legislature). Further south, across the road, is the National Afrikaans Literary Museum, topped by an imposing clock tower and with a statue of President Brand in front, while on the corner of Fontein Street is the Supreme Court, completed in 1906, where Free State civil and criminal cases are tried. Finally, diagonally opposite on the corner of St George's Street is the Old Presidency.

6

Old Presidency

17 President Brand St • Tues–Fri 10am–noon & 1–4pm, Sun 2–5pm • free • ☎ 051 448 0949

The **Old Presidency** was built on the site of the home of **Major Henry Warden**, the founder of Bloemfontein. The current building dates from 1886 and was designed in a hybrid style that combines Renaissance and Scottish baronial elements. Occupied by three successive presidents (Johannes Brand, F.W. Reitz and M.T. Steyn), today it is a museum devoted to their lives and achievements, with paintings, furniture and ornaments bringing a convincing Victorian feel to the building. It is also used for art exhibitions, concerts and theatre performances.

National Museum

36 Aliwal St • Mon–Fri 8am–5pm, Sat 10am–5pm, Sun noon–5pm • R5 • ☎ 051 447 9609, ⓦ nasmus.co.za

To the east of President Brand Street is the **National Museum**, well worth a visit for its good dinosaur fossil collection, the 260,000-year-old Florisbad human skull and an impressive reconstruction of a late Victorian Bloemfontein street. There's also an interesting exhibit on the township of Batho, birthplace of the ANC, which includes a replica of a typical Batho house and interviews with township residents.

First Raadsaal Museum

95 St George's St • Mon–Fri 10am–1pm, Sat & Sun 2–5pm • Free • ☎ 051 447 9609, ⓦ nasmus.co.za

Bloemfontein's oldest building, the **First Raadsaal** is a small thatched pioneer cottage that was built In 1849 by Henry Warden (see above) as the town's first school, but used later as a church and then an assembly hall for the first parliament. Inside, and in a grander adjacent building, is a rather dry exhibition on the history of the establishment of Free State.

The small **King's Park** gardens are wedged between Loch Logan and the zoo, and are a lovely spot for a picnic or an afternoon stroll, especially when the roses are in bloom in summer; Bloemfontein is sometimes known as the "city of roses", and over four thousand of the colourful bushes have been planted in the park.

Bloemfontein Zoo

Daily: Oct–March 8am–6pm; April–Sept 8am–5pm • R45 • ☎ 051 405 8484

Occupying the western half of King's Park and accessed from Henry Street, **Bloemfontein Zoo** has been criticized for the many enclosures that are either empty and

6

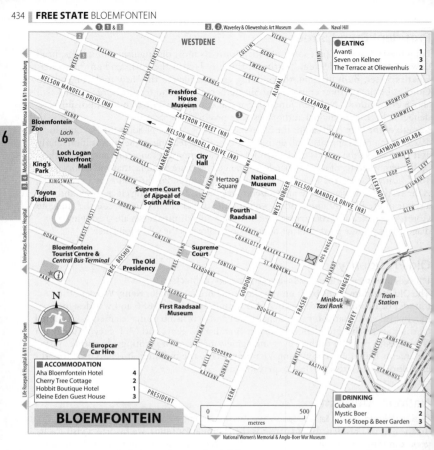

● **EATING**

Avanti	1
Seven on Kellner	3
The Terrace at Oliewenhuis	2

■ **ACCOMMODATION**

Aha Bloemfontein Hotel	4
Cherry Tree Cottage	2
Hobbit Boutique Hotel	1
Kleine Eden Guest House	3

■ **DRINKING**

Cubaña	1
Mystic Boer	2
No 16 Stoep & Beer Garden	3

BLOEMFONTEIN

0 — 500
metres

▽ National Women's Memorial & Anglo-Boer War Museum

overgrown or contain just one lone animal. However, a new zoo is currently under construction in Kwaggafontein, about 10km southwest of the city centre, and is expected to open in 2019. It will be big enough to build larger enclosures for the animals, some of which (waterbuck, zebra and eland) will be able to roam freely in the Kwaggafontein Game Reserve.

The waterfront and stadium

On the opposite site of Loch Logan lake to the zoo, the **Loch Logan Waterfront Mall** boasts shops, cafés, several chain restaurants and a cinema (ⓦloch-logan.co.za). Connected to the mall is the **Free State Stadium**, currently known as the Toyota Stadium, which was originally built for the 1995 Rugby World Cup, but is also used for football.

Freshford House Museum

31 Kellner St, Westdene · Mon–Fri 10am–1pm, Sat & Sun 2–5pm · R10 · ☎ 051 447 9609, · ⓦ nasmus.co.za

To the north of the city centre, just across Nelson Mandela Drive, the **Freshford House Museum** is a beautifully maintained late Victorian house from 1897, designed by architect John Edwin Harrisson as a home for himself and his wife Kate. Owned by the National Museum since 1982, the interior has been impeccably refurbished in period style, giving an insight into the everyday life of a Bloemfontein professional at the beginning of the twentieth century.

National Women's Memorial and Anglo-Boer War Museum

Monument Rd • Mon–Fri 8am–4.30pm, Sat 10am–5pm, Sun 11am–5pm • R10 • ☎ 051 447 3447, ⊛ wmbr.org.za

Just over 2km south of the centre, in an industrial part of town, a sandstone needle pointing skywards marks the **National Women's Memorial and Anglo-Boer War Museum**. Unveiled in 1913, this stands as a memorial to the 26,370 Afrikaner women and children who died in British concentration camps during the second Anglo-Boer War, also known as the South African War of 1899–1902. The suffering depicted in the museum isn't an exaggeration, but it is a little heavy-handed. Two cursory panels on concentration camps for Africans are a post-apartheid afterthought that at least provides a partial record of the more than 14,000 black South Africans who died during their incarceration.

Oliewenhuis Art Museum

16 Harry Smith St, 2km north of the centre off Aliwal St • Mon–Fri 8am–5pm, Sat & Sun 9am–4pm • Free • ☎ 051 011 0525, ⊛ nasmus.co.za

Located on Grant's Hill, the **Oliewenhuis Art Museum**'s collection includes a surprisingly good range of South African sculpture and painting and is housed in the former residency of the Governor-General of the Union of South Africa from 1942 to 1961. It is a beautifully light, neo-Cape Dutch manor set in 30 acres of large, attractive gardens, surrounded by wild bush traversed by short walking trails. Even if you're not interested in the gallery, it's still worth having tea at *The Terrace*, the café on the lawn (see p.436) – its trees and fountain make it the most harmonious location in town, and there's art here too, most notably the quirky African Carousel.

ARRIVAL AND DEPARTURE

BLOEMFONTEIN

By plane Bram Fischer International Airport (☎ 051 407 2200, ⊛ airports.co.za) is located 10km east of town on the N8; there are pricey SAA flights between here and the major cities, and budget flights to Cape Town by Mango. There are airport shuttles and taxis just outside the airport building which meet the arrivals of flights. The following car rental agencies are based at the airport: Avis ☎ 051 433 2931, ⊛ avis.co.za; First Car Rental ☎ 051 430 0390, ⊛ firstcarrental.co.za; National Alamo ☎ 051 433 3577, ⊛ nationalcar.co.za; and Tempest ☎ 051 433 2146, ⊛ tempestcarhire.co.za. Some of the above also have downtown offices, and Europcar is at 123 President Boshoff St, 750m southeast of the central bus terminal, ☎ 051 448 4530, ⊛ europcar.com.

By bus Translux, Intercape, City to City and Greyhound buses pull in at the central bus terminal at the Bloemfontein Tourist Centre on Park Rd, 500m south of Loch Logan

Waterfront Mall. Bear in mind that those buses stopping In Bloemfontein on longer journeys – between Cape Town and Johannesburg, for example – may arrive/depart during the middle of the night.

Destinations: Cape Town (8 daily; 12hr 20min); Durban (3 daily; 9hr); East London (4 daily; 7hr 30min); Johannesburg (22 daily; 5hr 30min); Kimberley (3 daily; 2hr 30min); Mossel Bay (1 daily; 11hr 15min); Pietermaritzburg (3 daily; 8hr 45min); Port Elizabeth (4 daily; 9hr 20min); Pretoria (8 daily; 6hr 30min); Upington (1 daily; 9hr).

Destinations: Cape Town (3–4 daily; 1hr 40min); Durban (2 daily; 1hr); Johannesburg (11 daily ; 1hr).

By train Trains operate from Bloemfontein Station (☎ 051 408 4843) on Harvey Rd, at the east end of Maitland St.

Destinations: Johannesburg (Wed, Fri & Sun; 7hr); Port Elizabeth (Wed, Fri, Sun; 12hr45min).

TOLKIEN IN BLOEMFONTEIN

Bloemfontein's biggest surprise is that it's the birthplace of **John Ronald Reuel Tolkien**, author of *The Lord of the Rings* and *The Hobbit*, a fact the city seems curiously reluctant to publicize. Tolkien's father, Arthur, left his native Birmingham to work in the colonies, eventually becoming manager of the Bank of Africa in Bloemfontein. Tolkien was born in 1892, in a house standing on the corner of West Burger and Maitland streets, a couple of blocks east of President Brand Street. When Arthur Tolkien died three years after Tolkien's birth, his wife returned to England with her two infant sons; their house was later torn down to make way for a furniture shop.

6

INFORMATION

Tourist information Inside the Bloemfontein Tourist Centre and central bus terminal at 60 Park Rd (Mon–Fri 8am–4pm; ☎ 051 405 8489).

GETTING AROUND

By taxi The minibus taxi rank lies one block west of the train station on Hanger St. The area around the station and the minibus taxi rank is regarded by some residents as the dodgiest in the city centre, but there have been few actual incidents; stay alert, and avoid the area at night. Fortunately, metered taxis usually gather outside the train and bus stations. Alternatively, you can phone for one: Bloem Taxis (☎ 051 433 7092, ☒ bloemtaxi.co.za), Rooikat Taxis (☎ 051 522 5446, ☒ rooikattaxi.com) and Uber all operate in Bloemfontein.

ACCOMMODATION

The suburbs of Westdene and Waverley just north of the centre and with easy access from the N1 highway are the best areas to stay. If you are driving through and need a bed for the night, phone guesthouses in advance, rather than just turning up.

aha Bloemfontein Hotel 101 Parfitt St, Park West ☎ 051 444 3142, ☒ aha.co.za/urbanhotelbfn; map p.434. A central, slick and affordable contemporary hotel with small, functional and stylish rooms, with a bar on the first floor. B&B and meals from local restaurants can be delivered. R830

Cherry Tree Cottage 12A Peter Crescent, Waverley ☎ 051 436 4334 ✉ cherrytree@imaginet.za; map p.434. A peaceful, a/c B&B set in a beautifully landscaped garden with views of the nature reserve on Naval Hill. The five thatched bedrooms each have their own separate entrances, the price includes a cooked breakfast and supper is served on request. R1100

★ **Hobbit Boutique Hotel** 19 President Steyn Ave, Westdene ☎ 051 447 0663, ☒ hobbit.co.za; map p.434. Inspired by Tolkien's *The Hobbit*, this is the best place to stay in Bloemfontein; a luxurious establishment filled with beautiful and comfortable antique furniture, with teddy bears tucked into every bed under handmade quilts. Excellent three-course dinners are available for small groups (phone by lunchtime). Book well in advance. R1300

Kleine Eden Guest House 2 Moffett St, Fichardt Park ☎ 051 525 2633, ☒ kleine-eden.co.za; map p.434. Well-maintained guesthouse with B&B, self-catering and family units. Rooms all have their own entrance and private garden and there's a small swimming pool. Breakfast extra. R730

EATING

While Bloemfontein is no culinary capital and there are few regional specialities to sample, you can still have a good and inexpensive meal here. Westdene's Second Avenue has a handful of restaurants and is safe to stroll about at night.

Avanti 53 Second Ave, Westdene ☎ 051 447 4198, ☒ avantirestaurant.co.za; map p.434. Bloemfontein's best Italian restaurant features mostly well-done classics, alongside a few more adventurous offerings like chicken panzerotti (R85) and "Italian spring rolls". There is a delicious array of focaccia as well. Booking recommended. Mon–Thurs 11.30am–10pm, Fri & Sat 11.30am–10.30pm, Sun 11.30am–3pm.

Seven on Kellner 7 Kellner St, Westdene ☎ 051 447 7928, ☒ sevenonkellner.co.za; map p.434. Upmarket dining in a fine old house, with a short but inventive menu that includes grilled meat and fish as well as imaginative wood-fired pizzas from around R95. Mon–Thurs noon–2pm & 6pm–midnight, Fri–Sat noon–midnight.

The Terrace at Oliewenhuis 16 Harry Smith St ☎ 051 448 6834, ☒ theterracebloem.co.za; map p.434. A pleasant location in the formal gardens of the Oliewenhuis Art Museum, leading onto a nature reserve, makes this Bloemfontein's nicest place for afternoon tea and cake (R25 per slice). Tues–Fri 9am–5pm, Sat & Sun 9am–4pm.

DRINKING

Cubaña 109 President Reitz St, Westdene ☎ 051 447 1920; map p.434. A bustling Latino restaurant and bar serving large portions of decent food such as quesadillas (R55) and meat platters. Later on in the evenings, cocktails (from R35) are served and DJs play Latino music. Wednesday is a rowdy student night. Daily 8am–2am.

Mystic Boer 84 Kellner St, Westdene ☎ 051 430 2206; map p.434. A great place to down a few tequilas, with pizzas available from around R75, and different music styles and special offers throughout the week. There's live music on Sundays. The best place in town for a night out. Mon–Fri 2pm–4am, Sat noon–4am, Sun 5pm–2am.

No 16 Stoep & Beer Garden 16 Second Ave, Westdene ☎ 051 430 2542; map p.434. Serves excellent gourmet burgers plus big portions of buffalo wings (R120) and ribs (R140), with a range of tasty basting sauces, but is mainly known for its Saturday-night bashes which go on into the small hours. Kitchen closes at 11pm. Tues–Sat 11am–4am.

DIRECTORY

Emergencies ☎ 082 911.

Hospitals The main state hospital is Universitas Academic Hospital (1 Logeman St, ☎ 051 405 3911, ⓦ universitas hospital.fs.gov.za), offering a free 24hr emergency ward, but you may wait hours and the level of care is variable. The private hospitals are a better choice: Mediclinic Bloemfontein, Kellner St, opposite the Mimosa Mall (☎ 051 404 6666,

ⓦ mediclinic.co.za); Life Rosepark Hospital, Fichmed Centre, Gustav Crescent (☎ 051 505 5111 ⓦ lifehealthcare.co.za).

Pharmacies Dis-Chem, Loch Logan Waterfront Mall, First Ave (☎ 051 411 6140; Mon–Fri 9am–6pm, Sat 8am–5pm, Sun 9am–2pm).

Post office Corner of Oos Burger and Charlotte Maxeke sts (Mon–Fri 8am–5.30pm, Sat 8am–1pm).

6

The Maloti Drakensberg Route

Hugging the mountainous border between South Africa and Lesotho for some 280km, the tarred **Maloti Drakensberg Route** offers some of the most scenic drives in the Eastern Free State, the Eastern Cape and the Drakensberg region of KwaZulu-Natal. It runs from **Phuthaditjhaba** (Witsieshoek) in the north to **Wepener** in the south, taking you past massive rock formations streaked with red and ochre, cherry orchards and sandstone farming towns. The highlight of the eastern Free State region is the **Golden Gate Highlands National Park**, which encompasses wide-open mountain country characterized by spectacular cliffs and overhangs. Nearby, the **Basotho Cultural Village** is worth visiting to gain some insight into Basotho traditions, while the closest village to Golden Gate is **Clarens**, a centre for arts and crafts and one of the most attractive of all the villages along the route.

Basotho Cultural Village

23km east of Golden Gate Highlands National Park and signposted from the main R712 road • Mon–Fri 9am–4.30pm, Sat & Sun 9am–5pm • R40 • ☎ 058 721 0300, ⓦ sanparks.org

The **Basotho Cultural Village** is a great place to learn about the traditional lives of the Basotho people, who have lived in the vicinity and just across the border in Lesotho

---

HIKING UP THE DRAKENSBERG ESCARPMENT

From the Free State, the easiest hiking access onto the high **Drakensberg Escarpment** – with views of some dramatic mountain scenery – is just southeast of the Golden Gate Highlands National Park. A five- to eight-hour return hike (depending on fitness and how leisurely you want to go) starts at the Sentinel car park (at 2560m), 7km above the *Witsieshoek Mountain Lodge* south of Phuthaditjhaba, and can only be reached with private transport. A 2.5-hour walk from the car park brings you to the foot of two sections of chain ladder, each approximately 50 rungs apiece, leading up an almost vertical rock face. From the top, you can make the final short onslaught to the chunky **Sentinel Peak**, the highest on the escarpment at 3165m. From here there are fantastic views of the 5km cliff face known as the Drakensberg Amphitheatre, the grand sweep of mountains dominating the Royal Natal National Park, while below are the Tugela Falls, at 948m the second-tallest waterfall in the world. This hike can be achieved relatively easily, but it's a tougher ten-hour climb if approached from the Mahai campsite in the Royal Natal National Park on the KwaZulu-Natal side (see p.398).

For those bitten by the mountain bug, other more serious hikes are available, including the **Amphitheatre Heritage Trail**, which is one of the most popular of the uKhahlamba-Drakensberg hikes and spans the Free State, KwaZulu-Natal and Lesotho. It also begins at the Sentinel car park and descends back down into the Royal Natal National Park. It's possible to spend up to a week on top of the escarpment, but the most popular option is to do 25km to 30km over three days; either by being fully equipped with camping gear, proper clothing, food and water, or by opting for a "slackpacking" excursion with professional guides and porters, and ready-prepared camps and meals. There are numerous other hiking options in the uKhahlamba-Drakensberg Park (see box, p.390).

6

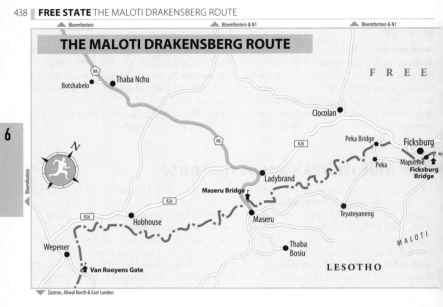

THE MALOTI DRAKENSBERG ROUTE

for centuries. The main display in the reconstructed village is a courtyard of beautiful Basotho huts, from organic circular sixteenth-century constructions to square huts with tin roofs, bright interior decor and European blankets and utensils. Visitors are taken on a 45-minute tour run by actors in traditional dress, meeting the chief, sampling traditional beer, hearing musicians play and seeing a traditional healer; you also learn about the curious spiral aloe, plants unique to the Drakensberg.

The views across the surrounding **QwaQwa Nature Park** are awesome, and the curio shop sells some quality local crafts (look out for raffia mats and baskets and the conical hats unique to this area). The open-air tea garden serves teas and, with advance booking, traditional food including *motoho* (porridge made of sorghum) and *dipadi* (toasted ground maize with a bit of salt and sugar). You can also stay overnight in traditional Basotho rondavel huts (see opposite).

Golden Gate Highlands National Park

300km northeast of Bloemfontein on the R712 • R176/day for hiking; driving through is free • ☎ 058 255 1000, ⓦ sanparks.org

The **Golden Gate Highlands National Park** was designated for its outstanding beauty rather than its wildlife. Although eland, zebra, mountain reedbuck and black wildebeest roam the hillsides, the real attraction here is the unfettered space, eroded sandstone bastions, grassy plateaus and incised valleys, which are part of the Drakensberg range (see p.388).

A number of hour-long rambles into the sandstone ravines start from the *Glen Reenen Rest Camp* and are fairly manageable; the only exception being a sometimes steep and physically challenging half-day walk up Wodehouse Kop, which offers great views back down across the park. The most strenuous hike, available for groups only, is the demanding two-day circular Rhebok Trail (R175), which reaches the highest and lowest points of the park; hikers need to book the basic overnight accommodation through South African National Parks (see p.65). Other activities at Golden Gate include horseriding (R100/hr), a two-hour guided walk to learn about medicinal plants (R40), and in summer you can swim in a natural waterfall pool close to *Glen Reenen*.

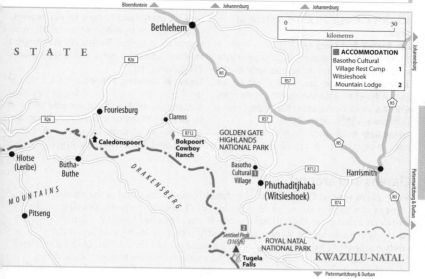

For those quickly driving through, two asphalted loops signposted off the main road take in fields populated by zebra and antelope, a carcass-strewn vulture feeding spot, and stunning views of the highest peaks of the Drakensberg.

ARRIVAL AND DEPARTURE

THE MALOTI DRAKENSBERG ROUTE

BASOTHO CULTURAL VILLAGE

Occasional **minibus taxis** run along the R712 between Clarens and Phuthaditjhaba via Golden Gate, dropping visitors off at the access road to the Basotho Cultural Village, from where it's a 2km walk.

GOLDEN GATE HIGHLANDS NATIONAL PARK

Golden Gate is easily reached on good, tarred roads from Bloemfontein (330km) and Johannesburg (320km). The same minibus taxis as above can drop off at *Glen Reenen*. There are no entry gates to the park, which is open 24 hours. Visitors with reserved accommodation who arrive after the office closes at 5.30pm can collect keys at the filling station.

INFORMATION AND ACTIVITIES

Tourist information There is an official Maloti Drakensberg Route website (Ⓦ malotidrakensbergroute .com), which is a useful source of advice about accommodation, activities and events across the area.

Hiking Drakensberg Hikes (Ⓦ drakensberghikes.co.za) organizes a whole range of slackpacking and hiking experiences in the uKhahlamba-Drakensberg.

ACCOMMODATION

BASOTHO CULTURAL VILLAGE

Basotho Cultural Village Rest Camp Ⓣ 012 428 9111, Ⓦ sanparks.org; map above. On the eastern side of Golden Gate, surrounded by huge sandstone mountains, the three cosy self-catering rondavels at the museum village are meant to resemble those of an eighteenth-century Basotho settlement. They sleep up to four, have electric blankets for chilly winter nights, verandas with magnificent views over the plains, and there's a communal braai and thatched lapa area. R870

THE ESCARPMENT

Witsieshoek Mountain Lodge End of the R57 Rd Ⓣ 058 713 6361 or Ⓣ 073 228 7391, Ⓦ witsieshoek .co.za; map above. Spectacularly set at 2283m above sea level, this is the highest lodge in the country. It has functional B&B rooms in chalets and bungalows, some with excellent mountain views, and there's a lounge with fireplace, restaurant and pub, and staff who can offer plenty of advice about hiking and even organize packed lunches. R1490

6

GOLDEN GATE HIGHLANDS NATIONAL PARK

Glen Reenen Rest Camp ☎012 428 9111 or ☎058 255 1000 on the day, ⊛sanparks.org. In the centre of the park, but right next to a road that has truck traffic all night. Camping, rondavels and basic four-bed cottages are available. As well as the provisions store, there's also a pool, picnic sites, a restaurant/bar and a filling station. Camping R230, rondavels R915, cottages R1495

Golden Gate Hotel ☎012 428 9111 or ☎058 255 1000, ⊛sanparks.org or ⊛goldengatehotel.co.za. This is the smartest place to stay in the park, with well-equipped self-catering chalets and comfortable rooms, most with fantastic views. The restaurant offers breakfast and dinner and there's a rooftop bar/coffee shop. Rooms R1140, chalets R1205

Highlands Mountain Retreat ☎012 428 9111 or ☎058 255 1000 on the day, ⊛sanparks.org. Away from the crowds, and beautifully located in the foothills off the Oribi Loop Rd, the *Highlands Mountain Retreat* offers luxury self-catering family log cabins with spacious verandas sleeping two to four people. R1650

Clarens and around

Some 20km west of Golden Gate Highlands National Park and at the northern-most point of Lesotho lies the tree-fringed village of **CLARENS**, the most appealing of the settlements along the Maloti Drakensberg Route. Founded in 1912, Clarens is especially remarkable for its dressed stone architecture, which glows under the sandstone massif of the Rooiberge (Red Mountains) and the Malotis to the southeast. The best time to see the village is spring, when the fruit trees blossom, or autumn, when the poplar leaves are turning. But at any time of year Clarens' relaxed air makes it a rare phenomenon in the Free State – a *dorp* you'd actually want to explore, or sip a sidewalk lager and simply hang out in. The scenery is a magnet for artists and photographers all year round, but especially during autumn when the leaves are ablaze in russet gold.

Clarens is an arts and crafts centre, with a number of studios and shops peppering the streets. If you arrive around lunchtime on a weekend there's a chance you'll catch some local live music at one of the streetside cafés around Market Square, effectively the town centre in the middle of Main Street.

Bokpoort Cowboy Ranch

4km east of Clarens and signposted from the main R712 road • ☎083 744 4245, ⊛bokpoort.com

The friendly **Bokpoort** provides outstanding horseriding onto the Drakensberg Escarpment, from where you can gaze across into Lesotho and view Southern Africa's highest peaks. Day visitors are welcome with advance reservations, or the farm itself has a range of accommodation, from en-suite chalets with fireplaces and kitchenettes (R800), to dorm beds (R200) in an old sandstone barn. If you're camping (R80), there's a good communal cooking and dining area. Reasonably priced meals, including breakfast and dinner, can be ordered from the farmhouse kitchen, while a small shop sells basics. Bokpoort's big draw is the memorable Western-style riding in deep, comfortable cowboy saddles on sure-footed horses. Short rides from the farmhouse (R400 for 2hr) take in San rock paintings and swimmable river pools, with the chance of seeing eland, zebra and springbok. Two-day riding trails into the mountains on the

---

SHOPPING IN CLARENS

The **galleries** in the village centre are great for gifts and souvenirs. Just west of the square, the excellent **Bibliophile Bookshop** (312 Church St; Tues–Sat 9am–5pm, Sun 9am–4pm; ☎058 256 1692) is a good place to stock up on books and a whole range of other desirables, including maps, artists' materials, and jazz and African music recordings. The most charming shop in town is **The Blanket Shop** (Sias Oosthuizen St; Mon–Sat 8.30am–1pm & 2–5pm; ☎058 256 1313), a genuine old-style general dealer that opened as **Di Mezza & De Jager Trading Store** in 1930 and is today run by octogenarians Gertie and Minnie, who can advise on quality woollen Basotho blankets (R250–1300) in various sizes and patterns.

Lesotho border (R2500) involve a 4WD vehicle carrying food and bedding (you sleep on mattresses in a remote mountain hut), and you ride about six hours a day. Other options on the ranch include mountain-biking, hiking, archery and pony rides for kids.

ARRIVAL AND DEPARTURE
CLARENS

Minibus taxis occasionally run along the R712 between Clarens and Phuthaditjhaba via Golden Gate Highlands National Park. More regular ones run between Clarens and Bethlehem, 41km to the north, which is on the N5 and is served by some of the intercity bus companies.

INFORMATION

Tourist information There is no official tourist information office, but Mountain Odyssey on Main St (Mon–Fri 9am–5pm, Sat 9am–2pm, Sun 9am–noon; ☎058 256 1173/1480, ⍟infoclarens.com) is a drop-in information office that also books accommodation and can help organize activities in the area. Clarens Destinations is another useful accommodation booking and information website (⍟goclarens.co.za).

ACCOMMODATION

Clarens Inn and Backpackers 93 Van Reenen St ☎076 369 9283, ⍟clarensinn.com. The cheapest place to stay, with the choice between a functional dorm, camping in pre-erected dome tents and tepees, a very basic honeymoon suite and a range of equally basic self-catering units sleeping up to eight people (from R200/person). Camping R400, dorms R180, suite R560

Cottage Pie 89 Malherbe St ☎071 686 0222, ⍟cottagepieclarens.co.za. In a lovely setting in a lush garden along a stream, there's a garden chalet and three rooms inside the thatched main house with kitchenettes. Rates are self-catering but excellent breakfasts are available on request and are served on the patio. R800

Lake Clarens Guest House 1-3 Lake Clarens Drive ☎058 256 1436, ⍟lakeclarensgh.co.za. Pretty rooms in a characterful old sandstone building overlooking a pond filled with geese, with breakfast served on a pleasant rose-covered terrace out front. There are a few cheaper rooms in an annex at the back, and a self-catering flat as well (R350/person). R1160

Red Mountain House 325 Market Square ☎058 256 1456, ⍟redmountainhouse.co.za. Centrally situated B&B that has rooms on the upper floor opening onto balconies with views onto the square and the mountains. Rooms have fireplaces and are luxuriously furnished with Persian rugs and Victorian antiques. R1310

EATING

On weekends, when the crowds arrive in town, most restaurants are packed and service can be slow, so best to book in advance or arrive early.

278 on Main 278 Main St ☎082 556 5208, ⍟278onmain.co.za/pages/restaurant. A good variety of sweet and hearty breakfasts (from R50), pasta, meat dishes, pancakes and desserts in an artsy interior, at the very end of the row of restaurants in the village. Daily 8am–8pm.

★**Clementines** Cnr Van Zyl and Church sts ☎058 256 1616, ⍟clementines.co.za. Booking is essential at Clarens' best restaurant, housed in an atmospheric old tin bus maintenance shed with its own garden. Try the steaks, a slow-food oxtail stew, or grilled local rainbow trout (R135), washed down with beer from the Clarens Brewery. Tues–Sun 11am–3pm & 6–10pm.

The Highlander Shop 3, Highlands Centre, Market St ☎058 256 1912. A cosy restaurant with a fire in winter and a terrace for when the weather is fine; it's especially recommended for its home-made pies, pizza, breakfasts and berry cheesecake (R42). Daily 8am–10.30pm.

DRINKING

Clarens Brewery 326 Market St ☎058 256 1193. Seven delicious beers (R40/pint) and a collection of ciders are proudly brewed on-site at this friendly biergarten, which also serves a few German-inspired dishes like bratwurst (R35). The perfect place for a drink in the sun, with cherry or apple juice free for kids. Daily 10am–7pm.

Ficksburg

FICKSBURG, 87km southwest of Clarens, is the centre of South Africa's cherry and asparagus farming. The town's sandstone architecture gives it a pleasant ambience, and it's a good place to make a stop halfway down the Maloti Drakensberg Route.

An annual Cherry Festival in the third week of November is the highlight of Ficksburg's calendar; it features a marathon, floats, stalls, a "cherry queen" competition and a popular beer festival (ⓦcherryfestival.co.za).

ARRIVAL AND DEPARTURE — FICKSBURG

By minibus taxi Minibus taxis from the Ficksburg Bridge/Maputsoe border crossing with Lesotho (24hr) on the eastern edge of town link Ficksburg to Bloemfontein (3hr 30min), Johannesburg (10hr) and other towns.

ACCOMMODATION

Bella Rosa Guest House 21 Bloem ⓣ 051 933 2623. A hugely popular and well-priced pair of Victorian sandstone houses set in a lovely garden, with 12 nicely furnished B&B rooms, some decorated with antiques. There's also a pub and a spacious restaurant with fireplace. R685

Ladybrand

LADYBRAND lies on the main route into Lesotho, just over 69km southwest of Ficksburg. It's one of the few small agricultural towns in the Free State that is booming, owing to its proximity to Lesotho's capital Maseru, just over 18km away. Many people working on projects in Lesotho stay in Ladybrand rather than in Maseru because of its calm and family-friendly village atmosphere.

ARRIVAL AND DEPARTURE — LADYBRAND

By bus and minibus taxi Minibus taxis run regularly between Ladybrand and the Maseru Bridge border crossing 16km away, as well as connecting to Johannesburg and Bloemfontein.

ACCOMMODATION

Cranberry Cottage 37 Beeton St ⓣ 051 923 1500, ⓦcranberry.co.za. One of the best and most popular options in town, offering 43 comfortable country-style rooms (some with kitchens) set in a rambling garden. There's a gym and spa here, and the owners have reams of information on day-trips and rock-art sites. R980

EATING

Cranberry's Restaurant 37 Beeton St ⓣ 051 923 1500. *Cranberry Cottage's* popular restaurant serves excellent international meals, including an assortment of seafood, pastas and grills like lamb chops (R110). In summer, guests are seated out on the candle-lit garden terrace by the pond, and it's also a good place to pop in for tea and some excellent cakes – sample the delights of their chocolate mud pie. Mon–Fri 7am–9.30pm, Sat 7.30am–9.30pm, Sun 7.30am–3pm.

★**Living Life Station Café** 1 Princess St ⓣ 051 924 2834. Ladybrand's former train station is now an attractive restaurant run by the charity, Living Life, which provides employment for women. The wonderful organic South African dishes, such as focaccia pizza (R60) and delicious salads, are made with ingredients sourced from the region and from the café's own garden. Locally made crafts are also on sale. Mon–Fri 7am–9pm, Sat 7am–4pm, Sun 7am–3pm.

Parys and the Vredefort Dome

The small town of **PARYS**, just off the N1 highway 300km northeast of Bloemfontein and just over 100km from Johannesburg, makes a good stopover on the long trek across the country, or an interesting day-trip from Joburg. The town, with its galleries, antique shops, adventure sports and the meandering Vaal River, is pleasant enough, but its main claim to fame is harder to spot as it's situated near **Vredefort**, the epicentre of a massive meteorite impact some two billion years ago. What remains of the huge 300km-wide crater is now South Africa's most abstract UNESCO World Heritage Site (it can only properly be seen from space), but by joining a tour (see box opposite) it is possible to get a good idea of what happened and to view what's left of the impact dome, the mass of molten rock that was thrust upwards after the meteorite struck.

6

THE VREDEFORT DOME

Some two billion years ago, an **asteroid** the size of Cape Town's Table Mountain slammed into Earth at a speed of 30,000 kilometres per hour, forming a 300km-wide crater. The impact at **Vredefort**, 10km south of Parys, vaporized the asteroid and part of the Earth's crust, melting, pulverizing and shattering rocks for kilometres around. It also forced rocks briefly down beneath the impact area before these rebounded, raising and upending rock layers to form a dome structure. Even though the Earth's surface has eroded about 10km since the impact, the weathered **concentric rings** of this dome can still be seen, forming the hills around Parys.

The dome area is best experienced on a **tour**, which takes in the view of the dome remnants and tracks down strange melt-rock formations. The operators offer a number of options (all must be prearranged and prices depend on the size of the group), but expect to pay in the vicinity of R150 per person for a 2hr walk or 4WD drive tour, and R400 for a half-day 4WD drive tour. *Dome Impact Tours* (62 Boom St, Parys ☎056 811 2078, ⓦdomeimpacttours.co.za); *Kopjeskraal Country Lodge* (off the R53, 6km west of Parys, ☎083 406 0841, ⓦkopjeskraal.co.za /tours); Vredefort Dome Info Centre (based at *Otters' Haunt Lodge*, Kopjeskraal Rd, Parys ☎056 818184 or ☎084 245 2490, ⓦvdome.co.za).

November is a good time to visit Parys, when outdoor enthusiasts descend on the town for dragon-boat racing and live music during the annual Parys Dome Adventure Festival (ⓦdomefest.co.za). The Parys Flower Festival also take place in November, at the end of the month.

ARRIVAL AND DEPARTURE
PARYS AND THE VREDEFORT DOME

By car An easy 110km drive from Johannesburg, take the N1 south and just after crossing the Vaal River take the R59 exit and follow it for 20km to Parys.

By bus Translux, City to City and Greyhound buses stop at the Sasol filling station on Breë St. Tickets can be purchased at the Shoprite supermarket on Philip St.

Destinations: Bloemfontein (4 daily; 5hr); Johannesburg (4 daily; 3hr).

INFORMATION
PARYS

Tourist information The Parys Info & Tourism Centre is at 30 Water St (Mon–Fri 8am–5pm, Sat 9am–1pm; ☎056 811 4000, ⓦinfoparys.co.za). The wedsite has lots of information about events and places to stay.

ACCOMMODATION

Art Lovers Guest House 89 Breë St ☎056 817 6515, ⓦartloversguesthouse.co.za. Seven spacious and artistically furnished suites with antique furniture, chandeliers and Persian carpets, plus nice personal touches like a glass of sherry to welcome guests. Breakfast is included and there's a restaurant for dinner. No children under 12. R1700

Secret Place 21A Venus Rd ☎056 811 5232, ⓦsecretplace.co.za. An elegant guesthouse infused with the flavour of France – it even boasts its own formal garden – with beautiful rooms decorated in a romantic, antique style. Each room is different: one has an outdoor shower, while another overlooks a herb garden. B&B R1100

EATING

O's Restaurant 1 De Villiers St ☎056 811 3683. Homey Boer comfort food like *bobotie* (R125) alongside more sophisticated fare like escargots and smoked chicken pasta, all served in a pretty and peaceful riverside garden. Bookings recommended. Wed–Sat 11am–10pm, Sun 11am–3pm.

Vetkoek Paleis & Kerrie Huis 62 Breë St ☎056 817 6833. Snack on Afrikaner *vetkoek*, deep-fried pastries with various fillings, at this local institution whose name means "fat cake palace and curry house". A *vetkoek* filled with mince curry will cost you R50. Normal breakfasts and pancakes are also served. Daily 8.30am–3pm.

Gauteng

JOHANNESBURG AT DUSK

Gauteng

Gauteng is South Africa's smallest region, comprising less than two percent of its landmass, yet contributing around forty percent of the GDP. Home to over twelve million people, Gauteng is almost entirely urban; while the province encompasses a section of the Magaliesberg Mountains to the east and the gold-rich Witwatersrand to the south and west, the area is dominated by the huge conurbation incorporating Johannesburg, Pretoria and a host of industrial towns and townships that surround them. Although lacking the spectacular natural attractions of the Cape Province or Mpumalanga, Gauteng has a subtle physical power. Startling outcrops of rock known as *koppies*, with intriguing and often lucrative geology, are found in the sprawling suburbs and grassy plains of deep-red earth that fringe the cities.

The older parts of Johannesburg and Pretoria are gloriously green in summer: both are among the most tree-rich cities on Earth, and Johannesburg, home to ten million of them, is proudly described by locals as the world's largest man-made forest. The ubiquitous jacaranda trees blossom in October, turning the suburbs purple.

Gauteng is dominated by **Johannesburg**, whose origins lie in the exploitation of **gold** (Gauteng means "Place of Gold" in Sotho). Although it has grown rapidly since the discovery of gold in 1886 to become the richest metropolis in Africa, it is a hectic city, home to extreme contrasts of wealth and poverty. The city has a reputation among both visitors and South Africans as a place to avoid, but those who acquire a taste for Joburg – something you can do in just a few days – are seduced by its energy and vibrancy, unmatched by any other city in South Africa. A highly cosmopolitan city, and the most Africanized in the country, Joburg boasts South Africa's most famous townships, its most active and diverse cultural life, some of its best restaurants and the most progressive nightlife.

Some 50km north lies dignified **Pretoria**, the country's administrative capital. Historically an Afrikaner stronghold, today it's a cosmopolitan mix of civil servants, diplomats and students from South Africa and around the world. Smaller and more relaxed than Johannesburg, Pretoria is an intriguing destination in its own right, with a range of interesting museums and historic buildings. The Gautrain rapid rail connection between Joburg and Pretoria was nothing less than a transport revolution when it opened in 2010, finally offering locals and travellers a safe and affordable alternative to the tedious traffic jams on the N1.

Less than an hour from the centre of Joburg, amid the rolling foothills of the **Magaliesberg Mountains**, is a series of caves and archeological sites making up the **Cradle of Humankind** World Heritage Site. Most famous of these sites are the **Sterkfontein Caves**, where some of the world's most important discoveries of pre-human primate fossils have been made.

TOWNSHIP HOUSE IN SOWETO

ighlights

Downtown Johannesburg Experience a ruly pan-African urban buzz at the heart of the ontinent's richest city. **See p.451**

Melville Hang out with Joburg's students nd hipsters in one of the city's few places where bars, cafés and decent restaurants line he street. **See p.463**

The Apartheid Museum, Joburg A owerful, inspiring journey through the South frican struggle for freedom. **See p.467**

Soweto tours Sample the vibrancy of South frica's most historically significant township. ee p.467

❺ **Live music** Make the effort and you'll find that Joburg has the best scene in the country. **See p.479**

❻ **The big match** Whether it's Chiefs v Pirates or Springboks v All Blacks, sport in Joburg is always big news. **See p.482**

❼ **Cradle of Humankind** A series of caves on the fringe of Johannesburg provides vital fossil evidence of human ancestry. **See p.482**

❽ **Voortrekker Monument and The Freedom Park, Pretoria** These two monuments are dramatic tributes to the old and new South Africa. **See p.492**

HIGHLIGHTS ARE MARKED ON THE MAP ON P.448

Johannesburg

Back in October 1886, when gold was discovered, what is now **JOHANNESBURG** was an expanse of sleepy, treeless veld. Now the economic engine of Africa, it's the sprawling, infuriating, invigorating home to six million people, but never the country's seat of government or national political power.

During the apartheid era, Johannesburg was the city in which black resistance and urban culture were most strident – Nelson Mandela and Walter Sisulu formed the country's first black law firm here in 1952 – while the democratic era has seen the city

HIGHLIGHTS

1. Downtown Johannesburg
2. Melville
3. The Apartheid Museum, Joburg
4. Soweto tours
5. Live music
6. The big match
7. Cradle of Humankind
8. Voortrekker Monument and The Freedom Park, Pretoria

become the vanguard of the gradual deracialization of South African society. The country's burgeoning **black elite** and **middle class** are concentrated here, and the city is a giant soup of ethnicities: Zulu and Sotho-speakers, Afrikaners and white English-speakers predominate, but Joburg culture is also enriched by immigrants from across Africa, as well as sizeable Indian, coloured, Chinese, Greek, Jewish, Portuguese and Lebanese communities. Joburg is an unpretentious, loud, ballsy city; outsiders are quickly accepted, and a pervasive social warmth keeps many of its more relaxed citizens from leaving.

Even so, there are still astonishing extremes of wealth and poverty here: mansions in verdant **suburbs** are protected by high walls and electrified fences, only a kilometre or two from overcrowded **shantytowns** such as the high-rise inner-city flatlands of Hillbrow and Yeoville, where hundreds of thousands of immigrants, mostly from Zimbabwe, have formed a teeming ghetto economy, since the formal job market cannot absorb most of them.

The bewildering size of Joburg can be daunting, and some visitors venture out only to the bland, safe, covered shopping malls and restaurants of the northern suburbs while making hasty plans to move on. However, once you've found a convenient way of getting around, either by car, on the new **Gautrain** trains and buses, or in the company of a tour guide, the history, diversity and crackling energy of the city can quickly become compelling.

The **central business district**, which in the 1990s was all but abandoned by big business fleeing crime and grime, is undergoing a slow rebirth, with crime rates dropping and investors moving in. New City Improvement Districts have been implemented to oversee the cleaning, sprucing up and guarding of the central areas, most effectively so far in Braamfontein and Maboneng; security guards and cameras can now be seen on many street corners and, as a result, it's now relatively safe to walk around the CBD during the day.

Shopping is Joburg's biggest addiction, and the city offers an abundance of superb contemporary African art, fashion and design. And then there are the **townships**, most easily explored on a tour but, in some cases, possible to get to under your own steam.

Joburg is also a great place to watch **sport**, with soccer, rugby and cricket teams commanding feverish support. The 2010 Football World Cup was headquartered in the city; the 100,000-seat FNB Stadium (formerly Soccer City) is a proud reminder of the event, and is regularly used for games, concerts and other gatherings.

Brief history

The city of Johannesburg dates back to 1886, when Australian prospector **George Harrison** found the main Witwatersrand gold-bearing reef. Almost immediately, this quiet area of the Transvaal became swamped with diggers from near and far, and a tented city sprang up around the site. The Pretoria authorities were forced to proclaim a township nearby: they chose a useless triangle of land called the Randjeslaagte, which had been left unclaimed by local farmers. **Johann Rissik**, the surveyor, called it Johannesburg, either after himself or after Christiaan Johannes Joubert, the chief of mining, or the president of the South African Republic (ZAR), Paul Johannes Kruger.

Mining magnates such as Cecil Rhodes and Barney Barnato possessed the capital necessary to exploit the world's richest gold reef, and their **Chamber of Mines** (a self-regulatory body for mine owners, founded in 1889) attempted to bring some order to the digging frenzy, with common policies on recruitment, wages and working conditions. In 1893, due partly to pressure from white workers, and with the approval of the ZAR government, the chamber introduced the **colour bar**, which excluded black workers from all but manual labour.

By 1895, Johannesburg's population had soared to over 100,000, many of whom were not Boers and had no interest in the ZAR's independence. Kruger and the burghers regarded these *uitlanders* (foreigners) as a potential threat to their political supremacy, and denied them the vote despite the income they generated for the State's coffers. Legislation was also passed to control the influx of black workers to Johannesburg, and Indians were forcibly moved out of the city into a western location. Before long, large shantytowns filled with black and Indian workers were springing up on the outskirts of Johannesburg.

The Anglo-Boer War

In 1900, during the Anglo-Boer War, Johannesburg fell to the British, who had been attempting to annex the gold-rich area for some time. At the same time, more black townships were established, including **Sophiatown** (1903) in an area previously used for dumping sewage, and **Alexandra** (1905). Bubonic plague erupted on the northern fringes of the city in 1904, providing justification for the authorities to demolish several Indian and African communities, including **Newtown**, just west of the centre.

Meanwhile, white mine workers were becoming unionized, and outbreaks of fighting over pay and working hours were a frequent occurrence. Their poorly paid black counterparts were also mobilizing; their main grievance was the ruling that skilled jobs were the preserve of white workers. Resentments came to a head in the **Rand Revolt** of 1922, after the Chamber of Mines, anxious to cut costs, decided to allow black miners into the skilled jobs previously held only by white miners. White workers were furious: street battles broke out and lasted for four days. Government troops were called in to restore order and over two hundred men were killed. Alarmed at the scale of white discontent, Prime Minister Jan Smuts ruled that the colour bar be maintained, and throughout the 1920s the government passed laws restricting the movement of black people living in the city.

Populating Soweto

During the 1930s, the township of **Orlando** became established southwest of the city, with accommodation for 80,000 black Africans; this was the nucleus around which **Soweto** evolved. By 1945, 400,000 black people were living in and around

GANDHI IN JOHANNESBURG

It was during the ten years that **Mohandas Gandhi** spent in Johannesburg between 1903 and 1913 that he first tested the philosophies for which he is famous. As an advocate, he frequently appeared in the Transvaal Law Courts (now demolished), which stood in what has since been renamed Gandhi Square in downtown Johannesburg. Defending mainly South African Indians accused of breaking the restrictive and racist registration laws, Gandhi began to see practical applications for his concept of **Satyagraha**, soul force, or passive resistance, as a means of defying immoral state oppression.

Gandhi himself was twice imprisoned, along with other passive resisters, in the fort in Braamfontein, on what is now Constitution Hill. On one of these occasions he was taken from his cell to the office of General Jan Smuts to negotiate the prisoners' release, but finding himself at liberty had to borrow the railway fare home from the general's secretary.

Gandhi's ideas found resonance in the non-violent ideals of those who established the **African National Congress** in 1912. Forty years later, only a few years after Gandhi's successful use of Satyagraha to end the British Raj in India, the start of the ANC's Defiance Campaign against the pass laws in 1952 owed much to his principles. In recent years, however, Gandhi's views on the struggle against oppression have come under scrutiny, with many questioning why his political activity in South Africa was aimed only at achieving equality for Indians. Particularly damning evidence of Gandhi's own racism is a series of letters sent to colonial authorities during his time in South Africa in which he referred to black Africans as "savages" and agreed with some segregationist policies that would offer Indians preferential treatment over the black African population. MuseuMAfricA (see p.457) contains displays on Gandhi's time in Johannesburg, as does Constitution Hill (see p.459), and he is commemorated with a statue on Gandhi Square.

Johannesburg – an increase of one hundred percent in a decade. In August 1946, 70,000 African Mineworkers Union members went on strike over working conditions. The government sent police in, and twelve miners were killed and over a thousand injured.

Forced removals of non-white residents from Johannesburg's inner suburbs, particularly from Sophiatown, began in 1955. Thousands were dumped far from the city centre, in the new township of Meadowlands, next to Orlando, and Sophiatown was crassly renamed Triomf (triumph). The **ANC** (see p.643) established itself as the most important black protest organization during this period, proclaiming the Freedom Charter in Kliptown, Soweto, that year.

During the 1950s, a vigorous black urban culture began to emerge in the townships, and the new *marabi* jazz and its offspring, the jubilant *kwela* pennywhistle style, were played in illegal drinking houses called *shebeens*. This was also the era of *Drum Magazine*, which celebrated a glamorous, sophisticated township zeitgeist, and introduced a host of talented journalists and photographers, such as Can Themba, Casey "Kid" Motsisi and Peter Magubane, to the city and the world. *Mbaqanga* music emerged later, with its heavy basslines and sensuous melodies capturing the bittersweet essence of life in the townships.

7

Resistance and democracy

The formation in 1972 of the **Black Consciousness Movement** (BCM) rekindled political activism, particularly among Soweto students. On June 16, 1976, student riots erupted in the township, and the unrest spread nationwide (see box, p.470). The youth's war against the State escalated in the 1980s, resulting in regular "**states of emergency**", during which the armed forces had permission to do anything they liked to contain revolt. Towards the end of the decade, the government relaxed "petty" apartheid, turning a blind eye to the growth of "grey" areas like Hillbrow – white suburbs where non-white South Africans were moving in.

The three years after Nelson Mandela's release in 1990 saw widespread political violence in Gauteng right up until the day before the first democratic national elections. However, as elsewhere in South Africa, the election on April 27, 1994, went off peacefully. The ANC won comfortably in Gauteng then, and retained control of the province in subsequent municipal and national elections. In the fiercely contested 2016 municipal elections, however, support for the ANC fell by almost ten percent compared to 2011. A growing feeling among urban voters that the ANC have not totally lived up to their promises and that they have turned a blind eye to corruption within local government, led to the loss of control of Johannesburg and Pretoria, the province's two largest cities, and the former is now led by a mayor from the opposition party the Democratic Alliance (DA). Black South Africans have indeed made steady inroads into positions of influence in business and politics, but, as an increasing number of township dwellers move to the suburbs, Johannesburg's infrastructure has struggled to cope: low-income housing is not being built fast enough, energy supply is wobbling as demand surges, and traffic is often hellish, though the Gautrain rail network has improved the situation along the north–south routes, while the efficient Rea Vaya bus network is also steadily expanding its routes northwards.

The central business district (CBD)

Johannesburg's **CBD**, the grid of streets and tightly packed skyscrapers just to the south of the Witwatersrand Ridge, is the most recognizable part of the city. For a century after the first mining camp was built, on what is now Commissioner Street, the CBD was the core of Joburg's buzzing commercial and financial life. Then there was the mass exodus during the crime-ridden 1980s and 1990s, and when the Joburg Stock Exchange moved out in 1999 in favour of Sandton, the city centre was all but written off. Today, however, Central Joburg is back on the map, with several regeneration projects having a profound effect on how the locals experience their city. A visit to the CBD offers the chance to see buildings and institutions with a fascinating history and get a taste of the bustle, sounds and thrills of a genuinely African city.

The Carlton Centre and around

Commissioner St • Centre and viewpoint daily 9am–5pm • R15; ticket office on the lower ground floor • Parking free for tower ticket holders • ☎ 011 308 2876

A good place to start exploring the CBD, the **Carlton Centre** complex has a lively shopping mall on the lower and underground floors and a convenient car park across Main Street. Its main attraction, however, is the **Top of Africa viewpoint** on the fiftieth

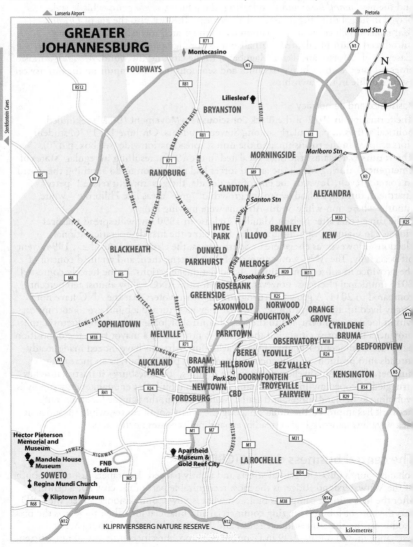

GREATER JOHANNESBURG

Lanseria Airport

Pretoria

Midrand Stn

R71

Montecasino

N1

FOURWAYS

R512

R81

Liliesleaf

BRYANSTON

R81

M1

R71

MORNINGSIDE

Marlboro Stn

WILLIAM NICOL

M9

RANDBURG

M5

N1

SANDTON

ALEXANDRA

Santon Stn

N3

R25

BRAM FISCHER DRIVE

MALIBONGWE DRIVE

BEYERS NAUDE

JAN SMUTS

HYDE PARK

BRAMLEY

KEW

M30

ILLOVO

BLACKHEATH

DUNKELD

M8

M5

PARKHURST

MELROSE

M20

M11

ROSEBANK

Rosebank Stn

R25

GREENSIDE

SAXONWOLD

NORWOOD

ORANGE GROVE

BEYERS NAUDE

BARRY HERTZOG

LONG FIFTH

HOUGHTON

CYRILDENE

SOPHIATOWN

OXFORD

LOUIS BOTHA

N12

MELVILLE

PARKTOWN

OBSERVATORY

M18

BRUMA

R71

KINGSWAY

BEREA

YEOVILLE

R24

BEDFORDVIEW

AUCKLAND PARK

BRAAM-FONTEIN

HILLBROW

BEZ VALLEY

N1

Park Stn

DOORNFONTEIN

R22

KENSINGTON

N3

R41

R24

NEWTOWN

CBD

TROYEVILLE

R14

FORDSBURG

FAIRVIEW

R29

M2

M1

M7

Hector Pieterson Memorial and Museum

SOWETO HIGHWAY

TURFFONTEIN

M1

M31

Mandela House Museum

FNB Stadium

Apartheid Museum & Gold Reef City

LA ROCHELLE

SOWETO

M5

M34

Regina Mundi Church

M38

N14

R68

Kliptown Museum

W12

W12

KLIPRIVIERSBERG NATURE RESERVE

0   5

kilometres

Sterkfontein Caves

7

N

SAFETY IN JOHANNESBURG

With Johannesburg's extremes of poverty and wealth, its brash, get-ahead culture and the presence of illegal firearms, it's hardly surprising that the city can be a dangerous place. Despite its unenviable reputation, it's important to retain a sense of proportion about potential risks and not to let paranoia ruin your stay. Most crime happens in the outlying townships, and the vast majority of Joburgers are exceedingly friendly; as in all major cities, taking simple precautions (see p.73 and below) is likely to see you through safely.

If you're wandering around **on foot**, the most likely risk of crime is from mugging. Although significant effort has gone into making the riskiest central areas safer – such as the installation of security cameras – you should remain alert when exploring the central business district (CBD), Braamfontein and Newtown, do your touring in daylight, use busy streets and never be complacent.

Joubert Park, Hillbrow, Berea and Yeoville should only be entered with a local guide who knows the area well. You're very unlikely to be mugged on the streets of Melville, Parktown, Rosebank or Sandton. If you want to walk around one of the riskier areas, study maps beforehand (not on street corners), don't walk around with luggage and avoid groups of young men. If you're carrying valuables, make a portion of them easily available, so that muggers are likely to be quickly satisfied, and avoid flashing around expensive jewellery or cameras. Never resist muggers. You're unlikely to be mugged on **public transport**, but, as always, stay alert, especially at busy spots such as Park Station and taxi ranks, and be extra vigilant when getting off minibus taxis. Waiting for buses in the northern suburbs is generally safe.

If you're **driving** around, there is a small risk of "smash and grab" theft or carjacking; keep all bags and valuables locked in the trunk, lock the car doors and keep windows up when driving after dark and in central areas. Always seek out secure – preferably guarded – parking; in Joburg this is in ample supply. Although urban legend suggests you can cruise through red traffic lights at night, this is dangerous and illegal; stop, keep a good distance from the car in front of you and be aware of anyone approaching the car.

Don't expect too much from the **police**, who normally have priorities other than keeping an eye out for tourists. In the city centre and Rosebank, **private guards**, identifiable by their yellow armbands and stationed on street corners, provide an effective anti-crime presence on the street.

oor of the Carlton Tower, Africa's tallest building (222m), which offers breathtaking iews of the centre of Johannesburg, and shows how the mines, mine dumps and city oncrete exist cheek by jowl. The adjacent *Carlton Hotel* was once the best hotel on the ontinent, but now stands empty after being closed in 1997.

Main Street

Main Street, partially pedestrianized for six blocks west of the regenerated Gandhi Square ear the Carlton Centre, is home to the offices of various mining companies and makes a reat introduction to Joburg's mining history. Industrial relics, such as trains, wooden ampmills and a headgear lift tower, have been placed along the road; walk right to the vestern end to see the fabulous 1940s Art Deco **Anglo American head office** buildings, onted by a fountain with a beautiful statue of a herd of springboks jumping over a pond. North of the courthouse, on the corner of Fox and Gerard Sekoto streets, **Chancellor ouse** is where Nelson Mandela and Oliver Tambo started their law firm in the 1950s. he ground-floor windows have a small exhibition about the history of the building, hile the impressive statue outside, based on the famous photo by *Drum* magazine's ob Gosani, shows a young Mandela shadowboxing.

Gauteng Legislature and around

rner of Rissik St and Albertina Sisulu Rd

he impressive **Gauteng Legislature** was built in 1915 as the City Hall and is fronted y huge palm trees. Beside it stands the city's daintiest little skyscraper, the ten-storey

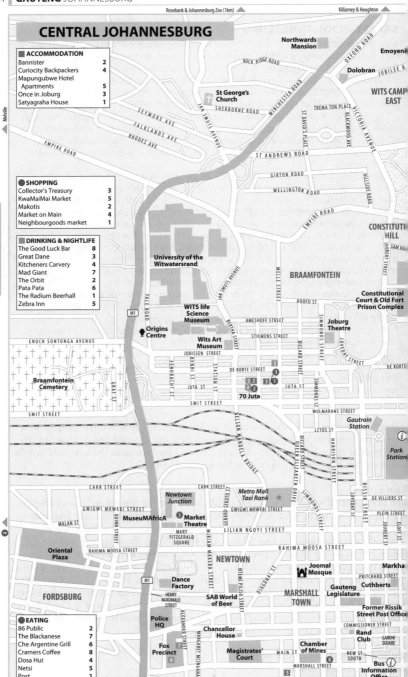

CENTRAL JOHANNESBURG

ACCOMMODATION

Bannister	2
Curiosity Backpackers	4
Mapungubwe Hotel Apartments	5
Once in Joburg	3
Satyagraha House	1

SHOPPING

Collector's Treasury	3
KwaMaiMai Market	5
Makotis	2
Market on Main	4
Neighbourgoods market	1

DRINKING & NIGHTLIFE

The Good Luck Bar	8
Great Dane	3
Kitcheners Carvery	4
Mad Giant	7
The Orbit	2
Pata Pata	6
The Radium Beerhall	1
Zebra Inn	5

EATING

86 Public	2
The Blackanese	7
Che Argentine Grill	6
Cramers Coffee	8
Dosa Hut	4
Netsi	5
Post	1
The Potato Shed	3

Barbican, built in 1931, which was saved from neglect and destruction when it was renovated in 2010. Directly opposite the Legislature, the former **Rissik Street Post Office** was not as lucky; squatters accidentally set it on fire in 2009. In 2016 it was announced that the building would be partially renovated, although plans for the future use of the building beyond this are still not clear. When this building was completed in 1897, it was the tallest in the city. Neo-Baroque in style, its fourth floor and clock tower were later additions, timed to coincide with the accession of the British king, Edward VII, in 1902.

Rand Club

33 Loveday St • Visits by prior arrangement only, book at least a week in advance • ☎ 011 870 4276, ✉ events@randclub.co.za, ⓦ randclub.co.za

The grandiose **Rand Club** is where mining magnates, nicknamed Randlords, have come to dine and unwind for over 130 years. Although the club was founded in 1887, the current building was completed in 1904 and is the fourth to occupy the site, as each successive clubhouse was replaced to reflect the members' growing wealth. The impressive hall with its stained-glass dome is surrounded by various dining rooms, a library and the *Main Bar*, home to the longest bar in Africa, which snakes around the room. The club hosts regular events where non-members can lunch, dine or drink at the club (all with prior booking). Visitors must observe the dress code: a shirt and smart trousers and shoes for men, smart casual for women.

Standard Bank Gallery

Corner Simmonds and Frederick sts • Mon–Fri 8am–4.30pm, Sat 9am–1pm • Free • ☎ 011 631 4467, ⓦ standardbankarts.co.za

At the superb **Standard Bank Gallery**, changing exhibitions consistently show off some of the best contemporary African art in South Africa. The gallery is especially good at uncovering new talent; keep an eye out for the annual exhibition by the Standard Bank Young Artist Award winner.

Ferreira Mine Stope

5 Simmonds St • Mon–Fri 8am–4pm, Sat 8am–1pm • Free

In the Standard Bank's head office, opposite their art gallery, it's possible to take a lift from the main concourse down to the **Ferreira Mine Stope**, an old mine access tunnel discovered when the building was being constructed in 1986. The plain rock face you see still bears pick-axe scars, and there's a simple but fascinating display putting the history of Johannesburg in context; look out for the old sepia photographs of the mine and early Joburg.

Diagonal Street

Diagonal Street, at the western end of Pritchard Street, lies at the heart of one of the most fascinating areas of the CBD. In the shadow of various concrete and glass behemoths, including the former Johannesburg Stock Exchange, is a street of old two-storey buildings, some of which date back to the 1890s; the lines of washing on the upstairs balconies show that they are still residential. The streets are home to a number of traders and shops peddling traditional medicines (*umuthi*), Sotho blankets and paraffin stoves alongside mobile phones. Though it might not feel so at first, the area is fairly safe, and with businessmen mingling with hawkers it has a very urban-African buzz. At the southern end of the street there are two fine statues of ANC heroes Walter and Albertina Sisulu.

Newtown

On the western edge of the CBD between Diagonal Street and the M1 motorway flyover, **Newtown** is an area of redevelopment where some of Johannesburg's cultural hot spots can be found, most notably the excellent Market Theatre. The striking

Nelson Mandela Bridge provides a swift link to the district from Braamfontein and the northern suburbs, while the large newly opened Newtown Junction shopping mall beside the bridge has breathed fresh life into the area, with a handful of new restaurants and the Work Shop New Town emporium showcasing local fashion and design.

MuseuMAfricA

Mary Fitzgerald Square • Tues–Sun 9am–5pm • Free • ☎ 011 833 5624

At the heart of Newtown is the massive **MuseuMAfricA**. The sheer size of the museum – formerly the city's fruit and vegetable market – can make it seem rather sparse and empty, and its deserted exhibition halls only compound the feeling. Don't let this deter you from visiting, however, as among the dozens of halls are some well-researched exhibitions that are worth seeking out. Among the best is *Joburg Firsts*, an exhibition filled with unusual details about life in early Joburg such as the story of the arrival of the city's first barmaid in 1886, who became an instant celebrity. Also look out for the imaginative re-creations of shacks from Joburg's lesser-known townships Alexandra and Thokoza, and the exhibit devoted to the history of South African political cartoons.

Market Theatre

Mary Fitzgerald Square, entrance at the eastern end of MuseuMAfricA, ⓦ markettheatre.co.za

The famous **Market Theatre** (see p.480) has been a reliable source of stimulating and often ground-breaking dramatic output since it launched in 1976. Weekly tours of the building (every Wednesday at 11am), highlighting the important role the theatre played in bravely traversing the black-white divide during the apartheid era, can be booked online. The Newtown Junction shopping precinct is just around the corner.

South African Breweries (SAB) World of Beer

On the corner of Helen Joseph and Miriam Makeba sts • Tues–Sat 10am–6pm, Sun–Mon 10am–4pm • R115 • ☎ 011 836 4900, ⓦ worldofbeer.co.za

The ninety-minute tour of the **South African Breweries (SAB) World of Beer** takes you through six thousand years of brewing history, which begs the question why SAB's ubiquitous end product, the anaemic, fizzy Castle lager, is so disappointing. Still, the reconstructed gold-rush pubs and 1960s *shebeen* are fun, along with the greenhouse where sample crops of barley and hops grow; use your two free beer vouchers to wash down a pub lunch on the balcony of the *Tap Room* bar and watch the city rush by.

Police Headquarters and 1 Fox Precinct

Fox St

At the infamous Johannesburg **police headquarters**, anti-apartheid activists were detained and tortured, and some fell to their deaths, having "jumped" from the tenth floor. After this, it's a pleasant relief to find the newly developed **1 Fox Precinct** which looks onto the building. Here a cluster of century-old warehouses has been transformed into a craft brewery and restaurant, foodhall-style market, beer garden, artist studios and live music venue. There's guarded parking by the entrance on 1 Fox Street.

Fordsburg and Oriental Plaza

The old Indian neighbourhood of Fordsburg lies just further west of Newtown, on the other side of the M1 flyover. At the centre of the neighbourhood is the vast **Oriental Plaza**, a hugely popular, Indian-owned shopping complex, selling everything from fabrics to spices and where haggling is *de rigueur*. Just beyond the Plaza, Mint Road is the scene of a colourful Asian market (Thurs–Sat evening from 5pm), with dozens of stalls selling knock-off DVDs and good Indian street food.

Johannesburg Art Gallery

Joubert Park • Tues–Sun 10am–5pm • Free • ☎ 011 725 3130, ⓦ friendsofjag.org

On the eastern side of Park Station, **Joubert Park**, named after General Piet Joubert (who lost the South African Republic general election to Paul Kruger in 1893), is the only inner-city green space but largely regarded as a no-go area.

The one sight you can visit here is the **Johannesburg Art Gallery**, housed in an elegant, predominantly nineteenth-century building accessed via King George Street (with safe parking). This is one of the most progressive galleries in the country, and regular exhibits include vast wooden sculptures by the visionary Venda artist Jackson Hlungwani that tower up to the ceilings. Elsewhere, there's a very South African mixture of African artworks and artefacts from the ceremonial to the purely decorative, and a range of European paintings, including some minor Dutch Masters. The special exhibitions are usually excellent, too.

The Maboneng Precinct

Between Commissioner and Main sts, bordered by Berea and Auret sts • ⓦ mabonengprecinct.com • Best reached from the M2 highway via Joe Slovo Drive (M31); take the R24 Albertina Sisulu Rd exit and follow signs to the right

Around Main Street, east of the city centre, several city blocks have been transformed into a hive of cultural activity, and are perhaps the best place to get a taste of the potential of the city centre, and how Joburg is changing for the better. It all started with **Arts on Main**, a former warehouse complex that now houses art workshops and galleries, an arts bookshop and a courtyard restaurant. It positively buzzes with people during the excellent **Market on Main** every Sunday, when clothing, accessories and healthy food are for sale.

Just 200m down the road, **Main Street Life** is a 1970s industrial building that houses the small POPArt Theatre (see p.480), the Bioscope art-house cinema (see p.480), the *Pata Pata* bar (see p.478), and a rooftop bar with great CBD views. Several other adjacent city blocks have also been renovated to house loft-style apartments and more than a dozen boutiques and small restaurants that attract a hip crowd, particularly on Sundays. Two blocks north, at the corner of Commissioner and Albrecht streets, is **The Cosmopolitan**, a colonial-era hotel that is now home to an art gallery, restaurant and a coffee shop which opens out onto a courtyard sculpture garden. The area is safe to visit even at night, with plenty of security guards around.

The central suburbs

Grouped around the CBD are various suburbs which, given Joburg's itinerant population and fast-changing demography, seem to be in a state of constant change. Some, particularly Hillbrow, Berea and Yeoville, were once the "grey areas" of Joburg, where apartheid first started to break down in the 1980s. The police turned a blind eye as large numbers of black people started moving from the townships into these previously all-white areas. Today, most white residents have left these neighbourhoods – though they still reside in leafy, residential Observatory, just east of Yeoville – while migrants from all over Africa have flooded in. The hectic street life of Yeoville, Berea and Hillbrow can be very exciting, but you should not venture into these areas at night and should consider going with a street-smart local or a guide during the day.

Braamfontein

It's not just for the transport facilities at Park Station that you might have cause to visit **Braamfontein** (ⓦ braamfontein.org.za), which starts at the main train station and extends north as far as Empire Road. Helped by its small size and clear physical boundaries, Johannesburg's prime student district has been regenerated after successful city improvement projects, increased policing and security, numerous new artworks nd dozens of office-space-to-budget-accommodation conversions. It's a fun place to tart exploring the new Johannesburg, especially on Saturday when the food market is n, and the developments in Braamfontein seem to fit comfortably in the urban fabric, vith plenty of local students livening up the scene.

'0 Juta and around

orner of Juta and De Beer sts • Ⓦ playbraamfontein.co.za/70-juta-street

A small development with a handful of fashion boutiques, shops, galleries and cafés, **'0 Juta** is where the regeneration of Braamfontein took off. Across the street, the istorical *Milner Park Hotel*, dating from 1906, is now home to the bohemian **Kitchener's** bar (see p.478), while a dozen other boutiques, cafés and restaurants have ince opened up along nearby De Beer and Melle streets. The best time to visit is on aturdays between 9am and 3pm, when the car park at 73 Juta Street is home to the ustling **Neighbourgoods market** (see p.481).

Constitution Hill and Old Fort prison complex

ubert St • Daily 9am–5pm, tours leave every hour and are included in the entrance price • R65–85 • ☎ 011 381 3100, Ⓦ www constitutionhill.org.za

7

Since 2003, **Constitution Hill** has been the home of the Constitutional Court, South Africa's highest court. Its hearings are fascinating for those interested in law or political cience: the Court must tread a difficult path between the constitution's array of opular rights and the frustrating realities of a state that is struggling to guarantee hem. The Court was built using the bricks of a demolished men's prison and is lecorated with over two hundred mostly excellent modern and contemporary South African paintings and sculptures, worth seeing in themselves.

The adjacent **Old Fort prison complex** was originally built by Paul Kruger in 1893 to e used as a prison. Following the Jameson Raid, ramparts were built around it and luring the second Anglo-Boer War the site was used as a military fort. From 1902 onwards it again became a prison and for the next eighty years was used to incarcerate nd torture mostly black prisoners who were jailed for breaking racist laws or fighting or their repeal. You can visit the spine-chilling **Number Four prison building** (the o-called "native" prison added in 1904), where Gandhi and Pan-Africanist Congress eader Robert Sobukwe were held, and the cell inside the original Old Fort where Mandela was kept briefly after his arrest in 1962.

The **Women's Jail**, built in 1910, is a grand Edwardian building that held black and vhite women prisoners in separate sections. The notorious serial poisoner Daisy de Melker was kept here when she was on death row, but major political leaders such as Winnie Madikizela-Mandela, Albertina Sisulu, Helen Joseph and Ruth First also ecame familiar with its cells. From the 1950s onward, most of the prison's inmates vere passlaw offenders, until the prison complex was finally closed in 1983. Rich in ymbolism, the Court and the prison complex provide a subtle but arresting estimony to the country's ongoing transformation, eloquently expressing the pride South Africans have in their new constitution and the democratic principles nshrined therein.

Origins Centre

ale Rd • Daily 10am–5pm • R80 • ☎ 011 717 4700, Ⓦ origins.org.za

On the campus of the University of the Witwatersrand, also known as "Wits", the **Origins Centre** uses a combination of films and exhibits to explain the African origins of umanity – where you can see a 75,000-year-old engraved ochre rock that's considered he world's first artwork – before moving on to its main focus: the beliefs, traditions nd rock art of the San people (see box, p.395). This is the museum's main strength, nd the displays give a useful overview for those intending to explore the San rock-art ites elsewhere in the country.

Wits Art Museum

Corner of Jorissen St and Jan Smuts Ave • Wed–Sun 10am–4pm • Free • ☎ 011 717 1363, ⓦ wits.ac.za/wam

Wits Art Museum presents the university's rich art collection, built up over seventy years, in exhibitions that change every month or so. It's especially worth checking out the West and Central African art, though the modern photography and other genres are equally fascinating. There's a very good café on-site, too.

Hillbrow

Smit Street marks the boundary of Joubert Park with infamous and densely populated **Hillbrow**, dominated by high-rise apartment buildings all crammed with people. Hillbrow has always attracted Joburg's new immigrants. Immediately after World War II, the typical immigrant was English, Italian or East European Jewish. These days, Africans from all over the continent are arriving in numbers, giving Hillbrow a uniquely pan-African atmosphere, with music from Lagos to Kinshasa to Harare pumping from the bars, clubs and markets that line the main thoroughfares. Along the many side streets, the scene is distinctly seedy, with drug pushers loitering outside lurid strip joints. The suburb is widely regarded as a no-go area for tourists, but the excellent **walking tours** by local NGO Dlala Nje, which leave from Shop 1, Ponte City, Saratoga Avenue (☎ 072 397 2269, ⓦ dlalanje .org, from R350), are a safe and fun way to visit Hillbrow and neighbouring Yeoville, while contributing to Dlala Nje's community centre and social projects. The walks visit the top floor of the fifty-storey Ponte City residential tower, renovated parks and apartment buildings, while the evening tours take in Yeoville's food and nightlife scene.

The northern suburbs

Safe, prosperous and packed with shops and restaurants, the **northern suburbs** seem a world apart from the CBD and its surrounds. The name is actually a catch-all term for the seemingly endless urban sprawl running over 30km from Parktown, beyond the N1

SIR HERBERT BAKER

South Africa's most famous architect, **Sir Herbert Baker**, was born in Kent, England, in 1862. Apprenticed to his architect uncle in London at the age of 17, Baker attended classes at the Royal Academy and Architectural Association. By the time he left for the Cape in 1892, Baker was already a convert to the new so-called **Free Style**, which advocated an often bizarre, but roughly historical, eclecticism. The young architect's favourite influences, which would crop up again and again in his work, were Renaissance Italian and medieval Kentish.

Once in the Cape, Baker met **Cecil Rhodes**, a contact which helped establish him as a major architectural figure in South Africa. The second Anglo-Boer War began in 1899 and Rhodes, assuming eventual British victory, sent Baker off to study the Classical architecture of Italy and Greece, hoping that he would return to create a British imperial architecture in South Africa. Baker returned to South Africa deeply influenced by what he had seen, and was summoned by **Lord Alfred Milner**, the administrator of the defeated Transvaal, to fulfil Rhodes' hopes.

Baker began with the homes of the so-called "kindergarten", the young Oxford- and Cambridge-educated men whom Milner had imported to govern the defeated territory. The result was the **Parktown mansions**, opulent houses lining the roads of Johannesburg's wealthiest suburb. Baker trained local craftsmen and used local materials for these mansions, pioneering the use of local *koppie* stone.

Baker's major public commissions were **St George's Cathedral** in Cape Town, the **South African Institute for Medical Research** in Johannesburg, and the sober **Union Buildings** in Pretoria, which express the British imperial dream – obsessed with Classical precedent, and in a location chosen because of its similarity to the site of the Acropolis in Athens.

Baker left South Africa in 1913 to design the Secretariat in New Delhi, India, returning to England on its completion, where he worked on South Africa House in Trafalgar Square, London. He was knighted in 1923; he died in 1946, and is buried in Westminster Abbey.

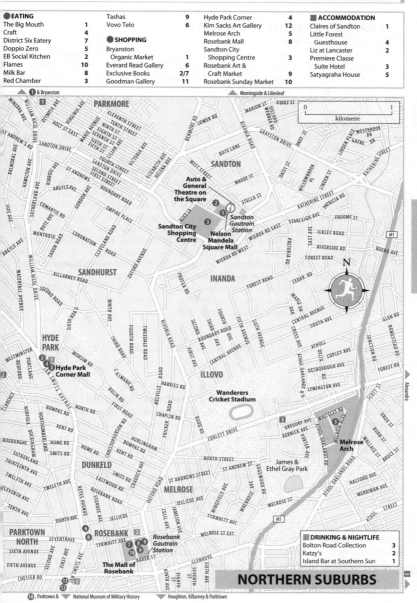

ring road and into an area known as **Midrand**, which is itself creeping toward the
southern edge of Pretoria. With the notable exception of Alexandra, this is a moneyed
area, where plush shopping malls are often the only communal meeting points, and the
majority of homes use high walls, iron gates and electric fences to advertise how
security-conscious a life the owners lead. Despite the often numbing sheen of affluence,
however, interesting pockets do exist, such as the centres of the suburbs of Melville,
Rosebank and Parkhurst. Most of the suburbs are close to major arterial roads and best

7

PARKTOWN'S RANDLORD MANSIONS

Parktown's main attraction lies in its distinctive architecture, largely the legacy of Sir Herbert Baker (see box, p.460). Baker's influence is still evident today in the opulent **mansions** of the Randlords, the rich mine owners, lining the streets. The Johannesburg Heritage Foundation (see p.474) runs regular tours, usually on Saturday afternoons, to some of the notable buildings in Parktown as well as to other districts in Johannesburg; and the Heritage Weekend (second weekend in September), also organized by the Foundation, features more tours and special events around the Parktown mansions and city centre.

High walls make viewing the buildings tricky on an independent visit, though most now have blue plaques with information outside. A good place to start is the area around Ridge Road, just north of the Randjeslaagte beacon, which marks the northern point of old Johannesburg. The *Sunnyside Park Hotel* here is a massive complex that Lord Alfred Milner used as his governor's residence from 1900. The best of the houses nearby are **Hazeldene Hall**, built in 1902 and featuring cast-iron verandas imported from Glasgow, and **The View**, built in 1897, with carved wooden verandas and an elegant red-brick exterior. To the north of Ridge Road, York Road curves to the left into Jubilee Road, with several palaces on its northern side; the neo-Queen Anne-style **Emoyeni**, at no. 15, built in 1905, is especially striking. At the corner of Jubilee Road and Victoria Avenue stands **Dolobran**, a weird and impressive house, also built in 1905. Designed by James Cope Christie (after Baker's original design had been rejected), it has an elegant veranda, an ornate corner turret, red Marseilles roof tiles and hallucinatory stained glass.

Crossing the busy M1 onto Rock Ridge Road, you'll reach the **Northwards Mansion**, built by Sir Herbert Baker in 1904 and home of the Johannesburg Heritage Foundation's offices. Unfortunately, there's no access along the road to Baker's own residence at no. 5. On the parallel Sherborne Road, you can see Baker's attractive St George's Church and its rectory, which mix Kentish and Italian features and were built in local rock.

---

explored by car, though the Gautrain, its bus routes and the Rea Vaya buses also offer easy access to some areas.

Parktown

The first elite residential area in Johannesburg, **Parktown** has retained its upmarket status despite its proximity to Hillbrow, which lies just southeast on the other side of Empire Road. The first people to settle in Parktown were Sir Lionel Philips, president of the Chamber of Mines, and his wife Lady Florence. In 1892, seeking a residence that looked onto the Magaliesberg rather than the mine dumps, they had a house built on what was then the Braamfontein farm. The rest of the farm was planted with eucalyptus trees and became known as the Sachsenwald Forest, some of which was given over to the Johannesburg Zoo a few years later. The remaining land was cleared in 1925 to make way for more residential developments.

Johannesburg Zoo

Roughly 2km north of Parktown, off Jan Smuts Ave • Daily 8.30am–5.30pm • R80 • ☎ 011 646 1131, ⊛ jhbzoo.org.za

Johannesburg Zoo is home to about two thousand species, including polar bears, gorillas, rhinos, white lions and red pandas. The zoo is slowly being spruced up, and it remains immensely popular, especially on warm weekends. The café beside the chimpanzee enclosure is an excellent spot for lunch.

Zoo Lake

Opposite the zoo, on the west side of Jan Smuts Ave

The park at **Zoo Lake** is a popular place for safe walking and picnicking that occasionally hosts outdoor performances, including an annual free concert in the first week of September. You can rent a rowing boat and pootle around the lake, or sample African cuisine at the lakeside restaurant *Moyo*, which has outdoor and indoor tables and plenty of peaceful, shady nooks.

National Museum of Military History

22 Erlswold Way • Daily 9am–4.30pm • R40 • ☎ 011 646 5513, ⓦ ditsong.org.za/militaryhistory.htm

The **National Museum of Military History**, next to the zoo, has a fascinating collection of intimidating tanks, guns and uniforms, and a display on Umkhonto we Sizwe (MK), the armed wing of the ANC – although the other liberation armies are conspicuous by their absence. The display focuses on the MK's commander, Joe Modise, who became Minister of Defence in the ANC government.

Melville

Together with Parkhurst, **Melville** is one of the more relaxed of the northern suburbs. When so many shops and restaurants in Joburg are tucked away in soulless malls, it's refreshing to find streets that are pleasant to walk along and full of cafés, secondhand bookshops and quirky antique dealers as well as a main drag (Seventh Street) lined with restaurants and bars for every taste.

Melville Koppies

North of Melville • Melville Koppies Central tours every Sun; check website for hours • R50 • ☎ 011 482 4797, ⓦ mk.org.za

The **Koppies** is a pleasant 3km-long hilltop park that is split into three distinct sections that contain hundreds of species of indigenous flora and fauna. Melville Koppies Central is a nature reserve that can only be visited on tours (starting on Judith Road opposite Marks Park; 3hr) and which is lovingly maintained by volunteers who weed

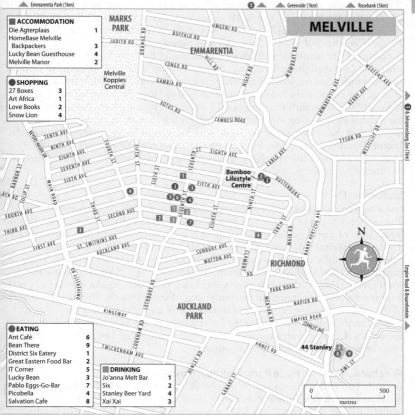

MELVILLE

■ ACCOMMODATION	
Die Agterplaas	1
HomeBase Melville Backpackers	3
Lucky Bean Guesthouse	4
Melville Manor	2

● SHOPPING	
27 Boxes	3
Art Africa	1
Love Books	2
Snow Lion	4

● EATING	
Ant Café	6
Bean There	9
District Six Eatery	1
Great Eastern Food Bar	2
IT Corner	5
Lucky Bean	3
Pablo Eggs-Go-Bar	7
Picobella	4
Salvation Cafe	8

■ DRINKING	
Jo'anna Melt Bar	1
Six	2
Stanley Beer Yard	4
Xai Xai	3

out tons of invasive non-African plants every year. Tours take in the archeological remains of both Stone Age and Iron Age settlements near the top of the hill. Flanking the reserve on either side, Melville Koppies East and West are public parks that are open daily from dawn until dusk; the main appeal of Melville Koppies East, reached from Zambesi Road (a short walk from the restaurants in the Bamboo Centre), is the hilltop, which offers fantastic views over central Joburg and the leafy suburbs. Melville Koppies West has a number of good walking trails – to get there, follow Ayr Road (off Melville's Main Road), which becomes Korea and then Arundel Road, and then turn right into the Third Avenue dead-end.

Emmarentia Park and Dam

Beyers Naude Drive · Daily 8am–5pm · Free · ☎ 011 782 7064

Emmarentia Park, a large spread of green parkland running north and west of the city for several kilometres, contains the beautiful **Johannesburg Botanic Garden** in its northeast corner. Situated beside Emmarentia Dam, a popular lake for paddling and rowing, the garden is noted for its wide-open spaces and routes for joggers, cyclists and walkers, which are safe during daylight hours when others are around. Apart from the fields, the botanical gardens have some attractive formal herb and rose gardens that are perfect for picnics. The main field is often used for concerts and festivals.

Sophiatown

West of Melville, the suburb of **Sophiatown** is unremarkable architecturally but significant in the history of apartheid – it was here that **Archbishop Trevor Huddleston**, the English cleric who established the UK Anti-Apartheid Movement, worked in the 1950s. When he died in 1998, his ashes were brought from London to be scattered in Sophiatown. For many years, Sophiatown was one of the few places within the city where blacks owned property, and as a result it became a creative whirlpool of culture, jazz, literature, cinema, journalism and political radicalism; Miriam Makeba had her musical roots here, and Huddleston gave the young Hugh Masekela his first trumpet. In the 1950s, the suburb was designated a white area by the government, which sent in the bulldozers, scattering some 65,000 inhabitants to Soweto between 1955 and 1960, regardless of their claim to the land and, with a degree of irony, renaming the suburb **Triomf**. Nothing of the original suburb remains apart from two houses, the old orphanage and the Christ the King Anglican church, from where Trevor Huddleston conducted his ministry.

Sophiatown The Mix

Corner of Toby St and Edward Rd · Mon–Sat 9am–4.30pm · R60; suburb tours R180 · ☎ 011 673 1271, ⓦ sophiatownthemix.com

The excellent Sophiatown visitor centre, **Sophiatown The Mix**, is located in a 1930s house (one of the few original buildings that have survived) and the contemporary Trevor Huddleston Memorial Centre (THMC) next door. The house contains exhibitions on the suburb, its culture, the music styles that were popular, "tsotsi" gang culture, and the area's destruction. Meanwhile, the THMC functions as a community centre and small business incubator that hosts regular events such as the Sophiatown Jazz Encounter on the last Friday of every month. There are good views of the suburb from the centre's roof terrace where a special community remembrance wall has been installed for residents of old Sophiatown to leave mementos detailing their experiences. The enthusiastic staff can provide walking tours of Sophiatown when called in advance.

Rosebank, Melrose, Hyde Park, Parkhurst and Greenside

Recently boosted by the renovation of its mall, the small suburb of **Rosebank**, a couple of kilometres north of Joburg Zoo, boasts one of the city's most appealing shopping malls, the Rosebank Art & Craft Market and a series of art galleries plus a Gautrain station. Just to the north of Rosebank, the two swanky suburbs of **Melrose** and **Hyde Park** also have malls as their main focus.

Not far to the west of Rosebank and the gracious but sleepy old suburb of Parktown North lies **Parkhurst**, which, along with Melville, is one of the few northern suburbs to boast decent street life – particularly on and around Fourth Avenue, which is full of upmarket cafés, restaurants, antique and interior design shops. West of Parkhurst is **Greenside**, another hip neighbourhood worth heading to for food and drinks.

Keyes Art Mile

19–21 Keyes Ave, Rosebank • ⓦ keyesartmile.co.za

Launched in 2016, Keyes Art Mile is a purpose-built hub for contemporary African art and design. At its centre is the immense new Trumpet building. The ground-floor shop fronts house art galleries and design showrooms, while on the rooftop is *Marble*, a popular restaurant and bar with great views over the suburbs. Next door is the landmark cylindrical **Circa gallery**, which faces its sister gallery **Everard Read** (ⓣ011 788 4805, ⓦeverard-read.co.za; map p.461), both known for their excellent contemporary art exhibitions. Five hundred metres further south at 161 Jan Smuts Avenue is the highly regarded **Goodman Gallery** (ⓣ011 788 1113, ⓦgoodman-gallery.com; map p.461), which represents globally renowned South African artists such as William Kentridge.

Sandton

Some 20km north of the CBD, **Sandton** is the archetypal northern suburb. It is outrageously rich, with plush shopping centres and endless rows of lavish villas. In the 1980s and 1990s, it became the retreat of choice for banks and large corporations fleeing the CBD. A stroll through the connected Sandton City and Nelson Mandela Square shopping centres, complete with a pseudo-Italian piazza crammed with restaurants and cafés, may make you shudder at the ostentation, but with cash to burn you'll have some fun.

At one end of **Nelson Mandela Square** is a large bronze statue of the man himself: sadly, it's a mediocre work, achieving neither a compelling likeness nor any originality of approach.

Liliesleaf

7 George Ave, Rivonia • Mon–Fri 8.30am–5pm, Sat & Sun 9am–4pm • R110; includes a guided tour • ⓣ 011 803 7882, ⓦ liliesleaf.co.za

Once a remote farmhouse but now swallowed up by Joburg's suburban sprawl, the **Liliesleaf** heritage site just north of Sandton is where the underground resistance movement had their headquarters and safe house until the police raid of July 11, 1963, when several important ANC and MK leaders were arrested. Mandela, who also spent time in hiding here as a caretaker, was serving five years in prison at the time but was sent to trial anyway, together with his comrades. The Rivonia Trial ended in life sentences on Robben Island for Mandela, Walter Sisulu, Ahmed Kathrada, Govan Mbeki and others, and sparked global interest in the ANC's struggle. The old farm and adjacent new buildings now house informative interactive displays about the house, key figures of the resistance, Mandela's stay, the arrests and the trial. There's an overland safari truck on display, used by the ANC to smuggle weapons into South Africa right beneath the seats of unsuspecting tourists. The site has a good café called *Cedric's*, after the farm's code name.

Alexandra

Jeff Mulaudzi's Alexandra Tours runs excellent 2–3hr bike tours • R450–550 • ⓣ 071 279 3654, ⓦ alexandratours.co.za • Based in the East Bank area, The Hub Presents offer s offbeat tours focused on local culture and food • From R450 • ⓣ 071 671 1227, ⓦ thehubpresents.co.za

The contrast between desperately poor **Alexandra**, just east of the M1, and the surrounding suburbs could hardly be greater. When it was founded, in 1912, this black township was one of the few places where black people could own property. The sense of ownership and independence helped Alex, as it's commonly known, to avoid the forced removals of former governments. Despite the simple grid design its map suggests, the township is actually a bewildering maze with overcrowded housing and a woeful lack of basic services such as sewerage and water. Half a million people live here in an area of less than eight square kilometres, with immigrants from places such as Mozambique, Malawi and Zimbabwe putting additional pressure on the township's inadequate infrastructure. In 2008, a series of riots was sparked when immigrants were attacked in Alexandra: the riots killed two people and injured forty more, and triggered further **xenophobic violence** elsewhere in the country.

"Exhilarating and precarious" was how Nelson Mandela described Alex when he lived here in the early 1940s after running away from the Eastern Cape to find work in Joburg as an articled law clerk. In those days, the township was well known for its gangsters as well as its developing political militancy, which saw **bus boycotts** preventing bus companies from raising their fares, one of the first examples of mass action by black people achieving political results. Alexandra has long been an ANC stronghold, and paid dearly for it until the collapse of apartheid, with ongoing warfare between Inkatha vigilantes and the ANC in the 1980s leading to one section of Alex being dubbed "Beirut".

While the old spirit of Alex lives on in the bustling streets on the western side of the polluted Jukskei River, the eastern bank is lined with new houses, some built by government funding and others by middle-class black homeowners looking to improve their quality of life but wanting to remain in the township. Not far from here a patch of land has been turned into a **cricket oval**; it's surreal to watch this most colonial of games being played against a backdrop of densely packed township shacks, with the skyscrapers of opulent Sandton peeking over the horizon beyond. While less popular than those of Soweto, tours of Alexandra are safe, authentic and very enjoyable, enabling visitors to learn about township life, just minutes from the malls of Sandton.

The eastern and southern suburbs

Among the oldest of the city's suburbs, and for years home to Johannesburg's Jewish and Portuguese communities, the eastern suburb of **Bezuidenhout Valley** (better known as Bez Valley) has changed dramatically in recent years and now has a predominantly black African population. Meanwhile, **Cyrildene**, to the northeast of Bez Valley, has become the city's new Chinatown, with dozens of Chinese supermarkets, businesses and authentic restaurants along Derrick Avenue.

The suburbs immediately **south of the city centre** were traditionally the preserve of the white working class. After the repeal of the Group Areas Act in 1990, black people started moving in; unusually in contemporary South Africa, many are wealthier than the original residents. South Joburg also has a large Portuguese population, and the very first Nando's restaurant was opened here in 1987 by a South African duo of Portuguese descent.

Gold Reef City

Northern Parkway, corner of Data Crescent, Ormonde (8km south of the city centre along the M1) • Wed–Sun 9.30am–5pm • 2hr mine tours at 9am, 10am, 11am, 2pm & 3pm • R190 • ☎ 011 248 6800, ⓦ goldreefcity.co.za

Gold Reef City is where old Johannesburg meets Disneyland: a large, gaudy, tacky entertainment complex built around the old no.14 shaft of the Crown Mines. Essentially a theme park, it has some points of interest, notably the old gold mine itself, into which you can descend 200m and get an inkling of what it's like to work underground.

You can wander round the streets filled with period houses, shops and museums, though most are generally disappointing, with the exception of those dedicated to early Johannesburg, such as Ohlthaver and Nourse House. Otherwise, the most enjoyable thing to do in Gold Reef City is to go on one of the thrill rides (for which you will need a Thrill Rider ticket), such as the Raging Rapids water ride and the terrifying Anaconda roller coaster. Various restaurants serve decent if pricey food, but the main focus of this section of Gold Reef City is the vast casino.

The Apartheid Museum

Northern Parkway, corner of Gold Reef Rd, Ormonde (Gold Reef City complex, 8km south of the city centre along the M1) • Daily 9am–5pm • R85 • ☎ 011 309 4700, ⊛ apartheidmuseum.org

The excellent **Apartheid Museum**, featuring separate entrances for "whites" and "non-whites" (your race is randomly assigned), is a world-class museum, delivering a sophisticated visual history that is distressing, inspiring and illuminating. The museum offers a nuanced insight into the deep social damage wrought by apartheid – and by colonial policies that long preceded it – and helps to explain the persistence of poverty and racial tension in the new South Africa. On the other hand, the museum's visual account of the jubilant advent of democracy serves to remind us how miraculous the transition was.

Allow at least two hours for the museum, three to four hours if you'd like to see all the exhibits in detail; there's a good lunch café and a bookshop on-site too. Also allow time to view the exhibition of photographs by Peter Magubane of the 1976 Soweto uprising, and don't miss the exhilarating short documentary on the State of Emergency during the mid-1980s, when a wave of mass demonstrations and riots, though violently suppressed, shook the resolve of the regime.

Klipriviersberg Nature Reserve

15km south of the centre on Ormonde Drive, Mondeor • Dawn–dusk • Free • ⊛ klipriviersberg.org.za

Few Joburgers know about this undeveloped, unspoilt parkland, just beyond the N12 in the suburb of Mondeor. Beyond the riverside picnic spot, there are easy valley trails on which you can spot zebras, wildebeest, hartebeest and other wildlife, as well as strenuous uphill hikes rewarded by wonderful views of the city to the north.

Soweto

South Africa's most famous township, **Soweto** (short for South West Townships), is a place of extreme contrasts. The area was home to two Nobel Peace Prize winners, yet suffers one of the highest rates of murder and rape in the world; it is the richest township in South Africa, home to a growing number of millionaires, but has some of the most desperate poverty; it is the most political township, yet has the most nihilistic youth.

VISITING SOWETO

The most convenient way to visit Soweto is with a **tour operator**. CitySightseeing Joburg's hop-on hop-off bus tour (see p.474) offers daily two-hour minibus tours around Soweto, departing from their Gold Reef City stop. Smaller outfits offer imaginative **alternative tours** such as jazz outings, walks around Orlando West and Diepkloof, visits to Sowetan artists or local churches, language immersion tours and homestays with locals.

For a more personal experience try Imbizo Tours (☎ 011 838 2667, ⊛ imbizotours.co.za), run by the irrepressible Mandy Mankazana. She runs three-hour, half-day and night tours, some including the Apartheid Museum and Alexandra township; particularly recommended are her evening *shebeen* crawls lasting up to five hours. Another highly recommended way to experience the township is on the **bicycle and tuk-tuk tours** offered by Lebo's Soweto Bicycle Tours – guests of Lebo's Soweto Backpackers get a discount (☎ 011 936 3444, ⊛ sowetobicycletours.com). Other local guides offering interesting tours include TKD Tours who lead walks through historic Kliptown (☎ 073 133 5234, ⊛ tktours.dube13@gmail.com), and Raymond Rampolokeng of Bay of Grace Tours (☎ 072 947 3311). Alternatively, you can visit independently using the safe Rea Vaya BRT bus system.

7

Southwest of the city centre, Soweto is huge, stretching as far as the eye can see, with a population estimated at between three and four million. Like any city of that size, it is divided into a number of different suburbs, with middle- and upper-class neighbourhoods among them. At first sight, it appears an endless jumble of houses and shacks, overshadowed by palls of smoke, though parts of it have a villagey feel. Apart from the Hector Pieterson Memorial and Museum, most of Soweto's **tourist highlights** are physically unimpressive, their fame stemming from historical associations. That history, however, is enthralling, not least because here it is told with a perspective and context rarely found in the rest of South Africa. For visitors it provides an insight not just into a place much mentioned in 1980s news bulletins for funerals and fighting, but into a way of life most Westerners rarely encounter.

A visit to Soweto with one of the many **tours** (see box, p.467) is the single most popular attraction in Johannesburg. Where once these had a whiff of daring and originality, a well-trodden tourist trail has developed, and unless you're content to follow the herds of minibuses and coaches around the conventional sights, visiting the same shantytowns and *shebeens*, it's well worth using an operator who mixes the highlights with lesser-known sights. Most outfits are keen for you to "meet the people", though conversations can tend to be strained and lead to your leaving a "donation" or buying local craftwork. While this gets a few tourist dollars directly into the townships, it often leaves visitors feeling pressurized and vulnerable.

At one time, taking yourself to Soweto would have meant a display of bravado bordering on foolhardiness, but it's now possible to visit the main sights **independently**. In Soweto, residents will stop to greet you or to chat, regardless of your colour. There are surprisingly few criminal incidents affecting tourists, though as ever it pays to remain vigilant; exploring less-visited areas by yourself, or going after dark, isn't recommended. If you want to drive to Soweto, you'll need good navigational skills – the lack of obvious landmarks amid kilometre upon kilometre of boxy little houses can be highly confusing. The Rea Vaya bus route from the city centre, which passes near Vilakazi Street, offers a good alternative to taking a minibus taxi to Soweto, which are more confusing than dangerous, as it isn't always easy to ascertain which part of the township they are heading for. Forming a cross with two fingers is the recognized minibus signal indicating that you want to go to "crossroads", which will bring you to the centre of Soweto. From here you can pick up another taxi to whichever sight you want to visit, though even in a taxi you may be let out on one of the main roads and have to walk a little way to reach your target.

Orlando West and Dube

Set in the northern part of Soweto, **Orlando West** and **Dube** qualify as two of its more affluent suburbs, with a number of sights and the greatest concentration of places to eat and drink. **Orlando East**, across Klipspruit Valley from Orlando West, was the first part of Soweto to be established in 1932, and the area is fairly easily accessible by car off the Soweto Highway (M70).

Hector Pieterson Memorial and Museum

8287 Khumalo St, Orlando West • Mon–Sat 10am–5pm, Sun 10am–4pm • R30 • ☎ 011 536 0611 • Using the Rea Vaya BRT bus from Joburg CBD, get off at Boomtown stop, and then walk or take the F4 feeder bus to Vilakazi St

The **Hector Pieterson Memorial and Museum**, opened in 2002, was named after the first student to be killed in the Soweto uprising (see box, p.470). Dedicated to all the students who died, the museum focuses specifically on the events surrounding and leading up to the 1976 Soweto uprising. The startling brutality used in the repression of student activists is depicted in video and pictures, including images from well-known photographers such as Peter Magubane and Sam Nzima.

RIGHT STATUE OF NELSON MANDELA IN FRONT OF THE UNION BUILDINGS, PRETORIA (P.492) >

The Mandela House Museum

8115 Vilakazi St, Orlando West • Daily 9am–4.45pm • R60 • ☎ 011 936 7754, ⓦ mandelahouse.com • Take the Rea Vaya BRT bus T1 from Joburg CBD to Boomtown; here, change to the F4 to Vilakazi St, or cross the bridge and walk a few minutes up the road

Vilakazi Street was once home to Nelson Mandela and Desmond Tutu. **Mandela's bungalow** is where he lived with Winnie in the late 1950s and early 1960s, before his imprisonment on Robben Island, and where Winnie lived until exiled to the Free State (from which she returned to an imposing brick house with high walls and security cameras, just down the road). On his release, Nelson insisted on returning to his old home, but its small size and lack of security proved too much of a strain, and he moved out of Soweto. The old bungalow displays some fascinatingly mundane memorabilia, including some original furnishings, a collection of Winnie and Nelson's photographs, and audiovisual displays describing living conditions in Soweto at the time Mandela lived there.

Regina Mundi Church

Near the junction of Klipspruit Valley (M10) and Potchefstroom (M68) roads • Daily 9am–5pm, outside church services • R20 • ☎ 011 986 2546, ⓦ reginamundichurch.co.za • Lakeview is the closest Rea Vaya BRT bus stop

The **Regina Mundi Church** is Soweto's largest Catholic church and was the focus of numerous gatherings in the years of struggle. Again, its impact owes more to historical aura than aesthetic appeal, although with so few large buildings in the township it has

---

THE SOWETO UPRISING OF 1976

The **student uprising** that began in Soweto in June 1976 was sparked off by a government ruling that **Afrikaans** should be used on an equal basis with English in black secondary schools. While this was feasible in some rural areas, it was impossible in the townships, where neither pupils nor teachers knew the language.

On June 16, student delegates from every Soweto school launched a mass protest march through the township and a rally at the Orlando football stadium. Incredibly, details of the plan were kept secret from the omnipresent *impimpis* (informers). Soon after the march started, however, the police attacked, throwing tear gas and then firing. The crowd panicked, and demonstrators started throwing stones at the police. The police fired again. Out of this bedlam came the famous photograph of the first student to die, Hector Pieterson, bleeding at the mouth, being carried by a friend, while his sister Antoinette, who now works in the Hector Pieterson Memorial and Museum (see p.468), looks on in anguished horror.

The police retreated to Orlando East, and students rushed to collect the injured and dead, erect barricades, and destroy everything they could belonging to the municipal authority, including beer halls. The attacks heightened the antagonism between the youth and older people who thought that class boycotts were irresponsible, given the students' already dismal employment prospects. Students accused their elders of apathy, which they attributed in part to drunkenness. In a society that has traditionally regarded respect for the old as sacrosanct, this was a historic departure.

In the days following June 16, all Soweto schools were closed indefinitely, thousands of police were stationed throughout the township, and police brutality continued unabated. In the face of worldwide condemnation, the government ascribed the violence to Communist agitation, citing as evidence the clenched-fist salutes of the students, though this was really an indication of their support for South Africa's **Black Consciousness Movement**, founded by Steve Biko (see box, p.333). Meanwhile, rebellion spread to other townships, particularly in Cape Town. In Soweto, schools did not reopen until 1978, by which time many students had abandoned any hope of formal education. Some had left the country to join the military wings of the ANC and PAC, while others stayed at home, forming "street committees" to politicize and police the communities. Others drifted into unemployment.

Now the armed struggle is over, the problems that face the former students of 1976 are manifold. As their parents warned, their lack of qualifications counts against them in the job market, even if June 16 is now a national holiday, during which they are praised for their role in the struggle. The street committees have dissolved, but the guns remain.

a certain presence. The caretaker shows visitors around; look out for the bullet holes left in the ceiling by the South African police, and the (black) Madonna and Child painting near the altar.

Kliptown Museum

Walter Sisulu Square • Mon–Fri 9am–4pm • Free • The Rea Vaya BRT feeder bus F5 travels from Lakeview to Klipspruitvalley Rd for Sisulu Square

The **Walter Sisulu Square of Dedication** is the site where the ANC's Freedom Charter was proclaimed to thousands in 1955. As well as sculptures and public artworks commemorating the event, the square is home to the **Kliptown Museum**, on its western side, which explains the history behind the Freedom Charter through photographs, documents and news clippings, and is worth a look once you've finished with the Hector Pieterson and Mandela House museums.

FNB Stadium

Nasrec, Soweto • Tours by appointment only • R60 • ☎ 011 247 5300, ⓦ stadiummanagement.co.za

Halfway between the CBD and Soweto in Nasrec and known as Soccer City during the 2010 Football World Cup, the **FNB Stadium** is Africa's largest stadium. A beautiful structure, it was designed by South African architects and built on top of an older football stadium that was used for Mandela's first speech after his release from prison in 1990. With earth colours on the exterior that blend in nicely with the adjacent mine dumps, the interior is larger than you'd expect, with 94,000 orange seats spread across three tiers. Unlike some other World Cup venues in South Africa, this stadium is no white elephant and regularly fills to capacity for matches, concerts and rallies. If you can't make it to a game, the sixty- to ninety-minute tours of the stadium are very worthwhile, taking in the players' rooms and VIP areas.

ARRIVAL AND DEPARTURE

JOHANNESBURG

BY PLANE

OR Tambo International Airport (☎ 086 727 7888, ⓦ www.airports.co.za), named after the ANC's greatest leader in exile, lies 20km east of the city centre. On the ground floor of the international arrivals hall there's a tourist information desk (daily 5.30am–10pm; ☎ 011 390 3614) and 24-hour facilities for changing money; ATMs, a post office and an internet café can be found on the first floor.

ONWARD TRANSPORT

Gautrain The fastest and easiest way to get to the city – especially during the dreaded morning and afternoon rush hours – is on the Gautrain rail link (daily 5.30am–8.30pm; see p.473), which takes 15min to reach Sandton station (R151, plus R15 card), where you can change for trains south to Rosebank and Park stations and north to Pretoria, or use the Gautrain feeder buses to Sandton's hotels.

Shuttle Buses EZ Shuttle (☎ 086 139 7488, ⓦ ezshuttle .co.za; R420–495) and Rhino Shuttles (☎ 010 010 6506, ⓦ rhinoshuttles.co.za; R450–525) offer a round-the-clock pick-up and drop-off service from the airport; book a day in advance.

Courtesy buses The more expensive hotels often provide courtesy buses, while most backpacker hostels and some smaller guesthouses or B&Bs offer free pick-ups (best booked when making your reservation) and sometimes free drop-offs back to the airport.

Taxis There are plenty of taxi touts floating around the arrivals hall proffering price lists with exaggerated (but usually negotiable) fares; however, you are better off using the taxi booking stand next to the tourist office in the arrivals hall. Make certain the driver knows where you're going before you set off, and get a quote beforehand. You should pay around R500 to get to central Joburg, Rosebank or Sandton, and no more than R600 to reach a far northern or western suburb. Uber also pick up from the airport, though it's best to arrange a pick-up point away from their meter taxi rivals who have been known to harass Uber drivers.

Car rental Standard car rental deals are available from the main companies such as Avis (☎ 011 573 0000), Budget (☎ 086 101 6622), EuropCar (☎ 011 390 3909) and Tempest (☎ 0861 836 737), which all have offices at both airports and in several city locations. It's often much cheaper to rent one of these company's cars using a broker website like ⓦ carhire.co.za. Alternatively, try Rent-a-Wreck, 343 Louis Botha Ave, Orange Grove (☎ 011 640 2666, ⓦ rentawreck.co.za). Beware of police checkpoints at the airport; heed all stop signs and speed limits or you risk getting fined.

7

Airline information All of the following airlines have ticket offices at OR Tambo International Airport: Air France/ KLM ☎ 011 390 8560; British Airways ☎ 011 441 8600; Lufthansa ☎ 086 184 2538; South African Airways ☎ 011 978 2888; and SA Airlink ☎ 011 451 7300. Qantas, 195 Jan Smuts Ave, Parktown North (☎ 011 441 8550), and Virgin Atlantic, 50 Sixth Rd, Hyde Park (☎ 011 340 3500), have offices in the city.

Destinations Bloemfontein (5–12 daily; 1hr); Cape Town (70 daily; 2hr); Durban (50 daily; 1hr); East London (9 daily; 1hr 25min); Hoedspruit (2 daily; 1hr); Kimberley (3–7 daily; 1hr 30min); Nelspruit (5–6 daily; 1hr 50min); Port Elizabeth (15 daily; 1hr 40min).

LANSERIA AIRPORT

Joburg's secondary Lanseria Airport (☎ 011 367 0300, ⓦ lanseria.co.za) is 30km northwest of the city centre and used by an increasing number of budget airlines. Taxis don't tend to wait at this airport and there's no public transport, so either organize a transfer with your accommodation or call a taxi (see opposite).

Destinations Cape Town (12–13 daily; 2hr); Durban (6–7 daily; 1hr); Upington (Mon, Tues & Thurs; 2hr); George (Fri & Sun; 2hr).

BY CAR

Toll roads The much-hated electronic road toll system on the N1, N3, N12 and R21 highways around Joburg and up to Pretoria charges all vehicles about R0.50 per kilometre. Rental cars are fitted with devices to register the toll payments; others must register beforehand at ⓦ nra.co.za.

Rush hour When driving to Pretoria, avoid the afternoon rush hour northwards (3.30–5pm), when travel time can double to 2hr; this is also when a quick 45min drive to OR Tambo Airport can turn into a two-hour ordeal.

BY BUS AND MINIBUS

Baz Bus (☎ 086 122 9287, ⓦ bazbus.com) operates 22-seater bus services from Johannesburg to Cape Town via the Drakensberg, Durban, the Eastern Cape coast and the Garden Route (4–5 weekly), stopping at hostels en route. The service is designed to be "hop-on hop-off", with overnight stops in Durban and Port Elizabeth.

Greyhound, Intercape and Translux These intercity buses arrive at Park Station in the centre of town. Once notoriously unsafe, Park Station has been significantly improved and the main concourse is big, open and secure, with information desks for all the bus companies. That said, it's not a good idea to walk around the surrounding area with a lot of luggage, so you're best off taking the Gautrain or a taxi to your final destination, or arranging a pick-up with your accommodation. Park Station has a number of car rental offices conveniently located on the upper concourse, usually listed under "Braamfontein" on their websites.

Destinations: Beitbridge (3 daily; 7hr); Bloemfontein (16 daily; 5hr); Cape Town (6 daily; 19hr 30min); Durban (16 daily; 8–11hr); East London (12 daily; 12hr 45min); Kimberley (5 daily; 6hr 30min); King William's Town (3 daily; 12hr 15min); Knysna (daily; 17hr); Kuruman (daily; 7hr); Ladysmith (2 daily; 5hr 45min); Mossel Bay (2 daily; 17hr); Nelspruit (6 daily; 5hr); Newcastle (daily; 5hr); Oudtshoorn (2 daily; 14hr 30min); Pietermaritzburg (16 daily; 7hr); Plettenberg Bay (daily; 17hr 30min); Port Elizabeth (4 daily; 13hr 15min); Pretoria (over 30 daily; 1hr); Mthatha (daily; 11hr 30min).

BY TRAIN

Intercity and Gautrain Long distance Shosholoza Meyl (ⓦ shosholozameyl.co.za, ☎ 011 774 4555) trains pull in at Park Station in the centre of town (see above) and tickets can be booked at the Shosholoza Meyl ticket office in Park Station. The Gautrain service is the fastest and most comfortable rail link to Pretoria (see opposite). Buy tickets and catch the Gautrain from the Gautrain Park Station at the corner of Wolmarans and Rissik sts (opposite the station's northern concourse entrance).

Destinations Cape Town, via Kimberley (Tues, Wed, Thurs, Fri & Sun; 26hr); Durban (Fri & Sun; 14hr); Port Elizabeth, via Bloemfontein (Wed, Fri & Sun; 20hr); Komatipoort via Nelspruit (Fri; 13hr); East London via Bloemfontein (Wed, Fri & Sun; 20hr).

GETTING AROUND

Johannesburg's **public transport** system is improving fast, with the Gautrain rail and bus network and the Rea Vaya Rapid Transit bus (BRT) system being very well received by city residents. Rea Vaya is steadily expanding northwards from its trunk routes to and from Soweto. However, driving still remains very much the order of the day in Joburg, though the CBD and some suburbs, notably Melville, are easily explored on foot. **Private taxis**, which should be booked in advance by telephone (see opposite), are an expensive option, as a simple journey to the CBD from the northern suburbs will cost at least R200. Fares on Uber are cheaper at around R130 for a similar trip.

BY CAR

Getting around The best way to explore Johannesburg is still by car. Although road signs can be poor and the local drivers pushy, familiarity with a few key roads, a GPS device or some careful map reading before you set out makes driving around relatively straightforward. In the city centre, the grid system does make navigation reasonably logical, though it's beset by one-way streets, and gridlocked traffic in rush hour. Be mindful of the bus lanes in the CBD; there are usually traffic police lying in wait to fine anybody who accidentally drives into one.

Routes The M1 connects the centre to the northern suburbs, crossing above Newtown on a flyover, through Braamfontein and Parktown, and heading into Houghton and Sandton, eventually turning into the N1 for Pretoria. South of the centre, the M1 is one of the best routes to Soweto. The next artery west of the M1, also useful for heading north, is Oxford Rd, which starts off in Parktown, and becomes Rivonia Rd once it enters Sandton. West again is Jan Smuts Avenue, which passes through Rosebank and Dunkeld before hitting Hyde Park.

Parking If you're travelling into the city centre by car, guarded parking can be found underneath Gandhi Square, in the Carlton Centre car park on Main St (connected to the centre via an underground passage; free parking if you have the ticket stamped at the Top of Africa office) or at the Newtown Junction mall.

BY BUS

Metrobus Most of Joburg's municipal Metrobus routes start and end at the main terminus in Gandhi Square, off Eloff St in the city centre. There's a bus information office in the Gandhi Mall on the southern side of Gandhi Square (Mon–Fri 8am–6pm, Sat 8am–2pm; ☎ 011 833 5918, ⓦ mbus.co.za), where you can pick up timetables. Buses only run between the suburbs and the centre, so are useless for getting from one suburb to another, unless they both lie on the same route to town. Most buses stop by 6.30pm, though a small number keep going until 9.30pm. At weekends very few routes have services and there are waits of at least an hour between buses. Fares (R10–25, depending on distance) should be paid to the driver; ensure you get a ticket as you may need to show it to a ticket inspector. Useful routes include the #67 to Melville and the #05CD to Rosebank and Sandton.

BRT The Rea Vaya Bus Rapid Transit (BRT) system (ⓦ reavaya org.za) is a fast and safe way to get from the CBD and Melville to Soweto as it uses dedicated roads and lanes; the high-floor buses stop at specially designed raised bus stops, which are clean, enclosed and well guarded. The T1 trunk line from Ellis Park in the CBD to Thokoza Park in Soweto has several feeder (F) bus routes, and links up with the C3 inner-city circular route. Handy for tourists, the C3 links the Johannesburg Art Gallery with the Old Fort on Constitution Hill, the Origins Centre in Braamfontein, Park Station, Rissik St, Newtown and the Carlton Centre, where you can transfer to the T1 to Soweto or the C1 to Maboneng. The C4 links Park Station to Milpark (for 44 Stanley) and Melville. You'll need a rechargeable smartcard, sold at the Park Station and Carlton Centre bus stops; you can also buy single journey tickets here (R15), as drivers do not carry cash; rides cost R12–25. Buses on the trunk routes run every 10–20min on weekdays from about 6am to 7pm, and every 20–30min at weekends

between 7am and 6pm; the inner-city circular route has buses every 15–20min on weekdays from 6am to 8.30pm, and every 15–30min at weekends between 7am and 5.30pm. The Rea Vaya website has handy maps showing the main city sights in relation to the bus stops.

Gautrain feeder buses The gold Gautrain feeder buses (ⓦ gautrain.co.za) serve all Gautrain stations except the airport station (Mon–Fri; R20, R6 if combined with a train journey); you'll need a preloaded Gautrain Gold Card to travel on them. Useful routes include: from Park Station to Parktown, from Rosebank Station to Hyde Park Corner mall and Melrose Arch mall, and from Sandton Station to the Montecasino complex in Fourways. Route information can be found at stations, bus stops and online; call ☎ 010 223 1098 for the exact arrival time of the next bus.

BY MINIBUS TAXI

Minibus taxis transport the vast majority of commuters, and cover the widest area. They can be picked up at taxi ranks or hailed mid-route using any one of a confusing array of hand signals. Generally speaking, if you're heading into town, point your forefinger upwards; if you want to go to a stop nearby, point downwards, then confirm with the driver if he is indeed heading your direction before you get in. Most minibuses travelling into the CBD terminate at Park Central Taxi Terminus. This is a hectic place and can be very intimidating: be vigilant and discreet with your valuables. Minibuses for Melville leave from rank #1, for Sandton from rank #2 and for Orlando West in Soweto from rank #9. Fares start at R9 for short rides.

BY TRAIN

Gautrain The rapid rail network (☎ 0800 428 87246, ⓦ gautrain.co.za) connects Johannesburg's Park Station to Pretoria via Rosebank and Sandton, with an airport line branching off at Sandton. Security is very tight, with guards at stations and on every train car. The system uses Gold Cards (R15) that can be purchased and charged with money at stations and used to pay for train travel, as well as on the feeder buses and for parking. Trains run daily from 5.30am to 8pm at intervals of 15–30min. The fare from Park Station to Rosebank is R19–27, to Sandton R22–30 depending on peak hours.

Metrorail The city's other suburban train system, Metrorail, has a poor security reputation, very limited services and is best avoided.

BY TAXI

The city's most reliable taxi company is Zebra Cabs (☎ 086 110 5105, ⓦ zebracabs.co.za), usually charging fixed rates of around R12 a kilometre, with a minimum of R50. The smartphone app Uber has extensive coverage in Joburg. When booking a taxi from any of the Gautrain stations, be aware of nearby taxi touts, who have a reputation for attacking rival taxi drivers.

7

7

BY TUKTUK
Sheshatuks (☎ 086 174 3742, ⓦ sheshatuks.co.za) in Sandton (at the Gautrain station) and Rosebank and E-tuktuk (☎ 072 316 8099, ⓦ e-tuktuk.co.za) in Melville scoot passengers around in small tuk-tuks; from R30 for short journeys.

INFORMATION AND TOURS

Tourist information The Joburg city tourism authority has an office in the Library on Sandton's Nelson Mandela Square (Mon–Fri 8am–5pm; ☎ 087 151 2950). The excellent city guide *Johannesburg In Your Pocket* (R40, ⓦ johannesburg.inyourpocket.com) is the best source of information for concerts, shows, exhibitions, sports and other events; it's available online, and at bookshops and accommodation across town.

Tours Gerald Garner (☎ 082 894 5216, ⓦ joburgplaces .com) and Chris Green (☎ 082 491 9370, ⓦ cashanafrica .com) are excellent local guides who can take you on tailor-made tours around the city centre, into the suburbs and beyond. Mainstreetwalks (☎ 072 880 9583, ⓦ mainstreetwalks.co.za), based in the *Curiocity Backpackers* hostel, has several interesting inner-city walking and cycling tours. The Past Experiences walking tour company (☎ 011 782 5250, ⓦ pastexperiences .co.za) is particularly good for those interested in art and architecture, offering tours of the Joburg CBD and Soweto, themed around street art, graffiti and shopping; these often use public transport, allowing for interaction with all kinds of Joburgers. On most Saturday afternoons the Johannesburg Heritage Foundation (☎ 011 482 3349, ⓦ www.joburgheritage.co.za) conducts historical walking and bus tours (from R150) to destinations across the city centre and the suburbs.

Bus tour The open-topped city tour buses run by CitySightseeing Joburg (☎ 086 173 3287, ⓦ citysightseeing .co.za) are popular and safe, with daily departures every 40min (30min at weekends), between 9am and around 3.30pm along two routes. The Red Route (2hr) from Constitution Hill travels via the CBD to the Apartheid Museum, Gold Reef City, Newtown, Braamfontein and then back to Constitution Hill. At the Apartheid Museum, you can join an additional 2hr tour through the main sights in Soweto. The Green Route (1hr) travels from The Zone at Rosebank to Constitution Hill via Joburg Zoo and the Military History Museum. Tickets purchased online cost R170 inclusive of the Red and Green routes (R420 including Soweto); from the booking office at Rosebank it's R20–50 more.

ACCOMMODATION

There's plenty of accommodation in Joburg's northern suburbs and in the city centre, both good options if you are relying on public transport. Melville is relatively close to the CBD and offers a characterful community with cafés, restaurants and bars within safe walking distance of a great number of guesthouses. Rosebank is well located at the heart of the northern suburbs, and has a decent selection of places to eat out and shop, plus a Gautrain station. Sandton has a wealth of pricey chain hotels aimed at business executives. It is also possible to stay in a guesthouse in the townships, though the most rewarding option is to stay with locals, something best arranged through an experienced tour operator (see box, p.467). The ⓦ johannesburg-guesthouses.co.za website is a handy portal for browsing and booking guesthouses based in and around Rosebank and Melville.

CBD & CENTRAL SUBURBS
Bannister 9 De Beer St, Braamfontein ☎ 011 403 6888, ⓦ bannisterhotel.co.za; map p.454. A classy budget hotel with small but fresh en-suite rooms. It's in the heart of Braamfontein's nightlife, at crawling distance from half a dozen bars, which can get noisy. R595

★**Curiocity Backpackers** 302 Fox St, Maboneng, CBD ☎ 011 592 0515, ⓦ curiocitybackpackers.com; map p.454. A basic but friendly hostel with spacious dorm and double rooms, set above a lively bar full of locals in the upcoming Maboneng Precinct. Plenty of activities are organized, from city walks and bike rides to pub crawls, bar concerts and volunteering. There's a free city-centre shuttle service and a tiny swimming pool. Dorms R170, doubles R390

Mapungubwe Hotel Apartments 54 Marshall St, Marshalltown, CBD ☎ 011 429 2600, ⓦ mapungubwe hotel.co.za; map p.454. Set in a former bank building, the first luxury hotel to open in the city centre for decades has an impressive foyer, stylishly furnished rooms and apartments, and a bar in the old underground bank vaults. Free CBD shuttle service. R1280

Once In Joburg 90 De Korte St, Braamfontein ☎ 08 625 0639 ⓦ onceinjoburg.co.za; map p.454. A colourful new backpackers hostel situated on a lively small square with several good places to eat nearby. There's a cool bar on the ground floor serving craft beers and cocktails. Dorm R285, doubles R885

NORTHERN SUBURBS
Claires of Sandton 42 8th St, Sandton ☎ 011 78 5481, ⓦ clairesofsandton.co.za; map p.461. Spacious comfortable and bright rooms, friendly staff and a big pool make this one of Sandton's most popular guesthouses. There's a decent selection of restaurants a few blocks away on 11th St. Singles R1045, double R1395

Little Forest Guest House 41 Fifth St, Parkhurst ☎084 503 8979, ⍟littleforestguesthouse.co.za; map p.461. Convenient for the boutiques and restaurants along Parkhurst's 4th Avenue, this charming and tiny guesthouse has five lovely en-suite rooms, most overlooking the garden and pool. R800

★**Liz at Lancaster** 79 Lancaster Ave, Craighall Park ☎011 442 8083, ⍟lizatlancaster.co.za; map p.461. A classy and very highly regarded guesthouse halfway between the restaurants and boutiques of Parkhurst's 4th Avenue and the upmarket Hyde Park Corner mall. Decorated with local art, the large rooms overlook a garden with a pool. R900

Premiere Classe Suite Hotel 62 Corlett Drive, Melrose North ☎011 788 1967, ⍟premiereclasse.co.za; map p.461. A calm, quiet and friendly hotel with comfortable suites and fully equipped kitchens. It's close to the Melrose Arch complex and the Wanderers Cricket Stadium. Long-term rates available. R800

★**Satyagraha House** 15 Pine Rd, Orchards ☎011 485 5928, ⍟satyagrahahouse.com; map 461. Peaceful guesthouse named after Gandhi's philosophy of satyagraha (non-violent civil disobedience). Gandhi lived here from 1908–09, and there's a small museum dedicated to his life. Vegetarian evening meals can be arranged. R2520

MELVILLE

★**Die Agterplaas** 66 Sixth Ave, Melville ☎011 726 8452, ⍟agterplaas.co.za; map p.463. Just a minute's walk from Melville's restaurants and cafés, this neat, tasteful guesthouse has balconied rooms with views over the Melville *koppies*, and more accommodation in a house across the road. There's a wonderful lounge, where the famed breakfasts prepared by chef Badia are served; non-guests are welcome as well (until 10am; 11am at weekends). R1040

Homebase Melville Backpackers 37 First Ave, Melville ☎011 482 5797, ⍟homebasesouthafrica .com; map p.463. Popular Melville hostel with dorms, family rooms and tiny chalets spread across two interconnected houses between Melville's Main and 7th streets. The chalets are clustered around a small pool overlooked by the hostel bar. Dorms R180, doubles R500

Lucky Bean 129 First Ave, Melville ☎082 902 4514, ⍟luckybeanguesthouse.co.za; map p.463. Run by the owners of the *Lucky Bean* restaurant (see p.477), this large guesthouse rests in beautifully tended and peaceful gardens a few blocks from Melville's main strip. R950

Melville Manor 80 Second Ave, Melville ☎011 726 8765, ⍟melvillemanor.co.za; map p.463. In an elegantly restored Victorian house, this welcoming, well-run guesthouse – with a pool and a great communal kitchen and dining area – is less than a minute's walk from the Melville restaurant strip. R750

NEAR THE AIRPORT

Airport en Route 97 Boden Rd, Benoni Small Farms, Benoni ☎011 963 3389, ⍟sa-venues.com/visit /airportenroutebenoni. A tidy, congenial budget lodge located 15min from the airport (pickups can be arranged) in the famously sleepy town where film star Charlize Theron grew up. Accommodation is in cosy, three-bed log cabins, some of which are en suite, and two rooms sleeping up to four people (R550); camping is also available. Camping R80, cabin R400

City Lodge OR Tambo airport ☎011 552 7600, ⍟clhg.com. Conveniently plonked right on top of the airport parking garage, this is the best value hotel within walking distance of the gates. Rooms are well sized, very quiet and overlook the Gautrain station. R1800

Emperors Palace Kempton Rd, on the corner of Bosch Av, Kempton Park ☎011 928 1000, ⍟emperorspalace .com. This gaudy Roman-themed casino complex is right next to the airport and has a choice of four hotels; the luxurious *D'Oreale Grande* with its beautiful pool terrace and gardens, the four-star *Mondior* and the more basic *Metcourt* and *Metcourt Suites*. There are free shuttles to the airport and a Gautrain bus service linking to the Rhodesfield station. Besides the 24hr casino, other entertainment options include two theatres, a cinema and a dozen restaurants. *D'Oreale Grande* R3840, *Mondior* R2900, *Metcourt Suites* R2060, *Metcourt* R1800

SOWETO

★**Lebo's Soweto Backpackers** 10823a Pooe St, Orlando West ☎011 936 3444, ⍟sowetobackpackers .com. One of the country's few black-owned backpacker hostels, with dorms, singles, doubles, camping and a great vibe when guests gather at the beach bar or around the fire pit for storytelling evenings on the last Thursday of the month. Walking, cycling and tuk-tuk tours, and volunteer opportunities in Soweto are also available. Camping R105, dorms R185, doubles R450

Lolo's Guest House 1320 Diepkloof Extension, Diepkloof ☎011 985 9183, ✉lolosbb@mweb.co.za. A smart and modern guesthouse run by former teacher Mrs Lolo Mabitsela in the historic Diepkloof district. There's a small garden, guarded parking and a conference room; tailor-made tours, including Soweto bar crawls, can be arranged. R700

7

EATING

Johannesburg has a huge range of places to eat out, with authentic French, Italian, Chinese, Greek and Portuguese restaurants, plus increasing numbers of African restaurants – not just township South African but also Congolese, Moroccan, Ethiopian and Cape Malay. Prices are higher than elsewhere in the country outside Cape Town and the

Winelands, and you can blow out in spectacular style, but an average meal out is still good value. The bulk of Joburg's restaurants are in the **northern suburbs**; the key places to try are Fourth Avenue in Parkhurst (west of Parktown North), Seventh Street in Melville, the junction of Greenway and Gleneagles in Greenside and at the Melrose Arch complex in Melrose. In the city centre dozens of small new restaurants are opening up around De Beer Street in Braamfontein and Fox Street in the Maboneng Precinct. Joburg's **shopping malls** are well stocked with takeaways and chain restaurants, though some top-notch venues do exist in malls.

CBD & CENTRAL SUBURBS

86 Public The Grove, 87 Juta St, Braamfontein ☎061 157 1823, ⓦ86public.co.za; map p.454. Bustling pizzeria, with weekend DJ sets, that opens out onto a youthful city square popular with students. More than 20 pizzas to choose from – the bacon, feta and avocado is the bestseller (R95). Daily noon–10pm.

The Blackanese 20 Kruger St, Maboneng ☎011 024 9455, ⓦtheblackanese.co.za; map p.454. Exciting African–Asian cuisine, where sushi and curries meet African flavours and ingredients. Come on Tuesday for the R130 all-you-can-eat sessions, or on Sunday for the seafood braai. Tues–Sun 11am–10pm.

★**Che Argentine Grill** 303 Fox St, Maboneng ☎011 614 0264; map p.454. Warm, welcoming and characterful Argentinean-owned steakhouse located in a former warehouse on Maboneng's main strip. The excellent steaks (R134–175) are cooked on a wood-fired grill in the restaurant's open kitchen, or try the home-made chorizo with chimichurri sauce for starters (R58) and wash it all down with perfect pisco sours from the bar (R65). Tues–Sun noon–11pm.

Cramers Coffee Main St, Marshalltown ☎011 833 2699, ⓦcramerscoffee.com; map p.454. A good place for a break on a tour of the sights along Main Street; excellent coffee, cinnamon buns and other snacks, plus free wi-fi. Mon–Fri 6am–5.30pm, Sat 7am–1.30pm.

★**Dosa Hut** 48 Central Rd, Fordsburg ☎011 492 1456; map p.454. One of several authentic options in the lively Indian district of Fordsburg, one block south of the weekend market, this South Indian restaurant serves masala dosa platters (R35), chicken *uttappam* (R55) and spicy fish curry (R75). Daily 10am–9.30pm.

Netsi 220 Rahima Moosa St, Shop 123, CBD ☎083 345 6789; map p.454. The converted Medical Arts building is now "Little Addis", home to dozens of Ethiopian shops, hairdressers and eateries. It looks a bit dodgy from the outside, but walk up to the second floor and ask for Netsi. Here, a delicious vegetarian platter for two (spongy injera bread heaped up with veggie snacks, eaten with your right hand) costs just R35. Mon–Fri 6am–5pm, Sat & Sun 6.30am–3pm.

Post 70 Juta St, Braamfontein ☎072 248 2078; map p.454. A hip little café serving healthy sandwiches (from R40), good coffee and home-made lemonade. There are large windows, and a stack of LPs from which to select the background music. Mon–Fri 6.30am–4pm, Sat 8.30am–2pm.

The Potato Shed, Newtown Junction, Newtown ☎010 590 6133 ⓦthepotatoshed.com; map p.454. Classy grillhouse named after its location in Newtown's century-old potato sheds near the Market Theatre. Try pairing the succulent fire-pit-roasted meat (R110–160) with one of ten different potato sides. Tues–Sat noon–10pm, Sun & Mon noon–4pm.

NORTHERN SUBURBS

The Big Mouth Nelson Mandela Square, Sandton ☎063 293 8869, ⓦthebigmouth.co.za; map p.461. This elegant, if pricey, seafood restaurant is among the best of the dozen or so restaurants clustered around the rather soulless, tourist-oriented Nelson Mandela Square. The inventive signature sushi menu is a winner – try the "reloaded" rainbow roll (R145) topped with spring onion, caviar, teriyaki and seven spice. Mon–Sat noon–11pm, Sun noon–10pm.

★**EB Social Kitchen & Bar** Hyde Park Corner ☎011 268 6039, ⓦsocialkitchenandbar.co.za; map p.461. Part of Hyde Park's much-loved Exclusive Books shop, the bar boasts a superb local wine list and good cocktails served with a bird's-eye view over the verdant northern suburbs. Meanwhile, the kitchen serves a pricey menu of contemporary tapas, entrées and larger mains, which can be eaten at the bar or in the adjoining restaurant. Mon–Sat noon–10.30pm, Sun noon–4pm.

Flames 67 Jan Smuts Ave, Westcliff ☎011 481 6000, ⓦwestcliff.co.za; map p.461. The terrace restaurant at the deluxe *The Westcliff* (part of the Four Seasons group) is perched on a steep hill, overlooking Joburg zoo and the lush green expanse of the northern suburbs. Come here for a weekend brunch (R595), sundowner cocktails or a fantastic meal, and enjoy the view and the sounds of the elephants and lions down below. Daily 10am–11pm.

★**Milk Bar** 19 Keyes Ave, Rosebank ☎010 594 5128; map p.461. Brightly patterned shweshwe fabrics, pot plants, vintage signs and colourful local crafts abound in this quirky Afrocentric café. Try the signature bunny chows (R65), chicken pregos (R65) and boerie rolls (R50), and drop by on Thursday and Friday nights for DJ sets and Mozambican beers. Mon–Fri 6.30am–6pm, Thurs & Fri 6.30am–11pm, Sat & Sun 8am–4pm.

Red Chamber Jan Smuts Ave, corner of Sixth Rd, Hyde Park Corner Mall, Sandton ☎011 325 6048, ⓦredchamber.co.za; map p.461. A long menu of the sual Chinese dishes including a good Peking duck (R212 or half a duck) and spicy aubergine with pork mince R115), served in plusher surroundings than you usually et in Chinatown. Daily noon–10.30pm.

ashas Oxford Rd, The Zone at Rosebank Mall ☎011 447 7972, ⓦtashascafe.com; map p.461. well-designed chain restaurant with a varied bistro nenu covering everything from breakfasts and sandwiches ɔ steaks and Turkish flat-bread wraps (R80–120). Book head to be certain of a table. Also in Melrose Arch and elson Mandela Square. Mon–Sat 7am–6pm, Sun .30am–4pm.

GREENSIDE AND PARKHURST

★ **Craft** 33 Fourth Ave, corner of 13th Ave, Parktown ☎011 788 7111, ⓦcraftrestaurant.co.za; map p.461. n informal pizzeria and grill restaurant for beer lovers, vith tables spilling out onto the pavements for optimal raft beer swilling and people-watching. The oven roduces magnificent pizza, priced from R95, plus pies, neat dishes and other wood-fired delicacies. Mon– hurs 7am–10pm, Fri & Sat 7am–11pm, Sun am–9pm.

istrict Six Eatery (D6) 35 Greenhill Rd ☎011 486 226; map p.461. Cosy and casual D6 is the best place in ɔburg to try authentic Cape Malay cuisine such as *bobotie* piced minced-meat bake topped with a savoury custard, 105), cooked up by charming owner and chef Grace ɔurie. Tues–Sat noon–10pm, Sun noon–3.30pm.

oppio Zero Corner of Barry Herzog and Gleneagles d, Greenside ☎011 646 8740; map p.461. npretentious and hugely popular Italian place with n eclectic menu. Breakfast (from R65) is a big draw, and ue omelettes are exceptional. Most pizzas and pasta shes are R70–100. Mon & Sun 7am–9pm, Tues–Sat am–10.30pm.

ovo Telo Cobbles Centre, Fourth Ave, Parkhurst ☎011 447 5939, ⓦvovotelo.com; map p.461. A calm nd classy bakery café serving tasty home-baked products nd light meals, such as vegetarian quiche (R76) and nicken and mushroom pie (R76). Also at the 44 Stanley ɔmplex. Mon–Sat 7am–9.30pm, Sun 7am–8pm.

MELVILLE

nt Café 11 Seventh St ☎076 476 5671; map p.463. classic Melville hangout, *Ant* has delicious crisp thin-crust zzas served with lots of toppings from R85, friendly rvice, a few comfy chairs on the pavement, and after all ese years still only accepts cash. Food is served till late ere. Daily noon–11pm.

ean There 44 Stanley Rd, Milpark ☎087 310 3100, • beanthere.co.za; map p.463. A bean roastery and café side a bright old warehouse, with a tiny garden terrace. ue coffee and freshly roasted beans are also available to

take away. Mon–Fri 7.30am–4pm, Sat 9am–3pm, Sun 9am–noon.

★ **Great Eastern Food Bar** 53 Rustenburg Rd, Bamboo Lifestyle Centre ☎011 482 2910; map p.463. Introducing adventurous Asian cooking and flavours that are new to South Africa, the self-taught chef here makes a selection of ramen noodle dishes (R130), seasonal dumplings, Korean fried chicken (R120) and sashimi tacos (R70) – plus plenty of vegetarian options. Mon 6–10pm, Tues–Sat noon–10.30pm, Sun noon–4pm.

IT Corner Seventh St, corner of Second Ave ☎011 482 6090, ⓦtheitcorner.co.za; map p.463. A boutique internet café with free wi-fi and excellent food and drinks; stuffed croissants for breakfast (R55), burgers (R70), carrot cake, crêpes and Moroccan mint tea. Daily 6.30am–7.30pm.

Lucky Bean 16 Seventh St ☎011 482 5572, ⓦluckybeantree.co.za; map p.463. A trendy place at the calm lower end of the street, with comfy sofas and an imaginative menu that includes ostrich burger (R105), vegan burgers (R95) and springbok pie (R100). Tues–Sun 11am–11pm.

Pablo Eggs-Go-Bar 2 Seventh St ☎063 335 9348; map p.463. Laidback cafe with a hipster aesthetic overlooking Melville's main drag. The all-day breakfast menu features eggs served every which way – the red or green shakshuka (R99) served on top of fresh Yemeni flatbread is famously good. Tues–Sat 6.30am–4pm, Sun & Mon 6.30am–3pm.

Picobella 66 Fourth Ave ☎011 482 4309; map p.463. This converted villa with a lovely porch is the best Italian place for miles; pizzas are served in a flash, with toppings such as spicy chicken strips, mushrooms and avocado (R68–98). Daily 8am–10pm.

★ **Salvation Cafe** 44 Stanley Rd, Milpark, between Braamfontein and Melville ☎011 482 7795, ⓦsalvationcafe.co.za; map p.463. This self-styled "food pharmacy" is located in a former industrial complex that now hosts various boutiques, restaurants and bars. There's an excellent chicken caesar salad (R89), the house breakfast burritos will fill you up for R80, and always leave space for their New York-style cheesecake (R44) before you leave. Daily 8am–4pm.

SOWETO

Soweto tours (see box, p.467) usually stop off for a meal in a local restaurant, bar or *shebeen*, and so long as you're not part of a huge group of tourists, it's not a bad way to meet some locals. If you're heading to Soweto under your own steam or with a local contact, any of the places below are worth checking out and will give you a warm welcome. Commonly, some kind of meat and *pap* is the main dish on offer, often alongside local favourites such as tripe or ox shin.

7

Chaf Pozi Corner of Chris Hani Drive and Nicholas St, Diepkloof ☎ 011 463 8895, ⓦ chafpozi.co.za. *Shebeen* chic at the foot of Soweto's iconic Orlando cooling towers; there's both traditional *pap en vleis* (cornmeal and meat) dishes (from R40) and sirloin steak available here – choose your meat of choice at the butchery and it gets grilled on the spot. Wed–Thurs 11am–6pm, Fri & Sat 11am–2am, Sun 11am–10pm.

Kofi Afrika 7166 Vilakazi St, Orlando West ☎ 084 665 2400. This cute coffee shop occupies the first-floor terrace of the quirky Box Shop, a two-storey building made from shipping containers at the top of Vilakazi St. There's a range of coffees to choose from, as well as some delicious smoothies, and you can buy bags of the signature Kofi Afrika roast to take home. Daily 7am–11pm.

Sakhumzi 6980 Vilakazi St, Orlando West, opposite the Mandela House Museum ☎ 011 536 1379, ⓦ sakhumzi.co.za. Once a small *shebeen*, the restaurant has completely taken over this residential home now, and is a great place to try typical "Kasi" Sowetan food (buffet R120). The lively streetside terrace is the best place in the area to enjoy drinks and watch rich Sowetans park their oversized cars. Daily 11am–11pm.

Wandie's Place 618 Makhalemele St, Dube ☎ 011 98. 2796 or ☎ 081 420 6051, ⓦ wandies.co.za. Situated 2km west of Vilakazi St, in the suburb of Dube, this was once Soweto's archetypal tourist-friendly *shebeen*, and is now the area's smartest eating spot, though it retains its popularity with locals. A buffet of local African food costs R120. Daily 10am–11pm.

DRINKING AND NIGHTLIFE

Joburg has the country's most racially mixed nightlife. There's a modest strip along **Melville's Seventh Street** (great fun for drinking), while weekend nights in more central Braamfontein and Maboneng are rather more lively. In many parts of the city, particularly the **northern suburbs**, old-school pubs and bars have been replaced by café/bar/restaurants commonly located in shopping centres. Irish theme pubs and sports bars are often packed and jovial, if not exactly cutting edge. You can visit some **Soweto** *shebeens* during the day (see above); at night it's wise to visit the townships in the company of a guide.

CBD & CENTRAL SUBURBS

Great Dane 5 De Beer St ☎ 011 403 1136; map p.454. A popular, grungy bar with a remarkable floor, consisting of R8000-worth of 5ct coins. There's no reason to sit – DJs get the crowd jumping around after 9pm, and the later it is the louder and more jam-packed it gets. Wed 7pm–4am, Thurs–Sat noon–4am.

★**Kitchener's Carvery** 5 De Beer St ☎ 011 043 0166; map p.454. The well-preserved pub in the former *Milner Hotel* has regular punters propping up the bar during the week, with hip youngsters taking over on Wed–Sat nights, when DJs and bands perform; funk and soul during the week, house and electro at weekends. Wed–Sat 10am–4am, Sun–Tues 10am–2am.

★**Mad Giant** 1 Fox Precinct, 1 Fox St, Newtown ☎ 011 492 1399, ⓦ madgiant.co.za; map p.454. A spectacular craft brewery that shares a building with the upmarket Asian-fusion *Urbanologi* restaurant. Choose from a pale ale, amber ale, pilsner or weiss and enjoy delicious lamb burgers (R80) from the grill in the beer garden. There's a shop selling Mad Giant branded merchandise, and behind-the-scenes brewery tours can be booked online. Daily 10am–10pm.

Pata Pata 286 Fox St, Maboneng ☎ 073 036 9031; map p.454. Named after a song made famous by local singer Miriam Makeba, this crowded ground-floor bar has a 1960s retro feel to it with mix of secondhand furniture to lounge on, a menu of African meals and a small stage for live jazz music on Fri & Sat. Daily 8am–11pm.

Zebra Inn 252 Albertina Sisulu Rd, corner of Kruger St, Maboneng ☎ 082 494 7763; map p.454. No need to head out to Kruger for your alcohol-soaked safari experience: take snapshots of the hundred trophy game heads crammed on the walls of this unmissable bar. It's also great escape from the hipsters draped around all the other bars in the area. Daily from noon till late.

NORTHERN SUBURBS

Bolton Road Collection Cnr Bolton Rd and Jan Smuts Ave, Rosebank ☎ 011 327 6104; map p.461. Part of Rosebank's fashionable Park Corner development, this hip restaurant and bar is a good place to try local craft gins with a build-your-own gin and tonic menu. The streetside tables fill up early on weekends. Daily 8am–midnight.

Island Bar Southern Sun Hyde Park First Rd, Hyde Park ☎ 011 341 8080; map p.461. A hotel bar with difference – this designer bar is perched on top of the Hyde Park Corner mall with excellent sunset views. Service slow, but the view makes up for it. Daily 6am–2am.

MELVILLE

Jo'anna Melt Bar 7 Seventh St ☎ 072 733 5966; map p.463. An attractive and busy open-fronted bar, with plenty of exposed brickwork, inventively decorated with the pressed iron panels traditionally used for ceilings. Jo'anna specializes in melted cheese with various toppings: cheddar with sweet mustard for example, for R49. There's craft beer, too. Tues–Sun noon until late.

ix 6 Seventh St, Melville ☎ 011 482 8306; map p.463. One of the more popular bars along Melville's nightlife strip, attracting a funky leftie and/ r gay cocktail-drinking crowd. Expect people dancing n any available space as the night proceeds, and don't miss the daily 2-4-1 happy hour from noon until 7pm. aily noon–2am.

Stanley Beer Yard 44 Stanley Rd, Milpark ☎ 011 82 482 5791, ✆ stanleybar.co.za; map p.463. Looking ke a cross between a barn and a garage, this is a wonderful hangout for beer lovers, with a dozen good craft beers, and live jazz music in the beer garden on Sunday afternoons. Tues–Thurs 3–11pm, Fri noon–11pm, Sat 11.30am–11pm, Sun 11.30am–5pm.

Xai Xai 5 Seventh St ☎ 011 482 6990; map p.463. A popular and grungy Mozambican-themed bar attached to the Portuguese restaurant *Nuno's*, serving up televised sports and cheap beer. The outside tables are great for people-watching and there's a relaxed bohemian atmosphere. Daily 9am–2am.

IVE MUSIC

ohannesburg dominates the South African music scene, offering a much wider spectrum of sounds than Cape Town or urban. Friday and Saturday nights are the busiest times for gigs, which are just as often held outdoors as inside clubs. oburg is always discovering superb new jazz talent, but established artists to look out for include the gifted vocalist mphiwe Dana, singer-songwriter Vusi Mahlasela, guitarist Carlo Mombelli and trumpeters Marcus Wyatt and Hugh asekela. The Orbit in Braamfontein is your best bet for live jazz. Indie and alternative acts worth catching live include esmond and the Tutus, The Brother Moves On, Urban Village, Jeremy Loops and BLK JKS. Kwaito, the hugely popular wnship-house genre, is rarely performed live except at major concerts. Hip-hop has a big following in the city – look out or rappers AKA, Cassper Nyovest and Ricky Rik – as does house music, with global stars like Durban-born DJ Black Coffee egarding Joburg as home. For classical music, the Linder Auditorium in the Wits University campus (entrance on Andrews Rd) in Parktown (☎ 011 717 3223, ✆ wits.ac.za) has regular concerts and is the home of the Johannesburg hilharmonic Orchestra. A useful **online gig guide** is provided by ✆ jhblive.co.za, and tickets are usually available via computicket.com or ✆ webtickets.co.za.

BD

The Good Luck Bar 1 Fox Precinct, Newtown ☎ 084 83 4413, ✆ goodluckbar.co.za; p.454. This gold-rush ra factory turned club has become the city's best live usic venue following the closure of the legendary assline. Promoting all genres of music from metal to ountry, Afrobeat and techno, it attracts an eclectic udience from all corners of the city.

The Orbit 81 De Korte St, Braamfontein ☎ 011 339 645, ✆ theorbit.co.za; map p.454. Much-loved jazz ub that is regarded as one of South Africa's best. There's stylish restaurant space on the ground floor, and a oncert room and terrace upstairs. Paid concerts dmission R100–150) every night and occasional omedy nights; see website for the weekly programme. ues–Sun 4pm–2am.

NORTHERN AND EASTERN SUBURBS

Katzy's The Firs, Rosebank Mall ☎ 011 880 3945, ✆ katzys.co.za; map p.461. A stylish and upmarket jazz bar and cigar lounge in the mall attached to the *Hyatt* hotel. There's live music (which veers more to the easy-listening than the innovative) five nights a week. Book ahead if you'd like to sit, and dress up a little. Tues–Sat noon–midnight.

The Radium Beerhall 282 Louis Botha Ave, Orange Grove ☎ 011 728 3866, ✆ theradium.co.za; map p.454. A charmingly shabby 1920s pub – one of the oldest in town – with live music every Friday and Saturday night (entrance from R100), a lively atmosphere and some tasty Portuguese food on the menu. Catch the Radium Jazz Band, a trio of piano, bass and drums, who perform every Friday. Daily 10am till late.

NTERTAINMENT

hannesburg has the best **entertainment** in South Africa, and draws top international performers. The Johannesburg ty guide *In Your Pocket* (✆ johannesburg.inyourpocket.com) has a handy online events guide that's updated weekly and eared towards foreign visitors. On Fridays, the *Mail & Guardian* carries cinema listings and articles on the main events, hile the *Daily Star* lists mainstream cinema and theatre. Otherwise, listen to local radio stations and check roadside osters and leaflets. **Tickets** for most events can be booked through Computicket (☎ 083 915 8000, ✆ computicket.com) r webtickets ✆ webtickets.co.za.

HEATRE, OPERA AND DANCE

uto & General Theatre on the Square Nelson andela Square, Sandton ☎ 011 883 8606, ✆ theatreonthesquare.co.za. A small, intimate theatre that offers mostly lightweight drama, some political theatre and a handful of mainstream music or cultural acts. It hosts a small jazz festival in January and there are regular free lunchtime concerts on weekdays too.

7

Joburg Theatre Loveday St, Braamfontein ☎ 0861 670 670, ⓦ joburgtheatre.com. Top venue offering a good mix of mainstream and more adventurous theatre, ballet and opera productions at an impressive four-stage venue, buried inside a huge brutalist block of concrete.

Market Theatre 56 Margaret Mcingana St, corner of Lilian Ngoyi St, Newtown ☎ 011 832 1641, ⓦ markettheatre.co.za. The venue for some of Joburg's finest stage productions – especially South African drama and contemporary dance; also celebrated for its innovative community theatre and the odd costly epic.

Montecasino Theatre Montecasino, corner of William Nicol Dr and Witkoppen Rd, Fourways ☎ 011 511 1988, ⓦ montecasino.co.za. Two stages for comedies, musicals and touring shows, and the huge 1800-seat Teatro at Montecasino which stages musicals and major concerts.

POPArt Theatre 286 Fox St, Maboneng ☎ 083 245 1040, ⓦ popartcentre.co.za. This tiny independent theatre prides itself on promoting the work of up-and-coming local writers with edgy, fringe productions often premiering here before going on to wider acclaim.

Soweto Theatre Cnr Bolani Link and Bolani Rd Jabulani, Soweto ☎ 011 930 7461, ⓦ sowetotheatre .com. Opened in 2012, the Soweto Theatre stages regular theatre productions as well as gospel and Afropop concerts. There's also a monthly open-air food and craft market on the first Saturday of the month.

CINEMAS

Bioscope 286 Fox St, Maboneng ⓦ thebioscope.co .za. An excellent art-house movie cinema in the Main Street Life complex where anything goes: environmental documentaries, Japanese splatter films, foreign film festivals, gay flicks and Asian movie nights that include food. Tickets cost R45.

Ster-Kinekor ⓦ sterkinekor.com. Cinema complexes in the Rosebank, Sandton and other malls. Their separate Cinema Nouveau brand, with a branch in Rosebank Mall has art-house films and regular festivals themed by country, which are sometimes free to visit. Otherwise tickets cost R55.

SHOPPING

Johannesburg is the best place in South Africa to buy arts and crafts, with excellent craft markets offering a plethora of goods, some of a very high quality. It is also home to over twenty major malls (typically open daily 8am–6pm), most depressingly anonymous, though the handful listed below are so plush that they merit visiting in their own right. The craft, music and book shops, galleries and markets below follow regular shop opening hours unless indicated otherwise.

MALLS

Hyde Park Corner Jan Smuts Ave, Hyde Park ⓦ hydeparkshopping.co.za; map p.461. A trendy and upmarket mall, awash with haute couture outlets. The excellent chain Exclusive Books has a large branch here, and the restaurants are much better than in other malls.

Melrose Arch Athol Oaklands Drive, Melrose North ⓦ melrosearch.co.za; map p.461. A well-designed city quarter, surrounded by tight security, with European-style streets, plazas, restaurants, bars, hotels and an upmarket mall, all built on top of a huge parking garage.

Rosebank Mall Corner of Baker St and Cradock Ave, Rosebank ⓦ rosebankmall.co.za; map p.461. One of the city's least soulless malls, with local design boutiques, craft shops, a daily African craft market and plenty of outdoor cafés and restaurants in the pedestrian streets of the adjoining The Zone centre. Famed for its food, art and craft market, every Sunday on the top parking deck. Right next to the Rosebank Gautrain station.

Sandton City Shopping Centre Corner of Sandton Drive and Rivonia Rd, Sandton ⓦ sandtoncity.com; map p.461. Linked to the opulent Nelson Mandela Square shopping centre, this enormous complex has a mind-boggling abundance of shops, plus a cinema.

CRAFT SHOPS, MARKETS AND PRIVATE ART GALLERIES

27 Boxes 76 4th Ave, Melville ⓦ 27boxes.co.za; map p.463. Built from shipping containers, this unusual centre houses dozens of small gift shops selling local crafts, art galleries, antique shops, secondhand book and music vendors and a regularly changing collection of pop-up stores. Closed Mon.

44 Stanley 44 Stanley Avenue, Milpark ⓦ 44stanley .co.za; map p.463. A deeply hip design and art complex between Braamfontein and Melville, with cafés, restaurants, exclusive South African fashion boutiques and shops selling antiques, furniture and gifts.

Art Africa 62 Tyrone Ave, Parkview ☎ 011 486 2052, ⓔ artafrica@tiscali.co.za; map p.463. Just west of the zoo, this shop has a very good selection of innovative and more familiar crafts from South Africa and the region, many ingeniously created out of recycled material.

Bryanston Organic Market Culross Rd, off Main Rd Bryanston ☎ 011 706 3671, ⓦ bryanstonorganicmarket .co.za; map p.461. Right-on collection of stalls selling lovely organic food, high-quality local crafts and handmade clothes. The market has a free shuttle-bus service picking up at the major Sandton hotels, and kid's crafting activities make it a family favourite. Thurs & Sat 9am–3pm.

JOHANNESBURG ARTS FESTIVALS

Art Week Joburg ⓦ artweekjoburg.co.za. Joburg hosts dozens of art exhibitions and other art-related events in the first week of September at venues across town, culminating in the three-day FNB Joburg Art Fair showcasing the best contemporary South African artists at the Sandton Convention Centre.

FNB Dance Umbrella Wits Theatre, Braamfontein ⓦ danceforumsouthafrica.co.za. Over ten days in February/March, Africa's largest festival of dance and choreography hosts international companies but also acts as the major national platform for work by South African talent.

First Thursdays Venues across Braamfontein and Rosebank ⓦ first-thursdays.co.za. Originally intended as a platform for late-night art gallery openings, this monthly event has grown to include DJ parties, book launches, pop-up bars and wine tastings hosted at more than a dozen art galleries in Rosebank and Braamfontein, including a street party at Keyes Art Mile.

Joy of Jazz Festival Sandton Convention Centre ⓦ joyofjazz.co.za. A weekend festival in early September that draws the cream of South African jazz, including the likes of Pops Mohamed and Hugh Masekela, along with international guest stars.

7

im Sacks Art Gallery 153 Jan Smuts Ave, osebank ☎ 011 447 5804, ⓦ kimsacksgallery blogspot.com; map p.461. A trove of magnificent rafts and traditional art from across Africa; the prices an be hefty, but the quality is consistently exceptional. losed Sun.

waMaiMai Market CBD; map p.454. This traditional edicine market is thought to be the oldest in Joburg, and me traders and spiritual healers have been working and ving here for generations. Most stalls specialize in muthi folk medicine, but there are plenty of local crafts well. While it's possible to visit on your own, it's much etter to go with a local guide, who can introduce you to e community and their traditions. MainStreetWalks, ased in nearby Maboneng, can organize visits ⓦ mainstreetwalks.co.za).

akotis 112 Helen Joseph St St, CBD ☎ 011 337 435, ⓦ makotis.co.za; map p.454. Traditional frican shweshwe designs sold by the metre at very ffordable prices, or as finished dresses and other lothing. Also sells colourful woollen Basotho blankets. losed Mon.

Market on Main 264 Fox St, Maboneng ☎ 011 334 947; map p.454. Food, design and entertainment at the rts on Main complex. All shops and restaurants in the Maboneng district are open on Sunday as well, making it e best time to visit. Sun 10am–3pm.

leighbourgoods Market De Korte St, Braamfontein ⓦ neighbourgoodsmarket.co.za; map p.454. A bustling arket selling mainly food, plus some art and design, in an ld parking garage. This is where the young and beautiful et their Balkan Burger fix. As the afternoon progresses, veryone somehow ends up on the terrace by the bar. at 9am–3pm.

osebank Art & Craft Market Rosebank Mall, 50 Bath ve, Rosebank; map p.461. Not to be confused with the unday market, this permanent and entertaining two-torey market has an impressive array of cottage-industry

African crafts and clothing. Bargaining is encouraged. Daily 9am–6pm, Fri 9am–7pm, Sat & Sun 9am–5pm.

Rosebank Sunday Market Rosebank Mall rooftop, Corner of Baker St and Cradock Ave, Rosebank ⓦ rosebanksundaymarket.co.za; map p.461. An excellent market with handmade African arts, souvenirs, fashion, jewellery, vintage bric-a-brac and more; held on the spacious top floor of the mall parking garage. There are also lots of food stalls. Sun 9am–4pm.

Snow Lion 12b Seventh St, Melville ☎ 011 482 2795, ⓦ www.snowlion.co.za, map p.463. Creative South African-themed T-shirts for children and adults (showing Mandela's smiling face or well-known South African brands), plus New Age artefacts. Daily 10am–9pm.

BOOKS & MUSIC
The Musica and Look & Listen chains, found in most malls, sell soul and rock import CDs, with small selections of local music. In the CBD there are dozens of small shops selling CDs of African sounds.

Collector's Treasury CTP House, 244 Commissioner St, CBD ☎ 011 482 6516; map p.454. For decades, the Treasury has been a book-lover's dream come true, with some two million secondhand books (including lots of Africana) stacked on shelves and left in random piles over several floors.

Exclusive Books ⓦ exclus1ves.co.za; map p.461. South Africa's biggest and best bookshop chain, with all the latest titles. There are branches in many malls, but the best shops are in Hyde Park Corner Mall (☎ 011 325 4298), Sandton City (☎ 011 883 1010) and Rosebank Mall (☎ 011 447 3028).

Love Books 53 Rustenburg Rd, Bamboo Lifestyle Centre ☎ 011 726 7408, ⓦ lovebooks.co.za; map p.463. A small but delightful bookshop selling African literature, imported novels and Joburg books. Comfortable seats, or visit the adjoining *Service Station* café.

SPECTATOR SPORT IN JOBURG

The biggest sport in Johannesburg is **football**, and there's a passionate rivalry between Joburg's two main teams, the **Kaizer Chiefs** and **Orlando Pirates** – for decades local derbies have pulled mammoth crowds of seventy thousand. Games against other local teams draw much smaller crowds, although it's worth trying to go to a home game against Pretoria giants Mamelodi Sundowns. Tickets are cheap, crowd violence is rare and the atmosphere exhilarating.

Ellis Park stadium in central Joburg (now officially the Emirates Airline Park) is a South African **rugby** shrine. As well as hosting international fixtures it's also home ground to the provincial **Emirates Lions** team. The best way to get there is on the park-and-ride system that operates for big games, with buses shuttling in from the Park Station Gautrain.

The major international **cricket** games, including five-day test matches, are played at the Wanderers Stadium (35 Corlett Drive, Illovo), also nicknamed the Bull Ring. The Gauteng provincial team, the **Highveld Lions**, also play their matches here.

DIRECTORY

Banks and exchange There are ATMs everywhere, but beware scammers: only use a safe indoor ATM and refuse any kind of help from strangers while using it. The main shopping malls have banks and exchange offices where you can change money.

Hospitals and ambulance services In any medical emergency, call the private Netcare 911 ambulance service on ☎ 082 911 (ⓦ netcare.co.za). Patients are taken to a Netcare private hospital, which will be expensive but more dependable than a public hospital. State-run hospitals with 24hr casualty departments include Johannesburg General Hospital, Parktown (☎ 011 488 3334/5), and Helen Joseph Hospital, Auckland Park (☎ 011 489 1011). Private hospitals include Netcare Milpark Hospital, Guild St, Parktown (☎ 011 480 5600), and Morningside Medi-Clinic, off Rivonia Rd in Morningside (☎ 011 282 5000). Private hospitals are

always the best option, but without proof of medical insurance, a hefty payment will be needed on admission.

Post offices Most major suburbs have a centrally located post office, often inside shopping centres or malls. There's a land-side post office at OR Tambo airport for last-minute mailings (sending a package up to 30kg to Europe by surface mail costs around R270, but can take three months to arrive). The main poste restante post office is on Rahima Moosa St in the CBD.

Swimming & gyms Public swimming pools around Johannesburg are not always in great repair, one exception being the outdoor, heated Olympic-sized Ellis Park pool (Mon–Fri 7am–7pm, Sat–Sun 8am–5pm; ☎ 011 402 5565). As for gyms, try the chain of Virgin Active gyms around the city (☎ 086 020 0911, ⓦ virginactive.co.za); some hotels will give you a voucher for a visit to the gym, or you can pay a single-visit fee of R180.

Around Johannesburg

Johannesburgers wanting to get away from it all tend to head northwest towards the ancient **Magaliesberg Mountains**, stretching from Pretoria in the east to Rustenberg in the North West Province. Formed over two billion years ago, the mountain range has steadily eroded over the millennia, so you won't see a horizon of impressive peaks: much of the area is farmland running across rolling countryside, with some ridges, cliffs, *kloofs* (gorges) and refreshingly wide vistas. A series of caves on the southeastern (Johannesburg) side holds some of the world's most important information about human evolution stretching back some 3.5 million years. These caves, including the renowned Sterkfontein Caves, are now protected as part of the **Cradle of Humankind**, one of South Africa's first World Heritage Sites.

The Cradle of Humankind

Covering some 116,000 acre, the **Cradle of Humankind** is the name given to the area in which a series of dolomitic caves has in the last fifty years or so produced nearly two-fifths of the world's hominid fossil discoveries. Given its accessibility and the

MRS PLES AND FRIENDS

Embedded in the dolomitic rock within a dozen caves in the area now called the Cradle of Humankind are the fossilized remains of **hominids** that lived in South Africa up to 3.5 million years ago. Samples of fossilized pollen, plant material and animal bones also found in the caves indicate that the area was once a **tropical rainforest** inhabited by giant monkeys, long-legged hunting hyenas and sabre-toothed cats.

Quite when hominids arrived on the scene isn't certain, but scientists now believe that the human lineage split from apes in Africa around five to six million years ago. The oldest identified group of hominids is *Australopithecus*, a bipedal, small-brained form of man. The first *Australopithecus* discovery in South Africa was in 1924, when Professor Raymond Dart discovered the **Taung child** in what is now North West Province. In 1936, australopithecine fossils were first found in the Sterkfontein Caves, and in 1947 Dr Robert Broom excavated a nearly complete skull which he first called *Plesianthropus transvaalensis* ("near-man" of the Transvaal), later confirmed as a 2.6-million-year-old *Australopithecus africanus*. Identified as a female, she was nicknamed **"Mrs Ples"**, and for many years she was the closest thing the world had to **"the missing link"**.

A number of even older fossils have since been discovered at Sterkfontein and nearby caves, along with evidence of several other genera and species. The most prominent recent discovery is the cache of 1550 bones which have been identified as a new species, named *Homo naledi*, and are thought to be 335,000 to 236,000 years old – thus placing *Homo naledi* in the same era as Homo sapiens. The discovery was made in 2013 inside two almost inaccessible chambers within the Rising Star (naledi in the Sesotho language) cave system. Some scientists believe that the unusual location of the bones is suggestive of ritualized behaviour, with a popular current theory being that *Homo naledi* deliberately disposed of their dead.

If you want to learn more and visit some of the caves and dig sites not open to the general public, try one of the excellent **tours** offered by Palaeo Tours (☎ 082 804 2899, ⓦ palaeotours .com) or Past Experiences (☎ 011 678 3905, ⓦ pastexperiences.co.za).

richness of the finds, it has now arguably overtaken Tanzania's Olduvai Gorge as Africa's most important paleontological site.

Sterkfontein Caves

Daily 9am–5pm, tours every half hour until 4pm • R165, or R190 including Maropeng Museum • ☎ 011 577 9000, ⓦ maropeng.co.za

The best known of the Cradle of Humankind sites are the **Sterkfontein Caves**, believed to have been inhabited by pre-human primates who lived here up to 3.5 million years ago. They first came to European attention in 1896, when an Italian lime prospector, Guglielmo Martinaglia, stumbled upon them. Martinaglia was only interested in the bat droppings, and promptly stripped them out, thus destroying the caves' dolomite formation.

Archeologist Dr Robert Broom excavated the caves between 1936 and 1951; in 1947, he found the skull of a female hominid (nicknamed "Mrs Ples") that was over 2.5 million years old. In 1995, another archeologist, Ronald Clarke, found "Little Foot", the bones of a 3-million-year-old walking hominid, with big toes that functioned like our thumbs do today. In 1998 an *Australopithecus* skeleton discovered here was the oldest complete specimen known, reckoned to be 3.3 million years old. There's a small museum that you can browse before being taken on a tour through the cave.

Wonder Cave

Tues–Fri 9am–4pm, Sat & Sun 9am–5pm • Tours depart on the hour • R100, R240 including the Rhino & Lion Nature Reserve • ☎ 011 957 0006, ⓦ rhinolion.co.za/wonder-cave-index • The caves are best accessed via the Rhino and Lion Nature Reserve – the alternative route is on a longer, rough dirt road

The only other cave with public access is the **Wonder Cave**, located within the Rhino and Lion Nature Reserve (see below) to the northeast of Sterkfontein. Also mined for lime in the 1890s, this cave hasn't revealed any paleontological finds, and the main focus of attention is the extraordinary stalactites, stalagmites and rimstone pools to be found in a huge underground chamber. Once you've descended into the cave by a lift, carefully placed lighting and marked trails make the experience theatrical and unashamedly commercial.

The Rhino and Lion Nature Reserve

Daily 8am–4pm • R160, R240 including the Wonder Cave • ☏ 011 957 0349, ⓦ rhinolion.co.za

The fourteen-square-kilometre **Rhino and Lion Nature Reserve** is really more a safari park than anything resembling a wilderness game reserve as found in other parts of South Africa, but it is Gauteng's best site for seeing large mammals. The main section of the reserve has white rhino, wildebeest, hartebeest and zebra roaming free, while the Lion and Predator Camp has several large enclosures containing lions, cheetahs and wild dogs. Elsewhere, there's a vulture hide, a series of hippo pools (located opposite the main gate) and a breeding centre. At the animal crèche, you can pet lion cubs – though you should realize that these animals usually end up on hunting game farms.

Maropeng Museum

Down the R400 turn-off from the R563, northwest of the Sterkfontein Caves • Daily 9am–5pm • R120, R190 with Sterkfontein Caves • ☏ 014 577 9000, ⓦ maropeng.co.za

Housed in a striking building, the Tumulus, half clad in grassy earth to simulate a burial mound, **Maropeng** ("returning to the place of our ancestors" in SeTswana) is an impressive museum dedicated to human origins and evolution. Visitors can take a short underground boat ride into the mists of time, and then browse through some child-friendly interactive displays and other exhibits explaining the history of human development. A room full of original hominid, plant and animal fossils, loaned from various institutions across South Africa, and a display on the recent *Homo naledi* discoveries provides a fitting finale.

ARRIVAL AND DEPARTURE	THE CRADLE OF HUMANKIND
By car The Cradle of Humankind can only be reliably reached by car: head west out of Johannesburg on the R47 (Hendrik Potgieter Rd) or M5 (Beyers Naude Drive), then	follow the N14 to the R563 junction. A few kilometres northwest along the R563 is a right turn to the Sterkfontein Caves turn-off.

ACCOMMODATION	
Forum Homini Kromdraai Rd ☏ 011 668 7000, ⓦ forumhomini.com. Set in a private game farm that's home to antelopes and hippos, this award-winning hotel has beautiful "cave chic" rooms overlooking a lake. The fantastic gourmet restaurant *Roots*, which serves set lunches and dinners, is worth the trip alone; plan to spend several hours eating here. Rates include meals. __R3500__	**Maropeng Hotel** Off the R400 ☏ 014 577 9100, ⓦ maropeng.co.za. The chic hotel next to the Maropeng Museum offers good value with full-board packages available that include museum entrance. Each of its classy earth-toned rooms has a patio commanding a dramatic Magaliesberg view. __R1300__

Pretoria

Gauteng's two major cities are just 50km apart, but could hardly be more different. With its graceful government buildings, wide avenues of purple flowering jacarandas, and stolid Boer farming origins, **PRETORIA** – or **TSHWANE** as the metropolitan area is now officially known – was for a long time a staid, sleepy city. However, since the arrival of democracy, the country's administrative and executive capital has become increasingly cosmopolitan, with a substantial diplomatic community living in Arcadia and Hatfield, east of the city centre, and a black middle class swelling the ranks of civil servants. Nowadays, most Pretorians are not Afrikaners, but Pedi and Tswana; and

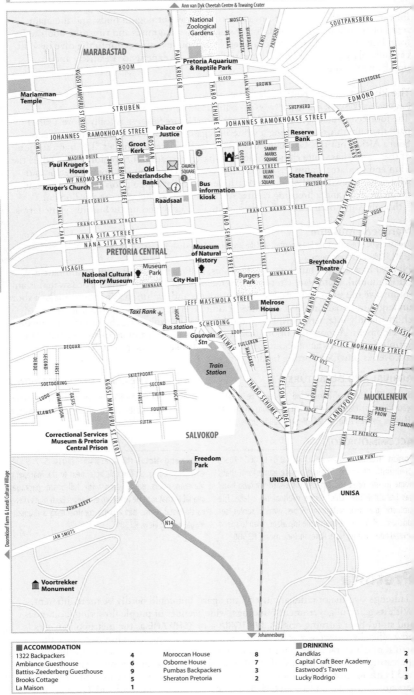

Ann van Dyk Cheetah Centre & Tswaing Crater

National Zoological Gardens

SOUTPANSBERG

MARABASTAD

Pretoria Aquarium & Reptile Park

Mariamman Temple

STRUBEN

BELVEDERE

EDMOND

JOHANNES RAMOKHOASE STREET

Palace of Justice

Groot Kerk

Reserve Bank

Paul Kruger's House

Old Nederlandsche Bank

Kruger's Church

Bus information kiosk

State Theatre

Raadsaal

PRETORIA CENTRAL

Museum of Natural History

Breytenbach Theatre

National Cultural History Museum

Museum Park

City Hall

Burgers Park

JEFF MASEMOLA STREET

Melrose House

Taxi Rank

Bus station

Gautrain Stn

JUSTICE MOHAMMED STREET

Train Station

MUCKLENEUK

Correctional Services Museum & Pretoria Central Prison

SALVOKOP

Freedom Park

UNISA Art Gallery

UNISA

Voortrekker Monument

Johannesburg

■ ACCOMMODATION		■ DRINKING	
1322 Backpackers	4	Moroccan House	8	Aandklas	2
Ambiance Guesthouse	6	Osborne House	7	Capital Craft Beer Academy	4
Battiss-Zeederberg Guesthouse	9	Pumbas Backpackers	3	Eastwood's Tavern	1
Brooks Cottage	5	Sheraton Pretoria	2	Lucky Rodrigo	3
La Maison	1				

PRETORIA

7

thousands of black students studying at the city's several universities have further diluted Pretoria's traditional Afrikaans roots. Connected to the Gautrain system, Pretoria is easily reached from Johannesburg and the airport, and the **nightlife** here is laidback and friendly.

Pretoria's city centre is a compact grid of wide, busy streets, comparatively safe to explore on foot. Its central hub is **Church Square**, where you can see some fascinating architecture; and there are other historic buildings and museums close by. To the north lie the vast **National Zoological Gardens**, while the Arcadia district is the site of the city's famous **Union Buildings** and the **Mandela monument**. On the southern fringes of the city is the remarkable **Voortrekker Monument**, and **Freedom Park**, a memorial that attempts to come to terms with South Africa's past conflicts. While Central Pretoria is fairly safe to walk around, you should be careful when wandering north of Church Square around busy Johannes Ramokhoase and Struben streets, and also be vigilant in the Sunnyside district, east of the CBD.

7 Brief history

Unlike Johannesburg, Pretoria developed at a leisurely pace from its humble origins as a **Boer farming community** on the fertile land around the Apies River. When the city was founded in 1855 by **Marthinus Pretorius**, who named it after his father, Andries Pretorius, it was intended to be the capital around which the new South African Republic (ZAR) would prosper. Embodying the Afrikaners' conviction that the land they took was God-given, Pretoria's first building was a church. The town was then laid out with streets wide enough for teams of oxen brought in by farmers to make U-turns.

In 1860, the city was proclaimed the capital of the ZAR, the result of tireless efforts by Stephanus Schoeman to unite the squabbling statelets of the Transvaal. From this base, the settlers continued their campaigns against local African peoples, bringing thousands into service, particularly on farms. Infighting also continued among the settlers, and violent skirmishes between faction leaders were common. These leaders bought most of the best land, resulting in the dispossession of many white trekkers, and also in the massacre of most of the animals of the region, particularly its elephants.

The Boer Wars

The British annexed Pretoria in 1877, and investment followed in their wake. Although the town prospered and grew, farmer **Paul Kruger**, who was determined not to be subjugated by the British again, mobilized commandos of Afrikaner farmers to drive them out, resulting in the first Anglo-Boer War (1877–81). After defeat at Majuba on the Natal border, the colonial government abandoned the war and ceded **independence** in 1884. Paul Kruger became ZAR president until 1903. However, his mission to keep the ZAR Boer was confounded by the discovery of **gold** in the Witwatersrand, which precipitated an unstoppable flood of foreigners. Kruger's policy of taxing the newcomers, while retaining the Boer monopoly on political power, worked for a while. Most of the elegant buildings of Church Square were built with mining revenues, while the Raadsaal (parliament) remained firmly in Boer hands. ZAR independence ended with the second Anglo-Boer War (1899–1902), but, despite the brutality of the conflict, Pretoria remained unscathed. With the creation of the **Union of South Africa** in 1910, the city became the administrative capital of the entire country.

In 1928, the government laid the foundations of Pretoria's industry by establishing the **Iron and Steel Industrial Corporation** (Iscor), which rapidly generated a whole series of related and service industries. These, together with the civil service, ensured white Pretoria's quiet, insular prosperity. Meanwhile, increasing landlessness among the black population drove many into the city's burgeoning **townships**. Marabastad and Atteridgeville are the oldest, and Mamelodi is the biggest and poorest.

After the introduction of apartheid by the National Party in 1948, Pretoria acquired a hated reputation among the black population. Its supreme court and central prison were notorious as the source of the laws that made their lives a nightmare.

Democracy

Mandela's **inauguration** at the Union Buildings in 1994 was the symbolic new beginning for Pretoria's political redemption. Through the 1990s, the stages of South Africa's revolution could be seen as clearly here as anywhere else: the gradual replacement of the diehards from institutions like the army and civil service, new faces in almost all the old government offices, the return of foreign diplomats and the influx of students.

Pretoria's metropolitan area was renamed **Tshwane** in 2005 by the city council, after a Tswana-Ndebele chief who ruled in the area before Boer settlers arrived, and dozens of city-centre streets have recently been re-named after resistance heroes. The central business district remains Pretoria, but the compromise is awkward, with most media, and indeed most citizens, still calling the whole city Pretoria. Many Afrikaners resent what they see as a spiteful and costly attempt to erase the city's historic origins from public memory, while many black Pretorians don't see why a post-apartheid, mainly black city should still bear a name deeply associated with racial oppression. It seems likely that the city will lug two names around for years to come.

Church Square

The heart of Pretoria is **Church Square**, surrounded by dramatic and important buildings. It was here that Boer farmers unharnessed their oxen when they came into town for the quarterly *Nagmaal* (Holy Communion) of the Dutch Reformed Church, turning the square temporarily into a campsite.

Indeed, nearly every important white meeting, protest or takeover the city has known happened in Church Square; the ZAR Vierkleur ("four colours") flag was lowered here in 1877 to make way for the Union Jack, only to rise again in 1881, after the British eviction from the republic; the British flag flew again in 1900 but was lowered for the last time in 1910; Paul Kruger was proclaimed head of state here four times, and thirty thousand people crammed into the square in 1904 for his memorial service. Such historical resonances are viewed differently by Pretoria's black community, and the square's central **statue of Paul Kruger** is for many an unwanted relic of a dismal past.

Raadsaal and the Old Nederlandsche Bank Building

On the southwest corner of Church Square, the old **Raadsaal** (parliament) was built in neo-Renaissance style in 1891, and still exudes the bourgeois respectability yearned for by the parliamentarians of the ZAR. Ask the security guard for a peek inside, and to look at the room where Paul Kruger spent most of his time during the final stages of the Anglo-Boer War.

Next to the Raadsaal is the **Old Nederlandsche Bank Building**, home of the tourist office (see p.494). Incredibly, it took a gathering of ten thousand people in 1975 and five years of deliberation to reverse a decision to demolish this building and the Raadsaal.

Palace of Justice

In the northwest corner of Church Square, the grandiose **Palace of Justice** was started in 1897 and, half completed, used as a hospital for British troops during the second Anglo-Boer War. Home to the Transvaal Supreme Court for many years after its completion in 1902, it was the location of the Rivonia Trial in 1963–64, which saw Nelson Mandela and other leaders of the ANC sentenced to life imprisonment.

Restoration work has revealed and repaired the splendid facade and balconies, although the new court is an ugly box sitting squatly in a street behind the Palace.

Queen Street Mosque

A small passageway off Queen Street brings you to the unexpected site of a bright white **mosque**, oriented at an angle to the city grid so as to face Mecca. Pretoria's Muslims, who reportedly got on well with Kruger, acquired the site in 1896, and the current building was constructed in 1927 by Cape artisans. The mosque is now hemmed in by ugly tower blocks, but is somehow all the more indomitable for that.

Lilian Ngoyi Square

Lilian Ngoyi Square is named after the anti-apartheid activist who was one of the leaders of the 1956 Women's March that started on this spot. Until 2006 this was called Strijdom Square, and was the site of a vast and horrific bust of the man himself. Prime Minister from 1954 to 1958, **Johannes Strijdom** began the wave of apartheid legislation that peaked under his successor, Hendrik Verwoerd, and was a firm believer in "white supremacy". Dramatically, on May 31, 2001, forty years to the day after the statue was completed, a structural fault caused it to collapse.

Paul Kruger's House and around

60 WK Nkomo St (formerly Church St) • Mon–Fri 8.30am–4.30pm, Sat & Sun 9am–4.30pm • R60 (South Africans R40) • ☎ 012 000 0010, ⓦ ditsong.org.za

Paul Kruger's House was built in 1884 by the English-speaking Charles Clark, described by Kruger as one of his "tame Englishmen", who mixed his cement with milk instead of water. Inside, the **museum** is rather dull, though you may find some interest in Kruger's effects, such as his large collection of spittoons. The *stoep* (veranda) is the most famous feature of the house, for here the old president would sit and chat to any white person who chose to join him. At the back is Kruger's private railway coach, built in 1898, which he used during the second Anglo-Boer War.

Opposite is a characteristically grim Reformed church known as **Kruger's Church**. The **Groot Kerk** (Great Church), on the corner of Madiba Drive and Bosman streets, is more impressive; its strikingly ornate tower is one of the finest in the country.

Melrose House

275 Jeff Masemola St (formerly Jacob Maré St) • Tues–Sun 10am–5pm • R20 • ☎ 012 322 2805, ⓦ melrosehouse.co.za

Opposite the restful **Burgers Park** (named after ineffective ZAR president Thomas Burgers, who was in office between 1873 and 1877), with its manicured lawns, you'll find **Melrose House**, an over-decorated Victorian domicile with a wonderful conservatory and interesting exhibitions. The house was built in 1886 for local businessman George Heys, who made his money running mailcoach services. Lord Kitchener used the house during the second Anglo-Boer War, and the treaty of Vereeniging that ended hostilities was signed inside.

Museum of Natural History

432 Paul Kruger St • Daily 8am–4pm • R30 • ☎ 012 322 7632, ⓦ ditsong.org.za

The grand **Museum of Natural History** is Pretoria's oldest museum and home to plenty of stuffed animals, bird exhibits, models of dinosaurs and casts of fossil remains (the original fossils can be viewed by appointment only). The museum's age shows and some of the exhibits could do with an update, or at least a good clean. The impressive bird exhibition containing the taxidermied bodies of 870 different African bird species, large and small, is strangely fascinating and for birdwatchers a definite highlight.

City Hall

Paul Kruger St

Forming an architectural ensemble with the Museum of Natural History directly opposite, the **City Hall** was built in 1935 in a mix of Greek and Roman architectural styles. The park in front of the building has a series of fountains and well-tended flowerbeds and statues of the city's founding fathers Andries and Marthinus Pretorius and – added in 2006 – founding grandfather Chief Tshwane.

National Cultural History Museum

149 Visagie St • Daily 8am–4pm • R35 • ☎ 012 324 6082, Ⓦ ditsong.org.za

The permanent exhibitions at the **National Cultural History Museum**, west of the City Hall, are eclectic to the point of being a bit unconnected: they include displays of San rock art, and a room showing work by J.H. Pierneef (1886–1957), one of the country's most famous artists, who is known for his dramatically stylized bushveld landscapes.

National Zoological Gardens

232 Boom St • Daily 8.30am–5.30pm • R110; cableway R25 one way, R35 return • **Night tour** Wed, Fri & Sat 6.30pm; R110 • **Camping tour** Fri & Sat 5pm; R165 • ☎ 012 328 3265, Ⓦ nzg.ac.za

Pretoria's spacious and recommended **zoo** houses rare species of antelope, a white rhinoceros, and a wide selection of South American as well as African animals. Next door, the **Pretoria Aquarium and Reptile Park** (included in the price) is less impressive, but nonetheless houses plenty of beasts, some weird and highly venomous. A cable-car ride takes you right over the zoo, across the Apies River and to the top of the ridge for fine views of the city. It's well worth trying to book one of the **night tours** (which run September 1–March 31), when you'll see some of the zoo's nocturnal creatures, like bats, owls and lions, at their most active; it's also possible to spend the night in the zoo on a camping tour (note that you'll need to bring all your own gear).

Mariamman Temple

Seventh St, Marabastad • Daily 9am–5pm • ☎ 012 358 1430

The scruffy streets of Marabastad, the city's first "non-white" area, lie to the west of the zoo and, while fascinating, can feel quite intimidating if visiting alone. Don't miss the intricately decorated Hindu **Mariamman Temple** from 1930, next to the market, which was built in Tamil style with a colourful Gorpuram tower, and is dedicated to the consort of the god Shiva, who protects against infectious diseases.

The Correctional Services Museum

Kgosi Mampuru St (formerly Potgieter St) • Tues–Fri 9am–3pm • Free • ☎ 012 314 1766, Ⓦ dcs.gov.za

The chilling **Correctional Services Museum** at Pretoria Central Prison, along the R101 towards Johannesburg, is well worth a visit. You'll see the notorious prison, where many famous political prisoners were held (and executed), on your right. Be prepared to walk past depressed-looking visiting relatives on your way in. Inside the museum you can see artwork made by prisoners, including a life-size statue of an inmate crawling towards an expressionless prison warder, who has his arms outstretched, ready to correct him. There are also exhibits of knives concealed in Bibles and shoes, files in cakes and so forth. Most alarming are the group photos of various forbidding-looking prison warders through the ages, which seem a strange sort of propaganda for the prison service. For a first-hand account of the conditions inside, Charles Herman Bosman's Cold Stone Jug is a fascinating collection of short stories about his four-year stay in this prison in the 1920s.

The Freedom Park

Salvokop Hill • Daily 9am–4.30pm, guided tours daily at 9am, noon & 3pm • R120 (South Africans R55) • ☎ 012 336 4000, ⓦ freedompark.co.za

Freedom Park, which winds its way around Salvokop Hill, is punctuated by a sculpture of ascending "reeds" that are dramatically illuminated at night. Started in 2000 in response to the Truth and Reconciliation Commission's (see box, p.650) call for new symbols to resolve past conflicts, the park is a courageous and successful attempt to create a memorial that speaks to all sections of post-apartheid society in South Africa. At the top of the hill is the Wall of Names, inscribed with the names of 75,000 victims of various South African conflicts, an eternal flame to the unknown soldier, and boulders representing important moments in the history of the country's nine provinces – Gauteng's rock symbolizes the peaceful marches in Soweto, Sharpeville, Mamelodi and other townships that were met by police violence. At the entrance to the park is the extensive //hapo museum, named after the Khoi word for dream, which tells the history of the country from an African perspective, particularly focusing on the impacts of colonialism and apartheid. The section covering the devastating effects of the mining industry on traditional ways of life has a wealth of archival footage and personal testimonies that are especially engrossing. Guided tours of the museum and park are included in the entrance price.

The Voortrekker Monument

Eeufees Rd • Daily: May–Aug 8am–5pm, Sept–April 8am–6pm • R70 • ☎ 012 326 6770, ⓦ vtm.org.za

A symbol of Afrikaner domination in the old South Africa, the **Voortrekker Monument and Museum** is a striking, austere block of granite, built in 1940 to commemorate the Boer victory over the Zulu army at Blood River on December 16, 1838 (see p.425). The monument is enclosed by reliefs of ox wagons, with a large statue of a woman standing outside, shaking her fist at imaginary oppressors. Inside, a series of moving reliefs depicts scenes from the Great Trek, and you can climb to the top of the tower for a peek down into the hall, or for dramatic views of the surrounding nature reserve. This has various hiking and mountain-bike trails, leading to lookout points over Pretoria.

The Union Buildings

In the Arcadia district, Pretoria's **Union Buildings**, the headquarters of the South African government, perch majestically on the main hill. Designed by Herbert Baker in 1910 to symbolize the union of Briton and Boer, the lashings of colonnades and lavish amphitheatre seem to glorify British imperial self-confidence. Nelson Mandela had an office here after his release from prison, and the buildings were the site of his inauguration as president in 1994. This was perhaps the first time their imperialist symbols were transformed, not least by the African praise-singers who delivered their odes from the amphitheatre, proclaiming Mandela as the latest in a long line of African heroes from Shaka to Hintsa, and beyond. The buildings are not open to the public, but you can walk around the terrace and the attractive gardens below to enjoy great views over the city. Just below the main terrace stands the 9m-high, wide-armed **Nelson Mandela statue**, unveiled the day after Mandela's burial in December 2013. The sculptors had added a small rabbit inside the sculpture's ear, referring to the time pressure they were under ("*haas*" in Afrikaans means haste as well as hare) but, although Mandela would probably have appreciated the joke, the humourless new guardians of the ANC had it removed because "Nelson Mandela never had a rabbit in his ear".

Pretoria Art Museum

Corner of Francis Baard and Wessels sts • Tues–Sun 10am–5pm • R22 • ☎ 012 344 1807, ⓦ pretoriaartmuseum.co.za

South of the Union Buildings, the **Pretoria Art Museum** is housed in a modernist pavilion overlooking a park. Inside is a modestly sized but excellent selection of South African and early Dutch-inspired art, modern photography, some works of "resistance art" by the likes of William Kentridge and a number of black artists, including Ephraim Ngatane and Gerard Sekoto.

Sunnyside and Pretoria University

Southeast of the centre, desegregated **Sunnyside** is the central suburb with the strongest African feel, with a lively street life, distinctive old houses and a multitude of cafés – though it's best not to walk around alone here. Robert Sobukwe Street is the busiest thoroughfare, brimming with bars and street hawkers. East of Sunnyside, the huge **Loftus Versfeld Stadium** is home to Pretoria's hugely popular sporting giants – the Bulls rugby team and the Mamelodi Sundowns football team – while further east still is the vast **Pretoria University**, with two worthwhile museums.

Mapungubwe Museum

Lynnwood Rd, Old Arts Building, Pretoria University campus • Tues–Fri 10am–4pm • Free • ☎ 012 420 5450, ⓦ www.up.ac.za

The small **Mapungubwe Museum** is dedicated to the remarkable archeological finds at Mapungubwe (see p.570), a hilltop fort near the Limpopo River that was the ancient capital of a major Southern African kingdom. Among the artefacts on display are a rhinoceros made from thin gold foil, figurines, jewellery and decorated pots, all at least seven hundred years old.

Anton van Wouw and Edoardo Villa Collections

Lynnwood Rd, Old Merensky Library, Pretoria University campus • Tues–Fri 10am–4pm • Free • ☎ 012 420 5450, ⓦ www.up.ac.za

The acclaimed Dutch-born sculptor **Anton van Wouw** was responsible for most of the brooding effigies of Afrikaner public figures from the 1890s to the 1930s that are scattered around the country, including the Kruger statue in Pretoria's Church Square and the Voortrekker Monument. The university's collection, in an elegant 1930s library building, includes two striking pieces, one of a mine worker, the other an accused man standing in the dock. Look out, too, for *The Guitar Player*, a feisty-looking woman strumming away with a trace of a smile on her face. Also on display here are dozens of impressive modern steel sculptures, spanning more than sixty years, by Italian artist **Edoardo Villa**, who was a prisoner of war in South Africa in 1947.

UNISA Art Gallery

Preller St, Kgorong Building, UNISA University campus • Tues–Fri 10am–4pm • Free • ☎ 012 441 5681, ⓦ unisa.ac.za/gallery

Travelling south of the centre on Elandspoort Road, you can't miss the enormous and head-shakingly ugly **UNISA**, South Africa's largest university, with more than 200,000 students – though most of them study by correspondence. The university's very good **art gallery**, inside the entrance building, hosts some of Pretoria's most innovative exhibitions of visual and conceptual art, as well as a permanent collection exhibiting young South African talent of all backgrounds.

ARRIVAL AND INFORMATION

By plane Johannesburg's OR Tambo International Airport (see p.471) is 55km to the southeast of Pretoria. The Gautrain (see p.472) connects the airport to Pretoria and Hatfield stations, with a change in Sandton or Marlboro, daily between 5.30am and 8.30pm; tickets from the airport to Pretoria or Hatfield stations are R174. The Airport Shuttle (☏ 086 1748 8853, ⊚ airportshuttle.co.za) also goes to Pretoria from OR Tambo and Lanseria airports for around R500, though it's often cheaper to ask your accommodation to arrange collection from the airport.

By train The Gautrain runs every twelve to twenty minutes (5.30am–8.30pm) from Johannesburg to Pretoria station, situated just south of the city centre and Hatfield

station. A ticket from Pretoria station to Sandton costs R49–68, to Rosebank R53–73 and to Park Station R55–76, depending on the time of day.

By bus Intercity buses stop beside the main train station, while minibus taxis from Joburg and other destinations arrive nearby at the corner of Jeff Masemola and Bosman streets.

Destinations Bloemfontein (10 daily; 7hr); Cape Town (6 daily; 20hr); Durban (18 daily; 9hr); Johannesburg (over 30 daily; 1hr); Kimberley (4 daily; 7hr); Nelspruit (6 daily; 6hr).

Information The tourist office is in the Old Nederlandsche Bank building on Church Square (Mon–Fri 7.30am–4pm; ☏ 012 358 1430).

GETTING AROUND

By bus Gautrain bus lines operate Mon–Fri and loop from Pretoria station through the city centre, while the suburbs, malls and embassies in Arcadia, Brooklyn and Menlyn are served by Gautrain buses from Hatfield station. (You can also take the Gautrain between Hatfield and Pretoria station for R27). The new A Re Yeng municipal bus service covers

Sunnyside, the CBD, Arcadia, Hatfield and Groenkloof. You'll need to register for a rechargeable smartcard at any of the main A Re Yeng stations to use the service.

By taxi Recommended local taxi firms are Rixi Taxi (☏ 086 100 7494, ⊚ rixitaxi.co.za) and Dial-a-Dove Taxi (☏ 012 323 2040). Most Pretorians prefer to use Uber.

ACCOMMODATION

Besides the many chain hotels, Pretoria has numerous guesthouses dotted around Brooklyn and Hatfield, offering good nightlife and easy access to Loftus Versfeld Stadium and the Gautrain station; Pretoria's Bed & Breakfast Association has a central booking site at ⊚ bbapt.co.za. As with Joburg, it's worth booking your first night before you arrive.

1322 Backpackers 1322 Arcadia St, Hatfield ☏ 012 362 3905, ⊚ 1322backpackers.com; map p.486. A popular hostel near the embassies and Hatfield's nightlife, with a kitchen, pool and travel desk. Just a short walk east of the Gautrain station. Dorms <u>R170</u>, doubles <u>R450</u>

Ambiance Guest House 28 3rd St, Menlo Park ☏ 083 280 0981 ⊚ ambianceguesthouse.com; map p.486. Provençal-styled guesthouse with spacious rooms that open out onto a garden. Two of the rooms come with kitchenettes, private patios and a braai stand. <u>R1020</u>

Battiss-Zeederberg Guesthouse Fook Island, 92 Twentieth St, Menlo Park ☏ 012 460 7318; map p.486. Comfortable B&B accommodation in the original home of eccentric Walter Battiss, one of South Africa's greatest twentieth-century artists, with brightly painted floors, unusual decorations and a distinctly Greek feel. <u>R800</u>

Brooks Cottage 283 Brooks St, Brooklyn ☏ 012 362 3150, ⊚ brookscottage.co.za; map p.486. A charming and elegant Cape Dutch-style home – a national monument – with five nicely furnished rooms, satellite TV and breakfast served on the porch overlooking the pool. <u>R900</u>

La Maison 235 Hilda St, Hatfield ☏ 012 430 4341, ⊚ lamaison.co.za; map p.486. A pleasant guesthouse in a mock castle dating from 1922, with lovely gardens and six Victorian-styled rooms full of antiques. It's a short walk from Hatfield Gautrain. <u>R1000</u>

★**Moroccan House** 435 Atterbury Rd, Menlo Park, ☏ 012 346 5713, ⊚ moroccanhouse.co.za; map p.486. Modelled on a Moroccan riad, the guest suites, each with a private terrace, are a riot of colour, decorated with fabrics, tiles and furniture imported from Morocco. The traditional breakfast served upstairs at the *La Terrasse Rooftop Café* is excellent. <u>R1450</u>

Osborne House 82 Anderson St, Brooklyn ☏ 012 362 2334, ⊚ osborneguesthouse.com; map p.486. A wonderfully elegant guesthouse in a restored Edwardian manor house with lovely furniture, big windows, wooden floors and a secluded pool with a deck – perfect for breakfasts in the sun. <u>R1300</u>

Pumbas Backpackers 1232 Arcadia St, Hatfield ☏ 012 362 5343, ⊚ pumbas.co.za; map p.486. Basic and friendly hostel with a choice of two dorms plus four private cabins and a small camping site arranged around a quiet back garden. A 5min walk from Hatfield Gautrain station. Camping <u>R100</u>, dorms <u>R180</u>, doubles <u>R350</u>

Sheraton Pretoria 643 Stanza Bopape St, Arcadia ☏ 012 429 9999, ⊚ sheraton.com/pretoria; map p.486. This good-value five-star hotel boasts all the usual *Sheraton* touches, but most importantly has the best views in town of the Union Buildings. If you can't afford a room with a view, head to the terrace beside *Tiffens Bar & Lounge* for high tea. <u>R1720</u>

EATING

★**The Blue Crane Restaurant & Bar** 156 Melk St, New Muckleneuk ☎012 460 7615, ⓦbluecrane restaurant.co.za; map p.486. A smart restaurant in a unique location, overlooking the lake and Austin Roberts Bird Sanctuary. The large menu includes lamb chops and oxtail (mains R120–170). Mon 7.30am–3pm, Tues–Fri 7.30am–10pm, Sat 9am–10pm, Sun 9am–3pm.

Bravo Pizzeria 1212 South St, Hatfield ☎012 362 0903; map p.486. A laidback cafe-style hangout staffed by friendly hipsters. The wood-fired pizzas are hard to fault – try their bestselling Sidewalk Vendetta pizza (bacon, feta and avocado R87); it's unlicensed, so bring your own booze. Mon–Sat 10am–9pm.

Café Riche 2 Church Square, CBD ☎012 328 3173; map p.486. Opened in 1905, this classic café overlooking the square is a must for a quick coffee or simple pub meal. It still has its original fittings, continental atmosphere and famously friendly staff. Daily 6am–6pm.

Crawdaddy's Cnr Middel & Dey sts, Piazza mall, Brooklyn ☎012 460 0889, ⓦcrawdaddys.co.za; map p.486. A popular Cajun-themed restaurant, serving chowder and surf-and-turf-style dishes such as prawns and calamari with a meat accompaniment (mains R90–135). Sun–Wed 11am–10pm, Thurs–Sat 11am–11.30pm.

★**Ginger & Fig** Jan Shoba St, cnr Lynnwood Rd, Brooklyn ☎012 362 5926, ⓦgingerandfig.co.za; map p.486. Delicious modern cooking in a shopfront "artisan eatery" run by ambitious young cooks. Everything here is home-made, free-range, organic and tasty – try the beetroot veggie burger (R90), a pear and blue cheese salad (R100) or some sweet-potato crisps. Mon 7.30am–5.30pm, Tues–Fri 6am–9pm, Sat 7am–3pm.

La Terrasse Rooftop Café & Deli 435 Atterbury Rd, Menlo ☎012 346 5713, ⓦmoroccanhouse.co.za; map p.486. Pretty little rooftop cafe serving beautifully presented authentic Moroccan cuisine. For lunch try one of the tagines, followed up by the fragrant orange blossom and Turkish delight cheesecake (R40). Mon–Sat 9am–5pm.

Papa's Real Food Duncan Yard, cnr Jan Shoba & Prospect sts, Hatfield ☎0012 362 2224, ⓦpapas restaurant.co.za; map p.486. A lovely place to linger, nestled in one of the interlinked courtyards that make up the quirky Duncan Yard centre, known for its antiques and decor shops. Choose from a simple menu of wraps, pastas, salads and steaks. Mon–Sat 8.30am–10pm, Sun 10.30am–3pm.

Pure 137 Thomson St, cnr Gordon Rd, Hatfield ☎012 342 1443, ⓦpurecafe.co.za; map p.486. A lovely café near the turn-off to the Polokwane highway, serving breakfast and lunch, cakes and coffee. The spring meadow salad (R82) is excellent, as is the stuffed aubergine (R80). Mon–Fri 7am–4pm, Sat 8am–3pm.

Tashas Design Square, cnr Bronkhorst and Veal sts, Brooklyn ☎012 460 2951, ⓦtashas.co.za; map p.486. A popular chain bistro with a beautiful, simple design and an extensive menu offering breakfasts, freshly squeezed juices, sandwiches, pasta and cakes; mains cost R90–160. Book ahead or expect to queue. Mon 6.30am–9pm, Tues–Sat 6.30am–10pm, Sun 7.30am–9pm.

★**TriBeCa** 220 Madiba Drive, CBD ☎012 321 8876, ⓦtribeca.co.za; map p.486. Excellent coffee, breakfast, cake and light meals, just northeast of Church Square. There are three more TriBeCa outlets in Pretoria, including one on the square in Brooklyn Mall that's a popular gay meeting place. Daily 7am–5pm.

DRINKING AND NIGHTLIFE

Most of the city's action is in Hatfield, Menlyn and, to a lesser extent, Brooklyn. **Hatfield**, next to the University of Pretoria campus, is where the students hang out, while the wealthy suburb of **Brooklyn**, southeast of the university, attracts an older, more upmarket crowd. Further east, Sun International's vast new Time Square casino development in **Menlyn** provides more flashy dining and entertainment options.

Aandklas Cnr Prospect Rd & Hilda St, Hatfield ☎12 362 3712; map p.486. Dark, grungy and thronged with students, this is Hatfield's largest and most popular bar. Rock and indie music rules at *Aandklas*, with local bands playing the large, partially open-air stage every Saturday night. Meanwhile the beer garden in the front is the choice destination for students looking for post-lecture drinks. Mon–Thurs, Sat 11am–2am, Fri noon–2am, Sun noon–midnight.

★**Capital Craft Beer Academy** Greenlyn Village Centre, cnr Thomas Edison & 13th sts, Menlo Park ☎012 424 8601, ⓦcapitalcraft.co.za; map p.486. Wholeheartedly committed to the craft beer cause, with more than 200 local and international beers on the menu. The sharing platters of Southern-style ribs (R220 for a kilo) are finger-licking good. Seating is beer-hall style and outdoor tables fill up fast. Tues 2pm–midnight, Wed–Sat 10.30am–midnight, Sun 10.30am–8pm.

Eastwood's Tavern 391 Eastwood St, Arcadia ☎012 344 0243, ⓦeastwoods.co.za; map p.486. A sprawling pub-restaurant near Loftus Versfeld Stadium popular with beer-loving sports fans; the atmosphere on match days is particularly raucous. Mon–Sat 8am–2am, Sun 8am–10pm.

Lucky Rodrigo Cnr The Hillside St & Alpine Way, Lynnwood ☎072 853 4468 ⓦluckyrodrigo.co.za; map p.486. Kitsch-cool bar whose eclectic 1970s interiors are a nod to the decidedly old-fashioned suburban corner on which it sits. Cheap beers and indie music attract a bohemian crowd. Tues–Sat 9am–1.30am.

ENTERTAINMENT

Pretoria lacks the dynamism and breadth of Johannesburg's arts and music scene, but there's still a fair amount going on. In particular look out for the Park Acoustics music festival held at the Voortrekker Monument on the first Sunday of every month (W parkacoustics.co.za). The *Pretoria News* is good for listings for theatre and cinema. Computicket (W computicket .com) is the big central ticket outlet for most arts and sports events.

Brooklyn Theatre 1 Greenlyn Village Centre, cnr Thomas Edison & 13th sts, Menlo Park ☎012 460 6033, W brooklyntheatre.co.za. A 400-seat auditorium that hosts regular classical music recitals, including performances by the Gauteng Philharmonic Orchestra.

State Theatre 320 Pretorius St ☎012 392 4000, W statetheatre.co.za. The city's main venue for dance, theatre, opera and classical concerts. Under the leadership of Hugh Masekela and then Aubrey Sekhabi, it also puts on an interesting programme of jazz and black theatre.

DIRECTORY

Banks Most banks are around Church Square and east along Helen Joseph St. Malls are also a reliable place to find ATMs.

Bookshops Exclusive Books has a branch at Brooklyn Mall, Bronkhorst St, Brooklyn (☎012 346 5864, W exclus1ves .co.za). Protea Book House, 1067 Burnett St, Hatfield (☎012 362 5683, W proteaboekhuis.com), offers a wide range of new and secondhand books.

Embassies and consulates Australia, 292 Orient St, Arcadia (☎012 423 6000); Canada, 1103 Arcadia St, Hatfield (☎012 422 3000); Ireland, 570 Fehrsen St, Brooklyn (☎012 452 1000); Lesotho, 391 Anderson St, Menlo Park (☎012 460 7648); Malawi, 770 Government Ave, Arcadia (☎012 342 0146); Mozambique, 529 Edmond St, Arcadia (☎012 401 0300); Namibia, 197 Blackwood St, Arcadia (☎012 481 9100); Swaziland, 715 Government

Ave, Arcadia (☎012 344 1910); UK, 255 Hill St, Arcadia (☎012 421 7500); US, 877 Pretorius St, Arcadia (☎011 431 4000); Zambia, 570 Ziervogel Ave, Arcadia (☎012 326 1854); Zimbabwe, 798 Merton Ave, Arcadia (☎012 342 5125).

Emergencies Private ambulance (Netcare) ☎082 911; ambulance & fire ☎10177; police ☎10111.

Hospitals Those with 24hr casualty services include Steve Biko Academic Hospital, Voortrekker Rd (☎012 354 1590), and Wilgers Hospital, Denneboom Rd (☎012 807 8100).

Pharmacies These can be found in almost every shopping mall; there are also 24hr pharmacies at Wilgers Hospital (see above) and the Muelmed Medi-Clinic, 577 Pretorius St (☎012 440 1457).

Post office Church St (Mon, Tues, Thurs & Fri 8am–4.30pm, Wed 8.30am–4.30pm, Sat 8am–noon).

Around Pretoria

The most absorbing sights in the vicinity of Pretoria are **Doornkloof Farm**, the former home of Prime Minister Jan Smuts, and the **Sammy Marks Museum**, an exquisite Victorian-era mansion built by the fabulously wealthy industrialist Sammy Marks. Further out, to the east of Pretoria, the mining town of **Cullinan** harks back to the pioneering days of diamond prospecting, while north of the city the **Tswaing meteorite crater** is a great place for a short hike. Those interested in wildlife conservation should not miss the **Ann van Dyk Cheetah Centre**.

Doornkloof Farm

Jan Smuts Ave, off Nellmapius Ave, Irene, signposted 20km south of Pretoria along the R21 • Mon–Fri 8am–4pm, Sat & Sun 8.30am–4.30pm • R20 • ☎012 667 1176, W smutshouse.co.za

Doornkloof Farm was the home of **Jan Smuts** for much of his life, including during his periods as prime minister of South Africa. His simple wood-and-corrugated-iron house is now a museum, which sheds light on one of South Africa's most enigmatic politicians. The massive library here reflects Smuts' intellectual range, while numerous mementos confirm his internationalism. Other displays focus on Smuts' role as one of the most successful commanders of Boer forces during the Anglo-Boer Wars. The surrounding farm is part of the museum, and features the pleasant 2.5km **Oubaas Trail**, leading from the house to the top of a nearby *koppie*, a walk the nature-loving Smuts took every day. Scattered near the house are various pieces of military hardware such as cannon and armoured vehicles – a little incongruously, given the declarations of peace and tranquillity posted along the trail and elsewhere.

Cullinan's Premier Mine

50km east of Pretoria · **Surface tours** Mon–Fri 10.30am & 2pm, Sat & Sun 10.30am & noon · 2hr · R115 · Booking required · ☎ 012 734 0081, ⓦ diamondtourscullinan.co.za · **Diamond Express train** R275 · ☎ 012 767 7913, ⓦ friendsoftherail.com

The quaint town of **Cullinan** is home to the **Premier Mine**, still worked today, where the world's largest diamond, the 3106-carat **Star of Africa**, was discovered in 1905. Mine enthusiasts can take a surface tour of the mine. The best way to visit is on the **Diamond Express** steam-train day-trip organized about once a month by Friends of the Rail, departing from Pretoria's Hermanstad depot at 8am and returning at 5.30pm, leaving enough time in Cullinan to wander the streets and have a relaxed lunch.

Tswaing Crater

Onderstepoort Rd, Soshanguve, off the M35 · Daily 7.30am–4pm · R25 · ☎ 076 945 5911, ⓦ ditsong.org.za/tswaing.htm

Tswaing Crater is one of the youngest and best-preserved meteorite craters in the world, a 1.4km-wide and 200m-deep depression created around 220,000 years ago. Tswaing means "place of salt" in Tswana, and the rich deposits of salt and soda around the edge of the shallow crater lake have attracted people since ancient times; artefacts up to 150,000 years old have been discovered here. Register at the visitors' centre on the main road before driving to the car park, from where a pleasant 7km trail crosses the veld to the crater, down to the lake and back; alternatively, park closer to the rim from where it's a short stroll to the crater.

Sammy Marks Museum

18km east of Pretoria, entrance off the Old Bronkhorstspruit Rd (opposite Savannah Country Estate), Donkerhoek · Tues–Sun 9am–5pm · R60 (South Africans R45) · Accommodation R800 · ☎ 012 755 9542, ⓦ ditsong.org.za

Zwartkoppies Hall, built in the early 1880s for the wealthy industrialist Sammy Marks, is a splendid example of the opulent tastes of Gauteng's early mining barons. Born in Lithuania in 1844, Marks arrived in South Africa aged 24 and set about seeking his fortune in the Kimberley diamond fields. By the time gold was discovered on the Witwatersrand, he had amassed sufficient wealth to build Zwartkoppies Hall. The hourly tours of the mansion reveal much about the incredible story of the rise and decline of the family fortune. Keen to sport the latest fashions, Marks spared no expense on antiques, porcelain, imported fabrics and silverware, even hiring Italian painters to decorate the walls to resemble satin. The upstairs billiard room, with its elaborately decorated ceiling, is one of the highlights of the house. Reasonably priced light meals and refreshments are available in the museum tea garden.

Ann van Dyk Cheetah Centre

West of Pretoria, just off the R513 towards Brits · **Cheetah run and tour** Tues, Thurs, Sat & Sun 8am · R400 · **Tours** Daily 1.30pm and Mon, Wed, Fri 8.30am; Tues, Thurs, Sat & Sun 1.30pm · R350 · Book in advance · ☎ 012 504 9906, ⓦ dewildt.co.za

The **Ann van Dyk Cheetah Centre** is a world-renowned conservation project. Its mission is to protect the cheetah by developing predator management policies with farmers, breeding cubs in captivity (over 750 have been raised to date) and then relocating them within game reserves. Other endangered animals bred and/or cared for at the centre include African wild dogs, vultures and brown hyenas. Visits include an educational tour of the centre and animal enclosures. Photographing cheetahs on the run is a big draw, and the early morning cheetah runs are a unique opportunity to experience the animals in close proximity. The conservation activities are partly funded by a cheetah adoption programme.

7

North West Province

WILDEBEEST IN MADIKWE GAME RESERVE

North West Province

South Africa's North West Province is one of the country's least-understood regions – renowned, among tourists at least, for the opulent Sun City resort and the Big Five Pilanesberg National Park, but not much else. Few people venture beyond these attractions to explore this area in greater depth; consequently, it can be curiously rewarding to do so. The old-fashioned hospitality of the myriad little *dorps* scattered throughout the region, and the tranquillity of the endless stretches of grassland and fields of *mielies* (sweetcorn) make a refreshing change after hectic Johannesburg and Pretoria.

North West Province extends west from Gauteng to the Botswana border and the Kalahari Desert. Along the province's eastern flank, essentially separating it from Gauteng, loom the **Magaliesberg mountains**, one hundred times older than the Himalayas and dotted with **holiday** resorts for nature-starved Joburgers. The **N4** from Pretoria cuts through the mountains to the main town of the northeastern part of the province, **Rustenburg**, gateway to the windswept **Kgaswane Mountain Reserve**, where you can hike high enough to gaze down onto the shimmering plains beneath. To the north lies the Big Five **Pilanesberg National Park** and the gaudy **Sun City** resort which sits on its doorstep. **Groot Marico**, further west along the N4, is a friendly *dorp* with powerful home-brews and laidback people to share them with. Further to the west lies the provincial capital of **Mafikeng** – famed for its siege during the second Anglo-Boer War – while near the Botswana border **Madikwe Game Reserve** is one of South Africa's undiscovered wildlife gems, a massive Big Five park which sees remarkably few visitors and boasts some superb game lodges.

Brief history

San hunter-gatherers were the province's first inhabitants; they were displaced 500–1000 years ago by cattle-herding Iron Age peoples from the north, who pitched their first settlements on low ground near watercourses. These settlements developed into stone-walled towns on hilltops; and by 1820 the largest, Karechuenya (near Madikwe), was estimated to have more inhabitants than Cape Town. By the nineteenth century, the dominance of the Rolong, Taung, Tlhaping and Tlokwa clans was established. European observers classified them all as **Tswana**, but it's unclear whether these people regarded themselves as very different from people further east classified as "Sotho".

The outbreak of intense **inter-clan violence** in the early 1800s was due to displacements caused by the expansion of white trekboers, and the growing availability of firearms. Victory went to those who made alliances with the new arrivals, whether **Griqua** from the Northern Cape or **Afrikaners** from further south. However, the clans' victories were short-lived and their Griqua and Afrikaner allies soon evicted them from their land and forced them into service. Various mini-states were formed until, in 1860, they were all amalgamated to form the **South African Republic** (ZAR), with Pretoria as its capital.

The first Anglo-Boer War (1877–81) left most of the province unaffected. Of far greater impact was the **second Anglo-Boer War** (1899–1902). As well as the celebrated **siege of Mafikeng**, where British and Tswana forces held out for 217 days against

Highlights

❶ The Magaliesberg mountains High above Rustenburg, in the Magaliesberg mountains, varied trails allow you to hike through savannah, rolling hills and rocky kloofs, and past sparkling streams. **See p.503**

❷ Sun City Las Vegas meets the bushveld at this unique fantasyland of hotels, slot machines, stage shows, elephant safaris, lush golf courses and a fun-filled water park. **See p.507**

❸ Pilanesberg National Park The most accessible Big Five park from Johannesburg and Pretoria, with beautiful landscapes in a former

volcano crater and terrific game viewing. **See p.508**

❹ Groot Marico One of the most characterful of South Africa's tiny *dorps*, or small farming towns, famed for its warm welcome, literary connections and the potency of the local fruit spirit, mampoer. **See p.511**

❺ Madikwe Game Reserve An often-overlooked Big Five reserve in the corner of the province; prepare to be pampered in some of South Africa's classiest wildlife lodges. **See p.512**

HIGHLIGHTS ARE MARKED ON THE MAP ON P.502

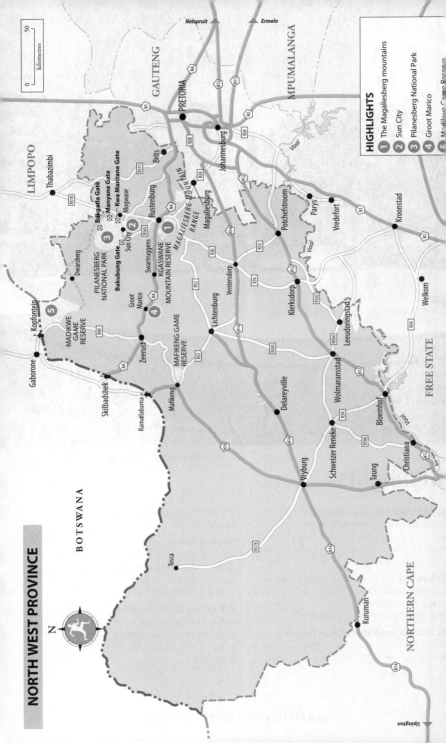

NORTH WEST PROVINCE

N

BOTSWANA

LIMPOPO

GAUTENG

MPUMALANGA

Nelspruit   *Ermelo*

PRETORIA

Thabazimbi

Brits

Johannesburg

Rustenburg

Bakgatla Gate
Manyane Gate
Kwa Maritane Gate
Mogwase

PILANESBERG
NATIONAL PARK

Bakubung Gate

Sun City

Magaliesburg

MAGALIESBERG MOUNTAIN RANGE

Dwarsberg

Swartruggens

KGASWANE
MOUNTAIN RESERVE

Groot
Marico

MADIKWE
GAME
RESERVE

Kopfontein

Zeerust

MAFIKENG GAME
RESERVE

Ventersdorp

Lichtenburg

Potchefstroom

Parys

Vredefort

Kroonstad

Klerksdorp

Welkom

Gaborone

Skilbadshek

Ramatabama

Mafikeng

Delareyville

Wolmaransstad

Leeudoringstad

Bloemhof

FREE STATE

Vryburg

Schweizer Reneke

Christiana

Taung

Tosca

Kuruman

NORTHERN CAPE

Upington

0   50
kilometres

Vaal

Vaal

Vaal

Vaal

R510
R511
R565
N4
R24
R28
R26
N12
N17
N11
M3
N1
R30
R53
R30
R502
R501
R52
R505
R504
R34
N18
N14
N12
N12
N12
R506
R378
N14
R49
N4
N4
N4
R27

Afrikaner troops, there were protracted skirmishes up and down the Vaal River. After the British victory, both Afrikaner and Tswana had their lands torched and many were thrown into concentration camps.

The Union Treaty of 1910 left the province, as the western part of the Transvaal, firmly in Afrikaner hands. Its smaller *dorps* soon became synonymous with rural racism, epitomized in the 1980s by the fascistic AWB led by **Eugene Terreblanche**, whose power base was here. In addition, the province played a relatively minor role in the national struggle against apartheid due to the absence of a significant black working class after the migration of many Tswana men to work in the gold mines of the Witwatersrand.

In 1977, the **Bophuthatswana Bantustan** homeland – or "Bop" – was created around Mmabatho in the western part of the province out of the old "native reserves", the poor-quality land into which Tswana had been forced. Far from being a long-awaited "independent" homeland for the black population in this area, Bop proved to be a confusing amalgamation of enclaves, ruled by the corrupt **Lucas Mangope**, who grew rich on the revenues from **Sol Kerzner**'s casinos in Sun City and Mmabatho and the discovery of platinum. Bophuthatswana's short life came to an end in March 1994, a month before South Africa's elections, when its army mutinied. Mangope called in hundreds of armed AWB neo-fascists to help quell the uprising, but the AWB – and Mangope – were ingloriously defeated.

The mining industry continues to dominate the province's economics, but in recent years there have been frequent and violent miners' strikes, most infamously in 2012 at the Lonmin mine in the Marikana area near Rustenburg (see p.504). Forty-four people were killed there, thirty-four of them by the South African Police, in the **Marikana massacre** (see box, p.506), the worst case of state violence against civilians since the Sharpeville shootings in 1960.

Magaliesberg mountains and around

Bordering Gauteng, the **Magaliesberg mountain range** is a popular weekend destination for Joburgers and one of the more distinctive parts of this largely empty and flat province. The mountain range gets its name from the Tswana chief **Mogale** of the Kwena clan. Kwena people lived here from the seventeenth century until 1825, when most were forced out by the Ndebele chief **Mzilikazi**. Afrikaner farmers continued the process of eviction, and today the dispossession and expulsion of the Kwena in the Magaliesberg is complete.

Great chunks of the Magaliesberg have been fenced off and turned into time-shares or resorts, but there are oases of unspoilt nature, in particular **Kgaswane Mountain Reserve**, accessed from the region's main town, **Rustenburg**; preserved in something like its previous natural state, it is well stocked with wildlife. It's also possible to partake of more extreme pursuits in the area, such as ziplining over gorges on the **Magaliesberg Canopy Tour**.

If you are driving north from Johannesburg for a safari in Pilanesberg or Madikwe, it is worth taking the scenic R24 and R563 through the Magliesberg mountains (rather than the N4 highway from Pretoria). There are plenty of quaint places to stop for lunch, or you can break up the journey by staying at one of the many countryside guesthouses.

VISITING NORTH WEST PROVINCE

Relentless sun alleviated only by torrential rain makes **summer** in North West Province something of an endurance test: aim to come here in **spring** or **autumn**. For the more adventurous, **camping** in the quiet and timeless veld is especially rewarding in this part of South Africa. **Tourist information** for the province is provided by the North West Parks & Tourism Board (☎0861 111 866, ⦿tourismnorthwest.co.za); its website has information and links to all of the region's parks. **Malaria** is absent throughout the province.

Magliesberg Canopy Tours

32km east of Rustenburg, from the R104 or R24 follow the signs for Sparkling Waters Hotel • Daily April–Aug 7am–3pm, Sept–March 6.30am–4.30pm • ☎ 014 535 0150 or ☎ 079 492 0467, ⓦ magaliescanopytour.co.za

One of the most thrilling ways to experience the Magaliesberg mountains is by zooming over its streams and gorges by zipline. The **Magaliesberg Canopy Tour** lasts around 2hr 30min and takes in ten ziplines, some up to 30m high, linked by eleven platforms that crisscross the beautiful Ysterhout Kloof. Advanced booking is essential. The minimum group size is two, the maximum eight. Tours leave from the booking offices in the *Sparkling Waters Hotel & Spa*.

Rustenburg

Some 120km northwest of Johannesburg lies the dreary platinum-mining town of **RUSTENBURG**, the oldest town in the former Western Transvaal. With its grid of prefabricated chain stores and shopping malls, the place is eminently missable. Still, you may end up having to stay if you're visiting the glorious **Kgaswane Mountain Reserve**, 7km south of town, or if you are looking for cheaper accommodation within a reasonable distance of the Pilanesberg National Park.

Rustenburg's historic centre is limited to two blocks of Burger Street, from Nelson Mandela Drive to Oliver Tambo Drive. Here you'll find two churches: the old **Anglican church**, dating from 1871, and the 1850 **Dutch Reformed church**. Facing the latter is the graceful 1935 town hall and a **statue of Paul Kruger** showing the president in his last days in exile in France, sitting grumpily in an armchair.

8

ARRIVAL AND INFORMATION   MAGALIESBERG MOUNTAINS AND AROUND

By bus and minibus taxi The daily Intercape bus (☎ 021 380 4400, ⓦ intercape.co.za, 2hr) from Johannesburg to Gaborone via Groot Marico stops in Rustenburg at the BP Garage opposite Waterfall Mall. Long-distance minibus taxis and the daily Bojanala bus (☎ 014 565 6550, ⓦ bojanalabus .co.za) from Mafikeng (3hr, not via Groot Marico) arrive at the terminal at the western end of Nelson Mandela Drive by Beneden St. Long-distance minibus taxis depart regularly, covering most of the province, including Groot Marico (1hr

30min; take the Zeerust taxi) and Mafikeng (3hr 30min), and also go to Lesotho (daily; 9hr). Bays are clearly marked with destinations, and tickets are available on the buses; it's best to check your options the day before you travel. When leaving the bus terminal, avoid its dodgy northern section.

Information The Rustenberg tourist office is on Kloof Rd and has maps and brochures for attractions and hotels across the province (Mon–Fri 8am–4.30pm, Sat 8am– noon; ☎ 014 597 0906, ⓦ tourismnorthwest.co.za).

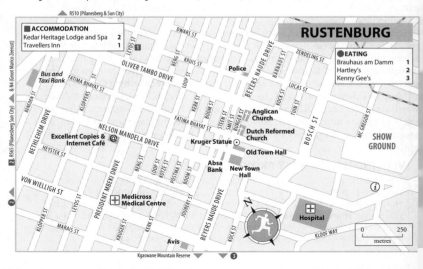

ACCOMMODATION

Rustenburg is a convenient base within easy reach of the mountains and the wildlife of the Pilanesberg, but you'll get the most out of the area by staying out of town. You can camp at Kgaswane Mountain Reserve (see p.506), but should always call first as sites are not always open. On the southern slopes of the mountain range, an 80min drive from Rustenburg or Johannesburg, are dozens of rural B&Bs and resorts, many with their own private hiking trails leading up the mountains.

MAGALIESBERG MOUNTAINS

Rustig 6km off the R401, between Hekpoort and Skeerpoort (take the R24 from Rustenburg or Joburg) ☎ 079 490 2690, ⓦ rustig.co.za. Part of a large working farm nestled at the foot of the Magaliesberg range with a network of craggy two-, four- and six-hour hiking trails leading to the top of the mountains right on your doorstep (open to non-guests). Choose from dorm beds, self-catering safari tents or one of three lovely rooms filled with period furniture in the main farmhouse. The restaurant overlooking the huge pool is the perfect spot for a post-hike drink. Doubles R1000, dorm R180, safari tent R1200

Steynshoop Mountain Lodge 10km off the R560, near the village of Hekpoort (take the R563 from Joburg or the R24 from Rustenburg; from the R560 junction follow the signs) ☎ 014 576 1035, ⓦ steynshoop.co.za. Two beautiful lodges situated 1km from each other on the mountain slopes looking down over the foothills of Gauteng. The peaceful Mountain Lodge has nine rooms (the luxury rooms are worth paying extra for the views) and the option of meals enjoyed in the intimate restaurant. The Valley Lodge is a Cape Dutch-style farmhouse with a choice of self-catering cottages. The 10km dirt road is doable in the average sedan car. Mountain Lodge R950, Valley Lodge R1200

RUSTENBURG

Kedar Heritage Lodge and Spa 20km northwest of Rustenburg in Boshoek, 500m off the R565 to Sun City ☎ 014 573 3218, ⓦ recreationafrica.co.za/kedar; map opposite. Set amid plentiful game and birdlife, this lovingly restored farmhouse once belonged to President Kruger, who's honoured by a small museum. The luxurious Afrikaner-style decor makes for a refreshingly tranquil rural getaway 20min drive from Pilanesberg National Park, and there's also a swimming pool, plus two suites with private plunge pools. Doubles R1130, suites R8525

Travellers Inn 99 Leyds St, Rustenburg ☎ 014 592 7658, ⓦ travellersinn.co.za; map opposite. Offering good modern rooms, with a large poolside dorm for backpackers. There's a fun rustic bar and good food, all a short walk from the town centre and bus stop. Gay and lesbian couples welcome. Breakfast R100 extra. Dorms R190, doubles R550

EATING

The charming farm restaurants through the valleys south of Rustenburg and along the southern flanks of the mountain range towards the Hartbeespoort Dam are the best places to stop for lunch or dinner. Otherwise pack a picnic and eat in the mountains. Rustenburg itself is dominated by fast-food joints, while there are more appealing restaurants at some of the hotels and in the town's main shopping centre, Waterfall Mall.

MAGALIESBERG MOUNTAINS

Brauhaus am Damm R24, 18km south of Rustenburg ☎ 087 098 0641, ⓦ brauhaus.co.za; map opposite. This brewery-restaurant, beside Olifantsnek lake, is especially popular at weekends when it provides one-hour brewery tours (call ahead, R50 including tasting and glass). Six types of tasty German beer are brewed here (half a litre costs from R35), and you can also buy it bottled to take away. The beer is served with tasty food, such as a meat or cheese platter (R80), or fried noodles, known as spaetzle (R35). Tues–Sat 11am–11pm, Sun 11am–3pm.

Die Ou Pastorie R560 in the village of Skeerpoort, 30km west of Pretoria ☎ 012 207 1027, ⓦ dieoupastorie.com. The pretty gardens of this former Victorian vicarage (pastorie in Afrikaans) fill up on weekend afternoons when live bands serenade diners and reservations are recommended. All ingredients are sourced from local farms and the homely fare is delicious. Try the home-made chicken liver pâté with rooibos jam (R60) or the famous duck (R145). Wed–Sat 7.30am–10pm, Sun 7.30am–4pm.

RUSTENBURG

Hartley's Rainhill Farm, 4km southwest of Rustenburg; follow Bethlehem Drive, turn right on Brink St, left on Watsonia Rd, right at the end ☎ 014 592 9202, ⓦ rainhill.co.za; map opposite. Tranquil, country-style pub and family restaurant. The pub area is called The Milk Shed, while The Pack House is the more formal, non-smoking restaurant. The food at both (R60–110) ranges from ribs and steaks to prawns and seafood platters – don't miss the farm's famous orange marmalade. You can also stay in the charming farm guesthouse. Mon noon–8pm, Tues–Fri 11am–9pm, Sat 11am–10pm.

Kenny Gee's 67 Brink St, cnr Kock St ☎ 014 592 8079, ⓦ kennygees.co.za; map opposite. The best central-ish option in Rustenburg, this non-chain restaurant serves good breakfasts (from R35), cheerful pub fare such as fish and chips, lasagnes, pies and daily weekday specials from as little as R37. There's modest partying too, with live music on Wednesdays and Fridays. Mon–Thurs 6.45am–10pm, Fri 6.45am–midnight, Sat 8am–3pm, Sun 9am–3pm.

8

MARIKANA

The 2012 **Marikana strike**, which ended on August 16 with the deaths of 34 miners at the hands of the South African police, had begun a week before on August 10 when 3000 workers downed tools demanding an increase in their minimum wage to R12,500 per month. Days earlier, the leaders of the National Union of Mineworkers (NUM), the biggest in Marikana, had flatly refused to support a strike, much to the resentment of its members. Soon after the wildcat strike began, men hired by the NUM allegedly shot at a group of strikers, killing two and injuring others, adding fuel to an already extremely volatile situation. The days that followed saw violence and intimidation flare up across the dusty streets of the impoverished Nkaneng informal settlement. More miners had downed tools, horrified by the NUM's apparent support for the mine owners, many of them carrying weapons in fear of more violent attacks. The situation reached boiling point on August 16 when hundreds of police officers, armed with thousands of rounds of ammunition, surrounded a rocky hill on the outskirts of the village where the striking miners had gathered. The police say they intended to disarm the men and coax them into ending the strike. However, the disproportionate show of force and almost constant miscommunication between officials and the men on the ground sowed the seeds for a disaster. Despite an official inquiry into the ensuing massacre, many questions about what happened that day in Marikana remain unanswered and numerous families still await the compensation and apologies promised them by the state.

DIRECTORY

Bank ABSA Bank at Waterfall Mall has an exchange office.

Emergencies Private ambulance (Netcare) ☏ 014 568 4338 or ☏ 082 911; ambulance ☏ 014 556 2073; fire ☏ 014 590 3334; police ☏ 014 590 3111.

Health Doctors and dentists are available at Medicross Medical Centre, on the corner of President Mbeki Drive and Von Wielligh St ☏ 014 523 5100.

Internet Excellent Copies & Internet Café, Nelson Mandela Drive, on the corner of President Mbeki Drive.

Shopping The 160-shop Waterfall Mall (Mon–Fri 9am–6pm, Sat 9am–5pm, Sun 9am–1pm; ⓦ waterfall mall.co.za), on Augrabies Ave 5km southeast of town, has the province's best shopping.

Kgaswane Mountain Reserve

7km south of Rustenburg • Daily: April–Aug 6am–6pm; Sept–March 5.30am–7.30pm • R40, plus R20 per vehicle • ☏ 014 533 2050, ⓦ tourismnorthwest.co.za/kgaswane

Kgaswane Mountain Reserve spans a spectacular forty-square-kilometre portion of the Magaliesberg and is dotted with rock formations, created by millennia of erosion, areas of dry veld and streams coursing through the valleys. The reserve's unique **flora** includes aloes indigenous to the Magaliesberg and the discreet *frithiapulchra*, a succulent with only its leaf tips exposed, flowering between November and March. The many crags are perfect for predatory **birds**; keep a lookout for the rare black eagle, Martial eagle and Cape vulture, as well as parrots and paradise flycatchers. Kgaswane is also home to eight hundred **antelopes**, representing most of South Africa's species, and also zebras. Predators are few in number and limited to caracal, aardwolf, black-backed jackals and the elusive leopard.

The reserve can be explored on foot or by bicycle (bring your own). There are two short trails for day hikes: the 5km **Peglarae Trail** follows a relatively easy path through rocky terrain and has most of the reserve's best features and views, while the shorter and flatter **Vleiramble Trail** (2km) leads to a viewing hut on the *vlei* (grassy valley) that is popular with birders. Longer walks follow the **Rustenburg Hiking Trail** (19.5km or 23.5km) and last two days and two nights. These must be booked in advance and are for groups of minimum 6 people, maximum 12 (there is an extra fee of R150 per person for the trail). You must bring your own food and sleeping gear to stay overnight in the trail's mountain hut.

ARRIVAL AND INFORMATION

KGASWANE MOUNTAIN RESERVE

By car You'll need your own vehicle to reach the reserve: take the R24 from central Rustenburg towards Johannesburg and turn right at the traffic lights just after the Waterfall

Mall (or just before the mall when coming from Joburg), and follow the road up the hill, turning left onto the signposted road to the reserve gate. Or follow Beyers Naude southwest across the highway and keep following Helen Joseph St. From here, the road winds dramatically up to the visitor centre in a broad valley near the mountaintop.

Information The Visitor Centre is in the middle of the park (can be closed in winter; check at the entrance gate), stocking useful maps and information on hikes and trails.

ACCOMMODATION

Camping ☎ 014 533 2050, ⓦ tourismnorthwest .co.za/kgaswane. There are 20 campsites spread through the reserve with stands available for up to 6 tents. Facilities are very basic with no electricity and no shops, so bring all your own supplies. The nights can get very cold in winter. Be vigilant about your possessions; unfortunately, thefts have been reported at some sites. Camping R60

Sun City

Day visitors R75, children R65 • ☎ 011 780 7855, ⓦ suninternational.com/sun-city

A surreal pocket of high-rise hotels and tinkling gaming machines in the endless bushveld, **SUN CITY** consists of four hotel resorts and a timeshare complex tightly packed together with golf courses, a water park and various other attractions. When entrepreneur Sol Kerzner began building the vast complex in the 1970s, the area was part of the Bophuthatswana Bantustan and therefore one of the few places in the country where you could **gamble** legally. Thousands visited from "across the border" to sample Kerzner's blend of gaming, topless shows and over-the-top hotels. However, now that gambling is legal in South Africa, Sun City has altered its focus, promoting itself these days as a **family destination** – indeed, if you have kids to entertain, this is an excellent place to bring them. The resort also makes a good base for exploring Pilanesberg National Park.

8

Cabanas and Waterworld

Daily 10am–5pm

Animal World, at the *Cabanas* hotel, is the area that young kids will enjoy most: it has a small zoo, horseriding, a crèche, an aviary with summer flying displays by hawks, falcons and owls, and a crocodile sanctuary. Behind it is **Waterworld**, a large artificial lake used for a range of watersports, from parasailing to waterskiing.

Sun Central

Daily 8am–10pm

The newly renovated entertainment complex **Sun Central** next to the towering triangle of *Cascades* hotel is the focal point of Sun City, with lots of family-oriented restaurants, arcade games, a bowling alley, a cinema, and the virtual reality Hall of Fame. Next to Sun Central you'll find a health spa and the renowned Gary Player Country Club golf course (green fee R790–890); book well in advance, as a waiting list of several months is not uncommon. The clubhouse overlooking the course is a nice spot for an afternoon drink.

Lost City and Valley of Waves

Valley of Waves daily: early May & mid-June to Aug 10am–5pm (closed mid-May to mid-June); Sept–April 9am–6pm • R120–160, children R70–85, free if you're staying at one of the hotels • Lost City Maze 9am–9pm • R120, children R60

The **Lost City** is the resort's showpiece, separated from the rest of the complex by the vibrating Bridge of Time. Inside is the **Valley of Waves**, a gigantic water park designed to look like a beach, complete with sand, palm trees, water slides and a machine producing 2m-high breakers suitable for surfing. Deeper into the acres of specially planted rainforest above the Valley, you'll find waterfalls, trickling streams and a network of explorable paths, all interspersed with "remains" of the Lost City, including the overpriced Lost City Maze. Overlooking the whole scene is the staggering *Palace of the Lost City* (see p.508); if you aren't staying at the hotel, the only way you can visit is by making a booking for afternoon tea or dinner.

ARRIVAL AND DEPARTURE

By car Driving from Pretoria or Joburg, follow the N4 past the Rustenburg turn-off, and turn right onto the R556, from where it's roughly 70km. Parking is near the Welcome Centre; when it's busy day visitors use the car park by the main gate and take the monorail to the Welcome Centre.

By minibus taxi Regular minibus taxis from Rustenburg to Mogwase pass the Sun City entrance, and daily shuttle buses operated by Ingelosi Tours (R1250 for two, R2100 for a group of six one way; ☎ 012 546 3827, 🖥 ingelositours .co.za) drive from OR Tambo International Airport, Sandton and Pretoria.

On a day-trip A large number of operators in Pretoria and Joburg (see p.474) offer day tours here; expect to pay at least R600 per person.

INFORMATION AND TOURS

Tourist information Sun City's Welcome Centre (Mon–Thurs & Sun 8am–7pm, Fri & Sat 8am–10pm; ☎ 014 557 1544) can provide maps, leaflets and details of special offers. There's also an information desk for the North West Parks & Tourism Board (Mon–Fri 8am–5pm, Sat 9am–4pm, Sun 9am–2pm; ☎ 014 552 2116).

Tours and adventure sports Mankwe Gametrackers (☎ 014 552 5020, 🖥 mankwegametrackers.co.za) has a desk at the Welcome Centre where you can book game drives, balloon flights and bush walks, as well as outdoor activities such as quad biking (R450–650) and archery (R300) that take place at the Letsatsing Reserve just outside Sun City. From the Welcome Centre you can also book a ride on the Zip 2000 (☎ 014 557 1544, 🖥 zip2000 .com, R600), a 2km zipline that is said to be one of the fastest in the world. The desk will arrange all transport.

ACCOMMODATION, EATING AND NIGHTLIFE

Sun City's hotels are all within a short distance of each other in the centre of the valley. Rooms can be booked through Sun City Reservations (☎ 011 780 7855, 🖥 suninternational.com/sun-city), but will be cheaper if arranged through a tour company as part of a package, or online. All hotels are enormous – *Cascades*, the smallest, has 243 rooms. You can eat at your hotel or at one of the many popular family-friendly South African chain restaurants.

The Brew Monkey ☎ 014 557 1681, 🖥 sun international.com. On the artificial beach overlooking the Valley of the Waves, *The Brew Monkey* has dozens of craft beers on tap and a pub food menu.

Cabanas ☎ 011 780 7810, 🖥 suninternational.com. Close to most of the kids' activities and with a relaxed atmosphere, this is the obvious base for families. The rooms are small but have recently been refurbished, and there's a good indoor pool and some reasonably priced restaurants. R2500

Cascades ☎ 011 780 7810, 🖥 suninternational.com. After the *Palace*, this is the resort's most comfortable place to stay, though the rooms and service are bland. A stylish pyramid-shaped high-rise with tropical decor and a mini rainforest and aviary, the outside lifts provide splendid views. The inviting pool and bar are for residents only. The quiet *Bocado* restaurant (☎ 014 557 5850), situated beside the pool, is known for its tasty Mediterranean food (R90–200) including Greek *kleftiko*, grilled prawns and meze, served amid lush subtropical palms. R3500

★**Palace of the Lost City** ☎ 011 780 7810, 🖥 sun international.com. Like something out of an *Indiana Jones* film, the vast *Palace* is a fantastically opulent and imaginative hotel – a soaring African jungle palace with towers, domes, extravagant carvings and sculptures. Rooms are large and beautifully furnished, and although a stay here is exorbitantly expensive, the experience is unforgettable. There are two recommended dining experiences available to non-guests at the hotel's classically furnished *Crystal Court* (☎ 014 557 4307): a sumptuous afternoon high tea (R235 per person, served 3–5pm) or à la carte dining in the evening (6.30–10pm). R5500

Soho ☎ 011 780 7810, 🖥 suninternational.com. The resort's original hotel houses its more adult attractions such as the main casino and a nightclub, so is a good choice if gambling is your main reason for visiting Sun City. The large, balconied rooms have great views of the golf courses and there are plenty of restaurants and bars, including the grillhouse and bar, *Legends* (☎ 014 557 3151). R4200

Pilanesberg National Park

Daily: March, April, Sept & Oct 6am–6.30pm; May–Aug 6.30am–6pm; Nov–Feb 5.30am–7pm • R65, plus R30 per person non-South African visitors' levy and R20 per car • ☎ 014 555 1600, 🖥 pilanesbergnationalpark.org

Adjacent to Sun City and home to a huge variety of animals, the **PILANESBERG NATIONAL PARK** is North West Province's biggest tourist draw. The artificially created reserve was, until 1979, occupied by farmers and the **Tswana** people, who were

unceremoniously evicted when **Operation Genesis** saw over six thousand animals shipped in from all over the country to fill the park. Just two to three hours' drive from Pretoria and Joburg, Pilanesberg is definitely the place to come to see some game if you're based in Gauteng and have only limited time. Like other game parks, you'll get the most from your visit if you stay in or near the reserve so that you're in the best position to head out at prime game-viewing time: at dawn, before the day visitors arrive

Don't let the crowds or the managed nature of the place put you off: the park offers game-viewing thrills aplenty, with a good chance of seeing all the **Big Five**, along with hippo, brown hyena, giraffe and zebra. The majority of antelope species are here, too, and there's a vast array of birdlife – over 365 species recorded so far. At night, some fantastic creatures emerge, including civet, porcupine and caracal, though you'll be lucky to spot them. The areas known for popular animals can become congested durin the day; the traffic disappears after dark, when only tour buses on night-game drives ar allowed in, making this one of the optimum times to visit the park (although be sure t bring warm clothes on winter nights).

Covering some 650 square kilometres, and with 200km of tarred and gravel roads, you'l need at least a full day to do Pilanesberg justice. The reserve is easily explored by car, especially with the official map (for sale at the gates and camp shops). The park's many beautiful hills – the result of an unusual volcanic eruption that occurred 1300 million years ago – are in some ways Pilanesberg's finest feature, though they are often ignored by visitors more interested in scouring their slopes for wildlife. Pilanesberg's natural focus, fo visitors and wildlife alike, is the alkaline **Lake Mankwe** ("place of the leopard"), whose goings-on are best observed from several walk-in hides. The various picnic spots and hide dotted around are ideal for breaking the drive – the hides in particular aren't used by man visitors and as a result can be cool, peaceful places to appreciate the natural surroundings. If you're self-driving, don't hesitate to ask the safari jeep drivers for sighting tips; they are a in radio contact with each other and know exactly what's going on.

ARRIVAL AND DEPARTURE

By car There are four entrance gates to the reserve; the most commonly used are Manyane, on the eastern side of the reserve near Mogwase, and Bakubung in the south, just to the west of Sun City off the R565.

On a guided tour Prices for day-trips from Gauteng average R1200 per person on a scheduled tour; private tours start at around R1600 for the day. Rates for overnight trips vary according to where you stay, but expect to pay upwards of R3500–4000. Ulysses Tours & Safaris (☏ 012 653 0018,

ⓦ ulysses.co.za) is a well-regarded and professionally r upmarket outfit based in Pretoria, which offers day-trips Pilanesberg every Saturday or otherwise on demand, fro R2050. While all activities can be booked on arrival, it's be to reserve them in advance either directly or through yo lodge to avoid missing out. The special activities organiz by Mankwe Gametrackers (see below) can usually incorporated into trips run by other operators, particularly you have the flexibility of a private tour.

INFORMATION AND ACTIVITIES

Information Both gates have boards with details of wildlife sightings, plus the official map and guidebook explaining the various habitats, enabling you to plan your journey around what you want to see. The Pilanesberg Centre in the middle of the park contains a café, gift shop and open-air restaurant, and a large terrace overlooking a watering hole often teeming with less timid wildlife.

Mankwe Gametrackers ☏ 014 552 5020, ⓦ mankw gametrackers.co.za. Sun City's activity operator offe spectacular balloon flights over the park (R4500), day a night game drives (from R550) and game walks (R60 Pick-ups from some of the resorts and lodges around t park are possible.

ACCOMMODATION

Pilanesberg's accommodation ranges from upmarket lodges where game drives are included in the price, to large, reso style complexes on the fringes of the park, and cheaper, more basic camps just outside the park gates. Camping is possi at Golden Leopard's *Bakgatla* and *Manyane* resorts. The more luxury lodges usually include all meals, game drives a walks in their rates, or can organize them for you; some may insist on two-night stays at weekends. *Bakubung* and *K Maritane* have shuttle buses every other hour to and from Sun City. Rates tend to be higher on weekends.

Bakgatla Resort Near Bakgatla Gate at the foot of Garamoga Hills ⓣ014 555 1045, ⓦgoldenleopardresorts.co.za. A large collection of reasonable chalets, safari tents with attached bathrooms and shady verandas, plus a big campsite. There's a decent restaurant and a large pool, too. Camping R200, safari tent R2050

Bakubung Bush Lodge Entrance next to Bakubung Gate ⓣ014 552 6000, ⓦlegacyhotels.co.za. The highlight at this lodge is the waterhole, a stone's throw from the restaurant with postcard views over the valley. Rooms are spacious and facilities include a pool, spa and a great restaurant, good for lunch even if you are not staying here. Rates include half board and a daily game drive. R4800

Ivory Tree Lodge Near Bakgatla Gate ⓣ014 556 8100, ⓦivorytreegamelodge.com. Luxurious lodge with stylish rooms (with en-suite toilets and showers outside), a health spa, conference centre and a rather hotel-like feel. R5700

Kwa Maritane Bush Lodge Near Kwa Maritane Gate ⓣ014 552 5100, ⓦlegacyhotels.co.za. A beautiful, upmarket resort in the park's southeast corner near Pilanesberg Airport, with decent rooms, a good restaurant and pool with views over to the reserve. Rates include half board and a daily game drive. R4450

Manyane Resort Just outside Manyane Gate ⓣ014 555 1000, ⓦgoldenleopardresorts.co.za. Low cost and convenience compensate for the distinctly un-bushlike atmosphere of the park's main camp. Stay in thatched chalets with a/c, safari tents, or bring a tent or caravan; there's also a restaurant, pool, mini-golf and walking trails. Camping R210, safari tent R1240, chalet R1800

Tshukudu Bush Lodge 8km from Bakubung Bush Lodge (parking is at the Bakubung Lodge from where you are chauffeured to Tshukudu) ⓣ014 552 6255, ⓦlegacyhotels.co.za. Watch big game at the water hole from your veranda at Pilanesberg's most exclusive lodge, located on a hilltop with sweeping views. The six picturesque thatched cottages offer luxury accommodation with sunken baths and roaring log fires; there's also a swimming pool and four new luxury suites. The lodge is unfenced – an especially memorable way to experience the reserve. No children under 12. Rates include full board and game drives. R9000

Groot Marico

GROOT MARICO, a tiny, dusty and characterful *dorp* resting contentedly by the banks of the Marico River, just south of the N4 and 90km west of Rustenburg, gained fame through Herman Charles Bosman's short stories based on his time as a teacher here. In mid-October, Groot Marico hosts the literary Bosman Weekend, drawing fans of one of South Africa's best-loved authors from far and wide – those unfamiliar with his work should start by reading the hilarious "In the Withaak's Shade", about an encounter with a leopard.

The local Tswana and Afrikaners are both short on English but long on hospitality, and the village is famed nationwide for its *mampoer* peach brandy and quintessentially laidback spirit.

Although prone to stultifying heat in summer (the best months to visit are March to May and September to November), the hills of the Marico district are good for hiking, and, when it all gets too much, the pristine river provides cool relief. The water of the Marico Oog ("Marico Eye"), a deep spring 20km south of town, is particularly clear and refreshing: festooned with water lilies and surrounded by beautiful dolomitic rocks, it makes a tranquil place for a picnic, and can be paradise for birdwatchers, with over four hundred species recorded here. It's also a favoured spot for scuba divers; contact the town's information centre for more details. Bear in mind that the dirt roads leading to the Marico Oog, and most of the town's accommodation, are in poor condition. While perfectly doable in a normal sedan, navigating them is nevertheless painfully slow.

Herman Charles Bosman Living Museum

rk St • Daily 8am–6pm • Free • ⓣ014 503 0085, ⓦmarico.co.za • Rondavels and camping from R60

Head to the tourist information centre to arrange a short tour of the modest **Herman Charles Bosman Living Museum**, a community project with reconstructed mud dwellings that were common in the area a hundred years ago and a quaint re-creation of the school where Bosman taught. There are two charming BaTswana homestead rondavels, where you can stay overnight; book ahead via the information centre to stay in the rondavels or to camp.

ARRIVAL AND INFORMATION

GROOT MARICO

By bus and minibus taxi The Intercape bus from Johannesburg/Pretoria (daily 3–4hr) to Gaborone in Botswana drops passengers off at the petrol station at the Groot Marico turn-off along the N4, a shady 20min walk north of the village centre. Minibus taxis travelling along the N4 from Pretoria or Rustenburg to Zeerust or Botswana also stop here.

Information The tourist information centre is on Paul Kruger St (daily sunrise to sunset; ☎014 503 0085 or ☎083 2722 958, ⍵marico.co.za), in an enclosure built by

Italian POWs in World War II. It's run by a couple with a wealth of knowledge about the town and its activities, who can arrange visits to the Bosman Living Museum and organize *dorp* tours which take in a *mampoer* distillery (see box opposite). Email in advance for help with accommodation. The adjoining *Art Factory* sells Tswana cultural artefacts, locally made Afrikaner crafts such as wooden pipes, whips and clocks, and books by Herman Bosman.

ACCOMMODATION

Djembe Guest Farm and Backpackers 3km south of Groot Marico ☎079 955 8119, ⍵bit.ly/Djembe guestfarm. Groot Marico's backpacker option has comfortable double rooms and a pleasant dorm room. There are shared kitchen facilities for self-caterers, or you can book meals. Pickups from the N4 and bike rental are possible. The place comes alive in the evening when travellers gather around the fireplace and the drums come out. Dorms R80, doubles R180

★**Evergreen River Guest Farm** 10km east of the village from the N4 Koedoesfontein exit ☎014 503 1057, ⍵facebook.com/evergreenriverguestfarm. Two

large, fully equipped self-catering cottages sleeping up to 6 people, each with a huge veranda from where you can enjoy expansive views of nothing but forest and mountain. There's excellent stargazing, birdwatching, fishing and swimming, and the farmhouse, where the owners live, has a small farm shop with nice local crafts and some useful basics. R1000

River Still Guest Farm 6km south of the village ☎083 272 2958, ⍵riverstill.co.za. Four charming self-catering cottages sleeping 2–8 people, down by the river in a secluded and heavily forested valley – just perfect for birders. Swimming in the river is possible, and there are canoes for rent and drumming sessions at weekends. R660

EATING

Most guest farms in Groot Marico offer self-catering facilities, and your hosts will usually already have a braai stand set up for you when you arrive. Bring your own charcoal and supplies as there isn't a lot to buy in town and shops can close early.

Wag n Biekie Corner Hendrik Potgieter St and the N4 ☎082 679 8517, ⍵sunbirdmedia.wixsite.com /wagnbiekie. Just off the N4 turn-off, this is a popular pit-stop for bikers, with non-stop sports on the TV and a beer

garden. The extensive pub food menu offers burgers (R45–R80), toasties (R30) and steaks, and there's a lively drinks list with some perilously strong *mampoer*-based cocktails on offer. Mon–Sat 8.30am–11pm; Sun 9am–5pm.

Madikwe Game Reserve

Gate fee R180; day visitor R70 extra · ☎018 350 9931, ⍵madikwegamereserve.co.za

Tucked up in the very north of the province near the Botswana border lies the 765-square-kilometre, malaria-free **MADIKWE GAME RESERVE**, one of South Africa's largest wildlife areas. The reserve was established in 1991 from reclaimed farmland, thanks to **Operation Phoenix**, which saw the reintroduction of over eight thousand animals. Today, Madikwe's largely low-lying plains of woodland and grassland are amply stocked with the Big Five, plus dozens of other mammals, including cheetah, wild dogs, spotted hyena and most of Southern Africa's plains antelopes. Twitchers won't be disappointed, with some 350 bird species recorded so far; the Marico River, on the eastern border, and the *koppies* scattered all around, are particularly rewarding birding areas.

Madikwe remains one of the least known of South Africa's large wildlife areas, even though there are more than twenty **lodges** here. It is also one of South Africa's most exclusive reserves. Only guests of its lodges may visit, there is no self-drive safari option and independent day visits are not allowed. All this makes for an uncrowded reserve with abundant wildlife and animal sightings. **Day visitors** must book a package through one of the lodges that includes a **game drive** and lunch.

MAMPOER

According to legend, a sePedi chief by the name of Mampuru introduced the art of distilling peach brandy to the Boers. Named **mampoer** in his honour, the fearsomely strong spirit has inspired locals and visitors ever since. In the old days the alcohol content was measured by throwing a chunk of lard into a sample: if it floated halfway, the *mampoer* was perfect. Today, you just hold a match over it – the higher and cleaner the blue flame, the better the brew. Any fruit can be used to make *mampoer*, but peach was the most traditional. Until 1878, much of North West Province's farmland grew peach trees solely for this purpose, though disease put an end to that and now most *mampoer* is made with citrus and wild fruits.

Another change was the ZAR government's distilling tax, and the new licensing system introduced in 1894, when thousands of *mampoer* stills were destroyed. A few, however, escaped detection. One local story recounts a farmer cleaning out his entire drainage system, but making no attempt to conceal fifteen barrels of *mampoer*. The inspectors found the barrels, split them open and poured the contents down the drain. Meanwhile, the canny farmer stationed his family in the field where the pipe ended with every container the household possessed, and managed to recover fourteen of the fifteen barrels.

To **sample** and buy *mampoer*, enquire at Groot Marico's information centre about taking a *mampoer* tour (from R250, including a farm lunch), which takes in two or more nearby farms where you can also see demonstrations of how the stuff is made.

RRIVAL AND DEPARTURE

MADIKWE GAME RESERVE

By car Road access to Madikwe is normally through Tau ate, 12km off the R49, although the reserve can also be approached from the east via Molatedi Gate. Whichever approach you take, you'll need to inform your lodge prior to rival. The park is 360km from Johannesburg.

By plane You can fly to the small airport inside the reserve on the two to three daily flights from Johannesburg (45min; around R3700). Book through the lodges or directly with Madikwe Air (☎011 805 4888, ⓦmadikwecharters.com) or Federal Air (☎011 395 9000, ⓦfedair.com). The lodges take care of transport to and from the airport.

CCOMMODATION

ccommodation rates at all lodges include full board, day and night game drives, and guided bush walks. There is no udget accommodation or camping. Prices listed are per person per night.

ci's Safari Lodge & Tree Lodges ☎083 700 2071, ⓦjacislodges.co.za. Two lodges whose sense of style, mfort and laidback luxury are hard to beat. The *Safari Lodge* verlooks a water hole on the Marico River and has a natural ck swimming pool nearby, while the *Tree Lodges'* rooms are uilt several metres off the ground around trees. **R6995**

adikwe Hills ☎018 350 9200; reservations ☎011 781 431, ⓦmadikwehills.com. Another gem, this one built ound a *koppie* close to the riverbank. There are pleasant odern rooms, a sundowner terrace and swimming pool with eat views, plus a gym, spa, and childcare facilities. **R9700**

ateya Safari Lodge ☎014 778 9200, ⓦmateya fari.com. Experience the ultimate in bush chic at these five luxurious suites, each with its own swimming pool, as well as indoor and outdoor showers. There's a spa and the lodge's excellent food is best sampled on the terrace overlooking the veld. No children under 16. **R13,200**

★**Mosetlha Bush Camp & Eco Lodge** ☎011 444 9345, ⓦthebushcamp.com. A bit cheaper than the other lodges and offering the most intense wilderness experience. There's no perimeter fence here and accommodation is in simple, open-sided log cabins with no electricity – the hot outdoor showers are delivered by an ingenious boiler and bucket system. What it lacks in luxury it makes up for in atmosphere, with the emphasis placed on game walks as much as drives. **R2595**

Mafikeng

hanks to its scrawny and desolate dryness, North West Province's Central Region feels specially remote, and there are few towns worth visiting. The provincial capital **Mafikeng**, 5km south of the Ramatlabama border post with Botswana, 100km from Groot Marico, and also known as Mahikeng, is a shopping and transport hub for the wide area f farmland that surrounds it. The government offices at the former Bophuthatswana apital of **Mmabatho**, now a suburb to the north of town, offer a unique portrait of the

vision of apartheid and its deep contradictions. However, Mafikeng remains most famous for Baden-Powell and the Boer siege of 1899–1900 (see box opposite).

Mafikeng Museum

Martin St • Mon–Fri 8am–4.30pm • Donation • ☎ 018 388 9000

The town's main attraction is the **Mafikeng Museum**, housed in the impressive former town hall, which was built in 1902, two years after the siege ended (see box opposite). There's a restored steam locomotive outside, in use from 1901 until 1971, during which time it pulled the Kimberley–Bulawayo Express. Inside, you'll find San hunting weapons and poisons, and a life-size re-creation of a traditional Tswana hut, complete with its trademark enclosed porch. The siege of Mafikeng is given a room of its own, filled with British imperial memorabilia, from weaponry to a collection of photos. There's also an exhibition on Sol T. Plaatje, who worked as an interpreter for the British. Plaatje's diaries are the only known record of the siege of Mafikeng written from a black perspective, and they help lend the museum's examination of the era some balance. Keep an eye out too for the fascinating exhibit on Mafikeng and the railways, which provides evidence of the connection between their spread from Cape Town and Rhodes' mission to colonize Africa.

Mafikeng Game Reserve

On the eastern edge of town • Daily: May–Aug 7.30am–6pm; Sept–April 7.30am–7pm • R40, plus R10 per car • ☎ 018 397 1675, ⓦ parksnorthwest.co.za/mafikeng_reserve • There are two entrances to the reserve, one 10km east of Mafikeng along the R49 towards Zeerust, the other 2km from the town centre, southeast along the R503

The 48-square-kilometre **Mafikeng Game Reserve**, is worth a quick drive around while in the area for its acacia-strewn bushveld landscape and herbivorous plains game, including giraffe, white rhino and buffalo. Cooke's Lake, in the reserve's western corner next to town, is a good spot for waxbill, colourful finches, waterfowl and mongooses.

THE SIEGE OF MAFIKENG

Mafikeng was besieged within three days of the start of the **Second Anglo-Boer War** (1899–1902) by generals Snyman and Cronje. **Colonel Robert Baden-Powell** (founder of the Boy Scouts) had the task of defending the town. This he did for 217 days, from October 16, 1899, until May 17, 1900, when relief arrived from Rhodesia and from the south. In the process, Baden-Powell became a British household name and hero, and the exuberant scenes of jubilation in London that greeted news of the relief gave rise to a new word in the English language: **maffick**, which meant to celebrate unduly.

Strategically, Mafikeng was irrelevant to the war; Baden-Powell's real achievement was to distract the six thousand Afrikaners besieging the town from fighting elsewhere. He relied heavily on the **Barolong** people for defence, labour and reconnaissance, but failed to record this either in his dispatches to London or in his memoirs, despite the fact that four hundred Barolong lost their lives during the siege – twice as many as the British casualties, some of whom are marked by white iron crosses in the town's **cemetery** on Carrington Street. Until the 1980s this was a whites-only cemetery, and today it still commemorates only the Europeans who died during the siege. The Barolong also received far fewer rations, and over one thousand subsequently died of starvation; they received none of the £29,000 raised in Britain for the rehabilitation of Mafikeng. To add insult to injury, not one Barolong was decorated for bravery, in contrast to the plentiful medals dished out to the British regiments, and none of the promises Baden-Powell made about land grants to them was ever kept. An important legacy of the involvement of the black population was the diary of the siege kept by **Sol Plaatje**, one of the first black writers to make an impact on English literature, who was later to become a founder member of the South African Native Congress, forerunner to the ANC.

ARRIVAL

By bus and minibus taxi None of the major intercity bus companies serves Mafikeng, but Atamelang (☎018 381 2680) runs a daily service to and from Johannesburg (4hr), while Bojanala Bus (☎014 565 6550) crawls once a day to and from Rustenburg (3hr). There are minibus taxis to most destinations within the province, as well as two to three daily services to Kimberley (5hr). The hassle-free bus and minibus taxi terminal can be found between Victoria and Hatchard streets on the northern side of town.

ACCOMMODATION

Ashden Lodge 1088 Jakaranda St ☎083 499 5108, ⓦashdenlodge.co.za; map opposite. A 10min drive from the city centre and overlooking the Mafikeng Game Reserve. The rooms spread through the attractive single-storey building are spotless and the location is blissfully quiet. The helpful owners will let you use the braai with prior arrangement (bring your own charcoal). **R750**

Cooke's Lake Chalets Cooke's Lake, access on Nelson Mandela Drive ☎018 386 6380, ⓦgoldenleopard resorts.co.za; map opposite. Near the city centre and overlooking the pretty lake with plenty of birdlife, these beautiful two-storey wood-and-thatch chalets make a most attractive place to stay. The reception building has a large, average restaurant overlooking the lake too. **R800**

Protea Hotel 80 Nelson Mandela Drive ☎018 381 0400, ⓦproteahotels.com; map opposite. Just north of the centre, Mafikeng's best hotel has comfortable rooms, a good pool, and cheerful staff. Their rather business-like *Mafika* restaurant is one of the better places to eat in town. Restaurant daily noon–10pm. **R1600**

EATING

Mafikeng is no culinary paradise, and your best option for good food is to eat at one of the hotels or fast-food joints scattered across town.

Buffalo Park Lodge 59 Molopo St, at the corner of Botha Rd ☎018 381 2159, ⓦbuffalolodge.co.za; map opposite. The small pub-restaurant at this family-run hotel is well run and popular with locals. The typical pub-style menu offers steaks, burgers, jacket potatoes and toasties. Mon–Sat 10am–9.30pm, Sun 10am–6pm.

DIRECTORY

Hospital Victoria Private Hospital, in Victoria St (☎018 381 2043), has walk-in doctors' clinics and a pharmacy.

Police Corner of Tillard and Carrington streets ☎086 001 0111.

Mpumalanga

LEOPARD, SABI SANDS RESERVE

9

Mpumalanga

Mpumalanga, "the land of the rising sun" to its siSwati- and Zulu-speaking residents, extends east from Gauteng to Mozambique and Swaziland. The province is synonymous with the Kruger National Park, the real draw of South Africa's east flank, and one of Africa's best game parks. Kruger occupie most of Mpumalanga and Limpopo's borders with Mozambique, and covers over 20,000 square kilometres – an area the size of Israel or El Salvador. Unashamedly populist, Kruger is the easiest African game park to drive around on your own, with many well-run restcamps for accommodation. On its western border lie a number of private reserves and game farms, called the Greater Kruger, offering the chance – at a price – to escape the Kruger crush, with well-informed rangers conducting safaris in open vehicles.

Apart from the irresistible magnet of big-game country, Mpumalanga also has som spectacular scenery in the mountainous area known as the **Escarpment**, usually passed through en route to Kruger. The most famous viewpoints – **God's Window**, **Bourke's Luck Potholes** and **Three Rondavels** – are along the lip of the Escarpment, the best of which is the Potholes. Descending the Escarpment on one of four mountain passes takes you into the tropical-fruit-growing and bushveld country of the **lowveld**, with impressive views back towards the towering massif of the Escarpment. Nearest to the Blydepoort Dam, at the base of the Escarpment, is the service centre of **Hoedspruit** (actually in Limpopo Province, but covered here because of its proximity to Kruger) with its own airport, a jumping-off point for safaris in the central and northern section of the park, as well as a number of priva game reserves. Note that **malaria** (see p.71) is a potential hazard in the lowveld and Kruger, particularly in summer.

There is great pressure on the land that lies between the mountains and Kruger: you'll see stretches of commercial tropical fruit farms, and very populous areas that were allocated for Sotho, Shangaan and Tsonga speakers during apartheid, where thousands of very poor people live harsh rural lives. Between here and the park itse lies a thick buffer of private game farms and wildlife reserves. Many of these reserv have taken down the fences that separate them from Kruger and animals roam free between the park and the reserves; it is here, in Greater Kruger, that you will find a plethora of safari lodges and camps, both the ultra-luxurious and the more reasonably priced.

WALKING SAFARI IN KRUGER NATIONAL PARK

Highlights

❶ Horseriding Head off on horseback to spot wild horses near Nelspruit, or on a big game safari in the Karongwe. **See p.530**

❷ Drive the R40 This road, which takes you along Kruger's western flank, is the best way to experience how rural Shangaan and Tsonga people really live. **See p.534**

❸ Aerial cable trail Glide in a harness through the air, over treetops and the river, on a 1.2km trail near Hazyview. **See p.534**

❹ Brushing an elephant Enjoy a close encounter grooming an elephant at the Hazyview Elephant Sanctuary. **See p.534**

❺ African meals at the Shangana Cultural Village Sample crocodile and unusual vegetables, cooked over open fires, and watch stirring traditional dances. **See p.535**

❻ Walking safaris in Kruger It's worth leaving behind the security of your vehicle for the thrill of potential close encounters with animals. **See p.542**

❼ Leopard-spotting The luxury camps in the Sabi Sands Game Reserve offer excellent opportunities to observe leopards. **See p.549**

HIGHLIGHTS ARE MARKED ON THE MAP ON P.520

9

The Escarpment

Four hours' drive east of Johannesburg International Airport is one of the city's favoured mountain retreats: the waving grasslands and luxury guesthouses of the Mpumalanga Drakensberg, generally known as the **Escarpment**. While most travellers visit the region purely because of its proximity to Kruger National Park, it provides some of the most dramatic views in the country, which can be enjoyed with little effort even if you are simply passing through en route to the park. This tour, known as the **Panorama Route**, can also be taken as an organized day-trip by numerous tour operators in Nelspruit (see p.527). The main draw of the Escarpment is the **Blyde River**

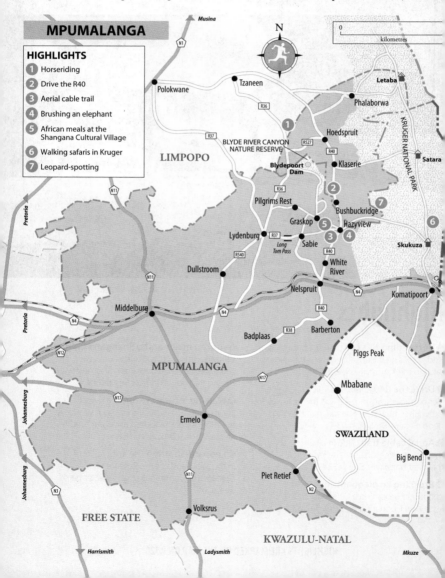

MPUMALANGA

HIGHLIGHTS

1. Horseriding
2. Drive the R40
3. Aerial cable trail
4. Brushing an elephant
5. African meals at the Shangana Cultural Village
6. Walking safaris in Kruger
7. Leopard-spotting

Canyon, whose dizzying views into one of the world's great gorges appear in countless South African tourist brochures, though it is often overshadowed by the allure of the game on the plains below.

Dullstroom

Unless your passion is fly-fishing, chances are you'll find the crossroads settlement of **DULLSTROOM**, some 209km east of Johannesburg, as unexciting as its name suggests, though it can be a useful place to stop on your way to Kruger National Park. The town is often proclaimed as "a drinking town with a fishing problem" – unsurprisingly, you'll find a thriving pub life here.

Birds of Prey Rehabilitation Centre

1km outside Dullstroom on the R540 • Daily 9am–4pm • R60, children R25 • Demonstrations daily 10.30am & 2.30pm • ☎ 082 899 4108, ⓦ birdsofprey.co.za

The **Birds of Prey Rehabilitation Centre** makes a worthwhile visit and is exclusively devoted to the housing, nourishment and rehabilitation of raptors, with very good daily flying demonstrations. The centre offers the opportunity to see magnificent eagles and other birds of prey close up and marvel at their lightness and agility.

ARRIVAL AND INFORMATION
DULLSTROOM

By car Dullstroom is 260km from Johannesburg's OR Tambo airport (3hr).

By bus City to City bus (☎ 015 781 1037; ⓦ busticket .co.za) leaves Johannesburg Station daily at 8am, arriving at *Tonteldoos Restaurant* at 12.30pm.

Tourist information Auldstone House, on the main road, Naledi Drive (Mon–Fri 8am–5pm, Sat 9am–4pm; ☎ 013 254 0254, ⓦ dullstroomreservations.co.za).

ACCOMMODATION

Critchley Hackle Lodge Teding van Berkhout St ☎ 013 254 0149, ⓦ urbanhiphotels.com. A gracious, country-style hotel, offering stone and brick cottages, each with a fireplace, and a veranda with outdoor seating. Facilities include a restaurant, a bar for after-dinner cognac, and there's also a patio for tea and scones. R2915

KlipHuisjes 264 Blue Crane St ☎ 079 610 2732, ⓦ kliphuisjes.co.za. Four self-catering stone cottage units, sleeping 2 to 6 people, in a beautiful garden. There are fires in the winter, good linen, a communal firepit for braaing, and it's close to the town's restaurants. R1290

EATING

Mrs Simpson's 94 Teding van Berkhout St ☎ 013 254 0088, ⓦ mrssimpsons.co.za. Enjoy fine dining at this busy country restaurant named after the woman who married Edward VIII. Their Dullstroom trout with garlic and almonds (R120), followed by malva pudding, is particularly recommended. Booking ahead essential. Daily 11am–3pm & 6–9pm.

Pickles & Things 86 Naledi Drive ☎ 013 254 0115, ⓦ picklesandthings.co.za. The best place in town for (fair-trade) coffee, this popular place serves up big breakfasts (R85) and home-made bread, and has an inviting garden. The deli at the front of the restaurant stocks smoked trout and other delicacies. Daily 7am–5pm.

DRINKING

Dullstroom Inn Cnr Teding van Berkhout and Oranje Nassau sts ☎ 013 254 0071/0, ⓦ dullstroom-inn.info. An Edwardian country inn, with a popular pub serving hearty meals and draught beer in front of a crackling log fire. Tends to be packed at weekends.

Lydenburg

Some 58km northeast of Dullstroom, along the R540, lies the humdrum town of **LYDENBURG**. Its main claim to fame is as the site of one of South Africa's major archeological finds; subsequently, the only reason to come here is to visit the museum.

9

Lydenburg Museum

In the Gustav Klingbiel Nature Reserve, 3km out of town along the R37 to Sabie • Mon–Fri 8am–4pm, Sat & Sun 8am–5pm • Free • ☎ 013 235 2213

In 1957, a young boy, Karl-Ludwig von Bezing, began collecting terracotta fragments found on his father's farm near Lydenburg. Pieced together by the archeologist Ray Inskeep, they were revealed as highly decorated mask-like heads, probably used for ceremonial purposes. Inskeep dated them to around 500 AD, making them some of the first figurative sculptures in Southern Africa. The original **Lydenburg Heads** are now in the South African Museum in Cape Town (see p.97), but high-quality replicas can be seen at the Lydenburg Museum, along with excellent displays on human activity in the area over the past million or so years.

Sabie and around

Lying on the R37 beyond Long Tom Pass, **SABIE** (pronounced "Saabie", like the car) is the centre of Mpumalanga's agroforestry industry. The extensive pine plantations that cover the surrounding hills look monotonous compared to the rich, jungly variety of the remaining pockets of indigenous woodland. It is a missable town, worthwhile as a stop only for the activities on offer in the surrounding area – Sabie is one of the best places in the country for mountain biking, valued for the intensity of the climbs and technical complexity of the trails.

Numerous **waterfalls** drop down the slopes outside Sabie. Just 7km from town, down the Old Lydenburg Road, you can visit three of the most impressive: **Bridal Veil**, **Horseshoe** and, appropriately at the end of the road, **Lone Creek Falls**. The loveliest of the three, Lone Creek is reached down a paved path that crosses a river and works its way back to the car park.

Mac Mac Falls

Falls 13km north of the town along the Graskop Rd • R20 • **Pools** 11km north of town • R10

The most visited of the falls around Sabie are the spectacular 65m **Mac Mac Falls**, named after the many people of Scottish descent who died looking for gold in the area and whose names appear on dozens of tombstones in the vicinity. While you can't swim in the inviting waterfall pool at the base of the falls, there is a river pool at the **Mac Mac Pools**, 2km before you reach the falls, where there's also a picnic and braai area, and the 3km **Secretary Bird walking trail**.

ARRIVAL AND INFORMATION
SABIE AND AROUND

Sabie is 60km from Nelspruit on a windy road, often slowed down by logging trucks.

By bus Public transport to Sabie is limited to minibus taxis plying the routes from neighbouring towns.

Tourist information The Tourist Office is on Main Road, in the centre of town, next to the *Wimpy* restaurant (Mon–Fri 8am–4.30pm, Sat 9am–1pm; ☎ 013 764 1177, ⓦ sabie.co.za).

ADVENTURE ACTIVITIES IN SABIE

With its forest, massive gorge and mountains, the Escarpment offers plenty of opportunities for adventure activities. Sabie River Adventures (☎ 013 492 0071, ⓦ sabieriveradventures.co.za) offer a wide range of activities that include white-water rafting and tubing, quad and mountain biking, ziplining, abseiling, archery and horse trails.

Induna Adventures is also recommended (☎ 013 492 0071 or ☎ 082 463 2334, ⓦ induna adventures.com) for **river rafting** on the Sabie River; its half-day trip (R400) takes two and a half hours, on Grade 2 and 3 rapids. It also specializes in mountain biking, taking you through forests and pine and eucalyptus plantations, and crossing the Mac Mac and Sabie rivers several times (R435 for 90min).

ACCOMMODATION

Hillwatering Country House 50 Marula St ☎013 764 1421, ⓦhillwatering.co.za. A renovated 1950s home, overlooking the Bridal Veil Falls, with four large bedrooms, each with its own veranda. The owners are welcoming and helpful, and serve an excellent breakfast. R1150

Merry Pebbles Holiday Resort 2km west from the centre on the Old Lydenburg Rd ☎013 764 2266, ⓦmerrypebbles.co.za. Go for the newer units at this resort, which offers camping as well as self-catering and en-suite chalets. The facilities include a big heated pool and a children's playground. Camping R240, chalet R2500

The Sabie Town House Guest Lodge 25 Malieveld St ☎013 764 2292 or ☎082 556 7895, ⓦsabietown house.co.za. B&B at the Sabie village fringe run by a friendly couple, Greg and Kate, who know a lot about activities in the area. There are 10 en-suite rooms (luxury, with Jacuzzi, or budget options) overlooking lush gardens, with sumptuous breakfasts on offer, an honesty bar and swimming pool. Doubles R1150

EATING

The Wild Fig Tree Cnr of Main and Louis Trichardt sts ☎013 764 2239, ⓦbit.ly/wildfigtree. South African dishes, including ostrich, kudu (R149) and crocodile, are the speciality at this pleasant restaurant – the best in town – with a wide deck to make the most of the weather. Mon–Sat 8.30am–9pm.

Woodsman Pub & Restaurant Main St ☎013 764 2204, ⓦthewoodsman.co.za. A licensed restaurant with a beer garden; the substantial menu includes breakfast (great Sunday brunch), pub lunches, and local specialities such as lamb schwarma, beef stew, ostrich and trout (R100). There's a cosy fire in winter. Daily 7am–10pm.

Pilgrim's Rest

Hiding in a valley 35km north of Sabie, **PILGRIM'S REST**, an almost too-perfectly restored gold-mining town, is an irresistible port of call for tour buses. With a collection of red-roofed, corrugated-iron buildings, including the characterful *Royal Hotel* brimming with Victoriana, the place is undeniably photogenic. But you can't help feeling there's little substance behind the romanticized gold-rush image, especially when the village nods off after 5pm once the day-trippers have been spirited away. If you do want to visit a real gold mine, you're best off heading to Barberton (see p.532).

Pilgrim's Rest stretches along its one main road and is divided into Uptown and Downtown. Commercialized **Uptown** has the greatest concentration of shops and restaurants and draws the bulk of tourists; **Downtown**, just 1km to the west, has a more down-to-earth atmosphere. Apart from souvenir hunting and lingering in the cafés and tea shops, the main activity in Pilgrim's Rest is visiting its handful of **museums** and its old cemetery – the best place to absorb the town's history.

Brief history

Pilgrim's Rest owes its origins to South Africa's first **gold rush**, which predates the uncovering of the great Gauteng seams. In 1873, Alex "Wheelbarrow" Patterson discovered gold here, though his attempts to keep his discovery secret were a total failure, and by the end of the year Patterson had been joined by 1500 diggers frantically working four thousand claims. Many diggers arrived malnourished, suffering from dysentery and malaria after punishing journeys. Those who survived could expect drab lives in tents or, if they struck lucky, more permanent wattle-and-daub huts. Mining slowed right down a hundred years later, and Pilgrim's Rest was declared a historic monument in the 1980s.

Diggings Site Museum

Graskop Rd • Guided tours only, daily at 10am, 11am, noon, 2pm & 3pm • R20, buy tickets from the tourist office (see p.524)

To get an authentic impression of the gold-mining days, head for the open-air **Diggings Site Museum** on the eastern edge of town, where you can see demonstrations of alluvial gold-panning and get a guided tour around the bleak diggers' huts and the remnants of workings and machinery from the early mining days.

9

Alanglade House Museum

Main St, Downtown • Guided tours only, daily 11am & 2pm • R20, buy tickets from the tourist office (see below)

If you want to see the lavish style in which the mine bosses and their families once lived, visit **Alanglade**, home to successive managers of the Transavaal Gold Mining Estates from 1915 – when it was built – until the mine's closure in 1972. It has been carefully restored to reflect the taste and style of the Barry family, the house's first occupants. The rooms contain much of the original Arts and Crafts furniture, selected by the fashion-conscious Gladys Barry, with hunting trophies dotting the pale walls. It reveals a sheltered way of life far removed from the conditions of the workers who supplied the family's wealth.

ARRIVAL AND INFORMATION

By car Pilgrim's Rest is 41km from Sabie and is easily accessed by car on the exceptionally winding R532, or on the R535 from Graskop, 17km away.

By minibus taxis There are no scheduled buses; minibus taxis run here from Sabie and Graskop.

PILGRIM'S REST

Tourist information The tourist office is signposted on the main road in Uptown, close to the *Royal Hotel* (Mon–Fri 9am–4.30pm, Sat–Sun 9am–4pm; ☎ 013 768 1060, ☯ pilgrims-rest.co.za); tickets for local museums can be bought here.

ACCOMMODATION

Pilgrim's Rest has a few restaurants and teashops that provide for the daily influx of visitors, all situated along the main road and, apart from the hotel, open only during daytime. Catering for the tourist trade, the food is nothing to write home about.

Royal Hotel Main St, Uptown ☎ 013 768 1100, ☯ pilgrimsrest.org.za/royal.htm. An historic hotel that dates back to the gold-rush days and brims with Victoriana; guests are mostly accommodated in restored houses on the main road. A visit to the pub is essential (see below). **R1034**

EATING

Pancakes at The Stables Main St, Uptown ☎ 071 634 7113, ☯ bit.ly/pancakesatthestables. Enjoy a beer or glass of wine with a light meal, such as springbok curry and rice (R70) or their house speciality – pancakes with a variety of delicious fillings. Tues–Sun 9am–7pm.

Peach Tree Creek Restaurant Royal Hotel, Main St, Uptown ☎ 013 768 1100. The nicest place in town, where you can soak up the atmosphere while having a steak and salad (R140) or an English breakfast. Daily 7am–8pm.

DRINKING

Church Bar Royal Hotel, Main St, Uptown ☎ 013 768 1100. The bar's history is enough to tempt you in: it started life as a wooden Catholic chapel in Cape Town, before being dismantled, sent to Mozambique, then transported by ox-wagon and re-assembled in Pilgrim's Rest. Linger over the fascinating old photos and enjoy a local craft beer (R25) and a chat with the locals while you're at it. Daily 10am–10pm.

Graskop

Some 17km east of Pilgrim's Rest, **GRASKOP** owes its place on the tourist map to *Harrie's Pancake Shop*, which serves much imitated but rarely rivalled crêpes, and attracts all the tour buses doing the Escarpment viewpoints. The town itself is very ordinary, with timber trucks rumbling heavily through, but its location close to the **Blyde River Canyon** is the major consolation.

Africa Silks Weavery and Showroom

Showroom Louis Trichardt St • Daily 8am–5pm • **Farm** 23km from Graskop, on the R533 • Guided tours daily 9.30am, 10.30am, noon, 2pm & 3pm • ☎ 013 767 1665, ☯ africasilks.com

The **Africa Silks Weavery and Showroom** is a notable village industry, and sells a range of products made by local African women from the silk of mopane silkworms. The silk-filled duvets, cushion covers and scarves are particularly fabulous. It's also possible to visit the farm where the silk is produced.

Big Swing

☎ 079 779 8713 or ☎ 082 574 2345, ⍟ bigswing.co.za • R430

Graskop's **Big Swing** is the best of all the big swings on the Escarpment – a 68m free fall done in under three seconds, on one of the world's highest cable gorge swings. After the drop, you "fly free" across the gorge on a 135m highwire "*foefie* slide", 130m above ground, to glimpse the Graskop Falls. It's also possible to swing tandem (R350). Book in advance – they will either pick you up or direct you to the gorge.

INFORMATION
GRASKOP

Tourist information Trips SA, at the *Graskop Hotel*, Cnr Hoof & Louis Trichardt sts (Mon–Fri 8am–4.30pm, Sat 9am–1pm; ☎ 013 764 1177, ⍟ graskop.co.za), can book accommodation, safaris into Kruger Park, adventure activities and transfers. They also have the clearest map of the region and provide decent activity brochures.

ACCOMMODATION

★**Graskop Hotel** Cnr Hoof & Louis Trichardt sts ☎ 013 767 1244, ⍟ graskophotel.co.za. One of the nicest places to stay on the Escarpment, with a personal and relaxed atmosphere. Though unprepossessing from the outside, it actually has a very stylish interior of retro furniture, African baskets, fabrics and sculptures. The rooms, some of which are in garden wings, are airy and decorated with simplicity and flair. Most importantly, there is a swimming pool. R1200

Sheri's Lodge & Backpackers 66 Oorwinning St ☎ 072 623 5583, ⍟ sherislodge.co.za. A clean and friendly backpackers, situated near the centre of town. Dorms and self-catering doubles are on offer, all in rondavels, and there's a kitchen, and a dining and entertainment area that boasts a pool table. Dorms R140, doubles R460

EATING

Canimambo Cnr Hoof & Louis Trichardt sts ☎ 013 767 1868, ⍟ canimambo.za.net. Excellent Portuguese and Mozambican cuisine, with a cheerful, informal atmosphere, and a fire in winter. There is spicy bean stew for vegetarians, while a carnivorous speciality is a marinaded rump steak (R135), though the Mozambican peri-peri chicken never fails to please. Daily 11am–9pm.

Harrie's Pancake House Cnr of Louis Trichardt & Church sts ☎ 013 767 1273, ⍟ harriespancakes.com. The legendary and well-signposted *Harrie's* serves the best sweet and savoury pancakes in town, with local specialities such as trout pancake (R90). There is a nice outdoor terrace, as well as an inside dining room with a roaring log fire in winter. Daily 8am–6pm.

Blyde River Canyon

There are few places in South Africa where you can enjoy such easily accessible and dramatic scenery as that of the colossal **Blyde River Canyon**, weathered out of strata of red rock and dropping sharply away from the Escarpment into the lowveld. The **Blyde River Canyon Nature Reserve** stretches from a narrow tail near Graskop in the south, and broadens into a great amphitheatre partially flooded by the **Blydepoort Dam** about 60km to the north.

The drive along the canyon lip

Viewpoints R10

The views of the canyon are wonderful from both above and below, but the nicest way to take in the vistas is on an easy half-day's drive along the canyon lip. Some 3km north of Graskop, the R534 makes a 15km loop past a series of superb **viewpoints**. The road winds through pine plantations until it comes to the turn-off to the **Pinnacle**, a gigantic quartzite column topped with trees, rising out of a ferny gorge. After another 4km the road reaches the sheer drop and lowveld views of **God's Window**, one of the most famous of the viewpoints; it's also one of the most developed, with toilets and curio stalls. The looping road returns to rejoin the R532, which continues north for 28km beyond the turn-off to reach **Bourke's Luck Potholes** at the confluence of the Treur and Blyde rivers – a collection of strange, smoothly scooped formations carved into the rocks by water-driven pebbles. If you only have time for one spot, this is the best choice, with an easy but rewarding 45-minute walk, though there are no facilities.

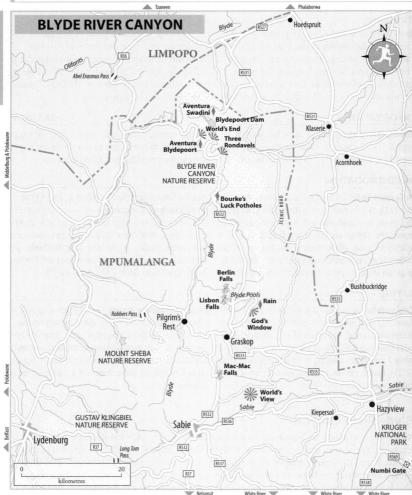

BLYDE RIVER CANYON

(Map labels:) Tzaneen, Blyde, R527, Hoedspruit, Phalaborwa, LIMPOPO, R36, Olifants, Abel Erasmus Pass, R531, Aventura Swadini, Blydepoort Dam, World's End, Three Rondavels, Klaserie, R531, Aventura Blydepoort, BLYDE RIVER CANYON NATURE RESERVE, Acornhoek, Bourke's Luck Potholes, R532, SCENIC ROAD, MPUMALANGA, Blyde, Berlin Falls, Bushbuckridge, Lisbon Falls, Blyde Pools, Rain, R533, Robbers Pass, Pilgrim's Rest, God's Window, Graskop, R533, MOUNT SHEBA NATURE RESERVE, Mac-Mac Falls, R535, Blyde, Sabie, World's View, Sabie, Kiepersol, Hazyview, GUSTAV KLINGBIEL NATURE RESERVE, R532, R536, KRUGER NATIONAL PARK, Sabie, Lydenburg, R37, Long Tom Pass, R532, R537, R569, Numbi Gate, R37, R538, Nelspruit, White River, White River, White River, Middelburg & Polokwane, Polokwane, Belfast, 0 kilometres 20, N

Another fine viewpoint lies 14km beyond, at the **Three Rondavels**. The name describes only one small feature of this cinemascope vista: three cylinders in the shape of huts with the meandering Blyde River twisting its way hundreds of metres below. No photograph does justice to the sheer enormity of the view, punctuated by one series of cliffs after another buttressing into the valley.

Three Rondavels to Blydepoort Dam

The 90km **drive** from the Three Rondavels viewpoint to the base of the canyon provides great views of the Escarpment cliffs rising out of the lowveld and can be easily fitted into your itinerary if you're heading to or from Kruger. The drive winds west to join with the R36 and heads north to begin its descent through the Abel Erasmus Pass and then the J.G. Strijdom Tunnel through the mountain, with the wide lowveld plains opening out on the other side. The road takes a wide arching trajectory to circumnavigate the canyon.

Blydepoort Dam and boat trips

26km from Hoedspruit; follow signs on the R531 for Forever Swadini Resort – the jetty is 5km beyond the resort • **Boat trips** daily 11am & 3pm • R150 plus R20 per person • Booking in advance essential • ☎ 015 795 5961, ✉ bookings@blydecanyon.co.za

At the heart of the Blyde River Canyon is the man-made **Blydepoort Dam**, most notable for the staggering views it gives of the canyon, looking up from the water. Here you can take a ninety-minute boat trip – probably the best way to experience the canyon – and view the spectacular mountain ravines and the Three Rondavels from below, as well as a number of impressive waterfalls. You'll also see the formations created by calcium deposits from the natural springs, and you may catch sight of hippos or crocs near the dam.

The lowveld

South Africa's **lowveld**, wedged between the Mpumalanga section of the Drakensberg and Mozambique, is part of a vast subtropical region of savanna that stretches north through Zimbabwe and Zambia as far as Central Africa. Closely associated at the turn of the last century with fortune-seekers, hunters, gold-diggers and adventurers, these days the South African lowveld's claim to fame is its proximity to the Kruger National Park and the adjacent private game reserves. The towns here all act as gateways to the park.

Largest of the lowveld towns, and the capital of Mpumalanga, is **Nelspruit**, accessible by air and bus (including buses from Maputo in Mozambique). East of Nelspruit, the N4 runs close to the southern border of the Kruger, providing easy access to its Malelane and Crocodile Bridge gates; the latter is just 12km north of **Komatipoort**, a humid frontier town on the border with **Mozambique**. From Nelspruit, you can also head 32km south to **Barberton**, with strong mining connections, or continue another 41km to **Swaziland**.

The R40 north of the provincial capital passes through **White River**, **Hazyview**, **Hoedspruit** and **Phalaborwa**, a series of small towns that act as bases for exploring Kruger. Each town is well supplied with accommodation, and has a Kruger entrance gate nearby; tours are available from some. The closest to Nelspruit and an entry point into the Park, Hazyview is now leader of the pack. Hoedspruit and Phalaborwa actually fall within Limpopo Province, but for the sake of continuity have been included in this chapter.

Nelspruit

Prosperous **NELSPRUIT** (nel-sprait), 358km east of Johannesburg on the N4, grew in the 1890s as a base for traders, farmers and prospectors, but there is little evidence left of these origins. Most of the old buildings have been ripped out and replaced by shopping malls and freeways, and the town has a bustling and prosperous feel. It's a major commercial centre, not only for the lowveld but also for shoppers from Swaziland and Mozambique. The municipality is called Mbombela, and you may see that name on some road signs, rather than Nelspruit.

The town also has the best **transport connections** in the province, including air links with Johannesburg, Cape Town and Durban, as well as to Maputo. Nelspruit also has an excellent hospital and all the facilities and shops you might need.

Lowveld National Botanical Garden

Signposted off the R40 to White River • ☎ 013 752 5531, ⊛ sanbi.org/gardens/lowveld • Daily 8am–5pm • R30

Nelspruit's major attraction is the **Lowveld National Botanical Garden**. Set on the banks of the Crocodile River, it is a delightful place to wander about, although it has begun to get a little run-down. Natural waterfalls and walks through rainforest

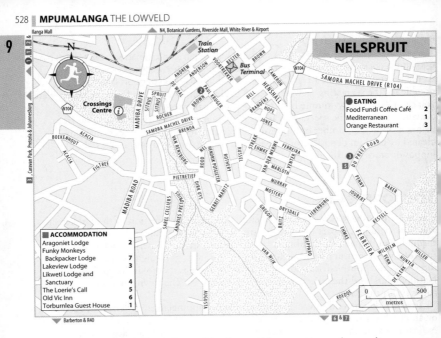

NELSPRUIT

Ilanga Mall | N4, Botanical Gardens, Riverside Mall, White River & Airport

Train Station
Bus Terminal

EATING
Food Fundi Coffee Café	2
Mediterranean	1
Orange Restaurant	3

Crossings Centre

ACCOMMODATION
Aragoniet Lodge	2
Funky Monkeys Backpacker Lodge	7
Lakeview Lodge	3
Likweti Lodge and Sanctuary	4
The Loerie's Call	5
Old Vic Inn	6
Torburnlea Guest House	1

0 — 500 metres

Barberton & R40

make a pleasant break from the midday heat, with **trees** grouped according to habitat and helpfully identified with labels. The garden specializes in **cycads** from around the world, and there's also a grove of baobabs from South Africa and other African countries. A useful brochure sold at the entrance gate has a map showing the highlights of the garden and the paths through it, and you'll find a tea room open for refreshments, as well as a restaurant with good views of the cascade waterfall.

Chimpanzee Eden

10km out of Nelspruit on the R40 to Barberton • Daily 8am–4pm • R190 • ☎ 079 777 1514, ⓦ chimpeden.com

The Jane Goodall Institute **Chimpanzee Eden** is dedicated to the rescue and rehabilitation of chimpanzees. There are currently three different chimp groups and enclosures, with viewpoints overlooking the forest. During the 45-minute tour you get to see the primates – many of them rescued from terrible conditions in places like Angola and Somalia – re-learning how to climb trees, foraging for food in the leaves, carefully grooming each other and establishing troop relationships. Light meals and refreshment are available from the restaurant before or after the tour. Book online well in advance, to be sure of a place.

ARRIVAL AND DEPARTURE   NELSPRUIT

By plane Flights, run by SA Airlink (ⓦ flyairlink.com), arrive at the tiny, thatched Kruger Mpumalanga International Airport (KMIA; ☎ 013 753 7500), 20km north of town off the R40 to White River. Unfortunately, flights to Nelspruit are among the most expensive in the country, and it may work out cheaper to fly into Johannesburg and continue here by car. All the major car rental companies, including Avis (☎ 013 750 1015), have rental desks at the airport. If you're not renting a car, your best option for onward travel is a private shuttle: Summit Tours and Safaris

(☎ 078 326 1041 or ☎ 071 445 6531, ⓦ summittoursand safaris.com) meets flights on request and provides reliable transfers into Nelspruit (or into Kruger and the private reserves, to Hazyview, and onwards from Nelspruit to Mozambique).

Destinations: Cape Town (daily; 3hr); Durban (2 daily; 1hr); Johannesburg (4 daily; 1hr).

By bus From Johannesburg, the City Bug (☎ 0861 33 44 33, ⓦ citybug.co.za) is the best option, with six departures daily 8am–6pm (4hr), leaving from OR Tambo Airport and arriving in Nelspruit at the BP garage in the Sonpark Centre, Piet Retief St, just south of the city centre. You'll need to arrange a taxi beforehand (it's too far to walk into town):

Edgars Taxi Service (☎072 147 1677) is recommended; alternatively, arrange for someone from your accommodation to meet you.

INFORMATION

Tourist information Lowveld Tourism (Mon–Fri 7am–6pm, Sat 8am–1.30pm; ☎013 755 1988, ⓦkrugerlowveld.com), at the Crossings Centre, corner of the N4 and General Dan Pienaar St, is the town's main tourist office. It provides maps and basic information, and arranges accommodation, including bookings for Kruger's restcamps, as well as day-trips with various tour operators.

ACCOMMODATION

Nelspruit's accommodation is largely geared towards business travellers, and none is close to restaurants. Most places have swimming pools, outdoor eating areas and tropical gardens. There are also some excellent options a few kilometres out, on farms, and a game lodge virtually at the airport.

Aragoniet Lodge 22 Aragoniet St ☎013 741 2233, ⓔaragonietlodge@vodamail.co.za; map opposite. Spotless and cheap self-catering in four rooms, in a convenient location, with a garden and pool, attractive mainly for the price. They can also arrange to have you collected from the bus or airport. R800

Funky Monkeys Backpacker Lodge 102 Van Wijk St ☎013 744 1310, ⓦfunkymonkeys.co.za; map opposite. Popular hostel with a licensed bar, pool table, shady veranda, swimming pool and broadband. It offers one- to three-day tours into Kruger and can arrange pick-ups from the town centre or airport. Dorms R150, doubles R390

Lakeview Lodge Take the Kaapsche Hoop road off the N4; the lodge is on your left after 4km ☎013 741 4312, ⓦlakeviewlodge.co.za; map opposite. Eleven thatched self-catering chalets in a rural garden setting, with a swimming pool, restaurant, caravan park and campsite. There's also a swimming pool and play area for kids, and a restaurant. Doubles R650, camping R260

Likweti Lodge and Sanctuary On the R538 between Nelspruit and White River, 5km from KMI airport ☎082 939 0629; map opposite. Planes are not allowed to fly over Likweti's 1400 acres of rocky outcrops and open plains, which are home to rhino, buffalo, zebra and giraffe. The lodge, set on a ridge, faces the sunrise, with supremely comfortable rooms and excellent breakfast. R2700

The Loerie's Call 2 Du Preez St ☎013 744 9507 or ☎083 628 7759, ⓦloeriescall.co.za; map opposite. This modern guesthouse, with a pool and subtropical gardens, offers upmarket en-suite rooms with private verandas, as well as an appealing lounge and terrace. It's often fully booked, so reserve well ahead. There is also a restaurant on-site and an upmarket spa. R3200

Old Vic Inn 12 Impala St, 3km from town ☎013 744 0993 or ☎082 340 1508, ⓦkrugerandmore.co.za; map opposite. Clean, comfortable doubles, en suite, luxury or budget options, and a dorm in a quiet backpacker hostel, with a pool, garden and walks in the adjoining nature reserve. There are also three self-catering units suitable for families. The owners can arrange transport from the centre of town and from the airport, and can organize tours, including to Mozambique and Kruger. Their in-house tour company is the one that will get you a bed right in Kruger Park; the tours are normally run by the owner himself. Extras include horseriding and a beauty salon. Dorms R135, doubles R480, self-catering R800

★**Torburnlea Guest House** Mataffin Macadamia Village, 5km east of town ☎072 884 8872,

HEADING INTO MOZAMBIQUE

Maputo is only 200km from Nelspruit, an easy journey by car on the N4, though there is one toll gate to pass through (R59). The Cheetah Express (☎013 755 1988; R300) is a **shuttle service** between the two cities – it leaves Nelspruit at 4pm daily; the journey takes three hours. Tickets can be purchased from the tourist office at the Crossings Centre (see above) and **visas** (R750 US & UK passport holders, R600 Europe) must be purchased beforehand at the Mozambique Consulate (19 Hope St; ☎013 753 2089). You'll need a whole day for this – arrive at the Embassy first thing to hand in your forms (including proof of accommodation booked in Mozambique), and collect your visa in the early afternoon. Visas can be issued at the border itself, but this can be unpredictable, so it's best to arrange your visa beforehand.

To find out how best to explore the Mozambican side of Kruger Park, east of Phalaborwa Gate, speak to the well-informed company Great Limpopo Wilderness Camps & Trails (☎021 701 7860, ⓦdolimpopo.com).

HORSERIDING NEAR NELSPRUIT

One of the best things to do around Nelspruit is horseriding, where you stand a good chance of seeing **wild horses** – or you can ride among plains game on a wildlife conservancy or reserve.

Kaapsehoop Horse Trails Kaapsehoop, 35km west of Nelspruit, off the N4 ☎076 108 0081, ⓦhorseback trails.co.za. Wild horses roam around Kaapsehoop, a mountainous, forested area close to Nelspruit; Kaapsehoop Horse Trails offer one-hour rides for beginners (R315), and two-hour (R550) and full-day (R980) rides for competent riders. There is very nice, reasonably priced self-catering accommodation (R660) at the riding centre, a café and shop, with friendly staff and a relaxed vibe.

Kwa Madwala Reserve 80km east of Nelspruit, off the N4 ☎082 779 2153, ⓦkwamadwala.net. Horserides are offered on this massive game conservancy, where you can ride among plains game (no predators or elephants); one-hour rides for beginners (R450), and a choice of two-hour (R600) and half-day (R970, including breakfast) rides for more experienced riders.

ⓦtorburnlea.co.za; map p.528. Pick of the Nelspruit guesthouses, *Torburnlea* is the panoramic beautifully renovated 1920s family home of friendly and informed hosts Andrew and Kim Hall, with a gracious colonial-style veranda looking from a hill onto orchards and sugarcane fields. The rooms are spacious and elegant, with luxurious fittings and linen, and you'll get fresh fruit juice and tropical fruit from the farm for breakfast. **R1800**

EATING

Food Fundi Coffee Café Pick N Pay Centre, 5–7 Sitrus Crescent ☎013 755 1091, ⓦthefoodfundi .co.za; map p.528. A local favourite serving really good coffee, home-made bread and craft beer, with a seasonal fresh menu of open sandwiches, wraps, cakes and salads. Their rooibos-smoked chicken sandwich with cashew nuts is very tasty (R55), as is the variety of all-day breakfast dishes. Mon–Fri 7.30am–6pm, Sat 8am–5pm, Sun 9am–2pm.

Mediterranean i'langa Mall, cnr Flamboyant and Bitterbessie sts ☎013 742 2235; Riverside Mall, White River Rd (R40) ☎013 757 0170, ⓦmediterranean seafood.co.za; map p.528. A popular seafood and sushi

choice, where you can try Greek-style Mozambican prawns (R199), or a whole fish baked, steamed or fried (R110). The menu is extensive – ask to see the display of fresh fish from the kitchen. Mon–Thurs & Sun 11.30am–9pm, Fri & Sat 11.30am–10pm.

Orange Restaurant 4 Du Preez St ☎083 628 7759, ⓦeatatorange.co.za; map p.528. Sleek wood, glass and steel restaurant, adjacent to *The Loerie's Call* guesthouse with a balcony providing panoramic views of the city and the mountains. The food is pretty good too: fine dining with an eclectic menu, from Norwegian Salmon to South African kudu (R150). Mon–Sat noon–3pm and 6–10pm, Sun 6–9pm.

DIRECTORY

Consulate Mozambique 19 Hope St (☎013 753 2089).
Emergencies Ambulance ☎082 911.
Hospital Mediclinic Nelspruit Private Hospital, 1 Louise St, Sonheuwel (☎013 759 0500).
Internet access There are internet cafés in the town's shopping malls.
Pharmacy Mopani Pharmacy, Crossings Centre (Mon–Fri 9am–6pm, Sat 9am–3pm, Sun 9am–1pm; ☎013 755 5566, out of hours ☎082 761 1603); i'langa Centre

(Mon–Fri 9am–6pm, Sat 9am–4pm, Sun 9am–1pm; ☎013 742 2225).
Post office 11 Voortrekker St (Mon, Tues, Thurs, Fri 8am–5pm, Wed 8.30am–5pm, Sat 8am–1pm); each shopping mall has a Postnet, which is easier to use than the post office.
Shopping There are three major malls in Nelspruit: Riverside Mall, towards White River heading north on the R40; the more central Crossings Centre; and i'langa Mall, to the west towards Johannesburg, off the N4.

Kruger's southern fringe

The N4 east of Nelspruit roughly follows the progress of the **Crocodile River**, which traces the southern boundary of Kruger National Park. For 58km to the tiny farming settlement of **Malelane**, the road travels within view of the Crocodile's riverine forest, passing lush, subtropical farmlands and the Dalí-esque

formations of granite *koppies*. Some 4km further on, the road turns off to Kruger's **Malelane Gate**, the most convenient entry point for *Berg-en-Dal* restcamp (see p.545). The only blight on the journey is the smoke stacks from the Malelane sugar-cane mill.

ACCOMMODATION	KRUGER'S SOUTHERN FRINGE

Buhala Game Lodge 12km east of Malelane Gate ☎082 909 5941 or ☎083 272 2150, ⊛buhala.co.za. A fabulous guesthouse on a mango, sugar-cane and papaya farm, on the banks of the Crocodile River, with views from a wooden deck across the slow water into Kruger, plus a swimming pool, a spa, and ten a/c elegant doubles. Day drives with a ranger into Kruger can be arranged from here for R1500 per person, as well as three-hour walks there for R825. It's also popular with golfers, as it's close to the exclusive Leopard Creek course, designed by Gary Player. **R4860**

Kwa Madwala Game Reserve Signposted off the N4, between Malelane and Crocodile Bridge gates ☎082 779 2153 or ☎013 790 4214, ⊛kwamadwala.net. A game lodge experience at B&B prices, set in a beautiful area of bushveld, dotted with granite hills and roamed by four of the Big Five. Accommodation at their main lodge, *Manyatta Rock Camp*, consists of chalets built into granite outcrops, and there's a nice pool and good views, though with farmland close by it doesn't have a totally wild feeling. Rates include dinner, bed and breakfast; game drives, microlight safaris and horseriding are extra. **R3600**

Barberton

BARBERTON, 36km south of Nelspruit, began its urban existence after **gold** was discovered in 1883. An influx of shopkeepers, hoteliers, barmen, prostitutes, even ministers of religion, soon joined the diggers in the growing frontier town, which consisted of tents, tin, thatch and mud, with nearly every second building functioning as a boozing joint. During the fabulous boom of the 1880s the mines slipped out of the grasp of the small-time prospectors and came under the control of the large corporations that still own them today. There are seven working **mines** around Barberton, each with its own recreational area for miners only, which means you won't find miners packing out public bars as in the wild days of old, and the whole place feels rather run-down these days.

This is the best place in the country, however, to take an **underground gold-mining tour**, in a working mine, or learn to do gold panning. This attraction aside, there's no real reason to detour to Barberton as it is sadly devoid of the charms it once had.

Barberton Museum

36 Pilgrim St • ☎013 712 4208 • Daily 9am–4pm • Free

You can explore the mining history of the town at the **Barberton Museum**; housed in a well-designed, modern building, the museum has good displays on the gold-rush era. The museum can also provide a map of the town's **Heritage Walk**, on which green and white signposts direct you to some historical houses and monuments, including the worthwhile Belhaven House and Stopforth House (R20 entrance fee for both these).

BARBERTON MINING TOURS AND TRAILS

Barberton Odyssey (☎079 180 1488, ✉barbertontours@gmail.com) offers tours down three fascinating **historical gold mines**, for which you will be provided with the necessary gear (4hr, R380) and a guided tour to **Eureka City**, a mining ghost town 7km from Barberton in the Mountainland Nature Reserve. The company also offers a three-hour guided motor geo-trail (R700) along the beautiful old Bulembu Road with several stops of geological interest along the way. The area is a **UNESCO geological heritage sight** as the nearby Mahonjwa mountains have a global reputation for being the best preserved ancient rocks on earth – 3.5 billion years old – with fossils recording the earliest life forms on the planet.

ARRIVAL AND DEPARTURE

By minibus taxi There is no scheduled public transport to Barberton, though from Nelspruit you can take a minibus taxi (36km).

On to Swaziland The closest crossing into Swaziland is south from Barberton along the N40 to Bulembu (daily 8am–4pm); the road is poor and should be avoided in summer unless you're in a 4WD vehicle. A better route is to head northeast to the crossing at Jeppes Reef/Matsamo (daily 7am–8pm), with views en route of the impressive Maguga Dam.

INFORMATION

Tourist information Crown St (Mon–Fri 8am–5pm, Sat 8am–1pm; ☏013 712 2880, ⓦbarberton.co.za).

Activities and tours Barberton Odyssey (☏079 180 1488) offers a guided historical walk of Barberton (free, not including entry to museums or tips for the guide), as well as mining and geological tours.

ACCOMMODATION

Aloe Ridge Guest Farm 10km north of Barberton on the R38 ☏082 456 3442, ⓦaloeridgeguestfarm.com. Peaceful and reasonably priced accommodation on an organic farm, with excellent birdwatching opportunities. The three rooms in the main house and two cottages are all furnished with wooden furniture, with cotton bedding, and do not have television. Doubles R570, cottages R1000

Mazwita Bush Camp 17km towards Nelspruit on the R40 ☏082 604 1190, ⓦmazwita.com. A small game farm with thatched rondavels, wooden walkways and a pool. It's all set within lovely hilly surroundings where you can walk, cycle or drive to view plains game in the bush without predator dangers. R1900

EATING

Die PlaasKombuis 73 De Villiers St ☏084 608 2643 or ☏076 154 9629, ⓦbit.ly/Plaaskombuis. Popular restaurant with an adjoining plant nursery and art gallery – sit on a top-deck veranda overlooking the nursery for a lovely view while you enjoy a tortilla wrap with fillings of your choice (R60). Mon–Sat 8am–9pm.

Victorian Tea Garden Market Square, Crown St ☏013 712 4985, ⓦfacebook.com/barbertonteagarden. This pleasant tea garden and restaurant, situated within a large white gazebo next door to the tourist information office, serves cheap toasted sandwiches (R25) outdoors, as well as tea and desserts. Mon–Fri 8am–5pm, Sat 8am–2pm.

Kruger's western flank – the R40

The **R40** heads north from Nelspruit along the western border of Kruger National Park, passing through some prosperous tropical-fruit-growing farmlands around Hazyview, but for the most part through densely populated and very poor African areas, the biggest conglomeration of which is called Bushbuckridge. It's a fascinating slice of busy, rural South African life, in which tiny brick houses and shacks exist alongside much more prosperous dwellings. It makes a stark contrast to wild, protected Kruger – a reserve that the majority of people in the area have never had the means to enter.

The R40 yields access to the private game reserves – **Sabi Sands**, **Manyeleti** and **Timbavati** – as well as the Kruger Park gates of Numbi, Phabeni, Paul Kruger and Orpen. Though marked prominently on maps, **Klaserie**, which lies on the border of Mpumalanga and Limpopo Province, is easily missed, being little more than a petrol station and shop, surrounded by a number of private game farms.

Continuing northwards into Limpopo, you reach **Hoedspruit**, a shopping and service centre that is good for access to several large private game reserves and to Orpen Gate (69km away). Further north is the mining town of **Phalaborwa**, a convenient 2km from Phalaborwa Gate into central Kruger and the rewarding camps of Letaba and Olifants.

Hazyview

HAZYVIEW, 43km north of Nelspruit, is a service centre for Southern Kruger, with **Phabeni Gate** situated a mere 10km from town. It's the last town in which to stock up with anything you need before reaching the major Paul Kruger Gate into Skukuza, Kruger's "capital", as well as the entrance to the Sabi Sands Reserve. It is a centre too for surrounding farms, with large shopping centres and busy roadside market stalls

9

DRIVING THE R40

If you're driving the **R40**, take special care as the road has many potholes that can easily damage a wheel, as well as wandering goats and cattle, oblivious pedestrians and a hair-raising combination of minibus taxis tearing along and heavy trucks travelling between Phalaborwa Mine and Mozambique. Given the potential hazards, don't travel along this route in the dark, and allow for a slow journey – it's a very busy road, with only a single lane in each direction.

selling fruit and goods to the surrounding, densely populated African areas. The town is one of the best bases for visitors who want to stay outside the park and take part in some adventure **activities** and **tours**, as well as view game. Hazyview is spread out, but **Perry's Bridge**, on the corner of the R536 and R40, is a central stop-off with a small complex of luxury shops, craft outlets and restaurants.

The Skyway Trails

Perry's Bridge Trading Post • R480 • ☎ 082 825 0209 or ☎ 013 737 6747, ⍈ skywaytrails.com

The **aerial cable way**, Skyway Trails, offers three-hour jaunts above the trees, on which you glide from platform to platform over the valley, securely clipped to a stout cable. Helmets and harnesses are provided and the guides are capable and fun. No skills are needed, other than a degree of calmness and a head for heights, and children aged 6–10 can ride with a guide. You meet at *Gecko Lodge*, 3km along on the R536 from Hazyview, where you are kitted up and given a short lesson before being transported to the hilltop where the trail begins. Book in advance (R495).

The Elephant Sanctuary

5km from Hazyview on the R536 road to Sabie • Brush Down R725 • R1120 • ☎ 079 624 9436, ⍈ elephantsanctuary.co.za. Book elephant activities ahead on the website

The **Elephant Sanctuary** offers the opportunity to touch and feed two orphaned elephants rescued from a culling programme. There's a variety of programmes which provide close interaction with the elephants, including the "Brush Down", where you groom the animals and feel the texture of their skin and ears, and "Trunk in Hand", where you walk alongside them, lightly holding their trunks. There is also a more immersive, full-day experience on offer.

ARRIVAL AND DEPARTURE   HAZYVIEW

By car The shortest and quickest route here from Johannesburg, 421km away, is via the N4 and Nelspruit (53km south).

By minibus taxi The only form of public transport serving Hazyview is minibus taxis.

INFORMATION

Tourist information Big 5 Country Tourism, Perry's Bridge, R40 (Mon–Sat 8am–7pm, Sat 8am–6pm, Sun 9am–3pm; ☎ 013 737 8191, ⍈ tours-tickets.co.za), is the best information office in Mpumalanga, and able to book accommodation, safaris into Kruger Park, adventure activities and transfers; it also has a branch in Graskop (see p.524). It publishes the clearest map of the region and has its own activity booklets; it also covers the Escarpment. You can purchase tickets online for almost everything worth doing around Kruger and the Escarpment, from gold-panning in Barberton to ballooning, horseriding or visiting animal rehab centres. Staff also offer game drives and walks in the Sabi Sands private reserve, as well as in Kruger.

ACCOMMODATION

Guesthouses here are set mostly in farmland strung along the roads radiating out to the neighbouring towns of Sabie (the R536), Graskop (the R535) and White River (the R538), as well as to Kruger's Paul Kruger Gate (the R40).

Bohms Zeederberg Country House 17km from Hazyview, on the R536 ☎ 013 737 8101, ⍈ bohms.co.za.

Well-run B&B chalets with an old-fashioned feel, set in subtropical gardens around a swimming pool, with magnificent views and walking trails to the river below. Wheelchair-friendly. R1848

Gecko Backpackers 3km from Hazyview on the R536 ☎082 342 6598, ⓦbackpackers-gecko.co.za. Situated next to *Gecko Lodge* (see below), with a swimming pool, camping, dorms and doubles, plus a funky bar and home-cooked meals. Transfers to and from Nelspruit, and trips of varying length into Kruger Park and the Escarpment are also available. Camping R85, dorms R180, doubles R430

Gecko Lodge 3km from Hazyview on the R536 ☎013 590 1020, ⓦgeckolodge.co.za. Probably the nicest setting in Hazyview, with lush riverine vegetation and a stream running through the grounds. Rooms are decent and well priced, and there is an on-site pub as well as a restaurant. The lodge is also the starting point for the aerial cable trails. R1190

Idle and Wild 6km from Hazyview, on the R536 ☎013 737 8173 or ☎082 381 7408, ⓦidleandwild .co.za. This mango farm in a lush valley on the banks of the Sabie River offers two thatched rondavels, a cottage (sleeping up to four) and two honeymoon suites (with their own spa bath) in the lush garden, as well as two en-suite bedrooms in the main house. All have kitchenettes, and there's a jacuzzi, sauna and swimming pool. Quad biking and river rafting on-site. Rondavels R1060, cottages R1215, doubles R1060

Nkambeni Safari Camp Numbi Gate, 25km south of Hazyview ☎013 590 1011 or ☎021 910 1780, ⓦnkambeni.com; map p.539. A large, popular safari camp just inside the Kruger park boundaries, offering a no-frills game-viewing experience at reasonable prices. Accommodation is in pleasant safari tents with indoor and outdoor showers, though a bit too close together. Massive buffet meals are served in an open-air thatched dining room overlooking the bush and swimming pool. Day and sunset safaris are available, though you can also use it as a base for self-driving in Kruger. Rates include half board. R2080

Numbi Main Rd ☎013 737 7301, ⓦhotelnumbi.co.za. An old-fashioned, comfortable place, right in the centre, offering camping, garden suites and hotel rooms. The grounds are shady and the hotel's restaurant serves excellent steaks. Camping R250, doubles R2780

Rissington Inn 2km south of town, just off the R40 ☎013 737 7700 or ☎082 327 6842, ⓦrissington.co.za. Relaxed, well run and informal, this large thatched homestead has fourteen rooms. The best are the garden suites, which have roofless outside showers, so you feel as if you are in a bush-lodge. There's also a swimming pool, a bar and a good restaurant. R2200

EATING

Kuka Perry's Bridge Centre ☎013 737 6957, ⓦkuka soup.co.za. Smart Afro-chic restaurant and cocktail bar with colourful, modern decor and indoor and outdoor seating. As well as meat and game dishes, such as kudu (R165), there are also decent salads. Daily 7am–10pm.

Shangana Cultural Village 4km out of town on the R535 to Graskop ☎013 737 5804/5, ⓦshangana .co.za. Delicious African dinners (R510; booking essential) cooked in massive pots over an open fire. The menu might include crocodile in spicy peanut sauce and beef and honey-glazed sweet potato, but vegetarians are also well catered for. You eat in huts and are served by women from the household. The meals form the climax of a village tour and an energetic display of dancing, all of which is included in the price; a minimum of fifteen people is required. Daily 5pm.

Summerfields River Café 4.5km out of town on the R536 Sabie Rd ☎013 737 6500, ⓦsummerfields.co.za. Beauty, harmony and healthy living are offered at this spa and restaurant on a rose farm. Breakfast and light lunches are served outdoors on a wooden deck next to the Sabie River, with fresh organic vegetables and salads grown on the property, while dinners at their indoor venue, the *Kitchen*, feature the likes of roast duck with pickled kohlrabi and potato bake (R1500). River Café, Mon & Sun 8am–11am & noon–3pm; Kitchen, Tues–Sat 8–11am, noon–3pm & 6.30–9pm.

DRINKING

Hippo Hollow Restaurant Hippo Hollow Country Estate, Perry's Bridge Centre ☎013 737 7752 or ☎072 752 0952. Enjoy a sundowner, or a meal using local seasonal food, on the expansive deck overlooking the Sabie River, while watching birds, elephants and hippos. Daily 6.30–10pm.

Orpen Gate

After Hazyview, the R40 passes through Bushbuckridge – although any bushbucks that might once have wandered here have long since been eaten and displaced by cattle and goats. People live crammed in at a density six times greater than the provincial average, a leftover from apartheid land divisions. Forty-five kilometres east from here lies **Orpen Gate**, the road heading east to Satara into the centre of the Park. Orpen is also the access point for the Manyeleti and Timbavati private game reserves.

Timbavati Safari Lodge Orpen Gate Rd, 20km from Open Gate ☎015 793 0415, ⓦtimbavatisafarilodge .com. The pick of the places to stay in the vicinity with space for couples or large groups in thatched Ndebele-styled huts, plus a pool, bar and pleasant outdoor dining with wholesome, hearty dinners under the stars. It has an established feel with well-tended grounds full of trees and tropical vegetation, and a lawn kept cropped by resident warthogs. The lodge has traversing rights into Manyeleti for their own game drives; these are rich in game with very few vehicles around to share the sightings, and thus superior in many ways to going into Kruger itself. The good value for money makes it a popular base for self-drives into Kruger; prices include half board. The visits into the traditional African village across the road are also worthwhile. R1550

Hoedspruit

Lurking in the undulating lowveld, 153km north of Nelspruit, with the hazy blue mountains of the Escarpment visible on the distant horizon, is the small but busy service centre of **HOEDSPRUIT** ("hood-sprait"). The town lies at the heart of a concentration of **private game reserves** and lodges, and is a good base for specialist **activities**, such as horseriding, rafting on the Blyde River, visiting animal rehabilitation centres and lazy hot-air ballooning over the bush. Hoedspruit is a significant arrival point for air travellers heading to Kruger and the nearby private reserves, which include Timbavati, Manyeleti and Balule.

Moholoholo Wildlife Rehabilitation Centre

17km from Hoedspruit, on the R531 between the R40 and R527, about 3km from the tarred turn-off to the Blydepoort Dam • **Tours** Mon–Sat 9.30am & 3pm, and during school holidays Sun at 3pm • R145 • Booking essential • ☎ 015 795 5236, ⓦ moholoholo.co.za

At the **Moholoholo Wildlife Rehabilitation Centre**, ex-ranger Brian Jones has embarked on an individual crusade to rescue and rehabilitate injured and abandoned animals, notably raptors, but also lions, leopards and others. Tours are informative and you get to see a lot of endangered animals close up. The centre is part of a wider reserve and both night drives and early-morning walks are offered, and there is also accommodation (see opposite).

Monsoon Gallery

Along the R527, near its junction with the R36 • Daily 8am–4pm • Free • ☎ 084 250 1233, ⓦ bluecottages.co.za

The **Monsoon Gallery**, 29km northwest of Hoedspruit, makes a good place to pause on your journey. Its great African arts and crafts shop has an absorbing selection of authentic artefacts, including ironwork and woodcarving from Zimbabwe, superb

---

ACTIVITIES IN AND AROUND HOEDSPRUIT

Hot-air ballooning is a fabulous way to appreciate the surrounding landscape, and recommended flights are offered by Sun Catchers, based near Hoedspruit (☎087 806 2079 or ☎082 572 2223, ⓦsuncatchers.co.za; R3680). Conditions have to be perfect, and flights are generally very early in the morning when the weather is at its most stable. They leave from different locations depending on the weather – you'll be advised in good time where to meet your flight, and when to set your alarm clock!

   Horseriding is on offer in Hoedspruit itself, at the Hoedspruit Wildlife Estate, where both beginners and experienced riders can view the reserve's game – zebra, giraffe and antelope, among others. Book through African Dream Horse Safaris (☎084 582 5442, ⓦafricandream horsesafari.co.za; 1hr R350, 2hr R450).

   For experienced riders, Wait a Little Safaris (☎083 273 9788, ⓦwaitalittle.co.za) offers the unforgettable experience of horseriding through big game country. Running from their base in the Karongwe Nature Reserve, 70km north of Hoedspruit, their **Big Five horseriding safaris** range from six to ten days, on highly disciplined horses, with first-class accommodation and food; the trails also venture into Makali Reserve, dependent on date and package. Prices start at R30,000 per person.

tapestries from the Karosswerkers factory near Tzaneen, Venda pots and jewellery, plus silk items, and African music CDs and books.

ARRIVAL, DEPARTURE AND TOURS
HOEDSPRUIT

By plane Hoedspruit airport, Eastgate, 14km south of town, is served by two daily flights from Johannesburg and daily flights from Cape Town, some direct, some via Johannesburg; both routes are run by SA Express (☎011 978 1111, ⓦ flyexpress.aero) and ticket prices are expensive. Car rental is available at the airport through Avis (☎015 793 2014, ⓦ avis.co.za). For transfers to game lodges from the airport, contact Eastgate Safaris (☎015 793 3678 or ☎082 774 9544, ⓦ eastgatesafaris.co.za), though most lodges send their own vehicles to meet guests.

By shuttle Ashton's Tours and Safaris (☎021 683 0234, ⓦ ashtonstours.com) runs a daily shuttle (R815) from Johannesburg OR Tambo Airport (6.45am daily & 11am Tues, Thurs & Sun) to Hoedspruit, and will pick up within a 5km radius of OR Tambo. It drops off in town, at the airport, or at your safari lodge; the journey takes just under six hours.

Tours Eastgate Safaris (☎015 793 3678 or ☎082 774 9544, ⓦ eastgatesafaris.co.za) offers a number of tours in the area, including a full-day game drive in Kruger National Park (R2310 per person for min 2 people, the more people in the group the less the cost).

ACCOMMODATION

★**Blue Cottages Country House** 27km from Hoedspruit on the R527 ☎084 250 1233, ⓦ bluecottages.co.za. Comfortable suites in a farmhouse filled with African artefacts and fabrics, set in an enticingly cool and colourful tropical garden; more modest, but also lovely, are the garden cottages. You can have dinner served in the garden or on the veranda, if you book in advance, and the adjacent *Mad Dogz Café* is open for light meals from 8am–4pm daily. R1140

Marepe Country Lodge Orpen Rd, on the R531 ☎072 520 9636, ⓦ marepecountrylodge.co.za. B&B accommodation in chalets and hotel-style rooms in a peaceful garden setting, with swimming pool. Bird-watchers will love it here, as they offer several birding tours. There is also a licensed restaurant and bar. R785

Moholoholo Forest Camp 26km from Hoedspruit, on the R531 ☎013 795 5236, ⓦ moholoholo.co.za. In the foothills of the Drakensberg Escarpment, this is an unshowy safari camp with plenty of game on the property. The price includes meals, a night drive, morning walk and a tour to the nearby wildlife rehabilitation centre. R3897

Phalaborwa

PHALABORWA ("pal-a-bore-wa"), 74km north of Hoedspruit, gives access to the central and northern part of Kruger Park. The name Phalaborwa means "better than the south", a cheeky sobriquet coined as the town developed on the back of its extensive mineral wealth. During the 1960s, the borders of the park near Phalaborwa suddenly developed a kink, and large copper deposits were found, miraculously, just outside the protected national park area. Mining actually began at Phalaborwa some time after 200 AD, and the **Masorini Heritage Site**, close to Phalaborwa Gate, is a reconstruction of an iron-smelting village.

ARRIVAL AND DEPARTURE
PHALABORWA

By plane SA Airlink (☎015 781 5823, ⓦ flyairlink.com) flights arrive daily from Johannesburg (1hr) at Phalaborwa Airport, a 5min drive from Kruger's Phalaborwa Gate, off President Steyn St, and virtually in the town itself. Unfortunately, this is one of the most expensive flights in the country. There are a number of car rental firms represented at the airport, including Avis (☎015 781 3169); alternatively, arrange for your accommodation to pick you up.

By bus There are seven bus schedules running daily from Johannesburg to Phalaborwa (ⓦ busticket.co.za); the journey takes about 6hr.

INFORMATION

Tourist information Sure Turnkey Travel, 73a Sealene St (Mon–Fri 8am–5pm; ☎015 781 7760, ⓦ phalaborwa .co.za), can make bookings for Kruger and help with accommodation and car rental.

ACCOMMODATION

Bushveld Terrace Hotel & Guest Lodge 2 Hendrik van Eck St ☎015 781 3447, ⓦ bushveldterrace.co.za. Enjoy a luxury hotel room with patio and bush or pool view, or one of the elegantly furnished rooms in the guesthouse,

9

ACTIVITIES AROUND PHALABORWA

Keen **golfers** shouldn't miss the chance of a round at the signposted Hans Merensky Hotel & Spa, Copper Road (☎015 781 3931/7, ⓦhansmerensky.com), where it's not unusual to see giraffes and elephants sauntering across the fairways, built over a vast area of indigenous bush (18 holes; hotel guest R150, day visitor R400). The hotel provides luxurious accommodation (B&B R1250) and there are three restaurants on site offering a breakfast buffet, light lunches and dinner.

You can whet your appetite before heading into Kruger Park with a 3hr **boat trip** with Kambaku Olifants River Safaris (booking essential; ☎082 889 4797 or ☎073 986 3190, ⓦolifantsriversafaris.co.za), on the Olifants River, frequently encountering game – including elephants – and guaranteeing sightings of crocs and hippos (R329, 8–11am or 3–5.45pm). Kruger Park's own activities, run from **Phalaborwa Gate** (☎013 735 3547), are definitely worth doing and must be booked in advance; they include 3hr morning and night drives (R385) and full-day drives (R645) and bush walks (R490).

some with their own bush view. There is also a swimming pool and a next-door restaurant (see below). R1500

Daan & Zena's 15 Birkenhead St ☎076 559 8732, ⓦdaanzena.co.za. Brightly painted and friendly en-suite self-catering rooms located in three neighbouring houses, with a/c and TV in each room, and three swimming pools to choose from. Breakfast available for R70. R500

Elephant Walk 30 Anna Scheepers St ☎015 781 5860 or ☎082 495 0575, ⓦaccommodation-phalaborwa .co.za. A small and friendly backpackers in a pleasant suburban home with a large garden, 2km from the Kruger Gate, with camping facilities and budget tours into the park, plus a booking service for Phalaborwa/Kruger

activities. Besides dorms and twins, they have four en-suite garden rooms, and a swimming pool in the garden. Breakfast is available for R75, if booked prior to arrival. Camping R128, dorms R155, doubles R730

Kaia Tani Guest House 29 Boekenhout St ☎015 781 1358, ⓦkaiatani.com. Almost at the gate into Kruger, this upmarket and comfortable B&B guesthouse is run by an energetic Italian couple, Paolo and Barbra, who can meet you at the airport. There is a lounge with library, a bar overlooking a rock swimming pool, a tropical garden, and lunch or dinner from the kitchen can be ordered too – a mixture of Mediterranean and African dishes. R1380

EATING AND DRINKING

Buffalo Pub & Grill 1 Raas Blaar Ave ☎015 781 0829. Meat lovers will love this place. The house speciality, Eisbein, is especially good – smoked pork shank slow cooked with an apricot and parsley glaze (R120). Mon–Sat 11am–11pm, Sun 11am–8pm.

Bushveld Terrace Restaurant 2 Hendrik Van Eck St ☎015 781 3447, ⓦbushveldterrace.co.za. Excellent if expensive, food in an atmospheric garden setting; try the tasty chicken and prawn pasta (R100). Mon–Sa 11am–11pm.

Kruger National Park

KRUGER NATIONAL PARK is arguably the emblem of South African tourism, the destination that best delivers what most visitors to Africa want to see – scores of elephants, lions and a cast of thousands of other magnificent animals roaming the savanna. A narrow strip of land hugging the Mozambique border, Kruger stretches across Limpopo Province and Mpumalanga, an astonishing 414km drive from Pafuri Gate, close to the Zimbabwe border in the north to Malelane Gate in the south, all of it along tar, with many well-kept gravel roads looping off to provide routes for game drives.

Visiting Kruger (see box, p.540) invariably means choosing between self-driving (staying either in the park itself, or in one of the nearby towns), an organized safari tour or staying on an exclusive reserve. How you experience the park will largely depend on your budget – the cost of accommodation is extremely wide-ranging – but regardless of whether you are roughing it on a backpacker tour, or in your own luxury riverside suite, your experience of Kruger, and its animals, is bound to be highly memorable.

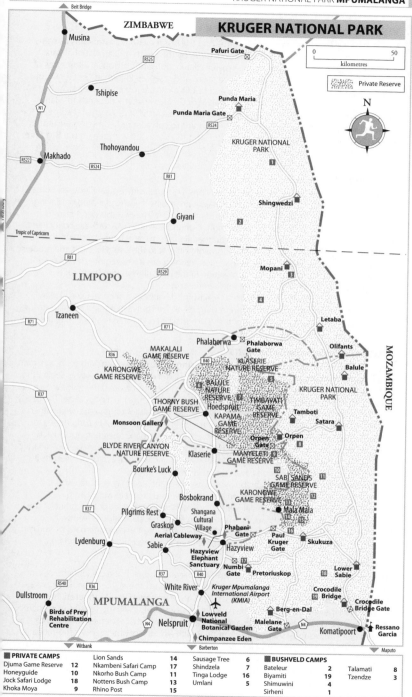

KRUGER NATIONAL PARK

ZIMBABWE

Belt Bridge

Musina

Pafuri Gate

R525

Tshipise

Punda Maria

N1

Punda Maria Gate
R524

KRUGER NATIONAL
PARK

Makhado

Thohoyandou

R522   R524   R81

Shingwedzi

Giyani

Tropic of Capricorn

R81

Mopani

LIMPOPO   R529

Tzaneen

R71   R71   Phalaborwa   Phalaborwa
Gate

Letaba

Olifants

MAKALALI
GAME RESERVE   R40   KLASERIE
NATURE RESERVE   Balule

R36   R37

KARONGWE
GAME RESERVE   BALULE
NATURE
RESERVE   KRUGER NATIONAL
PARK

THORNY BUSH
GAME RESERVE   Hoedspruit   TIMBAVATI
GAME
RESERVE   Tamboti

Monsoon Gallery   KAPAMA
GAME
RESERVE   Satara

BLYDE RIVER CANYON
NATURE RESERVE   Klaserie   Orpen
Gate   Orpen

MANYELETI
GAME RESERVE

Bourke's Luck   SABI SANDS
GAME RESERVE

KARONGWE
GAME RESERVE

Bosbokrand

Pilgrims Rest   Shangana
Cultural
Village   Mala Mala

Graskop   Phabeni
Gate   Paul
Kruger
Gate   Skukuza

Lydenburg   Aerial Cableway   Hazyview

Sabie   Hazyview
Elephant
Sanctuary   Numbi
Gate   Pretoriuskop   Lower
Sabie

Dullstroom   White River   Kruger Mpumalanga
International Airport
(KMIA)   Crocodile
Bridge   Crocodile
Bridge Gate

R540   R36   R37   R40

Birds of Prey
Rehabilitation
Centre   MPUMALANGA   Lowveld
National
Botanical Garden   Berg-en-Dal   Ressano
Garcia

Nelspruit   Malelane
Gate   N4   Komatipoort

Chimpanzee Eden   N4

Witbank   Barberton   Maputo

MOZAMBIQUE

N

0   50
kilometres

Private Reserve

■ PRIVATE CAMPS		Lion Sands	14	Sausage Tree	6	■ BUSHVELD CAMPS			
Djuma Game Reserve	12	Nkambeni Safari Camp	17	Shindzela	7	Bateleur	2	Talamati	8
Honeyguide	10	Nkorho Bush Camp	11	Tinga Lodge	16	Biyamiti	19	Tzendze	3
Jock Safari Lodge	18	Nottens Bush Camp	13	Umlani	5	Shimuwini	4		
Khoka Moya	9	Rhino Post	15			Sirheni	1		

9

VISITING KRUGER NATIONAL PARK

Kruger National Park, stretching for 414km along the border with Mozambique, remains South Africa's biggest wildlife draw. The park is run by the South African National Parks (SANParks; **w** sanparks.org), while on its western flank, thousands of square kilometres of land are divided into privately administered farms and reserves, known as Greater Kruger. As far as wildlife is concerned, the private and public areas are joined in an enormous, seamless whole. How you experience the park – or Greater Kruger – depends to a large extent on what you can afford; at the top end, expect exclusivity and a greater sense of the wilderness, while those on a tight budget may want to consider either a self-drive visit or an organized tour. Whatever you choose, don't get too obsessed with seeing the **Big Five** – wildlife-viewing always involves an element of luck, and the very experience of being in Kruger is undeniably exciting in itself.

GETTING TO THE PARK

Johannesburg has the best transport connections to Kruger, with regular flights and buses, as well as organized tours. It is also the best major entry point, if you're planning on driving yourself. If visiting from **Cape Town**, your best option is to fly the two-thousand-odd kilometres to get here – though prices are high as only one airline (SAA; **w** flyaaa.com) offers (daily) flights. A cheaper option is to take a budget flight from Cape Town to Johannesburg, rent a car from OR Tambo Airport and head straight off east to the park. Nelspruit, the modern capital of Mpumalanga, boasts the best transport connections in the region, and makes a good jumping-off point for the southern section of the park; flights arrive into Kruger Mpumalanga International (KMI), 20km north of the town.

The other airports serving the park are at Hoedspruit, Phalaborwa and Skukuza, all with expensive daily flights to and from Johannesburg (SA Airlink; **w** flyairlink.com) and all with car rental facilities. You might choose one of these airports if it is closest to the section of the park you wish to explore.

BUDGET AND MID-RANGE OPTIONS

Kruger is designed for **self-driving** and **self-catering**; if you're travelling with young children, on a budget, or want to manage your own time, this is likely to be the best way of seeing the park's animals. There are restaurants and shops at each of the camps, and the roads are a mix of tarred and dirt, making it possible to explore the whole of Kruger in a normal car. The park's popularity does mean that you are likely to share major animal sightings with several other motorists, some of whom may behave badly – hogging the sightings, or making noises to frighten the animals. A number of game drives are run by the park, operating out of each camp, which offer a greater chance of spotting the more elusive animals. On the plus side, it is very exciting when you are able to find animals yourself and watch them at your leisure. It's also possible to explore Kruger on a walking safari (see box, p.542).

Accommodation in the park can be over-subscribed, and you may want to consider staying in nearby Hazyview or close to an entry gate, where there are well-priced accommodation options, and then either driving into Kruger each day, or taking one of the organized game-drives. Another option is to stay in a backpackers' lodge in Nelspruit, Hazyview or Phalaborwa, all of which offer their own trips into the park; alternatively you can take a three-to-four-day trip with a tour operator from Johannesburg (see box, p.543).

LUXURY OPTIONS

With more to spend, choosing a private reserve in Greater Kruger is the obvious choice (and it's worth noting that some are more reasonably priced than others). The three major private reserves are **Sabi Sands** to the south (see p.549), and **Timbavati** and **Manyeleti**, both of which adjoin the central section of the national park (see p.549). With no tarred roads, and no self-driving, the private reserves offer a much greater sense of the wilderness, and you can be assured that you won't be sharing your sightings with a bunch of other cars. Accommodation is often in very romantic rooms or luxury "tents", overlooking the savanna or a river, and you'll be taken out on game drives in comfortable, open-topped 4WDs, with plenty of information and photo opportunities provided. Several of the luxury camps also cater for children, offering special kids' safaris and activities.

KRUGER FLORA AND FAUNA

Among the nearly 150 species of **mammals** seen in the park are cheetah, leopard, lion, spotted hyena, wild dog, black and white rhino, blue wildebeest, buffalo, Burchell's zebra, bushbuck, eland, elephant, giraffe, hippo, impala, kudu, mountain reedbuck, nyala, oribi, reedbuck, roan antelope, sable antelope, tsessebe, warthog and waterbuck. Rhino poaching remains an ongoing problem; despite many campaigns and plans of action, nothing seems to staunch the steady flow towards decimation, with at least two rhinos killed here every day.

The staggering 507 **bird species** include raptors, hefty-beaked hornbills, ostriches and countless colourful specimens. The **birders' "Big Six"** are the saddle-billed stork, kori bustard, martial eagle, lappet-faced vulture, Pel's fishing owl and ground hornbill. SanParks has a good birding page overviewing the different areas and species with details of bird hides (Ⓦ sanparks.org/groups/birders/accounts.php).

Keep your eyes open and you'll also see a variety of **reptiles**, **amphibians** and **insects** – most rewardingly in the grounds of the restcamps themselves: there's always something to see up the trees, in the bushes or even inside your rondavel. If you spot a miniature ET-like reptile crawling upside down on the ceiling, don't be tempted to kill it; it's an insect-eating gecko and is doing you a good turn. If, however, you have a horror of insects or frogs, stay away from Kruger in the rainy season (Nov–March).

Common among the three-hundred-plus **tree** species are the baobab, cluster fig, knobthorn, Natal mahogany, monkey orange, raisin bush, tamboti, coral tree, fever tree, jackalberry, leadwood, marula, mopane, lala palm and sausage tree.

Brief history

It's highly questionable whether Kruger National Park can be considered "a pristine wilderness", as it's frequently called, given that people have been living in or around it for thousands of years. **San hunter-gatherers** have left their mark in the form of paintings and engravings at 150 sites so far discovered, and there is evidence of farming cultures at many places in the park.

Around 1000–1300 AD, centrally organized states were building stone palaces and engaging in **trade** that brought Chinese porcelain, jewellery and cloth into the area, but it was the arrival of white **fortune-seekers** in the second half of the nineteenth century that made the greatest impact on the region. African farmers were kicked off their traditional lands in the early twentieth century to create the park, and hunters and poachers made their livelihoods here decimating game populations.

Paul Kruger, former president of the South African Republic, is usually credited with having the foresight to set aside land for wildlife conservation. Kruger figures as a shrewd, larger-than-life character in Afrikaner history, and it was **James Stevenson-Hamilton**, the first warden of the national park, who cunningly put forward Kruger's name in order to soften up Afrikaner opposition to the park's creation. In fact, Stevenson-Hamilton knew that Kruger was no conservationist and was actually an inveterate hunter; Kruger "never in his life thought of animals except as biltong", he wrote in a private letter, and it was his tenacity rather than Kruger's, that saved the animals that hadn't been shot.

The park was extended into Mozambique with the establishment of the Great Limpopo Transfrontier Park in 2000, and two border posts linking Kruger to Mozambique have been created, one right at the north of the park at Pafuri near *Punda Maria Camp*, the other at Giriyondo, between *Letaba* and *Mopani* camps.

ESSENTIALS   KRUGER NATIONAL PARK

Opening hours Daily: April, Aug & Sept 6am–6pm; May–July 6am–5.30pm; Oct & March 5.30am–6pm; Nov–Feb 5.30am–6.30pm.

Entry Fee R304 per day (SA residents R76).

Internet Available at *Berg-en-Dal* and *Skukuza*.

Petrol stations At all main restcamps (petrol and diesel); legitimate petrol/fuel/garage cards are accepted, as are Visa, Mastercard and cash.

9

ARRIVAL AND DEPARTURE

Johannesburg is the city with the best connections to Kruger, by both land and air. An easy option if you are flying in or ou of Johannesburg is to see the park as part of a tour that starts and ends in the city (see box opposite). Alternatively, rent car at the airport for the easy five-hour drive to the park; the airport is on the N4 motorway to Kruger.

By plane The four local airports servicing Kruger are KMI (see p.528) for the southern section; Skukuza (see p.546) in the park itself; Hoedspruit (see p.537) for the central and northern sections; and Phalaborwa (see p.537) for the northern section. Car rental is available at each airport, or you will be picked up by your safari lodge. Unfortunately, flights to airports near Kruger are pricey; all are operated

by SA Airlink (◌ flyairlink.com), SA Express (◌ flyexpre .aero) and CemAir (◌ flycemair.co.za)

By bus Regular buses service Nelspruit, Hoedspruit an Phalaborwa from Johannesburg; from these towns, you ca book on one of the many Kruger tours on offer at th backpacker lodges: the *Old Vic Inn* and *Funky Monkeys* Nelspruit and *Elephant Walk* in Phalaborwa can arrange tou

---

BUSH WALKS, GAME DRIVES AND WALKING TRAILS

Whether you're staying in Kruger or not, you can still join one of the early morning, mid-morning, sunset or night **game drives** organized by the park (R280–390). These drives are one of the cheapest ways of accessing the park, but the viewing is good because of the height of the open vehicles. The drives leave from every camp in the park (book at reception or, even better, when you make your reservation) and, for those staying outside the park, from these entrance gates: Crocodile Bridge (☎ 013 735 6012), Malelane (☎ 013 735 6152), Numbi (☎ 013 735 5133), Paul Kruger (☎ 013 735 5107), Phabeni (☎ 013 735 5890) and Phalaborwa (☎ 013 735 3457).

For those staying inside the park, three-hour **game walks** (R575) are conducted every morning at dawn from each camp. Groups are restricted to eight people, so it's worth booking beforehand. Kruger also runs several three-night **wilderness trails** in different parts of the park. Undertaken under the guidance of an experienced ranger, these trails pass through landscapes of notable beauty with diverse plant and animal life. They don't bring you any nearer to game than driving, and are really about getting closer to the vegetation and smaller creatures. Groups are limited to eight people staying in the same camp, comprising four rustic, two-bed huts, served by reed-walled showers and flush toilets; simple meals are provided. You walk for five hours in the morning, return to camp for lunch and a siesta, and go walking again for an hour or two in the evening, returning to sit around a campfire. The trails are heavily subscribed; you can **book** up to eleven months in advance through SANParks (✉ specialisedreservations@sanparks.org). The cost is around R4500 per person, including accommodation and meals.

In addition, there are three **backpacking trails** where you carry your own stuff on a guided, three-night walk (R2700): the Olifants River Trail, following the course of the Olifants River; the Lonely Bull Trail, which leaves from *Mopani*; and the Mphongolo Trail leaving from *Shingwedzi*. These trails offer one of the ultimate adventure wildlife experiences in Africa – sleeping out in the wild every night with no facilities.

More expensive, and easier to get a booking on, are the two- or three-night walking safaris in a magnificently wild concession near Skukuza, run by Rhino Post Walking Safaris (3 nights R13,790; ◌ isibindiafrica.co.za) with Plains Camp as its base (see p.551). These have the option of a sleep-out in a treehouse, where you spend the night cosily bedded on an elevated platform, able to see the stars and hear the sometimes chilling sounds of the night. Of the same calibre is Jock's Safaris (see p.551), which offers a luxury walking and camping experience, deep in the Kruger Park (R5405 per person per night).

There are also a number of cheaper walking trails within Greater Kruger, accessed from Hoedspruit and with organized departures from Johannesburg. Transfrontiers (☎ 015 793 0719, ◌ transfrontiers.com) offers four-night walking safaris for R7500, using a camp in Balule, where the Big Five roam; accommodation is in safari tents or chalets. Another recommended operator is Africa on Foot (☎ 021 712 5284, ◌ africaonfoot.com), which runs a combination of walking and driving trails in the Klaserie area, adjoining the Timbavati Reserve (R3295 per person per night). This area is wild and lovely, and their safari camp very pleasant; you walk for two to four hours in the morning, and enjoy game drives in the afternoons and evenings – the combination of safaris should allow you to see more game.

DRIVING IN KRUGER

When driving, only approved roads should be used; don't drive on unmarked roads and never drive off-road. In heavy rainfall some roads become unusable; check ⓦ sanparks.org/parks/kruger for the latest information. Do buy a Kruger map showing all the marked roads. Roads have numbers rather than names; some are tarred, some are dirt. Speed limits are 50km/hr on tar, 40km/hr on untarred roads and 20km/hr in restcamps; speed traps operate in some parts of the park. Never leave your car (it's illegal and dangerous), except at designated sites. If you're trying to get from one part of the park to another, note that although it's far more fun driving inside, the **speed limit** makes it a slow journey – the rule of thumb is to estimate that you will be driving at 25km/h between camps – and you're bound to make frequent stops to watch animals. Bicycles and motorbikes are not allowed.

CHOOSING YOUR ROUTE

The public part of Kruger can be roughly subdivided into three sections, each with a distinct character and terrain of its own. If your time is limited, it's best to choose just one or two areas to explore, but if you're staying for five days or more, consider driving the length of the park slowly, savouring the subtle changes in landscape along the way. The southern, central and northern sections are sometimes referred to as "the circus", "the zoo" and "the wilderness" – sobriquets that carry more than a germ of truth. Each camp is like a small village within a vast area, with *Skukuza* in the south the largest.

Southern Kruger The south has the greatest concentration of game, attracts the highest number of visitors, and is the most easily accessible part of the park if you're coming from Johannesburg.

Central Kruger The central areas offer excellent game viewing, as well as two of the most attractive camps in the park at *Olifants* and *Letaba*.

Northern Kruger The north has fewer animals, being drier and flatter, but an increased sense of wilderness, especially at *Punda Maria* camp and the lovely Pafuri River area. It is probably best for your second visit to Kruger.

WHEN TO VISIT

Kruger is rewarding at any time of the year, though each season has its advantages and drawbacks. If you don't like the heat, avoid **high summer** (Dec–Feb), when temperatures are in the mid- to high thirties, with short thunder showers; a lot of the accommodation is air-conditioned, however. At this time of the year, everything becomes green, the grass is high,

KRUGER TOUR OPERATORS

There are many **tours** to Kruger, several of which depart from Johannesburg. Prices given below are per person unless otherwise noted, and most include park entry fees, meals and transport to and from Johannesburg. Backpacker hostels in Nelspruit, Hazyview and Phalaborwa also run tours into Kruger at reasonable prices. In addition, in the Nelspruit and Hazyview area are some excellent tour guides who will take you into the Park, or organize trips in Mpumalanga. When choosing a tour from Johannesburg, a minimum of three nights (ideally four) is advisable to allow for the long journey time (six to seven hours to get from Joburg into the park), more opportunities to view game, and more drives.

★**Nguni Africa** ☎082 221 4177, ⓦnguniafrica .co.za. An extremely knowledgeable and personable guide, Andrew Hall is based in Nelspruit and can put together a package for you to see Kruger, and beyond if necessary. He has a great passion for the lowveld, where his ancestors were pioneers, and runs trips into the park in a Land Rover, where you'll be assured of spotting plenty of game, even on a day-trip (from R6800 including meals and fees); the exclusivity of the experience, rather than being in a vehicle with several strangers, is an attractive bonus. He also offers airport or lodge transfers.

Outlook African Wildlife Safaris ☎079 473 2443, ⓦoutlook.co.za. A number of options departing from Joburg, where they have a nice guesthouse not far from the airport that's ideal for before and after your safari. Options include camping in Kruger (4 days/3 nights R6360) or a combo of Kruger and private game lodge (two nights camping in Kruger and one night in a Lodge; R13,725).

Viva Safaris ☎071 842 5547, ⓦvivasafaris.com. Departing from Joburg, and geared towards a price-conscious market, Viva's trips offer all you might want from a Kruger experience (and include a stop at Blyde River Canyon, too). Of the different packages they offer, the most attractive is one night in *Tremisana Bush Lodge* in Balule, where there is plenty of game, and two nights at *Marc's Camp*, which gives you a more rustic, closer-to-nature bush experience, though there are fewer animals (3 nights R15,790).

9

animals are born and birds and insects are prolific. There's little rain during the **cooler winter** months of April to August; the vegetation withers over this period, making it easier to spot game. Although daytime temperatures rise to the mid-twenties (days are invariably bright and sunny throughout winter), the nights and early mornings can be very cold, especially in June and July, when you'll definitely need a very warm jacket and woolly hat. **September and October** are the peak months for wildlife viewing.

ACCOMMODATION

At most of the fourteen main **restcamps** inside Kruger, the sounds of the African night tend to get drowned out by air conditioning and the merriment of braais and beer. Nearly all camps have swimming pools, electricity, petrol stations, shops (though they don't stock much in the way of fruit or vegetables), restaurants and laundrettes. The restcamps are pleasant, but hardly wild, with walks around the edges, labelled trees to help you identify what you see on drives, and plenty of birds and smaller creatures around the camps themselves. You'll find thatched rondavels, each with an outdoor eating area, facing communally towards each other rather than out towards the views. The best rondavels are on the camp perimeters or directly facing onto rivers.

GAME VIEWING AND PICNIC SITES IN SOUTHERN KRUGER

GAME VIEWING

Berg-en-Dal The focus of the camp is the Rhino Trail along the perimeter fence (with Braille facilities), meandering under riverine trees along the Matjulu dam, where there are resident crocodiles and nesting fish eagles. Game includes white rhino, leopards and lions, and plenty of kudu. Some say this is the best camp from which to set out on a guided morning walk because of the likelihood of encountering white rhino, and the pretty scenery.

Crocodile Bridge Try the tarred H4 north and dirt S25 east for elephant, rhino and buffalo. For cheetah, among the best places are the open plains along the S28 Nhola Road. If you're pushing north to *Lower Sabie*, it's worth taking the drive slowly, as this area, dotted with knobthorn and marula trees, is known for its herbivores, which include giraffe, wildebeest, zebra and buffalo, as well as ostrich, warthog and the magnificent black sable antelope. You should also keep your eyes peeled for predators such as lion, cheetah, hyena and jackal.

Lake Panic Only a twenty-minute drive (7km) from *Skukuza* (see p.546), Lake Panic has one of the best bird hides in the park, where you'll see herons, kingfishers, ducks, geese, dikkop and African jacanas, as well as hippos and crocodiles.

Lower Sabie The must-drive roads here include the H10 for lion and cheetah, the S130 for white rhino and the H4-1 for leopard. Sunset Dam, just outside *Lower Sabie*, is a favourite sunset spot, where you can get really close to the water, and is worthwhile at any time of day.

Pretoriuskop A decent focus for a day drive is Transport Dam, on the H1-1, a good place to see buffalo and elephant, and there's invariably other game to be found.

Skukuza Most people drive along the Sabie River to *Lower Sabie*, on the H4, one of the best places to see game. The tangled riverine forest, flanked by acacia bush and mixed savanna, is the most fertile and varied in the park. Another great drive is northeast on the H1–2 to Tshokwane picnic site, stopping at Elephant, Jones, Leeupan and Siloweni water holes. The area around *Skukuza* is also one of the best places to see endangered African wild dogs; worth trying is the S114 between *Skukuza* and *Berg-en-Dal*, the S1 between Phabeni Gate and *Skukuza*, and the H11 between Paul Kruger Gate and *Skukuza*.

PICNIC SITES

One of the park's nicest picnic sites is at **Afsaal**, between *Berg-en-Dal* and *Skukuza* on the H3, a good focus for a day drive. Once here, look out for the African scops owl, which sleeps in a tamboti tree nearly every day – the tree is marked so that you can try to spot the camouflaged bird. There's a shop on-site.

Another top picnic spot is **Mlondozi**, north of *Lower Sabie* on the S29, which overlooks a dam from a thatched *lapa*, with some tables and chairs under trees. **Tshokwane** picnic site, 40km north of *Lower Sabie* on the H10, is much busier, but you can buy meals here.

TOP 5 ACTIVITIES

Kruger has, unsurprisingly, an abundance of activities that will make your time in the park memorable. Here's our pick of the very best on offer.

Rhino gazing at Pretoriuskop With over eleven thousand living in the area around the camp, this is a particularly fabulous place from which to spot both white and black rhinos. See p.546

Rhino Post Walking Safaris Head out into the wild on foot on a two- or three-day walking safari, with the option of sleeping in a treehouse. See p.551

Wildlife viewing at Sunset Dam, Lower Sabie Get close to the water for some prime hippo and crocodile spotting – great at any time of the day. See box opposite.

Birdwatching at Pafuri picnic site Northern Kruger at its best, with massive thorn trees and the Luvuvhu River making this the park's top birding spot. See box, p.548

Leopard-spotting in the Sabi Sands Undoubtedly one of the best places in the world to see leopards in the wild, helpfully close to the well-connected town of Nelspruit. See p.549

Just about all restcamps have a campsite (with shared kitchen and washing facilities), which provides the park's cheapest accommodation, but the stands are generally very close together, and you may not get shade. Sites for caravans and camper vans are available wherever there's camping and often have a power point. Most camps have furnished permanent safari tents and huts in configurations usually sleeping two to four people. These are fully equipped, with shared communal kitchens and ablutions. Bungalows and cottages sleep up to six people and come in several variations, with fully equipped kitchens and bathrooms. For a more rustic experience, head out to one of the handful of **bushveld camps** away from day-to-day trivialities and the tourist pack. The bushveld camps have accommodation of the same standard as the main restcamps, but accommodate fewer people, and are far smaller. They dispense with shops and restaurants, but are within reasonable reach of the restcamps. Kruger's restcamps and bushveld camps are administered by SANParks (☎ 012 428 9111 or ☎ 082 233 9111, ⓦ sanparks.org/tourism/reservations) – **bookings** can only be made in advance online, by email or telephone. Advance bookings are a necessity – book as early as possible, especially for school holidays and weekends, and don't turn up without a booking and expect to find accommodation. Even with advance booking, anticipate that you will most likely have to take any camp that is available, as demand far outstrips supply. Booking opens eleven months in advance.

SOUTHERN KRUGER RESTCAMPS

The so-called circus is the busiest section of the Kruger, with its hub at *Skukuza*, the biggest of all the Kruger camps, and *Lower Sabie*, one of the most popular. Apart from containing some of the best places for seeing large quantities of game, southern Kruger is also easily reached from Johannesburg along the N4. At peak times of year, the area buzzes with vehicles jostling to get up close anywhere that big cats are sighted – events which always seem to induce bad human behaviour. As with all restcamps in Kruger, book in advance with SANParks (☎ 012 428 9111 or ☎ 082 233 9111, Mon–Fri 7.30am–5pm, Sat 8am–3pm, ⓦ sanparks.org).

Berg-en-Dal In the southwest corner of the park, 12km northwest of Malelane Gate ☎ 013 735 6106/7. Attractively set among *koppies* in a shallow grassy basin, *Berg-en-Dal* overlooks the Matjulu stream and dam, and has modern, fully equipped bungalows sleeping three people, or family cottages sleeping six, all landscaped among indigenous bushveld vegetation and widely spaced to provide privacy. Facilities include a beautifully positioned swimming pool, a shop with a good range of food, restaurants, a petrol station and a laundry. The area is known for rhinos. Camping R330, bungalows R1450, cottages R2490

Crocodile Bridge 12km north of Komatiport on N4 ☎ 013 735 6012. The least impressive of Kruger's restcamps – its position at the very southern edge of the park, overlooking sugar-cane farms, does nothing to enhance your bush experience. However, old hands say this is a tremendously underrated camp as there is a high density of general game, and you have an excellent chance of seeing the Big Five. Moreover, it is quiet and has a lovely campsite with plenty of big trees for shade. Accommodation includes camping, two-bed permanent tents and en-suite bungalows sleeping two to three, with cooking facilities. Amenities are limited to a laundry and filling station, and a shop selling basic supplies. Camping R330, tents R640, bungalows R1450

★**Lower Sabie** 35km north of Crocodile Bridge ☎ 013 735 6056/6057. Usually fully booked, *Lower Sabie* occupies game-rich country, with an outlook over the Sabie River, which places it among the top three restcamps in the Kruger for spotting animals. One of its biggest attractions is the large wooden viewing deck

9

> ## GAME VIEWING AND PICNIC SITES IN CENTRAL KRUGER
>
> **N'wanetsi River Road** One of the best-known drives in the park is along the S100, with a stop at N'wanetsi Picnic Site, and beautiful scenery of riverine trees and open acacia savanna. It passes through a variety of terrain, which, besides being scenic, means it attracts large herds of buffalo, giraffe, zebra, wildebeest, kudu and waterbuck and, in their wake, big cats. The S100 is one of the best roads to try to find lions.
>
> **Satara** Rewarding drives are the Timbavati River Road (S39) and the drive east of *Satara* along the S100, which snakes along the N'wanetsi River towards the Lebombo Mountains, marking the border with Mozambique.
>
> **Tshokwane picnic site** About halfway along the tarred road between *Satara* and *Skukuza*, the area around this picnic site can be good for lions, hence the number of motorists usually present.

outside the restaurant (open to day visitors) where you can have a snack while often watching elephants crossing the river in front of you. Accommodation includes camping, luxury safari tents, bungalows and guest cottages, some with river views. There's a *Mugg & Bean* restaurant, a shop, a swimming pool, a filling station and a laundry. Camping R330, tents R1600, rondavels R640, bungalows R1400, cottages R2490

Pretoriuskop 9km east of Numbi Gate ☎013 735 5128/5132. The area surrounding Pretoriuskop is good for predators. However, given the dense bush, game viewing can be disappointing, and you may only see larger species such as kudu and giraffe. Accommodation here consists of en-suite cottages and guesthouses, bungalows and cheaper huts, and camping with shared ablution and cooking facilities. The camp has a *Wimpy* restaurant, a snack bar, a shop, a laundry, a semi-natural rock swimming pool – one of the most beautiful in Kruger, with a surrounding garden and picnic area – and a petrol station. Around the perimeter fence at night, you're almost certain to see patrolling hyenas, waiting for scraps from braais. One feature of the camp is the tame impala that wander freely around. Camping R330, huts R640, bungalows R1415, cottages R2490

Skukuza 12km east of Paul Kruger Gate ☎013 735 4265/4196. Kruger's largest restcamp accommodates over a thousand people and lies at the centre of the best game-viewing area in the park. Its position is a mixed blessing; although you get large amounts of game, hordes of humans aren't far behind, and cars speeding at animal sightings can chase away the very animals they are trying to see. Accommodation is in a range of en-suite guesthouses, cottages and bungalows, or more cheaply in huts, safari tents and campsites, with shared ablutions and kitchens. *Skukuza* is the hub of Kruger; with its own airport (SA Airlink, private airlines and charters) and car-rental agency, and its sprawling collection of rondavels and tent village, it resembles a small town and all the cars can be irksome. There are two swimming pools, and a deli café with internet facilities, plus a post office, a bank, a petrol station and garage, a *Cattle Baron & Bistro* steakhouse and

a really good library (Mon–Fri 8.30am–4pm & 7–9pm, Sat 8.30am–12.45pm, 1.45–4pm & 7–9pm, Sun 8.30am–12.45pm & 1.45–4pm) with a collection of natural history books and exhibits. Golf at *Skukuza* is also a draw, where you'll have to sign an indemnity form in case of bumping into wildlife on the course. There is a special area designated for day visitors, with its own swimming pool and picnic area. Camping R330, tents R640, bungalows R1400, cottages R2490

CENTRAL KRUGER RESTCAMPS

Game viewing can be extremely good in the "zoo", the rough triangle between *Orpen*, *Satara* and *Letaba*, which is reckoned to be one of the global hot spots for lions. At *Olifants* you'll find the Kruger's most dramatically located camp, with fantastic views into a river gorge, while *Satara* is one of the most popular – its placement is ideal for making sorties into fertile wildlife country. It is estimated that there are about sixty lion prides in this central area, but, even so, you may not be lucky enough to see one. As with all restcamps in Kruger, book in advance with SANParks (☎012 428 9111, ✆sanparks .org/parks/kruger).

Balule On the southern bank of the Olifants River, 41km north of Satara and 87km from Phalaborwa Gate ☎013 735 6606/7. A very basic satellite to *Olifants* (11km to the north), *Balule* is one of the few restcamps where two can stay for R500 without resorting to camping. The restcamp has two sections, one consisting of six rustic three-bed rondavels and another of fifteen camping and caravan sites. Each section has its own communal ablution and cooking facilities. You can forget about a/c; the only electricity is in the fence to keep out lions, and paraffin lamps are provided for lighting. Guests have to bring their own crockery, cutlery and utensils, and must report to Satara or Olifants at least half an hour before the gates close. Camping R330, rondavels R475

Letaba 52km east of Phalaborwa Gate ☎013 73 6636/7. *Letaba* is set in *mopane* shrubland along the Letaba River. Old and quite large, the camp is beautifully located on an oxbow curve, and though very few of the rondavels afford a view, the restaurant does have great vistas; you can spend a day just watching herds of buffalo mooching around, elephants drifting past and a host of other plains game. There is a full range of accommodation and the camp offers the usual shopping and laundry facilities, a *Mugg & Bean* restaurant, a swimming pool, a vehicle-repair workshop, and an interesting museum, Elephant Hall, with exhibits on the life of elephants, including a display on the Magnificent Seven, bulls with inordinately large tusks that once roamed the area, with six pairs of their tusks on display. Camping R330, tents R640, rondavels R790, bungalows R1400, cottages R2490

Olifants 80km east of Phalaborwa Gate ☎013 735 6606/7. With a terrific setting on cliffs overlooking the braided Olifants River, *Olifants* is reckoned by many to be the best restcamp in Kruger. It's possible to spend hours sitting on the benches on the covered look-out terrace, gazing into the valley whose airspace is crisscrossed by Bateleur eagles and yellow-billed kites cruising the thermals, while the rushing of the water below creates a hypnotic rhythm. You can eat at the *Mugg & Bean* restaurant, and there's a shop and a laundry. This is also promising country for spotting elephant, giraffe, lion, hyena and cheetah, and you should look out for the tiny klipspringer, a pretty antelope that inhabits rocky terrain, which it nimbly negotiates by boulder-hopping. Bungalows R1650, cottages R2360

Orpen and **Maroela** Right by Orpen Gate, 45km east of Klaserie ☎013 735 6355. Recommended mainly if you're arriving late and don't have time to get further into the park before the camp gates close. However, *Orpen* is very good for game viewing, because the substantial Timbavati Private Game Reserve lies to the west, so you're already well into the wilderness once you get here. There's a water hole right in front of the camp, and animals come and go all the time. The camp is small, peaceful and shaded by beautiful trees; facilities include a petrol station, a shop and a swimming pool overlooking a water hole, and accommodation is in bungalows and en-suite guest cottages, with communal kitchens. If you want to camp, you'll need to go to the small *Maroela* satellite camping area, overlooking the Timbavati River, approximately 4km from *Orpen*. You must report to *Orpen* reception to check in before going to the campsite, which has electricity. Camping R330, bungalows R1360, cottages R2490

★**Satara** 46km due east of Orpen Gate ☎013 735 6306/7. *Satara* ranks second only to *Skukuza* (92km to the south) in size and the excellence of its game viewing. Set in the middle of flat grasslands, the camp commands no great views, but is preferable to *Skukuza* because it avoids the feeling of suburban boxes on top of each other. Very busy in season, accommodation ranges from camping, through bungalows and cottages arranged around lawned areas shaded by large trees, to secluded guesthouses; besides a shop, petrol station, laundry and an AA vehicle repair workshop, there's also a swimming pool, pizzeria and café. *Satara* itself is usually good for sighting grazers such as buffalo, wildebeest, zebra, kudu, impala and elephant; the night drives are particularly recommended. Camping R330, bungalows R1455, cottages R2490

Tamboti Turn left 2km after Orpen and continue for 1km ☎013 735 6355. Not far from Orpen Gate, *Tamboti* is Kruger's only tented camp. You sleep in tents in a tranquil position on the banks of the frequently dry Timbavati River, set among apple leaf trees, sycamore figs and jackalberries. From the tents, elephants can often be

GAME-VIEWING TIPS

- The best times of day for game viewing are when it's cooler, during the early morning and late afternoon. Set out as soon as the camp gates open in the morning and go out again as the temperature starts dropping in the afternoon. Take a siesta during the midday heat, just as the animals do, when they head for deep shade where you're less likely to see them.
- It's worth investing in a detailed **map of Kruger** (available at virtually every restcamp) in order to choose a route that includes rivers or pans where you can stop and enjoy the scenery and birdlife while you wait for game to come down to drink, especially in the late afternoon.
- **Driving really slowly** pays off, particularly if you stop often, in which case switch off your engine, open your window and use your senses. Stopping where other cars have already stopped or slowed down is probably the best strategy you could choose.
- Don't embark on overambitious drives from your restcamp. Plan carefully.
- **Binoculars** are a must for scanning the horizon.
- Take **food and drink** with you, and remember you can only use toilets and get out at the **picnic sites**, where there's always boiling water available, braai places powered with gas, and, at some sites, food or snacks for sale.

9

seen just beyond the electrified fence, digging in the riverbed for moisture, hence the camp's popularity. Each walk-in tent has its own deck overlooking the river, but best of all are numbers 21 and 22, which enjoy the deep shade of large riverine trees, something you'll appreciate in the midsummer heat. The tents have fridges and electric lighting, while all kitchen, washing and toilet facilities are in two shared central blocks (bring your own cooking and eating utensils). R640

NORTHERN KRUGER RESTCAMPS

You won't find edge-to-edge game in the northern section, the least visited of Kruger's regions, but you do get a much stronger feeling here of being in the wilds, particularly after you've crossed the Tropic of Capricorn north of *Mopani* camp and hit *Punda Maria* camp, which still has the flavour of an old-time outpost in the bush. As with all restcamps in Kruger, book in advance with SANParks (☎ 012 428 9111, ⓦ sanparks.org/parks/kruger/).

Mopani 42km north of Letaba ☎ 013 735 6535/6. *Mopani* overlooks the Pioneer Dam, one of the few water sources in the vicinity, which attracts animals to drink and provides an outstanding lookout for a variety of wildlife, including elephant, buffalo and antelope. This is a sprawling place in the middle of monotonous *mopane* scrub, with en-suite accommodation built of rough-hewn stone and thatch, and a restaurant and a bar with a good view across to the dam. Other facilities include a shop, a laundry and a petrol station; the swimming pool, one of the best in the park, provides cool relief after a long drive. Bungalows R1450, cottages R1450

★**Punda Maria** 71km beyond Shingwedzi ☎ 013 735 6873. Kruger's northernmost camp is a relaxed, tropical outpost near the Zimbabwe border. It is the least-visited camp and is unpretentious and peaceful. There's less of a concentration of game up here, but this isn't to say you won't see wildlife (the Big Five all breeze through from time to time). The real rewards of *Punda* are in its landscapes and stunningly varied vegetation, with a remarkable nine biomes all converging here, which also makes it a paradise for

birdwatchers, notably along the Pafuri River. The landscape around *Punda* has many craggy sandstone cliffs, the hilltops crowned with giant baobabs, some as old as 4000 years. Accommodation is camping, in safari tents with communal cooking and ablution areas, or en-suite fully equipped bungalows. The camp has a restaurant, a small shop, a petrol station, a swimming pool and a bird hide. Camping R330, bungalows R1020, tents R1045, cottages R2450

Shingwedzi 63km north of Mopani ☎ 013 735 6806/7. A fairly large camp featuring a campsite, square, safari tents, brick huts and a few older, colonial-style whitewashed, thatched bungalows, as well as a cottage and a guesthouse, sited in extensive grounds shaded by *pals* and *mopane* trees. From the terrace you get a long view down across the usually dry Shingwedzi River. Look out for the weavers' nests with their long, tube-like entrances hanging from the eaves outside reception. Camping R330, huts R570, bungalows R1270, cottages R1850

BUSHVELD CAMPS

If you want to stay at a bushveld camp, book as early as possible, as demand for the bush experience they offer is pretty high. Note that the camps are out of bounds to anyone not booked in to stay. Most offer walks, night drives and hides. As with all camps in Kruger, book in advance with SANParks (☎ 012 428 9111, ⓦ sanparks .org/parks/kruger/).

★**Bateleur** About 40km southwest of Shingwedzi restcamp ☎ 013 735 6843; map p.539. Off the beaten track, in the remote northern section of the park on the banks of the frequently dry Mashokwe stream. The camp has a timber viewing deck, excellently placed for views of game coming to drink at a seasonally full water hole. The nearby Silver Fish and Rooibosrand dams also attract game, as well as birdlife in prodigious quantities. There are ten cottages; each has its own kitchenette and fridge, with electricity provided by solar panels. R2360

★**Biyamiti** 41km northeast of the Malelane Gate and 26km west of Crocodile Bridge Gate ☎ 013 735 6171; map p.539. *Biyamiti* lies on the banks of the Mbiyami

---

GAME VIEWING AND PICNIC SITES IN NORTHERN KRUGER

Red Rocks Loop The S52 southwest of Shingwedzi is a favoured road for elephant sightings; if you drive it in the early morning, look out for leopards.

★**Pafuri picnic site** 46km north of *Punda*. This picnic site should on no account be missed, as it's here that you'll experience the true richness of northern Kruger, and it is rated as the top birding spot in the park. The site is a large area under the shade of massive thorn trees, leadwoods and jackalberry trees on the banks of the Luvuvhu River and is the ultimate place for lunch. An interpretation board gives a fascinating account of human history in the area. There are braai facilities, a constantly boiling kettle to make your own tea, and the attendant can sell you ice-cold canned drinks.

iver; its proximity is one of the main advantages of this ery southerly camp, and the surrounding terrain attracts arge numbers of game including lion, elephant and rhino. here are twenty cottages, all with fully equipped itchens. **R3000**

himuwini About 50km from the Phalaborwa Gate on he Mooiplaas Rd ☎013 735 6683; map p.539. *himuwini* lies on the upper reaches of the Shimuwini Dam, which is filled by the Letaba River. Situated in *mopane* and ushwillow country, with sycamore figs along the banks of he river, this peaceful camp is not known for its game but ; a perennial favourite among birdwatchers. It's an xcellent place for spotting riverine bird species, including sh eagles. Accommodation is in fifteen cottages (nine of which are especially nice). **R2360**

irheni Roughly 54km south of Punda Maria ☎013 735 6860; map p.539. *Sirheni* is on the bank of irheni Dam. It's a fine spot for birdwatching, beautifully ucked into riverine forest, with some game also passing hrough the area. The big draw is its remote bushveld tmosphere in an area that sees few visitors. There are

twenty cottages, all en suite and equipped with kitchens. The camp's two bird hides are a great pull. **R2360**

Talamati About 31km south of Orpen Gate ☎013 735 6343; map p.539. Lying on the banks of the usually dry Nwaswitsontso stream, the mixed bushwillow woodland setting of *Talamati* attracts giraffe, kudu, wildebeest, zebra and predators like lion, hyena and jackal, as well as rhino and sable antelope. Two hides within the perimeter of the camp overlook a water hole, where game viewing can be excellent. The camp has twenty cottages arranged in an L-shape along the river in a forest of leadwoods and russet bushwillows. **R2720**

Tsendze Rustic Camp 7km south of Mopani ☎013 735 6535/6; map p.539. The back-to-basics *Tsendze Rustic Camp* caters for those who wish to escape the typical Kruger camp vibe. There is no electricity here – the lighting in the ablutions is from a solar battery system and hot water in the outdoor showers is from gas geysers. There are thirty camping sites (sites 14, 15 and 16 are best), but as each is surrounded by trees and scrub the atmosphere is wild and rustic. The nearest shop is at *Mopani*. **R330**

Private reserves – Greater Kruger

Kruger's western flank is comprised of private reserves, whose boundaries with Kruger are unfenced – the whole zone is often referred to as **Greater Kruger**. Within each reserve are a number of gorgeous safari lodges, each on a large tract of land. Some establishments have three different lodges on their properties, each one different in character, and with some price variations.

It's in these private reserves that you'll find utterly luxurious and romantic accommodation, fabulous food and classic safaris on Land Rovers, where you'll see plenty of big game, smaller animals and birds. All lodges follow the same basic formula: full board, with dawn and late-afternoon game drives conducted by a ranger, assisted by a tracker, in open vehicles. Afternoon outings usually turn into night drives following sundowners in the bush. In winter months you'll be given blankets on the vehicle and even hot water bottles in some places, to cope with the cold. Dinners are inevitably lamplit, around a fire, in the open. Several offer bushwalks, usually after breakfast, and most overlook water holes, rivers or plains, so that you can look out for animals during the time you're in camp, when you're not lazing around the pool, making use of the spa or gym facilities or perusing their collection of animal books on gigantic sofas.

The **Sabi Sands reserve** (⬥sabi-sands.com) is one of the best places in the world for seeing leopards and lions. **Sabi Sands South** is the most exclusive of all the game-viewing areas in South Africa, not only because of the superb game, but also because of its proximity to Nelspruit, and by car it's a two- to three-hour easy run to the lodges from KMI airport. **Sabi Sands North** is cheaper, and the game is good, but access is more difficult. From the R40 you turn east at Acornhoek, travelling along dirt roads through traditional African villages for a couple of hours to reach the lodges. **Manyeleti**, north of Sabi Sands, is easily accessed from Orpen Gate; **Timbavati**, accessed off the R40 Hoedspruit/Eastgate turn-off, is easy to reach, with less travelling on dirt roads than to reach Sabi Sands North.

Even easier to reach, but as a result closer to roads and the sounds of civilization, are the private reserves abutting the R40, and accessible from Hoedspruit – Kapama, Thorneybush, Balule and Karongwe.

9

ACCOMMODATION   PRIVATE RESERVE!

Prices are undeniably very steep in the private reserves – you're paying for the African wilderness experience and for rangers who are dedicated to showing you as much as possible. Prices quoted below include all mea' and all game activities. You need to book ahead, and get driving instructions to your camp, as no pop-i' are allowed.

MANYELETI

Honeyguide 4km from Orpen Gate ☎015 793 1729, ⓦhoneyguidecamp.com; map p.539. One of the more reasonably priced camps, and the only one to offer tented accommodation at each of its two locations, *Khoka Moya*, which takes children and is contemporary in design, and *Mantobeni*, which has more of a traditional safari camp feel. With a lack of tented gardens, the camps maximize the bush feel, and although they don't have views of a river or a water hole, they make up for it with attentive staff and superb rangers and trackers. Each tent is enormous and has its own bathroom with double showers and basins. The best thing about *Honeyguide* is that there is an imaginative children's programme, and great tolerance of children of all ages. Rangers will take your kids off your hands and make casts of animal tracks in the bush, teach them about wildlife and in the evenings sit them on cushions around the campfire. Meals are plated, and all beverages, including wine, are included in the price. R9850

TIMBAVATI

Shindzela 33km inside the reserve, accessed from Timbavati Gate ☎087 806 2068. Mon–Fri 8am–5pm, ⓦshindzela.co.za; map p.539. *Shindzela's* draw is its small size, affordability and walking opportunities. It is a twelve-bed unfenced, no-frills tented lodge, with early morning walks of two to four hours, or game drives if you prefer. They also offer transfers from Johannesburg. R3800

★**Umlani** Close to Orpen Gate, accessed from Orpen Rd ☎021 785 5547, ⓦumlani.com; map p.539. Eight reed-walled huts overlooking the dry Nhlaralumi River, each with an attached open-topped bush shower, heated by a wood boiler (there's no electricity). *Umlani* (meanin "place of rest") isn't fenced off, the emphasis being ver much on a bush experience, and windows are covered wit flimsy blinds so that you get to hear all the sounds of th night. The decor is simple, as is the food, though it delicious and you don't end up overstuffed. Altogethe *Umlani* delivers a much more satisfying experience of th wilds than many other places, and offers very good valu Check out their specials for some great deals. R7560

SABI SANDS NORTH

Djuma Game Reserve ☎013 735 5555 or ☎083 57 1660, ⓦdjuma.com; map p.539. The best of *Djuma* camps is *Vuyatela*, combining a hip, contempora African feel with township art and funky fittings, plu good wildlife spotting. Each five-star suite has its ow plunge pool and mini-bar. Moreover, there is a librar gym and wellness centre for massages and beaut treatments. *Djuma* is one of the more socially minde establishments, with traditional village trips organize during the day between game drives, and they suppo preschools in Dixi village. R12,300

Nkorho Bush Camp ☎013 735 5367, ⓦnkorho.com map p.539. A small, family-operated outfit in thin wooded grassland, *Nkorho* scores on affordability. The are six simple chalets with showers, catering to maximum of sixteen guests. The communal are comprise an open-air lounge, a bar with a pool table an an African fantasy of a *boma* – constructed from gnarle tree trunks – where evening meals are served around a open fire. The swimming pool overlooks a producti' water hole. R9190

WILDLIFE IN THE PRIVATE RESERVES

If it's **leopards** you're after, Sabi Sands is best, especially in the south, where they have become quite blasé about people and vehicles. Timbavati is much quieter and wilder than Sabi Sands, and is known for its large herds of **buffalo**, with plenty of lions and elephants, though it's not good for viewing leopards and cheetah. Timbavati's name is associated with the extraordinary phenomenon of **white lions**, and while you may see some prides carrying the recessive gene which makes them look a little paler, the last sighting of an adult white lion was in 1993 – though a dozen cubs have been born since, but with the high mortality rate, it is not known whether the two which were doing well in 2010 have survived. Manyeleti has a good spread of all game, with some stirring landscapes of open grasslands and rocky outcrops, where it borders Kruger. During the apartheid days, Manyeleti was the only part of Kruger that black people were allowed in, and consequently is far less developed than the other reserves, with little accommodation, which works to its advantage in that there are fewer vehicles about.

SABI SANDS SOUTH

Lion Sands ☎011 880 9992, ⓦlionsands.com; map p.539. One of the top game lodges in Sabi Sands, with accommodation in suites, with bathrooms that couldn't be more romantic, overlooking the Sabi River. *River Lodge*'s eighteen suites come with their own butler, combined with terrific game viewing. The food is top-notch, and the two swimming pools, heated in winter, are placed right next to the river so you can hang out and watch the hippos. Close to River Lodge, and actually in the Kruger itself, is *Tinga Lodge*, with gorgeous riverside suites, each with a deck and heated plunge pool overlooking the water. *River Lodge* **R19,950**, *Tinga* **R23,740**

★**Nottens Bush Camp** ☎082 414 2711, ⓦnottens .com; map p.539. Four decades old and still resisting the temptation to expand, this family-run outfit feels as if you are staying on a sociable friend's farm. Meals are served around a fire, or on a massive deck that acts as a viewing platform. The camp houses just eight elegantly decorated private suites facing the plain and lit by paraffin oil lamps (with mosquito netting on windows and doors). The lack of electricity in the bedrooms is meant to bring guests into better contact with the bush. It offers very good value for a five-star game-viewing experience, and has a swimming pool where you can actually swim laps, next to the massage room. **R10,390**

BALULE

★**Sausage Tree** Balule Nature Reserve, off the R40, 22km north of Hoedspruit ☎015 793 0098, ⓦsausagetree.co.za; map p.539. The pick of the crop of safari camps in Balule Reserve. Balule is well stocked with all the big game, and has the lovely Olifants River defining its northern border, though you are aware of the R40 not far away. *Sausage Tree* represents great value for money; the game drives are excellent, the rooms are comfortable with every detail thought through, and meals are served on the deck, which is set high up with long views across the bushveld. It is also a small camp with very personalized attention, so that you begin to feel like one of the family, sitting around the roaring campfire. **R5900**

PRIVATE CAMPS CLOSE TO SKUKUZA

★**Jock Safari Lodge** Kruger National Park, 38km from Skukuza ☎013 010 0019, ⓦjocksafarilodge.com; map p.539. Fabulous location in a game hotspot deep in the southern Kruger, at the confluence of two seasonal rivers. Majestic riverine trees shade the twelve thatched luxury suites: choose a north-facing room if you can, where you can doze on the sunny daybed on your private deck above the river bank. The lodge also has a spa, a small gym and a library with internet. *Jock* also offers a two-night package of walking with a ranger and staying over at a rustic camp. Watch for specials which can be a third cheaper. **R15,444**

★**Rhino Post Walking Safaris and Plains Camp** ☎035 474 1473, ⓦisibindi.co.za; map p.539. Two safari camps on this magnificent, wild concession near *Skukuza*, offering different experiences. *Rhino Post Lodge* has eight suites built out of stone, wood and thatch, above a sandy riverbed, while *Rhino Walking Safaris* has four super-comfy safari tents, in the wilderness area. Simply furnished in a pioneer style, the camp is marvellously peaceful with a maximum of eight guests, has been built without concrete or trees cut down, and is solar powered. For an ultimate wilderness experience, walk with a superbly informed armed guide to the tree-house overnight camp, which has basic beds under mosquito nets set on high wooden platforms, where you hear all the African night sounds. **R10,280**

Limpopo

BAOBAB TREE AT DUSK, MESSINA

Limpopo

Limpopo Province is considered by many to be South Africa's no-man's-land: a hot, thornbush-covered area caught between the dynamic heartland of Gauteng to the south and, to the north, the Limpopo River, which acts as South Africa's border with Zimbabwe and Botswana. The real highlights of Limpopo are often overshadowed by the busy N1 highway (also known as the Great North Road), South Africa's umbilical cord to the rest of the continent, which dissects the province. But this is where you'll find vast open spaces with wildlife galore, and breathtaking mountainous landscapes covered in mist, all accessible at lower prices than elsewhere in the country. Culturally, Limpopo also stands out: seven of South Africa's eleven official languages are spoken here, and you stand a good chance of meeting people from the majority of the country's ethnic groupings while travelling around the province. The region is also well endowed with a remarkable and ever-increasing number of wildlife and nature reserves, housing a multitude of elegant species of antelope and some Big Five animals, particularly rhino and leopard.

The eastern side of the province is lowveld, dominated by the 70km-wide strip of Kruger National Park abutting the Mozambique border. This part of Limpopo is covered, along with Kruger itself, in the preceding chapter. The principal attractions of the rest of the province lie in its three wild and distinctive **mountain escarpments**. The best known of these is the **Drakensberg** Escarpment, making the descent from highveld to lowveld through lush forests in the Letaba to the west of Kruger.

Polokwane, the provincial capital, lies west of the Drakensberg along the N1, while further to the west lies the sedate **Waterberg** massif, a region dedicated to wildlife conservation and offering malaria-free Big Five game viewing. In the north, parallel to the Limpopo River and bisected by the N1, are the subtropical **Soutpansberg Mountains**, and the intriguing and still very independently minded **Venda** region, a homeland during the apartheid era, to the east. North of the Soutpansberg are wide plains dominated by surreal baobab trees, much in evidence along the N1 as it leads to the only border post between South Africa and Zimbabwe, at Beitbridge. Hugging the border to the west, stifling hot **Mapungubwe National Park** provides a fascinating insight into what is now recognized as Africa's earliest kingdom.

Brief history

The first black Africans arrived in South Africa across the Limpopo River some time before 300 AD. The various movements and migrations, and of course trading, ensured a fluidity in the people who established themselves here, and the historical and cultural ties to the north are, as you might expect, stronger in this region than in other parts of South Africa. Traditional arts and crafts such as **pottery** and **woodcarving** are still an important part of life; and **witchcraft** is still encountered in many places.

Malaria in Limpopo p.558
The Louis Changuion Trail p.562
VhaVenda history and culture p.568

Venda and Tsonga arts and crafts p.570
Mapungubwe and other archeological sites p.572

SAN ROCK ART, MAPUNGUBWE

Highlights

❶ Exploring the Letaba Experience this otherworldly area of lush forests, subtropical fruit plantations and upmarket country-house guesthouses, and the quirky, time-warped village of Haenertsburg in its midst. **See p.561**

❷ Horseriding in the Waterberg This mountain range offers some of South Africa's finest wilderness riding and horseback safaris, with outrides among zebra and giraffe, and the occasional rhino tagging along. **See p.564**

❸ Soutpansberg Mountains Spend the night in the mountains watching the magical display

of stars above, and let the soothing sound of the gushing waterfall gently lull you to sleep. **See p.567**

❹ Venda crafts Explore the remote, simple villages of the mystical Venda region and discover its skilful and distinctive art, pottery and woodcarvings. **See p.570**

❺ Mapungubwe archeology Climb the Hill of Jackals and see the remains of Africa's earliest kingdom, then continue to the fantastic nearby San cave paintings. **See p.572**

HIGHLIGHTS ARE MARKED ON THE MAP ON P.556

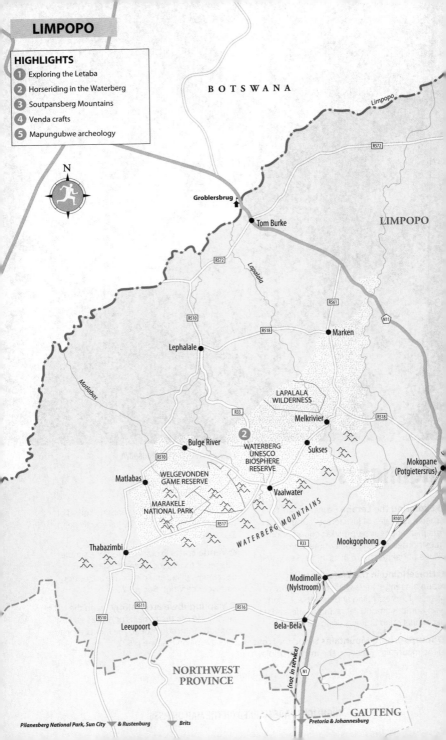

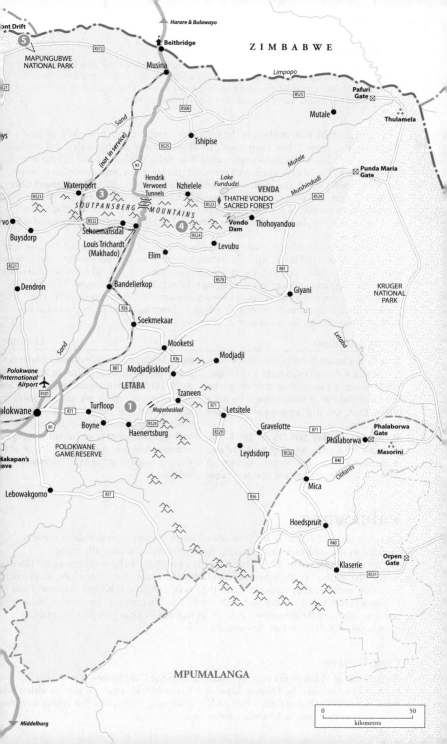

> **MALARIA IN LIMPOPO**
>
> Parts of eastern and northern Limpopo are considered intermediate risk areas for **malaria** from October to May. During this period you are advised to take prophylactics and exercise caution against mosquitoes if you are travelling in the lowveld, including Kruger National Park, or north of the Soutpansberg Mountains to the Zimbabwe border.

10

The arrival of the **Voortrekkers** in the early nineteenth century brought profound changes to the region. Their route roughly followed that of the N1 today, and brought about the founding of the towns now called Bela-Bela, Modimolle and Polokwane, among others. The Voortrekkers who ventured this far north were determined people, and their conflicts with the locals were notoriously bitter. In 1850, at **Makapan's Cave** off the N1 near Mokopane, several thousand Ndebele were starved to death by an avenging Boer commando, while further to the north, in 1867, Venda troops forced the Voortrekkers to abandon the settlement they had established at **Schoemansdal** in the Soutpansberg.

In the twentieth century, the apartheid years saw several large chunks of the province hived off as homeland areas, with Venda becoming notionally independent and Lebowa and Gazankulu self-governing. Today the contrasts between the old homelands and the white farming areas are manifest throughout the province, and poverty, HIV and corruption at council level are rife. However, in municipal elections in 2016, the Democratic Alliance and Economic Freedom Fighters managed to chip away at the ANC's dominance in the province's 22 councils.

GETTING AROUND LIMPOPO

By car Cutting through the middle of Limpopo, the N1 is fast and easy, if often busy with trucks. It's a toll road, with 11 toll stops (known as plazas) from Pretoria to the border with Zimbabwe at Musina (466km). The cost is between R8–42 each stop (depending on the distance between them).

By bus and minibus taxi Citiliner, City to City, Greyhound and Translux buses ply the N1 between Johannesburg/Pretoria and Musina, stopping at Polokwane and Louis Trichardt and other towns along the N1. Translux also runs buses between Johannesburg and Tzaneen via Polokwane. The Tzaneng Shuttle Service (☎ 084 369 6293, ⌨ tzanengshuttleservice.co.za) runs from Pretoria's Hatfield Gautrain station to Tzaneen and back via Polokwane (Wed, Fri & Sun; 4hr 30min; Polokwane R300, Tzaneen R350). In addition, these and other routes are covered by minibus taxis between any moderately sized town; the best way to find out where they're going and when they depart is to enquire at the taxi rank.

Polokwane

Lying almost dead centre in the province of which it is the capital, **Polokwane** was founded in the gold-rush period during the 1880s and was originally called Pietersburg. Renamed in 2003, Polokwane is a northern Sotho word meaning "Place of Safety". It's mostly an administrative and industrial centre, but it does have an excellent museum, and if you're heading towards the lowveld or central Kruger National Park, Polokwane is the point to connect with the R71 to Phalaborwa. The similar-looking one-way streets in the downtown area are all laid out in strict grid pattern, making navigation, especially by car, almost impossible.

Civic Square

At the heart of Polokwane's busy, compact CBD is the **Civic Square**, a park area bounded on two sides by Landros Mare and Thabo Mbeki streets. Streets on either side are abuzz with the bustle from street traders competing with stores and selling anything from top designer gear to Chinese enamelware.

Bakone Malapa Open-Air Museum

9km southeast of town on the R37 • Mon–Fri 8am–4pm • R12 • ☎ 015 295 2432 or ☎ 073 216 9912

Polokwane's one sight really worth seeing is the **Bakone Malapa Open-Air Museum**. A simple but genuine project, it succeeds in conveying some of the old way of life of the local Bakone people – a grouping within the Northern Sotho – where many flashier examples have fallen short. A village of huts has been built in the traditional style, and ten people live permanently on site, working on crafts such as pottery and leatherworking through the day. One of them also acts as a guide, and will explain the different activities you see, as well as the architecture, history and legends of the site.

Polokwane Game Reserve

Silicon Rd, along the R37 near the stadium, 5km south of town • Daily May–Sept 7am–5.30pm, last entry 3.30pm; Oct–April 7am–6.30pm, last entry 4.30pm • R23, car R35 • ☎ 015 290 2331

If you're not heading to Kruger, the 8000-acre municipal **Polokwane Game Reserve** is a good place to spot white rhino, and eland, sable and tsessebe antelope, plus giraffe and zebra, more than a dozen other mammal species and three hundred bird species. The well-kept trails through fertile grassland are suitable for regular cars, and there are hiking trails of 5–21km, too.

ARRIVAL AND DEPARTURE

POLOKWANE

By plane SA Airlink (☎015 288 0164, ⓦflysaa.com) flies from Johannesburg O.R. Tambo (Mon–Fri 3 daily, Sat & Sun 2 daily; 1hr) to Polokwane International Airport, on Gateway St off the R101, just over 5km north of the city (☎015 288 1622). All the city's car-rental firms have offices at the airport, including Avis (☎015 288 0171,

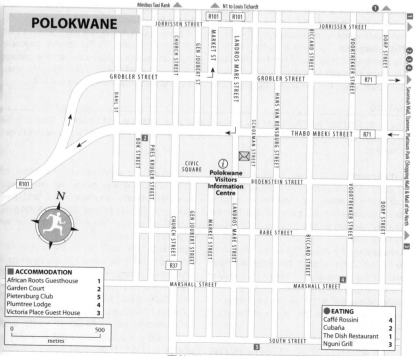

Bakone Malapa Northern Sotho Open-Air Museum & Polokwane Game Reserve

10

Ⓦ avis.co.za), Europcar (☎ 015 288 0097, Ⓦ europcar.com), and First Car Rental (☎ 015 288 1579, Ⓦ firstcarrental .co.za), while taxis line up outside (Easycab ☎ 079 430 4844, Ⓦ easycabpolokwane.co.za).

By bus All intercity buses with Citiliner, City to City, Greyhound and Translux from Johannesburg to Polokwane

(7 daily; 5–6hr) go via Pretoria. They arrive/depart on Thabo Mbeki St near Civic Square, and most also stop at the Mall of the North and Savannah Mall. Through services that terminate at destinations north of Polokwane stop at the Shell Ultra City on the N1 east of the centre. The Tzaneng Shuttle Service (see p.562) stops at Savannah Mall.

INFORMATION

Tourist information The municipal Polokwane Visitors' Information Centre (Mon–Fri 7.30am–5pm, Sat 9am–1pm; ☎ 015 290 2010, Ⓦ polokwane.gov.za) is on

Civic Square, and can help with information about the city's accommodation, attractions and transport, and stocks an array of brochures and maps.

ACCOMMODATION

Given that Polokwane is frequented by business people during the week, discounted rates can be had at most places at weekends.

African Roots Guesthouse 58a Devenish St ☎ 015 297 0113, Ⓦ africanroots.info; map p.559. On the corner of Oost St at the eastern edge of the city centre, this is a relaxed, tasteful spot with immaculate and stylish rooms given character by local and foreign works of art selected by the designer proprietors. The breakfast restaurant also serves evening meals on request. **R800**

Garden Court On the corner of Thabo Mbeki and President Kruger St ☎ 015 291 2030, Ⓦ www.tsogo sunhotels.com; map p.559. Large modern hotel complex, a short walk from Civic Square. The rooms are predictable but decent, and there's a good restaurant for breakfast (extra) and other meals, and an outdoor pool. **R1420**

Pietersburg Club 119 South St ☎ 015 291 2900, Ⓦ pietersburgclub.co.za; map p.559. Four blocks from Civic Square, this traditional gentlemen's club was founded in 1902 and today offers comfortable and elegant B&B

rooms, some with garden-facing verandas ideal for sipping sundowners. The club also has an excellent restaurant, and the "members only" sign at the club entrance refers only to residents of Polokwane. **R1010**

★ **Plumtree Lodge** 138 Marshall St ☎ 015 295 6153, Ⓦ plumtree.co.za; map p.559. Not far from the centre, this is one of the city's oldest and most efficiently run lodges, with smart rooms set in high-ceilinged villas around a large compound and garden, a poolside bar, and breakfasts to die for. This is probably the friendliest and most comfortable place to stay in town. **R1140**

Victoria Place Guest House 32 Burger St ☎ 015 295 7599, Ⓦ victoriaplace.co.za; map p.559. Situated a short walk east of the centre, this Victorian-style guesthouse consists of fourteen stylish rooms in three separate buildings and a self-catering section across the street. Known especially for its hearty breakfasts. **R1450**

EATING

True to its functional role, Polokwane has no shortage of chain restaurants and takeaways. Many of these can be found at the city's two largest malls: Savannah Mall and the Mall of the North, both on the western fringes of the city.

Caffé Rossini Shop 19 Savannah Mall, Thabo Mbeki St ☎ 015 296 1533; map p.559. Classy, contemporary café serving breakfasts, tasty light lunches, including paninis and wraps (R65–90), quiche and salad (R49), and delicious cakes and pastries. Mon–Sat 7.30am–6pm, Sun 8am–3pm.

Cubaña Shop 16 Platinum Park Centre, 1 Pamelo St, ☎ 015 297 1296; map p.559. Part of the Latino chain with a Cuban soundtrack, and a menu from breakfast burrito (R73), to quesadillas (R55), and huge plates of nachos serving two (R115). Simpler, fish, chicken and burgers are available too, and there's a creative cocktail list. Daily 9am–2am.

★ **The Dish Restaurant** 96 Burger St, on the corner of Rissik St ☎ 079 553 3790; map p.559. A delightful café,

restaurant and bar in an old house with creative decor and outside tables in a large garden. *Dish* serves cakes sandwiches and salads and hot meals such as home-made chicken pie (R55) and fillet steak with mussels and garlic sauce (R110). Mon 9am–5pm, Tues–Fri 9am–10pm, Sat 9am–2pm, Sun 11am–2pm.

Nguni Grill 28 Morris St, on the corner of De Wet Drive ☎ 015 296 1790; map p.559. This proper steak house serves generous portions of rumps, fillets and sirloins with delicious sauces, plus other meat dishes like lamb shanks (R190) and oxtail (R150), and there's seafood and Mexican options too, although little choice for vegetarians. The all-you-can-eat Sunday lunch carvery (R150) is popular and should be booked in advance. Daily 9am–11pm.

Letaba

East of Polokwane, the **Letaba** is a forested, lush, mountainous area, contrasting very sharply with the hot lowveld and bushveld abutting it east towards Kruger and west towards Polokwane. It marks the first dramatic rise of the Drakensberg Escarpment as it begins its sweep south through Mpumalanga. The forest begins around the mountain village of **Haenertsburg** and follows two very scenic parallel valleys to Limpopo's second-largest but missable town, **Tzaneen**. The valleys are filled with lakes surrounded by dark pine forests, sparkling rivers, misty peaks and, towards Tzaneen, subtropical crops such as macadamia nuts and avocados. With some very comfortable and beautifully located guesthouses, farm-stalls and tea rooms, hiking trails and trout fishing, the Letaba is in many ways an attractive, less-well-known alternative to Mpumalanga's crowded highlands, and is a popular weekend destination for Gauteng families.

10

Haenertsburg

Mellow **Haenertsburg** lies 60km from Polokwane, high on a hillside tucked away behind the R71 as the road winds down into the thickly wooded Magoebaskloof Valleys. Once an old gold-rush village, Haenertsburg has wonderful views over the area known as the Land of the Silver Mist; that is, when it's not covered in a light carpet of mist that gives it its nickname. With few fences or gates to protect private property, the village has a quaint, time-warped feel to it, and the **main street**, Rissik Street, is lined with various olde-worlde shops, including a secondhand bookshop, art gallery and antique and curio shops. The village's iconic pub is named after Iron Crown, the peak that rises above Haenertsburg to the south and, at 2126m above sea level, is the highest point in Limpopo. The Magoebaskloof and Haenertsburg Spring Fair (Ⓦ springfestival .co.za) is in the third week of September, when the valleys are coloured with beautiful azaleas and scented crab apple and cherry blossoms.

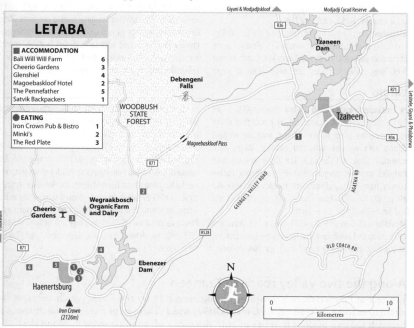

10

THE LOUIS CHANGUION TRAIL

Named after the local historian who laid out the original hiking trail in 1993, the 10km circular **Louis Changuion Trail** runs south of Haenertsburg through beautiful grasslands and indigenous afromontane forest, offering stunning panoramic views of the Drakensberg Escarpment, Ebenezer Dam and Iron Crown peak. It's well worth setting time aside to hike this trail, which takes roughly four hours at a leisurely pace. Look out especially for the blue swallow, Methuen's dwarf gecko and the delicate and endangered Wolkberg Zulu butterfly. Maps are available at the tourist office and can be downloaded from ⓦ magoebasklooftourism .co.za/hiking.

ARRIVAL AND INFORMATION

HAENERTSBURG

By bus The Tzaneng Shuttle Service runs three times a week between Tzaneen and Pretoria (see p.558), stopping at Haenertsburg on request. Regular minibus taxis travelling between Polokwane and Tzaneen also stop in the village.

Information The Magoebaskloof Tourism Association office (☎ 083 442 7429, ⓦ magoebaskloooftourism.co.za, Mon–Fri 8am–5pm, Sat & Sun 8.30am–noon) is at *The Pennefather* complex on Rissik St, and hands out useful free hiking maps.

ACCOMMODATION

There are plenty of places to stay in the Haenertsburg area, and the two roads to Tzaneen are littered with B&B signs. The ones listed below are the most convenient for visiting the town; for accommodation along the two routes, see opposite.

Bali Will Will Farm D3 Rd, off the R71 ☎ 015 276 2212 or ☎ 072 196 8125, ✉ baliwillwill@gmail.com; map p.561. About 1.5km into the hills west of Haenertsburg, this is a beautiful and peaceful spot (and a working farm) with B&B rooms in the farmhouse and two self-catering flats in an old farm building. There's also a shady area for camping at the back with showers, a kitchen area and a braai. Camping R250, doubles R700

Glenshiel 2km east of Haenertsburg on the R71 ☎ 015 065 0300, ⓦ glenshiel.co.za; map p.561. *Glenshiel* is one of the finer old country lodges in South Africa, with roaring fires, deep sofas, antiques and good food. A major

programme of refurbishment is due to end in July 2018. Set in an old farmhouse surrounded by lush pine forests and a number of hiking trails, this is an ideal place to chill out for a couple of days. Rates include breakfast. R1490

★**The Pennefather** Rissik St ☎ 015 276 4885, ⓦ thepennefather.co.za; map p.561. Conveniently located for the start of the Louis Changuion Trail, and named after Haenertsburg's original mining company, *The Pennefather* consists of six gold-mining-style cottages lining a small courtyard, with self-catering facilities, open fireplaces and small verandas. Breakfast is available in the café in the bookshop at the complex from 9am. R960

EATING

★**The Iron Crown Pub & Bistro** Rissik St ☎ 072 424 9912; map p.561. A quaint and busy pub that is the focal meeting place in the village, with an elegant dining area on one side and outdoor tables with mountain views out the back. The above-average food includes gourmet burgers (R60–85), authentic Indian curries (from R60), and some pub classics like steak and ale pie (R110). Mon 4pm–2am, Tues–Fri 10am–2am, Sat 9am–2am, Sun 9am–3pm.

Minki's Rissik St ☎ 015 276 4781; map p.561. A modern coffee shop and lunchroom overlooking the main crossing in town: it also sells art and craft supplies. It serves

excellent coffee and freshly baked goods, such as Belgian waffles, as well as light meals like the prego steak roll (R65) and oven-baked trout (R90). Mon–Fri 8.30am–4pm (closed Wed), Sat 8am–4.30pm, Sun 8am–3pm.

The Red Plate Rissik St ☎ 083 305 2851; map p.561. A couple of doors down from Minki's and with a shady terrace overlooking downtown Haenertsburg, *The Red Plate* serves an array of tasty salads, burgers, toasted sandwiches and wraps for lunch, and more sophisticated mains, such as freshly caught trout (R75), steaks, and pork or lamb chops (R65–90), for dinner. Wed–Sat 9am–9pm, Sun–Tues 9am–4pm.

Along the two valley roads to Tzaneen

Just east of Haenertsburg is a turning off the main R71 for the R528, which offers an alternative route to Tzaneen via **Georges Valley Road**. There is, in fact, little to choose between the two options in terms of both distance and stunning scenery. Along the

Georges Valley Road lies a memorial to the Scottish author and colonialist **John Buchan**, who visited the area in 1902 and described it in glowing terms the following year in his book *The African Colony*. Further along, the tranquil **Tzaneen Dam** is an atmospheric spot for swimming and picnicking.

Taking the R71 along the Magoebaskloof Valley will lead you through the winding hairpin bends of the dramatic **Magoebaskloof Pass**, which climbs to a height of 1400m and then drops 600m from the highveld down the escarpment to the lowveld over a distance of just 6km. The grand *Magoebaskloof Hotel* (see below) is a good place from which to start exploring: there are several hiking trails (ranging from easy to steep), including an attractive 1.5km waterfall walk and a 5km trail through the neighbouring Lesodi forest, home to the beautiful Knysna turaco bird and the noisy samango monkey. After the turn-off to the Debengeni Falls, the valley becomes broader, the rolling hillsides covered with huge stands of citrus, avocado, kiwi and banana trees.

Cheerio Gardens

4km out of Haenertsburg, off the R71 • Free • Tearooms daily 9am–5pm • ☏ 083 355 0835, ⓦ cheeriogardens.co.za

The tranquil **Cheerio Gardens** were established by keen botanist Sheila "Box" Thompson on her father's farm after she was discharged from the army in 1946. At first she wanted to grow South African indigenous plants, but the valley proved to be too cold so she imported deciduous and blossoming trees and shrubs from the northern hemisphere. Today the gardens make a peaceful place for a wander among the mass of pretty cherry trees, while the tearooms – set next to a small pond – are a good place to stop for delicious home-made cakes and scones. The gardens are one of the venues for the Magoebaskloof and Haenertsburg Spring Fair at the end of September when the plants are at their most colourful. You can also do a spot of trout fishing in one of the many ponds, and there are some self-catering cottages (see below).

Wegraakbosch Organic Farm and Dairy

4km out of Haenertsburg, off the R71 • Mon–Fri 7am–5pm, Sat & Sun 7am–noon • Tours at 10am, booking recommended • R60 • ☏ 082 853 8754 or ☏ 071 687 5218

Along the same dirt road as Cheerio Gardens, the **Wegraakbosch Organic Farm and Dairy** is another wonderful piece of backwoods life, with geese and ducks wandering freely among the rustic-looking farm buildings. The one-hour tours give you an opportunity to see the cheese being made, from the milking of the cows and goats to the stirring of curds. This is all done in traditional style over an open fire in huge copper cauldrons, without any electrical or mechanical devices. After the tour you get a chance to sample the freshly made cheese, with an optional glass of wine.

ACCOMMODATION   ALONG THE TWO VALLEY ROADS TO TZANEEN

Cheerio Gardens 4km out of Haenertsburg off the R71 ☏ 083 355 0835, ⓦ cheerio.co.za; map p.561. A range of eight different self-catering cottages sleeping two to six strategically placed around the Cheerio Gardens, with lots of privacy, beautiful mountain views, and with loads of character and homely atmosphere. Breakfast is available at the tearooms from 9am where there's also Wi-Fi. R700

Magoebaskloof Hotel 10km northeast of Haenertsburg on the R71 ☏ 015 276 5400, ⓦ magoebaskloof.co.za; map p.561. This large hotel boasts the most spectacular view in the area from its restaurant deck, and from all the balconies. The 68 rooms and self-catering apartments are spacious and comfortable, and there's a pool, two bars and restaurant. Mountain bikes can be rented, there's a short walking trail to a nearby waterfall, and picnic baskets can be arranged. R1400

Satvik Backpackers Georges Valley Rd, 4km from Tzaneen ☏ 084 556 2414, ⓦ satvik.co.za; map p.561. Down a steep dirt track, this is an unusual and appealing backpackers' lodge, housed in old workers' shacks, with a range of basic rooms, some self-contained, others sharing a shower block and communal kitchen with campers. There's a picturesque waterside bar and braai area, and various walking trails on the vast property. Camping R85, dorms R140, doubles R350

10

Modjadji Cycad Reserve

19km northeast of Modjadjiskloof, turn off the R36 at signpost 5km north of the village • Daily 8.30am–6pm • R10, car R20 • Guided walk R155 per person • self-catering rondavels R620 • ☎ 015 781 0690, ⓦ africanivoryroute.co.za

The area around the village of **Modjadjiskloof**, 30km northeast of Tzaneen on the R36, is the traditional home of the famous **Rain Queen**, the hereditary female monarch of the Modjadji people, who, according to legend, has the power to make rain – a useful talent in the frequently parched north. Currently however, there is no queen in post, but her royal kraal is up the mist-covered mountainside in the **Modjadji Cycad Reserve** (also known as the Modjadji Nature Reserve), where a special form of ancient cycad – the unique Modjadji cycad – flourishes. You can visit for the day, and there are picnic and braai areas and well laid-out walks taking you from the cycad forest steeply down to the grasslands below, with some fine views, although often obscured by mist. You can also rent five traditional rondavels with a communal kitchen (see above).

Waterberg

Rising out of the plains to the west of the Great North Road, the **Waterberg** was until recently one of the least known of South Africa's significant massifs. However, it has been "discovered" by Johannesburgers, and is now a hugely popular weekend destination. Once an area of lakes and swamps – hence its name – the elevated plateau can often seem as dry as its surrounding northern bushveld, yet it harbours a diversity of vegetation and topography that for years supported extensive farming and cattle-ranching. In recent times, the majority of the old ranches have been converted into private reserves catering either for the hugely lucrative hunting market, or less profitable game viewing, with white rhino often the star attraction, along with giraffe, large antelope and leopard. Today the entire area, some 14,500 square kilometres of both private and publicly owned land, is encompassed in the **Waterberg Biosphere Reserve**, designated as such by UNESCO in 2001.

As a game-viewing destination, the Waterberg makes a decent alternative to the lowveld areas around Kruger National Park, with the important advantage that malaria isn't present. It has impressive credentials as a vast area of true wilderness, and it is certainly a lot less commercialized than Kruger. **Vaalwater** – the only settlement of any size – is located at the heart of the region, and to the west of Vaalwater are two large game reserves that are home to the Big Five: **Marakele National Park** and the privately owned **Welgevonden** reserve. North of Vaalwater is the highly regarded **Lapalala Wilderness Area**, where the biosphere reserve was originally instigated.

The only reserve you can visit for a game-viewing day-trip under your own steam is Marakele National Park; Lapalala Wilderness Area can be visited with a guide from *Waterberg Cottages* (see p.566). Otherwise, to gain access to the reserves, large or small, you'll almost always be expected to book into accommodation on the reserve itself; as most accommodation in the Waterberg is on reserves, this is generally hard to avoid.

Vaalwater

The small farming town of **VAALWATER** offers the visitor little more than a couple of useful places to stay and eat, and an orientation point on the R33, which connects the N1 at Modimolle with Lephalale. Vaalwater marks the junction between the R33 and the tarred road to Melkrivier and Marken. The **Zeederberg Homestead**, 1.5km northwest of the main crossing along the R33, beside the Spar supermarket, was the town's first settlement and home to the legendary Zeederberg stagecoaches that used to crisscross Limpopo and Zimbabwe to service settler outposts. Today, the Zeederberg Centre offers a filling station, the tourist office, good self-catering accommodation, a café and an excellent crafts shop.

Lapalala Wilderness

55km north of Vaalwater; turn left down a dirt road at the Melkrivier junction on the R518 Marken Rd • Guided day safari R600, including lunch • ☎ 014 755 4395, ⓦ lapalala.com

Providing sanctuary for endangered and rare animals, the 244-square-kilometre **Lapalala Wilderness** area has developed into one of the foremost conservation projects in the country. It was the first private game reserve in South Africa to obtain the highly endangered black rhino, and it is now equally well known for its Wilderness School, which introduces some three thousand children a year from all over Africa to the principles and practices of conservation during week-long courses. To visit Lapalala on a **day safari**, book through *Waterberg Cottages* (see p.466).

10

Marakele National Park

Near Thabazimbi, 85km west of Vaalwater, or leave the N1 at Bela-Bela and follow the R516 to Leeupoort and then the R511 to Thabazimbi • Daily May–Aug 6am–5.30pm, Sept–April 6am–6pm, day visitors daily 7am–4pm • R176 • Sunrise/sunset game drives and walks R240 • ☎ 014 777 6928, ⓦ sanparks.org/parks/marakele

In the mountains to the northeast of the mining and hunting town of **Thabazimbi** lies the 670-square-kilometre **Marakele National Park**, reached via a 12km tarred road from Thabazimbi (where there's a shop for provisions and a filling station). At its core is the **Kransberg**, a striking assortment of odd-shaped peaks, plateaus and cliffs. The fauna includes varied populations of antelope including tsessebe, roan, sable, red hartebeest, eland, kudu and waterbuck, leopard and brown hyena. Larger game, such as elephant, white and black rhino, and lion, have also been introduced – many from Kruger National Park. Birding is excellent here, with more than 400 species – the highlight being eight hundred breeding pairs of the endangered Cape vulture.

If staying overnight, you can join one of the excellent two- to three-hour organized sunrise and sunset drives or bush walks, which are arranged at reception at the main gate close to Bontle Rest Camp. **Day visitors** are restricted to a small area, which includes Kransberg, with its inspiring views, and to specific times (7am–4pm). The roads do not require a 4WD.

Welgevonden Game Reserve

25km west of Vaalwater on the tarred R517 towards Thabazimbi, abutting Marakele • only accessible to overnight guests, R120 conservation fee per night • ⓦ welgevondengamereserve.org

Privately owned by an association of landowners, the 380-square-kilometre **Welgevonden Game Reserve** is managed as one large conservation area, which strictly regulates how many lodges can be built and the number of visitors to the park. This results in some fantastic undisturbed and relatively easy-to-view wildlife throughout the entire area, including the Big Five, a host of antelope and a plethora of colourful birds. All sixteen lodges in Welgevonden have their own unique features, such as bush spas, romantic fireplaces, outdoor showers, and granite swimming pools, and while some accommodate just one or two small groups, others have multiple rooms. With well-qualified and experienced game guides at hand at all times, there's no question that this is an expensive place, with all-inclusive rates hovering around R4500 per person per day. However, there are often midweek specials and discounts over the winter season. No private vehicles are allowed inside the reserve; you park at the gate and your lodge will pick you up.

ARRIVAL AND INFORMATION   **WATERBERG**

By car The most direct route from Gauteng to Vaalwater is via the N1, turning off on to the R33 at Modimolle. Other parts of the Waterberg, such as Marakele National Park, can be accessed from Bela-Bela on the N1 further south.

By minibus taxi The only public transport to Vaalwater from Modimolle is by occasional minibus taxi.

10

Tourist information The Waterberg Tourism information office is in the Zeederberg Centre on the R33 In Vaalwater (☎ 014 755 3535, ⓦ waterbergtourism.co.za, Mon–Fri 9am–5pm, Sat 9am–1pm), and has information on accommodation and activities in the region.

ACCOMMODATION

MARAKELE NATIONAL PARK

Bontle Rest Camp 2km from the main gate ⓦ sanparks.org/parks/marakele. The shaded campsite has a fully kitted kitchen and ablution blocks, the obligatory braai area, and the option of a power point. There are also pre-erected safari tents on wooden decks with verandas that sleep two with proper beds, en-suite bathrooms and small kitchens. Camping R285, safari tents R1315

Tlopi Rest Camp 17km from the main gate ⓦ sanparks.org/parks/marakele. A self-catering camp on the banks of the Matlabas River, with romantic luxuriously equipped tents sleeping two hovering on stilts over the water's edge, and the secluded Motswere Guest Cottage, an old farmhouse with four bedrooms, just a few kilometres away. Cottage R2495, safari tents R1445

WELGEVONDEN GAME RESERVE

Jamila Game Lodge ☎ 014 754 8946, ⓦ jamilalodge .co.za. A good, friendly option in the northern region of the reserve. It has five spacious chalets with wooden decks and outdoor showers, a pool, and nearby is a busy watering hole visited by birds, antelope and the occasional elephant. Like all the places, you need to book in advance and will be picked up at the main gate. Rates include game drives and all meals. R8195

VAALWATER AND AROUND

Ant's Nest & Ant's Hill North of Vaalwater, turn off the R33 at 19km and 11km respectively ☎ 087 820 7233 or ☎ 083 287 2885, ⓦ waterberg.net. Two super-luxurious lodges, offering all-inclusive pampering in the wild. Activities include horseriding, mountain biking, game drives and bush walks, and each day ends with a sundowner at a beautiful viewpoint. Successful breeders of sable antelope and passionate about conservation, the owners are happy to share their vast knowledge and experience. Rates are all-inclusive. R9750

★ **Horizon Horseback** Triple B Ranch, 24km north on the R518 to Melkrivier, then right onto the gravel road to Sterkstroom and continue for another 4km ☎ 083 419 1929, ⓦ ridinginafrica.com. A well-established and highly professional outfit with 60 horses and 32,000 acres of beautiful bushland inhabited by hippos, giraffe, zebra and antelope. There's lovely lakeside accommodation in individual chalets, and also a magical lantern-lit bushcamp with a pool and great views. Suitable for riders of all levels, activities include horseback game-viewing, cattle-mustering, polocrosse and a cross-country course. Rates are all-inclusive. R5810

Lindani Off the R518 around Melkrivier, 36km north of Vaalwater ☎ 083 631 5579, ⓦ lindani.co.za. On a 31-square-kilometre reserve, *Lindani* comprises eight secluded and attractive thatched self-catering lodges sleeping between four and eighteen people, and a tented camp with twin accommodation and shared ablutions and kitchen. What makes *Lindani* unique is the many hiking and mountain-biking trails crisscrossing the reserve, which guests are free to use unsupervised, making this an ideal spot to explore the bush at your own pace. With tranquil picnic spots along rivers and the potential for encountering giraffe and various antelope, it's not surprising this is one of the most popular game lodges in the Waterberg. Minimum stay two nights. Lodges R780, tented camp R560

Waterberg Cottages Triple B Ranch, for directions see Horizon Horseback (above) ☎ 014 755 4425, ⓦ waterbergcottages.co.za. Pleasant self-catering accommodation in five old farmhouse buildings on a working Bonsmara cattle ranch; some are small thatched cottages sleeping up to four, while the farmhouses can accommodate a couple of large families and there's a swimming pool. The unpolluted wide-open skies above make this an ideal spot for stargazing (two-hour star tours are on offer), and there are walking trails marked out in the bush. R800

Zeederberg Cottages Main Rd in Vaalwater, behind the shops and filling station ☎ 082 332 7088, ⓦ zeederbergs.co.za. The best choice in Vaalwater town, set around a large, relaxing garden with a pool. The cluster of comfortable self-catering cottages includes a Zulu-style rondavel. Guests have access to the kitchen and living room in the main house and all meals are available on request. R900

EATING

The only places to eat in the Waterberg are in Vaalwater itself, so you'll need to be self-catering or staying at one of the game lodges. Vaalwater also has the Waterberg's only banks and shops, including the Spar supermarket.

VAALWATER

The Hunter's Hide Main Rd, 200m south of the main crossing on the R33 ☎ 072 279 9255. A simple bush-style pub, with TVs for watching the rugby and an outdoor wooden deck where all the lodge employees hang out on their evenings off. The filling menu includes burgers (R50), baked spuds with toppings like creamed spinach (R50), and pizzas (R80), and there's plenty of cold beer. Mon–Sat 7.30am–midnight, Sun 7.30am–9pm.

★**Seringa Café** Zeederberg Centre ☎ 014 161 0643. The best place in town for lunch or a coffee, with outside tables under huge shady trees on the grass. It's often very

busy and service can be slow, but it's worth it if you are passing through Vaalwater. The menu offers breakfasts, cakes and pastries, and can include light meals like grilled chicken breast with coconut (R60), and hearty soups such as lentil and bacon (R35) in winter. Mon–Fri 7.45am–3.45pm, Sat 8.15am–2.30pm.

SHOPPING

Beadle Triple B Ranch, for directions see Horizon Horseback (opposite) ☎ 014 755 4002, ⓦ beadle.co.za. A community project for skills-training and sustainable employment, where you can watch the trainees applying intricate beadwork on to leather items, such as belts, bracelets and sandals, in the workshop. Next door is a tearoom and a shop where you can buy the goods. Mon–Fri 7.30am–5pm, Sat & Sun 7.30am–1pm.

★**The Black Mamba Company** In the Zeederburg Centre ☎ 073 701 0543, ⓦ blackmambacompany.webs .com. Next to the Spar supermarket and *Seringa Café*, this excellent gallery sells beautiful crafts from throughout Southern Africa, including basketware, wooden carvings and jewellery, as well as books and nature guides. Mon–Fri 9am–4pm, Sat 9am–1pm.

10

The far north

The northernmost part of Limpopo Province is a hot, undeveloped rural region that has much in common with Zimbabwe. Its essential geographical features are the **Limpopo River**, the border between South Africa and Zimbabwe (and, further west, Botswana), and the alluring **Soutpansberg mountain range**, aligned east–west just to the north of the area's main town, Louis Trichardt (also known, and often signposted, as Makhado), an unremarkable settlement and not worth a stopover.

Perhaps the most distinctive area is the **Venda** region, formerly an "independent" homeland under apartheid. Although economically impoverished, it remains rich in tradition, art and legend. East of the Venda lands is the northern tip of **Kruger National Park**, a less-visited but intriguing part of the park (see p.538); there are two entry gates to the park here, at **Punda Maria** and **Pafuri**.

Both the Limpopo River and the Soutpansberg range lie in the path of the N1 highway, which crosses into Zimbabwe at **Beitbridge**. About 70km west of here, the **Mapungubwe National Park** encompasses a UNESCO World Heritage Iron Age site which for archeology buffs is probably the area's most enticing attraction. Mapungubwe is considered as one of the first indigenous kingdoms in Southern Africa, and the long-term goal is to develop a tri-border heritage site that will also incorporate parts of Botswana and Zimbabwe along the Limpopo.

The Soutpansberg

The **Soutpansberg**, an impressive range of hills, particularly when approached from the south, attracts sufficient rainfall to create a subtropical climate, and spectacularly lush farms along the southern slopes produce a range of exotic crops such as avocados and macadamia nuts. In other parts, the rocky *kloofs* and green hillsides offer unspoilt mountain retreats, shaded by up to 580 different species of tree, and the home of monkeys, small antelopes, warthogs and some raptors. The uniqueness of the area led to it being designated as part of the 30,700-square-kilometre UNESCO Vhembe Biosphere Reserve in 2009 (ⓦ vhembebiosphere.org), which reaches north to the Zimbabwe border and east to Kruger National Park.

The N1 highway bisects the range, passing through Louis Trichardt, situated in the southern shadow of the mountains, then climbing over a low pass and descending through a pair of tunnels on the northern side. Once over the escarpment, the highway runs north across mostly empty baobab plains to **Musina** and the **Limpopo River**.

10

ARRIVAL AND DEPARTURE

By bus and minibus taxi Citiliner and Greyhound buses heading to Musina stop in Louis Trichardt, and minibus taxis service Polokwane and other neighbouring towns.

THE SOUTPANSBERG

ACCOMMODATION

139 on Munnik Guest House 139 Munnik St, Louis Trichardt ☎083 407 0124, ⍟139onmunnik.co.za. A comfortable, upmarket guesthouse on a quiet street in the northern part of town, with cosy rooms and a pool in a shady garden. The on-site *Sticky Toffee Coffee Shop* serves light lunches and cakes and dinner on request. R950

★**Leshiba Wilderness** 36km west of Louis Trichardt along the R522 ☎011 483 1841, ⍟leshiba.co.za. Located in a spectacular valley atop the mountain range, *Leshiba* is a truly unique experience, well worth the long uphill drive (safest in a 4WD, or book a R225 transfer from the car park at the bottom of the mountain). The renowned artist Noria Mabasa has used the ruins of old rondavels to create a replica Venda village, alive with plump sculpted figures that guests can admire when lounging by the pool or enjoying the quirky accommodation – each one different with absolutely no straight lines. There are also two regular thatched safari-style rooms with their own plunge pools. Rates include all meals. R4500

★**Madi a Thavha Mountain Lodge** 10km west of Louis Trichardt on the R522 ☎015 516 0220, ⍟madiathavha.com. A beautiful fair-trade lodge on the southern slopes of the Soutpansberg, where the lovely villas and guest rooms are furnished and decorated with local crafts. There's a guest lounge, swimming pool, and guided day-trips and birding walks. It even has an onsite art gallery, Dancing Fish, which promotes Venda crafts and artists. Rates include breakfast and other meals are available. R1370

The Ultimate Guesthouse 8.5km north of Louis Trichardt, turn off the N1 at Bluegumsport Rd ☎015 517 7005, ⍟ultimategh.co.za. The eighteen units here range from B&B rooms to self-catering cottages scattered around lovely gardens with excellent birdwatching, a swimming pool and nine-hole putt-putt course. The pleasant restaurant has a crackling fire in winter and good mountain views from the terrace. R680

Venda

To the east and north of Louis Trichardt lies the intriguing land of the **VhaVenda** people, a culturally and linguistically distinct African grouping known for their mystical legends, political independence and arts and crafts. **Venda** was demarcated as a homeland under the apartheid system in the 1950s, and became one of three notionally independent homelands in South Africa in the late 1970s (though never

---

VHAVENDA HISTORY AND CULTURE

The people who today call themselves **VhaVenda** are descended from a number of ancient groupings who migrated from the Great Lakes area in east-central Africa in the eleventh and twelfth centuries. Their identity gelled when a group under Chief Dimbanyika arrived at Dzata in the northern Soutpansberg, where a walled fort was later built. From here, they consolidated their power in the region, fending off attack from a number of different African groupings (including the Voortrekkers, whom they drove from their settlement at Schoemansdal in 1867). Although the VhaVenda suffered a reverse at the hands of the Boers in 1898, the onset of Anglo-Boer War prevented that victory being consolidated.

The **culture** of the VhaVenda is a fascinating one, steeped in mysticism and vivid legend. One pervading theme is water – always an important concern in hot, seasonal climates, but a resource in which Venda is unusually abundant. Lakes, rivers, waterfalls and lush forests all form sacred sites, while legends abound of *zwidutwane*, or water sprites, and snakes who live at the bottom of dark pools or lakes.

Many VhaVenda **ceremonies** and **rituals** still hold great importance, with the most famous being the python, or *domba*, dance performed by young female initiates. Naked but for jewellery and a small piece of cloth around their waists, the teenage girls form a long chain, swaying and shuffling as the "snake" winds around a fire to the sound of a beating drum – another sacred object in Venda – often for hours on end. Your chances of seeing it performed are limited. The genuine thing is most common during spring; Heritage Day around the end of August or the beginning of September is a good time for celebrations.

recognized as such by the UN). Of all the homelands, Venda was one of the least compromised, keeping both its geographic and cultural integrity, and largely being left to mind its own business during the dark years of apartheid. Nowadays, its boundaries have regained their former fuzziness within Limpopo, but the region has retained its strong, independent identity.

Aside from a sprinkling of accommodation in Thohoyandou (see below), you'll find almost no tourist-oriented infrastructure whatsoever in Venda, but travelling here can be wonderfully rewarding.

10

The R523 west from Thohoyandou

Some 70km east of Louis Trichardt on the R524, **Thohoyandou** is a chaotic place with fruit markets and street vendors but nothing much else to see – if you're heading on to Kruger, you'll be thankful that the road bypasses the centre of town. However, if you head west of Thohoyandou, through a valley traced by the R523 road along the northern side of the Soutpansberg, you'll find the lush forests, waterfalls and mountains that give Venda its mystical atmosphere – this is the most appealing core of VhaVenda history and legend.

Driving from Thohoyandou, climb out of town to the north and then west, leaving the suburbs to get among the elevated green scenery which lies enticingly ahead. You'll pass the **Vondo Dam**, created in the mid-1980s and surrounded by pine forests, then climb over the **Thathe Vondo Pass**. Over the summit, a small shack marks the entrance to a network of forest roads that take you into the area containing the most important lake in Venda, **Lake Fundudzi**, and the **Thathe Vondo Sacred Forest**, an area of dense indigenous forest which contains the burial ground of Venda chiefs. In the past you could only look at both from afar, as getting closer was a matter of deep sensitivity and you had to gain permission from the VhaVenda chief. Today, access is unrestricted but there isn't a readily available map showing you the network of roads around the forest, and some of them require 4WD, so you may be better off organizing a local **tour guide** from *Khoroni Hotel* (see below). Beyond the crest of the Thathe Vondo Pass, the R523 follows the **Nzhelele River** down a valley of scattered but mostly unbroken settlement for about 60km.

ARRIVAL AND INFORMATION

By minibus taxi Frequent minibus taxis run between Louis Trichardt and Thohoyandou.

Information The best place to get information about the area is from one of the established accommodation options such as *Shiluvari Lakeside Lodge* (see p.570) or *Khoroni Hotel*, both of which have lists of tour guides in the area.

ACCOMMODATION

Khoroni Hotel Mphephu St, Thohoyandou ☎015 962 4600, ⓦwww.khoroni.co.za. Set in the heart of downtown Thohoyandou, surrounded by trees, but not far beyond the road and tatty shopping mall. The hotel makes a living through its casino and conference facilities but also has a pool, and decent rooms. The Malingani Restaurant here is the best place to eat in town (daily 6.30–10.30am, 12.30am–3.30pm, 6.30–11pm). Breakfast is included in the rates. R1270

Naledzi Lodge 1 End St, Shayandima, 6.5km west of Thohoyandou off the R524 ☎015 964 1777, ⓦnaledzilodge.co.za. Popular with parents visiting their kids at the nearby University of Venda, a simple place offering eighteen motel-like B&B rooms around a large lawned garden, with the option of ordering in evening meals from local fast-food outlets. R525

Elim and around

Southeast of Louis Trichardt, only 23km along the R578 lie some areas that used to form part of the self-governing Tsonga homeland of **Gazankulu**. These feature the vibrant roadside action typical of such rural areas – most notably at **ELIM**, a cluster of stalls, minibuses and hoardings on the site of a long-established Swiss mission hospital.

10

VENDA AND TSONGA ARTS AND CRAFTS

The **Venda** and **Tsonga** regions have a strong reputation for **arts and crafts**. The best known of these are clay pots distinctively marked with angular designs in graphite silver and ochre. Also growing in status are woodcarvings, ranging from abstract to practical – the best of these can be imaginative and bold, though many are unfinished and overpriced. You'll also come across tapestries, fabrics, basketwork and painting. Finding your way to these **craft villages** can be quite an adventure, as they are widely scattered and the roads are poor, so the Ribolla Tourism Association, behind the Swiss mission hospital in Elim (Mon–Fri 8.30am–4.30pm; ☎ 015 556 4262, ✉ ribollata@mweb.co.za), has set up a demarcated **art route** in the area, and hands out free maps of the route. It also has knowledgeable guides to take you around. Alternatively, try the **shops** selling craft products at the *Shiluvari Lakeside Lodge* (see below) and at *Madi a Thava* (see p.568).

Continuing on the R578 from Elim crossroads, towards the town of **Giyani**, you'll come upon a series of rural arts and crafts workshops (see box above). The traditions and skills in arts and crafts are not dissimilar to what you find in Venda, and most of the workshops and small factories have simple, rural roots, making the trip to see them a worthwhile adventure. *Shiluvari Lakeside Lodge* (see below) can help with guides to arts and crafts workshops in the area, and sells products from many of them in its exquisite and well-stocked crafts boutique.

ACCOMMODATION   ELIM AND AROUND

★ **Shiluvari Lakeside Lodge** A short way from Elim; turn left at the hospital junction towards Thohoyandou, and follow the signs down a gravel road to the left ☎ 015 556 3406, ⊛ shiluvari.com. The peaceful *Shiluvari Lakeside Lodge* has lawns running down to the edge of Albasini Dam and great views over the water to the Soutpansberg. There are large rooms in the cottages in the gardens, and lakeside rondavels, all decorated with local art. The owners have strong links with the local community and have helped set up the art route (see box above) and can organize local guides. Tasty three-course dinners are available in the *Wood-Owl* restaurant. R1230

Mapungubwe National Park

Daily April–Oct 6.30am–6pm; Sept–March 6am–6.30pm, last entry for day visitors, two hours before gates close • R176 • Sunset and night drives R275, guided walks R420 • ☎ 015 534 7925, ⊛ sanparks.org/parks/mapungubwe

In the far north of Limpopo, the **Mapungubwe National Park** is a UNESCO World Heritage Site, primarily due to its famous Iron Age site known as the Hill of Jackals, thought by some experts to be the site of the first kingdom in Africa. The park is situated at the confluence of the Limpopo and Shashi rivers, where South Africa, Zimbabwe and Botswana meet, and is well worth a detour if you have even the faintest interest in archeology. The park is divided into an eastern and a western side connected only by the main road, with a large plot of private land in between. The main entrance is on the eastern side nearest Musina, which is also where you'll find the Hill of the Jackals and most of the accommodation.

The park offers excellent game viewing with a scenic backdrop of unusual sandstone formations, mopane woodland, riverine forest, and a landscape scattered with otherworldly baobab trees and housing wildlife such as elephant, giraffe, white rhino, plus various different antelope, including eland and gemsbok. If you're lucky, you may spot predators such as lion, leopard and hyena, and there are over four hundred bird species including the African fish eagle, kori bustard, tropical boubou and the magnificent pel's fishing owl.

You can explore the park in your own car, and 35km of the gravel roads are suitable for regular cars, while another 100km can be negotiated in a 4WD. There are also morning and evening three-hour guided game drives and walks for overnight visitors. A restaurant and curio shop are located at the main gate.

10

Hill of the Jackals

Heritage Tour at 7am, 10am & 3pm from the main gate • R230 plus park fee • Book at the main gate or on ☎ 015 534 7925

The **Hill of the Jackals** is one hour's drive from the main entrance, and, to visit, you need to join a two-hour **Heritage Tour**. A knowledgeable guide will talk you through the finds from an archeological dig in front of the hill, before climbing steps up to where the king and his extended family lived. It held a spiritual and mythological importance to local Modimo people long before it was "discovered" in 1932, when a local farmer climbed the dome-shaped granite hill and found various remains, including a tiny one-horned rhinoceros and a bowl, both made out of gold. It is thought that the years 1000–1300 AD were the heyday of a civilization centred at Mapungubwe. Prior to this, the Khoi and San people both left their footprints in the area with numerous sites of important rock art. Most impressive of these is found on land outside the national park (but still within the UNESCO World Heritage Site) at *Kaoxa Bush Camp* (see below).

Mapungubwe Museum and Interpretive Centre

Daily 8am–4pm • R55 plus park fee

The amazing domed and vaulted **Mapungubwe Museum and Interpretive Centre** near the park's main gate houses an informative exhibition, and has won awards for its architecture. However, owing to conservation and security worries only a few of the original gold items found at the site are on display here, but you can see a replica of the golden rhino, and guides bring the Mapungubwe story to life.

Kaoxa Bush Camp

Nestled in between the eastern and western section of Mapungubwe National Park is the privately owned Kaoxa wilderness area housing **Kaoxa Bush Camp**, a beautiful rustic camp set upon a hillside overlooking the confluence of the Limpopo and Shashi rivers across to Zimbabwe and Botswana. Stretching down to these two rivers, the camp is frequently visited by animals from Zimbabwe and Botswana, and signs at the camp make it clear that elephants have right of way. In contrast to the national park, visitors are free to move around independently (after signing lengthy indemnity forms) – on foot or by car. Bearing in mind the many hungry animals you may encounter, it's a good idea to seek advice before setting off. The only area that you're not allowed to explore by yourself is the amazing rock-art site with its unique locust images, which one of the camp staff will take you to.

ARRIVAL AND DEPARTURE   MAPUNGUBWE NATIONAL PARK

By car There are several routes to the park. The entrance gate lies around 60km west of Musina and the N1 along the R572 road to the Pont Drift border post with Botswana. Another option is to leave the N1 at Polokwane further south and take

---

MAPUNGUBWE AND OTHER ARCHEOLOGICAL SITES

As one of the early melting pots of Southern Africa, Limpopo has a number of important **archeological sites** where excavations have helped piece together a picture of the different people who inhabited the land for thousands of years. Some of the most interesting sites are at places where iron was smelted, as the development from what was essentially a Stone Age culture to an Iron Age culture, with its associated improvement in tools for cultivation and war, was a vital part of the migration of African tribes into South Africa around 1500 years ago. The presence of slag and other wastes provides the strongest clues – the iron itself seldom survives the processes of erosion. Some of the most revealing excavations have taken place at **Thulamela**, inside Kruger National Park not far from the Punda Maria Gate, **Bakone Malapa Open-Air Museum** outside Polokwane (see p.559), **Makapan's Cave** near Mokopane (see p.558), **Masorini**, also in Kruger, not far from Phalaborwa (see p.537), and the single most important site in Limpopo Province, **Mapungubwe** (Hill of the Jackals), west of Musina (see p.570).

the R521 via Dendron, Vivo and Alldays and turn right on to the R572 at the park's boundary and follow it to the gate; the distance from Polokwane using this route is about 215km. Note that the nearest fuel stop is in Musina and Alldays, so ensure tanks are filled on the way to the park.

By public transport The only public transport to the park is by a few minibus taxis from Musina. However, in practice this is only really useful if you are visiting the Museum and Interpretive Centre or joining the Heritage Tour, then moving on.

ACCOMMODATION

Kaoxa Bush Camp Off the R572 ☎ 072 536 6297, ⓦ kaoxacamp.com. Accommodation at the camp comprises three rustic stone cottages with breathtaking views from large terraces, which compensate for the fact that there's electricity but no a/c (and it gets very hot here). There are also three comfortable furnished safari tents with equally wonderful views. All the accommodation is self-catering, with shared kitchen and dining facilities. Cottages R920, safari tents R725

SANParks Accommodation ☎ 012 428 9111 or ☎ 015 534 7925, ⓦ sanparks.org/parks/mapungubwe. There are a number of different accommodation options within the park. The beautiful *Leokwe Rest Camp*, 11km from the main gate, has spacious cottages, a natural rock pool, and is close to a viewpoint overlooking the confluence of the Limpopo and Shashi rivers. *Tshugulu Lodge*, 23km from the main gate, has a guest lodge sleeping up to eight and a cottage for four; *Limpopo Forest Tented Camp*, 40km from the main gate, has twin en-suite tents and a shared kitchen; *Vhembe Wilderness Camp*, 13km from the main gate, has four simple cabins and a communal kitchen and is within walking distance of the Limpopo River; and *Mazhou Camping Site* is 40km from the main gate close to Limpopo Forest Tented Camp and is fully equipped including power points. Camping R305, Leokwe cottages R1475

10

Lesotho

THE MALOTI MOUNTAINS

Lesotho

Entirely surrounded by South Africa, the aptly named "mountain kingdom" of Lesotho (pronounced "Le-su-tu") is proudly independent and very different in character from its dominant neighbour. Whereas the Rainbow Nation next door is, in many respects, distinctly European, laidback Lesotho prides itself on its staunchly African heritage. Few people in the highlands of this fabulously beautiful and rugged land speak English or Afrikaans, though language isn't a barrier since the country's inhabitants – the Basotho – count among the most hospitable people in Southern Africa. Another refreshing physical (and psychological) contrast is the almost total absence of fences, which means you can trek into the upland regions at will.

11

Travelling almost anywhere in Lesotho is an adventure: there are no highways or slick intercity buses here (nor any timetables), though the tarred **road network** is good, covered by rickety minibuses held together in some cases by little more than prayers. For many Basotho, **ponies** are the preferred method of transport, particularly in the highlands. You can experience this too from pony-trekking lodges all over the country.

Lesotho is the only country in the world that lies entirely above an altitude of 1000m, earning it the nickname "the kingdom in the sky". Even the sandstone **Lesotho lowlands** – which form a crescent along the country's western rim – would be highlands anywhere else. It's here that you'll find all the nation's major towns, including the busily practical capital of **Maseru**, with its very African mix of new glass buildings, honking taxis and dusty streets, which began life as a tax-collection centre for the British administration. Lowland attractions include the weavers of **Teya-Teyaneng**, extraordinary caves near **Mateka**, rock paintings at **Liphofung**, and the mountain fortress at **Thaba Bosiu**, established by Lesotho's founder, King Moshoeshoe I.

At around 1400m above sea level, sandstone gives way to basalt, which forms the bulk of the ruggedly beautiful **Lesotho highlands**. Up the steep, twisting roads that lead into the mountains you can visit the engineering masterpieces of the **Katse** and **Mohale dams**, ski in the Maloti Mountains, fish from rivers everywhere and, above all, wander through the countryside, dividing your time between remote villages of simple stone-and-thatch huts and the peaceful solitude of the mountains. Three protected areas in particular are worth the effort of getting to: **Ts'ehlanyane National Park** and **Bokong Nature Reserve**, both in the Front Range of the Maloti Mountains and easily accessed by saloon car, and the remote **Sehlabathebe National Park** in the east of the country, offering gloriously rugged hiking terrain.

Lesotho's **winter** runs from May to July, when it often snows in the highlands and sometimes in the lowlands too. Although the days are usually clear and warm, it

PONY TREKKING NEAR MALEALEA

Highlights

❶ **Pony trekking** The ideal way to see Lesotho, following paths from village to village through spectacular mountain scenery and past towering waterfalls; you can also walk alongside while the pony takes your luggage. **See p.586**

❷ **Thaba Bosiu** Fabulous views from the hilltop fortress from which Lesotho's greatest king, Moshoeshoe I, defended his kingdom against attackers. **See p.588**

❸ **Maletsunyane Falls** A dramatic 200m waterfall plunging into a vast gorge deep in the remote highland region, reached on foot or by pony. **See p.592**

❹ **Highlands Water Project** Take a tour inside Africa's second-highest dam at Katse, visit the power plant at 'Muela, and learn about Lesotho's ambitious water project. **See p.597**

❺ **"Roof of Africa" route** The winding road from Butha-Buthe to the Sani Pass meanders through dramatic mountains and valleys, and passes one of Africa's few ski resorts. **See p.600**

❻ **Sehlabathebe National Park** A wonderfully remote mountain reserve with superb hiking. **See p.608**

HIGHLIGHTS ARE MARKED ON THE MAP ON P.578

gets extremely cold at night and ice can make driving hazardous in the highlands, while snowfall blocks even tarred highways for days at a time. **Spring** (Aug–Oct), when the snow melts, is a beautiful time, with new plants sprouting up everywhere. November to January is **summer**, when Lesotho gets most of its rain, often torrential, turning dirt roads into mudslides. Still, when it isn't raining the weather is usually sunny and the landscape is coloured in vivid shades of green. **Autumn** (Feb–April) is one of the best times to visit, as it doesn't usually rain much and temperatures are moderate. Whatever the time of year, Lesotho can be very cold at night, particularly in the highlands, and prone to rapid weather changes, for which it's always wise to be prepared.

Brief history

Lesotho exists because of the determined efforts of one man, **Moshoeshoe I** (1786–1870), to secure land for his people in the face of intense social upheaval and the insatiable land-hunger of others. Before the arrival of Moshoeshoe's ancestors, around 900 AD, the San inhabited Lesotho unchallenged. Today the San are gone, exterminated in 1873 by the last of many British campaigns against them. However, they left their mark in the country's rock paintings and elements of their tongue in the Sesotho

HIGHLIGHTS

1. Pony trekking
2. Thaba Bosiu
3. Maletsunyane Falls
4. Highlands Water Project
5. "Roof of Africa" route
6. Sehlabathebe National Park

LESOTHO

BORDER POST OPENING TIMES

Monantsa Pass	8am–4pm	Makhaleng Bridge	8am–4pm
Caledonspoort	6am–10pm	Tele Bridge	8am–10pm
Ficksburg Bridge	24hr	Ongeluksnek	8am–4pm
Peka Bridge	8am–4pm	Qacha's Nek Gate	8am–8pm
Maseru Bridge	24hr	Ramatseliso's Gate	8am–6pm
Van Rooyen's Gate	6am–10pm	Ngoangoana Gate	8am–4pm
Sepapu's Gate	8am–4pm	Sani Pass	6am–6pm

language (including seemingly impossible buzzes and clicks), while traces of their vaguely oriental features and paler skin can still be discerned in some Basotho faces.

The Basotho first settled the fertile plains that today form the Lesotho lowlands and South Africa's Free State, before going on to colonize the mountains. They farmed these plains relatively peacefully for centuries, but by Moshoeshoe's time, tribes from elsewhere had forced thousands of Basotho off their land.

Moshoeshoe became chief in 1820 and established himself on a mountaintop near **Butha-Buthe**, where he became patron to many refugees in search of safety. However, after a particularly vicious attack on Butha-Buthe in 1824, Moshoeshoe decided it was no longer safe and trekked south with his followers in search of a better mountain. He found one at **Thaba Bosiu**, which, though attacked repeatedly, was never taken. Moshoeshoe earned an almost mythical reputation for wisdom and generosity among ordinary Basotho that survives to this day.

The Europeans in Lesotho

The kingdom was encroached upon by land-hungry Europeans from the 1840s onwards, and the **Orange Free State** government invaded in 1858, their soldiers destroying Morija before launching a failed attack on Thaba Bosiu. They nonetheless captured plenty of farmland, whose acquisition was sanctioned by a British treaty in 1860. In 1865, the Orange Free State government cited Basotho cattle theft as the pretext for a new conflict, though few could deny Moshoeshoe's bitter assertion that "my great sin is that I possess a good and fertile country". The ensuing **Seqiti War** resulted in the destruction of Basotho crops, forcing Moshoeshoe into a humiliating treaty in 1866 that signed over most of his remaining good land. The war resumed in 1867, and was halted only by the British taking over what was left of the kingdom as the protectorate of **Basotholand** in 1868. The Treaty of Aliwal North in 1869 restored Moshoeshoe's land east of the Caledon River but left the rest with the Free State, where it has remained to this day – a loss that still stings.

Moshoeshoe died in 1870 and the British handed Basotholand to the Cape administration a year later, which began taxing its new subjects, establishing a series of hut tax-collection points that have since grown into Lesotho's small towns. Discontent turned to open rebellion in 1879, when the Cape government decided to confiscate all Basotho firearms. The result was the **Gun War**, one of the few colonial-era conflicts in which the locals prevailed; the prize for the victorious Basotho was the resumption of direct rule from Britain in 1884.

Independence

Along with Bechuanaland and Swaziland, Basotholand rejected incorporation into the union of South Africa in 1910, with **King Letsie II** instead helping found the South African Native National Congress (later the ANC) in 1912. During the following years, the monarchy and chiefs' position declined, partly because British reforms forced their uneasy conversion into a junior arm of the colonial civil service, but also because social changes at work in the region, like migration, urbanization and rising education levels, proved too much for them to adapt to. In 1960, when **Moshoeshoe II** was crowned king, independence politics were in full swing, spearheaded by Pan-Africanist Ntsa Mokhele's Basotho Congress Party (BCP), and rivalled by the more conservative Basotho National Party (BNP). After narrowly winning the 1965 elections, the BNP led newly named Lesotho to **independence** on October 4, 1966. However, after losing the 1970 election, prime minister Leabua Jonathan annulled the result, declared a **state of emergency**, and carried on ruling until he was toppled in 1986 by a **military coup** led by Major General Metsing Lekhanya. Lekhanya ordered the **expulsion of the ANC** from Lesotho and signed an agreement that year with apartheid South Africa for the **Lesotho Highlands Water Project** (see box, p.597) – Africa's biggest engineering project to date, aiming to divert much of Lesotho's ample water resources to the thirsty South African province of Gauteng.

11

LESOTHO TRAVEL BASICS

RED TAPE AND VISAS

Visas are not required for most citizens of Western Europe and the US. If you've travelled through a **yellow fever zone**, you'll need an International Certificate of Vaccination against yellow fever. The standard entry permit is for 14 or 28 days; should you need an extension, visit the Department of Immigration on Assisi Road in Maseru (☎2232 3771).

ROAD TAX

A "road fund" **fee** of M30 is payable when entering Lesotho by car.

TOUR OPERATORS

Lesotho's tourist infrastructure remains sketchy in some areas, and arranging activities such as pony trekking and visits to the natural parks can be time-consuming, especially without your own transport. If you're short on time, consider an **organized tour**. *Malealea Lodge* (see p.605) in the southwest offers some innovative pony trekking and 4WD combinations, while the *Trading Post Guest House* in Roma (see p.590) is the best source of information on mountain biking and can put together customized tours. Coming from South Africa, Thaba Tours (☎+27 33 701 2888, ⓦthabatours.co.za) in Underberg specializes in overland trips in Lesotho via Sani Pass, pony trekking, biking and hiking.

MONEY

Lesotho's currency is the **loti**, plural **maluti** (M), divided into 100 lisenti; the loti is tied to the South African rand (R1=M1). You can also use South African rand throughout Lesotho, but you cannot use or exchange maluti anywhere outside Lesotho (apart from in some border towns such as Ladybrand), so make sure you use them up or exchange them before leaving.

FOOD

The Basotho staple **food** is *papa*, maize meal which is boiled and stirred until it resembles stiff, white mashed potato. An alternative is *nyekoe*, brown beans mixed with sorghum and wheat. Both are fairly bland but filling and usually served with some kind of *nama* (meat) and *moroho*

In 1990, Lekhanya sent Moshoeshoe II into exile and installed Moshoeshoe's son on the throne as **Letsie III**, but a year later Lekhanya was himself ousted by Major General Phisona, who then gave way to a **democratically elected government** led by Mokhele's BCP in 1993. Letsie stood down in favour of his father in 1995, but Moshoeshoe II died in a car crash the next year, and Letsie regained the throne.

In 1997, the BCP split with Mokhele and most of his cabinet, breaking away to form the Lesotho Congress for Democracy (LCD). The following year Mokhele's health deteriorated and he was forced to step down just before the **1998 elections**, which his successor Pakalitha Mosisili won by a landslide. Opposition parties cried foul amid widespread allegations of **vote-rigging**, and in July and August, crowds gathered outside the Royal Palace in Maseru demanding that the results be overturned – these protests subsequently developed into a **mutiny** by Lesotho Defence Force soldiers. In September, under the flag of a Southern African Development Community (SADC) peacekeeping force, **South African troops** crossed the border, and fierce fighting took place around military bases and at the strategically vital Katse Dam. Meanwhile, thousands of demonstrators protested at what they regarded as South Africa's heavy-handed intervention, and a large number of shops and offices across the country were looted and burned. After the 1998 riots, Lesotho's electoral system was changed to combine majority voting and proportional representation: eighty parliamentary seats are elected by the first-past-the-post system, forty through proportional representation. Despite some scandals and unrest, subsequent elections have taken place with little incident.

(leafy vegetable – usually spinach or cabbage). On the street, you'll find *dipapata*, delicious steamed bread, and a fried snack called *makoenya* or fat cakes.

PHONE NUMBERS

Lesotho's **country code** is ☎ 266. There are no **area codes**. To call collect, dial the international operator on ☎ 109. If dialling South Africa, you should include the +27 international code.

BOOKS AND MAPS

The Morija Museum (see p.604) and some lodges sell books on Lesotho; a number of these lodges also stock a very good 1:250,000 **topographical map** of Lesotho that marks most trails. The Department of Lands, Surveys and Physical Planning on Lerotholi Road, near the corner of Constitution Road in Maseru (☎ 2232 2376), is the only place where you can buy the really detailed 1:50,000 maps, essential for serious hiking if you don't take a guide.

WEBSITES

ⓦ **gov.ls** The Lesotho government's portal with national news and links to its ministries.

ⓦ **publiceyenews.com** An independent local website with news, politics, business and events.

ⓦ **seelesotho.com** A wealth of information about the history, culture, flora and fauna of Lesotho, plus tips on where to visit and how to get there.

ⓦ **sesotho.web.za** The first stop if you are interested in learning Sesotho, with guidance on greetings and basic phrases in addition to references for Sesotho publications. There's an online dictionary too.

ⓦ **visitlesotho.travel** Lesotho's official tourism website has maps, accommodation and restaurant listings, driving route tips and contact details.

PUBLIC HOLIDAYS

January 1 New Year's Day
March 11 Moshoeshoe Day
Good Friday
Easter Monday
May 1 Workers' Day
May 25 Heroes' Day

July 17 King's Birthday
Ascension Day (Thursday)
October 4 Independence Day
December 25 Christmas Day
December 26 Boxing Day

Current challenges

Aside from politics, there are some promising economic opportunities for Lesotho. **Mining** brings in significant revenue: since reopening in 2004, the diamond mine at Letseng has discovered four of the world's largest diamonds, and has the potential to provide up to fifteen percent of Lesotho's GDP in the coming years. The government continues to attract funding from international donors to battle poverty. And the royalties from the **Lesotho Highlands Water Project** are guaranteed for the foreseeable future.

However, a number of gargantuan challenges remain. **Poverty** is entrenched, particularly in rural areas where the majority rely on small-scale agriculture. It was these areas that were pushed to the brink of emergency in 2007 when Lesotho suffered its worst **drought** in thirty years, resulting in a government appeal for food aid from the international community. **Environmental degradation** remains an issue too, ever visible in the numerous erosion-caused gullies, or dongas, across the country. And economically, Lesotho is still recovering from the massive losses in its textile exports, caused by Chinese competition, and suffers very high levels of **unemployment**. Most devastating of all is the scourge of **HIV/AIDS**; with 23 percent of the population HIV positive, the prevalence of the pandemic in Lesotho is the highest in the world after Swaziland; at one point life expectancy for the nation had plummeted to 43 years, and it now stands at around 50. Corruption, incompetence and political infighting have seriously hindered progress in all these fields, and the future prospects of the mountain kingdom depend on overcoming these challenges.

ARRIVAL AND DEPARTURE

By plane Flights to Lesotho only run from Johannesburg. South African Airlink operates three flights a day (1hr) to Moshoeshoe I International Airport, 18km southeast of Maseru. Taxis and a shuttle bus (M100) connect the airport with the city.

By bus There are no intercity bus services from South African cities to Lesotho's main overland border at Maseru Bridge (2km from Maseru city centre); to reach it, you have to change to a minibus taxi at Ladybrand.

By minibus taxi There are frequent minibus taxis throughout the day from Johannesburg, Bloemfontein and Durban, and less frequently from a host of smaller towns in the Free State and North West Province to various border crossings in Lesotho's western lowlands – particularly Maseru Bridge, Ficksburg Bridge (near Maputsoe) and Caledonspoort (near Butha-Buthe). All these places have plentiful onward transport connections within Lesotho, with shared taxis shuttling between the border and the nearest towns. It's also possible to enter Lesotho from the south via the spectacular Sani Pass by taking a 4WD car, a minibus taxi or hired transport from Underberg in KwaZulu-Natal (see p.390).

By car Travelling to Lesotho by car, you have a choice of fourteen border crossings, with varying opening times (see map p.578). Easiest to reach are the western lowlands crossings, including Caledonspoort (the closest to Johannesburg, an easy 350km, 4–5hr drive), Ficksburg Bridge and Maseru Bridge. The main crossings get very busy with returning migrants around weekends, and it may make sense to take a detour via a smaller crossing. If you've rented a car in South Africa, you'll need the agency to provide paperwork for crossing the border (this usually costs R500 extra, and some agencies also charge an additional cross-border fee) – also check whether the insurance covers you for Lesotho, especially for gravel roads and in winter.

SOME SIMPLE SESOTHO

The Basotho language is **Sesotho**. It can be tricky to speak, as spellings rarely correspond with pronunciation – a legacy of the bizarre nineteenth-century transcription by French missionaries, in which locals take a perverse pride. For more information about Sesotho and tips on learning the language, see ⓦ sesotho.web.za.

BASICS

Yes	*E* ("aye")
No	*E-e* ("ai-ai" as in the ai of hair)
Thank you	*Kea leboha* ("Kiya lee-bowa")
Today	*Kajeno* ("Ka-jen-noo")
Tomorrow	*Hosane* ("Ho-san-nee")
Yesterday	*Moobane* ("Mow-ban-nee")
Where is …?	*E kae …?* ("O kai …")
Where can we stay?	*Nka lula hokae?* ("N-ka dula o kai")
Where are you going?	*U ea kae?* ("Oo ya kai")
Where are you from?	*U tsoa kae?* ("Oo tswa kai")
How much?	*Ke bokae?* ("Ke bo-kai")
I speak Sesotho a little	*Ke bua Sesotho ha nyane* ("Ke boo-a Sesotho han-yaney")

GREETINGS AND RESPONSES

Hello (informal)	*Khotso* ("Khot-so" – literally "peace")
Hello (to one)	*Lumela* ("Do-mela")
…father (used to address any man)	*Ntate* ("N-dar-tay")
…mother (used to address any woman)	*Me* ("Mmeh")
…brother (used to address any boy)	*Abuti* ("A-boo-ti")
…sister (used to address any girl)	*Ausi* ("A-woo-si")
Hello (to many)	*Lumelang* ("Do-melang")
How are you? (formal)	*U phela jooang* ("O pela jwan")
I'm fine (formal)	*Ke phela hantle* ("Ke pela hank-le" – with a clicked *k*)
Goodbye (said by person leaving)	*Sala hantle* ("Sala hank-le" – literally "stay well")
Goodbye (said by person remaining)	*Tsamaea hantle* ("Ts-my-ya hank-le" – literally "go well")

GETTING AROUND

By car Lesotho has a good tarred road network, though it's hard to avoid dirt (and often boulder-strewn) roads when heading to more out-of-the-way places. Thanks to a newly tarred road between Mokhotlong and Sani Pass, the main route from Maseru north is smooth all the way to the border. The beautiful road from Leribe to Katse Dam is also tarred, as is the road from Maseru to Thaba-Tseka; as the gravel road between Thaba-Tseka and Katse can be handled by saloon cars this makes a big two- or three-day loop from Maseru via Thaba-Tseka and Katse to Leribe possible. The southern route from Maseru is tarred all the way to Qacha's Nek. Fuel costs roughly the same as in South Africa; unleaded is readily available in Maseru, but can be scarce elsewhere. When approaching a police roadblock, be sure to wait at the stop sign until you are waved through. The speed limit is 80km/h, and 50km/h in urban areas. Hitching is much safer than in South Africa and is a good way to get around.

By minibus taxi Inexpensive minibus taxis are the main form of public transport, and run on major routes, at least until early afternoon.

By bus Slower and even less comfortable, but safer than minibus taxis and very inexpensive. Buses simply leave when they're full, and operate just like minibus taxis.

Maseru and the central districts

11

A convenient entry point from South Africa, and the country's most sophisticated urban centre by far, **Maseru** is a handy first stop for exploring Lesotho, and is the place to fill up on supplies and organize onward transport. Apart from a few elegant colonial sandstone buildings, there's not a great deal to see here. However, if you're in town for a few days there are plenty of excursions into the surrounding countryside, including to **Thaba Bosiu**, the so-called "Mountain of the Night" where the founder of the nation, Moshoeshoe I, ruled for almost fifty years.

Further afield, **Roma** is the country's academic centre, surrounded by beautiful sandstone hills and with a historic Catholic mission. South of Roma, a road ascends into the **central highlands** – one of the most striking drives in the country. At the end of the road, the village of **Semonkong** has a superb lodge, the spectacular **Maletsunyane** waterfall nearby and a wide variety of outdoor activities on offer. Continuing along the A3 east of Roma, a wonderful tarred road heads up into Lesotho's **Central Range**, with particularly spectacular driving between the impressive Mohale Dam and **Thaba-Tseka**.

Maseru

Sprawling **MASERU**, the nation's capital and only big town, spreads east from the Caledon River, which marks the border with South Africa. Maseru was established by the British in 1869 as the administrative centre for newly annexed Basotholand, but Britain put as little effort into developing the town as it did the rest of the country, no doubt expecting it to become just a minor South African town when Basotholand was incorporated into South Africa.

Surrounded by sprawling shantytown suburbs, the city has grown swiftly over recent years, poverty in Lesotho's rural areas having driven people to the capital in search of a better life. Few have found it yet, and the city has a high unemployment rate. Yet Maseru's compact centre has all the marks of an upwardly mobile African city, with slick fashions and mobile phones much in evidence.

Maseru's older buildings, as well as some stylish new ones, are built from well-crafted local **sandstone** – from which the city gets its name – though a number of ugly concrete box buildings diminish the effect and, unfortunately, dominate the skyline. Most of the city's daytime action happens on or around **Kingsway**, the road that runs through town, becoming increasingly downmarket and lively as it heads east towards the cathedral. Compared with most towns and cities in South Africa, Maseru is relatively safe, and as long as you take the **safety precautions** you would in any other African city, you can walk around here comfortably by day. It's not advised to walk around at night, however.

11

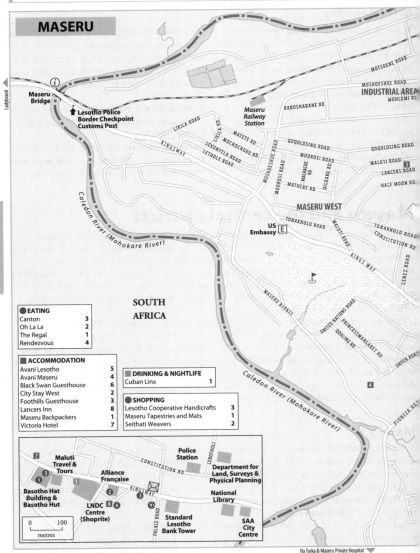

MASERU

EATING
Canton	3
Oh La La	2
The Regal	1
Rendezvous	4

ACCOMMODATION
Avani Lesotho	5
Avani Maseru	4
Black Swan Guesthouse	6
City Stay West	2
Foothills Guesthouse	3
Lancers Inn	8
Maseru Backpackers	1
Victoria Hotel	7

DRINKING & NIGHTLIFE
Cuban Linx	1

SHOPPING
Lesotho Cooperative Handicrafts	3
Maseru Tapestries and Mats	1
Seithati Weavers	2

Maseru's landmarks

The town's most famous landmarks used to be the trio of neo-traditional thatched buildings at the west end of Kingsway. Unfortunately, the **Basotho Shield** building, which housed the tourist office, burnt down in 2011; what remains is the **Basotho Hut**, home to the *Regal* restaurant (see p.587), and the appropriately shaped **Mokorotlo (Basotho Hat) Building**, housing the well-stocked Lesotho Cooperative Handicrafts shop (see box, p.588). The main part of town lies east of here along Kingsway, though there's not much to see other than a handful of colonial-era buildings: the **Alliance Française** (Mon–Thurs 9am–1pm & 2–7pm, Fri 9am–1pm & 2–5pm, Sat 8.30am–1pm; ☎2232 5722) in the former library at the corner with Pioneer Road, the former **Anglican church**

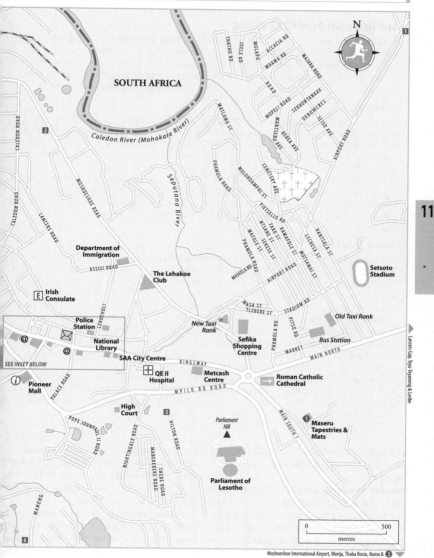

Moshoeshoe International Airport, Morija, Thaba Bosiu, Roma &

next to it, and the 1891 **Resident Commissioner's House** (now a government department), on the left beyond the towering **Post Office** building. Kingsway comes to an end at the traffic circle by the impressively large sandstone **Roman Catholic Cathedral**, where it splits into Main North Road and Main South Road.

ARRIVAL AND DEPARTURE

MASERU

By plane Moshoeshoe I International Airport (☎ 2235 0777), 18km southeast of town off Main South Rd (the A2 towards Mafeteng), is served by daily flights from Johannesburg (3 daily; 1hr) by South African Airlink

(☎ 2235 0418, ⓦ flyairlink.com). Private taxis (see p.586) and the shuttle company Airport Shuttle and Tours (☎ 5885 5527, ✉ airportshuttle@ymail.com) charge around M100. Alternatively, wait for an infrequent minibus taxi at the

HIKING AND PONY TREKKING

Hospitable and almost entirely fenceless, Lesotho is a **hiker's paradise**. It's possible to set off into the hills and walk for as long as you like, with no prospect of an angry farmer yelling at you to get off his land – quite a change from South Africa. In more remote areas, locals get around by pony, and **pony trekking** – which can be arranged at most tourist-oriented lodges and two of the three national parks – is an undoubted highlight of any trip to the country.

HIKING

Always **prepare adequately** before setting out, and bring supplies for at least a day more than you think the hike will take. Be warned that in the highest reaches of the highlands there are very few villages; lovely as this is, it's also risky, so make sure someone knows where you've gone, and don't hike in remote areas on your own. Lesotho's weather is notoriously fickle – be prepared for all eventualities.

Bring enough cash (you can't count on rural banks changing money), a torch, plenty of food (there aren't many shops in remote rural areas), a water container, water-purifying tablets, an all-weather cooker with fuel (don't count on finding firewood), a genuinely waterproof tent, a sleeping mat and a very warm sleeping bag. A compass and map (see box, p.581) are also invaluable.

PONY TREKKING

A number of lodges and other places offer **pony trekking** (no previous equestrian experience needed) though only a few are well organized, the best being the *Malealea Lodge* (see p.605), *Semonkong Lodge* (see p.593) and *Maliba Lodge* (see p.599). Semonkong, Mokhotlong, Bokong and Ts'ehlanyane are all high up; the others are lower down, with less variable weather conditions, though the terrain is harder on the ponies.

Costs vary according to group size, but tend to average M300 per person for short two-to-four-hour trips; for overnights, count on an extra M120–200 per person per day, which can include a pack horse as well as accommodation. A full-day's ride typically involves six or seven hours (10–15km) in the saddle, so overnight trips can be quite strenuous. Children under 12 are not usually allowed on overnights.

Wherever you go, make sure you bring a wide-brimmed sunhat, sun protection cream, waterproof gear, swimwear in summer, and a water bottle (and, if you're staying overnight, a sleeping bag, a mat and a torch; you can usually pay a bit extra for locally cooked meals to be provided).

---

airport gate. Avis/Budget (☎ 2235 0328, ⓦ avis.com) and Europcar (☎ 2235 0299, ⓦ europcar.com) have offices at the airport.

Overland from South Africa Minibus taxis from South Africa terminate at the Maseru Bridge border crossing. Walk over the bridge and complete the formalities, then either walk or catch a minibus taxi or a "4 plus 1" (saloon taxi – four passengers plus one driver) for the 2km ride into town (both M6.50).

By bus Intercity buses from within Lesotho drop you on Stadium Road, 10min walk east of the city centre, or M6.50 by minibus or local taxi. Walking by day with luggage is safe, if a somewhat amusing sight for locals. Most buses leave from the chaotic bus station between Market St and Pitso Ground, northeast of the cathedral roundabout.

Destinations Bokong (3hr); Leribe (1hr 30min); Mafeteng (1hr 30min); Mokhotlong (6hr); Morija (1hr); Qacha's Nek (7hr); Quthing (3hr); Roma (45min); Semonkong (3hr 30min); Teya-Teyaneng (45min).

By minibus taxi Minibus taxis arriving from elsewhere in Lesotho will drop you at one of two chaotic ranks, both within a few hundred metres of the cathedral. Minibus taxis to and from the south depart from the New Taxi Rank (also known as Sefika Taxi Rank), next to the Sefika Shopping Centre on Moshoeshoe Rd. Minibus taxis to and from the east and north use the Old Taxi Rank, 200m east of the bus station. Regular minibus taxis and 4 plus 1s link both taxi ranks to the city centre.

GETTING AROUND

The city centre is compact and easy to get around on foot during the day; at night it's recommended to take a taxi. There are lots of **minibus taxis** running up and down Kingsway and into the suburbs, from just before dawn to around 8pm. At night, **private taxis** are the only option; operators include Superb Taxis (☎ 2831 9647), Moon Lite Taxis (☎ 2231 2695) and Perfect Taxis (☎ 2232 5222).

INFORMATION

Tourist information The Lesotho Tourism Development Corporation has tourist information booths at Maseru Bridge at the border with South Africa (daily 8am–5pm; ☎2231 2427), and in the Pioneer Mall on Pioneer Rd (Mon–Fri 9am–6pm, Sat 9am–3pm, Sun 9am–1pm; ☎2833 2238).

ACCOMMODATION

Maseru is the only place in the country where there's much choice of accommodation, offering everything from camping to luxury suites in plush hotels. The central options, on or near Kingsway, are the most practical if you don't have your own transport.

Avani Lesotho Hilton Rd ☎2224 3000, ⓦminorhotels.com; map p.584. Maseru's largest and smartest accommodation option, this resort has comfortable (if smallish) rooms with TVs and good views over town, plus loads of sports facilities, a health spa, casino, cinema and several good restaurants. M1591

Avani Maseru 12 Orpen Rd ☎2231 2434, ⓦminorhotels.com; map p.584. The second of the town's *Avani* hotels, with decent rooms in soothing, well-tended garden surroundings, which are popular with locals in the evenings. There is also a good restaurant and a large, attractive swimming pool. M1320

Black Swan Guesthouse 28 Manong Rd, Hillsview ☎+27 72 580 4614 (South Africa), ⓦblackswan.co.ls; map p.584. Located in a quiet residential neighbourhood, this hotel has sixteen clean and attractive rooms and a small indoor pool set around a tidy compound with a duck pond. M880

City Stay West 221 Moshoeshoe Rd, Maseru West ☎2232 4215, ✉citystaywest@gmail.com; map p.584. A boutique guesthouse north of the centre near the industrial area; the elegant rooms with sandstone brick walls are nicely decorated with sleek bathrooms. M770

Foothills Guesthouse 121 Maluti Rd, Maseru West ☎5870 6566, ⓦfoothills.co.ls; map p.584. This colonial-style sandstone house offers simple, homely accommodation in a quiet part of town; in addition to the six comfortable and spotless rooms, there are a couple of self-catering chalets. M600

Lancers Inn Kingsway, corner of Pioneer Rd ☎2231 2114, ⓦwww.lancersinn.co.ls; map p.584. Maseru's most central, characterful and pleasant place to stay, set in an attractive complex around a sandstone building. There are well-priced and comfortable rondavels and chalets with en-suite bathrooms, a pool and a good beer garden and restaurant, all set in pretty gardens. M1025

Maseru Backpackers Airport Rd ☎2232 5166 or ☎2700 5453, ⓦlesothodurhamlink.org; map p.584. The best camping option in Maseru is run by an Anglican centre, with clean shower blocks and a well-equipped kitchen, plus comfortable four-bed rondavels and decent backpacker accommodation in small dormitories. The site, signposted as "Lesotho Durham Link" just beyond the old airport, overlooks the Maqalika Dam; they can arrange a number of outdoor activities. Camping M100, dorms M180, rondavels M700

Victoria Hotel Kingsway ☎2231 3687, ✉reservations@hotelvictoria.co.ls; map p.584. This plain concrete hotel towering over Kingsway, opposite the Basotho Hat Building, offers comfortable if unremarkable rooms, a good pool, a restaurant and a club; it caters to business travellers, so discounts are often available on weekends. M850

EATING

As you'd expect, Maseru has the best selection of restaurants in Lesotho. Several pricey, upmarket places can be found in the Lesotho and Maseru *Avani* hotels.

Canton Moposo House, Kingsway ☎2231 2003; map p.584. Despite the tacky interior, this is an excellent Chinese restaurant, spread across two floors. Try Lesotho-style stew or Chinese dumplings (M30), fried beef (M65) or duck. Mon–Thurs & Sun 9.30am–9.30pm, Fri & Sat 9.30am–11pm.

Oh La La Kingsway, corner of Pioneer Rd ☎6335 6570; map p.584. With terrace seating in the garden of the Alliance Française, this rondavel houses the best café in town, with fresh sandwiches on baguettes (M30), croissants, crêpes (ham and mozzarella M38), pastries and pies, plus good coffee and fresh juice. Mon–Fri 7.30am–9pm, Sat 7.30am–8pm, Sun 9am–4pm.

★**The Regal** Kingsway ☎2231 3930; map p.584. The best non-hotel dining experience in the country, *The Regal* specializes in Mugali cuisine traditionally prepared for royalty. It has a stylish dining room and balcony on the first floor of the thatched Basotho Hut building, and serves dishes like lamb korma (M110), butter chicken (M90), vegetarian *paneer tikka* and seafood. Mon–Sat 10am–9.30pm.

Rendezvous Lancers Inn, Kingsway ☎2231 2114; map p.584. Maseru's classiest restaurant (King Letsie is known to dine here regularly), with an African- and French-themed menu and a candlelit atmosphere. There's a spicy peri-peri chicken burger for M65, Thai curry for M75, and delicious local mountain trout. The outdoor seating is popular at lunchtime. Daily 7am–11.30pm.

11

HANDICRAFTS IN MASERU

Woollen bags, carpets, tapestries and traditional Basotho hats are the most sought-after crafts in Lesotho. The Basotho Hat Building in the city centre is home to the impressive **Lesotho Cooperative Handicrafts shop** (Mon–Fri 8am–5pm, Sat 8am–4.30am; ☎ 2232 2523; accepts credit cards; map p.584), which has a small selection of books published by the Morija Museum. You'll find a few more crafts, mostly woven Basotho hats (*mokorotlo*), sold on the pavements around this end of town. Good handicraft outlets on the outskirts of town include **Maseru Tapestries & Mats** (☎ 2231 3975; map p.584) just off Main South Road, which has handwoven tapestries and carpets; and the similar **Seithati Weavers**, 8km out along Main South Road (☎ 2231 3975; map p.584).

DRINKING

Maseru isn't known for its nightlife, and the city centre tends to empty after dark. Still, there are a handful of bars that can keep you entertained well into the wee hours.

Cuban Linx First floor of LNDC Centre, Kingsway ☎ 5890 2377; map p.584. Trendy bar that serves a selection of vaguely Cuban-themed food like mojito lamb chops (M90) and pork ribs, in addition to the usual cocktails (from M38) and plentiful quantities of Maluti beer. If you can stand the constant blaring of taxi horns, eat and drink alfresco on the balcony. Mon–Wed 10am–11pm, Thurs–Sat 10am–4am, Sun 1–11pm.

DIRECTORY

Banks and currency exchange The main branches and ATMs of Standard Lesotho Bank, Nedbank and First National Bank are on Kingsway. The best place for foreign exchange is the Standard Bank on the ground floor of the Standard Lesotho Bank Tower, on Kingsway.

Embassies and consulates South Africa, corner Kingsway and Old School Rd (☎ 2222 5800, ⓦ www.dirco .gov.za); USA, 254 Kingsway (☎ 2231 2666, ⓦ maseru .usembassy.gov).

Gym The Lehakoe Club, on the corner of Parliament and Moshoeshoe roads (☎ 2223 2300), offers exercise classes, indoor and outdoor pools, squash, tennis and a well-equipped gym, all open to non-members.

Hospitals Queen Elizabeth II Hospital, Kingsway (☎ 2231 2501); Maseru Private Hospital, Thetsane Rd (☎ 2231 2276).

Internet Newland Internet Café, on Kingsway opposite

the Post Office (Mon–Fri 8.30am–5.30pm, Sat 8.30am–3.30pm, Sun 9am–2pm).

Pharmacy MHS Pharmacy, LNDC Centre, Kingsway (☎ 2232 5189).

Police Constitution Rd (☎ 5888 1024).

Post office Kingsway (Mon–Fri 8am–4.30pm, Sat 8am–noon).

Supermarkets A large, well-stocked Pick 'n Pay supermarket can be found in the Pioneer Mall on Pioneer Rd (Mon–Sat 8am–8pm, Sun 8am–5pm).

Travel agents Flight ticketing and Intercape bus tickets are available through South African City Centre Maseru Travel on Kingsway (☎ 2231 4536, ⓔ mampek .maserutravel@galileosa.co.za), and Maluti Travel & Tours, next to First National Bank on Kingsway (☎ 2232 7172, ⓔ valentinem.maluti@galileo.co.za). Intercape bus tickets are sold at the Shoprite supermarket in the LNDC Centre.

Thaba Bosiu

About 20km east of Maseru • M40 • ☎ 2835 7207

Although you're unlikely to spend much time in Maseru itself, there are a number of rewarding places to visit within easy reach of the capital. **Thaba Bosiu** is Lesotho's most important historical sight, a steep mountain with a large flat top that was the capital of the kingdom in the days of Moshoeshoe I. It is a place of great significance to the people of Lesotho and the burial ground of the country's kings, and well worth a visit.

Moshoeshoe I trekked with his followers from Butha-Buthe to Thaba Bosiu in July 1824 in a bid to settle somewhere far from the warrior clans then terrorizing the flat plains to the north and west, and somewhere that would be extremely hard for anyone to capture. Thaba Bosiu, with its crown of near-vertical cliffs, good grazing and seven or eight freshwater springs on top, fitted the bill perfectly, and despite numerous attacks, the mountain was never taken (see box opposite). The name means "Mountain of the Night", perhaps because, as legend has it, Moshoeshoe first arrived there in the evening, and immediate protective measures took all night to install. A more compelling reason, and the one most Basotho prefer, is that the mountain, which does not look particularly high or impressive by day, seems to grow inexorably as night falls, becoming huge and unconquerable.

Visiting Thaba Bosiu

An official guide from the visitor centre will walk you up the steep **Khubelu Pass** (or "Red Pass"), a cleft in the cliffs marked by two flagpoles, where the Afrikaner General Louw Wepener was killed trying to storm the mountain in 1865 (see box below), and on to the remains of Moshoeshoe's **European house**, built for him by a deserter from the 72nd Seaforth Highlanders, David F. Webber. From here, it's a short walk to the remains of Moshoeshoe's royal court and then to the **royal graveyard**, where the tombs of Moshoeshoe I and most of his successors are marked with simple stone cairns. On the eastern edge of the plateau you get a great view of **Qiloane**, a strange cone-shaped mountain with a large nodule on the top, which was apparently the inspiration for the national headdress, the distinctive Basotho hat (*mokorotlo*).

At the bottom of Thaba Bosiu is a small **cultural village** (daily 6am–10pm; M20; ☎ 5022 1962, ⓦ thevillage.co.ls), essentially a collection of reconstructed traditional huts; it's worth a look, but if you've spent any time in up-country Lesotho, huts like these will already be familiar to you.

11

TAKING THABA BOSIU

In 1828, the Ngwane were the first to attack Thaba Bosiu, but were decisively beaten, after which they never troubled Moshoeshoe again. **Mzilikhazi**, King of the Ndebele, who later conquered much of modern-day Zimbabwe, tried to take the mountain in 1831, but his men were defeated by a mass of great boulders flung down from the top by the Basotho; Moshoeshoe is reputed to have sent the Ndebele a large number of fat oxen after their defeat, an unprecedented move for a victorious chief – as if to say that he understood that their attack had been inspired by hunger and that he wanted to help them out.

There followed a twenty-year period of relative calm, during which time Moshoeshoe would receive visitors wearing a beautifully tailored dark-blue military uniform, complete with cloak, and offer them tea from a prized china tea service. He allowed the French missionary **Eugene Casalis** to establish a mission at the bottom of the mountain in 1837, and employed him as his secretary and interpreter. In 1852 a British punitive force led by the Cape governor **Sir George Cathcart** didn't even make it as far as the mountain, instead being attacked a short distance away by Moshoeshoe's well-armed troops, who forced their hasty withdrawal. **Afrikaner forces** fighting for the Orange Free State (OFS) made a brief attempt on Thaba Bosiu in 1858, but came back in 1865 in a more determined manner, armed with heavy artillery, and began steadily shelling the mountain, launching two simultaneous assaults a few days later. Eight men made it to the top, but were seriously wounded as soon as they did so, and speedily retreated back down. A week later, more Afrikaner troops and the OFS president turned up, and another assault was launched. **General Wepener** led his men right to the top of the Khubelu Pass, but he was shot at the top and mortally wounded. The Basotho then mounted a counterattack, and the Afrikaners withdrew. They continued the siege for a month, though, during which time most of the livestock on Thaba Bosiu died of hunger and the Basotho became so short of bullets that they melted down the shells being fired at them to make home-made ones.

Although they won this battle, the Basotho lost the war, and Moshoeshoe signed a humiliating treaty in 1866 that surrendered most of Lesotho's farmland to the OFS. Four years later the old king died and was buried on the top of Thaba Bosiu, and two years after that Lesotho was annexed to the Cape Colony.

11

ARRIVAL AND DEPARTURE

By car To get to Thaba Bosiu by car, take Main South Road from Maseru, turning left 4km beyond the cathedral at the Engen petrol station. Follow this road for 10km and turn left at the T-junction for another 3km. Alternatively, follow Main South Road further towards Roma and follow signs to Thaba Bosiu.

By bus and minibus taxi During the day, frequent minibus taxis run here from Maseru's New Taxi Rank (45min).

INFORMATION

Tourist information At the foot of the mountain, just outside the cultural village (Mon–Fri 8am–5pm, Sat 9am–5pm, Sun 9am–1pm; ☎2835 7207, ✉m .mokuku@ltdc.org.ls). Contact them a day in advance and they can arrange ponies for a pleasant guided 2hr trip around the main sights on the mountain (M200). There's also another 2hr route taking in some rock paintings and cave dwellings. Outside opening hours you're officially not allowed up the mountain, but there's nothing to stop you.

ACCOMMODATION

Mmelesi Lodge ☎5050 0115, ✉mmelesilodge @yahoo.com. A pleasant lodge, next to the mountain and within walking distance of the visitor centre. It has a braai area, and comfortable en-suite rondavels at the back. Their *Mokhoro* restaurant serves moderately priced dishes such as burgers (from M35) and sole fillet (M75). <u>M700</u>

Thaba Bosiu Cultural Village Just below the mountain ☎5022 1962, 🌐thevillage.co.ls. Forty stylish thatched rondavels on manicured grounds, complete with all the amenities of a modern hotel, plus kitchenettes (the cultural village has a bar and restaurant if you'd rather not cook). They're often booked out for conferences, so be sure to call in advance. <u>M950</u>

Roma and around

About 30km from Maseru along a good tar road, the mission town of **ROMA** enjoys a beautiful location amid sandstone foothills and is home to the **National University of Lesotho**, which began life in 1945 as Pius XII College, run by the Roman Catholic Church. Between 1964 and 1971 it was the university of all three of the former British Southern African protectorates, now Lesotho, Botswana and Swaziland.

A kilometre or so further up the road is **Roma Mission**, most of which was built by French missionaries after 1862. Though grander than its counterpart in Morija (see p.602), the mission is a little run-down, and there's not much reason to linger.

The road to Semonkong

The road from Roma to Semonkong is one of the most spectacular in Lesotho, with superb views as you climb into the highlands. At **Moitsupeli**, 18.5km beyond Roma, look ahead towards the twin summits of the appropriately named **Thabana-li-Mele** (Breast Mountains). After the next village of Ha Dinzulu, the road continues to climb, peaking at 2000m at Nkesi's Pass and then dropping down to the village of **RAMABANTA**.

ARRIVAL AND DEPARTURE

By bus and minibus taxi Several buses and dozens of minibus taxis travel daily between Maseru and Roma, making this one of the busiest public transport routes in the country; taxis from here also run to Semonkong (2hr 30min). Minibus taxis to Roma depart from the New Taxi Rank in Maseru and take around 45min.

ACCOMMODATION

ROMA

Trading Post Guest House Signposted off the main road 2km before the centre of Roma ☎5024 5001, 🌐tradingpost.co.za. The best accommodation in Roma, built in 1903 as a trading store by John Thomas Thorn, and lived in by his family until recently. It's now run by a group of mountain-biking enthusiasts, who have bikes to rent (M250/half day, including a guide) and can organize tours of the region. The guesthouse offers luxury rondavels, en-suite doubles and comfortable dorm rooms with shared bathrooms, plus a self-catering cottage and camping. Decent meals are available by prior arrangement, and there

are two small swimming pools. Camping M120, dorms M200, doubles M700

RAMABANTA
★ **Ramabanta Trading Post Lodge** ☎ 5844 2309, ⓦ tradingpost.co.za. Sister establishment to the *Trading Post Guest House* and also an old trading post, whose lovely grounds offer stunning views of the surrounding mountains. Accommodation is in seven immaculate rooms in converted stables, each slightly different. There are also three luxury rondavels sleeping up to five, backpacker accommodation in six-bed dorms and a campsite. Meals are available and hikes and pony rides can be arranged, as can 4WD adventures (in your own car) staying overnight in villages. Camping M110, dorms M200, doubles M725

Semonkong and around

Crossing the Makhaleng River and the 3000m-high Thaba Putsoa mountain range from Maseru brings you to the curiously straggly town of **SEMONKONG**. The region was inhabited by the San until 1873, when – after a series of **genocidal campaigns** against them by the British – the last of Lesotho's San were finally exterminated by an expedition led by a certain Colonel Bowker. The town itself began life in the 1880s following the Gun War as a refuge for displaced Basotho from the lowlands. It offers a few basic stores, plenty of **bars**, and even a post office and bank, though you can't rely on either. If you're here in winter, try to catch the local **horse races** organized once a month on a Saturday; check with Semonkong Lodge for the exact dates.

Ketane Falls
From the lodge in Semonkong (see opposite), it's a day's hike or pony trek west (see box below) into the pretty Thaba Putsoa mountains to the pristine 120m **Ketane Falls**. The falls are inaccessible by any other means of transport, and the pony trek is considered one of the best in the country. The falls can also be visited on a popular multi-day pony trek from *Malealea Lodge* (see p.605).

Maletsunyane Falls
The dramatic **Maletsunyane Falls** (or Le Bihan Falls, after a French missionary) are a pretty one-hour walk downriver from Semonkong. The dramatic falls, the highest single drop in Southern Africa, plunge nearly 200m down a sheer cliff into a swimmable pool, whose mist gives the falls their name: "Smoking Water". There's a steep path down to the bottom, where you can swim or camp. The pool usually freezes by June, but the waterfall keeps going all winter, spraying the surrounding rocks with ice, and forming an impressive ice cage over the pool.

ACTIVITIES AROUND SEMONKONG

Working in conjunction with the local community, *Semonkong Lodge* offers a bewildering choice of **outdoor activities**, ranging from short walks through town and along the river in search of bald ibis, to abseiling and adventurous pony treks lasting several days staying overnight in basic huts. Advance booking is required for overnight rides. Semonkong boasts the longest commercially run **abseil** in the world, a 204m descent down the Maletsunyane Falls (M1085). It's an electrifying thirty-minute descent, just metres away from the crashing water. You'll be given training on a small cliff near the lodge before taking the challenge the next day, and receive photos of the experience afterwards.

There is also a variety of **pony treks**, from short jaunts visiting nearby sights to overnight expeditions. Per-person costs work out cheaper in larger groups; the maximum is fifteen people; couples pay M400 per person for a full day's ride. Overnight trips, including the guide and pack horse, are around M1220 per person for one night and M1890 per person for two nights. For overnight hikes, pack horses are optional but recommended. For day-trips on foot, a guide costs M130 per day.

ARRIVAL AND DEPARTURE

SEMONKONG AND AROUND

By car The 130km drive from Maseru to Semonkong takes about 3hr by car. This road, and the one from Semonkong to Qacha's Nek, have been asphalted and are fantastic drives.
By bus and minibus taxi From Maseru, buses and minibus taxis trundle up the winding road to Semonkong several times a day (3hr 30min), terminating in the village centre, 15min walk from the lodge. Taxis to Qacha's Nek also leave from here (3hr).

ACCOMMODATION

★**Semonkong Lodge** 1km south of the village centre beside the Maletsunyane River ☎2700 6037, ⊕semonkonglodge.com. One of the best lodges in Lesotho, this laidback and well-run place enjoys a spectacular location in a leafy gorge on the banks of the river. It offers en-suite doubles and a dormitory in cosy thatch-and-stone buildings, with fireplaces in most rooms. There's also a campsite, several kitchens for self-caterers, a great bar with pool table, and delicious meals (including vegetarian options). But the main reason for staying here is the immense selection of outdoor activities on offer (see box opposite). Wi-fi access costs extra. Camping M150, dorms M250, doubles M1300

Ha Baroana

About 45km east of Maseru, a few kilometres north of Nazareth village • Daily 8am–5pm • M10

Ha Baroana has what were once some of the finest rock paintings in the country. They are still interesting, with discernible figures of animals, dancers and hunters, but they have been damaged by guides who throw water at them to make them more visible for tourists. The easiest way to get to the paintings is along a difficult dirt road, signposted off the main road. After 3.5km you'll reach the village of Ha Khotso; take the second turning on your right and then continue straight on for another 3km to Ha Baroana. The attractive **visitors' centre** provides a (compulsory) guide to accompany you on the fifteen-minute walk down into the gorge.

Thaba-Tseka

The road from Mohale Dam (see box below) to **THABA-TSEKA** is a dramatic one, peaking in the heart of the Central Range at the 2860m **Mokhoabong Pass**, before descending to the town, which is over 2200m above sea level – although once here there's very little in this 1980s purpose-built administrative centre to detain you. The magnificent route from Mohale Dam has been asphalted, and it's now easy to drive from Maseru via Katse and Thaba-Tseka to Leribe, or vice versa, in two to three days.

ARRIVAL AND DEPARTURE

THABA-TSEKA

By bus and minibus taxi A number of buses and minibus taxis operate between Maseru and Thaba-Tseka (4hr); in Thaba-Tseka, they'll pick you up from anywhere along the main road.
By car With your own vehicle you could tackle the spectacular road to Mokhotlong and the Sani Pass, but it's not one you should attempt in anything other than a 4WD. The fairly flat gravel road to Katse is suitable for ordinary saloon cars.

MOHALE DAM

About 80km east of Maseru and signposted off the A3, **Mohale Dam** was completed in 2004 as Phase 1b of the Lesotho Highlands Water Project (see box, p.597). Unlike the astonishing engineering grace of Katse Dam (see p.597), Mohale is little more than an enormous pile of concrete-faced rubble, the highest of its kind in Africa, whose 145m-high barrier holds back almost a billion cubic metres of water. Connected to the Katse Dam by a 32km-long tunnel, its main purpose is to feed more water north towards South Africa. A **visitor centre** (Mon–Fri 9am–noon & 2–4pm, Sat & Sun 10am–noon & 2–4pm; ☎2293 6217), with a stunning location overlooking the lake, runs daily **tours** (M30) of the site on demand. There are cruises (M500–600 for two people) on the lake, taking in Thaba-Chitja Island and the dam wall. The visitor centre is difficult to reach without your own transport but is well signposted: follow the signs 6km beyond Mohale Camp on the A3.

ACCOMMODATION

Buffalo's Hotel At the western side of Thaba-Tseka ☎ 5080 4386, ✉ senatentabe@leo.co.ls. A neat compound of twelve comfortable rooms set back from the main road. The bar is popular with the locals, and there's a decent restaurant serving buffet dinners. M600

Mohale Lodge Near Mohale Dam, Likalaneng ☎ 2700 9199, ✉ res.mohalelodge@lhda.org.ls. This modern if somewhat bland hotel near the impressive Mohale Dam, which is visible in the distance, enjoys spectacular views of the surrounding mountains. M1160

Mohale oa Masite Lodge Near the centre of Thaba-Tseka, along the main road ☎ 2290 0980,

w mohale-oa-masite.co.ls. A pleasant, business-like but friendly hotel with en-suite rooms and a separate self-catering wing with a big kitchen, though there's also a restaurant and a bar. Popular with the 4WD crowd crossing Lesotho. M600

Motherland Guesthouse One street back from Mohale oa Masite ☎ 2890 0404, w motherland guesthouse.co.ls. A tidy and well-managed two-storey hotel with well-appointed rooms, good heating and modern facilities. It's the only hotel in town with any sort of garden, and the restaurant has a slightly better selection than most. M700

11 The northern districts

The route north from Maseru right the way round to the **Sani Pass** takes in the best of Lesotho's lowlands and highlands. The road is tarred the whole way, and although it's breaking up in places, it's fine for 2WD vehicles except in winter. The dramatic winding road from Sani Pass down the mighty Drakensberg into South Africa, however, is dirt, for which 4WD is strongly advised.

Teya-Teyaneng

TEYA-TEYANENG (usually abbreviated to "T.Y.") means "place of shifting sands", after the way the nearby river changes its course from time to time. T.Y. is the **crafts capital** of Lesotho, specializing in all manner of weavings (see box below), from jerseys to elaborately designed wall hangings.

ARRIVAL AND DEPARTURE   TEYA-TEYANENG

By car The scenic A1 Main North Road takes you through sandstone mountain-studded lowlands.

By bus and minibus taxi The bus and taxi rank is 100m east of the main highway on the road to Mapoteng. There's

plenty of transport to and from Maseru (40min) and further north to Leribe (45min) and Butha-Buthe (1hr), and you rarely have to wait long.

ACCOMMODATION AND EATING

Blue Mountain Inn A couple of hundred metres past the post office and its transmitter ☎ 2250 0362,

w bmilesotho.com. A spacious and well-run hotel with two blocks of unremarkable rooms; only the smarter

---

THE WEAVING INDUSTRY IN TEYA-TEYANENG

There are three weaving outlets in Teya-Teyaneng (all open daily 8am–5pm; call if no one is around). The most central is **Setsoto Design** (☎ 5808 6312, w setsotodesign.com) in town, where you can see tapestries being made. A good selection of woven products and crafts is sold in the adjacent shop: expect to pay around M1800 for a large tapestry and M2000 for a rug. Credit cards and online orders are accepted. Three kilometres south of town, on the left as you come in from Maseru, look for signs to the small showroom of **Hatooa Mose Mosali** (☎ 2250 0772), which translates as "women must stand up and work hard". There's a fairly limited range in stock but its catalogue displays some very special wall hangings, which you need to order as they take a week or two to make. For the best choice of products, head to **Elelloang Basali Weavers** (☎ 5851 0992, w africancrafts.com/artist/elelloang), about 5km north of town on the road to Leribe (the last building in town, constructed from recycled cans), where you'll find an extensive range of wall hangings, floor rugs, table mats and bags (from M400).

"executive" rooms have wi-fi. It also has a restaurant serving tasty meals (M60–120), plus a pizzeria, three bars, a clean pool and a large lawn with shaded tables. M900
Ka Pitseng Guest House Signposted below the main road as you approach the town from Maseru ☏ 2250

1638. A more modest option than *Blue Mountain Inn*, with a small garden, clean rooms and a decent restaurant that serves a selection of traditional Basotho dishes and drinks (including mutton tripe, steamed bread and sorghum with beans) on request (M150). M680

Ha Kome Cave Village

About 2km from the village of Mateka • Daily 8am–4.30pm • M43 • ☏ 5854 7673

Ha Kome Cave Village is an increasingly popular tourist destination, and well worth the short detour from the northern main road. Seven quaint and inhabited mud dwellings sit under a huge rock overhang, looking more like igloos or West African mud architecture than anything usually found in Southern Africa.

At the modern **visitor and crafts centre**, visible on approach from the main road, an obligatory guide accompanies you on the ten-minute walk down to the site, where the ladies living in the huts will happily show you their dwellings and pose for photos.

11

ARRIVAL AND DEPARTURE
HA KOME CAVE VILLAGE

By bus and minibus taxi Getting to the caves is easiest via Teya-Teyaneng, where you can pick up fairly regular minibus taxis to Mateka, 19km to the southeast; from here it's an easy 30min walk down the hill to the visitor centre and Kome.

By car The caves are signposted along the road from Teya-Teyaneng to Mateka; turn right onto the gravel track behind the football field in Mateka to find the road going downhill to the visitor centre. For a scenic option from Maseru, turn right onto the B31 after 4km, signposted to

Sefikeng and Kome Cave Village; this road climbs up a steep series of hairpins to Lancer's Gap, an extraordinary ridge with a great gap in the middle through which the road passes, so named because a Lancers regiment was allegedly ambushed and defeated in it during the Gun War. From Thaba Bosiu (30km away), there's also a decent, direct gravel road; however, the steep stretch of road between Sefikeng and Mateka could be problematic for saloon cars in bad weather, when you should only approach from Teya-Teyaneng.

Leribe (Hlotse)

Some 15km east of Maputsoe, a messy border town opposite Ficksburg in South Africa that's only good for its transport connections, **LERIBE** is a dilapidated but still pleasant little town, officially called **Hlotse** but more commonly known by the name of the surrounding district. It was founded in 1876 by an Anglican missionary, Reverend John Widdicombe, and suffered repeated sieges during the Gun War. With some effort, it's possible to view excellent **dinosaur footprints** at the turn-of-the-twentieth-century **Tsikoane Mission**, just over 7km south of town. To get there, turn off the main road at the white Tsikoane school sign and ask for directions to the mission, where you can tip a local to guide you up the steep slope to the rock overhang above the church. Here you'll find a large chunk of rock that fell from the overhang, which has dozens of clear three-toed Lesothosaurus footprints of varying sizes; the negative prints can be seen on the overhang ceiling.

Leribe Craft Centre

Mon–Fri 8am–4.30pm, Sat 9.30am–1pm; outside official opening hours call and someone will open up • ☏ 5877 0251

The **Leribe Craft Centre**, at the major intersection on the main road, sells wonderful mohair scarves and shawls (M200–450), blankets and tablemats made by women with disabilities, plus maps, postcards and a few books about Lesotho and its history.

ARRIVAL AND DEPARTURE
LERIBE (HLOTSE)

By car The highway from Maseru passes to the south of town, and between the two petrol stations you'll find the main intersection. The road on the

left if coming from Maseru leads up the hill to the town centre.

By bus and minibus taxi The taxi rank is reached along

11

CULTURE AS FASHION: THE BLANKET AND THE HAT

In a region of Africa where **traditional dress** has all but died out, Lesotho stands out as the exception. The **mokorotlo** (Basotho traditional hat) is not widely worn these days, admittedly, though you'll still regularly see its distinctive cone and bobble. Apparently modelled on the shape of Qiloane Mountain near Thaba Bosiu, and made of woven straw, the *mokorotlo* has become the standard Basotho souvenir, sold in every craft shop, usually for less than M100.

More prevalent than the *mokorotlo* is the Basotho **blanket**, made from high-quality woven wool and worn all over the country in all seasons. European traders started bringing these from England to Lesotho in the 1860s, though nowadays they are made in South Africa.

The symbols woven into the blankets were originally English design, but acquired significance for the Basotho over time; maize cobs were associated with fertility, for example. Young brides are supposed to wear a blanket around their hips until their first child is conceived, and boys wear different blankets before and after circumcision. The ubiquitous Fraser's Stores, which you find all over the country, first established themselves by selling blankets, and still stock them today; otherwise, The Blanket Shop, originally called Di Mezza & De Jager Trading Store, just across the border in Clarens (see box, p.440), is a great place to see a collection of historical blankets, as well as modern ones. Good ones (made of pure wool) cost M400–600, a fortune by local standards.

Although they have always been foreign imports, and are the commodities on which many European trader fortunes have been built, the blankets remain quintessentially Basotho, and a source of national pride.

the road branching off at the *Mountain View Hotel*. There's plenty of transport, though if you're heading south it may be quickest to grab a seat on one of the frequent minibuses west to Maputsoe (10min) and change there.

ACCOMMODATION AND EATING

Bird Haven Jlisimeng II, three streets east of the main crossing ☎ 5954 3030, 🌐 birdhavenleribe.com. A more homely option than Leribe's other hotels, with five charming rondavel chalets with kitchenettes and private bathrooms in a suburban garden, plus a two-room cottage and one room in the main house. **M700**

Mountain View Hotel Just up the road from the main intersection ☎ 2240 0559, 🌐 mvhlesotho.com. A range of rooms in the main buildings and in chalets and rondavels scattered around the pleasant gardens.

The restaurant serves tasty meat and fish dishes, and light snacks. There's also a lively bar, which is especially busy at weekends. **M750**

Naleli Guest House 2km from the centre along the old road north to Butha-Buthe ☎ 2240 0409, 🌐 naleliguesthouse.co.ls. The classiest accommodation in town, with a set of nicely furnished rooms that overlook a well-tended garden and terrace. The restaurant serves chicken and chips (M40) and ribs, with outdoor seating in warm weather. **M700**

The road to Katse Dam

To the east of Leribe rises the impressive Front Range of the Maloti Mountains. The region is at the heart of Phase 1a of the ambitious **Lesotho Highlands Water Project** (see box opposite), whose centrepiece is the massive dam and reservoir at **Katse**. The 100km A8 highway built for the dam from Leribe is a remarkable journey almost worth making for the drive alone, rising steeply up from the lowlands and over the 3090m **Mefika Lisiu Pass**, before reaching the Bokong Nature Reserve and dropping down to Katse Dam.

Bokong Nature Reserve

Just off the A8 • Daily 8am–5pm • M15 • Guides M30/day • Horses M150/half day, M250/day • ☎ 2246 0723

Established as part of the Highlands Water Project (see box opposite), and a paradise for high-altitude hikers, the breathtaking **Bokong Nature Reserve** features the dramatic **Lepaqoa Waterfall**, which freezes in winter to form a column of ice.

The reserve's **entrance** is next to the **visitor centre**, along the highway 3km beyond the pass. Perched dramatically on the edge of a 100m cliff overlooking the Lepaqoa valley, the visitor centre offers a 45-minute walk along a poorly marked footpath to the top of the Lepaqoa Waterfall, as well as guides and horses for hire. Call to enquire about the two- to three-day pony-riding or hiking trips across the plateau, 32km north to Ts'ehlanyane National Park.

Katse Dam

Visitor centre Mon–Fri 7am–5pm, Sat & Sun 9am–2pm • **Dam wall tours** Mon–Fri 9am & 2pm, Sat & Sun 9am, 11am & 2pm • M30 • **Botanical gardens** Mon–Fri 7am–5pm, Sat & Sun 9am–2pm • M30 • ☎ 2291 0377, ⓦ lhda.org.ls

Katse village, a former engineers' village overlooking the lake, is drab and boring, with uniform box-like houses. But the massive **dam** below (see box below), which holds back nearly two billion cubic metres of water, really is impressive, even if you aren't usually interested in engineering. To find out more, head for the **visitor centre**, with its bright blue roof, just before the village and dam. The hour-long **tours** take in the tunnels running from inside the dam into the mountainside, as well as the road on top, from where you can look straight down the wall.

During initial excavations it was discovered that the bedrock was seismically unstable, so a moveable joint was incorporated into the dam's base, allowing it to flex. Even so, the rapid filling of the reservoir caused a series of minor **earth tremors**. This was all to be expected, said the engineers, but not by the inhabitants of Ha Mapaleng, where a tremor ripped a 30cm-wide, 1.5km-long gash through the village. The local prophetess explained that a huge **underground snake** had been disturbed by the dam's construction and that the entire village would be gobbled up. No one hung around to find out, and the village was eventually relocated 1km away.

Situated in the village and overlooking the dam lake, the **botanical gardens** are beautiful to visit, with several "Afro-alpine" ecosystems represented on the sloping terrain, attracting colourful birds. It's something of a refugee camp for thousands of critically endangered spiral aloes rescued from the construction sites and thieves, and a programme to plant seedlings of spiral aloes and montane bamboo is under way.

ARRIVAL AND DEPARTURE
THE ROAD TO KATSE DAM

BOKONG NATURE RESERVE
By bus and minibus taxi The reserve can be reached from Leribe on minibus taxis that run regularly to Katse; ask to be dropped off at the visitor centre, 100m off the main road. If the minibuses returning from Katse to Leribe are full, try a minibus going 15km east to nearby Ha Lejone and pick up transport there.

THE LESOTHO HIGHLANDS WATER PROJECT

Lesotho's abundance of water but shortage of cash and Gauteng's monetary wealth and water poverty is the rationale for the stunningly ambitious **Lesotho Highlands Water Project** – Africa's largest engineering venture to date. The essence of the project is to dam Lesotho's major south-flowing rivers, then divert the water north through gravity tunnels (the longest in the world) via a hydroelectric power station at 'Muela to the Ash River, north of Clarens in South Africa, from where the water flows into the Vaal and to Gauteng. For this, South Africa pays Lesotho royalties of around R60 million a month.

The treaty formalizing the project was signed in 1986, although without much popular consultation or assessment of the environmental impact. Various compensation arrangements have been put in place for villagers affected by flooding, though there are grumbles that these promises have not been met.

The project's first phase, which concluded in 2004, saw the construction of the 185m-high Katse Dam, an underground hydroelectric plant at 'Muela, tunnels to the Ash River, and all the road infrastructure. Facilities were developed at Liphofung Cave, Katse and the nature reserves as part of this phase, the idea being that local communities would benefit from tourism revenues. It also saw the construction of Mohale Dam on the Senqunyane River, linked to Katse reservoir by tunnel. In 2014 the second phase of the project kicked off, entailing the construction of the 2.2-billion-litre Polihali Dam in Mokhotlong district, which will transfer water through another tunnel to Katse reservoir; completion of this new dam is expected in 2024.

11

KATSE
By bus and minibus taxi Public transport arrives at and departs from the taxi rank at the entrance to Katse village. There are daily buses to Maseru, leaving around 6am (7hr), and minibus taxis every few hours to Leribe (3hr). There are also several buses and minibus taxis every day to and from Thaba-Tseka, 2–3hr south along a good gravel road.

ACCOMMODATION AND EATING

PITSENG
Aloes Guest House Follow the signs from the A8 ☎ 2700 5626, ✉ aloesguesthouse@gmail.com. Dreary Pitseng, on the A8, is notable only for this stylish guesthouse, which offers thatched bungalows set around a grassy compound with a small pool, self-catering facilities and food served on request. Camping and dorm beds are also available. Quadbikes, pony trekking and guided hikes can be arranged. Camping M90, dorms M195, doubles M690

BOKONG NATURE RESERVE
Reserve accommodation Contact the LHDA Nature Reserves Booking Office in Butha-Buthe ☎ 2246 0723. Camping is possible throughout the reserve, and there are also two stone-and-thatch rondavels close to the falls (each with four single beds) with a shared kitchen and bathroom; both come with gas and bedding. Five large chalets are next to the visitor centre, where a basic restaurant serves meals on request. Advance booking for the restaurant, accommodation and ponies is recommended. Camping M100, rondavels & chalets M450

KATSE
Katse Lodge Katse village ☎ 2291 0813. The lodge has drab rooms with fine views of the lake and its impressive birdlife, and a good restaurant serving a decent selection of meals. There are also a number of cheaper dorm rooms and apartments in the compound. The hotel can arrange boat cruises (M330/15min), biking, pony trekking and hiking. Dorms M399, apartments M1018, doubles M1198

Butha-Buthe

BUTHA-BUTHE (meaning "Lie Down") has a frontier feel – noisy, dirty and dusty – and offers little reason to stay, although it makes a good base for visiting nearby attractions. The town was founded in 1884 because the local chief refused to go to Leribe to pay taxes, necessitating a new tax centre nearer his residence. Butha-Buthe attracted traders from the outset, and is one of the few towns in Lesotho with a sizeable Muslim Indian community.

Butha-Buthe Mountain, just east of town, is where Moshoeshoe I had his first stronghold before retreating to Thaba Bosiu in 1824. It's a stiff but not particularly difficult climb and the summit provides tremendous views. You can cut the hiking distance by catching a minibus taxi as far as Ha Mopeli.

ARRIVAL AND DEPARTURE ⠀⠀⠀⠀⠀⠀⠀⠀⠀⠀⠀⠀⠀⠀⠀⠀⠀⠀⠀⠀⠀⠀⠀⠀⠀BUTHA-BUTHE

By bus and minibus taxi There are frequent buses and minibus taxis from the main crossroads in town to Maseru (1hr 30min), Katse (3hr) and Leribe (30min), and two to three a day to Mokhotlong (4hr).

ACCOMMODATION

Crocodile Inn Hotel Hospital Rd ☎ 2246 0223, ✉ crocodileinn@yahoo.com. The only central place to stay, the basic *Crocodile Inn*, next to the hospital, has shabby en-suite rooms and better rooms in rondavels. There are two bars, which attract dedicated drinkers until well into the morning, and an inexpensive restaurant. M602

Likileng Lodge 1km out of town, on the left-hand side of the road if heading towards Oxbow ☎ 2246 0686, ✉ likilenglodge@tsebo.co.ls. The best accommodation in town, set in a large compound in a quiet residential area. The en-suite rooms are clean and functional, and there's a bar and a restaurant serving tasty meals. M500

Ts'ehlanyane National Park

Daily 8am–5pm • M30, plus M10 per vehicle and M10 if staying overnight • Horses are available for hire by prior arrangement M108/half day, M390/day • ☎ 2246 0723 or ☎ 2244 4207

An asphalt road starting 9km southeast of Butha-Buthe leads 32km southeast into the western scarp of the Front Range, following a very picturesque valley. Covering

56 square kilometres of extremely rugged hiking terrain at the confluence of the Ts'ehlanyane and Holomo rivers, **Ts'ehlanyane National Park** is intended to protect several areas of ecological importance, particularly the indigenous **Leucosidea sericea woodland** known locally as *Ouhout* or *Che-che* – one of Lesotho's very few forested areas. Equally rare are stands of montane bamboo. **Mammals** present include mainly duikers, baboons and serval cats, and the fenced-in mountain opposite the *Maliba Lodge* is home to a herd of huge eland antelope. There's also the endangered *Metisella syrinx* butterfly, bearded vultures (lammergeiers) and ground woodpeckers. The **best time to visit** is in spring, when the small yellow flowers along the riverbanks that give their unpronounceable name to the reserve are in flower. The highlight for serious hikers and pony trekkers is a spectacular 35km trail linking the park with Bokong Nature Reserve to the south (see p.596), with swimming possible in streams along the way.

ARRIVAL AND DEPARTURE
TS'EHLANYANE NATIONAL PARK

By minibus taxi There are regular minibus taxis from Butha-Buthe to the national park gates (1hr).

ACCOMMODATION

11

★**Maliba Lodge** ☎ +27 31 702 8791, ⊕ maliba-lodge .com. Inside the national park, this deluxe private lodge has Lesotho's best accommodation in six beautiful thatched "Mountain Lodge" chalets, each with underfloor heating, fireplaces, and a private balcony with views of the protected forest and mountains. There are also riverside rooms in four sleek lodges sleeping up to eight, and smaller huts. The lodge arranges pony-trekking tours in the national park (M450/person for up to 2hr, M700 for up to

4hr) and village visits (M300), and there are maps for hiking and 4WD trips. Massage and other treatments are available in the spa. Rates for huts and suites include meals; the lodges are self-catering. Riverside lodges M1540, huts M2480, chalets M3990

National Park accommodation ☎ 6303 5012. There's accommodation in a basic guesthouse near the park's reception, which sleeps six people, or in three-bed dormitories. Dorms M150, doubles M450

'Muela

Power plant Tours daily 9am & 2pm · M30 · **Visitor centre** Daily 9am–noon & 2–4pm · ☎ 2248 1221 or ☎ 2248 1211, ⊕ lhda.org.ls

Northeast from Butha-Buthe, the A1 road begins to climb into the Maloti Mountains. After 22km, you reach the small settlement of Khukhune where a road on the right leads up to **'MUELA**, an integral part of the Lesotho Highlands Water Project (see box, p.597). Here the water flowing down the delivery tunnel from Katse Reservoir to South Africa powers an underground hydroelectric station that supplies all of Lesotho with electricity. The real attraction lies underground, and **tours** of the power plant (run by the visitor centre) take you past the three large turbines that power much of Lesotho.

Liphofung Cave Cultural Historical Site

3km off the main road north, 7km beyond the 'Muela turn-off · Daily 8am–4.30pm · M30

The **Liphofung Cave Cultural Historical Site** consists of a large sandstone overhang boasting an impressive series of San **rock paintings**, from whose images it gets its name, "Place of the Eland". The site is well worth a visit and is also significant for the Basotho in its role as a hideout for the young Moshoeshoe I. Guided tours start from the visitor centre, where you can also see three traditional Basotho huts.

ACCOMMODATION
LIPHOFUNG CAVE CULTURAL HISTORICAL SITE

Liphofung Visitor Centre ☎ 2700 9477. At the site's visitor centre are a couple of delightful self-catering rondavels that each sleep four people, plus three larger chalets sleeping six in three bedrooms. You can camp as

well, though there are no real facilities so it's best to be self-sufficient. Camping M50, rondavels M250, chalets M450

Mamohase Rural Stay B&B Signposted off the main road just south of Liphofung, then 2km down a tough dirt track ☎5805 8438 or ☎5804 5597, ⓦmamohaseruralstay.com. Run by a local Basotho family, this is the place to get a good feel for what life is like in rural Lesotho. Accommodation is in mud-walled rondavels, simply but adequately furnished, with

bucket showers and an outdoor toilet. Visitors are welcome and encouraged to participate in the family's daily activities, which can include cooking over an open fire, working in the fields or helping herd the sheep. Half board M700

Oxbow

The A1 into the highlands is one of the most dramatic roads in Lesotho, passing through some particularly striking sandstone cliffs before twisting tortuously up a chain of heart-stopping hairpins into the basalt. Some 20km beyond Liphofung, past **Moteng Pass** (2820m), **OXBOW** is a string of unremarkable buildings in a narrow valley. In winter, the place is packed out with South Africans looking at snow. Between June and August, **skiing** is the main draw 16km up the road from Oxbow, where AfriSki (June–Aug daily 9am–4.30pm; ski pass M450/day, equipment rental M395/day) has a fun intermediate ski slope with a modern ski lift and snow-making equipment.

ARRIVAL AND DEPARTURE
OXBOW

By bus and minibus taxi Without your own vehicle, the best way to get in and out of Oxbow is to catch one of the passing buses or minibus taxis heading south towards Mokhotlong (2hr 30min) or west towards Butha-Buthe (1hr 30min); they will pick you up by the side of the road.

ACCOMMODATION

AfriSki Mahlasela Basin ☎5954 4734, ⓦafriski.net. About 10km up the road from Oxbow, at 3220m, this fledgling resort overlooking the ski slope is popular with South Africans in winter. Accommodation must be booked via the central reservation office; prices rise during the winter skiing season, when there's a minimum stay of three nights. The 250 beds on offer range from basic backpacker dorms to very comfortable self-catering en-suite rooms,

and there are apartments available for larger groups. Dorms M155, doubles M820

New Oxbow Lodge Oxbow ☎+27 51 933 2247 (South Africa), ⓦoxbow.co.za. This lodge along the bank of the Malibamatso River has comfortable, warm rooms, a well-stocked bar, and a restaurant serving reasonably priced meals. There's good trout fishing to be had, and wonderful hiking in any direction. M700

The Roof of Africa route

The scenic road from Oxbow to Mokhotlong is often called "the Roof of Africa route", peaking at **Tlaeeng Pass** (3251m) and passing the ugly **Letseng diamond mine** en route. The road is fully tarred, although the extremes of temperature and heavy mining trucks here have caused damage, and there are numerous potholes. As the road climbs into the Maloti Mountains, it winds its way past waterfalls and tiny stone villages, skirting narrow ridges from where you can see for miles on either side. Allow around two and a half hours to drive the 95km between Oxbow and Mokhotlong.

Mokhotlong

Perched on the banks of the scraggly Mokhotlong River, the wind-blown town of **MOKHOTLONG** ("Place of the Bald Ibis") was once known as the "Loneliest Place in Africa", and it's easy to see why, since it still gets cut off from the rest of civilization for days or weeks at a time in winter. Mokhotlong began life as a remote police outpost in 1905 and gradually evolved into a trading centre for the region's highlanders, but remained isolated from the rest of Lesotho for years, with radio contact only established in 1947. An airstrip was constructed in 1948 and a rudimentary road link built in the 1950s, but Mokhotlong continued to get the bulk of its supplies by pony from Natal, via Sani, for a long time afterwards. Even today it feels remote, with locals usually riding into town for a shop and a drink on ponies, resplendent in their gumboots and blankets. It's also the only town of any size in eastern Lesotho and a good place to stock up on supplies if you are using the Sani Top border post.

ARRIVAL AND INFORMATION

By bus and minibus taxi Getting to Mokhotlong's main crossroads is easiest on one of the several minibus taxis a day from Butha-Buthe (4hr), or one coming from Sani Top (1hr); minibuses from Mokhotlong to Sani Top usually continue down the pass to Ha Makhakhe near Underberg, returning several hours later; additionally, *Sani Mountain Lodge* (see p.602) has a shuttle service between their lodge and Underberg.

Bank There's a Standard Lesotho Bank ATM in town.

ACCOMMODATION

Farmers' Training Centre 2km north of town ☎ 2292 0235. Basic and cheap dorm accommodation in blocks, with clean rooms and shared bathrooms. The highlight is the pleasant and quiet location on the edge of town; get someone to show you the way. No food available. M80

Molumong Guest House 20km southwest of town along the road to Thaba-Tseka ☎ 5099 9843, ⓦ molumong.wordpress.com. A rustic 1920s place with plenty of character and fantastic mountain views. The main house is self-catering (though meals can be cooked on request), with very cosy doubles and a great lounge to relax in. There are also dorms, and a campsite. The lodge offers inexpensive pony trekking, and is a good base for hiking. It can be reached on the minibuses from Mokhotlong to Ha Janteau. Camping M100, dorms R108, doubles M450

Polihali Lodge Molumong Village, 20km down the road to Thaba-Tseka ☎ +27 083 254 3323 (South Africa), ⓦ polihali.wordpress.com. Although at the time of writing this lodge was little more than a sparsely furnished house with a couple of bedrooms, renovations were under way to transform it over the next few years into a hub of outdoor activities, including hiking and pony trekking, with a pub on-site. The remote location offers stunning mountain views, and while the double rooms in the house are self-catering with a fully equipped kitchen, home-cooked Basotho meals are also available on request (book in advance). Doubles R360

St James Lodge 12km along the road from Mokhotlong to Tsaba-Tseka ☎ 5920 5113. In the grounds of the St James Mission, this self-catering lodge offers pleasant en-suite rooms, cheaper rondavels with separate bathrooms, and camping. Pony trekking, cultural visits to the village and a church tour are all available. Camping M80, rondavels M300, doubles M700

Senqu Hotel On the edge of town as you enter on the A1 ☎ 2892 0330. This is the town's most upmarket hotel and some of the rooms are very nice, complete with fireplaces and small sitting areas (request one with a balcony and a good view). The restaurant is the best place to eat in town, and there's a bar too. M650

Sani and around

The gravel road to **SANI** branches off the main road to Mokhotlong 5km before town, and twists its way in spectacular fashion for nearly 60km along the Sehonkong River, peaking at **Kotisephola Pass** (3240m) before dropping to 2895m at **Sani Top**, a few kilometres from the South African border.

At Sani Top there are plenty of rewarding hikes, including a stiff 12km climb up **Thabana Ntlenyana**, at 3482m the highest point in Southern Africa and walkable in a day if you start early. Also tough but stunningly beautiful is the 40km **Top-of-the-Berg** hike to Sehlabathebe National Park, which takes about four days.

The descent from Sani, down the dramatic, hairpin-bend-filled **Sani Pass** into South Africa (see p.390), is only advisable with a 4WD car. In winter, the pass is frequently blocked by snow or ice. Talk of tarring the road has horrified off-road enthusiasts across the subcontinent, and isn't likely to happen soon.

ARRIVAL AND INFORMATION

By bus and minibus taxi Getting to Sani is only possible in good weather; if it's been snowing, you can forget it. Some five minibuses run daily (Mon–Sat; 1hr) from *Sani Mountain Lodge* to Mokhotlong. On the South African side, *Sani Mountain Lodge* (see p.602) runs a shuttle service between Sani Pass and Underberg, leaving the pass at 9.30am and 1.30pm and making the trip back up at 11am and 3pm; it costs R350/person, and must be booked in advance. At least two minibus taxis run Mon–Sat between Underberg and Ha Makhakhe near *Sani Mountain Lodge*,

11

where they are met by Basotho minibuses heading over the pass and on to Mokhotlong in Lesotho.

Crossing the border The border, between *Sani Mountain Lodge* and Sani Pass, is open daily from 6am to 6pm; the Lesotho side stays open slightly later to let vehicles from South Africa through.

ACCOMMODATION

Sani Mountain Lodge At the top of Sani Pass, just inside Lesotho ☎078 634 7496, ⓦsanimountain.co.za. The cliff-edge setting here is certainly hard to beat, with awesome views into KwaZulu-Natal. There's a pub with hearty food on offer, while in the evenings you can sit on the balcony and watch the sun set over the mountaintops. Rooms sleeping up to six are in attractive rondavels with fireplaces, and there's camping and backpacker accommodation available. Guided hikes and horseriding (R140/hr) can also be arranged. Camping M105, dorms M275, doubles M589

Sani Stone Lodge Signposted 5km from the border ☎5900 2441, ⓦsanistonelodge.co.za. A locally run guesthouse and backpacker hostel that offers sweeping views into the valley from its comfortable en-suite rondavels, which come with two double beds and fireplaces. There is also a dorm with a kitchen, plus a bar and restaurant (order in advance). The owners can organize traditional dances, as well as hiking and horseriding. They can also fetch you from the border – the road is for 4WD only. Dorms M190, doubles M600, rondavels M1100

The southern districts

The country's **southern districts** can't match the mountains of north and central Lesotho for sheer scale, but they do hold some dramatic countryside that is relatively easy to visit – especially on horseback from the excellent tourist lodges at **Malealea** and **Semonkong**. The nineteenth-century mission town of **Morija** is perhaps the most historic in the country. It also has dinosaur footprints in the vicinity, as does **Mohale's Hoek** and, more accessibly, **Quthing**, further south. Northeast of here, past the town of **Qacha's Nek**, the isolated delights of **Sehlabathebe National Park** are so remote as to make visits there a true adventure.

Morija

Set at the foot of the Makhoarane Plateau, 44km from Maseru, the pleasant little town of **MORIJA** houses the country's main museum and Lesotho's oldest building, church and printing press. The town was established in 1833 at Moshoeshoe I's behest as the country's first Christian mission, and granted to three missionaries of the Paris Evangelical Missionary Society. The bucolic setting, attractive accommodation and easy access make it a good base for exploring western Lesotho.

Lesotho Evangelical Church
In the middle of the village • Usually open on Sundays

The large, red-brick **Lesotho Evangelical Church**, with its impressive teak-beamed roof, was begun in 1847. This is the third church built on the site, using the labour of Pedi economic migrants on their way to Cape Colony, though its tall steeple was only built in 1905. Interestingly, the pillars inside were made from old ships' masts, transported here by ox-cart from Port Elizabeth.

Maeder House Gallery
Next to the Evangelical Church • Flexible hours; call if no one is around • ☎5051 7512

Most of Morija was razed to the ground by Afrikaner troops in 1858, and almost the only building left standing was the historical **Maeder House**, built in 1843 and the oldest building in the country. It's now used as a gallery selling striking modern paintings, mosaics and wonderful pottery by Patrick Rorke and crafts by other local artists. There's an **art centre** for local children and visiting artists, and any donations of art books or supplies are very welcome. An adjacent building houses the historic

RIGHT SANI PASS (P.601) >

printing works, which have produced Basotho literature since the 1860s as well as the country's oldest newspaper, *Leselinyana la Lesotho* (Little Light of Lesotho), which has been in almost continual publication since 1863.

Morija Museum

Just uphill from the Evangelical Church • Mon–Sat 8am–5pm, Sun noon–5pm • M30 • ☎ 2236 0308, ⓦ morija.co.ls

The bright-yellow **Morija Museum** is an excellent reason for coming to town. The exhibits, displayed in a large room and an adjoining hallway, are a stimulating combination of geological and fossil finds, meteorite fragments, ethnographic material and historic items connected with Moshoeshoe (see p.578) and his contemporaries. The museum also sells a range of books including the recommended *Guide to Morija* (M30), and can organize tours of the village and surroundings, taking in the church and Maeder House Gallery. The museum **archive** is the best collection of books on Lesotho anywhere. Curator Stephen Gill is the main authority on Lesotho's history and culture.

In the last week of September and the first week of October the museum organizes the **Morija Arts and Cultural Festival**, the largest and most significant event of its kind in the country, where traditional music, jazz, dancing, horse races and crafts mix with theatre, cinema, sport and children's events.

ARRIVAL AND INFORMATION

By bus and minibus taxi Getting to Morija is easy, with buses and minibus taxis running throughout the day from Maseru (1hr). There's no bus or taxi rank; transport finishing in Morija drops you outside the post office close to the museum, while minibuses running from Maseru to Mafeteng and Mohale's Hoek drop off and pick up on the highway 1km west of the centre.

Tourist information Morija Museum (see above) also doubles up as the town's tourist information.

MORIJA

Activities Pony treks can be arranged through *Morija Guest Houses* (see below) or the museum, and range from one-hour jaunts (from M150) to day-trips (from M630). The best of various walking trails from Morija leads to an impressive sets of avian dinosaur footprints on one side of a large rock halfway up the Makhoarane Plateau, 45min beyond the guesthouse. Guides are available for these walks; there are no fixed prices.

ACCOMMODATION AND EATING

Café Mojo Behind the Morija Museum ☎ 5910 4153. The museum's tea shop, in a traditional rondavel in the lovely gardens, offers coffee, sandwiches and good pizzas (from M30); enjoy them sitting on the terrace with valley views. Tues–Sat 8am–5pm, Sun 10am–4pm.

Lindy's B&B ☎ 2236 0732, ⓦ lindysbnb.co.ls. Two cottages sleeping up to four, up the hill above the museum (follow the white stones); one is historical and one is new, and while they're nicely furnished, they don't enjoy the attractive grounds or view of nearby *Morija Guest Houses*. Lunch and dinner can be ordered in advance. M760

★ **Morija Guest Houses** ☎ 6305 7431, ⓦ morijaguesthouses.com. One of Lesotho's most attractive lodgings,

set in a dramatic spot at the top of town (follow the white stones from the museum). The beautiful thatched house contains several comfortable rooms with shared bathrooms, plus a fully equipped kitchen, lounge, and veranda with fantastic views over the surrounding area. Just below the guesthouse stand several attractive and cosy self-catering Basotho cottages. Mountain bikes are for rent at M80/hr, and the guesthouse can arrange a number of activities in the area, including birdwatching and horseriding. Meals can be provided by prior arrangement. Arrive by public transport and pay M200 for the best available bed, in any room. All rates are per person. Wi-fi costs extra. M620

Malealea

The bustling minibus taxi stop at **Motsekuoa**, 10km south of Morija, marks the turning for the village of **MALEALEA**, one of the best-known places in Lesotho thanks to the hugely popular *Malealea Lodge & Pony Trek Centre* (see opposite). Now a spacious forested compound, set in a spectacular spot in the foothills of the Thaba Putsoa range, the lodge was originally a small trading store established by the British adventurer Mervyn Bosworth-Smith in 1905. It was Bosworth-Smith who wrote the words on the

ACTIVITIES AROUND MALEALEA

Malealea Lodge (see below) runs a series of **guided pony treks**, from short jaunts to as many days as your bottom and wallet can stand, with nights in basic huts equipped with gas cookers, kitchen utensils and floor mattresses. Trips can be arranged at short notice. **Costs** vary according to where you go and group size, but count on around M500 for a full day and night, plus M120 for village accommodation, or M15 per hour of hiking. Riders cannot weigh more than 90kg, you must have medical insurance, and luggage is limited to 12.5kg including food. A good alternative to the pony trekking (which can be quite hard on the body if you're not used to it) is simply to **walk** and use a pony as a pack animal. The pony can carry four people's packs, provided they're not excessively heavy.

Short trips include **village walks** and a consultation with a traditional healer (*sangoma*). Longer day-trips, either afoot or in the saddle, go to Botsoela Waterfall (a beautiful four-hour trip that's recommended for saddle-sore, novice riders; from M290), Pitseng Canyon and its rock pool, San rock paintings, and the Gates of Paradise Pass along Matelile Ridge.

11

brass plaque at the top of the magnificent Gate of Paradise Pass, 6km before the lodge: "Wayfarer, pause and look upon a gateway of Paradise".

ARRIVAL AND DEPARTURE   MALEALEA

By bus and minibus taxi A daily minibus taxi leaves from Maseru's New Taxi Rank at around 11am direct to the gates of *Malealea Lodge* (85km; 2hr). Otherwise, you can take one of the hourly taxis from Maseru to Mafeteng and change at Motsekuoa (1hr), where you'll find onward taxis to Malealea (1hr).

ACCOMMODATION

★**Malealea Lodge & Pony Trek Centre** ☎+27 82 552 4215 (South Africa) or ☎5018 1341, ⓦ malealea .com. Simple but comfortable accommodation in huts, chalets and rondavels spread out in a pretty forested compound. The lodge is always a lively place; next to the dining room (set meals served at set times) is a great little bar and most evenings guests congregate around an open fire outside. Every afternoon a local choir and band perform for guests, the latter bashing out tunes on home-made instruments. The local community benefits greatly from the lodge through employment and special projects funded by the Malealea Development Trust, and visitors can experience heart-warming hospitality when venturing out. Meals are optional: breakfast M90, lunch M100, dinner M160. Camping M120, huts M390, farmhouse rooms M640, rondavels M800

Mafeteng and around

The bustling town of **MAFETENG**, 18km from Van Rooyenshek **border post**, will be the first place you come to in Lesotho if crossing from Wepener in the Free State. It means "the place of Lefeta's people", after the son of a French missionary Emile Rolland, who was the district's first magistrate and was nicknamed Lefeta, or "he who passes", by locals, who regarded him as virtually Basotho except for the fact that he skipped (or "passed by") initiation. The only building of any interest is the **District Administrator's office** on the main street, worth a quick look for the carved animal heads studding its front wall.

Thabana Morena Plateau

About 20km east of Mafeteng is the impressive **Thabana Morena Plateau**, which makes a good excursion, though you'll need your own transport. Rising above the village of the same name, it rewards those who make the steep hour-long climb with good views of the Free State plains to the west and the Thaba Putsoa range to the east.

ARRIVAL AND DEPARTURE   MAFETENG AND AROUND

By bus and minibus taxi As befits a border town, Mafeteng has a very busy bus station at the main crossroads in the centre of town where you can easily find transport north to Morija (30min) and Maseru (1hr 30min), and southeast to Mohale's Hoek (45min), Quthing (1hr 30min) and beyond (numerous buses and minibus taxis daily each way).

ACCOMMODATION AND EATING

Golden Hotel To the right of the highway from Maseru, just before you enter Mafeteng proper ☎ 2270 0566, ✉ pulephakifi@gmail.com. The anonymous-looking *Golden Hotel*, which sits right on the road, offers functional en-suite rooms and a dining room serving pizzas and meat dishes. <u>M650</u>

Mafeteng Hotel & Restaurant On the south side of town down the small street near the telecommunications tower ☎ 2270 0236, ✉ hotel mafeteng@gmail.com. Looks like a 1960s airport control tower, but offers pleasant and spacious en-suite rooms, all with satellite TV, plus some cottages in a secluded garden and a good swimming pool. It's a good idea to ask in advance if the loud disco will be active when you plan to sleep here. Its restaurant is the best place to eat in town, with a range of moderately priced meat dishes. <u>M520</u>

Mohale's Hoek

MOHALE'S HOEK, a short distance from the little-used Makhaleng Bridge border post, is a rather bedraggled little town, but it has a decent hotel and some interesting sites in the surrounding hills, including some well-preserved **dinosaur footprints**. Mohale was Moshoeshoe's younger brother, appointed to look after the area by the king as part of his bid to wrest control of the district from chief Moorosi. There are still quite a few of Moorosi's Baphuthi clan here, though, whose language is in some ways closer to Xhosa than Basotho. There's nothing to see or do here apart from the excellent drive, walk or pony trek into the little-visited **Mokhele Mountain Range** (see below).

Mokhele Mountain Range

Ten kilometres east of Mohale's Hoek, the beautiful and little-visited **Mokhele Mountain Range** is perfect for a drive, walk or pony trek, available from *Mount Maluti Hotel* (see opposite). To get here, travel a few kilometres south on the main road to the little village of Mesitsaneng; turn left at the signpost for the primary school and head 11km east along a rough dirt track to the historic French **Maphutseng Mission**, in whose roof locals once hid from attacking Boers. When the road bends sharply to the left, branch right down a smaller track and you'll see a plateau a short walk away, where you'll find some **dinosaur footprints** and the remnants of an inscription recording their discovery in 1959.

DONGAS AND SOIL EROSION IN LESOTHO

One thing you'll quickly notice about Lesotho is that the entire country is virtually **treeless**. Indeed, the country – once the grain basket of the region – is in deep ecological trouble, and acres of irreplaceable topsoil, loosened by decades of over-farming, are washed away down its rivers each year.

The problems began with the expropriation of the best land by the OFS in the 1860s, which forced the Basotho to start farming hilly areas that had previously only been used for winter grazing. This process continues to this day, and you will even see crops being grown at over 2000m in districts like Semonkong and Mokhotlong. Mountains are no substitute for fertile plains, however, and Lesotho has been a net importer of food since the 1920s.

The ecological effect of the unrelenting cultivation of the Lesotho mountains has been devastating. The soil fertility has plummeted and, more seriously, huge quantities of topsoil are simply washed away in each summer's rains. In many places so much topsoil has gone that great ravines called **dongas** have opened up. Though they often look green enough, the remaining soil tends to lie close to the surface rock, making it useless for serious cultivation.

Efforts to slow this process have been under way for some time, most noticeably through the terracing of hillside fields. For one of the best examples of how simply dongas can be reclaimed, ask to be shown the way to the Musi family donga (M30 per person) in the village beside *Malealea Lodge* (see p.605) – reclamation of the donga began two decades ago by Fanuel Musi, and is now carried on by his grandson and wife.

ARRIVAL AND DEPARTURE　　　　　　　　　　**MOHALE'S HOEK**

By bus and minibus taxi Buses arrive at the busy station in the centre of Mohale's Hoek, while minibus taxis congregate on the main street near the Engen petrol station – between them and the buses you should be able to find transport heading both north to Maseru (2hr) and south to Quthing (1hr) throughout the day.

ACCOMMODATION AND EATING

Mount Maluti Hotel ☎ 2878 5224, ⓦ hmmlesotho .com. Comfortable rooms with TVs, plus a bar, tennis court and swimming pool, all in a quiet garden setting. The hotel restaurant is the best place to eat in southern Lesotho and offers decent cuisine including superb pizzas (M60–90) fresh from the oven. **M750**

Quthing and around

QUTHING, also known as **Moyeni** ("Place of the Wind"), is a curious split-level town established by the British after the Gun War in 1884. The town itself is messy, though it has an attractive setting beside a river gorge, with views of the surrounding hills improving as you climb to the upper part of town.

11

Dinosaur footprints

Daily 8am–4pm • M10

The most accessible **dinosaur footprints** in Lesotho are very near the lower section of Quthing. On the road to Mount Moorosi, about 400m from the junction to Quthing town centre, look out for the shed-like building with the thatched **visitor centre** beside it on the left of the road. The shed protects a variety of clearly discernible footprints, and there's also a limited range of handicrafts for sale.

Masitise Cave House

A few kilometres west of Quthing • Mon–Fri 8.30am–5pm, Sat & Sun 8.30am–2pm • M10 • ☎ 5875 8187, ⓦ masitisecavehouse.blogspot.com

The extraordinary **Masitise Cave House** is well worth a visit. It was built into the side of a rock overhang in 1866 by the Swiss missionary D.F. Ellenberger – whose *History of the Basuto: Ancient & Modern*, published in 1912, was the first study of its kind. The house has been converted into a museum and contains interesting displays on the history of the Quthing area, the Ellenbergers' fascinating home, and an explanation of the dinosaur footprints located in the ceiling of one of the rooms. To find it, turn right off the main road from Mafeteng at the "Masitise Primary" sign and follow the rutted road past the church; the curator, Aaron Ntsonyana, will guide you around.

ARRIVAL AND DEPARTURE　　　　　　　**QUTHING AND AROUND**

By bus and minibus taxi Daily buses and numerous minibus taxis run north from the bus stop at the main crossroads to Maseru (3hr), and less frequent services head northeast towards Qacha's Nek (4hr). You'll also find minibus taxis heading for the nearby Tele Bridge border post (daily 8am–10pm) where you can pick up transport to Sterkspruit in the Eastern Cape.

ACCOMMODATION

Fuleng Guest House In town, near the first hairpin bend to upper Quthing ☎ 2275 0260, ⓔ info.fuleng guesthouse@gmail.com. Good-value rooms in simple rondavels around a concrete courtyard (although check as they vary in standard), or more luxurious and stylish rooms with TVs. Rondavels **M500**, rooms **M570**

Mountain Side Hotel About 100m down the dirt track just beyond Fuleng ☎ 2275 0257, ⓔ mina.shata@gmail .com. The intimate *Mountain Side Hotel* has adequate rooms, though the cheapest ones come with (warm) bucket baths. There's a cosy private bar, a friendly public one and a bright, pleasant restaurant with a tasty fixed menu. **M600**

Mount Moorosi and around

Just over 40km beyond Quthing, the small town of **MOUNT MOOROSI** was named after a chief who moved to the region in the 1850s. He was an ally of the San and had several San wives, but made an enemy of the British. British troops attacked his stronghold in 1879, but he held out for eight months until soldiers used scaling ladders on the steep cliffs and finally captured him, after which they cut off and publicly displayed his severed head. **Thaba Moorosi**, where the main battle took place, is 1km or so further along the main road on the right. The site is marked by stone slabs on which British soldiers sent to catch the chief engraved their names. It's quite a tricky climb, though, so be sure to let someone in Mount Moorosi know where you are going.

Shortly after rounding Thaba Moorosi, the main road leaves the Senqu River and heads swiftly into the highlands through the impressive **Quthing Gorge**, peaking after about 10km at the **Lebelonyane Pass** (2456m), with superb views. A far less used route into the highlands than the northern road to Mokhotlong, the mountain road to Sehlabathebe is ruggedly beautiful; some would say it is the most rewarding drive in the country.

Qacha's Nek

11

Some 90km east of Mount Moorosi at **Sekake**, the asphalted road rejoins the southern banks of the Senqu. It's a beautiful, undulating drive, though once you reach the approach to **QACHA'S NEK** you'll see the depressingly familiar soil erosion and dongas (see box, p.606). Named after chief Moorosi's son Ncatya, Qacha's Nek was an area famed for its banditry when the British founded the town in 1888 in an attempt to forestall the kind of trouble they'd experienced with chief Moorosi. Many of the "bandits" were in fact desperate San, hounded from their homes and having no means of survival; this left the British unmoved, and they hunted them to extermination throughout the 1860s and 1870s. Moorosi's Baphuthi people had started moving there in the 1850s, rapidly wiping out all the game and turning the land over to grazing and cultivation instead. The area has unusually high rainfall, and the weather conditions favour conifers, including a few massive Canadian redwoods, giving Qacha's Nek an atmosphere completely different from most of virtually treeless Lesotho.

There's little to see in town, except the elegant **St Joseph's Church** at its eastern end, but the surrounding mountainous countryside is great for **hiking**.

ARRIVAL AND DEPARTURE   QACHA'S NEK

By bus and minibus taxi Qacha's Nek is an important border town and there's usually plenty of public transport heading southwest towards Quthing from the petrol station in the centre of town. There are daily minibus taxis to and from Maseru that take up to 7hr, though when heading towards Qacha's Nek, you may need to change in Semonkong. On the other side of the border you'll find transport (roughly hourly) heading for the Eastern Cape town of Matatiele, from where it's easy to find buses and minibus taxis on to Kokstad and beyond.

ACCOMMODATION

Letloepe Lodge If coming from the border post, turn right at the roundabout ☎ 2295 0383, ✉ bookings @letloepelodge.com. The town's best accommodation, is due to reopen in 2018. Set at the bottom of the Letloepe cliff, it offers en-suite rondavels with TVs, some with kitchenettes, and there's a restaurant with set meals. They also have cheaper backpacker accommodation in twin or triple rooms with shared bathrooms. Dorms **M140**, doubles **M420**

Nthatuoa Hotel The first building on the left as you enter Qacha's Nek on the main road from Quthing ☎ 2295 0260, ✉ nyalleng.makhetha@yahoo.com. A variety of en-suite rooms in a red-brick building, all perfectly comfortable though clearly aimed at business travellers; you're also welcome to pitch a tent for free, though they'd like you to pay for breakfast in the restaurant. All other tariffs include a substantial breakfast, and their restaurant also serves lunch and dinner. **M600**

Sehlabathebe National Park

About 80km northeast of Qacha's Nek • No fixed hours (call in advance) • M30 • ☎ 5710 1633

The oldest nature reserve in the country, and on UNESCO's World Heritage list since 2013 as part of the Maloti-Drakensberg Park, **Sehlabathebe National Park** is remote and difficult to access, but peaceful and stunningly beautiful. Set on the border with South Africa in the southern reaches of the Drakensberg at an average altitude of 2400m, the park is best known for its prolific birdlife, excellent trout fishing, waterfalls, rock paintings and seemingly endless open spaces just perfect for hiking. There are also a few game animals: baboons, rhebok, eland, the secretive oribi antelope, mongoose, otters, wild cats and jackals. In good weather you probably won't be in any hurry to leave, but at any time of year mist and rain can emerge out of nowhere, even on the finest of days, so come prepared.

ARRIVAL AND INFORMATION

SEHLABATHEBE NATIONAL PARK

By minibus taxi or car To get to the park from the Lesotho side of the border you'll need either a 4WD or to catch one of the infrequent minibus taxis from Qacha's Nek, which take around 3hr.

On foot The only other way into the park from the Lesotho side is to hike 40km along the Top-of-the-Berg route from Sani Top. From South Africa, it's a day's walk to Sehlabathebe through the southern section of South Africa's uKhahlamba-Drakensberg Park along a dramatic path starting at Bushman's Nek, 38km from Underberg in KwaZulu-Natal.

Sehlabathebe Ranger Station The ranger station in Sehlabathebe Village (☎5710 1633) has information about the park and hikes. If you want to do some serious hiking, go to the Department of Lands, Surveys and Physical Planning in Maseru (see box, p.581), where you should be able to pick up some detailed maps of the area.

11

ACCOMMODATION

Camping is permitted anywhere in the park, provided you get a permit from the lodge. Wherever you're staying, you'll need to be self-sufficient in food.

Sehlabathebe Lodge Near the park gate ☎2231 1767 or ☎5853 7565. There are basic dormitory rooms in this new lodge, which has self-catering facilities and can sleep around seventy people. They have a few gas heaters, but if the place is busy (which it rarely is), heating can be an issue. M250

Swaziland

UMHLANGA REED DANCE

Swaziland

A tiny landlocked kingdom, Swaziland is surrounded on three sides by South Africa, with Mozambique providing its eastern border along the Lubombo Mountains. Although South Africa's influence predominates, Swaziland was British protectorate from 1903 until its full independence in 1968, and today the country offers an intriguing mix of colonial heritage and home-grown confidence, giving the place a friendlier, more relaxed and often safer feeling than its larger neighbour. Though Swaziland still feels a lot more commercialized than, say, Lesotho, its outstanding scenery, along with its commitment to wildlife conservation, makes it well worth a visit. With a car and a bit of time, you can explore some of the less trampled reserves, make overnight stops in unspoilt, out-of-the-way villages and, if you time your visit well, take in something of Swaziland's well-preserved cultural traditions.

Swaziland is also something of a draw for **backpackers**, with an inexpensive network of minibus Kombi taxis covering all corners of the country, and some good backpacker lodges to boot. There are also plenty of adventure activities on offer – from mountain biking and horseriding to whitewater rafting and treetop canopy gliding. Swaziland has six **national parks** exemplifying the country's geographical diversity, all offering good-value accommodation. Those parks without the larger, more dangerous mammals mean that visitors can explore the reserves on foot, horseback or by bike, a unique opportunity to become truly intimate with this African landscape and her inhabitants, at a minimal cost. While not as efficiently run as South African national parks, the Swazi reserves are less officious, and many people warm to their easy-going nature.

Laidback **Mbabane**, the country's tiny capital city, makes a useful starting point, although many will choose to head straight down to the attractive central **eZulwini Valley**, home to the royal palace and the **Mlilwane Wildlife Sanctuary**. With your own transport, or a bit of determination and public transport, you can venture further afield, to the ruggedly forested highveld of the northwest with hidden waterfalls and ancient rock formations, or up to the fantastically beautiful **Malolotja Nature Reserve**, with its fabulous hiking country, soaring valleys and cliffs.

Summers are hot, particularly in the eastern lowveld. **Winter** is usually sunny, but nights can be very chilly in the western highveld around the Malolotja Nature Reserve. In summer, rainfall is usually limited to short, drenching storms that play havoc with the smaller untarred roads. Note that Swaziland's eastern lowveld, including Hlane Royal National Park, is **malarial (see p.71)** during the summer months (Nov–May).

Brief history
The history of Swaziland dates back to the **Dlamini** clan and their king, **Ngwane**, who crossed the Lubombo Mountains from present-day Mozambique in around 1750.

WHITE RHINOCEROS, MKHAYA GAME RESERVE

Highlights

❶ Royal festivals The spectacular ceremonies of Ncwala and Umhlanga are colourful affirmations of Swazi national identity. **See p.625**

❷ Malandela's Homestead A collection of buildings bursting with creativity, including the eccentric performance space and live music venue House on Fire, and Gone Rural, one of Swaziland's best arts and crafts outlets. **See p.627**

❸ Bushfire Festival At the end of May each year this immensely popular music festival highlights the best local acts and draws plenty of high-profile acts from across the region. **See p.627**

❹ Myxo's cultural tours, KaPhunga Get a true taste of life in rural Swaziland – this enterprising project allows you to live as part of a village for a few days. **See p.628**

❺ Mkhaya Game Reserve Swaziland's best wildlife experience, where you can walk with rhino before sleeping in luxurious open-sided cottages in the bush. **See p.630**

❻ Whitewater rafting on the Great Usutu As action-packed as anything south of the Zambezi – wild ride down Swaziland's largest river. **See p.631**

❼ Malolotja Nature Reserve A wild, rugged and breathtakingly beautiful reserve attracting hundreds of different bird species, with a network of trails perfect for hiking. **See p.634**

HIGHLIGHTS ARE MARKED ON THE MAP ON P.614

Pushed into southeast Swaziland by the Ndwandwe people of Zululand, the clan eventually settled at Mhlosheni and then Zombodze in the southwest, where Ngwane reigned precariously, under constant threat of Ndwandwe attack. His grandson, **Sobhuza I**, was forced to flee north from the Ndwandwe, but they in turn were defeated by the Zulu king Shaka in 1819. Sobhuza then established a new capital suitably far from Shaka in the eZulwini Valley, and made peace with the Ndwandwe by marrying the king's daughter.

SWAZILAND

BORDER POST OPENING TIMES

Ngwenya/Oshoek	7am–noo...
Sandlane/Nerston	8am–6p...
Sicunusa/Houdkop	8am–6p...
Mahamba	7am–10p...
Lavumisa/Golela	24...
Mhlumeni/Goba	24...
Lomahasha/Namaacha	7am–8p...
Mananga	7am–6p...
Matsamo/Jeppe's Reef	7am–6p...
Bulembu/Josefdal	8am–4p...

HIGHLIGHTS

1. Royal festivals
2. Malandela's Homestead
3. Bushfire Festival
4. Myxo's cultural tours, KaPhunga
5. Mkhaya Game Reserve
6. Whitewater rafting on the Great Usutu
7. Malolotja Nature Reserve

0 20
kilometres

CHOOSING THE KING

Swazi monarchs are always men of the **Dlamini** family, and over the course of their reign they marry a number of women carefully selected from different clans to cement national unity. In theory, the king marries women from increasingly important families as he goes along, which means that the son of the last wife is always a strong contender for the succession. In practice, however, other wives with older sons are also in with a chance, resulting in unrest and power struggles every time the king dies. After his death, the royal council, or *liqoqo*, selects the new **Queen Mother**, who rules as regent until her son is old enough to take charge. She usually has to work hard to ensure her position against ambitious uncles. The main advantage of this awkward process is that by the time the new king is old enough to rule, he and his mother have generally garnered enough support for him to do so effectively.

Sobhuza's power grew as he brought more and more clans under his wing. His alliance with the newly arrived Afrikaners in the 1830s, forged out of mutual fear of the Zulu, was continued by his son **Mswati II** (after whom the Swazi people are named), who stretched his kingdom north to the Sabi River and sent raiding parties as far as the Limpopo River and east to the Indian Ocean.

Europeans arrived in greater numbers throughout the 1880s, after the discovery of gold in neighbouring Transvaal and at Piggs Peak and Forbes Reef in Swaziland. Mswati's son, **Mbandzeni**, granted large chunks of his territory in concessions to the new arrivals, emboldening Britain to ignore his claims to most of the rest; by the time Swaziland became a protectorate of South Africa in 1894, there was precious little land left. After their victory in the Second Anglo-Boer War, Britain assumed control of the territory and retained it until 1968.

After World War II the British invested in their protectorate, establishing enormous **sugar plantations** in the northeast and an **iron-ore mine** at Ngwenya in the highveld (today, the country's major export is sugar). Meanwhile, **Sobhuza II**, who had become king of the Swazis in 1921, concentrated on buying back his kingdom, and had acquired about half of it by the time independence came in 1968. The Swazi aristocracy managed the transition to independence skilfully, with its Imbokodvo party winning every parliamentary seat in the first elections. In 1973 a radical pan-Africanist party won three seats, prompting Sobhuza to **ban political parties** and declare a state of emergency, which technically has been in place ever since.

12

SISWATI PHRASES

BASICS

Yes	*Yebo* (also a casual greeting)	**It's nice/tasty**	*Kumnandzi*
		Today	*Lamuhla*
No	*Cha*	**Tomorrow**	*Kusasa*
Thank you	*Ngiyabonga*	**Yesterday**	*Itolo*

GREETINGS AND RESPONSES

Hello (to one)	*Sawubona*	**Goodbye (said by person leaving)**	*Sala kahle*
Hello (to many)	*Sanibona*		
How are you?	*Kunjani?*	**Goodbye (said by person remaining)**	*Hamba kahle*
I'm fine	*Ngikhona*		

TRAVEL

Where is... ?	*Iphi I... ?*	**Where are you going?**	*U ya phi?*
Where can we stay?	*Singahlala kuphi?*	**How much?**	*Malini?*

SWAZILAND TRAVEL BASICS

MONEY

Currency is the **lilangeni** – plural **emalangeni** (E) – which is tied to the South African rand (1 rand = 1 lilangeni). The rand is legal tender in Swaziland, so you won't have to change any money, but note that emalangeni are not convertible outside Swaziland.

PHONES AND PHONE NUMBERS

The **country code** for Swaziland is ☎268, followed by the destination number (there are no area codes). The code for phoning out from Swaziland is ☎00, followed by the country and area codes and finally the destination number. To arrange a **collect call**, dial ☎94.

Swaziland has only one mobile phone network – MTN – which generally works well throughout the country. You can easily buy a chip for your phone in Mbabane.

PUBLIC HOLIDAYS

January 1
Good Friday
Easter Monday
April 19 (King Mswati III's birthday)
April 25 (National Flag Day)
May 1 (Workers' Day)
Ascension Day

July 22 (King Sobhuza II's birthday)
August/September (Umhlanga Dance Day)
September 6 (Independence Day)
December/January (Ncwala Day)
December 25 (Christmas Day)
December 26 (Boxing Day)

RED TAPE AND VISAS

Nationals of most Commonwealth countries (excluding Bangladesh, India, Pakistan and Sri Lanka), the US, Canada, South Africa, Australia and all EU countries are granted 30 days on entry, and may apply for a further 30-day extension. Other nationals must obtain visas before arrival. Swaziland's embassies are in Mbabane (see p.621).

TOUR OPERATORS

The country's biggest **tour operator** is Swazi Trails (☎24162180, ⊕swazitrails.co.sz), next to the Mantenga Craft Centre (see p.621), which offers tours to the royal village and game parks along with whitewater rafting, quad biking, caving and other activities. There are also a handful of smaller local operations, including Taman Tours (☎4163370, ⊕tamantours.com), which runs tours to different parts of Swaziland, and All Out Africa (☎24162260, ⊕alloutafrica.com), which organizes a selection of adventure tours such as river tubing on the Ngwempisi River, and also helps find volunteering opportunities within the country. The tourist office in Mbabane (see p.619) keeps information on other tour guides.

WEBSITES

⊕**biggameparks.org** Provides information on three of the country's most visited reserves, the Hlane, Mlilwane and Mkhaya parks, with practical information about activities, and an accommodation booking site.

⊕**swazi.travel** Hosted by Swazi Trails, with an efficient online accommodation booking service, reams of information about shopping and restaurants, and details of tours and activities around Swaziland.

⊕**thekingdomofswaziland.com** Swaziland's official tourism website is packed with useful information, including hotel listings.

After Sobhuza's death in 1982 a period of intrigue ensued, with the Queen Mother Dzeliwe assuming the regency until deposed by Prince Bhekimpi, who ruled until 1985, purging all the opposition he could. The current king, **Mswati III**, the son of one of Sobhuza's seventy wives, was recalled from an English public school to become king in 1986, and parliamentary elections were held in 1987. New opposition began to emerge, most notably the **People's United Democratic Movement** (PUDEMO), which has strong support among Swazi workers. But in general Swazis are proud of their distinctive kingdom, and as a result calls for change are tempered by an unwillingness to show disloyalty to the king or to expose Swaziland to what many see as the predatory ambitions of South Africa.

Thus the maintenance of tradition and appeals to broad nationalism have been key components of Swazi royalty's strategy to retain power. Although Mswati III is sometimes said to favour reform, the authorities have worked hard to keep dissent bottled up through sporadic police repression; opposition leaders have been prevented from speaking freely in the media, and poor turnouts marked the "elections" of 1993, 1998, 2003, 2008 and 2013. In 2011, demonstrations triggered by the "Arab Spring", calling for **multi-party democracy** and condemning the government's mismanagement of funds, were stopped in their tracks with the arrest of demonstration organizers. Currently Swaziland is the only country in Southern Africa not practising multiparty democracy, though it seems only a matter of time before it is coerced by the other regional powers into doing so.

ARRIVAL AND DEPARTURE SWAZILAND

BORDER CROSSINGS

Crossing the border is fairly easy – you simply show your passport and pay E50 in road tax. There are eleven border posts with South Africa and two serving Mozambique. The most convenient ones are listed below:

Ngwenya/Oshoek (7am–noon) is the most popular, the closest to Johannesburg and the easiest route to Mbabane. Can be very busy during holidays and weekends.

Sandlane/Nerston (8am–6pm) is a good alternative 15km further south, roughly 70km from Johannesburg.

Sicunusa/Houdkop (8am–6pm) is just off the N2 from Piet Retief in the southwest, which leads to the wonderfully scenic and fast MR4.

Mahamba (7am–10pm) in the south, runs lots of traffic from N2/Piet Retief and beyond.

Lavumisa/Golela (24hr) in the southeast, close to the KwaZulu-Natal coast, is the second-busiest crossing.

Mhlumeni/Goba (24hr) is a busy crossing into Mozambique and the main route for traffic from the southern half of South Africa, so expect lots of lorries.

Lomahasha/Namaacha (7am–8pm) is the second crossing Into Mozambique, passing through Hlane Royal National Park and the scenic Lebombo Mountains.

Mananga (7am–6pm) leads to Kruger and the busy Lebombo border between South Africa and Mozambique.

Matsamo/Jeppe's Reef (8am–8pm) in the north, handy if you're coming in from Kruger Park and Nelspruit.

Bulembu/Josefdal (8am–4pm), via Piggs Peak in the north, is the most spectacular crossing in the country, but the bad road makes it difficult in an ordinary car.

BY PLANE

The $200 million King Mswati III International Airport (also known as Sikhuphe Airport) near Hlane was completed in 2014, superseding the airport at Matsapha as the main international hub. Airlink Swaziland (📞 25186155, 🌐 flyswaziland.com), a partner of SAA, flies three times daily to and from Johannesburg (1hr). A shuttle bus runs three times daily from the airport to Mbabane (E50), with stops in Manzini (E25) and Ezulwini (E44).

BY BUS

Several bus companies run a regular service in large, comfortable minibuses between South Africa and Swaziland. The two best are TransMagnifique (📞 24049977, 🌐 goswaziland.co.sz) and Exclusive Shuttle (📞 24043315, 🌐 exclusiveshuttletours.com), which run two daily buses between Mbabane and Johannesburg (4hr; E600 and E500 respectively), stopping at OR Tambo Airport and Sandton. TransMagnifique also runs a weekend bus to Nelspruit and Kruger National Park Airport (E400) and a bus to Durban (E780) on Fridays and Sundays. Book in advance online. Swaziland Cultural Tours (📞 76426780, 🌐 swaziculturaltours.com) run buses on request to Nelspruit (E370) and Maputo (E450). For an extra cost, you can include lunch and visits to markets and natural reserves en route. A cheaper option is to catch Kombi minibuses (see below), which ply the main routes into Swaziland from Johannesburg and Nelspruit, and depart when they are full.

GETTING AROUND

By car Driving is the best way to see Swaziland; distances are small the main sights are near tarred roads, and the major travel roads are in good condition. Self-drive exploration of the Swazi game reserves is a thrilling, and affordable, alternative to guided tours. Most dirt roads are passable with an ordinary vehicle in dry months. Driving standards, however, are poor – two of the last four ministers of transport have died in road accidents. Also, the general speed limit of 80km/h outside towns is universally ignored and rarely enforced. Car rental outlets are at the airport (see p.619).

By Kombi minibus Swaziland is crisscrossed by a network of Kombi minibus routes that covers almost every corner of the country. The Kombis leave when full from stations in the main towns, and cover the main routes linking the towns, calling at set stops along the way. Some walking to get to your final destination is likely, so make

12

sure you're traveling light. Kombi travel is cheap – a ticket from Mbabane to *Malandela's* in the eZulwini Valley costs E15. Ask at the local bus station about the best route to get to your destination. The stations are organized by destination, so all Kombis to, say, Manzini will leave from one corner of the station, and to Big Bend from another. Although buses tend to get quite packed, they are a great way of meeting people.

Mbabane

Tucked into the jumble of granite peaks and valleys that makes up the Dlangeni hills, Swaziland's administrative capital, **MBABANE** (pronounced "M-buh-ban"), is small, relaxed and unpretentious, with a population of only about 100,000. Named after a local, eighteenth-century chief, Mbabane Kunene, the city roughly marks the point where the mountainous Southern African highveld descends briefly into middleveld, before bottoming out further east as dry lowveld.

There's not much to do in Mbabane, but it's more agreeable than hectic Manzini, and it is a good base to stock up on supplies or plan your trip. It's a useful central transportation hub if you're without your own transport: the Mlilwane Wildlife Sanctuary (see p.624) lies not far south, and the royal village of Lobamba (see p.624) makes an easy day-trip – useful if you're here when the *Umhlanga* or *Ncwala* ceremonies take place and everything nearer the village is fully booked.

Mbabane's hilly **centre** is a low-key jumble of office blocks, markets and malls that you can very easily explore on foot – which is just as well, as driving here can be stressful without a sound grasp of the street layout and confusing one-way system.

Gwamile Street is the closest the city has to a main street; running south into the central business district (CBD), it's lined in parts by colonial administrative buildings which are attractive to look at, but can only be entered on official business. At the end of Gwamile Street, on the banks of the Mbabane River, lies the daily **Swazi Market** where fresh fruit and vegetable stalls make for a colourful scene.

The main focus of the city centre, however, is the sprawl of shopping malls down the hill from Gwamile Street. Most of Mbabane's main shops, banks and services are located in either **Corporate Place** or the more upmarket **Mall** and **New Mall**.

Note that Central Mbabane empties at night, and **muggings** are a risk for those wandering the streets alone. If you're going out after dark, arrange for a taxi to pick you up.

SIBEBE ROCK TRAILS

About 10km north of Mbabane along the Pine Valley road is Swaziland's most famous geological feature, a huge granite dome called **Sibebe Rock**. Situated among the Mubuluzi Mountains, the area boasts springs you can swim in and a network of trails leading to various breathtaking viewpoints. Rising 300m above the Mubuluzi River Valley, the vast slabs of granite are very steep and dangerous in places, but among the scattered boulders at the summit are Bushman paintings indicating that the rock was inhabited by humans thousands of years ago. While the hard, coarse surface of the granite offers more grip than other types of rock, it can be very dangerous, so a guide is essential for any ascent.

Stop in at the community-run visitors' centre at the base of the rock to organize your hike (E30; ☎ 24046070), or contact *Maguga Lodge* (see p.634) to arrange a trip with their excellent guide Sipho Mnisi (E175, including transport from Maguga). For an adrenaline-fuelled ascent up the front face of the rock dome, Swazi Trails (see p.616) offers a challenge it describes as "the steepest walk in the world". It also organizes **caving trips** in the same mountain range, which involves a lot of squeezing through narrow spaces and navigation by little more than a head torch and the encouraging words of your guide – it's a memorable adventure for those who don't mind enclosed spaces and a few bumps and scratches.

12

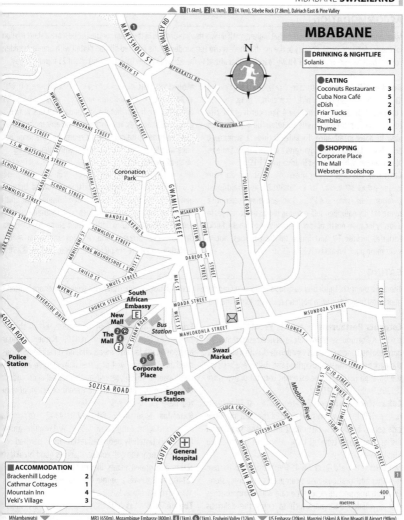

▲ 1 (1.6km), 2 (4.1km), 3 (4.1km), Sibebe Rock (7.8km), Dalriach East & Pine Valley

MBABANE

■ DRINKING & NIGHTLIFE
Solanis	1

● EATING
Coconuts Restaurant	3
Cuba Nora Café	5
eDish	2
Friar Tucks	6
Ramblas	1
Thyme	4

● SHOPPING
Corporate Place	3
The Mall	2
Webster's Bookshop	1

■ ACCOMMODATION
Brackenhill Lodge	2
Cathmar Cottages	1
Mountain Inn	4
Veki's Village	3

12

Mhlambanyatsi ▼   MR3 (650m), Mozambique Embassy (800m), 4 (1km), 6 (1km), Ezulwini Valley (12km), ▼ US Embassy (20km), Manzini (36km) & King Mswati III Airport (90km)

ARRIVAL AND DEPARTURE

MBABANE

By plane King Mswati III Airport (☎ 25184390) is about an hour and a half's drive east of the city. A shuttle service runs three times daily, or you can rent a car. Avis (☎ 23335299) and Budget (☎ 23335299) are at the airport, Europcar is at the Engen Garage on Main Road (☎ 24040459) and Affordable Car Hire (☎ 24049136) on Corporate Place.

By Kombi Kombi buses and minibuses from South Africa stop at the main bus station on Dr Sishay Road beside Corporate Place. From here you can catch minibus Kombis to Manzini and Piggs Peak, and local buses within the Mbabane area. Kombis plying the Mbabane–Manzini route leave from the western side of the bus station.

INFORMATION AND GETTING AROUND

Tourist office The Mall (Mon–Fri 8am–5pm, Sat 9am–1pm; ☎ 24042531). Has maps, brochures and a list of recommended tour guides. They can also help with hotel bookings (free).

By Kombi Kombi minibuses leave from the bus station near Corporate Place.
By taxi Your hotel can recommend a trusted driver. Private taxis congregate near the bus station.

ACCOMMODATION

Mbabane's accommodation is somewhat limited, with no worthwhile options in the town centre. The best are a short minibus journey or taxi ride away, notably to the north, where you're surrounded by the forested hillside dotted with granite boulders. For real backpacker options, you'll have to look further ahead to the eZulwini Valley (see opposite) about 25 minutes away.

Brackenhill Lodge Mountain Drive, off Fonteyn Rd ☎ 24042887, ⓦ brackenhillswazi.com; map p.619. Luxurious B&B on a quiet hillside 4.5km north of the city centre. The comfortable rooms are often full so it's a good idea to book in advance. Facilities include a swimming pool, lovely hiking trails, a gym and a steam room; dinner is also available when ordered in advance. **E1050**

Cathmar Cottages 3km north of Mbabane on Pine Valley Rd ☎ 24043387 or ☎ 76080820, ⓔ shieldguest @yahoo.com; map p.619. A laidback place offering a range of fully equipped self-catering rooms and cottages in a lovely location north of town with views of Sibebe Rock. Facilities include TV and fridge in the cottages, and a swimming pool; breakfast is E75. **E550**

Mountain Inn 4km southeast of Mbabane off MR ☎ 24042781, ⓦ mountaininn.sz; map p.619. A efficient, family-run hotel with good facilities aimed a groups and families. It is located on an airy mountainside plot, and the upstairs breakfast room and the large poc have wonderful views over the eZulwini Valley. **E1480**

★ **Veki's Village** Mountain Drive, Plot 881, off Fonteyn Rd ☎ 76036396, ⓔ vekisvillage@gmail.com; map p.619. Eleven self-catering apartments tucked between indigenous gardens and the wooded hillside. Each unit i decorated with a personal touch – handmade wooden furniture or colourful paintings, and some have a smal fireplace and private patio. A pool and braai area i available, and there are plenty of trails to explore. **R750**

EATING

There are plenty of quick and easy food options at Corporate Place mall downtown, otherwise your choices are limited t good local favourites, with nothing really breaking the mould.

Coconuts Restaurant Siphefu St ☎ 24111716; map p.619. A Portuguese/Mozambican-styled restaurant with good seafood and a spacious wooden deck with a view over the park below. The various grilled fish dishes are best; try the Garoupa (E160), or the excellent coconut prawn curry (E125). Daily 10am–10pm.

Cuba Nora Cafe Corporate Place ☎ 78062964; map p.619. In the sunny food court of the mall, this little café serves breakfasts, tasty light meals and some local dishes like goat curry (E110). Mon–Sat 7am–9pm, Sun 8am–6pm.

★ **eDish** Somhlolo Rd ☎ 24045504; map p.619. Despite its rather odd location above a computer part supply store, this is an unexpectedly cool little café with comfy couches and a wooden deck on which to enjoy the delicious gourmet sandwiches – try the oxtail (E75) or blue arugula (E50). Freshly baked pastries and good coffee make this a great place for breakfast as well, and there's free wi-fi. Mon–Sat 8am–5pm.

Friar Tucks Mountain Inn, 4km southeast of the cit centre ☎ 24042781; map p.619. Rather standar international à la carte meals and, on certain days, hous specialities, such as well-prepared baby chicken and Swaz goat casserole (E150), served in a vaulted cellar or outdoor overlooking the pool. There's a decent selection of wine too. Daily 12.30–2pm & 7–9.30pm.

Ramblas Mantsholo Rd ☎ 24044147, ⓦ rambla swaziland.webs.com; map p.619. A favourite amon locals, this tastefully decorated restaurant is perched on breezy hill near the golf course. It serves good breakfast pizzas and grilled meats like rump steak and pork rib (E140), and there's a jungle gym to keep kids occupiec Mon–Fri 8am–late, Sat 8.30am–late.

Thyme The Mall ☎ 76251861; map p.619. Downstairs i The Mall, along the central walkway, this is the place to g for good coffee. The well-prepared breakfasts includ granola (E42) and French toast (E34), and there ar excellent salads for lunch. Daily 8am–5pm.

DRINKING AND NIGHTLIFE

Nightlife in Mbabane is limited during the week and only slightly livelier at weekends. For the best nightlife, however, mos locals head out to the eZulwini Valley, especially to *Malandela's* (see p.627), where local and international bands ofte headline at the House on Fire. Women travellers on their own are likely to encounter some unwanted attention in bars an clubs, but the pestering probably won't be aggressive or persistent.

Solanis Dzeliwe St, Cnr Jojo and Jekwa sts ☎ 24045352, ⓦ solanis.co.sz; map p.619. The hottest spot to swing your hips in Mbabane, even drawing weekend crowds from Johannesburg. Excellent live DJs, braai meat on the menu,

and a cool, friendly crowd. Cover charge on the weeken only (E100), and extra when there's a visiting artist (E150 Take a taxi, as it's a little out of the way and not in the bes area. Mon–Thurs 9am–midnight, Fri–Sun 24 hours.

DIRECTORY

Banks Most banks are found in Corporate Place. Branches include First National, Nedbank and Standard. Hours are generally Mon–Fri 9am–3.30pm & Sat 9–11.30am.

Bookshops Webster's at 120 Dzeliwe St (Mon–Fri 7.45am–5pm, Sat 7.45am–1pm; ☎ 24042560; map p.619).

Embassies Mozambique, Princess Drive (☎ 24043700); South Africa, New Mall, 2nd floor (☎ 24044651); US, Corner of MR103 and Cultural Center Drive, eZulwini (☎ 24179000). Note that the UK's representation in Swaziland is a Pretoria-based consul; for details, see ⓦ fco.gov.uk.

Emergencies Fire ☎ 933; Police ☎ 999.

Hospitals Mbabane Clinic Service (private), Mkhonubovu Street (☎ 24042423); Government Hospital (public), Lusuftu Rd (☎ 24042111).

Internet access Real Image Internet, Tsekwane St (Mon–Fri 8am–5pm, ☎ 24091000).

Pharmacy Green Cross in The Mall (Mon–Fri 8.30am–5.30pm, Sat 9am–2pm, Sun 10am–1pm; ☎ 24043450, ☎ 76268630).

Post office The main post office is on Mahlokohla St (Mon–Fri 8.30am–4pm, Sat 8.30–11am), and there's a smaller one in the Swazi Plaza.

The eZulwini Valley

After passing through Mbabane from the Ngwenya border, the smooth, four-lane **MR3** winds down the steep sides of **Malagwane Hill** in a series of sweeping curves made hazardous by crawling lorries and reckless minibus taxis. The road then heads off southeast along the eZulwini Valley, but unless you're bound directly for Manzini and beyond, take the turning to the right not long after the foot of the hill onto the older and quieter **MR103** – also known as the eZulwini Valley Road – which links most of the main sights of the **eZulwini Valley** (Place of Heaven). In the 1960s a succession of casinos, strip joints, hotels and caravan parks sprang up here, catering mainly for South African tourists. When gambling became legal in South Africa in the mid-1990s, however, the number of pleasure-seekers dropped; the tourist industry had to start looking beyond the noise of the slot machines and karaoke to the valley's cultural and natural assets. Places such as the **Mantenga Cultural Village** were developed, while the royal residences of **Lobamba** and **Ludzidzini**, as well as **Mlilwane Wildlife Sanctuary**, became more recognized as attractive to visitors. The latter, in particular, is one of Swaziland's main attractions, with its range of accommodation and numerous activities, including hiking trails and game viewing from a mountain bike.

12

The Mantenga Valley

The first five kilometres or so of the **eZulwini Valley Road** take you past a strip of glossy, anonymous-looking and hugely overpriced casino hotels. Turning south along Mantenga Drive (signposted to *Mantenga Lodge*) will take you to the much more interesting **Mantenga Valley**, which follows the course of the Lusushwana (or Little Usutu) River. Most prominent in the valley is the twin-peaked **Lugogo Mountain**, also known as "Sheba's Breasts", which featured in H. Rider Haggard's famous adventure novel *King Solomon's Mines*. Further along, on the western horizon, Execution Rock is a stark reminder of the days when murderers and thieves were punished by being forced to jump off the rock to certain death below. Just beyond the turning to the Mantenga Valley is the **Gables Shopping Centre**, which boasts ATMs, banks, fast-food restaurants and a large supermarket.

Mantenga Craft and Lifestyle Centre

Mantenga Drive, less than 1km from the northern turn-off from the eZulwini Valley Rd • Daily 7am–7pm; ☎ 24161136

The **Mantenga Craft and Lifestyle Centre** consists of a selection of craft shops set around a large, pebbled courtyard shaded by an enormous rubber tree. The shops specialize in more exclusive and individual crafts than found in many other parts of Swaziland,

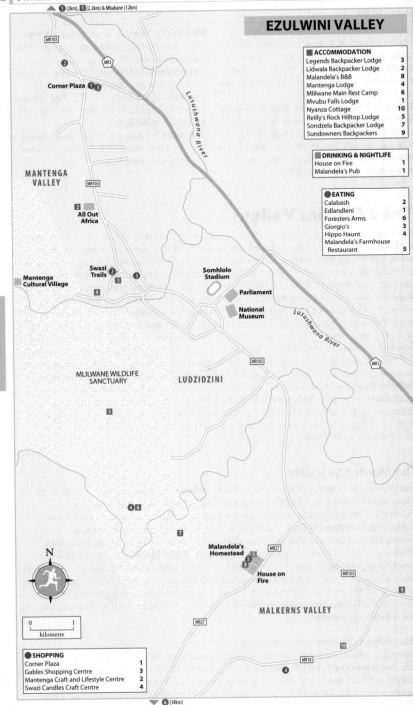

EZULWINI VALLEY

ACCOMMODATION

Legends Backpacker Lodge	3
Lidwala Backpacker Lodge	2
Malandela's B&B	8
Mantenga Lodge	4
Mlilwane Main Rest Camp	6
Mvubu Falls Lodge	1
Nyanza Cottage	10
Reilly's Rock Hilltop Lodge	5
Sondzela Backpacker Lodge	7
Sundowners Backpackers	9

DRINKING & NIGHTLIFE

House on Fire	1
Malandela's Pub	1

EATING

Calabash	2
Edlandleni	1
Foresters Arms	6
Giorgio's	3
Hippo Haunt	4
Malandela's Farmhouse Restaurant	5

SHOPPING

Corner Plaza	1
Gables Shopping Centre	3
Mantenga Craft and Lifestyle Centre	2
Swazi Candles Craft Centre	4

including African Fantasy artwork, silver-smithing, and beautiful and quirky carvings and sculptures, all sold at fair prices. There is also a wine shop and a couple of restaurants that invite a long, easy afternoon under the dappled shade. Try *Pizza Vesuvio*'s tasty, thin-crust pizza (E70) baked in a wood-fired oven right in front of you, or the excellent-value menu at *The ArTea Tree*, offering healthy alternatives like a lentil burger on a sweet-potato fritter (E55). Both stay open until 10pm.

INFORMATION

Tourist information At the far end of the Craft Centre, the main booking office for Swazi Trails also doubles as the country's best tourist office (daily 8am–5pm; ☎ 24162180 or ☎ 76020261 after hours, ⓦ swazitrails .co.sz), which can help you with accommodation booking and trip planning. As Swaziland's leading tour operator, Swazi Trails organizes a wide range of cultural and adventure trips including a half-day arts and crafts trail, whitewater rafting (see box, p.631), mountain biking and adventure caving.

THE MANTENGA VALLEY

ACCOMMODATION

Legends Backpacker Lodge Across from Mantenga Craft Centre ☎ 24161870, ⓦ legends.co.sz; map opposite. Rather run-down but friendly, with dorms sleeping twelve, ten doubles, a yard for camping, internet access and a communal kitchen. It's a great place to base yourself if you're on a tight budget and want easy access to all that the valley has to offer. Camping E90, dorms E175, doubles E475

★ **Lidwala Backpacker Lodge** On the eZulwini Rd just before the Mantenga Valley turn-off ☎ 24171791 or ☎ 76905865, ⓦ lidwala.co.sz; map opposite. A great backpackers' place above the All Out Africa responsible travel company office (see box, p.616). Made up of comfortable four- and six-bed dorms, a few en-suite doubles and a grassy area for camping, there's also a fully equipped kitchen, a library and computers with internet access. A stream runs through the grounds creating a soothing, verdant space. Camping E100, dorms E180, doubles E590

Mantenga Lodge From the Mantenga Craft Centre, continue along a dirt road for about 200m (follow the signs) ☎ 24161049, ☎ 76025266, ⓦ mantengalodge .com; map opposite. Nestled between Sheba's Breasts, this is a stunningly located, family-run lodge with 28 en-suite rooms. There are a handful of cosy chalets on the valley-side, as well as a pool, terrace bar and top-notch restaurant with especially good views of Execution Rock. E976

Mvubu Falls Lodge Off the MR3, about 6km from Mbabane ☎ 24044655, ⓦ mvubufalls.com; map opposite. Down a rather rough dirt road, this small lodge consists of a row of impeccable, reasonably spacious rooms with parking just in front and views over lush, well-kept grounds from a small terrace. There's a swimming pool, and a little further on, the all-wood bar and restaurant feels pleasantly secluded, and has the tumbling river as a constant soundtrack. E1150

EATING

Calabash Nyonyane Rd, Lobamba ☎ 24161187; map opposite. One of Swaziland's most upscale restaurants, serving an excellent range of fresh seafood and specializing in German, Swiss and French dishes such as beef tartare (E155) and proper Wiener schnitzel for E125. It's old school, with decor to match, but the quality remains high. Daily 12.30–2.30pm & 6–10.30pm.

★ **Edlandleni** Near Mvubu Falls, signposted off the MR3 2km west of the Mantenga turn-off ☎ 76184103; map opposite. This eclectically decorated restaurant, set on a grassy slope with a river running below, is the most interesting dining option in the area. Dolores Godefroy, local chef and activist for seasonal, local food, offers a range of traditional Swazi dishes, including *umbidvo wetintsanga* (pumpkin shoot and groundnuts in *mealie* porridge), fresh corn bread, peanut chicken stew and variously spiced and grilled beans, veggies and meats. Out of season and weekdays, call in advance to check the restaurant is open. On summer Sundays she hosts a buffet lunch by the river with live music (E150). Daily noon–3pm & 6–10pm.

Foresters Arms 27km southwest of Mbabane, Just before the small town of Mhlambanyatsi, on the back road to the Sandlane border post ☎ 24674177 or ☎ 24674377, ⓦ forestersarms.co.za; map opposite. Even if you don't plan to stay, this fine hotel, picturesquely set in a pine forest clearing, is well worth a detour for its outstanding restaurant. The meals are mostly made from home-grown and locally sourced produce such as hearty farm-style chicken and corn soup, unusual but mouth-watering tropical salmon, and delicious lamb confit with bean cassoulet. On Sundays, people from all over the country pour in to feast on the hotel's superb buffet lunch (E180) — you'll need to book ahead to be sure of a table. Daily 7am–10pm.

Giorgio's Corner Plaza, eZulwini ☎ 24162427; map opposite. An Italian café serving all-day breakfasts at a good price, including a well-loaded fry-up for E65. Lunch and dinner options range from basic pizzas (E90) and pastas (E65) to daily grilled meat specials. Mon–Fri 7am–6pm, Sat 7am–4.30pm, Sun 8am–3.30pm.

12

Mantenga Cultural Village

Daily 8am–5pm • E100 • ☎ 24161151, ⊛ sntc.org.sz

Mantenga Drive ends at the grand entrance to the tiny **Mantenga Nature Reserve**, only really worth visiting for its cultural village. This open-air living museum replicates a nineteenth-century Swazi homestead with sixteen beehive huts, all built in traditional style using wooden frames joined by leather strips, reed thatch, cow dung and termite-hill earth. Cattle and goats wander about, and there are often demonstrations of traditional activities and crafts. Twice daily (11.15am & 3.15pm) an enchanting thirty-minute traditional music and dance performance takes place in a small open-air arena, telling a story of Swazi soldiers in the Anglo-Boer War, and the love and witchcraft they encounter when they return home.

Although the cultural village is the main attraction of the nature reserve, it's worth finding time to follow the short trail to the scenic 95m **Mantenga Falls** with its pretty **picnic** and **swimming spots**; it's a signposted fifteen-minute walk from the café.

Lobamba

Some 20km south of Mbabane, at the heart of the eZulwini Valley, the small royal village of **LOBAMBA** was originally built in 1830 for King Sobhuza I, and became the royal kraal (residence) of Sobhuza II. The **Houses of Parliament** are situated here, and must be one of the few in the world to have cattle grazing undisturbed in surrounding fields.

National Museum

Next door to the Parliament building • Mon–Fri 8am–4.30pm, Sat & Sun 10am–4pm • E80 • ☎ 24161179

A paved road to the north of the MR103 leads to the **National Museum**, which provides a helpful potted history of the country through displays of cultural artefacts, a mishmash of old photographs of Manzini and Mbabane when they were one-horse towns, and sweaty British administrators in full colonial regalia. The only really interesting item in the natural history wing is a replica of a sixteenth-century head of Krishna that was discovered nearby. It was all that was found of what was a full-bodied statuette, and the find has been interpreted as an indication of the high level of trade with the East at the time. Outside the museum stands a life-size re-creation of a traditional Swazi homestead. Remarkably, given their size, these huts are actually portable.

Somhlolo stadium

In front of the Parliament and Museum

Lobamba's **Somhlolo stadium** is the country's venue for major events and football matches, which are usually highly entertaining. For a few emalangeni on a Sunday afternoon you can treat yourself to genial games of occasional great skill, with a good-humoured and vociferous crowd. Consult the local *Times of Swaziland* for details, or ask locally.

Ludzidzini

On the other side of the MR103 from Lobamba, the village of **LUDZIDZINI** is the kraal of the present king, Mswati III, and the Queen Mother. Ludzidzini cannot be visited or even photographed at all except during *Ncwala* (around New Year) and *Umhlanga* (end Aug/early Sept), when permission must be obtained (see box opposite).

Mlilwane Wildlife Sanctuary

Daily 24hr • E50 • ⊛ biggameparks.org

For many visitors to Swaziland the highlight of the eZulwini Valley is **Mlilwane Wildlife Sanctuary**, with its relaxed atmosphere and attractive, game-filled plains. The name Mlilwane refers to the "little fire" that sometimes appears when lightning strikes the

NCWALA AND UMHLANGA

The most sacred of Swaziland's ceremonies, **Ncwala** celebrates kingship, national unity and the first fruits of the new year. Its timing coincides with the new moon in November, when a group of selected men travels to the ancestral home of the Swazi people on the shores of the Indian Ocean to collect foam from the waves. While they are there, the *Ncwala* ceremony begins in Lobamba, with songs and rituals performed until the afternoon of the full moon in December/early January, when the six days of the full *Ncwala* begin. Young Swazi men gather branches of the *lusekwane* tree, from which they build a bower for the king. Warriors gather and sing songs that can only be sung at this time, while the king dances with them. On the sixth day, objects representing the previous year are burnt on a massive bonfire, and prayers are offered to Swazi ancestors. The ceremony ends amid raucous singing, dancing and feasting. Visitors are allowed to attend most of *Ncwala*, but photography is prohibited during certain times (a free permit is also required; contact the Ministry of Information, PO Box 642, Mbabane; ☎ 24054000, ⓦ gov.sz), so be sure to ask first to avoid having your camera smashed.

The **Umhlanga** is a **fertility** or reed **dance** that gets its name from the large reeds brought to the residence of the Queen Mother by young women to repair her kraal, usually in late August or early September. The sixth and seventh days are the most spectacular, when you can watch up to 25,000 young women, dressed in elaborate and carefully coded costumes, sing and dance before the king and Queen Mother at Lobamba, giving the king an opportunity to pick a **new wife**. The former king, Sobhuza II, invariably plucked a new mate from the bevy of young beauties and racked up a total of seventy wives during his lifetime. His successor, Mswati III, now in his 40s, has proved a little more restrained with only thirteen wives so far.

12

granite mountains. As well as offering good game viewing and activities, Mlilwane is an easy alternative to staying in Mbabane or on the eZulwini strip. Given its popularity, it's wise to book ahead if you intend to stay overnight.

The reserve holds a special place in the history of wildlife conservation in Swaziland; it was here that Ted Reilly (see box, p.626) first realized his dream of a sanctuary for Swaziland's fast-disappearing **wildlife**. Mlilwane's animals are mainly herbivorous, and include zebra, bountiful numbers of antelope and the sanctuary's emblem, the warthog. There's also the occasional crocodile and hippopotamus, which means you still need to be cautious if viewing the game on foot, bike or horseback.

ARRIVAL AND DEPARTURE

MLILWANE WILDLIFE SANCTUARY

By car To get to Mlilwane take the turning from the eZulwini Valley Rd, signposted about 1km beyond the turn-off to Ludzidzini. From here it's 3.5km along a dirt road to the entrance gate, where you pay your entrance fee – if arriving after 6pm entry fees are paid at the main restcamp the following morning. Note that you'll need to show both your entry and accommodation receipts in order to leave the sanctuary again, or they may charge you twice.

By shuttle bus There is a daily shuttle bus that runs between *Sondzela* backpackers and Malandela's Homestead, leaving Sondzela at 8am (see p.626) and Malandela's about half an hour later.

INFORMATION AND ACTIVITIES

Maps The park office, easy to spot in the middle of the main restcamp, sells maps of cycling and hiking routes in the sanctuary (E25).

Guided trails Guided walks and game drives are available through the park office at the main restcamp. There are also guided mountain-bike tours and horseback trails, both fairly relaxed ways of taking in the park's attractions. For those with a little more horseback experience, fully catered overnight trails involve camping in caves and rustic trail camps in the more remote parts of the reserve. For details, contact Big Game Parks central reservations (see p.626).

Self-guided trails Over 40km of road enables you to drive through the park to view game. There are also a number of good cycling routes running throughout the park; the main restcamp rents out mountain bikes (E130/hr). The best of the self-guided walking trails is the Macobane Hill Trail, a gentle, four-hour hike through the mountains. The more adventurous can climb to the top of Nyonyane, the "Execution Rock", which rises so prominently in the north of the reserve. Whichever route you choose to take, it's important you tell a ranger of your plans before heading out; they keep track of who's out on their own and come out to find you if you're not back by dusk.

ACCOMMODATION

The reserve offers a wide variety of accommodation, which should be booked through Swaziland Big Game Parks Central Reservations (☎ 25283944, 🌐 biggameparks.org), though *Sondzela* (see below) can also be booked directly.

Main Rest Camp About 3.5km from the gate ☎ 25283992; map p.622. Accommodation is basic but well kept, including a campsite, traditional beehive villages, two- and four-person rondavels and larger family cottages. A few fearless animals move freely around the camp's centre, and, slightly removed, there is a very welcome swimming pool. Self-catering and B&B options available. Camping E125, rondavels E860

Reilly's Rock Hilltop Lodge On a hilltop about 30min drive from Main Rest Camp; map p.622. A lovely colonial home full of antiques and hardwood furniture, and with a wrap-around veranda, situated on a hilltop surrounded by woodland and prolific birdlife. With only six rooms, it's more upmarket than a guesthouse but more rustic than a game lodge, and guests can enjoy fantastic views over the Mdzimba Mountains, and wander round the impressive gardens that surround the house. Rates include half board. E2410

Sondzela Backpacker Lodge 20min walk from Main Rest Camp ☎ 25283992; map p.622. A friendly place firmly established on the backpacking circuit, with dorms, doubles, and comfortable adobe rondavels sleeping two overlooking the valley, all with communal ablution facilities. Camping is also an option (tents only), and there's a lush garden, bar and large swimming pool. This is a rare chance to overnight in a nature reserve at budget prices, and they offer pickups from Malandela's Homestead. Camping E110, dorms E125, doubles E420

EATING

You can only buy basic supplies at the Main Rest Camp, so if you've opted for self-catering accommodation it's best to stock up at the Gables Shopping Centre (see p.621) beforehand.

Hippo Haunt At the Main Rest Camp; map p.622. The only restaurant at Mlilwane serves up some good grilled meats on the Swazi braai (E120), a delicious chicken tikka focaccia sandwich (E70), and buffet dinners on busy nights (E190). There's also a well-stocked bar. The restaurant overlooks an artificially created pond, which is home to hippos, crocs and a huge variety of birds, and is a superb place to while away a few hours. Daily 6.30am–10pm.

Sondzela Backpacker Lodge A 20min walk from Main Rest Camp ☎ 25283992; map p.622. Inexpensive breakfasts (E45) and dinners (E75) are available at *Sondzela*, served in front of the campfire. There's only one dish on offer – such as stewed impala prepared in cast-iron pots over an open fire – in addition to a vegetarian option. Dinner must be ordered in advance. Dinner daily 6pm.

12

THE SWAZI CONSERVATION STORY

Swaziland owes the creation and survival of three of its major wildlife sanctuaries – Mlilwane, Mkhaya and Hlane – to **Ted Reilly**, who was born in Mlilwane in 1938, the son of a British Anglo-Boer War soldier who had decided to make the country his home. As Reilly was growing up, Swazi wildlife and its natural habitats were coming under serious threat from poachers and commercial farmers. In 1959 Reilly lobbied the colonial government to set aside land for parks, but was defeated by farmers who wanted the land for commercial agriculture. Undeterred, he turned his Mlilwane estate into a park anyway, and set about cultivating a relationship with **King Sobhuza II**. After Swazi independence Sobhuza became much more powerful, and Reilly's connection to him lent weight to his nature conservation efforts.

Despite rickety finances, the **Mlilwane Wildlife Sanctuary** opened in 1961, and the restocking and reintroduction of species has continued ever since. Meanwhile, Sobhuza asked Reilly to help stamp out poaching at Hlane. Reilly's tough approach resulted in shootouts with the poachers, earning him the praise of some, but the enmity of many.

Reilly's dependence on his royal links has also generated controversy, and some critics also assert that Reilly subordinates wildlife management principles to the needs of the tourist industry. Reilly's answer to his critics is simply to point to the three game parks his company runs. It's a powerful argument – without Reilly, the parks would not exist. Ted Reilly still lives at Mlilwane and remains active in Swazi conservation.

Malandela's Homestead

1km southeast of the Mahlanya junction, off the MR103 · **Homestead** Daily 11am–3pm & 6pm–late · ☎ 25283115, ⓦ malandelas.com · **Gone Rural** Mon–Sat 8am–5pm, Sun 9am–5pm · ☎ 25504936, ⓦ goneruralswazi.com · **House on Fire** Tickets E50–80, gigs from 8pm · ☎ 25282110, ⓦ house-on-fire.com · **Bushfire Festival** Day ticket E380–480, whole festival E760 · ☎ 25282040, ⓦ bush-fire.com

The scenic Malkerns Valley, lined with pineapple and sugar-cane fields, is home to **Malandela's Homestead**. Initially just a collection of rustic farm buildings, it has now developed into a lively family-run arts and crafts venue that attracts locals and visitors alike to its top-of-the-range gigs, performances and exhibitions, while its pub and restaurant always seem to be filled to capacity. One of the highlights of the homestead is Gone Rural, one of the most successful and creative **local handicrafts projects** in Swaziland; the colourful and well-designed woven mats and baskets on sale here are made by a huge network of women working from villages all over the country.

Over the last three days of May, House on Fire is the venue for the hugely successful **Bushfire Festival**, with great musicians like Hugh Masekela, Johnny Clegg and Ladysmith Black Mambazo headlining in the past, and with camping on fields next to the homestead. Tickets can be bought via the website.

INFORMATION   MALANDELA'S HOMESTEAD

Tourist information All Out Africa is next door to Gone Rural (Mon–Sat 8am–5pm, Sun 9am–5pm; ☎ 25283423, ⓦ alloutafrica.com); along with organizing tours, it has a good array of tourist information leaflets and wi-fi.

ACCOMMODATION

Malandela's B&B ☎ 25283448, ⓦ malandelas.com; map p.622. Delightful Afro-chic double rooms built in natural and recycled materials, with lavish breakfasts served on a terrace facing sugar-cane fields, a pool and an exuberant yet immaculate garden. It tends to be full when there's a concert happening at House on Fire (see below), so advance booking is essential. <u>**E820**</u>

EATING AND DRINKING

Malandela's Farmhouse Restaurant ☎ 25283115; map p.622. Situated under a large thatched roof and offering an interesting daily blackboard menu, including stews, game and fresh fish dishes, plus a fabulous range of salads (E60). The restaurant's outdoor dining area leads onto a large open grassed area that's great for kids to play in and which looks over sugar-cane fields and distant mountains. Daily 9.30–11am, noon–3pm & 6–9.30pm.

DRINKING AND NIGHTLIFE

House on Fire ☎ 25282110, ⓦ house-on-fire.com; map p.622. This creative amphitheatre-like performance space doubles as an art gallery and music venue, and is worth checking out for contemporary African crafts and its riotous design. With live gigs most weekends – mostly up-and-coming local talent, with the occasional big international act – this is the heart of Swaziland's nightlife, drawing great crowds every weekend. Most shows start at 8pm.

Malandela's Pub map p.622. Adjoining the restaurant, this cosy pub has local craft beer on tap from the Thunderbolt brewery next door and is a popular spot for locals to watch rugby and football on cable TV. Daily 9am–10pm.

12

Along the MR4

The idyllic **Nyanza Farm** (☎ 76085779 or ☎ 76214181, ⓦ nyanza.co.sz), situated on the MR4 a few kilometres from the MR103 junction, is an appealingly cluttered working farm roamed by friendly dogs, cats, geese, turkeys, peacocks, horses and Jersey cows. A little further along the MR4 is the **Swazi Candles Craft Centre** (daily 8am–5pm; ☎ 25283219, ⓦ swazicandles.com), which in addition to a dedicated store producing and selling a bewildering array of brightly patterned wax candles also encompasses a number of local crafts outlets, including the colourful Baobab Batiks (☎ 25283242, ⓦ baobab-batik .com), the mohair weavers of Rosecraft (☎ 25504384, ⓦ tsandzaweaving.com) and Kwazi Swazi (☎ 25283110), selling books, art and a good selection of music. A charming coffee shop, *Sambane* (☎ 25283466, ⓦ sambanecafe.com), serves excellent all-day breakfasts, quality burgers (E75), light snacks and a tempting selection of freshly baked treats (E45).

ACCOMMODATION **ALONG THE MR4**

Nyanza Guest Cottages Nyanza Farm ⓣ76085779 or ⓣ76214181, ⓦnyanza.co.sz; map p.622. Simple yet delightful self-catering accommodation in two spacious, rustic cottages sleeping five, at the bottom of a farm track, plus a lodge with a double room and bunk beds suitable for groups. This is a great place for animal lovers and kids who want the hands-on experience of a real family farm. Riding lessons with expert instructors are offered. Doubles E930, cottage E820

Sundowners Backpackers At the MR103 junction to the Malkerns Valley, 9km west of Manzini, behind Sundowners Lodge ⓣ76878941, ⓦswazisundowners.com; map p.622. A laidback backpackers with tidy dorms, four decent doubles and some grassy areas outside for camping (tents can be rented for an additional E10). There's also a pool and a pleasant bar. Trips to various attractions and activities can be organized. No credit cards. Camping E70, dorms E120, doubles E250

Manzini

MANZINI is Swaziland's largest city and its commercial hub. Almost all of the country's industrial and commercial sector is based in or around here, and the city is dominated by office blocks and malls obscuring its few attractive edifices. With a rising crime rate and an atmosphere far less relaxed than Mbabane, Manzini would be an eminently missable place were it not for its outstanding **market** (Mon–Sat) on the corner of Mhlakuvane and Mancishane streets, which is best on Thursday morning when traders from neighbouring countries come to town. Much of Manzini's market is devoted to fruit and vegetables, household goods and traditional medicines, while an upper section that spills onto the steps below sells **crafts** and **fabrics**. The crafts selection is bigger, more varied and much better value than any other market in Swaziland, while the fabrics – from Zimbabwe, Congo and Mozambique – are hard to find elsewhere in the country.

ARRIVAL AND DEPARTURE **MANZINI**

By bus Buses from all over the country and South Africa pull in at Manzini's busy main bus and taxi rank at the end of Louw St, just north of Ngwane St.

By plane King Mswati III airport (ⓣ25184390) lies 57km east of the city; the shuttle service from the airport runs three times daily (E25).

ACCOMMODATION

The George Hotel Corner of Ngwane and Du Toit St ⓣ25052260, ⓦtgh.sz. A comfortable business-class hotel offering spacious en-suite doubles with plush soft carpets; though some rooms are showing their age. Facilities include a pool, three restaurants, a bar, and a beauty salon and spa. E1300

KAPHUNGA VILLAGE CULTURAL TOURS

An ambitious community tourism project in **KaPhunga** village, about 55km into the mountains southeast of Manzini, provides an excellent off-the-beaten-track opportunity to see the real rural Swaziland. The village is the second-highest settlement in the country and spreads over the top of a mountain rise with absolutely breathtaking views of the valley below – sugar-cane fields galore and the Lebombo Mountains in the distance. Myxo Mdluli has built a mini homestead with authentic huts here, but separate from the main village so that there's a certain amount of privacy for both visitors and villagers. You're encouraged to stay at least one night and sleep in the traditional Swazi way, on a mattress on the hut floor. Facilities are fairly basic, and there is no electricity, but the gorgeous and authentically rustic setting makes this more than adequate. During the day visitors can join in whatever is going on in the village, such as building projects, farming work, brewing beer or helping at the local primary school. Two-day trips (one night) to KaPhunga, including full board, transport from Manzini and contributions to the village, cost E1796 per person. Extra nights can be arranged. Day-trips including transport and meals cost E1350 per person. To book, contact Myxo on ⓣ25058363 or ⓣ76044102, ⓦswaziculturaltours.com.

EATING

Tandoori Express In the bus station, next to KFC ☏ 25058936. Some of Manzini's best food is to be had at this innocuous takeaway in the bus station, which does at least offer plastic chairs on which to enjoy its delicious kormas, biryanis, curries and tandoori chicken (E50). Daily 8am–5pm.

The south

Approaching Swaziland from one of its border crossings in the south is an excellent idea if you're travelling from northern KwaZulu-Natal through to the Kruger National Park or Mpumulanga. The scenery, particularly along the drive between **Mahamba** and Manzini through the **Grand Valley**, is really superb, and the road passes near most of the historical sites of the Swazi royal house. The south is also home to the **Mkhaya Nature Reserve**, Swaziland's most upmarket reserve and a sanctuary for the rare black rhino.

Mkhaya Game Reserve

35km east of Manzini on the MR8, 6km past Siphofaneni · Pick-up at 10am and 4pm · ☏ 25283944, ⓦ biggameparks.org

Mkhaya Game Reserve is situated along a turn-off from the wonderfully named village of **Phuzumoya** ("drink the wind") in classic lowveld scrubland, filled with acacia and thorn trees. A sanctuary for the rare **black rhino**, Mkhaya also accommodates **white rhino**, and numerous antelopes such as nyala, sable and eland. In 2016, the reserve's elephants were sold to US zoos to avoid almost certain death as a result of the devastating drought, but plans are in place to reintroduce new individuals. In addition, Mkhaya operates as a refuge where endangered species such as **roan antelope** and **tsessebe** are bred. Rubbing shoulders with them, in the reserve section closest to the road, are herds of **Nguni cattle**.

INFORMATION   MKHAYA GAME RESERVE

Essentials Book your visit to Mkhaya through Swazi Big Game Parks Central Reservations (☏ 25283944, ⓦ biggameparks.org). Day visits cost E790 (minimum two people), including lunch. Day visits and overnight stays at Mkhaya must be booked in advance (see above), and you can't tour Mkhaya in your own vehicle, but must arrange to be met at the gate (10am or 4pm) from where you'll drive in convoy to the reserve's ranger base and the starting point of the first game drives – Kombi buses from Manzini to Big Bend stop at the gate; ask for the Phuzamoya shop drop.

Game Drives Day visitors are taken on a game drive from the ranger base, and you'll have a high chance of encountering much of the big game. A generous lunch at the main camp is included in the price. For overnighters, morning and evening game drives are included in the accommodation price, and a sunrise walking safari can also be organized. Unlike game reserves in South Africa, Mkhaya's experienced Swazi rangers have few qualms about stopping in the middle of a game drive and inviting visitors to get out of the vehicle and walk quite close to white rhino.

ACCCOMMODATION

Stone Camp ☏ 25283944, ⓦ biggameparks.org. The reserve's only camp makes up for the lack of elevation in the reserve with an atmospheric bush setting beside the dry Ngwenyane river bed. Accommodation is offered in seductively luxurious open-plan and open-sided thatched stone huts with en-suite toilets and showers, which give you a wonderful sense of sleeping right in the bush. Beautifully prepared three-course meals are served around a large campfire in the main part of the camp, under the shade of a massive sausage tree (its seed pods look like sausages). Price includes meals and three guided game drives. E5290

The northeast

Northeast Swaziland is dominated by sugar plantations stretching into the distance, shimmering from the constant water spray, wreaking havoc with the water table – and leaving many locals without, hence the need for the new Maguga Dam (see p.634) – but earning the country valuable foreign exchange. Three large tracts of bush – **Hlane**, **Mlawula** and **Mbuluzi** – have been preserved as wildlife and nature reserves, and these are the main attractions for visitors to this region, together with the smaller **Shewula Nature Reserve**. They all form part of the **Lubombo Conservancy**, a grouping of protected land in the **Lubombo Mountains** that runs along Swaziland's eastern border and provides fantastic views of both Swaziland and the western fringes of Mozambique.

For mountain bikers, the Lubombo reserves organize a hugely popular annual marathon that hurtles riders along game trails and rugged jeep tracks through all three reserves.

The most direct and obvious route to the reserves from Mbabane and Manzini is to follow the signposted and tarred road towards Siteki for 100km and 65km respectively. Turning north roughly 10km before Siteki leads to the reserves listed below.

Mbuluzi Game Reserve

Daily 6am–6pm • E45 • ☎ 2383 8861, ⓦ mbuluzigamereserve.co.sz

Privately owned and little known, **Mbuluzi** is about 1km off the Manzini–Lomahasha road, and straddles the road to Mlawula Nature Reserve. Set in classic lowveld bush, it encompasses two perennial rivers, riverine forest and some rocky precipices, and is a quietly special landscape that has created a loyal following. The park has recently been restocked with game, including hippo and giraffe, which you can view in your own vehicle – a 4WD is recommended – or on a bike. The absence of predators in Mbuluzi also means that you can walk along a network of clearly demarcated **trails**.

ARRIVAL AND DEPARTURE   MBULUZI GAME RESERVE   **12**

By car 10km past Simunye on the MR3.
By Kombi Minibus Kombis from Manzini and Simunye to
the Lomahasha border stop at the Maphiveni junction, from where it's a 15min hike to the gate.

ACCOMMODATION

Campsite ⓦ www.mbuluzigamereserve.co.sz. The campsite is situated in the northern section of the reserve, close to the Mbuluzi River. Facilities include a shower block and the obligatory braai area. Book in advance. **E110**

Lodges ⓦ www.mbuluzigamereserve.co.sz. Mbuluzi's accommodation consists of six privately owned self-catering lodges set well apart and located along forested
riverbanks in the southern section of the reserve. They range from luxury-tented camps at Tambuti, to a rustic stone cottage, *Leadwood Lodge*, to the ultra-modern bush hideaway, *Imfihlo Lodge*. Most feature creature comforts such as swimming pools, DSTV and a/c. Three of the lodges sleep eight, one sleeps six and one five, and a studio cottage sleeps two. Book well in advance. **E1240**

Mlawula Nature Reserve

Daily 6am–6pm • E30 • ☎ 23838885, ⓦ sntc.org.sz

The largest single protected area in the Lubombo Mountains is the 165-square-kilometre **Mlawula Nature Reserve** south of the Mbuluzi River, where you can spend some time exploring a network of self-guided hiking **trails**. As well as climbing into the

---

WHITEWATER RAFTING

One of the most exhilarating things you can do in southern Swaziland is to **whitewater raft** on the beautiful Great Usutu River, located in the east of the country near the Mkhaya Nature Reserve. It's a great river for rafting and one of the few where you can take a trip in a two-man "croc" raft. The route runs for 15km in summer (a bit less in winter), and crosses over rapids classed in grades two to four. The scenery en route is stunning, but hard to appreciate once you hit the rapids, which leave you paddling like crazy and doing your best not to fall in the water. Trips include pick-ups from various points in the eZulwini Valley and en route to the river as well as a picnic lunch; they cost E1300 for a half day and E2200 for a full day. Contact Swazi Trails (☎ 24162180, ⓦ swazitrails.co.sz) for bookings and further information.

SHEWULA MOUNTAIN CAMP

Although isolated and time-consuming to reach, **Shewula Mountain Camp** (booking essential ☎76051160, ⓦshewulacamp.org; E440) is well worth the effort with its spectacular setting at one end of the Lubombo plateau. To get here, take a bumpy dirt road eastwards into the mountains for 16km, from a turn-off 10km north of the Mubuluzi junction on the Manzini–Lomahasha road. Here, the local Shewula community manages a well-run camp with stupendous views west across northeast Swaziland and even, on a clear day, to the skyscrapers of Maputo to the east. It also offers an interesting insight into rural life in Swaziland. Accommodation is in seven rondavels (which sleep up to five people), with bunks or doubles, some with communal ablution facilities, but there Is no electricity, and cooking in a large kitchen/dining area is done on gas. **Activities** include guided hiking through Shewula Nature Reserve to the Mubuluzi River (E50/person) or a two-hour visit to the nearby village where there's a school for AIDS orphans and a local crafts centre (E40/person). If you don't want to self-cater, meals can be arranged in advance (breakfast E60; dinner E100).

mountains and onto the plateau at the top of the Lubombo range where unique species of ironwood trees and cycads grow, the trails wend their way around the river, heading for caves, a waterfall and a hyena pool, and hikes vary in length from two to eight hours. The trails could do with better maintenance, and the bush throughout the reserve is quite dense, which prevents you from seeing much game; birdwatching is the real draw here. Guides are available to lead you on the hiking trails.

The Mlawula stream and more substantial Mbuluzi River both flow through some spectacular valleys in this reserve, and Stone Age tools over one million years old have been found along their beds. **Antelope**, **zebra** and **wildebeest** congregate near the water, but so do **crocodiles**, so resist the temptation to swim.

ARRIVAL AND INFORMATION
MLAWULA NATURE RESERVE

By car Turn east off the Manzini–Lomahasha Rd at the Maphiveni junction and continue past Mbuluzi Reserve until the sign to Mlawula Reserve. There's a second gate on the eastern side of the reserve, close to the Mhlumeni/Goba border crossing from Mozambique, on the main road to Siteki.
By Kombi Minibus Kombis from Manzini and Simunye to

the Lomahasha border stop at the Maphiveni junction, from where it's a 4km hike to the main Mlawula Nature Reserve gate. Kombis linking the Mhlumeni/Goba border crossing to Siteki stop outside the gate.
Information You can pick up leaflets at the park gate but no supplies, so stock up at the supermarket in Simunye.

ACCOMMODATION

Magadzavane Chalets ☎23435108, ⓦsntc.org.sz. Each of the twenty modern en-suite thatched rondavels, near the gate by the Mozambican border, comes with a spacious veranda offering fabulous views of the valley. They are all fully kitted with stove, fridge and TV, and the site also encompasses a pool and restaurant. Book in advance. **E900**

Siphiso Campsite ☎23435108, ⓦsntc.org.sz. A shaded site next to the Siphiso River, with a toilet and shower block and braai stands. There's also an area for caravans, and two thatched shelters that are handy should the weather turn nasty. Book in advance. **E100**

Hlane Royal National Park

Daily 6am–6pm • E40 • ⓦ biggameparks.org

Some 67km northeast of Manzini, **Hlane Royal National Park** is the largest of Swaziland's parks. Formerly a private royal hunting ground, the main attraction here is the presence of big game, including **elephant**, **rhino**, **lion** and **leopard**. Hlane has a large population of easy-to-spot elephants and rhino in the northern area of the park, which you can also visit in your own vehicle, and rhino-sighting is virtually guaranteed. Other animals in this section include giraffe, zebra and waterbuck.

Various **southern enclosures** contain lion and leopard, along with some more elephant and rhino. Although the enclosures guarantee lion sightings, the animals are well habituated to vehicles and look completely uninterested. Hlane is also home to the largest population of tree-nesting vultures in Africa, including the white-backed vulture and the endangered Cape vulture.

ARRIVAL AND INFORMATION
HLANE ROYAL NATIONAL PARK

By car The entrance to Hlane is roughly 7km south of Simunye, off the Manzini–Lomahasha Rd.

By Kombi Kombis running between Manzini and Simunye stop 300m from the park gate.

Guided tours Birding or game tours on foot (E225 for 2hr 30min) are available any time during the day from the reception at Main Camp. You can join a guided tour in one of the park's Land Rovers (E350 for 2hr 30min), with sunrise (5.30am) and sunset (4.30pm) tours also available (E370 for 2hr 30min). The more adventurous can head out for a sunrise cycle (E280 for 2hr) or an overnight hike, fully catered and staying over at a basic bush camp (E1445). Bookings at Main Camp reception.

ACCOMMODATION

Bhubesi Camp 14km from Main Camp along a dirt track ☎ 23838868, ⓦ biggameparks.org. These four-person self-catering stone cottages overlook a dry river and feel much more remote than the main campsite, though they do have electricity. **E1000**

Ndlovu Main Camp ☎ 23838868, ⓦ biggameparks.org. Situated near the gate, with large self-catering thatched cottages that sleep up to eight people and en-suite rondavels sleeping two. There's no electricity (paraffin lamps and gas cooker are provided), but the basic but adequate accommodation provides a relaxed setting, allowing you to focus on the wildlife. **E990**

Ndlovu Camping Area Main Camp ☎ 23838868, ⓦ biggameparks.org. Open camping ground with plenty of soft grass and trees using a communal kitchen and ablution block (with hot water) and plenty of firewood available in the braai area. **E125**

EATING

Ndlovu Restaurant Main Camp. A large thatched restaurant and lounge area, with a wide deck overlooking a nearby watering hole that attracts rhino, elephant and giraffe. There's a reliable à la carte menu offering the usual gamut of chicken and steak (E110), as well as a buffet at dinner time (E190). Unless there's a large group staying, the wide deck is fairly relaxed, with plenty of trees and shady spots to sit. Daily 7am–8pm.

12

The northwest

The highveld of the **northwest** is unquestionably the most beautiful region of Swaziland, with rolling hills perfect for hiking, countless sparkling streams, a sprinkling of waterfalls and some wonderful accommodation.

Most visitors to the northwest are en route to or from Kruger National Park (see p.538), but beautiful **Phophonyane Nature Reserve** is only 64km north of Mbabane and well worth a visit, too. The most spectacular – and rugged – entrance into the country is via the Bulembu road from Barberton in Mpumalanga where you can follow the fascinating Makhonjwa Geotrail, a series of eleven detailed panels at stops along the route that illustrate the three-billion-year geological history of the area, and with it, how the world was formed. Four-hour guided tours are available with geologist Dave Mourant (E100 ⓦ wildfrontier.co.za).

Phophonyane Nature Reserve

40km south of the Matsamo border • Daily 8am–4.30pm • E30 • ☎ 24313429, ⓦ phophonyane.co.sz

The enchanting, private **Phophonyane Nature Reserve** is situated five slow kilometres away from the MR1, making it best reached with your own transport (public transport drops off on the main road, from where it's a hike to get here). The five-square-kilometre reserve's carefully laid-out **trails** ensure a good couple of day's exploring, and take in the Phophonyane Waterfall on its northwestern side and several well-located viewpoints with impressive vistas over the valley below. The vegetation is subtropical and attracts hundreds of colourful **bird species**, while animals include mongoose, bushbaby, otter and numerous varieties of snake, though all are hard to spot. The **lodge** in the reserve is easily the most beautiful place to stay in Swaziland (see below); if outside your budget, it's still worth stopping here for a short hike and a meal in the thatched restaurant.

ACCOMMODATION	PHOPHONYANE NATURE RESERVE

★**Phophonyane Nature Reserve** ☎24313429, ⓦphophonyane.co.sz. The five secluded two-person safari tents, set on the ancient rock right next to the Phophonyane River, are the most atmospheric option here, with bathrooms in separate huts a few steps up the slope. There are also family cottages sleeping up to five, and two gorgeous interpretations of traditional Swazi beehive huts. The reserve has two pools; one with salt water next to the restaurant, while the other blends into the rocks beside the river and looks out onto the mountains. Tents E1400, Doubles E2050

Nsangwini rock art

Komati Valley • E30 • From the Mbabane–Matsamo Rd follow the Muguga Dam Loop Rd eastwards, following signs down a dirt road turn off to the east; the hike begins after 7km

A thirty-minute hike down a mountainside trail in the Komati Valley will lead you to a wide expanse of rock art, found in a rock shelter dramatically perched over the Komati River Valley, with breathtaking views of the mountain. The rock art is estimated to be around 4000 years old, and is absolutely mind-boggling; you'll find that the longer you look at the rocks, the more you see, including human figures in a trance-like dance holding spears, and the sacred preying mantis. To visit the site you need to hire a guide from the Nsangwini community, who are well informed. You can find one waiting in a shelter at the start at the hiking trail, or you can book a guided walk though *Maguga Lodge* (E180, see below). The road to the start of the hike has some rather bad patches; a high-clearance vehicle is recommended.

Maguga Dam

On the Maguga Dam Loop Rd, eastwards off the Mbabane–Matsamo Rd • Information Centre daily 8am–5pm • Free • ☎ 24371056

The hydroelectric **Maguga Dam** sits snugly in a lowveld dip surrounded on all four sides by the often mist-covered mountains. The dam, primarily constructed to provide water for the vast sugar-cane plantations downstream, was completed in 2002 and filled in 2006. You can ponder the vastness of the construction at the on-site café, while the **information centre**, on a ledge overlooking the dam, shows a short video about the dam's history.

Many people come to Maguga Dam to fish for bass, but the area also makes for some good hiking. The surrounding countryside is spectacular, and there are trails leading to "the Gap" on the Nkomati River, a point at which the river flows through naturally occurring holes and fantastic formations in the rock. Contact *Maguga Lodge* (see below) to arrange a local guide.

ACCOMMODATON	MAGUGA DAM

Maguga Lodge Next to the Maguga Dam on the Maguga Dam loop road ☎24373975, ⓦmagugalodge .com. A scenic location with 33 comfortable, if dated, en-suite rondavels overlooking the dam. The best choice is the fully equipped campsite right near the water's edge. There are relaxing boat trips on the dam (E170/person) to see the area's rich birdlife, as well as various hikes, visits to a local homestead and fishing expeditions. The pool and the restaurant both offer an impressive view, especially at sunset. Camping E170, rondavels E1240

Malolotja Nature Reserve

Daily 6am–6pm • E30 • ☎ 24443241, ⓦsntc.org.sz

Swaziland's least touristy park, the easy-going **Malolotja Nature Reserve** offers awesome scenery and some of the finest hiking in Southern Africa. This is a place to come for rugged, wild nature and tranquillity, rather than for game spotting. The mountains here, among the oldest in the world (3.6 billion years old), are covered in grassland and graced by myriad streams and waterfalls, including the 95m-high **Malolotja Falls**.

UP IN THE TREES

An alternative way of experiencing the reserve is through **Canopy Tours** (☏ 76606755, ⓦ malolotjacanopytour.com; E650 for two and a half hours), which involves gliding on wires between elevated forest platforms while securely kitted out with lots of tackle. You can't really see much wildlife while whooshing along, but there's a good adrenaline kick when stepping off the first platform. Tours include a light lunch. Booking is essential; tours start from the reserve's reception building. The first begins at 8.30am and the last at 2pm.

Nearly three hundred species of **birds** are found in Malolotja, with an impressive colony of the rare bald ibis just by the waterfalls. You'll have to look harder for **game**, although wildebeest, blesbok and zebra are often visible, and there are leopards lurking somewhere in the gaping tracts of mountain and valley. Malolotja's small network of roads passes some fine viewpoints and picnic sites, but to really savour this park's rugged wilderness and see its waterfalls you'll need to hike. **Trails** range from easy half-day excursions to epic seven-day marathons, with basic campsites available en route (see below). **Forbes Reef Gold Mine**, a few kilometres south of the reserve's main entrance on the main tarred road, can be visited alone, but take care on the slippery banks; you can find it using the map you get on arrival at the main entrance.

ARRIVAL AND INFORMATION

MALOLOTJA NATURE RESERVE

By Kombi Minibus Kombis between Mbabane and Piggs Peak stop at the main gate, which is clearly signposted on the Mbabane–Matsamo Rd.

Information and supplies Brochures and maps are available from the reserve's reception building, 500m from the main entrance gate. The reception also houses a nice

restaurant (daily 8am–4pm; ☏ 76606755), and there's a curio shop that sells basic provisions, but it's wiser to stock up in Piggs Peak or Mbabane.

Climate If you're on a long hike during the summer, be prepared for hot days; however, temperatures drop dramatically in winter, when the nights can be freezing.

ACCOMMODATION

Campsites ☏ 76606755, ⓦ sntc.org.sz. For those attempting longer hikes, there are 21 scenic overnight camps scattered around the reserve, all with natural water sources but few other facilities (except braai areas), so you'll need to bring all your own equipment. Camps 11 and 12 are near Malolotja Falls. Book in advance. **E70**

Main Restcamp ☏ 76606755, ⓦ sntc.org.sz. Fifteen tent sites with hot water in a communal ablutions block, and braai areas, as well as thirteen comfortable log cabins, each sleeping up to five people and kitted out with their own fireplaces. The cabins are a short walk from the main reception so you can eat at the restaurant there if you don't fancy cooking. Book in advance and ask for a cabin in the front row for uninterrupted views. Camping **E100**, cabins **E600**

Sobantu Guest Farm and Backpackers ☏ 86053954, ⓦ sobantu-swaziland.net. Tucked away on a rural hillside, but with easy access to both Malolotja and Magugua dam, this low-key backpackers consists of four rondavels scattered on a grassy slope, with rocky hills leaning just behind, while the main house has several very basic double rooms and dorms. The small kitchen and comfortable lounge with a large satellite TV are decorated with a nice creative touch, and the bar area, with pool table and central fireplace, is a treat. Service can be very laidback, but the honest, friendly ambience, and stunning location will make it a winner for the open-minded. Excursions are offered throughout the area. Tents **E80**, dorms **E120**, doubles **E300**, rondavels **E400**

Ngwenya glass factory

On the MR3, west of Motshane • Daily 8am–4pm • ☏ 24424053, ⓦ ngwenyaglass.co.sz

Barely 5km along the MR3 from the Ngwenya/Oshoek border, follow the signs to where one of Swaziland's best-known exports, **Ngwenya glass**, is made. The products, which range from attractive wine glasses to endless trinkets in the shape of rotund animals, are made from recycled glass and produced by highly skilled workers; it's well worth stopping here just to see them blowing and crafting the glass from the viewing balcony above the roaring furnaces. The adjoining gift shop and **café** are usually swamped by coach-loads of tourists.

QUEUING TO VOTE IN THE FIRST POST-APARTHEID ELECTION, 199

Contexts

History

Recent fossil finds show that *Homo sapiens* existed along Africa's southern coast over fifty thousand years ago. The descendants of these nomadic Stone-Age people – ochre-skinned San hunter-gatherers and Khoikhoi herders (see below) – still inhabited the Western Cape when Europeans arrived in the fifteenth century. By the time of the Dutch settlement at the Cape in the mid-seventeenth century, much of the eastern half of the country was occupied by people who had begun crossing the Limpopo around the time of Christ's birth.

The stage was now set for the complex drama of South Africa's modern history, which in crude terms was a battle for the control of scarce resources between the various indigenous people, African states and the European colonizers. The twentieth century alone saw the endurance of colonialism, the unification of South Africa and the attempts by the white minority to keep at bay the black population's demands for civil rights, culminating in the implementation of South Africa's most notorious social invention – **apartheid**. Ultimately, multiracialism has been victorious and, despite numerous problems, South Africa's lively elections are proof that democracy is still alive.

The first South Africans

Rock art provides evidence of human culture in the subcontinent dating back nearly 30,000 years and represents Southern Africa's oldest and most enduring artistic tradition. The artists were hunter-gatherers, sometimes called Bushmen, but more commonly **San**. The most direct descendants of the late Stone Age, San people have survived in tiny pockets, mostly in Namibia and Botswana, making theirs the longest-spanning culture in the subcontinent. At one time they probably spread throughout sub-Saharan Africa, having pretty well perfected their **nomadic lifestyle**, which involved an enviable twenty-hour working week spent by the men hunting and the women gathering. This left considerable time for artistic and religious pursuits. People lived in small, loosely connected bands comprising family units and were free to leave and join up with other groups. The concept of private property had little meaning because everything required for survival could be obtained from the environment.

About two thousand years ago, this changed when some groups in present-day northern Botswana laid their hands on fat-tailed sheep and cattle from Northern Africa, thus transforming themselves into herding communities. The introduction of livestock revolutionized social organization, creating the idea of ownership and accumulation. Social divisions developed, and political units became larger and centred around a chief, who had important powers, such as the allocation of pasturage.

These were the first South Africans encountered by Portuguese mariners, who landed along the Cape coast in the fifteenth century. Known as **Khoikhoi** (meaning "men of men"), they were not ethnically distinct from the San, as many anthropologists once believed, but simply represented a distinct social organization. According to current thinking, it was possible for Khoi who lost their livestock to revert to being San, and for San to lay their hands on animals to become Khoi, giving rise to the collective term "Khoisan".

30,000 BC	500 BC	500 AD	1488
Hunter-gatherers occupy Cape Peninsula	Khoikhoi sheep herders drift southwards into South Africa, eventually reaching southern coast	Tall Bantu-speaking farmers cross Limpopo River and begin dispersing down South Africa's east coast	Bartholomeu Dias becomes first European to set foot on South African soil at Mossel Bay

Farms and crafts

Around two thousand years ago, tall, dark-skinned people who practised mixed farming – raising both crops and livestock – crossed the Limpopo River into what is today South Africa. These **Bantu-speaking** farmers were the ancestors of South Africa's majority African population, who gradually drifted south to occupy the entire eastern half of the subcontinent as far as the Eastern Cape, where they first encountered Europeans in the sixteenth century.

Apart from having highly developed farming know-how and a far more sedentary life than the Khoisan, the early Bantu speakers were skilled craft workers and knew about mining and smelting metals, including gold, copper and iron, which became an important factor in the extensive network of trade that developed.

The Cape goes Dutch

In the late fifteenth century, Portuguese mariners led by **Bartholomeu Dias** first rounded the Cape of Good Hope, but it was another 170 years before any European settlement was established here. In 1652, *De Goede Hoop* and two other vessels of the **Dutch East India Company**, trading between the Netherlands and the East Indies, pulled into Table Bay to set up a refreshment station to resupply company ships.

Despite the view of station commander Jan van Riebeeck that the indigenous Khoi were savages "living without conscience", from the start, the Dutch were dependent on them to provide livestock, which were traded for trinkets. As the settlement developed, Van Riebeeck needed more labour to keep the show going. Much to his annoyance, the bosses back in Amsterdam had forbidden him from enslaving the locals, and refused his request for slaves from elsewhere in the company's empire.

This kicked off the process of colonization of the lands around the fort, when a number of Dutch men were released in 1657 from their contracts to farm as free burghers on land granted by the company. The idea was that they would sell their produce to the company at a fixed price, thereby overcoming the labour shortage. The move sparked the first of a series of Khoikhoi–Dutch wars. Although the first campaign ended in stalemate, the Khoikhoi were ultimately no match for the Dutch, who had the advantage of superior mobility and firepower in horses and guns.

Meanwhile, in 1658, Van Riebeeck established slavery at the Cape via the back door, when he purloined a shipload of slaves from West Africa. The Dutch East India Company itself became the biggest slaveholder at the Cape and continued importing slaves, mostly from the East Indies, at such a pace that by 1711 there were more slaves than burghers in the colony. With the help of this ready workforce, the embryonic Cape Colony expanded outwards, displacing the Peninsula Khoikhoi, who by 1713 had lost everything. Most of their livestock (nearly fifty thousand head) and most of their land west of the Hottentots Holland Mountains (90km southeast of present-day Cape Town) had been swallowed by the Dutch East India Company. Dispossession and diseases like smallpox, previously unknown in South Africa, decimated their numbers and shattered their social system. By the middle of the eighteenth century, those who remained had been reduced to a condition of miserable servitude to the colonists.

1652	1657	1658	1679
Dutch East India Company establishes supply station at Cape for trade ships sailing to Indies	Company releases indentured labourers to farm as free settlers	First slaves introduced at Cape and within fifty years slaves outnumber settlers	Castle of Good Hope completed

THE TREKBOERS

Like the Khoikhoi, impoverished white people living at the fringes of colonial society had limited options. Many just packed up their wagons and rolled out into the interior, where they lived by the gun, either hunting game or taking cattle from the Khoi by force. Beyond the control of the Dutch East India Company, these nomadic trekboers began to assume a pastoral niche previously occupied by the Khoi. By the turn of the nineteenth century, trekboers had penetrated well into the Eastern Cape, pushing back the Khoi and San in the process.

As their lives became disrupted and living by **traditional** means became impossible, the Khoisan began to prey on the cattle and sheep of the trekboers. The trekboers responded by hunting down the San as vermin, killing the men and often taking women and children as slaves. After the British occupation of the Cape in 1795, the trekboer migration from the Cape accelerated.

Rise of the Zulus

While in the west of the country trekboers were migrating from the Cape Colony, in the east equally significant movements were under way. Throughout the seventeenth and eighteenth centuries, descendants of the first Bantu-speakers to penetrate into South Africa had been swelling their numbers and had expanded right across the eastern half of the country.

Nowhere was this more marked than in **KwaZulu-Natal**, where, prompted by pressures on grazing land, chiefdoms survived by subduing and absorbing their neighbours. By the early nineteenth century, two chiefdoms, the Ndwandwe and the Mthethwa, dominated eastern South Africa around the Tugela River. During the late 1810s a major confrontation between them ended in the defeat of the Mthethwa. Out of their ruins emerged the **Zulus**, who were to become one of the most powerful polities in Southern Africa. Around 1816, **Shaka** assumed the chieftaincy of the Zulus, whose fighting tactics he quickly transformed.

By 1820, the Zulus had become the dominant regional power and by the middle of the century had established a centralized military state with a forty-thousand-strong standing army. One of the strengths of the system lay in its ability to absorb the survivors of conflict, who became members of the expanding Zulu state. Throughout the 1820s, Shaka sent his armies to invade neighbouring territory. But in 1828 he was stabbed to death by two of his half-brothers, one of whom, Dingane, succeeded him. Dingane continued with his brother's ruthless but devastatingly successful policies and tactics.

The rise of the Zulu state reverberated across Southern Africa and led to the creation of a series of **centralized Nguni states** as well as paving the way for **Boer** expansion into the interior. In a movement of forced migrations known as the **mfecane**, or difaqane, huge areas of the country were laid waste and people across eastern South Africa were driven off their lands. They attempted to survive either in small groups or by banding together to form larger political organizations.

To the north of the Zulu kingdom another Nguni group with strong cultural and linguistic affinities with the Zulus came together under **Sobhuza I** and his son Mswati II, after whom their new state **Swaziland** took its name. In North West Province, a few hundred Zulus under **Mzilikazi** were displaced by Shaka and relocated to Matabeleland, now southwestern Zimbabwe, where they re-established themselves as the **Matabele**

1713	1795	1816–1828
Khoikhoi dispossessed of livestock by settlers and reduced to servitude	Company goes bust and English becomes official language when British take over	Shaka assumes chieftainship of Zulus and forges militarized regional power in southeast

kingdom. In the Drakensberg, on the west flank of KwaZulu-Natal, **Moshoeshoe I** used diplomacy and cunning to establish the territory that became the modern state of **Lesotho**.

The Great Trek

Back in the Cape, many Afrikaners were becoming fed up with British rule. Their principal grievance was the way in which the colonial authorities were tampering with labour relations and destroying what they saw as a divine distinction between blacks and whites. In 1828 a proclamation gave Khoi residents and free blacks equality with whites before the law. The **abolition of slavery** in 1834 was the last straw.

Fifteen thousand Afrikaners (one out of ten living in the colony) left the Cape to escape the meddlesome British. When they arrived in the eastern half of the country, they were delighted to find vast tracts of apparently unoccupied land. In fact, they were merely stumbling into the eye of the **mfecane** storm – areas that had been temporarily cleared either by war parties or by fearful refugees hiding out to escape detection. As they fanned out further they encountered the Nguni states and a series of battles followed. By the middle of the nineteenth century, descendants of the Dutch had consolidated control and established the two Boer states of the **South African Republic**, aka the Transvaal (now Gauteng, Mpumalanga, North West Province and Limpopo) and the **Orange Free State** (now Free State). Britain recognized the independence of both of these states in the 1850s.

The Anglo-Boer War

Despite the benefits it brought, the discovery of gold (see box below) was also one of the principal causes of the **Anglo-Boer War** (more often referred to locally as the South African War, in recognition of the fact that South Africans of all colours took part). Gold-mining had shifted the economic centre of South Africa from the British-controlled Cape to the South African Republic, while at the same time Britain's European rival, Germany, was beginning to make political and economic inroads in the Boer republics. Britain feared losing its strategic Cape naval base, but perhaps even more important were questions of international finance and the substantial British investment in the mines. London was at the heart of world trade and was eager to see a flourishing gold-mining industry in South Africa, but the Boers seemed rather sluggish about modernizing their infrastructure to assist the exploitation of the mines.

GOLD AND DIAMONDS

In the 1850s Britain wasn't too concerned about the interior of South Africa. Its strategic position aside, South Africa was a chaotic backwater at the butt-end of the empire. Things changed in the 1860s, with the discovery of **diamonds** (the world's largest deposit) around modern-day Kimberley, and even more significantly in the 1880s, with the discovery of **gold** on the Witwatersrand (now Gauteng). Together, these finds were the catalyst that transformed South Africa from a down-at-heel rural society into an urbanized industrial one. In the process great fortunes were made by capitalists like Cecil Rhodes, traditional African society was crushed and the independence of the Boer republics ended.

1820s	1820s	1834
As defence against Shaka, Nguni states form in Swaziland, Lesotho and Matabeleland	British settlers arrive at Port Elizabeth as bulwark against Xhosa on eastern frontier	Abolition of slavery leads many Boers to leave Cape and establish two republics

In any case, a number of Britons had for some time seen the unification of South Africa as the key to securing British interests in the subcontinent. To this end, under a wafer-thin pretext, Britain had declared war and subdued the last of the independent African kingdoms by means of the **Zulu War of 1879**. This secured KwaZulu-Natal, bringing all the coastal territories of South Africa under British control. To control the entire subcontinent south of the Limpopo, Britain needed to bring the two Boer republics under the Union flag.

During the closing years of the nineteenth century, Britain demanded that the South African Republic grant voting rights to British miners living there – a demand that, if met, would have meant the end of Boer political control over their own state, since they were outnumbered by the foreigners. The Boers turned down the request and war broke out in October 1899. The British command believed they were looking at a walkover: in the words of **Lord Kitchener**, a "teatime war" that would get the troops home by Christmas.

In fact, the campaign turned into Britain's most expensive since the Napoleonic Wars. During the early stages, the Boers took the imperial power by surprise and penetrated into British-controlled KwaZulu-Natal and the Northern Cape, inflicting a series of humiliating defeats. By June, a reinforced British army was pushing the Boers back, but the Boers fought on for another two years. Lord Kitchener responded with a **scorched-earth policy** that left the countryside a wasteland and thousands of women and children homeless. To house them, the British invented the **concentration camps**, in which 26,370 Boer women and children died. For some Afrikaners, this episode remains a source of bitterness against the British even today. Less widely publicized were the **African concentration camps** which took 14,000 lives. By 1902, the Boers were demoralized, and in May the Afrikaner republics surrendered their independence in exchange for British promises of reconstruction. By the end of the so-called teatime war, Britain had committed nearly half a million men to the field and lost 22,000 of them. Of the 88,000 Boers who fought, 7000 died in combat. With the two Boer republics and the two British colonies under imperial control, the way was clear for the federation of the **Union of South Africa** in 1910.

Migrant labour and the Bambatha Rebellion

Between the conclusion of the Anglo-Boer War and the unification of South Africa, the mines suffered a **shortage of unskilled labour**. Most Africans still lived by agriculture: to counter this, the government took measures to compel them to supply their labour to the mines. One method was the imposition of **taxes** that had to be paid in coin, thus forcing Africans from subsistence farming and into the cash economy. Responding to one such tax, in 1906 a group of Zulus refused to pay. The authorities declared martial law and dealt mercilessly with the protesters, burning their homes and seizing their possessions. This provoked a full-blown rebellion led by Chief Bambatha, which was ruthlessly put down, at a cost of four thousand rebel lives. Armed resistance by Africans was thus ended for over half a century. After the defeat of the **Bambatha Rebellion**, the number of African men from Zululand working in the Gauteng mines shot up by sixty percent. By 1909, eighty

1843	1860s	1879
British annex Natal, settlers arrive and indentured Indian labourers brought to work cane fields	Discovery of world's biggest diamond deposit at Kimberley	Britain declares war on Zulus, suffers humiliating defeat at Isandlwana, but eventually wins

percent of adult males in the territory were away from home, working as migrant labourers. **Migrant labour**, with its shattering effects on family life, became one of the foundations of South Africa's economic and social system, and a basic cornerstone of apartheid.

Kick-starting Afrikanerdom

In a parallel development, large numbers of **Afrikaners** were forced to leave rural areas in the early part of the twentieth century. This was partly a result of the war, but also of overcrowding, drought and pestilence. Many Afrikaners joined the ranks of a swelling poor **white working class** whose members often felt despised by the English-speaking capitalists who commanded the economy, and threatened by lower-paid Africans competing for their jobs.

In 1918 a group of Afrikaners formed the **Broederbond** ("the brotherhood"), a secret society to promote the interest of Afrikaners. It aimed to uplift impoverished members of the **volk** ("people") and to develop a sense of pride in their language, religion and culture (see box below). The Broederbond would come to dominate every aspect of the way the country was run for half a century.

During the early twentieth century, a number of young Afrikaner intellectuals travelled to Europe, where they were inspired by fascism. It was around this time that Afrikaner intellectuals began using the term **apartheid** (pronounced "apart-hate"). Among those kicking their heels in Germany in the 1920s and 30s were **Nico Diederichs**, who became a minister of finance under the Afrikaner Nationalist Party; **Hendrik Frensch Verwoerd**, apartheid's leading theorist and prime minister from 1958 to 1966; and **Piet Meyer**, controller of the state broadcasting service, who named his son Izan ("Nazi" spelled backwards – he later claimed this was sheer coincidence).

NEW WORD ORDER

In the late nineteenth century, white Afrikaans-speakers, fighting for an identity, sought to create a "racially pure" culture by driving a wedge between themselves and coloured Afrikaans-speakers. They reinvented **Afrikaans** as a "white man's language", eradicating the supposed stigma of its coloured ties by substituting Dutch words for those with Asian or African roots. In 1925, the dialect of Afrikaans spoken by upper-crust white people became an official language alongside English, and the dialects spoken by coloured people were treated as inferior deviations from correct usage.

For Afrikaner nationalists this wasn't enough, and after the introduction of apartheid in 1948, they attempted to codify perceived racial differences. Under the **Population Registration Act**, all South Africans were classified as white, coloured or African. These classifications became fundamental to what kind of life you could expect. There are numerous cases of families in which one sibling was classified coloured with limited rights and another white with the right to live in comfortable white areas, enjoy superior job opportunities, and be able to send their children to better schools and universities.

With the demise of apartheid, the make-up of residential areas is slowly (very slowly) shifting – and so is the thinking on ethnic terminology. Some people now reject the term "coloured" because of its apartheid associations, and refuse any racial definitions; others proudly embrace the term as a means of acknowledging their distinct culture, with its slave, East Indies and Khoikhoi roots.

1886	1899–1901	1910	1912
Discovery of gold around Johannesburg	Britain defeats Afrikaners in Anglo-Boer War to gain total hegemony over South Africa	Boer republics and British colonies merge into Union of South Africa	ANC forms to fight for universal suffrage

In 1939, the Broederbond introduced a scheme that, in the space of a decade, launched ten thousand Afrikaner businesses, some of which are still among the leading players in South Africa's economy.

Africans' claims

Despite having relied on African cooperation for their victory in the South African War and having hinted at enhanced rights for black people after the war, the British excluded them from the cosy federal deal between themselves and the Afrikaners. It wasn't long, in fact, before the white Union government began eroding African rights. In response, a group of middle-class mission-educated Africans formed the **South African Native National Congress** (later to become the ANC) in 1912 to campaign for universal suffrage. In 1914, the leaders went to London to protest against the 1913 **Natives' Land Act**, which confined the black majority to less than ten percent of the land. The trip failed and the Land Act became the foundation for apartheid some 35 years later.

Through the early half of the twentieth century, the ANC remained conservative, unwilling to engage in active protest. In response, a number of alternative mass organizations arose, among them the **Industrial and Commercial Union**, an African trade union founded in 1919, which at its peak in 1928 had gathered an impressive 150,000 members. But in the 1930s it ran out of steam. The first political movement in the country not organized along ethnic lines was the South African Communist Party, founded in 1921 with a multiracial executive. While it never gained widespread membership itself, it became an important force inside the ANC.

Throughout the 1930s, the ANC plodded on with speeches, petitions and pleas, which proved completely fruitless.

Young Turks and striking miners

In 1944, a hotheaded young student named **Nelson Mandela** with friends **Oliver Tambo**, **Walter Sisulu** and **Anton Lembede** formed the **ANC Youth League**. The League's founding manifesto criticized the ANC leadership for being "gentlemen with clean hands". The 1945 annual conference of the ANC adopted a document called "**Africans' Claims in South Africa**", which reflected an emerging politicization. The document demanded **universal franchise** and an end to the **colour bar**, which reserved most skilled jobs for white people.

In 1946 the African Mineworkers' Union launched one of the biggest strikes in the country's history in protest against falling living standards. Virtually the entire Gauteng gold-mining region came to a standstill as one hundred thousand workers downed tools. Prime Minister Jan Smuts sent in police who forced the workers back down the shafts at gunpoint.

The following year Nelson Mandela took his first step into public life when he was elected general secretary of the ANC.

Winds of change

For years, the white government had been hinting at easing up on segregation, and even Smuts himself, no soft liberal, had reckoned that it would have to end at some point. The relentless influx of Africans into the urban areas was breaking the stereotype of them as rural tribespeople. The government appointed the **Fagan Commission** to

1913	1918	1920s	1930s
Land Act gives white South Africans (20 percent of population) 92 percent of the land	Afrikaner secret society, Broederbond, forms and Nelson Mandela born	Agatha Christie surfs at Muizenberg, Cape Town	Orlando township, the nucleus of Soweto, begins evolving

look into the question of the **pass laws**, which controlled the movement of Africans and sought to keep them out of the white cities unless they had a job.

When the Fagan Commission reported its findings in 1948, it concluded that "the trend to urbanization is irreversible and the pass laws should be eased". While some blacks may have felt heartened by this whiff of reform, this was the last thing many whites wanted to hear. Afrikaner farmers were alarmed by the idea of a labour shortage caused by Africans leaving the rural areas for better prospects in the cities, while white workers feared the prospect of losing jobs to lower-paid African workers.

The National Party comes to power

Against this background of black aspiration and white fears, the Smuts government called a **general election**. The opposition **National Party**, which promoted Afrikaner nationalism, campaigned on a *swart gevaar* or "black peril" ticket, playing on white insecurity and fear. With an eye on the vote of Afrikaner workers and farmers, they promised to reverse the tide of Africans into the cities and to send them all back to the reserves. For white business they made the conflicting promise to bring black workers into the cities as a cheap and plentiful supply of labour.

On Friday May 28, 1948, South Africa awoke to a National Party victory at the polls. Party leader **D.F. Malan** told a group of ecstatic supporters: "For the first time, South Africa is our own. May God grant that it always remains our own. It is to us that millions of semi-barbarous blacks look for guidance, justice and the Christian way of life."

Meanwhile, the **ANC** was driven by its own power struggle. Fed up with the ineffectiveness of the old guard, the Youth League staged a coup, voted in its own leadership with Nelson Mandela on the executive and adopted the League's radical Programme of Action, with an arsenal of tactics that Mandela explained would include "the new weapons of boycott, strike, civil disobedience and non-cooperation".

The 1950s: peaceful protest

During the 1950s, the National Party began putting in place a barrage of laws that would eventually constitute the structure of apartheid. Some early onslaughts on black civil rights included the **Bantu Authorities Act**, which set up puppet authorities to govern Africans in the reserves; the **Population Registration Act**, which classified every South African at birth as "white, native or coloured" (see box, p.642); the **Group Areas Act**, which divided South Africa into ethnically distinct areas; and the **Suppression of Communism Act**, which made any anti-apartheid opposition (Communist or not) a criminal offence.

The ANC responded in 1952 with the **Defiance Campaign**, aimed at achieving full civil rights for blacks. During the campaign, eight thousand volunteers deliberately broke the apartheid laws and were jailed. The campaign rolled on through 1952 until the police provoked violence in November by firing on a prayer meeting in East London. A riot followed in which two white people were killed, thus appearing to discredit claims that the campaign was non-violent. The government used this pretext to swoop on the homes of the ANC leadership, resulting in the detention and then **banning** of over one hundred ANC organizers. Bannings restricted a person's movement and political activities: a banned person was prohibited from seeing more

1939	1948	1949	1952
World War splits Afrikaners, with future prime minister John Vorster among those supporting Germany	National Party wins election and goes full throttle on segregation	Government bans inter-racial marriage and sex, followed by slew of other discriminatory laws	Mandela leads Defiance Campaign against apartheid legislation

THE FREEDOM CHARTER

- The people shall govern.
- All national groups shall have equal rights.
- The people shall share the nation's wealth.
- The land shall be shared by those who work it.
- All shall be equal before the law.
- All shall enjoy equal human rights.
- There shall be work and security for all.
- The doors of learning and culture shall be opened.
- There shall be houses, security and comfort.
- There shall be peace and friendship.

than one person at a time or talking to any other banned person; prohibited from entering certain buildings; kept under surveillance; required to report regularly to the police; and could not be quoted or published.

The most far-reaching event of the decade was the **Congress of the People**, held near Johannesburg in 1955. At a mass meeting of three thousand delegates, four organizations, representing Africans, coloureds, whites and Indians, formed a strategic partnership called the Congress Alliance. ANC leader **Chief Albert Luthuli** explained that "for the first time in the history of our multiracial nation its people will meet as equals, irrespective of race, colour and creed, to formulate a freedom charter for all the people of our country". Adopted at the Congress of the People, the Freedom Charter (see box above) became the principal document defining ANC policy.

The government rounded up 156 opposition leaders and charged them with treason. Evidence at the Treason Trial was based on the Freedom Charter, described as a "blueprint for violent Communist revolution". Although all the defendants were acquitted, the four-year trial disrupted the ANC and splits began to emerge. In 1958 a group of Africanists led by the charismatic **Robert Mangaliso Sobukwe** (see box, p.326) broke away from the ANC to form the **Pan Africanist Congress (PAC)**, arguing that cooperation with white activists was not in the interests of black liberation.

Sharpeville

On March 21, 1960, Sobukwe and thousands of followers presented themselves without passes to police stations across Gauteng and the Western Cape. At **Sharpeville** police station, south of Johannesburg, the police opened fire, killing 69 and injuring nearly 200. Most were shot in the back.

Demonstrations swept the country on March 27. The next day Africans staged a total stay-away from work and thousands joined a public pass-burning demonstration. The day after that, the government declared a **state of emergency**, rounded up 22,000 people and banned the ANC and PAC. White South Africa panicked as the value of the rand slipped and shares slid. Some feared an imminent and bloody revolution.

Later that month, Prime Minister Hendrik Verwoerd was shot in the head by a half-crazed white farmer. Many hoped that, if he died, apartheid would be ditched. But Dr Verwoerd survived, his appetite for apartheid stronger than ever. More than anyone,

1955	1958	1960
Mass non-racial meeting drafts the Freedom Charter, which becomes policy of ANC	New prime minister Verwoerd creates ten ethnic "homelands", the cornerstone of Grand Apartheid	Sixty-nine Africans shot dead at anti-pass law protest; government bans anti-apartheid opposition

Verwoerd made apartheid his own and formulated the system of **Bantustans** – notionally independent statelets in which Africans were to exercise their political rights away from the white areas. The aim was to dismantle the black majority into several separate "tribal" minorities, none of which on its own could outnumber whites.

In 1961 Nelson Mandela called for a national convention "to determine a non-racial democratic constitution". Instead, Verwoerd appointed one-time neo-Nazi John Vorster as justice minister. A trained lawyer, Vorster eagerly set about passing repressive legislation that circumvented the rule of law.

Nelson Mandela saw the writing on the wall. "The time comes in the life of any nation when there remain only two choices: submit or fight. That time has now come to South Africa. We shall not submit," he told the BBC, before going underground as commander in chief of **Umkhonto we Sizwe** (Spear of the Nation, aka MK), the newly formed armed wing of the ANC. The organization was dedicated to economic and symbolic acts of sabotage and was under strict orders not to kill or injure people. In August 1962 Mandela was captured, tried and with nine other ANC leaders he was handed a **life sentence**.

Apartheid: everything going white

With the leadership of the liberation movement behind bars, the 1960s was the decade in which everything seemed to be going the white government's way. Resistance was stifled, the state grew more powerful, and for white South Africans, businessmen and foreign investors life seemed perfect. For black South Africans, poverty deepened – a state of affairs enforced by apartheid legislation and repressive measures that included bannings, detentions without trial, house arrests and murders of political prisoners.

The ANC was impotent, and resistance by its armed wing MK was virtually nonexistent. But as South Africa swung into the 1970s, the uneasy peace began to fray, prompted at first by deteriorating black living standards, which reawakened industrial action. Trade unions came to fill the vacuum left by the ANC.

The **Soweto uprising** of June 16, 1976, signalled the transfer of protest from the workplace to the townships, as black youths took to the streets in protest against the imposition of Afrikaans as a medium of instruction in their schools. The protest spread across the country and by the following February, 575 people (nearly a quarter of them children) had been killed in the rolling series of revolts that followed.

The government relied increasingly on armed police to impose order. Even this was unable to stop the mushrooming of new liberation organizations, many of them part of the broadly based **Black Consciousness Movement**. As the unrest rumbled on into 1977, the government responded by banning all the new black organizations and detaining their leadership. In September 1977, **Steve Biko** (one of the detained) became the 46th political prisoner to die in police custody.

The banned organizations were rapidly replaced by new movements and the government never again successfully put the lid on opposition. By the late 1970s business was complaining that apartheid wasn't working any more, and even the government was having its doubts. The growth of the black population was outstripping that of the white; from a peak of 21 percent of the population in 1910, white people now made up only 16 percent. This proportion was set to fall to 10 percent by the end of the century. The sums just didn't add up.

1961	**1962**	**1966–1970s**
South Africa leaves Commonwealth and becomes republic; ANC launches armed struggle	ANC leadership jailed for treason on Robben Island	3.5 million black Africans and coloured people forcibly removed from "white" areas

Total Strategy

It was becoming clear that the deployment of the police couldn't solve South Africa's problems, and in 1978 defence minister **Pieter Willem (P.W.) Botha** became prime minister in a palace coup. Botha adopted a two-handed strategy, of reform accompanied by unprecedented repression. He devised his so-called **Total Strategy**, which aimed to draw every facet of white society into the fight against the opponents of apartheid. This included military training programmes in white schools, propaganda campaigns, the extension of conscription, and political reforms aimed at co-opting Indians and coloured people.

Despite this, the 1980s saw the growing use of sabotage against the apartheid state. Botha began contemplating reform and moved Nelson Mandela and other ANC leaders from **Robben Island** to Pollsmoor Prison in Tokai, Cape Town. But he also poured ever-increasing numbers of troops into African townships to stop unrest, while intimidating neighbouring countries. Between 1981 and 1983, the army launched operations into every one of the country's black-ruled neighbours, Angola, Mozambique, Botswana, Zimbabwe, Swaziland and Lesotho.

In 1983 Botha came up with another scheme to shore up apartheid: the so-called New Constitution in which coloured people and Indians would be granted the vote for their own racially segregated – and powerless – chambers. For Africans, apartheid was to continue as usual.

Around the same time, 15,000 **anti-apartheid** delegates met at Mitchell's Plain in Cape Town to form the **United Democratic Front** (UDF), a multiracial umbrella for 575 opposition organizations. The UDF became a proxy for the ANC as two years of strikes, protest and boycotts followed.

Towards the end of the decade, the world watched as apartheid troops and police were regularly shown on TV beating up and shooting unarmed Africans. The Commonwealth condemned the apartheid government, the United States and Australia severed air links and the US Congress passed legislation promoting disinvestment. An increasingly desperate Botha offered to release Mandela "if he renounces violence".

Mandela replied: "I am surprised by the conditions the government wants to impose. I am not a violent man. It was only when all other forms of resistance were no longer open to us that we turned to armed struggle. Let Botha … renounce violence."

As events unfolded, a subtle shift became palpable: Botha was the prisoner and Mandela held the keys. While black resistance wasn't abating, Botha was now also facing a white right-wing backlash. The ultra-right Conservative Party was winning electoral support and the neo-Nazi Afrikaner Weerstandsbeweging (Afrikaner Resistance Movement, aka AWB) was darkly muttering about civil war.

Crisis

In 1986, Botha declared yet another **state of emergency** accompanied by assassinations, mass arrests, detentions, treason trials and torture. Alarmed by the violence engulfing the country, a group of South African businessmen, mostly Afrikaners, flew to Senegal in 1987 to meet an ANC delegation headed by **Thabo Mbeki**. A joint statement pressed for unequivocal support for a negotiated settlement.

1970	1976	1978
Black Africans stripped of SA citizenship and assigned to impoverished ethnic "homelands"	Police shoot dead over 600 during countrywide protests, which start in Soweto schools	Hawkish former defence minister P.W. Botha becomes president

In 1988 Mandela was rushed to Tygerberg Hospital in Cape Town, suffering from tuberculosis. Although he was better by October, the government announced that he wouldn't be returning to Pollsmoor **Prison**. Instead he was moved to a prison warder's cottage at **Victor Verster** (now Drakenstein) Prison just outside Paarl. Outside the prison walls, Botha's policies had collapsed and the army top brass were telling him that there could be no decisive military victory over the anti-apartheid opposition – and that South Africa's undeclared war in Angola was bleeding the treasury dry.

At the beginning of 1989, Mandela wrote to Botha from Victor Verster calling for negotiations. The intransigent Botha found himself with little room to manoeuvre. When he suffered a stroke, his party colleagues moved swiftly to oust him and replaced him with **Frederik Willem (F.W.) De Klerk**.

De Klerk made it clear that he was opposed to majority rule. But he inherited a massive pile of problems that could no longer be ignored: the economy was in trouble and the cost of maintaining apartheid prohibitive; the illegal influx of Africans from the country to the city had become unstoppable; blacks hadn't been taken in by Botha's constitutional reforms, and even South Africa's friends were losing patience. In September 1989, US President George Bush (the elder) told De Klerk that if there wasn't progress on releasing Mandela within six months, he would extend US sanctions.

De Klerk gambled on his ability to outmanoeuvre the opposition. In February 1990, he announced the unbanning of the ANC, the PAC, the Communist Party and 33 other organizations, as well as the **release of Mandela**. On Sunday February 11, at around 4pm, Mandela stepped out of Victor Verster Prison and was driven to City Hall in Cape Town, from where he spoke publicly for the first time in three decades. That May, Mandela and De Klerk signed an agreement in which the government undertook to repeal repressive laws and release political prisoners, while the ANC agreed to suspend the armed struggle. As events moved towards full-blown negotiations it became clear that De Klerk still clung to race-based notions for a settlement: "Majority rule is not suitable for South Africa," he said, "because it will lead to the domination of minorities."

Negotiations

The **negotiating** process, from 1990 to 1994, was fragile, and at many points a descent into chaos looked likely. Obstacles included violence linked to a sinister element in the apartheid security forces who were working behind the scenes to destabilize the ANC; **threats of civil war** from heavily armed right-wingers; and a low-key war of attrition in KwaZulu-Natal between Zulu nationalists of the **Inkatha Freedom Party** (IFP) and ANC supporters, which had already claimed three thousand lives between 1987 and 1990.

In April 1993 it looked as if it would all fall apart with the **assassination** of Chris Hani, the most popular ANC leader after Mandela. Hani's slaying by a right-wing gunman touched deep fears among all South Africans. A descent into civil war loomed, and for three consecutive nights the nation watched as Mandela appeared on prime-time television appealing for calm. This marked the decisive turning point as it became obvious that only the ANC president could stave off chaos, while De Klerk kept his

1980s	**1983**	**1989**	**1989**
Botha floods townships with troops and sends army into neighbouring countries	Government cracks down further on opposition after formation of ANC-proxy, United Democratic Front	Botha rebuffs Mandela's appeal from prison for negotiations "to avert civil war"	Botha suffers stroke and is replaced by F.W. De Klerk, who unbans ANC

head down. Pushing his strategic advantage, Mandela called for the immediate setting of an election date. Shortly afterwards the date for elections was set for April 27, 1994.

The 1994 election

The election passed peacefully. At the age of 76, Nelson Mandela, along with millions of his fellow citizens, voted for the first time in his life in a national election. On May 2, De Klerk conceded defeat after an ANC landslide, in which they took 62.7 percent of the vote. Of the remaining significant parties, the National Party fared best with 20.4 percent, followed by the Inkatha Freedom Party with 10.5 percent. The ANC was dominant in all of the provinces apart from **Western Cape** and **KwaZulu-Natal**. One of the disappointments for the ANC was its inability to appeal broadly to non-Africans.

For the ANC, the real struggle was only beginning. It inherited a country of 38 million people. Of these it was estimated that six million were unemployed, nine million were destitute, ten million had no access to running water, and twenty million had no electricity. Among black adults, sixty percent were illiterate and fewer than fifty percent of black children under 14 went to school. Infant mortality ran at eighty deaths per thousand among Africans, compared with just seven among white children.

The Mandela era

Few people in recorded history have been the subject of such high expectations; still fewer have matched them; Mandela has exceeded them. We knew of his fortitude before he left jail; we have since experienced his extraordinary reserves of goodwill, his sense of fun and the depth of his maturity. As others' prisoner, he very nearly decided the date of his own release; as president, he has wisely chosen the moment of his going. Any other nation would consider itself privileged to have his equal as its leader. His last full year in power provides us with an occasion again to consider his achievement in bringing and holding our fractious land together.

Mail & Guardian, December 24, 1998

South Africa's first five years of democracy are inextricably linked to the towering figure of **Nelson Mandela**. On the one hand, he had to temper the impatience of a black majority that, having finally achieved civil rights, found it hard to understand why economic advancement wasn't following quickly. And on the other, he had to mollify many fearful white citizens. The achievements of the government, however, were more uneven than those of its leader.

The overriding theme of the Mandela presidency was that of **reconciliation**. Perhaps the highlight of this policy was in May and June 1995, when the rugby union World Cup was staged in South Africa. **The Springboks**, for many years international pariahs due to their whites-only membership, sporting Springbok colours – events won, watched by Mandela, portrayed in Clint Eastwood's 2009 film *Invictus* (based on a book by John Carlin).

The most significant sideshow of the period was the **Truth and Reconciliation Commission**, set up to examine gross human rights abuses in South Africa between 1960 and 1993 (see box, p.650).

The **New Constitution**, approved in May 1996, ensured that South Africa would remain a parliamentary democracy with an executive president. One of the most progressive constitutions in the world, it incorporated an extensive bill of rights.

1990	1994	1999	2007
Mandela walks to freedom	Mandela votes in election for first time and becomes president when ANC wins	Thabo Mbeki succeeds Mandela	Mbeki replaced as president by Jacob Zuma, at the time facing bribery and racketeering charges

THE TRUTH AND RECONCILIATION COMMISSION

As you type, you don't know you are crying until you feel and see the tears on your hands.

Chief typist of the transcripts of the TRC hearings
as told to Archbishop Tutu

By the time South Africa achieved **democracy** in 1994, it was internationally accepted that apartheid was, in the words of a UN resolution, "a crime against humanity", and that atrocities had been committed in its name. But no one could have imagined how systematic and horrific these atrocities had been. This emerged at the hearings of the **Truth and Reconciliation Commission** (TRC), set up to investigate gross abuses of human rights under apartheid. Under the chairmanship of Nobel Peace laureate, Archbishop Desmond Tutu, the commission examined acts committed between March 1960, the date of the Sharpeville massacre, and May 10, 1994, the day of Mandela's inauguration as president.

Evidence was heard from victims and perpetrators under a provision that amnesty would be given in exchange for "full disclosure of all the relevant facts". Unsurprisingly, the commission found that "the South African government was the primary perpetrator of gross human rights abuses in South Africa". It confirmed that from the 1970s to the 1990s the state had been involved in criminal activities including "extra-judicial killings of political opponents". Among the violations it listed were torture, abduction, sexual abuse, incursions across South Africa's borders to kill opponents in exile, and the deployment of hit squads. It also found that the ANC (and a number of other organizations, including the PAC and IFP) was guilty of human-rights violations.

There was considerable criticism of the TRC from all quarters. Many felt that justice would have been better served by a Nuremberg-style trial of those guilty of gross violations, but Tutu argued that this would have been impossible in South Africa, given that neither side had won a military victory.

Despite the victory of liberal democratic principles, South Africa still displayed a singular lack of the trappings associated with civil society. Crime, sensationalized daily in the media, continued to dog the country. In the closing stages of the ANC's first five years, the police were reporting an average of 52 murders a day, a rape every half hour (including a frightening rise in child rape), and one car theft every nine minutes.

Mr Delivery doesn't

In 1999 **Thabo Mbeki** succeeded Mandela as president of South Africa. A hopeful media dubbed Mbeki "Mr Delivery", believing that this clever, well-educated technocrat would confront poverty and build schools, hospitals and houses – and at the same time create badly needed jobs. Mbeki's business-friendly policies produced healthy **economic growth**, expanded the black middle class and created a small coterie of mega-rich black entrepreneurs. But it did little for the poor fifty percent of the population, and the gulf of inequality became wider than ever.

The poor also bore the brunt of Mbeki's misguided policies on **AIDS**. Holding the view that there was no link between HIV and AIDS, he blocked the provision of **anti-retrovirals** in state hospitals, causing over 330,000 deaths and the birth of 35,000 HIV-infected babies.

2009	**2010**	**2011**
Charges against Zuma dropped on eve of general election; ANC wins by landslide	SA stages successful football World Cup and unleashes vuvuzela on unsuspecting planet	South Africa joins BRIC (Brazil, Russia, India and China), club of the most important developing nations

And like the virus, **corruption** seemed to be infecting society, the most far-reaching example being the arms deal, in which the ANC government bought military equipment that South Africa's own defence force deemed unsuitable and too expensive. Newspapers alleged that the defence minister at the time was bribed and that a massive donation was paid to the ANC.

While money was squandered on arms, a raft of **social problems** festered. At the beginning of 2007, eight years after Mbeki assumed power, eight million people were living in shacks, millions had no water-borne sewerage and unemployment was running at forty percent. Disquiet at the slow pace of change was growing, and **protests** erupted on the streets of the townships. In 2005 alone, there were six thousand protests, and at the end of 2007 Mbeki was unseated by his party.

His replacement was the controversial former deputy president, **Jacob Zuma**, who was facing charges of bribery, fraud, racketeering, money laundering and tax evasion. A supreme populist, he portrayed himself as the people's president fighting off a conspiracy by an Mbeki-led elite. Miraculously, just two weeks before the April 2009 elections, top-secret recordings surfaced, purporting to prove that former president Mbeki had interfered in the Zuma case and charges against Zuma were dropped.

As expected, the Zuma-led ANC **won by a landslide**, while the Democratic Alliance (DA), the official opposition, increased its proportion of the vote. Support for the two main parties split down broadly racial lines, with the ANC getting most of its support from Africans and the DA from white and coloured voters. Given the ANC's overwhelming dominance of South African politics, it perhaps comes as no surprise that South Africa's most significant post-Mandela politics has taken place away from parliament – inside the ANC itself or on the streets.

After the vuvuzelas

For a brief period during 2010, South Africans united in a fever of vuvuzela-blowing euphoria, during the highly successful staging of the **Fifa World Cup**. But there was a return to politics as usual once the visitors had left and the country had returned to work – or not, as in the case of a million public-sector workers who staged a three-week strike in August over pay increases and housing allowances. Trade union leader **Zwelinzima Vavi** attacked the ANC for leading South Africa on the path to becoming "a predator state" in which an "elite of political hyenas increasingly controls the state as a vehicle for accumulation". These have turned out to be prescient words, following revelations of "state capture" by the Guptas, a powerful trio of Indian brothers with a high level of influence over Zuma.

Vavi's views represented the feelings of millions of South Africa's poor and dispossessed, who, nearly two decades after winning democracy, were still waiting for its economic fruits to be delivered. During Zuma's first two years of tenure, frustration with the ruling party accelerated. There were twice as many service-delivery protests in just 2009 and 2010 than there had been in the previous five Mbeki years.

By 2011, forty percent of South Africa's municipalities had been hit by popular street protests and there were attacks on Zuma from inside his own party. ANC Youth League leader **Julius Malema**, who had helped replace Mbeki with Zuma, now viciously attacked the president as being "worse than Mbeki", leading to Malema's

2012	2013	2014
Forty-four striking miners are shot in the back by police in the Marikana Massacre	South Africa and the world mourn the passing of Nelson Mandela – and of an era	Public Protector orders President Zuma to repay some of the R200m of taxpayers' money spent on upgrading his private residence

expulsion from the ANC and his formation of a new populist party the **Economic Freedom Fighters** (EFF).

Meanwhile, dissatisfaction festered in the platinum mines, with workers staging a **wildcat strike** at the Marikana mine in 2012. In an echo of the 1960 Sharpeville massacre (see p.645), one of apartheid's darkest hours, police fired on and killed 44 strikers at Marikana and wounded many more. Most of those killed in the **Marikana Massacre** were shot in the back – just as they had been at Sharpeville – delivering massive political capital to Julius Malema, who made a point of appearing at Marikana and proffering his support to the miners following the bloodshed. Malema traded on his working-class credentials all the way to the 2014 general election.

While mineworkers were dying in the cause of decent living conditions and millions of citizens were struggling to make ends meet, President Zuma was using taxpayers' money – over R200m of it – to refurbish his private residence at **Nkandla** in rural KwaZulu-Natal. With **Nelson Mandela's death** on 5 December 2013, the nation – and the world – mourned, not just because it had lost one of the country's greatest statesmen, but also because his passing symbolized the passing of an idealistic era that had promised a new dawn for South Africa. When President Zuma took the podium during the ten-day state memorial service, he was booed by sections of the crowd, in reaction to the dark clouds of corruption hanging over him.

These clouds proved to have a silver lining, however, when South Africa's political system demonstrated an encouraging robustness. The **Nkandla scandal** was widely reported by the independent media, and, perhaps more importantly, it was referred to the office of the Public Protector, a constitutional watchdog that protects citizens against abuses of state power. Despite official attempts to derail her investigations, the fiercely courageous Public Protector, **Thuli Madonsela**, delivered a measured report in 2014, in which she found, among other things, serious flaws in the tendering process for the upgrade of Zuma's home and numerous violations of the government's ethics code. She ordered Zuma to pay back millions of rands.

Strangely, the Nkandla scandal did little to dent the ANC's performance in the **2014 general election**. Despite losing some support, much of it to Julius Malema's EFF which won 25 seats, the ANC still managed to win the poll by a very healthy 62 percent majority. Nonetheless, many in the party realize that the ANC needs to be more responsive to the country's workers and the disenchanted dispossessed, and less tainted by allegations of corruption, if it is to maintain its support. Zuma is increasingly perceived as a liability to his party and the country, and as a leader who is trampling on the principles championed by Mandela, but the wily 75-year-old may well cling to power until the end of his term in 2019.

The local elections of 2016 were worrying for the ANC, with the party losing Johannesburg, Pretoria and Port Elizabeth to the DA. The following year, Zuma fired the well-respected finance minister, Pravhin Gordhan, prompting discontent in the ANC ranks and nationwide demonstrations as two credit rating agencies downgraded South Africa to "junk" status. Consequently, the ANC will likely see their support drop again in the 2019 general election. A DA government is less likely, however, as its image of being a white party persists – despite having a black leader, the Soweto-raised Mmusi Maimane.

2014	2015	2016
ANC wins general election by landslide	Aiming to "decolonize" education, #RhodesMustFall movement topples Cape Town University's prominent statue of Cecil Rhodes	The Democratic Alliance retains Cape Town in local elections, led in the Western Cape by former party leader Helen Zille

Music

Music from South Africa has a deserved following. The country has some of Africa's most diverse recorded music and its music industry is among the continent's most developed. It doesn't take much effort for an interested listener to encounter anything from indigenous African sounds that have remained largely unchanged for the last two hundred years, to the latest Afropop as well as a variety of white pop styles that would not be out of place anywhere in the Western world.

Gospel

Choral harmony and melody are perhaps black South Africa's greatest musical gifts to the world, and nowhere are they better manifested than in its **churches**. In the mainstream Catholic, Anglican and Methodist denominations a tradition of choral singing has evolved that has taken the style of European classical composers and loosened it up, added rhythm and, as always, some great dance routines.

In the Pentecostal churches, the music is more American-influenced, yet the harmonies and melodies remain uniquely South African and intensely moving. Pentecostal gospel music is the main recorded style; look out for groups like **Lord Comforters**, **Joyous Celebration**, **Pure Magic**, **Lusanda Spiritual Group** and the powerful **Rebecca Malope** (see box below).

Kwaito and hip-hop

South Africa's definitive youth sound, **kwaito**, has been around for about two decades. DJs importing dance music in the early 1990s, so the story goes, found white clubs unresponsive to Chicago house, and discovered that clubbers preferred the records slowed down from 45 to 33rpm.

In an accurate reflection of the depressed and nihilistic mood of township youth culture, *kwaito*'s vibe tends to be downbeat, and the music frequently carries a strong association with gangsterism and explicit sexuality.

Some artists worth looking out for include **Tokollo** (ex-TKZee), **Mzekezeke**, **Kabelo**, the hard-rock-influenced **Mandoza**, and the matchstick-chewing, gangster-styled **Zola**. **Kalawa Jazmee**, a record label started by Oscar Mdlongwa, aka **DJ Oskido**, was been responsible for several successful *kwaito* groups including **Trompies**, **Bongo Maffin** and the self-consciously retro **Mafikizolo**.

REBECCA MALOPE

Diminutive **Rebecca Malope** is South Africa's biggest-selling music star, enjoying years at the top of the **gospel scene**, with only stadia able to hold her fans, every album going gold or platinum, popular magazines full of her photos, views and story, and everyone knowing the lyrics of her songs. Well, nearly everyone that is, for Rebecca Malope is virtually unknown outside Africa.

The daughter of a Sotho father and Swazi mother, Rebecca was born in Nelspruit, Mpumalanga, in 1969, and soon began singing in the local Assemblies of God church, where her grandfather was a pastor. Her initial recordings were mostly forgettable bubblegum pop. She was spotted in Joburg by **Sizwe Zako**, who became her lynchpin keyboard player. Under his tutelage and, so she says, because of letters from fans pleading that she sing God's songs, Rebecca returned to gospel in 1990, where she has been amply rewarded.

Rebecca's musical formula, engineered by Zako, who also produces, rarely varies. The songs are anthems characterized by swirling keyboards and excellent backing singers, and are delivered in her tremendous, soaring and sometimes husky voice, accompanied by dramatic gestures.

BRENDA FASSIE

Kwaito killed the careers of many of the 1980s pop stars, but the late **Brenda Fassie** managed not only to survive the new music, but to thrive on it. Brenda was South Africa's true pop queen and the one local artist whose music is still pretty much guaranteed to get things going on the dancefloor, wherever you are in the country.

Brenda began her career in the early 1980s as the lead singer for **Brenda and the Big Dudes**, enjoying a string of bubblegum hits, including the classic "Weekend Special", which for years was a South African disco anthem. Her sound mixed *kwaito*, *mbaqanga*, gospel and her own extraordinary persona, earning massive and deserved success.

During the 1990s, while some contemporaries produced comfortable material aimed more at middle-class and middle-aged audiences, Brenda made a point of hanging out with the youth in Soweto and in Hillbrow, Johannesburg's fastest-paced inner-city patch. The result was a lesbian affair that thrilled the tabloids, a bad crack habit, a tendency to lose the plot completely on stage – and the best music she had ever produced.

Tragically, her many demons eventually caught up with her, and after falling into a two-week-long coma, which even saw President Thabo Mbeki coming to her hospital bedside, she died in 2004. Her funeral was a massive media event that witnessed an outpouring of grief exceeding that attending the deaths of most "struggle" veterans.

Local hip-hop artists are more likely than their *kwaito* counterparts to use English, and tend to come from middle-class backgrounds instead of the townships – as a result of which they can afford to spend more on production. Among the notable hip-hopsters are "township techno" wunderkind **Spoek Mathambo**, **Optical Illusion**, **Cashless Society**, **Zubz**, **Lions of Zion** (who, as their name suggests, blend hip-hop and reggae), comedian and rapper **Ifani**, and **Pro**, who is rated for the creativity of his lyrics

House, rap and reggae

DJ-mixed South African **house** attracts practitioners and fans from all parts of the country's racial and cultural divisions, but it is black DJs such as **DJ Fresh**, **DJ Ready D**, **Glen Lewis**, **DJ Mbuso**, **Thibo Tazz**, **DJ Fosta** and **Oskido** who for years have been garnering attention from the local media. The recordings they mix with are generally international sounds from Europe and beyond, while **Pex Africah** is renowned for his use of traditional African sounds.

South African **rap** has enjoyed sustained popularity since the early 1990s, remaining mostly ghettoized within the coloured community of the Western Cape (apart from the likes of the Soweto-born Spoek Mathambo). Heavily influenced by African American rappers, the performers often exude a sense of being "Americans trapped in Africa". Pioneers of the style were the heavily politicized **Prophets of Da City**, whose members included rapper Shaheen Ariefdien. Other performers who have come up are **Brasse Vannie Kaap** (who rap in Afrikaans), **Reddy D** and **Godessa**, while Cape Town-based record and production company, African Dope, has enjoyed success with acts such as **Teba**, **Funny Carp** and crossover jazz–Latin–hip-hop–funksters **Moodphase5ive**.

What is unusual as regards the place of **Lucky Dube** (who died tragically in 2007 in a hijacking) in the local **reggae** scene is the total lack of successful emulators. An energetic disciplined and talented live performer, Dube could also deliver a falsetto like Smokey Robinson's, which added a distinct twist to his otherwise familiar roots reggae sound.

Neo-traditional music

As with *kwaito*, the instrumentation in **neo-traditional music** is really just a backdrop to the lyrics and the dance routines. One of its major stars is the Shangaan singer **Thomas Chauke**, perhaps the single bestselling artist in any neo-traditional genre.

Hailing from Limpopo province, he makes heavy use of a drum machine and an electronic keyboard and often picks out some intricate lead-guitar work to complement his vocals.

Zulu neo-trad is pervasive, both in its a cappella form, known as *iscathamiya*, and as a vocal/guitar-based style called *maskanda*. For particularly fine examples of the art, look out for **Phuzekhemisi**, **Shiyani Ngcobo** and the late, great **Mfaz'Omnyama**. Another star of the neo-traditional scene is the queen of Ndebele music, **Nothembi Mkhwebane**. As well as being a talented and veteran performer, Nothembi, who sings and plays electric guitar, is also known for her sensational outfits, decorated with typically intricate Ndebele bead and metalwork.

Jazz

Jazz has been popular in South Africa for decades, and you can almost always find performances in Johannesburg or Cape Town on virtually any weekend, and sometimes midweek too. It was **South African jazz** that was the music most associated with the struggle against apartheid, especially after the music's main exponents went into self-imposed exile in the 1960s.

Jazz's roots in the country are much older than this, harking back to the emergence of *marabi* music in Johannesburg's African slums some time after World War I. During World War II, American swing became popular and fused with *marabi* into a new style usually referred to as African jazz. This remained predominant throughout the 1940s and 1950s, and produced the first South African musical exile in vocalist **Miriam Makeba**, who initially sang with the **Manhattan Brothers**.

The next development was a move in the direction of the American avant-garde, the two early, prime exponents of this in South Africa being the **Jazz Epistles** and the **Blue Notes**. Legislation prohibiting mixed-race public performances caused most of the Epistles to individually leave South Africa in the early 1960s, while the Blue Notes departed en masse in 1964. Some exiled South African jazzers detached themselves from their roots, while others such as **Hugh Masekela** reinterpreted their township influences. Back home, old-style African jazz as performed by the **Elite Swingsters** and **Ntemi Piliso's Alexandra All Stars** remained popular.

In the 1970s and 1980s, various South African strains were fused with funk, soul and rock influences to produce a more accessible, populist brand of jazz, from bands such

LADYSMITH BLACK MAMBAZO AND THE ISCATHAMIYA SOUND

The best known of South Africa's many neo-traditional musical genres is Zulu *iscathamiya* (or *mbube*), the distinctive male a cappella choral style made internationally famous by **Ladysmith Black Mambazo**. The style originated among Zulu rural migrants in urban hostels following World War I, and by 1939 the first commercial hit, "Mbube" by Solomon Linda and His Original Evening Birds, had been recorded, eventually selling over 100,000 copies. The song was later reworked as "The Lion Sleeps Tonight", which became a number one hit in both the US and UK.

In 1973, after recording for the SABC for several years, Ladysmith Black Mambazo made their first commercial release, *Amabutho*, for the Gallo label. It quickly sold over 25,000 copies (gold-disc status in South Africa), and since that time the group has recorded over fifty others, most of which have also gone gold. Following their collaboration with him on *Graceland*, Paul Simon produced their *Shaka* Zulu album, which sold 100,000 copies around the world and took *iscathamiya* to the international stage. In 1997, Ladysmith Black Mambazo extended its Afropop credentials with *Heavenly*, an album that featured collaborations with, among other international artists, Dolly Parton. Following the exposure of their song "Inkanyezi Nezazi" in a British TV advertisement for Heinz baked beans, the group went on to sell over a million units in the UK, an all-time record for a South African act. In 2013 they won their fourth Grammy Award, this time in the best world music category, for their album *Live: Singing for Peace Around the World*.

as **Sakhile**, **The Drive** and the **Jazz Ministers**. Following the end of apartheid, the surviving exiles began to trickle back and a new, younger generation of jazz musicians yet again married old local traditions with contemporary international trends.

Post-apartheid, a large group of new jazz names emerged that includes vocalists (**Gloria Bosman**, **Judith Sephuma**, **Sibongile Khumalo**), saxophonists (**McCoy Mrubata**, **Zim Ngqawana**), keyboard players (**Paul Hanmer**, **Themba Mkhize**), guitarists (**Jimmy Dludlu**, **Selaelo Selota**) and the odd trumpeter (**Prince Lengoasa**, **Marcus Wyatt**). Although many of the stars of this new generation emulate the smooth style of the Earl Klugh school, there are others whose tastes are considerably more muscular. Three artists that have come to the fore over the last decade or so are the talented Eastern Cape singer **Simphiwe Dana**, who fuses jazz, soul and traditional music, pianist **Bokani Dyer**, and vocalist **Tutu Puoane**.

Afropop

Afropop is a catch-all category, yet it's arguably where many contemporary South African artists sit most comfortably. Afropop is characterized by a knack for combining local African styles with Western popular influences, the ability to attract a multiracial audience, and the eschewing of computer-generated backing in favour of instruments.

Afropop goes back to Miriam Makeba's first American recordings in the early 1960s. More contemporary examples would include Paul Simon's 1987 *Graceland*, a collaboration with Ladysmith Black Mambazo and other local African artists; and the music of **Juluka** and **Savuka**, two bands led in the 1980s and 1990s by Johnny Clegg, whose melding of mainstream pop harmonies with Zulu dance routines and a touch of *mbaqanga* gained great popularity both in South Africa and in France. The music of bubblegum-pop queen **Yvonne Chaka Chaka** from the 1980s and 1990s could also be deemed Afropop. Artists who have subsequently adopted similar formulas include **Jabu Khanyile**, **Vusi Mahlasela**, **Ringo Madlingozi** and **Busi Mhlongo**.

The most successful proponents of the style are Cape Town-based **Freshlyground**, who, because of their broad appeal and engaging sound, were chosen to accompany Shakira in jamming to a billion viewers at the opening and closing ceremonies of the **2010 Fifa World Cup**. The group are still going strong, with plenty of live performances – their bedrock – and an album *The Legend* released in 2013.

White pop and rock

English-speaking South Africans have successfully replicated virtually every popular Western musical style going, and some have found fame in the outside world. Among the first and most famous of these are the alternative rockers the **Springbok Nude Girls**, who performed as the opening act for U2 during their 2011 tour of South Africa. Many local artists, such as **Dave Matthews**, **Seether**, **Just Jinger**, the **Parlotones** and **Wonderboom**, have achieved some international success, but many other gifted performers are mostly celebrated in South Africa, including string-maestro **Steve Newman** and **Tananas**, a string trio Newman plays with for a couple of months each year. A new Cape Town talent worth catching is folk-pop singer **Jeremy Loops**, who reached number one in the South African iTunes chart in 2014 with his artistry on loop pedal, guitar, harmonica and beatbox.

Like South African jazz, **Afrikaans music** is another world unto itself, with a multitude of sub-categories and a long list of heroes and heroines. From the late 1920s until the 1960s American country was its greatest outside influence, but by the early 1970s it looked to the lighter end of foreign pop and in particular Eurodisco. A long line of bouncy Afrikaans pop stars ensued, while a more sober side was represented by the light operatic style of Gé Korsten, probably the single most popular Afrikaans artist of the period.

ENTER DIE ANTWOORD

Die Antwoord (meaning "the answer") was an overnight sensation – an unknown crew from Cape Town that stormed the internet. Rapping in lowlife Cape Flats slang known as *zef*, they represented the voice of the Mother City's mean streets. That was the story, at least.

Their success was real enough: in February 2010, internet traffic to their website (⊛die antwoord.com), which was streaming their debut album *o*, was so heavy (fifteen million hits) that it crashed. Their signature foul-mouthed lyrics aside, there's nothing crude about their artistry. If you aren't convinced, note the tight machine-gun vocals (likened by *Rolling Stone* to "Eminem's 'Lose Yourself' on mescaline"), the slick art direction, the careful choreography and the cool Keith Haring-esque graphics on their video *Enter the Ninja*. The second and third albums, *Ten$Ion* and *Donker Mag*, were released on their own label, Zef Recordz, which they founded in 2011.

Far from being the band that came in from the Flats, Die Antwoord (frontman Ninja, helium-voiced Yo-landi Vi$$er and DJ Hi-Tek) is the latest surreal vehicle for Waddy Tudor Jones (Ninja), whose previous excursions included hip-hop rig Max Normal and the Constructus Corporation. Jones's history of taking on personas has led detractors to grumble that Die Antwoord "aren't real", while fans declare him a creative genius. Does it matter? The fact is, Die Antwoord deliver an unmistakably Cape Town sound that cooks.

Rumours of their demise abounded in 2017, but everything about these masterful image manipulators, who can be seen on the big screen in Neill Blomkamp's *Chappie*, should be taken with a pinch of sout.

Following the end of apartheid, a general concern about the future of the Afrikaans language and culture spurred a revival of interest in Afrikaans music. There is undoubtedly more stylistic variety now than ever before: witness the house/disco of **Juanita**, the heavy rock of **Karen Zoid** and **Jackhammer**, the modernized *boeremusiek* of the **Klipwerf Orkes**, and the Neil Diamond-esque songs of **Steve Hofmeyer** (the bestselling Afrikaans music artist). More recent sounds are the punk-rock riffs of **Fokofpolisiekar** and the studied banality of rapper **Jack Parow**. The Fokofpolisiekar documentary *Forgive Them for They Know Not What They Do* gives a sense of the challenges faced by rock bands in the still-conservative Afrikaans cultural universe.

New wave dance and electronica

Like Afropop, **new wave dance and electronica** is a catch-all phrase, in this case to describe a menagerie of sounds unleashed on South Africa's dancefloors over the past decade or so, and which began making their mark after 2010 in clubs in the US, Britain and the rest of Europe. Local musicians such as **Spoek Mathambo**, **DJ Mujava**, **Culoe De Song**, **Markus Wormstorm**, **Sibot** and Ibiza favourites **Goldfish** have been pumping out their blend of local sounds at the world's nightspots – and getting signed up by international labels. Mathambo offers an edgier take on the fusion of African and Western sounds in his "township tech", which merges lo-fi guitars, hip-hop beats and electronic noodling, along with sophisticated wordplay in English and several African languages.

Although global in flavour, the sounds are still distinctly South African, incorporating Afrobeat, *kwaito*, *mbaqanga* and anything else that's to hand. Most successful at riding the new wave so far are foul-mouthed zef-rappers **Die Antwoord** (see box above).

Discography

In the reviews on the following pages, items marked with an asterisk are international releases. Other items are South African releases, issued either by local labels or by the South African operations of international labels.

CROSS-GENRE COMPILATIONS

Various Artists *The Rough Guide to the Music of South Africa* (World Music Network). Excellent cross section of sounds combining big names with some interesting less-known musicians.

Various Artists *Mzansi Music: Young Urban South Africa* (Trikont). Fifteen-track collection that captures the city beat of Mzansi's (South Africa's) youth.

Various Artists *Putumayo Presents: South Africa* (Putumayo). A nicely varied selection of artists ranging from the Soweto Gospel Choir to Afrikaans rockers.

MBAQANGA

Mahlathini and the Mahotella Queens *The Best of Mahlathini and the Mahotella Queens* (Gallo). Perfect introduction to the sound of this most stomping of *mbaqanga* outfits.

Soul Brothers *Ezinkulu, The Best of The Soul Brothers* and *The Early Years* (Gallo). If *The Best of* whets your appetite, investigate *The Early Years*, a series comprising the classic first twelve albums, recorded in the 1970s and early 1980s.

Various Artists *From Marabi to Disco* (Gallo). A mini-encyclopedia of the development of township musical style from the late 1930s to the early 1980s.

Various Artists *The Indestructible Beat of Soweto* (Earthworks). Superb compilation, mainly featuring 1980s *mbaqanga*.

GOSPEL

IPCC *Ummeli Wethu* (Gallo). An excellent offering from one of South Africa's most popular gospel choirs.

Lusanda Spiritual Group *Abanye Bayawela* (Gallo). The biggest-selling album from a gospel music sensation.

Vuyo Mokoena & Pure Magic *Greatest Hits* (EMI). Simply wonderful melodic gospel-pop, featuring the silky lead vocals of Vuyo Mokoena.

Rebecca Malope *African Classics* (Sheer Legacy). A retrospective album that makes a good introduction to the gospel queen.

Solly Moholo *Abanye Bayawela Motlhang ke Kolobetswa "Die poppe sal dans"* (CCP). A beautiful release from the country's finest Sotho gospel artist.

Joyous Celebration *Various* (Sony, SA). Umpteen albums (and still proliferating: 21 by 2017) of classic gospel.

Various Artists *Choirs of South Africa* (Roi Music). Gospel anthems sung by mass choirs with exuberance and power.

Various Artists *Rough Guide to South African Gospel* (World Music Network). A comprehensive survey of South African gospel going back to the 1950s.

KWAITO AND HIP-HOP

Bongo Maffin *Bongolution* (Sony Music). A fine release from a popular group which combines Jamaican-style ragga lyrics with *kwaito* beats.

Brenda Fassie *The Queen of African Pop* and *Memeza* (CCP). The former is a posthumous survey covering the entire career of South Africa's very own Madonna; the latter, featuring the massive hit "Vuli Ndlela", was Brenda's most commercially successful effort.

Kabelo *And the Beat Goes On* (Universal). A monster hit from one of the biggest *kwaito* stars.

Mafikizolo *Sibongile* (Sony Music). Good solid melodies that are well sung and harmonized. The trio's female vocalist, Sibongile Nkosi, is outstanding.

Makhendlas *Jammer* (CCP). Features two massive hits, "Emenwe" and "Ayeye Aho", from the brother of *kwaito* pioneer Arthur Mafokate. Makhendlas tragically shot himself after killing a troublesome fan after a gig in 1998.

Malaika *Malaika* (Sony Music). Hugely successful, this is very much in the style pioneered by Mafikizolo but features even more contemporary African-American influences.

Mandoza *Nakalakala* (CCP). Not only was this album massively popular with African urban youth, the title track has been one of very few *kwaito* recordings to truly cross over into the white pop arena.

M'Du *No Pas No Special* (Sony Music). A popular album from one of *kwaito*'s most enduring stars.

Skwatta Kamp *Khut En Joyn* (Nkuli). A fairly relentless first offering from the *enfants terribles* of the local hip-hop scene.

TKZee *Halloween* (BMG). Complete with trademark catchy anthems and R&B-based sounds, this is a solid early (1998) offering from these popular *kwaito* artists.

Various Artists *Cape of Good Dope Volumes 1 & 2* (African Dope Records). Eclectic mix showcasing the label's performers, including Max Normal (an earlier incarnation of Die Antwoord's Ninja).

Various Artists *Yizo Yizo Volumes 1–3* (CCP). The soundtrack to South Africa's hippest TV drama, with cuts from virtually every major *kwaito* artist.

Zola *Mdlwembe* (EMI). The first solo album of "Mr Ghetto Fabulous", full of menacing rhythms.

RAP AND REGGAE

Lucky Dube *Prisoner* (Gallo). Lucky Dube's reggae album *Prisoner* was at one time South Africa's second-bestselling album ever, full of stirring Peter Tosh-style roots tunes.

Prophets of Da City *Ghetto Code* (Universal). South Africa's rap supremos' finest release, full of tough but articulate rhymes and some seriously funky backing tracks

NEO-TRADITIONAL

Amampondo *Drums for Tomorrow* (Melt 2000). South Africa's most famous marimba band deliver a fine and well-produced set here, full of their distinctive Xhosa melodies and powerful polyrhythms.

Ladysmith Black Mambazo *Favourites* (Gallo). A fine greatest hits selection from the group's first decade in the 1970s and early 1980s. *Congratulations South Africa: The Ultimate Collection* (Wrasse). This double CD is a mixed bag of Afropop and 1990s *iscathamiya*, including "Inkanyezi Nezazi", which gained the group plenty of new fans after being used in a Heinz baked-beans advert.

Mfaz'Omnyama *Ngisebenzile Mama* (Gallo). The title means "I have been working, Mum", and is amply justified by this superb set, featuring some of the best *maskanda* ever recorded.

Nothembi Mkhwebane *Akanamandl' Usathana* (Gallo). Beautiful guitar-driven sounds from the Ndebele music queen, with a cover showing Nothembi in one of her impressive traditional outfits.

Phuzekhemisi *Imbizo* (RPM). Like its successors, this debut by the reigning *maskanda* champion features stunning guitar work, great vocals and murderous bass lines.

Ringo *Sondelani* (CCP). A superb modern reworking of traditional Xhosa sounds by this bald Capetonian heart-throb, including the hit track "Sondela", which has become one of South Africa's most popular love songs.

Shiyani Ngcobo *Introducing* (Sheer Sound). Fine *maskanda* album aimed at a foreign audience, and thus with far more variety than a domestic offering would feature.

Women of Mambazo *Mamizolo* (Gallo). Beautiful *iscathamiya* melodies and harmonizations, not rendered by the usual male line-up but by a female group led by Nellie Shabalala, the late wife of Ladysmith Black Mambazo leader Joseph Shabalala.

JAZZ

Abdullah Ibrahim *African Marketplace* (Discovery/WEA). Ibrahim's best album – a wistful, nostalgic, other-worldly journey.

Gloria Bosman *Tranquility* and *Very Best Of* (Sheer/Limelight). A young and compelling jazz vocalist, Bosman juggles African and American styles with consummate ease.

★ **Hugh Masekela** *Hope* (Nashville Catalog/eOne). Jazz trumpeter and political exile under apartheid, Masekela treated Washington D.C.'s Blues Alley to this hot set in 1993, even including a Fela Kuti cover.

Jimmy Dludlu *Essence of Rhythm* (Universal). Dludlu is the essence of smooth jazz, and is one of South Africa's most popular representatives of the commercially successful jazz style.

Manhattan Brothers *The Very Best of The Manhattan Brothers* (Sterns). Classic recordings cut between 1948 and 1959 by this seminal vocal quartet, who crossed African-American secular harmonies with indigenous influences.

Miriam Makeba *Her Essential Recordings* (Manteca). A kind of Xhosa Billie Holiday who went into exile under apartheid; the jazz chanteuse's trademark hit "Pata Pata" and "Click Song", sung in the clicking Xhosa language, both feature here.

Moses Taiwa Molelekwa *Genes and Spirits* (Melt 2000). Fascinating jazz/drum 'n' bass fusion by a talented young pianist, who died tragically in 2001.

Paul Hanmer *Trains to Taung* (Sheer Sound). Constructed around Hanmer's dreamy, acoustic piano-based compositions, this album is now considered a classic.

Robbie Jansen *Nomad Jez* (EMI). Great album from veteran saxophonist Jansen, playing with other luminaries of the local jazz scene.

Sibongile Khumalo *Ancient Evenings* (Sony Music). Classically trained opera singer, Khumalo takes on jazz and a variety of traditional melodies on this wonderful album.

Various Artists *Amandla!* (ATO). The soundtrack to Lee Hirsch's excellent 2002 documentary about music's role in the fight against apartheid features the likes of Hugh Masekela, Miriam Makeba and Abdullah Ibrahim.

Winston Mankunku *Crossroads* (Nkomo/Sheer). Sinuous, upbeat township jazz from the veteran Cape Town saxman.

Zim Ngqawana *Vadzimu* (Sheer Sound). Ngqawana is one of the most revered figures in local jazz, despite being the antithesis of the smooth style that currently dominates.

POLITICAL

Mzwakhe Mbuli *Resistance is Defence* (Earthworks). Great sample of the militant lyricism of the people's poet, including a moving ode to Mandela's release.

Various Artists *South African Freedom Songs* (Making Music Productions). Superb double-CD set documenting the "struggle music" that helped power anti-apartheid resistance.

AFROPOP

Bayete *Umkhaya-Lo* (Polygram). A seminal fusion of South African sounds with laidback soul and funk, spiced with beautifully soothing vocals.

Busi Mhlongo *Urban Zulu* (Melt 2000). An immaculately produced Zulu *maskanda*-pop classic from the late jazz vocalist.

Freshlyground *Ma'Cheri* (Freeground Records/Sony BMG). Voted Album of the Year at the 2008 SA Music Awards, *Ma'Cheri* showcases the most enduring of South Africa's Afro-popsters.

Johnny Clegg *In My African Dream* (Universal). Clegg's mix of white pop harmonies and township rhythms has gained him a multiracial following in South Africa.

Ladysmith Black Mambazo *Heavenly* (Gallo/Spectrum). An inspired foray into Afropop, with versions of various pop classics plus vocal collaborations with Dolly Parton and Lou Rawls. Paul Simon's *Graceland* also famously features their dulcet tones.

Vusi Mahlasela *Silang Mabele* (BMG). Lush harmonies and melodies from this sweet-voiced township balladeer.

Yvonne Chaka Chaka *Bombani* (Teal) and *The Best of Yvonne Chaka Chaka* (Teal, SA). *Bombani* bombed, yet is Yvonne's most intricate and interesting release, mixing a range of traditional styles and featuring wonderful melodies. *The Best of* is pretty much all the 1980s disco-style Yvonne you need.

WHITE POP AND ROCK

Jeremy Loops *Trading Change* (Sheer Sound). Debut folk album, which shot to number one on the South Africa iTunes chart in 2014.

Just Jinger *All Comes Around* (BMG). Unexpectedly racking up sales of over 50,000 copies, this classic 1997 release demonstrated that local English rock was far from dead.

Mango Groove *The Best of Mango Groove* (Gallo). Mango Groove's mixture of white pop leavened with a touch of pennywhistle/township jive was briefly – from the late 1980s up to the dawn of democracy – the most commercially successful sound in South African music.

Springbok Nude Girls *Apes with Shades* (Sony Music). A recent release from one of South Africa's most popular white rock bands, led by Arno Carstens.

Various Artists *The Best of SA Pop Vols 1–3* (Gallo). Three double CDs covering all the biggest radio hits of the local English pop scene from the 1960s to the early 1980s.

AFRIKAANS

Anton Goosen *Bushrock* (Gallo). Goosen is one of South Africa's finest songwriters and performers. His style might best be described as Afrikaans folk rock. *Bushrock* is his one English-language album.

Fokofpolisiekar *Swanesang* (Rhythm Records/The Orchard). One of South Africa's most successful live bands has helped redefine Afrikaner identity for the post-apartheid generation with its punk-rock-influenced sound, while outraging the conservative establishment, starting with their name which translates as "fuck off police car".

Johannes Kerkorrel *Ge-Trans-To-Meer* (Gallo-Tusk). The late Kerkorrel was the leading light of the Afrikaans alternative scene of the 1990s, his brand of angst-laden pop also popular in Holland and Belgium.

NEW WAVE DANCE AND ELECTRONICA

BLK JKS *Mystery* (Secretly Canadian). The band (pronounced: "black jacks") that performed at the 2010 football World Cup kick-off. *Mystery* features their dizzying excursions across a succession of genres, from indie rock to psychedelia, tinged with traditional South African sounds.

Culoe De Song *Exodus* (Soulistic Music). Deep House for grown-ups, De Song's intoxicating tracks take their time to reach a lush climax, gradually piling on textures such as electro beat, looped chanting and animal-like calls.

Die Antwoord *O* (Rhythm Records). Signature album of the zef rave rap style that brought the trio to the world's attention, featuring their addictive – and plain weird – anthem track *Enter the Ninja*.

Felix Laband *Deaf Safari* (Compost Records/GoodToGo). Spacey folk-rock-tinged electronic tone poems spliced with old TV soundtracks as well as jazz and classical samples to generate chilled, minimalist mindscapes that justify repeated listening.

Goldfish *Perceptions of Pacha* (Pacha Recordings/Finetunes). Cape Town-based duo, who weave acoustic sounds into their predominantly electronica-based grooves to crank out one addictively Ibiza-style track after another.

Spoek Mathambo *Father Creeper* (Sub Pop). It's not always an easy listen, but Mathambo's 2012 album, showcasing his boundary-blasting "township tech" in all its language- and genre-switching glory, captures the pulse of township streets.

Various *Zoo City: The Soundtrack* (African Dope). The album that accompanied Lauren Beukes' novel of the same name (see p.663) showcases some of the contemporary exponents of South African electronica in an attempt to evoke the gritty atmosphere of Joburg's Hillbrow.

With contributions by Rob Allingham

Books

For a country with a proportionately small reading and book-buying public, South Africa generates a substantial amount of literature, particularly on the uncomfortable subjects of politics and history. Titles marked ★ are particularly recommended.

HISTORY, SOCIETY AND ANTHROPOLOGY

Ian Berry *Living Apart*. Superbly evocative and moving photographs spanning the 1950s to 1990s, which chart a compelling vision of the politics of the nation.

Richard Calland *Anatomy of South Africa: Who Holds the Power?* An incisive dissection of politics and power in South Africa during the first decade of the twenty-first century, from one of the country's most respected commentators. In 2013, Calland wrote a sequel, *The Zuma Years*.

John Carlin *Playing the Enemy: Nelson Mandela and the Game that made a Nation*. Gripping account of Nelson Mandela's use of the 1995 rugby World Cup to unite a fractious nation in danger of collapsing into civil war. Also published as *Invictus*, the title of the Clint Eastwood film, which starred Matt Damon and Morgan Freeman.

Paul Faber *Group Portrait South Africa: Nine Family Histories*. Fascinating account revealing the complexities of South Africa past and present, through the histories of nine South African families of different races, backgrounds and aspirations. Includes photos and illustrations.

Andrew Feinstein *After the Party: Corruption, the ANC and South Africa's Uncertain Future*. A personal account of how South Africa's government has lost its way, by a former ANC member of parliament.

★**Douglas Foster** *After Mandela: The Struggle for Freedom in Post-Apartheid South Africa*. Former editor of *Mother Jones*, Foster brings together political analysis and street-level accounts based on interviews recorded over six years to create one of the past decade's most interesting and penetrating accounts of a country poised between liberation and decline.

Hermann Giliomee and Bernard Mbenga *A New History of South Africa*. A comprehensive, reliable and entertaining account of South Africa's history.

★**Peter Harris** *In a Different Time: The Inside Story of the Delmas Four*. Brilliantly told true historical drama about four young South Africans sent on a mission by the ANC-in-xile, which ultimately led them to Death Row. As their defence lawyer, Harris had unique and sympathetic insight into their personalities and motivations. Also published as *Just Defiance: The Bombmakers, the Insurgents and a legendary Treason Trial*.

★**Antjie Krog** *Country of My Skull*. A deeply personal and ripping account of the hearings of the Truth and Reconciliation Commission. Krog, an Afrikaner former-ABC radio journalist and poet, reveals the complexity of horrors committed by apartheid.

★**J.D. Lewis-Williams** *Discovering Southern African Rock Art* and *Images of Power: Understanding Bushman Rock Art*. Concise books written by an expert in the field, full of drawings and photos.

Hein Marais *South Africa Pushed to the Limit*. An assessment of why the privileged classes remain just that, with a handful of conglomerates dominating the South African economy and how this relates to Jacob Zuma's rise to power.

Greg Marinovich *Murder at Small Koppie*. A meticulously researched account of the Marikana Massacre and its ongoing repercussions.

★**Noel Mostert** *Frontiers: The Epic of South Africa's Creation and the Tragedy of the Xhosa People*. An academically solid, brilliantly written history of the Xhosa of the Eastern Cape, and their tragic fate in the frontier wars against the British.

★**Pieter-Louis Myburgh** *The Republic of Gupta: A Story of State Capture*. A page-turning exposé of the dodgy deals that have gone on behind the scenes during Zuma's presidency, covering the Gupta family's influence on the governing party.

★**Thomas Pakenham** *The Boer War*. The definitive liberal history of the Anglo-Boer War that reads grippingly like a novel.

Charlene Smith *Robben Island*. Comprehensive and well-written account of Robben Island from prehistoric times to the present, including coverage of its most notorious period – as a prison for opponents of apartheid.

Allister Sparks *First Drafts: South African History in the Making*. A marvellous cross section of incisive writings about South African politics and history during the first decade of the twenty-first century written as he saw it at the time without the benefit of hindsight, by one of the country's most eminent journalists.

Desmond Tutu *No Future Without Forgiveness*. The Truth and Reconciliation Commission as described by its chairman. The book offers essential insight into one of South Africa's most unlikely heroes.

Frank Welsh *A History of South Africa*. Solid scholarship and a strong sense of overall narrative mark this publication as a much-needed addition to South African historiography.

Francis Wilson *Dinosaurs, Diamonds & Democracy: A Short, Short History of South Africa*. Brilliant account that packs two billion years into 128 pages, making it the perfect bluffer's guide to South Africa's history.

★**Nigel Worden, Elizabeth van Heyningen and Vivian Bickford-Smith** *Cape Town: The Making of a City*. The definitive account of the social and political development of South Africa's first city from 1620 to 1899. A companion volume covers the twentieth century.

AUTOBIOGRAPHY AND BIOGRAPHY

J.M. Coetzee *Boyhood: Scenes from Provincial Life* and *Youth*. Two riveting and disquieting accounts of growing up in a provincial town, and the author subsequently finding his way in the world, both in South Africa and London. Coetzee won the 2003 Nobel prize for literature.

★**Sindiwe Magoma** *To My Children's Children*. A fascinating autobiography – initially started so that her family would never forget their roots – that traces Magoma's life from the rural Transkei to the hard townships of Cape Town, and from political innocence to wisdom born of bitter experience.

★**Nelson Mandela** *Long Walk to Freedom*. The superb bestselling autobiography of the former South African president. Mandela's generosity of spirit and tremendous understanding of the delicate balance between principle and tactics come through very strongly, and the book is wonderfully evocative of his early years and intensely moving about his long years in prison.

★**Greg Marinovich and João Silva** *The Bang Bang Club*. Compelling account of the photographers who covered the bloody unrest in the townships at the end of apartheid, including the late Kevin Carter.

★**Benjamin Pogrund** *How Can Man Die Better? The Life of Robert Sobukwe*. The story of one of the most important anti-apartheid liberation heroes. The late leader of the Pan Africanist Congress and a contemporary of Nelson Mandela, Sobukwe was so feared by the white government that they passed a special law – The Sobukwe Clause – to keep him in solitary confinement on Robben Island after he'd served his sentence.

Anthony Sampson *Mandela, The Authorised Biography*. Released to coincide with Mandela's retirement from the presidency in 1999, Sampson's authoritative volume competes favourably with *Long Walk to Freedom*, offering a broader perspective and sharper analysis than the autobiography.

Stephen Taylor *Defiance: The Extraordinary Life of Lady Anne Barnard*. Biography of the Georgian-era socialite who spent five years in Cape high society beginning in 1797.

Chris van Wyk *Shirley, Goodness and Mercy: A Childhood Memoir*. A memoir of growing up in a working-class coloured family in Johannesburg during the apartheid era with humorous and poignant touches.

THE ARTS

Marion Arnold *Women and Art in South Africa*. Comprehensive and pioneering study of women artists in South Africa – both the successful and the neglected – from the early twentieth century to the present.

David Coplan *In Township Tonight: South Africa's Black City Music and Theatre*. Classic, updated in 2008, that traces local music from its indigenous roots through slave orchestras and looks at its humanizing influence in the harsh environment of the townships.

Thorsten Deckler, Anne Graupner and Henning Rasmuss *Contemporary South African Architecture in a Landscape of Transition*. Lavishly illustrated coverage of fifty outstanding South African architectural projects completed since 1994, all of which, the authors say, display a sense of South African identity.

Stephen Francis and Rico Schacherl *Madam and Eve*. Various volumes of witty cartoons conveying the daily struggle between an African domestic worker and her white madam in the northern suburbs of Johannesburg, these cartoons say more about post-apartheid society than countless academic tomes.

Steve Gordon *Beyond the Blues: Township Jazz of the Sixties and Seventies*. Portraits, in words and pictures, of the country's jazz greats such as Kippie Moeketsi, Basil Coetzee and Abdullah Ibrahim (Dollar Brand).

★**Andy Mason** *What's so Funny?: Under the Skin of South African Cartooning*. Insightful and fascinating wade through the history of South African visual satire from the colonial period to the present.

Ralf-Peter Seippel *South African Photography: 1950-2010*. South Africa's history has provided a rich vein of material for photographers and this volume covers the work of some of the country's most celebrated lensmen whose work is divided into three periods: apartheid, struggle and freedom.

Paul Weinberg *Then & Now*. Collection by eight photographers, tracing the changes in their subjects and approaches as South Africa moved from apartheid into the present democratic era.

Sue Williamson *South African Art Now*. A survey of South African art from the "Resistance Art" of the 1960s to the present, covering movements, genres and leading artists such as Marlene Dumas and William Kentridge, by one of the country's most influential commentators and an accomplished artist in her own right.

★**Zapiro** A series of annual cartoon collections by South Africa's leading, and always excellent, political cartoonist. Jonathan Shapiro, aka Zapiro, consistently reveals what needs to be exposed in satirical, hard-hitting and shocking cartoons (ⓦzapiro.com).

TRAVEL WRITING AND PHOTOGRAPHY

Richard Dobson *Karoo Moons: A Photographic Journey*. If you need encouragement to explore the desert interior of South Africa, these enticing images should do the trick.

Sihle Khumalo *Dark Continent, My Black Arse*. Insightful and witty account by a black South African who quit his well-paid job to realize a dream of travelling from the Cape to Cairo by public transport.

Julia Martin *A Millimetre of Dust: Visiting Ancestral Sites*. Sensitively crafted narrative that begins on the Cape Peninsula and takes the author, her husband and two children on a journey to important archeological sites in the Northern Cape, raising ethical, ecological and philosophical questions along the way.

Dervla Murphy *South from the Limpopo: Travels Through South Africa*. A fascinating and intrepid journey – by bicycle – through the new South Africa. The author isn't afraid to explore the complexities and paradoxes of this country.

★**Paul Theroux** *Dark Star Safari*. Theroux's powerful account of his overland trip from Cairo to Cape Town, with a couple of chapters on South Africa, including an account of meeting writer Nadine Gordimer (see p.665).

SPECIALIST GUIDES

G.M. Branch *Two Oceans*. Don't be put off by the coffee-table format; this is a comprehensive guide to Southern Africa's marine life.

Hugh Chittenden (ed) *Roberts Bird Guide*. The definitive, and very weighty, reference work on the subcontinent's entire avifauna population: if it's not in Roberts, it doesn't exist.

Richard Cowling and Dave Richardson *Fynbos: South Africa's Unique Floral Kingdom*. Lavishly illustrated book which offers a fascinating portrait of the *fynbos* ecosystem.

Richard D. Estes *Safari Companion: A Guide to Watching African Mammals*. A vital handbook on African wildlife, with fascinating information on the behaviour and social structures of the major species. Highly recommended for anyone wanting to go beyond the checklists.

★**Mike Lundy** *Best Walks in the Cape Peninsula*. Handy, solidly researched guide to some of the peninsula's many walks, and small enough to fit comfortably in a backpack.

L. McMahon and M. Fraser *A Fynbos Year*. Exquisitely illustrated and well-written book about South Africa's unique floral kingdom.

Willie and Sandra Olivier *Hiking Trails of Southern Africa*. Guide to major hikes, from strolls to expeditions lasting several days, throughout South Africa with information and where to get permits.

Colin Paterson-Jones *Best Walks of the Garden Route*. Handy for accessing some of South Africa's premier coastline and forests, along the Garden Route.

Steve Pike *Surfing in South Africa: Swells, Spots and Surf African Culture*. The essential guide to everything you need to know about riding the waves along the country's 3000km coastline, written by veteran journalist, surfing aficionado and founder of the definitive surfing website ⓦ wavescape.co.za.

Ian Sinclair, Phil Hockey and Warwick Tarboton *Sasol Birds of Southern Africa*. Comprehensive volume full of photos geared to the field, with useful pointers to aid quick identification.

Chris and Tilde Stuart *Field Guide to the Mammals of Southern Africa*. One of the best books on this subject, providing excellent background and clear illustrations to help you recognize species.

★**Philip van Zyl** (ed) *John Platter South African Wines*. One of the bestselling titles in South Africa – an annually updated pocket book that rates virtually every wine produced in the country.

FICTION

Tatamkhulu Afrika *The Innocents*. Set in the struggle years, this novel examines the moral and ethical issues of the time from a Muslim perspective.

Mark Behr *The Smell of Apples*. Powerful first novel set in the 1970s recounts the gradual falling of the scales from the eyes of an eleven-year-old Afrikaner boy, whose father is a major-general in the apartheid army.

★**Lauren Beukes** *Zoo City*. Winner in 2011 of the Arthur C. Clarke award for science fiction, this cyberpunk-style novel is set in an alternative Johannesburg where convicts are sentenced to be "animalled"– to have an animal familiar attached to them.

Herman Charles Bosman *Unto Dust*. A superb collection of short stories from South Africa's master of the genre, all set in the tiny Afrikaner farming district of Groot Marico in the 1930s. The tales share a narrator who, with delicious irony, reveals the passions and foibles of his community.

André Brink *A Chain of Voices*. This hugely evocative tale of eighteenth-century Cape life explores the impact of slavery on one farming family.

★**Michael Chapman** *Omnibus of a Century of South African Short Stories*. Comprehensive collection of South African tale-telling, starting with San oral stories and working up to twenty-first-century writing, including work by Olive Schreiner, Alan Paton, Es'kia Mphahlele and Ivan Vladislavic.

★**J.M. Coetzee** *Age of Iron* and *Disgrace*. In a *Mail & Guardian* poll of writers, *Age of Iron* emerged as the finest

CRIME FICTION

South African **crime fiction** was a rarity prior to 1994, but the post-apartheid era has seen the genre blossoming, with a number of local crime writers, among them Margie Orford, Roger Smith and Deon Meyer, making a splash internationally. So marked is the emergence of the home-grown crime novel that it has spawned a flurry of academic studies pondering its nature and asking why it is happening precisely now. The notion that it is somehow a response to South Africa's sky-high crime rates doesn't wash, given that Scandinavia and Japan – with their low crime rates – have both also experienced a recent boom in crime fiction.

One possible explanation for the genre's post-apartheid explosion is that previously, when the police were regarded as instruments of a repressive state, a storyline with a sympathetic protagonist who was also a cop would have been difficult to navigate. Another suggestion is that the crime thriller offers an opportunity to examine South African society – a niche previously occupied by the political "resistance novel". As one commentator remarks, South African crime fiction is often a "whydunit?" rather than a "whodunit?" Others speculate that in the crime novel resolution and catharsis are possible – symbolically, at least, making up for the failures of the Truth and Reconciliation Commission (see box, p.650) to deliver justice, and for the inadequacies of the country's overburdened judicial system. Whatever the reason, the popularity of the form suggests that, for readers and writers, crime does pay.

TEN KILLER SOUTH AFRICAN CRIME WRITERS

Joanne Hichens *Divine Justice*. Cape Town, dark humour and extreme characters – among them a fanatical preacher with a penchant for amputees – provide the backdrop for private eye Rae Valentine's search for missing jewels, as the body count grows.

Angela Makhowa *Red Ink*. Journalist-turned-investigator Lucy Khambule is asked to write the biography of a serial killer in a world of Joburg bling where the murders mount, and nothing is what it seems.

James McClure *The Song Dog*. One of a series of novels that pair up white detective Tromp Kramer and his black sidekick Mickey Zondi, by one of the rare apartheid-era crime writers, who is now regarded as the father of the genre in South Africa.

★**Deon Meyer** *Thirteen Hours*. This offering from South Africa's hottest crime writer is, as usual, a riveting read, and will appeal to backpackers especially – one thread follows Detective Benny Griessel's quest to find and save the life of an American overlander on the run from Cape Town gangsters after her travelling companion has been murdered.

Mike Nicol *Payback*. Hard-boiled thriller, one of several by established novelist Nicol (who has been compared to Elmore Leonard and Cormac McCarthy),

follows a pair of gun-runners drawn back from retirement into Cape Town's dark underworld.

Sifiso Nzobi *Young Blood*. Exploration of the attractions of crime – cars, money, women – for a young man finding his identity in Umlazi township in KwaZulu-Natal, and his struggle to break free from its tentacles.

Margie Orford *Water Music*. One of the Clare Hart novels by internationally acclaimed writer Orford, this engrossing read, set in picturesque Hout Bay, delves into the dark depths of child abuse.

Michele Rowe *What Hidden Lies*. Expertly crafted police procedural, in which Detective Persy Jonas winkles dark secrets from the inhabitants of several close-knit Cape Peninsula communities, after a floating body is discovered.

Roger Smith *Mixed Blood*. Relentless noir thriller set on the Cape Flats, and written with a brutal eloquence that requires a strong stomach as it traverses the ugly landscape of a violence-ruled gangland. *Mixed Blood* and another Smith novel *Wake Up Dead* have been optioned for Hollywood productions.

Diale Tlholwe *Counting the Coffins*. South Africa's first magical realist murder novel has Detective Thabang Maje navigating corruption and crime on the mean streets of Joburg.

South African novel of the 1990s. The book depicts a white female classics professor dying from cancer during the political craziness of the 1980s. She is joined by a tramp who sets up home in her garden, and thus evolves a curious and fascinating relationship. But even better is *Disgrace*, a disturbing story of a university professor's fall from grace, set in the Eastern Cape. No writer better portrays the

ever-present undercurrents of violence and unease in South Africa.

Achmat Dangor *The Z Town Trilogy*. A well-respected South African Indian writer once shortlisted for the Booker Prize, Dangor sets this novel during one of apartheid South Africa's many states of emergency, which is burrowing in intricate ways into the psyches of his characters.

Tracey Farren *Whiplash*. Powerful, acclaimed, and by turns relentless and funny, debut novel written in the voice of a Cape Town prostitute coming to terms with her past and present on her own personal walk to freedom.

Damon Galgut *In a Strange Room*. Galgut has scooped several literary awards: *In a Strange Room* was shortlisted for the 2010 Man Booker Prize for fiction. Unusually for Galgut, it's set outside South Africa and describes the global travels and relationships of a protagonist named, like the author, Damon. Quirky, beautifully written and highly readable.

Nadine Gordimer *July's People*. This controversial work by Nobel Literature Prize winner Gordimer was first banned by the apartheid regime for being subversive and later temporarily removed from schools by the ANC-governed Gauteng education department for being "deeply racist, superior and patronizing". Published in the 1980s when revolution in South Africa looked increasingly possible, it tells the story of a liberal white family rescued by its gardener July from a political deluge, and taken to his home village for safety.

Lily Herne *Deadlands*. South Africa's street-smart answer to *Twilight* follows the adventures and romance of 17-year-old Lele as she navigates the shattered, dystopian and zombie-infested suburbs of a post-apocalyptic Cape Town.

Pamela Jooste *Dance with a Poor Man's Daughter*. The fragile world of a young coloured girl during the early apartheid years is sensitively imagined in this hugely successful first novel.

★**Alex La Guma** *A Walk in the Night and Other Stories*. An evocative collection of short stories by this talented political activist/author, set in District Six, the ethnically mixed quarter of Cape Town razed by the apartheid government.

Anne Landsman *The Devil's Chimney*. A stylish and entertaining piece of magical realism set in the Karoo town of Oudtshoorn in the days of the ostrich-feather boom.

Sindiwe Magona *Mother to Mother*. Magona adopts the narrative voice of the mother of the killer of Amy Biehl, an American student murdered in a Cape Town township in 1993. The novel is a trenchant and lyrical meditation on the traumas of the past.

Songeziwe Mahlangu *Penumbra*. Semi-autobiographical debut novel that etches a unique vision of Cape Town through the eyes of a young man employed by a large insurance company. Torn by turns between mindless web-surfing, drug-induced mania and charismatic Christianity, Manga charts his course through the Mother City.

★**Dalene Matthee** *Circles in a Forest*. A descendant of Sir Walter Scott, Matthee powerfully evokes the bygone world of woodcutters dodging wild elephants in the forests of the Garden Route.

Zakes Mda *Ways of Dying*, *His Madonna of Excelsior* and *The Heart of Redness*. The first is a brilliant tale of a professional mourner, full of sly insights into the culture of black South Africa; *Madonna* focuses on a family at the heart of the scandalous case in the Free State in which nineteen people from the small town of Excelsior were charged with sex across the races; while *Heart*, which won the *Sunday Times* Fiction Prize, weaves the historical story of the Eastern Cape cattle killings with a contemporary narrative.

Brent Meersman *Reports Before Daybreak*. This moving novel and its sequel, *Five Lives at Noon*, follow an interconnected group of disparate characters through apartheid-era Cape Town.

★**Es'kia Mphahlele** *Down Second Avenue*. A classic autobiographical novel set in the 1940s in the impoverished township of Alexandra, where Mphahlele grew up as part of a large extended family battling daily to survive.

Barbara Mutch *The Girl from Simon's Bay*. This follow-up to the UK-based South African writer's excellent debut, the Karoo-set *Housemaid's Daughter*, is a romantic tale set a century ago in nautical Simon's Town.

★**Alan Paton** *Cry, The Beloved Country*. Classic 1948 novel encapsulating the deep injustices of the country, by one of South Africa's great liberals. With tremendous lyricism, the book describes the journey of a black pastor from rural Natal to Johannesburg to rescue his missing son from the city's clutches.

Sol Plaatje *Mhudi*. The first English novel by a black South African writer, *Mhudi* is set in the 1830s, at a time when the Afrikaner Great Trek had just begun. It's the epic tale of a young rural woman who saves her future husband from the raids of the Ndebele, who were then a powerful state in the Marico region.

Linda Rode and Jakes Gerwel (ed.) *Crossing Over*. Collection of 26 stories by new and emerging South African writers on the experiences of adolescence and early adulthood in a period of political transition.

★**Olive Schreiner** *Story of an African Farm*. The first-ever South African novel, written in 1883. Though subject to the ideologies of the era, the book nonetheless explores with a genuinely open vision the tale of two female cousins living on a remote Karoo farm.

★**Ivan Vladislavic** *The Restless Supermarket*, *The Exploded View* and *Portrait with Keys: Joburg and What-What*. *The Restless Supermarket* is a dark and intricate urban satire from the exciting Croatian–South African writer, about Johannesburg's notorious Hillbrow district during the last days of apartheid. *The Exploded View* is a collection of four interlinked pieces, a great follow-up from a writer who's unrivalled at evoking the contradictions and fascinations of Joburg, while *Portrait* is not so much a novel as an account, in a series of numbered texts, of the city that inspires Vladislavic's imagination.

Language

South Africa has eleven official languages, all of which have equal status under the law. In practice, however, **English** is the lingua franca that dominates politics, commerce and the media. If you're staying in the main cities and national parks you'll rarely, if ever, need to use any other language. **Afrikaans**, although a language you seldom need to speak, nevertheless remains very much in evidence and you will certainly encounter it on official forms and countless signs, particularly on the road; for this reason we give a comprehensive list of written Afrikaans terms you could come across (see opposite).

Unless you're planning on staying a very long time, there's little point trying to get to grips with the whole gamut of **indigenous African languages**, of which there are nine official ones and several unofficial ones. Having said that, it's always useful to know a few phrases of the local indigenous language, especially greetings – the use of which will always be appreciated even if you aren't able to carry your foray through to a proper conversation (see box, pp.668–669).

The nine official African languages are split into four groups: **Nguni**, which consists of Zulu, Xhosa, siSwati and Ndebele; **Sotho**, which comprises Northern Sotho, Southern Sotho (or Sesotho) and Tswana; **Venda** and **Tsonga**. Most black people speak languages in the first two groups. In common with all indigenous Southern African languages, these operate under very different principles from European languages in that their sentences are dominated by the noun, with which the other words, such as verbs and adjectives, must agree in person, gender, number or case. Known as concordal agreement, this is achieved by supplementing word stems – the basic element of each word – with prefixes or suffixes to change meaning.

The Nguni group, and Southern Sotho, both contain a few **clicks** adopted from San languages, which are difficult for speakers of European languages. In practice, most English-speaking South Africans sidestep the issue altogether and pronounce African names in ways that are often only approximations.

English

South African English is a mixed bag, one language with many variants. Around thirty-five percent of white people are mother-tongue English-speakers, and South African English has its own distinct character, as different from the Queen's English as is Australian. Its most notable characteristic is its huge and rich vocabulary, with unique words and usages, some drawn from Afrikaans and the African languages. The hefty *Oxford Dictionary of South African English* makes an interesting browse.

As a language used widely by non-native speakers, there is great **variation in pronunciation** and usage – largely a result of mother-tongue interference from other languages. Take, for example, the sentence "The bad bird sat on the bed", which speakers of some African languages (which don't distinguish between some of the vowel sounds of English) might pronounce as "The bed bed set on the bed". While some English-speaking purists may feel that their language is being mangled and misused, linguists argue that it is simply being transformed.

Afrikaans

Recognized as a language in 1925, **Afrikaans** is a dialect of Dutch, which became modified on the Cape frontier through its encounter with French, German and English settlers, and is peppered with words and phrases from indigenous tongues as well as African and Asian languages used by slaves. Some historians argue, very plausibly, that Afrikaans was first written in Arabic script in the early nineteenth century by Cape Muslims.

Despite this heritage, the language was used by Afrikaners from the late nineteenth century onwards as a key element in the construction of their racially exclusive ethnic identity. The attempt, in 1976, by the apartheid government to make Afrikaans the medium of instruction in black schools, which led to the Soweto uprising, confirmed the hated status of the language for many urban Africans, which persists to this day.

Contrary to popular belief outside South Africa, the majority of Afrikaans-speakers are not white but coloured, and the language, far from dying out, is in fact understood by more South Africans than any other language. It's the predominant tongue in the Western and Northern Cape provinces, and in the Free State it is the language of the media.

Afrikaans signs

Bed en Ontbyt	Bed and breakfast	**Perron**	Platform (train station)
Dankie	Thank you	**Plaas**	Farm
Derde	Third	**Poskantoor**	Post office
Doeane	Customs	**Regs**	Right
Drankwinkel	Liquor shop	**Ry**	Go
Droe vrugte	Dry fruit	**Sentrum**	Centre
Eerste	First	**Singel**	Crescent
Geen ingang	No entry	**Slaghuis**	Butcher
Gevaar	Danger	**Stad**	City
Grens	Border	**Stadig**	Slow
Hoof	Main	**Stad sentrum**	City/town centre
Hoog	High	**Stasie**	Station
Ingang	Entry	**Straat**	Street
Inligting	Information	**Strand**	Beach
Kantoor	Office	**Swembad**	Swimming pool
Kerk	Church	**Toegang**	Admission
Kort	Short	**Tweede**	Second
Links	Left	**Verbode**	Prohibited
Lughawe	Airport	**Verkeer**	Traffic
Mans	Men	**Versigtig**	Carefully
Mark	Market	**Vierde**	Fourth
Ompad	Detour	**Vrouens**	Women
Pad	Road	**Vrugte**	Fruit
Padwerke voor	Roadworks ahead	**Vyfde**	Fifth
Pastorie	Parsonage		

The Nguni group

Zulu (or isiZulu), the most widely spoken black African language in South Africa, is understood by around sixteen million people. It's the mother tongue of residents of the southeastern parts of the country, including the whole of KwaZulu-Natal, the eastern Free State, southern Mpumalanga and eastern Gauteng – as well as South Africa's president, Jacob Zuma. Some linguists believe that Zulu's broad reach could make it an alternative to English as a South African lingua franca. Don't confuse Zulu with **Fanakalo**, which is a pidgin Zulu mixed with other languages. Still sometimes spoken in the mines, it is not popular with most Zulu-speakers, though many white South Africans tend to believe it is.

For all practical purposes, **siSwati**, the language spoken in Swaziland, is almost identical to Zulu, but for historical reasons has developed its own identity. The same applies to **Ndebele**, which shares around 95 percent in common with Zulu. It broke off from Zulu (around the same time as siSwati) when a group of Zulu-speakers fled north to escape the expansionism of the Zulu chief Shaka. Ndebele is now spoken in pockets of Gauteng, Mpumalanga, Limpopo and North West Province as well as throughout southern Zimbabwe.

Xhosa (itself an example of a word beginning with a click sound) was Nelson Mandela's mother tongue. Today it is spoken by some eight million South Africans, predominantly in the Eastern Cape though with some speakers in the Western Cape, most of whom are concentrated in Cape Town.

The Sotho group

Northern Sotho dialects, which are numerous and diverse, are spoken by around 2.5 million people in a huge chunk of South Africa that takes in the country around the Kruger National Park, across Limpopo to the Botswana border and south from there to Pretoria. **Southern Sotho**, one of the first African languages to be written, is spoken in the Free State, parts of Gauteng, as well as Lesotho and the areas of the Eastern Cape bordering it.

Tswana, also characterized by a great diversity of dialects, is geographically the most widespread language in Southern Africa, and is the principal language of Botswana. In South Africa its dialects are dispersed through the Northern Cape, the Free State and North West Province.

As with the Nguni languages, the distinctions between the languages in the Sotho group owe more to history, politics and geography than to pure linguistic factors; speakers of some Northern Sotho dialects can understand some dialects of Tswana more readily than they can other Northern Sotho dialects.

Pronouncing place names

The largest number of unfamiliar **place names** that visitors are likely to encounter in South Africa are of Afrikaans origin, followed by names with origins in the Nguni group of languages. Afrikaans and English names are found across the country, while African names tend to be more localized, according to the predominant language in that area. Nguni group pronunciations generally apply in the Eastern Cape, KwaZulu-Natal, parts of Mpumalanga and Swaziland, while Sotho group names will be found in North West Province, Limpopo, the Northern Cape, Free State and parts of Gauteng. Sometimes you'll encounter names with Khoisan derivations, such as "Tsitsikamma" (in which the ts is pronounced as in "tsunami"). The pronunciation tips below are intended as a guide and are neither comprehensive nor definitive.

BASIC GREETINGS AND FAREWELLS

ENGLISH	AFRIKAANS	NORTHERN SOTHO
Yes	Ja	Ee
No	Nee	Aowa
Please	Asseblief	Hle.../...hle
Thank you	Dankie	Ke a leboga
Excuse me	Verskoon my	Tshwarelo
Good morning	Goiemore	Thobela/dumela
Good afternoon	Goeiemiddag	Thobela/dumela
Good evening	Goeinaand	Thobela/dumela
Goodbye	Totsiens	Sala gabotse/sepele gabotse
See you later	Sien jou later	Re tla bonana
Until we meet again	Totsiens	Go fihla re kopana gape
How do you do?	Aangename kennis?	Ke leboga go le tseba?
How are you?	Hoe gaan dit?	Le kae?

Afrikaans

In common with other Germanic languages, Afrikaans has a number of consonants that are **guttural**. Apart from these, most consonant sounds will be unproblematic for English-speakers. However, Afrikaans has numerous vowels and diphthongs, which have rough English equivalents but which are frequently spelled in an unfamiliar way – take, for example, the variation in the pronunciation of the letter "e" in the list below.

VOWELS AND DIPHTHONGS

a as in Kakam*as*	**u** as in p*u*p	**eu** as in K*eu*rboomstrand	**u** as in c*u*re
aa as in Br*aa*mfontein	**a** as in c*a*r	**i** as in Cal*i*tzdorp	**e** as in ang*e*l
ae as in H*ae*nertsburg	**a** as in c*a*r but slightly lengthened	**ie** as in D*ie*pwalle	**i** as in p*i*ck
		o as in Bont*e*bok	**o** as in c*o*rk, but clipped
aai as in Smitswinkelb*aai*	**y** as in dr*y*	**oe** as in Bl*oe*mfontein	**oo** as in b*oo*k
au as in *Au*grabies	**o** as in bl*o*w	**oo** as in Kl*oo*f	**oo** as in b*oo*r
ar as in G*ar*ies	**u** as in b*u*rrow	**ou** as in *Ou*drif	**o** as in wr*o*te
e as in Bont*e*bok	**er** as in rubb*er*, but clipped	**u** as in W*u*ppertaal	**i** as in p*i*ck
		ui as in Nelspr*ui*t	**a** as in g*a*te
e as in Clar*e*ns	**e** as in ang*e*l	**uu** as in S*uu*rbraak	**o** as in wr*o*te
ee as in Riebe*e*ck	**ee** as in b*ee*r	**y** as in Vanrhynsdorp	**ai** as in p*ai*n
ei as in Bloemfont*ei*n	**ai** as in p*ai*n		

CONSONANTS

d as in Suikerbosran*d*	**t** as in run*t*	**tj** as in Ma*tj*iesfontein	**k** as in *k*ey
g as in Ma*g*ersfontein	guttural **ch** as in the Scottish lo*ch*	**v** as in Nyslvlei	**f** as in *f*ig
		w as in *W*aterkant	**v** as in *v*ase

Nguni group

The clicks in Nguni languages are the most unfamiliar and difficult sounds for English-speakers to pronounce. The three basic clicks – which, as it happens, occur in the names of three places featured in the Wild Coast of the Eastern Cape (see p.337) – are: the **dental click** (transliterated using "c", as in the Cwebe Nature Reserve), made by pulling the tongue away from the front teeth as one would when expressing disapproval in "tsk tsk"; the **palatal click** (transliterated "q", as in Qholorha Mouth), made by pulling the tongue away from the palate as you would when trying to replicate the sound of a bubbly cork being popped; and the **lateral click** (transliterated "x", as in Nxaxo Mouth), made by pulling away the tongue from

SESOTHO	TSWANA	XHOSA	ZULU
E!	Ee	Ewe	Yebo
Tjhe	Nnyaa	Hayi	Cha
(Ka kopo) hle	Tsweetswee	Nceda	Uxolo
Ke a leboha	Ke a leboga	Enkosi	Ngiyabonga
Ntshwaerele	Intshwarele	Uxolo	Uxolo
Dumela (ng)	Dumela	Molo/bhota	Sawubona
Dumela (ng)	Dumela	Molo/bhoto	Sawubona
Fonaneng	Dumela	Molo/bhota	Sawubona
Sala(ng) hantle	Sala sentle	Nisale kakuhle	Sala kahle
Re tla bonana	Ke tla go bona	Sobe sibonane	Sizobanana
Ho fihlela re bonana	Go fitlhelela re bonana gape	De sibonane kwakhona	Size sibonane
Ke thabela ho o tseba?	O tsogile jang?	Kunjani?	Ninjani?
O/le sa phela?	O tsogile jang?	Kunjani?	Ninjani?

the side teeth. To complicate matters, each click can be pronounced in one of three ways (aspirated, nasalized or delayed) and may change when spoken in combination with other consonants.

VOWELS

a as in KwaZulu	a as in father	**o** as in Umkomaas	a as in tall
e as in Cwebe	e as in bend	**u** as in Hluhluwe	u as in put
i as in Kwambonambi	ee as in flee		

CONSONANTS

dl as in Dlinza	aspirated ll as in the Welsh Llewellyn	**ph** as in Mphephu	p as in pass followed by a rapid rush of air
g as in Haga-Haga	hard g as in hug	**r** as in Qholorha	guttural ch as in the Scottish loch
hl as in Hluhluwe	aspirated ll as in the Welsh llewellyn (though often pronounced like the shl in shlemiel by English-speakers)	**ty** as in Idutywa	approximately the initial sound in tube

Sotho group

VOWELS

a as in Thaba	a as in father	**o** as in Mantsebo	o as in bore, but curtailed
e as in Motsekuoa	e as in he	**u** as in Butha	u as in full

CONSONANTS

j as in Ha-Lejone	y as in yes	**ph** as in Maphutseng	p as in pool
hl as in Hlotse	aspirated ll as in the Welsh Llewellyn (often pronounced like the shl in shlemiel by English-speakers)	**th** as in Thaba	t as in tar

Glossary

Words whose spelling makes it hard to guess how to render them have their approximate pronunciation given in italics. Where *gh* occurs in the pronunciation, it denotes the **ch** sound in the Scottish word "loch". Sometimes we've used the letter "r" in the pronunciation even though the word in question doesn't contain this letter; for example, we've given the pronunciation of "Egoli" as "air-gaw-lee". In these instances the syllable containing the "r" is meant to represent a familiar word or sound from English; the "r" itself shouldn't be pronounced.

African In the context of South Africa, an indigenous South African

Aloe Family of spiky indigenous succulents, often with dramatic orange flowers

Apartheid (apart-hate) Term used from the 1940s for the National Party's official policy of "racial separation"

Assegai (assa-guy) Short stabbing spear introduced by Shaka to the Zulu armies

Baai (buy) Afrikaans word meaning "bay"; also a common suffix in place names, eg Stilbaai

Bakkie (bucky) Light truck or van

Bantu (bun-two) Unscientific apartheid term for indigenous black people; in linguistics, a group of indigenous Southern African languages

Bantustan Term used under apartheid for the territories for Africans

Bergie A vagrant living on the slopes of Table Mountain in Cape Town

Black Imprecise term that sometimes refers collectively to Africans, Indians and coloureds, but more usually is used to mean Africans

Boer (boor) Literally "farmer", but also refers to early Dutch colonists at the Cape and Afrikaners

Boland (boor-lunt) Southern part of the Western Cape

Boma An enclosure or palisade

Boy Offensive term used to refer to an adult African man who is a servant

Bundu (approximately boon-doo, but with the vowels shortened) Wilderness or back country

Burgher Literally a citizen, but more specifically members of the Dutch community at the Cape in the seventeenth and eighteenth centuries

Bushman Southern Africa's earliest, but now almost extinct, inhabitants who lived by hunting and gathering

Bushveld Country composed largely of thorny bush

Cape Dutch Nineteenth-century, whitewashed, gabled style of architecture

Ciskei (sis-kye) Eastern Cape region west of the Kei River, declared a "self-governing territory" for Xhosa-speakers in 1972, and now reincorporated into South Africa

Cocopan Small tip truck on rails used to transport gold ore

Coloured Mulattos or people of mixed race

Commandos Burgher military units during the Frontier and Boer wars

Dagga (dugh-a) Marijuana

Dagha (dah-ga) Mud used in indigenous construction

Dassie (dussy) Hyrax

Disa (die-za) One of twenty species of beautiful indigenous orchids, most famous of which is the red disa or "Pride of Table Mountain"

Dominee (dour-min-ee) Reverend (abbreviated to DS)

Donga Dry, eroded ditch

Dorp Country town or village (from Afrikaans)

Drift Fording point in a river (from Afrikaans)

Drostdy (dross-tea) Historically, the building of the *landdrost* or magistrate

Egoli (air-gaw-lee) Zulu name for Johannesburg (literally "city of gold")

Fanakalo or **fanagalo** (fun-a-galaw) Pidgin mixture of English, Zulu and Afrikaans used to facilitate communication between white foremen and African workers

Fundi Expert

Fynbos (fayn-boss) Term for vast range of fine-leafed species that predominate in the southern part of the Western Cape (see box, p.111)

Girl Offensive term used to refer to an African woman who is a servant

Gogga (gho-gha) Creepy-crawly or insect

Griqua Person of mixed white, Bushman and Hottentot descent

Group Areas Act Now-defunct law passed in 1950 that provided for the establishment of separate areas for each "racial group"

Highveld High-lying areas of Gauteng and Mpumalanga

Homeland See Bantustan

Hottentot Now unfashionable term for indigenous Khoisan herders encountered by the first settlers at the Cape

Impi Zulu regiment

Indaba Zulu term meaning a group discussion and now used in South African English for any meeting or conference

Inkatha (in-ka-ta) Fiercely nationalist Zulu political party, formed in 1928 as a cultural organization

Jislaaik! (yis-like) Exclamation equivalent to "Geez!" or "Crikey!"

Joeys Affectionate abbreviation for Johannesburg

Jol Party, celebration

Jozi Affectionate abbreviation for Johannesburg

Kaffir Highly objectionable term of abuse for Africans

Karoo Arid plateau that occupies a large proportion of the South African interior

Khoikhoi (ghoy-ghoy) Self-styled name of South Africa's original herding inhabitants

Kloof (klo-ef; rhymes with "boor") Ravine or gorge

Knobkerrie (the first "k" is silent) Wooden club

Kokerboom (both the first and last syllable rhyme with "boor") Quiver tree – a type of aloe found in the Northern Cape

Kopje Dutch spelling of *koppie*

Koppie Hillock

Kraal Enclosure of huts for farm animals or collection of traditional huts occupied by an extended family

Kramat (crum-mutt) Shrine of a Muslim holy man

Krans (crunce) Sheer cliff face

Laager (lager) A circular encampment of ox wagons, used as fortification by *voortrekkers*

Lapa Courtyard of group of Ndebele houses; also used to describe an enclosed area at safari camps, where braais are held

Lebowa (lab-o-a) Now-defunct homeland for North Sotho-speakers

Lekker Nice

Lobola (la-ball-a) Bride price, paid by an African man to his wife's parents

Location Old-fashioned term for segregated African area on the outskirts of a town or farm

Lowveld Low-lying subtropical region of Mpumalanga and Limpopo provinces

Malay Misnomer for Cape Muslims of Asian descent

Matjieshuis (mikeys-hace) Reed hut

Mbaqanga (m-ba-kung-a) A genre of music that originated in Soweto in the 1960s

Mbira (m-beer-a) African thumb piano, often made with a gourd

MK Umkhonto we Sizwe (Spear of the Nation) The armed wing of the ANC, now incorporated into the national army

Mlungu (m-loon-goo) African term for a white person, equivalent to *honkie*

Moffie (mawf-ee) Gay person

Nek Saddle between two mountains

Nguni (n-goo-nee) Group of southeastern Bantu-speaking people comprising Zulu, Xhosa and Swazi

Nkosi Sikelel 'i Afrika "God Bless Africa", anthem of the ANC and now of South Africa

Nyanga (nyun-ga) Traditional healer

Outspan A place set aside for animals to rest; can also mean to unharness oxen from a wagon

Pass Document that Africans used to have to carry at all times, which essentially rendered them aliens in their own country

Pastorie (puss-tour-ee) Parsonage

Platteland (plutta-lunt) Country districts

Poort Narrow pass through mountains along river course

Pronk (prawnk) Characteristic jump of springbok or impala

Protea National flower of South Africa

Qwaqwa Now-defunct homeland for South Sotho-speakers

Raadsaal (the "d" is pronounced "t") Council or parliament building

Restcamp Accommodation in national parks

Robot Traffic light

Rondavel (ron-daa-vil, with the stress on the middle syllable) Circular building based on traditional African huts

SABC South African Broadcasting Authority

Sangoma (sun-gom-a) Traditional spirit medium and healer

Shebeen (sha-bean) Unlicensed tavern

Shell Ultra City Clean, bright stops along major national roads, with a filling station, restaurant, shop and sometimes a hotel

Sjambok (sham-bok) Rawhide whip

Southeaster Prevailing wind in the Western Cape

Spaza shops (spa-za) Small stall or kiosk

Strandloper Name given by the Dutch to the indigenous people of the Cape; literally beachcomber

Stoep Veranda

Tackie Sneakers or plimsolls

Township Areas set aside under apartheid for Africans

Transkei (trans-kye) Now-defunct homeland for Xhosa-speakers

Trekboer (trek-boor) Nomadic Afrikaner farmers, usually in the eighteenth and nineteenth centuries

Umuthi (oo-moo-tee) Traditional herbal medicine

Velskoen (fel-scoon) Rough suede shoes

Vlei (flay) Swamp

VOC Verenigde Oostindische Compagnie, the Dutch East India Company

Voortrekker (the first syllable rhymes with "boor") Dutch burghers who migrated inland in their ox wagons in the nineteenth century to escape British colonialism

ZAR Zuid Afrikaansche Republiek; an independent Boer republic that included present-day Gauteng, Mpumalanga and Limpopo provinces and which was Britain's main opponent in the Anglo-Boer War

Food and drink

Amarula Liqueur made from the berries of the marula tree

Begrafnisrys (ba-ghruff-niss-race) Literally "funeral rice"; traditional Cape Muslim dish of yellow rice cooked with raisins

Biltong Sun-dried salted strip of meat, chewed as a snack

Blatjang (blutt-young) Cape Muslim chutney that has become a standard condiment on South African dinner tables

Bobotie (ba-boor-tea) Traditional Cape curried mince topped with a savoury custard and often cooked with apricots and almonds

Boerekos (boora-coss) Farm food, usually consisting of loads of meat and vegetables cooked using butter and sugar

Boerewors (boor-a-vorce) Spicy lengths of sausage that are *de rigueur* at braais

Bokkoms Dried fish, much like salt fish

Braai or **braaivleis** (bry-flace) Barbecue

Bredie Cape vegetable and meat stew

Bunny chow Originally a curried takeaway served in a scooped-out half loaf of bread, but now often wrapped in a roti

Cane or cane spirit A potent vodka-like spirit distilled from sugar cane and generally mixed with a soft drink such as Coke

Cap Classique Sparkling wine fermented in the bottle in exactly the same way as Champagne; also called Méthode Cap Classic

Cape gooseberry Fruit of the physalis; a sweet yellow berry

Cape salmon or **geelbek** (ghear-l-beck) Delicious firm-fleshed sea fish (unrelated to northern-hemisphere salmon)

Cape Velvet A sweet liqueur-and-cream dessert beverage that resembles Irish Cream liqueur

Denningvleis (den-ning-flace) Spicy traditional Cape lamb stew

Frikkadel Fried onion and meatballs

Hanepoort (harner-poort) Delicious sweet dessert grape

Kabeljou (cobble-yo) Common South African marine fish, also called kob

Kerrievis (kerry-fiss) See Pickled fish

Kingklip Highly prized deepwater fish caught along the Atlantic and Indian ocean coasts

Koeksister (cook-sister) Deep-fried plaited doughnut, dripping with syrup

Maas or **amasi** or **amaas** Traditional African beverage consisting of naturally soured milk, available as a packaged dairy product in supermarkets

Maaskaas Cottage cheese made from *maas*

Mageu or **mahewu** or **maheu** (ma-gh-weh) Traditional African beer made from maize meal and water, now packaged and commercially available

Malva Very rich and very sweet traditional baked Cape dessert

Mampoer (mum-poor) Moonshine; home-distilled spirit made from soft fruit, commonly peaches

Melktert (melk-tairt) Traditional Cape custard pie

Mielie Maize

Mielie pap (mealy pup) Maize porridge, varying from a thin mixture to a stiff one that can resemble polenta

Mopani worm (ma-parny) Black spotted caterpillar that is a delicacy among Africans in some parts of the country

Mqomboti (m-qom-booty) Traditional African beer made from fermented sorghum

Musselcracker Large-headed fish with powerful jaws and firm, white flesh

Naartjie (nar-chee) Tangerine or mandarin

Pap (pup) Porridge

Peri-peri Delicious hottish spice of Portuguese origin commonly used with grilled chicken

Perlemoen (pear-la-moon) Abalone

Pickled fish Traditional Cape dish of fish preserved with onions, vinegar and curry; available tinned in supermarkets

Pinotage A uniquely South African cultivar hybridized from Pinot Noir and Hermitage grapes and from which a wine of the same name is made

Potjiekos or potjie (poy-key-kos) Food cooked slowly over embers in a three-legged cast-iron pot

Putu (poo-too) Traditional African *mielie pap* (see above) prepared until it forms dry crumbs

Roti A chapati; called rooti in the Western Cape

Rusks Tasty biscuits made from sweetened bread that has been slow-cooked

Salmon trout Freshwater fish that is often smoked to create a cheaper and pretty good imitation of smoked salmon

Salomie Cape version of a *roti*; unleavened bread

Sambals (sam-bills) Accompaniments, such as chopped bananas, green peppers, desiccated coconut and chutney, served with Cape curries

Samp Traditional African dish of broken maize kernels, frequently cooked with beans

Skokiaan (skok-ee-yan) Potent home-brew

Smoorsnoek (smore-snook) Smoked *snoek*

Snoek (snook) Large fish that features in many traditional Cape recipes

Sosatie (so-sah-ti) Spicy skewered mince

Spanspek (spon-speck) A sweet melon

Steenbras (ste-en-bruss) A delicious white-fleshed fish

Van der Hum South African *naartjie*-flavoured liqueur

Vetkoek (fet-cook) Deep-fried doughnut-like cake

Waterblommetjiebredie (vata-blom-a-key-bree-dee) Cape meat stew made with waterlily rhizomes

Witblits (vit-blitz) Moonshine

Yellowtail Delicious darkish-fleshed marine fish

Small print and index

A ROUGH GUIDE TO ROUGH GUIDES

Published in 1982, the first Rough Guide – to Greece – was a student scheme that became a publishing phenomenon. Mark Ellingham, a recent graduate in English from Bristol University, had been travelling in Greece the previous summer and couldn't find the right guidebook. With a small group of friends he wrote his own guide, combining a contemporary, journalistic style with a thoroughly practical approach to travellers' needs.

The immediate success of the book spawned a series that rapidly covered dozens of destinations. And, in addition to impecunious backpackers, Rough Guides soon acquired a much broader readership that relished the guides' wit and inquisitiveness as much as their enthusiastic, critical approach and value-for-money ethos. These days, Rough Guides include recommendations from budget to luxury and cover more than 120 destinations around the globe, from Amsterdam to Zanzibar, all regularly updated by our team of roaming writers.

Browse all our latest guides, read inspirational features and book your trip at **roughguides.com**.

Rough Guide credits

Editors: Alice Park, Joe Staines, Ros Walford
Layout: Anita Singh
Cartography: Ashutosh Bharti, Deshpal Dabas
Picture editor: Aude Vauconsant
Proofreader: Jan McCann
Managing editor: Keith Drew
Assistant editor: Shasya Goel

Production: Jimmy Lao
Cover photo research: Marta Bescos
Editorial assistant: Aimee White
Senior DTP coordinator: Dan May
Programme manager: Gareth Lowe
Publishing director: Georgina Dee

Publishing information

This ninth edition published February 2018 by
Rough Guides Ltd,
80 Strand, London WC2R 0RL
11, Community Centre, Panchsheel Park,
New Delhi 110017, India
Distributed by Penguin Random House
Penguin Books Ltd, 80 Strand, London WC2R 0RL
Penguin Group (USA), 345 Hudson Street, NY 10014, USA
Penguin Group (Australia), 250 Camberwell Road,
Camberwell, Victoria 3124, Australia
Penguin Group (NZ), 67 Apollo Drive, Mairangi Bay,
Auckland 1310, New Zealand
Penguin Group (South Africa), Block D, Rosebank Office
Park, 181 Jan Smuts Avenue, Parktown North, Gauteng,
South Africa 2193
Rough Guides is represented in Canada by DK Canada, 320
Front Street West, Suite 1400, Toronto, Ontario M5V 3B6
Printed in Singapore
© Rough Guides, 2018
Maps © Rough Guides

688pp includes index
A catalogue record for this book is available from the
British Library
ISBN: 978-0-24130-630-7
The publishers and authors have done their best to ensure
the accuracy and currency of all the information in **The
Rough Guide to South Africa**, however, they can accept
no responsibility for any loss, injury, or inconvenience
sustained by any traveller as a result of information or
advice contained in the guide.
1 3 5 7 9 8 6 4 2

MIX
Paper from
responsible sources
FSC   www.fsc.org   FSC™ C018179

Help us update

We've gone to a lot of effort to ensure that the ninth
edition of **The Rough Guide to South Africa** is accurate
and up-to-date. However, things change – places get
"discovered", opening hours are notoriously fickle,
restaurants and rooms raise prices or lower standards. If
you feel we've got it wrong or left something out, we'd like
to know, and if you can remember the address, the price,
the hours, the phone number, so much the better.

Please send your comments with the subject line
"Rough Guide South Africa Update" to mail@uk
.roughguides.com. We'll credit all contributions and send a
copy of the next edition (or any other Rough Guide if you
prefer) for the very best emails.

ABOUT THE AUTHORS

James Bainbridge grew up in Shropshire, UK and lived on a few continents before his wife-to-be persuaded him to swap London for her home patch of Cape Town. Seven years later, they're based among the good schools and high fences of the city's leafy southern suburbs. When he's not dropping the kids at crèche, James covers Africa and beyond for numerous publications.

Hilary Heuler is a freelance journalist, researcher and travel writer who has spent the last decade or so exploring and writing about Europe, Asia and nearly half the countries in Africa. When not braving potholes and cramped public transport, she can be found at home in bustling Nairobi with her husband, son and three dogs.

Barbara McCrae was born in Zimbabwe, and taught African literature at the University of Natal. She lived in London for fifteen years authoring the Rough Guides to Zimbabwe and Botswana, South Africa and Cape Town and the Garden Route, before returning to live in South Africa after the release of Nelson Mandela. She lives close to the beach in Cape Town, where she swims, rides and climbs mountains to keep sane.

Greg de Villiers is a South African food photographer and writer living between Cape Town and Buenos Aires. He's never happier than when exploring a corner of the endlessly astounding continents he now calls home. See his photography at ⓦgregdevilliers.com.

Louise Whitworth is a British travel writer with a passion for big cities and long train journeys. In 2007 she ended an eight-month, round-the-world train trip with a six-year stay in St Petersburg. In 2013 she succumbed to the charms of the South African sunshine and now calls Johannesburg home.

Lizzie Williams has been working and travelling in Africa for more than twenty years; first as a tour guide on overland trucks across the continent and now as a guidebook author. She's written more than forty titles on African countries for various publishers and regularly contributes to magazines and websites on all aspects of African travel. When not on the road, Lizzie lives in beautiful Cape Town.

Acknowledgements

James Bainbridge: Thanks to Joe, Ros, Olivia and Keith at Rough Guides for your excellent briefing and editing skills. Also to everyone on the home front for cups of tea and patience as the deadlines, deadlines within deadlines and extensions loomed – especially my in-laws for the many hours of babysitting.

Hilary Heuler: Many thanks to Derek Alberts for the much-needed lifts and Lesotho travel advice, to Derryl and Elsa in Himeville for all their help, and, as always, to Elaine and Brian Agar in Durban for their incomparable hospitality and moral support.

Barbara McCrae: Thanks to editor Joe Staines and everyone else who helped with this edition, both with information and in the making of the book. Also thanks to those readers who wrote in with helpful feedback.

Greg de Villiers: I'd like to thank Mercedes, who traipsed around Swaziland with me, and our soon-to-be-born baby, who was privileged to get her first contact with a white rhino from the safety of her mum's belly. Thanks to everyone who helped and advised us on our travels, notably Patrick Ward at the Mountain Inn, Jacques Robbertze at Big Game Parks, Saga Dlamini and Rod de Vletter at Phophonyane, Dolores Godeffroy at eDladleni, Bongani Mbatha at Mkhaya and Tal Fineberg at Mbuluzi.

Louise Whitworth: A special thank you to the inimitable Laurice Taitz and her team at *Johannesburg In Your Pocket*, your enthusiasm for the city is inspiring. Also to Candice Morawitz of Legacy Hotels, Santa van Bart, Lynnie Kriel and Di Sparks. Finally, of course, I couldn't have done it all without the help of John Bowker – thank you for your patience, enthusiasm, excellent driving and spirit of adventure.

Readers' updates

Thanks to all the readers who have taken the time to write in with comments and suggestions (and apologies if we've inadvertently omitted or misspelt anyone's name):

Angelika Bucher; Arlene Fischer; Adrian Tahourdin; Sue Wall.

Photo credits

All photos © Rough Guides, except the following:
(Key: t-top; c-centre; b-bottom; l-left; r-right)

Index

Maps are marked in grey
Places in Lesotho are indicated by (L); in Swaziland by (S)

Map symbols

The symbols below are used on maps throughout the book

-----	International boundary	★	Transport stop	Garden		Mountain range
-----	Provincial boundary	P	Parking	Mountain refuge/lodge		Mountain peak
-----	Chapter division boundary	⊠	Gate	Battle site		Cave
	National route	♦	Place of interest	Ruins		Hot spring
	Road	✉	Post office	Hide		Waterfall
	Pedestrian road	@	Internet access	Castle		Lighthouse
	Unpaved road	⊞	Hospital	Golf course		Vineyards
	Steps	ⓘ	Information centre	Monument		Church (regional)
	Footpath	E	Embassy	Museum		Church (town)
	Wall	Λ	Campsite	Stately home		Building
	Ferry		Fuel/gas station	Swimming pool		Market
	Railway		Border crossing post	Picnic site		Stadium
	Cable car		Hindu temple	Viewpoint		Park
	Tram line		Mosque	Crocodile park		Christian cemetery
	Bridge		Synagogue	Nature reserve		Beach
	Airport					

Listings key

■	Accommodation
●	Eating
■	Drinking/nightlife
●	Shopping